The Pursuit of Victory

By the Same Author

Guide to the Manuscripts in the National Maritime Museum

(with Alan Frost) *The Journal of Daniel Paine 1794–1797*

Portsmouth Dockyard Papers 1774–1783:
The American War

(joint editor) *British Naval Documents 1204–1960*

Shipbuilding Timber for the British Navy:
Parliamentary Papers 1729–1792

ROGER KNIGHT

The Pursuit of Victory

*The Life and Achievement
of Horatio Nelson*

BASIC
BOOKS

A Member of the Perseus Books Group
New York

Copyright © 2005 by Roger Knight
Maps copyright © 2005 by John Gilkes

Published in 2005 in the United Kingdom by Allen Lane, an imprint of
Penguin Books Ltd.

The acknowledgments on pp. 818–20 constitute an extension of this
copyright page.

A CIP catalog record for this book is available from the Library of Congress.
ISBN-10: 0-465-03764-X
ISBN-13: 978-0-465-03764-3

05 06 07 08 / 10 9 8 7 6 5 4 3 2 1

Dedicated to the memory of
Admiral of the Fleet Lord Lewin of Greenwich
1920–1999

Contents

III   PASSION AND DISCREDIT
1798–1801

IV   ADULATION AND DEATH
1801–1805

V   THE TRANSFIGURATION

CONTENTS

Illustrations

Endpapers: *Nelson's Flagship at Anchor* by Nicholas Pocock

(*Plate Section One*)

1. *Racehorse* and *Carcass* in the ice, 4–8 August 1773, by John Cleveley
2. View of Bastia from the *Victory*, watercolour by Ralph Willet Miller, May 1794
3. Frances Nelson, 1798, by Daniel Orme
4. Emma Hamilton in 1800 by Johann Heinrich Schmidt
5. Nelson leading the boarding party on to the Spanish ships of the line at the Battle of Cape St Vincent, 14 April 1797, after James Daniell
6. Nelson before the attack on Santa Cruz, July 1797, by an unknown artist
7. Nelson's reception at Fonthill, December 1800
8. *A Jig around the Statue of Peace; or, All Parties Reconciled*, cartoon by W. Holland, 6 October 1801
9–12. The Battle of the Nile, 1 August 1798, 'At Evening', '10 O'Clock', 'Midnight', 'The Ensuing Morning', by Robert Dodd
13. Merton by Thomas Baxter

(*Plate Section Two*)

14. Captain Horatio Nelson, 1781, by J. F. Rigaud
15. The Reverend Edmund Nelson, 1800, by Sir William Beechey
16. Captain William Locker by Gilbert Stuart
17. *Midshipmen Studying between Decks On Board the 'Pallas', May 1775* by Gabriel Bray
18. Cuthbert Collingwood
19. Prince William Henry, later the duke of Clarence, *c.* 1791, by Richard Cosway.
20. Admiral Viscount Hood by James Northcote
21. Rear-Admiral Thomas Fremantle, after Domenico Pellegrini

Charts and Text Illustrations

Note on the Text

Quotations from contemporary documents are based on the originals as closely as possible. Capitals and spelling have been retained as written, except in the case of 'Jemmy' Jameson, the master of the *Boreas*, whose spelling in his log was so wayward that making sense of it required decryption skills. Abbreviations have been clarified by the addition of letters within square brackets. Punctuation has had to be inserted very occasionally for the sake of clarity. Where documents have been quoted from printed sources, the editing and alterations of their authors inevitably have had to be used.

MONEY VALUES

The value of money in Nelson's time is difficult to establish because the relative value of particular commodities changed significantly over a long period of time. Regional price variations and the widespread custom of part-payment of wages by non-monetary means further complicate the picture.

The table in Rodger (*Command of the Ocean*, xxiv–xxv) shows the pay of a junior naval captain at various dates from the seventeenth century to the early twenty-first. A captain was paid £200 in 1807 and £58,000 in 2003, which suggests that the value of the pound sterling has risen by a factor of about 290. This common-sense approach has much to commend it, though some historians would argue that the difference in the value of the pound between those days and today is much greater.

Acknowledgements

Hunting down Nelson manuscripts has taken me to far and interesting places. The most distant and beautiful was the Huntington Library in San Marino, California, where I held a Visiting Fellowship in 2001 for a month's productive work and stimulus from discussions with other fellows, and where I was made welcome by Roy Ritchie and his staff. At the William L. Clements Library at the University of Michigan in Ann Arbor, John Dann and his colleagues cheerfully and enthusiastically made available their expertise and their wonderful eighteenth-century British collections, and staff at the Houghton Library at Harvard University were similarly helpful. Nor should I forget my two-months in 1993 as the Alexander Vietor Visiting Fellow at the John Carter Brown Library in Providence, Rhode Island, during a bracing New England spring, which gave me time to read widely as well as giving me respite from museum administration, and which enabled me to approach this book with a firm framework of ideas on the Revolutionary and Napoleonic wars. A belated thanks is due to Norman Fiering and his staff, as well as to all these American scholars, archivists and librarians.

Archives and libraries in the United Kingdom, large and small, were supportive and efficient, and the National Archives at Kew and the British Library a pleasure to visit and swift to produce their documents. At the other end of the scale Christine Hiskey at Holkham in Norfolk, and Andrew Helme and Sue Miles at the Nelson Museum in Monmouth, smoothed the way to many documents. Matthew Sheldon at the Royal Naval Museum at Portsmouth not only produced documents efficiently but gave me ideas for other sources. Assistance beyond the call of duty came from Francesca Altman of the Norwich Castle Museum and Gallery, Jane Cunningham of the Photographic Survey, Courtauld Institute of Art, and Richard Draisey of the Devon Record Office. Valuable help by e-mail from Adrian Webb at the Hydrographic Office at Taunton and Roger Bettridge at the Centre for Buckinghamshire Studies enabled me to gain access to their collections.

Former colleagues at the National Maritime Museum gave up their time freely. Pieter van der Merwe helped with pictures and was full of ideas; Richard Ormond and Roger Quarm were always on hand, while David Taylor has been unfailingly helpful. Gillian Hutchinson and Brian Thynne answered a stream of questions about charts. For help with the manuscripts produced in the Caird Library I have to thank Daphne Knott, Andrew Davis, Kiri Ross-Jones, among all the others, for producing manuscripts; on occasions they went to great lengths to help. Gill Davies and the librarians gave great service. Margarette Lincoln and Nigel Rigby have been supportive, while it was a great comfort to be able to call upon the expertise of Brian Lavery and Liza Verity. Colin White generously and consistently shared his knowledge of Nelson documents, and was particularly helpful in providing transcripts from papers in the National Archives of Scotland. I must also thank Kevin Hall, who kept me afloat electronically throughout this project. At the Greenwich Maritime Institute at the University of Greenwich, where I now teach, Sarah Palmer, Dean Surtees and Suzanne Bowles put up with my absences, for the writing of this book ensured that this visiting professor was exactly that and no more.

References and ideas have come from many people and I thank Huw Bowen, Robert Clark, Jonathan Coad, Charles Consolvo, Gerald Draper, Michael Duffy, Dan Finamore, Ron Fiske, Iain Hamilton, Susan Harmon, Noah Heringman, Richard Hill, Margaret Hunt, Peter Le Fevre, Iain Mackenzie, Boye Meyer Friese, Janet MacDonald, Ruddock Mackay, Campbell McMurray, Lawrie Phillips, Marie Mulvey Roberts, Victor Sharman, Ann Shirley, Bill Vaughan, Tim Voelcker and Clive Wilkinson. I have had help of a more practical kind from Alan Borg, Nicholas Courtney, Anthony Cross, Chris Gray, Patricia Haigh, Derek Hayes, Gillian Hughes, Tim Lewin, Mike Palmer, Tony Sainsbury, Chris Ware, Dennis Wheeler and Glyn Williams. Lady Glenconner very kindly showed me around Burnham Thorpe. Lord Cottesloe attempted to locate the revealing diary of his ancestor, Thomas Fremantle. Susie and Paolo Nesso in Florence tried hard to locate the streets through which Nelson passed in Pisa and Leghorn, while the Reverend Donald Thorpe, from his temporary base in the English Church in Taormina, provided information on the last days of the Bridports in Sicily. From Cadiz came advice from Agustín Guimerá and Gonzalo Búton; their enthusiasm for the subject of Trafalgar led them to put on a delightful and most instructive conference in Cadiz in 2002.

No one can approach a life of Nelson without being aware of Tom Pocock's sustained contribution to the subject, not least for maintaining interest in Nelson in less fashionable times by his Trafalgar dinner at the

Garrick Club, which I have been privileged to attend for more years than both he and I would care to admit. Terry Coleman has been most supportive, and though I do not share all his scepticism about Nelson, I have benefited from his finely honed reasoning. Two long-established scholars in the field of naval history, whom I have known for many years, Julian Gwyn and Dan Baugh, made Nelson letters available to me. Julian, now Emeritus Professor of History at the University of Ottawa, proved, to my great surprise, to have been related to Nelson. Dan's visits from Cornell University have always been stimulating; when staying at my house, over breakfast, lunch and tea, he gives me invigorating, week-long seminars on eighteenth-century naval history, full of wisdom. John Hattendorf's long friendship has been similarly instructive. He kindly read an early draft of the first chapters and gave me encouragement just when it was needed. Michael Stammers, that man of Norfolk, helped me with eighteenth-century Norfolk life. Marianne Czisnik's thorough scholarship was always provoking and helpful and she generously made her newly awarded Ph.D. thesis available to me as I wrote the last chapters. For Nelson's complicated medical history I have had the benefit of Leslie Le Quesne's advice, transmitted over a long series of agreeable lunches with him, at which good cheer belied the sometimes gruesome subject of conversation. And it is sad to record my thanks to the late David Syrett, whose extensive eighteenth-century knowledge and gritty common sense were always available, and who will be sorely missed.

Two people gave up their time to read the script in full. Alan Pearsall, an old colleague at the National Maritime Museum and my mentor for thirty-five years, who not only taught me what was correct but also what was right, gave me as ever the benefit of his unrivalled knowledge. Nicholas Rodger had only just finished his seven-year travail with his magnificent *The Command of the Ocean* when he agreed to read my bulky script. I am grateful to both of them. No author is more indebted to an editor than I am to Stuart Proffitt at Penguin, and I owe also a great deal to his colleagues, Liz Friend-Smith, Richard Duguid and especially Donna Poppy. Thanks to John Gilkes for drawing the charts and to Elizabeth Wiggans for compiling the index.

My greatest thanks are due to my wife, Jane, who made writing this book fun and possible. When I had written half the book, she, an historian trained, joined in to help after her retirement from a long career in Whitehall. We sailed in the tracks of Nelson, went together to the archives, walked the north Norfolk coast and drove over the plains of Ohio to Michigan. With Patricia Haigh she explored the streets of Pisa and Livorno and visited Bronte, while I wrote at home. Without her help and support this book would not have been ready for the bicentenary of Trafalgar.

Finally, two eminent figures from the past at the National Maritime Museum at Greenwich have influenced this book. Katherine Lindsay-McDougall, Custodian of Manuscripts at the National Maritime Museum in the 1950s, was the last person at the museum who did serious work on Nelson. It has been a pleasure to get to know her as a distinguished predecessor. For sixteen years I was able to observe closely the late Admiral Lord Lewin, when he was a trustee, then Chairman of Trustees, at the National Maritime Museum. I would refer those who might feel that Nelson's qualities of naval leadership were unique to the concluding chapter of Richard Hill's *Lewin of Greenwich* (2000). The similarities in style of these two officers in managing difficult situations and getting the best out of people are startling. Dedicating this book to Terry Lewin is not merely a gesture of formal respect but a heartfelt tribute to an inspirational man, who, though I did not realize it at the time, gave me a model of leadership with which to approach the complexities of writing about Horatio Nelson.

Blackheath, December 2004

Introduction

It is an old saying, 'Show me the company a man keeps, and I will tell you his character.' Why not on a similar principle, 'Show me the correspondence which a man receives, and I will show you what manner of man he is.'

Sir John Barrow, *Life of George Lord Anson* (1839)[1]

It was my good fortune to have under my command some of the most experienced officers in the English Navy, whose professional skill was seconded by the undaunted courage of British sailors.

Nelson's speech at the dinner at the Beaufort Arms, Monmouth, 19 August 1802[2]

Nelson's success in hard-fought battles against the navies of France, Spain and Denmark, together with his adulterous love affair with Emma Hamilton, have made him one of the few historical figures about whom there have been several books in print at any time in the last 200 years. The first biography followed the Battle of the Nile and was published, probably, in 1801, and there was a steady succession of biographies after his death.[3] In 1990 a bibliography published by L. C. Cowie lists over 1,300 books on the broader subject of Nelson and the American Revolutionary and Napoleonic wars. Of these, over a hundred are biographies, but, he comments disapprovingly, 'Not a single biography of Nelson possesses proper bibliography, references and footnotes.'[4] This is no longer the case, for the list of titles has grown since Cowie wrote those words, but an early declaration of the principles of this book is necessary.* Why another biography?

* References in Nelson biographies started appearing soon after 1990, but the first full biography with extensive footnotes to original documents (Coleman, 2001, 2002) appeared after I had started work on this book. The recent volume by John Sugden, covering Nelson's career to 1797, has also taken a rigorous and detailed view of manuscript sources.

There are three ways in which this book differs from those that have gone before. First, it draws upon original, primary sources, and documents printed in volumes that have been carefully selected for their accuracy. Yet many of Nelson's letters remain unknown. The Nelson Letters project run by the National Maritime Museum and Royal Naval Museum has demonstrated clearly that many documents have remained hidden from view.* In some areas of Nelson's life a picture emerges from these documents that is completely different from the one to be found in those biographies that repeat traditional stories from secondary sources. Second, this biography takes account of correspondence to, as well as from, Nelson. So many letters and official papers written by Nelson have survived that if one does not search for the point of view of others in the story, it is very easy to take Nelson on his own terms. This has been done many times by previous authors. The third purpose of this book is to ask why Nelson was so successful. It argues that it is not possible to understand his brilliant victories without an understanding of the British Navy, its resources, government and politicians, the navies of Great Britain's enemies and a host of other considerations. Only once these broader and deeper factors are appreciated can one then ask how Nelson reached such extraordinary heights as a leader of men and as a controller of great fleets. Placing him more firmly in his historical context inevitably throws more light on those around him. He was above all a professional seaman; and it was the seamen and their qualities, and the intricacies of the relationship between them and their officers, upon which Nelson's victories rested. A French naval officer was later asked what had made the greatest impression upon him at Trafalgar.

The act that astonished me the most was when the action was over. It came on to blow a gale of wind, and the English immediately set to work to shorten sail and reef the topsails, with as much regularity and order as if their ships had not been fighting a dreadful battle. We were all amazement, wondering what the English seamen could be made of. All our seamen were either drunk or disabled, and we, the officers, could not get any work out of them. We never witnessed any such clever manoeuvres before, and I shall never forget them.[5]

How can these men be left out of the story?

I have attempted to spurn the speculation that so many of the biographers of this complex man have used to paper over the gaps in the evidence. In

---

* I should like to acknowledge the help of Dr Colin White over the last four years.

any case, by returning to the documents many new aspects of Nelson's life can be revealed. Yet writing history and biography is a humbling process, and, in spite of thousands of documents, it is often difficult to penetrate the inner life of Nelson. The style of his letters is open and informal, yet only for short periods, usually under intense strain, does he reveal his true feelings. Even though many letters survive between him and his wife, Fanny, it is still not clear why and when they drifted apart, or if, indeed, they had ever been close. His relationship with Emma Hamilton is a deeper mystery. Few of her letters survive, many of them destroyed by Nelson himself. Why and how, for instance, did she goad him into a jealous fury after the birth of their child Horatia? Only novelists and screenplay writers can write with complete conviction and certainty about such matters. We are, however, on firmer ground when we examine the thoughts and opinions of those around him, especially those to be found in private correspondence between third parties. But in order to do that we need, in turn, to understand the multitude of figures in Nelson's world. For that reason the Biographical Sketches section provides more than 200 portraits of the main characters in this story.

The core of my research has been taken, as far as possible, from archives in Britain and the United States. The principal collections are in the National Archives (the Public Record Office at Kew), the British Library and the National Maritime Museum, Greenwich, with important additions in the Nelson Museum at Monmouth, the Royal Naval Museum at Portsmouth and the Wellcome Library for the History and Understanding of Medicine. In the United States the William L. Clements Library at the University of Michigan at Ann Arbor, the Houghton Library at Harvard University and the Huntington Library in San Marino, California, contain Nelson letters brought together by collectors in the first half of the twentieth century.

These document collections have been supplemented by books of reproduced documents. Although there is some fine scholarship amongst these volumes, they contain major pitfalls, especially those published in the nineteenth century. Early panegyric works built an emotional and imaginative scaffolding around Nelson that rivalled the one surrounding Nelson's Column in Trafalgar Square when it was erected in the early 1840s. The first to be published, in 1806, was James Harrison's *Life*, in which the author selected documents under the supervision of Lady Hamilton, but the most inaccurate and fanciful was published in 1809 in two volumes by James Stanier Clarke and John McArthur: *The Life of Admiral Lord Nelson, KB, from His Lordship's Manuscripts.*[6] Clarke and McArthur were responsible for creating more myths about Nelson than any other authors.

William Nelson, Horatio's unscrupulous clergyman brother, who inherited the title and owned the papers, worked hard to ensure that the best face was put on Nelson's life. McArthur, admiral's secretary and naval prize agent, and purser of the *Victory*, had already been working on a biography. Through the prince of Wales, the newly created Earl Nelson ensured that 'a person of rank' should also be associated with the book.[7] The prince of Wales's chaplain, James Stanier Clarke, was finally agreed upon as a joint author. McArthur had the advantage of knowing Nelson well, and he was helped by many of Nelson's colleagues and friends.* This enormous work, bolstered by the transcripts of many of Nelson's letters and supported by over 700 advance subscribers, was never meant to be anything less than a monument to a dead hero. Not surprisingly, the narrative was heavily embellished. It gave rise to many stories still extant today. Much of its inaccuracy is the result of omission, but the authors were not above adding their own evidence and stylistic improvements to Nelson's words. The result is completely untrustworthy.[8]

This reputation for untrustworthiness is hardly new. William James, whose massive 1820s history of naval operations during the American Revolutionary and Napoleonic wars is still widely used today, asserted that 'Clarke and McArthur's *Life of Nelson* is not of the slightest authority.'[9] The authors, he wrote, 'seldom indulge in their own remarks without making a perfect braggardocio [*sic*] of their hero ... Much, indeed, has the memory of this great man suffered by the overweening zeal of his biographers.'[10] In preparation for writing the book, Clarke went to sea in about 1807 in the *Vestal*, for he knew little of naval life. A junior officer in the ship recalled:

Captain Graham of the *Vestal* was a perfect boy for fun; and he loved to get up a laugh at our author's expense. He used to concoct anecdotes and stories of Nelson, and have them ready cut and dried, and tell them as occasion served, or oftener get somebody else to tell them, as if by accident, after dinner. On these occasions Clark[e]'s eyes would sparkle; and he would lay down his half-broken biscuit, and listen; and then he he would say with a chuckle, '*that will do for my book*'. Then out came his memoranda, and down it went with his ever-ready pencil. All the time we were absolutely expiring, and Graham's look and command of countenance were irresistible.[11]

---

* After the publication of the *Life*, McArthur affected the name M'Arthur, presumably to draw attention away from his Scottish origins. In all official documents he appears as McArthur.

Documents from Clarke and McArthur have not been quoted in this book.

Victorian standards of biography and historical accuracy were not generally high.[12] An honourable exception is Sir Nicholas Harris Nicolas's impressive seven-volume edition of *The Dispatches and Letters of Lord Nelson*, published in 1844. But it is a work that needs to be used with care. The scarcity of documents from Nelson's early life leads to uneven coverage: the first volume covers thirty-six years, while the remaining six volumes contain documents from the last eleven years of his life. Nicolas also omits passages showing Nelson's weaknesses. Occasionally, he elides the surname and uses only an initial when Nelson was passing judgement and Nicolas did not want the subject's descendants to be offended.* Nicolas also over-punctuates Nelson's flowing prose in a way that is out of keeping with modern standards and tastes. The original letters are generally bereft of punctuation, particularly those written in haste, and some editing is necessary for sense and clarity. Nicolas indicated when he had to rely on less reliable sources (in particular, those letters transcribed by Clarke and McArthur), doing so only when the originals were not made available to him. He also prints some letters from the anonymously published two-volume *The Letters of Lord Nelson to Lady Hamilton: With a Supplement of Interesting Letters by Distinguished Characters* (1814), the publication of which first damaged Nelson's reputation by revealing the true nature of his relationship with Emma Hamilton. In general, however, Nicolas published very little correspondence between Nelson and Emma.[13]

Nicolas also used letters written to Nelson that were in the possession of John Wilson Croker, who had been first secretary of the Admiralty between 1809 and 1830. In about 1817 these papers were advertised for sale. With the agreement of Lord Liverpool, the prime minister, and Lord Melville, the first lord of the Admiralty, Croker employed someone to pose as an amateur collector in order to purchase them from, as he termed them, 'low greedy people'. Croker used government money and his purpose in buying them was to keep them out of the public domain. He was as much concerned about any material that related to Naples as about the scandal of Nelson's relationship with Emma Hamilton. Some thirty years later Nicolas came to know of these documents and asked Croker if he could include them in his great work. In February 1845 Croker wrote to Sir Robert Peel, the prime minister, for agreement to this proposal; having taken Melville's advice,

---

* For instance, in Nicolas, I, 58, 28 Jan. [1782], Nelson, in a letter to his brother William, refers to R [odney] as 'a great liar', and the many references to the heavy drinking of Charles Sandys are similarly disguised (e.g., I, 110, 24 Sep.; 112, 23 Nov. 1784).

Croker thought it best to lend the documents to Nicolas, 'destroying, of course, anything scandalous in itself or detrimental to the reputation of Lord Nelson'. We do not know if Croker destroyed anything. Melville and Croker were also averse to the original purchase becoming known, for 'the very act of having bought them would be prima facie evidence that there was something very scandalous which required so unusual a proceeding'.* Peel agreed that the papers in Croker's custody should be made available to Nicolas.[14] Late finds of additional documents account for the chaotic organization of Nicolas's seventh and largest volume, with the weight of administrative documents in the two years before Trafalgar finally over-whelming him: he omits hundreds of letters from this period, especially those that exist only as letter-book copies. Nevertheless, when used with care, Nicolas's seven volumes remain the most valuable published source for Nelson's life.

Nicolas's work dominated writing on Nelson for 150 years, and the apparent completeness of *Dispatches and Letters* perhaps inhibited more searching biographical interpretation. Other documents, however, appeared in print at sporadic intervals. Thomas Pettigrew's *Memoirs of the Life of Vice-Admiral Lord Viscount Nelson* appeared in 1849, publishing many letters from Nelson to Lady Hamilton and raising further doubts in the minds of Victorians about the morality of their relationship. In 1893 Alfred Morrison privately published his two-volume *The Collection of Autograph Letters and Historical Documents Formed by Alfred Morrison*. These documents ensured that the world knew in detail about Nelson and Emma Hamilton, and confirmed that he was the father of her daughter Horatia. They are accurately done, with only occasional traces of invasive Victorian editing. H. C. Gutteridge's *Nelson and the Neapolitan Jacobins*, published by the Navy Records Society in 1903, is a fine piece of work, an attempt to arbitrate a scholarly controversy of the time that caused intense emotion.[15] In 1932 Warren R. Dawson edited *The Nelson Collection at Lloyd's*, but this is a random selection of documents that reflected the collecting of an institution over many years. Geoffrey Rawson's *Letters from the Leeward Islands* (1953) contained many letters not previously in print. In 1958 George Naish edited the 600-page volume *Nelson's Letters*

---

* Subsequently these papers were purchased by the great Victorian manuscript collector Sir Thomas Phillipps. The National Maritime Museum bought them in 1946, and they now comprise the Phillipps–Croker Collection. There is a letter by Croker of 17 Aug. 1846 in the Duke University Perkins Library, Special Collections (File 1845–8, Perkins Add. Box 4), about a further tranche of Nelson's papers that Croker discovered in 1846, in addition to those made available to Nicolas on 21 Feb. 1845. I am grateful to Dr Iain Hamilton for this reference.

to His Wife. His editorship depended almost entirely upon the deep knowledge of Katherine Lindsay-MacDougall, at that time the Custodian of Manuscripts in the National Maritime Museum.[16] The high standard of scholarship in this volume makes it possible to bypass many of the absurdities of Clarke and McArthur. Other letters by and to Nelson are published in a variety of books and journals, principally in the volumes of the Navy Records Society.

In the twentieth century two biographies dominated the field. In the 1890s Alfred Thayer Mahan, a United States naval officer, brought a professional eye to *The Life of Nelson: The Embodiment of the Sea Power of Great Britain.* While clothed in late-Victorian assumptions and written, as its title implies, with an underlying political agenda, it still retains an authority that makes it worth reading. The other biography is Carola Oman's *Nelson,* published in 1946. Thorough and full of fresh material, although it now appears over-coloured, it went through many editions and was recently reissued in 1996. Forty years ago I turned to these two books when I wrote, as an undergraduate, a paper for the Dublin University History Society. Not long after I read my paper, on 8 March 1966, I heard, from my rooms in Trinity, the early-morning explosion caused by the IRA that destroyed the top of the Nelson Pillar in O'Connell Street. From these beginnings I made my career in naval history, although I turned away from Nelson to study how the British sailing navy was built and how it worked.

Nelson, however, was never far away, especially when I was Custodian of Manuscripts in the National Maritime Museum in the 1970s and 1980s. Important collections of his letters and associated documents were under my care. Every other week someone came into the Museum Reading Room with a Nelson letter, wanting confirmation that it was an original. Only once, I believe, were the owner's expectations realized. I purchased few Nelson manuscripts for the Museum, since collector's prices were then (as they are now) more than any museum could afford. But it was also difficult to escape Nelson when sailing over many years, whether in the Medusa Channel off the Essex coast, beating through the grey waters of the Sound off Copenhagen or anchored in Agincourt Sound in the Maddalena Islands off Sardinia. Thus, when a chance came to write again about Nelson after my departure from the museum in 2000, I turned back to the questions that had fascinated me in the 1960s.

I have benefited from working in the early years of the twenty-first century. Access to public and private archives is now enormously enhanced by information technology, and documents are produced with exemplary speed. Helpful staff ensure that working in such institutions is a far greater pleasure than when I first began to use documents in the late 1960s, a change of attitude emphasized by the newly built and well-designed facilities at the Public Record Office and the British Library. A further advantage is that several reference works of critical importance have been published since the early 1990s. Jan Glete's *Navies and Nations* and David Lyon's *Sailing Navy List*, both of which appeared in 1993, provided reliable information on the ships of the Royal Navy, in much greater detail than in previous works. In the next year two books did the same for the naval officers of the period: the first was David Syrett and Richard Dinardo's *The Commissioned Sea Officers of the Royal Navy 1660–1815*; the second, Roger Morriss's *Guide to British Naval Papers in North America*, tracked the diaspora of British naval papers that took place primarily before the Second World War. The consolidated edition of the *Naval Chronicle*, published in 1998–9 – in which the editor, Nicholas Tracy, reduced forty volumes of gloriously jumbled contributions, published between 1799 and 1819, to five, organized by subject and indexed – has been similarly valuable. It is difficult to imagine or remember writing eighteenth-century naval history without these volumes, although the electronic databases that are now beginning to appear will give researchers of the future even further advantage.

Although a number of recent historians have used the present accessibility of documentary sources, this is still not to say that all the best books on Nelson are modern. Sir Julian Corbett's *The Campaign of Trafalgar* (1919), for instance, remains a central work. In the main, I have relied upon those that use original documents and that are well referenced. The battles have received a great deal of detailed recent attention. Nelson's victory at the Nile has been illuminated by the work of Michèle Battesti in *La Bataille d'Aboukir* and of Brian Lavery in *Nelson and the Nile*, both of which appeared in 1998. Peter Goodwin's *Nelson's Ships 1771–1805* (2002) has wrung the logs and technical records dry. But there exists besides a wider body of scholarship, from Britain and many other countries, about naval power and conflict in Nelson's lifetime, and a much clearer view of the perspectives of other nations is now possible. The first full conference of French and British naval historians took place at the Sorbonne in 1984; since that time, they have met regularly, while other meetings included Spanish and Dutch historians. The translation into English of Ole Feldbæk's book gives the Danish view of the Battle of Copenhagen. By incorporating as much of this wider scholarship as I can, I hope to make better sense of Nelson's achievement. My debt to many others who have written about these times, and about Nelson himself, will be obvious from the references and Bibliography.

It is worth, nevertheless, quoting an example of how secondary sources can, over 200 years, distort the story. It concerns the first days of Nelson's naval career. Based on a reasonable spread of biographies from Robert Southey to recent works, the story, with variations, runs thus: on 27 November 1770, on 1 January 1771 or in March 1771, the young Nelson, lost and bewildered, alighted from the coach at Chatham and was unable to find his ship, the *Raisonable*.[17] He knew no one and wandered around for a long time until he was given a meal by a kind-hearted officer, who then found a boat across the River Medway to take him to his ship. When he eventually did get on the ship, the captain, his uncle Maurice Suckling, who had agreed to take him aboard, was not there. For at least a day nobody would speak to him.[18]

The log and muster books in the Public Record Office tell a different story. Captain Suckling joined the *Raisonable* at Chatham on 23 November 1770. 'This day I made my appearance and ordered the pennant to be hoisted,' he wrote in his log. Suckling supervised the fitting out of the ship, which had been 'in Ordinary', or reserve. Other officers joined in the following weeks. On 11 December the lower masts were hoisted in. On 1 January 1771 Suckling took care to enter his nephew in the muster book, thus establishing his place and seniority, which were to be of vital significance. It was not until 15 February 1771 that the ship moved twelve miles down the River Medway to Sheerness. Here, in the lowest reach of the river known as 'Blackstakes', she took on further stores and her guns. On 23 April she sailed out of the Medway and anchored at the Nore.[19] The muster book records that the next day, 24 April, 'Horace Nelson, Midshipman', joined the ship, and, as was the custom, his place of origin was identified as 'from Wells'; the date is entered clearly in a column headed 'Made his Appearance'.[20] Further, the direct way to the ships 'at the Nore' in the Thames estuary was on a sailing vessel from the London river; assisted by the tide, a constant succession of vessels serviced the warships lying there. In the 1770s it was the obvious and by far the cheapest method of travel.[21]

Musters when the ship was at a naval base were taken by dockyard clerks from the clerk of the cheque's department. They were documents that enabled seniority to be recorded and discipline maintained; together with the pay books, they determined pay. Late-Victorian and early-twentieth-century historians regarded these books with disdain. 'False musters, fraudulent time and bogus certificates were not only winked at but were in the regular order of things,' railed one of them, writing in 1929.[22] Although they sometimes take a little interpreting, the muster books constitute as firm a piece of evidence as the navy, a mature and successful eighteenth-century bureaucracy, could generate. It is beyond the bounds of probability that young Horace was sent to Chatham two months after the ship had left for Sheerness, twelve miles down the River Medway. It is even less likely that Maurice Suckling, the captain of a newly commissioned 64-gun ship, who had been ashore on half-pay for some years, under pressure from the Board of Admiralty to get his ship commissioned, would not have been on board continually throughout these weeks. He would certainly have been present when she sailed, with an incomplete and untrained crew, the three miles from Sheerness to the buoy of the Nore in the Thames estuary. Nelson arrived just at the time when all the preparations for a commission were being completed, the usual point at which 'the young gentlemen' joined the ship.* It is much more likely that his joining was well organized and timed, and that his presence was not noticed among the bustling crew, with a complement of 500 officers and men much more concerned in getting the ship in a condition to sail. Maurice Suckling turned his attention to his young nephew when he had the time. The romantic view of the small, lost boy at Chatham has been accentuated and gilded by successive biographers over the last 200 years. I have, in general, ignored such myths, rather than used up space to discredit them, but some have taken root so strongly that their origins need some explanation.

The intervening two centuries from the time of his death make it easier to avoid the legends and to examine the 'hero' more rigorously than in previous generations. Fifty years ago, Michael Lewis, the professor of Naval History at the Royal Naval College at Greenwich, felt uneasy. 'As a nation,' he wrote, 'we have done our best to kill him with kindness. We have taken him to our hearts as a National hero, and have modelled with our own hands a kind of super-waxwork which not only bears little relationship to the real article, but is so remote from life – and possibility – as to be slightly ludicrous, and certainly damaging to any real man's long-term reputation.'[23] The theme is echoed more brutally in Barry Unsworth's recent fictional examination of the Nelson legend in *Losing Nelson*. The main character, besotted by the idea of Nelson, who represents everything that he is not, is confronted in the last pages by the cold reality of the man in Naples, who says, 'Heroes are fabricated in the national dream factory. Heroes are not people.'[24]

---

* Twenty-two years later Josiah Nisbet, Nelson's stepson, joined the *Agamemnon* at Blackstakes, after two months of commissioning ((UK)NA: PRO, ADM 36/11358, 30 Mar. 1793).

Prologue

You do nothing by halves either to enemies or friends.
Lord Minto to Vice-Admiral Lord Nelson, 18 May 1803[1]

Ten miles off Alexandria in Egypt, at twenty-two minutes to five on the afternoon of 1 August 1798, two signals were hoisted to the masthead of His Majesty's 74-gun ship the *Vanguard*.[2] The thirteen signal lieutenants on the surrounding ships of the squadron commanded by Rear-Admiral Sir Horatio Nelson, squinting through their telescopes in the bright late-afternoon light, read these signals as the flags fluttered to the masthead. The first signal consisted of a top flag of double vertical stripes of blue and yellow, and a bottom flag with one horizontal stripe each of blue, white and red. This was Signal No. 53. By checking the tables in their signal books, issued to the Mediterranean Fleet by Admiral Sir John Jervis, the lieutenants quickly calculated that the first signal meant 'Prepare for Battle.' The second signal amplified the first: a blue and yellow flag, with an all-red one beneath, denoting Signal No. 54: 'Prepare for Battle: when it may be necessary to anchor: with a Bower or Sheet anchor Cable in abaft [by the stern], and springs etc.'[3]

These two signals heralded a battle that was to be a turning point in Horatio Nelson's life. It would also have a profound long-term effect upon the navy in which he served and upon the French Navy against which he fought. The signals transmitted Nelson's decision to fight the French fleet anchored in Aboukir Bay immediately. The lateness of the hour meant a night action in barely known and shoaling waters. The French fleet had been sighted by Captain Samuel Hood of the *Zealous* just over two hours before, at two thirty. Yet it is unlikely that Nelson hesitated very long over the decision, or that his captains were surprised by it. To sail into Aboukir Bay at this hour was a risk; but he had experience of the complexities of Mediterranean winds and land breezes, which often meant that the winds blew parallel to the shore; and he knew the outline of the bay and its shoals more certainly than historians have previously suspected.*

The long two-month search by Nelson for the fleet of French ships escorting the transports that had taken Napoleon's army to Egypt was over. Throughout the squadron the prospect of immediate action turned frustration into elation. Captain Sir James Saumarez in the *Orion* recorded that he and his officers felt: 'utterly hopeless, and out of spirits' when they heard the news, as they sat down to dinner, that the French fleet was not at Alexandria. An hour later, as the table cloth was being removed, the signal sighting the French fleet was reported: 'All sprang from their seats, and only staying to drink a *bumper* to our success, we were in a moment upon deck.'[4] There could not have been an action that night, however, had Nelson had anything less than total confidence in the ability of the officers and men in his ships. The signal to anchor by the stern could have been given only to ships with crews who were at a high pitch of efficiency and morale, with captains who were well briefed.† Anchoring by the stern, rather than by the bow, meant that the ship, running before the wind, would maintain its course, keeping the ships broadside to broadside with the French ships. Each would come to a halt as it sailed, rather than slowly swinging round into the wind to its bow anchor, during which time its vulnerable bows would be open to a withering French fire.[5] But even in the steady north-north-west breeze that blew the British ships into Aboukir Bay, stern anchoring was a complex operation.

When the signals were identified, every crew was galvanized into action, for those ships nearest the land were only an hour's sailing from the waiting French. The sweating crews had to unbend the hemp cable from the bow anchor. It was enormous and unwieldy; a 74-gun ship had a cable with a circumference of twenty-two inches and a total weight of over twenty tons. The crew ran it along one of the lower decks, pushed it through a stern gun port, passed it along the side of the ship, where it was supported at intervals by thin rope-yarn lashings, before making it fast to the same anchor at the bow of the ship. The rest of the bow cable had to be laid along the deck so that it ran out easily, and the end made fast around the

---

* It seems likely that a sketch of Aboukir Bay was taken from a French brig by Captain Thomas Troubridge of the *Culloden* and forwarded to Nelson by Captain Benjamin Hallowell shortly before the battle (Malcolmson, 'Aboukir', 292–7).

† Nelson had issued an order on 8 June on anchoring by the stern; the procedure had clearly been discussed in detail (Ross, 212–13, 227–8). The *Vanguard* used her heavy 'bower' cable, though most ships used their lighter 'stream', or 'sheet', cables (e.g., NMM, ADM/L/V/28; ADM/L/G/64; (UK)NA: PRO, ADM 52/3550).

mizzen mast.[6] Shorter ropes known as 'springs' were then attached to the cable so that the ship could be swung at an angle to the anchor cable to enable the guns to be trained at the anchored French ships.* The anchor and cable, thus prepared, had to bring a considerable floating mass, still pushed on by the wind, to an abrupt stop. The *Vanguard* was 168 feet long on the lower deck, had a carrying capacity of 1,600 tons and was ballasted with 349 tons of iron and shingle. There were 971 tons of equipment and stores, including the concentrated mass of the guns: the 32-pounder gun and its carriage weighed over three tons, the 18-pounders over two, and the total weight of all her guns was 187 tons. Crew, their sea chests and bedding came to another forty-five tons.[7] With such stresses on a wooden ship, the chances of damage to the rigging and equipment, and of injuries to the crew, were very high.

The timing of the operation had to be perfect. Each ship had to hold its fire and set all sail, in order to get into an attack position as quickly as possible. The topmen had to furl the sails, at speed, to help slow the ship; this would prevent over-straining or parting the stern cable. Only the most disciplined of crews could achieve such a very delicate manoeuvre; to do so 'within half-gun-shot distance' of the enemy was unprecedented.[8] Only when the sails were furled and the cables were in place could the British ships open fire. This nerveless performance by several hundred men on each ship was critical to the overwhelming success of the battle that lay ahead. How critical can be judged by the fate of the three British ships that bungled the operation: one was lucky and came to no harm; between them the other two had 100 men killed and 200 wounded.[9]

The rear-admiral who took this risk so readily was two months short of his fortieth birthday. Nelson was of medium height, with a thin frame and fair hair. His movements were rapid; he was, according to one younger officer, 'quick and active in everything he either said or did'. He had lost his arm over a year before at the landing in Tenerife and the sight in his right eye two years before that in Corsica. His drawn face reflected a long history of severe tropical illnesses as well as his driven personality. In sum, there was not much polish to him, as there was with so many naval officers at this time. Nelson had, concluded the same officer, 'not much either the appearance or the manner of a gentleman'.[10] There were traces of a Norfolk accent; another young officer noted that Nelson always called his captain,

---

* It is not clear how the crew managed to attach the spring to the cable, or at what point in the operation this was done. It can be assumed a spring was made ready on each side of the ship to run to a windlass in the bows.

Edward Berry, 'Ed'ard'.[11] He was exceedingly young to be in command of a squadron so far from home, and one with a responsibility of this magnitude. Indeed, because of his apparent inexperience, there had been much criticism of his appointment to the command by senior admirals, particularly by those who had been passed over.

Perhaps the most elusive aspect of Nelson's character to chart 200 years later is his quality of effortless leadership. He established a reputation for looking after his crews early in his career. No seaman could doubt his absolute physical courage, as he had recently gone to extreme lengths to demonstrate this: three times in the last eighteen months he had been in the thick of desperate hand-to-hand fighting, and had even boarded a Spanish ship of the line. Probably no flag officer had done this since Sir Edward Howard in 1513 in the reign of Henry VIII.[12] He was also fearless in situations when moral, rather than physical, courage was required. For many years he had demonstrated that he cared little for custom in an age when precedent was a powerful agent in government and society. A young officer, William Hotham, looking back many years later, remembered that 'He was perhaps more generally beloved by all ranks of people under him than any Officer in the Service, for he had in a great degree the valuable but rare quality of conciliating the most opposite tempers and forwarding the Public Service with unanimity amongst men not of themselves disposed to accord.' He admired Nelson's ability for 'sound judgement and an instant decision'.[13] Nelson's most remarkable characteristics in these nervous, pre-battle hours were his calmness and certainty.[14] Another young officer, William Layman, whose career was both made and then accidentally destroyed by Nelson,* also recalled that Nelson was

a most extraordinary man, possessing opposite points of character; little in little things, but by far the greatest man in great things he ever saw: that he had seen him petulant at trifles, and as cool and collected as a philosopher when surrounded by dangers, in which men of common minds, with closed countenances, would say, 'Ah! What is to be done?' It was a treat to see his animated and collected countenance in the heat of the action.[15]

Signals 53 and 54 were the prelude to the Battle of the Nile, which made Nelson's name known throughout Europe. He was fêted at home and

---

* Nelson persuaded Layman to withhold certain evidence at the court martial over the loss of Layman's ship. In turn, just before Trafalgar, Nelson promised to help him. Captain William Layman was never employed again and committed suicide in 1826 (Tracy, *Naval Chronicle*, II, 160).

abroad, and for the rest of his life experienced constant adulation, privately from Emma Hamilton or publicly from the crowds that gathered whenever he appeared. As his fame increased and the burdens of his commands grew heavier, the tensions in his character became more evident; yet, as Samuel Taylor Coleridge described admiringly, 'never was a commander so enthusiastically loved by men of all ranks, from the captain of the fleet to the youngest ship-boy. Hence too the unexampled harmony which reigned in the fleet, year after year, under circumstances that might well have undermined the patience of the best-balanced dispositions, much more of men with the impetuous character of British sailors.'[16] Nelson's achievements in battle are legendary, but what he achieved by decisions made in the quiet of his cabin and by his leadership of men in lesser-known dangers and difficult situations is no less remarkable. And he did this, in Coleridge's words, with a 'temper [which] was constitutionally irritable and uneven'.*

---

* Coleridge was later secretary to Sir Alexander Ball when governor of Malta, at a time when Ball had effectively left the navy and was prepared to talk freely.

I

Youth and Disappointment

1758–1793

I

Burnham Thorpe

September 1758–April 1771

I was born September 29th, 1758, in the Parsonage-house, was sent to the high-school at Norwich, and afterwards removed to North Walsham; from whence, on the disturbance with Spain relative to the Falkland Islands, I went to Sea . . .
    Rear-Admiral Lord Nelson, 'Sketch of My Life', 15 October 1799[1]

The north Norfolk coast is low and indeterminate, its shingle banks, creeks and salt marsh washed and shaped by strong tides. It is a place of great beauty, in the winter left to seabirds and seals and in the summer used by recreational sailors and visited by tourists. Today the sole port is Wells-next-the-Sea, navigable for small coasters and fishing boats at high tide, and then with local knowledge and a good chart; the channel heads northwards from the town quay for two miles, through marsh and mudflats, before the open sea is reached.

At the time of Nelson's birth in 1758 this coast presented a different and busier picture, for it formed the entrance to and exit from the countryside to the south, providing the only practical and economic way of transporting heavy goods in and out of north Norfolk. At the head of each creek was a long-established small port, at, from west to east, Thornham, Brancaster, Burnham, Wells, Blakeney and Cley-next-the-Sea. On the rising ground behind these ports, along the rivers that formed the creeks, were small market towns that gathered produce before export and distributed imported goods after their shipment by sea. Near the River Burn, to the south of Burnham Overy Staithe on the creek, is Burnham Market (sometimes called Burnham Westgate), and near the coast are the villages of Burnham Overy, Burnham Norton and Burnham Deepdale.

A little further inland, to the south and east of Burnham Market, is the village of Burnham Thorpe, Nelson's birthplace and his home for the first twelve years of his life. His father, Edmund Nelson, was the rector of the parish, as well as of two neighbouring defunct parishes, Burnham Ulph and Burnham Sutton. A mile to the east of the parsonage at Burnham Thorpe lay the boundary of the largest estate in Norfolk, Holkham, owned by Thomas Coke, a well-known Whig landowner and famed as one of the great eighteenth-century improvers of farming. Wells lies five miles to the east past the main gates of the estate. Nelson was born only two and a half miles from the thriving small port of Burnham Overy Staithe, which was 'navigable for vessels of 60 to 80 tons up to the Staithe, where the spring tides rise 9 or 10 feet, and where a considerable trade in coal and corn is carried on, as well as in oysters, of which there is an excellent bed in the offing, where 5 boats and 15 fishermen are regularly employed'.[2]

It is difficult today to imagine any sizeable vessel in these muddy creeks, yet many small, shallow-draughted craft, designed to sit easily on the mud when the tide was out, passed in and out of these harbours throughout the year. An illustration of a large vessel using one of these harbours is provided in 1801, coincidentally by a cousin of Nelson, who commanded the *Furnace*, a 76-foot long, 170-ton Royal Navy gun brig, with a draught of over eight feet. The *Furnace* was navigated into Blakeney on a high spring tide. The name of the captain of this gun brig, part of the fleet of small vessels in home waters guarding the shores against French invasion, was Lieutenant Maurice William Suckling. Suckling was an indifferent young officer, prone to drinking, who had inherited an estate in Suffolk. During the long months of boredom when nothing was happening, he allowed his crew 'to labour for the Gentlemen & Farmers in the neighbourhood of Blakeney', while he also lent seamen to local merchants to navigate their vessels in and out of the harbour. Bringing the vessel into the creek was, however, a misjudgement, for the gun brig was just too big for it: none of the spring tides rose high enough to float her out and she remained there for some months. While the ship was marooned on the mud, Suckling visited his estate in Suffolk and 'sometimes remained there more than a week', to the disgust of his fellow officers. He was unable to obey orders to bring his ship to sea and was court-martialled.* Suckling was dismissed his ship and left the navy.[3]

All these communities were dependent upon the sea. The light soils and low rainfall of north Norfolk favoured the growing of barley of high quality,

---

* Suckling produced a letter from Nelson testifying to his good character, which, 'in consideration of the high character given him by Lord Nelson', resulted in the lesser charge of negligence being proved, rather than disobedience of orders. Nelson concluded his letter of 8 Sept. 1801 to Suckling: 'Whatever fate awaits you I shall always feel myself your attach'd relation' ((UK)NA: PRO, ADM 1/5358).

used for brewing beer. During the eighteenth century the production and sale of this crop, and the malt that was extracted from it, continually increased owing to drainage improvements, liming and marling, with yields per acre increasing dramatically.[4] Most of it went to London, to supply the population that was growing prodigiously, but considerable amounts also went north to that other great centre on the east coast of England, Newcastle, from which these small ports received coal in return. This fuel was much needed in the winter in Norfolk, which had no spare wood to burn, when fires were needed to combat the intense cold of the winter north-easterly winds. Each year several thousand tons of barley went out of Wells and Burnham, and several thousand tons of coal came in.[5] Every necessity of life also came through these ports. With increasing frequency towards the end of the century, regular packet boats transported people and their goods.[6] Wine and tobacco came from London, as did grocery wares, soap and iron. Salt was imported from Spain, most of it via other, larger ports in England, particularly King's Lynn. In peacetime goods came directly from countries across the North Sea.[7] Dutch and occasionally French spoken by sailors, as well as the accents of Tyneside and London, could be heard on the quay of Burnham Overy Staithe. During Nelson's early years north Norfolk was also beginning to be accessible to the rest of the country by road. From 1750 the turnpikes had expanded quickly and had reached King's Lynn by 1770.[8] In 1778 another Norfolk clergyman, Parson Woodforde, recorded that relatives had taken no more than a day to travel the hundred miles in a post-chaise from London to his village just outside Norwich.[9]

The mid eighteenth century was a prosperous and innovative time for East Anglian agriculture. The population of Burnham Thorpe, a parish of 2,321 acres with a population in the region of 300, grew during the forty-six years in which Edmund Nelson was rector, with baptisms exceeding burials by seventy-five.[10] The village is recorded as having a market every Saturday.[11] Much of the land around the village was owned by Thomas Coke and farmed by tenant farmers, among whom Coke spread the new ideas of crop rotation. He was by no means, however, the only agricultural innovator; indeed, modern agricultural scholars are inclined to think that Coke's improvements were aesthetically driven and for the improvement of game.[12] Coke did not mix much with the middling sort, and his politics kept him away from the Tories of the county, of whom Edmund Nelson was one. The Nelson family knew the more modest Sir Mordaunt Martin of Burnham Hall in Burnham Market, 'the first to introduce mangel-wurzel and saintfoin into this county, where he greatly improved the growth of potatoes and other vegetables'.[13] Coke spent five years experimenting with potatoes, persuading his labourers, with difficulty, to follow his example. Hostility to the new crop was overcome later only by high prices of other crops caused by bad harvests or the French wars.[14]

The extensive Nelson family straddled the ranks of the English 'middle class', in the later eighteenth century a confusing, expanding and rapidly changing term.[15] Edmund Nelson, born at East Bradenham on 19 March 1722, with, in his own words, 'a weak and sickly constitution', was educated 'at a school in the County' before going to Caius College, Cambridge. His father, also called Edmund, had been to Eton, the provosts and fellows of which 'gave him the Vicarage of Sporle'. The older Edmund's father-in-law, John Bland, lived in Cambridge and 'began the world with very little, but by industry in Trade . . . Acquired Considerable fortune'; Bland purchased for his son-in-law 'the next presentation and perpetual advowson of Hilborow in Norfolk in 1735'.[16] Edmund, Nelson's father, was ordained in 1745 and married Catherine Suckling, three years younger than him, in May 1749. The younger Edmund could provide no money, for on his father's death at Hilborough in 1747 he had to give up all the profit from the living at Hilborough to pay his father's debts. Later in 1749 the newly married couple 'went to housekeeping at Swaffham', then lived in a 'hired house at Sporle', coming to the living of Burnham Thorpe in November 1755, presented through the Suckling family.[17]

The couple had eleven children, though the first two, Edmund and Horatio, died in infancy in 1750 and 1751 at Hilborow. George, the tenth to be born, also died very young in 1766. Horace (he did not call himself Horatio until 1777) had two elder brothers: Maurice, born in 1753, and William, born in 1757, both of whom have long and continuing parts in his life. Horace Nelson was born on 29 September 1758. Two more brothers died as young men: Edmund was born in 1762 and died in December 1789 of consumption. Suckling Nelson, who was apprenticed to a draper in Beccles, set up in the trade but failed; he eventually went into the Church and succeeded his father at Burnham Thorpe, dying in 1799. Horace had one elder sister, Susannah, born in 1755, and two younger sisters, Anne and Katherine ('Kitty'), born in 1760 and 1767 respectively. The two eldest were apprenticed at eighteen, Susannah to a milliner in Bath and Anne to a lace warehouse in London.[18] Horace's mother died at the age of forty-two, leaving the impractical Edmund with eight children.

Edmund Nelson was a man of middling means, by no means the impoverished country parson that he is often said to be. He was dependent on the tithes paid by his prospering parishioners. With the living came a 'glebe', an area of land of twenty-nine acres in the village, on which he grew corn and vegetables. His wife left him money, including the considerable sum of £908.6s.8d. in 'Old South Sea Annuities', which gave him a useful sum from annual interest, probably at 4 per cent.[19] He was able to employ four servants, while in his later years his income allowed him to go to Bath for long periods to escape the cold Norfolk winters

Of his eleven children, seven died before Horace; only William, Susannah and Kitty were to outlive him. In spite of the relative prosperity of north Norfolk, away from the crowded, unhealthy towns, death in the middle of the eighteenth century was still random and sudden. Horace came into the world at a dangerous time for young children. As was the custom, he was christened privately a week after he was born, in case he died, and publicly five weeks later on 15 November 1758. As a parson's son he would be familiar with the ritual of death, carefully recorded in the Burnham Thorpe parish records. In his first decade infant deaths averaged over four a year; in 1769 seven infants died. Infant deaths as a proportion of all baptisms in the 1760s and early 1770s were 42 per cent; almost every other child born in the mid century did not survive infancy. Catherine Nelson's first child lived only two days, her second less than four months and George, the tenth, for six months.[20] During Nelson's lifetime this rate dropped dramatically, and by the end of the century only one child in Burnham Thorpe died for every ten born.[21]

It would be wrong, however, to paint a picture of an overall rise in prosperity, for the living standards of farm labourers in Norfolk, as well as in those counties further from London, were falling. The employment of labourers became increasingly short term and casual, often spread thinly among the poor in order to keep them from claiming on the poor rate, always a concern of landowners and farmers.[22] They suffered badly when prices rose at the onset of war, a fact that worried Nelson in the early 1790s.[23] In 1801 the inhabitants of Blakeney were keen that Lieutenant Maurice Suckling kept his ship there, for they held 'themselves indebted to the position of the *Furnace* for these two years past for keeping down a spirit of revolt occasioned by the high price of provisions'.[24] Times of dearth weakened the sick and old. In 1796, for instance, a time of scarcity, thirteen people died at Burnham Thorpe. Other dangers included malaria, 'the ague', which was common, particularly where mosquitoes flourished in wet and marshy areas, of which there were several in Burnham Thorpe near the River Burn, which flows near the site of the rectory. In the early summer of 1779 in the parish of Weston Longeville near Norwich, some twenty-five miles from Burnham Thorpe, Parson Woodforde applied rough and ready

7

measures when his boy 'had another touch of the Ague': 'I gave him a dram of gin at the beginning of the fit and pushed him headlong into one of my Ponds and ordered him to bed immediately, and he was better after it and had nothing of the cold fit after it, but was very hot . . .' Four years later the doctor administered quinine bark to Woodforde's maid.[25] Smallpox was common and menacing, though by the 1790s it was fought with inoculation, itself dangerous in the early days of the treatment.[26] Parish registers all over England carry evidence of rapid and abrupt mortality. The randomness of death was a fact of life.

What social advantages the Nelson children possessed came from their mother. She was the great-niece of Sir Robert Walpole, the first prime minister, a fact of little political consequence in England in the 1760s, but which provided a clear social niche in Norfolk. She was the daughter of Dr Maurice Suckling, the rector of Barsham in Suffolk, who had died in 1729 when she was young. She had two successful, self-made brothers, Maurice and William Suckling, both of whom helped Nelson at critical times in his career. William was appointed as a clerk in the Excise and by 1762 he was assistant to the collector for the department of Inward Customs, based in the Customs House in London. Inward Customs had the considerable task of collecting the duties on tens of thousands of tons of incoming goods in the Port of London, the Customs House was crowded and busy at all times. By 1776 William had risen to deputy collector of Inward Customs. As the 'Collector-Inwards' was a senior peer who had no duties beyond collecting a sizeable sinecure, the business was the responsibility of the deputy collector; through his department passed cash, as well as deposits and bonds representing enormous sums of money, critical to the successful financing of the government. He was, effectively, the equivalent of a permanent under-secretary today, at the head of a large department of government. Suckling also had the job of 'Computer of Unrated Duties' on East India Company goods.[27] William worked his way up to the top of his profession, living in a substantial house in rural Kentish Town on the outskirts of London. Unexciting and bureaucratic though his career may seem, it enabled him to assist Nelson at the time of the American Revolutionary War. The most important early help, however, came from William's elder brother, Captain Maurice Suckling, RN, who planned and organized Horace's first eight years in the navy.*[28]

---

* The Nelson family had some previous connections with the navy. One of Edmund Nelson's cousins, William, was educated at Eton 'but proving Irregular was sent to sea under Adm. Geary, and died'. One of Edmund's brothers had married a relation of Admiral Lord Shuldham (RNM MS 1957/85, fols. 3, 7). Sir Robert Walpole's brother Galfridus was a captain of 1706,

Born in 1726, Maurice Suckling went to sea at the outbreak of the 1739–48 War with Spain, 'under the patronage of Sir Rob. Walpole his great uncle', as Edmund Nelson wrote in his history of the family.[29] Suckling had a faultless, rather than a brilliant, career. He was made post-captain at the start of the Seven Years War, spending the years up to 1760 on the Jamaica Station in command of the 60-gun *Dreadnought*. He saw little action but survived the climate. He returned with prize money in 1760, coming ashore on half-pay at the end of the war in 1763, having caught the eye of Admiral Lord Hawke. For seven years of peace he stayed at his home at Woodton in Suffolk, forty miles south-east of Burnham Thorpe.[30] In 1760 he married his cousin, the Honourable Mary Walpole, but there were no children and she died in 1764. This was critically important for Edmund's children, for they inherited his money when he died in 1778. He left Horace's three sisters £1,000 each and each of the brothers £50. The rest went to his own brother, William Suckling.

As a result, Horace's sisters were soon to move up the social and financial scale, (although Anne died young and unmarried in November 1784). In 1780 Susannah married a Wells merchant, Thomas Bolton, who traded in corn, malt and coal. In September 1781 he left for Ostend, followed by his wife a few months later, with assistance from the young Edmund Nelson; but the venture seems not to have been a success and the Boltons returned in February 1783, settling in Norwich. Bolton later had continual money problems. Kitty, the youngest, married George Matcham, a prosperous East India merchant; they lived at Barton Hall near by for a time and then moved away from Norfolk.[31] Their marriage was a happy and successful one.

The rest of the Nelson family were colourless and ordinary. William was seemingly stolid and large, while Maurice was honest, dull and disorganized.[32] Of the brothers, Horace was clearly the lively one. His early years were spent in the village, a community that would have given him the foundation for the easy relationships he was to have with seamen in his later career. At the age of ten he went to the Grammar School in Norwich and a year later to Sir John Paston's School in North Walsham. A school-fellow recalled many years later: 'Nor do I forget that we were under the lash of Classic Jones, as arrant a Welshman as Rees-ap-Griffith, and as keen a flogger as Merciless Busby of Birch-loving Memory. Your Lordship was in the Second Class when I was in the First. Your station was against

one-time treasurer of Greenwich Hospital and an MP, who died in 1726. Like Nelson after him, he too lost his right arm in action and continued to serve for some years after his arm had healed (Charnock, *Biographia Navalis*, III, 376).

the wall between the parlour door and the chimney.'[33] He learnt French – unsuccessfully – from a master named Jemmy Moisson. His later letters are sprinkled with literary and classical references, particularly from Shakespeare.

Nelson wrote almost nothing of his early years, nor did anyone else record family life. His silence has encouraged authors to repeat undocumented and unlikely stories of his childhood, illustrating early courage and a sense of honour. Lacking proper evidence, biographers have speculated on Horace's psychological development in the 1760s on the basis of his behaviour in later years. A long-held view, repeated in a recent biography, has attributed the pattern of his relationship with women to the early death of his mother. He made only two references to his mother in hundreds of extant letters, both written when he was at sea, lonely during his final command of the Mediterranean fleet. One was an offhand, apologetic remark at the end of a letter in 1803, when there had been some discussion of obtaining intelligence from dissident Frenchmen: 'I would not,' he wrote to a diplomat, 'upon any consideration, have a Frenchman in the Fleet, except as a prisoner. I put no confidence in them . . . Forgive me; but my mother hated the French.' The other was to an old Burnham friend: 'the thought of my mother brings a tear to my eye.'[34] He kept her memory and her link with him deep within him.

It has also been suggested that Nelson's search for approval and recognition has its roots in his membership of a large family, in which he had to fight for attention. His patience in later years with William Nelson, a grasping man whose ambition outran his abilities, and who behaved appallingly for almost all his life, has also been attributed to the young Nelson's relationship with an older brother.[35] This speculation upon the dynamics of a large family does little to account for William Nelson's later selfishness, ambition or greed, or his disdain for all his brothers except Horace, or how the dull Maurice was honourable and respected.[36] It remains a mystery how Nelson acquired such spectacular physical courage, continual aggression and ruthlessness, and, above all, extraordinary self-belief. These qualities did not come from Edmund Nelson. Nelson's father was learned and whimsical but doubting, negative and critical. Never in the best of health, he nevertheless lived to a great age. Judging by his letters to Nelson in the 1790s when Nelson's naval career was flourishing, praise did not come easily from him. Nelson was loyal and protective towards his father, but seems not to have been influenced by him. A succession of naval officers during his early career was to be much more influential in shaping his character. The first of these was his uncle Maurice Suckling. On

17 November 1770, at the beginning of the Falklands Islands crisis, Suckling was given command of a 64-gun ship, the *Raisonable*. It was a natural opportunity for the third son of a country parson to go with his uncle.

Nelson's later rise to fortune caused him to mask his provincial origins. In his 'Sketch of My Life', which he wrote for the *Naval Chronicle* when he was forty-one, he summarized his life in Burnham Thorpe in sixty words. As he saw it, his life began when he went to sea at the age of twelve.

2

The Navy in 1771

Recollect that you must be a Seaman to be an Officer: and also that
you cannot be a good Officer without being a Gentleman.
Vice-Admiral Lord Nelson to Midshipman Charles Connor, c. 1803[1]

Several landmarks in the history of the Royal Navy fell in the early months of 1771. In January Lord Hawke, the most successful admiral of the Seven Years War and since 1766 the first lord of the Admiralty, had resigned his post because of ill health. The first lord was the political head of the navy, with a seat in the cabinet, and he headed the Board of Admiralty. Lord Sandwich now succeeded Lord Hawke and was to be in office for the next twelve, controversial years. But these months were dominated by the mobilization of the navy against Spain over the issue of sovereignty of the Falkland Islands in the southern Atlantic. Since the end of the Seven Years War the navies of France and Spain had been rebuilding at a rapid rate for some distant time when they hoped to retake territories from over-mighty England. In 1771, however, they were far from ready, and in the face of a determined British government France would not support the weaker Spain in the confrontation with Britain. The islands were potentially an important staging post on the route around Cape Horn to the Pacific. By late January the Spanish government had effectively climbed down, although the mobilization of the fleet was still proceeding. One month later the army was reduced to its peacetime establishment, but the arming and refitting of the fleet continued until formal agreement was reached between Britain and Spain in mid April.[2] The gateway to the Pacific had been secured. As if to underline the importance of this confrontation, on 16 July 1771 Captain James Cook's ship, the *Endeavour*, moored in Gallion's Reach in the Thames, having completed its first momentous voyage, redrawing the map of the Pacific and signalling the redefinition of the navy's commitments for the next 200 years.[3]

The Royal Navy had been growing for a number of years, for it had new conquests to defend at the end of the Seven Years War in 1763. Britain had gained control of North America and India, in addition to four valuable West Indies sugar islands, at the expense of France. Spain made over Florida and conceded the right of English settlers to cut logwood in Honduras. In spite of the great gains, the British were wary for the rest of the 1760s. The early-eighteenth-century policy of stationing cruising ships on foreign stations continued: they watched the activities of France, especially in India; there were also concerns over Russia and Sweden.[4] Warships were expanding in size and numbers; dockyards, victualling and ordnance facilities were being enlarged.[5] In 1771 the navy had 126 ships of the line at its disposal, measured at 350,000 tons carrying capacity, although their condition and thus their effectiveness as a fighting unit was a political issue then and remains an historical debating point today. The British government had also raised taxes in the American colonies to pay for the army established there; the discontent that this caused was soon to have great consequences. Already by the early 1770s the prime minister, Lord North, was imposing financial stringency. The Seven Years War had been costly. He faced pressure in the cabinet from Lord Sandwich, who had an increasing naval establishment to maintain.

The Board of Admiralty was at the apex of the navy. It was the job of this board, composed of politicians and serving officers, to translate the strategic wishes of the cabinet into reality. Advised by the professionals in the Navy Board, they issued the regulations, ordered ships to be built and decided which ones would go to which parts of the world. Above all, the first lord appointed and promoted the officers of the navy, and every person who held the post during Nelson's lifetime was embarrassed by the pressure of applicants. Competition was strong for every officer place in every ship, and would become more intense by the end of the century. Far more boys wanted a naval career, and with it the possibility of prize money, than there were positions. Many midshipmen went to sea and came ashore soon after, when they could see no way ahead, particularly at the end of a war when the number of ships in commission decreased sharply. Many who rose to great offices of state, whose careers would be intertwined with Nelson's – such as Sir George Rose, who became senior secretary of the Treasury or Sir Evan Nepean, secretary of the Board of Admiralty – had started their careers in the navy and had then dropped out. Timing was everything: promotion hardly occurred outside war or mobilizations. 'In the opening years of a war there was a severe shortage of officers of all ranks, and promotion was rapid ... The ideal was to be born about twenty years before the outbreak of a major war, to contrive (in spite of the small number of H. M. Ships in commission) to get the qualifying sea time in peacetime, and to pass for Lieutenant just as war broke out – ready to profit from the acute shortage of officers of all ranks.'[6] This is exactly what Nelson did, reaching senior naval rank at just the right moment.*

Although the sea officer saw himself as a gentleman, he was seen by other parts of society as 'on the margins of gentility'. Army officers purchased their commissions, ensuring that the rich and aristocratic alone could join the fashionable regiments: only in the artillery and engineers was entry open to talent. Similarly, the sea officer belonged to a 'skilled, semi-bourgeois profession'.[7] Knowledge of seamanship and navigation had to come before social respectability. The way to promotion was, as in the rest of British eighteenth-century life, by means of patronage and interest: a senior officer brought on younger officers, often connected to their senior by family or through professional connections. Throughout the navy these very loose groups of officers were constantly changing from ship to ship and from commission to commission. 'Any settled ship's company tended to become a cohesive unit, in effect the following of her captain, and the connections thus established lasted, in many cases, throughout the professional lives of patron and follower.'[8] Inevitably, politics and political favours became caught up in the navy's appointments and promotions, but patronage within the service was largely controlled by officers who knew that if they appointed a favoured aristocratic duffer, he would be found out sooner or later; and thus professional skill and potential of a young officer counted for a great deal within the navy. Political interference in appointments was fended off to a remarkable degree. Much has been written about the political corruption of Lord Sandwich, but his appointment books, kept from 1771 to 1782, demonstrate that ability was a prerequisite for career advancement. For instance, one of Nelson's future fellow officers (and no friend to him), Robert Calder, was recommended by 'Lord Despenser' and on another occasion by 'Lord Bute', and Archibald Dickson was supported 'by Lord Marchmont'; but these are outnumbered by examples such as Gabriel Bray, who was recommended only by 'His father in Deal'.[9] In total only a fifth of captains 'made post' had influential sponsors outside the navy or kinsmen within it.[10] The first lord had frustrated many aristocratic applicants, which, as a result, added to his numerous political

---

* Rodger's analysis of 10 per cent of all officers, 1690–1815, shows that the best time to have been promoted lieutenant in the whole of the eighteenth century was the 1770s. Between 1770 and 1774 35 per cent of lieutenants made flag rank; it was a unique period.

enemies.* It was no better for his successors. Lord Howe, first lord in the 1780s, assured the House of Lords 'that patronage was not so desirable as might be imagined, and that he was sure, out of twenty candidates, for an appointment, to disappoint nineteen, and was by no means certain of pleasing the twentieth'.[11]

As we shall see, Nelson navigated his way through the navy of the 1770s and 1780s successfully, partly through luck but mostly through Maurice Suckling's advice and influence. The young man added to this early advantage through observing and learning from some good officers, chosen by Suckling. He was not alone in entering the navy at the age of twelve, for the earlier a midshipman started, the quicker he would go up the ladder. The long delay in promotion to flag rank was already evident by the middle of the eighteenth century. Pressure on parents to enter their sons early in order to advance them to captain was very real. To be an admiral demanded early captaincy, and there was little chance that a boy would make admiral at an active age unless he had reached post-captain in his twenties.† Only a handful of officers went up the ladder faster than Nelson, who was not yet twenty-one when he was made post-captain.

The character and quality of midshipmen were closely observed within the confines of a ship of war by officers and men alike, and they were at the beck and call of the lieutenants. William Falconer's *The Midshipman*, written in the 1760s, describes the life well: 'Hark! Yonder voice the MID to DUTY calls! . . . And damns the power allowed to a white lapel.'[12] There were some obvious requirements, among them willingness to take responsibility, physical courage when going aloft or taking charge of ships' boats in high winds, sufficient intelligence to grasp navigational principles and to pass the lieutenant's exam. Another essential was the ability to mix well within a midshipmen's mess, of which there would be several, usually situated down in the orlop deck, just above the hold. Seniority counted for a good deal even within a mess, and some organization was needed since there were expenses involved, which could be a source of friction.[13] It was a tough life at an early age, but one that was far from the traditional picture of disorder, quarrelling and skylarking drawn by John Masefield a hundred

---

* Rodger's analysis finds that of 1,812 qualified lieutenants who applied for commissions, 762 succeeded. Of the 323 backed by noblemen, 123 (38 per cent) were successful, as were 195 out of 440 (44 per cent) of those without aristocratic backers or influential officers. Of 923 applications on behalf of post-captains for promotion, only 203 came with powerful patrons. There is no appointment analysis for 1779.

† Nelson's later opinion that this was too young was recorded in the rollicking memoirs of George Parsons (*Reminiscences*, 247).

years ago, a view that has dominated the idea of the eighteenth-century navy until recent years.[14]

From their earliest days on board, midshipmen took part in the governance of the ship and their link through the lieutenants to the captain was a personal one. As a contemporary manual put it: 'The first object of every captain in His Majesty's navy on his appointment to a ship must be to have those officers with him whose dispositions he is acquainted with, and upon whose abilities and attention his character, comfort and happiness are, in great measure dependant.'[15] In larger vessels, the 'Divisional' system had developed in mid century, as ships became much larger and crews more numerous. Petty officers and seamen were divided into divisions, 'subdivided into squads with a midshipman appointed to each, who are respectively to be responsible for the good order and discipline of the men entrusted to their care'.[16] It was invaluable training for later responsibility. When Lord Howe was choosing his midshipmen in 1792, he wrote to his flag captain, Sir Roger Curtis, that he wanted those who had been with him before so that they had become 'a little accustomed to our peculiarities'; and Howe had plenty of those.[17] The midshipman's importance and role were emphasized by one captain who made a case to keep his together, bound in personal loyalty to him, as 'the discipline of the ship cannot be so strictly kept up as they form a very necessary part of the system of organisation in a man of war.'[18] Cuthbert Collingwood, Nelson's lifelong friend, was an innovator where training was concerned and made his midshipmen 'mess with the common men, where we lived with them for three months, performing all the offices of the ship boys such as cooking the victuals'. Indignant at first, one young midshipman, Jeffery Raigersfeld, saw the wisdom of this unusual order: 'And I am very glad I was so placed, as it gave me a great insight into the character of the seamen.'[19]

Patience and good humour were needed in a sea officer from an early age to deal with the heavily bureaucratic nature of naval life. His life was governed by *Regulations and Instructions Relating to His Majesty's Service at Sea*, first published in 1731 and frequently revised thereafter; they were otherwise known as the 'General Printed Instructions'. Through this exacting document the Admiralty imposed its discipline upon commissioned officers. The ultimate bureaucratic weapon was the court martial, but there were many lesser ways of guarding against fraud and slackness. Accounts had to be passed and logs had to be completed and submitted before pay was advanced. As in every large bureaucracy, opportunities existed to play the rules. For instance, when Nelson's brother William went to sea with him to the West Indies as chaplain in 1784, Nelson tried to have him paid for his duty on the ship after William had returned home. Technically, he argued, the chaplain was still appointed to the ship. Over a year later Nelson sent a note to the Navy Office, which was responsible for pay, certifying that William had served as chaplain to date, 'during which time he regularly performed divine service except when he was absent upon leave'. This was true, but William's 'absence on leave' comprised most of the commission. Two years later, when Nelson returned to London, William had still not been paid for his absent time. The navy had closed the loophole. Nelson wrote to his brother: 'I have this day been to the Navy Office about it, & have seen the order of the Admiralty against paying any chaplain who's bore of a Ships Book if he is absent from her.'[20]

In addition to the rules governing their own behaviour, sea officers were subject to those of other bureaucracies. They had a vital role to play when ships were being fitted for sea and so had to deal with the dockyards that built and maintained their ships. These, together with the industries and contractors supporting them, constituted the largest industrial organization in England, employing many thousands of shipwrights and other workers, all administered by the Navy Board in London. At the head of the board, made up of professional shipwrights and civil servants, was a naval captain, the comptroller. The organization extended beyond Britain, for the board was responsible for more yards overseas. Before he was thirty Nelson had visited those at Gibraltar, Halifax in Nova Scotia, English Harbour in Antigua and Port Royal in Jamaica, as well as the East India Company's dockyard in Bombay. As lieutenant and captain, he also had a detailed knowledge of the Victualling Board and its strict rules and accounts, through which men and officers were fed, even though each ship had a purser to oversee the detailed administration of provisioning. As a young officer during wartime, he did his share of press-ganging men too and would have known something of the laws surrounding it. Finally, an officer needed considerable knowledge of gunnery, and of the regulations of the Ordnance Board that contracted for the thousands of guns used by the navy.

An ambitious sea officer needed to acquire a knowledge of many things, in addition to a familiarity with the systems. One was the requisite social graces. Nelson's advice to the father of one of his midshipmen was 'Dancing is an accomplishment that probably a Sea Officer may require. You will see almost the necessity of it, when employed in Foreign Countries.' In the same letter he wrote 'French is absolutely necessary.'[21] Nelson himself, in spite of one major effort, failed to achieve a mastery of the language. Finally, there was the need for good health. This Nelson seldom had, a weakness inherited, perhaps, from his father. His susceptibility to disease, in particular the malaria that revisited him repeatedly in his career, influenced his path through the navy.

Nelson did, however, have the great advantage of serving almost entirely in small ships as a midshipman and young officer. In the sixteen years of continuous service before the start of the American Revolutionary War, he spent only twenty-one months in ships of fifty guns or over.[22] This kept him out of the factions that built up from time to time in the officer corps, but particularly during the American Revolutionary War. Had he been appointed as, say, a lieutenant in a ship of the line in the Channel fleet during these years, he would inevitably have been drawn into the political and professional feuds that in some cases lasted the length of a career. Since his progress was so rapid, he was never in a mess or a wardroom long enough to get drawn into personal or group conflicts; before his first command, he had served in nine ships, well above average. Serving in smaller ships also gave more opportunities for initiative, for learning the art of getting the best sailing performance out of a ship by adjustments to the ballasting or rigging and for gaining experience, at an early age, of the complex task of running a successful ship of any size.

The firmest guide for the young officer was, however, the idea of 'Honour'. One contemporary definition of the word was 'The Desire of Fame, or the Applause of Men, directed to the end of public Happiness', and this driven quality certainly applied to Nelson.[23] But 'honour' conveyed many meanings. First, that the word or promise of an officer should be followed to the letter. Second, that an acknowledged standard of physical and moral courage existed, from which there could be no deviation. From this it followed, for example, that a ship stand and fight an enemy of equal weight and guns. A sense of honour crossed national boundaries and, though it was to change later, it often governed hostilities. Honour allowed no second chance. In 1763, for instance, a marine lieutenant was dismissed the service for 'Allowing himself to be kicked out of a coffee house' at Portsmouth.[24] One senior admiral made a delicate analogy: 'The honour of an officer may be compared to the chastity of a woman, and when once wounded can never be recovered.'[25]

Its code, however, provided support for a sea officer to see him through difficult and frightening moments. 'An officer needed a powerful moral force to steel himself in the face of death, and he found it in the code of honour.'[26] The code led to occasional duels between officers. In the 1780s, when Nelson was commanding the *Boreas*, two of his midshipmen fought a duel. According to the law, had one of them died, the other would have hanged, although the Admiralty was always reluctant to punish those who were protecting their honour. It would not, however, have reflected well on the commanding officer.

Yet honour often sat uneasily with the prospect of prize money, the system by which the officers and crew of a warship would share the value of a captured enemy warship or merchant ship. The case for prize money was brought before the nearest vice-admiralty court, although complicated or very valuable cases usually were heard, many months later, in the main vice-admiralty court in London. These courts, intepreting the great body of Admiralty law, went through the process of 'condemning' a prize – that is, deciding whether a captured ship was a lawful prize and, if it was so proved, awarding the captors a proportion of the value of the captured ship and cargo. Not only were there disputes with owners over prizes, but the system also generated friction between officers and their crews. Sometimes a prize was taken by more than one ship, or a different ship, or other ships were in sight, enabling them to argue that they were in part responsible for taking the vessel. A captain would get a quarter, the admiral in command of the station would receive one eighth; while more junior officers and crew received their share on a diminishing scale.[27] An eighteenth-century sea officer was almost invariably faced with decisions which determined whether he would gain honour or prizes. Very often these priorities conflicted. For instance, in blockading a French port, a captain might place his ship off a point that he knew was frequented by enemy merchant shipping, instead of taking a forward position to watch the enemy fleet. To contemporaries, it was clear what was meant by a successful frigate captain: it was not the man who kept his station to prevent enemy warships from sailing, thus meeting British strategic aims; rather, it was the one who accumulated the most prize money.[28]

Without this lure of sudden fortune, the parents of young midshipmen would scarcely have fought so hard to get their sons into the navy. Nelson was in no way immune from prize-money ambitions in his early career, though several biographers have attempted to emphasize his disinterest.[29] In his early career Nelson was quite clearly prepared to take risks to his reputation for these rewards. When he captained the *Albemarle* in the middle of the American Revolutionary War, he just missed his chance to go to the East Indies, a station well known for enriching sea officers, through an accident to the ship. To have gone there, he wrote ruefully to his brother William, 'I should have liked exceedingly'.[30] He tried again to get appointed there just before the beginning of the French Revolutionary War in 1793.[31] What the East Indies Station meant to some sea officers is best summarized by one of Nelson's mentors and patrons, Admiral Lord Hood, who wrote in 1784 that he had refused the command of the East Indies Station because 'I should run a great risk of losing that character, which has cost me forty years to obtain, and besides, had I lived, I must have returned poorer than when I went out, unless I did one of two things, either connive at trade in the King's ships, or plunder government by contracts, neither of which I could bring myself to do.'[32] By contrast, Admiral Sir Edward Hughes – commander-in-chief in India before and during the American Revolutionary War, under whom Nelson served when a midshipman – became immensely rich from prize money, freight money and East India Company presents, and had no such scruples.

The relationship between money and honour was complex in another way. Prize money translated into status when an officer was back on shore, enabling him to become a gentleman, a member of an elite. Officers themselves drew a particular distinction between fighting officers and those responsible for administration, even though some of the latter, including the comptroller of the navy, were themselves sea officers. This jealousy rarely went beyond occasional abusive behaviour by young officers, but it led to some difficult situations. In 1773, when the king reviewed the fleet at Spithead for the first time, a great row erupted between the captains of the twenty-three ships present and the Navy Board over precedence. The captains wrote to the Admiralty Board: 'The Line of March established for the reception of the King having been taken into consideration, they are unanimously of opinion, That it is highly derogatory to the Honour of their Corps that the Navy Board shall take precedence of any of the Captains in the said Line.' Sea officers might have been a broad social group, but there were strong feelings about who was senior.* One of the twenty-three captains who signed this letter was Maurice Suckling of the *Triumph*. When a young captain, Nelson was particularly sensitive to his status as a sea officer, and the issue of seniority with administrators arose several times in his career, particularly in the 1780s; it is significant that he kept a copy of the 1773 captains' letter.[33]

This antagonism between officers and administrators was never so marked as the bitter rivalry between 'the pen and the sword' that so damaged the French Navy.[34] A major problem encountered by the aristocratic French fighting officer and those responsible for shore-side administration was that there were very few links between them. British sea officers,

---

* Nelson would have been present had he not gone with the Arctic Expedition in early 1773. See Chapter 6.

on the other hand, developed many. Nelson, for instance, had two such connections. The first was his uncle, Captain Maurice Suckling, who, after his career at sea, was made comptroller of the Navy Board in 1775. Judging from his performance in office, there is no reason to imagine that Maurice Suckling was anything other than very able.[35] The other was Nelson's brother Maurice, who started his career in the Audit Office in the Excise in 1768, his place secured by William Suckling. When Maurice Suckling became comptroller, he put forward young Maurice Nelson for a purser's post and in Lord Sandwich's appointment book, in his lordship's own hand, is a note against Maurice's name: 'Appointed to the *Swift*.'[36] For some reason, Maurice never went to sea. Instead, on 1 November 1775 Captain Suckling appointed him to the Navy Office as one of the clerks in the Office for Bills and Accounts.* Maurice did not have to pay the usual premium for the office, but Suckling 'gave him to understand that he must consider it as a gift of two hundred pounds'.[37] The young clerk's particular tasks were to examine the expenses of sea officers engaged in impressing seamen and their contingency accounts, to calculate the interest on navy bills and to make up the accounts called for by Parliament. He attended at the office from '10 or 11 until the business of the day is finished' and earned £60 a year as salary and another £68 in fees and gratuities. It was a dull, narrow life that would have suited neither Horace nor Horatio Nelson.

Underpinning the naval effort were the increasing national wealth and population; these had grown since the beginning of the century and would continue to do so at a faster rate for the rest of Nelson's lifetime. The basis of the wealth was Britain's capacity to trade, which was interdependent with the navy and provided the all-important reserve of skilled seamen. This wealth was taxed indirectly through Customs and Excise and was generally well administered, which in turn gave the government such solid credit that it could borrow when it liked.[38] By contrast, the French and Spanish governments experienced continual credit crises through the eighteenth century. No other country could match the sophistication and speed of the credit machinery available to government from the City of London. A system of redeemable navy bills enabled the Navy Board to buy the best-quality timber, hemp and pitch in the Baltic. Admirals and captains on foreign stations thousands of miles from London purchased stores or

---

* Maurice managed to do both the Excise and Navy Office jobs concurrently until 1779, when, according to the Commission on Fees, 'he was given to understand that the increase of Business, would in future require a more constant attendance, [so] he found it necessary to resign his Place in the Excise' (NMM, CAD/D/11).

provisions on bills drawn on London. One contemporary naval historian exulted: 'That our trade is the Mother and Nurse of our Seamen; Our Seamen the Life of our Fleet; And our Fleet the Security and Protection of our Trade: And that both together are the WEALTH, STRENGTH, and GLORY OF GREAT BRITAIN.'[39]

The reserve of seamen led to a great advantage over France and Spain, rooted in the consistently increasing number of British merchant ships throughout the eighteenth century. All trades expanded in peacetime, especially the 'coasting' trade around British and European waters, as well as in the East and West Indies. The Newfoundland fishing fleets also flourished. At the peak of the American Revolutionary War, of a total of 151,090 seamen, 93,000 were in the navy.[40] France and Spain, both of which ran systems of registers rather than impressing seamen, could not match these manning levels. The total of French seamen for the American Revolutionary War has been calculated at between 62,000 and 64,000.[41] For the same period the Spanish register of seamen contained 47,000 names.[42] Brutal though the British system of impressment was, it brought new young men rapidly into seafaring at the beginning of every war and over time even produced a surplus of seamen. One historian has concluded that 'In the long run, therefore, it seems that war itself was Britain's principal "nursery of seamen", a training ground for thousands of landsmen and boys drafted into the maritime services during hostilities.'[43]

Nevertheless, in the 1770s and 1780s the French Navy enjoyed something of a golden age – until it was starved of funds by a bankrupt government and handicapped by the chaos of the revolution. In the 1760s and 1770s the French government, never consistent with its financial support for its navy, gave it the resources it needed. From the beginning of the American Revolutionary War in 1775 the British Navy was out-built, and in subsequent summer campaigns, particularly in 1779 and 1780, its ships of the line were badly outnumbered in the Channel. In these years the French achieved their most spectacular eighteenth-century strategic success when they denied the British Navy the capacity to sustain British forces in North America, leading to their defeat by Washington and the loss of the American colonies. France enjoyed some geopolitical superiority too, for, having north, south and west coasts, it was in a position to dominate the Atlantic as well as the Mediterranean. The French invariably received news and orders in the West Indies before their British counterparts, who had much further to sail into the prevailing south-westerly winds down the Channel. For instance, when Nelson was in the West Indies at the beginning of the

American Revolutionary War, two British frigates were surprised by a sudden French attack because the British captain had no knowledge of the French declaration of war.[44]

Against these advantages, France, in spite of its immense forests, still depended upon naval stores from the Baltic, which the British were often able to intercept in the Strait of Dover. A foundation of British policy and strategy in wartime was to deny the enemy access to Baltic timber, hemp and iron. Britain also had the benefit of better-protected harbours on its south coast, which, with the fierce Channel tides, provided a good basis to counter French invasion attempts. Britain possessed more effective governmental and financial advantages. It had in the Admiralty and Navy Board a more integrated and efficient naval administration. The system of victualling its seamen was cheaper and provided better-quality provisions than its French counterpart.

British warships and crews were employed on active sea service for far longer periods than the French from the Seven Years War onwards. Fleets and squadrons spent extended periods at sea, cruising and escorting convoys, blockading the enemy and performing the many tasks to maintain superiority at sea. In general, the French and Spanish fleets spent much more time in port; the extra months and years of sea-time kept British crews at a much higher level of fitness and discipline. This training, and the traditions that became established during it – such as rivalry between ships in manoeuvres and sail handling – resulted in a margin of superiority that was to be of critical importance in the American Revolutionary and Napoleonic wars. Constant striving for faster teamwork, particularly in the handling of guns, resulted in a consistently faster rate of British fire. It was under such seagoing conditions that, given a talented and committed captain, 'the real, natural discipline of the service' could flourish.

The most important factor in the continuing success of the British navy was the relationship that existed between the eighteenth-century naval officer and the seamen who manned His Majesty's warships. One authority has described the sea officer of the Seven Years War as 'hoping to persuade', rather than 'expecting to command'.[45] From the middle of the century, as the navy became a much larger organization, some of the old ties and certainties between officers and men were lost. Before it increased in size, the navy had been 'relatively informal and free of class interest'; by contrast, 'the late eighteenth-century naval community was much more formalized and stratified.'[46] In the main, however, a tradition of tolerance and humanity prevailed. Outstanding captains ran their ships on enlightened principles, unlocking the force of motivation.* Nelson found the secret early. Here he had no special advantages, although his friendships and connections with two commanding officers at the Nore, Robert Roddam and William Locker, ensured that he obtained seamen of good quality. Much has been made by some biographers of the number of men from Norfolk in some of his ships, and the special relationship that he had with them, but they were not there in very significant numbers.[47] Captains with political and landed connections did better, such as Admiral Boscawen and his officers and men from Cornwall in the Seven Years War, called by Mrs Boscawen 'the little Navy of your own making'.[48] The qualities that made Nelson a natural leader were those of openness and ease of being with people. From this stemmed his inborn ability to trust his officers and men. At the end of the American Revolutionary War in 1783, there was considerable trouble on board other ships over delays in paying off crews; but the entire crew of the *Albemarle* declared that they would serve under Nelson immediately if he could get another ship.[49] Nelson was to excel in his leadership of seamen.

---

* This judgement takes in a large literature, back to Masefield. The number of capital punishments declined significantly, as did the number of lashes inflicted per crime (Gilbert, 'Mutiny', 118). He finds only eleven cases of large-scale mutiny between 1756 and 1796, usually under the stress of mobilization or paying off ships after a war. See also Wareham, 202–27; Hay, Chapter 4.

3

Horace Nelson, Midshipman
May 1771–April 1777

In this ship [the *Worcester*] *I was at sea with convoys till April 2nd 1777, and in very bad weather. But although my age might have been a sufficient cause for not entrusting me with the charge of a Watch, yet Captain Robinson used to say, 'he felt as easy when I was upon deck, as any Officer in the Ship'.*

'Sketch of My Life', Rear-Admiral Lord Nelson describing himself as acting fourth lieutenant in the *Worcester*[1]

As the young Nelson came down the Thames on the falling tide on 23 April 1771, the wind was blowing moderate west-south-west. The weather became squally with rain, when the colour of the sea in the estuary takes on a dark, metallic grey.[2] With a following wind, a sailing tender rolls with the short, steep seas, by far the worst motion for seasickness. To the south lies the high ground of the Isle of Sheppey, with the fortifications of Garrison Point at the mouth of the Medway. The low Essex shore disappears into mud flats. From Greenwich to the Nore is a forty-mile journey. The tender headed for a group of anchored ships near the lightship 'at the buoy of the Nore'.

The word 'Nore' seems almost to have vanished from the English language. For 400 years it was known as the area in the middle of the Thames Estuary, just north of Sheerness. Since 1732 Trinity House had stationed a lightship there to guide ships through these difficult waters.[3] To the navy, however, the 'Nore' also meant a much wider area covering the estuary, the Medway and the southern North Sea, an area in the charge of the 'Commander-in-Chief at the Nore', or in peacetime a more junior officer known as 'the Senior Naval Officer at the Nore'.* In Nelson's lifetime

---

* The Nore Command closed in 1961, and the knowledge and use of the word disappeared with it.

much of the operations and industry of the navy was generated from the royal dockyards of Deptford and Woolwich on the Thames, and Chatham and Sheerness on the Medway, as well as from private shipyards on both rivers. In his early career, at least, when his ships were smaller, Nelson was to start most of his commissions from the Nore rather than from Portsmouth or Plymouth, and much that he saw on 23 April 1771 would become familiar.

Here was the old Spanish 60-gun ship the *Conquestadore*, captured at Havana in 1762 at the end of the Seven Years War, which served for many years as the commander-in-chief's flagship and was moored at the Nore for long periods. When the American Revolutionary War broke out in 1775, she would act as a receiving ship, where pressed men would be held before being transferred to the ship in which they were to serve. The smaller ships in the group were the *Crescent* (32), the *Glasgow* (20) and the *Tamar* sloop of sixteen guns.[4] Also at anchor were two 64-gun ships, the *Augusta* and the *Raisonable*. It was the *Raisonable* for which Nelson was headed. The day before, she had sailed three miles out into the estuary from the River Medway. On board the crew were checking and stowing the anchor cables, although when the weather moderated the next morning the sails were hung loose to dry. That day, the lieutenant noted in his log, the fresh breeze and squalls returned, and the seamen were 'Employed about the rigging'.[5] In this seasonable, changing weather Nelson stepped aboard his first ship.

As the confrontation with Spain was now resolved, the Admiralty decided to pay off the *Raisonable* a month after Nelson joined, and Captain Maurice Suckling, his officers and crew transferred to the newer and larger *Triumph* (74).[6] Suckling saw that a prolonged period of peace attached to a guard ship was unlikely to instil in his young midshipman a fondness for naval routine. He therefore took the not unusual step of finding Horace a berth in a merchant ship in the West India trade, for naval officers often served in peacetime in Britain's expanding merchant navy. Suckling used the good offices of a former master's mate of the *Dreadnought*, John Rathbone, with whom he had served in the Seven Years War on the Jamaica Station.[7] Rathbone was now the master of the *Mary Ann*, trading to Jamaica. It is not clear when the voyage started, for through his period in the *Triumph* Nelson was mustered 'in lieu', so that he would continue to be paid, though not victualled. The merchant ship returned in the summer of the next year, reaching Gravesend on 17 July 1772.[8] Edmund Nelson recorded that the ship also went to other islands than Jamaica.[9] Most British ships in the West Indies trade at this time were between 150 and 300 tons, with a crew of between fifteen and twenty.* Nelson would have made the voyage as the equivalent of an apprentice, for which Suckling would have undoubtedly paid Rathbone a sum proportionate to the usual apprentice's premium. He came back influenced by his fellow seamen against the navy. 'It was many weeks before I got in the least reconciled to a Man-of-War, so deep was the prejudice rooted; and what pains were taken to instil this erroneous principle in a young mind!'[10]

On his return from the West Indies, Nelson rejoined the *Triumph*, 'on the 13th mooring off Princes Bridge at Chatham', opposite the dockyard.[11] Maurice Suckling was now 'the Senior Officer in the River Medway and at the Nore', a position he liked well enough to ask Lord Sandwich to keep him there.[12] Peacetime business occurred at no great pace. Matters of leave, docking ships and a few courts martial run through his correspondence with Philip Stephens, the secretary to the Board of Admiralty. Some excitement arose on 1 September when the 90-gun *Prince George* was launched at Chatham Dockyard and the French ambassador came on board the *Raisonable*, where he was saluted with fifteen guns.[13]

After the freedom of the Atlantic, it was time for Nelson's formal instruction, and Suckling shrewdly provided some motivation in getting Nelson down to his studies. In the 'Sketch of My Life' Nelson recalled that 'it was always held out as a reward, that if I attended well to my navigation, I should go in the cutter and the decked longboat, which was attached to the Commanding officer's ship at Chatham'.[14] For the next nine months he learnt the skills of handling and sailing small vessels. These are not easy waters, with strong and confusing tides and sandbanks that extend well out into the Thames estuary. The longboat worked hard, for the ship needed constant fresh water. Other ships needed men to assist in fitting out; those men needed to be ferried in boats under midshipmen, a task organized by the lieutenants (the rank immediately under the captain). There were four in the *Triumph*, a reduced number, as it was peacetime. The fourth lieutenant wrote methodically in his log on 16 October: 'Lent a mid. & 7 men to the *Greyhound* cutter at Sheerness,' and on 23 November: 'sent the longboat to the Nore with a party of marines for the *Endeavour* storeship'.† The longboat had to be

---

* This average is based on a search of the Naval Officer Shipping Lists for Jamaica and other islands for the 1770s, although there are none surviving for mid 1771 to mid 1772 ((UK)NA: PRO, CO 142).

† This was Cook's ship, which had taken stores to the Falkland Islands garrison in 1771 and was then repaired at Woolwich Dockyard. On 3 Dec. 1772 she departed for the Falkland Islands for a second supply voyage.

repaired in the yard at the end of November and the *Goodwill* cutter came up from Sheerness 'fitted up as a tender for the Senior Officer here'. 'Lent a mid. and 19 seamen to HM ship *Portland*. Sent them by the *Goodwill* cutter to Sheerness.'* On other occasions Nelson headed down the Kent coast to the North Foreland and down the Swin, parallel with the Essex coast, or up the Thames to London, probably with messages to and from Suckling as the 'Senior Naval Officer, Nore'.[15] As well as seamanship he learnt the infinite satisfaction of handling boats under sail and oar. He now had a small crew to command and to motivate. These two modest vessels, longboat and cutter, were his first independent commands.

Suckling's next plan for Nelson's training undoubtedly demanded some influence. The *Carcass* was a small, strongly built ship, fitting out at Sheerness in the early spring of 1773 for an expedition to the Arctic. She was a bomb vessel, designed to carry two very large mortars used in the bombardment of shore fortifications, and because of the recoil of these large guns was strongly built. She had been selected because the strength of her hull could withstand the pressure of the Arctic ice. With her was another bomb vessel, the *Racehorse*, to be commanded by Constantine Phipps, the leader of the expedition. Its purpose was to prove whether there was open sea beyond the ice north of Spitsbergen, at eighty degrees north. These seas were well known to European whalers up to that latitude. There had been a similar expedition in the 1740s when the *Furnace* and *Discovery* had tried to find a route to the North West Passage. It had recently been determined at the Royal Society that the ice at eighty degrees north was formed from fresh water from Spitsbergen's rivers, since it was not thought possible that ice could be formed from seawater. It was the additional spur of French interest in an expedition that persuaded the first lord of the Admiralty, Lord Sandwich, himself a fellow of the Society, to send two strengthened bomb vessels north for the summer.

The *Carcass* was to have a carefully selected crew of only eighty and the Admiralty sent orders to Captain Skeffington Lutwidge that specifically forbade taking servants: 'none but effective men shall serve . . . no others be entered for her, we have given orders for the officers to be paid an allowance, by bill equal to the amount of wages of the numbers of servants they are respectively entitled to.'[16] The seamen were experienced men, mostly in their thirties.† How was a sixteen-year-old to go? According to

---

* Cuthbert Collingwood was serving in the *Portland* at this time (Owen, 190).
† The muster shows that the ordinary seamen were aged between eighteen and twenty-five, while all the able seamen were over thirty ((UK)NA: PRO, ADM 36/756).

Nelson, he persuaded Lutwidge to let him be his coxswain; more likely it was Suckling's influence, for he was the senior naval officer while the ship was being fitted out and Lutwidge would report to him: besides, a seaman was entered as coxswain in the muster book only five days after Nelson joined.[17] But whoever was responsible, Nelson's selection for the voyage is the first indication of his restlessness, enthusiasm and ability.

The aristocratic Constantine Phipps, later to be a member of the Board of Admiralty and in 1790 Lord Mulgrave, had powerful connections. He and Sir Joseph Banks, the president of the Royal Society, had been at Eton together. In spite of the Admiralty instruction to take only effective men on the voyage, Phipps also allowed another Etonian friend to embark on the *Racehorse*, the young William Windham, later to be influential in Nelson's career, though Windham suffered from seasickness and was landed at Bergen.[18] Preparations were elaborate and the ships well equipped; both had fresh-water distillation equipment. The crews had special clothing and victuals, including the new 'portable soup', dried meat that when soaked and boiled provided a nutritious hot beverage. Two seamen from Greenland whalers were to be taken as pilots in the ice. The boats had the capacity to take the crews of both ships should they be trapped in the ice. They carried chronometers designed by John Harrison, which were still being tested, since Harrison had not yet been awarded all his prize money by the Board of Longitude. The *Carcass* also carried one made by John Arnold, who had to come on board at the Nore just before she sailed to attend to it; it had stopped 'for want of being sufficiently wound up'.[19] Eventually they set off to the north on 4 June, reaching Spitsbergen after a passage of twenty-four days.

The two ships anchored in a small bay near the Magdelena Hook at the north-east point of Spitsbergen. Time was spent taking sights, watering and obtaining the best information from British whalers on the state of the ice. The weather was mild and sunny, and on 5 July they turned north. They soon encountered ice. For two days they tried to go further, but no opening was found. Three days later the master of the *Carcass* noted in his log:

Found the ice clogging us on every side. The Com[m]and[e]r sent the Pilots on board again with orders to get out the Ice if Posable. Hoisted up the boat and got the Ice Anch[o]r and warps and warp[e]d and Bore the ship ahead between the Ice with the Ice Poles. At 7 sent the Com[m]and[e]r['s] boat on board and there spring up a Breeze from the NE. Set Steering sails. At 4am got clear of the Ice. At 8 am saw the Ice driving on us. Got out the Boats & Tow[e]d the Ship with Difficulty clear of the Ice. At 9 got a Breeze at WSW and stood from the Ice hoist[e]d in the

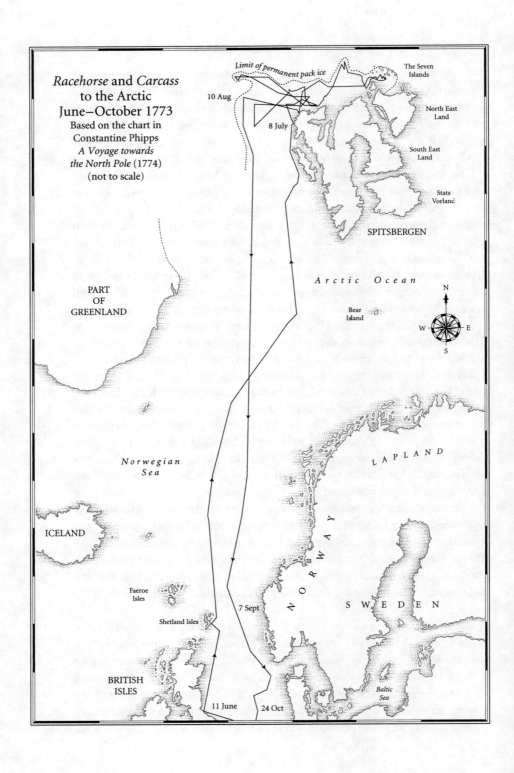

Racehorse and *Carcass*
to the Arctic
June–October 1773
Based on the chart in
Constantine Phipps
*A Voyage towards
the North Pole* (1774)
(not to scale)

Limit of permanent pack ice

The Seven
Islands

10 Aug

8 July

North East
Land

South East
Land

Stats
Vorland

SPITSBERGEN

PART
OF
GREENLAND

Arctic Ocean

Bear
Island

N

W   E

S

*Norwegian
Sea*

LAPLAND

ICELAND

N O R W A Y

S W E D E N

Faeroe
Isles

7 Sept

Shetland Isles

Baltic
Sea

BRITISH
ISLES

11 June   24 Oct

Boat . . . [10 July] Fresh gales with thick Fog. PM entered the Ice to the No[rth]ward. Employ[e]d working between Large fields of Ice. Midnight lost sight of the Com[m]and[e]r and Fir[e]d guns every hour as signals. Saw the Com[m]and[er] and bore away for him Round a large field of Ice, at 11 joined him.[20]

Phipps concluded that the ice 'was one compact impenetrable body'.[21] The ships now went to Fair Haven at the north of Spitsbergen, where scientific work was pursued, while the crew hunted, dried the sails or carried out the never-ending maintenance. The weather was brilliant. One expedition member described the rays of the setting sun: 'sometimes they appeared of a bright blue, like sapphire, and sometimes like the variable colours of a prism, exceeding in lustre the richest gems in the world, disposed of in shapes wonderful to behold, all glittering with a lustre that dazzles the eye, and fills the air with astonishing brightness.'[22] For a sixteen-year-old, it can only have been an intoxicating experience.

On 18 July Phipps tried again to enter the ice, this time to the east. There was, of course, slow progress, though they managed by their reckoning to get to 80° 48' N by 27 July. They investigated several openings in the ice, some of them two or three miles long. Again the weather was fine, the scene breathtaking. 'The whales were seen spouting their fountains towards the skies, and the fin fish followed their example . . . the whole prospect was more pleasing and picturesque than they had yet beheld in this remote region. The very ice in which they were beset looked beautiful, and put forth a thousand glittering forms.'[23]

The *Racehorse* and the *Carcass* were now near the straits that divide Spitsbergen from North East Land. The area was rich in wild life. On 27 July the lieutenant 'shott a seahorse and Tow[e]d it on board. It weigh[e]d about a Ton weight & measured 11 foot long.' Lutwidge records that 'a large white Bear coming over the ice towards the ships, was shot and brought on board the *Racehorse*.'[24] By 2 August the ships were locked in the ice, according to the master of the *Carcass*: 'Both ships beset by the Ice as far as we could see from ye Mast head.' On 4 August the two ships were cutting their way through the ice to the west, but, as the master described it, 'the Ice Close in on us so fast that it closed up what we cutt.' On 5 August three large bears came alongside. 'Shot all three and Skin[ne]d them. Found the large one to measure 6' 9" from head to tail.' Lutwidge's journal makes it clear that they were shot from the ship.[25] The next day 'A Bear came close to the Ships on the Ice but on the People going towards him he went away.' Later that day they shot one and sent it to the commander.[26]

No record exists of Nelson venturing alone on the ice to shoot a bear.*

The ships were now in real danger. Drifting with the ice, they were now to the north-east of Spitsbergen, and the pilots were beginning to fear that they would be trapped in the ice for the winter. Phipps ordered the crews of both ships to prepare to abandon ship and to put provisions in the ships' boats. The weather was still mild, Lutwidge remarking in his log that 'the weather was remarkably warm at noon, the tar running upon the side, anchor stocks etc where the sun shone on them, yet the water on the opposite side where the ice was removed was freezing on the surface.'[27] On 7 August the crews started the long haul of the boats over the ice towards the open sea. Nelson was given charge of the *Carcass*'s four-oared cutter and twelve crew, 'and I prided myself in fancying I could navigate her better than any other boat in the ship'.[28] The next day they pulled the boats four miles. They found open water to the west and the ice loosened sufficiently for the *Racehorse* and the *Carcass* to make progress enough to overtake the boats. On 10 August a NNE wind allowed the ships to force their way through the ice, and open sea was reached. One of the crew on board the *Carcass* wrote: 'Then festivity and jollity took place of abstinence and gloomy apprehension and before they arrived at Spitsbergen, there was not a sailor on board with a serious face.'[29]

After a rest at Spitsbergen, the ships set off south in late August. There were still dangers in continuous heavy weather, and the low waist of the *Carcass* was swamped many times by green water. The ships were separated; but eventually on 21 September the *Carcass* was anchored in the Yarmouth Roads and by mid October she was paid off at Deptford.[30] If Nelson ever wrote at length about the impact of the Arctic, the document has not survived. He had had the opportunity to observe some strikingly effective leadership. Constantine Phipps was notably strong and took more than his share of the physical exertions, leading by example, which was unusual for an aristocrat. The popular first lieutenant of the *Carcass*, John Baird, also set a powerful example. An anonymous observer singled him out: 'his conduct was always calm, and his orders resolute. He never was heard, during the whole voyage on the most pressing emergencies, to enforce his commands with an oath, or to call a sailor by any other than his usual name.'[31]

Nothing illustrates Maurice Suckling's care of the young midshipman

---

* Nelson's part in these incidents is not recorded. His central role was first indicated by Clarke and McArthur, though they attribute the story to Lutwidge (Clarke and McArthur, I, 21–2; Sugden, 73–6). The oil painting by Westall is based on their account (NMM, BHC 2907).

more than the speed of Nelson's next appointment. Two weeks after being paid off from the *Carcass*, he was entered on the books of the *Seahorse*, an old 24-gun frigate captained by George Farmer. Farmer had himself been a midshipman under Suckling in the *Dreadnought* in the West Indies at the beginning of the Seven Years War. At the end of October Nelson joined the *Seahorse* at Portsmouth, where she was being fitted out for a voyage to the East Indies. Here he made two long-term friendships. Thomas Troubridge entered as an able seaman in the *Seahorse*; he was the son of a London baker, and his and Nelson's careers would be closely intertwined. Charles Morice Pole was a midshipman on board the 50-gun *Salisbury*, commanded by Commodore Edward Hughes. On 19 November both ships set sail for the Cape of Good Hope for the first stage of their long passage.* The voyage was very slow, broken at first by the usual week in Madeira to replenish the stores. The ships did not reach the Cape until 3 March.[32]

At the Cape, damage to the *Seahorse*'s rigging from rolling in the swell was repaired, and they sailed on to Madras. It was a dull, 53-day passage. A month out from the Cape the *Seahorse*'s crew caught fifteen sharks, 'but lost a hook by one of them'.[33] 'People healthy in both ships except a few scourbatics [scurvy cases],' reported Hughes. 'I have directed constant Bathing in the Warm Latitudes every Evening by the Surgeon's recommendation, which has prov'd very usefull I am sure, assisting both the Perspiration and the Digestion.'[34]

Tedious though this six-month voyage was, there was much for Nelson to learn. He first experienced the resource and improvisation required to make a ship self-sufficient on a foreign station, experience that was to stand him in good stead. At the Cape, for instance, the *Seahorse*'s forge had to be sent on shore to repair iron work needed for the rigging. Before the end of the year, her fore and main masts had to be hauled out by the main yard of the *Salisbury*. She had to be careened, scraped and caulked; sun awnings had to be made.[35] In the *Seahorse*, Divine Service was held regularly, which was something Nelson had not previously encountered. There were further lessons in the stresses of commanding a ship on a long voyage. Hughes appointed a further lieutenant to both ships at the request of Farmer, 'particularly on this voyage where the many changes of Climate subject even both to be frequently incapable of Duty, what I have experienced in my own Ship the Master and one lieutenant having been long at watch and watch'.[36] Symptomatic of this strain was the arrest on arrival at Madras of

---

* Hughes kept Sandwich especially well informed since he had on board the *Salisbury* Robert Montagu, Sandwich's son by his mistress Martha Ray.

the *Seahorse*'s first lieutenant, James Drummond. Drummond's own log records: 'Capt. put Lieut. Drummond under an arrest & suspended him from all duty pr. Order of the Commodore.' He was found guilty of 'Drunkenness, sleeping on his watch, insolence to his captain and disobedience of orders' and dismissed the service.[37]

The two years of Hughes's tenure as commander-in chief, East Indies, have been described as 'undisturbed by anything except rumour', though there was much suspicion of French ambitions in India after the crushing British success in the Seven Years War.[38] Certainly, Nelson spent a great deal of time in port, for sixty per cent of the time that he was on the station his ship was not at sea. From May to September 1774 the ship was 123 days at Madras. This avoided the cyclone period, at its worst in June.[39] A further stay of over three months followed for ship maintenance at Kedgeree (Kedjeri) at the mouth of the Hooghli (Hugli). Nevertheless, the *Seahorse*'s humdrum escorting role, protecting trade especially from the Maharatta ships, was not without incident. The Maharattas from Gujarat, north of Bombay next to the border of present-day Pakistan, using the southern ports of Severndroog (Suwarnadurg) and Gheria (Vijayadurg) to the south of Bombay, were at this time in contention with the East India Company over territory. The *Seahorse*'s first task was to take the Company's coin and silver from Calcutta to Bombay. She set out on 30 January 1775. On 19 February two ketches were seen sailing after a British ship; both were flying the colours of Hyder Ali, at that time an ally of the East India Company. But there was sufficient doubt in the captain's mind to challenge them. This was the first time that Nelson experienced naval guns fired with real purpose.

We immediately Tacked and stood after them, at 8 fired several shot to bring one of them too, thinking her to be a Marratta, at 9 one of the ketches sent her boat on board us and told us they belonged to Hadir Aly, but as the [other] ketch did not bring too, nor shorten sail, and several other vessels heaving in sight, which we imagined to be consorts, we kept firing round and grape shot at her until noon. Broke 6 panes of glass in chace. At noon ketch brought too & struck her colours, we hoisted out the cutter and sent her with an officer on board, who found her to be one of Hadar Aly's armed cruisers, at half past 2 hoisted the cutter in and made sail. Upon examining the shot racks: 57 round shot 9 lbs, 15 grape shot 9 lbs, two double headed hammer shot, 25 round shot 3 lbs & two grape shot 3 lbs.[40]

This incident, with shots being fired at the ketch's rigging, was, nevertheless, a demonstration of the advantage of aggression from a position of strength, which Nelson was to copy many times.

The *Seahorse* was now sent into the Persian Gulf to convoy East India Company ships and to protect Company interests. She escorted the *Betty*, most likely a 'country' ship rather than an East Indiaman, bound from Bengal to Bussorah (Basra). At this time of the year there were fair winds from the north-east monsoon, but it was a long journey of 1,400 miles from Bombay to Bushire, on the north side of the Gulf, 250 miles from its head. Nelson later claimed, with more regard for alliteration than strict accuracy, that he 'visited almost every part of the East Indies, from Bengal to Bussorah'.[41] Had he actually been to Bussorah, he would have found himself in the middle of a war between the Persians and the Turks, for Turkish forces were under siege. Bussorah is 100 miles from the sea, not far from where the rivers Tigris and Euphrates join. The East India Company agent had left the city in a smaller Company vessel, and when he eventually arrived in the Bushire Roads he found nine British vessels at anchor. On 16 July the *Seahorse* left with a convoy of eight of them, in light, contrary winds and great heat. By now the south-westerly monsoon was blowing, and it took two weeks to get to Muscat, at the southern entrance to the Gulf. 'Brackish' water taken aboard at Bushire as well as the extreme heat made the majority of the crew sickly, though all recovered.[42] The convoy reached Bombay on 15 August. Further cruises took place, sometimes in company with other warships. The *Seahorse* went to Madras and then, from 23 October to 1 November 1775, was anchored at 'Trincomalee on the island of Ceylon'. She visited Goa and Anjenjo (Anjutenga), ports in southern India, returning to Bombay before the end of the year for repairs. Here, most likely, as Nelson related twenty-four years later to the writer Cornelia Knight, 'he won £300 at a gaming table; but he was so shocked at reflecting that had he lost them, he would not have known how to pay them, that from that time to this he has never played again.'[43]

At this point Nelson fell very sick, almost certainly with malaria. On 14 March 1776 he was discharged from the *Seahorse* by order of Edward Hughes.[44] He took passage in the homeward-bound *Dolphin*, captained by James Pigott, 'whose kindness at that time', Nelson recalled, 'saved my life'.[45] There is little doubt that he was very ill, although he was not mustered with the ten other invalids who were brought aboard the ship from the hospital in Bombay. The voyage took five months. Captain Pigott was new

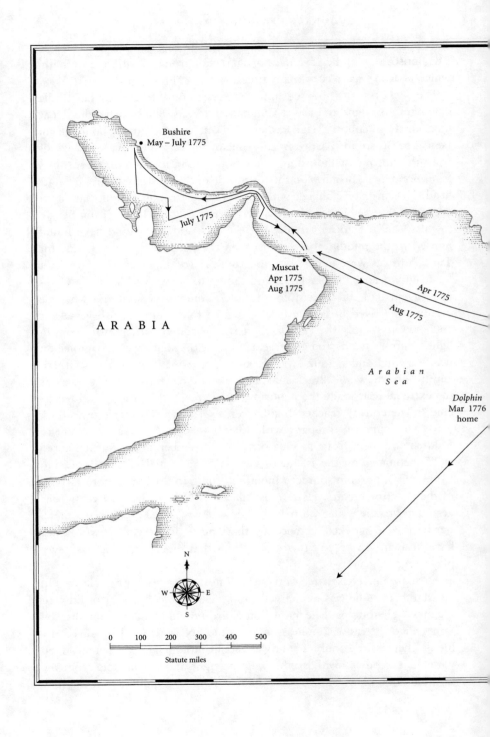

Bushire
● May – July 1775

July 1775

Muscat
● Apr 1775
  Aug 1775

Apr 1775

Aug 1775

ARABIA

*Arabian
Sea*

Dolphin
Mar 1776
home

N
W ⊕ E
S

0   100   200   300   400   500

Statute miles

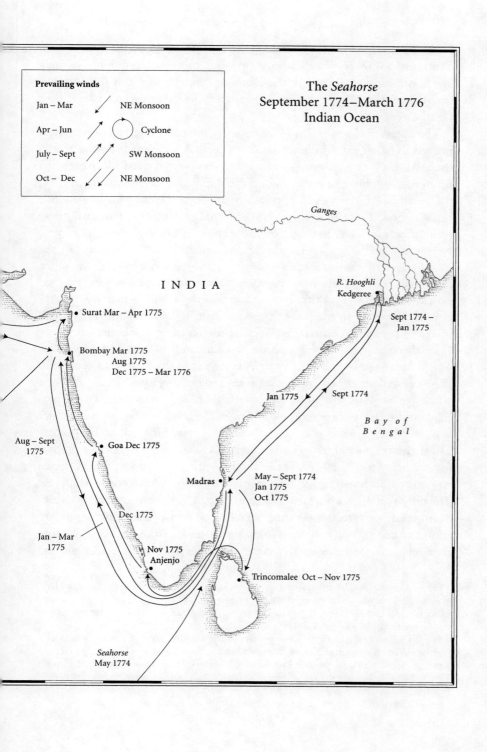

The *Seahorse*
September 1774–March 1776
Indian Ocean

Prevailing winds

Jan – Mar   NE Monsoon

Apr – Jun   Cyclone

July – Sept   SW Monsoon

Oct – Dec   NE Monsoon

Ganges

I N D I A

R. Hooghli
Kedgeree

Sept 1774 –
Jan 1775

Surat Mar – Apr 1775

Bombay Mar 1775
Aug 1775
Dec 1775 – Mar 1776

Jan 1775   Sept 1774

Aug – Sept
1775

Goa Dec 1775

*Bay of
Bengal*

Madras

May – Sept 1774
Jan 1775
Oct 1775

Dec 1775

Jan – Mar
1775

Nov 1775
Anjenjo

Trincomalee   Oct – Nov 1775

Seahorse
May 1774

to the ship and only in command to take the ship home; all the midshipmen had remained in Bombay with the previous captain. No one of Nelson's age and rank was aboard.[46] The *Dolphin* leaked badly and for a month stayed in Simon's Bay.* It was an extremely low point in the career thus far of a very young man.†

The illness that was the cause of his early return to England nevertheless proved to be an extraordinary stroke of luck. A war was brewing, and at the start of every eighteenth-century war there was a need for lieutenants for newly commissioned ships. For a midshipman who had served his time, the best place to be was in London, where he could take his lieutenant's examination. From now on, every naval officer took part in an intense promotion race. The *Seahorse* did not return to England until July 1777. Nelson's friend Thomas Troubridge continued in her, remained in the East Indies and was not made a lieutenant until January 1781. He was still a midshipman when Nelson had been a captain with a year's seniority, reached post-captain four years after Nelson and was 175 places behind on the captain's list in 1783 at the end of the American Revolutionary War.[47] These mixed fortunes unquestionably affected the later careers of both men.‡

By the time the *Dolphin* approached England, Nelson had recovered. The ship arrived at Spithead on 31 August 1776. She then went around to the Nore and on 16 September was anchored in Long Reach in the Thames, when Nelson was last mustered aboard her.[48] He had been away from England for thirty-three months. For over a year hostilities had been under way with the American colonies, which were arming, aided by France. Throughout England naval and military establishments were busy preparing the army for North America. On 25 April 1776 an Order-in-Council was issued authorizing the seizure or destruction of American shipping. The only sign of this warfare evident in Britain was the successful activities of American privateers, operating from French ports. Gradually the government ensured that all merchant shipping was escorted by convoy.[49] A more particular change in Nelson's circumstances was that Maurice Suckling had

---

* There has been considerable speculation as to whether Nelson was healthy enough to have gone ashore at Simonstown (Fawcett, 36–7; Pryce-Lewis, 355–9).
† From Clarke and McArthur (I, 9) comes the story of the 'radiant orb' that inspired him on the voyage home. 'Well, then, I will be a hero . . .'
‡ At a key point in their careers, July 1796, Sir John Jervis, later Lord St Vincent, would have promoted Troubridge before Nelson, but was unable to do so because of Troubridge's lack of seniority. Jervis wrote to the first lord of the Admiralty: 'I sincerely lament that Captain Troubridge is so low on the list of captains, for he is capable of commanding the fleet of England, and I scarce know another.' In the same letter he described Nelson as 'an excellent partisan' (Jervis to Lord Spencer, 27 July 1796, Corbett, *Spencer Papers*, II, 43).

finally come ashore. He had been appointed comptroller of the navy by Lord Sandwich on 12 April 1775. Although this change had not directly increased Suckling's capacity to advance his nephew, his position as head of the Navy Board gave him an unrivalled and up-to-date knowledge of an increasingly fast-moving situation. Further, as comptroller, he would be a member of the board that interviewed midshipmen for their lieutenant's examination.

In September 1776 Nelson had over six years' service and he could have taken the lieutenant's examination when he left the *Dolphin*.[50] Why did Suckling not examine him there and then and find a lieutenant's berth for him?* He may have concluded that six months' sickness should not morally have counted within the six years' qualifying time. Nelson was only just eighteen; candidates were supposed to be twenty. A more radical possibility is that Suckling felt that he might not pass the examination. Nelson's seamanship may have been good (we have only his own word for it), but there was more to the examination than being handy in a boat. In the event, it was decided that before the examination Nelson should go back to sea for a short period. With the outbreak of war a convenient shortage of lieutenants existed and an opening soon presented itself. On 29 September the Admiralty wrote to Vice-Admiral Sir James Douglas, the commander-in-chief at Portsmouth, directing him to appoint a well-qualified midshipman as fourth lieutenant of the 64-gun *Worcester*.[51] On 8 October Nelson joined the ship at Portsmouth, armed with letters from Suckling, and met her captain, Mark Robinson, who was due to take a convoy down to Gibraltar and to escort one home. The next day Robinson introduced him to Sir James Douglas.[52] Nelson, while still rated a midshipman, thus became acting fourth lieutenant of the *Worcester*. Suckling, as usual, chose well. He picked an experienced captain. Robinson, now aged fifty-one, seems to have been a down-to-earth character.† He took care of his acting lieutenant at Portsmouth, dining ashore with him on a number of occasions. On 11 October they dined with Philip Varlo, the mayor of Portsmouth and a friend of Robinson. As Maurice Suckling held one of two Portsmouth seats, doubtless Nelson was introduced as the nephew of the sitting MP.[53]

---

* Nelson's passing certificate for lieutenant ((UK) NA: PRO, ADM 107/6, fol. 386, 5 Apr. 1777) incorrectly totals his time of service at sea in the *Raisonable, Triumph, Carcass, Seahorse* and *Dolphin*. The certificate gives six years, three months one week and six days; it should total six years, two weeks, and five days.

† In a letter to the Admiralty in April 1777 Robinson referred to 'Horace' rather than 'Horatio' Nelson. This may have been the last time 'Horace' was used in Nelson's life ((UK) NA: PRO, ADM 1/2390).

Nothing but tough sailing into hard, cold winds could be expected in the winter in the Western Approaches and the Bay of Biscay. The *Worcester* was short-handed, with only just over half her usual complement aboard, although as the enemy now consisted of American privateers no enemy ships of comparable size were at sea. The *Worcester* went particularly well to windward and in heavy weather.[54] Robinson thought a good deal of her and had written to the Board of Admiralty to say so: 'an exceedingly easy seaboat . . . sails by the wind with single reef'd Topsails and Top Gallant sails nine knots . . . Upon the whole, Sir, I have so good an Opinion of the *Worcester*'s Sailing that I should think myself highly favored if His Majesty's Service would admit of their Lordships indulging me with another Cruise.'[55] Nelson was to gain a very active four months' experience from Robinson's quarterdeck, and he earned his captain's trust.

Escorting a convoy in European waters was not an unusual task for a 64-gun ship, as ships of this class were beginning to be regarded as of insufficient size to take their place in the line of battle. By the beginning of the American Revolutionary War the navy had to use them for convoy duty because it was very short of frigates: most of these were now in North American waters, and Lord North's government was slow in ordering new ones to be built.[56] Forty-five vessels made up the convoy that left Spithead, escorted by the *Worcester*, on 4 December 1776. Most of the merchant ships were between 100 and 150 tons, about a tenth the size of their escort. The majority carried hardware stores, hides, iron, salted fish, wheat and rice to Portugal and the Mediterranean, but some took ordnance stores for the garrison at Gibraltar.[57]

Hard southerly winds ensured that progress was very slow. It took the convoy four days to get down to Falmouth, where the ships had to stay a week in the Carrick Roads within Falmouth Harbour, finally getting away on 16 December. With 'hard gales' and 'squally' continually noted in the *Worcester*'s log, they did not reach Gibraltar until 9 January 1777.[58]

Once at Gibraltar, Robinson wrote to the British consul at Cadiz, James Duff, to see whether any ships there needed to be picked up for the journey home, a letter that Nelson took ashore.[59] For over a month the *Worcester* replenished and victualled in Gibraltar Bay. On 15 February, in strong gales with the ship double reefed, signals were flown and Robinson tried to get the homeward convoy to sea, but 'the ships in the Bay did not make the least motion towards coming out.'[60] At 3 p.m. the *Worcester* was 'Taken aback with a heavy squall of wind and rain which carried away the main yard. Came on to blow extreamly hard at SW & WSW so that we could not clear the land either one way or the other.' The crippled ship managed to beat north for Cadiz, where they were guided into safety by a fishing boat.[61] Robinson reported to the Admiralty that 'During our Stay at Cadiz the Spanyards behaved to us with the Utmost politeness and civility.' On 23 February he obtained a replacement spar from the dockyard at Cadiz.[62] Two years later England and Spain were at war.

Once the ship's carpenter had finished the work on the spar, and other storm-damage repairs on the merchant ships had been completed, the convoy got under way again on 3 March. Those ships with perishable fruit had gone ahead. The journey home still took a month, for further damage was sustained by some of the merchant vessels that had to be repaired en route. On the 25th they saw the Scilly Isles, at which point the convoy began to disperse, much to Robinson's irritation, as he reported to the Admiralty: 'Many of them Steered their own Course and took no notice of my signals that were made nor would they come near of us for fear (as I apprehended) of having their men impressed.'[63] The *Worcester* moored at Spithead on 3 April.

Within six days of anchoring, Nelson was in the Navy Office in Crutched Friars in the City of London taking his lieutenant's exam. He was examined by Maurice Suckling, the comptroller, and two even more senior captains, John Campbell and Abraham North. According to the certificate, dated 9 April 1777, 'he appears to be more than twenty years of age', although in reality he was only eighteen and a half. He had served for well over the requisite six years. He produced certificates from Captains Suckling, Lethbridge, Farmer, Pigott and Robinson 'of his Diligence etc he can Splice, Knot, Reef & Sail, and is qualified to the duty of an Able Seaman and Midshipman'.[64]

The next day he was appointed as second lieutenant to the *Lowestoffe*.[65] He went immediately down to Sheerness where she was fitting out, was mustered for the first time on 12 April, and two days later was back in London to meet his father.[66] From the Navy Office Nelson wrote a breathless, affectionate letter, tinged with anxiety, to his brother William, who was studying for his degree at Cambridge:

I suppose you have not heard of my Arrival in England yet . . . but I have been so full of business in preparing to set out again, that I have not had time to write. I passed my Degree as Master of Arts on the 9th instant (that is, passed the Lieutenant's Examination) & Receiv'd my Commission the following day, for a fine Frigate of 32 Guns. So I am now left in [the] World to shift for myself, which I hope I shall do, so as to bring Credit to myself and Friends . . .[67]

At the foot of the page he mischievously wrote to his lazy brother: 'NB if it is not too troublesome turn over.' Then followed earnest instructions: 'Where we shall go at present, I know not, but w[h]ere ever it is, I will always write to you. If you ever chose to write, inclose either to Mr Suckling, or my Brother, as in all probability they will know where we are gone. I leave London on Wednesday evening, so shall always be glad to hear from you.'

The first chapter of Nelson's seagoing career was over and he had done well. Passing the lieutenant's exam was by no means automatic, even when the comptroller of the board was a relation. Historians of previous generations have criticized the fairness and effectiveness of these examinations. More realistically, a modern authority has suggested that a 'fast track' promotion system was achieved by circumventing regulations rather than by any corrupt practice.[68] Many biographies relate that Suckling only revealed that he was the candidate's uncle to the other two examiners after the examination, a crude attempt at representing the fairness of the exam as beyond reproach, for it is beyond credibility that the other two examining captains did not know that Nelson was related to Suckling.[69]

Whatever the nature of the examination, there can be no doubt of the quality and variety of Nelson's training. Many successful officers never went outside the Atlantic Basin and the Mediterranean throughout their careers. Nelson, exceptionally for peacetime, had sailed 45,000 miles. Suckling had shrewdly picked sympathetic captains of ships who were engaged on duties that would give useful experience to his nephew. Further, although Nelson served for a total of twenty-one months in big ships, he never had to endure for long the spit and polish or the drudgery of a guardship. Nor did he suffer the tribulations of a junior in a large midshipmen's mess. In small ships he was always actively involved, with initiative demanded daily; and in the *Carcass* and *Worcester* especially he had shown his restiveness, energy, quickness and ability.

By the time he was thirteen he had crossed the Atlantic and had seen the West Indies. Before he reached the end of his teenage years he had been trapped in Arctic ice, spent long hours at the foretop of a frigate off India and watched a vicious Atlantic squall bring down the main yard of a 64-gun ship. He had seen real danger and observed how men reacted to it. He had endured severe illness and loneliness. He had experienced the endless tedium of ocean voyages. It is difficult to see how he could have been better trained, or his horizons broadened further, before he took on the responsibilities of a lieutenant in His Majesty's navy.

4

Lieutenant to Captain:
The West Indies
April 1777–November 1780

Captain Nelson's constitution is rather too delicate, but such minds,
My Lord, are most devoutly to be wished for Government's sake.
General John Dalling to Lord George Germain, secretary of state for
the American colonies, 29 June 1780[1]

'On the tenth April 1777 received a Commission appointing me Second
Lieutenant of His Majesty's Ship *Lowestoffe*, went down to Sheerness on
the twelth and found the ship fitting for sea.'[2] These were the first words
that Nelson wrote in his first official log. His early entries are long and
detailed, full of the minutiae of seamanship, although they tail off to a
modest length after a month or two. He would now keep an official record
for the rest of his career. At Sheerness he found not only the ship but also
his captain, William Locker, whom he had met five years earlier when
Locker was commanding the *Thames* frigate in home waters. Locker had
been a lieutenant in the Channel fleet during the Seven Years War and was
present at Edward Hawke's spectacular victory at Quiberon Bay in 1759.
He had served on Hawke's flagship after the battle, the period when the
Channel fleet had completely dominated the French by blockading their
fleet in Brest so that it was ineffective for the second half of that war.
Hawke's skilful aggression had coloured Locker's naval philosophy, who
passed on directly to Nelson a sense of the dash and confidence of Hawke.
Locker's influence went, however, much further, for he was an open, honest
man. His son described him as 'one of the most natural people I ever knew,
and this gave him a very agreeable tone to all he said and did'.[3] Nelson was
lucky to come under the influence of such a man when he was at his most
impressionable.

Locker came from an academic family and was a man of learning and
taste, with a keen sense of history and an interest in the arts, aware of the
special times in which he lived and determined to record them. Not many

eighteenth-century naval officers sent their lieutenants to have their portraits painted.[4] He was to commission portraits of Lieutenants James Macnamara and Charles Morice Pole, both of whom were to become close friends of Nelson. Now, in April and May 1777, while the ship was being prepared and Nelson went to London to impress men, he sat, at Locker's expense, for J. F. Rigaud.* The three-quarters-length portrait, unfinished until Nelson's return over three years later, has left us the remarkable image of the unlined and confident face of the young Nelson.[5] He felt an affection and a respect for Locker that went beyond that of a usual protégé and patron relationship. When they reached the West Indies, Nelson, concerned by the poor state of Locker's health, promised to look after his affairs, 'should anything happen to you (which I sincerely pray God, may not) . . . I think I have served faithfully the best of friends . . . All the services I can render to your family, you may be assured shall be done, and shall never end but with my life.'[6] Nelson served with Locker for only thirteen months, but the two became lifelong friends; the many letters he wrote to Locker until the latter's death in 1800 attest to this.

The spring of 1777 was stormy, and strong winds delayed the *Lowestoffe*'s fitting out.[7] When she finally left Sheerness on 3 May under double reefs, the boat she was towing was swamped and lost.[8] Following this excitement the wind died and it took a full week for the ship to reach Spithead. After a week of loading boatswain's and carpenter's stores from Portsmouth Dockyard, the *Lowestoffe* fired two guns to gather up her convoy and they were off to Madeira, thence to Jamaica.

At this point in the American Revolutionary War the only hostile ships were American privateers: France did not enter the war until July 1778 and Spain until June 1779. The Admiralty was quick to react to the powerful West India Committee of Merchants when it pressed for protection of trade. Almost all warships coming and going to the West Indies now accompanied convoys of merchant ships. Every effort was made to keep the convoys sailing regularly and, once they had sailed, to keep ships together.† Insurance policies required ships to 'take instructions'. Even

---

* A number of these portraits were presented to Greenwich Hospital and are thus in the National Maritime Museum. There are also two of Locker, by Gilbert Stuart and Lemuel Abbott. In 1793 Locker also presented a picture of the Battle of Quiberon Bay to the Hospital (Hattendorf *et al., Documents*, 541).

† The Admiralty urged the comander-in-chief, Jamaica, to send regular convoys because of pressure from the West India Committee of Merchants ((UK)NA: PRO, ADM 2/562, 11 June 1779, Stephens to Parker).

so, there were many reasons – particularly, as we have seen, the risk of impressments of crews in their home ports and the slow speed of many ships sailing together – for merchant ships to break ranks and finish the voyage on their own.[9] The American privateers had initially been very successful. By February 1777 they had taken 250 British West India merchant ships and four major West India merchant companies in London had collapsed.[10] The rebels did not have it all their own way, however, particularly in the Caribbean itself. Merchants in the islands fitted out their own armed vessels against American shipping and were particularly effective in intercepting the trade between the neutral islands and the North American mainland. In 1777 the governor of the Leeward Islands believed that these privately financed ships were of 'infinitely more service' than the navy in attacking the Americans.[11] One of these merchants in Jamaica, a Scotsman named Hercules Ross, owned three such vessels; he also acted as a victualling agent to the navy in Kingston. He was to become one of Nelson's prize agents, long-term friend and correspondent.

There were good grounds for the government to be concerned. The mercantile interest was politically powerful at Westminster, but of greater importance was the fact that the profits from sugar fuelled the economy more than any other single commodity. Governments of the day financed their wars mostly by borrowing, rather than by raising taxes. If the West India trade suffered too much from losses to enemy shipping or from loss of territory in the islands, then credit and government borrowing suffered. Jamaica, towards which Nelson was now heading, was a vital possession.[12]

While much of the *Lowestoffe*'s role was in defence of trade, the other major task of a 32-gun frigate was to pursue enemy warships and privateers, and to take American merchant ships as prizes. The *Lowestoffe*'s first confrontation occurred in the Atlantic. On 2 July, fifty-six leagues from their landfall in Barbados, a sail was sighted and the ship went after it. Locker entered into his log: 'At 1 fired 8 six pounders at the Chace boat, hove to, sent the Lieutenant on board, boat returned with the Master, remained on board the Lieutenant & 8 men. Made sail at 1/2 past 3, joined the convoy. Sent the Mate & 5 hands on board the Schooner on suspicion of her being American property.' Many similar entries followed, but it may have been this occasion that Nelson recollected when he wrote the 'Sketch of My Life' in 1799. The first lieutenant had failed to board the prize because of heavy seas and Nelson pushed his way in front of the master into the ship's boat to attempt the boarding. 'I know,' he wrote, 'it is my disposition, that difficulties and dangers do but increase my desire of attempting them' – a telling statement.[13] The hesitant first lieutenant was Charles Sandys, whom Nelson was to befriend.* Two days later Locker's entry reads: 'At 3 pm came too in Carlisle Bay [Barbados] . . . the convoy all safe and finding the Schooner no[t] American property delivered her up.' Nelson was to have many such prize money disappointments.

The *Lowestoffe* reached Port Royal, Jamaica, on 19 July 1777. After three weeks of maintenance and provisioning, the ship was off again, cruising against the enemy in the Windward Passage, the straits between Cuba and St Domingo to which the greatest concentration of French, Spanish and British merchant ships were drawn. It was difficult sailing in the teeth of strong trade winds from the north-east. The French had the advantage of their nearby bases at Cap François (now Cap-Haïtien) and Môle Saint-Nicholas.[14] The *Lowestoffe* did not shelter in port for the hurricane months of August and September, but set off on 9 August amid squalls and thunder and lightning. Once on station, she chased and boarded, sometimes several times a day, with constant work for the lieutenants in hoisting the ship's boats in and out. Later, in the calms of November and December, the ship's boats often had to tow the captured vessel. Locker's success rate was not high, and the value of the captured cargoes low. On the Jamaica Station as a whole forty-three American ships were taken for the three months of March, April and May 1778, small vessels with the regular cargoes of molasses, fish, lumber, flour, rice, tobacco and barrel staves carried between the American colonies and the islands.[15] There were no rich pickings of sugar ships bound for Europe, for war had yet to be declared against the French or Spanish.

Some of the American ships were very fast, particularly the privateers; often ex-slavers, they were built for speed. Many of the smaller ones were rigged 'fore and aft', rather than with square sails, since they could sail much closer to the wind. The *Lowestoffe*'s log, for instance, on 11 September 1777 records: 'Saw a sloop to the SW, bore away and gave chace. Find the Chace outsailed us: shortened sail and hauled our wind.'[16] It was not easy to find and detain American merchant ships, which disguised themselves and carried false papers. In any case, a ship at a distance was always difficult to identify. On one occasion Locker wasted six 12-pound shot, chasing and firing at an American ship that turned out to have been made a prize already by HM sloop *Diligence*.[17] Much effort was expended by officers and crews in keeping their ships at maximum efficiency, mending

---

* Richard Westall was inspired to paint this incident in the 'elevated' style: Nelson enters a heaving boat in mid Atlantic as though he were crossing a dance floor (NMM, BHC 0421).

rigging and cleaning the ships' bottoms, which necessitated long stays in Port Royal. The slowness of his ships was the constant cry of the commander-in-chief at Jamaica, Admiral Sir Peter Parker, who wrote to the Admiralty of the privateers: 'many have escaped by outsailing some of our foul vessels, which proves the utility of the scheme their Lordships have adopted to sheath some Frigates with copper. A few on this station would clear these seas of Privateers, and besides the annoyance to the Trade of the Rebels.'[18]

This was Parker's main concern for the first half of 1778. Although Jamaica was the great prize for the French, the station itself was something of a strategic backwater and did not warrant ships of the line. The Leeward Islands Station was the first line of defence for Jamaica, and in this war great British and French fleets were to meet there in action time and again. Parker's flagship, the *Bristol*, had only fifty guns; the rest were frigates and sloops and any other suitable ships that could be purchased from the prize court or from local merchants. In Nelson's time there were only two 64s in Jamaican waters: Cornwallis's *Lion* and the *Ruby*, which became Parker's flagship in November 1779. Only once, briefly and indecisively, on 20 June 1780, were they in action against equal force.[19] Parker's other tasks were comparatively small scale. He had the constant problem of maintaining small vessels, which were being worn out by hard sailing, converting the best of the prizes for use in his small squadron. He had to gather convoys to return to England, deal with impressment difficulties with the Jamaican Assembly and attempt to make up the shortages of naval stores. There were always too few shipwrights in Port Royal Dockyard.[20]

Small ships aided the promotion of younger officers, and Nelson was to gain his first command early. It is likely that it was Locker's recommendation to Parker that led to Nelson's transfer from the *Lowestoffe* to third lieutenant of Parker's *Bristol*, which he joined on 2 July 1778.* Nelson was promoted rapidly, over the heads of older lieutenants. For instance, Robert Deans and John Pakenham, first and second lieutenants of the *Bristol*, were much older and senior by thirteen and nine years respectively. When Deans was moved two months later to a command, Parker moved Nelson to first lieutenant, over Pakenham. They were then joined by a new third lieutenant, James Macnamara, who had first been made lieutenant as far back as 1761.

Nelson now succeeded in gaining the good opinion of Admiral Parker,

---

* Locker fades slowly from the story since he became ill several times, finally getting permission to return home after being diagnosed with 'a most violent scourbatic disorder' in mid 1779 ((UK)NA: PRO, ADM 1/241, 1 May 1779, Parker to Stephens).

who took him under his wing for the next three years and was responsible for his rapid promotion. Simultaneously, Parker advanced Cuthbert Collingwood's career at the same rate. Collingwood was a lieutenant in the *Hornet* sloop under an incompetent and cowardly captain, Robert Haswell, but three times in the next two and half years Parker was to move Collingwood into vacancies created by Nelson's moving upwards. Parker and his family undoubtedly prospered in the navy; his reputation has suffered at the hands of Victorian historians, but both he and his wife were kind and accessible to the young officers on this station.* Twenty-seven years later, Collingwood was able to write to him ten days after Trafalgar that 'two of your own pupils, raised under your eye, and cherished by your kindness, should render such service to their country'.[21]

By the summer of 1778 relations with France were fast deteriorating. Preparations for Jamaica's defence went ahead. Parker reported to the Admiralty in June that 'the militia are training and all ranks of the people are perfectly easy,' and relations with the civil powers were good at this time. He received orders from London to 'examine and seize all American ships although under the protection of a foreign power'.[22] France entered the war with no warning. Parker did not hear of the declaration of 14 July until 27 August. The *Minerva* (32) and the *Active* (28) were surprised by French warships, captured and taken into Cap François, their captains killed or dying soon after the action. Parker immediately seized all French ships in Port Royal. The governor of Jamaica laid an embargo on trade with the French. Preparations were made for the defence of Kingston, which, as Parker reported to the Admiralty, had gone on 'with a laudable spirit'.[23]

Nelson's stay in the *Bristol* was to last only five months, a largely uneventful period, although the ship took several French prizes, cruising in company with the newly arrived *Ruby* (64), *Niger* (32), *Lowestoffe* (32), the sloop *Porpoise* (16) and the brig *Badger* (14). In a show of strength the small squadron cruised near the French base at Cap François, 300 miles away. Immediately after Nelson was made a first lieutenant in September, a vacancy occurred. The captain of the *Ruby*, Michael Everitt, had been killed in June, causing a further shift of officers. Nelson had done sufficiently well to be rewarded when a vacancy arose. Back in Port Royal by 21 December,

---

* As a returned prisoner of war, hungry, in rags and unwashed, Bartholomew James remembered being immediately sat down at Parker's table (Laughton, *Bartholomew James*, 67). In the old *Dictionary of National Biography* Parker was described by Sir John Knox Laughton as 'unscrupulous as any of his contemporaries in the abuse of patronage', while Michael Lewis called him 'a notorious old jobber' (*Social History*, 214–15).

Parker made Nelson captain and gave him his first command, the little *Badger*. Nelson had been a lieutenant for a mere two years and eight months. He was two months past his nineteenth birthday.

After a three-week refit, during which he met John Tyson, the purser of the ship, who was to remain a lifelong friend, Nelson set off west in the *Badger* to visit the coast of the Spanish mainland in the Gulf of Honduras (present-day Belize). His task was to warn British settlers there of the impending war with Spain, likely now to join with France. The Spanish had never managed to eject the settlers who had established themselves from the 1740s in the Bay of Honduras and the Mosquito shore.[24] With their slaves, they had developed a lucrative trade in mahogany, which was popular for European furniture. Logwood, the other tree cut by the settlers and used in the process of dying cloth, was by then of declining importance.[25] The settlers had good relations with the local Mosquito Indians, always inclined to rebel against their old imperial masters. Many of the British settlers were Scots, independent-minded, suspicious of any authority, though they were under the loose control of the superintendent of the coast, who in turn was under the nominal control of the governor of Jamaica.[26] Nelson wrote later that he was there 'to protect the settlers from the depredation of the privateers'.[27] However, the visit of the *Badger* was designed to ensure that Spain took no liberties in the present delicate diplomatic situation.

The passage of 400 miles from Jamaica was relatively easy because the prevailing north-east winds were fair. Nelson's first task was to deliver orders to the superintendent at Prinaw Creek, at the mouth of the Black River, where the settlers were mainly concentrated.* But the cruise became demanding navigationally, especially when near the mainland coast. A young lieutenant, Bartholomew James, was in the Black River a few months later; he described the entrance to the river as 'dangerous beyond description, as the frequent north winds oblige ships to seek safety by running to sea, and the difficulty of landing – the river being defended by a dreadful bar – makes it still more uncomfortable'.[28] Nelson worked his way east, sailing to windward, along the coast to False Cape, visiting British settlements. Reaching Cape Gracias à Dias, he turned and came back along the coast via Rattan Island. He sounded as he went, often using the boat, sailing in shallow waters and frequently negotiating reefs. He met only one other

---

* There were nearly 500 settlers and up to 2,000 slaves in 1786, most of them from the Black River, at the time when they had to be evacuated after the 1786 Convention with Spain ((UK)NA: PRO, ADM 1/243, 16 Oct. 1786).

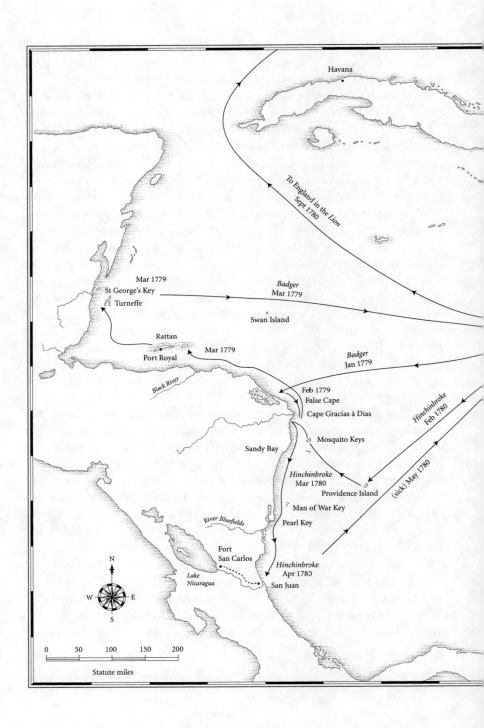

Havana

To England in the Lion
Sept 1780

Mar 1779
St George's Key
Turneffe

Badger
Mar 1779

Swan Island

Rattan

Mar 1779

Port Royal

Badger
Jan 1779

Black River

Feb 1779
False Cape
Cape Gracias à Dias

Hinchinbroke
Feb 1780

Mosquito Keys

Sandy Bay

Hinchinbroke
Mar 1780
Providence Island

(sick) May 1780

River Bluefields

Man of War Key

Pearl Key

Fort
San Carlos

N

*Lake
Nicaragua*

W   E

S

Hinchinbroke
Apr 1780
San Juan

0   50   100   150   200

Statute miles

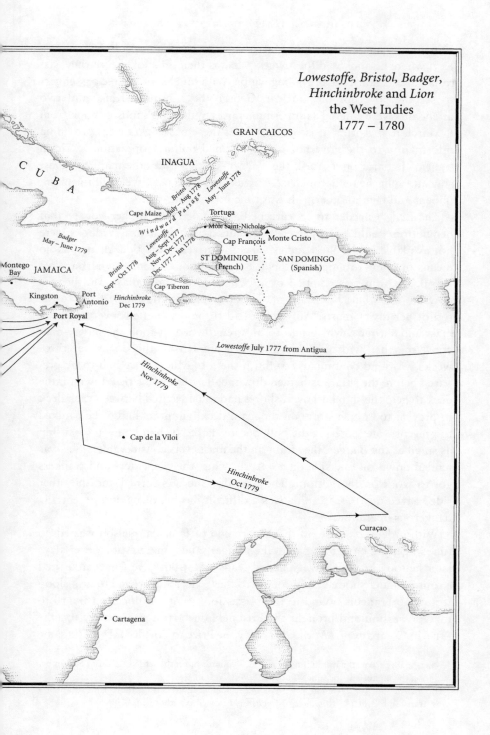

Lowestoffe, Bristol, Badger,
Hinchinbroke and *Lion*
the West Indies
1777 – 1780

GRAN CAICOS

INAGUA

C U B A

Bristol
July – Aug 1778

Lowestoffe
May – June 1778

Cape Maize

Windward Passage

Tortuga

Môle Saint-Nicholas

Lowestoffe
Aug – Sept 1777
Nov – Dec 1777
Dec 1777 – Jan 1778

Cap François ▲ Monte Cristo

ST DOMINIQUE
(French)

SAN DOMINGO
(Spanish)

Badger
May – June 1779

Bristol
Sept – Oct 1778

Cap Tiberon

Montego
Bay

JAMAICA

Kingston

Port
Antonio

Hinchinbroke
Dec 1779

Port Royal

Lowestoffe July 1777 from Antigua

Hinchinbroke
Nov 1779

• Cap de la Viloi

Hinchinbroke
Oct 1779

Curaçao

• Cartagena

ship, a local Spaniard. In late March 1779 he headed north to St George's Key, where he anchored for a week.* It was then time for the journey east to Jamaica, against the prevailing winds. With him he took three passengers to see the governor of Jamaica: 'George the Mosquito King' and two attendants were entered as supernumeraries in the ship's muster book from 8 March to 7 April.[29] It is probable that these passengers were providing information to the governor about planned military operations. Within sight of Jamaica on 1 April, the *Badger* 'carried away the main top mast stay and split the main top mast. Carried away the peak tye, split the main, unbent and bent another.'[30] It was time for another refit.

The *Badger* needed to be 'careened', or hauled over on her side, so that her bottom could be inspected, maintained and cleaned. Dry docks were not available in the West Indies, since, with very little tide, there was no means of filling or emptying them. Alongside the careening wharf at Port Royal, the ship was emptied of all guns, stores and ballast, and heaved down to the wharf by means of very large blocks and tackle fixed to the top of her lower masts. All rigging had to be dismantled save the lower mast and shrouds, which had to be strengthened. It took the ninety-man crew, together with caulkers and carpenters from the dockyard, three weeks, working continually, to finish the job. Much more had to be prepared before the ship was hauled down: ballast had to be tied down on the deck to help the ship heel over, shores had to be secured between each deck to prevent too much strain on the main deck; gunports had to be caulked to prevent water entering the hull; pumps had to be handy. Even for a ship as small as the *Badger*, the strain on the masts was considerable.† She was hauled down on one side on 11 April, when the carpenters and caulkers got to work on the bottom. The next day she was turned and the other side heaved down. Careening was a difficult, hectic, tiring and potentially dangerous operation.

With orders to cruise off the eastern end of Jamaica, Nelson wasted no time in getting back to sea, and the *Badger* sailed on 22 April. Seven days later he took his first prize. The log reads: 'At 3 pm gave Chace at 4 fired a four pounder shotted and brought to the Chace. She proved to be a sloop from Cap François bound to the Mississippi. Sent an officer on Board to take possession and brought the Prisoners on board. At 6pm lay too the Prize in Company. 30 April: Sent away the Prize to Port Royal.'[31] The same

---

* When Spain entered the war in June 1779, the Spaniards burnt the settlement on 15 September and took the inhabitants prisoner (Pocock, *Young Nelson*, 46).
† The instructions for careening a 74-gun ship calculate the strain on the masthead at forty tons (transcript from *The Romance of English Harbour* [no author, n.d.]).

day he wrote to Locker: 'I know you will be pleased with this little earnest of success, but we have had a good deal of plague with her. Two days before we could find the French papers, at last found them in an old shoe.'[32] The ship was *La Prudente* of ninety tons, with a nine-man crew, carrying sugar, coffee, taffia (a spirit made from molasses) and other articles.[33] The prize was small but the cargo valuable.

Yet the taking of *La Prudente* would, in the end, put Nelson out of pocket. Once the ship reached Port Royal, his first task and that of his friend and agent Hercules Ross was to prove to the vice-admiralty court that the ship was lawfully taken.[34] But if the owners could prove the ship to be Spanish, the cargo from and bound to a Spanish port, then the prize would not be 'condemned', for Spain had not yet formally joined the war. Using the evidence of the papers found in the old shoe, Ross had to convince the judge that the ship was French, that she was sailing from a French port and that her Spanish papers were not genuine. Ross testified as follows to the court:

That the officers of his Majesty's sloop *Badger* aforesaid, suspecting the papers to have been procured and then exhibited as a Cloak for French property, made a further search, in consequence of which they found – concealed low down among the cargo of the said sloop *La Prudente* – an old shoe containing a number of letters and other papers all written in the French language and dated from Cap François a few days preceding.[35]

The judge, however, found against Nelson and the *Badger*. The case seems to have turned on the fact, as Parker reported to the Admiralty, that the owners were 'naturalised subjects of Spain, residing at New Orleans'.[36] The strong circumstantial evidence found in the old shoe, of which Nelson was so confident, was discounted. Ross's expenses for the trial, which he submitted to Nelson, were £37.15s.3d. *La Prudente* sailed free.[37] Nelson was never to make his fortune from prize money; perhaps this early unsuccessful experience blunted his enthusiasm.

Through May, Nelson was cruising north of Jamaica, escorting local convoys and investigating strange ships. He chased another American brig, but she was caught before the *Badger* could reach her by another British warship, the new and larger *Pomona* (28). On 2 June he was anchored in Montego Bay when four ships from a convoy from England came in, escorted by the 20-gun *Glasgow*. Nelson now had an opportunity to show his presence of mind.

At 6pm saw the alarm of fire on board the *Glasgow*, sent our boats and two boats belonging to the merchantmen, with Buckets and men to their assistance. 1/4 past 7 pm was got through the Quarterdeck and up the main rigging. The Boatswain employed in receiving the men from the *Glasgow*. Captain and officers of the *Glasgow* on board the *Badger*. At 1/2 past eight she was cut adrift and drove out to sea. At 12 there was an explosion on board the *Glasgow* and she immediately sunk: some of the men were burnt: and the Master at 7am departed this life (name James Cobby).

So ran the *Badger*'s log.[38] This incident so printed itself on Nelson's mind that he recalled it when he wrote the 'Sketch of His Life' over twenty years later. The *Glasgow*'s captain was honourably acquitted by the court martial, but the purser's steward, Richard Brace, who had knocked over a candle when stealing some spirits, received 'a hundred lashes for being the cause through carelessness of the ship being burnt'.[39]

The *Badger* carried on cruising north of Jamaica, with little incident other than a tough chase on 14 June when Nelson expended fifty-six rounds of shot and forty-two of grape upon a strange sail. A game of bluff and counter-bluff ensued. The ship turned out to be a British privateer; her master thought the *Badger* was French. Nelson arrived back at Port Royal to find that the squadron was by now reinforced with the 50-gun *Salisbury*, Sir Edward Hughes's old flagship from the East Indies days. He discovered that on 11 June Parker had appointed him captain of the *Hinchinbroke* (28) though the ship was not yet in port. Parker put Nelson's time to good use until his ship arrived. A large French fleet under Admiral le comte d'Estaing was at the Leewards, and there were several thousand French troops in the islands, causing much haste and bustle in Kingston. Invasion was a real possibility. Martial law was declared. Booms were laid, fireships prepared, ships positioned – all these tasks were overseen by Nelson. The emergency, however, was soon over, for d'Estaing turned northwards to the American colonies. In late August Parker received orders to commence hostilities against Spain.[40]

The *Hinchinbroke* finally arrived at Jamaica, and on 1 September 1779 Nelson assumed command of her. This moment was a critical point in Nelson's career, for she was a sixth-rate ship, which meant that Nelson was now a 'post-captain' – that is, he had been 'made post', achieved the full rank of Captain. He was entered on the list of Captains and the date of his seniority established. Promotion up the list would now follow automatically. He was just under twenty-one. The *Hinchinbroke* was not much of a ship: a French prize captured in 1778, she was to founder off

Jamaica only two years after Nelson left her. Her hull was rotten and her rigging was continually troublesome.

Parker's first task for Nelson was to cruise to the southward to identify any increased Spanish activity. He set out towards Cartagena on the South American mainland on 5 October, checking also to see if there were ships of war in the Dutch port of Curaçao. When he turned back to Jamaica after three weeks with nothing to report, he joined the *Niger* and the *Penelope*, taking two merchant ships as prizes. He was by now at the eastern end of Jamaica. The ship beat into the north-easterly for several hundred miles, and her rigging started to show strain. With her foremast sprung, he took her into an anchorage just on the northern coast at Port Antonio. He was again to be unlucky with prize money. He wrote to Locker: 'We took four Sail, for which I shall share about £800 sterling.'[41] But two of the prizes were disallowed by the vice-admiralty court.[42]

On his return to Port Royal in mid December, Nelson found an expedition in preparation. General Dalling, the governor of Jamaica, had conceived a strike against the Spanish mainland. Pushing back the increasingly weak Spanish empire had long been a British ambition. A recent success had been an opportunistic expedition by six ships, commanded by Captain John Luttrell of the *Charon* (44), which had captured the town of Omoa on the mainland on 19 October; they had had the great fortune to seize the Spanish Register ships loaded with silver.[43] Had Nelson stayed with the *Lowestoffe*, he would have had a share in this rich haul. Spanish territory seemed undefended, and intelligence of a series of Indian rebellions across Spanish territories was now reaching the British.*[44] Dalling had determined on the bold stroke of attacking the fortress of San Juan and proceeding up the river to Lake Nicaragua, and then on to the Pacific to create a naval presence on the west coast of the mainland. In the words of one contemporary, 'The colours of England were, in their imagination, already on the walls of Lima.'[45]

Dalling was an impetuous man with a big idea. The main problem was that no one had real local knowledge of the conditions or geography of San Juan or Nicaragua. Dalling had outline approval from Lord George Germain, the secretary of state for the American colonies, to attack the Spanish mainland, but he did not have the support of Parker, with whom he was currently embroiled in a serious dispute over the navy and army

---

* Luttrell had also taken the island of Rattan and Parker wrote to the Admiralty with the idea of establishing it as a centre for British trade ((UK)NA: PRO, ADM 1/242, 5 Nov. 1779). A British colony had been tried in the 1739–48 War with Spain without success (Pares, 103–4).

prize money from the Omoa expedition.* Parker also disapproved of the expedition, since it took soldiers away from the defences of Jamaica. Nevertheless, he offered the command of the ships to Nelson, who replied, 'I am obliged to you for the good opinion you entertain of me which I hope will always continue.' He followed this pleasantry by a request for authority over the seamen in the transports.[46] He seemed, at least in a letter to Locker, sceptical of success: 'How it will turn out, God knows.'[47]

The expedition forces gathered in Kingston, and Hercules Ross raised supplies. Some regular soldiers from the 79th Regiment and two loyalist American regiments were available, but success depended upon the larger numbers of irregulars, who were of doubtful quality. Major Polson, dull and conscientious, made up to lieutenant-colonel for the duration of the expedition, commanded the land forces. The newly arrived lieutenant-governor, Archibald Campbell, a brigadier-general with a distinguished record, was not impressed with the quality of the troops, although they were in good health.[48] 'The irregulars were drawn up in a ragged line, half-clothed and half-drunk, they seemed to possess the true complexion of buccaneers . . . I thought it good policy to order ten guineas for them to be drunk in grog on board their transports and embarked them with three cheers to the great satisfaction of the town of Kingston.'[49] It was not an auspicious start.

The convoy, consisting of a transport, two brigs, three sloops, a tender and the *Hinchinbroke*, set off on 3 February 1780.[50] It took seven weeks to get to San Juan River. Having called at Providence Island to pick up pilots, armed settlers and Indians, Nelson made his landfall on 14 February at Cape Gracias à Dias, which he knew from the *Badger* cruise. There he rendezvoused with more troops from the 79th Regiment and with Indians. He disembarked the troops for three weeks while the carpenters constructed the prefabricated flat-bottomed boat for the journey up the river. After further delays in gathering soldiers from the Black River, settlers and more Indians, he sailed south.[51] Nelson had no knowledge of this shoal-ridden shore, though it had been charted, and he proceeded slowly, anchoring every night. The *Hinchinbroke* and the *Penelope*, one of the brigs, ran aground on reefs, both getting off by the next day. These delays were to prove important, for the end of the dry season was approaching. On 24 March the convoy arrived at the harbour at the mouth of the San Juan;

---

* Unusually, the bullion captured by the British had been aboard Spanish ships within the harbour, thus blurring the rights of the army to booty on land and the navy to prize money at sea.

according to the surgeon with the expedition, Thomas Dancer, the men were 'in general good health, and in great spirits'.[52]

Nelson's orders from Parker were to disembark the soldiers, the irregulars, the handful of settlers, some of their slaves and 200 Indians. At this point, his direct involvement was to cease: others were to take the soldiers up the river. But when Nelson saw some of the boats capsize on starting the journey upriver, he asked for volunteers, took the *Hinchinbroke*'s boats and put them and himself at Colonel Polson's disposal, his regard for the colonel and his young officers apparently having grown during the sea voyage. They started upriver on 28 March. The boats and canoes rowed and paddled hard upriver against the stream, but were obstructed as much by shoals as by the current. Away from the coast, conditions became difficult, with the heat and the hostile jungle against them. On 9 April the expedition took a Spanish outpost; according to Thomas Dancer, 'hardly any wounded'. The next day Nelson narrowly escaped being bitten by a snake.[53] On 11 April they finally reached the castle of San Juan, an imposing seventeenth-century fort, built on a hill next to the river. Nelson, supported by a young Irish engineer officer, Edward Despard, was for a quick assault, but the cautious Polson, after so many setbacks, decided upon a more traditional siege. Nelson and Despard worked the 4-pound guns up to high ground and opened fire. Not long afterwards the rains began with tropical force.

What fighting took place was mild, with only three killed and nine or ten wounded.[54] The humid conditions, however, began to take their toll. Dysentery was rife. Nelson's condition was made worse by a violent return of malaria, but that was clearly not all that was wrong. By now reinforcements of regular soldiers arrived from the mouth of the river, and the attacks and cannon fire had more weight. Nelson was weak and lying in his tent. Further reinforcements arrived and with them a letter from Parker in Jamaica, appointing Nelson to a new ship, the *Janus* (44). He was to be succeeded in the *Hinchinbroke* by Cuthbert Collingwood. Such an order Nelson could not ignore. He was taken downriver to the ships, borne swiftly by the river, which was swollen with the rain. The fort surrendered to Polson. Damp and ill supplied, it was 'worse than any prison, and, as one would suppose, calculated only for the purpose of breeding infection'.[55] It offered no comfort or shelter to its conquerors. The Mosquito Indians deserted. Although the waters of Lake Nicaragua were invitingly near and Spanish military resistance was crumbling, the expedition could go no further.

Collingwood had come to the mouth of the river with the third convoy of reinforcements. On 30 April Nelson signed his last entry, an incomplete one, in the *Hinchinbroke*'s log with a shaky hand and was carried off to Port Royal.[56] The officers and crew of the *Hinchinbroke* were very sickly. The first lieutenant had died a week before Nelson had reappeared from the interior. When Collingwood took over, there were seventy seamen sick. He eventually 'buried 180 of the 200 which composed it'. The crews of the transports also died and some of the ships sank at anchor.[57] Collingwood returned to Jamaica, but, because Parker found it difficult to gather enough transports and ships to bring the remains of the expedition back to Jamaica, he had to make a further passage to and from the San Juan River. A more harrowing experience in a post-captain's first months can hardly be imagined.[58] Few could disagree with Collingwood's verdict on the expedition:

The plan was formed without a sufficient knowledge of the country, which presented difficulties that were not to be surmounted by human skill or perseverance. The river was difficult to proceed on from the rapidity of the current, and the several falls over the rocks, which intercepted the navigation, and the climate was deadly; no constitution could resist its effects.[59]

Sixty-nine army and naval officers died. Out of 1,800 soldiers and sailors in the expedition, only 380 survived.[60] Of those that did, many suffered subsequent poor health. Twenty years later, a survivor, Benjamin Rogers, wrote to Nelson. He had 'not enjoy'd twelve months sound health together ... my two brothers likewise that were there, linger'd many years after, and the eldest (which was your Lordship's clerk) died about eight or nine years ago, the other I buried at Portsmouth five years since.'[61] Parker's order to Nelson to take command of the *Janus*, which took him out of the jungle, almost certainly saved his life.

Unquestionably, the expedition was under-resourced. Any eighteenth-century West Indies amphibious expedition could expect a high sickness rate from dysentery, malaria or yellow fever. Sickness rates for amphibious forces arriving in the Caribbean in the three middle wars of the eighteenth century were fully appreciated by the British; they 'typically rose to 30% within three months of arrival, up to between 40% to 50% after six to eight months and steadied to around 25% for immune survivors'.[62] Even when the British captured Havana in 1762, the victory was a near-run thing because of sickness. In this case Governor Dalling was blamed for the disaster; the Jamaican Assembly demanded his recall and he left Jamaica for London. His deputy, Archibald Campbell, took over as governor.

Nevertheless, the decision to mount the expedition at the beginning of a war with Spain was, in principle, a shrewd move. One is left wondering at the presence of three Mosquito Indians in Nelson's previous voyage undertaken in the *Badger*, delivered to the governor in April 1779, for the Indians were consistently hostile to the Spaniards. Did Nelson play any role in the planning of the expedition? As it turned out, Spanish military resistance to the San Juan expedition was minimal. But the expedition was planned against a background of dissension in Kingston, when army and navy were not at one, and when the town was under martial law. Had the San Juan River been reached in the dry season, the expedition might well have succeeded. Later in the war, Campbell was successful in Central America with a force of irregulars and Indians, defeating the Spanish at Black River in 1782.[63]

Nelson landed at Port Royal an emaciated figure. At the suggestion of William Cornwallis, he did not go to the hospital, where there was great danger of further infection. Nelson had befriended Cornwallis, captain of the *Lion* (64), shy, fourteen years older and very well connected, when he had arrived at Jamaica with a convoy in July 1779, and they had lodged together when not at sea.[64] Nelson was restored to some health by his housekeeper, Cuba Cornwallis, a former slave who had taken Cornwallis's name, as many African women in Jamaican domestic service did at this time.[65] Her herbal remedies restored vitamin C to his body. From there he was taken to Admiral Parker's house, where he was cared for by the admiral and his wife. Most recent medical opinion does not ascribe his dramatic illness to the usual yellow fever, for the symptoms do not agree with those of the crew of the *Hinchinbroke*, described by Collingwood on 17 May in his log: '86 men exceedingly ill with fevers, fluxes and scorbutic ulcers'. Nelson is likely to have suffered from a debilitating combination of diseases, of which the most certain was his recurring malaria.[66] Medical opinion is divided upon which the other might have been; the strongest candidate is water-borne typhoid, undoubtedly complicated by malaria, a diagnosis made more likely by no mention of fluxes or diarrhoea.*

Even though the *Janus* was waiting for him, Nelson did not recover

---

* I have been guided in this opinion by Professor Leslie Le Quesne, who in turn has talked to specialists in tropical diseases; see Kemble, 117–19, 120–21; Christie, 132–6. The description of typhoid in Christie fits the evidence, including the long duration of the illness, and the later symptoms of polyneuritis (to be distinguished from peripheral neuritis) in Nelson's arms and side. The fact that Nelson did not fall sick at the sieges of Bastia and Calvi in 1794 and 1795, when there was a lot of sickness, points to the fact that he may have built up immunity to the disease. See also the long discussion of medical opinion in Sugden, *Nelson*, 810–11.

sufficiently to assume command. Through the hot and sticky summer months he tried to return to duty, but towards the end of August he was examined by the surgeons from the hospital, who recommended his return home, finding:

From repeated attacks of Tertian and Quartan Agues, and those now degenerated into Quotidian, attended with bilious Vomitings, Nervous headaches, Visceral Obstructions and many other bodily infirmities, and being reduced quite to a Skeleton, we are of opinion his remaining here will be attended with fatal consequences . . .[67]

Parker ordered Nelson to England, writing to the Admiralty that he doubted 'whether he will Live to get Home'.[68]

Nelson was moved into the *Lion*, with his servant Frank Lepee, where William Cornwallis cared for him. The ship left Port Royal on 5 September. The voyage lasted nearly three months, because the *Lion* was an escort for a large convoy, that slowly gathered 140 merchant ships. The convoy sailed around the western end of Cuba, where it picked up the strong, northerly current that helped it against the north-east trade wind; it also sometimes produced dangerous conditions, described by a contemporary as 'raising a high, short, and disagreeable sea, which tumbled about us sadly', setting his ship 'from fifty to seventy-five miles to the northward every twenty-four hours'.[69] As the convoy passed in the vicinity of Havana, the warships took the precaution of hoisting Spanish colours. By 22 September they were off Cape Florida.[70] Only eleven days later the West Indies were struck by a ferocious hurricane, reckoned the worst in the century; late in the season, it took an unusual track. A week later it was followed by another. Twelve ships were lost; twenty-two were seriously damaged.* Hundreds of officers and men were drowned, many known to Nelson.[71]

Although the manner of his departure was a low point, Nelson in the last three years in the West Indies had achieved a reputation for courage and leadership, although he had not been successful with prize money. His relationships with army officers were unusually cordial. The *London Gazette*, reporting on the expedition, recorded that 'He was first upon every occasion, whether by Day or by Night, there was scarcely a gun fired but was pointed by him or Lieutenant Despard.'[72] Nelson had impressed Parker, a senior admiral. General Dalling wrote to Lord George Germain praising

---

* The *Badger*, for instance, was dismasted and driven on shore on the north side of Jamaica, though she was later salvaged.

his achievement, asking Germain 'to manifest a Satisfaction of his conduct' and requesting that Nelson should command another expedition 'for the Southern Ocean', if one were to come about.[73]

Nelson had displayed, for the first time, individualism, and he had very early promotion to show for it. Of his contemporaries, only Charles Morice Pole had made post-captain at a younger age. But the young man's certainty and confidence were now emerging, and his enthusiasm and charm had influenced his seniors and peers. In going up the San Juan River, Nelson had ignored his admiral's order, but Parker had chosen to interpret the young officer's disobedience as initiative. In early 1779 Nelson had also revealed early signs of temper and ruthlessness at what he considered the insubordination of the master of the home-going merchant ship *Amity Hall*, who quite rightly had protested at the pressing of his crew. Because of this altercation, Nelson pressed two seamen, overstepping the convention that allowed ships en route for England to keep their men, an action that had worried Locker and Parker.[74] But a real concern shows through Parker's official report to the secretary of the Admiralty: 'I wish much for his recovery. His abilities in his profession would be a loss to the service.'[75] At Spithead on 25 November 1780 Nelson was discharged from the *Lion*. He went straight to Bath for treatment. Ahead of him were many months of illness and fatigue, and it was well into the next year before he was again fit to resume his career.

5

Albemarle

November 1780–March 1784

*My situation in Lord Hood's Fleet must be in the highest degree flatter-
ing to any young man. He treats me as if I was his son, and will, I am
convinced, give me anything I can ask of him: nor is my situation with
Prince William less flattering.*

Nelson to Captain William Locker, 25 February 1783[1]

*. . . the ridiculous expedition against Turk's Island, undertaken by a
young man merely from the hope of seeing his name in the papers,
ill-depicted at first, carried on without intelligence, and hastily abandoned at last for the same reason that it ought not to have been
undertaken at all . . .*

James Trevenen, first lieutenant of the *Resistance*,
to his mother, 5 April 1783*

At Bath, Nelson drank the waters three times a day, was given purgatives
and was not allowed wine. He met other officers, read the papers avidly
and wrote to William Locker asking him to send an up-to-date *Navy List*.[2]
He tried unsuccessfully to persuade Locker, who was himself not well, to
come down to Bath. He was joined by an old friend of Locker, James Kirk,
who had come ashore many years before and was now a commissioner of
the Victualling Board. Kirk brought his wife to Bath for a cure, although
the surgeons could do nothing for her. In March he planned to travel
to London with the Kirks, stopping to stay with Robert Kingsmill near
Newbury.[3] The path of Nelson's recovery was erratic. By mid February he
wrote cheerfully to Locker that he had recovered the use of his limbs,

---

* Trevenen was in any case angry because Nelson's attack on Turk's Island had delayed the
arrival of the *Resistance*'s prizes at Port Royal until after peace had been declared. By then the
prizes were worth much less (Lloyd, *Trevenen*, 56).

though his left arm was still numb. In March and May he made journeys to London, staying with his uncle William Suckling.[4] A week after the second visit he wrote that he was now perfectly restored to health, though he would still remain in Bath for a period.[5] Then his condition deteriorated again.

The state of Nelson's health was to fluctuate markedly, as was the process whereby he was to obtain his next sea appointment. More captains had been appointed than there were ships in commission, and many were unemployed even in the middle of a war. Lord Sandwich's appointment book for this time shows eighty applicant captains still without a ship. The book was divided into three columns: 'Name', 'Recommended By' and 'For what'. Nelson's name first appears here in an undated entry in Sandwich's own hand: 'Horatio Nelson', 'Himself', 'Employment'. Nothing happened. Two pages further on there is another entry, in the hand of an Admiralty clerk. This time in the 'Recommended By' column the name 'Mr Jenkinson' is entered.[6] No more powerful patron lived in the land.

Charles Jenkinson was the secretary-at-war and a close confidant of the king. Horace Walpole described this minister as 'the director and agent of all his [the king's] secret counsels'. He was in the tight circle around the prime minister, Lord North, and, in the opinion of one authority on North's government, 'his influence was out of all proportion to his departmental standing.'[7] Sandwich, weakened within the government by lack of naval success and attacks in Parliament, could not ignore a request from this quarter; besides, Jenkinson controlled a great many appointments in which Sandwich himself would have an interest and their correspondence is heavily sprinkled with patronage business. There is no evidence that Jenkinson and Nelson ever met, but on 12 February 1781 Jenkinson wrote the following letter to Lord Sandwich:

I am earnestly desired to recommend to your Lordship Captain Horatio Nelson, late of His Majesty's Ship *Hinchinbrook*, to be employ'd; this Gentlemen is the Nephew of the late Comptroller of the Navy Mr Suckling & bears as I am assured a very good Character; I shall be much obliged to your Lordship if you will have the Goodness to comply with this request.[8]

There is thus no mystery as to why Sandwich appointed Nelson. Who, however, could have persuaded Jenkinson to write the letter? Jenkinson had served one year on the Board of Admiralty, in 1776/7, and thereafter for nine years he was a lord of the Treasury and well acquainted with the 'Deputy Collector, Inwards' at the Customs House in London, who was none other than Nelson's other uncle, William Suckling. Suckling wrote to Jenkinson about a ship for Nelson in April. He was assured by Jenkinson that he had already written to Sandwich 'strongly recommending Captain Horatio Nelson for Employment'.[9]

It is likely too that Suckling, as the most senior customs official, knew many of the officials in the Admiralty and Navy offices.[10] He was part of the governmental patronage network and had constant business with the navy as officers arrived from abroad with dutiable goods. Thus, in the autumn of that year, Vice-Admiral Robert Roddam, commander-in-chief at the Nore, received a letter from Suckling to pass on to Nelson, daily expected there in his new ship, the *Albemarle*. The admiral seized the chance to write back to such an important correspondent: 'you may depend on my good offices to your nephew Captain Nelson as I shall have the greatest pleasure in countenancing any body from you, particularly one so nearly related as Captain Nelson and at any time without Ceremony you may let me know your wishes.' For good measure the admiral asked, 'Will you be so good as to let me know what is a Tidewaiters place in fee, what's the duty and income as I want to get something of a Fixture for a person about 45 either in the Customs, Salt or Excise and how the best mode of Application?'[11]

While politicians and officials corresponded, Nelson's use of his limbs was still impaired.[12] During his visit to London in March he sought more sophisticated medical advice. He saw Robert Adair, surgeon-general to the army and to George III. Nelson also saw Lord Sandwich on 6 May, when the first lord assured him of a ship when one was available. He was still not well, writing to his brother: 'I have entirely lost the use of my left arm, and very near of my left leg and thigh.'[13] The condition improved, though he was to experience later relapses.

The lobbying finally bore fruit and Nelson was appointed to a frigate. On 15 August he saw her at Woolwich, making his first entry in his log: 'came down and put the ship in commission'.[14] The *Albemarle*, barring only the *Hinchinbroke*, performed worse than any other ship Nelson was ever to command. She was a French prize and consequently narrow in the beam; as a result, she heeled too much and thus would not go well to windward.[15] At first, when she was in dock at Woolwich having her hull sheathed with copper, Nelson liked the look of her lines and wrote enthusiastically to his brother William, but he soon realized her weaknesses and made a half-hearted attempt to obtain a larger frigate.[16] After a month's rerigging and taking on stores, the *Albemarle* made her way downriver to Long Reach, where she got in her guns; and on 14 October, there being no wind, she was towed down on the tide, assisted by men from Greenwich Hospital and from the Royal Yacht.[17] She came to anchor at the Nore the next day.

Nelson now set about the difficult task of raising men. Most came from London, though a small minority were Norfolk men from Wells. He sent some pressed men ahead to the receiving ship, Admiral Roddam's *Con-questadore*, at the Nore and in return forty came from her on the admiral's order, 'in equal proportion letting the Able and Ordinary be good and the Landsmen healthy . . . among the forty you will send a man for carpenter's mate.'[18] Several times Nelson commented on the quality of the crew: 'They are, in my Opinion, as good a set of Men as I ever saw; indeed, I am perfectly satisfied with both Officers and Ship's Company. All my marines are likewise Old Standers.'[19]

On 20 October Admiral Roddam received Admiralty orders for the *Albemarle* to be put in immediate readiness for sea. Three days later Nelson received his own orders. With the *Argo* (44) and the *Enterprise* (28) under his command, he was to go to Elsinore (Helsingborg) in Denmark, the rendezvous for British merchant ships from all ports in the Baltic, to collect the last of the season's merchant ships, before the winter ice froze, and convoy them to the Downs.[20] The Baltic convoy was one of the navy's unsung but essential tasks, for the merchant ships that came across to British ports carried the naval stores of hardwood and mast timber, hemp, pitch, tallow, Stockholm tar and Swedish iron essential to the existence of the British Navy and a merchant fleet.

In the meantime, Roddam received intelligence that three homecoming East Indiamen were passing the Downs and would soon come up the Thames estuary. He ordered the *Albemarle* to intercept them and press more men for the receiving ship. This would be difficult: the Indiamen were large and well manned, and would put up considerable resistance, repelling a ship's boat by force if necessary. Force would need to be met by force. Roddam specified that the ships were to be boarded, but that force was not to be used. Not unexpectedly, Nelson queried his orders.[21] The East Indiamen, to avoid detection, were passing through the Nore at night. With a new and untrained crew, in the confined and shallow waters of the Thames estuary with its fast flowing tides, it would be a difficult encounter. But the *Albemarle* found them and went alongside one of them. The log of the first lieutenant, Martin Hinton, for 29 October, gives the best account:

Rece[ive]d intelligence from a Tender that a number of E[as]t. Indiamen (whose men were not impressed) was coming up the River & they would not suffer any

Tenders or Boats to Board them . . . Bro[ugh]t to & hove a great strain on the Best Bower. Carried away the messenger. Rove a purchase & carried it away. Finding our efforts to weigh of no effect & 4 sail of Indiamen abreast, some above us. Cut the cable leaving 20 fa[thom]s, anchor Buoy and buoy rope behind. At 10 made sail after the above ships. At 11 hail the Headmost & ordered them to bring to, but having all their men on board they would not until we compelled them to anchor, firing 26 nine p[ounder]s shotted at their masts and rigging. We likewise bro[ught] to 3 others & anchored ourselves alongside the Headmost of them. At 12 sent the boat on board the *Haswell* whose men had not been pressed. They threatened resistance & til Daylight was given them to consider on it. At 5 am Weighed and run alongside the *Haswell* upon which her men entered for H.M. Service and accordingly Embarked in the Tenders.[22]

This act of impressment, ruthless though it was in taking men who had already been away from England for three years, was nevertheless typical of the time. Apart perhaps from firing at the rigging, Nelson was within his rights, although a number of officers found themselves in legal trouble when they overstepped the mark. In this case, neither the captains of the East India ships nor the Company itself protested. Nelson gathered up the *Argo* and the *Enterprise* and headed east across the North Sea to Denmark.

The importance of the Baltic convoys increased in 1781 and 1782. Britain was facing hostility from Russia, Sweden and Denmark, because of her insistence on her right to search neutral ships. Russia, under Catherine the Great, had brought these countries together to form the League of Armed Neutrality in July 1780. Though the alliance was hostile, it fell some way short of actually waging war. But the French had developed a river and canal route for transporting masts to Brest through Holland and France, thus evading the British blockade in the Channel. So desperate was the British government to prevent naval stores getting to France in neutral Dutch ships that it engineered a declaration of war against Holland.[23] The objective for both the British and Dutch, now hostile to each other, was the successful maintenance of their respective trades in the North Sea, particularly in naval stores. Protecting British merchant ships from Dutch warships and frigates thus added a further task to the already overstretched British Navy.

Elsinore, at the top of the Sound, was twenty-five miles north of Copenhagen. In 1781 seven British convoys sailed into the seaport and five left it bound for home. Nelson's was the last homeward convoy of the year, and it had little to contend with except the weather, no small enemy in the North Sea in winter.

The *Albemarle* reached Elsinore on 4 November. The next day Nelson wrote to inform the Admiralty that, in the opinion of the British consul, it would not be possible to bring the last ships home – there were still forty that would not reach Elsinore until Christmas and 'waiting for those few would endanger an Immense Fleet at this late season of the year'.[24] During the month-long wait it was very cold. The *Albemarle* lost seven men who deserted by taking the cutter and who no doubt found better-paid berths on the waiting merchant ships.[25] In November the convoy was joined by the newly completed ship *Sampson* (64), commanded by Archibald Dickson, a captain with five years' seniority, who therefore superseded Nelson's command of the convoy. Frosts set in and the masters of the merchant ships became restive, concerned that they might become frozen in the ice for the winter. On 7 December some ships sailed before Dickson was prepared to go. The next day he brought 192 out of the Kattegat.[26]

For the first day the wind was fair, as the convoy sailed north-west from the Sound to the northerly tip of Denmark, then headed west for the high land of Flamborough Head, where convoys generally divided, north for the Tyne or south for London. Winds from the south-west, prevalent at this time of year, meant that these convoys of heavily laden ships were beating into the wind across the North Sea. The weather was recorded as 'Fresh gales and squally'. By 11 December the convoy had scattered and the *Albemarle* could sight only forty-six ships, none of which were the other warships. Only one potentially hostile ship was sighted. On 13 December Nelson had his first real experience of the *Albemarle*'s shortcomings: a cutter was seen to leeward of the convoy. He chased it for an hour, but 'finding we could not come up with her', he returned to the convoy.[27] After four days of strong winds the scattered convoy made the English coast. Three overladen merchant ships had foundered.[28] The North Sea convoys customarily dispersed without notice, for fear of losing their crews to the press gangs. In a letter to Philip Stephens, the Admiralty secretary, from the Yarmouth Roads (which he reached on 17 December), Nelson commented that very few of the ships 'paid the least regard to any Signals that were made for the better conducting them safe home'.[29] He could hardly have been surprised, since he had only just taken the men off the East India Company ships in the Thames estuary. Archibald Dickson also wrote a report to the Admiralty, concluding, 'I hope their Lordships will be pleased to make my complaint public that the merchants may know the irregular conduct of the masters of their ships.'[30]

At Yarmouth, with the wind still blowing from the south, the *Albemarle* lay at anchor with the rump of the convoy, including twenty-eight contracted by the Navy Board that had naval stores for Portsmouth and Plymouth dockyards. He assured Stephens that he would sail to the Downs the 'instant the wind blows from the west'.[31] While lying there, he had a brief visit from his brother William during a lull in the boisterous weather.[32] He reached the Downs on 2 January and delivered his convoy, which by this time had grown to sixty-five ships, to the admiral commanding, Rear-Admiral Francis Drake. Then he waited for orders.[33] He also lost an anchor and cable, causing a small altercation with another rear-admiral, Sir Richard Hughes, stationed in the Downs in the store ship *Dromedary*. Hughes wrote to ensure that Nelson had made every effort to sweep for and retrieve the lost equipment. Nelson's indignant reply foreshadowed their future troubled relationship: 'I am very sorry you should have so bad an Opinion of my conduct as to suppose that every Effort has not and would not be made to sweep [for] the anchor.'[34] His reaction to criticism bordered on petulance. It was not the way to address a rear-admiral, but then, as we shall see, the easy-going Hughes did not conform to the idea that Nelson believed appropriate for a naval officer of that rank.

On 26 January 1782 disaster struck. The Downs are very exposed when the wind swings round to the north. A violent northerly squall caused the *Brilliant*, one of five East Indiamen that Nelson had just received orders to escort down to Portsmouth, to drag her anchor and be swept down on to the *Albemarle.* In heaving seas, the *Brilliant* slowly dragged past, each ship repeatedly grinding the other's hull and smashing masts and rigging. The *Brilliant* was lightly laden with 145 tons of iron, copper and lead, and full of troops destined for India, but she was bigger, stoutly built and higher out of the water than the *Albemarle*.[35] She caused extensive damage to the warship, mostly to the rigging, though the quarter galleries by the stern also suffered badly. The bowsprit, foremast and several yards went over the side and were quickly cut away to ensure that they did not damage the hull by hitting it as the ship rolled. The stern anchor and cable went overboard. The incident lasted only five minutes. Nelson reckoned he was lucky that the ship did not founder.[36] He had suspected that he was about to be ordered to the East Indies, but now the prospect of a long voyage, with its promise of prize money and freight money, was suddenly gone. Instead he could contemplate two months in Portsmouth Dockyard with the ship under repair.

The battered *Albemarle*, jury-rigged and now herself in need of an escort down the Channel since there was intelligence of a French frigate off Beachy Head, arrived at Spithead on 2 February. For the whole of 7 February, Nelson had the galling experience of watching the East India convoy pass the *Albemarle* as it headed out to sea. On 11 February she sailed into Portsmouth Harbour.[37] Nelson oversaw repairs, but found time for a two-week visit to London in late February and early March, during which he saw his physician Robert Adair, for he still had periodic bouts of illness. Adair's prognosis, however, was good. Nelson also saw to some family business. Thomas Bolton, married to his sister Susannah, wanted to sell the stocks left to her by Maurice Suckling. Since the money was in trust, Nelson was required to sign a Power of Attorney. He quieted his brother William's fears on the matter, unwisely trusting to Bolton's financial judgement.[38]

Her repairs complete, the *Albemarle* set sail on 6 April 1782, with orders to escort a convoy to Quebec carrying much needed supplies for the British garrison. Nelson feared that the climate would do his health no good. He thought about applying for a change of command, but North's government had finally been defeated and Keppel, whom Nelson did not know, was the new first lord of the Admiralty. He wrote to Locker: 'Many of my friends have advised me to represent my situation to Admiral Keppel, and they have no doubt but he would give me other orders, or remove me.' He was introduced to Admiral Barrington at Portsmouth: 'it is from that quarter, could I stay long enough in port, that I expect a better Ship.'[39] Nelson was wise in leaving the matter where it was. Keppel's appointments, in the short time that he was in office, were very much driven by party politics.[40] Nelson judged that he was more likely to have lost his ship than to have gained a new one.

By 17 April the *Albemarle* was anchored in Cork Harbour, where North Atlantic trade convoys assembled and took on final stores and victuals. The commodore of the convoy was Thomas Pringle of the *Daedalus* (32), a Scot whom Nelson came to know and befriend. The convoy, of 'between thirty and forty sail', got under way on 26 April.[41] The weather was fresh and provided plenty of work for the escorts. The *Albemarle* had to stand by one of the merchant ships for two days when her main yard carried away 'in a hard gale of wind', thus parting company from the *Daedalus* and most of the convoy.[42] Nelson sailed on with only four merchant ships. For the last ten days of May, the little convoy was enveloped in fog, and for much of the time had only light airs. To alert ships hidden by poor visibility, drums were beaten and bells rung; at night a gun was fired every hour. Nelson's log reflects considerable anxiety as they approached Newfoundland. On 23 May '150 fathoms were sounded, but no ground'. It was with relief on 27 May that the ship picked up the St John's pilot, and, with a great deal of firing of guns, he got all his four ships in.[43] It was a remarkable feat of navigation, successful largely due to the experience of his master,

The *Albemarle* in North American waters,
May – November 1782

Donald Trail, of whom Nelson wrote in the following year, 'He is the best
Master I ever saw since I went to sea.'[44]

The *Albemarle* did not stay long at St John's, which Nelson called 'disagreeable'.[45] The convoy resumed its journey to Quebec with thirty-two
ships on 17 June. They reached the Island of Bic, half way up the
St Lawrence and 160 miles from Quebec, on 2 July; here the *Albemarle* left
the convoy, spent two days replenishing wood and water, and then headed
down the St Lawrence again.[46] Nelson had orders to cruise against enemy
shipping off the New England coast, with a chance for prize money.

For the two months that he was on station, from mid July to early September, he had indifferent luck. The American Revolutionary War had entered its last months, and news of the negotiations between the French, British and Americans in Paris had reached North America by August. The commander-in-chief of the Halifax and North American Station, Rear-Admiral Robert Digby, was in two minds about his cruising policy due to the confused state of politics in London. He knew of a strong resolution of the House of Commons against the continuation of the American Revolutionary War, but was without Admiralty orders to desist from capturing rebel shipping. He chose to continue as before.[47] Moreover, British naval superiority in New England waters had recently been lost: following the Battle of the Saints in the West Indies in April 1782, the defeated French West Indies fleet, under Admiral le marquis de Vaudreuil, had sailed north to refit at Boston.

Nelson's first prize was a schooner laden with Madeira, which had been taken by an American privateer; he sent it to Quebec with a prize crew. His most frequent quarry were the New England fishing boats, but even they were hard to catch. On one occasion 'he chased one, but she cut away her masts and scuttled the boat.' More remarkably, he captured a fishing schooner called the *Harmony* in Boston Bay, took her in tow and used her for a month, with the cooperation of the master, Nathaniel Carver. Nelson then had a rude shock. On 15 August, when the morning mist had burned off, the *Albemarle* found herself very close to five men-of-war, four ships of the line and a frigate, which turned out to be part of Vaudreuil's fleet coming out of Boston. Nelson, heavily outnumbered, had to run for it. There followed a hectic ten-hour chase, the later part through the night. Guided by Carver, Nelson took the *Albemarle* over the shallow St George's Banks, 100 miles ESE of Cape Cod, on whose north-west edge the shoals range from twelve to eighteen feet. Carver would have known these waters: they were rich fishing grounds. Nevertheless, the course carried a considerable risk, because the *Albemarle*'s draft was more than twelve feet. The French ships of the line held back. When they were out of sight, Nelson backed the sails and challenged the still-chasing frigate, at which point the Frenchman thought the better of it and rejoined the larger ships. 'Our escape I think wonderful,' he recounted to Locker, 'they were upon the clearing up of a fog within shot of us and chased us the whole time about one point from the wind.'

Nelson had clearly got the best out of the *Albemarle*'s weak sailing qualities, and her year-old copper sheathing and clean bottom, which the French frigate would not have had, helped her speed. To repay his help,

Nelson gave Carver back his fishing vessel and a certificate that allowed the schooner henceforth to fish unmolested.[48] In return for this generosity, Carver later brought him out meat and fresh provisions. During this cruise, and for the only time in his life, Nelson and his crew suffered badly from scurvy, as they had had only salt beef to eat since leaving England. Nelson wrote to Locker: 'In the end, our cruise has been an unsuccessful one; we have taken, seen and destroyed more Enemies than is seldom done in the same space of time, but not one arrived in port. But, however, I do not repine at our loss.'[49]

On 8 September, Nelson headed back to Quebec, which took ten days. In the dry cold air of the city his health improved, and he and his crew shook off the scurvy. It was in Quebec that he lost his heart, as far as we know for the first time. Mary Simpson was the daughter of the provost-marshal of Quebec. They are likely to have met at one of the garrison balls, he then twenty-four and she twenty-two. Nelson's infatuation started and continued at a high pitch; Mary, still young, was not so smitten. According to Alexander Davison, at that time a merchant whom he had befriended in Quebec, he met Nelson walking up from the river, determined to propose to the young woman. Davison dissuaded him. Short of a fortune as Nelson was, such a move would have seriously interrupted or ended his naval career.[50] Since the source for the story is Clarke and McArthur, its more dramatic elements are less than likely.* His passion was broken off by the departure of the *Albemarle*. The Quebec shipwrights had been at work caulking for a month; if the ship did not get out of the St Lawrence by the end of October, she would be locked in the ice for the winter.[51]

Nelson expected to be sent home, but instead he was ordered to take a convoy of transports to New York, where every available ship was needed to evacuate 20,000 British troops, equipment and stores, and many thousands of loyalists; the task would take a year to complete.[52] Nelson left Quebec in mid October 1782, picking up the convoy at the Isle of Bic, and by 12 November was beating up towards New York. He moored in the East River three days later. In New York he found a directionless and worried British garrison. Washington's army was surrounding the city, which had been ravaged by fire, food shortages and years of military occupation. With the British defeat at Yorktown over a year before, on 18 October 1781, the war was effectively lost, and American patriots were

---

* In Quebec Nelson undoubtedly met Davison, later his close friend and prize agent. The story of Davison dissuading Nelson from marriage is in Clarke and McArthur (I, 76), who embellish the incident with dialogue.

flocking back to the city to reclaim property – it was a time of 'frayed tempers and tense confrontations'.[53] The loyalists were beginning to take matters into their own hands. Tit-for-tat atrocities were committed by both sides. Morale problems had affected the navy, which saw that it had no role left beyond the taking of French and American shipping for prize money. 'Money is the great object here,' Nelson reported to Locker; 'nothing else is attended to.'[54] The trapped British armies at Charleston in South Carolina and New York weakened the British negotiating position in Paris. But dangers still existed. The Battle of the Saints in April had reprieved Jamaica, but the French could still capture West Indies islands, useful cards at the final negotiating table.[55] Nelson had predicted to his father the previous October that he could well be in the West Indies again.[56]

In mid November, against the unpromising background of an unsuccessful war and a violent and disturbed New York, Nelson met Rear-Admiral Samuel Hood, who was to become the second of his three naval patrons. Hood had a large and loyal following in the navy, for as the son of a Somerset vicar he had had to work his way to the top through the system of 'interest'. Many of those whom he encouraged were from the politically powerful Linzee family of Portsmouth into which he had married.* In the previous two years the rise in Hood's fortunes had been dramatic. Only two years earlier he had been a captain and resident commissioner of Portsmouth Dockyard, with the particular trust of the king. Then in November 1780 he was sent to the West Indies by Sandwich as second-in-command to Admiral Rodney. He had brilliant success in battle against Admiral le comte de Grasse at St Kitts in January 1782; and he was a successful but frustrated subordinate to Rodney at the Battle of the Saints in April. Both efforts were rewarded in September with an Irish peerage.[57]

Hood was ambitious and talented; his letters, well constructed and well expressed, show a fine mind. 'Everything from him is so clear it is impossible to misunderstand him,' Nelson wrote to William Locker some years later.[58] Hood was also outspoken: throughout his career he made 'acerbic criticisms of inadequate military colleagues'.[59] He criticized Rodney for his conduct at the Battle of the Saints, not without reason, and he was to do the same to the new commander-in-chief, the newly appointed and not very effective Admiral Hugh Pigot, described by one modern authority as 'amiable,

---

* It was notable that five captains in Hood's division at the Battle of the Saints in 1782 were still with him in the Mediterranean fleet in 1793 (Wilkinson, 'Nelson Network', 232). His Portsmouth connections extended beyond sea officers, for his secretary in North America was the son of Edward Hunt, formerly master shipwright at Portsmouth and by this time surveyor of the navy (Nicolas, I, 69, 19 Nov. 1782, Nelson to Locker).

idle and corrupt'.[60] Captain Thomas Pasley, a long-term friend of Nelson, met Hood in 1782. 'He was', wrote Pasley in his journal, 'full of complaints and sarcastical observations to the prejudice of Admiral Pigot, his Commander-in-Chief. Dissatisfied and mortified at not being indulged with the command, he courts popularity by censuring the chief commander – I have ever thought him a dangerous Second and I am now clearly convinced of it.'[61] Nelson was fortunate to have had the uncomplicated William Locker to learn from in his impressionable early years, and to have come under the influence of Hood in his more experienced twenties. Hood was one of the few senior officers to come out of the American Revolutionary War with his reputation enhanced, and was to be at the centre of naval affairs for the next decade and beyond. This meeting of two ambitious officers in mid November 1782 could not have been timed better for the young captain's career.

In spite of his recent success, Hood knew little about the West Indies, having first been there in early 1781. Now, in November 1782, his orders were to prevent the junction of the French and Spanish fleets, which would greatly increase the threat to the British islands. Vaudreuil left Boston on 22 December 1782 with twelve ships of the line and with General le comte de Rochambeau's victorious troops from Yorktown on board. The British anticipated that they would join Admiral Josef Solano, the Spanish commander, who was at Havana with a squadron of twelve ships of the line. French and Spanish troops were positioned on San Domingo. At Cadiz forty ships of the line, with troops, under d'Estaing, were ready to sail for the Caribbean. Where would these fleets rendezvous? Which passage would they take? Nelson had knowledge of these waters, as had his second lieutenant, Joseph Bromwich. Hood engineered the transfer of the *Albemarle* to his fleet from that of Admiral Digby, with whom she was due to travel home. He took Nelson's advice,[62] writing on 22 November to Pigot: 'Captain Nelson of the *Albemarle*, who has been cruising about the Caicos Channel for ten or twelve weeks at a time, does not remember to have seen a ship of any burthen coming to Hispaniola by that passage. The reason against the Channel inward is doubtless strong and good, as the making of it from the northward must depend upon the longitude being exact, and the French, I believe, are not adept in that knowledge.'[63] The best chance of interception was a little to the westward off Cape Samana at the eastern point of Hispaniola.

Hood's fleet of thirteen ships of the line made a fast passage south to arrive off Cape Samana on 5 December. He sent Nelson to look into the harbour at Cap François to see if the French fleet was there, which it was not.[64] For the next month Nelson cruised with the fleet to the north of San Domingo, checking neutral ships and taking the occasional prize. On 20 January 1783 he chased three ships and was chased in turn by another, but she proved to be friendly: 'made the private signal which she answered'.[65] Five days later he captured his biggest prize to date, the *Queen of France*, at one o'clock in the morning: she was a mast ship, bound from Boston to Cap François to support Vaudreuil's fleet, with 300 troops on board; by Nelson's calculation she was worth £20,000, but the fleet was near, the admiral a mile away, and their presence heavily diluted his share of the prize money.[66] He wrote to Locker with feeling: 'They do not deserve to share for her: we had chased to leeward, and she had passed every Ship in the Fleet without being noticed.'[67]

There now followed the first of several episodes in his career in which Nelson demonstrated that his aggressive spirit could overcome his better judgement. Some way from the main fleet he met the *Resistance* (44), commanded by Captain James King, from whom he heard that the French had just captured Turk's Island, some eighty miles to the north. With the *Tartar* (28), which joined a few hours later ('I ordered to put herself under my command') and a 16-gun ship, the *Drake*, commanded by Captain James Dixon, they anchored off the island. Nelson sent a party ashore to demand surrender. The French refused. 'During the night we fired several Guns as we saw several lights to annoy them,' the log reads.[68] The discontented *Tartar* sailed off in the night and at five in the morning Nelson landed 160 seamen and marines under Captain Dixon, the two remaining ships firing at the town in support of the landing force. Nelson's report to Hood reads very lamely: 'Upon their getting within shot, I was very much surprised to see a battery of three guns open upon them. Captain Dixon at this time observed that the guns were fought by Seamen, and that the Troops were waiting to receive him with several field-pieces; and that they had a post upon the side of the hill with two pieces of cannon. With such a force, and their strong situation, I did not think anything farther should be attempted.'[69] The action went on for an hour, but fortunately he had only half a dozen men wounded. Success is often attendant upon initiative, but with poor intelligence and no element of surprise, he took a risk too far. Hood is unlikely to have been pleased, especially as peace was so close.

In the event all the British speculation about the intentions of the French and the Spanish was completely wrong. Vaudreuil and Solano had agreed to rendezvous far to the south near Caracas. Vaudreuil took a course well to the east, evading both Hood's fleet and also that of Pigot, who was cruising with twenty ships of the line off Martinique. The French fleet sailed

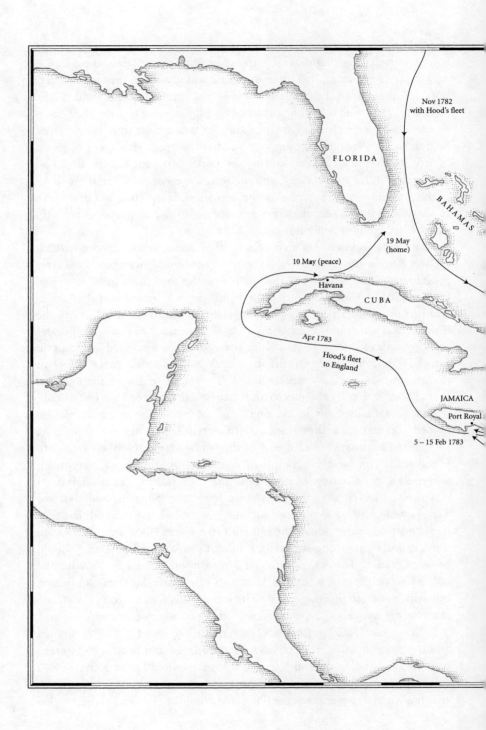

Nov 1782
with Hood's fleet

FLORIDA

BAHAMAS

19 May
(home)

10 May (peace)

Havana

CUBA

Apr 1783

Hood's fleet
to England

JAMAICA

Port Royal

5 – 15 Feb 1783

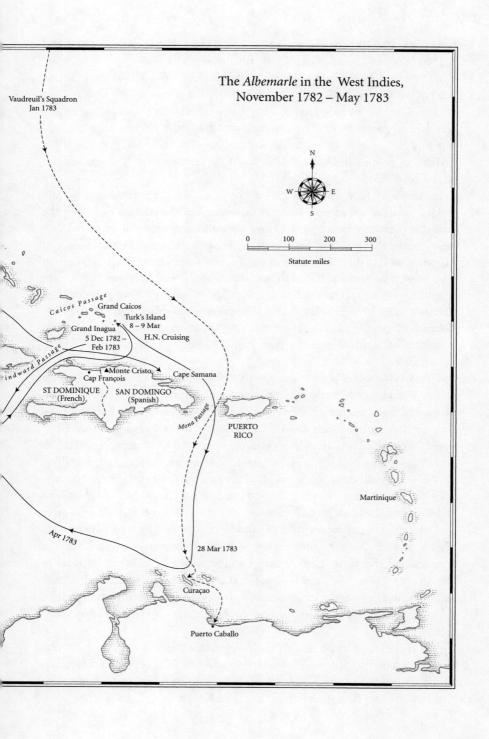

The *Albemarle* in the West Indies,
November 1782 – May 1783

N
W E
S

0   100   200   300
Statute miles

Vaudreuil's Squadron
Jan 1783

Caicos Passage   Grand Caicos
Turk's Island
Grand Inagua   8 – 9 Mar
5 Dec 1782 –   H.N. Cruising
Feb 1783

Windward Passage

Monte Cristo
Cap François   Cape Samana
ST DOMINIQUE   SAN DOMINGO
(French)   (Spanish)

Mona Passage
PUERTO
RICO

Martinique

Apr 1783

28 Mar 1783

Curaçao

Puerto Caballo

towards the South American mainland, and then split, half to Caracas and half to Puerto Caballo, a small port further west.[70]

At the end of February, Hood took his fleet, which had been at sea for twelve weeks, back to Jamaica and left his frigates to search for the enemy. The *Albemarle* sailed south, and on 29 March at last found half of Vaudreuil's force. Nelson tried one or two harbours further on and could not find the rest, so he returned to Jamaica with the intelligence. On his arrival on 7 April he learnt that news of the peace treaty had reached the island on 3 April.

Rodney's victory at the battle of the Saints in April 1782 is generally judged to have saved and secured Jamaica. Yet the danger of losing the island, even while peace negotiators were talking, was still very real, not least to those who took part in these wearisome operations. Pigot and Hood, who did their best to find the French fleet, could not have known that French political will and financial resources were wearing thin. From the middle of 1782 French diplomats had been attempting to persuade the Spanish to end the conflict, but the Spanish were still intent on wresting Gibraltar from the British. The French and Spanish admirals' plans for the conquest of Jamaica were at best half-hearted, and the threat failed to materialize.

The *Albemarle* set off for home with Hood's fleet on 26 April, calling on the way at Havana, arriving at Spithead on 25 June 1783.[71] The past two years had been an enriching experience for Nelson. The cruise has been described as 'rather a sad one, it is best briefly told' and his ship 'an unlucky one'.[72] True, Nelson, his officers and the crew had not accumulated much prize money, nor had they reached the lucrative East Indies. Had they done so, Nelson would most likely have had the patronage of Sir Edward Hughes, about to retire as a very rich man, and it might well have proved a dead-end in his career. Instead, he had met and impressed Samuel Hood, a younger and more important figure than Hughes, with another fifteen years' service ahead of him. Nelson's health too was much improved by his time in Canada and the West Indies. From London he wrote to Hercules Ross in Jamaica: 'I have closed the war without a fortune; but I trust, and, from the attention that has been paid to me, believe that there is not a speck in my character. True honour, I hope, predominates in my mind far above riches.'[73]

The real benefit to Nelson of the *Albemarle* commission, however, was the opportunity to develop his leadership abilities. He continually mentions in his letters to Locker how content he is with his officers and men. For nearly two years he had only one change in his officers, and few in his men.

He lost one seaman, who fell overboard and drowned on the first Atlantic crossing.[74] Ten seamen were punished in two years, and only a minority of these for insubordination. When the ship was paid off, he proudly wrote to Locker, 'The whole Ship's company offered, if I could get a Ship, to enter for her immediately.'[75] This was a reputation within the navy worth more than prizes, and it was the first inkling that Nelson might be special enough to stand out from among other talented young contemporaries.

In late July in London, Nelson was ill again and planning to go to Norfolk, as he wrote to William: 'a few days, however, I hope will allow me to get from my Room, and as soon as I get a little strength.'[76] But it was not until late August that Nelson went home to Burnham Thorpe, accompanied by his brother Maurice.[77] Now the war was over, there was an opportunity to travel to France, and he set off with James Macnamara, whom he knew as a fellow lieutenant in the *Bristol*, intending to learn the language, for French could be more than useful for diplomacy, questioning prisoners or making sense of intelligence. Before leaving England, they called on mutual friends from their time in the *Lowestoffe*: William Locker, Sir Peter and Lady Parker in Essex and Charles Sandys (who was not in). From Dover they had a fast passage of three and a half hours across the Channel to Calais. Macnamara, who was at least fifteen years older than Nelson and was never to go to sea again, had some French but was loath to stay where there were no English people at all, and he wanted to go to St Omer. Nelson sought something better, so they then took an aimless tour around northern France. They endured a slow and uncomfortable chaise south-west towards Boulogne, staying at a 'miserable' inn in Marquise, then on to Boulogne, Montreuil and Abbeville, where they failed to find lodgings.

France fascinated and repelled Nelson. With his countryman's eye he admired the agriculture, 'the finest corn country that ever my eyes beheld, diversified with fine woods, sometimes for two miles together, through noble forests . . . this is the finest country for game that ever was.'[78] He had fun in identifying the landlords whom Lawrence Sterne had described in his *Sentimental Journey*, published in 1768. But he thought little of the roads, the cleanliness of the inns and the chaises 'which have no springs'. At Montreuil he noted that 'there are no middling class of people: sixty noblemen's families lived in the town, who owned the vast plain around it, and the rest very poor indeed.' Nelson's verdict to Locker after his travelling was 'O what a transition from happy England.'[79]

Then they headed north again to St Omer, where Macnamara had originally wanted to go. Nelson admitted to Locker: 'I must do Captain Mac the justice to say that it was all my doings, and in a great measure against his advice.' In St Omer, against expectations, they found a 'a large City, well paved, good streets and well lighted'. They lodged with the family of Jacques Lamoury, a master potter, possibly in the rue de Dunkerque.[80] He observed to Locker that there were 'a vast number of English at this place; I visit but few of them'. The exceptions were 'two agreeable young ladies, daughters, who <u>honour</u> us with their company pretty often . . . Therefore I must learn French if 'tis only for the pleasure of talking to them, for they do not speak a word of English.'[81] In his copy of Chambaud's *A Grammar of the French Tongue* he inscribed: 'Horatio Nelson began to learn the French Language on the 1st November 1783.'[82] But two months later he wrote to his brother William: 'French goes on but slowly, time can only make me master of it, and that a long one, some years probably.'[83]

Nelson never mastered French. Too many English people were staying in St Omer, and study was neglected. Nelson had dinner with Captain William Young, twenty-seven places higher on the captain's list than Nelson. Young was a diminutive man, of considerable intelligence and polished manners, and a good linguist; later he was to serve on the Board of Admiralty and became a valued friend.[84] Two other captains, Alexander Ball and James Shephard, were also in the town, but Nelson did not meet them: 'In consequence of some punctilio', wrote Samuel Taylor Coleridge many years later, 'as to whose business it was to pay the compliment of the first call, they [Nelson and Ball] never met, and this trifling affair occasioned a coldness between the two naval commanders, or in truth a mutual prejudice against each other.'[85]

Two other young ladies also proved to be a distraction. They were the daughters of an English clergyman named Andrews. With the elder, Elizabeth, Nelson fell, as in Quebec, swiftly and heavily in love. 'I must take care of my heart, I assure you,' he wrote to Locker. Christmas passed. On 14 January 1784 he wrote asking William Suckling for an allowance of £100 a year so that he could get married. This was a steep demand, though Suckling made a note on the letter indicating that he was prepared to help. Nelson also asked his uncle to use his influence with his seniors in the Treasury: 'either . . . Lord North or Mr Jenkinson, for to get a guardship, or some appointment to a public office, where the attendance of the principal is not necessary, and of which they must have a number to dispose of? In the India Service I understand . . . their Marine Force is to be under the command of a Captain in the Royal Navy; that is a situation I should like.'[86]

Before Suckling could reply, Nelson suddenly came back to London. He gave a number of reasons for his return. 'Some little matters in my Accounts obliged me to come over,' he wrote to Locker. To his brother William he said that he needed 'a little good advice from some of the London Physicians'.[87] More than likely he had been refused by Elizabeth Andrews. Prospects for a half-pay captain were not good, and he had but £150 a year. Nelson's return may also have been prompted by the news he received in late November from Burnham Thorpe that his elder sister Anne had died suddenly at Bath. His letters show that he worried about the effect it might have on his family, and on his father in particular.[88] He came back to find the general election of 1784 in progress, which unexpectedly gave the young William Pitt a strong majority, the first of several elections that led to his seventeen-year tenure as prime minister. A reluctant Samuel Hood had been persuaded to stand against Charles James Fox and another Foxite candidate at Westminster; Nelson may have assisted Hood during the election. After the change of ministry, any prudent naval officer with ambition would have paid his respects to the new first lord of the Admiralty, Lord Howe, to ensure that his availability for service was known. Nelson managed to see Howe within a week of his return to London.* On 18 March 1784 he was appointed to the command of the 28-gun frigate *Boreas*.[89]

* The appointment to a ship forestalled Nelson's possible acceptance of an invitation from le comte de Deux Ponts, whom he had met in the last days of the war off Puerto Caballo, to come to Paris to learn the language and enjoy himself (Bl., Add. MSS, 34903, 23 Mar. 178[4], 'Dunponty' to Nelson).

6

Boreas and the West Indies

March 1784–July 1786

Thus circumstanced, your Memorialist is obliged to keep himself con-
fined to your Majesty's Ship, which, added to the unhealthiness of a
West India climate, has much impaired your Memorialist's health . . .
he thus ventures to lay before his Royal Master, not only the sufferings
of his faithful servant, but also the iniquitous practices carried on by
the alienated Americans, and their adherents in the British Colonies,
in contempt to the Laws, and to the infinite prejudice of the Commerce
of Great Britain.

Captain Nelson's 'Memorial' to the king, 29 June 1785[1]

For a 26-year-old captain, any peacetime command was a plum appointment. Half a dozen ships were being paid off every month: at the beginning
of 1784 there were 202 in commission; by December this had been reduced
to 140, with a total of 2,230 officers available to man them.[2] Nelson had,
however, caught the eye of powerful backers. Hood had seen the potential
of the young captain of the *Albemarle*, and his word had been enough to
convince Howe, who, as first lord of the Admiralty, made all appointments.[3]
The *Boreas* was by reputation a good ship. She had spent most of her career
in the West Indies, taken part in the Battle of Grenada in 1779 and had
captured a French prize soon afterwards. For seven months in 1782 she
had been in dock at Woolwich having a major repair and was now in good
condition.[4] In 1783 she had gone out to the West Indies under the command
of one of Keppel's appointments, Captain John Wells. Now she was paid
off but rigged and ready to sail, moored in the Thames at Long Reach. On
24 March 1784, a day of snow squalls, Nelson came on board and took
command.[5]

Though he still had ambitions to return to the East Indies, Nelson soon
found that he was destined for the West Indies again, this time to the
Leeward Islands Station rather than to Jamaica. A peacetime command was

likely to be dull. Regular intelligence reports had to be sent to the Admiralty on the movements and numbers of French ships in this jittery, suspicious post-war period. British trade interests needed to feel that naval support was present, to keep the West India Committee of Merchants in London content. The flag was required to be shown to other European nations, for the French, Spanish, Danes and Dutch all possessed islands, and the Swedes were to purchase St Barthélémy from the French in 1785. These humdrum tasks were important, for in the prosperous 1780s the tropical produce of the West Indies contributed over 20 per cent of the value of British imports, of which the most important was sugar. The Leeward Islands were major producers, particularly Barbados and St Kitts, where Nelson was to spend much time in the next three and a half years.

Very quickly Nelson learnt that a peacetime command incurred considerable obligations, flattering though some of them might seem. He was expected to convey Lady Hughes, the wife of the commander-in-chief, Rear-Admiral Sir Richard Hughes, together with her rather plain daughter. These guests would have to be entertained in some style, and at Nelson's expense. Commissioning a ship for an overseas service was always expensive. He purchased elaborate tableware: '2 very long best Blue Edged long dishes, 1 long tureen, 4 quart decanters etc'.[6] He also agreed to take his older brother William as the ship's chaplain, though the plan was for him to stay only for a few months.[7] William Nelson's duties did not appear to be onerous: 'Divine Service' for the ship's company was noted only three times in the captain's log. To judge by the tone and detailed gossip in the letters that Nelson sent after William's return to England, the clergyman seems to have fitted in with the ship's company well.[8] Nelson complained endlessly to him about Lady Hughes. 'I have a fine talkative woman for you to converse with,' he wrote ironically, and in a later letter he wrote dismissively of mother and daughter: 'What a specimen of English beauty. They are neither of them grown handsomer since you left them.'[9]

None of these obligations matched the complexities of choosing which young men he should take as midshipmen or captain's servants. The *Boreas* was allowed a complement of four midshipmen, two master's mates and perhaps seven captain's servants, but he found that he had to exceed this number many times over, eventually agreeing to take thirty 'young gentlemen'.[10] He was besieged by powerful men who wished to get their sons and nephews on board the ship for training and to gain seniority. Lords Howe and Hood were responsible for his appointment, but admirals Leveson-Gower and Hyde Parker, his friends William Cornwallis and Charles Morice Pole also pressed him to take their nominees, as did captains

Sir John Jervis and Douglas. From outside the navy he agreed to take the sons of two Irish peers.[11] Nelson described Courtenay Boyle to his father, the earl of Cork and Orrery, as 'amiable in the truest sense of the word . . . his charming disposition will make him many friends'; this was a fair prediction, and Boyle rose to be a vice-admiral, as did the other young Irishman, John Talbot.[12] By contrast, Joseph James Beale was a 'gunner's son . . . behaves vastly well . . . he is very attentive, sober young man as can possibly be', as Nelson reported to Beale's patron, William Cornwallis.[13] Nelson helped a few of them financially, as he had done for some on the *Albemarle*. A number of these young men lasted the whole voyage of three and a half years; others lasted no more than a month. A few were on the books for a very short time before they were invalided. Some of the older ones moved up fast, while the younger were captain's servants through the voyage. Thomas Orde, whose father, John Orde, was governor of Dominica, joined in the West Indies and came home at the end of the commission. A couple of others were taken on just before the voyage home. The *Boreas* was no exception in taking so many young men; in 1785 Nelson wrote to William Suckling that 'Every captain is so crowded with younkers [youngsters] that we cannot ask each other.'[14]

This was, of course, also an advantage to him, for an ambitious young captain needed able and well-trained junior officers about him to create his 'interest'. In any case, Nelson felt strongly about the training of young officers, for it was the 'basis of a well regulated service and want of a proper Nursery for them is well known severely felt in the last war'.[15] He was not the only officer to think in these terms; Hood wrote in 1783: 'we shall have scarce a Lieutenant that will know his duty . . . we have so many ignorant Boys . . . which from being any time ashore will of course become more ignorant.'[16] Nelson ensured that 'the young gentlemen learnt and did the duty from rigging the topgallant mast to stowing the ballast. They were never confined to any [one] part of the Service.'[17] His first lieutenant in the *Boreas*, James Wallis, remembered:

He never suffered the ship to remain longer than 3 or 4 days in any island at a time. She was always on the wing, and when it happened that any of the other ships were in company, he was always forming the line, exercising, chasing etc . . . he encouraged Music, Dancing and Cudgeling and Young Gentlemen acted plays which kept up their spirits and kept their minds employed.[18]

But there were simply too many midshipmen and captain's servants on the *Boreas*. Too many were too old and had already served their time, but without the right amount of time as midshipman and master's mate to enable them to sit their lieutenant's exam. Joseph Bromwich had served as acting lieutenant for eighteen months in the *Albemarle*; others were twenty, and George Andrews, the brother of Elizabeth Andrews to whom Nelson had lost his heart, was twenty-one. Almost all of them came on board as unpaid captain's servants. After the commission the Navy Board made difficulties when it came to the lieutenant's exams of these young men. Nelson's reply, drafted with some warmth, shows the pressures that the system was under:

The rated Mates had each been near Twenty years at sea [and] been for years Lieut[enant]s in the late war but had not had the good fortune to be confirmed. The Mids. were young men who had altogether or nearly served their time & without fortunes . . . all had nearly an equal portion of rated time given them. The Poor Ones I only disrated with their own consent and the Younger rated in their Room were bound in Honor to make their pay as good as before. Honourable Courtenay Boyle I have understood did make Mr Bishop in whose room he was rated a present when the ship was paid off.[19]

That tensions existed between these young men, intent on gaining the right seniority, is attested to by a duel early in the cruise between two midshipmen. Thomas Stansbury fought George Andrews when the *Boreas* was at Barbados in February 1785. The cause of the quarrel is unrecorded. Andrews survived a ball lodging in his stomach and left Barbados hospital in mid April.[20] Nelson put Stansbury and his second in irons, and they were discharged from the *Boreas*.[21]

The cruise started badly. The ship went aground coming out of the Thames and was stranded until the next tide.[22] Gales with snow followed at the Nore, then a rash foray in the Downs when he freed, as he claimed, some Englishmen on a Dutch East Indiaman whom he wanted for his crew. He told Locker that he had received Admiralty backing for this seizure, but the Admiralty were far from supportive and Admiral John Montagu, commander-in-chief at Portsmouth, ordered the pressed men to be discharged.[23] To add to his troubles, as he reported to Locker, he had a riding accident when ashore at Portsmouth during which he just escaped serious injury.[24]

For a month the *Boreas* lay at Spithead, moving ballast, taking on stores and men. Thirty-three officers, midshipmen and accompanying ladies were to form a crowded quarterdeck. Lady and Miss Hughes were joined by Mrs Peers, the wife of the purser.[25] At last, on 18 May, the *Boreas* sailed, put briefly into Plymouth Sound on 22 May because of adverse winds, and then with a fair wind sailed south, reaching Funchal in Madeira on 1 June, where she lay at anchor for a week taking on supplies and wine. The eighteen-day Atlantic passage was fast. The only incident, six days out, was the sighting of a foreign warship, which turned out to be French; Nelson, energetic as ever, cleared the ship for action – just in case. On 26 June the *Boreas* was anchored in Carlisle Bay, Barbados, the traditional point of entry for the West Indies and the base for the commander-in-chief, Leeward Islands Station. Admiral Hughes was saluted with fifteen guns, and the ship also 'made the signal for Lady Hughes' to come ashore; Nelson lost not a moment in getting her off the ship.[26]

In the period immediately after the hurricane season, all the ships on the Leeward Islands Station would meet at Carlisle Bay for orders from the commander-in-chief, after which they would disperse to their cruising areas. The squadron was now reduced to its peacetime level: at the beginning of 1784 sixteen ships were on the station; by June there were eleven; and at the beginning of the next year only seven.[27] Hughes's flagship was the 50-gun *Adamant*; Cuthbert Collingwood had the *Mediator* (44); and Charles Sandys, who had been first lieutenant of the *Lowestoffe*, commanded the *Latona* (38). The *Champion* (24), *Unicorn* (20), *Falcon* (14), *Fury* (16) and *Rattler* (16) made up the rest of the squadron. The *Rattler* was commanded by Wilfred Collingwood, Cuthbert's younger brother, and Nelson was to cruise in company with her for considerable periods, but he was to see little of Cuthbert, who in 1784 and 1785 spent August, September and most of October in Grenada, while Nelson was in English Harbour in Antigua.

Aside from the Collingwoods, Nelson thought little of his fellow captains. He was fond of Charles Sandys, and he repeatedly wrote to William Locker about the young ladies to whom Sandys lost his heart and about his weakness for the bottle, always, in Nelson's words, 'between Bacchus and Venus'. He feared that the combination of alcohol and the climate would kill Sandys.[28] From the start of this commission he suffered fools not at all. He wrote a waspish letter to Cornwallis: 'As to this Station I dislike it as Much as ever. The Admiral I shall say nothing about. His captain's name is Kelly ... an ignorant, self sufficient Man, the others are ignoramus's.'[29]

The *Boreas*'s arrival in June was just a month before the hurricane season, when ships had to find shelter. She soon sailed to English Harbour, Antigua, 'a close, unwholesome place', according to another officer, but very safe, affording protection from the constant easterly trade winds and hurricanes.[30] A pilot was required every time a ship entered. Once through the

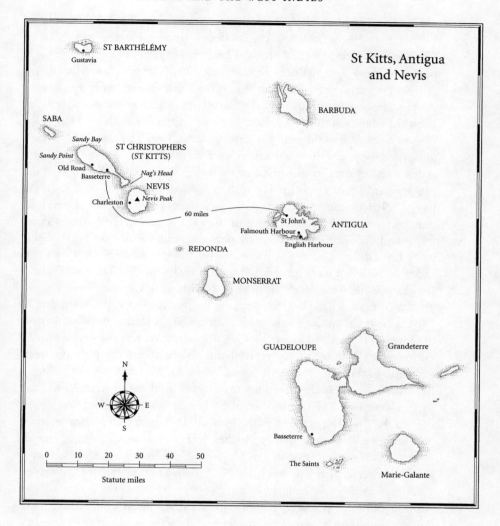

entrance and into Freeman's Bay, it encountered a windless area where it needed to be warped further into the harbour; bollards and rings on shore, as well as anchored buoys, were used for this purpose.[31] English Harbour was critical to the maintenance of British sea power in the West Indies, and the government had invested in a sizeable garrison to defend it. Dominating the harbour were very extensive fortifications, and when Nelson was there large army barracks were being built on Shirley Heights above the harbour. Nelson called English Harbour 'this vile place', though for safety he made sure that he was always there in the hurricane months.[32]

He soon found trouble. When Nelson sailed into English Harbour in February 1785, he found a commodore's pennant at the masthead of Charles Sandys's ship, the *Latona*. This pennant represented the intention of the resident commissioner of the dockyard, Captain John Moutray (a civilian appointment without an Admiralty commission), to be recognized as the senior officer at English Harbour, second-in-command of the Leeward Islands Station to Admiral Hughes. Effectively, this downgraded Nelson's position as the senior frigate captain afloat. The cause of Nelson's annoyance was the navy's hazy rules governing civil and military precedence, no clearer in this instance than they had been in the case of the Navy Board in 1773 and never to be resolved in the time of the sailing navy.[33] Nelson immediately took the pennant as a slight. He maintained that he recognized no precedence of the civil administration over a commissioned officer, for Moutray, though a captain twenty-six years senior to Nelson, did not have a commission for this position. Nelson wrote to Sandys: 'Your not having been on board since my arrival has been I take it for granted the Reason of this neglect, for I believe Captain Sandys is too good an officer to have neglected paying me that respect which is my due.'[34]

Nelson was not going to allow his position on the station to be weakened, arguing to Hughes and others that he, not Moutray, was the senior officer, even though Moutray had received the orders about the pennant from Rear-Admiral Hughes.* 'I never looked upon Mr Moutray in Commission,' he wrote later to Hughes, 'and my reasons for thinking so were, having sat as President of many Court-Martials, when he was upon the spot, acting only in the Civil Department of the Navy.'[35] In a draft that Nelson marked 'not sent', he wrote furiously to Hughes, 'otherwise any Captain upon <u>half pay</u> may take the direction of His Majesty's Squadron . . . the Service never shall be lowered by my suffering the Navy Board to take rank of Officers of Commission . . . and whenever I receive your order to receive Commissioner Moutray's Broad pennant, I shall with great readiness obey it and enter Commodore John Moutray and his <u>retinue</u> upon the Books of His Majesty's Ship under my command.'[36]

Had Nelson actually sent this high-handed note, even the easy-going Hughes might have had to take disciplinary action. Perhaps Nelson calculated that Hughes would not involve the Admiralty. But other letters passed

---

* Sugden (272–7) discusses the affair in fine detail and finds that, in any case, Moutray had a specific commission from the Admiralty, dated 25 July 1783, that designated him 'Commander-in-Chief, in the absence of a flag officer or senior captain' (277, n. 4). Whether Nelson, as the senior captain, would have accepted that as authority in view of his later actions on the issue of the ascendancy of commissioned officers over civilians is a moot point.

between them, and the commander-in-chief wrote to the Admiralty on the matter.* Eventually Philip Stephens, the Admiralty secretary, replied to Hughes, representing their lordships' irritation, though they chose this time not to make an issue of it:

Relative to the refusal of Captain Nelson . . . to receive orders from Mr Moutray as Commissioner of the Squadron during your absence . . . whatever he might think respecting Mr Moutray's Appointments he would have done well to have submitted his Doubts to you instead of taking upon himself to controul Mr Moutray in the Exercise of the Functions of his Appointments. But as Mr Moutray is probably now upon Passage to England, the Establishment of a Commissioner of the Navy at Antigua being retrenched, it is unnecessary for their Lordships to send any particular Instruction for preventing anything of the nature abovementioned from happening in future.[37]

The first lord of the Admiralty, Lord Howe, wanted to air this problem no further, unsurprisingly, since he was engaged in his own civil–military struggle with Charles Middleton, comptroller of the Navy Board, over whether Middleton should be promoted to rear-admiral while still in an administrative post. Howe was to resign on the issue in 1788. But Howe did not forget the faults of others. This was the first of a number of incidents concerning Captain Nelson on the Leeward Islands Station that would exasperate him and others at the Board of Admiralty.

Nelson's relationship with Hughes, his commanding officer, defined much of the *Boreas*'s commission. They had experienced a brief, irritable passage of arms three years before over a lost anchor from the *Albemarle* in the Downs, and this set the early tone of the relationship between the two men. Hughes was a faintly ridiculous figure and was chiefly known in the navy for an unfortunate accident: in pursuing a cockroach early in his career he had pushed a fork in his own eye, and was thus one-eyed. The kindest remark that Nelson made of him was 'his easy temper had made him the dupe of some artful people.' Hughes was wary of his fluent, assured junior. It is noticeable that from early 1786 Nelson warms to Hughes and appreciates his kindness; but by that time Hughes was known to be leaving the West Indies and was doing exactly what Nelson wanted.[38] He was the

---

* Hughes had himself been resident commissioner at Halifax Dockyard between 1778 and 1780 and had a more relaxed attitude to this continuing hierarchical problem. Tension between the civil and the military powers, bad enough on occasion in England, often flared up on foreign stations, far from Admiralty control. There were concurrently very similar problems on the North American Station (Webb, 'North American Waters 1783–1793', 19–34).

first in a long line of senior officers who discovered the difficulty of having Nelson as a subordinate.

Yet Nelson was developing a rare ability to push insubordination to the limit without offending his senior officers personally, or, at least, for only a short period, and he used charm and frankness, which he was to do for the rest of his career. Commissioner Moutray, whose life he made very difficult, still invited him to his house in English Harbour. Both he and Cuthbert Collingwood idolized Moutray's wife, Mary, who was much younger than her husband. 'What a treasure of a woman,' he wrote to his brother William. After she had departed for England in March 1785 with her sick husband, Nelson wrote again to William: 'I went once up the Hill to look at the spot where I spent more happy days than in any one spot in the world. E'en the trees drooped their heads, and the tamarind trees died, all was melancholy: the road is covered with thistles; let them grow.'[39] There was a strong desire for the unattainable, similar to what he had felt for Mary Simpson in Quebec and Elizabeth Andrews in St Omer.

However, the major theme of Nelson's time in the West Indies was now emerging in the shape of a battle of wills over illicit trade in the West Indies by American ships. The issue dominated Nelson's life for the next two years, even following him ashore after the commission. This lengthy struggle has usually been portrayed as one of young, virtuous naval officers against corrupt officials, but in truth it was a more complex issue than good against evil. With the war now lost, Americans were by definition outside the British empire; this reversed the situation that had existed before the war when their ships and merchants had a monopoly on trade. Even so, the political wisdom of legislating to put the former colonies outside the British mercantile system was closely argued and fought at Westminster; but during the short-lived Fox–North government an Order-in-Council was signed on 2 July 1783 outlining the new system.* American produce could be exported into the British West Indies, and West Indian rum, molasses, coffee, coconuts, ginger and pimento could be exported to the United States, 'but the trade in both directions was to be reserved to British subjects, using British-owned and British-built vessels with British crews'.[40] The West Indies colonies were 'thunderstruck'. One estate manager in St Kitts wrote that the restrictions 'took place very unexpectedly, and at a time when there was little Lumber or Provisions in the Island'.[41] They thought it unjust

---

* Taking maritime commerce as a whole in the eighteenth century, this period can be seen as an anomaly, and strict enforcement of the navigation laws was not the norm (Baugh, 'Maritime Strength', 206–15; Harlow, 488; Duffy, *Sugar and Seapower*, 13).

that merchants in Britain could trade with the former American colonies. The West Indies had, after all, fought loyally on the British side during the war.[42]

In the immediate post-war years the islands depended on the eastern coast of North America for a reliable and cost-effective supply of food and timber, particularly barrels of salted low-grade fish to feed slaves. Returning ships exported sugar, molasses and rum. The Leeward Islands and Barbados were particularly dependent upon this trade in provisions, for the population of the islands was swollen by slaves and food was scarce. The early 1780s was a particularly bad hurricane period: ground crops had been devastated, and 15,000 slaves died in Jamaica from storm and want of food. The islanders saw continuing trade with the new United States as necessary for survival, and it was a time of violent feelings.*

Nelson and the Collingwoods worked hard over the next two years in trying to enforce the new Order-in-Council, with very little support at first from other servants of the king. Opposition to Nelson came as much from the other two agencies of the British Crown, the island governors and the customs, as from West Indian merchants and American shipowners. The governors were under pressure from the legislative assemblies of the islands to allow trade in American ships. The customs saw its own powers eroded by presumptuous young naval officers and argued that naval ships had no right to arrest ships on suspicion of smuggling unless the captain was in possession of a 'Deputation' issued by customs – this authorized the navy to seize and seek the condemnation of suspected illicit traders. Not until an Act of Parliament in 1786 'for the further increase and encouragement of Shipping and Navigation' did the Admiralty and the Board of Customs in London agree that a strict prohibition of American ships was to be supported. The 27th section of the Act enabled naval ships to arrest ships without a 'Deputation' from the customs, thus settling the argument.[43] The friction in the Leeward Islands should not be seen in isolation, for there was much confusion and conflict on the issue elsewhere in the empire, and much argument between the governors and customs officials.[44]

From October 1784, for the next eighteen months, Nelson was totally absorbed in trying to stop American ships trading with the islands. Irritated by the complacency of his senior officers, bored with routine and angry at

---

* In 1784 and 1785 riots had occurred in Barbados and St Kitts, and a customs officer was tarred and feathered. Displays of disloyalty were common; both Nelson and Collingwood took action against ships flying an illegal Irish flag (Nicolas, I, 16 Mar. 1785, Nelson to Locker; O'Shaughnessy, 241; Hughes, *Collingwood*, 17; (UK)NA: PRO, ADM 52/2179, 22 Apr. 1785).

the flouting of British law by the former colonists, he and the Collingwoods were determined to enforce the will of Parliament. Shipmasters from the United States were equally determined to trade without detection by obtaining false registers that would make them island-registered ships, thus allowing them to present themselves, if challenged, as British-built. In fact, the first American vessel had been challenged well before Nelson arrived in the West Indies, according to the *North Carolina Gazette*, in May 1784 at Basseterre, St Kitts. The British captain involved is likely to have been Wilfred Collingwood.[45]

Nelson did not make his first move until October of that year, after the hurricane season, when the entire Leeward Islands squadron rendezvoused as usual at Carlisle Bay in Barbados. With Cuthbert Collingwood supporting him, Nelson confronted Hughes, who pleaded ignorance of the 1783 Order-in-Council legislation, as Nelson recounted:

The Admiral stopped me from proceeding, by asking me if I had got the Act of Navigation, that no Instructions had been sent from the Admiralty to him about those matters. I observed, that the Act of Navigation was furnished, I believe, to every Officer in the Navy, as were a number of Maritime Laws, in a book entitled 'The Statutes of Admiralty'. Hughes immediately issued an order to his captains: 'You are hereby authorised and required to proceed against all attempts of illicit trade by the American . . . as the Act of Navigation commands and directs.'[46]

On 17 November the first mention of intervention occurs in the *Boreas*'s log: 'Several Americans who we ordered not to enter received coals and water.'[47] This, of course, was the stock method by which American vessels were beginning to get around the system that was forming up against them, declaring either that they were distressed for food and water or that their vessels were in need of repairs. Word of the new stand taken by the three captains began to reach the American newspapers.

Hughes, however, began to waver in his support for Nelson. The *Boreas* and the *Rattler* went north for an initial cruise, but they found a further order from the commander-in-chief at St Kitts; the president there had persuaded him that the navy was exceeding its brief. The governors, faced with the continuous, delicate balancing act that they had to perform with the assemblies of the islands, were never likely to enforce the Order-in-Council. This time Hughes ordered his captains to ensure that American ships remained in the harbours while 'the Governor (or his Representative) shall think proper to admit the said Foreigner into the Port or Harbour of the Island where you may then be; you are on no account to hinder or prevent such Foreign ships or vessels from going in accordingly, or to interfere any further in her subsequent proceedings.'[48] Nelson dug in his heels. He opposed a direct, written order from his commanding officer. A short but furious correspondence ensued between Captain Nelson and Governor Shirley. Nelson concluded his attack against the Customs officers by disowning the authority of the civil power: 'If the Presidents wish to know the situation of any vessel coming into the Roads, and send an Officer of a certain rank to enquire on board the *Boreas* I shall take care he is answered by an officer of equal rank, and such information as is proper he should know be acquainted with.'[49]

Shirley was not used to this sort of language. His reply was short: 'I felt myself so Hurt and Insulted by the contents . . . that I shall immediately transmit it to your admiral.'[50] Nelson immediately changed his tone, though without backing down from his position. Nelson could not resist a remark in a later letter to Locker: 'Mr Shirley I soon trimmed up and silenced.'[51] These easy-going administrators, however, soon saw that the political wind was slowly blowing Nelson's way, as politicians and administrators in London reached agreement on the degree of coercion needed to enforce the Order-in-Council, copies of which were finally sent out from the Admiralty in May 1785. The Admiralty secretary, Philip Stephens, wrote a letter on 10 May to Hughes that left no doubt: he was 'to cause the same to be complied with so far as may depend upon you and the Commanders of His Majesty's Ships under your command'.[52]

Even when the servants of the Crown could, with difficulty, be persuaded to support the Order-in-Council, there remained the problem of enforcing it. After an initial period of four months Nelson issued a public proclamation on 1 May 1785, making it known that he would seize American ships as prizes. The next day he took the *Eclipse* of Philadelphia, which was crewed entirely by Americans, though registered at St Kitts. The case came to the Admiralty prize court on 17 May.[53] Nelson's right to seize the ship without the authority of the customs was challenged by the Crown lawyer, but Nelson argued his case in court, without legal help, and won. In doing so, he gained the backing of the Crown lawyer, who supported him henceforth. He then stepped up the pressure and arrested four ships at Nevis on 19 May.[54] A judge on board the *Boreas* heard the case and again Nelson won, again pleading his own case. The four ships and their cargoes were condemned as prizes to the *Boreas* and sold. Hughes kept out of the business. On 24 May he sailed into the Nevis Roads in his flagship *Adamant*, and left as soon as he could, at ten thirty the next morning.

Having won the first round, Nelson now came under severe legal and social pressure. The American captains went on shore, whipped up local merchant support and writs were issued against Nelson for the sum of £4000, claiming that the prize judgment was made under duress. The first lieutenant of the *Boreas*, James Wallis, wrote later that the Americans claimed that they were in 'bodily fear, with a man with a drawn sword standing over them, meaning the centinel of the cabin door, and other falsities'. Nelson was compelled to remain on the ship, which the islands' legal officials frequently boarded with the intention of arresting him. Wallis sent them away with, as he recalled, 'fair words'.[55] Nelson now considered that complaint to senior officials in the West Indies was worthless and took an extreme and risky step by going over the heads of his seniors. On 20 March 1785 he wrote to the highest possible authority: Lord Sydney, the home secretary, responsible for colonial administration.[56] By June, isolated and worried, with nothing to lose, he went further: he sent a long, detailed 'Memorial' to the king.[57] This junior captain was not going to hide his talents and efforts. He showed, for the first time in his career, his capacity for ruthlessness and the extent of his ambition, and that he was prepared to risk all.*

While the letters were on their way to London, the game of cat and mouse continued. Knowing these waters well, the American masters were adept at dodging His Majesty's ships. Nelson combated this by sailing at night, in particular the very short distance between St Kitts and Nevis, arriving at an anchorage at first light. Between 30 June and 5 July 1785 he went back and forth between the two islands each day, coming in on four of those days early in the morning: the log for 5 July reads: '5am: came to anchor in Nevis Roads in 4 fathoms'.[58] Sometimes the owners and masters were able to prove that they were indeed British ships. For instance, in July the *Gillon* brig, owned by a Thomas Erskine, was seized but returned.[59] The ships that were condemned were sold.[60] As Nelson wryly remarked, 'The Admiral seemed much pleased when I paid him his prize money,' although neither Nelson nor Hughes, nor indeed the crew of the *Boreas*, received all of it.[61]

In the late summer of that year Nelson received a reply to his letter from Lord Sydney, written on 8 August from Whitehall. Sydney wrote, surprisingly, 'I should have answered your first letter by the April packet had it not been reported at the time that you had died in the West Indies

---

* This step is seen as less extreme by Sugden (299, 826), who presents evidence that Nelson wrote these letters as a result of the advice from Crown lawyers. Even so, Nelson risked antagonizing those immediately senior to him in the navy, as well as naval officials in London.

soon after the date of it.' But the real news came at the end of the letter: 'His Majesty has been pleased to direct that the Law Officers of the Crown should defend the suit on this occasion. Further you can also appeal if the decree should be unfavourable.' Once the full legal and financial weight of the Crown was on Nelson's side, the legal threats from the American masters and the other islanders at Antigua, St Kitts and Nevis began to melt away. Nelson wrote to Sydney, 'The lawyers on the side of the prosecutors declaring they would no longer be concerned against me.'[62]

It took some time before the political will of the government in London became effective. The opinion of the Admiralty lawyer Sir William Scott on the navy's right to uphold the customs search was sought. Scott traced the rights back to the Navigation Acts of 1662 and cast some doubts on the navy's case. Nelson wrote for advice to his influential uncle in the Customs, William Suckling, showing a powerful grasp of the complexities of the law.[63] Scott's academic opinion came to nothing. The Admiralty, the Treasury and the Board of Customs then devised the procedure by which captains of warships carried the 'Deputation' issued by customs. In November 1785 the Board of Admiralty wrote to Hughes telling him that 'Commissioners of Customs will be desired to furnish ... Deputations to the several Captains and some of the officers of the ships under your command.' Two months later Stephens wrote again with a strengthened letter, directing Hughes 'to order them to exert themselves diligently in the execution thereof' and instructing him to say that the documents were being sent out from London.[64]

The shift in political thinking in London was of little avail in Carlisle Bay, however. When Nelson sailed south to Barbados in March 1786 he seized two ships, the *Jane and Elizabeth* brig and the schooner *Brilliant*, and was for ten weeks again embroiled in legal argument, during which he fell out with the judiciary and Governor Parry.[65] He was unable to bring the case to court. On 21 May the *Boreas* sailed, as he recorded in the log, 'brig in company, schooner in tow' and took the prizes to Nevis, where they were condemned.[66] Nelson would be pursued by these cases long after he had come ashore in England at the end of the commission; other prizes would be seized, but this was effectively the end of the affair.*

Nelson had many other tasks. One was surveying potentially useful

---

* Tension was also lessening because of rising West Indies prosperity and a reduction on the duty on rum entering Britain, thus reducing the importance of the American trade. Production of rum doubled between 1784 and 1785, with Britain taking the greater share (Clements, Sydney Papers, 'A Comparative View of the Trade to Jamaica from the Continent of America in the Years 1784 and 1785 and before the War' [1786]).

anchorages, information wanted by both the navy and by the governors of the islands.[67] On one occasion Nelson had to ensure that an over-inquisitive French frigate did not survey British anchorages similarly, by anchoring very close to her to prevent any sounding. The master's log relates: 'At 3pm went past a French frigate . . . At 4 am weighed and came to sail. At 9am near Sandy Point, Beat to Quarters & cleared ship . . . found French frigate here, out pinnace and sent her on shore with a lieutenant.' French ships were also reminded when they did not observe the courtesies of saluting the British flag in British waters. 'Fired three guns at a French sloop for not coming to us.'[68] Nelson was punctilious in marking the king's birthday and accession to the throne (19 January and 27 October), and on 30 May the restoration of Charles II in 1660 was marked by seventeen guns.

Relations had to be established with the Swedes, who had now taken over the island of St Barthélémy, only forty miles to the north of St Kitts. Six months later the Swedish king declared the island and its new capital, Gustavia, a free port, so as to attract trade and hence revenue for his expensive new colonial island. American ships came flocking in with American produce, which the Swedes re-exported to the British islands.[69] Nelson paid a courtesy visit to the new governor, Baron von Rajalin, on 14 February 1786, saluting him with thirteen guns.[70] Some weeks later the governor increased the irritation of the British authorities by announcing that he would grant asylum in St Barthélémy to debtors wanting refuge from any other island. Governor Shirley protested that this was against the interests of the British government, and on 13 July Nelson delivered a formal complaint to the governor at St Barthélémy, telling him that he had information that British slaves were also seeking asylum on Swedish soil. Von Rajalin denied all knowledge of such activity. Lacking support from the islands' assemblies, Shirley was unable to back up his threatened sanctions, and the Swedish island continued to represent a sizeable loophole in British measures against American ships.[71]

From May 1785, however, courtesy visits of a different kind began to intervene. Frances Nisbet was a young widow with a five-year-old son, Josiah. The daughter of a Nevis judge, William Woolward, who had died six years before when Frances was twenty-one, she had married the doctor, Josiah Nisbet, who had nursed her father through his last illness. When he in turn became ill, the couple returned to England, where young Josiah was born. Dr Nisbet died soon afterwards and Frances, who had inherited very little money from her deceased father and husband, appealed for help to her uncle, John Herbert, the president of Nevis, and she and Josiah went back to Nevis to live with him. Herbert was a rich man, himself a widower, although the liquidity of his fortune, dependent upon the price of sugar and the state of next season's crop, was changeable. Frances, the needy relative, helped with his continuous and extravagant entertaining. Her portrait at that time shows a thin and sensitive face, lacking in humour and rather worried, an image of someone whose life had not hitherto gone smoothly. She was slightly older than Nelson, accomplished as a piano player and as a French speaker. He wrote to his brother William: 'Her sense, polite manners, and to you I may say, her beauty, you will much admire: and although at present we may not be a rich couple, yet I have not the least doubt we shall be a happy pair: the fault must be mine if we are not.'[72] This careful assessment is in marked contrast to his emotional extravagance only seven months before when he had written to his brother about Mary Moutray.

The courtship with Fanny proceeded slowly and had to be fitted in when the *Boreas* visited Nevis. Nelson threw himself into writing long letters during his absences, to which Fanny did not always respond. He began a letter of April 1786: 'I will not begin by scolding you although you deserve it for sending me such a letter. Had I not known the warmth of your heart, by the epistle I might have judged you had never seen me.'[73] On another occasion: 'Never was a poor mortal more disappointed at not receiving a letter.'[74] Since they started meeting at the height of the illicit trade issue, naval business caused long gaps in the frequency of their meetings, quite apart from the danger of arrest Nelson at one point faced should he go ashore. No evidence exists as to Fanny's contentment on Nevis before she met Nelson, but her attachment seems constant and genuine. He wrote: 'it must be real affection that brings us together, not interest or compulsion which makes so many unhappy.'[75] His letters show flashes of irritation, reflecting her anxiety, for she worried about his seizing of American ships. This brought her a lecture about neglect of duty: 'Had I taken your advice,' he wrote to her in May 1786, 'and not seized any American I should now have been with you, but I should have neglected my duty which I think your regard for me is too great for you to have wished me to do. Duty is the great business of a sea officer. All private considerations must give way to it however painful it is.'[76] He was particularly low in spirits at English Harbour in August 1786 ('I have found nothing lately . . . but vexation and trouble') when his letters reflect some passion: 'Have you not often heard, that salt water and absence always wash away love? . . . every morning . . . I have had six pails of salt water at daylight poured upon my head, and instead of finding what the Seamen say to be true, I perceive the contrary effect.' But it is affection rather than love that dominates his letters: 'My thoughts are too big for utterance; you must imagine everything that is tender, kind and truly affectionate has possession of my whole frame.'[77] 'So much for marrying a sailor. We are often separated but I trust our affections are not by any means diminished.'[78]

Marriage for a 28-year-old naval officer, without substantial prize money or an inherited fortune, was inevitably a matter of calculation. There was a strong presumption in the navy against early marriage without money to sustain it.[79] A bride's dowry was thus a considerable factor. One of the few advantages of the West Indies Station was the number of available wealthy young women. Frances Nisbet was likely to inherit a considerable fortune, for Herbert was at this time estranged from the younger members of his family. But because of the unpredictable nature of his fortune, Herbert asked them to wait for two years. He had no objection to Nelson.[80] For the moment Nelson also tried to raise money from his uncle William Suckling, who promised to help, although not with any great enthusiasm.[81]

The attraction of staying at Nevis in the company of Fanny probably prevented the *Boreas* from reaching English Harbour by the beginning of August 1785 for the hurricane months. The log of the master, James Jameson, begins to get distinctly nervous, going into unusual detail on the weather. '1 August: very hot and sultry.' The *Boreas* lost her anchor in the Nevis Roads. '3 August: Slipped the best bower cable being a fine time in the hurricane [season].' Nelson, however, was not going to have another lost anchor against his name. The ship returned to Nevis and recovered it the next day. He did not sail again until 8 August. 'Most part of this 24 hours having thunder, lightning and rain. Very black.' It was well that the ship reached English Harbour by 10 August, for a particularly vicious hurricane blew on the 25th. 'At 10 am', Jameson wrote, 'blows a hurricane from NE. Night came, calm for 1/2 an hour, the wind shifted to the SE and blow a hurricane. Everybody on deck in readiness to stand by. Let go the anchors and cut the masts away. At 6am made fast. Lost one cutter and all her oars by this gale. Lost 27 leather buckets.' A day later it was 'Black with rain. People about the rigging.'[82] It was worse elsewhere. Nelson wrote to Locker soon after: 'At Martinique we have a flying report that everything is destroyed.'[83]

As ever, the effort to keep the ship seaworthy was constant and the 1785 hurricane season, some three years after the ship had been docked and repaired at Woolwich, was the time to empty and careen her. She had struck a reef when surveying in Crawl Harbour in November of the previous year, so her bottom needed checking. No damage was found, but Jameson noted: 'We found a little abaft the main mast in the bottom a spike hole through her bottom that had been left from one of the standing shores when the ship was last in dock.'[84] The rigging likewise required overhaul. Nelson wrote to Fanny at the end of the year from English Harbour: 'The main mast is so badly sprung that there was great danger of our losing it and our sails and rigging are tore to pieces. The carpenters of the Dock Yard say it is not safe to carry to Barbados but I have determined to try, as soon as the weather moderates, for well we know that if a person does not perform what he promises, the world is very apt to say he never did intend to do it.'[85] The ship did sail and was back in English Harbour for a week's repairs in January.[86] Besides attention to her condition, almost as much effort had to be expended in keeping her in the best sailing trim possible. Nelson determined early in the commission that the *Boreas* sailed best with her bows a couple of inches deeper than her stern. The crew had shifted seven tons of ballast forward when at Spithead.[87] With 150 men consuming provisions, which constituted a considerable portion of the weight of her ballast, full and empty casks in the hold had to be shifted constantly.[88]

The feeding of 150 men, though the immediate responsibility of the purser, Daniel Peers, needed constant attention from Nelson himself. It was a particular problem in the 1780s, since a large residue of victuals from the American Revolutionary War needed to be consumed, and they were not in good condition.[89] Provisions in casks and barrels were the mainstay of the crew's diet, but this naturally tended to deteriorate.* During the *Boreas*'s refit at English Harbour in 1785, nearly 15,000 pounds of bread were condemned.[90] Ship's victuals were much in demand by the local population. Whenever the *Boreas* or the other ships came into English Harbour, they would be surrounded by boats selling milk, fruit and vegetables, which the black population would barter with the crew for salt meat and biscuit. The seamen's diet was supplemented by fish and also by the inhabitants of the hold. In the *Mediator*, Cuthbert Collingwood's ship, according to the young midshipman Jeffrey Raigersfeld:

By eight in the morning, generally four or five rats were ready cleaned and spread out as butchers dress sheep for the inspection of amateurs . . . and they were found nice and delicate eating; so that this captain of the hold's fishing, for he caught them by a hook and line, became a source of profit. As for the rats, they fed off the best

---

* Soon after, when Nelson was senior naval officer in the Leeward Islands, he ordered all ships on the station to have fresh beef, 'one beef Day in the week, taking care that it is purchased at the lowest price' (NMM, LBK/33, 6 Dec. 1786).

of the ship's provisions, such as biscuit, flour, peas etc and they were as full as good as rabbits, although not so large.[91]

Water was also difficult to keep sweet in the hot West Indian sun. When ships were anchored off the islands water casks were filled daily, but when the ship was at sea it was often not possible to fill them for weeks at a time.[92] Herein lay the root cause of many problems for the eighteenth-century sea officer on the West Indies Station. While water could go off, and beer was not issued for the same reason, rum was unaffected. By the watering of rum, to make grog, the navy hoped to satisfy seamen and control drinking. The *Regulations and Instructions* were specific: captains were not to 'suffer the seamen to drink in drams (undiluted) the allowance made to them of any kind of spirituous liquor in lieu of beer'. Smuggling liquor on board carried an automatic twelve lashes.[93] Combined with the boredom of a peacetime cruise, made worse by the enervating discomfort of the hurricane months, cheap West Indian rum represented an inherent discipline problem.

The *Boreas* has been cited as the one unhappy ship that Nelson commanded, as evidenced by the high incidence of flogging. Unquestionably Nelson flogged more men in the *Boreas* than he had in any ship before, and it was not until sixteen years later, in the *Victory*, that he was to flog more severely.[94] But what is meant by 'high' and what was an 'acceptable' level of severity in the late-eighteenth-century navy?[95] Though the ship generally had a nearly full complement of 180, there was a steady changeover of men over the three and a half years. The total number of individuals who served in her in this period was 334, of which twenty-one (6 per cent) deserted. Eighty-two of the 334 (24.5 per cent) were flogged a total of 118 times, which over forty-two months of the cruise approached an average of nearly three a month. Of this number of floggings, only a dozen were for more than the stock twelve lashes. Some were given fewer than twelve, especially where matters such as personal hygiene were involved. Two cases of thieving occurred, one of absence without leave and one of leaving duty ashore; and late in the cruise, Thomas Watts, the purser's steward, was given six lashes 'for giving liquor to the Quartermasters'. On 20 August 1785 John Mor, the carpenter of another ship, was punished through the little 'Fleet' at English Harbour, being given twelve lashes for bad language to his officers and eleven more for 'imprudence at the gangway'.[96]

On board the *Boreas* most lashes were given to a hard core of persistent offenders. Twenty-one were punished fifty-five times, 47 per cent of all punishments. At the start of the commission Thomas Johnson was flogged round the fleet 'for mutinous expressions at different times', and only three months later received two dozen more lashes for drunkenness and threatening the boatswain. John Gill was flogged five times during the cruise for different instances of drunkenness, fighting and disobedience. Perhaps the sharpest illustration of the impact of alcohol was Nicholas Stevens, a Liverpool man who joined the ship in April 1784, aged twenty. He was clearly a man of ability and Nelson made him his coxswain – very much a personal appointment. Yet Stevens was flogged five times during the cruise. Trouble arose regularly when he was ashore, and every time it was caused by drink: 'drunkenness and disrespect to officers', 'disobedience' and 'fighting'. He was clearly a good man at sea, but was disrated and left the ship at the end of the cruise as he began, an able seaman.[97]

During the three years the ship was at English Harbour, over half the floggings took place in only two months of the year: each August and September, the hurricane months. In sweltering heat and humidity, the seamen had to work hard at refitting the ship, and the temptations of cheap and available rum and slipping away were too great. 'Bringing spirituous liquors on board' and 'going out of the dockyard gate without leave and staying some time' earned the set punishment of twelve lashes; the same was meted out for drunkenness. August and September of 1786 were markedly worse than the two previous years, with an increase in insubordination ('mutinous behaviour') and 'fighting in the yard'. The ten-week stay in Carlisle Bay between March and May 1786 was also a bad period.[98] By contrast, when at sea in the good months, early in the cruise, and when there was the possibility of prize money, only one man was flogged in the six months between the end of October 1784 and the end of April 1785. This was for insubordination, when William Waters was punished 'for striking the Master at Arms'.[99]

Nelson did not have a strong set of officers to enforce discipline, although he appeared to be satisfied with them, judging by the affectionate tone in which he wrote of them to his brother William. The first lieutenant, James Wallis, was efficient, but eccentric; the second, Digby Dent, had no great talent. The master, 'Jemmy' Jameson, was experienced, but he was afflicted by gout and recovering in Nevis during the ship's long stay in early 1786 at Barbados. For the middle six months of 1786 Nelson had no commissioned officer of marines, for the second lieutenant, Theophilus Lane, was invalided to the hospital in Barbados in April 1786, while the first lieutenant, John Hobbs, did not join until October 1786; during these months there was a steady number of marine punishments (twenty-nine), mostly for insubordination. Another weakness appeared to be his boatswains, the warrant officers who had the most critical influence on discipline afloat.

Nelson had four boatswains during this commission, of whom John Scotland served longest, from the time he was made up from able seaman in April 1784 to his disappearance in Barbados twenty months later. It is difficult to judge whether Scotland was a strong boatswain. A number of instances of insubordination to him occurred; one of the earliest was in October 1784, when he was threatened by the troublemaker Thomas Johnson.[100] Eighteen months later, on 12 April 1786, during the long stay in Barbados, Thomas Golding, a seaman, was given twelve lashes for 'stealing and destroying the boatswain's stick', no doubt provoked by the use of the stick on the men for petty offences or to make them work harder, known as 'starting'.[101] Two days later Scotland was leading a press gang ashore at Bridgetown when he shot dead a merchant seaman named James Elliot. Pursued by the civil authorities, Scotland disappeared, protected by Nelson aboard the *Boreas*. Governor Parry asked Hughes to find the boatswain; Nelson protested that he had not been seen. The matter went back to London, for Hughes received a letter from the Admiralty referring to Governor Parry's attempt to apprehend the boatswain of the *Boreas* and directing Hughes to find out 'how it happened that the Boatswain was suffered to make his escape'.[102] Only Captain Nelson knew, but, to his seniors and the civil authorities, he protested unblinkingly that he did not.* When the hue and cry had died down, only then did Nelson find a satisfactory boatswain, a Portuguese seaman named Joseph King, according to Nelson, 'one of the best Boatswains I have seen in His Majesty's Service'. King finished the commission and served with Nelson through the 1790s.[103]

The use of the lash on a peacetime cruise can be expected to be high, and higher than in wartime. The crew of the *Boreas* were hardened, volunteer seamen, prepared to take risks for acquiring drink. They knew exactly what to expect for specific misdemeanours. Crews in wartime were raised in an atmosphere of urgency and danger, and were composed of a large majority of pressed, untrained men with the hope of prize money. In the Leeward Islands as a whole between 1784 and 1793 the average number of punishments was significantly higher than that on the same station after the war with France started.[104]

---

* This incident has recently been uncovered for the first time by John Sugden (320–29), on whose work this brief summary depends. It is important in that it shows the lengths to which Nelson and many other sea officers of the time were prepared to go to defend their crews. James Elliott is entered into the *Boreas*'s muster book as a captain's servant for one day before he died, perhaps, as Sugden suggests, as a ploy to represent Elliott as a crew member so that Scotland could be tried by court martial rather than by a Barbadian court ((UK)NA: PRO, ADM 36/10528, 14–15 Apr. 1786).

Nelson took a strong line over insubordination, but, while the personality and style of the captain was by far the most important factor in the discipline of a ship, other factors, including the calibre of his officers, have to be taken into account. Wilfred Collingwood, commanding the small *Rattler*, was twice as severe as Nelson; Charles Sandys also flogged more than him. Not surprisingly, Kelly, Hughes's flag captain, seems to have run the *Adamant* as a very easy ship indeed. Cuthbert Collingwood was the most lenient of all.[105] As we have seen, over the three years of the *Boreas*'s commission the incidence of flogging was variable. After the 1797 mutinies, attitudes hardened, and as an admiral Nelson would later command ships with much harsher regimes. But his time in the *Boreas* showed that he was prepared to flog as hard and as often as necessary for a subordinate crew.

At the same time Nelson exercised paternal care over the crew. Not many captains would have written to the postmaster-general in London, as he did in October 1785, about the welfare of his crew:

The enormous price of letters received in this country is so very far above whatever a petty officer can afford to pay, much more the poor Seaman . . . since my serving here I have paid much more largely for letters than my fortune will allow of, for the Comforts of the Seamen hearing from their Wives and families, and at this moment are laying in the Post Office at St Johns near 100 letters which they can never afford to pay for; nor have I the means to relieve their distress . . .[106]*

Nelson also took a notable amount of care over the health of his crew. James Wallis claimed that 'not a single officer or man died out of her whole complement. A similar instance of health can scarcely be produced.'[107] Wallis's recollection was faulty. In a letter of October 1784 Nelson refers to a fever 'which carried off several of the *Boreas*'s ship's company' and by the time of this letter two men were entered in the log as having 'departed this life'.[108] In fact, three seamen and one marine died during the three and half years, one of whom, John Farrell, a seaman, fell out of the longboat and drowned when the *Boreas* was anchored in the Nevis Roads.[109] Wallis also noted that Nelson took particular care of the health of the young gentlemen and administered purgative medicines. For the West Indies at this time the *Boreas* was indeed a healthy ship.

Far from being routine or relaxing, this peacetime cruise put Nelson

---

* This problem was solved ten years later by the introduction of a penny post for 'Non-commissioned officers, seamen and Private Men in the Navy and Army, whilst on service' (35 Geo. III. c. 53, 5 May 1795).

under great stress. Some of the most remarkable facets of his character were revealed for the first time in the *Boreas*. His capacity for pushing a case to extremes is well illustrated by his battle with the island merchants and American shipowners, where his self-belief and his conviction that his cause was just kept him from buckling under social or legal pressure or compromising with lawyers. Combined with a lack of respect for his senior officer, it led him to calculated confrontation with his seniors. This success was not achieved by skills in negotiation, though he used his charm when he wanted to, but by an absolute confidence. His winning manner after his successful assertiveness over Moutray, Hughes and Shirley displayed a high degree of manipulation. He wrote knowingly to Locker that Hughes was 'a good natured blunderer who can be disobeyed with impunity if one is careful'.[110] His determined ambition would lead him to repeat this behaviour again and again throughout his career; half a dozen weak senior officers would be similarly swept aside, and he would quarrel even with the stronger ones, including those who helped him most. He was not a good second.

As a young officer who had fought long and hard against the Americans, and on the losing side, Nelson was not going to turn a blind eye to the law as laid down by Parliament. He was not alone in feeling that continued American commerce was an injustice: he had the Collingwoods on his side, and probably the other younger captains. Yet underlying Nelson's high moral and legal stance was his constant effort to bring himself to the notice of those who could influence his career. Nelson was highly indignant when the lackadaisical Hughes was congratulated by the Board of Admiralty for bringing the American trading under control, although a letter to the commander-in-chief of the station was the orthodox measure of conveying Admiralty approval. Nelson wrote to Locker: 'I feel much hurt that . . . another should be thanked for what I did against his orders. I either deserved to be sent out of the Service, or at least have had some little notice taken of me.'[111] For the first time intense ambition was leading him to take risks within his profession: writing to the king and the secretary of state on the question of the illegal trade in American ships, circumnavigating not only his commander-in-chief but the Board of Admiralty, was extremely risky. In the short term he got away with it; but those at the top of the Admiralty had long memories.

All of this was achieved with the high level of anxiety from which he would always suffer, an integral part of his driven personality. His awkward and disrupted courtship of Frances Nisbet also contributed to this vulnerable side of his temperament. Towards the end of his time in the West

Indies his health was undermined, and that can only have clouded his judgement. But these pressures did not break him, in the way that many officers were broken by sickness and the loneliness of command. Nelson's belief in himself was to be tested again at the end of 1786 and in the early months of 1787. This time he did not do so well.

7

Senior Naval Officer, Leeward Islands

August 1786–November 1787

Their Lordships . . . are much disappointed and dissatisfied at the little Attention you have shewn to the Rules and Practice of the Service as Well as the Directions contained in the 10th & 11th articles of the General Printed Instructions . . .*

Philip Stephens, secretary to the Board of Admiralty,
to Nelson, 9 March 1787[1]

By August 1786 Nelson seemed to have solved most of his problems. The illicit trade issue was virtually over and the hostility to him dying away, except in Barbados, and American merchant ships were still being seized. Nevis and Fanny provided a happy refuge. Sadly, Cuthbert Collingwood had just left for England; his good advice would be greatly missed. But his departure was offset by the fact that Sir Richard Hughes was to return home. Hughes was by now rather a pathetic figure, as well as the subject of much gossip: he had been seeing rather a lot of an unmarried lady since his wife had gone to live with their recently married daughter on another island.† His successor was expected to be a senior captain, Sir Richard Bickerton, but he had not yet arrived from England.

When Hughes departed for England on 1 August 1786 the 28-year-old Nelson was therefore the senior naval officer on the Leeward Islands Station.[2] He was now not only responsible for the ships and their deployment, but also for the dockyard at English Harbour. As a result of government retrenchment after peace, the post of resident commissioner,

---

* 'When the Ship arrives at the Port where she is to be laid up, he is to send the Original General Muster-Book to the Comptroller of the Navy, signed by himself' (*Regulations and Instructions Relating to His Majesty's Service at Sea*, Article X, 'Captain or Commander').

† Hughes's next and last appointment was commander-in-chief, North America, based at Halifax, where he again had to deal with the problem of American ships and illicit trade (Webb, 'British Squadrons', 29–31).

previously held by John Moutray, had not been continued, and thus the charge of the dockyard fell to Nelson. This part of his job was not going to be easy. Two years before he had taken a stance over the seniority of the fighting service over the civil administration of the navy by his aggressive attitude on the question of Moutray's pennant. This was not the way to bridge the social and professional divides between the fighting and the civil sides of the navy, when higher authority was several thousand miles away. Even Hughes had had to exert himself to ensure that his directions to the dockyard were obeyed.[3] Commissioner Moutray had got on well with his dockyard officers, and when he returned to England in March 1785 he wrote to them thanking them for their efforts with elaborate courtesy. He ended his letter: 'Accept my best Wishes for your Prosperity,' an all too accurate remark in view of subsequent events.[4]

Nelson did not let matters rest for long. Within a month of Hughes's departure, he peremptorily ordered the dockyard officers to tighten up their security. No 'foreigners' were to be allowed into the yard. It was 'of great national importance' that foreign vessels, even when in distress, should not be allowed in, and they were to be sent round to St John's on the other side of the island.[5] His correspondence with the dockyard officers marked the start of a confrontation with them of some months' duration. It was a time of particular stress. Nelson's health was not good. The morale of the *Boreas*'s crew was low. In December 1786 and the following January there were eleven floggings for drunkenness and fighting.[6]

It was not an ideal atmosphere in which to renew his acquaintance with the 21-year-old Prince William Henry, the third son of the king, who arrived at Dominica on 3 December 1786 in command of the frigate *Pegasus*. Hood had introduced Nelson to the prince in New York in November 1782. The prince was impulsive and weak. His father had hoped that a sea career would mature the volatile young man, and he particularly wanted him to be treated in the same way as any other young officer. The king enlisted Hood's help to tutor the prince. 'My eye shall constantly be kept upon His Royal Highness,' Hood wrote to the King in 1782, 'and to the utmost of my power will be watchful not only to encourage every laudable point, but to check & restrain whatever I may see amiss.'[7] In spite of the attentions of this very senior watchdog, the prince had quarrelled with his immediate commanding officer, Captain Napier. A year later, a disappointed monarch wrote to Hood, 'Your dispositions seem to have been very judiciously made ... but men cannot be disposers of events, and still less on so unstable an element as the sea ... William has ever been violent when controlled.'[8] Nelson had last seen William at Windsor before the prince had travelled to the Continent for two years, when he had developed his boorish and outrageous behaviour still further. In spite of the king's early wishes that the prince should receive no special treatment, he had been made a lieutenant in June 1785 on his return from the Continent; after only nine months he had been given his first command.* Spoilt, temperamental and barely experienced enough to stand a watch, the prince had been allocated a first lieutenant, Isaac Schomberg, to help him. Schomberg, thirteen years older than the prince, was a protégé of Hood and had been recommended by him. The task needed a diplomatic temper and finesse, but Schomberg proved to be nearly as obstinate as the prince.

The arrival of royalty in the Leeward Islands was marked by parties and balls, which Nelson did not like, as he was immediately thrown into a hectic social round that often continued until daybreak.[9] The prince caused immediate difficulties. The first problem arose over regulations concerning the ship's muster books; in itself of no great importance, it was none the less a bureaucratic triviality that was to cause lasting damage to Nelson's reputation. When a ship arrived at a dockyard, the clerk of the Cheque of the Dockyard, the officer who handled finance, or his deputy, would muster the ship's company; according to regulations, a copy of the muster book would be handed in to him by the captain. This book was then forwarded to the Navy Board so that a check could be made on the crew for pay and discipline purposes. When the *Pegasus* arrived at English Harbour, the prince refused to make up the ship's muster book and hand it in to the muster master, Archibald Dow, the deputy naval storekeeper. Dow wrote two long and respectful letters to Prince William, pointing out that a 'perfect muster' was the 'only official means by which to account to the Navy Board'. The prince wrote back that he would not be subject to instructions from the Navy Board and that they would 'not be attended to by any Military Officer in His Majesty's Service without having previous Instructions from the Admiralty for that purpose'.[10] Where did the young prince get these inflexible ideas of the inferiority and separation of the civil side of the navy? The Board of Admiralty was in no doubt: from the same officer who had caused a similar difficulty over Commissioner Moutray's pennant. The Board's secretary, Philip Stephens, wrote to the prince: 'Captain Nelson has very much misinformed your Royal Highness.'[11] Stephens did not mince

---

* The king's experiment with Prince William Henry has recently been described as 'astonishing if not subversive' in view of the great difference between his royal status and that of a sea officer (Rodger, 'Honour and Duty', 430). The next royal naval officer was Alfred, the first duke of Edinburgh, Queen Victoria's third son, who entered a vastly more aristocratic navy in 1858.

his words to Nelson. Their lordships were disappointed by his authorizing the prince 'to disregard the Applications of the Deputy Muster Master to be furnished with a perfect Muster Book'. Additionally, he pointed out Nelson's illogical position: why had Nelson not refused to do the same for his own ship? 'Their Lordships are the less able to judge of your motives . . . as they conclude you have not been wanting yourself in furnishing such a Book upon your first Arrival on the station.'[12] The muster books were not delivered until the *Pegasus* reached England.

Relations with the dockyard officers at English Harbour were to worsen. In mid February 1787 Nelson directly accused them of dishonesty. Stores had been purchased without his permission. When requested to sign bills for payment, Nelson had asked to see the original vouchers in order to check the amount of money for which he was to sign. This time it was Archibald Dow who refused to produce the relevant document, for the yard officers claimed through precedent that Nelson's initial authorization for the purchase of stores was not necessary. 'This refusal', Nelson replied angrily, 'I hold as a high mark of disrespect and Neglect of Duty: and you are to take notice that the Officers of the Yard do wait upon me at 10 o'clock tomorrow Morning with the Original Vouchers that those Stores were supplied & attested Copies for me to keep, that I may be assured that no alteration [was made].'

The yard officers were responsible to the Navy Board; Nelson was responsible to the Admiralty. He could not have it both ways, and it was a battle he did not win. At the same time, he made matters worse by ordering the *Boreas*'s boatswain, Joseph King, who had suffered an accident, to be entered in the yard as a sailmaker's assistant.* Again the matter went back to London, from the yard officers to the Navy Board. Nelson was later criticized for this appointment by the Admiralty and for ignoring the complaints of the yard officers.[13] He replied to Philip Stephens hotly: 'I know not of remonstrances – I never allow inferiors to dictate.'[14] The temporary appointment of King to the dockyard was a perfectly sensible move, and could have been achieved through friendly relations. The immature Nelson's bull-headed attitude had yet to be tempered by the power of persuasion, which could overcome the niceties of protocol.

Troubles piled upon troubles. These small battles were as nothing to the difficulties that developed on board the *Pegasus* between the prince and his

---

* King had previously been a sailmaker and a vacancy had arisen in the dockyard. Nelson could cite precedent, for Admiral Parker had appointed the master of the *Bristol* to be master attendant at Jamaica ((UK)NA: PRO, ADM 1/241, 7 Mar. 1779, Parker to the Admiralty).

first lieutenant. Friction had started almost immediately in January and February 1787 when the prince took over command of the ship at Halifax Dockyard in Nova Scotia. He later reported to the king that Schomberg had 'proceeded with regularity, but wished to carry on the duty of the ship entirely, and particularly whenever I found fault, would reason and shew this was not wrong. I highly disapproved of his conduct, but from diffidence and from the novelty of my situation I could not muster resolution to inform him of his impropriety and want of respect.'[15] Diffidence and Prince William Henry were not often mentioned in the same sentence.

The prince found in the Leeward Islands not, as he might have expected, a commander-in-chief in his fifties but a sympathetic 28-year-old captain. Here was a situation that the prince could exploit. Nelson knew none of the background, but he recognized tensions immediately. As a precaution, he noted down in rough form what happened at his first meeting with the prince, whose skilful manipulation started in the first minute of conversation. Delivering a packet to Nelson from the Admiralty, he immediately asked what was in it; then he asked whether he was still under Commodore Sawyer's instructions from the North American Station, or Nelson's. Very soon he moved the discussion to the centre of his frustrations. 'He enquired', wrote Nelson,

how I was officered & having told him very well, he said I wish I could say so, for although I think mine know their duty that they gave themselves such airs that he could not bear them. Do you know that they would not go to the Ball which Governor Parry gave me at Barbados, which I think a breach of great contempt for me? I told H.R.H. that I could not suppose they could mean anything disrespectful to him, that every other consideration was out of the question; it was too much their Interest to wish to disoblige him.[16]

The prince then mentioned Schomberg as the particular problem, but nothing further was said at that first meeting. The next day Nelson witnessed a quarrel between the prince and his first lieutenant over an order that the prince had issued for the men to wear their blue jackets to mark the arrival of a French frigate. Schomberg replied that the weather was too hot. Nelson noted:

The manner in which this was spoke made a greater impression upon me than all that happened afterwards, for I plainly saw all was not right. The next day Captain Brown of the *Amphion* told me he saw that Schomberg and the Prince would not long be friends & hoped that I would endeavour to prevent a court martial from happening in the *Pegasus* that he feared I should have a disagreeable time of it.[17]

The atmosphere of impending disaster deepened when the *Boreas* and the *Pegasus* reached English Harbour a few days later. The prince organized his living arrangements on shore so as to have the ear of Nelson continuously and alone. When the *Pegasus* moved to the careening wharf, Nelson offered the prince the commanding officer's house; the prince accepted, provided that Nelson stayed there too. Nor did the prince any longer dine with his officers, for, as he wrote in a long and self-justifying letter to the king, 'I had made and shall ever observe this rule, that whenever two captains or any strangers dine with me to have that day no officer of the ship at my table.'[18] To Nelson he gave a different explanation for Schomberg's absence: his 'Lieutenant could not be spared from the duty of the ship'.[19]

Prince William Henry's behaviour has been blamed on Nelson, a judgement influenced by the fact that Nelson was apt to discourse at length on the lack of discipline among naval officers. Thomas Byam Martin, a captain's servant in the *Pegasus*, recalled many years later that 'A change took place in the conduct of our royal captain on reaching the Leeward Islands station, which to this day I have never been able to account for'; and Byam Martin was highly critical of the petty restrictions that the prince put on the officers of the ship.[20] Nelson saw that it was affecting his own relationships. 'The Lieutenant of the *Pegasus* I saw was displeased with me,' he noted ruefully, and 'the officers of the *Boreas* told me that they attributed H.R.H.'s change of conduct to me.'[21] Thus, he must have been aware of the trouble that the prince was continually causing.* Nelson had received no special instructions, as Lord Howe, would have seen no need to instruct a sea officer on his duty. Nelson instinctively assumed that the prince had to be backed, whatever the circumstances. Nelson discarded sixteen years of naval experience, training and, indeed, honour for some possible social and, perhaps, career advantage in being so close to a prince of the realm. In a letter to his brother William he wrote of the prince: 'In every respect, both as a Man and a Prince, I love him. He has honoured me as his confidential friend; in this he shall be not mistaken.'[22] Ambition and naivity overcame common sense and fairness. Nelson was not to know for some years that his failure

---

* For instance, Nelson reversed one of the prince's eccentric orders, when he had refused to sign a warrant for the payment of men from other ships who had worked on the *Pegasus* ((UK)NA: PRO, ADM 241/1, 24 Jan. 1787, Nelson to the dockyard officers).

to deal with the prince authoritatively was to cause the king severe displeasure. For the rest of his life he was never able to shake off this handicap.

Matters came to a head between the prince and Schomberg in mid January 1787. The immediate cause, appropriately, was trivial – the punishment of a seaman and a marine 'for hanging up their clothes between decks'. There followed a furious correspondence between two obstinate men. 'It is', wrote the prince on 12 January, 'incumbent in you to promote and rigidly follow all directions and orders you may from time to time receive from me as your Commanding Officer; and by no means whatsoever make the least objection, as it is directly contrary to the respect which is ordered and directed by the Articles of War.' Two days later the prince put Schomberg under arrest, though he was free to move about the ship; and, in spite of a conciliatory gesture by Schomberg, disagreement broke out again between the two men over a boat going ashore without the captain's knowledge.[23] Schomberg made a direct request to Nelson, though not through Prince William, as he should have done. It was at this point that Nelson made a disastrous decision. He ordered the prince to put his first lieutenant under arrest. He claimed later he did this to protect Schomberg from his captain.[24] Worse still, the third lieutenant of the *Pegasus*, William Hope, was drawn into the conflict. The prince, seeing new demons, now imagined that Hope was the root of all the trouble. All the while, the arrival of the new commander-in-chief, still expected to be Sir Richard Bickerton, was daily anticipated.*

Nelson had let a personal squabble escalate. A court martial would have broken Schomberg, engulfed the prince in controversy and reflected disastrously on Nelson. He was by now completely subservient to the prince, concerned only to flatter his manipulative junior officer. In late April Nelson wrote the prince a letter that barely resembles that of a commanding officer: 'In appointing Mr Wallis to the command of her [the *Rattler*], I hope I acted as you wish me.'[25] He then sent the prince a blank lieutenant's commission, which, as the prince commented, 'you in your usual polite and civil manner authorised me to fill up'.[26] How far Nelson's judgement had been warped is demonstrated in a letter to Locker on 13 February, when he almost casually mentioned that 'Schomberg will, I have no doubt, be broke . . . in short, our service had been so much relaxed during the War, that it will cost many a court-martial to bring it back

---

* Had he come out to the Leeward Islands, it is doubtful whether (the older) Bickerton would have improved the situation. Nelson had earlier commented to Locker that he thought Bickerton seemed 'to carry it very high with his captains' (Nicholas, I, 57, 5 Feb. 1782).

again.'[27] The manipulative behaviour of the prince had completely turned the head of the young captain from Norfolk. A dangerous combination of inexperience and rigid respect for royalty blinded him to the obvious step of dissuading Schomberg from applying for a court martial, which was Schomberg's only recourse as an appeal against a senior officer.

Perhaps Nelson imagined that the Admiralty could remain in ignorance of the whole episode, at least until it was over, for he made yet another very serious misjudgement by not informing the board of what was going on. He had not bargained for the interference of John Orde, an ambitious and well-connected naval officer senior to Nelson, at that time governor of Dominica. Orde wrote directly to Lord Howe, who replied on 20 June:

The total Silence which has been observed in every other Quarter, towards this Board & the separate members of it . . . I had inferred that the cause of dissatisfaction on all sides had been privately removed . . . No notice has been taken in any official Return, that an Officer has ever been under suspension. The tenor of your letter therefore, gives me inexpressible Concern . . . It is by no means clear to me that Capt. Nelson's very injudicious conduct in many other instances, may not have proved the cause, or support at least, of the disinclination to temperate resolutions . . .[28]

Nelson was able to ease the tension after the sudden death of Wilfred Collingwood on 21 April by appointing his first lieutenant, James Wallis, into the *Rattler*, promoting his second lieutenant, Digby Dent, into Wallis's place and bringing Hope out of the *Pegasus* into the *Boreas* in Dent's place. 'I am delivered', wrote the prince to the king, 'from an officer of the most violent, obstinate, and quarrelsome disposition.'[29] (Hope was to have a distinguished naval and political career, rising to vice-admiral with a knighthood.) On 20 May Nelson ordered the *Pegasus* and the *Rattler* to Jamaica. At a different station the prince's ship would no longer be under the command of Nelson, and in Jamaica there would be the requisite number of captains to enable a court martial to be convened. This was an order for which Nelson would be much criticized. Again, he was directly pressurized by the prince, who was much later to write: 'in my opinion, Nelson, we were both to blame, you in sending the *Pegasus* and the *Rattler* down to Jamaica, and me in asking and proposing it.'[30]

The tense atmosphere in the *Pegasus* can only be imagined. On arrival at Jamaica the situation was defused very swiftly by the commodore, Alan Gardner. That he was shrewder than all the players in this minor drama is borne out by the smooth style of his long letter to their lordships ('by every means in my power to heal and conciliate').[31] Moreover, he did it with the help of his captains, one of whom was Brown of the *Amphion*, who had warned Nelson of the hornets' nest in the *Pegasus* in December of the previous year. Gardner persuaded Schomberg to withdraw his request for a court martial, although there were by this time signs of Prince William losing his nerve, as he realized that he had few witnesses to support his case. A relieved Board of Admiralty sent Gardner a congratulatory letter; his actions had met with 'the entire approbation of their Lordships'.[32] Schomberg then returned to England.*

In this anxious and unhappy period, Nelson married Frances Nisbet at her uncle's house on Nevis. Yet again the prince had his way with Nelson, for he precipitated the timing of the marriage by insisting upon giving the bride away. He reported to Hood: 'Nelson introduced me to his bride: she is a pretty and sensible woman, and may have a great deal of money if her uncle Mr Herbert thinks proper, poor Nelson is over head and ears in love ... I wish him well and happy, and that he may not repent the step he has taken.'[33] A cautionary note was also struck by the young captain's servant from the *Boreas*, Thomas Byam Martin, writing many years later that Frances had 'at that time some beauty, and a freshness of countenance not common in that climate'; but he added critically, 'there was so remarkable an absence of intellectual endowment as to make it evident that Nelson's sagacious eye was content to dwell upon the blooming cheeks, without going in search of the better graces which give permanence to conjugal felicity.'[34] Was this a judgement of hindsight or was there something obviously wrong from the start of Nelson's marriage? Nelson was in a more than usually anxious state at the time. In addition to the conflicts among his officers, the legal disputes generated by the island merchants had not entirely dissipated. When political pressures ashore threatened him a dozen years later at Naples, he was, of course, again to seek the solace of female company, in more dramatic circumstances.

Over the spring of 1787 Nelson's health had been steadily deteriorating, and this cannot have helped his judgement. In the previous summer he seems to have had a recurrence of malaria.[35] A surgeon from the hospital at English Harbour wrote on 21 July: 'I am therefore clearly of opinion that an immediate removal to another climate is highly necessary.'[36] At the

---

* The prince added his own bad-tempered postscript to the story by refusing to insert the words 'his complying with the General Printed Instructions' on Lieutenant Hope's certificate, without which he could not be paid. The prince was only persuaded to conform by the first lord of the Admiralty (NMM, LBK/33, 17 May 1787, Prince William to Philip Stephens; HOO/2, 24 July 1787).

time of his wedding the prince commented to Hood that Nelson 'is more in need of a nurse than a wife. I do not think he can live long.'[37] Thomas Byam Martin said that Nelson was of so 'wasted and emaciated an appearance that those eligible to promotion made no concealment of their expectation of an early vacancy'.[38] One young midshipman who saw him just before his departure remembered that 'it was not expected he could live to reach England, and he had a puncheon of rum for his body in case he should die during the voyage.'[39] On the eve of his departure to England, James Young from the hospital advised him to 'be particularly careful in guarding against the cold as you draw towards the Soundings' and to 'wear warm clothes and thick shoes'.[40] Yet, in spite of these worries, Thomas Graham, the *Boreas*'s surgeon, recalled more than a dozen years later that 'tho' you were frequently under the pressure of sickness . . . notwithstanding these repeated attacks of fever . . . your constitution was radically good.'[41]

One more situation was to test him. At the end of April a seaman, William Clark, was court-martialled. On two previous occasions in 1786 Clark had attempted to desert from Wilfred Collingwood's *Rattler*.[42] He deserted again and was automatically condemned to death. Nelson extracted the maximum drama from the case to point up the force of the law. All available boats in English Harbour were ordered alongside the *Rattler*, each manned with an officer, armed seamen and marines. The officers and crew were summoned on deck and told of 'the Nature of the Crime the Prisoner was guilty of, and the fatal consequences attending the same, in order to render them constantly Mindful of the Fidelity and Service done for their King and Country'.[43] The man was brought forward for execution: and at that point, at the request of the very sick Wilfred Collingwood (he was to die within the week), Nelson pardoned him. He went too far. The rule was that 'Commanders-in-Chief may suspend the execution of sentences of death until they receive superior orders, no right of pardoning in matters of a capital nature are vested in them'; the final decision of clemency lay only with the king. Then Nelson, still only the temporary senior naval officer on the Leeward Islands Station, went further still and discharged Clark from the navy, which was to bring a severe admonition.[44] Philip Stephens, writing on behalf of the Board of Admiralty, was blunt. 'You will see', he wrote, 'that you had no authority to pardon the man; and I am now to acquaint you that if you had been invested with such authority the man being pardoned had no right to the further indulgence of being discharged from His Majesty's service and that consequently the reasons you have offered are insufficient.'[45] Nevertheless, Clark was formally pardoned.[46]

At the end of May Nelson received the order to prepare the *Boreas* for the voyage home.[47] The ship was now in poor repair. On two consecutive days in February Nelson had entered into his log: 'The ship makes a great deal of water.'[48] Before she sailed for England her rudder had to be unshipped and the timber supporting it had to be removed, and she had spent much of April alongside the wharf in English Harbour. May was taken up with farewells at Nevis. The *Boreas* then returned to Antigua, where final pieces of business were completed and the sick seamen from the hospital were embarked for the passage home.[49] At last his relief, Commodore William Parker, arrived on 3 June.[50] Nelson set off the next day, while Fanny and her son, Josiah, with her uncle, John Herbert, returned in the *Roehampton*, a West Indiaman, more comfortable than the crowded warship and with less risk of infection from invalids being given a passage home in the *Boreas*.[51] The *Boreas* made good speed, anchoring four weeks later on 5 July at Spithead. Nelson's first call was on Samuel Hood, now commander-in-chief at Portsmouth. It was not a comfortable interview, the first of a number that Nelson was to have with his patron during years of growing estrangement.[52]

July was a difficult month, relieved only when Nelson sat on a court martial on the 19th, where he met a number of friends, including Charles Morice Pole.[53] The main discomfort was a succession of letters from Philip Stephens, conveying the Board of Admiralty's displeasure on a range of issues during *Boreas*'s commission, including Prince William's muster books, the affair of William Clark and Joseph King's appointment to the dockyard at English Harbour. His application to be paid at the rate of senior naval officer after Hughes had gone was turned down.[54] He complained without success to Hood about delays to the men's payment.[55] The promotions of Wallis and Dent were not confirmed.[56] He answered each of Stephens's critical letters carefully and, in some cases, defiantly.

Captain Nelson had acquired a reputation for exceeding his authority, and it is likely that Lord Howe was determined to teach him a lesson. Instead of receiving the expected order to pay off, on 17 August Nelson was told to proceed from Spithead to the Nore.[57] From late September the *Boreas* took up station deep in the Thames estuary, seven miles from land, to impress men from incoming merchant ships – they were needed to serve in the crisis with the Dutch, which had been brewing over the summer. Nelson encountered a great deal of disciplinary trouble on board, including desertion and drunkenness. In twenty-five days, fifteen of the *Boreas*'s crew received twelve lashes at the gangway for various offences of drinking and disobedience.[58] It was certainly unusual for a ship returning from a long overseas commission to have to do impressment duty, crisis or no crisis. The comptroller of the Navy Board, Charles Middleton, was surprised: a letter to Nelson of 17 August starts 'Taking it for granted that the *Boreas* would have been paid off soon after her arrival . . .'[59] Fanny recalled in later years that Nelson was so low that he talked of joining the Russian Service: 'he was so dissatisfied at the ill-usage particularly when at the Nore that I am certain that he would never have gone to sea if he had had a fortune.'[60]

Then suddenly the diplomatic crisis with the Dutch was over. The *Boreas* was ordered into Sheerness, and on 30 November Nelson and what crew remained were paid off. He was not to tread the decks of his own ship again for five years. However, behind the scenes, there was worse than the admonitory letters from Philip Stephens. One letter that Nelson did not see was written by Howe himself to Hood and was, as usual, abominably drafted. It was indeed chilling:

I am sorry Captain Nelson, whom we wished well to, has been so much wanting in his endeavours, which I think could not have failed of success if they had been judiciously exerted, to dissuade the Prince from the idea of going so prematurely to Jamaica . . .[61]

Nelson, missing the common-sense advice of Cuthbert Collingwood and far from the wisdom of Samuel Hood, had tackled a difficult task while labouring under a number of false assumptions. Winning the battle over illicit trade confirmed his self-belief. But more was necessary for successful command of a station, including a political sense that he had yet to develop. Had Schomberg's court martial taken place, the careers of the central players in the drama would have been fatally hurt and the credibility of Lords Howe and Hood with the king badly damaged. It would be some three years before Nelson could bring himself to accept that he had misjudged the situation.

8

Half-pay in Norfolk
December 1787–December 1792

Although I am set down here in a Country Life, Yet (and although Happily Married) I always shall as I ever have done be ready to step forth whenever service requires or my Friends may wish me to serve. Fame says you are going out with a command. If in either Actual Service, or a Wish of Yours to accept of one under your Command who reveres & esteems you. I am ready and willing to go Forth and by a strict adherence to Your Orders as my Superior and Wishes as any Friend prove Myself worthy of the friendship.
Captain Nelson to Captain William Cornwallis, 8 October 1788[1]

Of all the periods in Horatio Nelson's life, the five years that he spent ashore have most puzzled his biographers. The Victorians, in particular, portrayed Nelson at this time as despairing at his inability to be given a ship. How could the navy have neglected his genius? Mahan quoted previous biographies to demonstrate their emotional overstatement: 'his latent ambition would at times burst forth ... at others, a sudden melancholy seemed to overshadow his noble faculties, and to affect his temper; at those moments the remonstrances of his wife and venerable father alone could calm the tempest of his passions.'[2] But the evidence suggests that only in 1790 and 1791, the last two years of this period, did Nelson feel ignored and deserted by previous friends and supporters. It also took him a long time to understand why he should be so ignored.

Some weeks passed before he could shake himself free of the *Boreas*. Purchases needed to be steered through the London or Chatham customs houses. Some of them were substantial, especially the rum for his brother William and the wine and rum for Locker.[3] Tensions among the crew after three and a half years at sea remained a problem. He wrote to the Admiralty about the purser's steward, Thomas Watts, who had threatened the master, Jemmy Jameson, with a civil action 'for improperly correcting him'. Civil actions at the end of a commission to settle old scores had long been a hazard for officers.[4] Nelson had given the steward six lashes at the end of 1786 for 'suttling', or distributing rum, 'to the Ship's company and making numbers of them drunk, and being impertinent'. To Philip Stephens Nelson strenuously defended Jameson. He had nothing good to say of Watts; had he himself been on board, he wrote, 'I should have punished him at the gangway.'[5] Dramatically, Nelson appeared at the Old Bailey on 17 December, where he spoke on behalf of the *Boreas*'s cooper, James Carse, who in a drunken fit of madness had murdered a woman in Shadwell, then a rough, seamen's district on the north bank of the Thames. Nelson gave evidence that Carse was of good behaviour when on board, that he had suffered from sunstroke and had been hospitalized, and that this was the cause of insanity. Carse was found guilty but escaped the death penalty.*

Service matters gradually receded, and Nelson and Fanny spent some time together. A school was found for Josiah, arranged by William Nelson, who by that time had the living at Hilborough, a small village in west Norfolk.[6] The couple spent a short period over Christmas 1787 with Fanny's uncle John Herbert, now in London, in a grand house in Cavendish Square. Both of them, particularly Fanny, felt the effects of the English winter, and they soon departed in early January for the milder climate of Bath, where they stayed for three months.[7] In mid January, however, Nelson was invited down to Plymouth for a few days by Prince William. Unamenable as ever to orders, the prince had sailed from Newfoundland to Ireland, instead of taking the *Pegasus* to Quebec. The king ordered the prince to stay in Plymouth for the same length of time as he had been absent from his station. This gave the opportunity for the prince of Wales and the duke of York, estranged from their father, to go down to Plymouth to celebrate William's return, which they did publicly and noisily, and to the king's displeasure.

Nelson reached Plymouth after the two older princes had left and was more likely to have been engaged in earnest consultation than carousing. He was there on the same day, 19 January 1788, that the prince sent another long letter to the Admiralty Board. On his arrival at Plymouth the prince had had further altercations on the subject of musters, this time with John Lloyd, the clerk of the Cheque of the Dockyard at Plymouth. 'Mr Lloyd objected to the book in an official manner,' he complained to Philip

---

* In spite of efforts to reprieve him two years later, Carse spent seven and a half years in Newgate. He was released on 22 April 1795 under a general amnesty to find men for the navy (Cryer, 3–7; BL, Add. MSS 34903, 11 Apr. 1789; Ramsay, 177).

Stephens, though the letter ended upon a note of considerable doubt and a request for advice.[8] After the stream of admonition from the Admiralty, Nelson was unlikely to have encouraged the prince to adopt his previous aggressive tone, but he was still in the prince's corner. To Locker he continued to trumpet the prince's improvement, finding him, 'everything I could wish – respected by all . . . those who were prejudiced against him acknowledge their error. I think a Lord of the Admiralty is hurt to see him so able.'[9] This was Rear-Admiral John Leveson-Gower, with whom Prince William had first sailed. Such comment was merely naval gossip, but the effects of Nelson's continued support for the prince were to be more serious. In a few months the worsening relationships within the royal family had much greater significance, as a consequence of George III's porphyria. While he was ill, he was unable to perform his duties as monarch, and during the following winter of 1788 and 1789 the court and leading politicians polarized into factions between the king and the prince of Wales. Had the king not recovered, Nelson's friendship with Prince William Henry might have reaped dividends, although during the worst of the political crisis, the prince was off the scene in the West Indies, this time commanding the *Andromeda*.[10]

After a holiday in Exmouth in Devon in May 1788, and a short visit to London in June, again to Cavendish Square, Horatio and Fanny made their way to Burnham Thorpe. Although Nelson made occasional, brief forays to London, they stayed in Burnham for the next four and a half years. Money was scarce. Nelson's half-pay of £100 a year, paid half-yearly through his agents, Marsh and Creed in London (less their commission of £1. 7s. 0d.), was supplemented only by allowances of a £100 a year to each of them from their respective uncles.[11] What little prize money he had won had been spent on the expenses of his previous commission.

Some of Nelson's financial correspondence survives from this period, in particular his account for general items with his brother-in-law Thomas Bolton, now a general merchant in Norwich. It leaves an impression of careful husbandry, with a few luxuries. In January 1789, for instance, he ordered forty-seven bottles of red port at 1s. 6d. a bottle, an order that was repeated in July, 4s. 6d. to be spent on a cake for Master Nisbet, Nelson's annual shooting licence for £2. 3s.0d. and, increasingly, various agricultural supplies. In mid 1789 Nelson's father contributed £100 to Bolton's account with Nelson.[12] In mid 1791 Marsh and Creed sent him a balance that showed that he had only £1. 2s. 0d. in hand.[13] Notes in his papers underline how much this was a preoccupation: from their agent in Antigua, Mrs Nelson's harpsichord, now in poor condition, might fetch ten pounds sterling.[14] He again applied unsuccessfully for pay as senior officer in the Leewards to Lord Howe and even raised the question of his extra expenses.[15]

Apart from money from their uncles, little financial support was to be had from the family. Nelson's younger brother, Suckling, and eldest brother, Maurice, at the Navy Office, were constantly in debt, and Edmund Nelson supported them both. In July 1788 Horatio went down to London on behalf of his father to sort out Maurice's debts.[16] The old parson could no longer afford to go to Bath for the winter for his health. Still serving his parish, he therefore moved near by into a small cottage at Barton Ulph, leaving Horatio and Fanny to live in Burnham Rectory.

Though Horatio and Fanny were visited by the Boltons and his sister Katherine and her husband, George Matcham, little evidence survives of their social life. He went coursing but 'seldom escaped a wet jacket and violent cold'.[17] Although Nelson took out a shooting licence, there is no evidence that he was asked by Mr and Mrs Thomas Coke to shoot at the great house at Holkham.* On 5 November 1788 Coke invited the whole county to a great party, 'a Fête at Holkham ... to commemorate the Glorious Revolution of 1688'. All the replies to the invitation survive at Holkham, as well as a list of invitees in a notebook. Many refused, a number pleading ill health to be excused from what was likely to have been a very cold occasion. Others took exception to the overtly political nature of the event, for a more symbolic Whiggish date could not be imagined. All the Nelsons in the county refused, with the exception of William, who, leaving his wife at home at Hilborough, was as ever looking for preferment. Fanny's refusal was perhaps more pointed than most: 'Captain Nelson's compliments to Mr and Mrs Coke and is sorry it is not in his power to accept their Invitation for November 5th.' She wrote another on behalf of herself and her father-in-law. Coke's notebook on the invitations, carefully arranged in alphabetical order, has a column 'Nature of Reply'. Against many names of those who refused is written 'Civil', 'Friendly' or 'Ill-health'; one was even marked 'insolent'. Against the two letters from the rectory at Burnham the entry reads 'No reason'.[18]

The Nelsons found satisfaction, however, in ground improvements and, with the help of the Matchams and the Boltons, the garden of the rectory was replanted. Today the only tangible trace of Nelson's half-pay years lies in the pond next to the site of the house, pulled down within Nelson's

---

* The earliest gun book at Holkham dates from 1793. Family tradition has it that a bedroom was used by Nelson, but this story is not supported by evidence. The other family tradition is that Nelson was asked to shoot at Holkham, but that he was considered such a dangerous shot that he was not asked again (Stirling, *Coke of Norfolk*, 216).

lifetime. The shape of an eighteenth-century warship can still be discerned in the pond, and there is sufficient evidence to be sure that it was under Nelson's direction that the stream was dammed and the pond formed.[19] His father wrote to his youngest daughter, Kitty Matcham, 'Your brother is well and I hope fixed up at Thorpe; a place he delights in, but I wish it was a little better accommodated to Mrs N, as a woman who would sometimes chose a little variety.' Fanny and her father-in-law got on well, but life in England after the warmth and luxury of Nevis cannot have been easy for her. The cold of the Norfolk winters was worsened by a large area of wet and swampy meadow next to the rectory. In another letter Edmund reported: 'Horace has been unwell for some days. Mrs N. takes large doses of the Bed.'[20] No evidence exists of the nature of their relationship, but there were no children.

The 130 miles between Burnham and London made the affairs of the navy seem very distant. Communication with the outside world was by the post and newspapers at the small town of Burnham Market just over a mile away. The post brought some pleasures. Occasional letters arrived from Locker, Collingwood, Cornwallis and others; on another occasion Nelson accepted a pair of birds as a present to Fanny from Thomas Graham, the *Boreas*'s surgeon.[21] Business with the Navy Board intruded, concerning the lieutenant's examination for some of the young gentlemen whom Nelson had trained on the ship.[22] He corresponded with Sir Charles Middleton at the board about an idea for devising a system of signals, but he did not pursue it. Such proposals were fashionable at the time; as Middleton discouragingly put it, 'The idea of signals has of late occupied the thoughts of many officers.'[23] He watched on the sidelines the deteriorating relationship between Prince William Henry and Lord Hood over Hood's continued support for Schomberg, in particular the latter's appointment to Hood's flagship, about which the prince wrote furious letters and to which Hood replied with diplomacy and firmness.[24] Nelson could only comment to Locker: 'He has wrote Lord Hood what I cannot but approve.'[25]

The Barbados merchants and shipowners were still pursuing Nelson in the courts for the seizure of ships. In early May 1788 he received a hurried note from his old friend Thomas Pringle: 'I have this morning got Rose's answer, which is that Captain Nelson is a very good officer, that he need be under no apprehension for that he will assuredly be supported by the Treasury.'[26] Two years later, however, there was a further flurry, when a writ was again served. Letters to George Rose at the Treasury and Philip Stephens at the Admiralty followed quickly, which elicited further assurances that the government would protect Nelson. He wrote to Thomas

Graham in June: 'I have been plagu'd by the seizures made whilst in the West Indies, a prosecution now ag[ains]t me for five thousand pounds sterling for one vessel. It is very true Government are defending me, but the unpleasantness still falls on me, such as being served with Notices and things of that kind, and may be arrested perhaps in the end if it should be given against me.'[27]

Another complex piece of Admiralty business that took Nelson's time and emotional energy while he was at Burnham was the matter of alleged fraud in the dockyard and naval hospital at Antigua. Long letters arrived at Burnham from the West Indies and London. The dispute had its roots in Nelson's confrontation with the English Harbour dockyard officers in early 1787. Both he and Prince William Henry had then been approached by two merchants, William Wilkinson and Joseph Higgins, who acted as naval agents, with accusations of long-term fraud against a former business partner, William Whitehead. Whitehead had been the Victualling Board agent in the island since the Seven Years War, but the allegations were to extend far beyond one individual. Nelson had believed Wilkinson and Higgins, and, in any case, having been blocked by the dockyard officers at English Harbour when trying to examine the original vouchers for the bills he was supposed to sign, he welcomed the chance to investigate them. Before he left the West Indies he wrote to Lord Howe and to Sir Charles Middleton at the Navy Board, detailing the financial irregularities of Anthony Munton, naval storekeeper and clerk of the Cheque.[28] Yet again Nelson went one stage further and wrote directly to the prime minister: 'gov[ern]ment has been defrauded in a most Scandalous and Infamous manner . . . There is no fixed price for anything in this country . . . I shall most probably be sail'd for England by the time you receive this letter, and shall always be ready to give every information you may wish to know of me.' His letter contained an enclosure that alleged the embezzlement of '£25 or £30 per centum of the expenditure <u>during the whole of the last war</u>'.[29] This was a serious allegation.

From 1784 a parliamentary commission had been sitting 'to enquire into the Fees, Gratuities, Perquisites and Emoluments, which are or have been lately received into the several Public Offices', and Middleton, as comptroller of the Navy Board, was orchestrating the examination into the navy departments. It was a propitious time to raise the issue of corruption. Nelson and Middleton exchanged letters throughout 1787 about the dockyard officers.[30] The accusations effectively implicated all the naval establishments in the Leewards Islands and Jamaica.[31] Nelson passed on Higgins and Willkinson's information to senior people in the Navy Office, Ordnance and Sick and Hurt departments.[32] By October 1788 Higgins and Wilkinson had provided Nelson with sufficient evidence to prove that Thomas Druce, the deputy agent victualler in Antigua, was defrauding the government. Middleton wrote to Nelson in late May 1789 informing him that the navy solicitor had been instructed to send for Wilkinson and Higgins 'to make good their charge'.[33] In late June 1789 the Victualling Board invited Nelson to London to appear before the board.[34] Nelson travelled down to London, accompanied by a servant.* Decisions were taken later that year by the Admiralty, which decided also to proceed against Thomas Druce. However, just as it appeared that enough evidence had accumulated to proceed against the accused, the case foundered. Civil proceedings against Higgins and Wilkinson in Antigua had resulted in the imprisonment of Wilkinson for debt, and soon after Higgins died; thus neither could get to England to substantiate their accusations.[35] The proceedings against Druce were abandoned. And by 1791 the attorney-general gave up the case against Munton, because of the delays caused by the death of Higgins and the imprisonment of Wilkinson.†[36]

But the effort was not entirely wasted. The Commission on Fees examined the evidence and demonstrated the flaws in the system of payment. It found that officials at distant stations, instead of receiving an adequate salary, received a commission, or 'poundage', on stores delivered. The enormous amount of matériel for the swollen number of ships passing through English Harbour during the American Revolutionary War was estimated at £365,305; Munton had benefited to the tune of £4,214.15s. 9d., remarkable for a man whose annual salary and allowances amounted to £345. The 'want of a general system' was the cause, concluded the commissioners; 'it justifies the most alarming apprehensions with respect for the administration and application of the National property.'[37] To Middleton's intense disappointment, these findings were not published, for William Pitt decided not to use the commission reports, and they were not made public for ten years. Nelson's letter of 2 May and the correspondence from Wilkinson and Higgins were printed as appendices to the commission reports, but not

* Nelson's expenses totalled £20. 16s. 8d. for the journey of 130 miles, including £16, 2s. 7d. for the hire of a post chaise, 6s. 10d. for the turnpikes and £1. 11s, 6d. for lodging: 'The other Expenses I have been at whilst in Town I find it impossible for Me to State, whatever the Board think fit to allow for myself & Servant will fully satisfy.' The Victualling Board were generous, for £35 was credited to Marsh and Creed ((UK)NA: PRO, ADM 114/26, 6 July 1789, Nelson to Victualling Board).

† In some notes Nelson stated that Munton was fined and imprisoned, but this seems to have been wishful thinking (NMM, STW/2, [n.d.], rough draft of Nelson's record of service). Munton, who had been appointed to the post in Antigua in 1779, was replaced in 1794.

until after Nelson's death.[38] But by then further commissions and large-scale reform had taken place and were continuing; the reforming process started by the Commission on Fees was eventually to regenerate the navy.[39]

The second half of Nelson's period ashore was dominated by the doubts and fears over his reappointment to a ship. His first brief letter applying for a ship in August 1788 was a formality. Howe had resigned, and Nelson offered his services to the new Board of Admiralty, now under William Pitt's elder brother, Lord Chatham. Since the naval member of the new board was Samuel Hood, Nelson could have expected some success with an application; he went down to London later that month, but he came away with no promises.[40] He reported to Fanny: 'He agreed with me that a ship in peaceable times was not desirable; but that should a disturbance take place I need not fear having a good ship.'[41] In the autumn, a year after coming ashore, he applied to William Cornwallis, who was about to command a squadron to the East Indies. Cornwallis demurred in a curious phrase: 'his fireside was so changed since that time, that he durst not venture to name him'. This almost certainly referred to the fact the first lieutenant of Cornwallis's ship was Isaac Schomberg.[42] Cornwallis did, however, promise to try for Nelson if more ships were sent out, and it seems that two years later there were plans to send Nelson out to the East Indies with Robert Kingsmill, now a senior captain, had reinforcements been needed.[43]

In the next year, 1789, as news came of the revolution across the Channel, very little movement took place in the navy. In March, Nelson again approached Lord Chatham, asking for the command of a guard ship; the first lord answered that 'it is not in my power to comply with your wishes'.[44] The prospect of Nelson's restless spirit having to cope with the dull, spit and polish routine of a 74 anchored for almost the entire year suggests that this was a wise decision. Nelson's frustration began to surface in his letters. To Locker he wrote: 'Not being a man of fortune is a crime which I cannot get over, and therefore none of the Great care about me. I am now [a] commencing Farmer, not a very large one, you will conceive, but enough for amusement . . . Is there any idea of our being drawn into a quarrel by these commotions on the Continent: whenever that may be likely to happen, I will take care to make my application in time.'[45] In August his agents, Marsh and Creed, politely enquired: 'do you expect a line of battleship or a frigate'?[46] In the autumn he approached Hood directly. He wrote a letter, (which does not survive) in which he appears to have suggested that the reason why he was out of favour with the Admiralty was that he had supported Hood in the 1784 election. Hood, finally, spelt it out in the clearest language:

I am ready to own that I have often with much pleasure heard your Zeal & exertions spoken of in the handsomest manner, whilst you was in the West Indies, respecting illicit trade; but I am equally sorry to say that I have as often heard you censured for the advice you gave (which is upon record at the Admiralty) for a refusal of the Complete Muster Book to the Naval Officer and for putting Lieut. Schomberg under an arrest.[47]

It is significant that he mentioned the issue of the muster book: this trivial business had proved more than an irritant to their lordships, who presided over a bureaucratic organization. Nelson had shown consistent disregard for well-proven practice and could not be trusted to exercise mature judgement. The same weakness had resulted in the Schomberg affair. Nelson had transgressed twice. Hood's letter finished on a curious note: 'should I have the power of assisting any wish of yours I shall embrace it with pleasure, but with respect to your appointment as a commander-in-chief that is totally beyond what I could attempt.' What had Nelson suggested to Hood? Had he reasoned that he had nothing to lose? Had his anxiety, or his self-belief, or both, made him lose his judgement? Had he asked for a distant station? Perhaps he still did not believe that he could have been wrong in supporting the prince. There is no record of Nelson's reaction to the letter.

It was a dark time. His brother Edmund, aged twenty-seven, died in December. 'Poor Fellow, thank God he went off perfectly in his senses,' Nelson wrote to his brother-in-law, Thomas Bolton.[48] Nelson organized the funeral; the expenses had to be met by his father. The winter was even colder than usual. Early in the next year he was soon to have proof that there was indeed an almost indelible black mark against his name. Knowing now that Hood would not help him, Nelson persuaded his friend Charles Morice Pole to ask Prince William Henry, the source of all his trouble, to go straight to Chatham. Pole wrote back with an encouraging note, for the prince had 'expressed in the highest terms his sense of your conduct – and desired you might be informed therewith'.[49] The prince raised it with Chatham, who refused to do anything. The new first lord was feeling the usual discomfort of pressure on available appointments. 'The list is so large already', Chatham wrote to one senior officer in August 1790, 'that I fear even in an extensive war many a brave and active officer must be left on shore.'[50]

By June 1790 Nelson gave vent to his frustration and anger directly to Prince William Henry (who had been made the duke of Clarence two years before), without any of the conventional compliments to be used with royalty: 'My not being appointed to a Ship is so very mortifying, that I cannot find words to express what I feel on the occasion . . . I am the more hurt, and surprised. Sure I am, that I have ever been a zealous and faithful Servant, and never intentionally have committed any errors; especially as till very lately I have been honoured by the notice of the Admiralty.'[51] Nelson's final effort in October was to get William Suckling to write to Charles Jenkinson, now made Lord Hawkesbury and president of the Board of Trade, who had secured his appointment to the *Albemarle* in 1781. Hawkesbury wrote to his fellow cabinet member Lord Chatham, but with no result.[52] Neither Howe nor Hood wanted this promising but flawed young officer in their fleet.*

Others were more favoured. Cuthbert Collingwood was thirty-one places behind Nelson in the list, but his breathless letters to his sister Mary from London conveyed the excitement of mobilization. 'Every body pushing their interest for ships. We who have none must be content to wait until those who have are out of our way, but I hardly think I can miss being employed very soon.' Two weeks later at the Admiralty Collingwood had run into a relative, Walter Stanhope, MP for Hull, 'who very civilly offered his services and I got him on the spot to appoint a meeting with Lord C[hatham] and gave him the name of four ships to request any one of them. He had his audience . . . and was told . . . that I should have one.'[53]

Nelson too travelled to the Admiralty, but could gain no audience. He found Hood at home. This time Hood was not only clear but blunt. He was not going to put Nelson's name forward, and further he told him that, as the latter recorded in a draft, 'the King was impressed with an unfavourable impression of me'.[54] The interview was brief, and Nelson was to have no contact with his patron for another two years. He at last realized that he was disastrously out of favour, as a comforting letter from his father, dated 11 October, makes clear: 'It seems necessary to call forth all your prudence and mature deliberation, how to act at this critical juncture so as to justify your own character and give no offence to either party. It ought certainly to be made known at least to particular persons, why you are so marked as to render any application fruitless.' He went on to suggest, unrealistically, that Nelson talk to Cornwallis and even to the prince of Wales, 'tho' I have no doubt but on the issue, all will come about' and correctly suggested that things would be different if a war were imminent.[55]

---

* At this time Nelson was 144th on the captains' list, out of a total of 466, calculated by seniority of appointment. This figure had increased by seventy-three as a result of the mobilizations (Steel's *Navy List*, Dec. 1791).

Having tried one more short letter to Chatham in late September ('My wish to be employed is so great...'), and another to his old captain of the *Carcass*, Lord Mulgrave, Nelson finally accepted in November that there was nothing more to be done.[56] On 15 November he wrote to Thomas Bolton: 'you will know of my return from being as ill-treated as any person could be for taking the part of the King's son ag[ains]t as gross calumny as could be utter'd.'[57]

He could take little comfort from other appointments made during the 1790 mobilization. Of his particular friends, Cornwallis was in the East Indies and Kingsmill had a 98-gun ship in Howe's squadron. Collingwood was given the *Mermaid* (32), 'on particular service abroad', and Troubridge the *Thames*, also a 32, 'under private orders'. Few of Nelson's protégés had made progress. Wallis had got nothing, nor had his temporary rank of commander been confirmed by the Admiralty. Only those who had others to speak for them had flourished. One of the *Boreas*'s lieutenants, Digby Dent, commanded the *Sultana*, a 16-gun sloop. Of the younger ones, Thomas Orde was a first lieutenant of a 32, Richard Hughes junior was aboard his father's ship, still the *Adamant*, as was William Hope. The duke of Clarence had a 74, though in general it was the older and more senior captains who were appointed to ships of the line. None of those who were to command in Hood's projected squadron were junior to Nelson, with the exception of John Knight, Hood's flag captain in the *Victory*, who had two years less seniority.[58]

For the next two years Nelson continued life as a modest country gentleman at Burnham Thorpe.[59] Most of life revolved around the family. Suckling Nelson went to Cambridge. His cousin 'L[ieutenan]t Suckling of the Artillery & his brother the Sailor' came to visit.[60] The Nelsons stayed with the Walpoles at Wolterton. He wrote a series of cheerful letters to his sister Kitty, now moved with her husband, George Matcham, from Norfolk to Ringwood in Hampshire, reporting news of Burnham families ('the Martins and the Crowes are all single'), the assembly at Aylsham, the price of property; nor did he miss the gossip of who danced with whom.[61] Three fine Norfolk turkeys were to be sent to William Locker. Later that year he wrote a letter of condolence when Kitty lost a child, reflecting the fatalism of the time: 'the loss of children is certainly to be expected and we are surprised that from so many complaints which they poor little things are subject to that so many are rear'd to mature age.'[62] In the spring of 1792 Nelson contemplated buying another horse through Thomas Bolton, anxiously enjoining him to 'attend to everything particular about him ... I should not wish knowingly to throw away my money on Horse Flesh.' He was 'so much afraid of getting another daisycutter' that he was willing to pay a farmer to examine him.* 'I can make shift with the Black Mare for a little time.' Perhaps because of the cost of the horse, he determined not to take out another expensive shooting licence.[63] There seemed little hope of further employment: in February 1792 Nelson noted in a letter to his brother William that the navy was to be reduced to 15,000 men.[64] He made a further visit to London in June 1792, this time to support the former master of the *Albemarle*, Donald Trail, who had been brought to trial at the Old Bailey, accused of cruelty aboard his ship, the *Neptune*, which had taken convicts to Australia.[65] The case was dismissed. He is likely to have called at the Admiralty; no ship was available.

But in the second half of 1792 the diplomatic situation between England and France began to deteriorate rapidly. In late October, Nelson again applied to Lord Chatham, with some covering letters to the prince for good measure.[66] Two letters in November and December from Nelson to Prince William Henry were still bitter about Hood: 'I certainly cannot look on Lord Hood as my friend; but I have the satisfaction of knowing, that I never gave his Lordship just cause to be my enemy.'[67] On 2 January 1793 the *Childers* brig, watching the French fleet off Brest, was fired on by one of the nearby French forts. Four days later Nelson saw Lord Chatham. He wrote to Fanny on 7 January 1793: 'Post Nubila Phoebus – your son will explain the motto – after clouds come sunshine. The Admiralty so smile upon me that really I am as much surprised as when they frowned. Lord Chatham yesterday made many apologies for not having given me a ship before this time, but that if I chose to take a 64 gun ship to begin with I should be appointed to one as soon as she was ready, and that I should as soon as it is in his power be removed into a 74.'[68]

Yet again Nelson's career had been on a knife-edge.† In the matter of appointments the easygoing first lord was led by the two naval members of the board, Hood and Commodore Alan Gardner, the latter, of course, the senior officer in Jamaica who had provided the solution to the Schomberg affair. The king too would have had an influence on the appointments of officers. The change of heart can be explained only by the sharp change of circumstances caused by the French threat. Hood could also see that this crisis was one in which risks had to be taken. The mobilizations of 1790

---

* A 'daisycutter' was slang for a horse that never lifted its feet off the ground.
† Thomas Troubridge, left behind in the *Seahorse* in 1776, was unable to take his lieutenant's exam until 1781, and was now 152 places behind Nelson in the captains' list (Steel's *Navy List*, Dec. 1793). When Nelson was given the *Agamemnon* (64), Troubridge had a 32-gun ship.

and 1791 had been against Spain and Russia; this one was against a France in possession of the Low Countries, and every statement coming out of Paris suggested that this situation was extremely dangerous. Aggressive young captains with war experience were needed now. Hood had been consistent in saying nearly five years before that 'should a disturbance take place [Nelson] need not fear having a good ship'.[69] And Nelson was now more senior, a factor in appointments that could not be ignored by the board, as protests over Nelson's later rapid rise were to prove. As every year passed older captains became unwilling to serve; by the end of 1793 Nelson was 101st on the captains' list, high enough to be given a large ship without serious favour being shown. Nelson talked to Sir Henry Martin, the comptroller of the navy: the *Agamemnon* (64), fitting out at Chatham, was decided upon. In early 1793 Nelson was thoroughly rested, with hardly a penny to his name and with everything to prove – and he had been given a fine ship. Except for only two brief pauses, Nelson would now be on active service until his death twelve years later.

II

Maturity and Triumph

1793–1798

9

The Navy in 1793

Lord Chatham was accused of indolence & rising late from his bed, so much so that they called him the late Lord Chatham. Surely if ever a First Lord of the Admiralty should be awake it is on the present occasion when our very existence depends on our Navy.

Sir William Hamilton to Captain Nelson, 31 January 1795[1]

After the débâcle of the American Revolutionary War, the navy put the ten years of peace before 1793 to good use. Following the short administration of Lord Shelburne and six months of the coalition of Charles James Fox and Lord North, William Pitt emerged at the end of 1783 as a strong prime minister intent on reform, but he did not in these years have strong first lords of the Admiralty. As he put together his first cabinet in 1783, he fixed upon the distinguished but taciturn Lord Howe, from whom he was always distant; while Howe took no interest in anything but naval matters. He turned out to be an irritable and isolated political colleague, unpopular in the House of Commons. With a high level of support from all corners of the House and a growing economy, Pitt paid off the naval debt of the previous war by keeping the Naval Estimates at an unprecedented high level; between 1784 and 1792 a total of over £23 million pounds was voted.[2] Working very closely with him – and behind Howe's back – was the comptroller of the navy, Sir Charles Middleton, whose relentless energy reinvigorated and reorganized the administration of the navy. In 1788 Howe resigned and was succeeded by Lord Chatham, William Pitt's elder brother. Clever (when young, he beat his younger brother at chess) but indolent, he filled the post loyally, assisted by Hood and Gardner, until the end of 1794.[3]

The political conflict that had rent the navy during the American Revolutionary War had now lessened. Throughout the eighteenth century a small number of naval officers were MPs, for active service was not a bar to a seat in the House. From mid century to 1820 about twenty were usually elected at each general election.[4] Twenty-three entered Parliament in 1784, in contrast to the army officers' fifty-four seats. A number of 'Admiralty boroughs', where naval officers were natural candidates, were controlled by the government of the day. The navy was thus never far from the centre of politics. The more influential naval members of Parliament were Samuel and Alexander Hood, John Jervis and William Cornwallis. As senior officers they felt the need to provide themselves with some political insurance, especially if they were serving on a foreign station. Lord Howe, for instance, had come hastening back from his unsuccessful command in North America in the early years of the American Revolutionary War to defend himself in person from political attacks. Professional rivalry was heightened by using the House of Commons as a stage. The dispute between Augustus Keppel and Sir Hugh Palliser after the Battle of Ushant in 1778 was fought out in Parliament before and after the courts martial of both admirals. From this disastrous quarrel stemmed many long rivalries, including that which existed between the Hoods and Jervis.

Some officers were in the House because they had a seat that had long been at the disposal of their family. William Cornwallis had been the member for Eye in Suffolk since 1768, when he was twenty-four. George Keith Elphinstone became the member for Dumbartonshire at the age of thirty-five and had unsuccessfully contested the seat when he was twenty-eight. For others the most pressing reason to secure a seat was to further their careers and to apply more leverage on the promotion process. Perhaps the most spectacular example in 1783 was the 32-year-old Captain John Orde, made governor of Dominica, a post he held until 1791; his elder brother was a confidant of Lord Shelburne.[5] Of those officers whom Nelson knew well, only Robert Kingsmill had been an MP, for Yarmouth, Isle of Wight, between 1779 and 1780. Kingsmill had felt so strongly about the Keppel–Palliser affair that he gave up command of his ship. The son of an army officer, he was again looking for a seat in 1784; but by then he had inherited estates and was a rich man.[6]

After the schisms of the American Revolutionary War, officers took more care in the 1780s to ensure that their service loyalty overrode politics. In 1793 Howe wrote to his confidant Roger Curtis of a very strident political opponent: 'Admiral MacBride's professional attentions cancel all recollection of his political Hostilities,' though Howe's capacity to remember faults in others leaves one in some doubt that he really meant what he said.[7] Much later one Tory naval officer wrote of Sir John Jervis: 'Although deep in politics and a deadly Whig, he had the good sense and propriety to keep his opinions under control when afloat.'[8] The political divisions eased when the domestic tensions caused by the unpopular war against the American colonists no longer existed, and when France, the traditional enemy, appeared as powerful and as threatening as ever.

Nelson had clearly been active to some degree in the Westminister by-election of 1784 when he returned from France, although the extent of his involvement is not known. He wrote to his brother William at the end of January: 'I have done with politics; let who get in, I shall be left out.'[9] Had someone held out hope of political advancement? He may have been referring here only to his support for Samuel Hood, who had been persuaded by Pitt – against his better judgement – to stand for one of the two Westminster seats against Charles James Fox and another Foxite candidate. Hood's chances were good, as he was one of the few admirals to have come out of the American Revolutionary War with an enhanced reputation. Unlike the rest of the country, this constituency was always vigorously and closely fought. Gangs of seamen, supporting Hood, shouted down Fox's supporters. Hood stood because of 'his sense of duty to the King and his long friendship with Pitt's family'; he later described it as 'the most arduous and unpleasant duty I ever took in hand'.[10] The results went to scrutiny, with Hood leading the poll. At this time Nelson's correspondence is full of comments on the political situation, some of them strongly felt, especially against Fox and his supporters. Fox had opposed the American Revolutionary War and wanted parliamentary reform and radical change. Nelson was, and always remained, an instinctive conservative. He was a supporter of Pitt at this stage in his career, possibly because of the influence of William Locker; in a letter to Locker, Nelson referred to 'your friend Mr Pitt'.[11] It is unlikely, however, that he could have had serious parliamentary ambitions. Most of the naval officers who won seats in this election were older and senior, and much richer.

A dozen years later, when Nelson was approached to see if he would stand in an election, it might have been a different story. By late 1795 he was thirty-eight, with a rapidly growing reputation, and he was approached to stand for Ipswich. Nelson would have had to acquire considerable prize money for election expenses. Ipswich was a borough that had a tradition of electing naval officers who supported government. Nelson's reaction was realistic. He replied that he would follow the Portland Whigs, who were about to join Pitt in government, and that all political approaches should be conducted through Lord Walpole, his relative, with whom he was in contact.[12] He listed the political naval officers who would support him: Hood, Cornwallis and Lord Hugh Seymour Conway. But, he said, he had won little prize money. Some negotiations clearly followed, but by April his father wrote to him: 'The Ipswich business I believe is at an end. A dinner though a good one was too little.'[13] In the 1796 election the Ipswich seat was won by Captain Sir Andrew Snape Hamond, the comptroller of the Navy Board, with Treasury support.[14]

It is difficult to understand today how an army or sea officer could ever combine being an MP with an active career, or to grasp what either of the services gained from the custom. Even lords of the Admiralty might take their ships to sea. In some cases, the dual role ensured that officers felt themselves to be people of consequence. Lord Cornwallis described another successful election at Eye in 1802, in which his brother William Cornwallis was not only re-elected but, because of the Peace of Amiens, had actually been able to attend the election. 'The Admiral got very drunk at the election, and the next day insisted upon my steward taking £500 towards defraying the expenses. Without having given a vote in the House of Commons for many years past, and perhaps never intending to give one again, no youth of one and twenty was ever more pleased at coming into Parliament. What unaccountable creatures we are.'[15] William Cornwallis had already been an MP for twenty-six years. In the total of thirty-nine years when he was an MP he was never known to speak in the House of Commons.*

Nelson had little party-political help early in his career. Being close to a powerful patron provided an advantage to a young officer, and that was promotion, but inevitably such a career would be affected for good or ill by the vagaries of national politics. This was shown when Keppel became first lord of the Admiralty in 1782 in the Shelburne and Fox–North administrations just before the end of the American Revolutionary War; he promoted many of his supporters in numbers that were unprecedented at that time.[16] Conversely, if the great man lost political power, the way forward for the young officer could be blocked. Howe on occasion grumbled about the lack of consideration given to his 'friends' when he was out of office, though it was by no means the case that promotion was always blocked by the opposing party.[17] Sandwich, for instance, was even-handed in appointing officers, which his political opponents took as a sign of weakness.[18] Nelson also managed to avoid this difficult political period in the late 1770s, because he was abroad in the West Indies with his patron William Locker. According to his son, Locker 'often congratulated himself that he

---

* In 1806 John Jervis, by then Earl St Vincent, suggested to the first lord of the Admiralty that if he should 'bring a bill into Parliament to disqualify any officer under the rank of rear admiral to sit in the House of Commons, the navy may be preserved' (Brenton, II, 316).

was abroad when the disgraceful schism divided the Navy between Keppel and Palliser . . . He had friends on both sides and lost none.'[19]

Locker's influence kept Nelson far from politics early in his career. In any case, Nelson's early promotion was so rapid that he never became too identified with the wardroom of any particular ship. Samuel Hood's patronage in 1782 did not diminish or change Nelson's relationship with his old patron. He was careful to explain in his letters to Locker from North America how Hood was treating him: in one, 'I am a candidate with Lord Hood for a Line of Battle ship'; in another, 'He treats me as if I was his son.'[20]

There is no doubting his affection and admiration for Locker, and the absolute trust between them is demonstrated by the openness of Nelson's letters. Some of them, however, read almost as if they were reports, and occasionally he puts a better gloss on events than the official documents support.* They are laced with gossip: who is getting which ship, people's health and other information useful in helping Locker with the junior officers whom he was trying to guide and push forward. It is striking too that Nelson took care to meet officers whom he did not know, but who were in Locker's following. For instance, he gives a vivid picture of a young captain, William Peacock, just promoted to a captured French frigate, but with indifferent health, whom he met for the first time on his arrival in New York: 'Peacock I saw and dined with the day I landed; I could not do less.' He did the same for a young lieutenant (not confirmed), Charles Pilfold: 'I have had him with me almost ever since my arrival.'[21]

Locker never reached high rank because of his poor health, but he was widely respected, and once taken under his wing Nelson remained there. Locker was not in a position to appoint, but his view of a young officer's competence and character was influential. His role has been described as that of a 'broker'. Judging by Nelson's letters, Locker's following at this time also included Robert Kingsmill and Charles Morice Pole, both to become admirals.[22] Nelson's friends at the beginning of the 1790s were officers who tended to be older, including William Cornwallis, Cuthbert Collingwood, Thomas Pringle and James Macnamara. Although he moved

---

* For instance, in April 1784, when commanding the *Boreas*, he pressed eleven English members of the crew of a Dutch East Indiaman. Nelson wrote to Locker: 'the Admiralty have approved my conduct in the business' ((UK)NA: PRO, ADM 51/125, 15 Apr.; Nicolas, I, 104, 21 Apr. 1784). But when the ship reached Portsmouth, the men were ordered to be discharged by the commander-in-chief, Admiral Montagu, and Nelson received a far from supportive letter from the Admiralty ((UK)NA: PRO, ADM 36/10526, 14, 20 Apr. 1784; BL, Add. MSS 34961, 15 Apr. 1784, Philip Stephens to Nelson).

on to other circles, Nelson's original patron was never forgotten. Fifteen years later, after the battle of St Vincent, Sir John Jervis would write to Locker, for they had served together under Hawke in the Seven Years War, referring to Nelson as Locker's pupil: 'your élève Commodore Nelson'.[23]

While Nelson was in the West Indies and ashore in Burnham Thorpe, Britain was heavily engaged in an intense naval arms race with France. Most of the navies of Europe built warships furiously in these years, to the extent that by 1790 the number of ships of the line throughout the Continent reached a total of 1,700,000 tons, a peak that was never again to be reached in the era of wooden sailing ships. Britain ended the American Revolutionary War with many ships of the line on the stocks, giving her an advantage over France. To match this effort, the French also continued building through the 1780s. If France and Spain combined as they had done between 1779 and 1783, the Bourbon powers would have at least 34 per cent more warships than Britain.[24]

With Charles Middleton to the fore, the infrastructure of the navy was reformed at every level. Repairs and maintenance on warships in the dockyards were achieved to a higher standard and at a faster rate than ever before by retaining shipwrights and unskilled men in employment at wartime levels.[25] New docks were built at Portsmouth and Plymouth; the ropery at Chatham was rebuilt and many other facilities repaired or expanded.[26] The administration of the dockyards was brought under greater control, and their ordering and accounting systems were radically improved. Slightly under three years' reserve of naval stores were in the dockyards at the beginning of 1793: nearly 60,000 loads of oak, 1,300 masts and over 5,000 tons of hemp as well as high levels of every other necessary material were in store.[27] Investment was put into the buildings of the Naval Victualling Yard at Deptford.[28] The potentially disastrous problem of damage to ships' iron bolts by electrolysis, caused by the wholesale adoption of copper sheathing in 1779, was also tackled throughout the fleet, by replacing all the iron bolts with those made of copper alloy. This programme, started in 1786, was largely complete by 1793, a speed that the French could not match.[29]

The improvement to gunnery in pre-war years was to become of great importance to the navy after 1793. The Ordnance Board and Office, which supplied guns to both the army and navy, were reformed fundamentally by Thomas Blomefield, a single-minded, ex-naval officer who was appointed as inspector of artillery and superintendent of the brass foundry at Woolwich in 1780. For the first time, a single officer was responsible for the testing (or 'proofing') of all guns. He discarded hundreds and contracted for great batches of new ones, although it has been estimated that it would have taken twenty-five years to have replaced every gun.[30] Blomefield's two important measures were his new gun designs and the introduction of the 'thirty-round proof': all guns had to be fired thirty times before they were then inspected and accepted from the contractors by the Board of Ordnance. This simple measure raised the specification and standards of all ordnance issued to the navy. The manufacturing process was improved, resulting in a reduction of the sulphur content of iron, making the material less brittle.[31] Although there were occasional gunbursts with old guns, with the resultant appalling casualties, no improvement would be more valuable to Nelson and the officers and men of the navy, which allowed them to fire as fast as they could with confidence.[32] French and Spanish gun foundries could not match British technology.* Napoleon himself reckoned that his navy was ten years behind the British; a modern estimate is twenty years.[33] Furthermore, British gunpowder was superior to that of the French and the Spanish.[34] As a result, British gunnery was to be spectacularly faster than anything possessed by the French in the wars to come.

Other innovations were important. The old method of firing a cannon with slowmatch was steadily replaced by the gunlock, a device that operated on the principle of the musket flintlock. The gunlock's great advantage was that it could be operated by pulling on a lanyard, enabling the gun captain to stand back, beyond the limit of the gun's recoil, positioning himself so that he could take a sight along the gun. Adopted universally after 1793, it was faster, safer and quicker; the French were still using slowmatch.[35] Blomefield introduced an improved long gun, the '1787 pattern'. By 1796 it was officially recorded that under ideal conditions a 32-pounder long gun could fire effectively at 1,400 yards, but at sea 400 was the limit of effective range.[36] The introduction of the carronade, however, made the greatest difference to British battle tactics. The carronade was a short, light, wide-calibre gun, known informally as the 'Smasher', with little recoil, and from 1796 mounted on a fixed carriage. It was first manufactured by the Carron Company in Scotland in the 1770s. The bores of the guns could be machined with greater accuracy because they were short, reducing 'windage', the space between the ball and the barrel. As a result less powder was necessary.[37] They could be fired much faster than long guns. By 1794 each

* The ineffectiveness of Spanish gunnery is corroborated by a story related by George Elliot, a midshipman at the Battle of the Nile. He fired a shot from a captured Spanish howitzer from the *Goliath*, which managed to disable a French frigate by jamming the round between the hull and the rudder. The Spanish gun 'could not throw a shot with enough force to pass through a ship's side' (Elliot, 16–17; see also Clayton and Craig, 109).

ship of the line had eight extra carronades established on their armament: a 74-gun ship had in fact eighty-two guns, with two 32-pound carronades on the forecastle and six 18-pounders at the stern.[38] The largest calibre carronades fired a 68-pound ball, devastating at short range, making a large, ragged and splintered hole in the enemy's hull, difficult for enemy carpenters to plug. As we shall see, from 1793 Nelson kept two 68-pound carronades with him, transferring them as he moved from ship to ship; these lethal giants were rare, even in the British Navy.[39] Carronades were, however, useless at long range; Nelson's tactics were to bring his ships as close as possible to the enemy before he opened fire.

Aggressive British admirals aimed to get close to their enemy, holding their fire until they were close, yard arm to yard arm. At this time fighting at close quarters dominated British naval tactics in general and Nelson's in particular. The French tended to fire with their long guns at greater range, particularly at rigging to impede the opposing ship's ability to manoeuvre. British tactics therefore demanded a test of nerve and morale during the dangerous approach when the British ships held their fire, the point at which they took most casualties. Through the 1790s carronades were successful. A persuasive advocate of their advantages, Samuel Bentham, wrote to St Vincent in 1801: 'I am of opinion that in many cases by the introduction of carronades, howitzers and mortars and in general of pieces of Artillery of light weight instead of the established long guns, Vessels of war may be made much more effective than they are at present.'[40] In some small vessels carronades became the primary armament, and, because of their lightness, ships sailed better and faster when armed only with carronades. This innovation was, however, taken too far. They were finally discredited in the War of 1812, when the *Essex*, an American frigate equipped only with carronades, was devastated by the long guns of the British frigate *Phoebe*. The American ship was damaged, unable to utilize its superior speed. The British ship kept out of range of its opponent's carronades, but close enough to use her own long guns.[41]

In this peacetime period the French made every effort to improve the naval balance in their favour. Between 1781 and 1786 the Marquis de Castries, the French minister of marine, carried out far-reaching reforms, including methods of officer selection, the establishment of a corps of specialist gunners, and improvements in seamen's health and clothing. He tried especially to contain the power of the sea officers by giving the administrators more responsibility.[42] Their navy was hampered by lack of sufficient trained seamen, still at the level of about 60,000, which is what it had been in the American Revolutionary War.[43] The 'grand projet' of the decade was the attempt to build breakwaters and establish a safe anchorage at Cherbourg for their fleet. Success would transform strategy and tactics in the Western Approaches. The first of the huge 'cones', made of oak and containing rocks, was sunk in June 1784. In August 1787 Captain John McBride visited the site and saw 10,000 men working with 500 lighters. The project worried the British naval authorities.[44] However, the political upheavals in France and the weakness of government finances, together with Channel tides and winter weather, ensured that the project was abandoned in 1789.[45] By this time the expansion of the French Navy was slowing, as government financial and tax reforms failed. Workers in Brest and Toulon dockyards were not paid; mutiny and unrest followed, and the shipbuilding programme came to a halt. Most would now accept the recent judgement of one senior scholar: 'The French navy began in 1790 a period of prolonged decline.'[46] French historians agree that the French had lost the naval race, even before the turmoil of the revolution had had its effect.[47]

England, blessed with an efficient tax system and an expanding economy, continued its naval programme of building and continuous maintenance. In 1790 the primary force behind change, Middleton, now a rear-admiral, resigned as comptroller, disappointed that Pitt did not implement the comprehensive reforms of the whole administration that he had worked on for most of the 1780s; but the effect of his reforms speeded three successive mobilizations over the next three years. The late spring of 1790 saw a rapid naval armament to face down Spain over an incident at Nootka Sound, in what is now Vancouver Island, British Columbia. The Spanish insulted and detained an English merchant captain engaged in fur trading and claimed the whole north-west coast of North America. British public opinion was behind Pitt, who ordered the fleet to be mobilized; at issue was the attempt to break the long Spanish monopoly of the Pacific. Between May and October 1790 forty-three ships of the line were commissioned and stored, in addition to the guard ships, and 55,000 men were raised. Lord Howe's fleet gathered at Spithead, with thirty-six ships of the line; coinciding with this crisis was the confrontation with Russia over the Black Sea port of Ochakov, when yet more ships of the line were ordered to the Downs under Hood.[48] By November 243 ships were ordered to be commissioned.[49] The result of this massive mobilization, achieved smoothly and quickly, was emphatic. Spain backed down on the question of the Spanish claim to North America; and France was in no political or financial condition to help her previous ally, although Pitt had to abandon the expedition against Russia in the face of parliamentary scepticism about its necessity or the likelihood of success.

Relations between Britain and France were formal and correct for the first two years of the French Revolution. English politicians watched events on the other side of the Channel 'with a mixture of surprise, regret and self-satisfaction'.[50] In 1792 Pitt felt that he could reduce the naval estimates for the first time since the American Revolutionary War. France was unlikely to be a threat with so much internal dissension. Between July and December 1792 the numbers of ships commissioned remained virtually constant at between 118 and 125, while the number of men borne remained at about 20,000.[51] In the second half of that year the diplomatic atmosphere began to change. French military success on the Continent became truly alarming. In September their armies were victorious in central Europe, swept into Savoy and Nice, and entered into the Low Countries after the battle of Jemappes. Holland was defenceless. The Convention in Paris, flushed with success, voted to execute Louis XVI.

By now Britain and France were engaged in a violent war of words. The September Massacres of 1792 began to harden British public opinion. On 21 January 1793 Louis XVI was guillotined. Pitt spoke in the House of Commons soon after the execution: 'the bloody sentence . . . was passed against the Sovereigns of all countries'.[52] On 1 February the Convention declared war on England and Holland. Political tensions in Britain were exacerbated by the government's attempt to drive a wedge between different members of the Whig opposition, and by fear of social and political unrest. This 'war of principle', as it was called, drove both countries to more extreme positions. 'In an atmosphere of national paranoia that anticipated the twentieth century, Britain and France committed themselves to a kind of total war.'[53] When fighting started, rumours of the execution of prisoners of war were current in Parliament, and six months later, in May 1794, the Convention indeed passed a decree declaring that prisoners of war were to be executed. By the end of 1795 this extreme revolutionary fervour and the corresponding British reaction subsided, and the traditions of eighteenth-century honour were to prevail over the new notions of total war. Nevertheless, the French continued to be perceived as a threat to a constitutional monarchy based on property. It is more likely that it was the intense xenophobia prevalent in these years that shaped Nelson's feelings against the French, rather than his time at his mother's knee, as has often been implied.[54]

Among the first tasks of the government after the declaration of war was raising seamen for the navy, at the same time, of course, as finding soldiers for the army. Because of Pitt's disarmament measures at the beginning of 1792 only 16,613 seamen remained in the navy at the end of the year.[55] By the middle of 1793 Parliament voted money for 45,000; in 1794 for 85,000; and in 1795 for 100,000. Seamen were needed quickly. Volunteers were sought for the King's Bounty (the inducement of money to enter the navy), and a press was ordered in January 1793. Impressment, however, was responsible for only a minority of seamen on board His Majesty's ships: between January 1793 and January 1795 it produced only 14,900 out of 76,900 seamen raised.[56] The long-established system of captains finding their own crews had proved less and less effective, so the government created a central Impress Service, headed by an admiral. In 1795 Pitt's government, desperate for men, was to introduce a new measure, the Quota Act, by which areas of the country were to raise a fixed number of men, seen by many as the first step towards conscription. It was notably unsuccessful.[57] The British Navy could only with difficulty fill its ships to their full complement. Nevertheless, France and Spain were always more disadvantaged in the coming war at sea: in the quality and quantity of their seamen, their guns and their ships. Nelson was fortunate to reach senior rank at just the right time, on the crest of a wave of British naval superiority.[58]

10

The Commissioning of the
Agamemnon
January–August 1793

We do hereby Impower and Direct you to Impress, or cause to be Impressed, so many Seamen, Seafaring Men, and Persons whose Occupations and Callings are to work in Vessels and Boats upon Rivers, as shall be necessary either to man His Majesty's Ships, giving unto each Man so impressed One Shilling for Prest Money.

Order to Horatio Nelson, Esq., captain of His Majesty's ship *Agamemnon*, by command of their lordships, 1 February 1793[1]

Preparations for getting the *Agamemnon* to sea ensured that Nelson was constantly on the move from the first week of 1793. Officers had to be appointed, applications from aspiring midshipmen decided upon. Obtaining officers required much negotiation, since the Admiralty was exerting an increasing control of appointments; but Nelson did well, considering that he had been out of touch for five years, and that many of the best young officers were already in ships that had been in commission since the 1790 mobilization. Most of all, however, Nelson needed men, for the complement of a 64-gun ship of the *Agamemnon*'s class was 500 and seamen were scarce. When he travelled up to Burnham in mid January manning was the most urgent aspect of his business. The easiest and cheapest way to bring men and goods from north Norfolk was by sea, for passenger ships sailed regularly from Wells to London, and some of Nelson's baggage was transported 'from Wells by the *Supply*, Robert Franklin, Master'.[2] Clothing, provisions and luxuries were purchased and sent on board. Nelson was keen to get a ship at Chatham, 'as it would be convenient on every account', and this influenced the decision for him to have the *Agamemnon* rather than any other 64.[3] On 12 January the Navy Board ordered the Chatham Dockyard officers to put the *Agamemnon* 'into condition for service at sea', and she went into dock before the end of the month.[4]

On 7 February, Nelson went to Chatham for two days to put the ship into commission.* With him was Martin Hinton, who had been his first lieutenant in the *Albemarle* ten years before. Hinton was the first in a team that Nelson built up and upon whom he came to rely; he had previously known all his officers except the surgeon. His second lieutenant, Joseph Bullen, had served with him in Nicaragua, while George Andrews, who had escaped death after his duel in the West Indies when a midshipman in the *Boreas*, was his third. Prince William Henry cooperated by releasing Joseph King, Nelson's boatswain, also from the *Boreas*. His old servant Frank Lepee was appointed coxswain; he was to take to drink and was discharged to another ship in October 1795.[5] Nelson managed to fend off William Nelson's interest in the chaplaincy.[6] He intended to take his cousin, the Reverend Robert Rolfe, on board the *Agamemnon*, but he did not arrive. (Later that year the chaplain's absence was questioned by the bishop of Winchester, who happened to be in Naples when the *Agamemnon* called there.)[7] He took the unsatisfactory Maurice Suckling, who had sailed in the *Boreas* as a midshipman. Nelson pressed Hood to promote Suckling to lieutenant, which he did in April 1794 when he rose to second lieutenant, but he and Nelson were to fall out. Three years later Nelson reported to Fanny that: 'Suckling seems again discontented. He is gone to the hospital by way of being, I fancy, clear of the ship.'[8] Suckling took to hard drinking, went home, progressed little further and a court martial ended his naval career.

Two of his 'young gentlemen' were to prove to be talented. From north Norfolk he took William Hoste and John Weatherfield, almost certainly at the request of, and no doubt with the approval of, the previously distant Thomas Coke of Holkham.† William Hoste was the son of Dixon Hoste, the parson of Tittleshall, some fifteen miles south of Burnham Thorpe. The older Hoste was a keen Whig and a close political ally of Coke. Young William was small and delicate, and prone to injury, and Nelson became very fond and protective of him. He was to gain a knighthood.[9] John Weatherhead was the son of another Norfolk parson, the former vicar of Ingoldisthorpe, near King's Lynn. Weatherhead, taller and stronger than Hoste, was by all appearances the more promising prospect, but he was to die four years hence, with many others, at Tenerife.

---

* There survives a note of Nelson's expenses when staying in London with G. Hulbert in 9–17 February 1793. Totalling £1.2s.0d., it included breakfast at 11d., a fire at 6d. and lodgings at 10 s.6d. (Wellcome 3676).

† In August 1794 Edmund Nelson reported to Fanny that Coke had inquired after Nelson, and had contributed five guineas at Wells to drink His Majesty's health; 'some say he is coming round' (Monmouth, E610, 5 Aug. 1794).

Two members of the family who also came with him were less promising. William Bolton, the son of his sister Susannah's clergyman brother-in-law, irritated Nelson at various times because of laziness, but Nelson eventually pushed him up to captain a frigate, resulting in a moderately successful career until 1815. Nelson's stepson, Josiah Nisbet, was to cause Nelson disappointment and hurt. Nisbet was troublesome and gauche. Nelson wrote to Fanny of her son two years later: 'I fear he will never be troubled with the graces. He is the same disposition as when an infant. However, he has many good points about him. He is in extraordinary good health, never sick.'[10] Only at the attack on Tenerife, when Nisbet saved Nelson's life by stemming the bleeding from his wounded arm, did the young man distinguish himself; otherwise his progression consisted of a series of disasters and confrontations, and he was unsuited to a naval career.

Nelson took particular care of these four young protégés, and he ensured they were carefully taught by a schoolmaster. The *Agamemnon* was a happy ship. Early in the commission, Joseph Emerson, the young surgeon's second mate, wrote enthusiastically to his brother: 'Captn Nelson made us a present of seven pounds the other day, because his son in law messes with us . . . The captain is a worthy, good man, much liked on board – is much of a gentleman. I don't think there is a ship in the navy better mann'd throughout.'[11] Nelson seemed satisfied. In early February he wrote to William Nelson: 'I have the pleasure of telling you that my Ship is, without exception, the finest 64 in the service, and has the character of sailing remarkably well.'[12]

Whatever the quality of Nelson's crew, quantity remained a problem. Before the end of January he sent a lieutenant and four midshipmen to seek out volunteers in every seaport in Norfolk. He tried to obtain men from the regulating captains in Whitby and Newcastle, a rich source of seamen since the north-east was the region that had experienced the greatest growth in the merchant shipping industry.[13] But the crew was assembled painfully slowly. 'I have only got a few men, and very hard indeed they are to be got,' Nelson wrote to his brother in early February.[14] By the middle of the month only sixty-two had been mustered; by the end of March only 185.

Nelson left for London from Hilborough on 4 March by the night coach.*

---

* On 4 March, Nelson wrote to Fanny: 'Never a finer night was seen last night and I am not in the least bit tired.' One biographer attempts, at least by implication, to link this to a fond farewell and sexual gratification (Coleman, 103). However, Nelson is referring to the night coach (Barker, 96–7; Langford, 398–9). In his next letter Nelson warns Fanny not to take the day-coach south: 'you will be tired to death' (Naish, 74, 12 Mar. 1793). See Parson Woodforde's experiences of the Norwich coach (Beresford, 121, 132, 151).

His matter-of-fact letters to Fanny, full of detailed instructions, indicate how hectic his departure had been. The tone was querulous when arrangements broke down. One letter starts 'You forgot to send my things . . . I have got a keg of tongues which I supposed you ordered, and also a trunk from Wells, Norfolk, and a hamper of 3 hams, a breast of bacon, and a face, not very well packed . . . However they will do.'[15] There was always the danger that without strict timing and the correct address, the ship might have to sail without important personal possessions and clothing. Nelson's main consignment of belongings did not come down from Wells by ship until 30 March, reaching him when the *Agamemnon* was anchored at Blackstakes at the mouth of the Medway.[16] Another did not arrive until early May, just before he sailed to the Mediterranean.[17]

A major domestic disappointment occurred at this time. Fanny's uncle, John Richardson Herbert, president of Nevis, died in January 1793, and the will had been proved. She was not the heiress it had seemed probable that she would be when they were married six years previously. Financial matters now had to be discussed by letter in cold detail. Nelson and Fanny had to abandon the idea of a legal career for Josiah, and the decision for the boy to accompany Nelson was taken only at the last minute. Almost simultaneously a letter came from the Treasury telling Nelson that money due from two prize cases from his time in the *Boreas* could not be recovered through official channels, but only through his own attorney.[18]

Progress on the refitting of the *Agamemnon* was slow, and she did not come out of dock at Chatham until 16 March, when she was moored 'by the Princes Bridge', where Nelson had spent many months nearly twenty years before.* On 23 March, as was customary, the *Agamemnon* was piloted down the Medway to Blackstakes by the master attendant of the dockyard, John Madgson, who brought with him the boatswains of three of the ships in reserve and eighty extra men to add to the handful of the *Agamemnon*'s crew.[19] Here, on 6 April, Nelson had the unusual task of sitting on a court martial of two pilots who had run a warship ashore; both were found guilty and sentenced to six months in the Marshalsea Prison.[20]

When he sailed from the Nore, Nelson had just over 350 men, of which only forty came from Norfolk. It was not until May that Nelson had secured 483 of his complement of 500.[21] However, the ship had just under 50 per cent able seamen in her crew, which was a high proportion of skilled men at the beginning of an eighteenth-century war.[22] It is likely that William

---

* Nelson's only request to the Navy Board during fitting out was for a six-oared yawl rather than a cutter (NMM, CHA/E/40, 26 Mar. 1793).

Locker had assisted in obtaining such a high proportion of skilled men, since from late 1792 he was senior naval officer at the Nore. By April, Nelson was content, writing to Fanny from the Nore: 'we are well officered and manned, the greatest comfort a captain can have.'[23]

There were further delays caused by waiting for orders from London; these were followed by a gale that kept the ship at the Nore. Finally the *Agamemnon* sailed to the Downs on 25 April, anchoring next to the *Cumberland*, the flagship of Rear-Admiral John McBride, for whom the crew gave three cheers. Nelson escorted a down-Channel convoy of seventeen ships to Spithead, arriving on 29 April. It is not clear when he knew that he was to go to the Mediterranean with the newly appointed commander-in-chief, none other than Admiral Lord Hood. He had had orders as far back as 12 March that the ship was to take on stores for foreign service.[24] While he was at the Nore, the rumour was that he was to escort the West Indies convoy.[25] At some point after his arrival at Spithead his Mediterranean destination would have been confirmed.[26] For Nelson, it was a good outcome. While he knew West Indian waters, and honour and prizes were likely, his health would have been at risk: many naval officers and seamen were to die there in the next two years. The Mediterranean would be less unhealthy, but the potential for reward from prizes would be far less, for they were likely to be small merchant ships that carried foodstuffs of relatively low value. The station held lower risks but fewer possibilities for reward.

Blustery weather followed; topgallant masts and lower yards were lowered to the deck. His brother Maurice took leave from the Navy Office to pay a visit. The *Agamemnon* was then ordered to cover the passage of the *Tisiphone* frigate, commanded by Anthony Hunt, which was escorting a transport with troops for Guernsey.[27] On 2 May, with sails heavily reefed, and with Maurice still on board since the weather was too rough for him to get ashore, Nelson set off south across the Channel.[28] He ventured as far south as Cherbourg and at Cap Barfleur caught his first sight of hostile warships. Anchored just to the south of the lighthouse were two frigates, one of thirty-two guns and another of twenty-eight, and two brigs. The small squadron hoisted sail and stood towards him, but when one of the brigs came out to have a closer look, she signalled to the others. All four French ships ran for the nearby harbour of La Hogue. The entrance to the harbour is beyond an area of flat sands, and little water would have been under the *Agamemnon*'s keel, whatever the state of the tide. Most captains with a newly commissioned ship would not have risked their ship in such waters. 'I had now to lament the lack of a pilot and not a man on the Ship had ever been on this coast, it blew a Strong Gale, we were close in with the rocks to windward and sand breaking under our lee. Had the ship touched the ground she must inevitably have been lost.'[29] There was a note of alarm in the log kept by the master, John Wilson: 'Our ship with all the sail she could carry: the strange ships made a great number of private signals which we could not answer . . . Run them near on shore under two little forts in the harbour of La Hogue our ship being within one quarter of a mile of the Rocks on the west side of the entrance of the harbour.'[30] Although Nelson had to turn back because of the shallow water, he did not give up. He reckoned that there were ten or twelve feet in La Hogue Harbour at low tide, and that the *Agamemnon* could get at the French ships when the tide was high. He sailed back to Alderney for a pilot, but could not persuade one to take him into La Hogue. Disappointed, he turned north for Spithead.

The *Agamemnon* had been given a useful four-day shakedown voyage in heavy weather. Nelson was to relish the independence of having the command of a 64-gun ship, and he was to refuse the offer of a 74 several times over the next three years. By the 1790s a 64 was used as a ship of the line only in exceptional circumstances. The *Agamemnon* was unquestionably fast, and this has often been given as the explanation for Nelson staying with his 'favourite' ship, but there were other reasons. Cuthbert Collingwood, who did not like 64s, explained to his sister: 'Their most common employment is convoy, which is a constant worry: in the line they are the weakest ships, for which reason when any detachment is made they are the ships.'[31] It was just this likelihood of being detached from the main fleet that appealed to Nelson. He was to exploit this freedom fully in the Mediterranean; an independent command of a small squadron was to be the means of his next promotion. Besides, there was less tedium and expense in entertainment than when lying with the rest of the ships of the line, and prize money was more likely. Many captains refused larger ships, particularly captains of frigates, and they constituted a very effective elite within the navy at this time.[32] The exploits and fame of captains such as Sir Edward Pellew and, later, Philip Broke (of the *Shannon*) were greater than those of many admirals, and often they became rich through prize money. In a sense, the *Agamemnon* was a compromise between independence and seniority. Nelson was not long in the Mediterranean before he was chasing French frigates. Until the loss of his arm in 1797, he was in the thick of every close action, conduct more akin to that of the captain of a frigate than that of a flag officer, which he was soon to become. Had Nelson not already been well up the promotional ladder by the time war broke out, it is likely he would have remained an elite frigate captain, and have become rich.

Final preparations for leaving for the Mediterranean were made. Nelson had already ordered his wine at the end of March from David Shephard, a wine merchant of Guernsey, recommended to him by Captain Thomas Pasley, who also had been fitting his ship, the *Bellerophon*, at Chatham.[33] Since Guernsey was outside the British customs area, it made a speciality of importing young wines, brought by Guernsey ships from Spain and Portugal. Having matured in cellars on the island, they were then sold in England, though duty could be avoided by sending the wine straight on to the ship.[34] Nelson first ordered thirty dozen of the best port and five dozen of the best sherry. Captain Hunt of the *Tisiphone* delivered to Nelson a further order of fifty dozen bottles of wine and fifteen dozen of port for the wardroom. With the mobilization, business was brisk, for the Guernsey wine merchant wrote to Nelson: 'I hope the wine will prove to be entirely satisfactory. Please make allowance for the Port being but lately Bottled the demand for that Wine for the Fleet being so rapid that we have no old stock in Bottles remaining.' Nelson was to entertain well. When he left the ship, thirty-two dozen bottles of port, twelve dozen of sherry and forty-two dozen empty bottles remained.[35] Fine foods for keeping a good table were also delivered, such as souchong tea, Turkish coffee, nutmegs and cinnamon.[36] Nelson's agents in London, Marsh and Creed, settled the bills.

Once Nelson knew that the *Agamemnon* was ordered to Spithead, he arranged that Fanny should stay with his sister and her husband, the Matchams, who now lived at Ringwood in the New Forest, thirty miles from Portsmouth. It is most likely that they visited Nelson at Spithead on 10 May. Josiah and Nelson bid Fanny goodbye; husband and wife were not to meet again for four years. 'I hope you all got home safely, you had a fine day,' he wrote to her. 'Josiah is in high spirits.'[37]

Vice-Admiral William Hotham's squadron of seven ships, part of Hood's fleet, sailed to St Helens. Hotham was in the 100-gun *Britannia*, Nelson's old friend Charles Morice Pole captained the *Colossus* (74) and William Young, whom Nelson had met briefly in St Omer ten years before, the *Fortitude* (74). A frustrating two weeks of what Nelson considered aimless cruising in light airs and hazy weather in mid Channel followed: 'I believe we are sent out for no other purpose than to amuse the people of England by having the fleet at sea,' he wrote to Fanny, 'for where we are placed the French it is not likely will have a fleet. The English are hum'd and the Fleet made fools of. We have spoke many neutral vessels from the French ports who tells us that Nantes, Bordeaux and L'Orient are filled with English prizes to the French privateers and frigates, this information makes us feel more uneasy.'[38]

Off the Lizard on 25 May 1793, the squadron joined Hood's fleet of thirty-six warships, and several convoys on the way to the East Indies, as well as those bound for Spain, Portugal and the Mediterranean. Before the end of May, and still within sight of the Scilly Isles, Nelson took the opportunity of demonstrating to the crew that the *Agamemnon* was to be a disciplined ship. He ordered that a seaman be given three times the permitted number of twelve lashes for theft; to the boy who aided him, he gave twelve.[39] Theft by seamen was damaging to morale in general and unpopular with the seamen themselves; at the beginning of a long commission it had to be stamped on. By 4 June the fleet was still only seven leagues from the Scilly Isles.

Hood commanded a formidable force of eighteen ships of the line, three 64s, one 50, fourteen frigates and ten support vessels – forty-six ships in all.[40] He took the opportunity, when the weather permitted, to exercise and manoeuvre his fleet. For long periods he flew a signal every ten minutes and harried his captains to keep close order. The *Agamemnon* was given two or three orders to keep her station more closely, while many more were sent to the *Berwick*, which had a notably weak captain, Sir John Collins, a sick man who was to die in the Mediterranean. Nelson was stationed at the rear of the formation, sent to chase any strange sails.[41] The official total of the complements of all the ships came to over 16,000 men, although it is more than likely that the actual number was less, a figure not including the army regiments aboard. Hood's ships were better than those that had been given to Howe for the Channel fleet.[42] Since he was on the Board of Admiralty and close to Lord Chatham, he was in a very good position when it came to selecting officers. Talented officers abounded. Many who rose to fame and distinction were there, although the junior flag officers, Hotham and Rear-Admiral Sir Hyde Parker, were not of the first calibre. Among the captains, as well as Pole and Young, were George Keith Elphinstone (later Lord Keith), Thomas Frederick, Thomas Foley, Archibald Dickson and William Waldegrave; the younger captains with smaller ships included the younger Samuel Hood, Robert Stopford, Thomas Troubridge, Benjamin Hallowell, Thomas Fremantle, George Hope and Thomas Byam Martin.[43] All these officers were to do well.

Despite the strength of Hood's fleet, the Mediterranean was not to rate highly in strategic importance in the calculations of Pitt and his cabinet during the first four years of war. Initially greater priority was placed on amphibious operations against the French West Indian sugar islands, while hopes and resources were also invested in operations in western France to aid French royalist resistance to Paris. The centre of attention, then, became the army in the Low Countries. Conscious of the mistake made in the American Revolutionary War of dispersing British naval effort around the world, the Admiralty kept the Channel fleet intact, and was to be rewarded by Howe's victory on 1 June 1794. The Mediterranean fleet was expected to act in concert with Austria against France, defending its huge territories in south-eastern Europe and northern Italy.[44] However, the British fleet was to prove impotent against the French armies that were to sweep down through Italy. And Austria's consistent lack of military success blunted the enthusiasm of British ministers for Mediterranean operations. Spain too was a potential problem. As a monarchy, it was still an ally of Britain against Revolutionary France, but there was little trust between the Spanish and English governments. If it changed sides, Spain's geographical position astride the Western Mediterranean would make the British presence there untenable. Thus the Kingdom of Naples and Sicily, ruled by King Ferdinand and his wife, Maria Carolina – daughter of the Austrian empress Maria Theresa, violently anti-France, anti-republican and pro-Austria – was an important ally and could be relied upon for troops and ships. Naples could also supply and support British naval ships, which otherwise had no base east of Gibraltar.

The naval tasks in the Mediterranean were many and various, and British warships were dispersed in the coming years, sometimes dangerously so, as successive commanders-in-chief tried to blockade ports, support land operations and convoy food to troops and ensure the safe passage of British trade to and from the Levant. But most important of all was the need to ensure the safe conveyance of food, water and supplies for large concentrations of soldiers and sailors. Conversely, it was also essential to capture the enemy's ships, or cargoes in neutral ships that were destined for French forces or coasts, in order to deny the enemy these vital ingredients for successful land hostilities. The corsairs of the Barbary States constituted another danger. British relations with these states were strained; the most recent treaties with them were signed as far back as 1762 and 1763. By contrast the French were on much better terms, with treaties in 1780 and 1781, with another to be signed with Tunis in 1795.[45] The armies and navies of both France and England were to find themselves dependent on the supply of grain and other provisions from the Barbary States.

With contrary winds that blew fresh at the end of May, Hood's fleet took over three weeks to get to Cadiz and did not arrive until 17 June, not surprising in view of the cumbersome number of ships. When he reached Cadiz, Nelson made full use of a four-day stay. The British officers dined on board the Spanish flagship of 112 guns with the commander-in-chief,

Admiral Langara, now an ally but within three years to become an enemy. Nelson toured the dockyard, which he had last seen in 1777, and admired the ships, but formed a strong opinion of the weakness of the fighting qualities and discipline of Spanish seamen. He wrote to Fanny: 'I am certain if our six barges' crews (which are picked men) had got on board one of their first rates they would have taken her. Therefore in vain may the Dons make fine ships, they cannot however make men.'[46] It was an important observation, to be confirmed several times in the coming years and a significant factor in British confidence when fighting the Spanish. He also saw a bullfight, of which he disapproved strongly.[47] He took the opportunity to buy some more wine and made the practical purchase, through James Duff, the British consul, of ninety-six chickens and twelve turkeys, together with a substantial quantity of grain.[48] Nelson meant to use his abundant dinner table as a means of communication with his peers and junior officers.

When the fleet reached the Strait of Gibraltar, the wind was once more against them. Thomas Byam Martin, in Hood's fleet as the new captain of the *Tisiphone*, related that Hood bet his second-in-command, Sir Hyde Parker, half a crown that the frigate could beat through the strait against the easterly breeze, if Byam Martin put up all the canvas that he could. 'We had gained very considerably to windward of the fleet when the breeze which had been very strong increased to a gale'; nevertheless, the frigate reached Gibraltar several hours before the rest of the fleet, such was a frigate's superiority over a larger ship in sailing close to the wind.[49] At Gibraltar the stay was likewise only four days, enough to take on water. On 28 June 1793 the *Agamemnon* set sail through the strait for Toulon.

I I

The Western Mediterranean:
Frustrated Subordinate
July 1793–July 1795

I hardly think this war can last, for what are we at war about?
Nelson to Fanny, 4 August 1793[1]

We are certainly equal to meet the French Fleet in any part of the Ocean & shall have no doubt did the conquest of the World depend on the event. But in the present situation of affairs a Naval Victory will not save Italy.
Captain Nelson to Sir William Hamilton, 26 February 1795[2]

The naval base of Toulon, and the threat that it posed to British interests, was to dominate eight of the eleven years remaining in Nelson's career at sea. It has a well-protected harbour, known to the British as the Inner Roads, with a further extensive anchorage to seaward, the Outer Roads, protected by a circular strip of land to the south. This ends at a high point called Cap Cépet, which would often appear in the *Agamemnon*'s log over the next three years. The immediate hinterland of the town is mountainous. Toulon's greatest weakness, however, was that its economy was not self-sufficient; surrounded by parched and mountainous countryside, it was dependent upon ship-borne grain. Nor were timber and other shipbuilding materials available locally. The forests of Provence had long been exhausted, and Corsica was by now the chief source of timber, while there was a busy trade with ships from Northern Europe, particularly Dutch, which brought mast timber, iron, tar and hemp from the Baltic. The supply to Toulon of food and stores was to be critical in the waters of southern France and Italy over the next three years of war.

The French Navy directly employed over half the adult male population of the town. At the peak of the American Revolutionary War the dockyard labour force consisted of over 4,000 skilled and unskilled workmen, although this figure includes unproductive convicts. In the spring of 1793

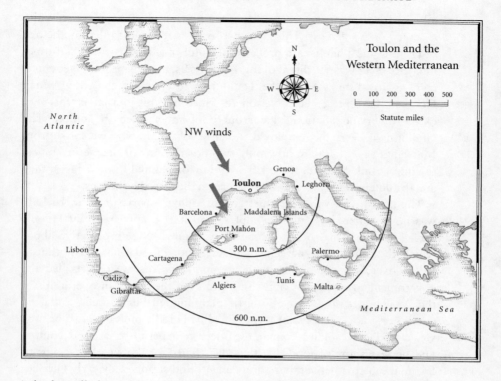

it had swelled to 6,000, an enormous number when compared with the total British dockyard workforce of 8,000 in six dockyards.[3] Formidable though it appeared, Toulon was vulnerable to internal dissension and external aggression. In 1793 the town was sharply divided between the municipality, dominated by the bourgeoisie, and the dockyard labour force, which had radical Jacobin sympathies. Both resented the Ministry of Marine, far away in Paris. From the late 1780s the weakness of the French royal finances had led to violence, strikes and poverty in Toulon. Divisions between the town and the navy, left and right, Catholic and Jacobin, were sharply drawn long before France slipped into civil war in 1793.

These civic power struggles became even more intense in 1792 when the Jacobins were swept out of power. In addition, the town was overrun with refugees, fleeing from fighting elsewhere in France; some estimates put the total population of the town at 50,000 by August 1793. As Hood's ships established a coastal blockade of Provence, food became scarce and the price of bread rose sharply. On 18 August some of the town's leaders contacted Hood about supplies of grain.[4] On 23 August he offered to defend the town on condition that the Republic was renounced and that all military installations were entrusted to him, an offer that was eventually accepted on 27 August. This great betrayal, as it was regarded by the rest of France, was a haphazard process; the number of royalists was 'a distinct minority . . . It was the threat of savage reprisals, not any profound commitment to royalism, that led the Toulonnais to clutch at the straw which Hood's offer represented.'[5] Nelson described it in his journal as 'this very extraordinary negotiation'.[6] He wrote to his father when off Toulon: 'The Guillotine is every day employ'd, a Master of a Ship who we spoke from Marseilles says there are now only two descriptions of people in France, the one Drunk & Mad, the other with horror painted in their faces, they are absolutely starving. Yet nothing brings them to their senses.'[7]

The British government's chief aim of aiding Austria in northern Italy was now rendered yet more complex, and it also appeared that Hood's forces were fighting to restore the French monarchy, an objective about which there was little agreement in England. Hood's natural optimism led to overconfident messages to London. His 'roseate reports' led the government to withdraw vital ships and send them to join operations in the West Indies, and over-optimistic planning led Pitt to believe that he could get 50,000 troops into Toulon.[8] But Hood's military position was weak. He lacked soldiers to man the fifteen-mile perimeter around Toulon, and he was short of food. He thus dispatched a number of his ships to Spain and Naples to obtain reinforcements and supplies. By early October he was writing to the British agent in Rome: 'In addition to my fleet, I have now to provide for 10,000 troops and all the inhabitants of Toulon, not one of which, I believe, has tasted animal food for several weeks.' Two weeks later he reported that 'the enemy has cut off the water from all the mills, the inhabitants of Toulon are in great want of flour.'[9] He also had to set up a temporary administration on shore, to which some of his admirals and captains now moved. Nelson's lack of French would have made him unsuitable for work there.* His second lieutenant, Joseph Bullen, went to a shore post, but Hood reserved the *Agamemnon* for another task. 'I may have lost an appointment by being sent off,' Nelson wrote regretfully to Fanny.[10]

Nelson's orders were, first, to deliver dispatches to the nearest British consul, in Oneglia (Imperia) in Italy, on the coast west of Genoa, for onward transmission to London and then to sail south to Naples. There

---

*Among those ashore at Toulon as an ally was the young Spanish admiral Gravina, who would be Nelson's opponent at Trafalgar (NMM, CRK/7/28, 1 Oct. 1793, Mulgrave to Hood).

he was to persuade Ferdinand, the king of Naples and Sicily, to hurry reinforcements of 6,000 troops to Toulon and, after completion of watering, to rejoin the fleet off Toulon.[11] The *Agamemnon* arrived in Naples Bay on 12 September, and Nelson found himself negotiating directly with Sir John Acton, an Englishman who was the king's first minister. He argued, successfully, that 2,000 troops immediately were worth more than 6,000 in a fortnight.[12] Four days later 2,000 Neapolitan soldiers set out in transports for Toulon. In a letter to William Suckling, Nelson claimed to have anticipated his instructions: 'the Lord is very much pleased with my conduct ... which I undertook without any authority from him.'[13]

The *Agamemnon*'s crew had to struggle with a great swell in the Bay of Naples to get water aboard. Nelson inspected the king's grenadiers and was dined by the physically dominating but coarse Ferdinand, whose interests in affairs of state were no match for his passion for hunting. His wife was a complete contrast. Maria Carolina was the daughter of the Empress Maria Theresa of Austria and sister of the recently guillotined Marie Antoinette. She and her daughters turned the head of one impressionable English midshipman, who described her: 'this energetic woman, whose slender and perfect form seemed to tread on air, while the tender animation of her sparkling eyes expressed a warmth of heart that prompted her (at least in my imagination) to embrace all around her'.[14] More objective and informed observers thought her ruthless and scheming. Nelson noted to his brother with pride that he was seated at the place of honour at the king's right hand.[15] Thus he met, for the first time, the 63-year-old Sir William Hamilton and his young wife Emma. For many years she had been Sir William's mistress, but they were married in 1791. They were an incongruous couple. Sir William, tall, saturnine and cultured, had been in Naples as minister plenipotentiary (not as full ambassador) for twenty-nine years. He was famous as a connoisseur and distinguished collector of Greek vases, with a collection already in the British Museum, a passion that left him constantly short of money. His published observations of the volcanic Mount Vesuvius, which he had climbed many times, had made his name further known, and he had been a Fellow of the Royal Society since 1767.[16] Emma, his second wife, was at the height of her startling beauty at twenty-eight. Though English society looked down on her humble origins and her questionable past, these social nuances were lost at the Neapolitan court, where she was a great favourite with the queen.[17] Nelson immediately took to both of them. He wrote to Fanny: 'She is a young woman of amiable manners and who does honour to the station to which she is raised.'[18]

The next day the *Agamemnon*'s log records: 'Came on board the British

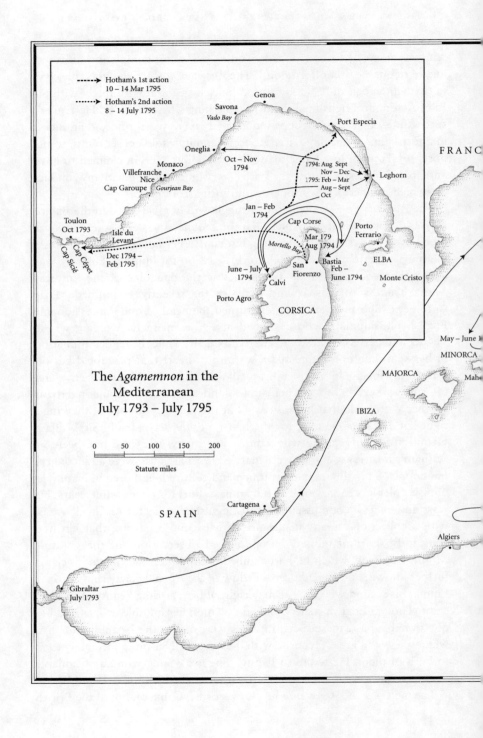

Hotham's 1st action
10 – 14 Mar 1795

Hotham's 2nd action
8 – 14 July 1795

Genoa

Savona
Vado Bay

Port Especia

FRANC

Oneglia

Oct – Nov
1794

1794: Aug Sept
Nov – Dec
1795: Feb – Mar
Aug – Sept
Oct

Leghorn

Monaco

Villefranche
Nice

Cap Garoupe   *Gourjean Bay*

Jan – Feb
1794

Cap Corse

Porto
Ferrario

Toulon
Oct 1793

Isle du
Levant

Mar 179
Aug 1794

Mortello Bay

Dec 1794 –
Feb 1795

Cap Cépet

Cap Sicié

June – July
1794

San
Fiorenzo

Bastia
Feb –
June 1794

ELBA

Monte Cristo

Calvi

Porto Agro

CORSICA

May – June

MINORCA

MAJORCA

Mah

The *Agamemnon* in the
Mediterranean
July 1793 – July 1795

IBIZA

0   50   100   150   200

Statute miles

SPAIN

Cartagena

Algiers

Gibraltar
July 1793

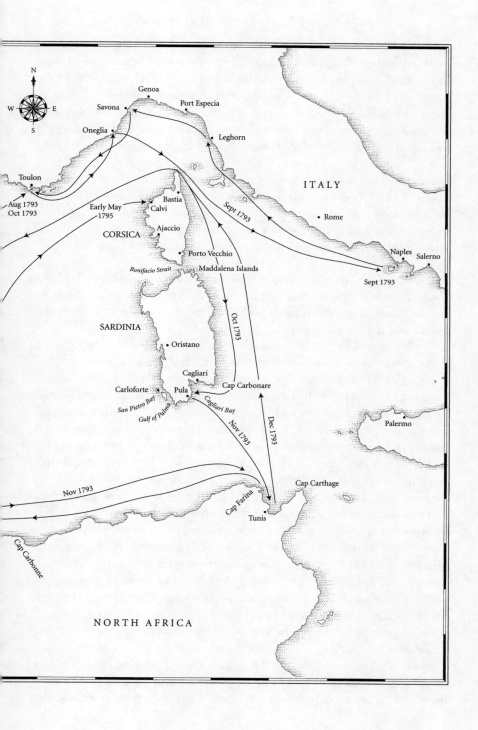

N
W • E
S

Genoa
Savona
Port Especia
Oneglia
Leghorn
Toulon
ITALY
Aug 1793
Oct 1793
Early May
1795
Calvi
Bastia
Rome
CORSICA
Ajaccio
Sept 1793
Porto Vecchio
Naples
Salerno
Bonifacio Strait
Maddalena Islands
Sept 1793
Oct 1793
SARDINIA
Oristano
Cagliari
Dec 1793
Carloforte
Pula
Cap Carbonare
San Pietro Bay
Cagliari Bay
Palermo
Gulf of Palma
Nov 1793
Nov 1793
Cap Carthage
Cap Farina
Cap Carbonne
Tunis
NORTH AFRICA

Ambassador and saluted him with 15 guns on his coming on board &
leaving the ship.'[19] All this ceremony, combined with the continuing swell
in the Bay, disrupted Nelson's continuing efforts to get water. While the
party was in full swing, he received intelligence from Sir John Acton, by
way of Sir William, of a French corvette off nearby Sardinia, together with
a small English prize and a convoy of two ships on their way from Smyrna
to Leghorn. He decided to leave immediately. He wrote in his journal:

although my ship was almost without water, casks on shore etc: Yet I considered
that the City of Naples looked what an English Man of War would do. I ordered
my Barge to be manned and sent the Ladies on shore & in two hours my ship was
under sail. I believe we carry with us the good wishes of Naples & of Sir William
Hamilton & Lady Hamilton in particular which I esteem more than all the rest . . .[20]

As a postscript he noted: 'if I am successful I return if otherwise to Toulon.'
Such a theatrical demonstration of British naval efficiency would be blighted
by the anticlimax of returning with nothing. He was not to meet the
Hamiltons again for five years.

The *Agamemnon* found nothing except two abandoned local craft, 'a
Polloco ship and a zebec' off the island of Monte Cristo. He sent them to
Leghorn with prize crews and appointed a Leghorn agent, Thomas Pollard,
from among the English merchant community.[21] He was beginning to send
in small prizes steadily and had already picked up two promising merchant
vessels, though getting them 'condemned' was not proving easy. The nearest
British vice-admiralty court was at Gibraltar, and delays in business sent
to London could take months and longer, so it is probable that British
warships sent their smaller captures to be condemned at the court at
Leghorn, a neutral port. From there Nelson also obtained most of the stores
and provisions for the *Agamemnon*. The ship usually anchored in the Roads
outside the port, but Nelson was liable to have French ships at anchor near
him. During this week's stay at the end of September, he watched with
fascination as the crew of a Revolutionary French frigate deposed their
captain and appointed officers from the crew. He wrote to Fanny with
amazement, tinged with admiration: 'What a state. They are mad enough
for any undertaking . . . I shall be surprised at nothing they may attempt.'[22]

Nelson was now ordered to Toulon, where he anchored on 6 October
and stayed for four days. He did not go ashore and would never set foot in
Toulon. Soldiers from the 69th Regiment, whom the *Agamemnon* was
carrying instead of marines, were landed and some of his crew went ashore
for stores; some stayed to help with the defence of the port against the

Revolutionary Army.[23] The *Agamemnon* was sent away again, this time on a mission to Tunis in a small squadron under Robert Linzee. The rendezvous was to be at Cagliari on the south-eastern point of Sardinia. On the way south, off Corsica, Nelson experienced his first serious action, of a ferocity that surpassed any encountered in his previous war. He came across a small squadron of strange ships, which at first he thought might be Neapolitan or Sardinian, and went after them through the night. At daybreak the leading ship, a large frigate, hoisted French colours. She later proved to be *La Melpomène*, a powerful 38-gun frigate. A chase developed between two fast ships, leaving the rest of the French squadron behind. In spite of the *Agamemnon*'s speed the French ship was even faster. 'Chace had superiority,' John Wilson, the master, noted in his log. By 'yawing' (altering her course temporarily to bring her stern guns to bear on the *Agamemnon*) Nelson 'could not get the foremost guns on her'. The log continues:

But whilst the Breezes continued fresh the Chace and ourselves left them fast. At 9 we ran into nearly a calm, the ships on the quarter bearing NW by W coming up fast with us. The Chace hauled up to join them. The Captain sent for the officers to consult them. Wore ship and laid our head to the Westward. The frigate made many signals to her Consorts who steered to join her. When they brought to hoisted out their Boats & sent them to her assistance. The Enemy were 4 frigates and a Brig. The Enemy from this time till noon had the option to bring us to action when they pleased. But we having our Main Topmast shot to pieces, main mast, mizzen mast and fore yard Badly wounded could not haul our wind till noon.[24]

Although the *Agamemnon* had managed to make her broadsides tell against the French frigate, she suffered considerable damage. Nelson had been bested in his first action of the war. As soon as he headed away from the French frigates, he began to justify the fact that his 64-gun ship had broken off an action with a frigate. The same day he sent a detailed letter to Hood that not only enclosed a copy of his log, but also a verbatim account of his consultation with his officers, a guard against criticism from his senior officers, in which much emphasis was put on their collective, though mistaken, judgement that the first of the other frigates coming up with them was a ship of the line.[25] He was later to learn from one of the French admirals cooperating with Hood in Toulon that his opponent was the 'finest frigate out of France and the fastest sailer'; and he commented to Fanny, 'we were unlucky to select her . . . Had she struck I don't think the others would have come down and I should have had great credit from taking her from such a superior force.'[26]

Had *La Melpomène* been caught before the wind died, the *Agamemnon*'s 24-pounders would have made short work of her; but the French gunnery, aimed at the rigging, did quite enough damage to disable and slow Nelson's ship. *The Agamemnon*'s mainmast and rigging were already weak.* If the other French frigates had decided to attack after the chase, it would have been a bloody fight, with high casualties, for the *Agamemnon* was outnumbered in guns and men. According to Nelson, the French frigate was in a sinking condition and had twenty-four men killed and fifty wounded, while one English crewman was killed and six wounded.[27]

Nevertheless, however powerful the French frigate, and however near their accompanying ships, Nelson had failed in his first action to bring an inferior ship to surrender. His feeling of relief at having got off so lightly was reflected in an unusual entry in his journal: 'How thankful ought I to be and I hope am for the mercies of Almighty God manifested to me this day,' and he copied a prayer by Addison from the *Spectator*. 'When I lay me down to Sleep I recommend myself to the care of Almighty God . . .'[28] More practically, he took the precaution of writing to his brother Maurice at the Navy Board to ensure that the exact details were known in that quarter.† He poured scorn on the Frenchmen: 'they certainly behaved very ill in not attacking me again, as to taking me I am of opinion that was no easy task. They had not the courage for the attempt.'[29] In spite of this bravado, the affair was embarrassing; it was not surprising that Nelson's official letter describing the action was not published in the *London Gazette*, as was the custom with successful actions.[30]

Linzee's squadron at Cagliari sailed south. In the neutral waters of Tunis Bay were three Spanish ships of the line, two frigates and a brig, as well as the *Duquesne* (74), a frigate and a brig, which were escorting a convoy.[31] Such a mixed gathering was to be encountered many times, since neutral ports were a marked feature of warfare in the Western Mediterranean, and British attempts to establish command of the sea were much circumscribed by them. All the European belligerent powers courted the bey of Tunis, for, as well as useful harbours, he possessed great supplies of wheat and cattle, which were of increasing importance as the war continued and more ships and troops were deployed. The French convoy at Tunis was destined for

---

* *The Agamemnon* received two 'fishes' for her mast from the stores in Toulon, and they were fitted on the passage south from Cagliari to Tunis ((UK)NA: PRO, ADM 51/1104, 9, 25 Oct. 1793). 'Fishing' a mast was effectively fitting a splint around it.
† More than six months later Nelson took particular pleasure in noting that three of the frigates had been captured (Nicolas, I, 403, 30 May 1794, to William Nelson). *La Melpomène* was captured on 10 August in Calvi.

17th Octr continued.

came on board our boat which
as a French boat which he ?
we might take out of the harbr
& between 2 & 300 killed ?
the Lt in moving her clear of
the Vessels. found her from Barcta
the Cargoe admitted to be French
but the bottom ? to be Genoese
in the afternoon stood under
Placrosa when we thought by
information to have found
some French Privateers.

from 18th to 21st making the
best of our way to Cagliari
in the Night of the 21st fell in
with 5 Sail of French Men of
War, four Frigates & a Brig
brought one of the Frigates to
Action but a Calm prevented
our capturing her the other
Frigates (I fancy found enough
to do to take care of themselves as
who appeard well hulled)
declind bringing us again to battle
although with such a superiority
they ought to have taken us
each had more Men than the
Agamemnon had on board- the
remainder of our compliment
being landed at Toulon - their
force united was as follows,-

70 - Nine Pounders
16 - Twelve Pounders
56 - Eighteen Pounders
28 - Thirty Six Pounders
_____
170 Guns - 1600 Men

Agamemnon.

12 - Nine Pounders
26 - Eighteen Pounders
26 - Twenty four Pounders
_____
64 Guns - 345 Men
_____
The Enemy superior to us
106 Guns - 1255 Men.

how thankful ought I to be
and I hope am for the Mercies
of almighty God manifested to
me this day = we lost only
only one Man killed & Six
wounded although my Ship
was cut to pieces, being obligd
to receive the Enemy's fire under
Every disadvantage believing
for a long time one of the Enemy
to be one of the line - My Thanks
& offerings to the Almighty
have been nearly in the same
words & certainly with the
same meaning. as those so
inimitably wrote in the
Spectator -

When I lay me down
to Sleep I recommend myself

Marseilles and brought food for the troops attacking Toulon; Linzee's mission was to try to persuade the bey to prevent the French from sailing with their convoy.[32] When Linzee called his captains for a council of war, Nelson's advice, as he related to Fanny, 'was to take the men of war and the whole convoy and then to begin negotiating'.[33]

It was the reaction of an impatient young officer, characteristically aggressive and, in the circumstances, unhelpful, for Linzee had clear orders from Hood not to attack the French ships in neutral waters. Hood knew well, as Nelson was to learn in future years, that long-term relations with the Barbary States were of greater importance than short-term advantage. In fact, Hood's plans, unknown to his officers, were far more machiavellian, for he had set a bait by sending the *Tisiphone*, of only twenty guns, to Tunis with a letter for the bey. Hood explained: 'I had fully calculated that the French admiral would, in the rashness of their republican feelings, have captured the *Tisiphone* – at any rate it was my plan to put temptation in his way; and if the bait had been taken, I was prepared at once to make a general sweep of the French ships of war out of every neutral port.'[34] He deliberately did not tell the captain. Unfortunately for Hood's plans, the *Tisiphone* saw the overwhelming French force, immediately turned back and never entered Tunis Bay. With Linzee's diplomacy clearly failing, the *Agamemnon* and the other ships in the squadron cruised in the waters off Tunis for nine days in the middle of November, hoping that the French ships would venture out of the neutral port. They encountered foul weather, with thunder, lightning and heavy rain, but found only neutral or friendly ships. As the squadron returned north, Nelson recorded in his log a hint of the subterfuge used against the enemy: 'Lost overboard a French ensign.'[35] Nelson used the customary ploy of disguising the nationality of his ship to get close to enemy or neutral shipping.

For the next three winter months, the *Agamemnon* cruised off Corsica with a small squadron, blockading the north Corsican ports of Calvi and Bastia. But dramatic events were unfolding at Toulon. By December 1793 it was clear that British forces could no longer hold the port; only Hood's unshakeable though misplaced optimism kept them there. The army officers, with whom Hood was not on good terms, had wanted an evacuation much earlier.[36] The expected attack by French troops, some of them led by the young major, Napoleon Bonaparte, came on 16 December. Hood used strong language about the quality of his Neapolitan officers: 'I am really sick of Neapolitan discipline – the strange and unaccountable panic that seizes his Sicilian Majesty's officers, for I have a high opinion of the men – made the retreat unavoidable.'[37] Nelson was to echo these sentiments in later years. Aided by a favourable breeze, warships and transports sailed on 18 December, in some confusion, overloaded with soldiers and with as many civilians as could be evacuated. Some ships had 1,500 soldiers on board 'and many beyond that number'.[38] An estimated 7,500 Toulon citizens escaped, including most of Toulon's political leaders; 300 Toulon citizens were shot without trial and 1,000 condemned to death by courts.[39]

Hood charged Captain Sir Sidney Smith with the destruction of the French fleet and storehouses. The high peak of Smith's brilliant but controversial career was to be the later defence of Acre against Bonaparte's troops in 1799; his unquenchable ego infuriated all his contemporaries in the officer corps. The destruction of the French ships was only partially achieved, a failure not immediately apparent to the British. When it was clear how many French ships had survived, Nelson did not fail to criticize Smith, at least in private: he wrote to Dixon Hoste, father of his midshipman William Hoste: 'Great talkers do the least, we see.'[40] Only part of the arsenal was burned, together with nine ships of the line and three frigates, although the British and Spanish managed to tow away twelve more. A modern French estimate is that 54 per cent of ships and 82 per cent of frigates and corvettes were taken or destroyed.[41] The Spanish commanders, always equivocal allies, ordered their sailors to hinder the operation, and the blaze was fought with great bravery by French political prisoners and convicts.[42] Toulon now became even more dangerous to British interests.* No longer divided politically, the dockyard made huge strides in recovery in a short time; by the end of 1794 there were 12,000 workers building a new French fleet. Very rapid progress was made only after the arrival in early 1796 of a new 'Ordonnateur du Port de Toulon', Antoine Grognard.[43] Those ships that remained unharmed formed the core of the fleet to be destroyed by Nelson at Aboukir Bay five years later.

Nelson was by now at Leghorn, dealing with the distraught evacuees, describing their situation in a distressed letter to Fanny: 'Fathers are here without families, families without fathers. In short, all is horror we hear . . . Each teller makes the scene more horrible.'[44] As the senior officer at Leghorn,

---

* It was here that Captain Samuel Hood (the younger) began to establish his reputation for consummate shiphandling, for he sailed the *Juno* frigate into Toulon, unaware that the British had left, and promptly ran the ship aground, whereupon 'a French boat from the shore boarded them, thinking that no resistance could be made in their situation. Then Captain Hood's most masterly and gallant conduct took place, by guying the mizzen boom so far to windward that backed the ship from the ground afloat . . .' He then sailed away through the fire of the French batteries, with the Frenchmen who boarded him as prisoners (Hutchinson, vii).

he reported on the situation at Toulon to the first lord of the Admiralty.[45] Hood's naval position was now much weakened, and he determined to take Corsica by force to gain a much needed Mediterranean base, while at the same time denying the French their supplies of shipbuilding timber.[46] To do this he would have to take the main strongholds of Bastia and Calvi. A race ensued to get to the island before the French could reinforce it.

Nelson's first task in this operation was to keep at sea with a small squadron of three frigates, the *Meleager*, the *Leda* and the *Amphitrite*, ensuring that no French ships reached Corsican ports. It was his first experience of the Mediterranean winter at sea, where severe conditions can rival those to be found anywhere in the world. One 74 was caught in a squall in December 1793 between Sicily and the coast of Africa; it lasted several hours: 'The storm staysails were blown from their bolt rope, and the ship during this prodigious gust lay with her main-deck guns in the water. The sea was one white sheet, and during the whole course of my servitude I never witnessed anything equal to it; and many who had been in the hurricane of 1780 in the West Indies, declared that this squall was equally terrible.'[47] The 74-gun *Berwick* lost her masts and rigging and had to return to Gibraltar.[48] The *Ardent* (64) blew up with no survivors. Nelson wrote to Locker in January that the *Agamemnon* had been fifteen days under storm staysails, 'such a series of bad weather I never experienced'.[49]

The *Agamemnon*, however, kept her station and the blockade was successful, in spite of French attempts to reinforce the island. On 18 January the *Leda* captured a small French frigate full of soldiers heading for Corsica.[50] Only one French frigate reached Calvi, when the *Agamemnon* had been driven to leeward in mid January.[51] Nelson combined the blockade with a series of raids on the small ports of the island to destroy any food supplies destined for the French defenders; he encountered little or no opposition. At San Fiorenzo, the village that gave its name to the large bay in the north-west of Corsica, he recorded in his log: 'destroyed all flour and corn at the place, burnt the watermill.'[52] After a brief journey to and from Leghorn for supplies, again in heavy weather, he resumed his attacks, burning vessels with food and wine supplies for the French. But strong winds and high seas continued, and on 6 February a seaman fell from the *Agamemnon*'s mizzen chains and was drowned. When conditions eased, Nelson was able to carry out operations in the bays and islands around Bastia, before hostilities against the town started in earnest. He met severe resistance in cutting out a prize off Capraia, a small island twenty miles east of Cape Corse, and six men were wounded.[53] In most of these minor operations Nelson personally led the soldiers and sailors ashore, rather than relying on more junior officers.

On 18 February, Hood landed forces at San Fiorenzo Bay, where the British fleet were to shelter for the next eighteen months. The landings were achieved without loss, and teams of British sailors first achieved prodigious exploits by hauling 18-pounders and mortars 700 feet up steep mountainsides.[54] The surprised French garrison, fired on from a great height, surrendered soon afterwards, though not before escaping across the island to Bastia.* Nevertheless, sickness among his soldiers and crews was beginning to worry Hood.[55]

On the far side of the island Nelson captured a defensive tower at Miamo, two miles to the north of Bastia. With the *Tartar*, commanded by the young Thomas Fremantle, covering the landing, Nelson went ashore with his first lieutenant, George Andrews, the captain and lieutenant of the 69th Regiment and sixty troops. The master noted in his log that the party marched '2 miles to a small village and [took] possession of it and [hoisted] the English flag with a great number of Civilians with our people with arms'.[56] Nelson noted in his journal that the French ran away.[57] It was easy enough if the local population was supportive, but, as he remarked shrewdly in a letter to Locker, 'If the Corsicans know their interests they will be happy with us, but they cannot bear dependence.'[58]

The siege of Bastia was never going to be an easy task, in spite of the early and optimistic opinions which Nelson sent to Hood, who himself had received encouraging intelligence reports about the shaky morale of the inhabitants. Hood wrote to William Hamilton: 'The French are in daily expectation of the town being taken.'[59] The town had a citadel, strong fortifications on most points, 4,500 troops and an estimated 14,000 inhabitants. In the event the siege lasted three months, from late February to late May 1794. British operations were marked by disagreement and ill-feeling between army and navy, with both services failing to appreciate each other's problems. So many soldiers on board ships took the place of marines that it was unclear whether they should obey army or navy orders. Inter-service relations had been soured in Toulon at senior level when the overall command had been disputed. Hood's mixture of impetuosity and arrogance did not endear him to any of the generals. Hood and the senior army commander, General Dundas, could not abide each other, and complaints

---

* It was here that the tower in Mortello Bay put up such resistance to British ships that it was copied for the coastal defence of southern England.

from both were sent back to London. Dundas was considered cautious even by his fellow army officers: Colonel Moore (later General Sir John Moore, who fell at Corunna in 1809) described him in his diary as 'perhaps not sufficiently enterprising'.[60]

The problems of command were further complicated by the civil arm of British rule in the shape of Sir Gilbert Elliot, who had been sent out by Pitt to take civil control of Toulon, and who had now been ordered to assume a similar role in Corsica as viceroy. His relationship with the military forces was ill defined, although he was given powers over the army by the Corsican constitution of 1794.* This inevitably led to conflict with the generals, and Elliot repeatedly sided with the navy in arguments.[61] Elliot and Nelson immediately took a liking to each other. Elliot's flattering letters show the political and diplomatic skills with which the older man handled Nelson. Through both sieges, conflict continued between Nelson and the strong-minded Colonel Moore.[62] At this time Nelson was thirty-five, Moore thirty-two; both were impatient and ambitious. An early foray by troops across the island from the bridgehead at San Fiorenzo was abandoned in early March, and a day later Dundas left the island in disgust.[63] Relations between the two services sank to a new low. In Hood's eyes, Dundas's replacement, General Abraham D'Aubant, was not much of an improvement. Nelson's alternative to the caution of the generals was, predictably, a direct assault on Bastia by seamen. He pressed these ideas on Hood, but the admiral could see that the situation did not warrant out-and-out aggression. Moore's opinion was that 'the enemy position is strong, the ground to be passed in order to attack them rough and much against the attacker'; after the siege was over, when walking over the battlements, he concluded 'if we had succeeded it must have been at great loss.'[64] The siege was therefore to develop in the classic style, inching closer to the walls, cutting off supplies, bombardment, ultimatums and flags of truce. These methods were to be successful.

From mid March the *Agamemnon* lay four or five miles off to avoid the dangerous squalls that occur near the coast when the prevailing north-west winds blow.[65] She made forays near the shore, bombarding the town heavily; her gunnery seems to have been accurate and French batteries were destroyed.[66] The ship's company, Nelson noted in his journal, 'behaved most amazingly well. They begin to look upon themselves as invincible, almost invulnerable.' However, a calm prevented his ship from getting close

---

* 'The Commission of the Viceroy is exactly the same as that of the Lord Lieutenant of Ireland, with patronage of the army etc.' (Thomas Fremantle to his brother Parry, 34).

to the town, allowing the French to repair their batteries, and the initiative was lost. The *Agamemnon* was now running out of stores, 'not a piece of canvas, rope, twine, or a nail in the Ship'; and her water reserves were running very low.[67] A gale struck, and she moved round to San Fiorenzo Bay on 19 March for six days, taking on supplies and leaving the blockade of Bastia to the *Romney*, the *Tartar* and the *Fox* cutter. On 21 March a council of war took place at which the most junior naval officer was Commodore Linzee; Nelson was not present. After long hours of argument, the army rejected the idea of a frontal assault. Hood argued for a landing and pushing batteries of guns up on to the hills above the town.

At the end of March, Nelson returned to Bastia, where Hood was anchored off in the *Victory* (100) with the *Princess Royal* (90) and the *Fortitude* (74). As these huge ships fired into the town on 3 April, 1,100 troops and 250 seamen and artillery were landed three miles from Bastia. They were unopposed. Nelson went with them, though confusion still reigned ashore over who was in command. His relationship with Colonel William Villettes, the army commander ashore, was good, but he found the situation exasperating: 'yet I am considered as not commanding the Seamen landed,' he wrote to Hood.[68] The seamen sweated the heavy ordnance up the hillsides, covered in rocky soil and coarse brushwood, to high positions above the town, a considerable task since there were at least fifteen guns and all large, including two 13-inch and two 10-inch mortars.[69] Nelson dispatched a ship to Naples for more gunpowder, shot and shells.[70] The *Agamemnon*, moored to the north of the town, under the first lieutenant, Martin Hinton, acted as support ship, and the remainder of the crew were put to making sandbags for the defence of the artillery positions.[71] In spite of barrages of fire from the town, in a week the British positions were established 800 yards from the nearest enemy redoubt, but still 2,300 yards from the centre of the citadel. Defensive works were dug in case of a French counter-attack, but none came. The French artillery fire was energetic, and the heights around the town were contested. On 11 April, Hood sent a flag of truce into the town with an ultimatum, which was refused.

The next day the barrage started. The French defenders had initial success. A floating battery, the *Proselyte*, made from a frigate brought out of Toulon, was towed in close to the shore, but it was sunk by red-hot shot from the town batteries, and boats had to go in to rescue the crew. Once British forces were established on shore, the siege became a process of attrition, with guns gradually moving nearer the town. With a need to conserve ammunition, the operation provided little excitement. On 12 May a boat tried to escape from Bastia under cover of darkness, but it was picked up by the English guard boats and her dispatches, thrown overboard, were found later by the newly promoted Lieutenant Maurice Suckling.[72] They confirmed that damage in the town was considerable, food was short and that if help did not arrive by 29 May, Bastia would fall. From the middle of May barrages increased. French boats tried to get into the town with food supplies; one succeeded. The struggle was finally over on 19 May. The French sued for an armistice, and a flag of truce was flown from the *Victory*. That evening British troops arrived from the force that had remained in San Fiorenzo under General D'Aubant; by 22 May negotiations between attackers and besieged were complete, and the next day Bastia was occupied.[73] Over 4,000 French troops surrendered to fewer than half that number of British soldiers and seamen. The *Agamemnon*'s shore party had suffered. Four seamen had been killed and seven wounded; among the latter was George Andrews.[74] Considering the number of men and inhabitants involved, casualties were light. Nelson noted the casualties in his journal: nineteen soldiers and seamen killed, thirty-seven wounded; estimate of the French killed 203, 540 wounded. British forces had used 1,058 barrels of powder, 11,923 shot and 7,373 shells.[75]

No frontal assault had been necessary, contrary to Nelson's belief, and his advice to rush the defences, drawn from his limited experience of land warfare, would have been costly in life and unlikely to have succeeded. No one doubted his aggressive spirit, which contrasted with that of some of the soldiers, and he and his ship's company had done well. But the recognition he received in Hood's dispatches did not meet his expectations.* A captain who had lost his ship, Anthony Hunt, had been sent ashore by Hood and had queried Nelson's authority over him. Nelson complained to Hood in late April, indignant that Hunt was mentioned ahead of him in the official dispatch to the first lord of the Admiralty, which Hunt was taking back to London.[76] Seven months later he wrote to William Suckling: 'I freely forgive, but cannot forget . . . I have got upon a subject near my heart, which is full when I think of the treatment I have received.'[77] Not for the first time, he became dissatisfied after the victory.

Hood now planned to turn to the similarly fortified town of Calvi on the west side of the island, but attention suddenly shifted to operations at sea. On 4 June the regenerated French Mediterranean fleet left Toulon, shadowed by the frigate *Dido*. Admiral Hotham and his ships of the line,

---

* Collingwood had felt similarly unrecognized by Lord Howe after the Battle of the 1st of June (Hughes, *Collingwood*, 9, 30 June 1794, to Sir Edward Blackett).

watching off the French coast, were outnumbered and retreated.* Hotham headed south for Calvi, fearing that the French would strike there. Hood's ships joined them, and the whole fleet turned north, Nelson with them. Hood dispatched the *Agamemnon*, not being a ship of the line, to bring the troop transports and victuallers round from Bastia to Calvi. Nelson was to command the naval forces. Now it was Hood's turn to lose the chance to bring the French fleet to battle off the French coast; the wind died for four days, and the French ships anchored defensively. He reported: 'I had the mortification to see every ship by the assistance of an infinite number of boats from Antibes and other places towed into the Bay of Gourjean within the shoals and under the protection of the Batteries.'[78] Back in Corsica, Colonel Moore remarked acidly in his diary: 'Lord Hood, on the report of eight sail of the line having got out of Toulon, thinks proper to assemble and cruise with seventeen. I have long been of opinion that his Lordship's zeal was not for his country, but to gratify his own vanity.'[79]

However, relations between the two services improved with the arrival of Major-General Sir Charles Stuart, with reinforcements, on 24 May; this gave renewed impetus to the Siege of Calvi.[80] On 13 June, Nelson's convoy set out from Bastia, arriving in San Fiorenzo two days later. He and Stuart agreed upon a suitable place to land troops and ordnance, and between 18 and 21 June they were landed in a tiny inlet at Porto Agro, south of Calvi.[81] The sailors sweated forty guns up the hillsides. Anchoring the ships was difficult, for the depth of water close to the shore was very much greater on the west side of the island, the sea bottom strewn with sharp rocks instead of the alluvial mud of the east coast.[82] And though high winds lasted only for short periods in summer, they were likely to come from the north-west, which made anchoring on a lee shore unsafe. Whenever there was a high wind, the ships proceeded to sea and the troops ashore were left unsupported. The *Agamemnon* was to lose two anchors here. Hardly had the soldiers been landed when her cable parted, with Nelson ashore; she was blown out of the bay and had to make her way north to San Fiorenzo, thirty miles along the coast. The anchor lay in fifty-three fathoms of water.[83]

The Siege of Calvi followed a very similar pattern to that of Bastia, and Nelson was on shore for almost the whole time. He reported the routine

---

* William Waldegrave wrote to Lord Spencer that Hotham 'seem'd much dispirited at the idea of what the world might think of his having fled before the Enemy. But every Officer of his is firmly convinc'd that it would have been downright madness to have acted otherwise' (NMM, Waldegrave Papers, Box 5, 11 June 1794). The young James Anthony Gardner, aboard the *Berwick*, was, in contrast, highly critical (Lloyd, *Gardner*, 109).

and excitements of the siege to Hood, now moored in San Fiorenzo Bay. A great deal of shot was expended. On 21 June, Hood sent him two able young captains, Benjamin Hallowell and Walter Serocold.[84] Nelson and Hallowell maintained a 24-hour watch at the advanced batteries, the start of a long friendship. General Stuart also slept every night at the advanced batteries, though they came under accurate fire, causing casualties to seamen and soldiers. Slowly the batteries were moved forward towards the town until two breaches began to appear in the town defences. On 7 July several men were killed, including Serocold, just as a new battery was being established. At seven in the morning of 12 July Nelson himself was wounded. Colonel Moore, whose batman was knocked over by the same shot, wrote: 'Captain Nelson was wounded by stones in the face. It is feared he will lose one of his eyes . . . the ball struck a heap of stones close to us.'[85] Nelson left his post for a day and made light of it.* Hood wrote him a sympathetic note, hoping 'you tell the truth in saying it is not much.'[86] A week later Nelson wrote in more detail to William Suckling about the injury: 'I can distinguish light from dark, but no object.'[87] To the surgeons William Chambers and Michael Jefferson, who gave Nelson a certificate on 9 August, it was obvious that he would never recover his sight in his right eye. His eyesight was to plague him, often painfully, for the rest of his life.[88]

With the heat at noon reaching exceptionally high temperatures, tempers were frayed. '. . . here it is called the Lion Sun,' Nelson wrote later; 'no person can endure it.'[89] His malaria returned. The army resented naval interference in their business. Fearing Moore's influence on Stuart, Nelson wrote an intemperate note to Hood: 'I wish Moore was 100 leagues off' (he concluded: 'Burn this letter'). The next day Moore was wounded, though not dangerously, 'by a stone tumbled from a wall'.[90] Hood himself was worn out 'with fatigue of mind and body', wanting to return home for a rest.[91] By the end of the siege Stuart was 'very unwell' and army relations with the navy had again deteriorated; those with Gilbert Elliot were even worse.[92] Stuart did not accept Elliot's authority and eventually left the island in disgust on 6 January 1795.[93] Stuart downplayed the naval contribution, and Nelson's in particular, in the official dispatches home. Even Hood and Nelson had their differences. Hood had to ask Nelson to rewrite his official journal, which contained gratuitous criticism of an army engineer captain by the name of Nepean. In a show of petulance to his

---

* The spot is today marked by a tablet set into the rock: '*Ici Nelson dirigeant le feu des batteries contre Calvi perdit un œil 12 Juillet 1794*' (Denham, 33; Chisholm, 269).

commander-in-chief, Nelson made the correction, which Hood had to rewrite again. Hood knew from experience that Nelson's criticism could make him an unnecessary enemy. The engineer officer's younger brother was Evan Nepean, under-secretary for war, already well known in the navy and soon to be first secretary of the Board of Admiralty.[94]

On 1 August the *Agamemnon* was lying off Calvi. Her log notes that the town, which was much damaged, was burning in two places, and on 3 August a flag of truce was flown.[95] A three-day gale started to blow and the *Agamemnon*'s cable parted yet again. The crew had to act quickly: 'up fore staysail and wore ship the gale increasing and the sea running very high.'[96] Negotiations with the French garrison were complete by 10 August. Corsica was secured.[97] Two days later Nelson returned to his ship, which was damaged by a collision with another ship in the gale when at anchor in San Fiorenzo Bay. More significantly, the crew were physically exhausted: on 11 August, when she was sent to Calvi, the commanding lieutenant ordered her cable to be cut, 'being weak-handed and not able to heave the anchor'. The same day she received onions and lemons from the *Victory*, as well as six bullocks. She had also to take on thirty-five sick men from ashore.[98] Other ships were also suffering from scurvy, while on shore almost half the 2,000 soldiers were sick.[99] Pausing only to retrieve some of the lost anchors, and obtain some of the captured gunpowder, the *Agamemnon* sailed from Calvi and soon 'was at single anchor in Leghorn Roads' for rest and recuperation for the men, and for storing and maintaining the ship.[100] On 9 September the surgeon of the fleet inspected the ship's company and 'found them unfit to serve at present [owing] to the weakness of the seamen'.[101]

Another piece of business in Leghorn that Nelson pursued was prize money, but the courts were not easily persuaded. Nelson had written to Fanny in September the previous year that 'Prizes are not to be met with except so covered by neutral papers that you may send in fifty and not one turns out good.'[102] If successful, prize and cargo were then sold by the agent at auction. Successful cases were, however, possible, and Nelson pressed strongly to get prize money paid in time. He could then distribute it to his crew, with consequent improvement in morale.[103] His irritation at the delays in payment led him to press for a British vice-admiralty court on the island of Corsica.[104] No fortune was to be made in the Mediterranean, as he explained to Fanny: 'Corsica in the prize way produces nothing but honour, far above the consideration of wealth. Not that I dislike riches, quite the contrary but would not sacrifice a good name to obtain them.'[105] To his brother William he wrote: 'I don't think I shall make prize money enough to purchase an estate.'[106] But he had some success: the first payment of £500 from Thomas Pollard appears in his accounts in July 1795.[107]

For the next six months Nelson sailed as part of Hotham's squadron watching for the enemy off Toulon and in the Gulf of Genoa, convoying merchant ships to and from friendly ports. In September the *Agamemnon* visited Genoa to deliver dispatches to Francis Drake, the British minister, for diplomatic relations were prickly with the Genoese Republic. Nelson was received in style by the doge.[108] Apart from that splash of colour, these months were recuperative and routine. Nelson had experienced a recurrence of his old ague, but his officers and crew suffered badly, mostly from first-time malaria. His lieutenants and midshipmen, including Suckling, Bolton and Hoste, recovered, but the death of young Lieutenant Moutray of the *Victory*, son of the Mrs Moutray worshipped by him in the West Indies, hit him hard, as it did Lord Hood, who was Moutray's godfather.[109] Nelson's second lieutenant, Wenman Allison, had a drink problem and was invalided in July 1795.[110] Off Toulon in October, Nelson still had seventy-seven on the sick list and those he considered hospital cases.[111] Of the complement of a 64-gun ship of 500, the *Agamemnon* rarely mustered more than 400.

Another winter at sea demanded more resilience than ever. The *Agamemnon* was beginning to show disturbing signs of wear, in spite of as good a refit as could be given at Leghorn.[112] Off Toulon, cruising with Hotham's squadron in a December gale, Nelson noted that 'the ship labours very much. Split main topsail in several places when hoisting main staysail. Carried away one of the main chain plates.'[113] In early February she spent a week in San Fiorenzo Bay shipping a new mizzenmast. Later that month the master's log reads: 'from a very high sea breaking into the head had washed overboard the steep tubs with 105 Double Pieces of pork . . . The ship pitching and rolling very heavy in the sea . . . straining her masts and rigging greatly.'[114] Off the south coast of France the winds blew from the east in the autumn, but in the winter and spring the mistral could blow for days from the north-west. Conditions in the Gulf of Genoa could be even more dangerous, where south-westerly gales would make anchoring at Genoa on a lee shore a danger and, once behind the Genoa moles, difficult to sail away from.[115] As Nelson wrote to Fanny, 'In the Channel the fleet goes instantly into Torbay, here we always keep the sea.'[116]

Nelson had hoped to go home, perhaps with Hood, who returned to England in early November. Hood still had Nelson's interests in his mind. He wrote to Nelson soon after he reached England: 'On getting out of my coach, Lord Chatham came to me, and I took the earliest opportunity of explaining to his Lordship the very illiberal conduct of General Stuart in not mentioning you in his public letter, and put into his hands your letter to me, with the accompanying Certificates, which he will show to the King, so that you may be perfectly easy on that subject.'[117] Ideally, Nelson would have liked to have had a new ship crewed by *Agamemnon*'s, thus raising Fanny's hopes in several letters that he would be home soon. Nothing, however, came of it. By November, Fanny realized that her expectations were false: 'My disappointment at not seeing you and my child as soon as you gave me some hope that I should is very great.'[118] Fanny saw the Hoods several times when in London, once going to the theatre with them. Hood, though by now seventy, intended to return to the Mediterranean, but he made a political miscalculation, for in his period of leave Lord Chatham resigned as first lord of the Admiralty, and Hood tried to browbeat the new first lord, Lord Spencer, into giving him more ships for the Mediterranean fleet. Hood's political moves to get Spencer overruled were ineffectual, and Spencer took the opportunity to dismiss Hood not only from the Mediterranean command but also from the Board of Admiralty.[119] It was a sad conclusion to a distinguished career and also ended any senior influence that might have brought Nelson to England.

From November 1794 William Hotham acted as commander-in-chief for just under a year. He was over-promoted and sick, though popular among his fellow officers, including Nelson; but adverse opinion on his ability was consistent: 'he was not fit to command in chief, but very able as a second.'[120] Writing to Collingwood, Nelson commented: 'Our admiral, entre nous, has no political courage whatever . . . but in other respects, he is as good a man as can possibly be.'[121] Back in England, Lord Howe, still on the active list, was near the mark: 'Hotham, I understand, feels very much the weight of having to do with foreign intercourse and correspondence; and is by no means in a State of Health for close mental investigations.'[122] The 60-year-old Hotham's shaky handwriting during this period indicates that he was not at all well. Discipline slackened. A serious mutiny took place on board the *Windsor Castle* in San Fiorenzo Bay days after Hood's departure, when the men demanded a change of officers, to which Hotham eventually agreed.[123]

When British and French squadrons finally met, the encounters were inconclusive. On hearing the enemy were at sea on 8 March, Hotham sailed with his squadron of eleven ships – two 64s, seven frigates and two sloops from Leghorn – convinced that they were bound for Corsica. Two days later he found that the French, with fifteen sail of the line and six frigates, were north-west towards Genoa. The weather was calm. Hotham made the signal for a 'general Chase' on 11 March, but the winds were so light that the British did not catch the French until two days later. As daylight faded, conditions suddenly changed. The wind got up and squalls, which enabled the English fleet to get into a close order of sailing, gave the French ships and their raw crews difficulties, and two of them had collided. The *Agamemnon* was in the van. At 5.16 on the evening of 13 March, Hotham made the signal to engage. The next morning was hazy with light breezes. At first light 'all the fleet was in company,' ran Nelson's log.

At Daylight one of the Enemy's line of battleships carry away his topmasts. The *Inconstant* coming fast up with this disabled ship . . . Hove seven Live Bullocks overboard, clearing decks. A 1/4 past 9 *Inconstant* began her fire upon the disabled ship. At Noon the action continued.

14th: Weather. Nearly calm. We kept up a constant fire upon the *Ça Ira* with several of the Enemy's ships bearing down on us . . . and as the ships got up the engagement became general but at a great distance on the larboard side the Enemy having the Wind. At 1/2 past we began to engage on both sides, as did the *Princess Royal*. At five minutes past 10 two of the Enemy's ships Struck their Colours, boarded them and hoisted English colours. They proved to be the *Ça Ira* of 80 guns and 1300 men and *Le Censeur* of 74 and 1000 men. The Engagement returned but at a great distance from the centre to the rear, saw that the *Courageux* and *Illustrious* had lost their main and mizen masts.[124]

This became known as Hotham's First Action. Conditions in the light winds, which inevitably dispersed the fleet, were not easy for the admiral. Much of the action was determined by the speed of individual ships, allowing Thomas Fremantle's *Inconstant* and the *Agamemnon* to come into action so early. Nevertheless, the *Ça Ira* would not have been taken had it not been for the 'masterly harrying' by the 36-gun *Inconstant*, which had three men killed and fourteen wounded.[125] Both Fremantle and Nelson went for the much larger *Ça Ira*. Their ships manoeuvred skilfully off her quarter and stern, which were crowded with soldiers destined for Corsica; and both had to disengage, the *Inconstant* because she received a shot on the waterline and the *Agamemnon* because French ships of the line came up, although she was also damaged. Nelson had done well: of his crew of 344, only five had been wounded. Other ships too had distinguished themselves. But Hotham, his fleet dispersed, signalled to disengage.

The French took the *Ça Ira* in tow, but she became separated from their main fleet. The next day saw a very tough engagement between the *Ça Ira* and *Le Censeur* and the *Captain* and the *Bedford* before the two French ships struck their colours.[126] Both put up a memorable defence, particularly the *Ça Ira*; after two days of battering, only her bowsprit was left intact. The two French ships lost 300–400 men, the English only a handful. After one attempt at rescue at dawn the next day, when they were beaten off, the French admiral decided to abandon his two disabled ships. Despite the lack of any decisive result, it had been a gruelling exchange of fire. Revolutionary zeal and passion was very evident, although French ship handling was consistently weak. The French officers were taken prisoner and made an impression on Sir Gilbert Elliot when he asked them to dine with him:

The Captain of the *Ça Ira* is an intelligent fellow & has something of the manners & language of a gentleman though these qualities do not overflow even in him. The rest are such ragamuffins as have seldom been seen out of France. They are horribly ugly with a strong Banditti, or rather hangman cast of countenance, & in manners & address are about the pitch of the mate of a Guineaman. They have fought resolutely, however, and have thus extorted a sort of respect.[127]

Some British ships were badly damaged, particularly the *Illustrious* and the *Courageux*. It was a struggle to get the two prizes back to port. For two calm days the *Agamemnon* towed *Le Censeur* before the cable broke nine miles off Port Especia (Spezia). In the gale of 18 March that followed the calm, the *Illustrious* foundered. On the 19th *Le Censeur* limped into Port Especia without assistance.[128] Vital stores were taken from the prizes, and damage was repaired. Hotham's dispatch to the Admiralty was precise. Fremantle showed 'a good proof of British enterprise' and was 'most ably seconded by Nelson'.[129] After the battle Nelson complained to Hotham that a Neapolitan 74-gun ship, the *Tancredi*, commanded by Francesco Caraccioli, had continually impeded the *Agamemnon*, but he refused Nelson's demand that he reprimand the Neapolitan officer.[130] Hotham received the unanimous thanks of both Houses of Parliament. Nelson praised his fellow captains ('one excepted') in his letter to William Locker; Hotham, he reported, commanded 'a Fleet half manned, and in every respect inferior to the Enemy'. George Andrews in particular did well, and Nelson did his best to push him for promotion.[131] There was little of his usual post-action frustration reflected in his letters to his family.[132]

On 27 March the fleet was back at Leghorn. At least one captain was wary of Nelson. Fremantle, who had in the opinion of many distinguished himself more than Nelson, made a tantalizingly cryptic entry in his diary: 'Dine at Currys . . . Nelson made me many *compliments*. I know why!'[133] In the opinion of Sir Gilbert Elliot, Fremantle's part in the action 'was one of the most distinguished actions which has happened in the war, & Capt. Nelson's 64 gun ship which succeeded Fremantle in the attack seems a little more than a frigate by that great ship.' Unknown to the officers on the Mediterranean Station, they were constantly under the gaze of Elliot, whose shrewd observations in his letters home were read by the most influential ministers. One of Elliot's oldest friends was William Windham, who had recently been made secretary-at-war with a seat in the cabinet, and it was to him that Elliot wrote a long letter not long after Hotham's First Action for his 'very private and confidential ear'. Hotham, Elliot wrote, 'is a gentleman [who] wants, I am persuaded, to do his duty in a day of battle. But he is past the time of life for action; his soul has gone down to his belly & never mounts higher now.' He urged Windham to use his influence to make Hyde Parker the commander-in-chief. More critically, he questioned the principle of strict seniority on the Admiral's List:

Admirals Hotham and Goodall are now before Hyde Parker in the Mediterranean, and without disparagement to either of them, it would be a very great point gained in the war to get over that difficulty . . . I write now as a very private friend & the matter is so delicate as to have doubt of its being quite justifiable from me to you. It seems hard, however, on the world that delicacy should stand in the way of its interests or safety, & that it should be impossible for anyone to say a useful or necessary thing.[134]

Unknown to either writer or recipient, this letter set in train a process that in two years would have a critical effect upon the career of Horatio Nelson.

Hotham's fleet went looking for the French fleet again in May and June 1795, then sailed west to Minorca to escort an important convoy eastwards. The fleet also made its presence known to the Spanish in Port Mahón, though by then little trust existed between them and the British: 'the Allies are a rope of sand,' Nelson had written to William Hamilton in February.[135] Hotham did not find the French. Off Minorca the fleet was joined by five ships of the line from England, commanded by Rear-Admiral Robert Man.[136] But by early July the French had themselves assembled a formidable fleet at Toulon. Nelson was ordered with four smaller ships to cruise in the Gulf of Genoa and to assist the Austrian Army in its offensive against the French. On 8 July the British sloop *Moselle*, south-east of Cap delle Mele, saw ships flying Spanish colours; they were French, hoping to decoy the British.[137] By late afternoon twenty-three sail of the enemy were seen, bearing WNW, five or six leagues away. Turning south towards Corsica, Nelson and his squadron were chased for over a day, leading the French towards Hotham's fleet in San Fiorenzo Bay. In light winds the French kept up the chase. 'Several Sail in Chace of Us, at 12 some of the Enemy's ships astern coming up fast firing signal guns to our fleet in San Fiorenzo. Nearly calm from 8 to 12.'[138] It was a tense moment, at which Nelson was at his best, the *Moselle* having to pass between rocks to avoid being taken by the French and the *Agamemnon*, which was covering her, very nearly not weathering Cap Corse. The crew of the *Moselle* prepared to burn the ship rather than let it fall into the hands of the enemy.[139] Hotham was watering and storing his fleet of twenty-two ships of the line. The wind was north-westerly, blowing right into the bay. Once the French ships realized they were considerably outnumbered, they left off the chase and headed west-wards. By nine that evening, taking advantage of the evening breeze off the land, the British fleet sailed out of the bay and started a long pursuit.

The night of 8 July brought a strong wind from the north, with a heavy swell, during which six ships split their topsails, but thereafter in calm or light airs, with the fleets in sight of each other, the French headed back to Toulon.[140] The two fleets crossed each other on opposite tacks. Hotham brought the British fleet towards the French and signalled 'General Chase'. Again the fast ships, well sailed or with cleaner bottoms, were far ahead of the rest of the fleet. Off the islands of Hyères they caught up with the sternmost French ships. The log of *Agamemnon*'s master has some unusual purple patches:

at Noon the Noble *Victory* and *Culloden* commenced the Action second by the dauntless *Cumberland* & Your Humble S[ervan]t, the Centre and rear of our Fleet at a great distance astern, with all sail set, light airs & clear, Our Van in Action.

14th. At 1 one of the enemy's ships struck to the *Victory*. Adml. Gave signal to discontinue the action. 1/4 before 3 hauled our wind & left off Chace, at the same time kept up a Constant fire on the Enemy's Rear as they passed us with all sail crowded standing into Fregus Bay.[141]

By this time the bulk of the French fleet had reached the Bay of Fréjus, taking advantage of the land breeze and the smoother water. Hotham's ships were still battling with the strong northerly wind further from the land. One observer recalls seeing the 90-gun *Blenheim*, 'a bad sailer and a crank ship, laying down under a heavy press of sail frightfully'.[142] Yet inshore, as so often in summer, it was calm and thus dangerous, so near to the enemy coast. This time Hotham's caution brought the action to a close almost before it had started. The *Victory*, always a fast ship, had taken the only prize, *L'Alcide*, but the French ship caught fire in her foretop and then exploded. The *Agamemnon* was only distantly engaged. This time Nelson was critical. Though measured in his comments to Locker, he wrote to Fanny: 'The risk might have been great but so was the object. Had Lord Hood been here he would never have called us out of action, but Hotham leaves nothing to chance.'[143] The engagement became known as Hotham's Second Action. Nelson later referred to it as a 'miserable action'.[144]

Nelson's ship had been very effective and his crew were content, even though only a modest amount of money was earned from their prizes. While his ambition grew, along with his reputation for resourcefulness and courage, his prospects did not, even though he had climbed up to seventh in the list of captains.[145] The frustration is evident in his letters, 'so much neglected and forgotten are we at home', he wrote to Locker.[146] The loss of Hood's influence was a blow. Letters sent home in the first half of 1795 show his depressed state of mind. He wrote to William Hamilton in February: 'I have the satisfaction of knowing the King approves of my conduct but as to rewards we know a Campaign in St James's is preferable to all others & most likely to be rewarded.'[147] He thought little of the Board of Admiralty. Two months later he wrote to his father, 'Lord Chatham did better than this sleeping. Nothing in this war has ever been half so badly managed as we find the new Admiralty.'[148]

Yet on 1 June 1795 Lord Spencer made him a colonel of marines. This sinecure did not come out of the blue. Nelson had discussed the idea with Hotham, who had put his name forward.[149] The colonelcy was conferred upon three senior post-captains, to be given up when flag rank was reached.[150] It carried the considerable allowance of £552 a year, and, just as important, recognition from London.[151] To Fanny, Nelson described the appointment as 'honourable and pleasant'.[152] From Bath his father wrote him a letter of less than enthusiastic congratulation. It was the first of many in the next few years, tinged with the scepticism often felt by those without ambition, and overlaid with the suspicion of corruption of those in high places:

the pleasure we feel in your appointment to the Marines, which perhaps we relish in a very high degree, as it is, the general voice, it is Well & properly given. How eminently does such a Situation shine above whatever is obtained by Interest, or bribery, when it falls upon the unworthy. May we begin to get somewhat anxious to know what effect this event may have upon the arrangement of your public matters, which you are the Sole best judge of.[153]

12

The Western Mediterranean: Independent Command

July 1795–December 1796

I came in here two days ago having searched St Fiorenzo in search of the Admiral who I found was got here frolicking.

Nelson to Fanny from Leghorn, 25 August 1795[1]

I am glad you have a little damped the ardour of Commodore Nelson respecting the republic of Genoa, he is an excellent partisan but does not sufficiently weigh consequences.

Sir John Jervis to Sir Gilbert Elliot, 25 July 1796[2]

At the end of July 1795 the *Agamemnon* was lying at Vado Bay, twenty miles west of Genoa. Nelson wrote Fanny a letter full of optimism and confidence:

What changes in my life of activity, here I am, commenced a co-operation with an old Austrian General, almost fancying myself charging at the head of a troop of horse. As nothing will be wanting on my part towards the success of the common cause I have no doubt that you will hear by autumn that we are in possession of 60 miles of sea coast, including the towns of Monarco and Nice. I have 8 sail of frigates under my command. The service I have to perform is important . . . I am acting not only without the orders of my commander-in-chief but in some measure contrary to them.[3]

Vado had been wrested from the French by the Austrian Army in June, and it was now that army's headquarters.[4] Less of a bay than, in Nelson's words, 'a bend in the land', its main advantage was that it afforded excellent holding for anchoring, 'a good deep clay bottom & plenty of fresh water'.[5] For the next four months, while the main fleet under Hotham watched Toulon, Nelson and his squadron were based at Vado, 140 miles along the coast to the north-east.[6] His task was to assist the Austrian Army's operations and to prevent supplies reaching the French Army. He had some good ships and officers in his squadron, including the talented young captains George Cockburn in the *Meleager* and Thomas Fremantle in the *Inconstant*. Cockburn was his senior captain, and Nelson developed a close working relationship with him, coming to rely on him when the *Agamemnon* was absent from the squadron.[7] Nelson was short of men, and he badgered the surgeon in Leghorn Hospital to get more off the sick list. The surgeon wrote to him with a hint of irritation: 'Captn. Nelson may be assured that I shall not keep them one Day longer in the Hospital than is necessary for their re-establishment.'[8]

Though Nelson put all his energies and inventiveness into this command, he and his squadron were not to be notably effective in helping the ailing Austrian Army. His efforts in the next months at trying to invigorate the old Austrian general Baron Joseph de Vins came to nothing. Admiral Hotham's corresponding lack of energy in the overall command of the station was frustrating: Nelson complained to Fanny before he started that Hotham had given him 'such orders as to be useless to the common cause'.[9] In spite of Nelson's initial optimism, success on land and sea was elusive. But he relished the independence of his squadron, writing to Collingwood at the end of August: 'My command here is so far pleasant as it relieves me from the inactivity of our Fleet, which is great indeed.'[10]

Nelson's main task was to enforce the blockade of French supplies along the coast. Various episodes, however, illustrate only moderate success. On 26 August 1795 his squadron attempted to cut out a corn convoy supplying the French Army at Alassio, and the *Resolise*, a French corvette, was captured, though the main purpose of the operation was not realized: the corn had already been landed and was guarded by French troops.[11] Four days later three 'gallies', recently captured at Alassio, manned by thirty-four men from the *Agamemnon* and ten from the *Southampton*, stopped three seemingly neutral, lateen-rigged vessels on a calm, moonlight night off Cap delle Mele. The strange vessels flew no ensigns and were lashed together. The British officers, Lieutenants George Andrews and Peter Spicer, assumed that they were neutrals waiting to have their papers inspected. Without warning, the British boats were fired upon. In all, seven men were killed and ten wounded. One of the unidentified vessels was taken 'after a most desperate action of three hours'.[12] Nelson wrote a long and angry letter to Francis Drake, the minister in Genoa, where the other two vessels had gone, demanding action. The only flag found on the captured vessel was Greek, yet 'Vessels firing and fighting without any Colours has ever been considered as Piracy, on this Ground the Republic of Genoa ought not to protect such people.'[13]

Although the partial success at Alassio could be excused, Nelson was more culpable in the second incident: it had been careless to let his men be surprised and killed. He received a short note from the kindly but sickly Hotham, his handwriting as shaky as ever: 'I cannot refrain from congratulating you upon your late success, notwithstanding your last enterprise did not in its consequence end so well.'[14] The admiral's generous remarks could not disguise the fact that the blockade was too easily evaded by neutral ships. Writing to John Trevor, the minister plenipotentiary in Turin, Nelson argued that Hotham ought to issue a proclamation hardening the terms of the blockade. Agents of the bey of Algiers were buying corn in Genoa and then sending it to Marseilles under his flag and passports. 'Half measures are mean and useless. We prevent the small coasting trade from Genoa and allow ten times as much from Barbary and other neutral ports.' So many neutral ships left Genoa bound for the French that one merchant started a rumour that Drake and Nelson were letting corn ships through for bribes.[15] By September, Drake managed to obtain the agreement of the Genoese government that only those vessels with a Genoese signature, countersigned by him, would be allowed through the blockade.[16] In general, however, the British had little satisfaction from the Genoese, who could sense that the French were winning the land campaign. Nelson could do little except write furious letters.[17]

The *Agamemnon* spent long periods anchored in the Leghorn Roads. Leghorn was a friendly port, as Tuscany was first at war with France and next in uneasy neutrality, before it was overrun by the French at the end of June 1796. Until then it was the main base for refitting and resupplying British ships in the Central Mediterranean, with its large English merchant community profiting considerably. At the head of this community was the consul, John Udney, who also worked as a partner in Thomas Pollard's prize agency.[18] They saw through the business of prizes with local merchants and supplied intelligence, as well as wine, and smoothed the way for the pursers of British ships to obtain the stores they needed: in July 1795, for instance, the *Agamemnon* took aboard twelve bullocks and 1,000 pounds of fresh beef.[19] Her first prolonged stay was in November and December 1794, when the ship was stripped of her masts and yards; her masts went on shore for repair.[20] She also took on a new bow cable, boatswain's and carpenter's stores. A year later she received another extensive five-week refit, the hold being completely cleared.[21] Nelson wrote to Fanny: 'I have lodgings on shore during the refitment of my ship and a French master, which with the amusements of the place fully occupy my time.'[22]

There were plenty of amusements. Leghorn was notorious for having in abundance the attractions to be found to a lesser degree in any major city seaport. It had an opera house and 'Scratch Alley', a lane where the low life was concentrated. James Anthony Gardner, a midshipman in the *Berwick*, left a rich account. He arrived at Carnival time. 'We were not long at anchor before the ship was surrounded by boats with musicians playing fine Italian airs and women singing most delightfully.' He managed to obtain leave with difficulty and with two others from his mess had a wonderful run ashore. They saw the 'old woman of enormous size, who was named the Boatswain of Scratch Alley. Saw a figure there I never shall forget, with a fine cap trimmed with a blue ribbon and a white frock on, a face like Vulcan with a long beard . . . he danced a fandango.' At Pisa, fifteen miles away, the Carnival was in full swing, but Gardner also saw the observatory and botanical gardens and climbed the Leaning Tower; he noted its former prosperity, which 'has greatly fallen off and grass grows in the streets'.[23]

British officers and men enjoyed their time at Leghorn. Perhaps not surprisingly, the muster books of the *Agamemnon* show that fifteen seamen deserted at Leghorn, a much higher number than at any other port.[24] Captain Thomas Fremantle, whose career was intertwined with Nelson's from their first meeting at the Siege of Bastia in February 1794 until Trafalgar, also kept a diary. 'Arrived at Leghorn,' he wrote on 25 February 1795. 'Hotham to my great joy orders me to anchor which I did directly go on shore. Dined with all the Lads at Curry's, went to the Comedie. Very bad.' The next day: 'take up my abode at the Lion Rouge, no room at Coulsons.'[25] Mixed with the pleasure of meeting his fellow officers in the entries in his diary are his invariably successful searches for women, a number of whom he met at the Leghorn Opera, introduced by John Udney. (Two years after this he married the eminently respectable Betsey Wynne.) Fremantle's entry for 30 September reads: 'Have serious conversation with some of the officers who stay on shore more than they ought to,' though from the evidence of the rest of his diary he did not seem to be in a strong position from which to deliver a stern warning.[26] The charms of the city affected even the scholarly Reverend Alexander Scott, later Nelson's chaplain and secretary, then on board the *St George* as chaplain to Sir Hyde Parker. When at sea many references in his journal mention Leghorn, to which he sent many letters. 'I think of nothing but my friends in Leghorn . . . It is moonlight tonight. Oh, how much I wish to go back to Leghorn.'[27]

Nelson formed a relationship with a woman in Leghorn that lasted for more than two years. Her name was Adelaide Correglia. Evidence about her is scarce, and we do not know what she looked like, though she was once referred to in a letter to Nelson as 'your little Adelaide'.[28] It seems that they met during the *Agamemnon*'s first refit. On 3 December 1794 Fremantle 'Dined at Nelson's and his dolly', which implies that she and Nelson shared lodgings, an impression strengthened by a postscript in a letter that Nelson wrote in the following February to Thomas Pollard: 'I desired to give my female friend ten echus in addition to my note left with her and paying her house rent if the letter is not received.'[29] In August 1795 Fremantle dined with Nelson and Adelaide aboard the *Agamemnon* in Vado Bay: 'Dolly aboard who has a sort of abscess in her side. He makes himself ridiculous with that woman.' A week later, again in Vado Bay, he dined with them and a month later a third time in Leghorn: 'Very bad dinner indeed.'[30] Adelaide has been described as both an intelligence agent and an opera singer; she was neither.[31]

Leghorn was, nevertheless, an important centre for gaining intelligence, as was Genoa, which also had an English community, or 'factory', as it was sometimes called.[32] Contact with London through the fleet with Gibraltar was provided by fast cutters that carried dispatches; in addition, British ships received instructions and information from the 'ministers plenipotentiary' (ambassadors were appointed only to major capitals) and consuls who were run by the Foreign Office. It was through them that naval commanders sent dispatches to London and received general news about the progress of the war and the political situation at home. The consuls at Leghorn and Genoa, John Udney and Joseph Brame, were in constant contact with Nelson at this time, and he corresponded with British ministers in the different Italian states. They included Francis Drake in Genoa, John Trevor and his assistant Thomas Jackson in Turin, William Wyndham in Florence and William Hamilton in Naples.

It was essential that the commander of a squadron knew the general intelligence picture as well as the day-by-day movements of enemy shipping. The two main subjects of intelligence messages were these: the state and readiness of the French fleet at Toulon; and early warning of the anticipated entry of Spain into the war as allies of France, which eventually happened in October 1796.[33] The most importance source of information was Francis Drake at Genoa. Drake was an important member of the intelligence network established by the spymaster William Wickham, now minister at Berne, whose objective was to coordinate counter-revolutionary activities against France.[34] The minister was able to channel information derived from his wide range of French contacts to Nelson. Nelson's relationship with Drake was close. In March 1796 Drake gave Nelson two cipher books with a numeral code and instructions upon how to use them; all their messages thenceforth were in cipher. Letters from Drake to Nelson were in one code, while those from Nelson to Drake were in another.[35] In July 1795 Nelson took Drake for a short cruise in the *Agamemnon* to Vado Bay, where they met John Trevor to have a conference with General de Vins.[36] Nelson was on shore at Genoa several times and dined with Drake, who once invited him ashore 'to take your chocolate with us'.[37] Trevor too was useful to Nelson. In early May 1796 he warned Nelson about French intentions towards Tuscany: they were 'disposed to treat Tuscany as an enemy'. From Trevor, Nelson heard about the emergence of the young French general Napoleon Bonaparte, who, Trevor added, 'if he was not a Jacobin I should call him a fine fellow for his Enterprise and Abilities.'[38]

Intelligence from a humdrum level was necessary as well – a task of the consuls or their agents, usually through dockside gossip. Simply by watching ships warping themselves out of any of the Mediterranean harbours to lie 'at single anchor' in the Roads outside, waiting for a fair wind, agents could glean useful information that could then be sent quickly by land to Nelson. This was particularly important because British ships could not formally blockade a neutral port such as Genoa and they had to keep at a distance.[39] The greater part of the trade that Nelson intercepted consisted of corn, sometimes in neutral ships sailing west to Marseilles, more frequently in Greek or Turkish ones. Drake at Genoa warned him of the routes that these ships were planning to take in order to evade the British coastal blockade, usually to the south of Corsica.[40] Valuable information could also be had from disaffected prisoners and fishermen. Nelson wrote to Jervis in July 1796: 'I have just anchored in Leghorn Roads. I have had a fishing boat on board. All quiet in Leghorn.'[41]

Much of the business with these ports related to disputes over prize money, especially when Genoese cargoes were involved. Many letters from the consuls are full of legal complications, and often they had to face deputations of Genoese merchants.[42] If matters could not be settled locally, papers had to be referred either to the vice-admiralty court in Gibraltar or even to the main court in London known as the 'Doctor's Commons'.[43] When two captains trusted each other, they might enter into an agreement, as Thomas Fremantle did in August 1796: 'The Officers and ships company agree to share all the Prizes taken with the Squadron under Capt. Nelson while the *Inconstant* remains under his command.'[44] Nelson at this time relied upon George Cockburn to deal with prizes. Cockburn had the advantage of speaking fluent French and possessed a legalistic mind: besides, as his father had been a bankrupt, he was very keen on making money. Nelson eventually left all the business to him. 'You know how to settle bills better than I do, therefore I shall say no more.'[45] Cockburn's enthusiasm for prize money led him into trouble; one case had to be referred to George Grenville, the secretary of state, in London.[46] 'Captain Cockburn has been much too precipitate,' Nelson wrote to Drake, 'although the evidence may be very satisfactory to Capt. Cockburn, it may not be quite so to a Court of Admiralty who like to have their regular forms gone through.'[47] In another case Cockburn had to compromise, since forty-one merchants in Genoa had claims on a disputed cargo; an understanding was reached and 'tedious litigation' was avoided.[48]

Political and legal complications led to great expense and long delays in the payment of prize money.* No one was going to make his fortune in such waters, although there are records of modest distributions to the officers and crews in Nelson's papers.[49] Much depended upon the price that the confiscated corn could fetch at public auction; by the end of the summer of 1795 Nelson noted that the harvest in France was good and that 'bread is by no means scarce or dear'.[50] However, corn was still in demand, since the Austrian troops also needed feeding, as well as British seamen and troops. Nelson seems to have been relaxed about prize money at this time. He was content to leave matters to Cockburn. By Nelson's calculation he should have received £4,349 between June 1794 and June 1796, but he actually received only £2,227.† Since the remainder was pending on Pollard's account, Nelson subsequently relied on Cockburn to sort it out. Nelson's account with Marsh and Creed shows small sums totalling £900 being paid in 1796 and 1797.[51] To William Suckling he was philosophical: 'If I save my pay for the *Agamemnon*, I should feel myself extremely fortunate. Everything is by comparison: except one or two line of Battleships, we are the only one who has got a pound; and they must, from the expenses of the Fleet, have spent a little fortune – so far I feel highly fortunate.'[52]

---

* Gilbert Elliot, as viceroy of Corsica, did, reluctantly, take it upon himself to judge prize-money cases: 'by Corsican tribunals which may terminate the business in a few weeks or by myself in the last resort' (NMM, CRK/5/21, 12 Aug, 1796, Elliot to Nelson).

† The example of the cargo of the *Spartano* – 2,375 sacks of corn sold on 28 March 1796 – shows how legal expenses, as well as the costs of guarding the corn and Pollard's 2 per cent commission, cut the value of prize money before it was available to Nelson and his crew by 40 per cent (BL, Add. MSS 34904, 28 Mar. 1796). Corn purchased for the use of the British Army was paid by bills drawn on the Commissary-General in London, which entailed more fees and delays in payment (Wellcome 3676, 31 May 1796).

The optimism of the summer gradually subsided. Hotham's blockade of Toulon failed hopelessly in the autumn when French squadrons under Rear-Admiral de Richery and Rear-Admiral Honoré Ganteaume escaped and played havoc with English trade.[53] The *Agamemnon* spent a period with the fleet off Toulon in heavy weather in October. She found few prizes, though valuable barrels of gunpowder were taken off some small vessels.[54] By early November the French armies were advancing eastwards along the coast, and the *Agamemnon* moved eastwards in front of them. It was bitterly cold. Back off Cap delle Mele in squally weather, 'with the sea running very high from the west, and the ship labouring very much', Lieutenant Peter Spicer and six men boarded a prize, but the cutter was swamped, and a man in it was drowned. The yawl was lost as well. The weather worsened; the *Agamemnon* lost her mizzen topmast; the prize lost her foremast. French boats came out from Alassio to retake the prize but were beaten off, and the two ships reached Vado Bay safely.[55]

On board, morale was beginning to decline. Several punishments for drunkenness were handed out. Nelson reported to the Admiralty on the cold: 'at present it is intense what could not have been expected in this Country, without snow but most intense frosts and northerly winds blowing hard.' On his own activities his report was optimistic: 'I scoured the coast between Monarco and Borgetta so completely that although I was unable to take one ship loaded with corn, yet I so forced the others into the Bays of Allassio and Languelia where they are so completely under the protection of formidable batteries that not less than three sail of the line could attempt to take or destroy them.' He took every opportunity to bring himself to the notice of the Board of Admiralty, writing to Evan Nepean, the new secretary of the Admiralty: 'I hope their Lordships . . . will think I have been right in giving them this information without it coming through the Admiral which is the proper Channel.'[56] Nelson became frustrated, pushing for a 'distinguishing pennant', a flag that the senior captain of a squadron would fly, which carried no higher rank or pay. He wrote in November 1795 to Francis Drake: 'I am the first officer who have Commanded the Squadron destined to cooperate with the Austrians and Sardinians who have been without a distinguishing pennant,' and asked Drake to use his influence, 'if you think proper to represent it will order me a distinguishing pennant from my having this Command or some other mark of favour.'[57] Nelson did not immediately get his way, for in January 1796 Spencer wrote to Nelson refusing his request for his distinguishing pennant: 'I know of no-one whose zeal & Activity in the Service is more deserving of distinction . . . but it will be impossible for me at present to recommend the adoption

Horatio Nelson by John Francis Rigaud. Commissioned by Captain William Locker, this oil painting was started in early 1777 before Nelson left for the West Indies as second lieutenant in the *Lowestoffe*, and was completed when he returned as a captain in 1780. The confident gaze and unlined face seem to date from the earlier sittings. Rigaud put the fort at San Juan in the background to mark Nelson's part in its capture.

Early influences: Nelson's father, the Reverend Edmund Nelson (*top left*, painted in 1800 by Sir William Beechey), rector of the parish of Burnham Thorpe for forty-six years. Edmund was sceptical and diffident, which led to a certain distance from his ambitious son. Captain William Locker (*top right*) by Gilbert Stuart, was captain of the *Lowestoffe* in 1777 when Nelson was second lieutenant. Although they served together for only fifteen months, Locker's influence on the young Nelson was considerable. They remained friends until Locker's death in 1800.

(*bottom*) *Midshipmen Studying between Decks On Board the 'Pallas', May 1775*. At the same time as Lieutenant Gabriel Bray made this sketch on board the *Pallas* (38), Nelson was a midshipman on the *Seahorse* (24), living and eating in similar dark conditions.

Cuthbert Collingwood (*top left*) met Nelson in 1773 and was to succeed him after Trafalgar as commander-in-chief in the Mediterranean. A shy, reflective man who was humane to his crew, he was not popular with his captains when he became an admiral. Prince William Henry, later the duke of Clarence (*top right, c. 1791*, by Richard Cosway). George III hoped that the navy would bring some discipline to his spoilt and capricious third son. Nelson's failure to deal with the prince's quixotic and extreme behaviour in the Leeward Islands in 1786/7 nearly cost him his career, and put him permanently out of favour with the king.

Admiral Viscount Hood (*bottom left*, by James Northcote), painted after his return from the West Indies at the end of the American Revolutionary War. Hood was a man of great ability, but also domineering and tactless, and Nelson's relationship with him was marked by many difficulties. Thomas Fremantle (*bottom right*) when he was made a rear-admiral in 1810. As a junior captain he had known Nelson well in the Mediterranean between 1794 and 1796, and he was to fight alongside Nelson at the battles of St Vincent, Tenerife, Copenhagen and Trafalgar.

(*top*) The *Agamemnon* cutting out French vessels at Port Maurice on the Riviera coast, 1 June 1796, by Nicholas Pocock. Nelson's operations attempted to prevent food and supplies reaching the French Army opposing the Austrians; on this occasion the squadron sent in boats and captured a bomb vessel, a brig and three ketches.

(*bottom*) The French Army enters Leghorn, 30 June 1796. The ships evacuating British citizens, commanded by Thomas Fremantle, can be seen on the horizon. Leghorn had been a base for maintaining British ships, and had provided rest and recreation for the British officers and seamen.

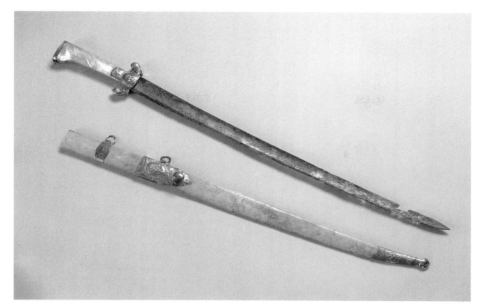

(*top*) The sword of Rear-Admiral Don Francisco Winthuysen of the *San José*, which was surrendered to Nelson at the Battle of Cape St Vincent. Nelson sent this sword to William Windham with the dispatch of the battle. It was later presented to the Corporation of Norwich, and is now in the Norwich Castle Museum and Gallery.

Gilbert Elliot, later Lord Minto (*bottom left*, by Thomas Lawrence, dated 1794). A Scottish lawyer and politician who had been sent out to the Mediterranean to be civil governor of Toulon, Elliot became viceroy of Corsica, where he met Nelson and became convinced of his talent for leadership. It was because of Elliot's influence that Nelson sent the Spanish sword to William Windham (*bottom right*, by Joshua Reynolds, 1787). Windham was MP for Norwich and secretary-at-war, as well as a close friend of Lord Spencer, first lord of the Admiralty.

Middle career influences: Sir John Jervis, later Earl St Vincent (*top*), by Lemuel Francis Abbott. This portrait, painted during the 1790s, shows Jervis's rough, tough and unyielding character, and it is easy to imagine him terrorizing his captains. However, he recognized Nelson's potential and prepared him for higher command, to which Nelson was promoted by Earl Spencer (*bottom left*, after John Hoppner). Pitt appointed Spencer first lord of the Admiralty in 1794, when Spencer had no experience of the navy. He and his wife, Lavinia, became great admirers of Nelson. Rear-Admiral Sir Alexander Ball (*bottom right*, by Henry Pickersgill) was not made a rear-admiral until 1805, but, as a captain at the Battle of the Nile and during the Siege of Malta, he was closely involved in Nelson's operations. St Vincent called him 'a thinking, judicious man without pomp and display'.

(*top*) The dismasted *Vanguard* being towed to safety by the *Alexander*, 21–23 May 1798, by Nicholas Pocock. Alexander Ball's seamanship and nerve saved Nelson's ship when he towed the *Vanguard* to a bay in the south of Sardinia, where a new mast was made and hoisted in. The arrival of the *Vanguard* at Naples, 22 September 1798 (*bottom*, by Giacomo Guardi). The sweep of Naples Bay can be seen clearly, as can the great castle of San Elmo that dominated the city.

Friends and rivals: Rear-Admiral Sir Thomas Troubridge (*top left*, by Sir William Beechey). Nelson knew Troubridge when a midshipman in the East Indies, but their friendship eventually turned to rivalry, largely because St Vincent felt that Troubridge was more talented than Nelson, and Nelson resented Troubridge's influence as a commissioner of the Admiralty between 1801 and 1804. Captain Thomas Foley (*top right*), the Welshman who led the squadron into Aboukir Bay in the *Goliath*. Nelson transferred to Foley's ship the *Elephant* at Copenhagen, but after the Peace of Amiens Foley suffered from ill health and stayed ashore.

Flag captains: Captain Sir Edward Berry, after Daniel Orme. Nelson appointed Berry as his flag officer in the *Vanguard* after his gallant behaviour at the Battle of St Vincent, and Nelson appreciated his role at the Nile: 'I shall never forget your support for my mind on the 1st of August.' But Nelson came to prefer Thomas Masterman Hardy (*bottom right*, by Domenico Pellegrini). Though painted after Nelson's death, this informal picture shows an unpolished, practical officer, on whose steady character Nelson came to rely.

of the measure.'[58] Nelson, however, did not give up writing to Spencer, and through the early months of 1796 he gave him regular reports of the campaign.[59]

On shore, the campaign was going badly for the allies. Despite heavy losses, the French were advancing rapidly. Nelson became utterly disillusioned with the Austrians, 'whose inactivity', commented Thomas Jackson to Nelson, 'is as unaccountable as it is prejudicial'.[60] On 24 November the French routed the Austrian Army at Loano, and Vado had to be abandoned. The squadron retreated down to Genoa. Anchored in the Roads for two weeks, the *Agamemnon* rolled in a great swell, with heavy squalls and then a thick fog. Anxiety about the state of the cables was reflected in the log. Further crew punishments followed, for drunkenness and fighting.[61] To cap all these misfortunes Nelson sent Lieutenant James Noble in the jolly boat into Savona for water, but the French were already in possession of the town and Noble, his crew and the boat were captured.[62] The *Agamemnon* now needed a refit and Nelson sailed to Leghorn, where he remained for five weeks.

At the end of November 1795 radical change took place in the Mediterranean fleet. Hotham struck his flag at Leghorn on 1 November, leaving Sir Hyde Parker in temporary command. At the end of the month the new commander-in-chief, Admiral Sir John Jervis, reached the fleet in San Fiorenzo after a fast passage from Gibraltar in an unaccompanied frigate. Now sixty, he was the most formidable and forthright of the senior admirals, known for his absolute standards of discipline. Harsh to officers and seamen alike, he often laced his comments with savage humour, although he was capable of great acts of kindness, which he usually executed in secret.[63] Jervis had been penurious during his early career, which contributed to his prejudice against the aristocratic young officers now coming into the navy in greater numbers.[64] He once referred to them as 'sprigs of nobility', and for the solemn and religious William Waldegrave, later Lord Radstock, he developed a particular dislike.[65] He terrified some captains. A year after Jervis's arrival, Betsey Fremantle described her husband's reaction to the news of an impending visit to his ship by the commander-in-chief, saying it 'made him quite nervous and miserable'.[66] Jervis enjoyed bullying. After one piece of obstructive behaviour among some of his captains, he called the offenders on board his flagship and, as he related with satisfaction to Evan Nepean at the Admiralty, gave 'them such a sit down, that, if it did not bring them to a stool, certainly made them piss and cry'.[67]

With unremitting attention to detail, Jervis drove himself as hard as he drove those he commanded. Furthermore, he was still smarting from his cool reception in Britain after he had commanded the successful expedition to the West Indies between 1794 and 1795, when he and General Grey were considered to have plundered rather too thoroughly the islands they had captured, and had had to endure the indignity of a motion of censure against him in the House of Commons.[68] He was to write Nelson later: 'No service I can ever perform will amount to what Sir Charles Grey and I did in the West Indies – and you have seen how well we were rewarded.'[69] Jervis had something still to prove. There is no denying the passion and commitment that he brought to his command; he was to set new standards.

Jervis's arrival – in Nelson's words, 'to the great joy of some and sorrow of others' – changed the whole scene.[70] He soon rid the Mediterranean fleet of older, weaker officers. Hotham had gone, Vice-Admiral Samuel Goodall, second-in-command to Hyde Parker, left the fleet immediately, while Hyde Parker himself and Robert Linzee, newly appointed to vice-admiral, left for England in April and May 1796 respectively.[71] Rear-Admiral Robert Man, coming from England with six sail of the line, failed to find a vital convoy, misinterpreted his complicated orders, stayed at Gibraltar and then sailed back to England. His actions were widely considered a failure of nerve and he never went to sea again. To Elliot, Nelson showed his frustration: 'Oh, our Convoy, Admiral Man, how could you quit Gibraltar?'[72]

Jervis turned his attention to his captains, identifying the weak ones and those whose ships were in 'a most undisciplined, disorderly state, the people incessantly drunk'. They included the *Victory* (100), the *Britannia* (100), the *St George* (90), the *Windsor Castle* (74) and the *Zealous* (74). From these ships Captains John Knight (whom Jervis called 'this imbecile') and John Holloway went quickly.[73] The captain of the *Zealous*, Lord Hervey, was 'no officer, having suffered everything to relax'; he had died in January of venereal disease.* Other officers were in hospital for the same reason.[74] Jervis wrote to Lord Spencer, 'I fear many of the young men of the fleet are in the same state, owing to too much sexual latitude in Leghorn before I took command.'[75] He expelled the many women on board ships of the fleet, one a hospital ship. 'I was under the necessity of sending the Matron, who

---

* Hervey was the son of Augustus Hervey, later earl of Bristol, who had set a striking standard of licentiousness when serving in the Mediterranean in the middle years of the century, elegantly described in David Erskine (ed.) *Augustus Hervey's Journal: Being the Intimate Account of a Captain in the Royal Navy Ashore and Afloat* (1953). Jervis informed John Udney that 'the remains of Lord Hervey were immediately placed in a lead coffin' (BL, Add. MSS 31166, 12 Jan. 1796).

was the Captain's Mistress, and all the Nurses down to Gibraltar. Women attached to the steerage of the *Victory* got 'drunk and practice[d] every abomination . . . Was I to relate to you', he wrote to Nepean, 'all the mean abuses, which have unavoidably come to my knowledge . . . you would be petrified with astonishment.'[76] Jervis also tackled corruption and waste of stores: 'every Magazine in Leghorn being full of His Majesty's Stores, insomuch that eighteen, out of twenty-two Bolts of Canvas purchased for the *Victory*, had the King's Mark upon them . . . if a sharp look out is not kept, all the Magazines in Europe will not supply the Wear, Tear and Embezzlement of the Fleet of England.'[77]

The morale and prospects of the younger, tougher officers rose accordingly. However much the *Agamemnon* needed refitting and repair in an English dockyard, this was no time for Nelson to return to England, in spite of protestations in his letters to his family that he would be home soon.[78] Nelson is likely to have met Jervis already, since Locker and Jervis had served together in the Seven Years War, but Nelson was not to see him until seven weeks after the latter's arrival, by which time the *Agamemnon* had finished refitting and maintenance in Leghorn.[79] She sailed into San Fiorenzo Bay on 19 January 1796. The log records: 'Manned ship and cheered Sir John Jervis.'[80] The relationship between Jervis and Nelson was soon marked by a businesslike familiarity. One envious captain remarked to Nelson, in words not far from the truth, 'you did just as you pleased in Lord Hood's time, the same in Admiral Hotham's, and now again with Sir John Jervis'; he received, Nelson reported to Fanny, 'a pretty strong answer'.[81]

Nelson was by no means the only young officer to have caught the commander-in-chief's eye, for Jervis's most promising protégé at this time was Thomas Troubridge, whom Nelson first knew as a midshipman in the *Seahorse* twenty years earlier. In July, Jervis wrote to the first lord that Troubridge 'was capable of commanding the fleet of England, and I scarce know another'. A month later he confided to Nepean that he had held back in recommending Troubridge to the Board of Admiralty: 'I am afraid of being thought a Puffer like many of my brethren . . . I never saw him before my arrival at San Fierenzo.'[82] Nelson knew Jervis's opinion.* At a low

---

* Jervis was a shrewd judge of character. He compiled a list of twenty-two of the best post-captains. Here is his list in its original order: Nelson, Frederick, Troubridge, Hood, Tyler, Garlies, Fremantle, Hallowell, George Hope, Morris, Grey, Cockburn, Matthew Henry Scott, Richard Bowen, Bayntun, Griffith, Thomas Rogers, Skynner, James Macnamara, Peard, Foley, Halliday. He added three masters and commanders: Rutherford, Winthrope, Dixon (NMM, NEP/7, 4, 5 Oct. 1796). All of them did well.

point two years later, Nelson wrote to Jervis about Troubridge: 'I well know he is my Superior'; whether he really thought this or was playing up to Jervis is difficult to say.[83] Other captains in the squadron who had impressed Jervis were Benjamin Hallowell, Nelson's companion in arms in Corsica, and the younger Sam Hood. Jervis had been a supporter of another promising young officer, Richard Bowen, for many years. Nelson's early seniority at the beginning of the American Revolutionary War above these promising officers, particularly Troubridge, was critical to his career, and Jervis regretted how low Troubridge was on the captains' list.

The sudden change of generation among the officers of the Mediterranean fleet caused by Jervis's trenchant personality and drive for efficiency gave Nelson his next chance.[84] Jervis immediately offered Nelson a choice of two ships. It was his first move in trying to keep an officer who had been on station for nearly three years, who could have insisted on returning home for leave after such a long period at sea. Nelson could have the 90-gun *St George* or the 74-gun *Zealous*, 'but it is probable that a seventy-four may better suit your active Mind than a ninety'.[85] Nelson had to weigh up the advantages of a larger ship in better condition, over the greater costs of captaincy and the lesser chance of prize money. The *St George* was slow and cumbersome. In what is likely to have been a long negotiation with Jervis, Nelson refused both ships, weighing his chances of promotion not only to commodore but to rear-admiral. By 20 January 1796 Nelson was honest with his wife and gave a fair indication of how matters were progressing: 'Thus, my dear Fanny, although I wish to get home, yet my fair character makes me stand forward to remain abroad, and I rather believe that Sir John writes home this day that . . . my flag on a promotion may be sent out.'[86]

By March 1796 promotion was again under discussion, and Nelson pressed hard, Jervis replying: 'The distinguishing pennant you shall most certainly wear, and now I am in possession of your further wishes, I will write to Lord Spencer upon the subject of them, in short, there is nothing within my grasp, that I shall not be proud to confer on you.'[87] A week later Jervis wrote to Spencer that Nelson was 'very ambitious of becoming a flag-officer, which does him the greatest credit, because of his having the Marines. Should the event happen, he is also very desirous to hoist his flag in the Mediterranean.'[88] Without waiting for the first lord's authority, Jervis promoted him.[89] He justified himself to Nepean: 'Circumstanced as I am I could not possibly avoid making Nelson an established Commodore and I rely on Lord Spencer's judgement to bear me out in it.' To Elliot he explained that he needed an officer of that rank to liaise with the Austrians.

'I have dubbed him a Commodore with a view to effectual cooperation.'[90] The broad pennant was hoisted at 8.30 in the morning on 9 April 1796.[91] The promotion was not confirmed by Spencer until September.[92] Nelson wrote long letters to Fanny about this upturn in his fortunes, some of them awash with barely suppressed excitement, some tinged with feelings of injustice and worries about expense. 'All this is certainly flattering and pleasant. These blossoms may one day bring forth fruit but I doubt it. My expenses here are too much and it is not the Marines that compensates.'[93]

Nelson remained aboard the *Agamemnon* and returned to winter cruising in the Mediterranean. For the first three months of 1796 he was watching off Toulon, where the French were working hard at rebuilding their fleet, for long periods. 'I was six days in sight of Toulon and could each day see a visible getting forward of their ships,' he reported to John Trevor in Turin.[94] The same difficult conditions prevailed, the same routine. On 18 February, south of Cap Sicié, there were 'light airs with a high sea, later calm. Saw 6 sail to windward, gave chace. Beat to Quarters & cleared for action.'[95] On this occasion the ships were friendly. A few days later, in the same conditions, light airs with a heavy swell, the *Princess Royal* and the *Excellent* lost steerage way and collided with each other. The *Excellent* had to make her way to Ajaccio, the British base in Corsica, for a new foremast and bowsprit.[96] Then it was the *Agamemnon*'s turn for misfortune. On 1 March it was blowing hard from the north-east with heavy rain and a high sea, followed at 8.30 in the morning by a sudden calm. The order was given to sail on another tack. As the ship wore round, she lost way and a large sea struck the stern, smashed the lower windows and carried away some of the quarter galleries. The next day the ship was taken aback again. The main topmast was sprung.[97] The *Agamemnon* was by then in a very weak state, and again made her way back to the Leghorn Roads.

As winter turned to spring, the land campaign restarted. Nelson's reports to Jervis demonstrated misplaced optimism. Jervis wrote to Elliot on 5 April that 'Capt. Nelson's intelligence from Genoa ... is very sanguine in his expectations of a vigorous campaign on the part of the Austrians.'[98] A week later the first of Bonaparte's Italian victories at Montenotte triggered another Austrian retreat. Genoa came completely under French influence and Leghorn was threatened, but the retreating Austrians still had to be supported. Nelson's letters report nothing but disasters. Nelson complained to John Trevor of Austrian delays, stressing 'the absolute necessity of punctuality in Joint attacks'.[99] The Riviera coast ports had to be blockaded rather than sustained. Nelson and his squadron, the *Meleager*, the *Diadem* and the *Peterel*, resumed their former coastal operations with a string of successful raids on enemy shipping. The first was a cutting-out operation at Finalle near Loano at the end of April, when four vessels were taken.[100] At the end of May the squadron captured vessels at Port Maurice. Moored under batteries, a small French convoy, consisting of a ketch, a gunboat and five transports, carried stores for the French troops besieging Mantua. As he knew this part of the coast well, Cockburn, in the 32-gun *Meleager*, went into Port Maurice first, accompanied by the boats from each of the ships. The defence put up a smart rate of fire. The *Meleager* anchored with her broadsides against the batteries. Then, as Cockburn later recalled,

The Commodore, desirous to place himself if possible within me stood under my stern designing to luff in between me and the principal battery. But as I had taken as close a position as the depth of water would allow he of course grounded under my stern, which gave us some inconvenience in the operation in which we were engaged in as of course our principal attention was then obliged to be given to get the *Agamemnon* off again.[101]

The *Meleager* drew six foot less than the *Agamemnon*. Neither Nelson's report to Jervis nor the *Agamemnon*'s log records this part of the engagement.[102] Five French vessels and a great many ordnance stores were towed away. In his report to Jervis, Nelson's praise of Cockburn was unusually handsome. He then began trying to persuade Jervis to give Cockburn the splendid French 44-gun prize frigate *La Minerve*, to which Jervis eventually assented.[103]

Yet, however much these raids could irritate and hinder the enemy, superiority at sea was never going to halt the military impetus that the French Army had built up. Bonaparte was then at his most brilliant. An account by Jacob Nagle, a lower-deck sailor with a strong, seamanlike gift for language, on board the *Blanche*, describes an ambush laid by Nelson just east of Vado in early June 1796:

After passing Vardo, the road leads a long shore for Genoa. Nelson having information that his [Bonaparte's] army was to pass that night along the road close to the water, he brought his squadron to an anchor close in shore, with springs on our cables, 2 sixty fours, 4 frigates, a twenty gun ship, and 2 sloops of war. We lay there during the night, but Boneypart having intilagance took a nother road through the fields and was past in the morning. We then took up our anchors and cruised a long shore.[104]

By the early summer it was clear from the *Agamemnon*'s condition that she needed to go to England for repair and refit. She would take a convoy to Gibraltar on the way. It was quite possible that Nelson could have gone with her. If he was to stay in the Mediterranean, he would need a new ship, and Jervis had been trying to find one for him since May. Captain John Sutton of the *Egmont* (74) was going to England, and Jervis tried to obtain his ship for Nelson; but Sutton refused the *Agamemnon*.[105] On 1 June Jervis wrote: 'I deplore the loss of your service . . . I will make another effort to keep you with me,' and then tried to exchange him with another captain, Sir Charles Knowles.[106] Jervis was keeping a close blockade of Toulon aboard the *Victory*, and letters between the two men occur regularly. Both assumed that flag rank was certain for Nelson and would not be long in coming. Jervis wrote on 11 May: 'as I cannot possibly do without you in the Gulf of Genoa, I am arranging the Fleet in two Divisions, for I will not have a third Commander, under the rank of Admiral, unless you are the Man.'[107] Further, he undertook not to take away Nelson's ships in the Gulf of Genoa: 'I shall not think it right, to remove the Squadron from the Gulf of Genoa, while there is a Ray of hope, that the Austrians will rally.' Jervis also agreed to Nelson's taking twenty days' leave.[108] It would be understating the case to say that Nelson had succeeded in his negotiations with the commander-in-chief.

In the event, a solution to finding Nelson a ship presented itself unexpectedly. The *Captain*, a 74, less than ten years old, had arrived on station, but her captain, John Smith, was ill; Jervis wrote, 'poor Smith is in such a deplorable state that his going to England can only save him.'[109] Smith was ordered back to England in the *Agamemnon*. She has often been represented as Nelson's favourite ship. Though in a letter to Fanny, he did refer to 'poor old *Agamemnon*', there is not a whiff of regret on Nelson's part about leaving the ship he had commanded for more than three years. Nor did she seem the happy ship that Nelson had described at the start of the commission. Before Nelson left her, ten seamen were flogged for drunkenness 'and bringing liquor on board without liberty'; one was given thirty-six lashes.[110] Forty-one officers and seamen transferred with him into the *Captain* on 11 June 1796.[111] All his lieutenants went to the new ship, except the unsatisfactory and hard-drinking Maurice Suckling, who had come into property and was going back to England.[112] Though John Wilson, the master, went home – he had been wounded in Hotham's First Action – most of his warrant officers also transferred, including his Portuguese boatswain, Joseph King, of whom Nelson thought so highly. His clerk, Philip Castang, Tom Allen, his servant, and all his boat's crew came to the *Captain*, as did Thomas Withers, the schoolmaster, who became a master's mate. Seven midshipmen also came with him. Nelson succeeded in persuading Jervis to allow him to keep Lieutenant Peirson of the 69th Regiment, whose Italian was invaluable.[113] He brought two sergeants, two corporals and fifty-nine privates with him. In all, 105 seamen and soldiers transferred with Nelson.[114] Two 68-pound carronades were slung out from the *Agamemnon* and into the *Captain*.[115]

Though a bigger and better ship had been procured, Nelson's promotion to rear-admiral was to take longer. On 13 July, Jervis wrote to Nelson with the disappointing news that Lord Spencer, while expressing a great desire to promote Nelson, 'confessed he could not face another promotion, he however has approved of the distinguishing pennant.'[116] Although he had said to Fanny that he would come back if he did not get his flag, Nelson accepted that Jervis was trying hard on his behalf.[117] Nelson was much better off in the *Captain*, which was younger than the *Agamemnon*, having first been commissioned in 1790, though it was over three years since she had been docked.[118] In addition, Jervis's efforts at getting sufficient naval stores to the Mediterranean were beginning to have some effect. The health of the seamen had improved, and Jervis's good relations with Elliot ensured that supplies for the fleet from Corsica were efficient.[119] The formation of the Transport Board in 1794 had improved the provision of merchant ships as naval transports and victuallers, though the Navy Board continued to resist Jervis's attempts to requisition stores centrally for his fleet.*

By early June the land campaign had gone so badly that Leghorn was surrounded by French troops. Plans were set to evacuate the English merchants and their families. 'The Consul, Factory and Emigrés are in the greatest alarm,' Thomas Fremantle reported to Jervis.[120] Austrian resistance crumbled, and on 27 June Leghorn fell. Nelson was delayed by light winds and Fremantle in the *Inconstant* managed the evacuation.[121] Hundreds of English citizens were transported to San Fiorenzo Bay in Corsica, 'distressed . . . some without a change of linen'.[122] From 2 July, Nelson put Leghorn under a tight blockade, as ordered by Jervis.[123] From the tone of Nelson's letters to Fanny, he was enjoying himself. 'Not a boat gets in or out or an inhabitant gets a dish of fish without coming on board to get a pass to fish for it.'[124] To Collingwood he wrote: 'This blockade is compleat, and we lay very snug in the north road as smooth as in a harbour.'[125]

---

* The Navy Board still insisted on the time-honoured practice of individual captains 'purchasing and vouching for, the Stores they are in want of' and that ordering on a fleet-wide basis by the admiral was unauthorized and would be charged to him personally (NMM, CRK/11/57, 11 May 1796, Jervis to Nelson). Jervis's contempt for the Navy Board, which came to a dramatic head when he was first lord of the Admiralty (1801–4), pre-dated his Mediterranean command, but these restrictions cannot have helped his relations with the administrators.

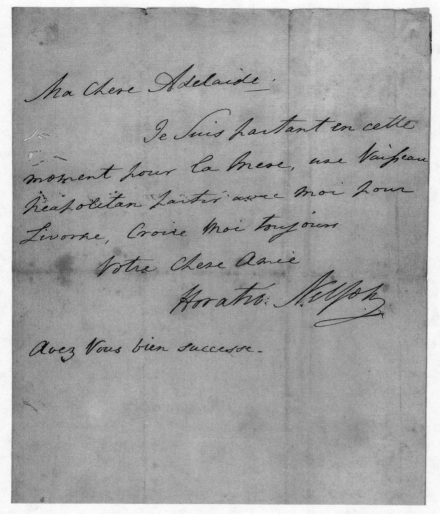

Draft of a note to Adeladie Correglia

Nevertheless, the evacuation of Leghorn brought to an end ships' maintenance and support, and disrupted both the intelligence network based there and the city's social life. Though the French were not far away, Fremantle's diary records on 16 June that he 'went to Pisa Baths, called on Adelaide who was quite recovered and looked well.' On 20 June, Thomas Pollard paid Adelaide £20 on Nelson's account.[126] On 25 June, aboard his ship the *Inconstant* just before the evacuation of Leghorn, Fremantle recorded that 'Adelaide came off in the evening.'[127] The ships carrying the English community sailed for Bastia. What happened afterwards to Adelaide is something of a mystery. In a letter of 13 July, Jervis wrote to Nelson: 'My compliments to la Belle Adelaide,' indicating that she had met the commander-in-chief. At some time in that month John Udney wrote to Nelson from Bastia and finished his letter: 'Compliments to your Passengere'; and in a letter five days later he wrote, 'It will then give me the sincerest saŦisfaction to obey your commands or that of your friend.'[128] In yet another letter from the same period, this time undated, but after the French occupation of the city, Udney sent a letter to Nelson at Leghorn, which is readdressed to 'Signora Adelaide Corellia, en Casa Carlo Turbato a Bagnio di Pisa'.[129] It is unlikely that he was there.

Nelson now threw his energies into planning the retaking of Leghorn, conceiving a combined operation and persuading Elliot of its feasibility. Elliot replied to Nelson on 30 July: 'I confess my mouth waters in being instrumental in driving the French out of Leghorn' and wrote ten days later to say that he had 'taken the necessary measure of having 3,500 [soldiers] embarked at Bastia to be employed in driving the French out of Leghorn'.[130] In a long letter to Jervis on 2 August from Leghorn Roads, Nelson painted a vivid picture of the situation in the city, since he had 'last night much conversation with an old fisherman . . . The people of Leghorn will not be put off any longer than the 10th or 15th. The French must go . . . these people represent them as a miscreant set of Boys without Cloaths or Shoes.'[131] His enthusiasm at full stretch, he proposed to Elliot that he should command both army and naval forces; after all, he was now a colonel of marines. Elliot swiftly discouraged the idea, as he could see the trouble that this would cause with the army: 'What you mention would blow us all up.'[132] Besides, the optimism created by a French reverse at the Siege of Mantua was soon lost by lack of further Austrian military success, and the plan was abandoned. By late August, Nelson had certainly been parted from Adelaide. On 21 August, Joseph Brame in Genoa wrote to him: 'Your message to Sig. Adelaide was immediately sent and any answers I may receive shall go herewith'; the next day the consul repeated the following message to Nelson: 'Your letter of 19th received: the enclosed for Sign. Adelaide was immediately sent & presume Capt. Sawyer will bring the answer.'[133] There remains only one very short, undated draft of a letter to Adelaide in clumsy French in Nelson's hand: 'Ma chere Adelaide, Je Suis partant en cette moment pour la Mere, une Vaisseau Neapolitan partir avec moi pour Livorne, Croire Moi toujours Votre Chere Amie, Horatio Nelson. Avez Vous bien successe.'[134]

We know that Adelaide had been on board the *Agamemnon* for a period. It was not unusual for women to be aboard ships in the Mediterranean fleet, especially after the evacuation of Leghorn. Some waggish advice to Nelson came from Jervis at the time: 'The factory will find themselves very happy under your protection, and all our fair countrywomen pent up in Italy will fly into your embraces.' In the same letter Jervis refers to a Mrs Newnham, obviously a lady with a reputation, 'but she must expect nothing more from me than Board & single lodging.'[135] Among the evacuees was Mrs Pollard, wife of Thomas Pollard, as well as the Wynne family, elderly parents and two daughters, Eugenia and Betsey. They came aboard Fremantle's *Inconstant* at the same time as Adelaide was on the *Agamemnon*. The Wynnes were comparatively rich, respectable and refugees, but it is unclear why they stayed so long and why Sir John Jervis did not pack them off to Gibraltar on the next convoy; he even encouraged the match between the poor, though well connected Fremantle and Betsey. She was to live on board a succession of British warships for fifteen months, marrying Fremantle in Naples in early 1797. How does this square with Jervis's biographer's description of his aversion to naval officers marrying? 'He said they were the first to run to port, and the last to come out of it.'[136] Yet Jervis did not object to Adelaide, and he liked the company of women. When Betsey Wynne and the rest of her family went to dine with him, 'the Admiral was on deck to receive us with the greatest civility and kindness, nothing stiff or formal about him . . . He desired we should pay tribute that was due to him at our entering his Cabin, this was to kiss him which the ladies did very willingly.'[137]

Whatever the number and identity of women on Nelson's quarterdeck, there were women forward with the crew. On board the *Captain*, half a dozen women and three children lived forward of the mast; they belonged, according to the muster book, to 'the Soldiers serving as Marines'.[138] Among his brother officers Nelson had a reputation for, at the least, a soft heart. Colonel Villettes, whom Nelson had met in Corsica, wrote to him on behalf of another army officer, Captain Alexander Sanderson of the 69th Regiment: 'he had brought a very pretty wife with him, I know he will be very thankful for your indulgence to come on shore when he is not particularly wanted and from what I heard you say on the subject, I suspect it will not be very difficult to obtain it from you.'[139] Another soldier, General de Burgh, teased Nelson: 'Your merits are pretty generally known, your deficiencies are I believe much less so; amongst the few that have ever come to my knowledge, hard-heartedness towards the fair sex is not included.'[140] From this scant evidence it seems that Nelson relished his independence from Fanny. Two years later, after the Battle of the Nile, Jervis was to write: 'Pray do not let your fascinating Neapolitan dames approach too near him, for he is made of flesh & blood & cannot resist their temptation.'[141] Jervis's correspondent was Emma Hamilton.

Another woman who was important to Nelson at this time was Frances Caffarena at Genoa, whose family supplied British ships with live cattle and lemons. Part of the merchant intelligence network, she wrote him a long series of fluent and amusing letters throughout most of 1796, and also provided him with translations of various Italian documents.* After the French had taken Leghorn in late June 1796, and the British ministers and consuls in northern Italy had fled, she was almost the only source of information ashore. Caffarena, an English woman married into a merchant family, was the mother of thirteen children and knew the business of the authorities in Genoa. She reported some lively exchanges with the Jacobins in the city, telling one of them to inform the French consul that 'I was an Englishwoman, that all my riches consisted in that title, nor would I change for all the Contributions his Army had gain'd.' She was extraordinarily well informed, being the first to tell Nelson about Spanish preparations for war in a letter of 30 July 1796: 'By a private letter from Cadiz to a friend of mine, they have fresh orders come to refit their fleet again for sea & orders for making every preparation by land,' news that was later confirmed by London. Remarkably, in the same letter she gives news of the war from the West Indies, Surinam, Sweden and Finland.[142] Nelson forwarded all of Frances Caffarena's letters to both Elliot and Jervis.† Jervis replied that 'Madame Caffarena is a charming correspondent and appears to possess a true English heart.'[143] Her business suffered badly when the French became dominant in Genoa, and her later letters to Nelson were full of news of financial distress and illness, but they were still informative and beautifully written.[144] It was to Frances Caffarena that Nelson was referring when he wrote to Gilbert Elliot in August that 'one old lady tells us all she hears, which is what we wish.'[145]

The occupation of Leghorn, less than seventy sea miles from Bastia, immediately gave the French a nearby port from which to attack Corsica,

---

* The Caffarena family was not well capitalized. One of the agent victuallers reported that her sons 'find much inconvenience in being four weeks out of £600 sterling' (NMM, CRK/6/153, 15 Aug. 1796, David Heatley to Nelson).

† Lady Jervis asked her husband to purchase some fine velvet from Genoa, a request that he passed on to Nelson, suggesting that Frances Caffarena's advice should be sought, but Nelson was unable to fulfil this errand (Naish, 338, 5 Sept. 1796; NMM, PAR/251 [n.d.], Nelson to Jervis).

even though the city was now blockaded by British warships. Jervis privately doubted the effectiveness of the British blockade.[146] To counter an invasion of Corsica, Elliot sent orders that British forces should occupy Porto Ferrajo on the island of Elba. Soldiers at Bastia were speedily gathered together in a convoy under the command of Thomas Fremantle in the *Inconstant*. According to that astute observer, Betsey Wynne, soon to marry Fremantle and now aboard his ship, he was 'quite in a fever as the success of this enterprise depends on him'. Off Porto Ferrajo, 'Commodore Nelson having joined us now has been a great relief to Capt. Fremantle.'[147] Fremantle noted the same day: 'The Soldiers very undetermined and very jealous of us.'[148] Nelson's authority had swept any friction away and his relationship with Major John Duncan, the commanding officer, was amicable, resulting in a well-organized operation. Although the inhabitants of Elba were friendly, sensible precautions were taken: 'during the time when I was necessarily employed on shore ... my First Lieutenant, Edward Berry, commanded the Ship, and placed her opposite the grand bastion, within half-pistol shot; and in such a manner as could not have failed, had we opened our fire, to produce the greatest effect.'[149] Doubtless the two 68-pound carronades were also loaded.

The occupation of Porto Ferrajo was useful to the British forces, but the allies were still very much on the defensive. France dominated the whole of the Riviera coast: the Republic of Genoa was nominally neutral, but was in no position to resist French political pressure. Nelson returned to blockading Leghorn and harrying the French Army by raids on shore, where it was well established.[150] The blockade was hurting Leghorn's trade, and the French were very soon unpopular. The problem remained of evacuating English merchants from Genoa.[151] Nelson's time, however, was mostly taken up by complex negotiations with the Genoese authorities over neutral shipping and prizes. In spite of his protests, the French brought in stores and reinforcements, and its army moved into Genoa. Correspondence became heated, particularly when Nelson's honour as an officer was called into question.[152] Occasionally neutrality was breached. Three of the crew tried to desert at Genoa, and Nelson sent in the barge and pinnace in pursuit by night; for good measure they brought out a French transport laden with ordnance stores.[153]

All intelligence sources now pointed to an invasion of Corsica from Leghorn. Jervis wrote from Toulon that not only did Madame Caffarena report this, but that 'we hear of nothing but the intended Descent in Corsica; Lord Bute, Mr Jackson and our spies assure us that it is to take place from Leghorn in small feluccas.'[154] From London there came increasingly reliable information that Spain was about to enter the war as an ally of the French. What no one in the Mediterranean knew yet was that the cabinet in London had decided to evacuate the Mediterranean: on 31 August 1796 the Board of Admiralty signed the order to evacuate British forces from Corsica to Gibraltar.[155] The order did not reach Jervis until 25 September, but from mid August he was already bringing his dispersed fleet together off Toulon in case he was caught by the combined fleets of Spain and France, or, as he wrote to Elliot, 'in case Langara and Rickery may attempt to cut me up'.[156] Events began to move fast. Nelson quickly secured another dangerously situated island, Capraia, anticipating a French occupation. He landed troops there on 18 September, without opposition. At this awkward point, the *Captain*'s foremast needed replacing. Fortunately, Nelson had just received the news that he was now offically a commodore, which meant that he had a captain under him.[157] So, with Captain Charles Stuart in command, the ship departed for Ajaccio on 27 September to have the new mast fitted, while on the same day Nelson transferred to the 64-gun *Diadem*, commanded by Captain Henry Towry, for just under three weeks, taking only James Noble, his flag lieutenant, and his servant, James Lenstock, with him.[158]

As predicted by intelligence, a small French expedition transported from Leghorn in feluccas evaded British warships and landed in Corsica on 19 October. Gathering support, the growing anti-British force arrived out-side Bastia on 21 October.[159] The evacuation of British forces from Corsica was now urgent. Nelson was well prepared for the embarkation of troops; under instructions from Gilbert Elliot in July, he had made plans for it in advance.[160] In the face of fractious but determined Corsicans in Bastia, but with the guns of five warships backing him up, Nelson opened negotiations and acted decisively. He quickly took Elliot and his baggage on board the *Diadem*, then landed troops, who occupied Elliot's house, from which the embarkation point could be defended. Under duress the Corsicans agreed to an ordered evacuation of those who wished to depart, together with their property. 'Our sailors had plenty of opportunities of displaying their gallantry; for it was not uncommon to see two or three of our ship's crew marching along with a female under each arm, convoying them safely to the place of embarkation.'[161] Boats transported people and goods from shore to ship night and day. Lieutenant William Day, the agent for trans-ports, received particular praise in Nelson's report to Jervis, and relations with the army were cordial. Even some army guns were rescued, although, as Nelson wrote to Fanny, 'the Army said it could not be done, and I was absolutely the last man who quitted.'[162]

Thus Porto Ferrajo on Elba was left as the only base occupied by English forces in the Mediterranean. Nelson escorted the transports there briefly, landing troops and ordnance, and then sailed to San Fiorenzo Bay to join Jervis and the rest of the squadron. The remaining troops were evacuated from Corsica on 23 October; as the last boats left the shore, the tower of Fornali, which had proved so difficult to take two and half years before, was blown up by Samuel Hood of the *Zealous*. By now the town of San Fiorenzo was surrounded by 4,000 hostile troops and irregulars, who fired sporadically from the shore as they left. It was an ignominious, if efficient, exit. On 3 November the squadron and convoy sailed for Gibraltar, passing Minorca, and then south along the Barbary shore, away from the Spanish coast. 'Bad weather and foul winds' resulted in a month-long voyage.[163]

Pitt's government was under pressure from the lack of success of its Continental allies, the armed landings in north-west France having come to nothing. Divisions within the government arose over the question of where to concentrate the effort. Henry Dundas, secretary of war, was the consistent proponent of action in the West Indies. Lord Spencer favoured a cautious plan of bringing ships back to the western approaches, for the fear of a French invasion was beginning to take root. With French gains in Italy nullifying local British naval superiority and no operational base east of Gibraltar, massive reinforcements would have been needed to maintain any sort of hold in the Western Mediterranean. The moment that Spain signed its offensive alliance with France, Gibraltar itself was under threat; the Admiralty order to Jervis to evacuate Corsica was signed only days after it did so.[164] At that point, unexpectedly, the Austrians were victorious in Germany. Even so, Pitt's government was short of money and looking for peace, and it was not only divided but vacillating. Disagreement, in particular between Dundas and Spencer, resulted in the reversal of the policy to evacuate Corsica, and on 19 October the cabinet countermanded the evacuation order, intending to offer Corsica to the Empress Catherine of Russia.[165] However, the order took time to reach the Mediterranean. As Jervis wrote to Spencer, it was, however, 'a great blessing that the evacuation of Corsica had taken place before I received the orders to maintain the Viceroy in the sovereignty of it.'[166] Once the French had overrun Italy and Naples had made peace, any further British naval effort in the Western Mediterranean would have been wasted. From the vantage point of Francis Drake, the English minister in Genoa (though at this time in Venice), the withdrawal seemed logical. He wrote to Nelson: 'I am persuaded that, situated as Italy is, we have nothing more to do here and that our fine Fleet may be more usefully employed elsewhere . . . Naples . . . and none of the other Maritime States of Italy either deserve or have Energy enough to avail themselves of our Protection.'[167]

Jervis, however, was mortified by the retreat. He knew the low level of competence of the Spanish Navy: if it had not been for Admiral Man's unaccountable action in taking his ships back to Spithead instead of reinforcing him, Jervis was sure of being able to deal the Spanish fleet a blow. 'I cannot describe to your Lordship', he wrote to Spencer, 'the disappointment my ambition and zeal to serve my country have suffered by this diminution of force . . . I have every reason to believe the Spanish fleet would have been cut to pieces; the extreme disorder and confusion they were observed to be in by the judicious officers who fell in with them leaving no doubt in my mind that a fleet so trained and generally well commanded as this is would have made its way through them in every direction.'[168] He had heard that his protégé Richard Bowen had captured a Spanish frigate of equal rate; there had been carnage on board the Spanish ship, while Bowen had not lost a man.[169] Nelson wrote to William Hamilton in Naples: 'To say I am grieved and distressed but ill describes my feelings on the receipt of the positive order for the evacuation of the Mediterranean.'[170] By the end of 1796, just at the point of evacuating the Mediterranean, confidence in the fleet was high. The men were at their peak with regard to training and efficiency, and in good health; Nelson noted that the fleet had been to sea for twenty-two weeks and was 'remarkably healthy'.[171] Assembled here were the next generation who were to achieve so much: Nelson, Collingwood, Troubridge, Berry, Hardy and Foley among many others. 'You have established so good a school for young officers,' wrote Lord Spencer to Jervis, 'that if a lad has anything in him, it must come out.'[172] Nelson put it more vividly to Fanny: 'his fleet is capable of performing anything and everything . . . I lament in sackcloth and ashes our present orders, so dishonourable to the dignity of England, whose fleets are equal to meet the world in arms, and of all fleets I ever saw I never saw one equal in point of officers and men to our present one, and with a Commander-in-Chief fit to lead them to glory.'[173]

Jervis reached Gibraltar on 1 December, but disastrous weather struck immediately. The *Courageux* (74) parted her anchors and was wrecked on the North African shore, with great loss of life.* Jervis took his fleet round

---

* The *Courageux* dragged her anchor when her captain, Benjamin Hallowell, was ashore attending a court martial. She drifted south, under the command of an incompetent and panic-stricken lieutenant, and was wrecked under the mountainous cliffs of the North African coast. Of her crew, 129 out of 593 were saved (Corbett, *Spencer Papers*. II, 78–80, 19 Dec. 1796, Jervis to Spencer).

to Lisbon for shelter. Three days later he again had to write to Spencer, this time to inform him of the *Bombay Castle* being lost on a sandbank going into the Tagus for shelter. The last weeks of 1796 were bitter. 'In any event,' Jervis had written to Nelson not long before, 'I am fortified in Lord Anson's motto, Nil Desperandum.'[174]

Nelson's first experience of independent command fell into two starkly contrasting periods. Under Hotham and Hyde Parker impetus had been lost, and even Nelson's aggressive spirit had relaxed on occasion. Jervis later claimed that the attractions of Leghorn blunted the resolve of the British fleet in 1794 and 1795. 'In truth, the war might have been carried into the enemy's country . . .', he wrote to Lord Spencer, 'but the miserable crapule [debauch] which occupied the minds of the chief and another flag officer, whose character is mistaken, occasioned these dire effects.'[175] The arrival of Jervis changed Nelson's career, though he did not slavishly copy the older officer. Discipline under Jervis was much more severe than under Nelson, who, by contrast, treated his officers in a frank and friendly manner. His relationship with Jervis was not as close as that with his other two patrons, Locker and Hood, but rested on respect. Jervis learnt that he could not do without Nelson, a situation that Nelson exploited to the full when pushing for promotion.

Recognition and praise had come from all quarters, and Nelson's letters during the autumn of 1796 richly reflect a new level of confidence and achievement. 'I am very happy to learn that Captain Nelson whose zeal, activity and enterprise cannot be surpassed, stands so high in your good opinion,' Jervis wrote to John Trevor in February 1796. 'I have only to lament the want of means to give him the Command of a squadron equal to his merit.'[176] Nelson visited the doge of Genoa for the second time on the question of neutral trade in September. He related to Fanny: 'The Doge was very curious about me. He asked my age, said he had heard much of me, that the blockade of Leghorn was strict beyond what he could have thought possible, at the same time publicly thanked me for my goodness on many occasions to Genoese vessels. It has hitherto been my good fortune to have combined the strictest rigor of my duty with gaining the goodwill of the parties interested. My conduct has been open: this has been my secret and it has answered.'[177] 'My character never stood higher than at this moment.'[178] In another letter: 'Sir John Jervis honours me with his confidence,' relating with pride that Jervis 'told Lord Spencer that the evacuation of Bastia was due to the firmness of conduct in Commodore Nelson'.[179]

Now that he had achieved promotion and reputation, there is no doubt that he was looking forward to some leave. His health had held up, but he was tired.[180] In September he suggested that he would be home by Christmas. In November he wrote to Fanny: 'This day I saw in reading a newspaper your name and my good father's as arrived at Bath. It is impossible to express what I felt at only seeing it and I trust the time will come when I shall see you there myself.'[181] Further exploits were to occur before that wish could be fulfilled.

13

La Minerve and the *Blanche* to Porto Ferrajo
December 1796–February 1797

. . . an arduous and most important mission.[1]
Nelson to Fanny, 9 December 1796

'Cockburn is in raptures in his *Minerve*,' ran a postscript in one of Jervis's letters to Nelson in August 1796.[2] By placing the ambitious and talented young captain in the fastest and most powerful French prize taken in the Mediterranean, the commander-in-chief had created a crack ship. *La Minerve*, a large frigate of thirty-eight guns, was thus the natural choice for one of the final tasks before the British Navy abandoned the Mediterranean: to bring out the last of the troops and naval stores from the Corsican operations, left behind on the island of Elba. 'The evacuation of Porto Ferrajo both in respect to time & manner I have left entirely to the judgement of Commodore Nelson and it cannot be in better hands,' Jervis wrote from Gibraltar on 10 December to Gilbert Elliot, who was at Naples, in a letter that Nelson took with him. Jervis was not confident that Thomas Fremantle, who was still in Elba in command of the squadron, could effect an efficient withdrawal, since other frigate captains there were senior to him.[3] He was particularly concerned about the military commander, General de Burgh. Jervis had written to Elliot: 'I entertain the highest opinion of the honour and integrity of General de Burgh, but inexperienced as he is in the business of such a complicated nature, diffident and doubtful, where prompt decision is requisite, I dread the moment of your final departure.' Nelson's 'firmness and ability will very soon combine and fix all of the parts of our force Naval and Military'.[4]

Nelson hoisted his broad pennant in *La Minerve* only ten days after reaching Gibraltar. She set off to Elba on 15 December in company with the 32-gun frigate *Blanche*. The smaller ship had been in Nelson's squadron since March 1796, but her crew had recently experienced the unsettling and unusual matter of having her captain, Charles Sawyer, court-martialled for homosexuality – 'having a fondness for young men and boys', in the words of Jacob Nagle, a seaman in the *Blanche*.[5] The court martial found that Sawyer had been found in bed with his coxswain several times; two midshipmen and a seaman were also involved.[6] This homosexuality had become known in the ship, the coxswain having denounced the captain publicly. The facts went beyond the ship as a result of a quarrel between the captain and his first lieutenant in the last rush of the evacuation from Corsica: at one point Sawyer ordered seven officers, including all the lieutenants, to be confined. Nelson and George Cockburn, the senior frigate captain, acted fast. Nelson told Jervis that 'the Captain [is] certainly not fit, in his present state of mind, to command that ship. I spoke to him fully, but he never once said "I am an innocent man." '[7] Sawyer was dismissed the service by the court martial on 10 October 1796. The case shocked many, but none more than Jervis, who had made Sawyer a post-captain in the West Indies in 1794: 'my consternation and indignation may therefore be more readily guessed, than described,' he wrote to Nelson.[8] Jervis immediately put the *Blanche* under the temporary captaincy of D'Arcy Preston, his nephew, and selected her for the voyage to Porto Ferrajo. Henry Hotham, the present captain of the *Dido*, a nephew of Admiral Hotham, had been appointed by the Admiralty to the *Blanche*. In Eugenia Wynne's opinion, Hotham was 'a handsome and a very young man'.[9] Jervis had misgivings: 'I rather incline to wish Hotham would stick to the *Dido*. Preston is a married, grave man, with a family of children, and will feel the less in consequence.'[10]

The voyage to Elba was chronicled in detail by Jacob Nagle. 'Sailing a long the Spanish shore we fell in with a Spanish coaster running a long shore. We brought her two and boarded hur. She was loaded with bales of silk, but over hauling hur log book we found there was two Spanish frigates crusing off Cathergreen [Cartagena]. Nelson ordered 7 bails of silk to be hoisted out of hur for a drink for the sailors and let hur go.'[11] Nelson had no time to put a prize crew aboard, but taking a part of the cargo, rather than observing the legalities of the prize-money system, was done more often than was admitted in the Admiralty. In these cases prize cargo would be sold informally and would never go near the prize courts. When shared, the money did not amount to a great deal, but such seizures boosted morale. Nelson and Cockburn would have taken care to have secured the agreement of all the other officers and the crew: legally a prize was as much their property as it was the commanding officer's.

The two Spanish frigates were soon sighted off Cape de Gata, and the ships closed as night fell. The action started at midnight. Cockburn's terse entry in *La Minerve*'s log summarizes the one-sided contest with the larger of the two, the *Sabina*:

Commenced action by firing a broadside into her. *Blanche* engaged the other. Mizzen mast of Spanish frigate fell. 20 past one [she] struck. Sent 1st Lieutenant to take possession of her. Her captain on board & gave up his sword. *Santa Sabina* 40 guns, 20 18 lbers, 286 men, took her in tow. Another Spanish frigate comes up and fires a broadside into her. Proves to be 2 line of battleships & a frigate.[12]

The Spanish ships were outmanoeuvred and outgunned. Cockburn's skilful handling of the ship brought his guns to bear so accurately that the *Sabina* was overwhelmed. She lost all her masts. Spanish casualties were exaggerated by Nelson, who claimed that 164 were killed, including all her officers except the commodore, Jacobo Stuart, a descendant of the duke of Berwick, son of James II, a claim that was repeated in the *London Gazette*.[13] More reliable is a source from Cartagena in the Admiralty papers that quotes fourteen Spanish killed and two officers and forty-odd wounded: 'her fire, the Spaniards say, was a perfect hell.' The main Spanish authority gives an even lower figure.[14] *La Minerve* had seven men killed and thirty-four wounded.[15] The smaller Spanish ship was similarly overwhelmed. 'In the *Blanche* we were not idel,' Nagle relates. 'We run as close alongside as we could without running on board of hur and gave hur a broadside fore and aft. We played so hot upon them, they run from there quarters ... Hur topsails and colours all came down by the run. When they did fire there guns they ware in such haste that there shot all went over us.'[16] Her captain, D'Arcy Preston, reported to Nelson that 'the Enemy made a trifling resistance and Eight or Nine broadsides completely silenced her.'[17] Both British ships were at their peak of discipline and training, but the two contests demonstrate vividly the weakness of the quality and quantity of Spanish seamen in the 1790s. From early in the decade the low state of the Spanish government's finances had undermined the marine registry to the point of collapse; the navy built fine ships and many of them, but it did not have the means to man them effectively.[18] Not until 1800 did the Spanish Navy take control of the marine registry by which warships were manned.

La Minerve put Lieutenants John Culverhouse and Thomas Masterman Hardy aboard the *Sabina*, with thirty men, and took her in tow. The Spanish commodore was taken on board *La Minerve*. At daybreak the next morning yet another Spanish frigate came up, and a further contest took place. After half an hour this Spanish frigate retreated, but then four more ships, which could only have been Spanish, were seen on the horizon. When near enough, they were identified as two ships of the line and a further two frigates. *La Minerve* was heavily outnumbered. Nagle on the *Blanche* noted of the Spanish ships: 'They all stood for Nelson. He, having the frigate in tow and seeing the 74 close on board, cut and run, at the same time gave the seventy four a broadside and the 30 men on board the prize gave hur a broad side and then struck. When taking possession they all gave chace after Nelson.' With the prize, two lieutenants and the prize crew all abandoned, *La Minerve* ran towards the African shore, her crew hard at work on her damaged rigging. The *Blanche* then found herself among a Spanish convoy and managed to escape. But she had to ignore signals from *La Minerve*, for she was surrounded by Spanish ships. '[We] dare not answer them,' noted Nagle, and then added admiringly, 'Nelson out run them all excepting one small frigate that could come up with him, but he got two long 18 pounders out of the gun room ports and two out of the cabin windows and two on the quarter deck, which was 6 long eighteens. When she would come about half gun shot, he would bore hur fore and aft. She would then drop a stern.' Even when Nelson retreated, he did it in style. Still with a southerly course, the Spanish ships were only three miles astern, but by six in the evening, with more damage repaired, *La Minerve* finally lost her pursuers. Sailing round the south of Sardinia, she reached Porto Ferrajo on 27 December 1796, three days before the *Blanche*.

At the end of this eventful week, Nelson displayed early signs of the leadership that was to become legendary. To Cockburn's masterly handling of his ship he gave full credit in his reports and also later generously presented him with a gold-hilted sword.[19] A more individual and significant gesture was made towards the crew of the *Blanche*. When she came to anchor, according to Nagle, 'Nelson came on board and ordered the capt[ain] to beat to quarters, and as we ware in a line before our guns, he came round the decks and shook hands with us as he went along and telling us he was rejoiced to find that we had escaped.'[20] Nelson was at pains to nurture a crew that was recovering from a notorious captain, but for a commodore to symbolize his relationship with the lower deck in this way was indeed remarkable. A greater contrast with the style and traditions of the Channel fleet, where in four months' time the great mutinies of Spithead and the Nore were to take place, cannot be imagined.

Nelson was to stay at Porto Ferrajo for a month, forced to delay by negotiations with the army commander, who had no orders to retreat to Gibraltar. Curiously, despite this being an evacuation, the army immediately put on a ball for 300 people at the theatre. Nelson reported to his brother that 'it was ball night, and being attended by the Captains, was received in due form by the General, and one particular tune was played: the second was "Rule Britannia".'[21] Eugenia and Betsey Wynne, still living on board Fremantle's *Inconstant*, were escorted by Nelson, Cockburn and Fremantle. 'We had to trot about in the dirt before we would arrive there,' Eugenia recorded, but the theatre 'was very prettily decorated. General de Burgh received us with great civility, we danced a great deal and amused ourselves very much.'[22] Dancing continued until three in the morning.

It is possible that Adelaide Correglia was also at Porto Ferrajo, although we know this only from a shred of later evidence and have no proof that she and Nelson met. This evidence comes in a letter George Cockburn wrote to Nelson in July 1797, after the final foray into the Mediterranean. He hoped that Nelson had again visited Porto Ferrajo, though 'not solely on account of Blue Skin for I should wish to have heard some news of your little Adelaide & all our other Italian friends'.[23] 'Blue Skin' was slang for any 'person begotten on a black woman by a white man'; no one knows who she was, but Cockburn looked back on this time and company with affectionate nostalgia.

A dozen ships of the squadron were anchored at Porto Ferrajo, as well as transports. Nelson first dispatched the *Inconstant* to Naples to fetch Sir Gilbert Elliot, in order to take him home via Gibraltar. The Wynnes travelled on the ship, with Betsey Wynne returning as Betsey Fremantle. Thomas Fremantle's hesitations had finally been overcome, and he married Betsey in Naples in a ceremony arranged by Lady Hamilton.[24] Stores and provisions needed to be collected and put on board the ships. *La Minerve*'s mainmast and mizzenmast had to be replaced. Nelson held several courts martial. The first two were of officers of the *Dromedary* store ship, including one for embezzlement and one for drunkenness on the captain's part. Captain Isaac Coffin, in command of the dockyard at Ajaccio, wrote of the 'constant state of intoxication Captain Harrison has appeared to me to be in for these last six months'.[25] Harrison was dismissed his ship.[26] On 30 December, Nelson and his officers condemned a seaman from the *Speedy* to death 'for frequent desertion and attempting to desert from the said sloop at Naples'.[27] Over ten years before, when senior naval officer in the Leeward Islands, Nelson had condemned William Clark and then pardoned him. He acted similarly in this case. Nelson wrote to Jervis that the seaman 'is a proper object for an example, for the Desertion of the present day from the Navy is too fast, but on the side of Mercy which I will know well your inclination [to be] . . . perhaps a Respite to this Wretch may have a proper effect, on the consideration of the gallant conduct of those Seamen who have

Agamemnon and *Captain*
July 1795 – September 1796

1796: Mar
Apr
May
Genoa
Savona
Port Especia
Loane
Alassio   Vado Bay
Oneglia   Cap Noli
Port Maurice   Feb 1796
San Remo   Aug – Sept 1795
Monaco   July 1795
Villefranche   Cap delle Mele
Nice   Leghorn 1795: Sept
May 1796   Oct
British blockade   1796: Jan
Cap garoupe   June 1796   July – Sep 1796   Mar
Gulf of Frejus
Oct – Nov 1795   Porto Ferrarjo
Toulon   July 1796
Isle du Levant   San Fiorenzo Bay   Capraia
Isle Portcros   1796: Jan   ELBA
Cap Sicié   Porquerolles   Apr
Nov 1795   June   San   Bastia
Feb – Mar 1796   Fiorenzo
Calvi

CORSICA

Ajaccio

Agamemnon, Captain and *La Minerve*
Western Mediterranean
July 1795 – May 1797

⟵—————— *Captain* escorting convoy, San Fiorenzo to Gibraltar Nov 1796
⟵·—·—·— *La Minerve* Gibraltar, Porto Ferrajo and back Dec 1796 – Feb 1797
⟵- - - - - *Captain* meeting the returning Porto Ferrajo convoy Apr – May 1797

IBIZA

Cartagena

SPAIN

To Cape St Vincent

Gibraltar   *La Minerve* Dec 1796

Captain Nov 1796

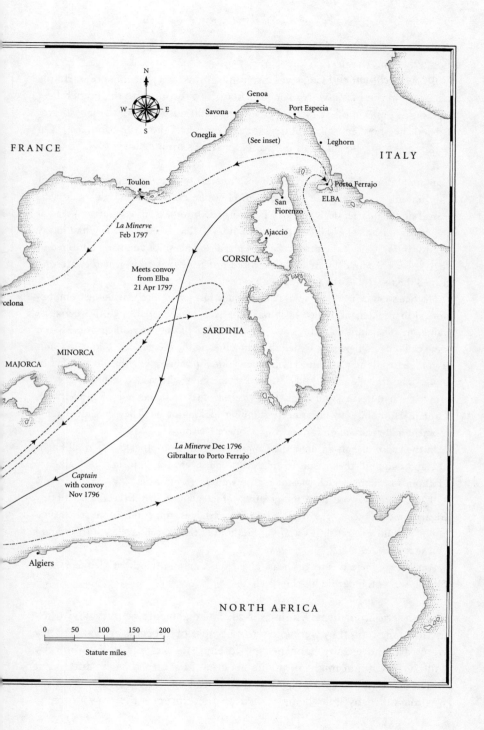

N

W   E

S

FRANCE

Genoa

Savona

Port Especia

Oneglia

(See inset)

Leghorn

ITALY

Toulon

Porto Ferrajo

La Minerve
Feb 1797

San
Fiorenzo

ELBA

Ajaccio

Meets convoy
from Elba
21 Apr 1797

CORSICA

celona

SARDINIA

MINORCA

MAJORCA

La Minerve Dec 1796
Gibraltar to Porto Ferrajo

Captain
with convoy
Nov 1796

Algiers

NORTH AFRICA

0   50   100   150   200

Statute miles

remained faithful to their King and Country.'[28] Some other seamen were flogged round the fleet.[29]

Of all the disruptions to naval discipline at this time, the most remarkable occurred in the *Blanche*. Nelson sent her off to reconnoitre the French fleet at Toulon, and she left Porto Ferrajo on 1 January 1797.[30] When she returned, her new captain, Henry Hotham, was to take over command. On 7 January 1797 he came on board. Nagle takes up the story:

Captain Hothom bearing the name of such a tartar by his own ships crew, that our ship mutinised and entirely refused him. He came on board, had all the officers armed on the quarter deck and all hands turned aft to hear his commission read at the capstan head. They all cried out, 'No, no, no'. He asked what they had to say against [him]. One of the petty officers replyed that his ships company informed us that he was a dam'd tartar and we would not have him and went forward and turned the two forecastle guns aft with canester shot.

He then went in his boat on board the commedore and returned with the Com[modore's] first leutenant. When on b[oar]d he [Lieutenant Charles Gill] ordered all hands aft. The ships company came aft. He called all the petty officers out, which were call'd by name, and pareded them in a line on the quaterdeck. 'Now, my lads, if you resist taking Capt[ain] Hothom as your capt[ain], every third man shall be hung.' The crew flew in a body forward to the guns with match in hand, likewise crowbars, handspikes, and all kinds of weapons they could get holt of and left him, Captain Hothom, and the officers standing looking at us. They consulted for a moment and returned on b[oar]d Commedere Nelson.

In the space of half an hour the Commedore came on b[oar]d, call'd all hands aft, and enquired the reason of this disturbance. He was inform'd of Capt[ain] Hothom's caractor, which was the reason we refused him.

'Lads,' said he, 'you have the greatest caracter on b[oard]d the *Blanch* of any frigates crew in the navy. You have taken two frigates supperiour to the frigate you are in, and now to rebel. If Capt[ain] Hothom ill treats you, give me a letter and I will support you.'

Amediately there was three chears given and Capt[ain] Hothom shed tears, and Nelson went on b[oard]d his ship.[31]

It was a serious incident. Mutinies in the late-eighteenth-century navy often involved the refusal by a crew to work because of a specific grievance. They were rare and usually happened on foreign stations, far from Admiralty control. A captain might persuade his crew to return to their duty, after which no action was taken against them.[32] But on this occasion the refusal was magnified by guns being turned on the officers – the crew probably making use of the carronades on the forecastle that were light and manoeuvrable.

The scene could not have been more dramatic. Porto Ferrajo is a small harbour where the surrounding hills form an amphitheatre; the crews of every one of the dozen ships in the harbour would have been watching intently. Nelson increased the tension by sending Lieutenant Gill on board to state what terrible retribution he could take against mutiny.* With timing of almost theatrical accuracy, Nelson then delayed coming on board the *Blanche* for half an hour, leaving time to sow doubt among the tense crew. His calmness and resolution shine through Nagle's account. His previous care with the crew now paid off. Yet he was taking a considerable risk in attempting to reach a compromise publicly in a highly charged situation: he had to rely on his sense that the personal trust that existed between him and the crew would overcome their collective anger. The situation was critical. Surrounded by hostile forces in the Mediterranean and a long way from higher authority, it would have been difficult to overpower a crew so obviously united. Very few officers of the time would have had the confidence to act as he did.[33] Not a word of the incident went back to London formally. Reputations, however, do not rest on official reports. It was the first sign in his career that he was an officer of extraordinary qualities.

Nelson's final task on Elba was to persuade the army to retreat with the squadron to Gibraltar, but General de Burgh had received no orders from Henry Dundas in London to leave the island, nor had Jervis's orders for him to withdraw, sent on 13 January by the *Hope* lugger, reached him.[34] William Wyndham, the minister from Florence, arrived to help, and Nelson also put his faith in Sir Gilbert Elliot being able to persuade the general to leave.[35] When Elliot arrived from Naples on 22 January in the *Inconstant*, Nelson and de Burgh sat down with him to make a final decision. Nelson made it clear to de Burgh when he arrived 'that this place is not to be kept on the consideration of its being any longer useful to His Majesty's Fleet ... I shall withdraw nearly all the supplies from this place whether the troops quit it or not, and reduce the Naval force here as much as possible.'[36] De Burgh could not be persuaded to leave; his orders, he wrote, 'were indisputably framed and issued, under circumstances very different from those of the present moment', although he would accept orders from Jervis as commander-in-chief of the Mediterranean.[37] Elliot, hoping to keep a

---

* Lieutenants Culverhouse and Hardy had been taken prisoner when the prize crew of the *Sabina* had been abandoned; Noble, Nelson's flag lieutenant, had been wounded in the action; this left the third lieutenant, Charles Gill, as the only lieutenant available.

British presence in the Mediterranean, declined to give him the order, hardly being in a position to do so as the viceroy of a dispossessed island.[38] Nelson wrote a delicately phrased letter to Lord Spencer, partly designed to cover himself in case of future trouble: 'the Army are not so often called upon to exercise their judgement in political measures as we are; therefore the General feels a certain diffidence.'[39]

Diplomats, soldiers and sailors could not decide who was in overall command, and an unsatisfactory compromise was agreed. The bulk of the stores and transports would go with Nelson, leaving a minimum naval force at Porto Ferrajo under Fremantle, enough to keep communications open with Tuscany and Naples.[40] In Gibraltar, Jervis was getting nervous, writing to General de Burgh in mid February, assuming that his January orders had reached him: 'every hour's delay increases the difficulty of your retiring down the Mediterranean ... I shall not be able to give you the protection I wish, and the elements will be less in your favour as the days lengthen, and the strong Levant Winds cease to blow.'[41]

The night before Nelson left for Gibraltar a final party was given by a convivial Cornish captain, Bartholomew James, on board his ship the *Dolphin*. It was James's birthday, and he noted in his journal: 'Gave a dinner for Commodore Nelson and the captains and the field officers of the army. Did not break up until 2 in the morning.' Not all the captains were there – Hotham, for instance, was absent – but they included: Cockburn (*La Minerve*, 38), Fremantle (*Inconstant*, 36), the younger James Macnamara (*Southampton*, 32), John Giffard (*Mignonne*, 32), Thomas Elphinstone (*Speedy*, 14), Philip Wodehouse, just made post-captain and at this point without a ship, and Isaac Coffin, who had been commissioner of the dock-yard at Ajaccio.[42] James was well known for eccentric festivity. In 1789 in the West Indies he had founded a dining society of thirty-one members called the Order of Marlborough, of which James was the grand master, or 'Sovereign', and the members were 'knights'. The society even had ribbons and stars and a special uniform.[43] In his old age James used to say that he was the first to knight Nelson, and it was on this particular evening that Nelson was initiated into the society as a 'knight'. There was much drink and noise. Betsey Fremantle observed good-humouredly: 'Colonel Drinkwater, Mr Hardman the Commissioner, and Captain Cockburn at the head of a rioting party of all the other captains.' She also observed a certain detachment about the commodore. 'Old Nelson very civil and good natured, but does not say much.'[44] Watchful, controlled, careful of his drinking, conscious of his responsibilities, a riotous party was one situation in which Nelson did not shine. His tolerance and informality with junior, but not necessarily younger, officers, were to be a key factor in his later success; this was in contrast to older commanders such as Howe, Hood and Jervis, or those of his seniority who stood on their dignity, like Robert Calder or John Orde.

On 29 January, Nelson sailed in *La Minerve*, accompanied by *Romulus* (36), *Southampton* (32), *Dido* (28), *Sardine* (16), *L'Utile* (16), the *Dolphin* hospital ship, the *Dromedary* store ship and twelve transports. He left Thomas Fremantle at Porto Ferrajo in command of two frigates, three sloops and two gunboats.[45] The next day, with the *Romulus* in company, Nelson left the convoy and sailed north to examine the state of French and Spanish warships in Toulon, Barcelona and Minorca. Five miles east of Barcelona he captured a Spanish merchant ship, the *Fillieca*, took stores out of her and burnt her.[46] The rest of the voyage was uneventful. On 9 February *La Minerve* arrived at Gibraltar, where she stayed for only two days, anchored in Rosia Bay. The Spanish fleet was out, and Nelson needed to get back to the *Captain*, for to miss an action under Jervis would be disastrous. Lieutenants Culverhouse and Hardy, and the seamen in the prize crew from the *Sabina*, returned on board, having been exchanged in a cartel from Spain. Jervis had positioned the British fleet well south of Cape St Vincent to 'enable [me] to go to his [Nelson's] assistance in case the Fleet of Spain should attempt to interrupt his passage through the Gut [of Gibraltar]'.[47]

Stores and water complete, Nelson set off in *La Minerve* in a strong Levanter, a fair wind for her course westward to the Tagus. She was under her staysails only and with her topgallant masts struck. Immediately, two Spanish ships of the line, the *Terrible* and the *Neptune*, slipped their anchors in Algeciras Bay and went after her. In these conditions, if the British frigate was not well handled, a larger, heavier ship might overhaul her. Once *La Minerve* had reached the Gut, Cockburn ordered the topgallant masts up and the reefs shaken out. At 3.15, a seaman, William Barnes, fell overboard from the main topsail yard when shaking out the reefs. The ship immediately hove to, and Thomas Masterman Hardy, the second lieutenant, lowered the jolly boat with a hastily gathered crew. There was no trace of the seaman, and the jolly boat was hoisted in by 3.30.[48] At this point the Spanish ships were three miles astern, according to the master's estimate.[49] *La Minerve* picked up her customary speed and shook off the big Spanish ships.

All this was observed from the shore from Gibraltar. One army officer, Lieutenant Cookson, wrote in his memoirs that once the reefs had been shaken out, 'in an instant she hove to in the wind all standing; and we all on Shore thought the Commodore meant to come back to avoid the Spanish ships of the line. But to our great surprise in 10 minutes she bore up and with a press of Sail stood out of the Gut and it appeared to us that the line of Battleships would cut him off.'[50] This account accords with Nelson's and Cockburn's logs.[51] The published account by Colonel John Drinkwater, on board the ship, and already a friend of Nelson, has been more influential. Drinkwater adds drama and draws all the attention to Nelson. When the jolly boat crew was pulling hard towards *La Minerve*, Drinkwater has Nelson saying, 'By G—, I'll not lose Hardy,' then ordering the mizzen topsail to be backed to stop the ship.[52] Yet the ship would have to be nearly stopped before the jolly boat could be hoisted into the water, or else it would have been swamped if launched at speed.[53] Whatever the opinion of those on shore, the handling of the ship was the responsibility of Cockburn and his officers, and the Spanish ships were a good three miles astern.

At this point in Nelson's career myths began to take hold. But it was also at this time that Nelson can first be discerned as having qualities quite out of the ordinary. Up to the beginning of 1796 he was one of a number of a gifted generation of naval officers, taking advantage of superior British naval resources and technology to best the French and Spanish navies. Though physically brave, aggressive and successful, nothing until now had marked him out from others with talent and ambition. George Cockburn noted many years later how Nelson invariably rose to the crisis, possessing 'powers of high exertions of intrepidity and talent whenever great occasions call for the exertion of the noble qualities . . . and blessed with a never failing kindness of heart'.[54] Before he left the Mediterranean in February 1797, Nelson had already discovered the foundation for his inspired leadership, which rested on winning goodwill and cooperation rather than instilling fear and obedience.

14

The Battle of Cape St Vincent and the Blockade of Cadiz

14 February–14 July 1797

The date of this letter reminds me of a day that methinks ought not to be forgotten & yet it is buried so deep that I never expect to see it rise again unless the usage of history should bring it forward. The truth is a certain Commodore had the audacity to run away with too large a portion of its laurels, otherwise I think it would at least have yielded the parties concern'd an anniversary dinner – But jealousy is the Devil whether in female or male . . .

Admiral William Waldegrave to Nelson, on the anniversary of the Battle of Cape St Vincent, 1805[1]

The Blockade of Cadiz has been and is the compleatist thing in Naval History.   Admiral Sir John Jervis to Evan Nepean, 21 May 1797[2]

By eight in the evening of 12 February *La Minerve* was through the Strait of Gibraltar and had lost sight of the Spanish ships.[3] She sailed into the night, her course north-west. The wind was still easterly and the visibility became hazy. In the dark, near Cape St Vincent, she passed through the Spanish fleet. The next morning Nelson sighted the British fleet and came up with it by noon. It had been considerably strengthened since he had left it two months before, for Rear-Admiral William Parker had reinforced Jervis on 6 February with five ships of the line from Lord Bridport's fleet off Brest.[4] Jervis already had a frigate watching the Spanish fleet and knew that the enemy was very near; he had signalled his fleet to be prepared for battle more than twenty-four hours before.[5]

Nelson immediately went on board the *Victory* to report the failure to bring the army out of Porto Ferrajo. Jervis sat down there and then to draft the withdrawal orders to General de Burgh; the *Fox* cutter set out immediately for Elba with these dispatches. At three o'clock Jervis signalled that the *Captain* should change position in the line with the *Goliath* so as to bring the latter near the centre of the line. She was captained by Sir Charles Knowles, who was ill, and Jervis had no confidence in him; later he referred to his 'notorious imbecility'.[6] With Nelson present, Jervis could now strengthen the rear of his line. Troubridge was to lead the van and Collingwood the rear: Jervis was playing to his strengths.

Aboard the *Captain* the broad pennant was hoisted, and the ship's company mustered to quarters. Nelson came aboard at 6.30, to be greeted by Ralph Willet Miller, the captain who had joined the ship only two days before Nelson had joined *La Minerve* in early December.[7] Miller was a pious, good-natured and technically minded officer and in the nine weeks in which Nelson had been absent he had imprinted his personality upon the crew. Significantly, Miller had concentrated on gunnery training, causing, as he wrote later, 'six guns to be drill'd every day, and being often present at the drill'.[8] This period had been marked by foul weather. For six days the *Captain*'s crew had striven unsuccessfully to haul the *Bombay Castle* off a sandbank at the entrance to the Tagus.[9] The *Captain* was one of several ships in the fleet that were short of water. Miller entered the amount of water on board daily in the *Captain*'s log; consumption varied between one and a half to two and a quarter tons a day.[10]

After some days of blowing from the east, during the night of 13 February the wind had come round to the south. By the morning of the 14th it was, according to Miller, 'a fine breeze at SSW ... with smooth water'.[11] The breeze was so steady that the sails, filled with wind, were motionless, 'just sufficient to cause all the sails to sleep', in the words of Midshipman George Parsons, aboard the *Barfleur*.[12] Although Jervis knew that the Spanish fleet was near, the hazy weather prevented any sightings, but he had reports of it at 9.30.* It was not until 10.30 that it was clearly sighted, by the *Captain*, four or five miles to the south.[13] It may be, as some claimed, that the poor visibility fooled Don José de Córdoba, the Spanish commander-in-chief, into thinking that Jervis had fewer ships than he actually did. Although the British were heavily outnumbered, mere numbers were misleading. Jervis's recent experience of the competence of the Spanish Navy, reinforced now by the knowledge that Nelson had overwhelmed the *Sabina* in December, led him to believe that boldness was the best course. Jervis had fifteen ships of the line. As the mist lifted and the Spanish approached, it was apparent that their fleet comprised twenty-seven ships, among them some of the

---

* Jervis's journal recorded the wind through the day as 'NNW, NwbyW and NbW' ((UK)NA: PRO, ADM 50/79). The master of the *Captain* records the wind as 'variable' all day (ADM 52/2825). In a moderate breeze the direction of the wind would be disturbed by the rigging and sails of these large ships in proximity.

biggest in the world, massively built of hardwoods from Spain's empire. Jervis formed his line very quickly, described by Parsons as

one of the most beautiful and close lines ever beheld ... The fog drew up like a curtain, and disclosed the grandest sight I ever witnessed. The Spanish fleet, close on our weather bow, were making the most awkward attempt to form their line of battle, and they looked a complete forest huddled together; their commander-in-chief, covered with signals and running free on his leeward line, using his utmost endeavours to get them into order; but they seemed confusion worse confounded.[14]

Córdoba had been caught unawares.[15] His large fleet had sailed out into the Atlantic escorting a small convoy of four ships laden with mercury for the mines of South America. It was an extraordinarily large escort for only four ships, but the cargo was of the utmost importance to the impoverished Spanish government, which needed the mineral to process silver into coin. Eight days before, the convoy had been just off Cadiz, but the strong easterly wind had blown the Spanish ships out to sea again. Córdoba thought that Jervis's fleet was in Lisbon, and he was unlikely to have known of Parker's reinforcement of five ships of the line: in any case, the Spanish commander-in-chief was seeking to avoid battle.[16] Now at last the wind was blowing WSW, enabling the Spanish ships to steer ESE towards Cadiz. Unaware of the proximity of the British fleet, earlier that morning Córdoba had signalled two of his ships of the line to turn back away from the British to cover the rear of the convoy. At 10.30, when Córdoba realized the danger and when Jervis saw his advantage, the Spanish ships were dispersed.

The British fleet was steering just west of south, almost at ninety degrees to the Spanish. Jervis held his ships in two close columns; according to Parsons, 'so beautifully close was our order of sailing, that the flying jib-boom of the ship astern projected over the taffrail of her leader.'[17] Just before eleven o'clock in the morning, Jervis ordered them into a single line of battle 'as convenient', allowing the fastest ships to go to the head of the line. The *Culloden* was first, followed by Thomas Frederick's *Blenheim* and William Parker's *Prince George*. Nelson in the *Captain* was in the rear division; only two ships were astern of him. There was no racing ahead; all the captains were under orders to set no more sails than those of the flagship. At 11.26 Jervis signalled No. 40, 'The Admiral means to pass through the enemy's line.'[18] The advance of the British ships towards the centre of the array of Spanish ships was, like the character of the commander-in-chief, deliberate and controlled.

As the British formed their line, the Spanish ships changed direction by wearing on to the starboard tack, they turned north and close-hauled, keeping to windward of the British. They had by now formed into four loose groups, with three near the flagship, the *Santissima Trinidad* (120), to the north, and a strong group to leeward.* Córdoba hoisted a series of signals to organize his ships into a line, but none was obeyed; it was a difficult manoeuvre, which would have caused some confusion even in the British fleet, with their superior signal discipline.[19] The result was confusion. Some of the Spanish were abreast of each other, which greatly increased the danger of hitting one another when firing at the enemy. Three of the Spanish, two 112-gun ships and a 74, failed to wear quickly enough and fell to leeward. At 12.10 the leading British ship, the *Culloden*, captained by Thomas Troubridge, reached a point between the two groups. Jervis signalled his line to tack in succession, northwards with a course converging on the Spaniards. Troubridge had anticipated the signal and tacked immediately the signal flag reached the *Victory*'s masthead. The rest of the fleet tacked in succession in the moderate breeze, not with the parade-ground precision favoured by the text books, but some quickly, some falling off to leeward and all, after the tack, trying to bring the line together as they sailed after the larger group of Spanish ships.[20] Troubridge now raced ahead. The *Culloden* was 'far ahead and to windward, kept all sail'.[21] At 11.58 the first ships in the line opened fire on the Spanish; at noon the *Captain* fired some long-range shots at a three-decked ship passing on the other tack.[22]

Nelson now made the move that made his name – unorthodox yet correct, beyond the confidence and powers of any of his contemporaries. He was in a good position to see that the leading Spanish ships were now turning towards the east, which might have enabled them to link up with the rear Spanish division. According to the logs kept on board the *Captain*, the time was 12.50; Jervis's admiral's journal recorded: '12.35: Comm. Nelson in Rear, tacked and joined the Van.'[23] Heavy smoke lay over the action, and the view from the flagship was much impeded, so that he could only assume that Nelson had tacked. In fact, Nelson ordered Miller to wear the ship out of the line. She swung to port in a large arc, turning dramatically away

---

* The central group consisted of the *Santissima Trinidad* (120), *Mejicano* (112), *Soberano* (74), *San Nicolas* (80), *San Isidro* (74), *Salvador del Mundo* (112), *San Ildefonso* (74); the second group, *Concepcion* (112), *Santo Domingo* (64), *Conquistador* (74), *San Juan Nepomuceno* (74), *San Genaro* (74); a third central group, *Glorioso* (74), *Firme* (74), *Atlante* (74), *San Jose* (112); the group to leeward, *San Antonio* (74), *Conde de Regla* (112), *Principe de Asturias* (112), *San Francisco de Paula* (74), *San Fermin* (74), *Oriente* (74) (from Gonzalez-Aller and O'Donnell, 74–5; Harbron, 168–73).

from the enemy. Wearing ('gybing' is the modern sailing term for fore-and-aft rigged vessels) was the only safe and sure way of moving a ship out of the line, since tacking involved bringing her head through the wind, which might stop her, or she might drift to leeward before getting up speed on the other tack, with the threat of colliding with the following ships. The *Captain* passed in front of the last ship, the *Excellent*, and Nelson put himself at the front of the British line ahead of Troubridge in the *Culloden*.[24] He did not signal the last two ships, *Excellent* and *Diadem*, to follow him (though as commodore he may have felt that this was within his power); that might have been a risk too far.[25] The *Captain* went straight for the *Santissima Trinidad*, and engaged two other three-decked ships. She was, however, followed by Cuthbert Collingwood in the *Excellent* and George Towry in the *Diadem*, which was only a 64. According to the master of the *Colossus*, the *Captain* at this point 'received the fire of 5 or 6 of the enemy's ships'.[26] To those aboard the *Captain*, it appeared that engaging these huge ships had the effect of forcing them back on their course and away from the rear division of Spanish ships, 'actually turning them as two Shepherd's Dogs wou'd a Flock of sheep', in Captain Miller's words.[27] Had the two separated groups of the Spanish fleet been able to concentrate, some semblance of defence might have been mounted. Collingwood had no doubt that Nelson's action prevented this when he wrote to him the next day: 'The highest honours are due to you, my dear friend. You formed the plan of attack. We were the accessories to the Don's ruin for [had] they had got on the other tack, the wou'd have been sooner joined & the business less compleat.'[28]

At 12.51 Jervis made Signal No. 41: 'The ships to take suitable station for their mutual support and to engage the enemy as arriving up with them in succession.'[29] He intended that the *Britannia* under Vice-Admiral Charles Thompson should take the rear ships over and join the mêlée, abandoning the line of battle.[30] Thompson did not comply, to Jervis's displeasure, although the *Britannia* was at this moment busy cutting away a damaged jib-boom.[31] Jervis took a calculated risk that superior English gunnery and discipline would outweigh the Spanish advantage in size and guns. The resulting close-quarter mêlée, with crews striving at a desperate pace to load and fire their guns as quickly as possible, was confused by noise and hidden by gun smoke. Rather later, 2.05, Jervis signalled: 'Fleet to engage the Enemy Close.'[32] Not surprisingly, conflicting accounts were recorded in the logs of the different ships. Parker's ship, the *Prince George*, recorded that the *Culloden*, then the *Blenheim*, opened fire first, followed by the *Captain*.[33] Not so, according to Philip Thomas, master of the *Captain*, who

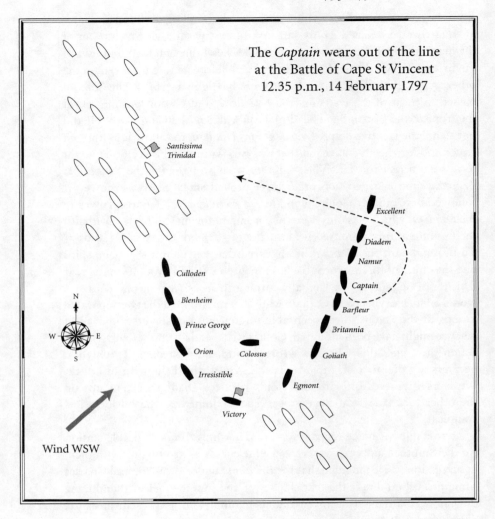

The *Captain* wears out of the line
at the Battle of Cape St Vincent
12.35 p.m., 14 February 1797

Santissima
Trinidad

Excellent

Diadem

Namur

Captain

Culloden

Blenheim

Barfleur

Prince George

Britannia

N

Orion   Colossus

Goliath

W   E

Irresistible

S

Egmont

Victory

Wind WSW

wrote that she was 'immediately engaged with the *Santissima Trinidad* and
two other three decked ships in which we were most nobly supported by
the *Culloden*, Captain Troubridge'. Not long after, they were joined by
Collingwood in the *Excellent*. Nelson and the crew had two periods of
respite of about ten minutes each when first the *Culloden* and then the
Blenheim passed between the *Captain* and the enemy ships. During these
intervals the crew replenished shot and repaired the tattered rigging.[34]

A close action could not last long. Damage to the ships or exhaustion of
the crews would bring it to a halt. Forty minutes after Jervis's close-action

signal the first Spanish ship struck her colours; a quarter of an hour later another followed. Jervis signalled to two ships, the frigate *Lively* and the *Diadem*, which were lying off, away from the action, to take possession of the prizes.

Soon after three o'clock Nelson had his second inspired moment when the *Captain*, with serious damage to her rigging and not much steerage way, was closely engaged with the *San Jose*. The Spaniard's mizzenmast was shot away, so that she too lost steerage way. The master takes up the story:

She then fell abreast of the *St Nicholas* to windward at 1/2 past 3, the *Excellent* passed us to windward engaging the *St Nicholas* within Pistol Shot as she passed by the latter luffing, and the *St Joseph's* mizzen mast having gone they fell on board each other. The *Captain* immediately luffed close alongside & prepared for Boarding, and having engaged very sharply for a few minutes in which time we had 17 men killed and wounded.[35]

Here was the direct assault, the Nelson trademark; most of the *Captain*'s casualties occurred in these few minutes, at point-blank range. The *Captain*'s casualties were one officer, three soldiers and twenty seamen killed, and eighty wounded.[36] Edward Berry, the first lieutenant, secured the *Captain* to the *San Nicolas*, and was first aboard the Spanish ship. Nelson ordered Captain Miller to stay aboard the *Captain*. Lieutenant Peirson and the soldiers of the 69th Regiment and seamen swarmed on to the Spanish decks. A soldier smashed the windows of the stern cabin, and Nelson was through after him. This determined rush overcame Spanish resistance. Realizing that the second Spanish ship was also for the taking, the boarding party rushed onwards, but there no one resisted. In an often described scene, the Spanish officers gave up their swords to Nelson, surrounded by his boat crew, all originally from the *Agamemnon*, there to protect the commodore. One of them, William Fearney, an able seaman from Tyneside who had served with Nelson for four years, put the swords under his arm 'with the greatest *sang froid*', as Nelson put it.[37] Jervis, observing from the *Victory*, recorded: '4.15: *Captain* alongside two of the Enemy's ships, observed them to hoist English colours.'[38]

Nelson left the scene almost immediately. The *San Nicolas* was on fire in the forehold, but the blaze was soon extinguished. The *Captain*'s boats were shot away, so Nelson signalled at 5.40 for boats to tow her.[39] Lieutenant John Culverhouse from *La Minerve* boarded the *San Jose* and found Nelson on her quarterdeck.[40] Nelson then left with Culverhouse, putting

Berry in command of the *San Jose* and Lieutenant Peter Spicer of the *San Nicolas*. The two Spanish prizes were not disentangled for another hour. With his flag lieutenant James Noble and his secretary Philip Carstang, Nelson went on board *La Minerve* at 4.30 and sailed to the *Victory* to confer with Jervis. It is not clear why he left so quickly. Perhaps he reasoned that he was of more use to Jervis aboard an undamaged ship. Underlying this rational response was perhaps the emotional need to see the commander-in-chief in order to justify his unorthodox actions and to be reassured. He received lavish praise and heartfelt thanks. In any case, Jervis did not trust his second-in-command, Charles Thompson, and the other rear-admiral, William Parker, was new to the fleet. By 5.15 Nelson was on board the *Irresistible*.[41] He was to fly his broad pennant on this newly refitted, recoppered ship for five weeks; her captain was George Martin, an old acquaintance from West Indies days. At 4.30 Jervis signalled to his dispersed ships to form the line 'in Close Order'. Firing ceased at five o'clock.[42]

It had been a five-hour battle. Four Spanish ships of the line were taken as prizes. The *Captain*'s gunnery had been devastatingly effective. She expended 146 barrels of gunpowder, 2,773 round, grape and double-headed shot, and 1,940 musket and pistol shot. She used one ton, seven hundredweight of junk, made of unpicked hemp rope, which formed the wads rammed home behind each shot. The highest number of shot (1,051) was from her twenty-eight long 32-pounders. Close action had lasted three hours, and, allowing for two periods of respite of ten minutes each, the height of the battle had lasted 160 minutes. This indicates a rate of fire of approximately one broadside every four and a half minutes. Her two short-range 68-pound carronades, so short that they were easily loaded and fired, fired 117 round shot, one every two and a half minutes.[43] The Spaniards had nothing to match it.

Nelson's action in breaking out of the line has generated deep and sometimes heated disagreement among commentators, especially those writing in the nineteenth century.[44] Did Nelson wear out of the line before Jervis made his signal? Not surprisingly, timings and interpretations vary from one ship's log to another, additionally, many entries were obscured by smoke from the firing of many hundreds of guns, so variations were sure to result when they were written up afterwards. If Jervis's journal can be believed – and he had more staff on his quarterdeck than any other ship to record signals and events – it can be taken that Nelson wore the *Captain* out of the line before Jervis made his signal, although recent historical opinion still maintains that Nelson did not act until 12.51 when Jervis made his Signal No. 41.[45] Some have seen this as a courageous move overturning decades of rigid adherence to the line of battle, but Nelson's time spent under Jervis's command meant that he knew the commander-in-chief's mind, which was similar to his own on the matter of close-range fighting with superior gunnery.[46] But how much of this historic, daring move was instinctive, fuelled by Nelson's ambition and competitive spirit? The sight of Thomas Troubridge, his rival for Jervis's good opinion, taking the honour of reaching the Spanish fleet first can only have been a powerful impetus within him for precipitate action.

Nelson's decision was not without precedent. At the end of his life, Jervis was to remember his mentor, Lord Hawke, who, as a young captain at the Battle of Toulon in 1744, had come out of the line in exactly the same manner. 'Lord Hawke, when he ran out of the line and took the *Poder*, sickened me of tactics,' he told his biographer.[47] In his report to the Admiralty, Jervis explained that he himself had not observed the rules during the battle: 'With the enemy unable to form a line, such a moment was not to be lost . . . I felt myself justified in departing from the regular system.'*[48] Collingwood had no doubt that the initiative came from Nelson, saying in his letter of congratulations the day after the battle, 'It adds very much to the satisfaction I had in thumping the Spaniards that I relieved you a little.'[49] Signal or no signal, disdain for the Spaniards or not, wearing out of the line in one of the smaller 74s and going for the largest ship of the Spanish fleet as a single ship was unquestionably a morally brave and physically courageous act.

There now followed an extraordinary race to establish the credit for the victory in the minds of the politicians in London. Jervis was to be sparing in his praise in his 'public letter', which would be published in the *London Gazette*, reluctant to pick any officer out. In his long, private letter to Lord Spencer he was relatively even-handed, although the greatest praise went to his favourite, Thomas Troubridge, with a special mention for Benjamin Hallowell, who had been aboard the *Victory*, having lost his ship.[50] Only

---

* The generally held, but mistaken, view is that the British line of battle was kept intact by the elimination of the initiative of individual captains, rigidly enforced by the Admiralty's printed 'Permanent Fighting Instructions'. In fact, the fighting instructions were contained in only one chapter of the *Sailing and Fighting Instructions*, which were heavily amended by the signals and instructions issued by each commander-in-chief. The orthodox view was challenged by Tunstall (6) and more comprehensively by Rodger ('Tactics', 292–4), who emphasizes the differing leadership styles of commanders-in-chief, and the shortcomings of the signal systems before the numeral system introduced by Howe. This would explain Jervis's reference to Hawke's flexibility, and his own decision at the Battle of Cape St Vincent to abandon the 'regular system' and to fight in a mêlée style.

when he was persuaded to do so by Nepean did Jervis commit himself to naming the flag officers publicly, and then not until 4 April.[51]

Nelson had previously felt indignation at being undervalued after an action, with neglect by Hood after the sieges in Corsica the most documented example. This time Nelson acted quickly to ensure that his version of events reached London first. The day after the battle he went on board the frigate *Lively*, which he knew was ordered back to England with dispatches and from the deck of which Gilbert Elliot had watched the battle. Elliot was not on board, but instead Nelson briefed Colonel Drinkwater, who had served under Elliot in Corsica and was an author of repute. (Within the year Drinkwater would publish a narrative of the battle that emphasized Nelson's role. Nelson later also wrote his own account, 'A Few Remarks Relative to Myself in the *Captain* . . .', which was as dramatic and fluent as anything by a journalist; to add weight, he had it signed by his captain, Ralph Willet Miller, and Edward Berry, who had also been on board the *Captain*.[52]) Nelson took precautions because he knew that Robert Calder, Jervis's flag captain, would be sent home with the victory dispatches. Nelson rightly did not trust Calder, whose long report of the battle to Lord Spencer mentions neither Nelson nor the *Captain*.[53] Jervis acknowledged that there was feeling between Calder and Nelson when he wrote later to Nepean about Calder: 'I will tell you honestly that he encouraged, nay originated, the faction ab[ou]t Nelson.'[54] Calder, however, was no match for the political skills of Sir Gilbert Elliot.

In what has usually been seen as a theatrical gesture, laced with sentiment for the county of Norfolk, Nelson presented the sword surrendered by the Spanish admiral to the city of Norwich. The gift was, however, a means to an end. Lieutenant Peirson of the 69th Regiment, who was wounded in the action, took it to London with Nelson's account of the battle. Peirson reported back to Nelson: 'I delivered your letter to Mr Windham, with the Sword, and put to the Post Office the rest.'[55] William Windham was a long-standing and close friend of Gilbert Elliot, as well as the MP for Norwich and a member of the cabinet as secretary-at-war. In view of the closeness of Elliot and Windham, it is difficult not to come to the conclusion that this shrewd gift was Elliot's idea. Windham's diary for 15 March 1797 reads: 'On coming home found Lieut. Pierson with letters etc from Commodore Nelson. To St James's late, where we went in to [the] King and left Nelson's account of his part in the action.'[56] Thus Nelson's account of the battle was seen immediately by the king.

Nelson's version of events was also the subject of a conversation between Windham and another of his long-time political friends, none other than

Lord Spencer, the first lord of the Admiralty. Two copies of Nelson's account are in Windham's papers. The first copy is the one signed by Nelson, Miller and Berry. A second has been transcribed carefully into the third person, giving it more objective authority. A note in a clerical hand carries a message from Spencer, who was ill at the time, to Windham:

Lord Spencer desires me to say to you that he thinks as you do about the propriety of putting the enclosed into the third person & he thinks no harm can arise from the Paragraph being left and the whole substance being allowed to remain as it was originally written. God bless you. Sometimes remember a convalescent & keep a great part of our conversation of today to yourself.[57]

Remarkably, Spencer therefore supervised the editing of Nelson's account for publication. It became the known version, rather than Calder's, and for the first time Nelson was headline news. Nelson's stratagem under Elliot's guidance for influencing government had succeeded brilliantly. For the politicians in power a more glorious gloss was put on the battle. The confidential conversation between the first lord of the Admiralty and the secretary-at-war is likely, as we shall see, to have paved the way for Nelson's rapid promotion fifteen months later.

Other means were used to spread the exploits of Commodore Nelson. Rear-Admiral William Waldegrave wrote privately to Spencer, including not only a full description of the *Captain*'s exploits but also a copy of the comic broadsheet celebrating the boarding of the two Spanish ships, 'Olla Podrida; or, Nelson's new art of cookery', which was circulating around the fleet.[58] A further copy of Nelson's account went to William Locker, who made sure it appeared in the *Sun* and the *True Briton*.[59] In addition to Peirson, some of the *Captain*'s officers went home and spread the word. Lieutenants Spicer and Noble were promoted and went to London to find a ship. Culverhouse obtained leave.[60] Peirson wrote to Nelson from London that the action of 14 February 'is represented on the Stage and when the broad pennant comes out on the Stage it was a general cry out, "Here comes the brave Comm. Nelson." Many could not believe you boarded . . . they drink your health in bumpers.'[61] The fame of Nelson's 'Patent Bridge for Boarding First Rates' spread quickly. It was no wonder that everyone made their bows to Fanny at the morning concert at Bath, while Edmund Nelson wrote to his son: 'Not only my acquaintances but people in General met me at every Corner with such handsome words . . . was obliged to retire from the public eye.'[62]

The publication of Nelson's account of the action caused trouble within the navy. In it Nelson had written: 'For near an hour, I believe, (but do not pretend to be correct as to time) did the *Culloden* and *Captain* support this apparently, but not really, unequal contest.'[63] Rear-Admiral Parker was chief among those who took exception to the statement that the *Captain* and the *Culloden* alone had taken the brunt of the Spanish fire for an hour. In fact, the *Blenheim*, the *Prince George*, the *Orion* and the *Diadem* were soon in the mêlée.[64] There was more to Parker's irritation than his good name, for prize money was at stake. The rear-admiral's ship, the *Prince George*, had also engaged with the *San Jose*. Parker was convinced that the Spanish ship was his prize; he wrote to his friend James Gambier: 'a three decker bearing a Rear-Admiral's flag struck to the fire of the *Prince George*, and from her disabled state [she] fell on board the same Spanish ship Commodore Nelson was on board of, upon the Quarter, upon the opposite side.' Parker did allow that the *Captain* and *Culloden* took more punishment than his ship or the *Orion*, but he doubted that the boarding was any more than luck: 'whether t'was exactly intended on the part of the Commodore, I am to learn.'[65] When Nelson's account (in the first person) appeared in the *Sun*, Parker wrote a long letter to Nelson protesting that it was biased. Nelson replied in an uncharacteristically short, formal letter, stating that 'it is impossible I can enter into the subject of your Letter.'[66] Parker took up the matter with the first lord, from whom he had an ameliorating reply: 'The variations in the accounts of an action at sea by different persons are so easily and naturally to be accounted for by the different situations in which the writers are at times placed ... that it is neither necessary nor fair to draw an inference from them that any intention has existed of disparaging the conduct of others.'[67] However, the damage had been done; there were those in the officer corps who sympathized with Parker; many years later his letter and Nelson's reply appeared in the *Naval Chronicle*.[68]

Despite this behind-the-scenes manoeuvring, however, no public dispute sullied the victory. Jervis failed to discern jealousy, or, as he put it to Nelson, 'as far as I can judge, the green Eyed Monster has not appeared in any Quarter.'[69] Nelson was made a knight of the Bath; he had made sure that Elliot knew that he did not want to be rewarded with a baronetcy 'without a fortune to support the Dignity'.[70] Eventually the thanks of the House of Commons were recorded for the flag officers, Vice-Admirals Thompson and Waldegrave, Rear-Admiral Parker and Commodore Nelson.[71] Jervis distrusted Thompson and despised Waldegrave, so that when they were offered baronetcies he was furious. 'For God's sake repair it if you can,' he wrote to Nepean. Jervis himself nevertheless secured an earldom, named, at the king's insistence Earl St Vincent, after his battle. Even then he grumbled to Nepean that he was unlikely to do better than the two Hood brothers, who were viscounts, since they 'had the protection of Mr Pitt's honour'.[72] Nelson was finally given his flag. Spencer approved a promotion of nine rear-admirals, all of eighteen years' standing, Nelson being sixth on the list.[73] Jervis's admiral's journal records on 2 April 1797 that at 4 p.m. 'Commodore Nelson hoisted his flag on board the *Captain* on his Promotion to the Rank of Rear-Admiral of the Blue, and saluted with 13 guns, returned 11 guns.'[74] Ninety-nine admirals were above him in the *Navy List*, active and retired.[75]

Private letters to Nelson demonstrated genuine pleasure. Gilbert Elliot wrote, as usual, in extravagant terms, as did Dixon Hoste, father of Midshipman William Hoste, from Norfolk: 'Your Character is declared unparalleled in History.'[76] Lady Parker, wife of Sir Peter Parker of West Indies days, wrote that 'your mother could not have heard of your deeds with more affection' and added that Jervis 'shall henceforth be my Valentine'.[77] His father's praise was for once unqualified: 'You, my Good Son, I see as a rare instance of personal Merit rewarding with self earned Laurels . . . all agree you merit the eulogies of the Country.'[78] Only Fanny struck a faintly discordant note. Martha Saumarez reported to her husband from Bath that she and Fanny were 'upon the most friendly terms – and her good spirits recruit mine – She would have preferred her Husband had not been made an Admiral so soon – 700 a year is a douceur that she thinks of greater value than being an Admiral's Lady.' Lady Saumarez added in a letter written a month later that Fanny had appreciated Saumarez's 'praise of Comdre. Nelson's service which she acknowledges with the more pleasure as it is not always that he has had so much justice done him – In this instance however he will have no cause to complain for his conduct in the Action is the subject of general admiration.'[79]

The Spanish Navy suffered terribly. According to Saumarez's account of the battle, 3,000 Spanish prisoners were put ashore.[80] The numbers of killed and wounded were frightful. From the captured prizes alone 280 were killed and 334 wounded, double the numbers inflicted on the entire British fleet.[81] Several of the other Spanish ships absorbed prolonged punishment, most notably the huge flagship *Santissima Trinidad*, with her 130 guns. For most of the afternoon of 14 February she had been battered by four British ships and dismasted, suffering 300 casualties. Repeated attempts to capture the ship had been beaten off, and she was only rescued by other Spanish ships of the line coming up. Córdoba wrote in the 'Parte del General Córdoba', his official report, 'Whoever considers . . . the rapidity and accuracy with which the English handle their guns, can imagine what must have been our conditions . . . after five hours fighting.'[82] Córdoba's report appeared in the *Madrid Gazette*, which caused great Spanish public anger. One of Jervis's intelligence sources in Cadiz wrote: 'we all expected there would have been a rebellion, the Mob being so exasperated that they stoned several of the Captains. The Admirals were ordered under arrest in their Houses, and the Captains and the Commodore under Arrest to the Isla.'[83] The court of inquiry found Córdoba and some of his officers guilty of negligence, though some were praised for their gallantry. The young Vice-Admiral Don Federico Gravina arrived at Cadiz to oversee the repairs of the Spanish fleet, and was appointed second-in-command to Admiral José Mazarredo; but the Spanish Navy was never again to constitute the same threat to the British.[84]

Nelson had sustained a blow to his abdomen. In the returns after the battle it was stated that Commodore Nelson was 'bruised, but not obliged to quit the deck'. Considering the physical exertion he went through during the boarding of the Spanish ships and reaching the flagship and the *Irresistible*, it cannot have been serious, but for some ten days he cannot have been completely well. Three days after the battle he begged to be excused from sitting on a court martial, probably as a result of a contusion, which he described to Elliot 'as of no consequence, unless an inflammation takes place in my bowels, which is the part injured'.[85] Ten days later, puzzlingly, he wrote that he was suffering from a suppression of urine.[86] He kept the news from Fanny. Later symptoms indicate that he possibly suffered a lumbar hernia (or rupture), which did not develop for some seven years, when it gave him pain when coughing when he had a cold.* He was still mentioning these symptoms as late as 1804.[87]

The British fleet retired to Lagos Bay, east of Cape St Vincent; extensive repairs were needed and Nelson was not to rejoin the rerigged *Captain* for five weeks. The fine weather that lasted for several days after the battle gave way to a severe gale; the *Irresistible*, the *Victory* and the *Salvador del Mundo* parted their cables.[88] On 2 March, Jervis maintained his strategic initiative by sending Nelson in the *Irresistible*, with a squadron of three

---

* Diagnosis after this length of time is bound to be uncertain. A lumbar hernia (first recorded in medical literature in 1803) is an uncommon but well-recognized condition, which is usually drawn to the patient's attention by a cough. It may have been that as a result of the wound he had a small tear in the attachment of his abdominal muscles to the iliac crest, and that over the years this gave rise to the rupture. It is also quite possible that the condition might have developed independently from the blow. (In these judgements I have been expertly guided by Professor Leslie Le Quesne; see also Hills, 'St Vincent', 84–9.)

ships of the line and four frigates, to cruise off Cape St Vincent.[89] They sailed in cloudy, blustery weather, usual for the time of the year: 'ship pitching very heavy' is recorded in the *Irresistible*'s log for 20 February.[90] The British had specific intelligence on two convoys: Nelson was 'to intercept a Convoy hourly expected from San Sebastian to join the outward bound West India trade, assembling at Cadiz: the late Viceroy of Mexico is also on his passage to Europe and several valuable ships from Buenos Ayres, La Vera Cruz, and other ports of Spanish America.'[91] Nelson wrote to his younger sister Kitty Matcham: 'I long to see England but whether ever I shall have that pleasure God only knows . . . I am not six times richer for the War but my road has hitherto been the path of Honour not of Wealth but I hope Riches will now flow in a gentle manner to me . . . I am going to look for the Viceroy of Mexico.'[92] But the Spanish treasure ships never arrived.

The blockade of Cadiz tightened as the repaired British ships were again sent to sea, with the damaged and demoralized Spanish fleet anchored in Cadiz Bay. Nelson sent a letter to the neutral American and Danish consuls that Cadiz should now be considered 'a Blockaded Port', but provided a frigate escort for fourteen neutral American merchant vessels, harassed by French privateers, leaving Malaga. This was wise politics, for relations between France and the United States over neutral trade were deteriorating and would soon result in the 'Quasi-War' between the two countries.[93] Sea control around the Strait of Gibraltar was one of the fruits of the victory of 14 February. Nevertheless, Earl St Vincent (as Jervis was called after 27 May) remained at a numerical disadvantage, with considerably fewer ships than those of the Spanish fleet that he blockaded. He badgered Spencer and Nepean for more ships and, realistic as ever, was never entirely confident of maintaining the blockade.[94]

St Vincent's most pressing task was to arrange the withdrawal of the army from Elba: 3,400 soldiers, their stores and guns, transports and convoying frigates, under the command of Thomas Fremantle, were still at Porto Ferrajo. Fremantle in the *Inconstant* had done well in the interval since Nelson had left at the end of January, picking up prizes in the winter seas off Italy.[95] Nelson's squadron, cruising between Cape St Vincent and Cape Spartel on the North African coast, had orders from St Vincent to prepare to sail into the Mediterranean to meet Fremantle's convoy.[96] But Nelson was now to sail into a hostile Mediterranean: French ships were able to leave an unblockaded Toulon, and the nights, needed for covering a retreat, were getting shorter. Dispatches had been conveyed between St Vincent and Fremantle in the *Fox* cutter, noted for its fast passages.[97] In mid March, St Vincent urged him to leave as soon as possible, informing him that he would send frigates to cover his retreat.[98] Critical timing would be required to meet the convoy and escort it past any French ships near Toulon or the coast of Spain. Intelligence reports of French ships of the line cruising off the southern coast of Minorca caused St Vincent to send larger ships than frigates, thus weakening his blockading force. On 12 April, Nelson received his orders to take the *Captain* and six ships of the line to meet Fremantle and escort the convoy to Gibraltar.[99] St Vincent wrote to Spencer that he was 'a little apprehensive for the fate of the garrison of Porto Ferrajo, this procrastination is a terrible thing in military operations, everything that can be done R[ear] Admiral Nelson will achieve.'[100]

When Nelson had left Elba at the end of January, the transports had been organized so that the embarkation of the soldiers would take no more than three days, due to efforts of Lieutenant Day, the agent of transports, who was made commander.[101] Fremantle was to take the convoy around the north of Corsica, then steer for Algiers; when at latitude 38 degrees north he would steer straight for Gibraltar.[102] Nelson knew this. Instead of trying to avoid a reported French squadron, on 19 April he passed Port Mahón 'within gunshot'. A strong north-westerly wind was blowing. The French ships of the line were not to be seen. Nelson wrote to St Vincent that the wind 'I fancy blew the French behind St Peter's Island in Sardinia . . . and this morning at 7, with inexpressible pleasure, I saw the convoy which I hope to see safe into Gibraltar.'[103] Nelson was lucky to have met the convoy in daylight. St Vincent reported to London with relief: 'The Rear Admiral, with his wonted precision, made his junction with Captain Fremantle soon after the latter had passed the Bocca of Bonifacio, in the most critical circumstances.'[104] The passage back to Gibraltar was slow and without incident, with west and south-west winds, sometimes heavy. Between 6 and 8 May, for instance, the convoy was blown backwards. On the morning of 8 May the *Captain*'s log records sixty-three sail in sight. Once in the safer waters off southern Spain, Nelson went ahead, leaving the escort to the other ships; on 19 May the *Captain* anchored in Gibraltar Bay; the convoy, large, unwieldy and slow, followed five days later.[105] The British withdrawal was complete, and it was lucky that no losses were sustained. Although a few frigates remained, for the first time for 130 years, in wartime, no British ship of the line was present in the Mediterranean.

Nelson sailed north after taking on stores, arriving off Cadiz on 24 May to find the British fleet anchored in regular lines in the shallow waters off the town. News of the mutinies in almost all of the Channel fleet at Spithead had reached the ships of the Mediterranean. This extremely serious mutiny over pay and discipline had broken out on 7 April, and on 16 April the men refused to put to sea; within a week Parliament had voted extra money for pay and unpopular officers had been put ashore. The trouble at Spithead was soon over, though the Nore mutiny, in late May, was prolonged and more severely punished, and affected operations against the Dutch Navy. Residual trouble remained in individual ships for a long time. St Vincent had already ensured that every captain in the fleet had read to his crew the Admiralty's letter of 18 April raising the men's wages.[106] As usual, his harshest judgements were for his officers: 'I dread not the Men, it is the indiscreet, licientious conversation of the officers, which produce all our ills, and their presumptive discussion of their orders they receive.' He blamed much of the officers' behaviour on the well-born among them: 'the rapid decline of young Men in this squadron whether from ill treated venereal complaints, or the Climate, is inconceivable.'[107] The *Theseus*, however, remained troublesome. Her ineffective captain, John Aylmer, and a bullying first lieutenant had administered harsh punishment; according to St Vincent, Aylmer was 'not fit to command', while the ship was 'in a most deplorable State of licentiousness and disorder'.[108]

The commander-in-chief acted quickly. Two days after Nelson returned to the fleet, he was ordered on board the *Theseus*, with Captain Miller and forty-two of his officers and crew. Aylmer and his officers were transferred to the *Captain*.[109] Few victuals were aboard the *Theseus*, and she was destitute of carpenter's or boatswain's stores.[110] Discipline was slowly restored. Within three weeks Nelson described to Fanny a piece of paper with an anonymous message that was found on the quarterdeck: 'Success attend Admiral Nelson, God Bless Captain Miller ... we thank them for the officers they have placed over us.'[111] Nevertheless, punishments aboard the *Theseus* continued to the end of June, with a series of lashings for insolence and drunkenness.[112] The crew was kept extremely busy stowing fresh stores and bringing aboard coal, wine, lemons, as well as 'three bullocks and sheep from Moorish vessels'; and, above all, loading as much of her capacity of 230 tons of water as there were water casks, all brought by transports from Lisbon and Gibraltar.[113] The crew of the *Theseus* was, nevertheless, still restless and noisy a few weeks later when Betsey Fremantle described them as 'the most tiresome, noisy, mutinous people in the world, they annoyed me amazingly, and Fremantle still more'.[114]

Another aid to discipline and good order was to keep within gunshot of the enemy to divert the attention of the crew from their grievances. St Vincent had placed the inner squadron of the blockading ships, mostly frigates, under Nelson's command. They were anchored close to the shore to provoke the Spaniards into coming out. Small Spanish gunboats and launches were active, keeping up a steady rate of fire. If the gunboats advanced, Nelson remarked to St Vincent, 'so much the better. If they venture from the walls, I shall give Johnny his full scope for fighting. It will serve to talk of better than mischief.'[115] Spanish batteries from the walls of Cadiz kept up an occasional, though not an effective, fire. In return, St Vincent ordered a gunboat to be fitted with large mortars at Gibraltar to shell Cadiz. The British frigates had to be constantly on the alert. In the *Blanche*, Joseph Nagle recalled, 'all hands at quarters during the night with the hatches laid over that no one was allowed to go below . . . The gunboats would come a[nd] lay off and keep firing at the ships laying at their anchors, but when we ware in side we could cut them off, but the batteries on either shore could fire at us.'[116]

It was a tough period for officers and crews, some in a state of serious discontent. In April the conditions were difficult for the largest ships, with the three-deckers seldom at anchor, sailing back and forth regularly some way offshore, while Nelson's smaller ships blockaded the entrance to Cadiz. St Vincent was concerned for 'the safety of my heavy-going and leewardly ships', the *Britannia*, the *St George* and some others. As he explained to Nepean, 'the coast forms a bight here which makes it difficult to obtain an offing [with] the wind upon the shore & a strong indraft'.[117] In a gale anchors would drag, and the watch was constant day and night. St Vincent described the conditions to Spencer: 'We have no relaxation in port . . . the officers are all kept to their duty . . . when at sea we do not make snug for the night, as in the Western Squadron, but are working incessantly by the lead to keep our position, insomuch mind and body are continually upon the stretch.'[118] In some ships the men were still very discontented; Betsey Fremantle, as observant as ever, noted that her husband was 'out of spirits which he is often on account of the impossibility of enforcing discipline'.[119]

Both St Vincent and Nelson were confident that the Spanish commander would be goaded into bringing his more numerous fleet out. However, the Spanish moved their fleet further down the Bay of Cadiz, out of range of the mortar boat.[120] Now only the civilian population remained in the line of fire. Women were evacuated out of the town.[121] In Nelson's opinion, 'Mazzaredo [Mazarredo] will be more than human if he can keep the Merchants of Cadiz in good humour.'[122] The Spanish Atlantic trade was brought to a standstill. More significantly, the blockade stopped the incoming corn trade. Merchant ships with corn from Hamburg and with salt provisions from North America were turned away. British frigates operated successfully off the North African coast against corn ships from the Barbary States. The price of bread corn in Cadiz rose to twice that of Lisbon.[123]

In spite of the very high stakes involved, a constant use of flags of truce enabled contact to be maintained between Mazarredo and St Vincent, and courtesies were elaborate. An early peace between the two countries was expected by both sides, and the Spanish admiral kept the blockading ships informed of general political news. Several rumours of the resignation of Pitt were carried out by the Spanish to the blockading ships.[124] Personal messages were also sent. Nelson received compliments from the Spanish admirals and particularly one from his one-time captive, Don Jacobo Stuart.[125] Intriguingly, he also received a letter from an agent ashore, Andrew Archdekin, about two cargoes of wheat that were apparently ransomed to the Spanish for 2,000 Spanish dollars; St Vincent was unlikely to have known about, or approved of, such a transaction.[126] Fishermen were constantly bringing St Vincent news of the state of Cadiz. He arranged a spy in 'a Moorish boat' to give him early warning of Spanish intentions, although he had little confidence in the information.[127] With such heavy traffic, it was important that the British guard boats could identify friend from foe; every night Robert Calder, now back from London, issued a password, or 'parole', and a 'countersign'.[128]

By the beginning of July, St Vincent attempted to increase the intensity of this low level warfare and ordered Nelson to carry out a night bombardment. During the night of 3 July a converted Dutch galliot, fitted with a 13-inch mortar and a 10-inch howitzer, was to be towed by ships' boats to a position in the entrance to the Bay of Cadiz, close to the north walls of the town. The *Goliath*, the *Terpsichore* and the *Fox* cutter were to be under way further out to sea in case of trouble. During the afternoon Nelson planned the position of the mortar boat with Miller. Starting at ten o'clock, with Nelson aboard, the mortar boat was towed by eight ships' boats and the rear-admiral's barge, guided by Miller. With some difficulty they found the planned position, and the mortar opened fire. The large gun did not function. Seeing this, the Spanish gun boats and launches, on the south side of the town, rowed around the lighthouse towards the British. Nelson, immediately appreciating the danger, ordered Miller to take some launches to counter this threat. He jumped into his barge, with Thomas Fremantle, and dashed off alone towards the enemy. As Miller gathered the launches, he heard the cry 'Follow the Admiral'. While the rest of the boats hung back, Miller went after Nelson. Simultaneously the two launches attacked two Spanish gunboats.

They were met with pistol shots. The stem of Miller's boat collided with his antagonist's quarter. Volleys were exchanged and the Spanish captain was killed. The Spanish attempted to pull away, but Miller turned to see the largest Spanish gunboat being boarded by Nelson and his crew and decided to go to his admiral's aid. The Spanish resisted bravely. It was desperate, hand-to-hand fighting with sword and cutlass. Nelson was nearly cut down twice, saved only by his coxswain, John Sykes, who was badly wounded in the arm. Miller and his crew boarded the other side of the Spanish gunboat, and she was taken. The rest of the British boats had by then come up to the action. The other Spanish vessels retreated into the rocks under the walls of Cadiz, pursued by Miller and five British boats. Having driven them off, he brought the boats to the bomb vessel. She was still in danger, and it was with great difficulty (because of the inexperience of the lieutenants in the rearguard boats) that she was brought under the protection of the ships standing off. Miller cut her cable and organized the boats to tow her back to the British squadron.[129] Two Spanish gunboats and a launch were taken to the British fleet; they were the only gains from an operation that failed.

The encounter was ruthless and bloody. While Nelson's dash provided inspiration and leadership, it was left to Miller to drive the rest of the Spanish to the shore and bring the British boats back in some order. The fighting demonstrated the superior fitness and determination of the British. One British seaman was killed and twenty wounded.[130] Nelson had been protected by his boat's crew. On board the Spanish gunboat, commanded by Don Miguel Irigoyen, eighteen out of twenty-six Spaniards were killed. Two days later Nelson reported to St Vincent that he had eighty-seven Spanish prisoners on board the *Theseus*, including Don Miguel Irigoyen; thirty prisoners had since died of their wounds.[131] The surviving prisoners were returned to Cadiz that day.[132] Nelson's attack was instinctive, although, judging by his notes to St Vincent earlier in the day, he had expected trouble: 'I wish to make it a warm night at Cadiz.'[133] But the operation was badly planned; his orders to the boats, under the command of some junior lieutenants, were perfunctory. The long months of blockade led him to underestimate the Spanish, not for the last time. Privately Miller was highly critical of Nelson. Miller had fixed the positioning of the gunboat, but Nelson at dusk 'sent me in again, to place a boat on the spot (a measure completely useless).' He found the boats initially rowing the wrong course, and with difficulty recovered the bomb vessel that had been abandoned. Miller was dissatisfied with the action: 'I cannot recollect it without a strong mixture of regret.'[134] Nelson's success earlier in the year may have made him feel invulnerable, and his inadequate preparations and actions off Cadiz bordered on the foolhardy.

For the crews of the blockading ships, bored, tired and, in some cases, with low morale, the action provided a boost to flagging spirits. St Vincent wrote an enthusiastic letter of thanks. Nelson's modesty was to the fore: 'Thank you for your flattering letter which as we all like I will believe as much of as I can.'[135] Nelson did not make the same mistake again. Two days later, on 5 July, the boats were deployed in three regular divisions, under the orders of captains rather than lieutenants, 'that we may expect a little more regularity'. This time Nelson left Miller to position the bomb vessel, much to the latter's satisfaction. The Spanish gunboats did not come out. They relied on shore artillery for their defence, the accuracy of which had improved. The mortar vessel was hit several times and Nelson ordered it to be withdrawn.[136] The next day St Vincent called off further bombardment, to the relief of Betsey Fremantle, who felt that 'it was sacrificing men for nothing'. Attacks by Spanish gunboats, however, continued.[137] Waspishly she added in her diary that the commander-in-chief hoped that the bombardment would bring him financial reward from the Cadiz authorities: 'he did it out of avarice as he heard 4 millions of paistres should be sent out to him.'[138] A week later Nelson felt encouraged to observe the hoisting of several red flags aboard the Spanish ships, the traditional colour for mutiny.[139]

Discipline in the anchored British fleet still continued to be a serious problem. While the excitements of the bombardment were taking place around the inner squadron, St Vincent had much else to attend to. Four seamen on William Parker's ship, the St George, were court-martialled and condemned to death. Two had been plotting mutiny – one confessed that a plan had been 'in contemplation for six months, in concert with the Britannia, Captain, Diadem and Egmont'. The other two were found guilty of homosexuality. St Vincent lost no time. They were to be hanged the following day, a Sunday, 3 July, the same day as the action against the Spanish gunboats. The gruff Sir Charles Thompson, St Vincent's second in command, objected strongly and publicly to hanging on a Sunday; St Vincent wrote immediately to Lord Spencer to request Thompson's early recall; he had already informed the first lord that Thompson had shown little initiative at Cape St Vincent.[140]

St Vincent chose to make examples of all four seamen. The two mutinous seamen represented a serious threat of conspiracy, although St Vincent had obtained his evidence by breaking the traditional confidentiality of confession to a chaplain. Had the homosexual incident taken place before the mutinies, the seamen involved would more likely have been given a large number of lashes rather than being hanged. Courts martial were unlikely to convict under Article 29 of the Articles of War, which covered the capital charge of homosexuality, since proof was difficult to obtain; but if convicted, the death sentence was more likely to be carried out than for any other crime.[141] In the navy as a whole only two officers were condemned to death for sodomy during these wars; one, in May 1797, provided the only example of the death of an officer by hanging.[142] Nor were troubles in St Vincent's fleet over yet, for in August there was another harsh hanging of a boatswain; unhappy with the prize money performance of his captain, he had spoken out against authority.[143] These months saw swift naval justice, with no appeals to the king. Instead of employing compromise, persuasion and encouragement, as Nelson had in the mutiny in the *Blanche* six months earlier, St Vincent struck down formal dissension at the heart of his fleet immediately and ruthlessly.

Discipline and religion went hand in hand in the hierarchical and confined life of an eighteenth-century warship. The rise in the outward show and practice of religion on board naval ships as a means of ensuring good order was increasing; Nelson, noted a later observer, was concerned that Divine Service should be understood by the men and that the chaplain's 'discourse should be sufficiently plain'.[144] However, for Nelson, discipline was a greater imperative than religion. He did not share Charles Thompson's religious qualms about hanging on a Sunday. He wrote to Robert Calder, St Vincent's flag captain: 'had it been Christmas Day instead of Sunday, I would have executed them. We know not what might have been hatched by a Sunday's grog; *now* your discipline is safe.'[145] He wrote in June to Fanny expressing his hope that the government would execute the mutineers at the Nore. 'If government gives in, what can we expect of this fleet? . . . Mankind are all alike and if these people find their brethren in England get their ignorant wishes complied with by being troublesome, it is human nature for others to take the same methods.'[146]

15

Disaster at Santa Cruz
14 July–4 September 1797

It was so dark . . . But really the enemy had every possible advantage,
and alas! What a number of glorious men fell, all cheering and crying
out 'Let us storm', but neither saw or knew the proper object.

Account of Captain Herbert Taylor, 2nd Dragoon Guards,
commanding an eight-oared cutter in the second attack on Tenerife[1]

I hope the Earl of St Vincent had thoroughly examined the intelligence
on which He detached Rear-Admiral Nelson to attack Santa Cruz;
I own the attempting Expedition on shore, without Troops seems
hazardous undertakings, and unless there is an almost certainty that
the Enemy have no military Force, ought not to be attempted, for I do
not wish for empty displays of valour when attended with the loss of
many Brave Men and no solid Advantage gained by their exploits.

George III to Lord Spencer, first lord of the Admiralty,
2 September 1797[2]

St Vincent now planned an extension to the blockade of Cadiz by an attack
on Spanish merchant ships at Santa Cruz on Tenerife, to be carried out by
a squadron of eight ships, the first independent expedition to be led by
Rear-Admiral Sir Horatio Nelson. The purpose of the attack was to capture
Spanish treasure in ships that, it was supposed, had been unable to reach
mainland Spain, but it cannot have been far from St Vincent's mind that
such an attack would also serve to occupy his still discontented seamen.
The plan was an echo of the dramatic victory of Admiral Blake in 1657,
when he too blockaded the Spanish in Cadiz. Blake then took all his ships
and destroyed the Spanish plate fleet and its bullion at Santa Cruz. Both
St Vincent and Nelson were aware of the historical precedent. The ships of
the viceroy of Mexico had been expected at Cadiz by British ships for some

months, and one of them had been captured. It was presumed that the viceroy had avoided the blockade by putting in at Tenerife.

It was unlikely that the garrison in the town of Santa Cruz could be taken unawares. Since the Spanish fleet was no longer at sea, raids by British frigates were already regular occurrences. In a night raid at the end of April 1797 Richard Bowen in the *Terpsichore*, accompanied by the *Dido*, cut out a Spanish merchant ship worth £30,000, although they failed to take a much larger ship, the *Princessa* from Manila, which was, according to Bowen, worth ten times as much.[3] A month later Benjamin Hallowell in the *Lively* and George Cockburn in *La Minerve* had done the same with a French corvette that had anchored near the town. Both these successes contributed to the feelings of the officers of St Vincent's fleet that the Spanish had no enthusiasm for this war, and that only determination was needed to overcome them. It was a line of thought strengthened by concern about incipient mutiny in the fleet and boredom with the blockade of Cadiz. The raid was of little strategic value, beyond inflicting economic damage on Spain by the capture of valuable specie.[4]

The idea for the expedition has traditionally been attributed to Nelson and appears to have come from a conversation over dinner with Troubridge in April, although ambitions to take the treasure ship had been current among the captains for some while. The day after his conversation with Troubridge, Nelson wrote a letter to St Vincent, brimming with enthusiasm rather than clarity, detailing the problems of the sea approach to the island. He anticipated difficulty in gaining support or soldiers from either General de Burgh or General O'Hara at Gibraltar. He had no information about the Spanish defences on land. He offered to lead a small squadron against Tenerife, but he pointed out to the commander-in-chief that with an operation such as this 'All the risk and the responsibility must rest with you.'[5]

St Vincent had already considered the idea of an attack on Santa Cruz while Nelson was escorting Fremantle's convoy from Elba during April and May 1797. His first priority was to keep the number of ships outside Cadiz to a level that would not prejudice the blockade, but he expected reinforcements. He wrote to Nelson in early June: 'the moment the expected ships arrive I will dash you off.'[6] Later in the month he informed Nelson: 'I have been examining young Longford, a sensible Lad, who was in one of the *Lively*'s boats; he is clear Santa Cruz may be carried with the greatest Ease.'[7] The view of a midshipman gained from a night raid, during which there was no landing, was hardly the level of intelligence that was needed before committing a strong force to a distant and potentially hazardous operation; but it was in this overconfident frame of mind that the expedition was conceived. Success was expected; no discussion or planning of what might happen if the first foray failed seems to have taken place.

St Vincent allowed Nelson to take the best of the captains from Cadiz with him. Two other 74s accompanied the *Theseus*. Troubridge, who was to lead the land forces, commanded the *Culloden* and young Samuel Hood was captain of the *Zealous*. Thomas Boulden Thompson of the *Leander* (50) was the one senior officer who had been to Santa Cruz before; but the *Leander* was late in joining and did not arrive until 24 July. The three frigate captains, Thomas Fremantle in the *Seahorse* (38), John Waller in the *Emerald* (36) and Richard Bowen in the *Terpsichore* (32) were the pick of the fleet. Finally, the fast sailing *Fox* cutter, captained by Lieutenant John Gibson, which had carried so many dispatches up and down the Mediterranean, was also included in the squadron. On 14 July, Nelson spent the whole day with St Vincent receiving his orders; he was to make 'a sudden and vigorous assault'.[8]

Next day at daylight the squadron set off to sail the 800 miles down the coast of Africa to Tenerife. Without soldiers or store ships, the operation could be only a raid and not a siege. On board the ships were scaling ladders for the walls of the forts, while the *Seahorse* towed a small vessel with a howitzer for bombarding them, in the charge of an artillery officer.[9] The ships picked up the north-east trade winds, a moderate and then a freshening breeze behind them; with the 'Canary Current' underneath them, the voyage took only five days before Tenerife was sighted. On 21 July the north end of the island was eight or nine leagues distant.[10]

A landing at Santa Cruz was a formidable undertaking, primarily because of the constant heavy surf generated by the Atlantic swell. Only the mole, built by the Spaniards immediately in front of the town, afforded any protection from it. The coast is almost straight and is exposed to easterly winds; the only landing place was at the mole. Off the town the depth of water plummets only a short distance from the shore, making anchoring impossible. At spring tides there is a tidal current of a knot that runs parallel to the shore, north-east with the rising tide and south-west with the falling tide. Steep mountains lie behind the town, making the winds very uncertain, particularly in summer; they sometimes blow with localized intensity for short periods, in a completely different direction from the prevailing winds, and often at night. Today the local fishermen call this wind 'the White Sheet' because of the churned-up surface of the water on a flat sea; later pilot books warned sailing ships away from the area.[11] Nelson possessed none of this local knowledge. It presented a very different proposition to

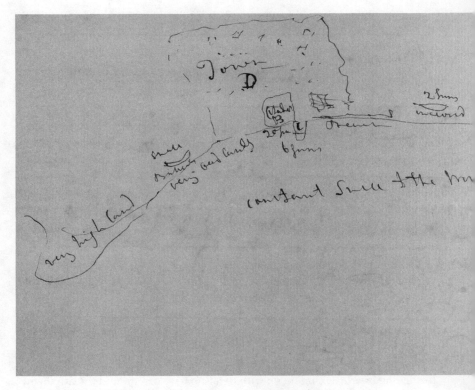

Nelson's sketch of the coast at Santa Cruz, Tenerife

his recent successful and bloodless operations in the tideless Mediterranean at Porto Ferrajo and Capraia.

Nelson knew little or nothing of the strength of the Spanish defences. While the line of forts along the shore was understood, no detailed information on the town, roads or interior was evident in the planning of the expedition. A small sketch survives in Nelson's papers, but its inaccuracy and lack of detail support the idea that the plan of attack was quite vague.[12] From Spanish sources we know that in all there were only eighty-four Spanish guns to oppose them, spread out over fifteen batteries along the shore and in the town of Santa Cruz. Twelve of them, however, were in the north-east fort of Paso Alto.[13] The town itself was a mass of narrow streets, defended by about 1,600 soldiers and civilians from all over the island. Only 400 of them were professional soldiers, although they were supported by over a hundred French sailors returned to the shore after the capture of *La Mutine*, the corvette taken by Cockburn and Hallowell in

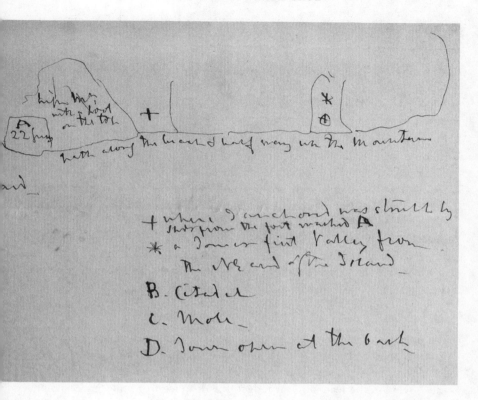

May. These forces were led by an experienced and determined professional soldier, Don Antonio Gutierrez, commandant general of the Canary Islands, a 68-year-old veteran of many campaigns. He had been in similar situations against the British in Minorca in 1756 and the Falkland Islands in 1771.[14] Gutierrez had very thin resources at his command, but they were backed up by natural defences: the current, the surf, the mountains and the heat.

Given that this expedition had been in the planning for three months, it is remarkable that there was no apparent effort by either St Vincent or Nelson to attempt the difficult task of obtaining detailed intelligence. Nor is it even clear why, if the cargo of the *Princessa*, moored off the town, was the objective, it was necessary to land at all; perhaps there was the presumption that the cargo had been landed. All previous successful operations against Santa Cruz, including Blake's, had not involved landing. Nelson planned the management of the boats before landing with care; but his plans were unformulated once British forces had landed. Captain Miller's account makes clear that the shore party was relying on 'very imperfect information given by a seaman of the *Emerald*, and a servant of Captain Fremantle's (neither of whom had been at Santa Cruz for five years)'.[15]

Without soldiers or siege weapons to wear down Spanish resistance (which, in any case, would have required a patience that was anathema to Nelson's style of warfare), the only hope of success was a sudden descent under the cover of darkness, landing forces on the beach at dawn. Nine hundred seamen and marines, drawn from all ships in the squadron, were to embark on the three frigates, with the ships of the line following three hours later. The sailors were to scale and overpower the forts to the east of the town and, having secured them, to make straight for the town. Nelson gave Troubridge very detailed orders on 20 July.[16] Timing was critical. The boats had to land the sailors undetected before dawn on the morning of 22 July.

While still many miles from Tenerife, the officers and seamen of the landing force transferred from the larger ships to the frigates during the morning of 21 July. They set off towards the distant shore that evening, led by Richard Bowen in the *Terpsichore*, with Troubridge on board. The operation went wrong from the start. The bomb vessel, towed by the *Seahorse*, had to be cast off before it was swamped. When it came to the decision to heave to, in order to put the seamen in the boats, Troubridge and Bowen in the lead ship misjudged the distance from the shore, for at sea mountains of great height and mass invariably look nearer than they really are. In the words of Ralph Miller, the laden boats were 'more leagues than intended miles from Santa Cruz'.[17] Careful planning to keep the boats together came to naught. In spite of rowing hard against the current, at dawn the boats were still a mile and a half from the proposed landing place. In Santa Cruz the alarm was raised instantly, and every advantage of surprise was lost. The sailors were already tired. Troubridge did not press on. The boats headed back to the frigates, which were coming up fast, as were the *Theseus* and the ships of the line. Troubridge, Bowen and Captain Oldfield of the marines conferred quickly with Nelson; they reckoned that if the landing force scaled the heights behind the fort, it could be shelled from there and could yet be taken. Nelson agreed. He ordered the landings to go ahead and the landing force to head for the Jurada Mountain behind the fort.[18] By now the north-east battery was fully alert. A direct assault against a prepared enemy in the battery was out of the question. The seamen were greeted by grapeshot as they landed through the surf.

The heights to which Troubridge and his force were moving overlooked the fort of Paso Alto. The Spanish commander immediately dispatched 200 of his best troops to seize other heights, which they did rapidly. He also sent troops to the town of La Laguna to ensure that the British did not penetrate inland.[19] The British seamen dragged two small field pieces up the steep sides of the mountain as the sun rose in the sky. The sailors became exhausted and dehydrated. No water had been brought; Nelson had specifically ordered the seamen to land 'with only their arms'.[20] Troubridge was extremely ill when he reached the top of the mountain; Miller thought he was going to die.[21] One exhausted seaman did die. It was immediately apparent that the climb was fruitless. The range of the small field pieces barely reached the fort from their position. Between the Jurada Mountain and Santa Cruz there was a steep valley, hidden from the shore. On the heights opposite were well-established Spanish troops, supplied with superior field pieces and with water. Half an hour before sunset, Troubridge ordered the landing force back to the ships for the second time that day. It was a pitch-black night and the slopes were precipitous. Two seamen lost their lives when they fell down the mountain.

The landing force reached the frigates at eight o'clock that night. Miller records that on coming on board he drank three cups of tea one after the other. The frigates sailed south into the night. Nelson had remained on board during the day; his frustration can be imagined. He was later to write that had he been in command ashore rather than Troubridge the result would have been 'a complete success'.[22] Fremantle, however, had brought away from the shore a German with recent knowledge of Santa Cruz, who appeared to give accurate figures for the number of defenders but, more importantly, described a vivid picture of panic and lack of morale among the Spanish forces in the town. Betsey Fremantle translated, and Fremantle took the information to Nelson. Here was intelligence, but was it accurate? The German's information encouraged Nelson to think that dash and daring could still carry the day.

Nelson now formulated a second plan, one that was completely different from the 22 July attack and that involved an element of deception. He would bring the ships to anchor in daylight by the north-east fort so that the Spanish would think that the attack would once more fall there. Under cover of darkness, the seamen would again embark in the boats, but this time make a concentrated central assault on the town by the mole. According to Miller, 'The Captains being all assembled in the Admiral's Cabin the guide was a second time examined before them, and the plan already fixed, determin'd by the Admiral to be put into execution.'[23] The decision was Nelson's alone, and he would stand by it by leading the landing force. It was one of the most foolhardy decisions that he ever made; the humiliation of the first attack had affected his judgement. In a later letter he admitted as much: 'My pride suffered.' The second attack was 'a forlorn hope, yet the honour of our Country called for the attack . . . I never expected to return.'[24] He was under no illusions about the danger of the operation. At eight o'clock that night he wrote a maudlin letter to St Vincent: 'tomorrow my head will probably be crowned with either laurel or cypress.' He tried to dissuade his stepson, Josiah Nisbet, who was to be an aide-de-camp, from accompanying him. William Hoste was to stay behind.[25] Among the officers the talk had been upbeat: Betsey Fremantle, who by now knew that she was pregnant, had no qualms: 'As the taking of this place seemed an easy and almost sure thing, I went to bed after they were gone apprehending no danger for Fremantle.'[26]

The second attack, on 25 July, was undermined by the sea conditions. Miller recorded that 'it was a star light, yet not a clear night, with little wind and a swell that became considerable as we approached the shore.'[27] The frigates anchored at five o'clock in the afternoon. The Spanish were meant to see great activity. At 7.30 the bomb vessel starting to shell the Paso Alto Fort, ineffectually as it was to prove.[28] At 10.30 Nelson, with Fremantle and Josiah Nisbet in his boat, led the boats off; more men were put into the *Fox* cutter, which was to follow behind the main landing party, to be landed at the mole after the first boats went ashore. To keep them together, the boats were roped to each other; each was loaded heavily with men, with scaling ladders lashed to their sides. Oars were muffled. Yet 300 yards from the shore they were discovered by a Spanish sentry on the end of the mole. An immediate cannonade was fired from the town. The log of the *Theseus* records the time as 2.30 in the morning.[29]

The boats were now cast off from each other, and the crews rowed hard for the shore, although it was so dark that little could be seen with precision. The force of the current parallel to the shore now had its effect, and the boats were split up; some never put their crews ashore.[30] A landing with concentrated force was now impossible. Only Bowen and his men reached the mole, which they stormed, immediately spiking the guns; but they were then mown down by grapeshot from guns further up the town. Captain Richard Bowen was killed. Other Spanish batteries situated to the east and west fired diagonally across the area by the mole. Several officers commented upon the pitch black, viewed from sea to shore. 'From the darkness of the night,' Troubridge later reported to Nelson, 'I did not immediately hit the mole . . . the boats were full of water in an instant and stove against the rocks.'[31] Miller, Hood and Waller also landed to the west of the mole, where they were swamped thirty yards out, wading chest high to the shore through the surf and under heavy fire from the shore. The *Fox*, coming behind the boats, crowded with men, received an unlucky heavy shot from a distant battery. She was struck below the waterline and sank quickly; nearly a hundred seamen and marines drowned as a result.

As Nelson stepped out of his launch, he was struck just above the right elbow by a musket ball; blood poured from a cut artery. Josiah Nisbet showed calmness and presence of mind. He sat Nelson down in the boat, staunched the blood and applied two silk neckerchiefs as tourniquets. The young lieutenant ordered five seamen to refloat the boat, which they did with difficulty, for the tide had receded. They rowed back, still under fire, as quickly as they could to the *Theseus*. On the way they picked up two or three of the *Fox*'s men from the sea. When the boat reached the flagship, Josiah called up to warn the surgeon that an amputation would be required. In spite of shock and his loss of blood, Nelson refused a chair to hoist him on board. He came up the side with one arm, with Nisbet immediately behind him in case he fell. Nisbet later recalled: 'On getting on the quarter-deck the officers as usual saluted him by taking off their hats, which compliment Nelson returned with his left hand as if nothing had happened.'[32] At no other time in his life did he demonstrate more vividly his mental and physical toughness. Thomas Eshelby, the surgeon, amputated the arm immediately, assisted by Louis Remonier, the surgeon's first mate. Eshelby entered in his journal: 'Compund fracture of the right Arm by a musket ball passing thro' a little above the Elbow, an Artery divided, the Arm was immediately amputated.'[33] It was a fortunate decision to operate quickly, for some naval surgeons of the time would have waited to perform the operation in the mistaken belief that the patient needed time to regain strength.[34] Nelson's arm was amputated high above the elbow. He was given opium after the operation and every night afterwards for some weeks.[35]

On shore, the landing parties made little progress. The loss of officers had its effect on the enterprise and courage of the seamen, who were out of their element and under heavy fire. The maze of streets baffled those who managed to drive the Spanish defenders back. The citadel at the landward end of the mole was impenetrable without the scaling ladders, which had been lost with the boats; ammunition was washed overboard or dampened by the surf. The sailors became disheartened, but, urged on by the officers, they formed a marching column. Troubridge, Hood, Waller and Miller managed to join up in the great square. At this point, according to a Spanish report, the British 'charging with Bayonets on the Canary Battalion killed 22, wounded 3 and took four prisoners'. The report claimed that the men 'rushed without orders . . . which very much displeased their officers'.[36] The British now had captured prisoners and muskets.

Local knowledge, however, was against the British, who found themselves under sniper fire. Guterriez had expertly placed field guns at the head of narrow streets. The British officers and seamen retreated into a convent, where the Spanish slowly surrounded them. There followed several hours of negotiation, with Troubridge attempting to bluff Guterriez by threatening to burn the town. By now the officers knew of the landing casualties and of the loss of the *Fox*, which had carried reserves of ammunition as well as of men. The British position was hopeless. After several rounds of negotiation involving, on the British side, bluster and bluff, Troubridge sent Hood to agree a capitulation. Guterriez was more than generous. He allowed the British force to withdraw without molestation as long as they sailed away from Tenerife and the Canary Islands without further attacks. This honourable agreement worked well, threatened only by the jeers of the French sailors from the *Mutine*, which nearly caused a renewal of conflict with the British seamen.[37] Food was sent by the governor to the British seamen. His offer of dinner to the officers was politely refused. Since so many boats had been lost during the landings, the Spanish provided three brigs and thirteen boats to return the sailors and the wounded to their ships.[38] Nelson exchanged courtesies with Gutierrez, offering to take back dispatches that he would deliver to the Spanish authorities at Cadiz. Ralph Miller was impressed: 'Indeed, however much it may have degenerated on the Continent, the Old Spanish Honour seem'd quite alive in Santa Cruz.'[39]

British casualties were very heavy. The total number of officers and men killed and drowned (153) was more than double the number of those who had lost their lives in the great battle off St Vincent (73). There were 110 wounded. No ship escaped casualties. The *Theseus* lost forty-six; the *Culloden* thirty-nine.[40] Some of these were among the brightest prospects in the navy. St Vincent's protégé Richard Bowen had seemed destined for high rank: he was buried at sea the next day.[41] John Weatherhead from Norfolk, popular, full of promise and recently made lieutenant, died on 30 July of a stomach wound.[42] Captains Fremantle and Thompson were wounded. Fremantle, who had a bad flesh wound in the arm, suffered much pain before he was back to health again, not least because the surgeon in the *Seahorse* was not competent. Once everyone was on board the ships sailed, but not before the Spaniards in the Paso Alto Fort fired some shots over the ships. One went through the *Seahorse*'s sails.[43] It was the final indignity.

The passage back to the fleet at Cadiz, against the wind and current, y will be able to give me a frigate to convey the remains of my carcase to England, God Bless you my Dear Sir & Believe me your most obliged & faithful

Horatio Nelson

You will excuse my Scrawl considering it is my first Attempt

Sir John Jervis K B.

Nelson's first letter written with his left hand

took three weeks.[44] Only ten days before, the journey south had taken a quarter of the time. In the long periods of calm the heat took its toll on the wounded. When the wind blew fresh from the north-east, it was uncomfortable; Betsey noted that Fremantle could not get out of his cot when there was any motion to the ship.[45] On board the *Theseus* Thomas Eshelby noted in his journal that Nelson's arm appeared to be progressing, although one of the ligatures, applied to the artery to prevent infection, had not come away. It proved later to have attached itself to a nerve and was to remain a problem for many weeks. Louis Remonier, the Frenchman who had been with Nelson from the *Agamemnon*'s time at Toulon as surgeon's first mate, sat up with the admiral for fourteen nights. Nelson was given opium every night.[46] He wasted no time in beginning to write with his left hand. From the *Seahorse* Betsey Fremantle wrote him a note, which he replied to on 6 August: 'he answered me a long note. He is astonishingly well.'[47]

By 16 August the squadron reached the fleet off Cadiz. St Vincent reported to Spencer that Nelson was 'in such health that nothing could prevent his coming aboard the *Ville de Paris*, he din'd with me & I have every ground of hope that he will be restored to the Service of his King and Country.'[48] On the same day Nelson wrote to St Vincent: 'A left-handed admiral will never again be considered as useful, therefore the sooner I get to a very humble cottage, the better, and make room for a better man to serve the State.'[49] For the outwardly tough St Vincent it was indeed a sad time: he confided to Spencer that 'my mind labours under too much anguish to enter into details upon this subject . . . It has been my fate during this war to lose the Officers most dear to me; by that of poor Bowen, I am quite unmanned.'[50] As a small compensation to Nelson, St Vincent made Josiah Nisbet captain of the *Dolphin* hospital ship and felt certain that peace with France and Spain would soon be signed.[51]

In spite of Nelson's vigour, his frame of mind was pessimistic and resigned. 'I shall not be surprised to be neglected and forgot,' he wrote to Fanny, 'as probably I shall no longer be considered as useful.'[52] It was obvious that both Nelson and Fremantle needed to return to England to recover from their wounds. In his admiral's journal St Vincent entered the comfortingly bureaucratic note: 'Rear-Admiral Nelson to proceed to Spithead in the *Seahorse* to acquaint the Secretary of the Admiralty of his arrival & wait there for further orders.'[53]

On 20 August, Nelson came aboard the *Seahorse*. He was 'in great spirits', according to Betsey Fremantle, although she added, 'I find it looks shocking to be without one arm.' He was accompanied by the surgeon Thomas Eshelby, who entered in his journal: 'The Sore on the Stump about the size of a shilling. One of the Ligatures not come away.'[54] The next day Betsey observed that 'though stout and hearty he is not free from pain.'[55] This cheerful mood did not last. The ship made little progress until the winds went round to the south and west on 27 August. Nelson described the voyage as 'very miserable'.[56] Eshelby recorded that, in spite of opium, Nelson experienced 'Twitching Pains at times particularly by Night'.[57] With many casualties aboard, Betsey complained: 'This ship is worse than an hospital, a number of sick and wounded from the *Theseus*, from morning tonight and from night to morning, you hear nothing but these unfortunate people groan.'[58] Fremantle was also still in great pain. In spite of Eshelby's attentions, Nelson's stump did not heal. He was not a good patient. On

26 August, Betsey noted that 'the Admiral is far from being well.' Towards the end of the two-week passage he was depressed, she noted on 31 August, the day the Scilly Isles light was sighted. 'The Admiral very low and wishes himself back to Cadiz.'[59] With a freshening breeze the ship's progress was rapid, past Portland on 1 September and then through the Needles Channel. Eshelby noted on 1 September that Nelson 'would not suffer the ligature to be touched'.[60] On Saturday, 2 September, the *Seahorse* anchored at Spithead. Nelson went ashore immediately after dinner and straight to Bath to seek assistance in the healing of his arm.

Yet even in disaster Nelson's luck had held. Had Gutierrez been a younger and more ambitious victor, he might have exacted more from his helpless British captives, even though it would have been difficult to hold prisoners with his small forces. How lucky Nelson had been in limiting the damage was understood by influential people in London. William Young wrote about the incident to Charles Morice Pole, but was not prepared to risk saying what he really thought in a letter. 'I must not give you my opinion of this expedition. We were however fortunate in not having mischief done to our Ships, and in getting some of our men off again, which the Spaniards, had they chose it, might have prevented.'[61] Later he wrote to Pole: 'The expedition was indeed a sad one. The Admiral must have been mortified.' He, like the king, questioned St Vincent's judgement: 'I should, like you, be glad to find a perfect Commander, but between ourselves, he who ordered this expedition, is on many accounts very far from being one.'[62] There was criticism of St Vincent around the Admiralty boardroom table, where he could count some political and professional enemies, William Young among them. With the numbers of ships at the blockade of Cadiz less than adequate, why had he dispersed his fleet in such a manner? Why had he not insisted that soldiers should accompany the expedition? In any case, it was too late in the season to send an expedition on a complex siege operation. St Vincent went on the defensive, writing to Evan Nepean: 'I was not deceived about the strength of Santa Cruz except that I did not expect the Crew of the *Mutine* who were not exchanged, the British subjects, and Americans would have joined in the defence, to them alone is to be attributed the failure in the gallant attack.'[63] In this debate, the notion established itself that the Spanish defenders numbered 8,000. The reputations of St Vincent and Nelson had been harmed. But the loss of his arm provided Nelson with a cushion against criticism of the Santa Cruz expedition. Lord Spencer wrote a sympathetic letter, referred to the 'glorious though unsuccessful attempt' and hoped that Nelson would call on him in London after his return from Bath.[64] When Nelson met Spencer at the Admiralty – their first meeting – there was a diplomatic silence when Nelson described his second attack on Tenerife.[65]

The landings at Santa Cruz were the last time that Nelson saw action ashore. He had participated in or led seven amphibious operations. As a subordinate, impatient of the steady attrition exercised by the army, he had taken part in the Nicaraguan expedition in 1780, and at the sieges of Calvi and Bastia on Corsica in 1794; these operations eventually achieved their objectives by patient, orthodox methods. As a young captain he had attacked Turk's Island at the end of the American Revolutionary War, failing humiliatingly because of lack of intelligence and forethought. At Elba and Capraia, from a position of overwhelming force, he had been well organized and successful without a shot being fired. Little had prepared him for the disaster at Tenerife. Nelson had no alternative to headlong, frontal assault, for officers and seamen were not trained for disciplined marching or infantry tactics. Seamen performed prodigious feats in hauling guns, in moving troops and in evacuating the army from difficult situations. One sea officer put it well: 'Few men, if any, are to be preferred to sailors at a rush or an assault, when headlong impetuosity and daring courage are required; but take them out of their ships, and marshal them on shore, and they will be found restless and unsteady, and particularly impatient of inactivity.'[66] In control of a more fluid situation at sea, in superior ships, better manned and gunned, taking the enemy head-on was an acceptable risk. On land, courage and will power were not enough. As St Vincent wrote to Nelson on his return to Cadiz, quoting Addison, 'Mortals cannot command success.'[67]

16

Recovery and High Command

September 1797–May 1798

*Addressed to that intrepid Admiral Sir Horatio Nelson on his arrival
from scenes of Danger and Glory to the Arms of His Family in this
City*

> *But ah what subject worthier to inspire*
> *The grateful Bard, and call forth all his fire*
> *That NELSON – form'd in every part complete*
> *Glorious alike in Conquest and Defeat . . .*
> *Our British Warriors, midst the Cannon's roar*
> *Seize lofty TENERIFFE, thy rocky shore*
> *Impetuous rush resistless in their course*
> *By Glory fir'd against superior force . . .*
> *And then O NELSON! Subject of our praise*
> *While conscious Worth shall gild thy future days*
> *Sooth'd with the blessings of domestic life*
> *A reverend Father, and a faithful wife.*
> *Bath Herald, 9 September 1797*

Nelson's first visit to Bath in 1780 for a cure had passed without public notice; his sudden arrival at the beginning of September 1797 was news. The Corporation of Bath congratulated him. Full accounts of the attack on Santa Cruz were in the three Bath newspapers; these were taken mostly verbatim from the London papers and written alongside reminders of the Battle of St Vincent. Those published later in the week were topped up by hurriedly written poetic tributes.[1] For this at least Nelson was happy and satisfied. 'My reception from John Bull has been just what I wish'd for,' he wrote to St Vincent. 'I assure you they never forget your name.'[2]

Nelson and Fanny had last seen each other on board the *Agamemnon* when he had set off for the Mediterranean nearly four and a half years before. She and his father were at Bath in their regular lodgings. Nelson had dispatched a letter to Fanny written with his left hand on 16 August when he reached the fleet off Cadiz. He did not tell her exactly what had happened, although it was clear that something serious was amiss; as usual he put the best face on things to save her anxiety. She may not, however, have received the letter by the time he reached her.[3] No evidence remains of the reunion, of its emotion, of Fanny's reaction to Nelson's amputated arm, of Edmund's relief, of Nelson's feelings at being in England and away from the fleet.

Nelson's immediate task was to have his arm, still very painful, dressed by Mr Nicholls, surgeon of the Bath General Hospital, which was done every day.[4] 'My husband's spirits are good,' Fanny wrote to William Suckling, 'although he suffers a great deal of pain.' William Nelson arrived at Bath a week later.[5] Letters came from Lord Hood and Lord Spencer. Replies were written mostly by Fanny, with short additions from Nelson in his left hand, his writing crabbed and irregular. Fanny wrote to Suckling: 'Such a letter from Lord Hood – it does him honour, and I have forgot the ill-treatment of former years – which My good man received from him.'[6] Lord Spencer wrote from Althorp that he would soon be in Town, but that Nelson was not to hurry away from Bath and that he should be careful of his wound.[7] Nelson wrote to several of the families of those who were still in the ships off Cadiz to let them know that they were safe, for which Ralph Miller later thanked him. Nelson's thoughtfulness had 'completely sav'd the torment of all those anxious fears to which the tenderness of a female bosom is so liable'.[8] However, he seems to have failed to write a letter of condolence to John Weatherhead's father in Norfolk, who first knew of his son's death by reading of it in the newspaper.[9]

In spite of the attentions of Mr Nicholls, the painful arm showed no sign of healing, and Nelson soon decided that he required the opinion of London surgeons. Fanny wrote to Maurice Nelson, who booked lodgings for them at No. 141 Bond Street. Still anxious about the impact of Santa Cruz on his career, Nelson ensured that his first visit was to Lord Spencer at the Admiralty. The first lord was sympathetic but particularly guarded in his opinion about the second attack. This was the first time that Spencer and Nelson had met, and it was clearly a satisfactory interview on both sides. They discussed Nelson's pension, 'the same as those of 1st June, £712 with deductions', and established that he would serve again: '–the Moment I am cured,' Nelson wrote to St Vincent in shaky, unformed handwriting, 'I shall offer myself for service and if you continue to hold your Opinion of me, I shall press to return with all the zeal, although not with all the personal ability I had formerly.'[10] Spencer reported immediately to St Vincent: 'I have had great pleasure in making acquaintance with Sir Horatio Nelson, & am very happy to have it in my power to inform you that he seems likely to recover entirely from the effect of his Wound, & to be able to serve.'[11] It was arranged that Spencer should take him to the king's levee at St James's Palace the following week: his investiture as a knight of the Bath was to take place after the reception.[12] For the supporters for his coat of arms he chose 'a British Sailor on the sinister side trampling on the colours of Spain, and on the dexter, a lion tearing them with his teeth. [The] motto is "Faith and Works".'[13] There is little reason to doubt the story that is often told of the levee. When the king observed that Nelson had lost his right arm, Nelson presented Captain Berry as 'his right hand'. To which the king replied, 'But your Country has a claim for a bit more of you.'[14]

For three months after his return, Nelson's arm was still very painful, particularly at night, and no plans could be made to go to sea until the ligature had come away from his arm and the wound healed. Throughout this time he attended to the multitude of tasks that had accumulated during his long absence.[15] First among them was to buy a house of his own. Roundwood, two miles north of Ipswich, was substantial, with a 'barn, stables, cow-house and other offices and a well-planted garden' together with fifty acres. Nelson was successful in the auction of 27 September: the house was purchased for £2,000 and the articles of agreement signed on 13 November.[16] He also instructed his agents to acquire £1,600 of 3 per cent consols and 5 per cent stock.[17] His purchases from Italy, 'bronze figures, oil, soap, some drawings and China', aboard the *Seahorse* were guided through customs by the third lieutenant, Edward Galwey, who managed to ensure that they were duty-free; Galwey added: 'I believe I told a lie.'[18] A sculpture (Nelson called it 'my Cleopatra') that had been left aboard the *Agamemnon* was retrieved by Thomas Fellowes, the *Agamemnon*'s purser, and forwarded to Nelson in London, a service that Nelson returned by writing on Fellowes's behalf, successfully, for an appointment to a new ship a few months later.[19]

Other naval business took his time. On 12 October he attended the Court of Examiners in the College of Surgeons when the damage to his right eye was assessed as 'equal to the loss of an eye and equivalent to the loss of a limb'.[20] He did not qualify for a pension for the loss of his eye, because he received a pension of £1,000 a year for the loss of his arm.[21] He corresponded with the other junior flag officers of the Mediterranean fleet, Charles Thompson, William Waldegrave and Robert Man, about their entitlement to freight money (the percentage of the value of merchant's specie transported by warship and a valuable source of income), which St Vincent did not intend to share with his junior flag officers. This dispute foreshadowed the later prize-money case between Nelson and St Vincent. It was debatable whether the freight-money case was worth giving to the lawyers, and Nelson took the trouble to gather the opinions of senior officers, such as Howe, Hood and Duncan, on their view of precedent in the matter.[22] Some prize-money cases from the actions around Corsica were still extant, but Nelson paid little attention to them, and the residue of business was cleared up by George Cockburn during the following year.[23]

Nelson also had to help his family. At his father's request he managed the transfer of the incumbency of the parish of Burnham Thorpe from his father to his younger brother Suckling Nelson. He had to endure the incessant pressure of his elder brother William Nelson, intent on using Nelson's fame for advancement in the Church. William was surveying vacancies at most of the cathedrals in southern England. 'I would give up a living for a Prebend,' he wrote loftily, 'if my income could be bettered, & you have my free leave to propose my giving up Hilbrough for a stall if it [does] not bring in £100 per annum additional.' William was not successful.[24]

The arm would not heal. 'The ligature is still fast to the nerve, and very painful at times,' Nelson wrote to St Vincent on 6 October.[25] The wound was seen every day for a month by an eminent surgeon, William Cruikshanks, who advised patience. So did William Nelson, who met a surgeon in Swaffham and, unusually, passed on some good advice. 'I mentioned particularly the apparent pain in your right hand,' William reported; 'he said it was a sure sign of a nerve being taken up with the artery, indeed he says it is hardly possible to avoid it, as there are so many and such small ones: that you must now have patience and all will do well.' On 19 October a further consultation took place with three of the most senior surgeons in London from the army, St Bartholomew's and St George's hospitals.[26] Again they advised caution. Having paid their fees, Nelson decided to employ young Michael Jefferson, the surgeon's mate who had attended his eye in Corsica; he had just been made up to full surgeon.[27] At last at the end of November the ligature finally came away and the pain decreased. By 13 December the wound had begun to heal and Jefferson was no longer required.[28]

Throughout these months the pace of the social life of the Nelsons was considerable. He came to know the first lord of the Admiralty. Nelson and Spencer were the same age, and the aristocratic Whig peer established a sympathetic relationship with the young rear-admiral. Spencer had come to office at the age of thirty-six with no previous experience of government and certainly with no knowledge of the navy, but not long after the Portland Whigs joined Pitt's government Spencer had been made first lord. One of his predecessors, Lord Howe, was impressed: 'Lord Spencer is a young man of singular probity and worth. Has much application, and I believe intelligent capacity. And those that have business or intercourse with him will find him to be of a most pleasing character.'[29] Spencer's wife, Lavinia, one of the great political hostesses of the age, became a great admirer of Nelson. He did not, according to her later recollections, cut much of a figure: the first time she saw him he was 'a most uncouth creature . . . He looked so sickly, it was painful to see him; and his general appearance was that of an idiot, so much so, that when he spoke, and his wonderful mind broke forth, it was a sort of surprise that riveted my whole attention.'[30]

In the first week of October, Nelson, Fanny and Gilbert Elliot, recently raised to the peerage as Lord Minto, dined with Lord Hood in the gracious surroundings of Greenwich Hospital, of which Hood was now governor. Hood's elegant wood panelled rooms overlooked the busy Thames. Minto reported to his wife that 'Nelson looks better and fresher than I ever remember him. His arm, however, is by no means well . . . He suffers a great deal of violent pain, and takes opium every night. He is impatient for the healing of the wound that he may go to sea again.'[31] In early October, Nelson saw Rear-Admiral William Young, now on the Board of Admiralty, who was a useful source of information at the highest level. After these occasions both Minto and Young wrote detailed descriptions of the state of Nelson's arm and ligature.[32] A week later Fanny held a family dinner for William Locker and his son.[33] For occasions like these the pheasants and partridges sent by Thomas Coke from Holkham came in useful.[34] When Lieutenant Edward Galwey visited, he wrote afterwards to Nelson regretting that he had been unable to thank him for 'his obliging offer of being one of your officers when employed' because of 'the numerous company at your Apartments'.[35]

Towards the end of the next month we catch a glimpse of the political machine at work and of some of the formidable individuals who were to press for Nelson's advancement. On 28 November, Nelson dined with the secretary-at-war, William Windham, at his Park Street residence in eminent company. Windham had invited a cabinet minister, Lord Loughborough, the lord chancellor, with whom Nelson had recently been in correspondence about the living of Burnham Thorpe.[36] Two of Windham's oldest political friends were there, Lords Minto and Cholmondeley, the latter the private secretary to the prince of Wales. The prince's former secretary was also present, Rear-Admiral John Willett Payne, and his brother Lord Lavington.

The final name noted in Windham's diary was 'Grenville'; this was less likely to have been the foreign secretary, Lord Grenville, than his elder brother Thomas, who was to be first lord of the Admiralty in 1806.[37] Although Lord Spencer was closely associated with this group of Whigs who had followed Lord Portland into Pitt's government, on this occasion he was not present. Here was Nelson's chance to widen his political support beyond Windham and Minto.

At eleven o'clock that night, he sat down to write an excited letter to Edward Berry. Having first congratulated Berry on his recent marriage, he went on to relay important news to his flag captain: he, Nelson, was to have the new 80-gun *Foudroyant* as his flagship; she finally was to be completed in January 1798 and commissioned in February. 'I am not perfectly at liberty about a First lieutenant, but I believe Galwey will be the man; Mr Vassall second, although a much older officer; but if they do not choose to stand as I like in the Ship, they may stay away; and so I have told Mr Vassall.'[38] The Admiralty might be bringing the appointment of officers under its control, but the Board could be influenced. He did not tell Berry that the ship was to return to the Mediterranean command under Lord St Vincent.[39] A week later Lady Spencer invited Nelson to dinner, as 'Lord Spencer wants to speak relative to your ship.'[40]

The day after Windham's dinner, Nelson was again in the limelight when he received the Freedom of the City of London from the lord mayor; he was presented with a handsome gold box, value a hundred guineas, and 'an elegant sword'.[41] The address was made on behalf of the lord mayor by the once notorious radical politician, John Wilkes, now living quietly as the city chamberlain. He referred not only to Nelson's gallantry at Tenerife and the 'severe and cruel wounds you suffered in the service of your country' but also to his custom of praising his brother officers and seamen and neglecting to mention himself, which he ascribed to a 'rare heroic modesty'. It was handsome recognition for the victory of 14 February and compensation for the Santa Cruz action that had been lost.[42]

Further celebrations followed with the news of Admiral Duncan's victory over the Dutch at Camperdown on 11 October. Duncan had captured eleven Dutch ships, mostly 64s, reversing the gloom engendered by the Spithead and Nore mutinies in the early summer. The capital was illuminated and the crowds rejoiced. Some, including Nelson, felt that Duncan received overmuch applause. Windham grumbled to a relative: 'For Lord St Vincent's victory, the greatest beyond all examples in naval annals, not a candle burnt.'[43] The king decided to celebrate all three major naval victories of the war on 19 December, in part to mirror the French who paraded regularly in Paris when they had something to celebrate, but also as a show of national unity and royal confidence. Parades, which could dissolve in disorder, had not hitherto been an aspect of British political life outside the rumbustious electioneering of the age. After the 1784 Westminster election the Foxites had paraded to snub Pitt's government, while in 1786 during a parade an attempt was made on the king's life. Outward show was not part of George III's style.[44] Nelson received his invitation: 'His Majesty has signified his Intentions of going to St Paul's Cathedral . . . to return thanks to ALMIGHTY GOD for the many signal and Important Victories obtained by His Majesty's Navy during the present War.'[45] Detailed printed instructions followed. The ensigns of the French ships captured at the 'Glorious First of June', followed by those of the Spanish captured at Cape St Vincent and then by Dutch colours from Camperdown, were to be marched to St Paul's and presented during a service of thanksgiving.

The procession was led by the band of the Chatham division of marines. Two hundred and fifty marching sailors symbolized the end of the mutinies. Members of both Houses of Parliament travelled in coaches to attend the service. Nelson shared a coach with an old friend, Rear-Admiral Sir Thomas Pasley, whom he had first met as a lieutenant when Pasley dined aboard the *Lowestoffe* in 1778; Pasley had lost a leg at the Battle of the First of June. They were accompanied by Sir Roger Curtis, Howe's flag captain at the same battle, who from this point was to befriend and admire Nelson.[46] The coach was surrounded by seamen and marines. The colours were presented early in the service, Sir Charles Thompson leading the officers presenting those of Spain. Behind him came Rear-Admirals Nelson and Waldegrave, followed by captains from the Mediterranean Station, including Sir Charles Knowles, John Sutton, James Dacres and Henry Towry. Their task was to hold the fly of the flag as it was paraded up the aisle.

The victor of the Battle of St Vincent was, of course, still at sea off Cadiz, continuing to grumble to Nepean about the quality of his officers. Since he had sent home the majority of those carrying the Spanish colours in St Paul's as unsatisfactory, it can be safely assumed that the commander-in-chief would not have enjoyed the occasion; in any case, he had a thoroughgoing dislike of ostentation. The crowds were appreciative, although there was some political demonstration and disorder in the margins. The *Bath Journal* reported that Pitt's carriage 'received considerable applause (though not unmixed with disapprobation from the multitude)', while 'some villains no doubt for the purpose of creating confusion and thereby plunder contrived to get an overdrove ox into the crowd. The beast was driven through

St Paul's churchyard.' Overall, the event succeeded; only the opposition *Morning Chronicle* called it a 'Frenchified farce'.[47]

With his arm now healed, Nelson's aim was to get to sea and back to the fleet off Cadiz as quickly as possible. News came from the Navy Board that the new *Foudroyant* was not going to be ready for some months, and the smaller, 74-gun *Vanguard*, refitting at Chatham, was substituted. Just before the Colours Ceremony at St Paul's, Nelson went to see his new ship, which was floated out of dock on 18 December. She had received a major refit that included new rigging.[48] Nelson left his officers to oversee the work on the ship; Berry and Edward Galwey arrived on the ship in the last days of 1797. Nelson took Fanny to Bath for Christmas, coming back to London in mid February, when the ship moved out to the Nore. It took much of January to ballast the ship and assemble a crew; this was easier than it usually would have been in the middle of a war, since several ships had paid off at Chatham and spare men were available.[49] When Nelson had seen the *Vanguard* in December, he requested that a screen bulkhead be moved forward to make his cabin bigger, as the living quarters in a 74 were small for an admiral and his staff. Moving the bulkhead would weaken the deck overhead, and the Navy Board took a month to come up with an idea for strengthening it, which the Board of Admiralty approved. Nelson also ordered seven ships' boats, appropriate for service in the Mediterranean, consisting of a launch, barge, pinnace, two yawls and two five-oared cutters. A month later Berry requested cushions and awnings for the barge; the Navy Board allowed these, as they were 'proper for a flagship'.[50] On 4 February the *Vanguard* sailed to Blackstakes at the mouth of the Medway, where she was provisioned and her guns hoisted in. Exactly a month later she sailed out to the Nore. Berry's new wife was getting used to her role; he wrote to Nelson: 'my wife and sister have become good seamen frequently accompanying me on board.' He added with some complacency: 'by the bye it is rather extraordinary not to have had one serious axident [*sic*] since the *Vanguard* has been commissioned.'[51] He would come to rue those words.

We have little knowledge of Nelson and Fanny's last weeks together in Bath. The newspapers were full of Pitt's new income-tax assessment. Nelson wrote at the time: 'I am sorry the King is so poor . . . now I hope all the Nation will subscribe liberally.' The lord mayor of London opened a subscription 'for the defence of the Country'. The mayor and Corporation of Bath subscribed £1,000. Lady Nelson gave £20 and Edmund Nelson £10.[52] Nelson baulked at subscribing himself, in lofty and improbable terms: 'I mean to debar myself of many comforts to serve my Country and

I expect great consolation every time I cut a slice of salt beef instead of mutton.' In the same letter he described a visit to the theatre when he sat in the Marquis of Lansdowne's seat in a box with the handsome 'Ladies of Bath'. Had he not been married, he mused to Mr Lloyd in London, 'I would not answer to being tempted.' This unguarded remark would seem to arise out of the ladies' interest in him, in spite of the loss of his arm. He was enjoying one of the by-products of fame.[53] This period of rest and repose had to end. By mid February it was time to return to London, lodging this time at No. 96 Bond Street.

Berry's letters to Nelson from the *Vanguard* are tinged with anxiety, champing at Admiralty delays more than was customary among sea officers during fitting out. After one complaint, he remarked to Nelson, 'Perhaps I'm rather impatient'.[54] Questions still hang over Berry's seamanship and capacity for command. His courage during the excitement of action had been witnessed at close hand by Nelson at the Battle of Cape St Vincent; but he was not a good choice. He shared Nelson's nervous energy and bravery, and the same fragile health; but he did not seem easy in an organizing role and it would become clear that he could not think clearly when in command in a crisis.[55] He reported that on 8 March he had 'upwards of three hundred women on board and not less than 150 supernumeraries besides the ship's company compleat. All the Females to go on shore tomorrow if we are paid – at all events I have set my Face against taking *one* to sea.' Four days later the crew was paid and the women disembarked. By 13 March the ship was in the Downs and two days later at Spithead.

In London, Nelson and Fanny were immediately embroiled in the rush of business to get to sea. Hurried correspondence had to be negotiated with the parents of boys wanting to go as midshipmen, or 'First Class Boys' as they were then known.[56] Personal effects and food for his table had to be purchased. His secretary John Campbell, at the Fountain Inn at Portsmouth, bought sixteen hundredweight of best butter, a hundred pounds of common salt, fifty pounds of salt fish, and live sheep, ducks, fowls and geese.[57] Sir Peter Parker, now commander-in-chief at Portsmouth, ordered a cutter to Guernsey for his wine.[58]

In early March, Nelson attended a dinner party given by Evan Nepean, first secretary to the Board of Admiralty. William Windham's diary again records an interesting and well-informed company, which included Vice-Admiral Lord Keith, just appointed to the Irish peerage, John Trevor, the former minister at Turin, Sir Andrew Snape Hamond, the comptroller of the Navy Board, and Mr Preston, 'of the India House'. Another guest, intriguingly, was 'Governor Phillip', who eleven years earlier as Captain Arthur Phillip had commanded the first fleet to Australia to found the settlement at Botany Bay. Phillip had just arrived back from St Vincent's fleet, where he had commanded the *Blenheim*. Then in his sixtieth year, he had been forced to give up his ship to Rear-Admiral Frederick, but he had the latest news from off Cadiz. Windham notes in his diary: 'Letters from Lord St Vincent about Spanish ships with quicksilver ships that had got out of Cadiz. Event agrees with opinion which Sir Horatio Nelson gave on Sunday last.'[59] Nelson's dinner-table judgements were being carefully noted by a government minister.

It was time for farewell dinners. Lady Spencer invited captains to dinner regularly, but her aristocratic hospitality did not extend to wives with whom she did not consider herself on calling terms. Many years later she described how, on this occasion, she allowed herself to be persuaded to break her rule by Nelson, who asked her to invite Fanny:

if I would take notice of her, it would make him the happiest man alive. He said he felt convinced that I must like her. That she was beautiful, accomplished; but, above all, that her angelic tenderness to him was beyond all imagination. He told me that his wife had dressed his wounds and that her care alone had saved his life. In short, he pressed me to see her, with an earnestness of which Nelson alone was capable. In these circumstances, I begged that he would bring her with him that day to dinner.[60]

It remains unclear as to why Nelson wished so much to have Fanny present on that occasion. The story may have been exaggerated in the telling by Lady Spencer after a distance of many years and in view of what happened to Nelson's marriage; but in persuading one of the most prominent aristocratic hostesses in the land to alter her social rules, Nelson was displaying social and political confidence.[61] Lady Spencer continued to admire him. To St Vincent she wrote: 'He is a very delightful creature & I hope I shall see him once more – tho' when I consider how little there is of him, I cannot be sanguine in such expectations.'[62]

From Evan Nepean, Nelson received on 17 March '12 setts of private signals', which were the identifying flag codes for his ships.[63] The secretary of the board was the centre of the naval intelligence network, and he, as well as the first lord, would brief Nelson on the latest situation – which was bleak. Almost all of Continental Europe had fallen under the domination of France, and most of her former enemies had made peace by the end of 1797; those that had not been conquered, such as Naples or Portugal, were under intense French pressure. Preparations for the invasion of England were being advanced in French Channel ports. At Toulon a major armament of warships and transports was assembling, although its destination could not be determined. The cabinet had not yet decided upon any major strategic moves, but an intense debate was continuing, prompted by a request from Austria, received on 1 April, for the return of a British fleet to the Mediterranean.[64] Lord Grenville, the foreign secretary, argued that a fleet should be sent to the Mediterranean again, to be based at Naples, which would bring about French intervention in the south of Italy, thus forcing Austria back into the conflict. Nelson knew little of these arguments when he hoisted his flag on board the *Vanguard* on 29 March, with orders to join St Vincent off Cadiz. On 1 April the ship moved down to St Helens off the Isle of Wight with a convoy of four large troop transports. Contrary winds forced them to wait there for a frustrating week until 10 April.[65]

That very week, on 6 April, the cabinet came to the decision to send St Vincent's fleet, or, at the commander-in-chief's discretion, a part of it, back into the Mediterranean. The Admiralty was not convinced of the seriousness of the mobilization at Toulon, but through April firmer intelligence arrived, including reports from northern Italian ports and Bastia. On 24 April a report was received from Lieutenant William Day, the same officer who had done so well at Porto Ferrajo a year before as agent for transports and whom Nelson had commended to their lordships. Day was still at Genoa; here was a specialist who could be counted on to know about transports. By now there was no doubt that an enormous expedition was in preparation, although it was unlikely to be ready in May and its destination remained a secret. The only man who had calculated this correctly was John Udney, the consul at Leghorn, who made use of merchant intelligence. In a letter of 16 April, which the Foreign Office did not pass to the Admiralty until 24 May, Udney argued that the great expedition was designed to threaten British interests in India. The statesmen in England still believed that Cadiz was the most likely destination. The turning point was reached on 1 May at a meeting between Spencer and William Day, by now promoted to captain, who had returned from Genoa overland in great haste. He confirmed that the transports were not seaworthy enough to pass westward through the Strait of Gibraltar into the Atlantic. Spencer realized that the French could be going to the Levant, 'though I can scarce believe it'.[66] Later that day the cabinet decided to reinforce St Vincent with ten ships of the line.[67]

Spencer wrestled with a strategic problem that had been encountered by many first lords before him: should the British fleet concentrate defensively in the Channel or should risks be taken by sending ships to foreign stations? It was known that Bonaparte was on a tour of inspection of Channel ports; Ireland was also at risk. Advice from the naval officers around the Board of Admiralty was cautious; not one was in favour of going back to the Mediterranean. In a long memorandum William Young weighed up the thin resources and the demands on them: 'With such a number only, must we not leave the whole of our coast defenceless whenever the fleet puts to sea?'[68] Lord Hugh Seymour and James Gambier, the other naval members of the Board, supported their colleague. Henry Dundas, the secretary of state for war, sent the tentative Spencer some characteristically blunt advice. 'Exercise your understanding and if your Board don't support your opinions and your measures, send them to sea.'[69]

Nelson's passage to join St Vincent off Cadiz was uneventful. The convoy stopped at Lisbon to take on water, wine, lemons and onions and arrived on station on 30 April. St Vincent had spent a long winter badgering his captains.* Writing to Spencer on 1 May, he said: 'I do assure your lordship that the arrival of Admiral Nelson has given me new life.'[70] The prickly Sir John Orde had been chief among the troublemakers. In October 1797 St Vincent had described Orde as 'an affected coxcomb' to Evan Nepean, although in January 1798 all seemed well on the surface when Orde had written to his wife: 'Lord St Vincent continues all goodness to me. He is a wonderful Officer and man.'[71] A month later relations had soured, for St Vincent wrote to Nepean: 'There is such a universal prejudice taken against Sir John Orde, by all the Captains of this Fleet, that it is really painful to place them under his orders, and I foresee something very serious will happen.'[72]

This unhappy set of relationships off Cadiz was inflamed further by St Vincent's decision to send Nelson immediately into the Mediterranean. He was put in command of a small reconnaisance squadron: this was composed of two of the best ships in the fleet, the *Alexander*, commanded by Captain Alexander Ball, and the *Orion*, commanded by Captain Sir James Saumarez, and three frigates. His mission was to find out whether the Toulon fleet was preparing to sail. As soon as Nelson had established the state of preparation of the French ships, he was to return to Gibraltar.[73] St Vincent made this decision immediately after Nelson arrived, writing to

---

* The unhappiness of the officers under St Vincent is indicated in a letter that Nelson received from John Wilson, the master of the *Captain*, describing the passage home from Gibraltar. 'We kept well to the westward to avoid Earl St Vincent, as Captain Aylmer is not very fond of serving under him, and few on board are fond, or willing to serve under Captain Aylmer' (BL, Add. MSS 34906, 18 Oct. 1797; also NMM, NEP/4, 30 Oct. 1797, St Vincent to Nepean).

the first lord on 1 May to tell him so. It was on the face of it a curious decision to send ships of the line, rather than frigates, on a reconnaissance mission: William Young at the Admiralty called it privately 'a most extra-ordinary measure'.[74] But St Vincent, who was anyway short of frigates, was determined to send Nelson, whose rank now required the larger ship. He thus anticipated a letter of 29 April from the first lord that he had not yet received. Spencer's letter contained a long appreciation of the strategic situation, although Spencer still did not know the destination of the French expedition. Towards the end he wrote: 'If you determine to send a detach-ment into the Mediterranean, I think it almost unnecessary to suggest to you the propriety of putting it under the command of Sir H. Nelson, whose acquaintance with that part of the world, as well as his activity and disposition, seem to qualify him in a peculiar manner for that service.'[75]

Sending Nelson to reconnoitre the Mediterranean was one thing; giving him the command of a further eleven ships of the line that St Vincent sent after him in late May was quite another. It is perhaps difficult at this distance to appreciate how Nelson's appointment to lead a substantial detached squadron was such a radical departure from precedent. It went against all the traditions embodied in the admiral's seniority list. Previous Boards of Admiralty had reached down the admiral's list before to pick out a talented individual, but never this far down. Two admirals protested: Rear-Admiral Sir William Parker was thirty-one places above Nelson; Rear-Admiral Sir John Orde senior by eighteen. It was too much for Orde, already bruised by St Vincent's tongue. He started a quarrel with St Vincent that embittered him for the rest of his career. Orde wrote to his wife in June: 'You will not wonder at what I say about disgust when I mention that Admiral Nelson . . . is the only Admiral in the Mediterranean where much is supposed to be going on, whilst I am here doing nothing but sitting daily a member of infernal court martials with Sir Roger Curtis, Sir Wm Parker and Admiral Frederick together with the most respectable old Cap-tains not favourites of Lord St Vincent.'[76] A month later he wrote: 'My officers and people felt hurt & mortified at the preference given a younger Admiral and the circumstance of course lowers my credit on all sides.'[77] Orde had become accustomed to being on the right side of political prefer-ment when he had been made governor of Dominica in the 1780s. His feelings of outrage at being passed over led to his challenging the com-mander-in-chief to a duel after his return to England. He published a pamphlet on the affair. For eighteen months he chased St Vincent around the country with duelling pistols and his second. Splashed all over the press, the affair brought the navy into ridicule: only the express order of the king to the Board of Admiralty stopped the duel from taking place.[78] Orde's obstinacy passed into obsession, and trouble over prize money between Orde and Nelson lay ahead. More than eight years later, in a long letter to the then current first lord of the Admiralty, Thomas Grenville, Orde claimed that 'even the Victory of the Nile would not probably have been less glorious had either Sir William [Parker] or myself been that day in command of the British Fleet.'[79] Orde's bitterness was to warp his judgement.

The politicians were presiding over a clumsy system, in which talent and leadership could not be substantively recognized. Since the 1740s promotion from senior captain to rear-admiral was an automatic progression; these promotions were made in groups of officers when it seemed that they might be necessary. Spencer's rate of appointments was erratic: in any one year they could range from nil to thirty-four.[80] William Young admitted candidly to his friend Charles Morice Pole: 'Lord Spencer's general wish is to employ as far as he can distinguish, those Officers who are the most deserving of employment, though the weight of influence will at times outweigh his good intentions.'[81] Any number of these officers could choose to be inactive or on shore, and a post-captain who had not served a prolonged time in that rank would not be offered active service at flag rank. Of the eighteen rear-admirals between Orde and Nelson, nine were active and already employed as flag officers, while six were unemployed; three were the naval members of the Admiralty Board. Talent was thin among the admirals above Nelson; there were no obvious alternatives, except, as Orde believed, himself. As William Young commented, St Vincent 'must be allowed to chose them, and we all know that a second in command may be the least fit to command a particular expedition . . . I do not wonder at older officers being hurt, because every man is disposed to think of himself qualified for everything; but the choice must be left to the Chief, though it is likely enough that he may chose wrong.'[82]

The key to Nelson's appointment lay in the series of premeditated moves that ensured that the right politicians were able to discern Nelson's talent. Minto had seen at first hand how lack of commitment by a senior admiral – Hotham – on a foreign station had damaged British interests and pointed out to William Windham the weaknesses of promoting by seniority. He then guided Nelson through the presentation of the Spanish admiral's sword to Windham and the publication of the account of the battle of 14 February. Nelson had attended the right dinner parties and impressed the first lord of the Admiralty as well as his wife. He could not have put his sick leave to greater use.

Nearly three years later, Nelson tried, characteristically, to improve his relations with John Orde: 'I can now assure you on my word of honour, that neither Earl St Vincent nor Lord Spencer were the original cause of my being sent to the Mediterranean. The arrangement was made in April 1797, a year before I was sent. It is plain that neither the First Lord of the Admiralty, nor the Commander-in-Chief, thought it right to tell you the causes which naturally sent me in particular to the Mediterranean.'[83] Had a political decision been taken as far back as the time of withdrawal from the Mediterranean for Nelson to return with a British squadron? How much had Nelson's Mediterranean experience been a factor in the decision? In a later letter to Sir Roger Curtis, a senior admiral who did not protest and who wished Nelson well, Nelson emphasized the 'five years not only in constant correspondence but in constant service on every part of the Coast of Italy' and insisted that there would have been no use in 'sending a person totally ignorant of the Coast and Politicks of Italy'.[84] If so, the decision would have been made by the senior politicians. It may have been the subject of the confidential conversation between Spencer and Windham in March 1797, although there is no evidence other than Nelson's letter to Orde. To those older admirals and captains off Cadiz, Nelson's appointment smacked of favouritism and corruption. In June 1798 St Vincent wrote to Nepean: 'There is such a faction against Nelson here, that I wish you would order all the Admirals above him to England, or elsewhere, immediately – the Service cannot go on, unless you do.'[85]

17

Chasing the French

3 May–1 August 1798

Your Lordship is to lose no time in detaching from your fleet a squadron under the command of some discreet Flag Officer into the Mediterranean with Instructions to him to proceed in quest of the said [Toulon] Armament, and on falling in with it . . . to take and destroy it.
Board of Admiralty's secret instructions to Earl St Vincent,
2 May 1798[1]

What an extraordinary People these are, no Plan too vast for their undertakings and the Magnitude of their operations confound and dismay all their adversaries, except us.
St Vincent to Evan Nepean, on the French, 13 July 1798[2]

'Sir John Orde is here giving fêtes etc,' Nelson wrote in an ironic aside to Fanny on his arrival at Gibraltar on 4 May 1798, 'but I have no turn for such things when we had better be alongside a Spaniard.'[3] In April hurried notes about clothes and trunks, financial arrangements and missing items, usual when he was getting away to sea, passed between them, impatient on his part, anxious on hers. Their letters gradually become longer, a relaxed correspondence between two people more confident now of their place in the world. At the end of the month Fanny moved from Bath, after a week at Kentish Town ('Mr Suckling as usual is very kind'), to the new house at Roundwood near Ipswich in Suffolk, where she made many improvements. Her letters tell of Ipswich society, of Nelson's father, who lived with her, indignation over the avoidance of the new income tax by the rich, of a new carnation named 'Admiral Nelson'. The details of Roundwood were lovingly spelt out: the deepening of the well, buying carpets and furniture. She and Edmund were critical of the Boltons, who were, as usual, short of money: 'they expect too much of you and he [Edmund] says to put me upon my guard . . . I must say they are cunning people.' It was a boring

life: 'Since I wrote last Monday little has occurred in our private lives . . .
Our good father . . . wants to be more amused.'[4] Nelson's letters are shorter
than hers, with service gossip, sometimes giving only outline information
in case the letter should fall into the wrong hands. He ends them formally,
always using the word 'affectionate' rather than 'love'; only once, on 1 May,
did he display a flash of emotion: 'With every affectionate wish which a
fond heart can frame'.[5] Perhaps this was in response to a letter she had
written a month earlier: 'Indeed I have always felt your sincere attachment
and at no one period could I feel it more strongly than I do at this moment
and I hope as some few years are past, time enough to know our dispositions, we may flatter ourselves it will last.'[6] Did this guarded exchange
hide some tension after his stay in England? Her letters remain long and
detailed, with her anxieties increasingly reflected: in early June she hopes
that St Vincent 'will never send you upon a service without a sufficient
force'; in early July she confesses her 'spirits are a little fagged'; and by
16 July she is writing of 'my extreme anxiety to hear from you'.[7]

When the *Vanguard* anchored in Gibraltar Bay, all hands were set to
heave fifty tons of ballast overboard and get water aboard. A hundred tons
of water had been previously transferred from the *Vanguard* to the *Theseus*
and the *Zealous*, which were blockading off Cadiz. With no naval support
available in the Mediterranean, every inch of space in the ship was needed
for stores. There were 210 tons of water now aboard. Unfortunately, Berry
also sent some spare topmasts ashore to the dockyard that would later be
needed.[8] By 7 May all was ready; at eight the next morning the small
squadron set sail in light winds. With Nelson were two men whom he
would come to know well, both commanding 74s. The captain of the
Alexander was Alexander Ball, recently sent out to St Vincent. He had
made an immediate impression. 'Your friend Ball is so good a fellow, I
class him with Troubridge, Hood and Hallowell,' the commander-in-chief
informed Evan Nepean.[9] Ball was the officer who wore the epaulettes of
which Nelson had disapproved in St Omer nearly fifteen years before;
Nelson had not seen him since and cordial relations took some while to
become established. The *Orion*, which had taken a full part in the Battle
of Cape St Vincent and to which the *Santissima Trinidad* had struck her
flag, was commanded by James Saumarez, from the Channel Islands. Courteous ('the civilest man I ever saw', according to Betsey Fremantle), sensitive
and deeply religious, he had a streak of irritability that kept him at a
distance from his fellow officers. He was never susceptible to Nelson's easy
charm.[10] With the three ships of the line were the frigates *Terpsichore* and
Bonne Citoyenne. The *Emerald* was to join later.

Nelson's task was modest enough. He was to sail to familiar waters. 'After ranging the coast of Provence, and the Western Riviera of Genoa (or before this object is accomplished, should you discover that the preparations upon those Coasts are in forwardness), to make the best of your way back to Gibraltar,' were St Vincent's orders.[11] The mission was intended to be only a short foray into hostile waters. The squadron's passage, firstly to the east and then to the north-east past Minorca, started slowly because of light winds. After ten days, moderate winds from the south-west picked up, and by 18 May the ship's estimated position was only sixty-five nautical miles from Cap Sicié by Toulon.[12] The winds fell light, but at noon on 20 May a fresh breeze blew from the north-west, the ships being close-hauled.

By nine that evening the wind had increased to 'fresh gales', and at ten the topsails were close reefed. At eleven topgallant yards and royal mast were brought down to the deck, and the fore and mizzen topsails were furled. Wales Clodd, the master of the *Vanguard*, entered into his log that at midnight 'strong gales' swung violently around from NE to WSW, with a heavy cross sea. It was not until half an hour after midnight that the order was given to bring in the main topsail. At the same time, the main topmast carried away, throwing two seamen overboard, while another fell on the booms below. At two o'clock in the morning the mizzen topmast went. By this time the ship was rolling heavily in 'exceeding hard Gales'; the foremast cracked and went overboard. The crew worked frantically to clear the mass of rigging. The next morning, the five-oared cutter was jettisoned, as it was entangled in the wreckage. The bowsprit was sprung in three places. A midshipman, Thomas Meek, was killed as the wreckage was being cleared. The best bower anchor, striking against the side of the ship, also had to be cut away.[13]

It had been a terrifying twenty-four hours at sea. The chaplain, Stephen Comyn, recalled in a letter to Nelson five years later that it was a night he would never forget.[14] Four lives had been lost. The ship had lost her foremast, with all its yards, and the main and mizzen topmasts and topgallant masts. By contrast, none of the other five ships in the squadron had suffered any major damage. Both the *Orion* and the *Alexander* had had sails blown out, but Saumarez and Ball had been more cautious with the amount of canvas they had set and their rigging was intact. The frigates had passed the night safely under bare poles.[15] Edward Berry claimed that the *Vanguard* had the worst of the storm: 'the other ships experienced the fury of the gale but not in the same degree as the *Vanguard*.'[16] Her new rigging, fitted at Chatham three months before, may not have been fully stretched, for the ship had experienced little hard weather since leaving England, apart from some squalls off Finisterre. Nelson may have heeded the advice he received from a previous captain, Charles Thompson, that the ship would sail better if her rigging was not too tight.[17] Once the rigging had started to unravel, the spars were given no support when the rolling started, and a whipping motion set up by the rolling caused the damage. Lack of experience was undoubtedly a factor. Neither the captain, Edward Berry, nor the first lieutenant, Edward Galwey, had served as senior officers of a ship of the line, while the master had not served in a large ship of the line.[18] William James, a naval historian writing in the 1820s, believed that 'the *Vanguard*'s was a very indifferent ship's company'; it was 'instinctively brave' but 'new and inexperienced'.[19]

The ordeal, however, was far from over, for, at first light, with the wind in the north-west on the beam, the only course the ship could steer was towards the rocky north Sardinian shore. With what little steerage way could be mustered without foresails, Nelson coaxed the ship around to starboard, and, with the help of 'a small rag of a spritsail', she 'wore' round away from the island. She was still making so much leeway that her course was more sideways than forward, but the immediate danger was past; by the morning of 22 May, Sardinia was thirty-five miles to the south-east. A sheltered anchorage had to be found for repairs; if Oristano Bay, halfway down the west side of the island, could not be reached, then they would have to make for the sound behind San Pietro Island at the south-west tip, which was well known for shelter. At 3 p.m. the *Alexander* took the *Vanguard* in tow, an operation of great danger to both ships, for in steep seas there was no possibility of launching a boat to take the tow rope between them. Allowing for the *Alexander*'s own leeway as she manoeuvred, Ball took her very close to Nelson's stricken ship, wallowing in the troughs and rolling on the crests of the steep seas. One of the crew of the *Alexander* heaved a line to which was attached the heavy tow rope, run out through a stern port and attached to tackles along one of the gun decks. The manoeuvre had to be done as slowly as possible so that the line could be gathered by the *Vanguard*'s crew and the tow rope made fast.

The shiphandling skills involved were considerable, and neither these nor the difficulties of towing in such conditions should be underestimated. Contemporary manuals advised against towing in steep seas; if the wind died away, both ships were in danger since the tension of the tow rope would pull them together.[20] Once under way, the *Vanguard* managed to hoist her mainsail on what was left of the mainmast. The crew were destined for another night of anxiety, this time from lack of wind, which fell light at nine. With the swell still high and powerful, the two ships drifted near the coast, high and rocky, with very deep water making anchoring impossible. For six tense hours there was no wind at all. The surf could be heard clearly against the rocks. Nelson conferred anxiously with Ball about whether he should cast off the *Vanguard* to save his own ship. Nelson 'repeatedly requested Captain Ball to let him loose; and on Captain Ball's refusal, he became impetuous, and enforced his demands with passionate threats'.[21] Ball refused to leave the *Vanguard* to probable destruction. The crew of the *Vanguard* made ready all the remaining anchors with spare cables.

The danger faded as quickly as it had arisen. At 5 a.m. on 24 May, a north-westerly breeze sprang up and the two ships managed two knots, and in the next hour three. At eleven o'clock that morning, coming into the San Pietro anchorage, the two ships anchored, then were lashed side by side. The *Alexander* had towed the *Vanguard* for twenty hours. Nelson was generous and open in his thanks to Ball; the experience removed any jealousy between the two men, and it chastened Nelson. Never before or again would his career be out of his control for so long and his reputation so dependent upon the determination and skill of others. He wrote an uncharacteristically confessional letter to Fanny: 'Figure to yourself a vain man on Sunday evening at sunset walking in his cabin with a squadron about him who looked up to their chief to lead them to glory . . . this proud, conceited man, when the sun rose on Monday morning his ship dismasted and himself in such distress that the meanest frigate out of France would have been a very unwelcome guest.'[22]

The next four days brought forth brilliant extemporary seamanship and shipwright skills from the crews of the *Vanguard* and the *Alexander*. With the *Orion* cruising offshore (they had lost contact with the frigates), the two ships' companies set about repairs. Nelson was to make a special point of commending the experienced ship's carpenter of the *Alexander*, James Morrison, to their lordships. Eight shipwrights were found among the crews of the other two ships. By lashing the *Vanguard* alongside the *Alexander* and using the latter's masts and yards, the stump of the foremast was hoisted out, and by the end of the day a jury-foremast, using splices and other spars, had been fitted. By the evening of 25 May the jury-foremast and the mainmast had both received a topmast, and the *Alexander* had been hauled away from the *Vanguard*, which now lay to single anchor. Every conceivable piece of timber was used (they even dismantled one of the gun carriages in the wardroom).

On shore the arrival of the three ships of the line caused consternation, for the Kingdom of Sardinia was fearful of the French threat. Saumarez went on shore, where he was received by the local commandant, de Nobili, but, in spite of courteous negotiations, the Sardinian explained that he was unable to render assistance because of an agreement between his government and the French. He nevertheless agreed to obtain some supplies as a proof of his goodwill, and three bullocks were swung aboard the *Vanguard* on 27 May. On the same day the commandant came aboard to meet the English admiral and seven guns were fired as a salute.[23] Again he explained his government's position and hoped that Nelson and his ships would soon depart, to which Nelson, having completed most of the repairs to the *Vanguard*, readily agreed. He set out to charm de Nobili and succeeded. Seven guns saluted the commandant as he left the ship, and, as he reported to the viceroy of Sardinia, 'I cannot express to His Excellency how many compliments, kindnesses and graces I received on board the sail vessels.'[24] At 5.30 a.m. on 28 May the *Vanguard* 'weighed and made sail standing out of the Bay'.[25] Commandant de Nobili ordered a nine-gun salute for Nelson's flag from the fort, an act that later earned him a reprimand from the king of Sardinia.[26]

Light winds again prevailed. Only twenty-five miles were made good in the next twenty-four hours. Nelson sailed slowly north towards Toulon. Shipboard routine was established again, although repairs were continuing. The master noted in his log that the armourer was at his forge, while the carpenters were still busy at the masts and rigging. Even so, the gun crews were exercised at every possible opportunity. On Sunday, 29 May, Divine Service was conducted aboard the *Vanguard*, a practice that continued throughout this commission. Anxious lookout was kept for the missing frigates.[27]

On 5 June, Thomas Masterman Hardy, commanding the 18-gun *Mutine* brig, brought dispatches from St Vincent with new orders. Nelson was to rendezvous with a squadron of ten 74s and a 50-gun ship off Toulon, led by Thomas Troubridge, take command of it, and then seek and destroy the French fleet, wherever it was in the Mediterranean. On 8 June the reinforcements appeared off Toulon.[28] Nelson's fortunes had been transformed once again: at a stroke, his buffeted reconnaissance squadron was transformed into a major fighting force. Indeed, had the *Vanguard* not been delayed by being dismasted he might well have missed Troubridge altogether.[29]

The reinforcement had been agreed in London at the cabinet meeting of 1 May. The next day orders were sent to Rear-Admiral Sir Roger Curtis, cruising off Ireland with a substantial squadron, to reinforce St Vincent off

Cadiz. So secret and important were these orders that Curtis was to sail twenty leagues away from the coast of Ireland before unsealing them.[30] It was a courageous political and strategic decision, for cabinet ministers were still divided upon the perceived objective of the Toulon armament. Their disagreement was to have near-disastrous consequences because information was not flowing freely between them. As a result, the uncoordinated government intelligence machine failed Nelson. At no time was he given any intimation that Egypt was even a possible destination of the French. Henry Dundas, the secretary-at-war, the most clear-headed in assessing the intelligence that was coming in from all quarters, received internal papers before the end of April indicating that Egypt could be the target.[31] Lord Spencer did not mention Egypt as even a faint possibility in his crucial letter of 29 April to St Vincent, after which neither London nor St Vincent was in touch with Nelson.[32] Wherever the French fleet was heading, St Vincent's fleet would have to intercept it. A half-sentence from the first lord of the Admiralty could have changed history.

The Levant and Egyptian intelligence had to be set against reports suggesting other possible destinations for the French fleet, particularly Ireland, which in May was experiencing outbreaks of violence and revolt; but it is still difficult to account for the cabinet's continuing disbelief of the possibility of Egypt as Napoleon's destination, and for the failure of ministers to entrust either St Vincent or Nelson with information on the widest range of possibilities. After all, France had long looked with envy at the contribution that India made to English wealth; her own ambitions were not new, and her own territory in India at Pondicherry cost her more to maintain than it contributed to her treasury. Since the end of the Seven Years War sporadic diplomatic confrontation had taken place between the two countries over India: this involved French forces on the Île de France (Mauritius) in the late 1760s and early 1770s; a hard-fought campaign there during the American Revolutionary War; and constant British edginess in the peace after 1783 in case the French reinforced their navy and army in India.[33] France saw advantage too in challenging Russia and Turkey in the Eastern Mediterranean. Whether such an expedition really had a chance of success against India puzzled statesmen then and historians since; a recent view was that 'the expedition was fundamentally an aggressive impulse followed by a weak divided government for domestic more than foreign-policy reasons, without serious calculations of its feasibility and likely results.'[34] Nevertheless, St Vincent began to sense the possibility of a French move against the Levant as early as the middle of June: 'I begin to think the Mosman Porte [Turkey] has ceded Egypt to them, & is to have it for the Islands they have taken from the Venetians – Egypt was an object of the old Government.'[35]

Other relevant intelligence was available in London. Lord Grenville, the foreign minister, received a letter from John Udney, the consul in Leghorn, making a clear argument for Egypt. Though this was written on 16 April, it was not until mid June that the Foreign Office, which was conducting secret negotiations with Russia, sent it to Dundas.[36] Other information received in June included an account from some Frankfurt academics of material and scholars being gathered for a French expedition to Egypt; and a proclamation by the French governor of Mauritius, 'in consequence of an embassy from Tippo Sultan inviting the inhabitants to enlist into his Services for the purpose of expelling the English from India'. It was at this point, 13 June, that Dundas became convinced that Egypt and India were the objectives. He wrote a persuasive, thirteen-page letter to Lord Grenville. However, Dundas's East India connections were well known, and his fellow ministers were still not convinced. Evan Nepean remained sceptical until as late as 28 June, when he received William Wickham's intelligence from Turin that Napoleon's fleet had received only three months' provisions, 'the first Intelligence which reached the Office in a shape which appeared worthy of attention'. He did not give it to Lord Spencer until 24 July.[37] All round, it was an inept performance.[38]

Sir Roger Curtis and his ships left Ireland and arrived at Cadiz on 24 May. Moving all his ships away from the coast to ensure that the Spanish did not see what was happening, St Vincent immediately dispatched Troubridge and his eleven ships to join Nelson. 'You must not suffer him to pass your squadron in the night if he is coming back to Gibraltar,' St Vincent wrote in Troubridge's orders.[39]

These ships can only be described as a crack squadron. All bar one of the captains were of the first quality, and, with two exceptions, they were young. St Vincent sent letters home that, in contrast to his usual complaints, extolled the virtues of these officers. To Nepean he remarked of his list 'a better cannot be employed'.[40] Nelson was later to call them 'the finest Squadron that ever graced the Ocean'.[41] He knew most of them well, had served under fire with the majority and knew the others by reputation. In recent weeks he had come to appreciate Ball and Saumarez. He knew Benjamin Hallowell (*Swiftsure*) from his time in Corsica. At Tenerife, Nelson had already commanded Troubridge (*Culloden*), Samuel Hood (*Zealous*), Ralph Willet Miller (*Theseus*) and Thomas Boulden Thompson (*Leander*). He knew the competent Thomas Foley (*Goliath*) from many months off Leghorn and Corsica, and the cautious Davidge Gould

(*Audacious*) from service at Corsica and during the two Hotham actions; at three separate points in the battle ahead Gould was to prove a weak link. John Peyton (*Defence*) had travelled out from England in the *Vanguard* with Nelson; and Peyton's father was six places senior to Maurice Nelson in the same department in the Navy Office. He knew by reputation only (further acquainted no doubt by an assessment from St Vincent) Henry D'Esterre Darby (*Bellerophon*), Thomas Louis (*Minotaur*) and George Blagden Westcott (*Majestic*).*

To Cuthbert Collingwood's intense disappointment, St Vincent did not include him. Later that year Collingwood complained bitterly in a letter to his father-in-law: the commander-in-chief 'knew our friendship; for many, many years we had served together, lived together, and all that ever happened to us strengthened the bond of our amity, but my going would have interfered with the aggrandisement of a favourite to whom I was senior, and so he sent me out of the way when the detachment was to be made.'[42] Saumarez was senior, and automatically should have been second-in-command, a position which St Vincent had wanted for Thomas Troubridge; but Saumarez, due to go to England, stayed with the fleet and Nelson bypassed the problem by not appointing a second.

In London, expectations began to mount, for ministers were confident of British superiority. 'This force, tho' somewhat inferior in number,' mused Henry Dundas on 18 June, 'is so decidedly superior to that of the Enemy in every other respect, that should the latter be overtaken before they reach Alexandria (the supposed part of their destination) the most sanguine prospect of success may reasonably [be] entertained.'[43] Critically, the ships with which Troubridge now joined Nelson were well supplied; even St Vincent pronounced himself satisfied in this respect. They 'have six months' provisions of all species on board, except bread and wine, of which they have as much as they can store ... their water kept up from day to day ... The whole of these ships are in excellent order, and so well officered, manned and appointed I am confident they will perform everything to be expected from them.'[44]

While Nelson was sailing north to his rendezvous with Troubridge, the French fleet, commanded by Vice-Admiral François-Paul de Brueys d'Aigalliers, but under the orders of Napoleon Bonaparte, set sail from Toulon on 20 May, gathering up detachments from Genoa and Civita Vecchia as it sailed south. Malta was to be captured on the way to secure

---

* All the ships bar the *Leander* (50) were 74s. The squadron now had thirteen ships of the line. The *Vanguard*, *Alexander* and *Orion* were joined on 8 June by *Culloden*, *Audacious*, *Bellerophon*, *Defence*, *Goliath*, *Majestic*, *Minotaur*, *Swiftsure*, *Theseus* and *Zealous*.

the route across the Mediterranean. Brueys did not have a strong fleet. It consisted of thirteen ships of the line, eight of them survivors of the firing of the French fleet on the night of 18 December 1793, when the British withdrew after the occupation of Toulon; they were, on average, twenty years old, three of them were over forty, while the *Conquérant* was over fifty.[45] They were not well manned – at only 77 per cent of their complement – while on board the French warships there were more soldiers than sea-men.[46] They escorted an enormous convoy of 280 transports, carrying in all 48,662 troops, as well as 300 women and civilians.* This cumbersome force sailed very slowly south between Sardinia and mainland Italy. On 8 June, the day Nelson was reinforced by Troubridge, the main convoy from Toulon was off Sicily; on 10 June, Bonaparte started his assault against the weak and divided Knights of St John at Valetta, who capitulated two days later. Malta now became a significant pawn in the power games of western European states. Bonaparte, however, stopped for only ten days, pillaging the wealth of the Knights and loading it into the flagship *L'Orient*, leaving behind troops to hold the island. The great armada set off again towards Alexandria on 21 June.

Nelson was now expected to find the French fleet. He had no idea as to its course or destination. Intelligence was never to catch up with him during the next two fast-moving months, and the long letters written in June to Nelson by Sir William Hamilton, the British minister in Naples, never reached him in time to be of use.[47] Nor is it clear when Nelson received his letter of 20 April from John Udney, in which Udney was as prescient as he had been in his dispatch to London: 'If France intends uniting with Tippoo Said against our possessions in India, the danger of losing half an Army in crossing the Desert from Egypt, would be no obstacle.'[48] Yet, by the middle of June, Nelson himself had in mind the possibility of Egypt as a destination for the French. According to Edward Berry, Nelson had 'no certain infor-mation respecting the destination of the Enemy's Fleet; he was left entirely to his own judgement'. Portugal or even Ireland could not be discounted, and within the Mediterranean, anywhere from Algiers to the Adriatic was a possibility.[49] Receiving early intelligence that the French were heading towards Sicily, Nelson sailed south along the coast of Italy, stopping at Naples for two hours to allow Troubridge time to go ashore for an interview with Sir William Hamilton and Sir John Acton, the first minister at Naples.

---

* Some of the civilians were scholars and administrators, for the French government and Napoleon wished to understand the new territory he intended to conquer, and to make Egypt prosperous and self-supporting, a base for wider action against British wealth and trade (Schroeder, 176–9; Lavery, *Nile*, 14–16, 18–20).

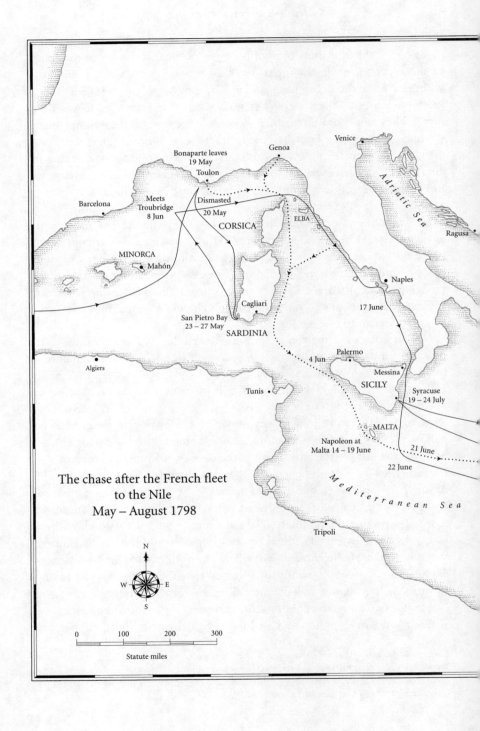

Venice

Genoa

Adriatic Sea

Bonaparte leaves
19 May
Toulon

Ragusa

Barcelona

Meets
Troubridge
8 Jun

Dismasted
20 May

ELBA

CORSICA

MINORCA

Mahón

Naples

Cagliari

17 June

San Pietro Bay
23 – 27 May

SARDINIA

4 Jun

Palermo

Algiers

Messina

SICILY

Tunis

Syracuse
19 – 24 July

MALTA

Napoleon at
Malta 14 – 19 June

21 June

The chase after the French fleet
to the Nile
May – August 1798

22 June

Mediterranean Sea

Tripoli

N

W   E

S

0   100   200   300

Statute miles

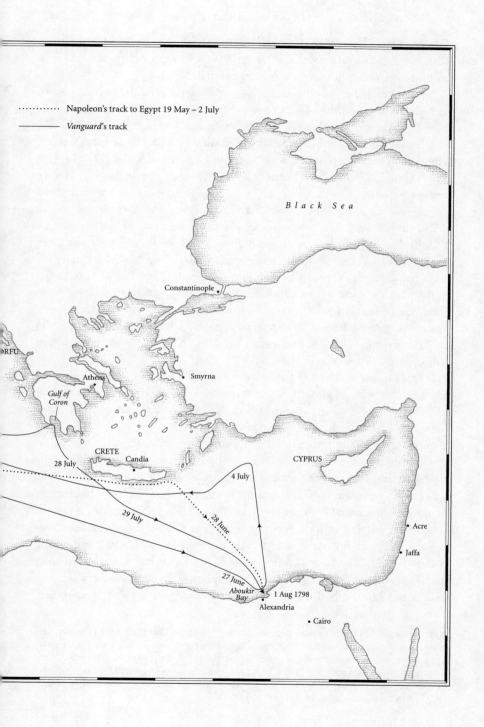

Napoleon's track to Egypt 19 May – 2 July
Vanguard's track

Black Sea

Constantinople

ORFU

Athens
Smyrna

Gulf of
Coron

CRETE
Candia

CYPRUS

28 July

4 July

29 July

28 June

Acre

Jaffa

27 June

Aboukir
Bay
1 Aug 1798
Alexandria

Cairo

Troubridge had no more than half an hour with Acton, putting questions with his usual directness, but receiving no certain information. Assistance with provisioning, however, was forthcoming.[50]

Nelson pressed on south, taking his ships safely through the tricky Strait of Messina on 20 June. As he passed Messina, the English consul, James Tough, informed him that the French had taken Malta.[51] Two days later a brig from Ragusa gave him intelligence upon which he placed great weight. The French had taken Malta, leaving behind a garrison and sailing the next day.[52] Had the French been heading for Sicily, surely the British would have known by now.* On that day, 22 June, four strange frigates were sighted sailing east. Cautiously he called back the *Leander*, which was investigating them, anxious that his ships should not get separated. He summoned Troubridge, Saumarez, Darby and Ball on board the flagship. He put three propositions to them as to which course to pursue: to Malta, to Sicily or, with the greatest emphasis on the last and leading question, 'Should the Armament be gone to Alexandria and get safe there our possessions in India are probably lost. Do you think we had better push for that place?' Their short, signed answers survive. Each one opted for Alexandria.[53] On 23 June, Edward Galwey, first lieutenant of the *Vanguard*, noted in his log: 'Alexandria, distance 200 leagues'.[54]

It was an inspired and extreme decision, laden with risk: and it was the right one. It was taken without prompting or information from London: but Nelson had wrongly assumed that the French fleet was well ahead of him. His squadron had in fact passed close to it on 22 June. His three frigates, which hadn't been heard from since the storm when the *Vanguard* lost her mast, were never more missed; by this time they were frantically trying to find Nelson off Sardinia and Naples, unable to calculate that he was heading eastwards.[55] The squadron was accompanied only by the tiny *Mutine*, commanded by Thomas Masterman Hardy. Nelson did not want to disperse his 74s to look for the enemy, for although his squadron was powerful, it was not large, and for that reason he kept it in close sailing order. In Berry's words: 'The smallness of our Squadron made it necessary to sail in close order, and therefore the space it covered was very limited; and as the admiral had no frigates that he could despatch upon look-out,

---

* The vice-consul in Genoa, James Bird, with his ear (like John Udney's) close to the merchant network of intelligence, thought that Egypt was the destination. As late as 12 July, Bird's opinion was reported to the Foreign Office by a sceptical Francis Drake: 'He suspects that the French will go to Alexandrette: I think he is mistaken in his conjecture and that we shall hear of them next in Paros in the Archipelago' ((UK)NA: PRO, FO 28/18, 'Advices, Intelligence, etc., from Vice-Consul James Bird, 1798-1803').

June 22ⁿᵈ 1798

The Vessel Spoke with this morning is from Malta one Day, he says the two frigates in Sight are french, that the french Colors and Garrison are in malta, that the Fleet Transports left it Six Days to Day, but they did not know when they were going, some said to Sicily —

with this Information what is your Opinion, do you believe under all Circumstances which we know that Sicily is their destination,

Do you think We had better stand for malta, or Steer for Sicily

Should the armament be gone to Alexandria and get safe there our Possessions in India are probably lost do you think we had better push for that place

Nelson's questions to his captains, 22 June 1798

added to the constant haze of the atmosphere in that climate our chance of descrying the Enemy was very much circumscribed.'[56] 'My want of frigates is extreme,' Nelson wrote to William Hamilton. When Captain George Hope of the frigate *Alcmene* reached Naples wanting water at the end of June, desperately trying to find Nelson, Hamilton went alongside and read those words from Nelson's last letter out to Hope.[57]

Nelson's squadron made good progress towards Alexandria with north-west moderate breezes behind it.[58] Nearing the city on 29 June, disappointment and frustration were the immediate reactions on the first sight of the harbour. Apart from some Turkish warships, only merchant shipping could be seen. Nelson sent Hardy forward in the *Mutine* to find the British consul, George Baldwin, but he was away on leave. His deputy, an Egyptian, was not sympathetic and poured scorn on the idea that the French could be heading towards Egypt. Nelson left Alexandria almost immediately, in spite of suspicions by some, including Saumarez, that they might have overtaken the French. Nelson did not have the patience, with his nerves stretched to breaking point, to wait to see if he had been right after all. Some years later Nelson was to write to George Baldwin: 'had I found you at Alexandria there can be no doubt but that I should have been off Alexandria when the French fleet arrived.'[59] Henry Dundas was nearer to the heart of the problem when he later commented to the foreign secretary, Lord Grenville: 'If we had not been too incredulous as to the object of Buonaparte's armament, I think such instructions would have been given to Sir Horatio as would have prevented him from leaving Alexandria after he had once reached it in the auspicious and promising way he did.'[60]

Nelson's despondency can be judged by the self-critical, doubting letter he sent to St Vincent, in spite of Alexander Ball's advice not to do so. 'I am before your Lordship's judgement (which in the present case I feel is the tribunal of my country) and if, under all circumstances, it is decided that I am wrong I ought for the sake of our country to be superseded . . . However erroneous [they] may be I feel conscious of my honest intentions which I hope will bear me up under the greatest misfortune that could happen to me as an officer, that of your Lordship's thinking me wrong.'[61] A lieutenant in the *Goliath* wrote home: 'Words will give but a faint idea of the Chagrins and disappointments Poor Nelson and we all felt before we were so fortunate as to fall in with the Republicans . . . Poor disappointed us.'[62]

Nelson left Alexandria on 30 June at eleven in the morning. At 3 p.m. the next day a lieutenant from a French frigate in advance of Bonaparte's fleet was rowed ashore to seek out the French consul.[63] By this time the Egyptian authorities were thoroughly alarmed, and the consul was forced to leave the city and stay with the French fleet. During the night of 1 July, Bonaparte and his troops landed. The next day they took the city with ease. Egypt, under weak Turkish rule, put up little resistance. Napoleon rapidly took his army inland and three weeks later had defeated the Egyptian Army near the Pyramids.

The anchorage for the French fleet was less successful, for the harbour at Alexandria was too shallow. Egyptian pilots would allow only 64s and lightly loaded frigates into the old harbour, and refused entry to the deeper-drafted 74s. Another option was for Brueys to take his fleet to Corfu in the Adriatic, now in French hands, where ships could lie safely under formidable battlements and could be resupplied. According to Brueys's orders all three – Alexandria, Aboukir and Corfu – were possibilities.[64] It is unclear whether it was Brueys or Bonaparte who favoured the last, although Bonaparte did not intend to remain long in Egypt and is likely to have wanted the fleet near him. The compromise was Aboukir Bay, to the east of Alexandria. On 7 July the French fleet moved there, anchoring in a two-mile line on the seven-fathom (forty-two feet) mark.[65] Brueys was short of water and provisions.

Nelson sailed north towards Turkey for four days. He tried, with little success, to pick up intelligence from passing ships, in an effort to cover the possibility that the French fleet could be heading towards Constantinople. On 4 July he turned back towards Italy. Galwey entered in his log: 'Messina 693 miles'.[66] The journey westwards was long and slow, with light, contrary winds coaxing 74-gun ships to windward for nearly three weeks. The state of morale can only be imagined, since Nelson wrote little during this period. The ships were running short of water. On 3 July the captain of the *Defence*, John Peyton, reported sick, requesting that he be allowed to leave his ship as soon as it reached a friendly port.[67] The crew of the *Vanguard* overhauled the anchor ropes. Divine Service was held regularly. On 12 July two seamen were given twenty-four lashes for being drunk, while two received six lashes.[68] The consumption of alcohol by the officers of the flagship peaked in the first week of July.[69] On 20 July the squadron slowly approached Syracuse on the south-east coast of Sicily.

Whatever his private feelings, Nelson's persistence and determination to find the enemy never wavered. During this period he called together a number of captains aboard the flagship for conferences; this, together with his own term for them, 'Band of Brothers', created a legend of leadership. Edward Berry provides the only contemporary description: 'It had been his practice during the whole of the Cruise, whenever the weather and circumstances would permit, to have his Captains on board the *Vanguard* where he would fully develop to them his own ideas of the different and best modes of Attack . . . every one of the Captains of his Squadron most thoroughly acquainted . . . they could ascertain with precision what were the ideas and intentions of their Commander without the aid of further instructions.'[70] Doubt has been cast upon the frequency of these meetings and whether some captains ever went aboard the flagship; Nelson has even been described as 'remote and isolated' in these months.[71] Yet Nelson kept closely in touch with his captains, and at least one full meeting occurred on 18 July as the squadron approached Syracuse. Lieutenant Galwey noted in his log: 'Made the Signal for all Captains'.[72] Berry's enthusiastic description conjures up a picture of fourteen captains of one mind and in full possession of Nelson's battle plan, and there can be no doubt that Nelson was developing an extremely effective consensual style of leadership. 'Unanimity,' James Saumarez entered in the journal he wrote for his wife, 'I believe greater never existed in any squadron.'[73]

As an admiral younger than several of his captains, Nelson had a very practical reason for adopting this approach. His control was instinctive, based on informality, frankness and discussion, and it rested on personal confidence, quickness of mind and a charm of manner. It contrasted sharply with the formal, hierarchical system of the late eighteenth century as practised, and not with overwhelming success, by the centralized commands of Rodney and Howe. Their control depended upon retaining, rather than sharing, information. Nelson came to the conclusion 'that the best way to control veteran subordinates was not to try'.[74] Nelson also had to solve the problem of appointing a deputy, often a difficulty in the management of a close-knit team. Troubridge had long been favoured by St Vincent; however, as already noted, he was very junior in the list of captains. Nelson needed to keep St Vincent content. Yet James Saumarez was senior captain. Nelson solved this problem by not acknowledging a second in command. He was uneasy about this situation, and his relationship with Saumarez suffered as a consequence. That, at least, was Saumarez's opinion, according to his biographer: 'Although Nelson carefully concealed his feelings towards Saumarez they were but too manifest by the chary manner in which he expressed himself.'[75] Had Nelson been killed in the forthcoming battle, an awkward situation might have arisen between Saumarez and Troubridge, even though they were friends.

Nelson conferred with some captains more than others, and gained support and ideas from the polished and well-read Alexander Ball, the thoughtful Saumarez, the aggressive Troubridge and the confident Samuel Hood. Nelson worked hard at his relationship with Saumarez, who noted in his journal for 29 June: 'I have passed the day on board the *Vanguard*, having breakfasted and staid to dinner with the Admiral.'[76] He acknowledged that Nelson's burden was heavy in an often-quoted remark: 'Fortunately I only act here *en second*; but did the chief responsibility rest with me, I fear it would be more than my too irritable nerves would bear.'[77] Saumarez did, however, think that he should have been recognized formally as second-in-command.

From 20 to 25 July the squadron 'moored in the harbour of Syracuse'.[78] Water in all the ships was low and replenishing took a full five days, as the supply of fresh water in quantity was not easily available. Fresh beef and vegetables were to be had from the first day, and all ships were issued with twenty live bullocks. Lemons and onions were plentiful, although bread was not.[79] To William Hamilton, Nelson railed against the treaty that the Kingdom of Naples had signed with the French, which put constraints on how much help could be given.[80] He was now certain that the French were to eastward, announcing to his captains that he would sail 'for Cyprus, Syria and Egypt'.[81] Letters of encouragement, emphasizing the continuing importance of finding the French, came from all quarters. Off Cadiz, Roger Curtis, one of the passed-over admirals, sent 'his warmest and sincerest wishes for every possible success . . . Our accounts of you have been various and contradictory that we pant anxiously for certain intelligence.'[82] James Tough, the consul at Messina, wrote to him a month before: 'The fate of this country depends intirely upon the fleet under your command.'[83] Sir William Hamilton in Naples wished for 'the destruction of this boasted Armament on which the future tranquillity not only of Italy but all of Europe seems greatly to depend'.[84] From the Admiralty Office in London, where anxiety about the expedition was beginning to rise, William Young confided to his close friend Charles Morice Pole: 'On the success, or destruction of Buonaparte's fleet [an] event of great moment, not to us alone, but to all Europe, may depend.'[85] The minister from Turin wrote to Nelson that '. . . the eyes of all Europe indeed are upon you.'[86] If these expectations were great, so was the burden on Nelson.

18

The Battle of the Nile
1 August–22 September 1798

I feel for Nelson. He has the whole Navy upon his Back, but the Public, less unmindful of his former Merits, and uninfluenced by professional jealousy, refrains from censuring his Misfortune, and looks forward with confidence, to a speedy and brilliant Reparation of it.
William Huskisson, under-secretary of state for war, to
Lord Macartney, 18 September 1798, more than six weeks after
the battle and a fortnight before the victory was confirmed[1]

When the British squadron finally sailed from Syracuse on 26 July, the wind was fair and soon increased in strength. As the ships passed the south-west coast of Greece, Nelson detached the *Culloden* into the Gulf of Coron (Messina) for more information. Troubridge came out of the gulf towing a captured French brig loaded with much needed wine, and in possession of firm information from the Turkish governor that the French were in Egypt.[2] Some certainty was at last possible, and the course was again set for Alexandria. On four successive days, over a hundred miles was sailed; 172 miles was entered in the log on 30 July. The same day the great guns and small arms were exercised on board the *Vanguard*.[3] Two days later, at ten in the morning, the leading ship, the *Alexander*, sighted the land around Alexandria. By the early afternoon, with the wind at NNW and the visibility clear, she signalled she could see only two Turkish ships of the line and six French frigates in the harbour.[4] Nelson committed nothing to paper, but the intensity of his disappointment after the strain of the previous two months can be imagined.

The gloom in the British squadron was to last only an hour. Foley in the *Goliath* and Hood in the *Zealous* took a more easterly course to see if the French fleet could be in the great curved, shallow bay at Aboukir thirty miles to the east of Alexandria. At 2.30 the masthead lookouts on the two ships, which were sailing close together, simultaneously saw thirteen French

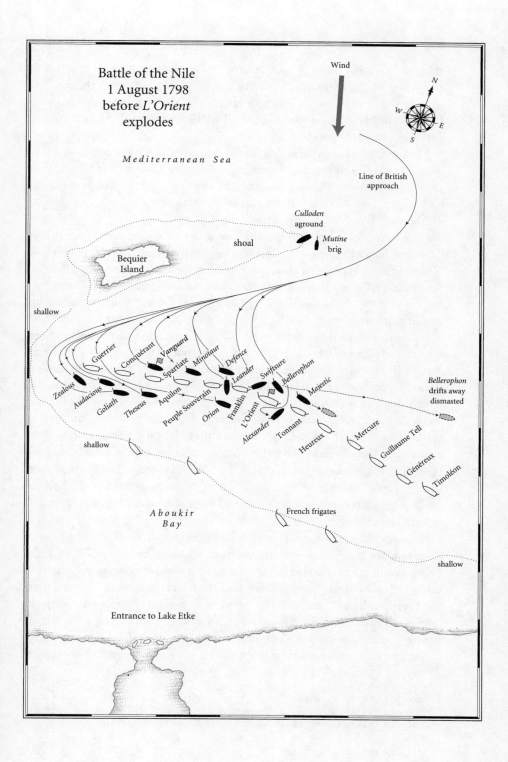

Battle of the Nile
1 August 1798
before *L'Orient*
explodes

Wind

N
W   E
S

Mediterranean Sea

Line of British
approach

Culloden
aground

Mutine
brig

shoal

Bequier
Island

shallow

Guerrier

Conquérant

Vanguard

Minotaur

Defence

Leander

Swiftsure

Bellerophon

Bellerophon
drifts away
dismasted

Zealous

Audacious

Goliath

Theseus

Aquilon

Spartiate

Peuple Souverain

Orion

Franklin

L'Orient

Alexander

Majestic

shallow

Tonnant

Heureux

Mercure

Guillaume Tell

shallow

Généreux

Timoléon

*Aboukir
Bay*

French frigates

shallow

Entrance to Lake Etke

ships anchored in a line at the western end of the bay. At that end of the bay was a castle, although its batteries were unable to protect the moored ships, as they were out of effective range. Signals were hoisted rapidly to Nelson's dispersed squadron. The *Zealous* cleared immediately for action and 'hove bullocks overboard'.[5]

The French had been surprised. The first and perhaps most unaccountable mistake of Admiral Brueys, aboard the 120-gun *L'Orient*, was that he had not stationed frigates offshore to warn of any approaching danger. Instead, they were moored in Alexandria Harbour and behind the main French fleet in Aboukir Bay. With the bright visibility and fresh northerly wind, Nelson did not hesitate, in spite of the shallow water of the bay and impending darkness; he had some knowledge of Aboukir Bay from a rough sketch and some rudimentary sailing directions in French that had been captured by Benjamin Hallowell in the *Swiftsure*. The directions read: 'half a league to the north-west of the castle are two low reefs of rock which break easily and are six cables round,' which the squadron would have to avoid.[6] The more prevalent north-westerly wind would have made it impossible to beat into the wind to reach the north end of the line, but a fresh breeze from NNW (Hood noted 'and sometimes more northerly') enabled Nelson to decide to attack the van and centre. He signalled his intentions to this effect.[7] Lieutenant Thomas Wilkes of the *Goliath* thought that the French were 'moored in a most masterly state of Defence'.[8] The immediate attack was one of the best risk-taking decisions that Nelson ever made in his life and would have been beyond the capacity of most commanders. He had complete confidence in his captains. He later claimed that he would not have ordered the immediate attack 'without knowing the men he had to trust to . . . that there was little room, but he was sure each would find a hole to creep in at'.[9]

Nelson could not have known exactly how much surprise had been achieved, for the French were in disorder.* Brueys had by this time little understanding with Bonaparte, on whom he was dependent for orders. The relationship between the two men had deteriorated to such a point that the French admiral has been described by a modern French authority as 'paralysed intellectually'.[10] It might appear that Brueys's ships were in a strong position, but doubts about the anchorage had been expressed by several French officers, who put forward a plan to reanchor them nearer

---

*From the north the French line was the *Guerrier* (74), *Conquérant* (74), *Spartiate* (74), *Aquilon* (74), *Peuple Souverain* (74), *Franklin* (80), *L'Orient* (120), *Tonnant* (80), *Heureux* (74), *Mercure* (74), *Guillaume Tell* (80), *Généreux* (74), and *Timoléon* (74).

the shore; the change was never put into effect. His ships were shorthanded and ill trained; dysentery and other illnesses were rife; crews were underfed and morale was low.[11] The lack of that crucial element of sea warfare in the Mediterranean, fresh water, had forced him to send valuable seamen ashore to dig wells, and from each ship twenty-five men had accompanied the shore parties to guard against hostile Arabs. Signals were made for them to return on board, which, according to the account of Admiral Blanquet, the French second-in-command, were 'only obeyed by a small number'.[12] The French signals used by Brueys were complex and unwieldy, and he could not make himself understood by other ships. Nor had the French taken two simple mooring precautions. No springs had been attached to the anchor cables of his ships, so that they could be angled to allow them to bring broadsides to bear on the advancing English ships. More important, only towards the rear of the line were there cables to prevent the attackers passing between the anchored ships; most of the line was unprotected. Brueys was undecided on whether to get under way, unsure if enough seamen were aboard each ship to do so. When he realized very late in the day that Nelson was coming straight into the bay, risking a night action, he had no choice but to stay anchored, make his ships ready for battle as best he could and wait.[13] At no time in Nelson's career was the margin of superiority between the British and French fleets so heavily weighted in his favour.

At 5.30 Nelson signalled 'to form the line as most convenient'.* All the careful preparations about the order of ships were abandoned. Hood in the *Zealous* and Foley in the *Goliath* raced for the honour of being the first ship into Aboukir Bay. Eventually Hood let Foley lead in, guided, according to one of his midshipmen, by a French atlas.[14] It was Foley who decided to sneak his ship inshore around the head of the line; Nelson could hardly have seen from the deck of the *Vanguard*, sixth in the line, that the French were at single anchor, and certainly not before Foley. According to George Elliot, a midshipman aboard the *Goliath*, Foley and the master, George Andrews, 'both looked at it, and agreed there was room to pass between the ship and her anchor . . . and it was decided to do it . . . I heard Foley say, that he should not be surprised to find the Frenchman unprepared for action on the inner side.'[15] In the words of Foley's family, 'so far was Lord Nelson from taking any credit for the thing that he told Sir Thomas Foley

---

* The order of sailing of the British line was: *Goliath, Zealous, Audacious, Orion, Theseus, Vanguard, Minotaur, Bellerophon, Defence, Majestic, Leander, Alexander* and *Swiftsure. Culloden* went aground.

after the action that he, Sir Thomas, had done it, but so hazardous did he, Lord Nelson, think it, that had he had a signal ready in time he would have stopped him.'[16] Foley's move took Hood, sailing just astern, by surprise; he expected 'to stick on the shoal every moment'.[17] Andrews states in his log baldly but professionally: 'At 15 minutes past 6 the *Goliath* being the leading ship crossed the van of the enemy's line and Commenced the Action.'[18] Bar Saumarez's *Orion*, every British ship was to anchor by the stern, though some more successfully than others.[19]

As a result of Foley's bold decision, the first five ships went around the head of the line. He was right. The French guns were not prepared on their port, landward side. At the head of the line the *Guerrier*, an old ship, absorbed broadsides from successive British ships as they passed. The *Goliath* did not position herself well, because when the anchor was dropped the cable 'kept slowly surging [i.e., slipping] through the stoppers . . . and ran out to the clench [end] placing us a little past the second ship of the line'.[20] Hood, in second place, took Foley's position alongside the *Guerrier*. A considerable distance had opened up between them and the third ship, the *Audacious*. Hardy in the little *Mutine* had tried to get local pilots on board the *Vanguard*; the flagship 'brought to', upon which the third in the line, Gould in the *Audacious*, followed suit.[21] By the time the *Audacious* came in, Foley and Hood had gained the upper hand over the first two French ships. Midshipman Elliot in the *Goliath* claimed: 'Before the fleet began to come in the two headmost ships of the line were destroyed . . . so that most of those ships got also in without injury.'[22]

At about the same time Troubridge in the *Culloden* went aground on the shoal and was to take no further part in the action. A rapid signal hoist by the *Culloden* warned the last two ships, *Alexander* and *Swiftsure*, which had looked into Alexandria and separated from the main fleet, of the danger of the shoal. Hood believed that the two last ships would have struck the shoal had not the *Culloden* shown where the danger lay so the *Culloden*'s bad luck 'may have been fortunate'.[23] Daylight was fading fast.

Cautious Gould in the *Audacious* soon secured *Conquérant*, already battered by the *Goliath*. He wrote a rapid note to Nelson: 'The Slaughter on board her is dreadful . . . we have but one killed.'[24] She was followed by Saumarez in the *Orion*. Going even further inshore to avoid the first three English ships, she was fired upon bravely by a French frigate; in one murderous broadside the French frigate was dismasted and sunk. The *Orion* immediately came into the wind and, exceptionally, anchored with her bow anchor on the quarter of *Peuple Souverain* and the bow of the *Franklin*.[25] Miller in the *Theseus* was the last to follow the ships inshore, anchoring just beyond the *Goliath* opposite the *Spartiate* and the *Aquilon*. Behind her, Nelson in the *Vanguard* saw that it was time to 'double' the line. He steered a course on the seaward side of the French line and anchored alongside the starboard side of the *Spartiate*, a ship that proved to be a tough and brave opponent, working her guns on both sides. Also in this duel was the *Aquilon*, which was pressing the *Vanguard* until Thomas Louis in the *Minotaur* anchored alongside her next to the *Vanguard*. The *Majestic*, captained by George Westcott, failed in its anchor drill; she 'did not bring up on letting go her anchor till she got her bowsprit foul of the bowsprit of *Heureux*, in which position she lay one hour, able to make use of but few guns'.[26] Westcott was killed in the first few minutes of opening fire; the *Majestic* lost her masts and suffered heavy casualties.

At 8.30 the *Spartiate* surrendered to the *Vanguard*.[27] At about the same time Nelson was struck on the right forehead by a missile. He fell into the arms of Edward Berry, with blood pouring from the wound. Nelson immediately thought the worst: 'I am killed. Remember me to my wife.' Taken down to the cockpit, he was soon seen by Michael Jefferson, the surgeon who had treated him in Corsica. Jefferson was hard at work with nearly thirty men waiting for treatment. Bleeding from wounds of the scalp is usually profuse; Nelson's injury was not life-threatening, but it gave him a severe shaking. 'The cranium bared for more than an inch, the wound 3″ long,' the surgeon recorded. There was no 'flap' of skin to blind him, as has often been asserted.[28] It is possible that the blow caused a concussive injury, for Nelson had splitting headaches at times in the weeks afterwards, but he suffered no loss of consciousness or loss of recent memory. Medical experts are still divided on the effect that this wound had on him.[29] His immediate reaction was not entirely rational, for he began to dictate a letter to the Admiralty, thinking it to be his last. He then, however, began to recover and soon came on deck to witness the climax of the battle.

The French flagship, *L'Orient*, was a three-decker giant of a ship. Two 74s at least were needed to take her on. At seven o'clock the *Bellerophon* under Captain Darby came into the line, but failed to anchor at an angle to *L'Orient*'s bow as intended, out of the line of fire of the great ship's guns. Instead, she found herself alongside the French flagship. Before she could open fire, *L'Orient* put two broadsides into her. Darby was wounded, and, on fire in several places, the *Bellerophon* drifted out of the line, nearly becoming the target for the two last English ships into the battle, the *Alexander* and the *Swiftsure*. In the darkness, for it was by now about eight o'clock, both ships anchored by the stern perfectly, with springs on the cable angling the ships on the quarters of *L'Orient* and the *Franklin* respectively.

Perhaps the most remarkable incident of this remarkable battle now took place: the destruction of *L'Orient*. Some years later Alexander Ball of the *Alexander* recounted that he 'had previously made a combustible preparation, but which . . . he had purposed to reserve for the last emergency . . . one of the lieutenants, without his knowledge, threw in the combustible matter.'[30] The *Alexander* was well placed for a member of her crew to throw combustible material through the stern windows. Lieutenant Lewis Davis of the *Swiftsure* recorded: 'at 3 mins past 9 observed the *L'Orient* on fire in her Starboard Quarter apparently in the Admiral's cabin but still engaging us and we firing all our Starboard foremost guns loaded with round and grapeshot at the place where she was on fire, at 1/4 past 9 the *L'Orient* still continued burning very rapidly and had spread all over the after part of the ship but still firing from her lower deck.'[31]

The combined efforts of the *Alexander* and the *Swiftsure* ensured that *L'Orient* continued to burn fiercely. By 9.15 it was obvious that the fire was unquenchable and would soon reach her magazines. At 9.20 the *Swiftsure* also stopped firing at her, and the French guns began to fall silent as every ship took precautions against damage from an explosion. She was upwind of *L'Orient* and, according to Lieutenant Davis, 'covered all the lower deck ports and got the people under cover of the decks'. *L'Orient*'s crew began to abandon her; the *Swiftsure* hauled fourteen French seamen from the water. Davis recorded: 'at 37 minutes past 9 the *L'Orient* blew up, and from the explosion a great many Splinters, fire etc blew on board of us but did not material damage.'[32] The *Swiftsure* was lucky to escape damage; the *Alexander* was out of the battle for two hours, dousing fires and heaving burning sails and rigging overboard.[33] In the words of Lieutenant Wilkes of the *Goliath*, 'the Battle recommences, the Roaring of the Guns, the Crashing of the Masts & the Shrieks of Wounded & the Jargon of surrendering Frenchmen fill up the remainder of this ever Memorable Night.'[34]

The *Franklin* opened fire five minutes after the explosion. 'At 42 minutes past 9 opened fire again on the *Franklin*,' noted Lieutenant Davis.[35] The *Franklin* struck twenty minutes later. Every French ship forward of *L'Orient* had now surrendered. Throughout the early hours of the morning exhaustion of the crews and damage to ships slackened the pace of the action to desultory fire only. Just before 3 a.m. firing ceased completely.[36] Nelson, shocked, exhausted and in pain, took no part in this phase of the battle, and, indeed, little could be done during the night, but before dawn at four in the morning he began to resume command. He sent a boat up the line ordering those ships capable of sailing to come forward to the rear of the French line. The *Goliath*, the *Theseus*, the *Zealous* and the *Leander* got under way in the light wind, now westerly. Only Davidge Gould, in the inappropriately named *Audacious*, the least damaged of the ships, failed to come forward. We know that Nelson thought very little of him.[37]

Some idea of the exhaustion of the crews at this point is described by Ralph Willet Miller of the *Theseus*: 'My people were also so extremely jaded, that as soon as they had hove our sheet anchor up they dropped under the capstan bars, and were asleep in every sort of posture, having been then working at their fullest exertion, or fighting, for near twelve hours.'[38] Lieutenant Wilkes described the scene: 'At Daylight we find our Victory Compleat, Immense wrecks in every direction . . . [our] killed & wounded have been great but nothing in comparison with the Enemy's.'[39] In fact, the battle was far from over.

The French ships at the rear of the line were under the command of Rear-Admiral Pierre-Charles de Villeneuve aboard the *Guillaume Tell*. Three were unscathed. Villeneuve was torn between sailing up to windward to help or staying in position in case the ships ahead were to drop back behind him. A third option was for the rear division to leave the scene and to constitute a continuing threat to the English fleet. At 5:05 the action started again.[40] The *Tonnant* was dismasted, although she had not surrendered, while *Heureux* and *Mercure* were soon aground. Firing against Villeneuve's ships continued for some hours, before he gave the order to sail and escape. The captain of the *Timoléon*, with severely damaged rigging, ran her aground and awaited an attack. At 11.30 a.m. two ships only, the *Guillaume Tell* and the *Généreux*, left the scene, although Hood in the *Zealous* attempted to cut them off.[41] Had Nelson not been wounded, he might have prevented even these two from escaping.[42]

It was not until the morning of 3 August that the *Tonnant* and *Timoléon* surrendered to end the most decisive naval battle of the eighteenth century. During the approach to Aboukir Bay, Nelson had hoisted only nine signals. His weeks of consultation and contact with his captains led to success once the battle started, when darkness and smoke precluded centralized direction and demanded initiative from his captains.[43] Significantly, the average age of Nelson and his captains was just under ten years younger than the admirals and captains who had fought at the Battle of the Glorious First of June, only four years earlier.[44] Risk-taking seamanship, complex anchoring manoeuvres, highly skilled crews, a rapid rate of fire and determination by every officer and seaman had devastated French naval power in the Mediterranean in under twenty-four hours. It was a battle in the style and tradition of Anson, Boscawen and Hawke – though taken to extremes –

rather than in the style of Howe or Rodney, with their laborious signal control.[45] It has lessons for command and tactics in today's navies.[46] When Howe heard of the great victory, it puzzled him: 'the most remarkable feature of the transaction consists in the eminently distinguished conduct of each of the captains of his Squadron. Perhaps it has never before happened, that every captain had equal opportunity to distinguish himself in the same manner, or took equal advantage of it.'[47]

Nothing was said officially about their setting fire to L'Orient, unsurprisingly in view of the code of honour against the use of anything but solid shot. Howe had voiced naval disapproval at Gibraltar in 1782 when pressed to use red-hot shot by an army officer. Howe had replied by asking if the officer had ever been in a naval action: 'On his replying in the negative, "Then", said his Lordship, "I think it, Sir, quite horrid enough, without having recourse to anything more . . . depend on it cold shot will effectually do the business."'[48] In a letter to William Locker three years earlier, Nelson himself had been critical of the use of heated shot, 'ordered positive by the Convention', although he noted that he thought the French officers ashamed of using it.[49] This use of incendiary devices at the Nile came to light in later years when Alexander Ball, as governor of Malta, described events to his secretary, Samuel Taylor Coleridge. Other evidence supports this explanation of the destruction of the French flagship. Midshipman Elliot recounted that 'the Alexander was the cause of the burning of L'Orient', but repeats a convenient story of paint being left in the French admiral's cabin.[50] The combustibles were dinner-table gossip: Cornelia Knight in Naples soon afterwards stated categorically that Ball was responsible, 'as his ship was nearest and chiefly instrumental to the blowing up of L'Orient'.[51] Seven years later Lady Bessborough recorded that 'Mr Pitt said that he [Sir Robert Calder] was one of a junto who gave out that Nelson deserved to be punished for the battle of the Nile, as it was in contradiction to all former naval tactics that they all swear by so much.'[52] After the battle the French protested against the English use of combustible material, but Benjamin Hallowell found that the French themselves had shells on board the Spartiate, which when tested afterwards 'continued to burn under water' and seem to indicate the early use of phosphorus, developed by the French in the 1780s.[53] Napoleon thought that carronades had been responsible for the burning of the L'Orient.[54]

French defence and tenacity had been of a high order, although outmanoeuvred and outgunned. Resistance from the newer and larger ships moored in the middle of the French line had been strong and their gunnery had caused high casualties on board the Bellerophon (forty-nine killed, 147 wounded) and the *Majestic* (fifty killed, 143 wounded). The *Vanguard* too sustained heavy casualties. William Faddy, the captain of marines, had been killed, while Lieutenants Vassall and Adye, and John Campbell, Nelson's secretary, had been wounded. Twenty-seven seamen and marines had been killed and sixty-eight wounded. In the fleet as a whole, sixteen officers and 202 seamen and marines had been killed, thirty-seven officers and 640 seamen and marines wounded out of a total of something under 8,000 men under Nelson's command.[55] Estimates of the French killed have traditionally varied between 3,000 and 4,000, but the latest estimate is 2,012; even this lower number was approximately ten times that of those killed in Nelson's fleet.[56]

In spite of the overwhelming superiority of Nelson's squadron in the Eastern Mediterranean, no one in the fleet could relax, for the squadron was nearly 1,000 miles from the nearest friendly dockyard facilities at Naples, and just under 2,000 miles from Gibraltar. Only three or four ships did not need urgent repairs. But time was found for a service of thanksgiving on board the *Vanguard* on 2 August, and immediate congratulations followed to Nelson from his captains. These demonstrated real affection, the most generous and emotional from Saumarez: 'the most glorious and compleat Victory ever yet obtain'd, the just Recompense of your Zeal, and the great Anxiety you have so long experienced before it pleased Providence to give you the sight of vile miscreants who have now receiv'd the just Punishment due to their Past Crimes.'[57] Saumarez called a meeting of the captains aboard the *Orion* to agree a subscription to present a sword to Nelson.* His portrait was to be painted and 'hung up in the room belonging to the Egyptian Club now established'.[58] The boisterous Benjamin Hallowell in an ironic but equally affectionate gesture had a piece of *L'Orient*'s mast made into a coffin for his admiral. Nelson sent dispatches to London with Edward Berry in the *Leander* and overland to India.[59] He mentioned no one by name, for 'in the Battle the conduct of every Officer was equal', as he remarked in his letter to his captains thanking them for the offer of the Egyptian Club sword.[60] The outstanding success of the action enabled him to avoid the awkwardness of selecting individuals for particular mention;

---

* The only surviving relics of the Club are the ornate swords with the hilt in the form of a crocodile, one of which was sold at Sotheby's recently (Downer, *Davison*, 46–52). Others are in the National Maritime Museum. Nelson's crocodile sword was sold by the Bridport family in 1895 but was stolen from Greenwich Hospital in 1900 and never seen again (Downer, 49; Cross, 'Offence against the Nation', 92–109). This was also the fate of the diamond chelengk given to Nelson by the sultan of Turkey to mark the victory, stolen from the National Maritime Museum in 1950.

but the only one to receive a formal honour for this battle would be Nelson himself.*

Nelson now took steps to secure his victory and to transport as many French prizes as he could to Gibraltar. He wrote to Alexander Davison in London appointing him sole agent of the prizes and to Maurice Nelson to tell him so.[61] He transferred the calm and solid Thomas Masterman Hardy, who commanded the *Mutine* brig, to the *Vanguard* as captain after Berry left with dispatches; it was to prove a durable combination of temperament between admiral and captain, although Hardy had established a reputation on his small vessel as a disciplinarian and flogger.† He acquired Ball's efficient secretary, John Tyson, his old purser from West Indies days, and found another position for his existing secretary, John Campbell, whom Nelson had never found satisfactory. Tyson provided faithful service for the rest of that war and was to become a close friend. Through Troubridge he negotiated with French forces on shore that they should take back 3,000 French prisoners, of which 1,000 were wounded. Nelson needed to get his damaged ships back to Gibraltar, but also to leave sufficient force off Alexandria to blockade Napoleon's army. He left Samuel Hood to command the three ships in best repair to maintain the blockade – the *Goliath*, the *Zealous* and the *Swiftsure* – as well as the frigates, which had finally caught up with the squadron.[62] He sent Saumarez back to Gibraltar with the six British ships escorting six French prizes, but he was forced to strip the *Mercure* and *Heureux* of their stores and burn them. It was exhausting work. Lieutenant Wilkes wrote home: 'since the battle we have been almost killed with fatigue refitting our ships and prizes.'[63] There were a few less demanding moments: on 13 August, Nelson wrote a curiously worded letter to Lady Hamilton, intending to both cajole and reprimand, reflecting the strain that he was under: 'I am penetrated with the Queen's condescension to think of such an Animal as I am, God Almighty has made me the happy instrument of destruction . . . Why will not Naples act with Vigor?'[64]

Almost three weeks after the battle, on 19 August, the *Vanguard* set off for Naples, with the *Alexander* and the *Culloden*. The damage to the hull and rudder of the last would take many months to repair, and her progress was impeded by a sail wrapped around her hull. Her slow speed held back

---

* The dispatches of Howe, St Vincent and Duncan had created extreme discord among their officers after their victories. Ross argues several times that Saumarez should have received 'some mark of distinction' (Ross, I, 227–8, 230, 273). Edward Berry eventually received the baronetcy traditionally given to the bearer of dispatches of a successful battle to London.
† On board the *Mutine*, with a crew of 120, men were flogged twice a week, with up to four men being flogged on the same day (Lavery, *Nile*, 114–15).

the other two ships.[65] The month-long passage was very slow, hot and uncomfortable, winds light and contrary. At times Nelson's health was frail, although observers did not feel that his head wound was serious. Before he set off from Aboukir, Samuel Hood had written that 'his wound in the head is not dangerous, but troublesome.'[66] Nelson's secretary, John Campbell, wrote to London soon after the battle that the wound was not serious and that he would be quite well in a week or ten days.[67] After a week the *Vanguard*'s course crossed that of Saumarez's ships. On 26 August, Saumarez went on board the *Vanguard* and spent half an hour with Nelson; he was 'happy to find him in perfect health. He will ever retain the mark on his forehead which he has so honourably acquired; mine is not in quite so distinguished a place.'[68] Saumarez had received a severe contusion on the thigh. Surgeon Jefferson took Nelson off the sick list on 1 September, but he was still not well. On the same day Nelson wrote to St Vincent, 'My head is splitting at this moment,' but this could be ascribed to nervous exhaustion.[69] Nelson's new secretary, John Tyson, wrote later of 'the pain in his heart, of which he suffered so much coming from Egypt'.[70] In the week before Nelson landed, however, he appears to have fallen seriously ill, possibly with a recurrence of malaria.[71] A general feeling prevailed that Nelson needed a rest. Back in London, old Lord Howe wrote to Roger Curtis, hoping that Nelson's 'state of health would oblige him to solicite relaxation from his splendid maritime excursions'.[72]

As Nelson sailed slowly westwards, the mood in London was one of disappointment and frustration. Edward Berry's dispatches had been destroyed when the *Leander* was captured by the *Généreux* off Crete. In late July, Lady Spencer had been fondly imagining how she would treat the captured Bonaparte, asking William Windham: 'what will be the best way of conducting myself when Buonaparte is dining at my right hand. Shall I do it in a sincere & a brutal style? Or in a false & a generous one?'[73] But by August early anticipation of success was weakening. 'The Publick are tired, absolutely fatigued with thinking of Buonaparte,' Colonel Drinkwater reported to Lord Minto on 9 August.[74] Later that month information that Nelson had missed the French fleet at Alexandria reached the Admiralty. One of the junior ministers reported: 'During this long Period our Hopes have been kept alive by Ten Thousand favourable Rumors, from every Quarter . . . we have at last an Account, not Official, but too Authentic I apprehend, that this favourite of Fortune [Bonaparte] reached Alexandria on 7 July and to complete our Mortification, the same Account adds that Nelson got there two Days before him.'[75]

By the middle of September several unverified reports of a victory, with both Nelson and Napoleon killed, arrived via Portugal and Constantinople; there were also reports in the French newspapers. Political anxiety was at a high pitch; Drinkwater by this time was referring to Nelson's 'unfortunate cruise'.[76] Newspaper opinion was now universally critical, with the opposition *Morning Chronicle* in particular pointing to Nelson's inexperience.[77] Fanny was tense and anxious. She wrote to Nelson on 11 September: 'The newspapers have tormented and almost killed me in regard to the desperate action you have fought with the French fleet. How human faculties can be brought to make others intentionally miserable I cannot conceive.'[78] On 20 September, William Young at the Admiralty was 'in anxious expectation' of a messenger from Deal, although he had received a message sent through the 'telegraph' that transmitted visual signals from towers built on hills between the Downs and London: 'Action near Alexandria, Admiral burnt two or three French ships, sank some, French and English ships driven on shore being dismasted, several French made perfect wrecks, one ship of 80 guns got to Malta, one of 74 to Corfu.' 'If this is not a forged paper,' he wrote confusingly to Charles Morice Pole, 'there can be little doubt of the truth.'[79] Seven weeks after the battle no clear picture existed in London.

While uncertainty prevailed in England, Nelson continued to make slow progress towards Italy, sailing with long two-day tacks against the north-westerly light airs. On 1 September the *Vanguard* saw the last of the *Orion* and the French prizes as they made their way to Gibraltar. On 11 September, 'inclinable to calm', the ships anchored off the Tower de Pharos at Messina. The wind sharply and suddenly increased three days later, with heavy squalls, then thunder and lightning. 'When handing the foretopsail', Galwey wrote in his log, 'the foremast went 10 or 12 feet from the deck, two seamen were killed & 2 lost overboard. Carried away the main topmast.' The *Thalia* frigate towed the flagship, the winds again falling light. On 19 September no more than eight miles was covered in twenty-four hours. The last days of the passage were spent rigging another jury-mast. Just before the ships reached Naples, the tow was slipped and the *Vanguard* sailed slowly into Naples Bay. On 22 September thirteen guns were fired as Sir William and Lady Hamilton came on board; this was, one sailor noted, 'before we let down our anchor or had time to prepare for their reception'.[80] An hour later twenty-one guns saluted Ferdinand, the king of Naples.[81]

Not until 2 October did Edward Capel arrive in London with a second set of official dispatches. Naples had heard the news first: the queen, Maria Carolina, put it precisely when she wrote to the Naples ambassador in London: 'Great hopes were entertained from his Bravery but no one could flatter themselves with so compleat a destruction.'[82] At Gibraltar the governor received the news late in the evening and insisted upon firing a twenty-one gun salute in the middle of the night, although he considerately informed the Spaniards beforehand.[83] Lord Spencer, criticized in recent weeks for his choice of command, collapsed with relief and emotion on hearing the news, his political reputation safe. According to Lady Spencer, 'His joy had mastered him.'[84] Her own relief was palpable: 'Joy, Joy, Joy, brave gallant immortalised Nelson.'[85] Spencer, Howe, William Young and Collingwood wrote to Nelson, as did Admiral Goodall, who was gleeful that he could get his own back on his doubting naval friends: 'knowing my attachment to you, how often have I been questioned, what is your favourite Hero about?' Even Sir Richard Hughes put pen to paper to Nelson: 'I think you have given them (as the Pugilists term it) a Dose in the Bread Bag.'[86] The politicians who had worked to get him appointed to command in the Mediterranean congratulated themselves. Thomas Grenville wrote to Spencer, 'I am ashamed almost to feel what a boaster he has made of me.'[87]

The newspapers piled superlative on superlative, and 'Rule Britannia' was sung after theatre performances, according to The Times, 'in a burst of patriotic exultation'.[88] An hour and a half long 'feu de joie' for the king and queen began with salutes from ships in Weymouth Bay.[89] The king, as ungracious as ever where Nelson was concerned, thought that the destruction of the Brest fleet would have been more advantageous. The prime minister, William Pitt, was more measured: 'The Accounts of Bonaparte's situation and prospects gathered from intercepted Letters are most satisfactory ... but I find great Doubts entertained about a Thanksgiving at St Paul's which I have submitted to the Archbishop.'[90] While no official ceremony marked the victory, a day 'of general thanksgiving' was declared on 29 November, and prayers were said in churches. A subscription was immediately opened at Lloyd's for relief of widows and orphans of the men killed. 'There is such a *tintamaire* all around here,' Lady Bessborough reported to Lord Leveson-Gower, 'with bells and squibs and bonfires.'[91] An ox was roasted in the market place at Norwich. In the Norfolk village of Western Longeville, Parson Woodforde gave his servants 'after Supper some strong-Beer and some Punch to drink Admiral Lord Nelson's Health on his late grand Victory and also all the other Officers with him and all the brave Sailors.'[92]

Nelson could reasonably expect to be made a peer for such a victory. Between 1780 and 1801 George III ennobled thirty-five politicians, judges and military commanders.[93] Pitt assured Lord Hood on 3 October that Nelson would be made a viscount, but Pitt had not allowed for the king, cautious of precedent, from whom Spencer received a letter written the same day: 'Sir Horatio Nelson is not rich and therefore declined being created a Baronet. This puts his getting a peerage quite out of the question, but is a reason that he should have a handsome pension settled on him.'[94] Only a skilful letter by Spencer, stressing 'the expectation of the public', managed to persuade the king that a barony, the most junior of the five ranks of the peerage, would be suitable for Nelson.[95] Hood was incensed, for he had already told Fanny that Nelson would be made a viscount. He wrote to Nelson about 'objections from a certain quarter', echoes of the king's displeasure of late 1780s.[96]

Putting the best face on it, Spencer wrote to Nelson three days later suggesting that a barony 'is the highest honour that has ever been conferred on an Officer of your standing in the Service & who was not a Commander-in-Chief'.[97] William Windham wrote in his diary: 'So Nelson is only to be a Baron. I am not sure that the decision is not right, on the principle of considering, not merely the merit and importance of the action, but the rank of the commander.' But to Spencer he suggested that Nelson ought to be somewhere between St Vincent, who was an earl, and Duncan, who had been made a viscount.[98] Six months later St Vincent had to write to Duckworth, just promoted to rear-admiral, but who wanted recognition for the capture of Minorca: 'Lord Nelson is the single instance, within my recollection, of a Sea Officer, detach'd by his Commander in Chief, receiving any Reward, for the performance of the Service he was sent upon, and there was so much brilliancy in the Exploit, that the country called loudly, for even a higher honor than that of an English Baron.'[99] Tributes were heartfelt in Parliament, with the speech of Lord Minto, Nelson's old friend, on 21 November receiving particular prominence. 'I have witnessed a degree of ability, judgement, temper and conciliation, not always allowed to the sort of spirit which without an instant's hesitation can attack . . . a superior French fleet moored and fortified within the islands and shoals of an unknown bay.'[100] In Austria the sense of relief was as great as in England. Haydn wrote the 'Nelson Mass' and in Vienna 'the government paper rose 5 per cent'.[101]

The strategic impact of the battle was dramatic. At a stroke it restored Britain's supremacy in the Mediterranean, which it held for the rest of the wars against France. It trapped Bonaparte and his army in the East for fifteen months and exposed the French colonies to recapture.[102] The Turks entered the war on the side of the allies and even allowed a Russian squadron through the Strait of Constantinople 'for this occasion only'.[103] The victory encouraged the Second Coalition of Britain, Austria and Russia against France, which had been brought together by Britain in the spring of 1798. But none of the political and diplomatic consequences brought about by the victory at the Nile were to endure. Although French ambitions in India were fatally weakened, only in 1800, when General Abercromby defeated the French Army in Egypt, was the threat to the East finally ended. While Turkey was brought into the Coalition, she was ineffectual. Lack of Russian military success in Central Europe caused her withdrawal from the alliance by late 1799. Napoleon managed to escape from Egypt back to France, and in the following year he defeated the Austrians at Marengo. They were defeated again by General Jean Victor Moreau at Hohenlinden.

The Battle of the Nile was, however, decisive in the long term. First, it opened up the Mediterranean to British trade and to other nations that had recently been excluded by French naval power. For instance, the United States minister to Spain urged his political masters, now engaged in a 'Quasi-War' with France, to send warships into the Mediterranean to enable American merchant ships to trade there, as 'the English have gained the complete command of the Mediterranean'.[104] But the greatest impact was upon the French Navy, for the absolute nature of Nelson's victory was a new phenomenon in European warfare. The French Navy never recovered, psychologically or materially, and the battle established a long era of British naval confidence. The two French ships that made their escape were captured soon afterwards; three of the prizes enjoyed long careers in the British Navy. For the first time the tonnage of the British battle fleet began to equal the combined total of France, Spain and Holland and by 1800 had surpassed it.[105] In this and subsequent wars Britain never abandoned the Mediterranean as it had done so abruptly in 1796. Malta came into British hands by September 1800, its refitting and repair capacity strengthening the British hold on the Western and Central Mediterranean; it became a British possession for 179 years. The Battle of the Nile, notes a French study written in 1988, is one 'of which French historians never speak'. It was 'the end of the French navy as a force capable of counterbalancing British power. It could not be put together again and Aboukir carried within itself the germ of Trafalgar.'[106]

III

Passion and Discredit

1798–1801

19

Palermo and Naples

22 September 1798–6 August 1799

His Majesty never disembarked on the Neapolitan shore & Lord
Nelson's ship has constantly served him for a palace. His Majesty . . .
insisted that the treaty which amounted to a general amnesty for the
past should be set aside and so positive was His Majesty that a number
of the principal leaders were arrested, strip[p]ed and put aboard vessels
guarded by his Britannic Majesty's Ships . . . this breach of faith has
given umbrage to some of His Britannic Majesty's Naval Officers who
seem to think that Lord Nelson has been too complaisant, and that he
has no right to make their ship the engine . . . of turpitude.

Report from Palermo, 9 August 1799, to Lord Minto, minister at
Vienna, and forwarded to William Windham, secretary-at-war[1]

After the Battle of the Nile, things changed irrevocably for Nelson. His
name was known throughout Europe. In Naples he was greeted by cheering
crowds. 'All confess him to be their saviour and deliverer,' Sir William
Hamilton reported to St Vincent. 'In short no words can express what is
felt here, and the consequences of this most important and well timed
action are incalculable.'[2] The immediate effect was practical. Within a week
of Nelson's arrival on 22 September 1798 Hamilton reported to St Vincent
that 'nothing that His Sicilian Majesty's dockyards and magazines can
possibly furnish has been denied them, and they will all be ready for sea in
a very few days.'[3] In fact, the squadron did not get to sea until 15 October.
Nelson explained to Spencer that the swell in Naples Bay and wrecked
masts had caused delays: 'I admit three weeks is a long time to refit a fleet
after a battle.'[4]

Some of the delay can be attributed to the receptions and balls in those
three weeks, with the lead given by the royal family. The contrast with the
strain of the last three months could not have been greater. Alexander Ball
reported to Saumarez that the king 'gave all the captains a very elegant

dinner on board one of his ships of the line. We dined on the poop; the party very select . . . After dinner, the King gave us a toast, "Sir Horatio Nelson and the brave English nation" with a salute from his lower deck guns. Sir William Hamilton gave us a fête which cost a thousand pounds. It was much admired for its taste and magnificence.'[5] Nelson struggled to get used to the extravagant and constant praise: on his fortieth birthday, as he reported to Fanny, '80 people dined at Sir William's, 1,740 came to a ball, 800 supped, conducted in such a style of elegance as I never saw or shall again probably.'[6] He wrote to St Vincent more formally of 'the most distinguished reception that ever, I believe, fell to the lot of a human being'.[7] To his sceptical father he commented with candour: 'it is enough to make me vain.'[8]

Yet Nelson still felt unappreciated by the British government. When he heard from Spencer that he was to be made only a baron, when for their victories St Vincent had been made an earl and Duncan a viscount, his long-held sense of grievance was strengthened and his indignation refuelled. Nor would prize money flow from the victory: he pointed out to Spencer that St Vincent, as commander-in-chief of the Mediterranean, though 2,000 miles from Aboukir Bay, would receive six times as much as he would. Nor could he promote his officers and use his influence.[9] 'All must go to Earl St Vincent I have no power to make a cook,' he remarked bitterly to Fanny.[10] He wrote directly to Pitt on behalf of his brother Maurice, who had 'served the King in the Navy Office for near 20 years with a Character unimpeachable', seeking to get him appointed a commissioner of the navy. Nelson never received a reply.[11] A year later nothing had happened, and in a letter to Maurice he hoped that Lord Spencer would do something 'handsome' for him.[12] The criticism he had experienced at the hands of jealous, passed-over admirals had now been answered by stunning success, but he was still sensitive on the subject. 'I grieve that any of our brother Officers should be hurt at my being sent up here,' he wrote to Sir Roger Curtis; 'I can, however, with truth say that I neither asked or Solicited for the honor.'[13] In December he wrote to Fanny that he felt St Vincent was jealous of him. 'Lord St Vincent is in no hurry to oblige now. I am got he fancies too near him in reputation. In short, I am the envied man.'[14] Coping with success can sometimes be more difficult than coming to terms with failure. Nelson's sensitivity prevented the glittering victory of the Nile from bringing him much satisfaction and happiness, and his sense of grievance did not diminish with time; six months later he remarked to Edward Berry: 'As to both our Honours, it is proof how much a battle fought near England is prized to one fought at a great distance.'[15] Only in Naples was applause and joy seemingly unalloyed.

Life in Naples was made infinitely more comfortable by Sir William and Lady Hamilton, with whom he lived when he was ashore.[16] Hamilton was by now only eighteen months short of his seventieth birthday and the previous year had already applied to the government for a pension. In spite of many years of frenetic collecting and possessing much physical energy, Hamilton was a curiously passive character, one of nature's bystanders. His recent biographer notes his 'ironic detachment, never expecting too much of either his nearest and dearest or of himself, and certainly not of the world at large whose opinions and behaviour he viewed on the whole with an amiable contempt . . . He was on the margins, his master overlooked him, he never had much clout.'[17] Hamilton had been in Naples for far too long and had 'gone native', wrapped up in the politics of an unstable court. His residence, the Palazzo Sessa, had become one of the main centres of the social and cultural life of the capital. At the most critical moments in Naples in the following year his age and his indecision led to periods of 'nervous prostration', rendering him useless to Nelson. Certainly Lord Grenville, the foreign secretary, had little opinion of Hamilton's capacity for independent judgement, reckoning that he 'takes any impression that is given him'.[18] His weakness of character allowed a dangerous vacuum to encircle the king and queen, and it was into this that Nelson was drawn.

Emma Hamilton could not have been more different. The most vivid of many colourful characters in Naples at this time, Emma always sought the centre of the stage; indeed, her life had the quality of a play. By means of her beauty, she had come a long way from the cottage on the Wirral in Cheshire where she was born. The details of her early years, not surprisingly, are hazy. It is possible, even likely, that she was a prostitute in London before she found her way in 1779 to Dr Thomas Graham, a 'vaudeville medical messiah'.[19] Here, it is said, she helped to market, largely unclothed, his 'Celestial Bed', an early exercise in medical electricity that claimed to end sterility and impotence, as well as other quack methods of rejuvenation therapy.[20] It was a position in which a talent for acting and singing was clearly an advantage. From here she became a kept woman, taken 'under the protection' of Sir Harry Featherstonehaugh, who abandoned her cruelly in 1782 when she was pregnant. Charles Greville, William Hamilton's nephew, was probably already having an affair with her before her abandonment; he took her under his protection and she became his mistress. Her daughter, Emma, was brought up in Cheshire.[21] Greville's finances and marriage prospects required him to be rid of her, and in 1786 she went out to Naples, where she became Sir William's mistress and, in 1791, his wife.

In Naples, Emma Hamilton was a celebrated hostess. Evenings at the

Palazzo Sessa generally ended with her presenting her 'Attitudes', in which, encouraged by her connoisseur husband, she portrayed characters from classical mythology. Her singing too was impressive, one of her listeners noting that she 'had no scientific knowledge of music, but an ear and a voice that left nothing to be desired. She was possessed of a great natural genius, which added to her beauty, had completely fascinated Sir William.' This was the opinion of Cornelia Knight, a writer and spectator at the Neapolitan court, and the Hamiltons' constant companion of the next two years; she concluded that Emma was 'a singular mixture of right and wrong'.[22] Emma could certainly be counted on to enhance the drama of any moment. When first she came on board the *Vanguard* to greet the victorious Nelson, she cried, 'Oh God! Is it possible!' Nelson was bemused, relating to Fanny that she 'fell into my arms more dead than alive. Tears however soon set matters to rights . . . the scene was in its way affecting.'[23]

The attraction between Nelson and Emma was not instantaneous; his early letters to her are awkward and ill phrased: 'your whole conduct has ever been to me so very much above my deserts that I am absolutely at a loss how to express myself.'[24] Emma was a confidante of the queen, and very soon the strong-minded royal came to dominate Nelson. The country parson's son first had his head turned by royalty in the form of Prince William Henry in the 1780s; in Naples it happened again. Within two weeks he was writing in fulsome terms of the queen and of her policy; within three months he was writing to Spencer that she 'again made me promise not to quit her and her Family till brighter prospects open upon her'.[25] Maria Carolina, daughter of the empress of Austria, Maria Theresa, was the driving force in the court, the government and foreign policy. Her husband, King Ferdinand IV, was no more than a cipher in the affairs of state, combining a great physique with equally evident moral and physical cowardice. His only political strength was unswerving support from the poor of Naples, the anti-Jacobin, fiercely Catholic *lazzaroni*, who saw him, with some reason, as one of their own.

Naples and Sicily, independent of Austria only since 1734, had long been in economic decline and dependent upon Spain. It was an unusually complex country: feudalism was an integral part of its structure, yet it had a powerful intellectual elite, driven by Enlightenment ideas, pushing for reform. The court was not opposed to reform, but the execution five years earlier of the queen's sister, Marie Antoinette, the wife of Louis XVI of France, created an unbridgeable rift between the elite and the monarchy.[26] The queen's thinking was dominated by hatred of the French Republic and personal vengeance for her sister.

The key to the foreign relations of the court of Naples was the queen's ambition to forge an Austrian alliance, and turn away from the traditional understanding with Spain, a new policy deeply unpopular with the governing classes.[27] Intellectuals, the bourgeoisie and merchants were completely separated from the court. It was a corrupt, unstable kingdom, which Nelson despised. It epitomized the worst of the states of the *ancien régime*, and was comprised of an emotional political mixture that led to violence at the slightest pretext. The tired and often sick Nelson was unprepared and ill equipped to deal with it successfully.

Nelson, however, was soon to get his instructions from London. Britain, with its allies Portugal, Turkey and Russia, all of which contributed squadrons to work with Nelson, now had to consolidate its hold on the Mediterranean. The day after the news of the Nile reached London, Spencer and the Board of Admiralty instructed its secretary, Evan Nepean, to send secret orders to St Vincent, with a copy to Nelson. The 'Principal Objects' that Nelson had to achieve were: to protect the coasts of Sicily, Naples and the Adriatic, cooperate with the Austrian and Neapolitan armies, cut off the French from their army in Egypt, blockade the French in Malta and cooperate with the Turkish and Russian squadrons that were trying to wrest Corfu from the French. It ended with a carefully phrased warning to Nelson: 'from the uncertainty of Events which may occur, much must of necessity be left to his discretion, but he should be particularly directed in every possible situation to give the most cordial and unlimited protection to H. M. Allies, to exert himself to the utmost to preserve a good Intelligence between them, and most carefully to avoid giving to any of them the smallest cause for Suspicion, Jealousy or Offence'[28]. Their lordships were only too well aware that Nelson, when a commodore, had had a history of upsetting the Italian states, particularly the Genoese, and that complaints in the past had reached Lord Grenville, the secretary of state.[29] They were not to know that Nelson would now go to the other extreme and embrace their 'Principal Objects' of 'cordial and unlimited protection' to Naples to an extent that went beyond the bounds of reason, and certainly beyond the interests of His Majesty's Government.

Most of those 'Principal Objects' were already established and well understood. 'Malta, Corfu and those Islands are my object after Egypt,' he wrote on 7 October to Spencer Smith, the British envoy in Constantinople and the brother of the effervescent Sir Sidney Smith, who had just been appointed to the command of a ship destined for the Mediterranean.[30] Captain Samuel Hood had been left by Nelson to blockade the French Army in Egypt with Russian and Turkish ships; these ships were also trying to take Corfu from French hands and Nelson sent Troubridge to Zánte to liaise with them.[31] Problems too abounded at Tripoli, where the bey of Tunis was supplying the French forces in Malta.[32] On 15 October, Nelson left Naples on board the *Foudroyant* to view Malta, which, prompted by the news of the Nile victory, had risen in rebellion against the occupying French Army. At this point Nelson believed that, once the French were ejected, Malta should be restored not to the Knights of St John but to the king of Naples. He soon found that the optimism in Naples over the early surrender of the French was not well founded, for their army in the fortifications above Valetta was already well supplied. A capitulation was unlikely for some time.[33] He left Alexander Ball to continue the blockade of Malta and returned to Naples.[34] Here the queen and Acton were plotting to advance against the French in Rome and Tuscany. Nelson urged action, encouraged by Hamilton, who argued 'the certainty of the intention of the French Republick to plunder this Kingdom'.[35] The way seemed clear, since a series of defeats over the summer of 1798 had left the French temporarily on the defensive. The opportunity was to be brief; no one had been able to prevent Bonaparte from landing at Frejus on 9 October after his journey back from Egypt. Then the coup of 18th Brumaire (9–10 November) took place, which overthrew the Directory and appointed Napoleon first consul. Although he did not yet enjoy total control of the government, Napoleon now essentially ruled France as a military dictator.[36]

The decision to send the Neapolitan Army under General Karl Mack von Leiberich to occupy Rome and Leghorn was taken in early November 1798. Nelson was present at long deliberations with the king, queen and Acton. With his usual enthusiasm Nelson described the army in a letter to Spencer as 'thirty thousand of the finest troops in Europe'. He was more cautious in a letter to General Sir Charles Stuart, with whom he had been under fire at the Siege of Calvi; he thought them 'fine young men, but with some few exceptions wretchedly officered'.[37] At the end of the month the Neapolitan Army marched north and unopposed into Rome. Nelson took troops on board to Leghorn, disembarking them on 29 November.[38] In Leghorn, Nelson fell out with General Naselli, who commanded the troops on board the British ships: he maintained that the Kingdom of Naples was not at war with France and refused to allow Nelson to seize the French privateers in the port. Nelson wrote: 'My feelings almost got the better of my prudence, however, I considered this a sacrifice necessary for the King of Naples.'[39] But Nelson's early optimism over Neapolitan success was utterly misplaced. Provoked by the invasion, the French declared war on Naples and marched against the Neapolitan Army in Rome, which melted away and fled in an undignified shambles, headed by the terrified king.* Fewer than a hundred Neapolitan soldiers were killed.[40] Nelson found it difficult to believe the lack of determination displayed by the Neapolitan forces, saying more than once that he felt as if he were in a bad dream. 'In short, all is corrupt,' he remarked to Ball.[41]

Within three weeks the French Army under General Jean Championnet was approaching Naples, where the *lazzaroni* and rival Republicans were rioting. Nelson now organized a rapid evacuation. He first took steps to prevent the Neapolitan Navy from falling into French hands, leaving the Portuguese squadron under Rear-Admiral Marquis de Niza with orders to burn the ships at Gaeta. According to Cornelia Knight, the king and queen did not board the Neapolitan ship commanded by the most senior admiral, Francesco Caracciolo, which also sailed to Palermo, because they did not trust the crew.[42] Nelson undertook to transfer the royal family to Palermo in Sicily, the alternative capital of the country, as well to remove some 600 Englishmen and women in transports.[43] With Nelson on board and Sir William keeping out of sight to allay the suspicions of the mob, Emma was responsible for ensuring that the royal treasure was safely on board the ship. The Hamiltons could take only their best vases and pictures.[44] The royal family slipped aboard the *Vanguard* while a dinner was in progress, for it was essential that the deeply loyal *lazzaroni* did not become aware of their escape. Although the king abandoned them, they were to provide resistance to the French soldiers. The flight of the king enabled the Neapolitan Republicans to set up the Parthenopæan Republic. They did not enjoy wide support and were entirely dependent upon French military power.

As darkness fell on Christmas Eve 1798, with a light breeze, the over-crowded ships sailed from Naples Bay. The following day the *Vanguard*'s crew was surprised by a violent squall, which blew out all the topsails; yet again a member of the crew was killed.[45] Conditions among the passengers were overcrowded and chaotic. The queen's youngest child, Prince Albert, suddenly died in Emma's arms. With all around her prostrate with sea sickness and misery, she proved herself in a crisis. St Vincent later wrote her a letter of exaggerated praise: 'I shall never cease to admire the magnanimous conduct of your Royal Friend and self, during the late severe Trials at Naples, and during your short voyage to Palermo. The Page of History will be greatly enriched by the introduction of this Scene in it, for the greatness of both your minds, and the firmness and ability, shown in the

---

* According to Admiral Caracciolo, it was lack of money to pay the troops that was the reason for the supine performance of the Neapolitan Army (Parsons, 3).

most critical situation.'[46] Nelson wrote her a note from the *Vanguard* inviting her, Sir William and her mother, Mrs Cadogan, to dinner: 'come and let us have as merry a Xmas as circumstances will admit.'[47]

It was a relief when the ships anchored off Palermo on 26 December, although the British had some difficulty in making out the loyalties in this baffling country. One seaman aboard the *Vanguard* noted that 'the people seemed happy to receive their King . . . rec'd Ashore with shouts of apparent joy from a numerous & polite concourse of People there being a vast quantity of carriages which followed the King in procession.'[48] A British government observer saw the queen and her family 'walking in the suburbs of Palermo with her family followed by a number of miserable wretches and some literally naked. Many of them kissed the ground she walked over and one in particular took up some of the dust & deposited it carefully in a box: but this apparent devotion I was told could not be constantly depended upon.'[49] In this revolutionary period, the loyalty of the majority of Sicilians was anything but assured. As Nelson observed of the French, 'it is their infernal principles I dread, not their prowess.'[50]

Nelson was to remain on shore at Palermo for five months, going to sea for only ten days in late May 1799. During his time on shore he transferred his flag from the *Vanguard* to whichever ship was available in Palermo Harbour. His refusal to move was in part due to the hold that the queen had over him; it appears that he was not yet emotionally involved with Emma Hamilton.[51] To stay on shore was the most effective method of maintaining communications with the widely dispersed forces he had to administer. These included a squadron of Portuguese warships, allies of the British; although his initial impression that they were 'totally useless' did not change, he appreciated the qualities of their commander, the Marquis de Niza.[52] A continuous correspondence had also to be maintained with St Vincent at Gibraltar, with Ball off Malta and with Troubridge, whom he sent off with newly arrived bomb vessels first to Malta and then to Alexandria to try to dislodge the French. The bey of Tunis had to be persuaded not to supply grain to the French, and he sent the *Vanguard* to Tripoli to reinforce his forceful letter: the English consul, Simon Lucas, reported that 'the ship & letter has frightened him to that degree that he would do anything in his power to oblidge the English.'[53] Nelson threatened them with the Portuguese ships at his disposal: 'That Nelson, who has hitherto kept your powerful Enemy from destroying you, can and will let them loose upon you, unless the following terms are, in two hours, complied with: the French consul was to be delivered on board a Portuguese ship.'[54] A month later the threat had to be renewed. He also ensured that the

Maltese forces besieging the French received grain from Sicily. Leghorn was evacuated. One success could be registered: Corfu fell to Russian and Turkish forces on 3 March 1799.

Above all, the security of Sicily had to be ensured. Nelson encouraged the government to raise 26,000 Sicilian militia in addition to regular troops. But on 10 March he was surprised and grateful to see that his request for troops had been answered by nearly 3,000 British soldiers under General Stuart, who arrived in Palermo from Minorca. Nelson wrote to Stuart: 'you have done more for the preservation of Sicily than all the Ministers could have in 7 years, indeed except Acton they are a sett of Coxcomical fools.'[55]

By April, Nelson was dissatisfied and wanted to get back to England. He wrote to Edward Berry, now in London after the ordeal of his capture in the *Leander*: 'I am in addition to my duty as an Admiral, become a Councillor and Secretary of State.'[56] St Vincent reported to Spencer in February 1799 'the discontents of Lord Nelson and Captain Troubridge: the former continuing seemingly determined upon relinquishing his command and returning to England, and the latter in such a state of despondency . . . that I really am put to my wit's end how to act'.[57] Troubridge was still affected by the *Culloden*'s grounding before the Battle of the Nile. Suitable senior commander replacements, however, were not easily found. Admiral Young, viewing the situation from the Board of Admiralty, wrote to his old friend Charles Morice Pole that there were few flag officers 'in whom much confidence can be placed'.[58] St Vincent discussed with Nepean who might undertake the defence of Minorca, but he could think only of Lord Keith, 'and the Squadron is not of size for a Vice Admiral, without putting Lord Nelson under his command, which would revolt his feelings.'[59] War weariness among naval officers in general can be discerned at this time. In another letter to Pole, Young lamented 'the sad want of spirit' in the officer corps in general.[60]

An additional problem for St Vincent was dealing with Sir Sidney Smith, who was appointed in October 1798 as senior naval officer in the Eastern Mediterranean, responsible to St Vincent, and also as a joint plenipotentiary with his brother, Spencer Smith, the minister in Constantinople. This unusual dual diplomatic and naval brief arose through an agreement between Spencer and Grenville, since the latter felt that a greater diplomatic effort was needed in the Levant after the Nile. Given the personalities involved, the arrangement caused a predictable amount of trouble. St Vincent tried to stop Smith's appointment, writing to Nepean: 'I want none of your "soi-disant" heroes, pray keep them all to yourself.'[61] Spencer's letter to St Vincent, informing him of Smith's appointment to his command, combines apology and firmness in equal measure.[62] Nelson, not unnaturally, took the appointment as a direct attack on his control of his station and on his reputation. To avoid further trouble, St Vincent put Smith 'under the immediate command of Admiral Lord Nelson', but with little effect.[63] Nelson's letters through the first five months of 1799 are peppered with rude remarks about Smith, 'the Swedish Knight' or 'the Great Plenipo'.[64] Smith, similarly, complained directly, to Grenville (which he was empowered to do) about Nelson's 'paroxysm of jealousy' and his 'extreme sensitivity'. Sir William Hamilton acted as intermediary, and an open breach was prevented.[65]

Throughout this period Nelson continually complained about his health. Apart from those letters to politicians and admirals with influence, those to friends reflect constant depression, although not 'listlessness' as some have suggested.[66] His wide range of responsibilities kept him very busy. To Sir Roger Curtis in January 1799 he wrote, 'God knows, since the battle I have not had one easy moment and what has brought me here adds not to my comfort . . . I want Rest, and a summer's residence in England will do me much good.'[67] To his old friend Lady Parker he wrote in February: 'I will venture to say a very short space of time will send me to that bourne from whence none return . . . After the Action I had nearly fell into a decline, but at Naples my invaluable friends Sir William and Lady Hamilton nursed and set me up again. I am worse than ever . . . You who remember me always laughing and gay, would hardly believe the change; but who can see what I have and be well in health?'[68] In May when at sea he wrote to William Hamilton complaining of 'headache, sickness and . . . want to rest', declaring that he had made it known to his squadron that if he was ordered to blockade Toulon, he would give up.[69] To Fanny he wrote in June: 'My health is tolerable, but my mind is full of sorrow, not for myself for I care not, but for my country and the world.'[70] That letter was written when he was sailing towards Naples; it was not the right frame of mind in which to face an intense political crisis.*

At the same time as attending to his wider strategic responsibilities, Nelson was under pressure to retake Naples from the French and the Republicans. Royalist forces under Cardinal Fabrizio Ruffo, a courtier rather than a priest, acting under the orders of the king, had been put

---

* A number of authors have followed Nicolas, who attributed Nelson's actions after the Nile to a change of behaviour brought about by the blow on his head during the battle, 'that morbid irritability of temper under which Nelson occasionally laboured during the remainder of his life . . . This change in his feelings . . . unhappily soon after extended towards his wife' (Nicolas, III, 194).

ashore in Calabria in February 1799, gathering as they went an indisciplined anti-Republican mob that gained in numbers as it marched on Naples. Ruffo was now closing in on the Parthenopæan Republic. In March almost all French troops were pulled out to move northwards, for the Austrians had at last declared war on France. At the end of March Troubridge was sent to blockade Naples, and on 3 April he took the islands of Procida and Ischia, just off the coast. A small mixed force of Russians and Turks had taken east-coast ports, including Brindisi and Bari; from there a few hundred disciplined Russian troops joined Ruffo's force, under the Chevalier Antonio Micheroux.[71]

The principal French danger was posed by the menace of a naval counter-attack in the Mediterranean, which became a reality when on 26 April Vice-Admiral Eustache Bruix, the French minister of the marine, evaded the British blockade of Brest, sailing with nineteen ships of the line and ten smaller ships. As usual the British assessments as to Bruix's destination were wide ranging: Minorca, Malta, Naples and Egypt were among them. Nelson added the capture of Palermo as a possible objective of the French, as did St Vincent.[72] Bruix sailed south. Off Cadiz, in blowing weather and on a lee shore, Lord Keith prevented the Spanish fleet from joining him.[73] On 12 May, Nelson received the intelligence that Bruix was heading through the Strait of Gibraltar, and the following day heard that the French were heading towards Minorca.[74] His immediate response was to concentrate his ships at the westerly tip of Sicily by the island of Maritimo (Marettimo) where he waited for Ball to arrive with reinforcements from Malta; 'Malta must trust to the Russians,' Nelson wrote to Hamilton.[75] Nelson expected his squadron to be summoned by St Vincent.[76] On 28 May he heard that Bruix was in Toulon. On 5 June, Nelson was joined by Rear-Admiral John Thomas Duckworth with four sail of the line; one of these was the *Foudroyant*, in which Nelson hoisted his flag. Since she had reached the Mediterranean, St Vincent had ensured that her crew had been under a new captain, William Brown, to enforce strict discipline; he wrote to Nelson, 'in the interim he will correct the vile state she has been in, ever since her Pennant was hoisted, although her crew is for its numbers well composed in point of bodily strength and seamanship.'[77]

Nelson hesitated. His orders now presented him with irreconcilable 'Principal Objects'. His concentrated force off Sicily was ideally positioned to maintain control of the Central and Eastern Mediterranean in the face of the new French naval threat. On the other hand, his powerful squadron could sway the balance at Naples. With Bruix temporarily neutralized in Toulon, Nelson could contemplate taking his reinforced squadron of eighteen ships to Naples. On 10 June, while the *Foudroyant* was anchored in the Palermo Roads, Ferdinand gave Nelson command of the expedition, his powers most clearly defined in the 'Instructions to the Troops', doubtless drafted by Acton and the queen. Nelson was to command the expedition; the crown prince, commanding Sicilian troops, was under Nelson's orders. The castles of Naples 'shall be speedily evacuated by the enemy and rebels, supposing any other measures besides that of force has to be used, the Prince Royal is authorised to pursue the intention at any cost.' When the French and Republicans capitulated,

the power of stipulating for their departure may be extended to several rebels, even to the leaders . . . [but] . . . in case of obstinacy shown on the part of the rebels shall be fix[e]d in the manner that Lord Nelson shall think most proper for the occasion and intent. The Prince Royal, when he shall have been advised by the said Lord Nelson, to whom His Majesty has given on this point the proper declaration, shall give his assent in the most convenient manner to the said resolutions, and shall dispose in consequence the necessary arrangements for the execution thereof.[78]

Acton wrote to Nelson on the same day of 'the Expedition which your Lordship will undertake, protect and direct'.[79] There can be no doubt that Ferdinand gave Nelson absolute authority over the expedition to Naples.

Still Nelson wavered. In Palermo 1,700 Neapolitan troops were embarked on his ships, but, after further intelligence from Naples, a decision was made that they were no longer needed, and the next day they were offloaded.[80] Nelson sailed with the fleet to his usual position off Maritimo, where for a further five days he waited for Bruix's squadron. While he waited, he idled his time gossiping with his officers. 'They told me such things of Palermo Ladies that I was all astonishment,' he wrote to Emma on 18 June 1799,

that one who is a Lady we saw oddly lifted up on the quarterdeck of the *Principe Reale* gives herself up for money. Price named a great deal more than I am sure she is worth. In short, we of your house know nothing . . . where have I been not to have known as much as these gentlemen, living in a house of virtue and goodness. There are others I only catched as they flew for I was thinking of other things much more interesting to me.[81]

It is a passage that betrays the beginning of an intimacy between Nelson and Emma. Many have argued that the love affair had not started, and that Emma did not influence Nelson in Naples: but the start of a relationship is often the most unnerving, and Nelson's temper was noticeably irritable in the weeks that followed.

While British ships of the line were waiting off Sicily, the streets of the capital witnessed violence and bloodlust on a scale remarkable even in Naples. Ruffo's unruly mob from Calabria, estimated at 60,000, had reached Naples on 13 June, meeting little resistance.[82] While the main French armies had left Naples, a residue of 500 or so troops remained in the great fortress of St Elmo that overlooks the city. Republican troops barricaded themselves inside the fortresses of Uovo and Nuovo; they too were waiting for Bruix's fleet to rescue them from their predicament. In the streets below, the Calabrians, assisted by the *lazzaroni*, slaughtered hundreds of citizens suspected of Republican sympathies over two days. Ruffo had little or no control over his army of liberation. It was later reported that they pillaged 4,000 houses, even that of Ruffo, 'their Commander-in-Chief who promised Paradise and heaven to them who died fighting for Royalty'.[83] On 15 June a junior British captain, Edward Foote, in the *Seahorse* frigate, which had been left on blockade duty in Naples Bay, secured a foothold at Castellamare with the help of Sicilian galleys, on the opposite side of the bay to the city. Thus, while the French and the Republicans controlled the strategic points, the rest of the city was out of their control.

It was at this point, on 16 June, that the nerve of the Republican troops in the fortresses of Uovo and Nuovo began to fail and they asked to negotiate terms with Cardinal Ruffo. He refused. Two days later, after further bombardment, a flag of truce was sent out from the Nuovo fortress to Micheroux, in command of the Russians. Acting without reference to Ruffo, Micheroux granted an armistice to the fortress early on 19 June; this was against the wishes of Ruffo, but he nevertheless let it stand. Negotiations then progressed from an armistice to a capitulation. There is every difference between an armistice, which is a short truce, and a capitulation, which is effectively a treaty. Ruffo involved Captain Foote, who also signed the formal capitulation on 22 June, with reservations. In every way the capitulation was premature, since not one of those who signed had the power to do so. Nor did anyone in Naples know when the expected French fleet was likely to appear in the Bay of Naples. The queen later described the capitulation to Emma Hamilton as 'a masterpiece of infamy'.[84]

By 21 June, Nelson, back in Palermo, heard that Ruffo had concluded an armistice. Acton and the queen now asked Nelson to go to Naples to secure the surrender of the castles. He agonized but agreed, reasoning it out in the following way to William Hamilton: 'I shall not be gone eight days. Sicily will be safe. I am full of grief and anxiety.'[85] After a hurried council meeting at Palermo, and having embarked Sir William and Lady Hamilton, the *Foudroyant* sailed for Naples the same day.[86] Neither the cowardly king nor Acton accompanied the squadron, preferring to control events from the safety of Palermo. In agreeing to go to Naples, Nelson finally came down on the side of high risk for potential gain; but it was more to the advantage of the royalist cause in Naples than to British strategic interests in the region.

Three days after the formal capitulation, Nelson's eighteen ships of the line anchored in Naples Bay, to the surprise of the inhabitants of Naples in general, who were expecting the French, and to the dismay of the Republicans in the forts. Nelson found a situation of considerable complexity. On the passage to Naples he had noted in a 'Memorandum on the Armistice' that 'All armistices signify that either party may renew hostilities, giving a certain notice fixed upon by contracting parties.'[87] He found at Naples, however, a signed capitulation. One visitor to the ships found him 'in a great passion which Sir William Hamilton endeavoured to appease'.[88] Nelson failed to agree with Cardinal Ruffo in a stormy meeting on board the *Foudroyant*, with both Hamiltons acting as interpreters between the two men. Nor was any military cooperation between them forthcoming. Chevalier Micheroux, representing the Russians, requested that he recognize the capitulation. Nelson argued that no one in Naples was empowered to agree to a capitulation. A further complication was that on 25 June, the day of Nelson's arrival, Admiral Caracciolo had been captured. The admiral had returned from Palermo, despairing of the behaviour of his king, and had defected to the Republicans.

The events of 26 June are difficult to unravel. In the early hours Nelson assured Ruffo through Hamilton that he would do nothing 'which might break the armistice'.[89] This was a compromise on Nelson's part, but he may have decided to leave the final decision on the capitulation to the king, which Ferdinand would make when he arrived. Besides, he had little control over events on shore, since Ruffo's Calabrese forces, if not Ruffo himself, were in control of the city. Thomas Troubridge was sent on shore with 500 British marines. It is clear that from this time suspects off the streets were also being brought on board the *Foudroyant*. Some years later Nelson received a letter from an English merchant in Naples at the time, Robert Smith: 'I was twice on the point of being murdered by those wild enthusiasts the Lazzaronis, once by the Labouring Tanners, between the two Bridges returning from purchasing Wines at Portros when I was seized by them, and carried on board yr Lordship's ship with the same wild Idea that hundreds of innocents were dragg'd away [suspected] of being a Jacobin. Being known by several officers on Board, Capt. Hardy instantly released me finding who I was.'[90]

Through the day the Republicans marched out of the forts of Nuovo and Uovo and were put aboard Neapolitan vessels in the bay. It is unclear who supervised the surrender, but there is general agreement that the Republicans marched out without military honours; were they, by doing so, trusting to the clemency of King Ferdinand? Nelson stated very firmly to Lord Spencer that 'I found a most infamous treaty entered into with the rebels in direct disobedience of his Sicilian Majesty's orders. I had the happiness of saving his Majesty's honour rejecting with disdain any but unconditional submission to rebels . . . The rebels came out of the castle with this knowledge, without any honours and the principal rebels were seized and conducted on board the ships of the squadron, the others embarked in 14 polaccas were anchored under the care of our ships.'[91]

Two days later, on 28 June, letters arrived from Palermo that prompted Nelson to harden his position. He ordered the polaccas to be brought under the guns of the British ships, and some of the political prisoners were put in confinement aboard the British warships in the bay, thus drawing them even further into the internal affairs of Naples.[92] It was at this point that Samuel Hood and Benjamin Hallowell protested strongly to Nelson. The scene was recalled by Charles Lock, the British consul in Naples. Hood 'ventured to suggest to His Lordship, whether it would not be deemed an Act of Treachery, the having decoyed them (his own word) on board the Vessels, under pretence of fulfilling the Convention'. The officers put forward the alternative of returning the Jacobins to the castle and then reducing it by force. 'His Lordship affirmed that he acted under the K of N's orders, that it was not his doing . . . and when Adm[ira]l Duckworth's presence & remonstrance emboldened them to press the matter more home to him, he said I see you are all against me. I am determined to obey my orders right or wrong, it shall be done. I will be obeyed. This shut their mouths & they proceeded to the Execution of His Lordship's commands.' The evidence of another British observer, the Italian-speaking John Rushout, corroborates this account: he describes the British officers on board the *Foudroyant* as 'strongly and openly against it. Nelson became agitated & irritated & insisted upon their not interfering.'[93] Nelson's consensual style of leadership had temporarily collapsed. At the same time he wrote to the king urging him to come to Naples.[94]

Legally Nelson had the right to reject the capitulation, but the captains' unease is the most powerful evidence that Nelson's judgement was warped.

The Republicans' understanding of the terms of the surrender as they marched out of the fortresses is not clear. Nor is it clear whether they left the fortress as a direct result of the softening of Nelson's line on the armistice and capitulation. Were the Republicans tricked? The most respected of the traditional English commentators judged that 'there is not the slightest proof of any foul play on Nelson's part' and was more inclined to blame Ruffo.[95] One authority blames Hamilton for misleading Nelson.[96] A recent detailed review concludes that 'it seems likely that it was Micheroux who took the initiative again and misinformed the rebels, if they were deceived at all.'[97] Others disagree, holding that at the least Nelson dissembled; a recent hostile critic has used the word 'duplicitous'.[98] No direct written evidence remains. The responsibility cannot, however, be shifted away from Nelson, who had the authority of the king for the entire operation of bringing Naples under control.

Nelson was also to fail the next test. The following day, 29 June, a boat from Cardinal Ruffo, 'guarded by ragged ruffians', brought Admiral Caracciolo to the *Foudroyant*. He was, according to midshipman George Parsons, who was in the party that guarded the prisoner, 'a short, thick-set man, of apparent strength, but haggard with misery and want'.[99] The Neapolitan Count de Thurn chaired an immediate court martial composed of Caracciolo's former colleagues. At 9 a.m. on 30 June the court assembled. The prisoner had unquestionably taken command of gunboats that had fired at Neapolitan royalist frigates. No witnesses were called.[100] Nelson requested that Rushout attend the court, but within minutes 'strangers were asked to withdraw'.[101] Caracciolo was found guilty. According to Rushout, a majority verdict ordered him to be hanged in two hours. The two Neapolitan officers in the minority wished to wait for the arrival of King Ferdinand before the execution was carried out.

Nelson rejected a plea for Caracciolo to be shot rather than hanged and for time to prepare himself for death.[102] Although legally in command of the Neapolitan forces, Nelson did not intervene, even when, according to Rushout, 'Caracciolo was brought out on deck to be transferred to the Neapolitan frigate, threw himself in a supplicating attitude & almost kneeling implored for Mercy & said "Misericordia son condonato" . . . but no notice [was taken] of his appeal & he was hurried away.'[103] Nelson himself said Caracciolo 'did not attempt to deny the justness of his sentence'. Midshipman Parsons remembers that 'the veteran, with a firm step, walked into Lord Nelson's barge.' Lieutenant Parkinson escorted Caracciolo to his Neapolitan flagship, where he was hanged and his body cut down and thrown into the water. Parsons recalls: 'The seamen of our fleet, who clustered on the rigging like bees, consoled themselves that it was only an Italian prince, and the admiral of Naples, that was hanging – a person of very light estimation compared with the lowest man in a British ship.'[104] Perhaps that feeling of British superiority was more important in the whole business than is generally realized. As Nelson dined on board *Foudroyant*, a gun was fired. 'Lady Hamilton starting up from the table with a wine Glass in her hand exclaimed: Thank God! That Gun announces the doom of a Traitor.' William Hotham, who witnessed these events, specifically blames Emma for her harsh influence in the decisions.[105]

To the forty-year-old Nelson, still instinctively a frigate captain, a swift example was necessary to address the political chaos then reigning in Naples. But was the speed of the hanging morally justified? Nelson had to weigh the possible imminent arrival of Bruix's squadron in the Bay of Naples. To wait for the arrival of the unreliable Ferdinand was a risk that he was not prepared to take. One judicious historian of a hundred years ago strove for a compromise historical verdict: 'Technically . . . this sentence cannot be impeached, but the haste with which he was executed is more open to criticism.'[106] It is difficult to see what such haste achieved. Caracciolo's sentence came from a court martial driven by politics; even though its legal basis was sound, its procedure, without witnesses, can hardly be seen as beyond criticism; his hanging without the signature of the king was unjustified and unnecessary.[107] The story of the dead admiral's bloated corpse floating past the *Foudroyant* two weeks later is well attested; this image of injustice, still strong, hangs over Nelson's judgement on the death of Caracciolo.[108]

The intervention of the British fleet in the demise of the Parthenopæan Republic on the events of the first six days was critical, but more violence and conflict were to come. The French troops in the fortress of St Elmo, presuming that any armistice had ended, resumed firing on 1 July.[109] Nelson directed hostilities against them, Troubridge commanded the land forces bombarding St Elmo, assisted by Ball and Hallowell. 'These are curious events when sea captains become generals . . . but Nelson observes that almost all the nobles are traitors,' Admiral Young commented back in London.[110] On 10 July, King Ferdinand finally arrived from Palermo and came aboard the *Foudroyant* at four in the afternoon the next day, saluted by twenty-one guns. On 12 July the French surrendered and Neapolitan colours flew from St Elmo. Troubridge brought 'the keys of the Castle and the French colours and presented them to His Sicilian Majesty'. Every ship in the bay saluted with twenty-one guns. Three days later the French prisoners were sent in cartel vessels under escort to Toulon.[111]

Nelson and his squadron stayed at Naples for forty days to ensure that royalist power was consolidated in the city. His reputation was to suffer further. None of this pomp and display could hide the fact that the Neapolitan prisoners were being examined and tried on board British ships, a process that had begun before the king arrived.[112] The officers, but not the captain, of the *Leviathan*, in which Rear-Admiral Duckworth flew his flag, took the highly risky step of writing to Emma on behalf of one family imprisoned aboard the ship. They asked her to present a petition to King Ferdinand to save their lives: 'because we have heard of many instances of your Ladyship's unbounded humanity, which we trust will plead an excuse (more powerfully than anything else can)'.[113] Emma, however, ignored all pleas for clemency; she was not going to sacrifice the queen's favour and her position at court for abstract principles. She even added the names of Republican prisoners to lists made by British officers.[114]

Parties and ceremonies continued on board the flagship. 'Things moved on in the same gay strain,' Parsons recalls, 'though many hearts were breaking with incurable sorrow, and many a brilliant eye was dimmed by incessant weeping; while famine, with its attendant miseries, reigned in the populous city of Naples.'[115] With the dramatically beautiful Bay of Naples as background, underlined by this highly charged atmosphere, it seems probable that an emotional, if not a physical, entanglement between Nelson and Emma was now developing. Lady Bessborough, the younger sister of Lord Spencer, reported in a letter of 11 August that year: 'My mother has received a letter of 12 sides from Ly. Hamilton (dated 15 July aboard *Foudroyant*) . . . Nelson is desperately in love with Ly. Hamilton.'[116] Emma wrote that letter at the height of the crisis, when Nelson's judgement was influenced by her harsh predilections as the mouthpiece of the queen.

During July, Nelson took a number of erratic decisions. He disobeyed the orders of Lord Keith, now the commander-in-chief, Mediterranean, since 10 June when St Vincent had resigned the command. Keith ordered Nelson to send part of his squadron to the defence of Minorca. Nelson refused this direct order: 'I have no scruple in deciding that it is better to save the Kingdom of Naples and risk Minorca.'[117] A marine private, John Jolly, was court-martialled for striking an officer during the operation against St Elmo; Nelson signed his death warrant but three days later commuted it and overruled Troubridge's protests.[118] (He had allowed the death of Caracciolo just over a week earlier.) In the middle of the month an altercation followed on the quarterdeck with Charles Lock, the consul at Naples, over Lock's accusations of cheating by the pursers of the fleet. Lock had been seeking the beef-provisioning contract.[119] Strains between

Emma Hamilton and Lock and his wife had led to poisonous relations in the court at Palermo.[120] Both men raised their voices; Nelson made Lock grovel by insisting that his accusation was sent to the Victualling Commissioners in London. This was not Nelson's usual style.

In response Lock wrote hostile letters home.[121] Gossip was repeated around London within the month. Lady Bessborough commented: 'I am miserable at the accounts I have read of the cruelties at Naples, but worst of all that my Dear Delightful Nelson should have let himself be drawn in to do so disgraceful an action as to annul a sign'd treaty upon the faith of which (whether good or bad) his enemies resign'd their arms. I hope the account is not true, as I have only read it in the newspapers, for I cannot bear it.'[122] Lady Holland, a Whig political hostess of great influence, noted in her journal: 'Naples now exhibits a scene of revenge more bloody than the Sicilian Vespers. The hearts of Frenchmen are brought as trophies to a cruel people . . . L[ad]y Hamilton has not been remiss in adding her quota to the barbarity which inflames every breast.'[123]

A further lapse in Nelson's political handling of the situation was brought to the attention of London by a shadowy British official called William Daniels. A letter was sent to William Windham in London, written from Naples days after Nelson had left:

It is well known that Lord Nelson is governed in his conduct by the advice of His Sic[ilia]n Majesty's Privy Counsellors . . . Lord Nelson is by nature so good that he cannot refuse anything when Majesty makes a request. His natural inclination operates with what he conceives it is his duty to grant. This good disposition, however, may produce many inconveniences. It is to be regretted that His Lordship has not with him some faithfull counsellor to guard him against political finesse. Our ships have been frequently employed to serve as Prisons to Sicilian & Neapolitan Gentry which to seriously reflecting men appears rather extraordinary should be permitted.[124]

This was an official, direct criticism of the naivety of Nelson, the inappropriate involvement of British ships in the internal affairs of another country and of William Hamilton as minister. Hamilton was to pay for his ineffectiveness.

The trials and executions continued for many more months. Emma received one report in mid September from Naples: 'The juncto of state proceeds so slowly in not hanging the guilty, nor freeing the innocent, occasions a great ferment in the people.'[125] Eight months later Charles Lock reported to Keith that 145 had been executed in Naples; 1,900 transported to France; between 700 and 800 sent to the island of Maritimo; and many had died in the unwholesome Neapolitan gaols.[126] By a modern estimate 8,000 were tried, more than a thousand exiled and several thousand put into prison. It was, however, the 120 executions in Naples that 'made the revolution's reputation'. Some were beheaded; the others were hanged, 'pushed from ladders while the urchins, the *tirapiedi*, clung to their feet'.[127] Some of those executed had European-wide intellectual reputations; the drawn-out bloodshed did the British cause in Europe no good.

Initial reactions from the Board of Admiralty were, however, sympathetic to Nelson. Spencer described the news from Naples as giving 'the most sincere pleasure to everyone here'.[128] The board approved of Nelson going to Naples but criticized him for ordering so many seamen ashore into the city, an action that might have crippled the capacity of the squadron to move rapidly to sea had the French fleet arrived. Their lordships, however, reserved their greatest criticism for Nelson's disobedience of Keith's order to leave Naples and sail to the defence of Minorca; they did not 'see sufficient cause to justify his having disobeyed the orders he had received from his commanding officer, or his having left Minorca exposed to the risk of being attacked without having any naval force to protect it'.[129] Nelson had disobeyed orders before; as the victor of the Nile he felt strongly enough to protest. He was lucky to get away with a reprimand.

One week at Naples out of a career of thirty-five years has besmirched the reputation of Horatio Nelson. In one sense, this judgement is unfair in that no single person can be blamed for the excesses in Naples in the summer of 1799. For part of the critical period, before British seamen had landed, Nelson was powerless in the city. What else could he have done?[130] A more cautious admiral would have stayed with his fleet to defeat Bruix and would not have gone to Naples, seeing it as a sideshow to the central issue of the French threat to the Mediterranean. A calmer admiral might have seen the political necessity of accepting the signatures of Ruffo and Foote on the capitulation, maintained the status quo ashore as much as possible until the king arrived and not allowed any sentences to be carried out on the authority of a British admiral. The cost might have been continued chaos in the city of Naples, but that price may have been worth it. It was Hamilton's job to point out these considerations, but there is little sign that the minister was concerned about anything except keeping the peace between Ruffo, Micheroux and Nelson.

Some of Nelson's misjudgement can be put down to lack of experience. He had been propelled to fame within the navy, in which the absolute authority of the hierarchy was underpinned by the Naval Discipline Act. In Naples he was facing irreconcilable political issues with only Thomas

Troubridge to advise him, an officer not known for restraint.[131] The quarter-deck, where he possessed absolute power, was his natural habitat, which is why his consensual style of leadership, which he developed during the Nile campaign the year before, was so remarkable. Fighting admirals of the time, and since, have not adapted well to the politician's role. Hood had never been comfortable, and was hopelessly indiscreet, in the House of Commons; Howe had been an ineffectual first lord of the Admiralty in the 1780s; St Vincent was soon to demonstrate his complete lack of political finesse in a disastrous period in the same office. Nelson made little impact in the House of Lords when he returned to England. Politics in the last years of the eighteenth century were not easily understood, with contradictory alignments across Europe, as Britain and France continued their global struggle. Revolutionary France was suppressing the Catholic peasantry at home and supporting it in Ireland: the year before Nelson was at Naples, the British government and army in Ireland had brought the rebellion of the United Irishmen to an end with as much severity as the royalist forces were to show in Naples and Sicily in 1799.[132] After five weary years of war, with continued Republican French success and influence on the Continent, compromise and compassion were not in the air.

Most of Nelson's action, or lack of intervention, in Naples in the summer of 1799 stemmed from his naive attachment, to the point of sycophancy, to Queen Maria Carolina and to the Naples royal family. He confused his allegiance to the ever ungrateful George III with a loyalty to another monarchy. He was seen, in Samuel Hood's reported words, to have 'decoyed' the Republicans out of their fortress. He took the unnecessary responsibility of hastening the hanging of Caracciolo. He did not possess the instinct to distance himself and his country from a damaging political situation, and allowed the British fleet to become far too involved with violence in another country, so that his ships, in the words of Daniels, the British official, became 'the engines of turpitude'.[133] Nelson's strengths were his speed of thought, powers of leadership and decisive action rather than the talent or patience required to reconcile political divisions. At Naples he was feeling undervalued and, at times, physically unwell; his thoughts may have drifted towards Emma Hamilton in the vacuum created by the weakness of Sir William. At critical periods Nelson was in a great rage, 'the torrent of his impetuosity', as Hamilton once described it.[134] Remarkably, within two years he was to show great subtlety, calmness and shrewdness as a commander-in-chief. But in 1799 Nelson was certainly not capable of cool calculation and independent moral judgement. For once, he did not measure up to his responsibilities.

20

Dalliance and Dishonour

7 August 1799–8 November 1800

We have nothing from England since October 24th: being in a corner, we are forgot.
Rear-Admiral Lord Nelson to Lord Elgin, Palermo,
21 December 1799

[Nelson] does not seem at all conscious of the sort of discredit he has fallen into, or the cause of it, for he writes still, not wisely, about Lady Hamilton and all that. But it is hard to condemn and use ill a hero, as he is in his own element, for being foolish about a woman who has art enough to make fools of many wiser than an admiral.
Lord Minto to Lady Minto, 23 March 1800[1]

During 1799 Fanny divided her time between visiting Bath with her father-in-law and improving the house at Roundwood in readiness for Nelson's return. Roof leaks and damp continued to be a problem.[2] Occasionally she visited London and the court, as she recounted to Nelson: 'Our Gracious King thought it was a long time since I heard from you . . . The Queen always speaks to me with so much condescencion that I like her very much.'[3] She raised the idea of coming out to join him in Palermo, but Nelson wrote back firmly emphasizing the difficulties of accompanying 'a wandering sailor'.[4] For the first part of the year they exchanged optimistic letters about acquiring a London house, but progressively Nelson's letters to her became less frequent and increasingly short and impersonal, then cruelly offhand, demonstrating little concern for her welfare. Usually he added an excuse that he was stealing time from his duties to write to her.[5] His only long letter described the celebrations in Naples on the anniversary of the Battle of the Nile.[6] When Ferdinand created Nelson duke of Bronte in August 1799, Nelson wrote to his father and brother, since he wished to secure 'the descent of the Nelson title & the Pension that goes with it'.

He made a gift of £500 to each of them from the grant of £10,000 from the East India Company.[7] There was little comfort here for Fanny. Nelson made it clear that he was unable to come home until the king and queen of Sicily were secure.

Fanny's disappointment turned to apprehension. At the beginning of the year, having received a letter from Emma Hamilton describing the nursing that Nelson required after returning from the Nile, Fanny wrote to Alexander Davison, Nelson's agent for the Nile prizes: 'I am nervous beyond description.'[8] In another letter in April she confided: 'Lord Hood expressed his fear that Sir W & Lady Hamilton would use their influence to keep Lord Nelson with them: they have succeeded . . . I am sadly hurt and out of humour.'[9] She became ill and was bled; eight ounces of blood were taken from her. '. . . anxiety will shake the strongest,' she wrote. She was ordered to see the doctors at Clifton.[10] Edmund Nelson too was far from well. 'I think it is hardly possible he can last long – his cough is painful to hear & he spits terribly,' she reported to Davison, while 'he won't have any of his children with him.'[11] The uncertainty was also affecting him. 'His extreme agitation upon hearing a Carriage or a knock at the door is quite distressing,' while news of Nelson from Davison was 'the only thing that keeps her good father alive'.[12]

In early August 1799 Edward Berry (now Sir Edward) and his wife stayed at Roundwood before he resumed his position as Nelson's flag captain.[13] At the end of the month Fanny was staying at Burnham and, in spite of cold, damp weather, seemed rather more cheerful. She dined twice with the Cokes in the great house at Holkham, and she wrote to Davison again. 'All hands expect My Husband home very soon.'[14] But by the end of the year her letters to Davison had became desperate: 'Can you tell me anything of My Dear Lord . . . tell me what you have heard.'[15] In December she met Captain Hardy, who was in London to seek a new command; he 'made us all happy with flattering accounts of your health'. Yet at the same time Nelson was writing to her 'I am almost totally blind.'[16]

Nor did the behaviour of her son Josiah Nisbet help this slowly deteriorating relationship. Nelson had always done his best for his stepson, even, in his own words, 'cheating' the system two years earlier to bring forward the date of his lieutenant's commission.[17] Using the credit he had gained from the Nile victory, Nelson pushed very hard for Josiah, who was given the command of the *Dolphin* hospital ship. Then Nelson wrote to Spencer and also persuaded a sceptical St Vincent to give Nisbet the command of the *Thalia* (36), a fine frigate.[18] Josiah, however, drank and kept bad company, and had little notion of commanding a ship. Nelson heard that Josiah messed in the gun room of the *Thalia* and let him know that it was 'very imprudent'.[19] 'I hope Captain Nisbet behaves properly,' he confided to Ball; 'he is now on his own bottom, and by his conduct must stand or fall.'[20] To St Vincent he wrote hoping that Nisbet would improve.[21] Nelson asked other officers to help, realizing that he had little influence on the young man. Troubridge tried, but gave up after Nisbet's 'strange & insulting conduct to me, & that so publicly . . . I could obtain no promise of any change. The only answer I could procure was that he knew it would happen, that you had no business to bring him to Sea, that he had told you so often, & that it was all your fault. I again pointed out to him in the strongest language, his black ingratitude to you.'[22] To Rear-Admiral Duckworth in Port Mahón Nelson admitted that Nisbet 'has by his conduct almost broke my heart'.[23] Duckworth was encouraging: 'you may depend upon it I shall be highly gratified to bring him round,' and in an optimistic letter in early December 1799 wrote: 'I augur much better of him than your Lordship.'[24] But Captain Nisbet disappointed them all. He never adapted to the responsibilities of command, bullying and behaving boorishly in a manner that was reminiscent of Prince William Henry in the West Indies. He insulted the *Thalia*'s master: 'Damn your eyes, you are no more an officer than the boatswain or carpenter . . . I want no master but a broom stick who I can make do as I think proper.' This incident was reported to the Navy Board.[25] The ship returned to England in October 1800. Josiah was never given another command.

For the five months after leaving Naples in August 1799, Nelson stayed at Palermo with the Hamiltons. An exception was a brief, sixteen-day voyage to Minorca in October, although Nelson never landed on the island. He left his comfortable surroundings in Palermo on 5 October to take a small squadron to convoy the outgoing trade towards Gibraltar, prompted by an intelligence report of the sighting of thirteen large ships off Portugal.[26] On his way past Minorca, he fell in with the *Bulldog* bomb vessel and received information from Duckworth that the Portugal sighting was false. On board the *Bulldog* was Edward Berry, who now regained his flag captaincy under Nelson. Nelson regretted losing Hardy, whose calm temperament complemented his own. Berry was in the same mould as his admiral, excitable, without Nelson's presence of mind under pressure. Nelson also feared that Berry's fragile health would oblige him, as he observed to Fanny, 'to fag and think of those things which my present excellent Captain Hardy takes entirely from me'.[27] At Mahón his ships were repaired; he wrote the 'Sketch of His Life' for the *Naval Chronicle*.[28] He conferred with General St Clair Erskine, in command in Minorca, about bringing troops to Malta, but the general saw 'difficulties in the clearest terms', as Nelson wrote to Sir William Hamilton. More intelligence reports brought unconfirmed news of French ships heading towards Malta. 'I am in a fever of anxiety about those ships.'[29] These two problems – lack of soldiers and the continued resistance of the French garrison in Malta – were to dog Nelson for the rest of his time in the Mediterranean.

From 1 September, Nelson was made temporary commander-in-chief, Mediterranean, although he appeared to have received no appointment letter, only his instructions.[30] St Vincent had returned to England in June but had not resigned as commander-in-chief.* Lord Keith, now acting for St Vincent, was unable to intercept Admiral Bruix in the Mediterranean and had followed the French fleet north to Brest; then he too had gone on leave in England. Admiralty instructions had not changed a great deal from those Nelson had received in May 1798 when he was first sent into the Mediterranean by St Vincent. Ships were still required off Genoa, Cadiz was to be blockaded, Minorca was to be defended and Malta captured. New clauses in his orders instructed him to support Sir Sidney Smith in the Eastern Mediterranean. Smith was managing to upset almost everyone except his brother, Spencer Smith, the minister at Constantinople.[31] Convoys were to be provided for the increased numbers of British merchant ships that were sailing to the Mediterranean to obtain grain because of bad harvests in northern Europe.[32] Privateers from the Barbary States infuriated Nelson: Algiers had reached a 'pitch of insolence', and he urged Spencer to take action: 'Terror is the only weapon to wield against these people.'[33]

These disparate objectives, and the lack of resources to achieve them, illustrated the extent to which the Mediterranean had become a sideshow for Pitt's government. British war strategy at this time lacked coherence, sharply reflecting the increasing disagreements in the cabinet between Lord Grenville, the foreign secretary, and Henry Dundas, the secretary for war. For six years Britain had failed to make any impact on the Continent. Dundas's thoughtful, questing mind no longer saw amphibious operations or Continental intervention as the way to defeat France, nor did he think it was now necessary to replace the French government; he wanted naval strength, expanded trade and new overseas markets to counter French Continental military power.[34] Grenville, as before, expected British troops in Italy to encourage a wavering Austria against France. Dundas won

---

* This untidy arrangement led to the long-running prize-money dispute between Nelson and St Vincent, for in October the Spanish treasure ships *El Thetis* and *Santa Brigida* were captured off Ferrol, just within St Vincent's command.

the support of Pitt and the intended operation against Malta suffered. A proposed Mediterranean expedition of 15,000 troops was cut to 5,000. The cabinet was in disagreement too over which power should occupy Malta when the French were defeated. The Kingdom of Naples and Sicily could be said to have a justifiable right to the island. The tsar of Russia, as grand master of the Knights of St John, had a highly disputable claim, but the British government needed to support Russia as a Continental ally because of the weakness of Austria. Lord Spencer reminded Nelson of the 'utmost importance . . . to the object of carefully avoiding to do anything which may raise any jealousies in the mind of the Emperor of Russia, who is particularly bent on this point of restoring under some new regulations the Order of Malta.'[35] The commander of the British troops in the Mediterranean, General Sir Charles Stuart, whom Nelson had fought alongside in Corsica, resigned in disgust when he learnt that the government intended to hand Malta to Russia.[36]

Conflicting priorities and a continued lack of resources made Nelson's position difficult. Typically, in his current frame of mind, he responded by maintaining his single, obsessive idea: that the Kingdom of Naples in general, and the royal family in particular, should be put before all else. Both he and Sir William Hamilton saw the rottenness of the regime, and the difficulty of achieving anything, including trying to persuade King Ferdinand to return to Naples; but none of this shook their loyalty, not least because it would have meant losing the queen's favour. Her influence was overwhelming, especially upon Emma; and Nelson was absent from the court for only three months during the whole of 1799. He was also subject to pressure from Acton, acting on behalf of the queen, who did not trust the Russians or the Turks.[37] Nelson considered the danger to Minorca, captured in 1798, as slight; as we have seen, at the time of the troubles in Naples he had disobeyed Keith, who had ordered him to send ships there. He tried hard to break the French hold on Malta, even though he believed that the island, while significant in protecting access to the Levant, was not useful for blockading Toulon.

The capitulation of the stubborn French force in the fortifications above Valetta was confidently expected by politicians in London, yet without troops and artillery the British could make little progress. The Maltese, marshalled and commanded by Alexander Ball, and the small number of British marines from the ships made no impression on the well-supplied French behind formidable defences. Nelson was anxious that, if the French counter-attacked, these forces would have to abandon the siege.[38] Maintaining a naval blockade in winter was wearing and difficult and needed plenty of ships; many of those on station were by now in a bad condition.[39] Supplies for the besieging forces were short.[40] At his desk in Palermo, Nelson wrote persuasive and emotional letters to the widest range of politicians and officers, and even to the tsar of Russia, but was thwarted at every turn.[41] The blockade was strengthened for a time by the Portuguese squadron commanded by the Marquis de Niza, but he was ordered back to Portugal in November and left on 18 December 1799.[42] He expected 5,000 Russian troops from Naples, but after months of hesitation their commander, Admiral Fedor Ushakov, of whom Nelson thought little, withdrew to Corfu in January 1800.[43] In December, at last, Brigadier-General Thomas Graham arrived with a small number of troops, a force that Graham himself described as 'totally inadequate to any serious attacks on the enemy's works'.[44] In November, Nelson wrote to Troubridge: 'I am almost in desperation about Malta.' In January a food supply crisis hit the besiegers, and corn ships were commandeered just in time by Troubridge. He reported dramatically to Nelson: 'I have this day saved 30,000 people from dying.'[45]

Nelson's letters led to friction with his superiors in London. The captain of the *Charon* hospital ship, having called at Palermo at the end of August, reported to the Admiralty when he arrived in England that he 'found Lord Nelson's Flag in a Transport' and that he had been given no dispatches to bring back to London. Nelson received a reprimand (which he described as 'a severe set-down') in October from Nepean: 'knowing as you must, their Lordships' anxiety to receive information of the events which have recently occurred, My Lords could not help feeling much surprised that he had not been charged with any letter or communication whatsoever from your Lordship to them.'[46] Nelson replied indignantly that he had sent two letters to London that day 'by cutter and courier', reminding their lordships that as he was a junior flag officer, 'without Secretaries, Interpreters etc, I have been thrown into a more extensive correspondence than ever, perhaps, fell to the lot of any Admiral, and into a political situation I own out of my sphere . . . that till after eight o'clock at night I never relax from business.'[47] He grumbled to Duckworth with the mixture of self-doubt and lofty confidence now common in his letters: 'I see clearly that they wish to show I am unfit for command . . . But, my dear Admiral, when the object of the actor is only to serve faithfully, I feel superior to the smiles or frowns of any Board.'[48] In spite of the shortage of ammunition, Nelson was ordered not to spend any money on stores and equipment for the troops: 'if nobody will pay for it', he wrote extravagantly to Spencer, 'I shall sell Bronte and the Emperor of Russia's box.'[49] Spencer had enough experience in dealing with his difficult admiral to know an empty threat. When Nelson protested about two promotions made by Sidney Smith, the board informed him that they had already approved the appointments in question. Nor did their lordships approve of Nelson awarding Troubridge a temporary broad pennant 'in very peculiar circumstances' and ordered him to strike it.[50] Nelson drafted a very strong letter to Spencer but probably did not send it: 'I am here working as a centre for our operations . . . My situation in this Kingdom is wonderful and I ought hardly to be told when I move or even think of it.'[51] It is difficult not to come to the conclusion that the Board of Admiralty, worried about the lack of success at Malta, knew of the involvement with Emma and felt that his presence on shore was untypical. He ought to have been at sea prosecuting the siege.

Nelson's duties had been intense and frustrating in the last six months of 1799, a period when he became completely entangled with Emma Hamilton. The court was closely observed by Lord and Lady Elgin, who passed through Palermo in October on their journey to Constantinople, where Elgin had been appointed ambassador. Lady Elgin wrote to her mother: 'You never saw anything equal to the fuss the Queen made with Lady H. and Lord Nelson, wherever she moved, was always by her side . . . Such a complete old devil as the Queen is, I never met with; she flattered us beyond credibility; to Lord N. it was the most fulsome thing possible. I never saw three people made such thorough dupes of as Lady Hamilton, Sir William and Lord Nelson . . . It is really humiliating to see Lord Nelson, he seems quite dying and yet as if he had no other thought than her . . . Is it not a pity a man who had gained so much credit should fling himself away in this shameful manner?'[52] Lord Elgin thought that Nelson looked 'very old, has lost his upper teeth, sees ill of one eye, and has a film coming over both of them. He has pains pretty constantly from his late wound in the head. His figure is mean, and, in general, his countenance is without animation.'[53] In September, Nelson wrote to Ball: 'We are all very unwell, the air of Palermo is very bad.'[54] Nelson seemed little cheered by his attachment to Emma Hamilton.

Life changed when Lord Keith arrived at Leghorn on 12 January 1800 to resume his command.[55] Nelson did not take kindly to Keith's resumption of his command, writing to Minto that 'Greenwich Hospital seems a fit retreat for me, after being evidently thought unfit to command in the Mediterranean.'[56] Keith was a Scotsman, twelve years older than Nelson with four years' seniority, and now a vice-admiral. He was chiefly known for taking the Cape Settlement from the Dutch in September 1795, a commission that had made him rich. He was not a disciplinarian; William Hotham, who had served under both St Vincent and Keith, recalled that 'though the one was strict and the other the reverse, it was pleasantest to serve with the first than the last.'[57] According to the younger Samuel Hood, Keith was 'too <u>great</u> to consult people who are informed of the local situation of the country, which he himself does not appear to have a right knowledge of'.[58] It seems that Keith failed to consult Nelson, and he took over the latter's official communication with the board. As a consequence, Nelson's workload and correspondence diminished.

At last, however, in mid January 1800 Nelson put to sea in the *Foudroyant*, meeting Keith in the *Queen Charlotte* at Leghorn. Admiral Young in London wrote to Keith complimenting him on 'a most judicious change of rendezvous, which nothing but the infatuation you mention would have prevailed being done before. I am grieved, as everyone must be, that a man who on other occasions has done so well should on this have so sadly exposed himself to ridicule and censure.'[59] Towards the end of January both admirals sailed for Palermo for a week's visit. Keith was appalled by the court: 'the whole was a Scene of fulsome Vanity and Absurdity all the long eight days I was at Palermo.'[60] They then continued to Malta. At sea Nelson's health troubled him. He wrote to Sir William Hamilton: 'I am far from Well and have half promised Jefferson to take an Emetic this evening.'[61] But there were grounds for optimism. Some of Bonaparte's senior officers returning from Egypt were captured on a ship heading towards France. According to William Hamilton, 'They threw the dispatches overboard but the weight not being sufficient they were fortunately saved & all the important letters were sent to England & copies sent to Lord Nelson'. The letters outlined 'the desperate situation of Buonaparte's army in Egypt'.[62] Relations between Keith and Nelson also improved. Admiral Young wrote to Keith: 'I am very happy to find you and Nelson on such good terms, and him so reasonable.'[63]

The six-month-old blockade of Malta finally met with good fortune. Only two days after Nelson and Keith reached the Maltese coast, the French attempted to bring troops and stores from Toulon into Valetta in the store ship *Commerce de Marseilles*, escorted by the *Généreux* (74), three frigates and a corvette. Nelson in the *Foudroyant* was accompanied by three 74s, the *Audacious*, the *Northumberland* and the *Alexander*. Some twenty miles north-west of Malta, the squadron became separated from Keith in a strong south-easterly wind. Early in the morning on 19 February, five strange ships were seen to the northwards. Davidge Gould in the *Audacious* was left to secure the *Commerce de Marseilles* and a frigate that struck her colours, while the *Foudroyant*, the *Northumberland*, the *Alexander* and the *Success* frigate chased after the French ship of the line with all speed to reach her before dark. Nelson and Edward Berry did everything to draw ahead of the *Northumberland*. The *Foudroyant*'s bilges were pumped, her sails wetted to increase their resistance to the wind, the shrouds slackened giving the masts play; a 32-pound shot was put in every hammock lashed to the windward rail to keep her as upright as possible. The midshipman who witnessed this tense chase also noted Nelson's sharp temper, adding: 'The admiral is working his fin [the stump of his right arm], do not cross his hawse, I advise you.'[64] For two hours after three o'clock, with the wind on the quarter, the 80-gun, 2,054-ton *Foudroyant* was logged at ten knots.[65] The *Success*, ahead of the ships of the line, caught up with the *Généreux* at four o'clock, positioned herself on her quarter and raked her decks with accurate fire. At 4.30 p.m., 'four miles only from Sicily, and a few leagues from Cape Passaro', the larger ships came up with her.[66] The *Foudroyant* fired two shots. The *Généreux*, completely outgunned, fired one broadside and hauled down her colours.[67]

The *Généreux* was one of the two ships that had escaped from the Battle of the Nile. To have captured her was a boost to Nelson's low morale. He wrote triumphantly to Minto: 'This, my dear Lord, makes nineteen Sail of the line and four Admirals I have been present at the capture of, this war.'[68] Even Fanny echoed the feeling distantly in London: 'The taking of the *Généreux* seems to give great spirits to us all.'[69] Rear-Admiral Jean-Baptiste Perrée had been killed by the *Success*'s fire and Nelson secured his sword. The prize had been loaded with troops for the relief of the French garrison at Malta. The captured store ship was now sent to Keith off Malta. The *Généreux* was escorted by the *Northumberland* and *Alexander* to Syracuse, from where a prize crew was to take her on to Port Mahón in Minorca. Nelson's secretary John Tyson went with her to oversee the prize money and found it politic to share the agency with Keith's secretary.[70] Keith was generous in his praise of Nelson in the *London Gazette*: 'His Lordship has on this occasion, as on all others, conducted himself with skill and great address, in comprehending my signals, which the state of the weather led me greatly to suspect.'[71]

Keith now left for Leghorn, leaving Nelson in command of the blockade. Only two days after the taking of the *Généreux*, Nelson acted with speed by holding a court martial at sea, an unusual event. He was determined to snuff out trouble in an accompanying sloop, the *Minorca*, whose discontented warrant officers had petitioned him against the 'barbarous' conduct of their captain. It was an unhappy ship, without a purser and short of rations, and with a high proportion of pressed men; Nelson acquitted the captain, although the court found 'some want of regularity in the ship'. He reprimanded the senders of the letter and sentenced them not to be promoted for two years.[72] For three weeks he cruised off the coast of Malta, sometimes moored in St Paul's Bay. By 17 March, however, he was back in Palermo, citing ill health, sending the *Foudroyant* back to Malta with Berry in command.

On 30 March the *Guillaume Tell*, the last survivor of the Nile fleet, tried to break out of Valletta Harbour on a moonless night during a southerly gale. Discovered and shadowed by the *Penelope* frigate under Captain Henry Blackwood, she was chased by the blockading squadron through the night. In contrast with the taking of *Généreux*, the battle was fierce and casualties high: the French ship, totally dismasted, with an estimated 200 killed, eventually surrendered.[73] The *Foudroyant* had eight killed and sixty-one wounded, and lost her foretopmast and mizzenmast.[74] One account is exceedingly critical of Edward Berry's captaincy of the *Foudroyant*; writing many years later, Midshipman Parsons felt that the performance of the crew 'had not appeared to me extremely commendable; in fact, she was not in a high state of discipline'.[75] Berry wrote to Nelson: 'All hands behaved as you would have wished, how we prayed for you God knows.'[76]

William Young, that shrewd observer on the Board of Admiralty, commented in a letter to Keith: 'Nelson must have been sadly mortified at not having been present when she was being taken: that will be a sort of crisis to his disease, and will certainly make him ill enough to come home, and perhaps for his own sake it is much better that he should. Lord Spencer's letter to you will show you that it was intended you should allow him to come if his health required it. I thought this had been mentioned to you long ago, and was much surprised at finding it had not.'[77] It was an accurate prediction. Four days after the capture of the *Guillaume Tell*, Nelson wrote to Keith: 'My Health is so very much impaired that a change of Climate is absolutely necessary and a temporary release from fatigue of Service, I therefore request that you will allow of my going to England.' It was the start of a long negotiation with Keith for a ship of war to take him home, for, as he ended the letter, 'I am sure, my Dear Lord, you would not think it right to send me home in a store ship or anything less than one of the large frigates for our family will not be less than six of us with innumerable servants.'[78]

Not only was it the end of Nelson's command in the Mediterranean, but also of William Hamilton's career, as he was effectively in disgrace and without a pension. He paid the penalty for his ineffectiveness during the troubles in Naples.[79] He was relieved by Arthur Paget, the new envoy extra-ordinary and plenipotentiary, who received a hostile welcome, particularly from Emma, on his arrival on 9 April. Paget described it to Grenville: 'I was represented as a Jacobin and coxcomb, a person sent to bully and to carry them ... back to Naples. Her Ladyship's language in general has been extremely indiscreet, representing Sir William as an ill-used man etc etc. She has however persuaded herself and others that I am only sent here for an interval, & that Sir William will resume his situation at Naples next winter ... I am sorry to say that Lord Nelson has given more or less into this nonsense.'[80] Emma's confidence in her husband's position was misplaced: it was a strained diplomatic handover. Hamilton wrote to his nephew Charles Greville that Paget's 'behaviour to me has been cold and reserved from the moment of his arrival, nor has he asked me any questions relative to this Court or country, and of which I must certainly know more of than he can, having been Minister at Naples before he was born.'[81]

Distance from reality marked these months. Nelson's long-time admirer Lord Minto wrote to his wife in exasperation at how little Nelson and the Hamiltons realized they were appearing ridiculous.[82] Minto was particularly critical of their obsession with foreign honours. Nelson sent the sword captured from the *Généreux* to the tsar of Russia. 'I presume to lay at your feet the sword of the French Admiral Perrée who I had the good fortune to capture in the *Genereux*, together with a large store ship with provisions and ammunition for the fall of La Villette [Valetta] ... this capture will doubtless much facilitate the fall of the place and enable me to see the Flag of the order flying in La Villette.' He wanted to secure the Cross of the Knights of St John for Emma, or, as the full title would have it, to create her 'Chanoiness of the Order of St John of Jerusalem'.[83] Spencer, among many in the higher reaches of government, was not impressed, writing to his mother: 'The Fêtes at Palermo are not quite to my Mind any more than the Dukedom of Bronti.'[84] Alexander Ball was much more level-headed than Nelson, for he too had been showered with Russian and Sicilian honours, but he wrote to Evan Nepean, 'I have seen too much of life to be tickled with a foreign feather. They are too light for estimation in England.'[85]

A day after taking formal leave from the court at Palermo, Sir William and his wife embarked on the *Foudroyant*, with eight other guests, including Cornelia Knight and servants, for a journey to Malta. With all French ships of the line destroyed or captured, Nelson reckoned it was safe to risk the Hamiltons on board. He informed Keith in Leghorn by a letter written on the morning of his departure.[86] Although the ship took stores, provisions and troops, including live cattle and 7,000 lemons and oranges, to the blockading ships, this was more in the nature of a farewell cruise. At least that was how Nelson remembered it, for at this point the relationship with Emma was beyond infatuation and had been consummated, almost certainly by January 1800.[87] It was during this cruise that their daughter, Horatia, was conceived. A year later he was to write to her: 'This day twelve months we sailed from Palermo on our tour to Malta. Ah! Those were happy times: days of ease and nights of pleasure.'[88]

After a week of light winds, a squally passage through the Strait of Messina and two days' sightseeing in Syracuse, the ship reached Malta on 9 May. The *Foudroyant* was moored in St Paul's Bay for a week. She was next moored off Valetta in light airs for one night, when at daybreak, on a windless morning, she was fired on and her foretopmast hit by French cannon fire from the fortress; she had to be towed quickly out of range. William Bolton, the officer of the watch, was apparently to blame.[89] For another week the ship lay in Marsa Scirocco Bay, at the south of the island; the party waited for the surrender of the fortress in vain. Nelson may have had fond memories of the time, but he was still not well. Alexander Ball wrote a brief note to Emma from the shore at this time, saying that Nelson was 'harassed and fatigued with anxiety. I am most thoroughly convinced that his Lordship's spasm is brought on by anxiety of mind. I therefore rejoice at your being on board, as I am sure you will exert your powers to keep up his spirits, and the worthy Sir William will contribute much to it.'[90]

Accompanied by the *Alexander*, the *Foudroyant* sailed from Malta to Palermo, arriving on 1 June for nine days of farewell festivities. On 5 June a total of 102 guns were fired in Palermo Bay saluting respectively the king's birthday, Arthur Paget, the Turkish ambassador, His Britannic Majesty's health and Sir William Hamilton. Five days later the *Foudroyant* took the Hamiltons' baggage on board and that of Queen Maria Carolina, who, by now 'more and more at odds' with the king, had decided to visit her family in Vienna, with her retinue of thirty-seven companions and servants. Again accompanied by the *Alexander*, the *Foudroyant* sailed for Leghorn, which she reached on 15 June 1800.[91] Eleven days later Keith arrived, flying his flag in the *Minotaur*. The commander-in-chief was surprised and displeased to see the two ships, for he had intended that neither ship should abandon the blockade of Malta. His patience with Nelson was wearing thin; he wrote to Paget at Naples on 20 June: 'I must go to Leghorn ... to be Bored by Lord Nelson for permission to take the Queen to Palermo, and Princes and Princesses to all parts of the Globe, to every request I have said that my Duty to the Nation forbids it.' When he learnt that on 8 June the French brig *Margueritte* had broken the blockade at

Malta and reached the garrison with supplies, he put the blame squarely upon his second in command: 'Had not Nelson quitted it [the blockade] and taken the ships off that station it might have fallen about this time.'[92]

From late April, Nelson had tried to persuade Keith to let him return to England in the *Foudroyant*, for the ship needed a refit. Keith had offered the *Culloden*, then a frigate.[93] Sir William would have been content with this.[94] Nelson hesitated, for he wanted to take the Hamiltons home in style. Keith decided instead that the *Foudroyant* should sail to Port Mahón for a refit. All Nelson's baggage and that of the Sicilian royal family was moved into the *Alexander*, in which he now flew his flag. He did not want to leave without the Hamiltons. But Emma had set her mind against returning by sea, at least in a small ship, and intended to go overland. From the evidence of her sterling behaviour during the flight from Naples aboard the *Vanguard* eighteen months earlier, she did not suffer from seasickness, although her pregnancy may have affected her health. It seems likely that she wanted to prolong her influence on the queen. On board ship too, with Nelson dominant on the quarterdeck, she might have judged that her influence over him would have lessened.

Yet an overland journey was not without danger, for on 14 June Bonaparte had decimated the Austrians at Marengo and the military situation in Italy worsened. Keith could therefore no longer spare a warship any larger than a frigate or a troopship for the journey home. It was thus agreed that the party should go overland, accompanying the queen to Vienna, and thence travel through Germany to England. According to Cornelia Knight, who accompanied Nelson and the Hamiltons, 'Lord Nelson is going on an expedition he disapproves, and against his own convictions, because he has promised the Queen . . . [he] is well, and keeps up his spirits amazingly. Sir William appears broken, distressed and harassed.'[95] Miss Knight's own morale was not good. She ended her letter to Edward Berry, 'If I am not detained in a French prison, or do not die upon the road, you shall hear from me again.'

On 12 July at 3 p.m. the queen disembarked in Leghorn from the *Alexander*, saluted by twenty-one guns. An hour later Nelson struck his flag.[96] It was an inglorious exit from his Mediterranean commission, during which his squadron had destroyed the French fleet. Major-General John Moore, with whom Nelson had crossed swords so many times in Corsica, now in Leghorn to conduct operations against Genoa, saw him again, writing in his journal: 'He is covered with stars, ribbons and medals, more like the Prince of the Opera than the Conqueror of the Nile. It is really melancholy to see a brave and good man, who has deserved well of his country, cutting so pitiful a figure.'[97] William Young in London, writing to Keith, regretted 'exceedingly that Nelson should have conducted himself so strangely. He is a little too old to be so led away by a woman. The Queen of Naples had been too much accustomed to have Officers and Ships attending to her to be satisfied with being told that the service of the Country required their being otherwise Employed; to attend on her she would consider as the best service on which they could be employed; it is very fortunate you were there to think better.'[98] The *Foudroyant*'s barge crew had real regrets, saying to Nelson: 'We have been along with you (although not in the same Ship) in every Engagement your Lordship has been in, both by Sea and Land, and most humbly beg of your Lordship to permit us to go to England, as your Boat's crew, in any ship or Vessel, or in any way that may seem most pleasing to your Lordship.'[99] His departure overland for England broke many of his long-held professional bonds and loyalties.

The fifteen-week journey across Italy, with a party of never fewer than fourteen, through Austria and Germany to Hamburg was expensive, at times comic, at others dangerous. High social moments were mixed with periods of seclusion. The queen's party, numbering more than sixty, left two days earlier for Ancona on the east coast of Italy. Nelson's coaches followed, making their way along roads crowded with refugees from the advancing French Army, as well as Neapolitan deserters, whom the travellers feared. The coaches passed within two miles of the French advanced posts. The Hamiltons were slightly hurt when their coach overturned; Nelson left their two fellow travellers, Cornelia Knight and Emma's mother, Mrs Cadogan, with the upturned coach, while he and the Hamiltons went ahead. After four days everyone reached Ancona. A small squadron of Russian frigates took the two parties, which now totalled eighty-five, on a four-day passage to Trieste. Nelson's frigate was commanded by Thomas Messer, an Englishman in the long-term service of the Russian Navy. Cornelia Knight wrote to Edward Berry: 'Lord Nelson talks often of the *Foudroyant*, whatever is done to turn off the conversation; and last night he was talking with Captain Messer of the manoeuvres he intended to make in case he accepted of another command. In short, I perceive his thoughts turn towards England, and I hope, and believe he will be happy there.'[100]

After nine days' rest, particularly needed by Sir William Hamilton, at Trieste, where Nelson was 'followed by thousands when he [went] out', the party set out for Vienna. The roads were steep and rough, the weather very hot, the accommodation simple, the mountains and countryside beautiful and dramatic. They reached the city on 18 August. The next day they were entertained by Lord and Lady Minto, as Minto was now ambassador to the court of the emperor and empress.[101] Lady Minto wrote to her sister: 'He is just the same as ever he was: says he owes everything to Lord Minto.'[102] Hamilton was still ill, in Minto's words, 'so feeble and so much reduced that I cannot see how it is possible for him to reach England alive'.[103] Partly because of Hamilton's health, the party was to stay there for five weeks. Invitations flowed in, including visits to the theatre with the Mintos, the audience applauding Nelson. Heinrich Fuger was commissioned to paint Nelson's portrait.[104] After ten days Hamilton had sufficiently recovered to take tea with the empress at the Schönbrunn Palace; Nelson and Lady Hamilton were officially presented at court.

On 6 September they travelled the short distance to Eisenstadt to stay with Prince Esterhazy. There they met Joseph Haydn, who admired Emma's singing and named a mass that he had already written after Nelson; it is still known today as the 'Nelson Mass'. 'It did not appear to me that the English nation was at all popular,' Cornelia Knight noted in her journal, but Austrian public enthusiasm for Nelson did not diminish during his stay.[105] Minto wrote to Keith: 'Lord Nelson has been rec'd here by all ranks with the admiration which his great actions deserve, & notwithstanding the disadvantage under which he presents himself at present to the publick eye . . . I who am a lover of naval merit & indeed a sincere friend of the man, hope we shall again hear of him in his proper element.'[106]

Minto's sympathetic wish highlighted uncertainty over the increasingly obvious relationship between Nelson and Emma. Nelson appeared from all accounts passive, led on social occasions by Emma. The expenses of the journey were enormous, totalling £3,431. Nelson drew £1,100 in bills in Vienna alone, though costs were shared with William Hamilton.[107] The attention that Nelson paid to Emma in public excited comment from British observers. She was by this time heavily pregnant. Such an old friend as Lady Minto did not think Nelson 'altered in the least. He has the same shock head, and the same honest, simple manners; but he is devoted to Emma; he thinks her quite an angel, and talks of her as such to her face and behind her back, and she leads him about like a keeper with a bear.' And, she added, 'he is a gig from ribands, orders, and stars.'[108]

Gossip was sharp and malicious. James Harris, a nephew of the Mintos, who saw the party at Eisenstadt, wrote to his parents that 'Lady Hamilton is without exception the most coarse, ill-mannered, disagreeable woman I ever met with . . . I could not disguise my feeling, and joined in the general abuse of her.'[109] Some idea of the reception that Nelson and the Hamiltons were likely to receive in England can be gained from the reaction of Sir

William's nephew Charles Greville, when he received a letter from Vienna. Greville, who clearly did not welcome any further drain on Hamilton's estate, wrote in exasperation to Sir Joseph Banks that the party was coming home

to my great sorrow with what they call the small reserve of the Establishment! 3 Neapolitan, 1 Roman, 1 Ethiopian: men 1 French, 1 Neapolitan, 1 Egyptian: women. How they will get to Hamburgh from Vienna, God knows. 8 more useless creatures could not be imported. I wish they had been 8 Konguroos. I would send them by Lannay [landau] to the Institute, but being Loyal Women and Men, they must be stowed as unprofitable curiousities. I had prepared a plan for cheap residence but this establishment confounds all![110]

After long farewells, especially to Queen Maria Carolina, Nelson and the Hamiltons set out on 26 September with their companions and servants for the two-day journey to Prague. There they stayed for two days, after which they continued to Dresden, travelling some of the way by boat down the River Elbe. They stayed a week, entertained by the British minister, Hugh Elliot, the younger brother of Lord Minto. Their reception at Dresden was more muted; only Nelson attended at court. The trio were observed at the minister's dinner table by Melasina St George, a guest of the Elliots: 'Lady Hamilton takes possession of him [Nelson], and he is a willing captive, the most submissive and devoted I have seen. Sir William is old, infirm, all admiration of his wife and never spoke today but to applaud her.' On the last day of their visit Emma's high spirits at dinner were again recorded: 'Lady Hamilton repeated her attitudes with great effect . . . declared she was passionately fond of champagne, took such a portion of it as astonished me, Lord Nelson was not behindhand, calling more vociferously than usual for songs in his own praise.'[111] Although it is the judgement of a non-admirer, this is the only time that Nelson was recorded as being anything like merry or boisterous after drink had been taken.

Now followed the quietest and quickest part of the journey. Two shallow-drafted barges with single sails, about eighty foot long, were hired to take the party the 375 miles down the Elbe to Hamburg, where, according to Hugh Elliot, a British frigate was available to take them to England. They set off on 10 October, passing through thirty customs stations, staying by night at poorly furnished inns; on occasion food was procured with difficulty, since it had been a dry summer with a poor harvest.[112] Five bridges had to be negotiated, with the barge crew lowering and rehoisting the masts of the two barges.[113] The party went ashore at Vockerode, ten miles south of Dassau, at Magdeburg and then at Hitzacker, not far from Hamburg. From there notice of the arrival of the party was sent forward by horse, and the barges finally arrived in Hamburg on the afternoon of 21 October 1800.

No British frigate was in Hamburg Harbour; this was hardly surprising in view of deteriorating British relations with Denmark, for the Elbe formed part of that country's southern border. Arrangements were made to hire a packet to take the party to England. In the meantime Nelson and the Hamiltons enjoyed the cosmopolitan atmosphere of Hamburg, a bustling city where merchants of different nations lived alongside each other. In contrast to the aristocratic Elliots at Vienna and Dresden, the British government here was represented by the consul, Alexander Cockburn, the brother of George, the dashing frigate captain with whom Nelson had combined so well in the Mediterranean. Dinner parties were given. Nelson even met a French general, Charles François Dumouriez, who had won the first French victories in the war in 1792 against the Austrians but was now estranged from Napoleon. Cornelia Knight, increasingly 'uneasy on many accounts' with the relationship of Nelson and Emma, gained some comfort by helping Nelson buy lace for Fanny.[114] She noted with relief that Nelson told her that he hoped that Sir William and Lady Hamilton would come to dinner, after which he and Fanny would go to bed, while the Hamiltons went on to their musical parties.[115] He was not yet contemplating the break up of his marriage.

At last the packet was ready to sail from Cuxhaven on the evening tide of 31 October. It reached Yarmouth after a stormy passage of no fewer than six days. The reception from the people of the town was remarkable, considering that it was more than two years after the Nile victory. Crowds formed instantaneously. The mayor and Corporation presented Nelson with the freedom of the town, 'some time since voted to him for his eminent services'.[116] He presented them with £50, though he was still short of cash.[117] He went to church with the Hamiltons for a service of thanksgiving. The infantry of the town paraded in front of the Wrestlers Arms, where he was lodging, 'firing feux de joye of musquetry and ordnance till midnight'.[118]

At some point in this hectic, noisy day he opened one of several letters from Fanny that were awaiting him. On 20 September Nelson had written to Fanny from Vienna, asking her 'to take a house or good lodgings for a very short time I shall be in London . . . where I shall instantly proceed and hope to meet you in the house'. He estimated that his arrival in England would be in the second week of October, but she did not receive the letter until 20 October.[119] The same day she sent letters to Nelson at both Harwich and Yarmouth, and, as she described it to Davison, 'begged My Dear Lord just to stop at his own door for a few Minutes and I would have everything ready to sett off with him'. He would then be able to see his father.[120] She sent a further letter inviting the Hamiltons to stay at Roundwood. But she heard nothing and by 30 October she was in London, lodging near Thomas Masterman Hardy in Duke Street. By then Hardy had heard that the party had been delayed in Hamburg for fifteen days.[121]

Still at Yarmouth, Nelson replied to Fanny on 6 November, telling her that the Hamiltons 'will accept your offer of a bed' and that the rest of the party and the servants would continue south to Colchester. They were to leave Yarmouth at noon the following day.[122] According to the *Naval Chronicle*: 'On leaving the town, the corps of cavalry unexpectedly drew up, saluted, and followed the carriage, not only to the town's end, but to the boundary of the county.'[123] When the carriage reached Roundwood, the house was deserted. Was it a genuine mistake? Was she showing disapproval in the only way she felt she could? Did she panic? Perhaps it was at that moment that she lost him.

By now the nerves of the reception committee in London were strained. Troubridge agreed with Hardy that the latter should travel to Yarmouth, as Hardy wrote to a relative: 'Notwithstanding all the Newspapers his Lordship is not arrived in town & when he will God only knows. His Father has lost all patience, her Ladyship bears up very well as yet but I much fear she will despond. He certainly arrived at Yarmouth on Thursday last & there has been no letter received by anybody. Should he not arrive tomorrow I think I shall set off for Yarmouth as I know only too well the cause of his not coming.'[124]

21

Separation

8 November 1800–March 1801

I want neither nursing, or attention, And had you come here, I should not have gone on Shore, Nor would you have come afloat. I fixed as I thought a proper allowance to enable you to remain quiet, and not to be posting from one end of the Kingdom to the other. Neither I live, or die, am Sick or Well I want from no-one, the sensation of pain or pleasure. And I expect no comfort till I am removed from this World.
Nelson to Fanny, quoted by Fanny in a letter to
Alexander Davison, 24 February 1801[1]

I am just returned from receiving the Sacrament – and I now say if at any future time My husband will make My house his home – I will receive him with joy; and whatever has passed shall never pass my lips – I pray God he may return to us, bound with laurels, and an Easy Mind.
Fanny to Alexander Davison, 15 March 1801[2]

The carriage drew up outside Nerot's Hotel in King's Street, St James's, on 8 November 1800. 'The noble Admiral,' the *Naval Chronicle* recorded, 'dressed in full uniform, with three stars on his breast, and two gold medals, was welcomed by repeated huzzas from the crowd, which the illustrious tar returned with a low bow. Lord Nelson looked extremely well, but in person very thin.' Nelson, with Sir William and Lady Hamilton on hand, met Fanny and his father in the hall of the hotel. It was a very public meeting, with no time for private talk; the first well-wisher, the duke of Queensberry, arrived ten minutes later and stayed for an hour. After dinner that night with the Hamiltons, which can only have been strained, Nelson and Fanny visited Lord and Lady Spencer.[3]

While all was joy and congratulations on the surface, widespread knowledge of Nelson and Emma's affair had long preceded their arrival. St Vincent, in command of the Channel fleet, had not seen Nelson since

May 1798; he called Nelson and Emma 'a pair of sentimental fools'.[4] Writing from Devon to Nepean on 9 November, he felt that Nelson was 'doubtful of the propriety of his conduct. I have no doubt he is pledged to getting Lady H. received at St James's and everywhere, and that he will get into much *brouillerie* ab[ou]t it.'[5] At the levee on 12 November the king barely acknowledged Nelson; this was unsurprising in view of the fact that he had been outmanoeuvred by Pitt and Spencer into giving Nelson a peerage. Nelson told Cuthbert Collingwood that 'His Majesty merely asked him if he had recovered his health; and then, without waiting for an answer, turned to General —, and talked to him in great good humour . . . not very flattering,' Collingwood commented, 'after having been the adoration . . . of Naples'.[6]

Nelson orchestrated his public appearances in London in the same fashion as he had in Naples: by defiantly wearing full-dress uniform. Displaying foreign orders *en masse* was not popular. After the Battle of the Nile, Gillray had lampooned him mercilessly in a caricature emphasizing a mournful, drawn face, his slight figure made smaller by the enlarged size of the medals, the chelengk from the sultan of Turkey dwarfing his hat. Nelson's shameless display of orders was matched, in the eyes of the powerful in London, by his brazen display of a mistress. The social climate in England at the turn of the nineteenth century has been described as one of 'ostentatious uxoriousness'; in contrast to earlier in the eighteenth century, politicians in power followed the fashion of the domesticity of the king and the probity of William Pitt, fearful of the supposed licentiousness of the Revolution in France.[7] Judging by Nelson's inability to push his relatives forward, he must have been seen as a political liability. He wrote to the younger Maurice Suckling: 'not one favour has to my knowledge been granted me since I came to England, and you may believe me, when I cannot get Nisbet a Ship, or my elder brother removed from being a Clerk in the Navy Office.'[8]

Nelson tried to counter gossip by being seen with his wife in the company of both the Hamiltons. The two couples, with Edmund Nelson, went to Covent Garden to see the musical entertainment *The Mouth of the Nile*, during which the party was much applauded. It was noted particularly by the *Morning Herald*: 'The hero of the Nile was in the front of the second box from the stage . . . Lady Hamilton being seated on his right, and Lady Nelson on his left.'[9] But when they went to Drury Lane Theatre on 24 November to see Kemble in a play called *Pizarro*, the *Morning Herald* reported that 'about the end of the third act Lady Nelson fainted away, and was obliged to be carried out of her box.'[10] The newspaper attributed the cause to the heat of the theatre, but many thought the cause to be extemporary lines from the leading actress on the subject of 'an injured woman's fury'.[11] 'So much was said about the attachment of Lord Nelson to Lady Hamilton, that it made the matter still worse,' wrote Cornelia Knight.[12] Fearful of being associated with scandal, she detached herself from Nelson and the Hamiltons, going to stay with the secretary of the Admiralty, Evan Nepean, and his family, thus ending a two-year friendship.

Yet Nelson was cheered by the public at large. On his way by foot from the Admiralty Office to Somerset House, he was mobbed in the Strand. Two days later his appearance in the cavalcade at the Lord Mayor's Show led to the crowd taking the horses from the carriage and pulling him to the Guildhall 'amid repeated huzzas. All the way he passed along Cheapside, he was greeted by the ladies from the windows with their handkerchiefs, and the loudest acclamations.'[13] The Corporation presented Nelson with a sword, studded with diamonds and with a gold handle in the shape of a crocodile. He took his seat in the House of Lords. On 3 December he was dined by the East India Company at the London Tavern. The company was distinguished: William Windham, as he noted in his diary, sat between Henry Dundas and Lord Macartney.[14] At some point Nelson met the prime minister. Pitt wrote to Grenville, his foreign secretary, giving measured approval for Nelson's dealings over Malta: 'Lord Nelson put into my Hand some days ago some letters which passed between him and the Emperor Paul; and which I think it is material you should see. Our admiral has perhaps gone unnecessarily out of his Way, and out of his Element, but I do not think he has given any grounds that can be fairly used against him.'[15] Nelson also met and impressed Henry Addington, then speaker of the House of Commons, who was to succeed Pitt as prime minister within two months. Addington described Nelson as a 'most extraordinary man: his view of the present state of Europe is that of a well-constructed & well informed mind, engrossed by & devoted to the Cause of the Country.'[16]

But friction between Nelson and Fanny was increasing. At one of Lady Spencer's dinner parties, Nelson 'never spoke during dinner, and looked blacker than all the devils', a situation that reduced Fanny to tears.[17] Towards the end of December he left her to make a short Christmas visit to Wiltshire with the Hamiltons; they stayed with a distant cousin of Sir William, the notorious but immensely rich, William Beckford. Beckford had lent the Hamiltons his London house in Grosvenor Square on their return, retiring to one of his many other properties. He spent his great West Indian fortune on collecting and is considered one of the first to reintroduce a taste for the Gothic into England. He was also a bisexual who created one scandal after another, a social outsider who encouraged Hamilton to lobby for a pension and a peerage, which he might inherit. The visit to Beckford's extraordinary 'pleasure building' near Salisbury, Fonthill Abbey, an enormous Gothic Revival structure built near the site of a medieval priory, added a layer of unreality to Nelson's changing life.

On 20 December the party arrived at Salisbury, where Nelson was greeted by the mayor and Corporation and given the freedom of the city. Afterwards Nelson and the party, which included the president of the Royal Academy and the architect, James Wyatt, in the words of the *Gentleman's Magazine* correspondent who accompanied them, 'partook of a cold collation with the body corporate'. Nelson's public performance demonstrated 'a feeling and generous heart, a quick discernment of occasion, and a popularity of manners'.[18] They spent two days at Fonthill Splendens, where Beckford actually lived – no one slept at the Abbey – and on the evening of 23 December the company boarded coaches 'as the dusk of the evening was growing into darkness'. Their short journey to the abbey was lit by torches. They entered through the Western Hall, with its massive 35-foot Gothic Revival oak doors, 'attended by Beckford's resident dwarf in livery'.[19]

It was an experience that outshone anything that Nelson had experienced in Europe. Fonthill Abbey never saw any other celebration; Nelson's banquet was the only one to take place there. It was lucky to take place at all, for part of the abbey had fallen down in May and throughout the autumn 500 men had laboured night and day to rebuild it.[20] The enormous Gothic Revival tower, lit inside by torches, had its fleeting moment of admiration and glory. The guests went to the West Hall for dinner, after which they left for a tour through its sumptuous rooms, their way lit by torches held by hooded servants. Emma then entertained the company with appropriate 'Attitudes' for one who was eight months pregnant. She 'appeared in the character of Agrippina, bearing the ashes of Germanicus in a golden urn, and presenting herself before the Roman people . . . Lady Hamilton [was] most classically graceful . . . in the last scene of this beautiful piece of pantomime.' Leaving the abbey, wrote the correspondent, 'he could scarcely help doubting whether the whole of the last evening's entertainment were a reality, or only the visionary coinage of fancy'.[21]

The party returned to London and reality reimposed itself. Nelson's early mentor Captain William Locker died on 26 December; his body was taken from Greenwich Hospital to be buried in the parish church at Addington, south of London; Nelson wrote a heartfelt letter to Locker's son John:

William Locker was, 'a man whom to know was to love, and those who only heard of him honoured'. Nelson followed the funeral cortège in his carriage and saw his first and most loved patron buried.[22] On 3 January 1801, according to one observer, 'Lord Nelson was at the Levee on Wednesday and at the Drawing Room yesterday – He was coldly received by the King, who merely observed that his Lordship had come to Town on Monday & was to hoist his Flag in the Channel Fleet, then turned and spoke to another.'[23]

From the moment that Nelson had stepped ashore at Yarmouth, he was anxious to get back to sea. He wrote from there to the first lord of the Admiralty: 'my health being perfectly re-established, it is my wish to serve immediately; and I trust that my necessary journey by land from the Mediterranean will not be considered as a wish to be a moment out of active service.'[24] Nelson afloat lessened political and social embarrassment, even though, according to Fanny, there was talk, even an offer, of his becoming a junior lord of the Admiralty.[25] When Nelson met Spencer he asked to serve under St Vincent, in spite of the fact that the two officers were engaged in the prize-money dispute over the Spanish treasure ships. St Vincent was not keen to have Nelson in his fleet, as he wrote to Spencer: Nelson should have 'a separate command, for he cannot bear confinement to any object; he is a partisan; his ship is always in the most dreadful disorder, and never can become an officer fit to be placed where I am.'[26] However, in the end it was decided that Nelson should serve in the Channel fleet under St Vincent. He was given the *San Josef*, the great Spanish 112-gun ship that Nelson had captured at the Battle of St Vincent: as Spencer remarked to St Vincent, 'which ship I consider (unless you had yourself wished for her) to be Nelson's peculiar right'.[27] St Vincent agreed: 'I always had the *San Josef* in view for my friend Nelson, who seems most highly flattered by it; the fear I have about him is, that he will tire of being attached to a great fleet, and want to be carrying on a predatory war (which is his métier).'[28] He was soon to fulfil this role, for the delicately balanced alliances that had maintained peace since 1793 in the north of Europe were unravelling rapidly.

Relations between Britain and the Baltic countries had been stable through the 1790s largely because of Russia's enmity towards France and the Revolution. As ever, good relations with Sweden, Russia and Prussia, as primary producers of timber, hemp and pitch to all Europe, were essential, as were those with Denmark, which controlled entry to the Baltic. The long-held and contentious claim of the British Navy to search neutral trading ships and to seize a vessel if the cargo was destined for an enemy had caused resentment but no problems until the 29-year-old crown prince took over power in Denmark in 1797. With his 'strong conviction of the need to uphold the prestige of Danish sovereignty and respect for its power', Danish warships began to contest the right of search.[29] Shots were fired by a Danish warship off Gibraltar in December 1799 and again in July 1800, when the Danish frigate *Freya*, protecting a Danish convoy in the Channel, was surrounded by five British warships and a short action ensued. The British government acted with speed. By August 1800 Vice-Admiral Archibald Dickson was in the Sound off Copenhagen with nine ships of the line, five gun brigs and four bomb vessels, accompanied by Lord Whitworth, the British diplomat who was able to negotiate an agreement between the two governments.[30] The price of St Petersburg 'clean' hemp paid by the Navy Board jumped from £35 a ton in 1798 to £42 in 1799; by July 1800, fuelled by speculation, it rose to £61.[31] The confrontation was a dress rehearsal for the battle of April 1801 that was to come.

The situation worsened when Tsar Paul briefly ordered an embargo on British vessels in Russian ports. Although it was soon lifted, Paul reimposed it on 6 November 1800, after he had heard that the British flag – alone – had been raised over the newly conquered Malta: British ministers had changed their mind over the importance of the island.[32] The mad Paul heightened the tension further by seizing British crews in St Petersburg and marching them inland, through the Russian winter, which caused widespread indignation in England. In London, funds were set up by the Russia Company for the relief of the seamen.[33] The tsar was now wooed by Napoleon. Statesmen of all the warring nations became concerned about strategic war materials, particularly hemp, for which there was no alternative supply. In London, Spencer convened a secret committee, which included Sir Joseph Banks and Sir William Scott, the lawyer, to develop alternative means of supplying hemp, possibly from Ireland or India.[34] On 16 December the Northern Convention, an agreement between the signatories to resist the right of search, was signed between Russia, Denmark, Sweden and Prussia.*

By early December the Admiralty was planning to send a squadron to the Baltic; St Vincent recommended to Spencer that Vice-Admiral Sir Hyde Parker should command it, as he was 'the only man you have to face them.

---

* The Northern Convention was similar to the Armed Neutrality of the American Revolutionary War. News of the Convention did not reach the British government until 13 January 1801. By 14 January embargoes were put on Russian, Danish and Swedish ships in British ports; two days later the Admiralty ordered British warships to sweep the seas to bring them in ((UK)NA: PRO, ADM 3/144, 16 Jan. 1801).

He is in possession of all the information obtained during the Russian armament, more particularly that which relates to the navigation of the Great Belt.'[35] Some suspected that St Vincent – or the 'Old Jesuit', as he came to be called – was putting forward Hyde Parker's name to keep him away from command of the Channel Fleet.[36] Cuthbert Collingwood's opinion of Hyde Parker at this time was 'a good tempered man, full of vanity, a great deal of pomp, and a pretty smattering of ignorance – nothing of that natural ability that raises men with the advantages of learned education'.[37]

On 9 January, Nelson and Fanny had jointly signed the document that sold Roundwood.[38] A short time later, the break came; perhaps the completion of this document was a significant factor in the timing of the separation. One morning Fanny's patience had snapped. The moment was witnessed by William Haslewood, Nelson's lawyer. He recalled many years later:

I was breakfasting with Lord and Lady Nelson . . . and a cheerful conversation was passing on indifferent subjects, when Lord Nelson spoke of something which had been done, or said, by 'dear Lady Hamilton'; upon which Lady Nelson rose from her chair, and exclaimed, with much vehemence, 'I am sick of hearing of dear Lady Hamilton, and am resolved that you shall give up either her or me.' Lord Nelson, with perfect calmness, said: 'Take care, Fanny, what you say. I love you sincerely; but I cannot forget my obligations to Lady Hamilton, or speak of her otherwise than with affection or admiration.' Without one soothing word or gesture, but muttering something about her mind being made up, Lady Nelson left the room, and shortly after drove from the house. They never lived together afterwards.[39]*

Letters still passed between them, irritable on Nelson's part, concerning the mundane arrangements of getting away on a commission.[40] Nelson set out from London on 13 January to join the *San Josef* at Plymouth, and he wrote her a note on his journey, as was his custom, to say that he had reached Southampton. But his abiding memory of this period was recalled three months later when he wrote to Alexander Davison, 'sooner than live the unhappy life I did when last I came to England, I would stay abroad for ever.'[41]

During the journey Nelson was in a state of high anxiety. After Southampton he stopped at George Rose's house, but he was absent. Nelson then

---

* On 24 January, Fanny gave up the rented house in London and went to stay in Brighton with William Locker's daughter (Naish, 573, 22. Jan. 1801, Fanny to Sarah Nelson).

had a malarial attack: 'various workings of my imagination', he wrote to Emma, 'gave me one of those severe pains of the heart that all the windows were obliged to be put down. The carriage stop'd and the perspiration was so strong that I was never wetter & yet dead with cold. However, it is gone off.'[42] After a stop at Honiton, where he saw the widow of George Westcott, one of his Nile captains, he reached Exeter, where he received the freedom of the city. On 16 January he called on St Vincent, now living ashore at Tor Abbey near Dartmouth while commander-in-chief of the Channel fleet.[43] The confident, trusting bond between them was lacking, with the prize-money dispute unmentioned but ever present. 'Nelson was very low when he first came here,' St Vincent reported to Nepean, '[he] appeared and acted as if he had done me an injury, and felt apprehension that I was acquainted with it. Poor man! he is devour'd with vanity, weakness, and folly; was strung with ribbons, medals etc and yet pretended that he wished to avoid the honors & ceremonies he everywhere met with upon the Road.'[44] But Nelson was on his guard in case St Vincent opened up on the subject of the prize-money case. He wrote to Davison: 'I am prepared with a broadside as strong (and backed with justice) as any he can send.'[45]

Much business needed to be settled. Sir Hyde Parker's letter announcing his command of the squadron for the Baltic arrived while Nelson was with St Vincent, and they discussed what he should do. Ideally, Nelson would have preferred the command of the Mediterranean, though Keith was still there. His next choice was to serve under St Vincent in the Channel. But Nelson agreed to serve under Parker in the Baltic. He was keen not to lose the deep-drafted *San Josef*, which he called 'the finest ship in the world' but which was unsuitable for the shallow Danish waters. St Vincent promised that he could return to her after the Northern expedition.[46] The relationship of the two men was improved by the meeting. Nelson wrote to Spencer asking the first lord to provide 10,000 troops 'to get at the Danish Arsenal'.[47] St Vincent wrote Nelson a jocular note a couple of days later: 'A thousand thanks for your recollection of My having yesterday liv'd sixty six years, and your wishes that the small remainder of my days may be well spent in your Company,' and he went on to suggest that Nelson pay some attention to 'the Lady's of Plymouth, Stonehouse & Dock ... you know how to tickle them.'[48] This was the St Vincent of old.

At Plymouth the *San Josef* was still in dockyard hands when Nelson hoisted his flag in her. Thomas Masterman Hardy had been on board since the turn of the year and had now been joined by all the officers, including William Bolton, Nelson's nephew, and George Elliot, son of Lord Minto. The ship moved out of the Hamoaze to Cawsand Bay on 22 January.[49] On

23 January, St Vincent received confirmation from Spencer that Nelson was to go as second-in-command to the Baltic, news that he sent on to Nelson.[50] When Nelson's baggage was opened he found complete confusion, with half his clothes left behind and many useless articles included. He wrote to Fanny: 'I could have done all in ten minutes and for a 10th part of the expense.'[51] They were the last – barely – civil words he wrote to her.

While anchored in Plymouth Sound in the huge Spanish-built ship, alone in his cabin, Nelson began the first of a long series of daily letters to Emma Hamilton. In the bitter cold, Hardy and the officers made ready for sea, the crew employed on the never-ending task of getting water aboard. Over the next month Nelson decided to leave Fanny; he also faced the prospect of being parted from Emma for several months. He had been with her, with the exception of three short intervals, since the middle of 1799, when he had become emotionally dependent upon her. For the first time in his life he began to express on paper what he felt rather than what he thought. The mood of the letters swung wildly. At first anxious about Emma's unborn child, he was joyful, loving, longing, then angry and jealous. The first sign of this outpouring to Emma comes in his letter of 25 January, which contains a sudden outburst against Fanny: 'Let her go to Bri[gh]ton or where she pleases, I care not; she is a great fool, and thank God! you are not in the least bit like her.'[52]

Then occurred the event that finally made up his mind. On 29 January, Emma gave birth to his child, a baby girl. He used a code in case letters were opened; he and Emma were to be called Mr and Mrs Thomson.* On 1 February, the day the *San Josef* sailed from Plymouth to Torbay, he wrote: 'I believe poor dear Mrs Thomson's friend will go mad with joy. He cries, prays, and performs all tricks, yet dare not show all or any of his feelings, but he has only me to consult with.'[53] Two days later: 'He hopes the time may not be far distant when he may be united for ever to the object of his wishes, his only, only love. He swears before heaven that he will marry you as soon as it is possible.'[54]

Fanny, meanwhile, now in Brighton, had received no reply to her letters to Nelson, although one had come from Sarah, the wife of William Nelson,

---

* A theory that Emma may have given birth to twins rests on an undated letter from Nelson to Emma printed in Morrison (II, 121): 'I daresay twins will again be the fruit of your and him [Thomson] meeting.' Morrison gives the date of this letter as 23 February 1801, without supporting evidence. However, the word 'twins' is by no means certain in the original letter (Clements, Smith Collection, n.d.). The word could be interpreted as 'theirs', which does not make immediate sense but then Nelson was not in a rational state when writing the letter. The idea that one child was given to the Foundling Hospital has recently been discounted (Edwards, 313–15; Pocock, 'Twins', 97).

to say that Lady Hamilton – 'her friend in Piccadilly' – had taken Sarah out to dinner. Fanny confided in Alexander Davison: 'I am certain some Mischief is brewing' and told him of how Emma had tried to hire one of her recent servants to be a butler to the Hamiltons and had mentioned the amount of the allowance that Nelson gave her. 'My housekeeper made some apologies for telling it to me, but as it was the talk of the kitchen she thought it was right for me to know it – none of us [I] believe like the servants to know our incomes. I can only say no Woman can feel the least attention from a husband more than I do.' Fanny had been further undermined by hearing from a third person of Nelson's opinion of her: 'he spoke of your <u>want</u> of <u>health</u>, your great dejection of spirits in short that you looked <u>miserable</u>.'[55]

Nelson was no more cheerful. 'It blows so hard,' he wrote to Emma, 'that I doubt if it will be possible to get a boat on shore, either to receive or send letters.' He was now redrafting his will in favour of Emma. Her next letters brought him news that the prince of Wales was coming to dinner. He wrote to her on 4 February, a letter suffused by violent and helpless jealousy. 'I know his aim is to have you for a mistress. The thought so agitates me that I cannot write. I had wrote a few lines last night, but I am in tears, I cannot bear it.'[56] The next day he instructed Emma to have the child christened at St George's, Hanover Square, choosing the name Horatia, with parents to be named (extraordinarily) as Johem and Morata Etnorb (Bronte spelt backwards). Horatia was cared for by a nurse, out of sight of society. Calmer, he wrote on 6 February, '<u>your letters are to me gazettes</u>, for as yet I have not fixed upon any, nor can they be half so interesting to my feelings,' putting forward further ideas for the christening. He also received a messenger with letters from Emma. 'Davison came while I was at dinner yesterday and gave me your letters. He says you are grown thinner, but he thinks you look handsomer than ever. I know he is a great admirer of yours. He says you told him to tell me not to send you any more advice about seeing company . . . I rest confident in your conduct.'[57]

On 10 February the 90-gun *St George* arrived in Torbay, a ship with three feet less draught than the *San Josef*. Spencer had decided Nelson would take her on the Baltic expedition, in which, as the first lord put it, he 'will do his part as the Champion of old England'.[58] The next day Nelson and his officers transferred to the smaller ship, in 'strong breezes from ESE and heavy swell'. For a week the ship lay in Torbay, with strong easterly gales. Topmasts were struck. Nelson found the ship, as he wrote to Emma, 'so completely uncomfortable you can have no conception how miserable she is'. For the most part he was isolated aboard: 'I am now of course very much by myself, for none ever come to me except at meals, or I send for either Hardy or [Edward Thornborough] Parker, and they are both so modest and well behaved that it is really a pleasure to have them aboard.'[59] He went ashore for two days, as the ship was 'neither wind nor water tight'.[60] It was an anxious, dangerous time, for easterly gales in Torbay put the ships on a lee shore: two cables were put on the anchor for safety. The wind later changed to the north-east, 'with snow at intervals, then continuous snow'.[61] Nelson reminded Emma: 'if a gale of wind comes from the East to South no boat can live in Torbay.'[62]

Still no orders came to move. Even Hyde Parker did not know what was happening, writing to Nelson, 'such is the uncertainty reigning in all departments . . . that I am as much in the dark as when your Lordship left town . . . as yet without a ship under my orders.'[63] In fact, there was more order in the Admiralty's method than was obvious to Parker. The minutes of the Board record for 12 February: 'Everything should be prepared but the Squadron should not assemble nor should any display of preparation be made till a very short time before it is to sail, that the expectation of it may not render the enemy more active in their preparations to resist it.' On 18 February, Nelson was finally ordered to Spithead.[64] From there he planned a short visit to London.[65]

This windy, freezing week at Torbay brought more strong words of frenzied jealousy and distrust of Emma, occasioned by a 'cruel' letter from her, which he burnt: 'you try to irritate me to say hard things, that you may have the pleasure of scolding me.' His eyes were not good. He drank 'nothing but water at dinner, and a little wine and water after dinner: I believe it has saved me from illness.'[66] He then discovered that the prince of Wales was, after all, to be entertained by the Hamiltons. On 18 February, Nelson wrote his most hysterically jealous letter yet. These letters were written with a violence that can still be discerned upon the page, with ink blots and words scratched out. 'I knew he would visit you . . . But his words are so charming that, I am told, no person can withstand them . . . Hush, hush, my poor heart, keep in my breast, be calm. Emma is true. But no-one, not even Emma, could resist the serpent's flattering tongue they all SAY and think, that Emma is like other women, when I would have killed anybody who had said so, must now hang my head and admit it . . . Tears have relieved me.'[67] The next day, 19 February, Nelson wrote five letters to Emma, all in the same vein.[68] 'I have been unwell all night, and horrid dreams . . . Sir Wm must be mad to attempt giving his wife the reputation of w[hor]e to the P[rince].'[69] The violence of his letters caused Emma to ask Sir William to reassure Nelson, which he did in a diplomatic letter on

19 February: 'I am well aware of the danger that would attend the Prince's frequenting our house . . . Emma would really have gone to any lengths to have avoided Sunday's dinner, but I thought it would not be prudent to break with the Prince.'[70] Sir William was trying hard to obtain a peerage and a pension through influencing the prince.

On the same day that Hamilton wrote this letter, Pitt's government fell and Spencer was replaced by St Vincent as first lord of the Admiralty. Thomas Troubridge became a junior lord of the Admiralty, which was to threaten his fragile friendship with Nelson and take their rivalry to new levels. 'Our friend Troubridge is to be a Lord of the Admiralty, and I have a sharp eye, and almost think I see it,' he commented to Emma, then saw advantage in the new situation. 'No, poor fellow, I hope I do him injustice; he cannot surely forget my kindness to him. When I am at sea I shall send my packets through him.'[71] Though Nelson had been on good terms with the previous administration, to have friends on the new board was to be a great advantage.

Nelson was in this state of panic-stricken despair about Emma when he received a letter from Fanny. She had heard from Josiah Nisbet (who had in turn been told by William Nelson) that Nelson's eye was inflamed: 'I offered to go to him and assured him he should find me an affec[tionate] Nurse,' she informed Davison.[72] She wrote on 20 February to Davison, in reply to a soothing letter from the agent; he had relayed to her the news that Nelson had spoken of her with affection. 'I hope in God all you say will prove true. My Mind has not yet recovered its Natural calmness – or do I think it ever will – I am now distrustful and fearful of my own shadow . . . My anxiety, My fondness for him all rushed <u>forth</u> . . . and offered to nurse him and that he should find me the same I had ever been to him faithful, affec[tionate] and desirous to do everything I could to please him . . . to this letter I have had no reply.'[73]

On 21 February the wind swung round to the north-west and the *St George* sailed up the Channel to Spithead in 'thick, foggy weather with rain'.[74] Once there he wrote to the Admiralty requesting three days' leave to go to London, which was immediately granted.[75] He also replied to Fanny with a letter of savage finality: now that her allowance of £400 a quarter had been arranged, she should keep away. It contained not a line of regret or explanation. As Fanny explained to Davison: 'You may surmise the consternation it threw me into: I own I never allowed myself to think any change was wrought in my favour, but I was willing [and] desirous to shew every attention which affection dictated.'[76] Bitterness and spite were welling up. Emma Hamilton used the cruel nickname for Fanny, 'Tom Tit', in a letter to Sarah Nelson. She and William Nelson placed themselves quickly in Emma's camp and were the first of Nelson's immediate family to abandon Fanny.* When Nelson reached London on 24 February, he wrote another letter to Fanny – 'upon the whole rather milder', she thought – repeating his desire that she keep away from London or Portsmouth.[77] 'Tom Tit does not come to town,' Emma wrote in triumph; 'she only wanted to go to do mischief.'[78] To Davison, Fanny wrote in bewilderment: 'Indeed, I shall never volunteer my nursing abilities again,' and she asked his advice: 'tell me honestly if you think silence is the best way, sometimes to answer harsh & severe letters undeserved.'[79]

Nelson's stay in London was brief, unrecorded by the press. He saw the Hamiltons and Horatia. It is likely he called at the Admiralty. He met Josiah Nisbet, for whom he tried to obtain a command. Nisbet received a warm welcome from Nelson. 'My Josiah is perfectly astonished,' Fanny related to Davison: 'when he returned from seeing my dear deluded Lord he told me he received him in the most affectionate manner, desiring him to be as much with him as he could – breakfast with me and I will get you a dinner wherever I dine – "Ah," said Josiah, "I told you all would be well, he has the best of hearts." ' This was the only crumb of comfort that Fanny could extract from the situation. She now thought of returning to London to give, as she put it to Davison, 'Miss Locker an opportunity of returning to some of her more cheerful acquaintances.'[80]

On his return to Spithead, Nelson wrote to Emma: 'Parting from such a friend is literally tearing one's own flesh; but the remembrance will keep up our spirits till we meet.'[81] On 1 March he wrote her three lengthy letters. In the first he refers to having been to a party with Emma. 'Would to God I had dined alone with you. What a desert we would have had.'[82] By the third of his letters, written at nine at night, he started dreaming of what might be: 'Now, my own dear wife, for such as you are in my eyes and in the face of heaven . . . I love, I never did love any one else. I never had a dear pledge of love till you gave me one, and you, thank my God, never gave to any body else . . . I burn all your dear letters, because it is right for your sake, and I wish you would burn all mine – they can do no good, and will do us both harm . . . My longing for you, both person and conversation, you may readily imagine. What must be my sensations at the idea of sleeping with you! It setts me on fire . . . I am sure my love & desires are all to you,

---

* Before Nelson left for the Baltic, he arranged for Sarah Nelson to go to London to look after Emma – and possibly to chaperone her – at his expense (Naish, 577, 581, 20 Feb., 7 Mar. 1801).

and if any woman naked were to come to me, even as I am this moment from thinking of you, I hope it might rot off if I would touch her even with my hand.'[83]

The next day the feeling of elation had gone. Emma had received a letter from Troubridge that had upset her. 'Damn all those who would make you false, but I know you will be true and faithful.' He again railed against the prince of Wales: 'if ever the Damned fellow is admitted into your Company then your Nelson is rejected.'[84] With the same feeling of dejection he wrote to St Vincent, as the *St George* was getting under sail, suggesting that this expedition would be his last service for the navy. St Vincent wrote back, 'appal'd . . . for God's sake do not suffer yourself to be carried away by any sudden impulse.'[85]

While anchored in the Downs, three days later, Nelson wrote a final, formal letter to Fanny at Brighton. He had done all he could for Nisbet, 'with little thanks from him . . . and he may again as he has often done before wish me to break my neck . . . therefore my only wish is to be left to myself and wishing you every happiness, believe me that I am your affectionate Nelson and Bronte.'[86] It was a short note, which, apart from the flash of bitterness about Josiah, betrays no feeling, not even anger. It reads like a sailing order. 'This is my Lord Nelson's letter of dismissal, which so astonished me that I immediately sent it to Mr Maurice Nelson . . . he desired me not to take the least notice of it, as his brother seems to have forgot himself.' (She endorsed it only much later, after receiving it back from Maurice Nelson.) Susannah Bolton also could not believe what had happened, writing to Fanny: 'Your conduct . . . is exemplary in regard to him & he has not an unfeeling heart. I sincerely love my Brother & did quite as Much before he was Lord Nelson & I hope my Conduct will ever be the same towards you as Mrs Nelson. I hope in God I shall have the pleasure of seeing you together as ever. He certainly as far as I hear is not a happy man.'[87] George Matcham too had kind words for her: 'We have seen nothing of the gay world . . . You must pay us charitable visits.'[88] Betsey Fremantle wrote in her diary: 'Lady Nelson is sueing for a separate maintenance. I have no patience with her husband, at his age and such a cripple to play the fool with Lady Hamilton.'[89]

On 5 March the *St George* sailed north from the Downs beating into a north-westerly wind, anchoring in the Yarmouth Roads two days later. The ship saluted Vice-Admiral Sir Hyde Parker flying his flag in the 90-gun *London*. Other ships joined, including the *Ganges* captained by Thomas Fremantle. Speed in getting the squadron to Copenhagen was now critical. Sir Hyde, as lackadaisical as in his Mediterranean days, seemed in no hurry to leave. The 61-year-old admiral had recently married a young bride of twenty-four; the newspapers sniggered, calling the new Lady Parker the admiral's 'sheet anchor'.[90] A ball to mark the departure of the squadron was arranged. Fremantle, even though he was a protégé of Parker, was critical, writing to his brother that he had dined with the vice-admiral, but 'until My Lady goes away I don't think we shall make much progress. They get up too late and all business in consequence is much delayed.' He felt that Parker was 'mortified at being tricked out of the Command of the Western Squadron'. Nor did Fremantle feel that everything was as well as might be on the flagship. 'The Captain of the Fleet [William Domett] is a very clever, intelligent Man but cannot act without directions and confidence. Sir H and he have never sailed together and it appears to me there is not that sort of communication between them so essential to the good of our Service.'[91]

Nor did Parker communicate with Nelson, who commented darkly in a letter to Davison: 'Sir H is on board sulky . . . his treatment of me is now noticed. I declare solemnly that I do not know I am going to the Baltic, and much worse than that I can tell you . . . Burn this letter.'[92] Nelson decided on action and told Fremantle, who wrote to his brother that Nelson 'will certainly determine Sr H. Nelson breakfasts at 7, anxious to sail immediately.'[93] Nelson wrote immediately to St Vincent on the lack of progress, but St Vincent did not approve, rightly, of more junior officers writing to the Board of Admiralty.[94] Troubridge warned Nelson not to write to the first lord, so Nelson wrote to Troubridge instead, with barely concealed sarcasm: 'I know, my dear Troubridge, how angry the earl would be if he knew I, as second in command, was to venture to give an opinion, because I know his opinion on officers writing to the admiralty. But what I say is in the mouth of all the old market-women at Yarmouth . . . Consider how nice it must be lying abed with a young wife, compared to a damned raw cold wind.' He added as a postscript: 'The *London* moving into a more commodious berth. The lady cannot go on board this nasty weather.'[95] Two months later Lady Malmesbury shrewdly commented to Lord Minto: 'no wise man would ever have gone with Nelson or over him, as he was sure to be in the background in every case.'[96]

Perhaps domestic jealousy accounted for professional sarcasm. Still Nelson could find no peace of mind. His letters to Emma now were becoming self-pitying as well as angry. The prince of Wales still troubled him, the language of his letters was still violent: 'never meet or stay if any damned whore or pimp bring that fellow to you.' The prize-money case with St Vincent was unfair and the case stacked against him. The next day he wrote: 'Your letters today have made me miserable . . . Good night, I am more dead than alive.'[97] His brother William visited the ship, as Nelson told Emma, 'so prying that I have been almost obliged to scold him'.[98] Two days later he was convinced of the machinations of William Hamilton: 'I see clearly, my dear friend, you are on SALE. I am almost mad to think of the iniquity of wanting you to associate with a set of whores, bawds, & unprincipled lyars. Can this be the great Sir William Hamilton?'[99] His jealousy and ill-humour were unabated.

St Vincent was told by Troubridge of Hyde Parker's delay and the reasons for it. The first lord wrote Parker a letter that was friendly in tone but menacing in intent: 'I have heard by a side wind that you have an intention of continuing at Yarmouth till Friday, on account of some trifling circumstances . . . I have, however, upon a consideration of the effect your continuance at Yarmouth an hour after the wind . . . sent down a messenger purposely to convey to you my opinion, as a private friend, that any delay in your sailing would do you irreparable injury.'[100] Nelson wrote gleefully to Troubridge: 'Now we can have no desire for staying, for her ladyship is gone, and the ball for Friday night knocked up by your and the earl's unpoliteness to send gentlemen to sea instead of dancing with nice white gloves.'[101] The squadron unmoored at dawn and sailed on 13 March.[102]

One of Nelson's last, depressed letters was to his agent William Marsh on the prize-money case with St Vincent. He repeated words that he had written to Emma the day before. It was 'enough to make a Dog sick, as to my Cause. I have only Justice & the Custom of the Service on my Side, agt. Me, Power, Partiality Money and Lies, this may carry it, scandal to the Country if it does. I blush for the party.' He added: 'Pray do not forget to send Lady Nelson her £400.'[103]

22

Copenhagen
March–2 April 1801

*His Lordship . . . made the most daring attack that has been attempted
this war (the Nile not excepted) . . .*
                Thomas Masterman Hardy to John Manfield, 5 April 1801[1]

*The nature of the battle of 2nd is I believe unparalleled in history, &
for enterprise & difficulties as well as the length of the contest (for we
were five hours in one incessant roar of cannon) infinitely superior to
the famous action of Aboukir . . . all our fleet engaged at Anchor by
the Stern, in the Nile stile . . .*
                Colonel William Stewart to Colonel Sir William Clinton,
                                                        6 April 1801[2]

The British government had been swift and effective in organizing a powerful squadron for the expedition against Denmark and Russia, and possibly
Sweden. Together these countries' fleets represented a considerable threat,
ninety-six ships of the line, at least on paper.[3] The crisis came at the same
time as two difficult political problems. On 19 February 1801, after eighteen
years in power, William Pitt resigned over the question of Catholic Emancipation, a measure to which George III could not agree. The king also fell
gravely ill in March, which delayed the swearing in of Henry Addington's
administration. But preparations and the issuing of orders for an expedition
to the Baltic did not falter. The objectives of the expedition required careful
drafting, for the destruction of the fleets of the northern powers was not
intended, as permanent alienation of the countries that provided the hemp,
timber and iron upon which British naval power depended had to be
avoided. Henry Dundas, the outgoing secretary for war, emphasized to
Evan Nepean, secretary of the Admiralty, that 'in our Baltick operations we
stand in a different predicament from what we do in every other. In others
we are upon the defensive and our force will be successful if we are able to

cripple the efforts of our enemy so as to baffle their hostile attempts, but in the Baltick we must act with vigor in the <u>Offensive</u>, for it is on such an exertion that the whole contest turns.'[4] Diplomacy with force was required.

The king, however, was determined that negotiations should succeed – the crown prince was after all his nephew – and that only in the last resort should force be used.[5] Lord Hawkesbury, the new foreign secretary, put it bluntly in a letter to Nicholas Vansittart, sent to Denmark as a special plenipotentiary: 'It cannot be expected that His Majesty's fleet shall proceed into the Baltic leaving the armament behind and depending for security against its possible hostility on no better ground than that of signature of such a Treaty . . . The Danish Armament must either be reduced or it must be rendered decidedly and actively friendly or it must be destroyed. The last of these is the mode to which His Majesty would be least willing to have recourse.'[6] Under these orders, Vansittart's task of coming to a last-minute accommodation with the Danes was almost impossible. Henry Dundas had stayed in office after Pitt had stepped down to issue the king's objectives to the Admiralty, which he did on 23 February. It was impossible to destroy shipping 'without exposing that City also to great damage . . . there is nothing His Majesty would have more at heart than to prevent its calamities being thus extended to the destruction and injury of unoffending individuals . . . that no injuries or damage whatever will be done to the town' if shipping was delivered up to the Fleet; but, if this demand was refused, to continue the operation 'without regard to the preservation of the Town'.[7] These confusing orders from king and government were to be important in determining the endgame of the coming battle.

Vansittart arrived in Copenhagen on 9 March to find that relations were so bad that communication had ceased between the Danish government and William Drummond, the British minister. Long discussions nevertheless took place, but the two nations were far apart on the question of the embargo placed on Danish ships, the rights of neutral ships, the state and significance of the Northern Convention and the influence of France and Russia. Diplomats alone were not going to make progress, and the talks broke up on 16 March.[8]

Final instructions to the Admiralty were not issued by Dundas until 14 March, the day after Parker's fleet had sailed from Yarmouth, and were hurried after them. If Denmark did not withdraw from the convention, Parker was to destroy the Danish fleet and dockyards.[9] After Copenhagen, Parker was 'to proceed to Reval . . . to make an immediate and vigorous attack upon the same . . . and to proceed successively and as the Season and other Operations will permit against Cronstadt . . . and to capture or destroy ships of war or other belonging to Russia wherever he can meet with them'.[10] Sweden was seen as less of a danger, partly through a well-founded report from Karlskrona of 'the despicable condition of the Swedish Navy'.[11] Sweden, as ever, was afraid of Russia, and Parker was 'to afford to Sweden every protection in his power against the resentment and Attacks of Russia'.[12]

Communications between the government departments had improved since the friction in 1798 before the Nile, and intelligence was flowing freely between them: every piece of information pointed to the need for speed. The Danes were far from ready to resist an attack on Copenhagen, not least because a third of seamen of the Danish fleet were Norwegians, who, because of the ice, could not sail for Copenhagen before April or May. In mid February intelligence was received by the Admiralty through the Foreign Office from the consul in Khristiansand: 'Le Prince Royal précipité toute et rien n'est prêt' [The Prince Royal hurries everything and nothing is ready], while the Danish Count Louvendale was travelling to the tsar of Russia: 'le Secrétaire Prussian assure qu'il sera bien reçu' [the Prussian Secretary is bound to receive him well].[13] Frederick Thesiger and Richard Cadman Etches, who had been in Russian service, provided information and charts, and Thesiger was assigned to the fleet.[14] Etches – described by Vansittart to Nelson as 'the most active & intelligent adventurer I ever met with – immediately set out to find out the state of the Russian fleet.[15] Etches's advice to Evan Nepean was to set off as soon as possible, for both the Russians and Danes 'completely dismantle their fleets for the Winter'.[16] The melting of the Baltic ice also imparted urgency, for the sooner it melted the sooner the fleets of the Northern powers could join into a formidable combined force. Dundas informed the Admiralty that the 'navigation of the Baltic will be open some weeks earlier than usual'.[17] Another useful source of local knowledge was Nicolas Tomlinson, who had been a captain in both the British and Russian navies and sailed with Hyde Parker on board the flagship. He was optimistic about the vulnerability of Reval (Tallinn) and the state of the Russian fleet, reminding Evan Nepean on 5 February in his 'Plan for Destroying the Russian–Danish Fleets 1801' that 'the ice is rotten and spongy in the Spring of the year, there is no danger, as in the Autumn, of its hurting or cutting the ships' bows.'[18]

Relations between Parker and Nelson were also frosty after the fleet sailed from Yarmouth, demonstrated by the barely suppressed indignation of Nelson's frequent letters to Troubridge in London. On 16 March, as the squadron neared Denmark, he wrote: 'I am yet in the dark, and am not sure we are bound to the Baltic.'[19] Parker gave orders for sailing and battle order, irritating Nelson by giving him weaker ships. Nine ships of the line, including the *London* and the *St George* (both 90s), five 64s and a host of smaller ships – fifty-six in all – set off.[20] Because of the hasty departure others had not yet arrived at the rendezvous at Yarmouth, and Parker left orders that the latecomers should join the fleet off the Slaw. They sailed north-east, with the wind in the north-west, '74s taking the bad sailing Gun brigs in tow', as Nelson noted in the journal that he kept in a very rough form until mid May.[21]

Nelson was again miserable, still tortured by jealousy over Emma and the prince of Wales. On 17 March he wrote with almost an hysterical force to her:

I dreamt last night that I beat you with a Stick on account of that fellow & then attempted to throw over [your] head a tub of Boiling hot Water, you may believe I woke in an agony and that my feelings cannot be very comfortable. I have no communication yet with my commander in chief. Lord Spencer placed him here & [he] has completely thrown me in the background . . . I guess that Lord St Vt. Recommended Sir HP in the strongest manner, because he wanted to get rid of him, they all hate me and treat me ill.[22]

He also worried about the prize-money case with St Vincent, which was coming to court.[23]

The weather worsened. Thomas Fremantle commanded one of the 74s, the *Ganges*. He wrote to his wife, Betsey: 'We have since we sailed experienced a second winter; it has snowed every day since; the ship's company are hacking from morning to night with coughs.'[24] Nelson noted critically on the second day out: 'The Fleet in general kept very badly their stations for altho' the Commander in Chief made the signal for close sailing yet scarcely one have kept their stations particularly the good going ships.' The wind increased and went to the north-east. By 15 March he noted: 'Fresh gales easterly with snow . . . Fleet scattered . . . *St George* the only ship in her station.'[25] By 15 March, Nelson counted only forty-eight ships in sight at noon.

The weather allowed little contact between Parker and Nelson. One of his young officers, William Layman, recalled later that at this point Nelson made a gesture towards the commander-in-chief when seamen in the *St George* caught a small turbot. Nelson, mindful of Sir Hyde's fondness for good living, had it rowed across to the flagship. Between the sleet and snow Nelson received a note from Parker telling him 'a little of his intentions'.[26] On 17 March, Parker sent the *Blanche* frigate to Elsinore with the dispatches containing the British government's latest ultimatum.[27]

By 19 March the *St George* passed the Skaw to turn south into the Kattegat. The weather improved finally and Nelson went on board the *London* to pay his compliments to Parker.[28] But on the 20th the wind increased and went round to the south-west. The squadron withdrew into the lee of the point known as the 'Kole' (today called Point Kullen) in the bay of Skälderviken, where they stayed for two days.[29] By 21 March only thirty-eight ships of the fleet were in sight, with many of the smaller bomb vessels and fire ships still to catch up with the main fleet.[30] Nelson noted in his journal with distaste: 'The swell as at Torbay.'[31] The wind blew hard enough for the yards of the *St George* to be struck. 'Much snow and ice about our rigging. I find it very sharp,' Nelson remarked in a letter to Troubridge.[32]

Hyde Parker and Nelson now debated which of two approaches to Danish waters was best: by the Sound past Copenhagen or through the Great Belt. It was not an easy decision. The new first lord of the Admiralty wrote a worried letter to Evan Nepean: 'if Parker passes the Belt, he certainly abandons Copenhagen. I fear he has not consulted Nelson; the plan should have been formed before he left Yarmouth, and the orders for carrying it into execution circulated the first favourable day after his departure from thence ... Should he proceed to Reval, the Swedes and Danes will unite their force, and occupy the Sound completely.'[33] Yet Parker undoubtedly faced difficulties. Information on the preparedness of the Danes was difficult to obtain. The timing and direction of a northerly wind for a southerly course down the Sound and Belt was critical. A southerly wind would then be needed in both cases to approach Copenhagen. Among those on board the flagship analysing intelligence was the Reverend A. J. Scott, who was rapidly learning Danish. He wrote to his uncle in England that 'we have certainly arrived here at least a fortnight before we were expected' and that most of the Danish warships were still in harbour. However, the three Crowns (Trekroner) islands, 'artificially formed and constructed ... are represented to be wonderfully strong. I believe however their chief strength consists in being almost surrounded by shoal water.'[34] He concluded: 'I fear there is a great deal of Quixotism in this business: there is no getting any positive information of their strength.'[35] These considerations may have contributed to Parker's lack of resolve throughout the next ten days.[36]

No one in the British fleet, least of all the pilots from merchant ships on board, was confident of the waters, for these large warships needed a depth of water far greater than that required by the merchantmen that usually navigated the Sound. In 1800 the Danish Navy had published an English translation of 'sailing Directions' for the Kattegat, but it contained few details on the Sound, beyond the fact that anchoring was safe: 'the Bottom being clear and good, it is safe enough for such Vessels that are provided with good Anchors and Cables, you may anchor almost every where you please.'[37] Parker had worked hard before he left Yarmouth to obtain the best chart from London, which he considered to be Lord Mulgrave's; nevertheless the *London* grounded hard on an unmarked shoal near Anholt Island in the Kattegat 'with only nineteen feet of water on it'.[38] Nelson sounded his way past it successfully.[39]

On 22 March the squadron worked their way south across the entrance to the Sound to anchor in the evening within sight of Kronborg Castle by Elsinore, which Nelson had visited on convoy duty twenty years before. On 23 March the *Blanche* returned to the squadron: further negotiation had been refused by the Danes. The diplomats had seen the Danish preparations for defences in Copenhagen and brought back gloomy news. Thomas Fremantle wrote to his brother: 'The Enemy have moved floating batteries all along the bank opposite to Copenhagen, and have likewise three Sail of the Line and two frigates at the Entrance to the harbour. All is determined War and we are waiting for a change of Wind to pass the Castle, I suppose . . . but I think from the disposition of Sir Hyde something will be attempted.'[40]

During 23 March the wind came round to the north-west. Only with this wind could the slow bomb and gun vessels catch up with the rest of the squadron, for they had become separated from the main fleet in the Kattegat; little in the way of bombardment of Copenhagen could be done without them.[41] Nelson conferred with Hyde Parker and Nicholas Vansittart, a conversation which he noted, but it was 'too import[ant] to be put [in this] journal'.[42] It seems clear from subsequent correspondence that at this meeting Parker wanted to wait for the Danish fleet to appear outside the Sound, which it would hardly have done, and Nelson later described this decision as 'a measure . . . disgraceful to our Country'. Nelson put forward the view that the tsar 'was the Enemy most vulnerable, and of the greatest consequence for us to humble'.[43] It was an important meeting and during it Parker's mind was changed, with Nelson gaining ascendancy over the senior officer. That day Parker wrote to the Admiralty that he wanted to go to Reval first to deal with the Russians before returning to Copenhagen because of 'the formidable disposition of Copenhagen'.[44] What was agreed between the three men was important enough for Vansittart to report it

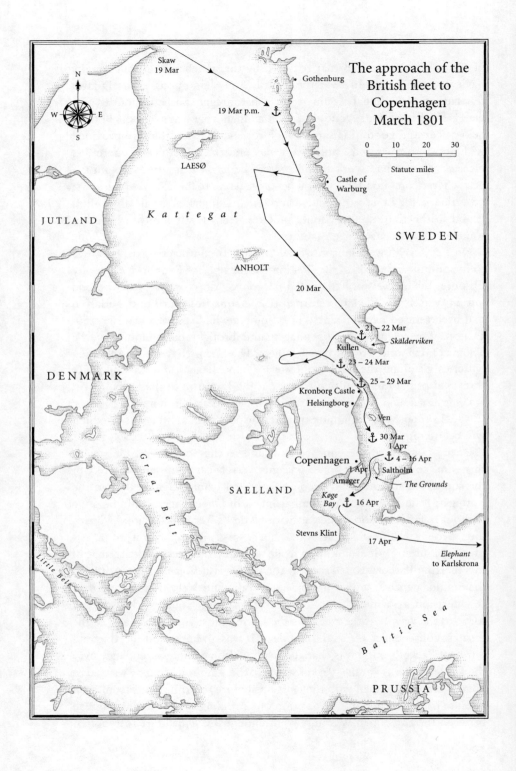

The approach of the
British fleet to
Copenhagen
March 1801

Statute miles
0   10   20   30

N
W   E
S

Skaw
19 Mar

Gothenburg

19 Mar p.m.

LAESØ

Castle of
Warburg

JUTLAND

Kattegat

SWEDEN

ANHOLT

20 Mar

21 – 22 Mar
Kullen   *Skälderviken*

23 – 24 Mar

DENMARK

25 – 29 Mar

Kronborg Castle
Helsingborg

Ven

30 Mar
1 Apr

Copenhagen   4   16 Apr
1 Apr   Saltholm

Amager   *The Grounds*

SAELLAND

*Køge
Bay*   16 Apr

Stevns Klint   17 Apr

Great Belt

Little Belt

Elephant
to Karlskrona

Baltic Sea

PRUSSIA

directly to the prime minister on his return, for the diplomat sailed in the *Kite* cutter to England immediately after the meeting.[45] Vansittart later reported to Nelson that Addington had been 'fully satisfied with the propriety of your advice & of Sir Hyde Parker's ultimate resolution, & that he considered your readiness to take on yourself the responsibility attaching on a deviation from your instructions, as not the least eminent among the service which you have rendered your country in so many years of glory.'[46]

The next day, 24 March, the wind was strong but favourable for going through the Sound. Hyde Parker still hesitated. He had been losing sleep through anxiety.[47] Nelson calmly observed in his journal that it was 'very squally all the afternoon but my Barometer rose very much, in the evening very fine'.[48] We now know that on 24 March the Danish defence was only half prepared; just seven of the eighteen Danish defence vessels were anchored in the King's Deep, while the others were still being warped into position.[49] The diplomats, particularly William Drummond, had been unduly pessimistic, and Parker did not seek intelligence from elsewhere.[50] That day Nelson met with Parker and read him a memorandum that he had drafted: 'Not a moment should be lost in attacking the Enemy, they will every day and hour be stronger . . . By Mr Vansittart's account, their state of preparation exceeds what he [Vansittart] conceives our Government thought possible.' He reviewed both routes with a masterly analysis, emphasizing the importance of destroying the Russian fleet, which he felt was the paramount objective; both Sound and Belt had their advantages and their risks, but, whatever happened, action had to take place immediately.[51] The 24th was a wasted opportunity. Had Parker sailed south through the Sound to anchor off Copenhagen at this time, a distance of under thirty miles, the city would have been defenceless.

Instead, Parker decided for the Great Belt. He had had the masters of four ships, including Thomas Atkinson of the *St George*, briefly survey the Belt in the *Kite*; they found the charts accurate.[52] On 25 March the squadron set off to the west, with the *Edgar* leading, commanded by George Murray, who had experience of this passage. The young Captain Robert Otway of the *London* then persuaded the commander-in-chief that he was not going to get through the Belt. The fleet was ordered to heave to, and Otway was sent on board the *St George* with a note to Nelson from Parker: 'having seriously reflected on our Plan of going up the Belt I find many reasons against the Idea'. He went on to invite Nelson on board the flagship for a further conference.[53] From Otway's recollection Nelson exclaimed: 'I don't care a d—n by which passage we go, so that we fight them.'[54] Nelson noted: 'Sir Hyde told me he was uneasy about going by the belt in case of accidents and therefore he thought of going by Cronenburg [Kronborg] to which I cordially assented ... and the fleet was tacked.'[55] Parker wrote to Nepean later: 'the want of Pilots in so intricate a Navigation with such a considerable Fleet ... determined me on the passage to the Sound.'[56] Fremantle commented to Betsey: 'as you may imagine there is a great diversity of opinion'.[57]

A decision to risk the Sound was now taken, with Nelson to command the attack against the city with lighter draft ships.* The objective of the attack was to gain command of the King's Deep, the channel that flowed alongside the city of Copenhagen and its dockyard. Once control had been gained, the bomb vessels could be positioned within range to bombard the city and the dockyard.[58] Any coolness between Parker and Nelson disappeared from the time of this decision.[59] Parker wrote to his wife: 'I must do his Lordship the Justice to say no man can have given stronger proof of Friendship than he has done in the very intricate business I have to do with.'[60]

The squadron sailed back to the Sound slightly to the south of the previous night's anchorage. Then the wind went to the south. Between 25 and 29 March the wind varied between SW and WSW, making the Sound impassable, giving the Danes vital time to man and organize their defences.[61] In the British fleet, battle preparations started in earnest. Nelson issued detailed orders to prepare to anchor by the stern, as at the Nile, with the cable led out through a stern port and back to the anchor at the bow; three ships had missed their station at the Nile, and captains were to take 'care to have that anchor hanging by the stopper only, as great precision is necessary in placing the ships'.[62] The *Elephant*'s log recorded: 'Hoisted out flat-bottomed boats, exercised them and sealed their guns & hoisted them in again.'[63] Nelson spent a day 'arranging and explaining to the different officers the intended mode of attack'. He noted in his journal: 'very unwell all day.'[64] On 27 March, while they waited for a favourable wind, Nelson transferred his flag from the *St George* to the smaller and more manoeuvrable 74-gun *Elephant*, a latecomer to the fleet that had not joined until 18 March.[65] She had fifteen inches less draft than the *St George*. Her captain

---

* When anchored off the Kole between 27 and 29 April in high winds, Nelson took a considerable risk in going aboard the *London* to go to the meeting with Hyde Parker when this was decided. 'The captain expressed a doubt of his lordship's being able, with the sea that was running, and having but one arm, to get into the boat. "But I am determined I will go," said Nelson. "Then," said Hardy, "I must put you into the boat as she lays on the booms, and hoist you out in her." This was accordingly done, with every proper and seaman-like precaution' (Brenton, II, 41).

was the quiet Welshman Thomas Foley, who had been first into Aboukir Bay less than three years before. 'Foley is very good to me,' Nelson wrote to Emma.[66] The same day he noted with satisfaction in his journal: 'Some vessels came through the Sound who report Consternation & Confusion at Copenhagen.'[67]

Parker meanwhile negotiated with the governor of Kronborg Castle, which dominated the Elsinore Passage, at that point only two miles wide. He made it clear that if the guns of the castle fired upon the British, it would amount to a declaration of war. The governor delayed and sent to Copenhagen for instructions. On 29 March, Parker informed Nelson: 'The enclosed note indicates a clear determination to oppose our Entrance into the Sound.'[68] On the morning of 30 March the log of the *Elephant* reads: 'At ½ past 5 weighed & made sail past Cronberg Castle. Danes opened heavy fire on the Fleet which had no effect and the Bombs of the Squadron returned their fire.'[69] Nelson noted: 'form[e]d our line steered our course ⅔ over towards the Swedish shore.'[70] Tomlinson reported that the ships ran down the Sound 'not three quarters of a mile from the Swedish shore; yet the generality of the shot from Cronberg Castle fell a quarter of a mile short.'[71] Boldness had paid off. The old distrust between the Danes and the Swedes led the Swedes to hold their fire.[72] Nelson wrote to Emma with relief that night: 'We this morning passed the fancied tremendous fortress of Cronenburg mounted with 270 pieces of cannon. More powder and shot, I believe, never were thrown away, for not one shot struck a single ship of the British fleet. Some of our ships fired; but the *Elephant* did not return a single shot.'[73]

The *Elephant*'s log continues: 'About 10 Anchored in 7 fath. Copenhagen Palace SW 1/2 W, Heren Island NNE. Passed the Sheet Cable out of the Larboard Stern port and bent it onto the anchor.' Foley followed the routine used at the Nile. 'The Commander in Chief & Lord Nelson went onboard the *Amazon* to reconnoitre.'[74] The land around Copenhagen is low and the fortifications are very difficult to discern from seaward. The current flowed north, strengthened at this time of the year by melting ice. To Emma he wrote comfortingly, 'It looks formidable to those who are children at war, but to my judgement, with ten sail of the line, I think I can annihilate them; at all events I hope to be allowed to try.'[75] Any doubts among the Danish defenders about British intentions were disappearing, as they anchored the last of their ships of the line, blockships and floating batteries in a line parallel to the shore.[76] The crews, many of them volunteers and pressed men, were given hurried instruction in gunnery drill.[77]

The British fleet now formed two divisions. Hyde Parker kept the larger ships, the *London* and the *St George*, although the latter's captain, Thomas Masterman Hardy, came aboard the *Elephant* as a volunteer. The rest of Parker's squadron consisted of four 74s – the *Warrior*, the *Defence*, the *Saturn* and the *Ramillies* – and two 64s – the *Raisonable* and the *Veteran*. With Nelson's *Elephant* were six other 74s: the *Defiance* (Rear-Admiral Thomas Graves), the *Ganges* (Captain Thomas Fremantle), the *Edgar* (George Murray), the *Bellona* (Thomas Boulden Thompson), the *Russell* (William Cuming), the *Monarch* (James Mosse). He also had three 64s, including his old ship the *Agamemnon* (Robert Fancourt), the *Ardent* (Thomas Bertie) and the *Polyphemus* (John Lawford). William Bligh commanded a curiously armed 54-gun ship called the *Glatton*, and the 50-gun *Isis* was captained by James Walker. Of the five frigates, Edward Riou's *Amazon* (38), Graham Eden Hamond's *Blanche* (36), and Samuel Sutton's *Alcmene* (32) were to distinguish themselves. One of the four sloops was commanded by Nelson's kinsman William Bolton. His powerful squadron was completed by seven crucial bomb vessels and two fire ships, as well as gun brigs and cutters.[78]

Nelson did not know his second-in-command, Thomas Graves, promoted to rear-admiral only in January, whose flag was in the *Defiance*; but several of his captains, Foley, Thompson, Fremantle and Murray, were old friends.[79] He had sailed with Thomas Bertie of the *Ardent* nearly thirty years before as a midshipman in the *Seahorse*. William Bligh, well known as captain of the *Bounty* at the time of the mutiny, commanded the *Glatton*, an adapted East Indiaman entirely fitted with 42- and 68-pound carronades. She was also equipped with 'carcasses', incendiary projectiles, which she was to use with some effect in the coming battle.[80] Nelson admired neither the *Ardent* nor the *Glatton*, 'for they sail so very heavy, that no rapid movement could be made with them in the Line or Order of Sailing'.[81] The *Agamemnon* was commanded by Robert Fancourt, who passed as lieutenant in the same year as Nelson but was not made captain until twelve years after him. In the short time Nelson knew Edward Riou, who captained the *Amazon*, he came to admire his seamanship, and he later became close with the captain of the *Alcmene*, Samuel Sutton. It was a team with more than its share of energy and resolution. Nelson wrote to Prince William Henry (now the duke of Clarence) after the battle: 'It was my good fortune to Command such a very distinguish'd sett of fine Fellows.'[82]

Before the Nile, Nelson had had months to build up confidence and understanding among the captains of his squadron: now he had hours. The night of 30 March was spent in surveying the Hollander Deep outside the Middle Ground and replacing the buoys that the Danes had removed.

The next day Hyde Parker called a council of war. Nelson brought only those captains whom he knew well, in addition to Graves as rear-admiral. Also present was Colonel Stewart, who commanded the riflemen taken aboard the *St George* at Spithead.[83] According to Stewart, Nelson exuded confidence, aggression and a disdain for the capabilities of the Swedish and Russian navies, which he called 'the total want of tactique among the Northern Fleets'. 'The energy of Lord Nelson's character was remarked,' the colonel recalled; '[he] kept pacing the cabin, mortified at everything which savoured either of alarm or irresolution.'[84] From this meeting Nelson rapidly issued his instructions, a model of precision at the same time as allowing flexibility. The van was to be led by the *Edgar*, the *Ardent*, the *Glatton*, the *Isis* and the *Agamemnon*. They were to anchor, firing on the enemy ships as they went down the line. They were to be followed by the *Bellona*, the *Elephant*, the *Ganges*, the *Monarch*, the *Defiance*, the *Russell* and the *Polyphemus*. Each Danish vessel, whether ship of the line or floating battery, was identified and matched by a British ship of equal strength, which would anchor opposite her opponent.[85] Gun boats and bomb vessels would remain at a distance.

Off Copenhagen the last of the line of Danish defensive ships was being moored in the King's Deep as the British ships came in sight. Only one of the eighteen Danish ships was a 74: another was a 64 and the rest were a mixture of much smaller vessels, some of them little more than floating batteries. The sizes of the guns were similarly varied, most of them 24-pounders, but some of them 36-pounders. Many of the vessels had no masts, which was to make them difficult targets from a distance. The ships positioned from the southern part of the line were the *Prøvestenen* (56), the *Wagrien* (48), the *Rendsborg* (20), the *Nyborg* (20), the *Jylland* (48), the *Sværdfisken* (20), the *Kronborg* (22), the *Hajen* (20), the *Elven* (6), the *Dannebrog* (62) and the *Sjælland* (74), the Danish flagship commanded by Commodore Olfert Fischer, who had command of the main part of the Danish line. To the north of the flagship was the *Charlotte Amalie* (26), the *Søhesten* (18), the *Infødsretten* (64) and the *Hjælperen* (20), which were just to the east of the Trekroner Fort, the Danes' most powerful defensive position.[86] A further seven ships were the other side of the fort to guard the entrance into the dockyard; they were not to play a part in the battle. Commodore Fischer was well aware that his stationary ships were easy targets for Nelson, who could repeat the tactics of the Nile by doubling his line; furthermore, as he explained well before the battle to the Danish Defence Commission, 'the enemy only has to destroy one or more ships in the line and then expose the others to raking fire.' He knew that his countrymen would fight bravely, but he did not expect to repel the British squadron.[87]

On 1 April the British fleet sailed south down the Sound on the north-westerly wind, anchoring five miles to the north of the Middle Ground, the shoal that was to dominate so much of the coming battle. That night, boats from the squadron again buoyed the Hollander Deep; they completed the task by 1.30 the next day. After a further consultation 'with a few chosen friends' on board the *Amazon*, Nelson returned at one o'clock to the *Elephant*. As he passed each ship, he shouted instructions. Midshipman W. S. Millard recorded in his diary: 'a squeaky little voice hailed the *Monarch* and desired us, in true Norfolk drawl, to prepare to weigh.'[88] At 2.30 p.m. Nelson's ships came southward against the northward current of between one and two knots, the same stream that was to keep Parker's ships out of the next day's battle.[89] Parker did in fact signal three 74s, the *Defence*, the *Ramillies* and the *Veteran*: 'On Lord Nelson getting under way, to weigh also, and to menace the northern part of the enemy's line, as well as to be ready to assist disabled ships coming out of action.'[90] They did not come far south enough. Nelson's division anchored to the south of the Middle Ground.

As soon as the ships were secured, Nelson invited his captains to dinner. According to Colonel Stewart, he 'was in the highest spirits, and drank to a leading wind, and to the success of the ensuing day'.[91] Afterwards he dictated orders to his clerks. Thomas Masterman Hardy was out in the boats, laying more buoys on the edge of the King's Deep on the west side of the Middle Ground. It was not an easy task, for the edge of the shoal was not easy to determine, and, being within earshot of Danish sentries, they had to keep their oars muffled. Nelson spent a restless night, asking every half hour if the wind was turning to the south, as he anticipated. In the night the wind shifted. By 4 a.m. it was exactly what was needed: 'SE, moderate breezes and cloudy.'[92]

The plan was simple in concept but difficult to accomplish because of the doubts about the depth of water. No ship was to be risked by doubling the anchored Danish vessels, as at the Nile, but, as at that battle, the squadron was to concentrate on one part of the line, then move up the line from the south, using their superior gunnery to force the enemy into submission. Once this was achieved, the bomb vessels were to move into the King's Deep, within range of the city, and bombard it. Instructions were issued to the captains. The pilots and masters were nervous, unclear about the line of the Middle Ground shoal in the King's Deep, but Alexander Briarly, master of the *Bellona*, volunteered to lead, and he transferred to

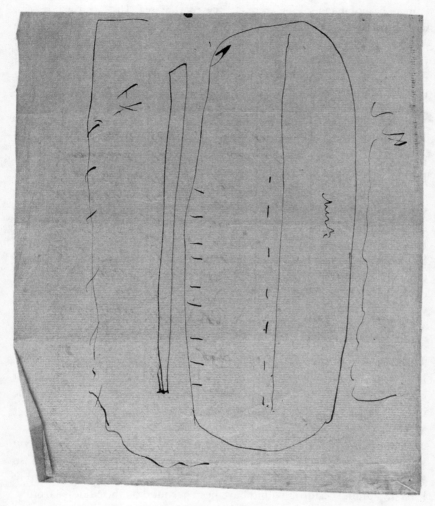

Nelson's sketch of his plan for Copenhagen

the *Edgar*. At 9.45 the *Elephant* hoisted her first signals: the *Edgar*, the *Ardent*, the *Glatton* and the *Isis* were to weigh anchor.[93] Ten minutes later the *Agamemnon*, the *Bellona*, the *Ganges*, the *Monarch*, the *Defiance*, the *Russell* and the *Polyphemus* were given their orders, and at 10.15 the general order to weigh was given. The *Edgar* led the ships through the King's Channel. Midshipman Millard in the *Monarch*, towards the end of the British line, described the scene:

A more beautiful and solemn spectacle I never witnessed. The *Edgar* led the van, and on her approach the battery on the Island of Amak and three or four of the southern-most vessels opened their fire upon her. A man of war under sail is at all times a beautiful object, but at such a time the scene is heightened beyond the powers of description. We saw her pressing on through the enemy's fire . . . our minds were deeply impressed with awe, and not a word was spoken throughout the ship but by the pilot and the helmsman.[94]

The British ships, with wind and current with them, did not take long to reach the Danish line. At 10.30 the *Prøvestenen*, the most southerly of the Danish ships, opened fire on the *Edgar*. One by one Nelson's ships formed into line. Ten minutes later Nelson's carefully drafted and rehearsed orders went wrong. The *Agamemnon* weighed anchor but was swept by the current on to the Middle Ground and stuck fast; her captain, Robert Fancourt, was later to be criticized by his fellow captains. At 10.50, five miles to the north, Sir Hyde Parker signalled the first three ships of his division to set sail for Copenhagen. The *Bellona* and the *Russell* also grounded on a westerly spur of the same shoal at 11.00 and 11.05, within 600 yards of the Danish line, which was at the extreme range for accurate gunnery. The ships, being aground, were motionless, which contributed to the accuracy of the fire, and both maintained their fire from this range for the duration of the battle. Two boats from the *Russell* were to take possession of the *Prøvestenen*. However, their firing was ineffective. Thomas Fremantle did not think that either 'could fire a shot with effect'.[95] Nelson described them as capable only of 'random shot'.[96]

As the ships moved north up the King's Deep, Nelson brought his instinct and experience to bear decisively. The pilot and master of the *Elephant* were convinced that the deep water was to the east of the stranded British ships, away from the city. Nelson overruled them. Had he not done so at least half of his squadron would have been aground on the Middle Ground. He ordered the *Elephant* and the ships that followed her to position themselves between the Danish line and the *Bellona* and the *Russell*, instructing them to take up different places from those planned. Nelson was observed throughout this day by Colonel Stewart, who was on the *Elephant*'s quarterdeck, 'except whilst employed [with] my carronade on the Poop or carrying Captain Foley's order to the different Decks . . . & never passed so interesting a day in the course of my life'. He recorded that Nelson's 'distress at the Pilot's refusing to take the ship closer to the enemy was very great & he called me down at the beginning of the day from the Poop to tell me the indignation he felt at the fellows refusing to go nearer than ½ less 5 which

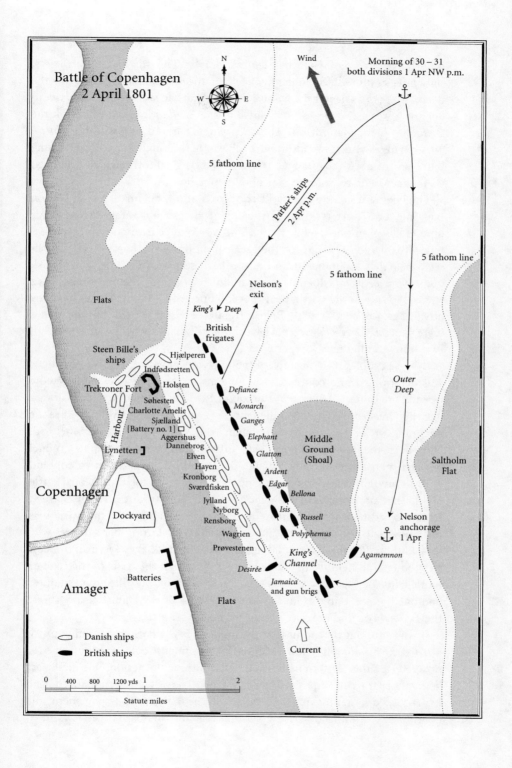

Battle of Copenhagen
2 April 1801

N
W E
S

Wind

Morning of 30 – 31
both divisions 1 Apr NW p.m.

5 fathom line

Parker's ships
2 Apr p.m.

5 fathom line

5 fathom line

Nelson's
exit

King's Deep

British frigates

Steen Bille's
ships

Hjælperen
Indfødsretten
Holsten
Søhesten
Charlotte Amelie
Sjælland
[Battery no. 1]
Aggershus
Dannebrog
Elven
Hayen
Kronborg
Sværdfisken
Jylland
Nyborg
Rensborg
Wagrien
Prøvestenen

Trekroner Fort

Harbour

Lynetten

Copenhagen

Dockyard

Amager

Batteries

Flats

Defiance
Monarch
Ganges
Elephant
Glatton
Ardent
Edgar
Isis
Polyphemus

Bellona
Russell

Desirée

King's
Channel

Jamaica
and gun brigs

Middle
Ground
(Shoal)

Outer
Deep

Saltholm
Flat

Nelson
anchorage
1 Apr

Agamemnon

Current

Danish ships
British ships

0   400   800   1200 yds 1   2

Statute miles

is within a fathom of what the *Elephant* draws.' The ship had, nevertheless, only three and a half feet under her keel, but the pilots did not realize that the deeper water was nearer the Danish line. Nelson had wanted the *Elephant* to anchor abreast the largest Danish ship, the *Sjælland*; instead he took the *Bellona*'s planned position. The *Elephant* anchored opposite the *Elven*, which had only six guns, although each was a 36-pounder, and two floating batteries 'of above 20 four & twenty Pounders'; the Danish ship fired at them, according to Stewart, 'for above three hours'.[97]

The enemy was, however, still 200 yards away, far further than Nelson had intended.[98] At that range the major British advantage, close-range gunnery, was nullified, while the 32- and 68-pound carronades were ineffective. This was to account for the great duration of the contest. The Danes were heavily outnumbered: in the southern sector of the line, 496 British guns faced 244 Danish guns; in the middle of the line, the margin was 352 to 202.[99] Only in the north, near the Trekoner Fort, did the Danes have the advantage, opposed only by British frigates. Nelson argued that the Danes were superior by 108 guns.[100] These totals fail to allow for weight of metal, rate of fire and gunnery experience.

By 11.45 all the British ships of the line were engaged. Danish resistance was determined and courageous. The guns of the Trekroner battery now opened fire on the *Defiance* at the top of the line. Fremantle in the *Ganges* lost his master and pilot, killed and wounded respectively, before he anchored at 11.35, but her opponent, the *Sjælland*, was overwhelmed. Moreover, the floating batteries were difficult targets, according to Colonel Stewart 'being without any rigging, mere hulks & as difficult to contend with as any batteries on shore'. One of the batteries 'held us a hard rattle for at least an hour more, nor did we make her strike till we discharged Round & grape from all guns in the Ship – her height above the water was not above six feet, & there was no possibility of hitting her – there were no less than 8 of these formidable batteries afloat, & they were all difficult to subdue, and held us a severer contest than even the hulls of the Line of battleships'.[101] Nevertheless the Danish ships took very heavy casualties, and one by one retired from the conflict. By 12.45 the Danish heavy ships, the *Dannebrog* and the *Sjælland*, were no longer effective.

It was at about this point that the anxious Hyde Parker, five miles away aboard the *London*, his view obscured by an immense column of gun smoke, ordered signal No. 39 to be hoisted: 'Discontinue the action.' He made it a general order to all ships by firing two guns. The *St George*, anchored near by, recorded in her log at 12.30: 'Discontinue the Action. Engagement still continues.'[102] Stewart described Nelson's reaction on board the *Elephant*:

After the Action had lasted about three hours, & we had fired about forty broadsides (we fired above 60 in all) he said to me 'Well, Stewart, those fellows hold us a better Tug than I expected, however we are keeping up a noble fire, & I'll be answerable that we shall bole them out in four if we cannot do it in three hours, at least I'll give it them till they are sick of it' – Our grand fleet was under Sail all this time, about two leagues on our Starboard beam, & as there a number of Croakers or what you may call Cautious men in it (names I shall not mention) the Signal was made for us to leave off Action . . . Ld N: however never answered it, & expressing his astonishment to me at the circumstances, turned & said what I have written above, in a most animated Manner – the only Signal which the hero kept flying was the very reverse viz 'for Close Action'.[103]

Only the frigates firing on the Trekroner Fort obeyed Parker's order. The *Amazon* weighed and ran towards Parker's ships, turning her stern towards the Danish guns: as she did so, her captain, Edward Riou, was torn apart by a Danish cannon ball. Rear-Admiral Graves on board the *Defiance*, also at the northern end of the line, with fine presence of mind, hoisted Parker's signal behind a sail so that Nelson could not see it, at the same time as flying the signal for close action. Parker's indecision and state of mind were underlined when he sent Captain Otway in a launch from the *London* to Nelson 'to ascertain the situation of affairs'. Otway's later claim that he was given 'verbal authority from Sir Hyde Parker that the battle should continue if he saw the probability of success' was academic, as the signal was ignored. The action continued while Otway was being rowed to the *Elephant*; by the time he arrived, it was clear that the Danes were weakening.[104] The most famous Nelson story of all – that Nelson put his telescope to his blind eye to see Parker's signal and said to Foley, 'I really do not see the signal' – is a myth.[105]

Still more Danish ships were put out of action.[106] By two o'clock most Danish ships had taken heavy casualties and damage; those that had not struck had only a small number of guns firing.[107] Although both the *Monarch* and the *Defiance* had, as described by Fremantle 'dreadful slaughter', all the British ships were intact and in action; even the grounded ships managed to keep firing.[108] At two o'clock the Danish vessels opposite the *Elephant* and the *Ganges* ceased firing. Nelson then decided to send a letter to the crown prince of Denmark.* Of all of Nelson's actions at the height

---

* Nelson's insistence upon sealing the letter with wax and candle, rather than using a wafer, which was quicker, seems well attested. He reacted to the idea of the wafer by saying, 'that will not do now – they will think we are afraid.' He then instructed Hardy's clerk to find his large seal, as opposed to a common seal (Brenton, II, 43). It seems likely from the pattern of anecdotes about Nelson that Brenton's source was Hardy.

of battle, this has caused the most controversy, for it is debatable whether he was in a sufficient position of strength to impose a truce. Later he repeatedly stated that his motive for the truce was 'humanity'.

Many British present at the action felt it was a *ruse de guerre*. Thomas Fremantle, whom Nelson asked to come aboard the *Elephant* for consultation, expressed the conundrum best. When he arrived on board, Nelson put into his hand 'a letter, which he meant to send immediately to the Prince in a flag of truce, threatening to burn every ship captured if the batteries did not cease firing. At this time he was aware that our ships were cut to pieces, and it would be difficult to get them out. We cut our cables and ran out. The ships were so crippled, they would not steer.'[109] Hardy had no doubt: 'the wind not sufficient to take off his Prizes and crippled Ships, he very deliberately sent a Flag of Truce on shore to say that his orders were not to destroy the City of Copenhagen . . . Political management was if possible greater than his Bravery [which] allowed him to get off all the Prizes that was not sunk or burnt, and his own ships, five of which at this time were on shore within gunshot of the Batteries.'[110] Peter Cullen, surgeon of the *Agamemnon*, which was far from the action, wrote in his journal: 'It was a grand manoeuvre of Lord Nelson obtaining the Truce, it gave us an opportunity of getting these Ships off the shoals, where otherwise we must have set fire to them.'[111] Even Colonel Stewart, at Nelson's elbow throughout the day, thought the truce 'was a masterpiece of policy of the little hero's, for victorious as we were, the narrowness of the Channel in which our ships were engaged & the commanding batteries on shore had left our Ships, six of which were aground, in a most perilous situation Ld. N. then commanded a cessation of hostilities.'[112] Nelson later defended himself, especially when the Danish commodore, Olfert Fischer, accused him of dishonour. Nelson was most eloquent in a letter to the British prime minister:

The Crown batteries, and the batteries on Armak and in the Dockyard, were firing at us, one half of their shot necessarily striking the Ships who had surrendered, and our fire did the same, and worse, for the surrendered Ships had four of them got close together, and it was a massacre. This caused my Note. It was a sight which no real man could have enjoyed. I felt when the Danes became my prisoners, I became their protector; and if that had not been a sufficient reason, the moment of a complete victory was surely the proper time to make an opening with the Nation we had been fighting with.[113]

To Emma, Nelson wrote: 'Nelson is a warrior, but will not be a Butcher.'[114] He was also aware that the British advantage was paper-thin, and he had in mind the contradictions between the force required by the British government and the conciliation desired by the King. In the midst of gunfire, smoke, death and suffering he applied peaceful *realpolitik* with quick thinking and calmness. It was one of his supreme battle decisions.

Nelson's letter was delivered by boat to the crown prince, who was watching the battle from the shore. The message was both vague and threatening; the word 'truce' did not appear. It stated that he had 'directions to spare Denmark when no longer resisting', but if fighting continued he would set the batteries that he had captured on fire 'without having the power of saving the Brave Danes who have defended them'. It ended: 'To the Brothers of Englishmen the Danes'.[115] The crown prince immediately accepted a truce and sent orders for a ceasefire to all his commanders. From his vantage point he could see that the battle was lost; he might now prevent the destruction of his capital.[116] By 14.30 the *Jylland*, the *Kronborg* and the *Sværdfisken* had been taken, and just before three o'clock the *Rendsborg* struck, then the *Indfødsretton*.[117] On the other hand, the *Monarch*, which had suffered badly from a gun burst, was under heavy fire from the guns of the Trekroner Fort. It was at this point that the *Defence*, one of Parker's ships that he had sent south hours ago, managed some shots at the Danish ships at extreme range. It was to be the only contribution from Parker's squadron. By now the Danish fire had all but died away and the British followed suit. A quarter of an hour later all firing had stopped and flags of truce were flying.

Immediately Nelson signalled all ships to leave the King's Deep and go to the Outer Roads, but several, their sails and rigging in tatters, had difficulty in withdrawing. The *Elephant* and the *Defiance* were aground. William Fothergill, the master of the *Cruizer* sloop, took charge of the *Elephant*, which did not get off until late that evening. She failed to heave herself off after 'starting 25 Butts of Water & sent part of the Bread on board a Brig when at 9 a brig brought us a Cable laid out on the larboard bow by which we hove off about ½ past 9'.[118] Otway was sent to take the *Holsten*, which had struck but refused to surrender, and he went on board the Danish commodore's ship, the *Sjælland*. Nelson followed Otway and met Fischer: 'both chiefs recognised each other, having both commanded frigates in the West Indies at the same time.'[119] Colonel Stewart emphasized the British predicament: 'by prolonging it [the truce] under one pretext or another, in four & twenty hours after, got our crippled ships off the shoals, & from under the guns of the enemies batteries, & also took possession of all our prizes, which otherwise we should have found some difficulty in doing.'[120]

Casualties were heavy on both sides. There were 254 British officers and seamen killed and 689 wounded. The two ships caught by the Trekroner Fort were worst hit; the *Monarch* with fifty-five killed and 155 wounded, and the *Defiance* twenty-two killed and forty-seven wounded. The *Edgar*, first into the King's Deep, had twenty-nine killed and 104 wounded. Eight were killed and eleven wounded aboard the *Elephant*.[121] According to Stewart, 'the poor *Monarch* particularly suffered & is nearly a wreck – it became a positive butchery on board her, till the interchange of Ld. Nelson's flag of truce slackened & at length stopped the fire from the enemy on the Crowns.'[122] Aboard the stranded *Bellona*, Thomas Boulden Thompson, her captain, lost a leg from a Danish cannon ball early in the action; her casualties were light, however, apart from the local devastation caused by the bursting of two 32-pounder guns, likely as a result of gunners loading double charges in the effort to fetch the range. Both guns were in the charge of Lieutenant Thomas Wilkes, a veteran of the Nile, but he suffered nothing more than being knocked down three times – 'black eyes & bruises are my only wounds.'[123]

The miseries of the Danish ships were not yet over. The *Dannebrog*, aground and on fire since the truce, blew up at five o'clock. Danish losses were considerably higher than those of the British: 367 Danes were killed and 635 wounded, of which a hundred later died from their wounds.[124] Fremantle was shocked: 'The carnage on board the Danish vessels exceeds anything I ever heard of; the *Ça Ira* or Nile ships are not to be compared to the massacre on board them. The people generally were carpenters, labourers and some Norwegian seamen.'[125] In addition 1,779 Danes were taken prisoner, although a month later Danish officers signed a document for the Navy Board in London to say that the total complement of the captured Danish vessels totalled 3,500 men.[126] For the Danes there was nothing less than admiration. Thomas Wilkes wrote home: 'I will do them the credit to say they fought well, far better than I have ever found the French or Spaniards.'[127] The battle gained them a lasting reputation. Some three years later, Alexander Ball in Malta was talking to his secretary, Samuel Taylor Coleridge, about naval gunnery; as usual, he made a note of the conversation. 'Sir A.B. assured me that the men on board our most glorious Warships often run from their Quarters tho' it was made a point to hush it up – that it was the British officers & our Discipline – yet believed their Men too braver and steadier than any other nation except Danes and Swedes.'[128]

After the battle Nelson felt little elation. He entered in his journal 'Our ship suffered a good deal, at night went on board the *St George* very unwell.'[129] Nor was the action immediately seen to be a victory. Stewart complained: 'Yet there are many people in this fleet, about Headquarters too, who think our victory bought infinitely too dearly – our damage in ships is certainly great, so much so that we fear four of them must be sent home, but even if that be the case I maintain the panic we have struck into our Enemy, the confidence which our tars now have overcoming anything after the difficulties we surmounted on this last action, well recompenses these and still more answer losses.'[130] For once, Nelson did not need to ensure his contribution was appreciated in London. He was confident enough to play the courtier in a disingenuous letter to the out-of-office Spencer, now in Bath: 'as your Lordship had the appointment of the Commander-in-Chief great merit must be due to you for your judicious choice, as to myself being second in command I had only to obey my orders and of course little merit can attach itself to me.'[131] Spencer wrote a fulsome letter from Bath – 'Lady Spencer, I need not tell you, is unbounded in her Joy' – and told Nelson that he had seized 'a very early moment to congratulate Lady Nelson and your venerable Father on your Glory & your Safety, for both of which they were necessarily so highly interested'.[132] Addington wrote to assure Nelson that 'every part of your Lordship's conduct is approved of by the King' and expressed 'his sentiments of admiration & of complete satisfaction.'[133]

Although forceful diplomacy attained its objective, Copenhagen was far from a perfect action and much less penetrating and spectacular than its obvious parallel, Aboukir Bay. However, the fleet, though damaged, was in a good-enough state to continue the pressure on the Russians. Stout Danish defence and tricky waters stifled the effect of boldness and dash, although Nelson's own performance was appreciated. His coolness and presence of mind excited much praise: 'he is the admiration of our whole fleet', wrote Stewart, 'beyond any officer now alive.'[134] In London his professional standing was beginning to be re-established after the Mediterranean discredit: 'You have greatly outstripped ourself,' St Vincent wrote, 'and all who have gone before you, the late most glorious conflict.'[135] However, the City of London honoured neither him nor his fleet, about which he long protested.[136]

Nelson underestimated the Danish defence and the capacity of their men to take punishment. The pilots misread the King's Deep and Hardy's dangerous work in surveying the waters during the previous night was wasted. The failure of the British line to anchor nearer the Danes was potentially disastrous. Stewart noted ruefully: 'we have examined the Channel since the action, for it is proved that we might have gone within pistol shot of their whole line; whereas we conceived it to be formed on the

Southern shoals & therefore gave it a <u>supposed necessary</u> wide birth – the contest had we been aware of this could have lasted one fourth of the time.'[137] Two British 74s and a 64 went aground and took no real part in the battle. Casualties were heavy, although, to put them into perspective, more British lives were lost by drowning when the *Invincible*, due to join the Baltic fleet, hit a shoal off Yarmouth called Hamond's Knowl at nine knots; of a complement of just under 600, only 190 were saved.[138] Copenhagen was the only one of Nelson's battles in which the close-range, devastating, engagement-winning carronades could not be brought to bear.

23

Commander-in-Chief, Baltic Fleet
April–June 1801

All my things on board the Blanche *being to sail in the evening when Col. Stewart arrives with an order for me to [be] Commander in Chief and for Sir Hyde Parker to return home, at 4 o'clock the* Blanche *sail'd & left me the Command to my great sorrow.*

Nelson's journal, 4 May 1801[1]

For a week relations between the two sides remained tense. The day after the battle, 3 April, Nelson visited his damaged ships in the morning. At noon Parker, unaccountably, sent Nelson ashore to negotiate with the Danes when he should have gone himself. Nelson spent two hours with the crown prince, who was accompanied only by an aide, Commander Hans Lindholm. Both leaders were free of the niceties of diplomacy and came to the nub of the issues quickly. Nelson's message was that England would never consent to 'this freedom and nonsense of navigation', pointing out that the result would be 'ruination to Denmark'; if the country pressed for free trade, Denmark would have no power to exact dues from ships sailing through the Sound; and his ultimatum to the prince was 'join us or disarm'. The prince insisted that he would never join Russia against England, pressed the fact that Denmark was a neutral trading nation and offered to mediate between Britain and Russia. Nelson fought his corner well. He obtained the concession that Denmark should now provision Parker's fleet; and he also raised the possibility of concluding an armistice rather than carrying out the British government's instructions of a full diplomatic agreement. Crowds had gathered on shore to see him. He wrote to Davison, 'I was received in the most flattering manner by all ranks ... No wonder I am spoilt. All my astonishment is that my head is not turned.'[2] This time, perhaps, it was not.

Despite the fact that the crown prince had absolute power, he had to take Nelson's proposals back to the Danish Privy Council. Nelson reported back to Parker at eight in the evening 'to communicate the result of my business, very tired'.[3] He also took care to write a long account of the meeting for the prime minister, Henry Addington.[4] The next day, while waiting for the Danish answer, he went with Fremantle to the *Bellona* to visit the gravely wounded Thompson. He wrote a letter of encouragement to the downcast captain of the *Agamemnon*: 'I have the highest opinion of all on board my old and good *Agamemnon*.'[5] The weather again became cold, with snow. The Danish Privy Council was split, and the Danish foreign minister, Count Christian Bernstorff, was no longer on speaking terms with the minister of finance.[6] On 5 April the crown prince appointed two negotiators, Commander Hans Lindholm and Major-General Frederik Walterstorff, both fluent in English, who went aboard the *London*. The answer from the Danes was, as Nelson noted, 'a very unsatisfactory note from Count Bernstoffe which Sir Hyde answer'd and all hope of negotiation seem'd at an end'. Parker presented the Danes with an ultimatum. He wanted a written assurance that the Danes would declare themselves neutral and that the British fleet could provision itself from any Danish territory. He gave them twenty-four hours to reply.

The situation of the British fleet was not strong. Fremantle, aboard the *St George* advising and drafting documents for Nelson, did not feel confident: 'I know and feel as a seaman', he wrote home, 'that great sacrifices in our present situation should be made, sooner than declare openly against them again. Should we begin with their bombs, little will be effected and our fleet must positively return to Leith or Yarmouth for water and stores ... we are now with above 100 prisoners each, eating and drinking us out.'[7] Parker finally sent away Robert Otway with dispatches for London with a gloomy prognosis. In London, St Vincent was determined not to send stores and reinforcements until, as he wrote to Nepean on 4 April, 'we are at a certainty as to his [Parker's] first stroke'.[8]

That night three of the Danish prizes were burnt; the British bomb vessels were prepared for action, opposite the city. As each hour passed without a diplomatic agreement, it looked more likely that British guns might again open fire at Danish ships and at the city of Copenhagen. Nelson's journal reveals that he was not confident of a settlement and was contemplating a resumption of hostilities. Early the next day, 7 April, he examined the position of the carefully placed bomb vessels, ordering the northerly part of the Middle Ground to be sounded, 'in case the Bombs are forced to retreat': then 'at 11 the flag of truce came on board with a nonsensical note'.[9]

The breakthrough came on 8 April. Nelson, Colonel Stewart and Reverend Alexander Scott, as secretary, went ashore. The wind was fresh, and Nelson recorded in his journal 'got wet through, sat all day debating and arranging an armistice'. During these long negotiations the crown prince heard that Tsar Paul had been assassinated, enabling him to soften his attitude. Nelson knew nothing of it, for he wrote in his journal at the end of the day: 'The Danes are afraid on each side both of us & Russia. Came on board at 10 o'clock wet through.'[10] Finally an armistice of fourteen weeks and fourteen days was signed on 9 April. The fourth article permitted the British fleet to obtain provisions not only at Copenhagen but also 'along the Coasts of the different Islands and Provinces of Denmark, Jutland included, with everything it may require for the health and Comfort of its Crews'.[11] Nelson took the agreement on shore for ratification by the Crown Prince. He 'returned on board at 6 o'clock very unwell, feverish. Under all circumstances I am sure our armistice is a good thing.' Late that night he wrote privately to Troubridge: 'I am in a fright at the decision about the minister's thought of this armistice. Be it good or bad, it is my own; therefore, if blamable [sic], let me be the only person censured.'[12] The next day, 10 April, Colonel Stewart set off for England with dispatches, and the news of the assassination of Tsar Paul in St Petersburg reached the fleet.[13] Two days later the Danish prisoners were sent ashore.[14]

The tension over, with Nelson tired and physically ill, his thoughts turned to home and he immediately slipped into the anxious state he had been in during February and March. Late at night he wrote a wildly scribbled, extravagantly phrased letter to Emma. Part of his anxiety was about Horatia, prompted by a conversation with one of the frigate captains, Graham Eden Hamond: Emma was to ensure that 'the Nurse had no bad disorders for he has been told that Capt. Hamond before he was 6 weeks old had the bad disorders which has tried his constitution to this day'.[15] Nelson was still plagued by jealousy of the prince of Wales: 'Gold, Silver & Jewels may be presents from Royalty, I can only send you a Sprig of Laurel & the friendship of a human & generous heart.' He dreamt of retiring to Bronte with Emma.[16] He continued to worry about his prize case against St Vincent.[17] He even thought about going home overland. From Lindholm, with whom he had struck up a friendship, he obtained a Danish passport, because 'it is my intention from my state of health to return to England in a very short time and probably by Lubec[k] and Hamburgh.'[18]

The British fleet now prepared to move south to the spacious anchorage of Køge Bay, later described by Nelson as 'an amazing Bay flat and a fleet may anchor in it 7 leag[ue]s from North to South, the ground good & clear from Rocks.'[19] Most of the fleet sailed cautiously south on the morning of

13 April. Both the 90-gun ships took out their guns because of the shallow water south of Copenhagen, the *London* bringing her draught to twenty-two feet and six inches. Most of the ships touched the ground; even the relatively shallow-draughted *Elephant* 'rubbed along the Ground' twice.[20] The *St George*, with Nelson on board, had to wait for assistance from a suitable vessel in the Copenhagen Roads. '. . . here we lay perfectly idle,' Nelson fretted, although on 14 April he wrote a letter to a distant relation, Isaac Preston, to whom he confided, in a more optimistic mood, 'I do not expect to fire another Gun in the Baltic.'[21] The next day an American merchantman was found to transport the *St George*'s guns, and to lighten her further she also put sixty tons of water aboard the *Desirée* frigate. The wind now went round to the south, preventing the *St George* from joining the fleet.[22] Fresh intelligence reached Parker, now anchored in Køge Bay, that the Swedish fleet was out, and he sent a note to Nelson suggesting that he hoist his flag again in the *Elephant*. Nelson received the message at six. Immediately he ordered a boat to be manned. Taking with him Alexander Briarly, the master of the *Bellona*, who was temporarily aboard and knew the waters, he set off at once. The *Elephant* was twenty-four miles away: Nelson urged on his men during a five-hour row into wind and tide. It was bitterly cold. Briarly said that 'his anxiety . . . lest the fleet should have sailed before he got on board one of them . . . is beyond all conception.' When offered a boat cloak, Nelson said: 'No, I am not cold; my anxiety for my country will keep me warm. Do you think the fleet has sailed?'[23] He threatened to row after the ships as far as Karlskrona if they had left Køge Bay. But they were still there.* Nelson reached the *Elephant* at eleven that night.[24] For this latest anxiety-fuelled drama, he suffered, unsurprisingly, as he told Emma, 'a terrible cold [which] struck me to the heart'.[25]

For three days in light south and westerly breezes the squadron sailed in search of the Swedish fleet, past Bornholm towards Karlskrona. On 19 April one of the frigates 'made the signal for a strange fleet in the NE going large with the wind on the Larboard Quarter. Signal for a general chace. At 11 saw they where [sic] at anchor in the outer part of the harbour of Carlscrone. Damn Them,' he scratched furiously in his journal.[26] Lieutenant Thomas Wilkes of the *Bellona* wrote home: 'We found them "too secure for even the Dashing Nelson to attack".'[27] The rest of the fleet began to catch up. Nelson debated the next move with Hyde Parker, who wrote: 'under all circumstances I do not feel I ought to proceed higher up the Baltic

---

* This is the incident used by Patrick O'Brian and retold in the film *Master and Commander* (2003), related by Jack Aubrey to his officers at the dinner table.

until I hear from England or that I am joined by Adm. Totty.'[28] The *St George* came up on 21 April and Nelson returned to her the next day.[29] Nelson then received reports that the new tsar of Russia had given directions for all hostilities to cease. Signs that the tension with Russia was easing had been apparent a week before, when Lindholm had written to Nelson informing him of the 'interesting news that the Emperor of Russia has offered to give up the English Vessels and the English goods detained in Russia when England will give up the Russian, Danish and Swedish vessels in her Ports. I hope that the Northern Business will soon be settled.'[30] The fleet sailed back to Køge Bay. Echoing the frustrations of a junior officer of any age, Lieutenant Wilkes wrote home: 'We are now, God knows why, steering a course back to Copenhagen.'[31]

On the passage back on 24 April, anchored off Moen Island in light winds, Nelson gave a dinner party to celebrate Emma's birthday. The captains were, as he extravagantly related to Emma, 'invited to assist at the fête of Santa Emma. In the morning Divine Service then as good a dinner and Wine as money can purchase, you may rely my Saint is more adored in this fleet than all the Saints in the Roman Calendar . . . there is certainly more of the Angel than the human being about you.'[32]

Nelson now made a determined effort to get home. He wrote formally to the Board of Admiralty on 25 April and to Troubridge three days later, describing his 'old complaint' – malaria: 'the two last [attacks] I had was going down to Plymouth with my brother, and a little one in Yarmouth Roads.'[33] On 2 May he wrote again: 'if I do not get from here in a very short time . . . I shall remain for ever. I am dreadfully pulled down.'[34] Parker reluctantly and sceptically gave him leave to return home, but, with his eye on St Vincent, whom he feared, he wrote to Nelson, saying, 'a little more Form necessary to Justify my giving the leave you Ask. I will therefore request you will desire your Surgeon to represent the State of your health, which letter you will be so good as to enclose with your application.'[35] For the first three days of May, Nelson made preparations to go home, loading his baggage into the *Blanche* frigate. On 4 May, Colonel Stewart arrived from England. Parker was recalled. Nelson, to his chagrin, was to be commander-in-chief.

Hyde Parker was astounded. Stewart had returned to the fleet with the thanks of the king, both Houses of Parliament and the Board of Admiralty: 'Their Lordships command me to send their congratulations on the honour you have acquired on the occasion, which I beg to add mine,' wrote Nepean to Parker.[36] Yet Stewart also brought Parker's recall. The soldier had arrived in London on 20 April with dispatches and is likely to have amplified their content to ministers. Addington, the new prime minister, had always preferred Nelson to Parker as commander of this expedition, and Parker had, after all, been appointed by the previous government.[37] Two days later the cabinet had decided that he should be recalled. Parker protested long and vehemently, asking for an inquiry, but to no avail.* According to William Young, now out of office and down in Bath, when Parker returned to London he complained of Nelson's disobedience, 'which will of course give rise to much party discussion', but Young echoed majority opinion: 'that it [the signal] was not obeyed is a most fortunate circumstance, for if we had not conquered on that day, it would have been such a triumph to the Danes and such a disgrace to our Navy . . . A drawn battle would have been a victory to Denmark.'[38] Some disagreed. Parker's old protégé Thomas Fremantle wrote to his brother in the summer: 'I hear he [Parker] bears his misfortune with great philosophy – I think they have used him cruelly.'[39]

The cabinet knew nothing of Nelson's illness, and the decision in any case was made before his malaria attacks of late April. Three weeks earlier Nelson had written to Davison to say that 'if the Admiralty would send me a commission as Commander-in-Chief, I would not now accept it.'[40] But with the prospect of command, Nelson rose to the challenge. When his request for leave became known in London in late May, the king asked for information. St Vincent delivered a crushing verdict on Nelson, referring to his hypochondria and his inability to accept the role of second in command: 'Lord Nelson, who is in the habit of complaining of ill health and stated it to be the cause of his taking that step, has, it appears, received considerable benefit from the additional responsibility which has recently been thrown upon him, and will, Lord St Vincent has no doubt, be able to continue in the command.'[41]

It was an answer that accorded with the king's prejudiced view of Nelson; but it nevertheless seems clear that Nelson had indeed suffered several debilitating attacks of malaria. On 2 May he wrote to Emma: 'I have been so very indifferent, and am still so weak, that I cannot take the journey to Hamburgh by land, or I should have been off long ago.'[42] To Troubridge, the one senior officer who would remember Nelson's first malarial attacks in India when they were both midshipmen, he wrote: 'my night sweats and

* On his return to England, Nelson wrote a long, friendly letter to dissuade Hyde Parker from pressing for an inquiry, citing the unfortunate experience of Sir John Orde after Nelson's appointment to the Mediterranean squadron in 1798. A grateful Parker wrote back: 'Many thanks for this proof of your friendship which be assured will never be forgotten by me.' (NMM, CRK/14/91, 8 July 1801, Nelson to Parker, Parker to Nelson; also CRK/8/150, 18 Aug. 1801, John McArthur to Nelson).

cough are much against me ... nothing could have been more gratifying under good health than this command ... but now it's too late.' His letter suddenly changes tone, from self-pity to anger, as if remembering that Troubridge was a member of the Board of Admiralty. 'I dare say I have tormented you so much on the subject that you say, "Damn him, I wish he were dead, and not plaguing me this way" – therefore, I never shall mention to you one more word on the subject.'[43]

On taking command, Nelson determined to sail north to show his ships to the Russians in Reval. Orders to attack Russia had been rescinded by Lord Hawkesbury, the secretary of state, on 16 April, but Sweden was still showing hostility, and as late as 12 June orders from the Admiralty remained unchanged: 'to omit no opportunity of annihilating the Naval Force of Sweden'.[44] It was still important to prevent the Russians and the Swedes from joining forces.[45] Nelson called it a friendly visit, but no one doubted its purpose as a show of force. Considerable disagreements remained between the courts of St Petersburg and of London. Not only was the right of search of neutral shipping unresolved, but 200 English merchant ships were still held in Russian ports, their officers and crews confined inland.[46] The ships were unloaded and the Russians had emptied the English merchants' hemp warehouses to renew the rigging of the Russian fleet. In London the price of St Petersburg hemp was £86 a ton, more than twice the price of 1799.[47] Thomas Fremantle, delivering dispatches to St Petersburg, was to inform Nelson at the end of May that 103 vessels were confined at St Petersburg, eighty-eight at Riga and ten at other ports. He painted a bleak picture: 'the Sails of the English ships are quite decayed and unfit for use having been so long without air.' Fremantle also reported that otherwise the Russian warships were not in a good state and unready for sea. Nelson's decision to push north was based on sound knowledge. In any case, the most senior officers in the Russian Navy were British, and they had been relieved of their commands and ordered to Moscow.[48]

At four in the afternoon on 4 May the *Blanche* sailed for England with Parker on board. Forty-eight hours later the fleet weighed anchor under Nelson's orders. The wind went round to the east, and the ships anchored in the lee of Falsterbo, the south-west point of Sweden. For two days fresh easterly winds blew. Nelson wrote to the Swedish admiral in Karlskrona a letter of menacing charm, sending it in a cutter: 'I beg, therefore, to apprise your Excellency, that I have no orders to abstain from hostilities, should I meet the Swedish fleet at sea, which, as it lies in your power to prevent, I am sure you must take this communication as the most friendly proceeding on my part.'[49] The Swedes wisely stayed in port under the guns of their fortifications.

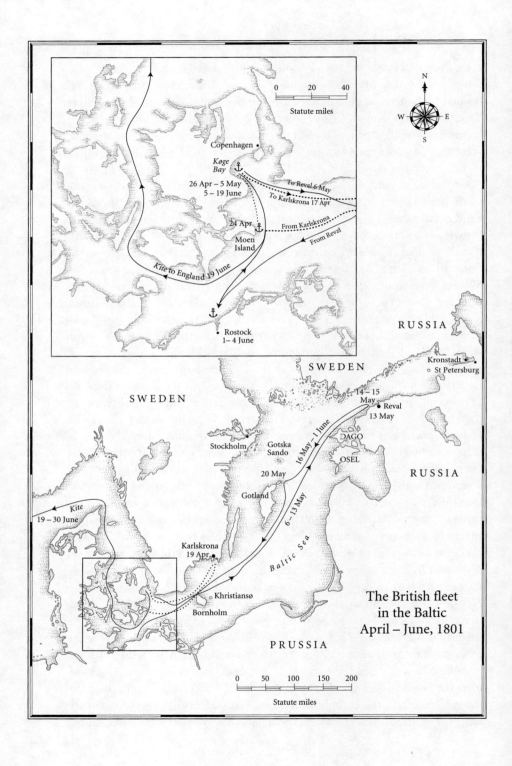

The British fleet
in the Baltic
April – June, 1801

Copenhagen

Køge
Bay
26 Apr – 5 May
5 – 19 June

24 Apr.

Moen
Island

To Reval 6 May
To Karlskrona 17 Apr
From Karlskrona
From Reval

Kite to England 19 June

Rostock
1– 4 June

RUSSIA

SWEDEN

Kronstadt
St Petersburg

SWEDEN

14 – 15
May

Reval
13 May

DAGO

OSEL

RUSSIA

Stockholm

Gotska
Sando

16 May – 1 June

20 May

Gotland

6 – 13 May

Kite
19 – 30 June

Baltic Sea

Karlskrona
19 Apr.

Khristiansø

Bornholm

PRUSSIA

0   20   40
Statute miles

N
W   E
S

0   50   100   150   200
Statute miles

The fleet made better progress when the wind blew from the south-west on 9 May. 'Came into the fleet a Russian lugger from Revel with dispatches answer'd them & sent her away,' Nelson noted in his journal. Among those letters was one to Count Pahlen, the Russian minister for foreign affairs and one of the chief conspirators against Tsar Paul. Assuring him of friend-ship, he was 'determined to show myself with a Squadron in the Bay of Revel . . . there shall be neither Bomb-Ship, Fire-Ship, nor any of the Flotilla, in order to mark the more strongly, that I wish it to be considered as a mark of the greatest personal respect to his Imperial Majesty.'[50] In a letter to Lord Carysfort, minister at Berlin, he was more belligerent: 'we have force enough to bid defiance to the whole Baltic fleet, but I hope that all will end amicably.'[51] Nelson left Captain George Murray off Bornholm with seven ships of the line and the small craft to watch the Swedes, where water was to be obtained from the two islands of Khristiansø and Fredericksø.[52] Murray was to be joined by a reinforcing squadron under Rear-Admiral Totty on 14 May.[53]

Still physically weak, Nelson did not leave his cabin during the whole passage,[54] writing to Alexander Davison that the weather was not 'very favourable for Invalids'.[55] Off the north end of Gotland on 11 May, Nelson sent the *Kite* brig ahead with dispatches to Reval. Receiving a favourable answer to his letter, he approached the town on 13 May, anchoring seven miles off. But the Russian fleet had departed. The early melting of the ice had allowed it to sail round to Kronstadt, where it had arrived on 7 May.[56] Nelson's reception from the Reval authorities was guarded. The local port commander allowed an unarmed vessel in for fresh meat, 'otherwise your squadron may not approach within cannon shot until the General of Div-ision Baron Orten has received orders on the subject.'[57] Nelson went ashore briefly, 'forced to row 7 miles', he complained to Emma, 'to make the formal visit to the Governor General & head of the Admiralty here. It cost me about 3 hours. They wanted me to dine on shore, but if I had been ever so well I would not. It is a horrid, nasty place, and nothing less than the arrival of the Emperor shall get me ashore again.'[58] He and Colonel Stewart drew maps of the harbour defences, while the *Kite* surveyed the channels into the harbour.[59]

On 16 May Nelson received his reply from Count Pahlen. In view of the confusion after the assassination, Nelson was unlikely to be accorded a formal welcome. The letter stated, reasonably, that His Imperial Majesty found the presence of the British fleet against the spirit of the pronounce-ments of the British government and requested it to leave. Nelson wrote a short note in reply and ordered his squadron to leave immediately, even though it was foggy, late in the afternoon and in strange waters. He steered south.[60] He wrote a tight-lipped note of explanation to Thomas Graves: 'As the Court of St Petersburgh did not think us very welcome guests, I determined to leave them as soon as possible.'[61] It was the only time in the Baltic when his diplomatic dealings carried the stamp of his ill-temper at Naples. Nor were their lordships satisfied: 'they cannot [but] feel some regret that your endeavours to mark your respect for His Imperial Majesty should not have been attended with success.'[62]

Nelson's sudden departure, without the usual courtesies, in itself perceived as threatening, prompted the new tsar, Alexander, and Count Pahlen to send Rear-Admiral Paul Vassilievitch Tchitchagov after him. He caught up with Nelson off Gotland on 20 May. The two admirals had a constructive discussion lasting six hours, with the Russian making a declaration that British merchantmen would pass unmolested in the Baltic; Nelson noted in his letter book, 'on such a Declaration being given on the part of his Imperial Majesty, my orders are clear and decisive to commit no act of hostility appertaining to the Emperor of Russia.'[63] He sent a reassuring note to St Petersburg.[64] An armistice was now effectively in place, and three days later Nelson applied the same pressure on the Swedish admiral in Karlskrona.[65] By now Nelson knew that Rear-Admiral Totty, with five ships of the line, was about to reinforce him.[66] Off Gotland, fortuitously, Nelson also met the newly appointed ambassador to St Petersburg, Lord St Helens, travelling in the *Latona* (38), and they had a three-hour meeting while the ships hove to.[67]

The diplomatic impasse was soon broken once the ambassador arrived in St Petersburg on 28 May. A week later St Helens wrote to Nelson with 'great reason to hope that this Government may ultimately be induced no longer to contest our rights of searching neutral vessels sailing under convoy & of seizing enemies property on board of neutral vessels'. St Helens was on terms of intimacy with the Russian minister, 'in order to defeat the intrigues of the Swedish party here'.[68] On 20 June he reported to Nelson that three days previously he had concluded a convention with an armistice of three months to allow it to be taken to London for ratification. He added that the tsar had invited Nelson to go to St Petersburg.[69] Nelson's skill and force when negotiating – from a position of strength, his mind now clear of complexities of the Neapolitan court, and without the distraction of Emma Hamilton – are striking. The brief Russian episode, successfully terminated without a gun being fired, was a measure of the potency of British sea power.

The risks and uncertainties that accompanied Nelson as he sailed north into the Baltic should not be underestimated. He had 18,000 men to feed.[70] In England supplies for ten weeks had been loaded on merchant vessels by 31 May, but as late as 11 June Nelson had heard only reports of victuallers lying at Yarmouth, ready to sail.[71] Even before the end of April the fleet began to run short of water; according to Fremantle, 'had we been under the necessity of proceeding to the Gulf of Finland, we should have been much straitened for it.'[72] The last British fleet to enter the Baltic had been in 1727, since when ships of the line were much larger, had a greater draft of water and had more numerous crews. He was heavily dependent upon British diplomats, consuls and local merchants to secure fresh beef and vegetables. When Admiral Totty came to reinforce Nelson, he could take on very little water: 'as it was necessary to keep the ships as light as possible, in order to pass over the Grounds, they could not take any supply of water in Copenhagen Road.' He hoped that he could obtain some at Bornholm.[73] This was solved at Khristansø and Frederiksø. When Totty arrived off Bornholm, he found the gun vessels in George Murray's squadron 'in want of fuel and cannot purchase any, as their bills are not negotiable'. In early June the governor of Bornholm refused to supply the British ships moored off with vegetables. Nelson wrote to Totty that as this was in contravention of the fourth article of the agreement with Denmark, he was to stop Danish vessels from leaving the island if no cooperation was forthcoming.[74] Scurvy made its appearance in the *Ramillies*, but lemon juice was issued on the advice of Dr Andrew Baird; it was there that Nelson became a convert to its use.[75] The fleet in general was short of bread and Nelson ordered a two thirds allowance.[76]

By 24 May the *St George* was anchored in Rostock Bay. Alexander Cockburn, consul at Hamburg, whom Nelson had met there the previous year, had offered to supply the fleet from Rostock soon after the battle.[77] Nelson invited Cockburn to send his proposals: 'it must be noticed that the lowest price & best provisions must both combine.'[78] On the arrival of the British fleet at Rostock, prices rose. Nelson saw that 'a combination has been entered into against us, to make us pay nearly double the market price for both beef and bread.'[79] He did not accept Cockburn's offer.[80] Instead, he ordered Richard Booth, purser of the *London*, to stay ashore to obtain the best prices; he would recommend to the Admiralty that Booth be paid a 2 per cent commission.[81] Danzig (Gdansk) now became the chief source of supplies, for on 26 May Lord Carysfort wrote informing Nelson that 'The Court of Berlin ... with the utmost readiness & every appearance of cordiality, has given orders all along their coasts upon the Baltic for the supply of your fleet.'[82] After more difficulties, cattle were eventually supplied from Danzig, purchased through an agreement by which the tallow and hides were returned to the seller, a task that had to be undertaken by the gun brigs, although when they were returned they were 'stinking, full of maggots and so very offensive' and only a third of the agreed value of the hides was retrieved.[83] Admiral Totty was also extremely careful, successfully obtaining bread for as little as 3d. a pound.[84] Nelson's previous experience with victualling contractors led him to keep a very firm financial hand on the supply of provisions.* He was also aware of the new first lord's views on these matters. In one of his frequent notes to Troubridge (who was forwarding letters to Emma Hamilton) he added a postscript as an insurance: 'Such iniquity, I fear, has been going on in Denmark that the Victualling must look out before they pay the horrid bills.'[85]

Nelson was still unwell. He wrote on 23 May: 'I am going home immediately or I shall be dead with a consumption, the keen air of the North has cut me to the heart. Graves has kept his bed for a month.'[86] Another soldier, Lieutenant-Colonel William Hutchinson, on his return to London, had informed the first lord that Nelson's health really was bad. St Vincent now changed his tune, writing to the king: 'a lamentable account of the state of Lord Nelson's health and spirits, insomuch that Lord St Vincent is very apprehensive, unless his Lordship is immediately reliev'd, his life will be in danger.'[87] St Vincent now had to find a successor to Nelson rapidly. After considering George Montagu and Henry Harvey, the board decided upon Charles Morice Pole.[88]

Nelson had to attend to a little more business. The duke of Mecklenburg, with a huge party, visited the St George in Rostock Bay.[89] A rumpus involving British officers ashore had to be smoothed over with Lindholm, who spent a day on board the St George.[90] More significantly, the Danes were infuriated by the news of the loss of their West Indies islands to Admiral Duckworth; as Lindholm put it to Nelson, 'from their idea that the Capitulation is severer than they could have expected.'[91] Colonel Stewart, in Copenhagen, observed the repair of Danish ships in contravention of the armistice, but they remained eager to appease Nelson. The crown prince sent Nelson wine and fruit from the royal hot houses, accompanied by a note from Lindholm expressing the hope that 'the present British ministry will treat this Nation in a just Manner and not pretend to despotise us because we are a Power of the second Rank.'[92] The Danes were sensitive

---

* Nelson was rewriting the rules, using Richard Booth ashore as a forerunner of the system of victualling that he used in the Mediterranean from 1803. In the event, Booth sought further help from Solly and Gibson, long-established English timber merchants in Danzig, which led to further complications in settling payment with the Victualling Board.

about their reputation. Walterstorff wrote later to Nelson, 'unfortunate as the war has been for Denmark, it has not shown the character of the Danes in an unfavourable light.'[93]

By early June he had heard nothing from the Admiralty for a month. 'My eyes are almost stretched out looking at the point of land where Ships come from,' he complained to Emma.[94] But his health was much improved. 'I am perfectly recovered,' he wrote to Emma on 10 June, 'and as far as relates to health I don't think I ever was <u>stronger</u> or in better health. It is odd but after severe illness I feel much better.'[95] To Alexander Ball in Malta he was less optimistic: 'I have been at <u>death's</u> door apparently in a consumption. I am now rallied a little but ... I know not whether I am really better and no-one will tell me, but all in the fleet are so truly kind to me that I should be a wretch not to <u>cheer up</u>.'[96] Fremantle wrote to his brother: 'Nothing can exceed Nelson's kindness to me, he is adored in the Squadron.'[97] Nelson's farewell message to the fleet came straight from the heart. He could not leave without

expressing to the Admiral's, Capt[ai]ns, Officers and Men how sensibly he has felt and does feel all their kindness to him and how nobly & honourably they have supported him in the hour of Battle ... that with the exception of the glaring misconduct of the Officers of the *Tygress* and *Cra*[c]*ker* Gun Brigs out of 18,000 of which this fleet is composed not a complaint has been made of Any officer or Man in it* ... the extraordinary Health of this Fleet under the blessing of Almighty God is to be attributed to the great regularity, exact discipline and chearful obedience of every individual in it.[98]

Vice-Admiral Charles Morice Pole arrived on 18 June, and the next day Nelson shifted his flag from the *St George* to the *Kite* brig (Captain Thomas Digby) and sailed for home. The *Kite*, steered through the Great Belt, was headed by light winds and took two weeks to reach Yarmouth.[99] With him went his secretary Thomas Wallis and Frederick Langford as his flag lieutenant. Amongst the fleet there were many regrets at Nelson's departure, for, whatever his state of mind, his popularity with officers and men was undiminished. Yet Thomas Masterman Hardy shrewdly observed of Nelson in a letter home: 'it is as much impossible for him to remain at home as it is for him to be <u>happy at sea</u> ... I am very comfortable with Adml Pole but

---

* Lieutenant William Davies of the *Tygress* was dismissed his ship for drunkenness and behaving in a 'Cruel, oppressive manner unbecoming the Character of a British Officer' ((UK)NA: PRO, ADM 1/5356, 13 June 1801). Lieutenant O'Brien of the *Cracker* escaped court martial.

I am not anxious to remain with him or any other Adm[ira]l (except Lord Nelson).'[100] Fremantle confided to his brother: 'Pole is very civil to me, he adopts Lord Howe's formality, which is not very ingratiating after Nelson's familiar manner, he is, however, a steady and honest good man.'[101]

Between April and June 1801 Nelson had retrieved his professional reputation as much by his achievements as commander-in-chief as by his presence of mind during the battle on 2 April. It was by no means assured that the new tsar would quickly reverse the anti-British stance of his father, or at least do so in time for the naval stores to be exported before the winter of 1801/2. The Swedes might have persuaded him otherwise. Nelson's fleet had strengthened the hand of Lord St Helens in the diplomatic negotiations that led to the end of the Northern Convention. In London in the second half of 1801 the price of Stockholm tar and flax fell dramatically, while St Petersburg hemp dropped from a peak of £86 to £43 a ton.[102] This time Nelson's public – if not his private – homecoming was uncontroversial and praise was warm. He had administered and fed a fleet in strange waters and stayed at sea, keeping clear of local personalities and politics, in contrast to the two years in Naples and Sicily, and his force had been absolutely welded to British policy and interests. In the opinion of Charles Greville, in a letter to Henry Addington, 'the late event in the Baltic has opened the eyes of many who considered Ld Nelson merely to be possessed of a rash Courage which rendered him fit only for forlorn hopes & the post of honor in desperate attacks.' He went on to attempt to persuade the prime minister to reward Nelson, recalling the previous occasion when Nelson had returned to England: 'he felt . . . a measure of personal injustice . . . it will hardly be credited that the Battle of the Nile, or any part of his command in the Mediterranean, was not mentioned or alluded to, in any of the occasions when Ld. N appeared in the presence; this I would not say if I did not know it from his own mouth.' Greville also lobbied for William Nelson to be made one of the chaplains to the king or to be given 'a stall in Westminster or Canonry Prebendary'.[103]

Nelson had been away from England for three and a half months and he returned to a troubled family. On 24 April his eldest brother Maurice had suddenly died of 'a brain fever'. Nelson had heard the news off Gotland when Lord St Helens had delivered a letter of genuine feeling from the comptroller of the Navy Board, Sir Andrew Snape Hamond: 'your favourite Brother's death . . . one of the most honourable and worthy men I ever knew and lament him when gone as a most irreparable loss.'[104] In a letter to Alexander Davison, Nelson was brusque: 'As the dead cannot be called back, it is of no use dwelling on those who are gone,' but he immediately undertook to ensure that Maurice's common law wife was financially secure.[105] Fanny was shocked, and worried too, for Maurice had been close to her. She wrote to Davison: 'I have truly lost a friend . . . my heart is full, too full . . . My good old Father feels this affliction sensibly.'[106]

Fanny still entertained hopes of a reconciliation, in spite of the 'final' letter of March. She wrote a letter of congratulation to Nelson when she heard news of the victory. She received nothing back and, as Edmund Nelson informed him, 'was heavily affected with her personal feelings at not receiving a line from your own hand'.[107] But Nelson had hardened his heart, asking Davison to ensure that she bother him no longer: 'a very liberal allowance to her, to be left to myself, and without any inquiries from her . . . my mind is fixed as fate; therefore you will send my determination in any way you may judge proper.'[108] Fanny wrote to Davison: 'My Lord Nelson will be grieved to hear of his Brother Maurice's death. He loved him most sincerely. I have not the happiness of hearing from My Lord. It hurt me too much even to mention it to you – Don't mention me in Yr letters, better not – pray do not.'[109] Rumours reached Edmund and Fanny of Nelson's determination not to live with Fanny: Edmund 'was so shocked he could hardly reach his chair'.[110] As a final act of loyalty, Fanny went from Bath to St James, where in his absence Nelson was invested as a viscount.[111]

The split between Nelson and Fanny was beginning to drive the family into opposing camps, which was shown when they met at Maurice's funeral. Fanny related to Davison: 'Mr Matcham would go to London and attend the funeral [at] Burnham. Mr N objects to that as Mrs M & Mr WN had a most terrible quarrel when he came from Plymouth.'[112] 'When the Revd Mr Nelson was last hear [sic] his conduct was so glaring that Mrs Matcham told her Husband that although she had determined not to know anything of My Lord Nelson's Conduct towards Me that as there was a party forming against Me, let the consequences be what it May she never wd desert me. Mr Matcham & William Nelson had a most violent quarrel – upon which the Revd WN told him Lord Nelson did not care for One of this family but himself and Children & that he had told him so.'[113] The Matchams and the Boltons tried to stay neutral. Nelson's elder sister Susannah, wife of the impecunious Thomas Bolton, wrote to Fanny in mid May: 'do not say you will not suffer us to take too much notice of you for fear it should Injure us with Lord Nelson. I assure you I have a pride, as well as himself, in doing what is right.'[114]

Avarice and ambition were uppermost in William Nelson's motives when he jumped into the Hamilton camp. Blandishments and discord came from

Emma Hamilton, often transmitted by his weak wife, Sarah. In a letter later that year Emma described Fanny as 'a very wicked, bad, artful woman', Edmund Nelson as 'unknowing', Josiah Nisbet as a 'villain': these three would, 'if this designing woman had had her way, have put you all aside'. She went on to sow doubts about the loyalties of the Matchams and the Boltons, who were still seeking neutral ground.[115] While Emma was prepared to use every weapon, the good-natured Sir William was more gentle. After the news of the Battle of Copenhagen arrived in London, the Hamiltons gave a celebratory dinner, which he described in a letter to Nelson: 'Your brother was more extraordinary than ever. He would get up suddenly and cut a caper, rubbing his hands, every time that the thought of your fresh laurels came into his head.'[116]

William Nelson's cynical behaviour goaded Fanny into her bitterest comments in her letters to Alexander Davison. William – 'to my knowledge' – had treated Maurice with contempt during his lifetime. 'We none of us thought an opportunity would so soon offer for William Nelson to show himself in his right Colours. He never, Never had a spark of affection for his Br Maurice – gain, gain is his Motto.'[117] 'So much Art, so much deceit – The Revd Mr W Nelson expressions of affection for his dear Brother Maurice almost distracts me . . . Mrs Matcham has just been telling me that she wishes her brother had left his father some little token of remembrance as he has been a heavy expense to him – but in my humble opinion not greater than the Revd.'[118] From Bath she wrote to Davison: 'Letters are received most days from the Revd. Mr W Nelson. I take myself out of the room (not but what I see them) – I am not surprised at his contempt of you . . . but I own when I hear his name mentioned I give an invol[untary] movement.'[119]

Fanny's letters to Davison become less angry with the family but more anguished, focusing on Emma Hamilton. 'No names are ever mentioned in his letters to his father – I mean the Lady of 23 Picc[adilly] or has he noticed me . . . I beg when you write to him not to mention me – so much has been said to him that I believe it has angered him instead of doing good . . . Never mention me at 23 Pic[c]adilly.'[120] Fanny's letter of 27 June protests: 'I did not mean the least coolness or indifference to my dear Lord.'[121] She poured her heart out to Davison:

When I heard on Sunday that my Dear Lord was hourly expect'd My heart was all thankfulness and pleasure, but a moment's unwelcome and intruding reflection made me truly a miserable and pitiable being. I love him. I would do anything in the World to convince him of my affection. I was truly sensible of My good fortune in having such a Husband. Surely I have angered him. It was done <u>unconsciously</u> and without the least <u>intention</u> I can truly say. My wish, My desire was to please him – And if he will have the goodness to send for me, I will make it my study to obey him in every wish or desire of his – and with cheerfulness – I still hope – He is affectionate and possesses the best of hearts – he will not make me Miserable . . . <u>and if you find</u> that you can <u>mention me</u> I will thank, I will esteem it the greatest favor you can confer on me. I shall feel myself under very great obligations. You or no one can tell my feelings in what I have suffered since My Lord left England.[122]

One can be sure that Nelson had seen little of this suppressed emotion and sadness, or of the love that lay behind it. It was too late to show it now.

24

Boulogne

July–October 1801

Today I dine with Adm. Graeme [commander-in-chief, Nore] *who has also lost his right arm, and as the Commander of the Troops has lost his leg, I expect we shall be caricatured as the lame defenders of England.*   Nelson to Emma Hamilton, 27 July 1801[1]

I do not at present see any prospect of getting at the Enemy & I most seriously hope we shall have Peace, I do not believe any Armistice is thought of: Preliminaries or nothing I hope is the plan.
                    Thomas Troubridge to Nelson, 2 September 1801[2]

While Nelson was in the Baltic, the minds of the lords of the Admiralty were turning towards the Channel. Concentrations of troops and flat-bottomed boats at the ports of Le Havre, Dunkirk and Boulogne were reported. On 6 April an intelligence source in Boulogne reported that an envoy from the first consul had arrived that afternoon to review troops, then numbering 1,500, and that lodgings for a further 1,800 men had been ordered. Fifty boats were in the port; it was thought that they were destined for Holland.[3] The possibility that they were to be used for the invasion of England ('Les Projets de Descente') was first contained in a report of 21 April. Tentative confirmation of invasion came from a high-level source in Paris on 25 April – the first consul was preparing to visit the troops along the coast near Dunkirk – even though this report cast doubt on the timing and viability of an invasion.[4]

A month before, Addington's government had made the first peace proposal to the French. The desire for peace in the country was strong, encouraged by spring wheat prices that were even higher than those in 1796, accompanied by unrest and rioting.[5] Initially Napoleon was in a strong position and had no need to make concessions, but from April several events led to an improvement in the British strategic and diplomatic position. The death of the tsar and the collapse of the Northern Convention were soon followed by French reversals in Egypt and Portugal. These developments reduced French pressure and loosened Napoleon's firm hold on events.[6] As peace negotiations dragged on through the spring, his unemployed armies gathered at the Channel ports.

In May, French invasion preparations began in earnest, and the British reintroduced the counter-invasion orders of 1797. The number of British sloops and gun brigs in the Channel Islands was increased. In southern counties cattle were driven inland, and main roads were blocked. On 21 June the official French government newspaper *Le Moniteur* published the first consul's threat of invasion.[7] Reports from Boulogne told of a press for seamen and the arrival of Contre [Rear] Admiral René Latouche-Tréville, commander-in-chief of the 'force naval de la Manche', to take command of the flotilla of flat boats. Intelligence, however, continued to throw doubt on whether Napoleon intended to invade. According to one source, senior French officers thought that the invasion plan was 'un projet chimérique'.[8] Did Napoleon really mean anything more than to intimidate the British government and public into accepting disadvantageous peace terms? However confident the British government was of resisting an invasion attempt, or of facing down Napoleon's bluff, it had to take measures to counter it.[9]

Nelson was soon caught up in these events. He came ashore at Yarmouth from the *Kite* at noon on 30 June, visiting the wounded from Copenhagen in the hospital there, arriving in London on 1 July, where he reported immediately to St Vincent.[10] He then visited Boxhill in Surrey with the Hamiltons for a few days, and afterwards they travelled to Staines for a 'quiet retreat in the country'. It is reasonable to suppose that it was during these days that plans were laid for Nelson to buy a house. Alexander Davison found him 'better in Health than I had reason to expect', although 'there yet remained a very troublesome disagreeable Cough'.[11] When staying there Nelson received an invitation from the prime minister to dinner – alone. 'You will find me with my family and without any other company.'[12] We have no record of their conversation, but it was followed immediately by two developments. First, by special 'remainder', Nelson was allowed to perpetuate his barony so that it could pass to the families of his brothers and sisters, thus preventing the extinction of his peerage. Addington made Nicholas Vansittart responsible for ensuring that 'the Barony of Nelson [was] expedited through the Offices'.[13] Second, Nelson agreed to be the 'Commander-in-Chief of a Squadron of Ships and Vessels employed on a Particular Service', responsible for the defence of the coasts between Beachy

Head and Orfordness against invasion.[14] It seems that a little gentlemanly horse-trading took place, the politicians reckoning that the prime minister would be more successful than St Vincent in persuading Nelson to go to sea again so soon after his return from the Baltic. Addington too is likely to have stressed the importance of Nelson's name and reputation as essential to quieten public fears in the face of the invasion threat from Napoleon.

The cabinet was overseeing other defence measures. Lord Cornwallis was appointed to the eastern command of the army. On 21 July all leave was suspended for the Horse Guards. The next day 4,730 volunteers were mustered in Hyde Park, watched by 30,000 spectators. St Vincent wrote to both Vice-Admiral Alexander Graeme, commander-in-chief at the Nore, and Admiral Skeffington Lutwidge, Nelson's old captain when he went as a midshipman to the Arctic and now commander-in-chief in the Downs, to ensure their cooperation with Nelson. They were to be responsible, as St Vincent put it, for 'what is generally understood to be the Port Duty'.[15] Nelson received detailed instructions from the Admiralty on 26 July 'to be employed on a particular service . . . in the defence of the mouths of the Thames and Medway, and all that part of the coasts of Sussex, Kent and Essex, comprised between Beachy Head and Orford Ness'. Once those arrangements were in place, Nelson was required to 'make such a disposition . . . as you may judge most advisable for blocking up or destroying, if practicable, the enemy's vessels and craft in the ports wherein they may be assembled, or if they should be able to put to sea, for destroying them'.[16] St Vincent left it to his commander on the spot to decide where such an attack should be made, but all the intelligence steadily coming into the Admiralty pointed to Boulogne as the main port in which the French invasion craft were gathering.[17]

The navy was overstretched, and the government was facing difficulties in finding extra vessels and manning them. It tried to get the Sea Fencibles, fishermen and others in coastal areas with sea experience, to go to sea with the navy, but they remained uncooperative, arguing that they had signed on for the defence of the country, not to attack the enemy. From the Admiralty, Thomas Troubridge wrote to Nelson: 'I most sincerely hope that the Fencibles will embark if not we will impress them but keep this to yourself.'[18] Channel pilots held out for more money.[19] Troubridge was trying to bring men down from Scotland.[20] The Treasury made sixteen revenue cutters available for Nelson's command.[21] Even Greenwich Hospital was emptied, but not with great effect. On board the *Unite* Captain Thomas Harvey had sixty-nine pensioners from Greenwich. He reported: 'Twelve of them have lost legs – the rolling of the ship on the weather tide is such that it is dangerous for them to attempt walking the Deck – not a man of them have a Change of Cloaths or linen – and in general they are very old and infirm men – many of them are sickly and scorbutic.'[22] This state of affairs even got back to Troubridge in London, and he advised Nelson: 'perhaps they would do better in one of the ships in smoother water.'[23]

Nelson's speed of movement and thought were rapid as he travelled from London to the Downs to take up his command. He took with him Edward Parker, now a captain, as aide-de-camp, reaching Sheerness by 27 July, where he hoisted his flag in, but did not board, the *Unite* frigate.[24] He used her for signalling to other ships for lieutenants in order to distribute his orders quickly. Nelson conferred with Vice-Admiral Graeme. He divided his ships into small groups and spread them widely: some in Hollesley Bay off the Suffolk coast, some off the Essex coast and some off the Swale and the Thames.[25] He also had to be diplomatic with his fellow commanders-in-chief, writing to Edward Berry, for instance, commanding the *Ruby* (64) but under the orders of Admiral Archibald Dickson, commander-in-chief, North Sea: 'Although by Admiralty orders I am not absolutely to take you under my command, yet I am authorised to give you any directions which I may think proper.' He sent Berry two revenue cutters, 'who must always be kept on the look-out, so that you may not be surprised in the night by an Enemy close to you'.[26]

Edward Parker described to Emma Hamilton the scene at Sheerness, where Nelson was 'received by the Acclamations of the People who looked with mild but most affectionate amazement at him who was once more going to step forward in defence of this Country . . . In the short time we were at Sheerness He regulated and gave orders for 30 of the Ships under his command, made everyone pleased, filled them with emulation and set them all on the Que Vive.'[27] Emma also received a letter from Nelson at Sheerness: 'Not one moment do I have to myself and my business is endless. I have not rose from my chair since 7 this morning.'[28] He was away at noon by post-chaise on 29 July, stopping at Faversham to attempt to enthuse the Sea Fencibles and later that night reached Deal.

Here Nelson paused to confer with Lutwidge, using the *Leyden* (64) as his flagship to convey orders; he was aboard for only one day. In all, he had over seventy ships under his command, including three 64s, three 50s and seven frigates, but most were small: eleven sloops, 32-gun brigs and seven of the all-important bomb vessels, each armed with two long-range mortars.[29] By September he had 148 vessels under his command.[30] Some of the larger ones, however, were still at the Nore, unable to sail because of lack of men. The next day, 31 July, he hoisted his flag in the *Medusa*, a new 38-gun frigate, just arrived in the Downs, captained by John Gore, whom Nelson had first met when Gore was a lieutenant in Corsica. With the *Greyhound* and *Spencer* revenue cutters in company, the ship set a southerly course for Boulogne, beating into the WSW wind. On 2 August he joined the squadron anchored off Boulogne. The slow bomb vessels had arrived two days before, straight from the Baltic.[31] In the nine days since Nelson had received his orders from the Admiralty, he had organized a credible force from what little was available, and had moved into an attacking position, in itself a remarkable achievement.

The next night, with the *Medusa* standing off, Nelson sent the gig inshore to reconnoitre and he himself went in the *Nile* cutter.[32] The situation was not unlike that at Copenhagen, with depth of water and range of the bomb vessels critical. Admiral Latouche-Tréville was aware that he was facing Nelson, for he informed his minister of marine of the fact on 2 August.[33] The French admiral had moored, in shallow water, a defensive line of six gunboats, five bomb vessels, armed with mortars, and eight launches in front of Boulogne harbour, in order to keep the British bomb vessels out of range of the town.[34] The French vessels 'were laying in twelve feet of water [at] high water, and at low water they were aground', reported one midshipman.[35] It was a summer position only; 'if the wind comes fresh at WNW they are lost,' Nelson informed Lutwidge.[36] As a consequence, the British bomb vessels, with relative deep draughts, had to keep their distance.[37] The French Army also manned land batteries on the high ground above and beside Boulogne to cover the line of gun vessels. With little wind there was no question of risking other ships within range of the French land ordnance. A long-distance naval bombardment was unlikely to be decisive. St Vincent was cautious in his expectations. He wrote to Nelson: 'our experience shows the uncertainty of sea bombardments.'[38] To Emma, Nelson was characteristically aggressive: 'The wind is too far to the Westward to allow our Bombs to go on the Coast this Morning or some of the Rascals should repent their vaporise[ing] nonsense.'[39]

At dawn the next day, 4 August, with light airs from the WSW, Nelson ordered five bomb vessels to move forward and open fire. They kept up the bombardment until nine that evening, firing 750 to 848 (variously estimated) shot and incendiary shells, or 'carcasses'.[40] After returning the initial salvos, the French did not resist, for the range of their guns was limited because of the inferior quality of their gunpowder. Nevertheless, the British sustained some casualties, including Captain Peter Fryer of the artillery, who was wounded 'by the bursting of a French shell'; an English bomb

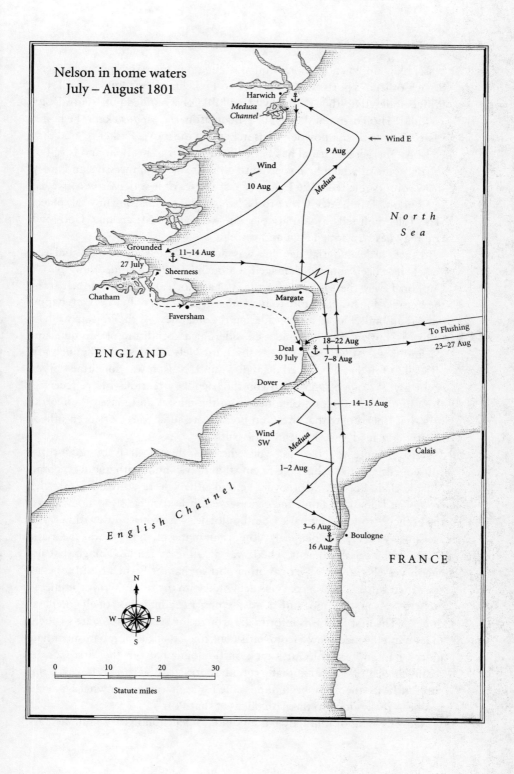

Nelson in home waters
July – August 1801

Harwich

Medusa Channel

D

← Wind E

9 Aug

Medusa

Wind

10 Aug

North Sea

Grounded

11–14 Aug

27 July

Sheerness

Chatham

Faversham

Margate

ENGLAND

Deal
30 July

18–22 Aug

To Flushing

23–27 Aug

7–8 Aug

Dover

14–15 Aug

Wind
SW

Medusa

Calais

1–2 Aug

English Channel

3–6 Aug

16 Aug

Boulogne

FRANCE

N

W   E

S

0   10   20   30

Statute miles

vessel blew up when its mortar burst, killing one man and injuring others. French official reports made out that no Frenchman was killed, but Troubridge doubted it: 'they deny any being kill'd or wounded but Neutrals say 16 kill'd. The Town not damaged.'[41] Boats from the *Medusa* kept the bomb vessels supplied with powder. Nelson kept on the move. Parker related that Nelson, 'energetic as usual has been rowing about in his Boat and is full of spirits, some of which he has given to all'.[42] It was an impressive and noisy show, observable from the English coast. News of it was swiftly conveyed to London. Troubridge wrote to Nelson as the bombardment took place: 'The Telegraph tells us you are playing away at the Miscreants. God send you may destroy both Town and vessels.'[43]

In fact, little material damage was achieved. Nelson claimed that ten vessels had been sunk or damaged; Latouche-Tréville claimed only two.[44] Captain Fryer, the captain of artillery, had not expected too much from the bombardment. He wrote to his senior officer at Woolwich: 'I am happy we did any mischief at all considering the smallness of the objects we had to fire at, but we certainly had a considerable expenditure of Ammunition – I find in the *Sulphur* 200 shells (by Lord Nelson's desire). The men are all well.' Only Fryer received a small wound. Nelson was solicitous, Fryer reporting: 'I cannot describe to you the friendly attentions I have received from him.'[45] Information obtained from the master and mate of a neutral brig that 'they knew that five Gun boats were sunk & six or seven others greatly damaged' may be nearer the truth.[46]

Nelson wrote to Nepean: 'The whole of this affair is of no further consequence, than to show the Enemy that they cannot with impunity come outside their Ports.'[47] Moreover, he and others were convinced that the troops and boats in Boulogne represented little danger. 'I do not believe the French Army will embark from Boulogne,' he wrote to Edward Berry.[48] Nelson saw that psychological, rather than material, damage was the main result of the bombardment. There was also the added advantage that no enemy vessels could escape to another port so that the French could concentrate their forces.[49] St Vincent was delighted with the result, writing immediately to Nelson: 'I cannot sufficiently express my admiration of all you have done.'[50] The first lord was informed, through the secretary of state's office, that an intelligence source from Paris confirmed that the bombardment had indeed had an impact: 'Our attack on Boulogne has put the First Consul so much out of Humour that Nobody dares to open their Lips on the subject. It has therefore been impossible for me to ascertain what Damage has been really done to the Armament at that Port.'[51]

Nelson's state of mind after the bombardment followed a familiar pattern. He had received another upsetting letter from Emma, and though it is not possible to be sure what caused his wrath, it seems that the purchase of a house was at issue. During the evening of 4 August he penned a furiously written, scratched and blotted letter to her: 'Buy the house at Turnham Green. I can pay for it. How could you be angry with me?'[52] As a consequence of this pressure, Nelson tried to get leave of absence from the Admiralty. Edward Parker explained to Alexander Davison: 'it is her alone who is persuading him to go to London to purchase her a Villa' and that his excuse to St Vincent for going was 'to plan a little expedition'.[53] The first lord wrote back to Nelson at once: 'The public mind is so very much tranquillis'd by your being at your post, it is extremely desirable that you should continue there.'[54] Troubridge also wrote the same day: 'Your being on the spot keeps the minds of all classes easy, & it seems to be the General Opinion & wish of all this B[oar]d, as well as HM Ministers that you should not quit your Post. I therefore intreat your Lordship not to make any request of that nature.'[55] This marked the beginning of an estrangement between Nelson and Troubridge, which the troubled Troubridge consistently tried to heal; during August he wrote nearly every day to Nelson. On 14 August Troubridge wrote defensively on the question of leave: '– as Admiral Dickson has only been absent I think 7 days for three years & had been refused at this critical time, I did not see how the Board could grant it.'[56] From Nelson's perspective, Troubridge had now moved into the centre of power and was subject to the same sort of criticism that Nelson had directed at all his superiors since the 1780s. Frustrated at this lack of understanding, Troubridge wrote back to Nelson: 'I wish you was a Member of this Board. In a short time you would see how difficult our task is: what at present seems simple cannot be done.'[57]

In spite of doubts about the threat from the troops and flotilla at Boulogne, Nelson maintained publicly that Napoleon still intended to invade. On 6 August, Nelson wrote to some of the captains of Sea Fencibles in Essex: 'There can be no doubt of the intention of the French to attempt the Invasion of our Country.'[58] Privately, however, Nelson was less confident. By early September he wrote to Lord Keith: 'The force collected at Boulogne about 20,000 men, and craft sufficient to carry them, but I can hardly believe they will be such fools as to make the attempt. They had better let us catch them half seas over.'[59]

Intelligence, however, still confirmed that Napoleon was making aggressive statements. St Vincent passed on news to Nelson on 10 August: 'Our advice from Paris says that the First Consul has declared himself Generalissimo of the Army of Invasion, and that we are to look to Flanders for the grand effort.'[60] St Vincent added: 'I have always been of opinion that the real attempt of the enemy will be made from the Dutch and Flemish harbours, because of the great number of flat-bottomed vessels constantly employed in the inland navigation of those countries, besides that there is always a large body of troops in them.'[61] If there was to be an attempt, Flushing (Vlissingen), a port covered by ships under the command of Admiral Dickson, seemed to be the most likely port of embarkation. Immediately after the bombardment of 4 August, Nelson tried to sail north and east to Flushing, but the wind was easterly and he turned back to Margate, although he sent some reinforcements to the blockading ships off the Dutch coast.[62] It was as well he did not reach Flushing, for St Vincent anticipated trouble from Admiral Dickson, an elderly admiral of the old school, and sent Nelson a firmly worded warning; Nelson knew that this meant, as he put it to a junior captain, that he was 'not to interfere with Admiral Dickson's cruizers'.[63]

Before Nelson left for Boulogne for the first attack, he had ascertained from the naval storekeeper at Deal that 'twelve or fourteen Flat-bottomed Boats would be ready to put in the water before the end of the week'. He now wanted them armed with 8-inch howitzers and 24-pound carronades.[64] The Ordnance could find no spare howitzers at first, and then only a few captured French ones; the Admiralty tried hard to expedite this order, but the Ordnance, as St Vincent explained to Nelson, 'are not so quick as our impatient spirit at this Board wishes them to be'.[65] Several of the bomb vessels off Boulogne had suffered damage after such a heavy use of their mortars and had to return to Sheerness for repairs.[66] A further attack on Boulogne was not feasible until these craft were ready to use their mortars again.

With the wind still in the north-east, there was no possibility of going to Flushing; instead Nelson took the Medusa up to Harwich on 8 August to see if the Sea Fencibles of Suffolk and Essex were more accommodating than those in Kent. Anchoring off the Bawdsey Sands, he took on a pilot to take the ship to Harwich. There she anchored outside the port, as the master noted, 'in Rowling Grounds – Fort Landguard Saluted ye flag with 19 Guns – which we returned in Equal Number'.[67] Nelson spoke to the Sea Fencible captains, but the men were still not prepared to go aboard a king's ship until danger really threatened the English coast. Nelson therefore ordered the revenue cutters from the Nore to various points on the Suffolk, Essex and Kent shores, 'ready to receive the Sea Fencibles whenever the time arrives that every man must come forth'.[68] Stores for the Medusa were ordered from Harwich naval yard.

The next day the wind was at ENE, which, the local pilots declared, made it impossible to tack out of the main channel. Nelson was fortunate that an experienced Admiralty surveyor was at Harwich at that moment; he had the most detailed knowledge of the Thames estuary available. Graeme Spence was the cousin of Lieutenant Murdoch Mackenzie, the first surveyor to undertake a comprehensive survey of the waters around the British Isles. Spence had nearly thirty years' experience of these waters.[69] At high tide he took the *Medusa* on a new south-easterly course from Harwich. 'Recd a Pilot who took charge of the ship . . . at . . . 1130 weighed and made sail over the Ness Flats,' noted the master in his log.[70] When the ship was in deep water 'at the buoy of the Gun-Fleet', Spence left the ship carrying a letter of recommendation from Nelson to Nepean, noting that the channel 'was never yet navigated by a Ship of War of this size'.[71] Spence named the channel after the *Medusa* on the Admiralty chart. Nelson immediately wrote a letter reporting his position to St Vincent, bragging of his knowledge of the Thames from his time as a midshipman.[72] But even Nelson was not exempt from the sea's disconcerting habit of punishing complacency. At seven o'clock that evening, with the tide low, the *Medusa* grounded on a mud bank off Sheerness. Two hours later she got off and anchored at the Nore in seven fathoms.[73]

During 14 and 15 August the *Medusa* beat down the Channel against south-westerly winds towards Boulogne. His planned second attack was well known to the French, for preparations were visible along the Kent coast. Troubridge wrote to Nelson: 'I see your Lordship's plans got into the newspapers. There is some active agent writing from your division.'[74] The Admiralty received information from their Paris source: 'I rather suspect that the private signals and Instructions for His Majesty's ships have been betrayed.'[75] Two days before the attack Latouche-Tréville sent the minister of marine 'Le plan figurative du l'attaque par l'Amiral Nelson'.[76] Even the prefect of Calais appeared to know. When an American applied to him for a passport, 'he immediately informed me, that Lord Nelson was going to make another attack, and until that was made, he would not permit me to embark.'[77]

Unable to mount an effective bombardment, Nelson turned to the idea of a surprise night attack, as he had done at Tenerife. Without troops at his disposal, he had no other option. Latouche-Tréville had reinforced his vessels with soldiers, as well as nets to prevent boarding; they were waiting and alert. The night of 15 August was moonless, 'light airs and cloudy weather'. The preparations and the initial attack are described in the *Medusa*'s log book:

Employed fitting out the boats. 8.10 hoisted boats out & armed them. 10.40 Manned the boats – dropped them astern in two subdivisions. 11.20 Boats assembled in 4 divisions, each division 14 boats commanded by Captains Somerville, Parker, Cotgrave & Jones, & 8 flat boats w. Howitzers in each commanded by Captain Conn. 11.30 Boats attack enemy's flotilla. 1.30 attack commenced by boats and howitzers 1.45 Musquetry ceased firing.

In the darkness the four divisions of boats immediately lost touch with each other. The tidal current, running parallel to the shore and at some states of the tide at one and a half knots, separated them further. The division under Robert Jones was swept past the French gunships and saw no action. The other three divisions attacked different parts of the line separately and at different times. Edward Parker's division reached the centre of the line, near the Mole, first, but his seamen and marines failed to board a brig, unable to penetrate the defensive netting rigged between the gunwales and the lower yards of the French vessels.

2.15 barge returned having 8 killed & wounded, manned her and sent her to the assistance of the other boats. At 3.0 the two flat boats, launch & 1 cutter returned. Captain Parker, Lieut[s]. Pelly & Langford, Mr Kirby Master, Hon. Anthony Maitland, wounded. Mr Wm Gore, Mid, Killed – several seamen & marines killed & wounded.

Casualties in Parker's division numbered twenty-one killed and forty-two wounded. Parker himself was severely wounded in the thigh. Isaac Cotgrave's boats were driven away, with five killed and twenty-nine wounded.

At 3 am the attack commenced on the enemy from another division. Employed getting the wounded on board. At 4.0 the firing ceased. Saw the boats returning from the attack. Hoist boats in at 4.15. Barge & cutter returned. W[illia]m Bristow, Master's Mate, killed. Small lugger taken. Several wounded men from the Revenue and Hired Cutters.[78]

In the third attack of the night Philip Somerville carried a brig near Boulogne pier, but she was moored with chains that could not be cut, and he and his men had to retreat with eight killed and fifty-five wounded.[79] French casualties were comparatively light, with eight killed and forty wounded during the whole night.[80] Nelson's ships left for the Downs by eight the next morning. The Medusa sent eighteen killed and twenty wounded to the hospital at Deal. While landing them, four of the crew deserted.[81]

(*top*) The *Racehorse* and the *Carcass* in the ice, 4–8 August 1773, by John Cleveley, who based his watercolour upon drawings by Philip D'Auvergne, a midshipman serving on board the *Racehorse*. The crews were ordered to haul the ships' boats over the ice towards Spitsbergen to reach the Dutch whalers before they returned south before the winter. Nelson had charge of one of the boats.

(*bottom*) View of Bastia in Corsica by Lieutenant Ralph Willet Miller, May 1794. Miller was later Nelson's flag captain at Santa Cruz and also one of his captains at the Battle of the Nile. This view shows the mountainous coastline that made Bastia difficult to capture.

Frances, Lady Nelson (*top*), sketch of 1798 by Daniel Orme. Nelson and Frances were married on the West Indian island of Nevis on 11 March 1787, when he was twenty-nine and she twenty-six. Nervous and anxious, Frances was the opposite of the confident and sensual Emma Hamilton (*bottom*), painted by Johann Heinrich Schmidt in Vienna in 1800. Nelson kept this portrait in his cabin.

Nelson leading the boarding party on to the Spanish ships at Cape St Vincent, after a painting by James Daniell. This print is dated 1 November 1798, although by this time Nelson's arm had already been amputated.

Nelson before the assault on Santa Cruz, explaining the method of attack. This watercolour may have been painted by Ralph Willet Miller, whose sketch of Bastia shows him to be a competent artist.

(*top*) Nelson's reception at Fonthill, December 1800. This print accompanied the account of the Fonthill visit that appeared in the *Gentleman's Magazine*.

(*bottom*) *A Jig around the Statue of Peace; or, All Parties Reconciled* by W. Holland, 6 October 1801, celebrating the Peace of Amiens. Nelson was used by caricaturists to symbolize the defence of Britain; here he holds hands with Napoleon. Fox and Pitt make up the circle.

The four phases of the Battle of the Nile by Robert Dodd. As is usual with representations of the battle, the sequence is dominated by the burning and destruction of *L'Orient*.

'At Evening'

'10 O'Clock'

'Midnight'

'The Ensuing Morning'

Merton, from the sketchbook by Thomas Baxter. Baxter painted a series of charming views of the house and gardens, as well as members of the Nelson family and Emma in graceful poses.

Opposed landings were always difficult, but every condition that had governed Nelson's second attack at night at Tenerife four years earlier was repeated at Boulogne, with almost exactly the same disastrous effect. Nelson's orders were as detailed as at Tenerife.[82] 'An affair with boats took place last night,' one of the artillery captains reported to his seniors; 'owing to the darkness of the night the Enemy being well secured with high boarding netting and moored with chains, the result was not so successful as was expected.'[83]

Many then and since have questioned Nelson's judgement in ordering the second attack at Boulogne, given that he was convinced that the forces in the port alone did not constitute an invasion threat. His orders from St Vincent had emphasized the need for an attack, yet the decision was unquestionably rash. He failed to recognize that his plans had been compromised, and he underestimated his opponents. His plan was simple in conception but complicated to execute, with boats rowing some distance across the current. He was again under stress, writing to Lutwidge on 14 August that 'his head was split with pain'; St Vincent was concerned at his fatigue.[84] Yet it is a mistake to see the night attack merely as compensation for the failure of the initial bombardment to break the French line, for Nelson had requested the shallow-drafted flat boats well before the first bombardment on 4 August. He was under pressure from politicians to make a showing, for they were concerned that Napoleon's activities in the Channel ports might be a diversion for an invasion of Ireland.[85] The government was still negotiating peace terms, and Napoleon was proving as tricky as ever. A reminder of the capacity of the British Navy to mount an attack on the coast of France, however costly in lives, was not necessarily regarded as a failure. Addington saw the action 'as the sort of cordial to the country which no-one has administered so consistently as yourself . . . fresh proofs of that spirit and determination which are perpetually confirming our naval superiority and perpetually disinclining the enemy to contest it'.[86] Troubridge wrote Nelson a letter of comfort: 'It is true a more Gallant Attack was never made or deserved success.'[87] Public opinion was, however, sceptical. Opposition newspapers throughout these months were doubtful of an invasion danger.[88] Lord Hood in Greenwich wrote to William Cornwallis that Nelson 'had taken the Bull by the Horns & to have sacrificed a great number of lives without an adequate object, for the bringing off a few gunboats could not be one, for they could be replaced in a fortnight. This I am told is generally said in Town where I go very seldom.'[89]

Among the criticism came a blackmail note. In early September, Nelson received a highly critical account of his orders in the recent attack, entitled

'Remarks by a Seaman on the Attack at Boulogne'. This so-called damning material would be published unless he enclosed 'by return of post a bank note for hundred pounds, to Mr Hill, to be left at the Post Office till called for, London'. Anticipating Wellington's 'Publish and be damned', Nelson wrote back a short note addressed to Hill at the Post Office: 'I defy you and your malice.' He then requested Nepean 'to send proper people to take up whoever comes for Mr Hill's letter'. No one was arrested.[90] A critique of actions throughout his career did appear in the *County Herald*, a newspaper with circulation around London, but it was ignored and created no stir.[91] St Vincent had never taken heed of newspaper comment. He wrote to Nelson: 'Sarcasm in Newspapers are a tribute every man who is placed in a high situation must submit to; it is evident that those I have read are levelled at the Administration of the Government, and intended to deprive the country of your eminent services.'[92]

Such lofty advice came at a low time. The wounds of Edward Parker and Frederick Langford saddened and depressed Nelson, particularly those of 'little' Parker, whom he described several times as a 'son'.[93] Langford recovered, but Parker's thigh never mended. Nelson and others nursed him ashore at Deal. Nelson wrote to St Vincent on 16 August: 'After all this sorrow for me, my health is not improved; my fever is very severe this morning.'[94] Nelson also found the motion of smaller ships in the short seas of the Channel made him seasick. Nicholas Vansittart wrote to Nelson: 'I should have hoped that the inconvenience of sea-sickness had been confined to us landsmen, or at least that the sea would have had more respect for one who has long been its Master.'[95] Nelson also confessed this to the first lord. A strong gale blew in early September, but Nelson was ashore.[96] St Vincent wrote: 'I rejoice that you are not afloat in this gale, for although I was never sea-sick, I have seen so much distress in those subject to it, that makes me feel most sensibly for your Lordship.'[97]

Sadness and worry over Parker did not prevent Nelson planning a further attack, this time on Flushing. Intelligence was still coming in of concentrations of troops and vessels there, and at Ostend and Dunkirk.[98] Troubridge distrusted some of the intelligence: 'I wish the Smuglers may be correct in general. They are great liars & mislead.'[99] But those serving under Nelson expected more action, for he issued orders on 20 August 'in which he assures all under his Command that the Enemy will not have long to boast of their security and that he will himself lead us in to certain Victory'.[100] Nelson, however, was now unusually cautious, for the strength of the tides and the intricacies of the sandbanks at the mouth of the Scheldt made Flushing a difficult target. Nevertheless, from 23 to 27 August Nelson took thirty assorted ships, including bombs and fire vessels, across to Flushing. He and Captain Gore took a close look at the port in a hired cutter, as he reported to Nepean, 'four or five leagues from our ships, and near three from the enemy'.[101] When he saw the navigational difficulties for himself he decided without delay to disperse his fleet, sending them back to their different stations of the Downs and off Margate.[102] Troubridge was also cautious: 'I was always of the opinion that the Flushing ships lay too high to be attacked with any prospect of success, our Pilots know nothing of the place, the Smuglers are in vessels of an easy draft of Water and come out on the flood & the Channells was Buoy'd . . . we are all glad you abided with your own judgement.'[103] Further attacks against other Dutch ports were later discounted.[104]

Then Emma and Sir William arrived in Deal on 27 August.[105] The next day Nelson shifted his flag from the *Medusa* to the *Amazon*, a frigate of a similar size, and for nearly three weeks he lived ashore with them. The Hamiltons were accompanied by Sarah Nelson, who wrote a series of gossipy, superficial letters to her husband. 'I should have been glad to have staid all night at Canterbury,' she related on 27 August, 'but am very glad we did not for before I was out of Bed, I heard your brother was coming in & we have had the pleasure of Break fasting with him & Capt. Hardy.' She and Lady Hamilton bathed often, and visited the Lutwidges and others in the vicinity: 'I am glad on your brother's account we are nowhere, for it is very blowing weather & he would be on Board if we were not here, he is very well & in good spirits'.[106] Emma had found a property for Nelson at Merton in Surrey, and he wrote immediately to William Haslewood, his solicitor, urging him to secure it.[107] She also took her turn at nursing Edward Parker. An unexpected visitor was Josiah Nisbet, still without a ship. Sarah wrote to William Nelson: 'I was at church, so I did not see him . . . your Brother did not ask him to stay to dinner, nor did my Lady see him, and I am glad I was out, for I never wish to see him again.'[108]

The Hamiltons left on 16 September, and Nelson settled back to the routine of running the squadron, although he was made miserable again by the course of Parker's grievous wound. Parker's leg was eventually amputated at the thigh, but, in spite of the attentions of Dr Baird, after rallying, the young man died on 27 September. Nelson wrote to Davison: 'I am grieved almost to death.'[109] Nelson paid for Parker's funeral and settled his outstanding debts. 'The Admiralty have refused to bury Capt. Parker. He might have stunk above ground or been thrown in a ditch,' he wrote bitterly to Emma; 'except in my own dear Emma, I can safely declare that I never found gratitude.'[110] From Troubridge came the comforting but uncomfortable advice: 'I feel much for your distress about Parker, but really you should not feel having sent him on Service, that any part of the misfortune attaches to you.'[111]

Nelson was not the only one to experience low morale. Naval discipline always suffered at a time of peace negotiations following a long war. Crews in the Irish squadron off Bantry Bay mutinied at this time following a report that the squadron was to be sent to the West Indies.[112] Nelson was accosted in the streets of Deal 'by a vagabond', as he described the man to St Vincent, for 'arraigning my conduct in being careless of poor Seaman's lives'. Troubridge sympathized: 'I rather think the improper growling conversations, held in the Ward Rooms, has caused the Seamen to Murmur, both in my opinion, without cause'. Troubridge's solution was to make the first lieutenants accountable for the conduct of the wardrooms: 'if he is found encouraging or suffering any improper talk, he should be erased from the List; some Example of this sort I see will be necessary.'[113] Nelson wrote to St Vincent: 'The Wardroom will prate, I believe, none of us can doubt, and it has its bad effects. The Boat service I believe is got very unpopular. Gore flogged some of his chaps severely for some very improper expressions.'[114] Exceptionally, two men were given thirty-six lashes for drunkenness on board the *Amazon*.[115] Stories of subversive handbills posted in Deal were circulating among Nelson's captains, though Troubridge doubted their authenticity.[116] Nelson began to lose confidence in the men he commanded, writing to Nepean that 'if I was to order a boat expedition it would be obey'd, certainly not in such a zealous manner as to give me confidence.'[117] But that was not how it seemed in London, from where Troubridge assured him: 'The Board & all the World are so thoroughly pleased & satisfied with all your Lordship's Arrangements, that all feel at their ease while you are afloat.'[118] Nelson was not to be cheered, concluding a note to Emma: 'I am very low. Bad weather.'[119]

Although Nelson's letters to Troubridge for this period have not survived, Troubridge's replies make it clear that Nelson was lashing out at his old friend. These two ambitious men were gradually drifting apart. 'I feel much distress'd at the part of the letter', Troubridge wrote on 20 September, 'which construe that this Board would envy any Success your Lordship might have, & feast on your failure. If I am right I will venture to say there never was a charge so unmerited on your real Friends & cannot persuade myself but some person has been poisoning your mind against us.'[120] Four days later Troubridge assured Nelson: 'if you had fail'd the envy, hatred & ill Nature of the World which you think would have been bestowed on us, would not have given us one moment's concern.'[121] Troubridge was feeling the strain of political office. He wrote to Nelson: 'I really wish myself out of this. I am ruining my health, & losing my Friends, tho' I feel conscious I have acted religiously upright.'[122] But Thomas Masterman Hardy took Nelson's part wholeheartedly: 'I left Lord Nelson three Days ago much displeased with the Admiralty for refusing him leave of absence, but I think they seem Determined to oppose him in everything he wishes. I begin to think Lord St V[incent] wishes to clip his Wings a little & certainly have succeeded a little in the affair of Boulogne. Troubridge like a true Politician forsakes his old friend (who has procured him all the Honor he has got) & sticks fast by the Man who is likely to push him forward hereafter.'[123]

The Peace Preliminaries for the treaty with the French were signed on 29 September; they were to be confirmed by the definitive treaty signed at Amiens six months later. But Addington was still keen that Nelson should stay at his post, although he agreed that Nelson could be on shore or even 'remove to London or elsewhere for a few days'.[124] Nelson quoted Addington's letter to Emma: 'it is of the utmost importance to the Interests of the Country that your flag should be flying till the Definitive treaty is signed. You will then have seen the ship safe into Port and may close with honor a career of unexampled success & glory.'[125] For Nelson this delay echoed the end of his *Boreas* commission when Lord Howe had kept him anchored in the Thames estuary for three months in 1787. On 13 October he was visited on board the *Amazon* by the warden of the Cinque Ports, William Pitt; now in opposition, he had time on his hands. Nelson wrote to Emma: 'Mr Pitt has just been on board and he thinks it very hard to keep me now it is all over.' Pitt found Nelson seasick and bored, but Nelson refused an invitation to dine at Walmer Castle.[126] He whiled away the time with a short cruise at the beginning of October and was required to keep his ships at sea 'to guard the trade'.[127] Finally, leave was granted on 23 October 1801.[128] Compared to some, Nelson had been treated well. William Cornwallis did not come ashore from his station off Brest for nearly another six months, in mid April 1802.[129]

The naval and military developments in August, September and October 1801 were governed by continuing peace negotiations. The cabinet – 'honourable but not very experienced men' – was taking decisions against deadlines set by Napoleon. The country at large was in full expectation of peace.[130] Napoleon's military success on the Continent had dimmed the brightness of Britain's diplomatic prospects. Although Britain remained dominant at sea and had consolidated its colonial power, particularly in the East and West Indies, it remained diplomatically isolated. The restoration to France of possessions in the Mediterranean, particularly Malta, and colonial conquests to Holland became the crucial negotiating points with Napoleon.[131] Behind the scenes and in Parliament many were critical of giving away too much. One correspondent wrote to Dundas: 'with Sicily, Malta and Minorca we sit upon the shoulders of all Europe.'[132] But the desire for peace overrode all objections. Pitt wrote to Dundas on 2 October: 'I find Windham (as might be expected) in Agonies, but the rest of the World, as far as one can judge, very much delighted with the peace.'[133]

Nelson was essentially an aggressive admiral who was always going to be uncomfortable at being used by Addington's government as a military icon to achieve diplomatic ends. The attacks on Boulogne can be seen as a culmination of a long war, driven by political, rather than military, considerations, chiefly the need to be seen to be taking the action to the French. Given the limited time and resources available, the attacks were unlikely to succeed, but they did, as Cuthbert Collingwood commented at the time, prevent the French from moving or concentrating their invasion forces. Having noted the difficulties of penetrating the sandbanks, Collingwood wrote: '[Nelson] will make a fair experiment, and at least let them know what they are to expect when they venture beyond them.'[134] After mid August 1801 patience and steadiness were required. Nelson had some justification for his frustration with his 'curious command', as he once called it, and he became tired and ineffective, anxious to be ashore with Emma.[135] For the Admiralty he was an irritable subordinate, one who took up an unreasonable amount of the board's time in encouraging and restraining him. The risk-taking admiral had transformed himself reluctantly into the steadfast defender. He did so only with unremitting protests.

IV

Adulation and Death

1801–1805

25

Peace and the Journey to Wales
October 1801–May 1803

I am confident, my Lord, your income is not, nor ever will be, equal to your generosity . . .

George Matcham to Nelson [14 February 1802][1]

[Lady Hamilton] talked very freely of her situation with Lord Nelson and of the construction the world may have put upon it; but protested that their attachment had been perfectly pure, which I declare I can believe, though I am sure it is of no consequence whether it is so or not. The shocking injury done to Lady Nelson is not made less or greater by anything that may or not have occurred between him and Lady Hamilton.   Lord Minto to Lady Minto, 18 April 1803[2]

For the next eighteen months – the duration of the Peace of Amiens – Nelson lived at Merton Place, his newly purchased house at Merton in Surrey, seven miles (fifty minutes by post-chaise) from the centre of London. Throughout the summer of 1801 Emma had been searching for a property for Nelson, and at her bidding he decided to purchase the house at Merton, sight unseen. In August, on the day that she arrived at Deal, Nelson wrote to William Haslewood, his solicitor, urging him to make haste:

I wish very much to have the place at Merton and agree that £9000 with the furniture should be given for it. You will take care the title is good. £3000 I can pay tomorrow and if necessary great part of the other very soon . . . The place I wish much to have and sailorlike a few pounds more or less is no object. I never knew much got by hard bargains. I approve of the Gentlemen's plan that went to see an estate, bought it as it stood, Dinner on the Table, the former owner eat as his guest.[3]

Nelson's pressure led to a fast purchase, and he returned from Deal to find Sir William and Lady Hamilton already in residence, having taken possession of the house in mid October. Sir William commented admiringly: 'a seaman alone could have given a fine woman full power to chuse & fit up a residence for him without seeing it himself.'[4] Hamilton had by now bought the lease on No. 23 Piccadilly, and this was officially his and Emma's home.[5] Predictably, Emma decorated Merton with enthusiasm, rather than with the understated taste admired by society. Lord Minto described Merton to his wife:

The whole establishment and way of life is such to make me angry, as well as melancholy; but I cannot alter it, and I do not think myself obliged or at liberty to quarrel with him for his weakness, though nothing shall ever induce me to give the smallest countenance to Lady Hamilton . . . She goes on cramming Nelson with trowelfuls of flattery, which he goes on taking as quietly as a child does pap. The love she makes to him is not only ridiculous, but disgusting; not only the rooms, but the whole house, staircase and all, are covered with nothing but pictures of her and him, of all sizes and sorts, and representations of his naval actions, coats of arms, pieces of plate in his honour, the flagstaff of *L'Orient* etc – an excess of vanity which counteracts its own purpose. If it was Lady H's house there might be a pretence for it; to make his own a mere looking-glass to view himself all day is bad taste.[6]

Nelson had written to her from the *Amazon*: 'I hope you will forever love Merton, sure nothing will be wanting on my part, from me you shall have everything you want. I trust, my dear friend, to your economy for I have need of it and [to] you I may say my soul is too big for my purse, but I do earnestly request that all may be mine in the house, even to a pair of sheets, towels etc.'[7]

Economy was indeed needed, for the days of thoughtless spending in Naples and during the journey across Europe were over. To meet the costs of Merton and these other demands, Nelson had sold stock in government funds to the value of £8,000 in November 1800; this had originally been purchased largely with the £10,000 granted by the East India Company after the Battle of the Nile. He realized a further £3,500 of stock in October 1801 and £2,127 of India stock in January 1802, although he still retained £1,000 in the 3 per cents.[8] He received £3,300 for the sale of Roundwood.[9] To raise the major proportion of the purchase price for Merton, Nelson accepted loans from Davison and John Tyson, although £2,000 borrowed from Tyson was paid back in January 1802. He also owed Mrs Graves, the previous owner of Merton, £2,000, which he agreed to pay, with interest, in October 1803.[10] In the second half of 1802 Nelson also turned to his brother-in-law, George Matcham, for £4,000 for the purchase of an adjoining property, Axe's Farm, and agreed to pay him the same interest that the government funds would have yielded.[11]

William Hamilton could lend nothing and could only just pay his share of expenses, for his debts were notorious, the greater part of them incurred at Naples and Palermo in the course of his business as minister; the government eventually repaid £8,268 to his estate in 1811 long after his death.[12] In September 1802 he still owed Nelson over £1,000, a debt that had started during the journey back from Italy.[13] Hamilton spent much of this period trying to lever a substantial pension from the government for his 37-year career as minister in Naples. He failed, receiving only a single payment of £2,000, and thus he was forced to sell the remaining part of his Italian antiquities. He was, however, scrupulous in sharing running expenses at Merton with Nelson, although, as he complained to his nephew Charles Greville, 'as fast as I get money in my banker's hands, the house-keeping draughts draw it off.'[14] For appearances' sake Hamilton had to continue the lease of the house at No. 23 Piccadilly, although he thought of relinquishing it, commenting, again to Greville, 'if we had given up the house in Piccadilly the living here would indeed be a great saving; but as it is we spend neither more nor less than we did.'[15]

Nor could Hamilton expect income from the estates in Pembrokeshire that he had inherited from his first wife. Charles Greville had been managing Hamilton's affairs for some years, and the land was not profitable. Greville had a number of schemes for improving Milford, including speculative building; this required capital that he did not have.[16] One of Hamilton's tenants was Richard Foley, the younger brother of Captain Thomas Foley, who had done so well at the Nile and at Copenhagen, and who also lived in Pembrokeshire. A new lease was under negotiation with the Foley family. Hamilton had visited Milford Haven the previous year on his return from the Continent, but he left all the business to Greville, writing to him: 'was I to take upon me the management of your plans there, I should rather do hurt than good.'[17] Hamilton, it seems, had little enthusiasm for his estates. He had written to Emma during his visit in 1801, shrugging off the problems with a joke: he had been given 'some good hints about getting money from our Estate without hurting futurity much and as the Irishman said, what has futurity done for us?'[18]

Early in 1801, when still on full pay, Nelson had estimated that his income was £4,000 a year.[19] He had spent freely when he was in command at Boulogne and in the Downs, complaining ironically to Davison in September: 'Since I left London it has cost me, for Nelson cannot be like others, near £1000 in six weeks . . . everybody knows that Lord Nelson is amazingly rich.'[20] Pay and table money from the Admiralty would take a long time to be settled by the Navy Board. Fanny still had to be paid her £1,800 a year.[21] The running expenses for Merton were heavy, particularly the food and wine accounts from local tradesmen: these averaged £65 a week between June 1802 and April 1803, totalling over £3,000 for the year, of which William Hamilton paid half.[22] Although Nelson presented his father with £500 in November 1801, he had to curtail his customary generosity to his family.[23] He sent Susannah Bolton £100 a year, for three years, for the education of her son, with more than a hint of irritation: 'all I desire is that you would not say or write me a syllable on the subject for I am sorry I cannot do more.'[24]

Prize money remained a potential source of income and Nelson attempted to claim his share still owing from his time in the Mediterranean in the mid 1790s, corresponding with John McArthur and meeting with George Cockburn.[25] He was depending on this to pay off the £2,100 due to Mrs Graves.[26] The second possibility was winning a greater share of the valuable Spanish prizes taken in October 1799, when Nelson was temporarily commander-in-chief of the Mediterranean and St Vincent was in England. His dispute with St Vincent came to the court of the King's Bench on 4 March 1801. Of the total of £651,694 from the two ships, St Vincent's claim, if upheld, would be £9,671.[27] Nelson corresponded anxiously with Alexander Davison, who was instructing the lawyers, and with Vice-Admiral Duckworth, who would also stand to share in a successful outcome for Nelson but was not a plaintiff. 'Our law suit with the Earl is going on,' he wrote to Duckworth, 'and on the part of his Lawyers with all the venom which is possible. As our cause is just I hope for success and shall pursue the means as far as my Lawyers think.'[28] A month later the case did not look promising. 'I dare say it will cost us a large sum of money . . . I find it very hard to fight ag[ains]t the first Lord. I much doubt if justice ought to be fair but blind, for I see her Eyes always turn'd to the rich & powerful.'[29] None of these indignant feelings were expressed in court, in which Nelson was represented by the Attorney-General. The case was conducted in a gentlemanly spirit, 'by no means of a pecuniary nature; but arose out of the different opinions that had been entertained on the subject, as to the custom of the service.' St Vincent's case was that his constitution had suffered from the 'unremitting service' on the station, and that he was still in command, merely on sick leave. The jury, 'under the direction of the Lord Chief Justice', found for St Vincent.[30] As expected, Nelson went to appeal.

Income from the estates in Bronte was never to materialize, and they were to cost Nelson far more than they earned, even though he had great hopes of them. We have it on Hardy's authority that Nelson was 'determined to reside there in peace'.[31] John Graefer, who had created the English garden for King Ferdinand at Caserta, whom Nelson sent as agent to Bronte, wrote a long letter in September 1801 warning Nelson not to expect too much, complaining of the laziness of the Sicilian farmers.[32] Six months later Graefer was still lamenting his lack of success, writing to Lady Hamilton: 'Tell My Lord, notwithstanding the Ingratitude of many of His ungrateful Vassalls not to give over the Introduction of English Agriculture, His Majesty & all rational being praise my Lord's Greatness in this pursuit.'[33] Then Graefer died in late 1802, leaving his widow as housekeeper.[34] However laudable the reforming ideas, no income resulted. 'I have never yet received one farthing from the estate,' Nelson wrote to the Naples banker Edmund Noble.[35] Noble's opinion was that the estates could bring £3,000 a year, but by 1803 even he had given up hope and recommended that Nelson should sell the estate.[36] Thus, in spite of hopes of greater riches, Nelson's finances were not yet equal to the demands that Merton and the constant, if not lavish, entertaining made on them.

If Emma put her heart and soul into the house, Nelson took a countryman's interest in the farm. He wrote to Thomas Bolton about the hay harvest: 'I shall not allow its being cut too soon, not in too great a hurry to sell but I mean to sell in the Cock or standing.'[37] He had two cows with calves, purchased by Bolton in Norfolk, driven down to 'be at the Pyed Bull at Islington on Sunday next'.[38] Later in the year, when he was away at sea, he sent Emma instructions on the spring planting of the fields, and in early 1804 a visitor reported to him: 'I was greatly pleased to see that worthy, faithful good woman Mrs Cadogan managing your House and Lands with as much cleverness as a skilfull Member of the Agricultural Society, the premises in the highest order, the cattle healthy, the Hay got in and stow'd away and the Dairy showing signs of plenty.'[39]

Merton, however, defined itself as much by its constant stream of visitors as by its decoration, garden and farm. By the time of its purchase all of Nelson's immediate family had become reconciled to Nelson's separation from Fanny. Even his father stayed at Merton in November 1802 before going back to Bath for the winter; he had warmed to the attentions of Emma.[40] The children of Nelson's brother and sisters spent long periods at the house when not at school.[41] Emma wrote to Kitty Matcham in December 1802: 'We are as happy as Kings & much more so, we have 3 Boltons, 2 Nelsons and only want 2 or 3 little Matchams to be quite en famille.' A near neighbour was Abraham Goldsmid, a rich and prominent supporter of the Royal Naval Asylum, who entertained lavishly. Emma reported: 'we had yesterday a magnificent fête of Mr Goldsmid's.'[42] In January 1803 Nelson wrote to George Matcham: 'Lady Hamilton gave a little Ball last night to the children. They danced till 3 this morning and are not yet up.'[43] Nelson's faithful secretary John Tyson, now rewarded with a clerical post as the clerk of the Survey at Woolwich Dockyard, stayed there frequently with his wife.[44] Nelson rarely went to London, although he spoke at infrequent intervals in the House of Lords and kept in contact with the prime minister.[45] His appearance at a levee at Buckingham House resulted in yet another snub from the king.[46] Nelson made clear his aversion to London to his banker, William Marsh: 'I have made it a point never to dine from my friends at Merton and in addition to those constantly with [me] my Brother & his family are on a visit. Did I ever deviate from this rule I have laid down I assure you that I would dine with you with the very greatest pleasure.'[47]

Merton's proximity to London did ensure that visitors came from further afield. Lord Minto describes a dinner attended by his brother Hugh Elliot, Charles Greville and Brigadier-General Graham, who had commanded the troops at the Siege of Malta.[48] From Nelson's days in Jamaica during the American Revolutionary War, Hercules Ross, Dr Benjamin Molesey and the ex-army officer from Ludlow in Shrophire, Richard Bulkeley, were entertained, as well as Bulkeley's midshipman son.[49] Of his captains at the Nile, Alexander Ball, now home from Malta, Samuel Hood, Thomas Louis and Thomas Foley came at different times. A young protégé from Copenhagen, William Layman, stayed for several days, and Frederick Langford (still wounded), Samuel Sutton and Alexander Scott for longer periods.[50] Even Count Wolterstorff, one of the Danish negotiators, spent a day at Merton on his way through London to the West Indies, where he was to negotiate the return of the captured Danish islands to Denmark.[51]

On his way home from his commission in April 1802 Thomas Masterman Hardy 'stole three hours today to go to Merton, where I saw his Lordship, Sir Wm & Lady Hamilton. They are all extremely well & her Ladyship was quite <u>angry</u> that I could not stay longer.'[52] Hardy was never won over by Emma Hamilton, but, since he wished to serve again with Nelson, he swallowed his principles by visiting Merton. A number of fellow officers, however, did not come. It is hardly likely that St Vincent and Troubridge were invited, but others who might be expected to have called did not. When Cuthbert Collingwood was on his way home to Northumberland after he struck his flag in early May 1802, for instance, he stayed in nearby

Egham and then in central London; he visited friends in Greenwich, but did not pay his respects to Nelson.[53]

In March 1802 a midshipman named George Parsons, who had served with Nelson on the *Foudroyant*, also visited Merton, although his welcome was distinctly guarded. Parsons had been made lieutenant by Lord Keith, returning from Egypt after the peacetime promotions had taken place. He wanted Nelson to persuade St Vincent to confirm his rank as lieutenant. Parsons knew Nelson's old servant Tom Allen, who brought him, apprehensively, to Nelson's study door.

The voice of Lord Nelson, denoting vexation, reprimanded my friend, and declared, most truly, that he was pestered to death by young gentlemen, his former shipmates. Tom pushed me into the room, and went in search of an able auxiliary, who entered the study, in the most pleasing shape – that of a lovely and graceful woman . . . His countenance, which, until now, had been a thunder-cloud, brightened . . . Lady Hamilton . . . set aside his scruples of asking a favour of the first Admiralty Lord, by dictating a strong certificate, which, under her direction, he wrote. 'Now, my young friend,' said her ladyship, 'send this to Lord St Vincent, at Brentwood, so as to reach him on Sunday morning.' My commission, as an officer, was dated the same as the aforesaid certificate.[54]

Underneath the surface of this contented domestic scene, tensions and uncertainty remained. It was not definite that Nelson would stay ashore. Rumours abounded that he might go to the West Indies or even Ireland, where his reputation as restorer of discipline and morale could be employed to calm the unrest in the crews after the mutinies in the ships off Bantry Bay. In January 1802 Hardy wrote to his cousin: 'Lord Nelson is determined not to be employed if he can help it. I think it by no means unlikely that they will make him hoist his Flag, particularly if the Bantry Bay business is not quite stopped as he is a popular man amongst us; however, we have reason to believe it is all settled at least for the present.'[55]

Further tension was caused by the continued exclusion of the Hamiltons from the higher levels of London society. Although the duke of Hamilton visited Merton, Hamilton's family in London would not receive them, which distressed Emma.[56] Charles Greville's sister explained the family policy to a friend: 'It was settled . . . that it could not be avoided noticing Ly H, without offence to Sr Wm or at least affecting his feelings . . . Sr Wm & Ly H. came to me one Morning, I explained that I could not be in their Society; but hoped He was assured of my affection; He was very kind, laughed & said He knew I was a Nun . . . Few Ladies visit Ly. H. except those [that] have been at Naples.'[57] The happiness of Nelson and Emma depended upon the patience, good humour and pragmatism of William Hamilton. The three-sided relationship was not without strain; the extent of his forbearance can occasionally be glimpsed when he let his feelings be known. For instance, writing to Charles Greville in January 1802, his vexation plainly shows: 'Nothing at present disturbs me but my debt, and the nonsense I am obliged to submit to here to avoid coming to an explosion, which wou'd be attended with many disagreeable effects, and would totally destroy the comfort of the best man and the best friend I have in the world.'[58]

Fanny was now living in London at No. 16 Somerset Street, near Portman Place.[59] In September 1801, through Davison, she had retrieved glass, china and table linen still in Nelson's possession.[60] In October she had visited Burnham to stay with Edmund and then visited Lord and Lady Walpole at Wolterton. From there she wrote a depressed, slightly sharp letter to her father-in-law: 'My visit to Burnham was one of duty rather than of pleasure and assure you it called forth all My feelings.' She rejected Edmund's idea of his living permanently with her, 'which from your conversation makes it impractical, the deprivation of seeing your Children is so cruel even in thought that it is impossible'.[61] Fanny was rejecting any middle ground. Edmund's reply was dignified and firm:

Be assured, I still hold my Integrity, and am ready to join you, whenever you have your servants in your London House . . . the Opinion of others must rest with themselves, and not make any alteration with us. I have not offended any man, and do not rely on my children's Affection that notwithstanding all that have been Said, they will not in my Old Age forsake me.[62]

Edmund was not going to side with either party. To Nelson he wrote: 'If Lady Nelson is in a hired house and by herself, gratitude requires that I should sometimes be with her, if it is likely to be of any comfort to her.'[63] He was as good as his word. In November 1801 he stayed with Fanny in Somerset Street, and went on to Merton on his way back to Bath.[64] Fanny tried one last time in December to persuade Nelson to live with her, writing to him at Davison's address: 'Do, my dear husband, let us live together . . . Let everything be buried in oblivion, it will pass away like a dream.' Her letter was returned to her, endorsed by Davison: 'Opened by mistake by Lord Nelson, but not read.'[65]

Only Davison and Edmund Nelson openly acknowledged being in contact with both parties. Nelson's father, at last, was now writing genuinely affectionate letters to Nelson. In March from Bath he hoped that his son would have an 'abundance of internal peace such as you have never yet enjoyed much of, but are now of an age to enjoy' and he still hoped 'I shall with the assistance of the May sunshine get able to travel, and smell a Merton rose in June.'[66] But Edmund Nelson, comforted by his youngest daughter, Kitty Matcham, died at Bath on 26 April 1802.

Nelson did not attend his father's funeral at Burnham Thorpe. He wrote long, detailed letters about the burial arrangements to George Matcham, who was at Bath: but they contained no expression of grief.[67] His father should be 'buried with all that respect and attention becoming his Excellent Life and the Worthy and Beneficial Pastor of his Parish for 45 years, no proper expence shall be wanting.'[68] To the end he treated his father remotely, as someone to be honoured rather than loved. He began to distance himself when he knew that his father was dying, writing to Matcham: 'Had my Father expressed a wish to see me, unwell as I am, I should have flown to Bath, but I believe it would be too late. However, should it be otherwise and he wishes to see me no consideration shall detain me a moment.'[69] Two days later, when he knew that Edmund had died: 'I am not yet fixt whether I shall go to Burnham, my state of health and what my feelings would naturally be might be of serious consequence to myself.'[70] Transporting Edmund's body from Bath on the long journey to Burnham was undertaken by George Matcham, and William Nelson bustled on to the scene to make the funeral arrangements. At the service he and Thomas Bolton represented the immediate family. Susannah Bolton described the scene to Fanny in a letter of 15 May 1802: 'The church was crowded, everyone lamenting as the death of a friend . . . Six clergymen attended as bearers . . . the farmers in the three parishes followed.'[71] No record of Nelson's feelings, if he wrote them to anyone, has survived. He pleaded ill health perhaps because he felt that he could not brave local and wider family disapproval for the abandonment of Fanny, only six months after her visit to Burnham. But it is also difficult not to come to the conclusion that Nelson felt guilty because of the moral contradictions of his own life and that he could not bring himself to bid farewell to a man whose religious principles had been staunch, and had been the foundation of his own upbringing.

With the death of Edmund the alienation of Fanny was complete. Susannah's letter of 15 May was her last to Fanny. She concluded: 'I am to Merton in about a fortnight, but, My dear Lady N., we cannot meet as I wished, for everybody is known who visit you, indeed I do not think I shall be permitted even to go to town.'[72] In January 1803 George Matcham reported to Nelson that Fanny was at Clifton and had called upon them, 'but did not come in nor make the least inquiry about us, but left a card and rolled off as she came in Lord Hood's carriage and four. We should have told her, as we have always declared, it is our maxim if possible to be at peace with all the world.'[73] Perhaps Fanny was demonstrating exactly where Lord Hood's sympathies lay. Edward Berry and his wife also continued to see her socially, and, while in Norfolk, Lord and Lady Walpole kept in touch with her.[74] The most faithful of her naval friends was Thomas Masterman Hardy. In June that year he reported to his cousin: 'I breakfasted this Morning with Lady Nelson. I am more pleased with her if possible than ever, she certainly is one of the Best Women in the World.'[75]

In July 1802 it was decided that the Hamiltons, accompanied by Nelson, would travel to Pembrokeshire to inspect Sir William's estates.[76] The expedition appears to have been planned on the spur of the moment. On 12 July 1802 Thomas Foley visited Merton, and it was on the same day that Nelson wrote a persuasive letter to the headmaster of Eton, requesting leave 'long before the regular vacation' for Horatio Nelson, son of William and Sarah Nelson, who were also to be of the party.[77] The Matchams, whom they were to meet at Oxford, planned to travel some way along the road with them to the west. Nelson wrote to George Matcham on 16 July to ask him to book dinner for eight at the Star Inn at Oxford on 21 July: 'be so good as to order it, but not to say for whom.'[78] Crowds were expected.

Oxford set the pattern for the next six weeks. Both city and university conferred honours, and Nelson attracted crowds at every appearance. The party travelled westward through Gloucester, then through Ross-on-Wye and Monmouth to the Welsh hills. At each town Nelson was fêted. At Monmouth, which he approached from the north by boat down the Wye from Ross, the Corporation wished him to stay longer. He promised to visit the town again on the return journey.[79] The coaches drove through the rough roads of the Welsh mountains, stopping at Brecon, where Nelson's reception was notably enthusiastic, diverting to the south to see the iron works at Merthyr Tydfil, then on to Carmarthen, reaching Milford by the end of July, in time to celebrate the fourth anniversary of the Battle of the Nile on 1 August.

At Milford, Nelson toured the town. The central purpose of the tour was to publicize William Hamilton's investment in the town and to attract money from others. The visit was managed by Charles Greville, who was already there to greet the party. Greville hoped to benefit further from government money that had been invested in shipbuilding there. Attracted by plentiful timber in the vicinity, the government had contracted with a local shipbuilder called Jacob to build warships, but in 1800 the shipyard had failed with the keels of three warships already laid down. The Navy Board had been forced to take over the failing business and had hired land from Greville for £250 a year. The expansion was not to be a success. These ships had been designed and their building overseen by the French émigré Jean-Louis Barallier, who had impressed Spencer's administration with his theoretical grasp of ship design. But the Frenchman's designs were a failure, he was not favoured by St Vincent's Board of Admiralty, and the ships were not launched until several years later.[80] The climax of the visit was Nelson's speech to the county gentry of Pembrokeshire at the New Inn. Nelson praised Tom Foley, pronounced the harbour fine, the dockyard and shipbuilding impressive.[81] At the behest of Greville and Hamilton, he included a plea for government help, but this public relations exercise fell on deaf ears. Milford flourished slowly and was formally established as a government shipyard by Order-in-Council only in 1809; it was moved to a more spacious site at Pembroke on the south bank of Milford Haven in 1813.[82]

Having been entertained by the Foleys and others, the party headed for home via Carmarthen, Swansea, Cardiff and Newport. They also visited Chepstow, where Nelson met timber merchants from the Forest of Dean, contractors with the Navy Board, who were unhappy, like almost everyone else, with the administration of the navy under St Vincent. Nelson also wrote a memorandum for reform of the forests, based on 'the conversation of gentlemen in the oak Countries'. The state of the forests was 'deplorable' and 'shameful'. For whom it was intended is not certain, but it followed the pattern of other memoranda intended for government that he was writing at this time.[83] After staying at Chepstow on 17 August, the party turned northwards, past Tintern Abbey, returning as promised to Monmouth. Here the Corporation fêted them thoroughly. On 19 August Nelson took a coach up the steep hill called the Kymin, which overlooked the town; in a small building at the top, where a dining club met weekly, a 'public breakfast' was held. Near by was, and still is, the remarkable 'Naval Temple', erected on 1 August 1800. Covered with medallions and inscriptions, it is dedicated to great names such as Boscawen, Hawke, Rodney and St Vincent, as well as Nelson.[84]

Nelson, the William Nelsons and the Hamiltons journeyed back from Wales by taking the road due north to Hereford, then further north to Ludlow to visit Richard Bulkeley. Bulkeley was a faithful and admiring correspondent who had immediately taken to Lady Hamilton. He wrote amusing letters, marked by an easy familiarity and a rough barrack-room humour stemming from his early association with the young Nelson.* The route home took in Worcester, then Birmingham, where they attended the theatre. Going south, they made a formal call on Lord Spencer at Althorp, then travelled through Towcester, St Albans, Watford and home to Merton on 5 September. The careful accounts kept by Nelson reveal it to be an expensive journey, with horses, turnpikes and inns accounting for most of the total cost of £481.3s. 10d.[85] Charles Greville travelled back to London separately, causing Hamilton's old friend Sir Joseph Banks to comment: 'I think you have done very wisely in preferring a route through Cornwall, where nature would arouse you at every step, to the artificial satisfaction of feasts, Mayors, & Aldermen, freedom of Rotten Boroughs etc.'[86]

The journey to Wales had led to increasing tension between Sir William and Emma. Hamilton, now in his seventy-second year, was increasingly feeling the strain: 'I by no means wish to live in solitary retreat, but to have seldom less than 12 or 14 at table, & those varying continually, is coming back to what was so irksome to me in Italy.' He then continued with a veiled threat: 'but I feel the whole attention of my wife is given to Ld N and his interest at Merton. I well know the purity of Ld. N's friendship for Emma and me, and I know how very uncomfortable it would make his L[ordshi]p, our best friend, if a separation shou'd take place, & am therefore determined to do all in my power to prevent such an extremity, which would be essentially detrimental to all parties, but wou'd be more sensibly felt by our dear friend than by us.'[87] Hamilton now spent more time on his own pursuits, in the British Museum or at the Royal Society.

The autumn of 1802 was not without its anxieties for Nelson. His eyesight had given trouble for much of the year. In October he consulted his old West Indian friend Dr Benjamin Moseley in London: 'I agree with you that (if the operation is necessary) the sooner it is done the better, the possible risk is for your consideration. I cannot spare very well another Eye.'[88] Fortunately no operation took place, though he was 'forbid writing'.[89] Money was becoming a problem. In March 1803 he took the unusual step of writing to Henry Addington, as a friend rather than as prime

---

* In July 1802 Bulkeley told a long, bawdy story over several letters about the sexual inadequacy of a mutual soldier friend, Tom Fowler, who married 'a Baron widow, an over match for him ... who if she could not have substance would content herself with a feather. Tom, I fear, carrys one at each end but the only one erect is on his head – the Middle piece is always drooping.' Nelson replied, 'Your description of Capt. Fowler made me laugh heartily' (NMM, CRK/2/86, 16 July 1802, Bulkeley to Nelson; BL, Add. MSS 34956, 13 Aug. 1804, Nelson to Bulkeley).

minister, giving a breakdown of his assets, asking for financial rewards equal to that of St Vincent and Duncan.[90] Nothing came of it.

Public events were intruding into their life at Merton. Peace was beginning to look uncertain; relations with France were deteriorating as Napoleon intervened in Switzerland, while Holland and Malta continued to be trouble spots.[91] Addington's government began to prepare quietly for war. In late November, Evan Nepean invited Nelson to a private dinner – 'tête-à-tête'.[92] Nelson told Minto on 26 November 1802 that it had already been decided that he was to have the Mediterranean command.[93] Nelson began to make more visits to London, speaking in the House of Lords in December. 'Our Hero was most graciously & particularly well received by her Majesty when he went with Sir Wm to the Drawing Room,' Emma reported proudly to Kitty Matcham.[94] Emma, of course, was not present.

In February 1803 an unlooked-for event brought Nelson again into the public eye when he was called as a character witness at the trial of Edward Despard, his companion in arms during the San Juan Expedition in 1780; he was accused of a conspiracy to overthrow the British government. In Central America the two young men had vied for the most honour, having similar characters and not dissimilar looks, both driven and thin. Now Despard had attempted to overthrow all that the conservative Nelson stood for. Despard had served as a soldier and colonial servant for thirty years, reaching the rank of colonel and returning to England only in 1790, when he was imprisoned for debt between 1792 and 1794. By now an extreme radical, he was among the crowd breaking Pitt's windows in Downing Street in 1795, chanting, 'No war, no Pitt, Cheap Bread.' He conceived a conspiracy, called by the judge a 'wild scheme of impracticable equality'.[95] Arrested with many others at a tavern in Lambeth in November 1802, he was brought to trial on 7 February 1803. Nelson told the court that Despard bore the character of a brave officer and an honourable and loyal man, impressing the jury. Richard Bulkeley, the only friend of Nelson who remembered Lieutenant Despard in 1780, wrote from Ludlow to Nelson: 'I cannot describe to you my inward emotions on reading your generous efforts in the sad and lost case of poor Despard, and I lament, as I am sure you do, that a man possessing such endowments and abilities as he does, should have been mad enough to employ them for the Attainment of any Object by such base and despicable means.'[96] But Despard was sentenced to death.[97] He wrote a heart-rending letter to Nelson on 15 February:

Swol[le]n I feel my heart to be with gratitude and my mind filled with sensibility of the great obligations I am under to you for the long and painful attendance you submitted to on the day and night of my trial, the character you were pleased to honor me with on that occasion, and the salutary effect for me which that character widely produced in prevailing on the jury to recommend me to His Majesty's mercy ... on my headstone the character given of me by Lord Nelson shall be inscribed upon it ... if your Lordship can with propriety interfere further on my behalf I need not ask you to do so.[98]

Nelson passed on Despard's petition to appeal against the sentence. Minto commented approvingly that Nelson 'behaved with a due mixture of generosity and private feeling with public propriety. He abominates and abhors him, and never took a step towards saving him except by forwarding a petition.' But from Despard's letter it is clear that Nelson was a powerful advocate for clemency, that he saw Despard after the trial, and that he had much private sympathy for the fallen army officer. Addington told Nelson that he and his family had wept over the letter.[99] But the king rejected the appeal, reflecting the feeling in a country still fearful of revolution. Bulkeley wrote again to Nelson that Despard 'ought not to be spared. The King owes to the country that the execution should take place'.[100] The evening before his execution Despard wrote to Nelson: 'the awful sentence is to take place tomorrow Morning early. My dearest Lord, I can say no more, my heart is too ful[l] and my mind distracted.'[101]

Despard was hanged before a large crowd on 21 February, with a dignified but defiant speech on the scaffold.[102] But even the conservative Bulkeley sent Nelson a five-pound note, asking that it be sent to Despard's family 'without saying anything about me'.[103] Emma visited Despard's inconsolable black wife, Catherine, with whom she could empathize, for Catherine was probably not formally married and was disowned by Despard's numerous and respectable army family: 'she did not know her, but went to comfort her, and found her much better since the body had been brought back to her.'[104] Perhaps she delivered Bulkeley's five-pound note.

More sadness followed. Sir William had lived an active life through the winter, but in March 1803 he fell ill, as he had done in the same month in the previous two years. This time he did not recover. He died at No. 23 Piccadilly early in the morning of 6 April in Emma's arms, with Nelson holding his hand.[105] Emma's reaction was an extended display of dramatic grief. John Tyson called the next day, relating to Nelson: 'I could not go upstairs nor indeed did I think it prudent, as your Lordship was out and her Ladyship was in such deep distress.'[106] To compound the sense of loss and sadness, Nelson's godson, Edmund, one of the Matcham boys, died of influenza at the same time as Sir William. 'In a house full of affliction,'

Nelson wrote to Kitty, 'I can readily conceive feelings so nearly similar to what we are feeling. I shall almost hate April. Look at the last three years. Good Mr Matcham has seen our Parent go out of the World and now his Own. I now trust that the work of Death will cease for many years. Lady Hamilton suffers very much.'[107]

Hamilton had signed his will on 31 March 1803. He left his money and what works of art he still possessed to Charles Greville and the estates in Pembrokeshire to his kinsman the marquis of Abercorn, from which income Emma was to be paid £800 a year during her lifetime, £100 of which was to be given to her mother. To Nelson he bequeathed a portrait of Emma, 'a very small token of the great regard I have for his Lordship, the most virtuous, loyal and truly brave character I ever met with'.[108] Minto commented to his wife: 'I have seen Lady Hamilton, who is worse off than I imagined, her jointure being £700 a year, and £100 to Mrs Cadogan for her life. She told me she had applied to Mr Addington for a pension.'[109] This was less than half the amount that Nelson had provided for Fanny. It was a low time for Emma. Thomas Masterman Hardy asked a pertinent question: 'How her Ladyship will manage to live with the Hero of the Nile now, I am at a loss to know, at least in an honourable way.'[110] She moved from No. 23 Piccadilly to nearby Clarges Street, as she could not live openly with Nelson at Merton. Nelson even thought of leasing Merton.[111] But, as it had been settled that Nelson was to have the Mediterranean fleet, by 17 May he was on his way to Portsmouth to take up his command.

This period in Nelson's life on shore has often been labelled 'Paradise' Merton, and he experienced some happiness, principally because Nelson's family had accepted his relationship with Emma. But, in truth, it was a bitter sweet time, framed by anxieties about social acceptance, tinged throughout by the uncertain peace, emnity towards Fanny, rows and tension between Sir William and Emma, and interspersed with worries over money and health. The deaths of Edmund Nelson and William Hamilton cast long shadows. Horatia, Nelson and Emma's daughter, who lived with a Mrs Gibson, could be seen only very occasionally and then under all sorts of pretence, usually quietly in London, although the little two-year-old girl was sometimes taken to Merton.[112] Even more poignant was that when Nelson went away to sea in May 1803, Emma was pregnant. He was to write to her from the Mediterranean in the spring of 1804: 'Kiss dear Horatia for me, and the other. Call him what you please, if a girl, Emma.'[113] But the child, a daughter, did not survive. The apparent simplicity and bliss of Nelson's domestic life at Merton were, in fact, artificial: 'Paradise' Merton was never without complexity and never without some sadness.

Nelson protected Emma's reputation as best he could by destroying almost all her letters to him, for which reason her feelings and personality are partially hidden from us. For years he declared himself to her in many letters of extravagant devotion. One younger naval officer who observed them emphasized the 'self-serving', rather than the symbiotic, nature of the relationship, commenting later: 'I for one, do not believe that passion was the paramount incentive. I consider that ambition was her inducement, vanity his. She was proud of having a Hero in her chains. He was vain at having so beautiful and extraordinary a woman attached to him. Of the two, his conduct was in every way the most culpable.'[114] But this calculated view of human relationships, while it has undoubted elements of truth, does not allow for the real love that undoubtedly existed between them. Only occasionally are there glimpses of Emma's feelings and her anxieties, very often at the end of letters. She concluded one, almost frantically, to Kitty Matcham in December 1802: 'I love him, adore him, his virtue, heart, mind, soul, courage, all merit to be adored & everything that concerns his Honer, Glory & happiness will ever be Dear.'[115] Two and a half years later she was to add a wistful postscript to a long, heartfelt letter to Mrs Lutwidge: 'I should like to say – how pretty it sounds – Emma Nelson.'[116]

26

The Peace of Amiens
October 1801–May 1803

We consider it incumbent upon us to acquaint you that ever since the
news of the Blessings of Peace reached us, we most anxiously looked
forward and daily expected to sail for England in particular when we
seen almost all the large shipping gone; seeing however no signs of our
going, in a warm, unwholesome Climate, confined and cut off from
our Wives, families and all the little we hold dear in this transitory life,
together with bad living it at once conspires to render our situations
miserable in the extreme, and the majority of the Ship's Company is
dissatisfied not ever knowing on what ground we are kept more than
any other Line of Battleship . . . Death itself would be preferable to
the being kept here 6 months longer.

Anonymous letter, dated 25 August 1802, Malta, found
in the cabin of the commander-in-chief, Mediterranean,
Rear-Admiral Sir Richard Bickerton.[1]

While Nelson rested at Merton, others toiled. Only when the definitive
Peace Treaty with France was signed in March 1802 were orders issued for
a full naval demobilization. While some politicians had doubts about the
peace, the population at large were enthusiastic. The navy had profited
from the war. Since the outbreak of hostilities in 1793, 1,260 French,
Spanish and Dutch warships had been destroyed or captured, to which
could be added seventeen from the Danes. Of those, a remarkable seventy-
seven had been ships of the line. In tonnage terms, at least, British battleships
were nearly on a par with those of the nation's three main rivals combined.[2]
It was now time, as Lord Hobart put it in his formal letter to the Admiralty:
'to take proper measures for relieving the Nation from the vast expense
incurred in the Naval Department . . . forthwith order home from Foreign
Parts (excepting the West Indies) and pay off and lay up all such ships . . .

as many . . . as may exceed the number of those that it may be thought necessary to keep established in time of peace.'[3]

This 'vast expense' quickly became the priority of St Vincent's tenure as first lord of the Admiralty, which lasted for three ill-tempered and damaging years from February 1801 to May 1804. No one doubted that the civil administration of the navy needed improvement, but few felt that aggression, bombast and political vindictiveness would lead to successful reform. St Vincent's views on corruption in the navy had been formed by Whig principles of economy rather than efficiency; in the words of one historian, 'he brought to the Admiralty a museum of attitudes many of which belonged to the seventeenth rather than the nineteenth century.'[4] His view of the Navy Board had been buttressed by his experiences with supplies when he commanded the Mediterranean fleet and by his time ashore in Gibraltar when he saw the workings of the dockyard there at first hand. He had written to Nepean in early 1799: 'I have already told you my Opinion, that although there is so much boast of Talent, and Ability at the Navy Board, the business in all its parts, was never so ill conducted, no, not in the corrupt time of Cockburne and George Jackson.'[5]

St Vincent thus came to the Admiralty in 1801 with rigid ideas on the degree of corruption practised by the navy, the dockyards and the contractors who built ships and supplied timber. He very soon picked a permanent quarrel with the Navy Board under its comptroller, Sir Andrew Snape Hamond, and personal relations became so fraught that the two officers, on whom the efficient working of the navy most depended, communicated only by letter. Contracts were cancelled. Dockyard officials were summarily dismissed, while, in an atmosphere of fear, droves of restless and dissatisfied skilled workers were turned out of the gates of the various dockyards. When war broke out again in May 1803 the situation was just short of disastrous.[6] Every type of naval store was in short supply. By June 1804, after St Vincent's resignation, the Navy Board reckoned it had less than three months' reserve of sailcloth, deals and copper, and only six months' of plank.[7] Outside the first lord's small circle, which included the two overbearing younger naval officers on the board, Thomas Troubridge and Captain John Markham, St Vincent's unpopularity was universal. His 'bigotry and meglomania' caused serious problems of morale in the dockyards, which reduced output to a fraction of what was possible and necessary.[8] Moreover, the violence of his methods and his language soon proved politically embarrassing to the government. St Vincent as first lord of the Admiralty was the wrong man in the wrong place at the wrong time. Speculation abounded throughout 1803 that St Vincent would be dropped by the prime minister. However, as Richard Bulkeley reported to Nelson in November 1803, the papers 'cease to talk of a change in the Admiralty. The Earl holds fast like a good dog. He can play the Spaniel to keep his berth and the Tyger to those who must tremble at his blusters.'[9] Bulkeley was not the only observer to note that St Vincent was too smooth with his seniors and too rough with his juniors.[10]

From December 1802 Nelson gave the government some support, speaking for the government's bill to set up the Commission of Naval Inquiry, which was to investigate irregularities, frauds and abuses in the naval departments and prize agency. Many saw the commission as a first move by St Vincent to abolish the subordinate naval boards over which he had little power. Nelson spoke in favour of setting up this commission, though he showed an uncharacteristic concern for the confidentiality of the merchants' accounts that might be examined, a theme that looks suspiciously as though it had been prompted by Alexander Davison. Nelson went on to criticize the shortcomings of the prize-money agency, a subject on which he was authoritative and persuasive.[11] He gave evidence under oath on prize money to the commission in April 1803, his chief criticism being the slow speed of distribution of the shares by prize agents, and he suggested that this should be limited to three months. He also proposed the establishment of an official prize agency office, and also that the prize agents' commissions should be calculated on the net, rather than the gross, proceeds. When the commission reported, it did indeed include many of Nelson's proposals, but the subsequent Prize Act of 1805 adopted only a few of the Commission of Naval Inquiry's recommendations.*[12]

Nelson also wrote assorted memoranda for Addington on problems in manning the Navy and of timber supply – full of directness and common sense but short on political calculation.[13] He offered ideas on the rapid manning of the navy: 'whatever objections may be made to my plan I am ready and I think able to defend it, therefore I shall not be prolix by answering what interested people may object to it . . . Not a soldier to be raised until the Fleet is manned, An Embargo to be laid on every Port in the Kingdom.' In addition, he proposed that no protections against pressing should be issued.[14] Nelson would have been hard put to persuade

---

* The 1805 Prize Act tightened the regulations for prize-agency fees and, following Nelson's proposal, limited the period in which prize agents could remit money to Greenwich Hospital for seamen to four, though not three, months. However, the Act did not establish a separate prize office. According to the main authority on prize money, there seems little doubt that Nelson was advised in the production of his memorandum by John Scott, who was to be his secretary in the Mediterranean (Hill, 144, 145–6).

Parliament to adopt these quarterdeck ideas. It is difficult to place him politically at this time. He was disillusioned with the aristocratic Pitt, who had never done anything for him or his family, and he felt at ease with Addington, the son of a doctor. Though a Whig, Addington was essentially conservative. Nelson's motives seem to have been to cultivate Addington in the expectation of a further naval command, should war break out. After all, he still owed over £2,000 to the previous owner of Merton and financial pressure to obtain an appointment to a profitable station still existed.*

During his eighteen months ashore Nelson developed close ties of friendship with the prime minister, which he used several times to try to obtain preferment in the Church for his brother William, who would now inherit his peerage. In February 1802 he wrote emotionally to Addington: 'I know . . . that you are pressed perhaps by superior claims certainly much superior to mine, but My Brother, my only Brother is with me and I feel his situation.'[15] He tried to exert some leverage on the prime minister at the time of the General Election in July 1802, when the two candidates in Norfolk, Thomas Coke of Holkham and Jacob Astley, were challenged at the last minute by Colonel John Wodehouse. Displaying political naivety, but with an eye to creating a sense of obligation, Nelson wrote to Addington:

Since I called on you this morning My brother has been strongly solicited to go into Norfolk to give his vote by both parties. I do not know how either of them are attached to you, Coke and Astley: certainly not, and perhaps not the other (Wodehouse). Be that as it may my Brother could not go to the expense of fifty pounds merely to give a vote, besides the fatigue of men or Journey but situated as I am with you, He will go with pleasure if you desire it, therefore say in two words Go or Not and who you wish him to vote for and Dr Nelson will be there on Monday, the expense of it will to oblige you I shall pay with pleasure.[16]

It is not known whether William went up to Norfolk, although the election was acrimonious and expensive, the result going, after scrutiny, to Coke and Astley.[17] The General Election made little difference to the political balance in Parliament. At the end of the year William still had no preferment, and Nelson displayed his frustration to Addington in full:

---

* When Nelson left for the Mediterranean in May 1803 he left his proxy vote in the House of Lords to Lord Moira, who wrote to Davison that he 'was bound to give his vote as his relations to the Ministry requires tho' it may be in contradiction to my own' (DRO/152M/c1803/02/59, 11 July 1803). However, Nelson regretted doing so (Nicolas, V, 13 Jan. 1804; VII, 39, 16 Sept. 1805, Nelson to Davison).

I have had my feelings and pretty strong ones the unexampled career of naval glory I have run thro' I had thought might have attracted the notice of a Great & Gracious Sovereign but the Gazette has never yet recorded the name of Nelson for anything to be given away. I own when I see other noble Lords' Brothers Gazetted, whose services I can scarcely trace, my feelings, my Dear Friend, are warm and I should burst was I to keep them unconfined. You saw and was kind to my feelings and I am ever your firmly attached friend.[18]

Friendship was no substitute for political weight in clerical appointments.

Nelson had no political ambitions, and when he first spoke in the House of Lords he seemed under-prepared and generally tended to wander off the point. He spoke for the peace in the debate of 21 December 1801, talking down the advantages of retaining Malta, Minorca and the Cape.[19] He had previously accepted the importance of Malta, if only to deny it to the French, but the retention of the island was a subject on which he was not consistent, possibly because his judgement was always warped when the claims of the Kingdom of Naples and Sicily were involved.[20] In the event the problem of Malta developed as the chief difficulty in the way of the continuance of the peace with France.

Unsure of Napoleon's intentions and now determined to hold on to Malta, Addington's government was nervous, and throughout the peace and during the rest of the 1803 Parliament reflected an anxiety by all members. Doubts were expressed most freely on 2 December 1802 in the debate on the 'Naval Estimates'. The government asked Parliament for a grant for 50,000 seamen – 20,000 more than the normal peace establishment. 'It was strange', commented Thomas Grenville, now in opposition, 'that the Government had not informed the House whether the Country was likely to be at war or at peace.' Grenville could see no signs of security for the country and was not inclined to oppose a vote for a greater number of seamen. In the same debate Sir Sidney Smith warned of the danger of invasion if the French should occupy Holland. 'Holland affords the means of sending over an army in one night. I assert it, because I know the voyage from England to Holland is but one night's sail.'[21] Fear of invasion was still, even during the peace, a constant political factor, but St Vincent's confidence was unshakeable. He wrote to Keith in July 1803: 'You will see by the debates in the House of Lords that some of our Brethren think the Invasion will be attempted immediately. I am not of that Number. Nevertheless it is good policy to make every possible preparation for the Event.'[22] By mid 1803 the Sea Fencibles and the coastal signal stations had been revived, ships were stationed in the Channel and in the Thames estuary, and a string of watching frigates was in position across the North Sea.[23] Most expert opinion agreed with St Vincent. Troubridge wrote to Nelson: 'there is much talk of invasion, for my own part I do not think it.'[24] Others, however, were worried. George Rose wrote to Nelson later in 1803: 'hazardous as the Navigation is I do not think it at all out of the questions but that an attempt may be made.'[25]

In order to break the military deadlock, both Britain and France were developing new weapons. Word of Robert Fulton's experiments in France with a submersible reached England. In November 1802 the House of Lords was cleared of strangers while this 'Diving Boat' was debated: it was alleged that the French could now 'blow up a first rate man of war with only fifteen pounds of powder'.[26] Nepean sent more information in a secret circular to senior admirals; the 'submarine vessel' could stay submersed for seven hours and move at two and a half miles an hour.[27] Experiments with rockets (or 'combustibles') were also under way after their successful use by Hyder Ali and Tippoo Sultan against European troops in India in 1799, although the British, knowing French strength in chemistry, hesitated to use them in case their lead should be overtaken.[28] There were fierce debates in 1804 on the best type of ships to defend the country from a French invasion, to which in his absence Nelson could not contribute, although he wrote a persuasive memorandum on the need for a flotilla of lightly built gunboats, a course that future governments were to follow.[29]

Distrust of France had also led Britain to maintain a strong Mediterranean squadron and disarmament during the peace had been gradual, almost imperceptible. At the end of 1802 it still consisted of eleven 74s, three 64s and forty-five smaller warships.[30] The commander-in-chief, Rear-Admiral Sir Richard Bickerton, experienced many problems during his time in command. Since 1801 he had had to oversee the transport of troops back from Egypt, as well as the evacuations of Elba and Minorca. He had also been required to convoy British trade between Gibraltar and Italy and the Levant. Cruisers from Algiers and Tunis had preyed upon merchant ships and protection was essential. Malta had to be fed by ensuring the supply of corn from Sicily. In addition, he was expected to watch Toulon, for the French were equipping an expedition to wrest back San Domingo from the slaves who had revolted in 1791. But Bickerton's chief problem was the paralysis of the dockyards caused by St Vincent's savage cuts and cancellation of contracts. In the Mediterranean ships were not relieved and their condition had deteriorated sadly. Bickerton's own flagship, the *Kent*, lost all her masts in a storm in December 1801 because her bowsprit and foremast were rotten.[31] Food became scarce by June 1802, by December he was reporting scurvy; and in January 1803 he described his situation to Nepean as 'almost destitute'.[32] Malta was relieved only by the eventual arrival of victuallers from England as late as April 1803.[33] He had to cope with crew sickness on a large scale, a situation worsened by the Admiralty order to give up the naval hospital, which led him to rely upon the army hospital. In March of 1803 he reported that 408 men were sick and that fifty-three of them had died, 'since the breaking up of the Naval Hospital in the month of May last'.[34] Bickerton was not well served by St Vincent's administration, nor was he able to hand over a fleet in good condition to Nelson, his successor as commander-in-chief.

Morale suffered too, the men restive at continuing to have to serve during the peace. In November 1802 the *Gibraltar* (84) was on passage from Malta to Gibraltar when the crew mutinied and attempted to persuade the rest of the squadron to follow their example. The situation was brought under control by the officers and marines. In Oristano Bay on the west side of Sardinia, the court martial condemned two seamen to death, and they were hanged from the yard arm.[35] Then in March, London became suspicious that Napoleon was going to use the expedition fitting for San Domingo for a sudden swoop on Egypt. Bickerton was informed by the Admiralty that he should send no more ships home until he was certain that the French ships from Toulon were through the Strait of Gibraltar, and that he was to make his dispositions according to this perceived threat: if the French ships did appear to steer east to Egypt, Bickerton was to exert his 'best endeavours to take or destroy them provided the force you may have with you at the time be sufficient to enable you to do so with a reasonable prospect of success'.[36]

Bickerton's ships had been surveying through the summer of 1802, and this painstaking work was to prepare the way for Nelson in the coming two years, but it was Captain Ryves's fortuitous discovery that would prove to be the most important of all. In December 1802 Bickerton was in the *Kent*, anchored in Oristano Bay, on the west coast of Sardinia.* He had informed Evan Nepean at the Admiralty that the anchorage was good and the bay 'not so likely to awake the jealousy of the French, from hence I can easily watch the proceedings of the French expedition'.[37] In the town of

---

* Nelson had considered the potential of the harbours of Sardinia as far back as 1796, when he had asked John Trevor, the minister in Turin, to find out about Oristano Bay, while he once anchored his squadron close to Cagliari in the south-east corner of the island (Monmouth, E987, 4 Mar. 1796, Nelson to Trevor). A copy of a printed survey of Oristano Bay surveyed by the master of the *Kent* in November 1802 is in the National Maritime Museum (NMM, G231:11/10).

Oristan he was told by the Sardinian commandant that a squadron of Tunisian warships was threatening the Maddalena Islands, off the north-east coast of the island. Bickerton ordered Captain George Ryves of the *Agincourt* (64) to the islands to protect the inhabitants. In doing so, Ryves stumbled upon an ideal anchorage, which he was ordered to survey; this quickly came to be known as Agincourt Sound.* Not only was it far enough north to enable ships to beat across the prevalent north-westerly winds to watch Toulon about 160 miles away, but it was accessible from both the north-west and the south-east, sheltered to the south by the main island of Sardinia and to the north by the islands of Maddalena and Caprera. The land around is low so that winds over the smooth waters of the anchorage were not fickle; but, above all, the bottom has soft mud, shelving gently to a depth of fifty feet, brought down to the sea by the River Surreo.[38] This mud held the anchors firm in the hard winter storms, making Agincourt Sound a rarity in the central Mediterranean, for most bays there are very deep, with rock or coarse sand and shell on the bottom, less likely to hold an anchor. The Sound was to serve as Nelson's main supply base for two years; there, throughout the year, victualling and store ships could safely offload provisions and stores into his warships.

By early 1803 the peace looked increasingly precarious. Addington's government – the same one that had agreed to the controversial peace a year earlier – was being provoked by Napoleon's continual aggressive moves in Switzerland and Holland, and by his exclusion of British trade from Continental ports. In the words of one modern historian: 'The British went to war simply because they could not stand being further challenged and humiliated by Bonaparte; France went to war because Bonaparte could not stop doing it.'[39] The first sign of rapid escalation was the king's message of 8 March, which contained a clear threat: 'as very considerable military preparations are carrying on in the ports of France and Holland, [His Majesty] has judged it expedient to adopt additional measures of precaution for the security of his dominions.'[40] By 1 April, St Vincent was telling Samuel Hood, commanding in the West Indies, that he should obstruct the arrival of French troop reinforcements.[41] By 7 May, Nepean wrote to

---

* Other anchorages in the Maddalena Islands and the Straits of Bonifacio were surveyed, particularly by the *Weazle* sloop, and progress in these tideless and translucent waters was fast. Nepean ordered that these bays should also be assessed for 'wooding and watering and how far these places may be capable of sheltering a fleet' ((UK)NA: PRO, ADM 2/1360, 1 Feb.; BL, Add. MSS 34935, 1 Feb. 1803, Nepean to Bickerton). The charts were taken back to London, engraved copies taken and twenty copies then sent out to the fleet (NMM, CRK/13/87, 26 Aug. 1803, Troubridge to Nelson).

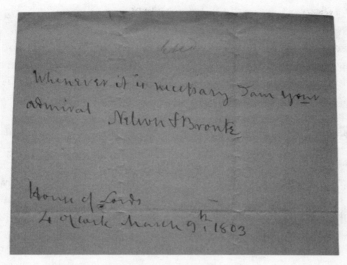

Nelson's note to Henry Addington, 9 March 1803

Richard Bickerton of the probability of hostilities and ordered him to hold himself 'in a constant state of readiness'.[42] Bickerton's final act in the peace was intelligent anticipation: without orders, and after judging the reaction of the French newspapers to the king's speech, he instructed one of his captains to bring twenty-two British merchant ships out of Leghorn to Malta before France declared war.[43]

The day after the king's speech, secure in the knowledge that he had already been chosen for the Mediterranean, Nelson sent the prime minister a reassuring note from the House of Lords: 'Whenever it is necessary I am your Admiral.'[44] In the following week St Vincent and Addington had to withstand furious visits and indignant letters from Keith, staying in London although serving as the port admiral at Plymouth. Keith was the senior admiral and his safe pair of hands contrasted favourably with Nelson's wayward performance in 1799 and 1800; thus he wrote to St Vincent on 11 March, expecting the Mediterranean command. Later that day he received a reply, offering him instead the North Sea. Keith responded furiously: 'I cannot help being hurt at a Junior Officer being sent to a command I so lately held, and I hope with credit.'[45] He stormed off to see Addington, who told Keith that Nelson's appointment had been 'a Cabinet measure'. 'I thought I had explained to your Lordship that Lord Nelson has been held in readiness more than a month past,' replied St Vincent, with unusual patience, 'I am nevertheless glad that this has been confirmed by such high authority.'[46] Keith could not bring himself to write a mollifying letter to the first lord until 17 March: 'I feared that some of my conduct had given offence to the Minister . . . [but] . . . Mr Addington and Lord Chatham both assured me Lord Nelson's name had been mentioned for some time past, but not in the event of a War, nor in competition with me . . . perhaps I should not have felt so much (as I confess I do) on this occasion.'[47]

Addington had appointed sensibly. Nelson had told Minto nearly a month earlier that the 'Government is under the greatest uncertainty whether they shall be forced to some hostile measure or not. One of those in contemplation has been to send him to the Mediterranean, by way of watching the armament and being ready if wanted. He says that he is thought fitter for that delicate service, as on the one hand he wishes the continuance of peace, and therefore is not likely to precipitate matters; and on the other hand Bonaparte knows that if he hoists his flag it will not be in joke.'[48] For once, Nelson knew what was going on. He had recently demonstrated that patience was not his strong suit; his flair and judgement were of greater use in the Mediterranean. Keith's methodical personality was more suited to the defence of the Channel and the North Sea. Moreover, with Nelson in the North Sea command, Emma Hamilton would almost certainly have been involved; with Nelson in the Mediterranean she would perforce be kept at a distance.

On 16 May 'The King's Most Excellent Majesty in Council' took the final step. An Order-in-Council was issued, ordering reprisals against French shipping, 'in consequence of the repeated insults and provocations which his Majesty has experienced from the Government of France . . . His Majesty's fleets and ships, as also all other ships and vessels that shall be commissionated [sic] by letters of marque . . . may lawfully seize all ships, vessels, and goods belonging to the French Republic.' A proclamation was issued to encourage seamen and landmen to enter the navy; another to prohibit British ships from making voyages to French ports; and yet another to enable the British to take Dutch ships.[49] Events now moved faster.

Preparations for war were in hand. On 9 March the 100-gun *Victory*, appointed to be Nelson's flagship, was floated out of Chatham Dockyard and into the Medway. She had been at Chatham for three years undergoing a 'large repair'; only the respite of the peace had allowed the hard-pressed Chatham shipwrights to complete such a complex job. After her service as Hood's flagship in the Mediterranean in the early 1790s, she had returned to Chatham in late 1797 and was docked in April 1800. Her repairs had cost the enormous sum of £70,000.[50] The *Victory* was not the largest ship that Nelson had commanded; for a month in 1801 the *San Josef*, nearly 300 tons heavier, had been his flagship, but, as we can still see today, the *Victory* was a formidable fighting machine. As well as her complement of 837 crew, there were often to be as many as 100 'supernumeraries' aboard. But the flagship had the space necessary for these additional volunteers and passengers – including Nelson's personal retinue of seven servants and his secretary; the flag captain's secretary and servants and the physician of the fleet. She was also known to be sea-kindly; a few months later Nelson wrote from the Mediterranean: 'this ship is so easy in a sea that we scarce feel a gale.'[51] The *Victory* was now thirty-eight years old, and it was unusual for a ship to be kept going for that length of time, but her sailing qualities were legendary and admirals vied with each other for her. Indeed, Lord Keith announced that he was going to have her, as she would not be ready in time for Nelson to take her to the Mediterranean. Nelson had to write a hurried letter to the first lord to ensure that she could sail with him.[52]

No effort was spared to get her to sea as soon as possible. The day after she was afloat, the *Victory* was put into commission by her first lieutenant, Robert Pettet. He borrowed 160 men from nearby ships, and fifty retired seamen from Greenwich Hospital were on hand: by the end of the day her main foremast and her bowsprit were in. On 11 April her captain, Samuel Sutton, arrived on board. Within five days nearly 400 tons of iron and shingle ballast had been loaded. Between 19 and 22 April gales prevented her from being moved downriver to deeper water in Long Reach, below the dockyard; she sailed there on 24 April 'under treble reefed topsails'. Under the eye of Thomas Atkinson, her master, she was loaded with boatswain's and carpenter's stores, provisions and guns. Artificers from the dockyard were still painting the main deck on 8 May. Three days later 360 seamen were brought aboard from various ships and tenders, and the borrowed men returned to their ships. On 14 May, John Madgson, the master attendant from the dockyard who had charge of the *Agamemnon* when she was commissioned only ten years before, came on board with dockyard men to assist. Delayed again for a day, this time by variable winds, the *Victory* sailed on 15 May. She dropped her river pilot at Garrison Point at the mouth of the Medway, picked up her pilot for the Downs, and sailed into the Thames estuary and up the Swin. At nightfall she dropped her anchor near the Whitaker Beacon. On 16 May she sailed south through the Downs, shortening sail to drop the pilot. She did not stop.[53]

Two days later Nelson received his 'Most Secret Orders' from the Board of Admiralty. He was to go straight to Malta in the frigate *Amphion* (36), put Bickerton and his ships under his command and confer with Alexander

Ball to make 'such arrangements as may be necessary with a view to the protection and security of that Island'. He was then to proceed to a position off Toulon that would 'be most proper for enabling you to take, sink, burn, or otherwise destroy, any Ships or Vessels belonging to France'. Another imperative was to watch the French in Genoa, guarding against the mounting of another expedition to Egypt, for Talleyrand, the French foreign minister, had bragged to Charles Whitworth, the ambassador in Paris, that the French reconquest of Egypt was only a matter of time.[54] Nor had Napoleon hidden his intention to invade Italy and occupy the south.[55] Nelson was to prevent any French ships that had been to the West Indies from re-entering the Mediterranean, protect Sicily and all the Turkish dominions, and observe strict neutrality with Spain while at the same time ensuring that a Spanish fleet should never join with a French one.[56] The Levant trade would need convoys and protection. The Mediterranean command, with its mixture of both defensive and aggressive objectives, was as complex as ever. Nelson would come to regard the destruction of the French Toulon fleet as the means by which the great aim of holding the Mediterranean could be achieved.

Nelson had more immediate problems. He did not want to leave the *Victory* behind, in case, once he had left, Keith succeeded in persuading St Vincent to let her stay in the Channel. But nor did he want her lack of readiness to become public knowledge. The Admiralty added further confusion to the commissioning by insisting that Nelson sail immediately to find Admiral Cornwallis off Ushant. They feared that the Brest fleet might outnumber him, in which case Nelson should leave the *Victory* with Cornwallis. Nelson wrote to Captain Sutton from the Admiralty to get his baggage on board the *Victory* and to buy sheep, hay, chickens and corn, 'for I may yet go out in the *Victory*'.[57] Yet Nelson's orders to embark on the *Amphion* were designed to ensure that he would get to Malta quickly. Her captain was Thomas Masterman Hardy, and she was in good order, having already had a shakedown cruise to Cork and back.[58] At 2.30 p.m. on 17 May the *Victory* anchored at Spithead, only thirty-eight days from her undocking. For the next two days the crew tightened the new, stretched rigging.[59]

On 18 May, Nelson arrived at Portsmouth, 'smothered with dust at exactly one o'clock', as he related to Emma. 'I found Hardy & Sutton waiting for me, they both agreeing with me, my flag is hoisted in the *Victory* to prevent without the Service absolutely requires it the indelicate removal of an admiral.'[60] He wrote to St Vincent immediately to tell him that 'if Admiral Cornwallis wants her – which is very improbable according to what I have heard – but if he does, I shall remove nothing from the Frigate but my cot.'[61] He dined with Hardy and Sutton, and with Captain George Murray, who was to be his captain of the fleet. Also present was his secretary John Scott. Nepean then wrote to give Nelson the freedom to go in either the *Victory* or the *Amphion*.[62] Troubridge wrote optimistically from London: '*Victory* is compleat and ordered to Spithead directly, we shall pay her advance there, & Bounty to such as are entitled. Sir Jam[e]s Saumarez writes to me to say she is the best Man'd ship that has been fitted this Armament. I wish I was on the Old *Culloden* to second you.'[63] Nelson was to take with him the new ambassador to Naples, Hugh Elliot, younger brother of Lord Minto, and Minto's son, George Elliot, who went out as a volunteer, hoping to pick up a ship and secure his promotion to captain.[64]

To Emma, Nelson wrote candidly: 'The *Victory* is in a pretty state of confusion and I have not moved my cot from the *Amphion*.'[65] He was short of crew – 'half manned', he complained to the commander-in-chief at Portsmouth, Admiral Lord Gardner, although by early June she was up to complement.[66] Nelson decided to go aboard the *Victory*.* One contemporary description ran:

As soon as he got on board, the anchor was weighed, but before they proceeded to St Helen's they found the ship running away . . . the crew which had been sent on board, consisted of all sorts of persons, some captured by the police, others released from prison etc. In short, there were few men who could either hand, reef or steer. It was coming on to blow hard and instead of being able to profit by the fair wind, it became quite necessary, for the safety of the ship, to take in nearly all the sail . . . The poor fellows, with long-tailed brown coats, were mostly floating about in the lee scuppers, in a most wretched state of sea sickness.[67]

The *Victory* proceeded slowly, accompanied by the *Amphion*, which immediately took a Dutch prize. On the other side of the Channel, they failed to find Cornwallis and the fleet off Brest. Chafing at the delay, Nelson waited for three days at the rendezvous point. Nelson complained to Addington in a long, personal letter, displaying his frustrations to the full while simultaneously indemnifying himself against future failure: 'I am aware of the importance of my getting to the Mediterranean and I think I

---

* Nelson considered the crew of the *Victory* inexperienced, for he noted in his private journal on the voyage across the Atlantic as the fleet crossed the Tropic of Cancer, 'Neptune performed the usual ceremony, near 500 persons in the *Victory* never before crossed the Tropic' (BL, Add. MSS 34968, 22 May 1805).

might safely have been allowed to proceed in the *Victory* . . . I can only work with such tools as my superiors give me.'[68]

When the weather moderated on 24 May, he and his retinue transferred into the *Amphion*. Her cramped quarters had to accommodate Captain George Murray, George and Hugh Elliot, and all their servants, as well as John McArthur, the *Victory*'s purser, and thirty-eight able seamen, forty-five in all. With him came his midshipmen but not the lieutenants.[69] The next day Samuel Sutton in the *Victory* found Cornwallis, who did not want to transfer to her, so the flagship followed in the *Amphion*'s wake and 'jogged along gently, but very majestically', the great guns and small arms exercising every day.[70] The confusion and muddle over, the *Amphion* made rapid progress towards Gibraltar. Hardy wrote to his cousin: 'His Lordship looks remarkably well and is in high spirits.'[71] Nelson was enjoying the prospect of resuming command in the Mediterranean.

27

Commander-in-Chief, Mediterranean

May 1803–January 1805

*Your lot off Toulon must be very hard without any Port to refresh at.
I thought it bad enough when we had Corsica & Leghorn ...*
Thomas Foley to Nelson, 25 August 1803[1]

*We have hardly a port to go to on this station. Naples is without the
track. The Spaniards are uncivil and lay very hard restraint upon our
communication. Malta is so far and, as well as Gibraltar, so out of the
way that, except the barren shores of Sardinia, we have no where to
thrust our noses. The consequence is that the greatest inconvenience
must and does ensue. We are without butter, wine, porter, nay, almost
no cloathes ... Lord Nelson expects them [the Toulon Fleet] out
constantly, but that is altogether doubtful.*
Captain John Whitby to Admiral Cornwallis [24? November], 1803[2]

Nelson's achievement over the next two years, during which hardly a gun
under his command was fired, was as remarkable as any of his battles.
It represented a concentration of effort and willpower that overcame
stretched, sometimes negligible resources, lack of shore support, little strategic guidance and almost no intelligence that did not come from his own
efforts, for, in contrast with the 1790s, French dominance across Europe
isolated the Mediterranean command from London. Napoleon's hold over
the countries bordering the Western Mediterranean was almost complete.
He had detached 15,000 troops into the southernmost part of Italy, the
Kingdom of Naples and Sicily; this allowed him to secure the Italian mainland by intimidating neutral states while at the same time threatening
Sicily and the countries across the Adriatic, the Morea (the Peloponnesian
peninsula and further north) and Turkey. Austria was exhausted. Spain
was insolvent and cowed. Only Russia, now an ally, actively supported
Britain, her ships and troops defending the Ionian Islands.[3] The French fleet

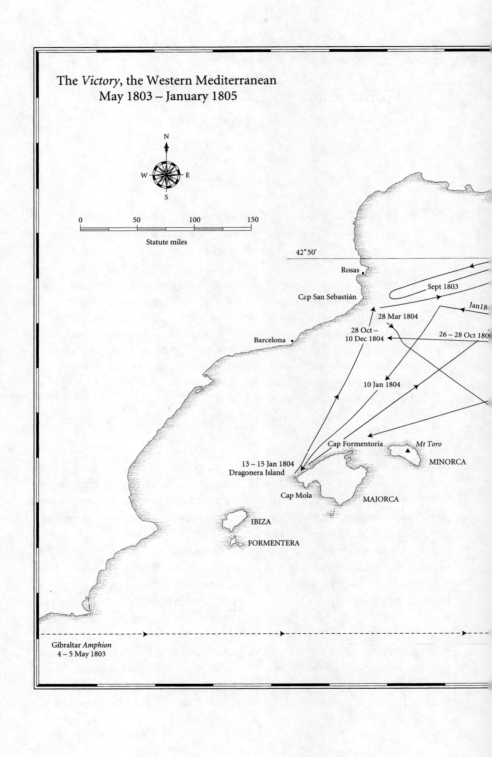

The *Victory*, the Western Mediterranean
May 1803 – January 1805

N
W   E
S

0   50   100   150
Statute miles

42° 50'

Rosas

Cap San Sebastián

Sept 1803

Jan18

28 Mar 1804

Barcelona

28 Oct –
10 Dec 1804

26 – 28 Oct 180

10 Jan 1804

Cap Formentoria   Mt Toro

MINORCA

13 – 15 Jan 1804
Dragonera Island

Cap Mola

MAJORCA

IBIZA

FORMENTERA

Gibraltar *Amphion*
4 – 5 May 1803

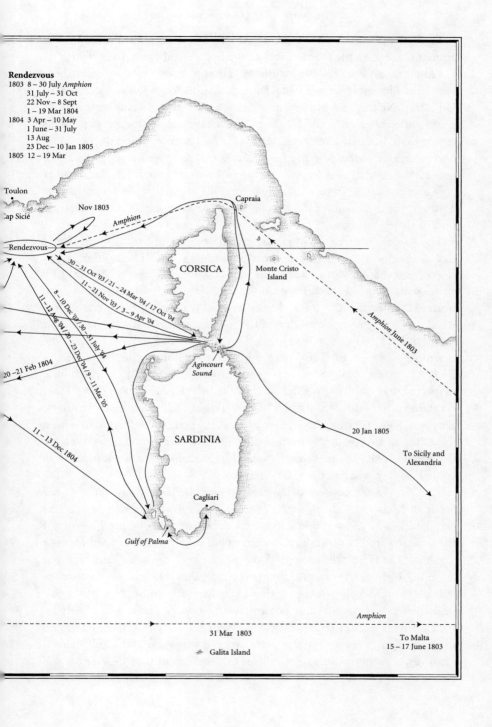

Rendezvous
1803 8 – 30 July *Amphion*
      31 July – 31 Oct
      22 Nov – 8 Sept
      1 – 19 Mar 1804
1804 3 Apr – 10 May
      1 June – 31 July
      13 Aug
      23 Dec – 10 Jan 1805
1805 12 – 19 Mar

Toulon

Cap Sicié

Nov 1803

Amphion

Rendezvous

30 – 31 Oct '03 / 21 – 24 Mar '04 / 17 Oct '04

11 – 21 Nov '03 / 3 – 9 Apr '04

8 – 10 Dec '03 / 30 – 31 July '04

11 – 12 Aug '04 / 20 – 23 Dec '04 / 9 – 11 Mar '05

20 – 21 Feb 1804

11 – 13 Dec 1804

CORSICA

Capraia

Monte Cristo
Island

Amphion June 1803

Agincourt
Sound

SARDINIA

20 Jan 1805

To Sicily and
Alexandria

Cagliari

Gulf of Palma

Amphion

31 Mar 1803

To Malta
15 – 17 June 1803

Galita Island

mobilizing at Toulon was poised to deliver a concentrated show of naval strength wherever the febrile mind of the first consul chose to apply it.

From his time in the *Agamemnon*, Nelson knew only too well how very difficult it was to blockade Toulon. As the *Amphion* sailed south to Gibraltar, Nelson had little idea of the solutions to his many problems as commander-in-chief. Yet he rose to this challenge, a steeper step in his career than any that had come before. He had been appointed to secure a decisive result: instead he produced a dogged, sustained campaign, diplomatically finessed, that kept Napoleon's European southern flank under constant pressure. It was as if his previous erratic performance in the Mediterranean had never happened. This time he was without the distraction of the Hamiltons.

The *Amphion* reached Gibraltar on 4 June, staying for no more than a day to take on stores and men for Malta. On 11 June, Hugh Elliot transferred into the *Maidstone* (32) and was taken to his post in Naples.[4] By 15 June the *Amphion* had arrived at Malta and was greeted with enthusiasm by the Maltese.[5] Bickerton and the fleet were at sea. Nelson stayed only three days, conferring with Alexander Ball, now formally installed as governor of the island. The *Amphion* was warped out of Valetta Harbour early in the morning on 18 June.[6] The *Victory*, by now at Gibraltar, had captured a French frigate and three merchant ships from the West Indies, which little suspected that war had been declared by the British government on 18 May. Captain Sutton estimated that Nelson would gain £4,000 from these prizes, but, with Nelson's usual bad financial luck, the prizes were captured within the limits of Cornwallis's station and Nelson would not therefore receive the admiral's share; otherwise he would have earned in a week more than enough to pay what he owed on Merton.[7]

The *Amphion*'s course to the rendezvous off Toulon lay through the Strait of Messina and up the Italian coast.[8] The three-week passage was dogged by light and variable north-west winds, and it convinced Nelson of the impracticability of Malta as a convenient base from which to blockade Toulon. 'The Fleet can never go there if I can find any other corner to put them in,' Nelson wrote to Addington on 28 June.[9] He had yet to discover that corner. On 8 July he met with Bickerton and his nine ships of the line near the rendezvous south of Toulon, just below the horizon.[10] 'Nearly all the fleet were perfect strangers to me,' Nelson later wrote to Emma, 'and therefore I can expect no particular marks of private friendship.'[11] It was, however, a smooth handover. Ball informed Nelson that Bickerton 'will attach himself to you by his implicit execution of your orders, and with a candid and open conduct. He is a safe officer and will never attempt to undermine his superior.'[12]

The business of blockade started. A court martial was held on board the *Donegal*.[13] A French corvette on passage to Athens was taken; she carried classical busts and bronzes that Nelson sent to Sir Joseph Banks in London for disposal as a prize.[14] On 31 July, the first day on station, the *Victory* was forty miles south of Cap Sicié.[15] Nelson kept his ships well away from the coast. Even so, within a week of arriving at the rendezvous French frigates had captured a schooner and two water transports.[16] 'It is not my intention to close watch Toulon, <u>even with frigates</u>,' Nelson informed one of his frigate captains, 'and I beg you will not keep too close to Sepet or Sicie in the night.'[17] Nelson had no margin of superiority over the French fleet refitting in Toulon, and he exercised proper caution, for he could not afford to lose any ships in a surprise foray from the port.

Nelson immediately sent Nepean a long analysis on the state of his ships of the line. Though its tone was cheerful, its message was gloomy, for the condition of only three, the *Victory*, the *Donegal* and the *Belleisle*, was 'most perfect in every respect'. The other six were urgently in need of docking and had masts and bowsprits that needed renewing. The *Monmouth* sailed so badly that she could not keep up with the others, so Nelson sent her 'to Naples to lay Guardship in case the Royal Family should again want the protection of the British Flag'. The *Madras*, he was told, 'is so bad in every respect that she or the *Agincourt* may toss up which will be the fittest to make a prison ship.' He ended: 'So much for my Fleet of the Line, take it in good humour as it is meant but I solemnly declare the Account I have given is correctly true.'[18]

William Mark was a bright, self-educated seaman, only twenty-one years old; rated in the muster book as 'AB', he worked as an assistant secretary to Bickerton and now transferred to the *Amphion*. On his second day he 'received an invitation to dine with Lord Nelson, and it was the most agreeable thing possible. There were several captains of my acquaintance there. Much was said on Mediterranean affairs and Lord Nelson showed me kind attention.' Nelson was, as usual, using his dinner table to gather information. Mark had been in the Mediterranean since 1801 and was well briefed. Nor had Nelson forgotten the value of the flamboyant gesture, for Mark remembered: 'It was only necessary to see him to be able to appreciate his extraordinary qualities. One day at dinner he sent for his steward and told him to get up the extra plate, because he should soon have to entertain the Prefect Maritime of Toulon, Admiral Gantheaume.'[19] Many officers of

Lord Howe's generation could not have conceived that the commander-in-chief, Mediterranean, should dine with a lowly clerk, rated an able seaman, however knowledgeable. Life aboard the *Amphion* was cramped. Mark commented: 'Much inconvenience was now endured by the flag being in a frigate, which, in addition to her crew, had on board the suite of the Admiral. The confusion was scarcely bearable.'[20] But at the end of July the *Victory* caught up with the squadron.[21] Nelson transferred his flag and Hardy came with him, Sutton moving to the *Amphion*.

Though Rear-Admiral George Campbell arrived in the *Canopus* (74) on 18 August, ships in good condition from England were still not forthcoming. Nelson received a jocular letter from Lord Hobart, secretary of state for war, explaining how Nelson's role was to act as deterrent: 'Your ships being crippled will not induce your friends at Toulon to come out. It was the port from whence they took their departure for Aboukir; and whilst the memorable events which took place there remain impressed on their minds, they will not encounter a Fleet under the command of Lord Nelson, if they can avoid it.'[22] He was to keep the sea in front of Toulon with his patched-up ships until nearly the end of October, in daily expectation that the French would depart.[23]

During these early months, Nelson, with his secretary John Scott and the Reverend Alexander Scott, his translator, established a voluminous correspondence.[24] In London his distant masters had to be kept informed. St Vincent and Nepean at the Admiralty were his usual correspondents, but after several lengthy letters to Addington, the prime minister directed him to correspond with Hobart. Communications with London were slow and haphazard. A dispatch took a month to be transported across Spain from Barcelona to Ferrol, while a cutter sailing hard from Plymouth to Sardinia could take as little as three weeks, but dispatches rarely reached Nelson rapidly.[25] In April 1804 some were lost when a small cutter, the *Swift*, was captured. Nelson wrote to Troubridge with icy irony: 'I know we are apt to blame our friends rather than strangers . . . I will not suppose that any dispatches of importance be sent in a vessel with 23 men.'[26] A year later William Marsden, by then secretary to the Admiralty Board, was to write to Nelson: 'It is quite unaccountable that you should have been 75 days without official dispatches, as many during that interval were forwarded to the Mediterranean.'[27]

However, Nelson was able to make use of a large network of British ministers and consuls around the Mediterranean. Letters were constant between the *Victory* and Hugh Elliot at Naples, and with Hookham Frere at Madrid. The Kingdom of Naples and Sicily was still neutral, although a large French army was within its borders. It was in British interests that its neutrality was at least maintained, and some provisions could be obtained in spite of French pressure on the kingdom. Thomas Jackson, minister to the court of Sardinia in Turin (and later in Rome), became an important correspondent when the French threatened Sardinia in 1804.[28] Nelson had briefly met William Drummond, the minister in Constantinople, in the hectic days before Copenhagen. Turkey was a natural ally. Nelson wrote to Emma: 'I am as popular there as ever . . . they want me to protect Morea and Egypt.'[29] Nelson also re-established contact with consuls all round the Mediterranean, some of them old friends; he reminded James Duff at Cadiz that it was twenty-seven years since they had first met.[30] Spiridion Foresti at Corfu, 'a very able man', in Nelson's opinion, was the main conduit to Turkey; 'from thence the passage of an express by land to Constantinople is twelve days'.[31] Foresti advised him of the need to supply frigates and brigs to convoy trade from the Adriatic, now infested with French privateers operating from the coast in southern Italy. Likewise, the safe conveyance of the Levant trade to the Strait of Gibraltar was the main concern of Francis Wherry at Smyrna. The roles of the consuls in the Barbary States – Perkin Magra in Tunis, Simon Lucas in Tripoli, John Falcon in Algiers and James Matra in Tangiers – were mainly political, countering French influence. Good relations with neutral states were critical so that cattle, corn and vegetables could be obtained for the fleet and Malta; they also needed to prevent North African cruisers from attacking British merchant ships. A long-running complication arose when two Moorish women were found in John Falcon's house and the bey of Algiers demanded his recall. Nelson sent Richard Goodwin Keats in the *Superb* (74) to resolve the confrontation, which he achieved, but not until the end of 1804.[32]

Napoleon now held sway over the Continent, making political and military intelligence more vital than ever. Nelson kept in touch with other admirals such as Edward Pellew and Alexander Cochrane, blockading off Brest and Ferrol.[33] Within the Mediterranean station he was well informed, particularly at local level. The most regular method of gaining intelligence was by having his frigates observe the position and readiness of the masts and rigging of the French ships in Toulon; merchants were another useful source for this, especially Edward Gayner of Rosas in northern Spain. What Nelson most lacked was accurate and timely information about the intentions of Napoleon, who was prone to change his mind and his strategy, particularly about the attempted invasion of England. Reports from London were of little use. Troubridge wrote from London in October 1803: 'I am equally puzzled with your Lordship about the destination of the

French fleet, some say Egypt, some Morea, others Ireland, Colonys, Brazils etc. I believe Bonaparte has puzzled himself.'[34]

Throughout 1804 Nelson's other main concern was whether Spain was likely to enter the war as an ally of France. Hookham Frere in Madrid irritated Nelson by his erratic reporting and analysis of the policy of the court of Spain. 'Yesterday I received a letter from Mr Frere,' he complained to Hugh Elliot in Naples in the spring of 1804, 'in which, after having put us so much upon our guard that we expected a Spanish War every day, the name of Spain is not mentioned; therefore, I must suppose the alarm is gone off.'[35] Nelson was thus reduced to using local information to draw wider conclusions. For instance, Charles Price, the consul at Cartagena, wrote to him in October 1803 confirming the usual Spanish problem of lack of money and men. The Spanish ships there 'stand in need of much repair, and this Arsenal very ill provided and in want of many articles . . . the difficulty they will find to get seamen, such is the aversion they have for the Service that they desert and conceal themselves in the Mountains.'[36] Off Toulon more than a year later Nelson picked up similar local intelligence: 'a Pilot came off accompanied by only one Man, both in a most wretched state and only keeping the Sea from apprehension of being prest for the fleet in Toulon. They assured me that 3 or 4 nights past every individual in the Shape of a Seamen both from the Vessels & houses were seized and sent to the fleet. This looks like a Move.'[37] To where remained a mystery.

Another concern was the destination of French troops in the south of Italy who seemed poised for a crossing of the Adriatic to land in the Morea or on the mainland opposite the Ionian islands. A long-held fear of the British government was that Napoleon still had designs on Egypt if sufficient transports could be gathered to convey the troops.[38] The first alarm occurred in September 1803: in Toulon eight French ships of the line, eight frigates and five or six corvettes were sighted with their sails bent, with two more ships of the line equipping.[39] Intelligence reported their destination to be either the Morea or Egypt.[40] But no move had been made by the end of September 1803, when Nelson reported confidently to St Vincent: 'I believe we are uncommonly well disposed to give the French a thrashing, and we are keen; for I have not seen a French flag on the sea since I joined the Squadron.'[41]

With his limited resources, Nelson set out to protect the vulnerable areas within his command. Captain John Gore of the *Medusa* was the senior officer at Gibraltar, and he had with him Samuel Sutton in the *Amphion*, covering the strait to keep it free of hostile privateers and to allow trade to and from England to pass. It was a privileged posting for both his

Boulogne captains, as rich prize money was more likely there than in the Mediterranean. Frigates were, however, needed everywhere, and Nelson was constantly juggling his scarce ships. He sent frigates to the Adriatic under Captain Edward Cracraft, described by Lady Elgin as 'a famous, dashing Rattle of about 35'.[42] Ceaselessly on the move in the large frigate *Anson* (44), Cracraft worked to cover any invading force that the French might send to the Morea and to protect English trade from privateers. On the eastern side of the Adriatic, he had to keep on good terms with Ali Pasha of Yanina, who ruled independently of the sultan in Constantinople; Cracraft needed naval stores from the region for use in Malta. By October 1803 he had two frigates and two sloops under him, and these ships worked tirelessly in convoying trade between ports in the Adriatic and to and from Malta, and sometimes to the Aegean.[43] On one occasion in 1804 the hard-worked *Anson* took a convoy to Constantinople.[44] Nelson reported to the foreign secretary, Lord Hawkesbury, in October 1803, 'with this force I think we have done all that is possible to serve the Morea & the Islands and to prevent that army going to Egypt.'[45] The situation in the Adriatic was eased by March 1804, when the first Russian frigates and troops arrived from the Black Sea in the Ionian islands; by August there were 9,000 Russian troops. By early 1805 Nelson was assisted by four Russian ships of the line and the same number of frigates, as well as smaller ships.[46]

For the next eighteen months Nelson was under constant pressure from consuls and ministers for warships for convoy duty. He complained about lack of frigates within days of reaching the rendezvous off Toulon at the beginning of August: 'I am absolutely in the very greatest distress for the service off Toulon,' he wrote to General Villettes at Malta.[47] William Drummond, minister at Constantinople, and Francis Wherry, consul at Smyrna, regularly demanded protection for the trade from their ports.[48] To Alexander Ball, who had suggested that Nelson send a frigate to show itself off Alexandria, he wrote a long letter, marked by some irritation, outlining the deployment of all his small ships.[49] By February 1804 Nelson wrote to Ball reckoning that he was ten frigates short.[50]

Discomfort was one of the costs of this control of the seas, for strong north-west winds blew constantly off Toulon. 'Such a place for storms of wind I never met with, and I am unfortunately in bad weather, always sea-sick,' Nelson told Davison. To St Vincent, of all people, he wrote: 'I am – don't laugh – dreadfully sea-sick this day, as it blows a Levanter.'[51] But there was cause for optimism. 'I never saw a Fleet altogether so well Officered and manned,' he wrote to Davison, 'Would to God the Ships were half as good, but they are what we call <u>crazy</u>.'[52] The fleet was healthy and in good humour. In early September 1803 Nelson wrote to a society that had sent the *Victory* bibles and prayer books, which had been distributed to the seamen: 'a ship where divine service is regularly performed is by far more regular and decent in their conduct than where it is not, and in this ship only 2 men have been punished for upwards of two months.'[53] Public worship was necessary for welfare and good order. Prize money in the early part of the commission also kept morale steady. In the first year Nelson estimated that his ships took £117,700 worth of prizes, of which the *Victory*'s share was £67,000.[54] But the prize money was to dry up: by January 1804 Nelson wrote to his sister Susannah: 'The French having no trade, but very little has been done in the Prize Way.'[55]

It blows hard from the north-west in the Gulf of Lyons in the late summer and autumn, and the fleet sought shelter to the westward, where the seas were smoother under the lee of the land near Cap San Sebastián off Barcelona. Nelson explained to Addington: 'my station to the Westward of Toulon, an unusual one, has been taken upon an idea that the French fleet is bound out of the Straits, and probably to Ireland.'[56] 'I shall remain till the French come out, if it is a year, provided our ships are not worn out,' he wrote on 3 September to Hugh Elliot.[57] During this time transports laden with wine, sent out by Mr Gibert, the British consul at Barcelona, failed to find the fleet, demonstrating the difficulty of replenishing the fleet at sea.[58] The situation became less critical when the *Prévoyante* store ship from England reached the fleet on 21 September. Her cargo of coal was particularly needed, for the ships were 'all very much in want of fuel'.[59] Fuel for cooking and the need for water determined the length of Nelson's periods at the blockade rendezvous.

Nelson's want of water finally became urgent. In early October he sent George Campbell in the *Canopus* to Sardinia to look for some and waited at the rendezvous for her return.[60] But on 24 October, as he noted in his private journal, 'The fleet being very short of water . . . determined to go to the Madalena Islands to Water.'[61] At some point during the autumn Nelson received from London the first printed copies of the surveys of the bays and islands of Sardinia carried out by Bickerton's ships during the peace, which enabled him to attempt the entry into Agincourt Sound. He timed his interruption of the blockade of Toulon to coincide with a week of full-moon nights when he felt that the French would not try to break out.[62] He nearly left it too late, for the passage to the Bonifacio Strait took him longer than he thought. He wrote that five days after leaving the rendezvous '[we] found ourselves 5 l[eague]s direct to leeward of the place we left last night. Made sail under close reef'd Topsails & kept course a very strong current against us but the fleet being absolutely in distress for water I am determined to persevere notwithstanding all the difficultys.'[63]

The wind was fresh, from the south-east, with 'light rain at intervals'.[64] His ships had Ryves's chart, as well as invaluable pilotage instructions from Richard Goodwin Keats on the course through the Bonifacio Strait.[65] Nelson tacked the fleet through the narrow channels, then along the strait to Agincourt Sound. 'We worked the *Victory* every foot of the way, from Asinara to this anchorage . . . under double-reefed topsails,' he reported to Ryves. By 3.15 p.m. on 31 October the *Victory* dropped her anchor; by six o'clock the whole fleet was in.[66] The next day Nelson sent Ryves a letter of thanks for his chart that crackled with relief: 'I individually feel all the obligation due to you for your most correct chart, and directions for these islands . . . This is absolutely one of the finest harbours I have ever seen.'[67] He described the chart to Nepean as 'the most correct thing I ever met with'.[68] It was Ryves's first attempt at surveying.[69]

Good relations with the Sardinians had already been established by Ryves, as well as by correspondence with Thomas Jackson at Turin to ensure the support of the court of the grand duke of Sardinia. Nelson sent Alexander Scott ashore to use his charm and fluency in Italian on the governor of Maddalena, who also came aboard the *Victory*.[70] The first week-long visit was a success, and Nelson thanked the governor in a letter just before the fleet left.[71] He was later to present the local church with a pair of silver candlesticks and a cross.[72] Moreover, the anchorage was safe – 'Trincomalee is not to be compared to it' – and provisions were available – 'Beef, mutton, poultry, and vegetables are in abundance and cheap.'[73] He took the fleet there seven times in the next fourteen months, making Agincourt Sound the main rendezvous point for victualling the fleet and for transports to replenish their stores. Thomas Masterman Hardy showed his usual caution, writing privately to his cousin: 'I have not been on shore nor Do I think I shall, it is a poor miserable place, not capable of furnishing us with fresh Provisions.'[74] But by November 1804 the use of Agincourt Sound was so efficient as a fleet rendezvous that Nelson could write home to the first lord: 'the fleet has been to Madalena to clear out our Transports and compleat our Wood & Water & prepare for a Winter's look out. We were five days at an anchor and came to sea compleat to five Months of every thing.'[75]

By the summer of 1804, however, as his fleet grew in numbers, Nelson also used the Pula Roads, to the west of the Gulf of Cagliari in the south-east corner of Sardinia. Although this anchorage was more exposed it

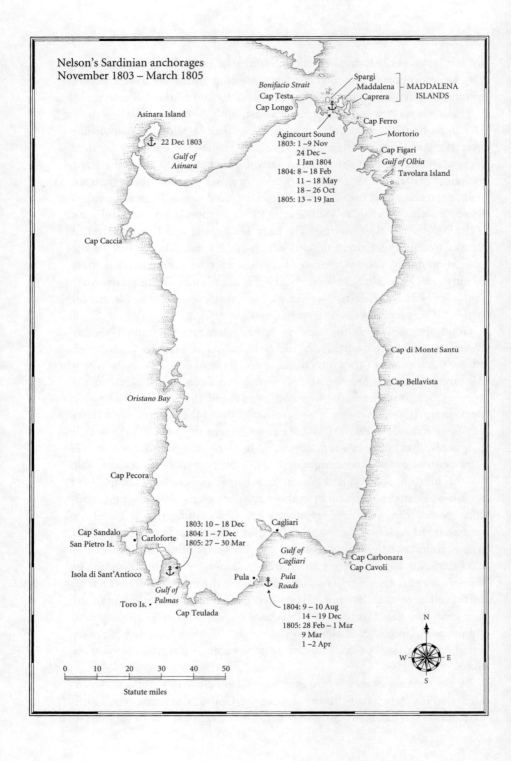

Nelson's Sardinian anchorages
November 1803 – March 1805

Bonifacio Strait
Cap Testa
Cap Longo

Spargi
Maddalena   — MADDALENA
Caprera   ISLANDS

Cap Ferro
Mortorio

Asinara Island

22 Dec 1803

*Gulf of
Asinara*

Agincourt Sound
1803: 1 –9 Nov
        24 Dec –
        1 Jan 1804
1804: 8 – 18 Feb
        11 – 18 May
        18 – 26 Oct
1805: 13 – 19 Jan

Cap Figari
Gulf of Olbia
Tavolara Island

Cap Caccia

Cap di Monte Santu

Cap Bellavista

Oristano Bay

Cap Pecora

Cagliari

1803: 10 – 18 Dec
1804: 1 – 7 Dec
1805: 27 – 30 Mar

Cap Sandalo
San Pietro Is.

Carloforte

*Gulf of
Cagliari*

Cap Carbonara
Cap Cavoli

Isola di Sant'Antioco

Pula

*Pula
Roads*

*Gulf of
Palmas*

Toro Is.

Cap Teulada

1804: 9 – 10 Aug
        14 – 19 Dec
1805: 28 Feb – 1 Mar
        9 Mar
        1 – 2 Apr

N
W   E
S

0   10   20   30   40   50

Statute miles

had a more reliable water supply through the summer drought. From August 1804 to April 1805 he used the Pula Roads six times, chiefly because, as he noted in his private journal, 'the river runs all year round . . . 20 ships can water at one time with arrangements as easy as two, for the River runs several hundred yards Parralel to the Beach.' At the height of the summer of 1804 he observed with satisfaction: 'The whole fleet compleat with water having got off 1300 tons of very fine water.'[76] He also made two visits to the Gulf of Palmas in the south-west corner of Sardinia, where bullocks were plentiful, while the transports used 'the snug cove' in the island of Asinara on the north-west tip of the island.[77] Nelson also moved from Agincourt Sound to the south of Sardinia because by the beginning of 1804 he was worried about the threat of a sudden French attack from Corsica. In January he believed that 10,000 men were gathered at Nice ready for an invasion.[78] He gave orders to ships in Agincourt Sound: 'their commanders should have the strictest orders to be vigilant during the night.'[79] He advised a frigate captain who was to stay in Agincourt Sound to keep alert for any signs of a French crossing of the Strait of Bonifacio: 'Keep a strict watch during the night, and have your guns loaded with grape.'[80]

From late 1803 Nelson almost never sent an official letter without extolling the strategic virtues of Sardinia in general and of Agincourt Sound in particular; and when he wrote home to people of influence he did not hesitate to emphasize the limited role that Malta could play.[81] To Addington he wrote that Sardinia was 'the Ceylon of the Mediterranean'.[82] The impossibility of defending Sardinia without a considerable army unit, with its attendant costs, was its great weakness as a permanent base. Even Nelson acknowledged this when the government offered to send a senior army officer to assess the possibilities of defending Cagliari and Maddalena, a scheme that Nelson eventually scotched.[83] But his faith in Sardinia as a temporary base for operations never wavered, for it produced a substantial amount of fresh provisions and cattle for the British fleet over the next two years, a supply that had been started and encouraged by Bickerton's ships during the Peace of Amiens.[84] As Nelson put it in early 1804: 'Spain will not give us live animals, Naples dare not, and Sardinia ought not.'[85]

Nelson had to adapt and develop the existing system for feeding the fleet blockading Toulon.* The Board of Admiralty's expectations of Malta as a

---

* Nelson evolved a quick check of the state of stores and water in the *Victory* by measuring the draft of the ship fore and aft, and the height of the middle port above the water (BL, Add. MSS 34967, 6 June 1804).

supply centre proved to be wildly optimistic, and the agent victualler there, Patrick Wilkie, was less than cooperative and lacking in initiative.[86] Malta possessed a fully developed yard, with a considerable ropery and store-houses that could be adapted to store provisions (though no dock), but it became a short-term liability, for the island could not feed itself.[87] The island's traditional source of food was Sicily, now under French influence. Alexander Ball wrote to Nelson in September 1803: 'The Sicilians will not give us Bullocks. We are obliged to send Transports to Tunis and Con-stantina for a supply under convoy, and if I had more means I would send to the Morea.'[88] The island thus became dependent upon North Africa, and even Odessa in the Black Sea, which meant that supplies took up valuable transports and also frigates to convoy them. To Thomas Trigge in Gibraltar, Nelson wrote: 'Sir Alexander Ball calls loudly upon me for protection of their trade of provisions. I have 4 for that service.'[89]

The Admiralty also hoped that Malta could supply seamen, which it had done in some numbers since the 1790s. Troubridge wrote: 'I am in hopes the Maltese will enter our Ships if properly managed and a little attention paid by the Captains to their Masses . . . I found them willing, hard working Men.'[90] Ball warned Nelson that there were none to be had, and London's optimism irritated Nelson. He replied to Ball that St Vincent and Trou-bridge 'think that the 900 men we are short of can be supplied by holding up my finger . . . you see how they attack me.'[91] On the usefulness of Malta in general, however, Nelson and Ball agreed to differ.[92] A worried Alexander Ball wrote a pained letter to the secretary of state's office: 'Lord Nelson declared that the Port of Malta was of little use; and he really seems to seek every occasion to justify this erroneous assertion. He now publicly says that he would as soon send a ship to St Helens as to Malta . . . It is true that ships have been a month after they arrived upon the Rendezvous before they have joined his Lordship, but that is not the fault of the distance from Malta.'[93] Nelson's opinion of Malta's usefulness might have been extreme, but, in winter especially, a genuine problem arose from its position to the south and east, 600 miles downwind of often fierce north-westerly winds.* Nelson wrote to Fremantle in January 1804 from near the rendez-vous off Toulon: 'I cannot generally speaking get even a frigate from Malta. The westerly winds are so prevalent and as they approach the Gulph of

---

* For an extensive discussion of the difference of opinion between Ball and Nelson on Malta, see Samuel Taylor Coleridge's 'Life of Sir Alexander Ball' in *The Friend* (Rooke, I, 571–80; II, 362–9). Coleridge concluded: 'I shall only add, that during the plague at Gibraltar [late 1804], Lord Nelson himself acknowledged that he began to see the possession of Malta in a different light' (Rooke, I, 579).

Lyons they are blown to the south end of Sard[ini]a.'[94] By the beginning of 1805 he stopped sending ships to Malta and ordered William Otway, the commissioner there, 'constantly to have stores sent out and the different ships made good at Sea, or at the Anchorages occasionally'. The *Camel* store ship at Malta was to be made 'as a floating storehouse', stationed at Agincourt Sound, with a clerk to account for expended stores, and manned with caulkers and artificers to repair the ships.[95] This was long before the modern idea of the 'fleet train' became standard practice.

Within the first few days of cruising off Toulon, Nelson wrote a persuasive letter to St Vincent demonstrating the impossibility of maintaining the blockade under the existing system. He needed a knowledgeable agent victualler afloat, dedicated to provisioning the fleet as a whole. He also needed a supply of cash: the complicated system of redeeming victualling bills on the London market was useless when it came to paying for supplies in places that were far removed from centres of British influence.[96] The Admiralty made a number of rapid changes, sending out £10,000 in Spanish dollars.[97] By early 1804 Richard Ford, the agent victualler afloat, had been sent to the fleet and the administrative load was taken off the commander-in-chief. Ford performed well and Nelson trusted him.[98] While supplies came from a number of ports, the nearest to the rendezvous was Rosas, north of Barcelona, where supplies, particularly onions and wine, were obtained by Edward Gayner, a Quaker wine merchant from Bristol resident there.[99]

Gayner proved particularly useful when a large naval store ship, the *Hindostan*, an ex-East Indiaman of 1,249 tons, bound from England and packed with naval stores, caught fire and sank on 2 April 1804 off Rosas. Gayner looked after the crew, paid a ransom for them and sent them back to the fleet.[100] This accident caused a break in the continuous flow of naval stores that Nelson needed, although the *Bronte* store ship was already on its way, loaded entirely with sails, cables and cordage.[101] This overall problem of supplying adequate naval stores to the fleet also exercised the Admiralty, for the shortage of hardwood, masts and hemp was now of general strategic concern. In August 1803 Troubridge wrote a troubled letter to Nelson (marked 'Most Secret') about the shortage of hemp and suggesting that Nelson obtain rope made in Malta from Adriatic hemp: 'the Ropemakers of the fleet could help the Maltese.'[102] By November, Nelson, under orders from London, wrote a 'most secret and confidential' letter to Captain Cracraft, commanding the squadron in the Adriatic, to find out what timber and hemp could be obtained from the Adriatic; he also wrote to Ali Pasha at Yanina for help.[103] Spiridion Foresti, the English consul in Corfu, reported to Nelson in January 1804 that supplies of timber were plentiful: 'with respect to woods, Ali Pasha has in his dominions very extensive ones, which produce timber for building ships of the line ... the Arsenal of Toulon was supplied from there in former times with timber ... hemp and flax can be grown.'[104] Canvas for sails and hammocks was obtained from Naples.[105] In spite of Nelson's reservations, Malta proved invaluable for making and supplying both new and twice-laid cables.[106] Eventually supplies came from as far away as the north coast of the Black Sea, where prices were low.[107] In March 1804 a merchant based at Malta, William Eaton, was dispatched to Odessa to obtain corn and naval stores, but he did not enjoy Commissioner Otway's confidence: 'Mr Eaton he will probably not prove the most fit person to have been trusted with a commission of such importance and magnitude.'[108] Nelson agreed: 'As Burke said of a noble Marquis, "a giant in promises, a pigmy in performances".'[109] Nelson sent Lieutenant Henry Frederick Woodman, the agent for transports at Malta, with two transports to accompany Eaton, who managed to contract for hemp and spars, and also buffalo meat, 'very coarse and very lean such as our Jacks are not used to'.[110] Woodman brought back a long and valuable intelligence report on the capacities of the north Black Sea coast, which Nelson sent on to London.[111]

Yet, in spite of the many problems and shortcomings, Nelson was able – with the support of the Admiralty, the Navy Board, the Victualling Board, his captains, his boatswains and carpenters, the consuls and merchants, the store ships and victuallers – to keep his fleet on blockade duty for 75 per cent of his time in the Mediterranean.* Since the British fleet had no margin of superiority over the French in Toulon, Nelson kept his ships together and did not detach them in ones or twos to replenish their water, which remained, as ever, the most pressing supply problem. He took all his ships of the line to provision and water together, leaving only frigates to watch the French.[112] Shortages of provisions did occur; on 1 January 1804, for instance, Nelson had to put the fleet on two thirds allowance of bread. But this did not affect operations.[113]

The arrival of Richard Ford in February 1804 signalled a significant improvement in both supplies from England and fresh provisions locally. In

---

* Of the 538 days between 30 July 1803 and 20 January 1805, when he left to chase the French, the fleet was at the rendezvous off Toulon or engaged in purposeful cruising for 404 days. Only seventy-four days were spent in the three Sardinian anchorages at Agincourt Sound, the Pula Roads or the Gulf of Palmas, while the balance of sixty days was taken up with passages between anchorage and station. Visits to Agincourt Sound lasted on average just seven days each ((UK)NA: PRO, ADM 51/1446; 51/4514; 51/1482; NMM, ADM/L/V/57).

the same month, when transports arrived in Agincourt Sound the *Victory*'s provisions were complete to a five months' establishment.[114] Taken as a whole, the period is one in which Nelson's crews were impressively healthy. Nelson wrote in his diary in October 1804, 'Not a man sick in the fleet'.[115] One sample of the muster books of some of Nelson's ships from this period reveals that no more than 0.5 per cent of the crews were sick at any given time.[116] Some scurvy was prevalent when Nelson arrived in July 1803, and it was dealt with quickly.[117] Nelson had learnt the healing effects of lemon juice from Dr Andrew Baird during his time in the Baltic, although he was unconvinced of its use as a preventative medicine. He wrote to Baird: 'The pernicious use & abuse of Lemon Juice, taken properly the finest anti-scourbatic in the World, but abused the destroyer of the strongest constitution. My use of it is perhaps in direct contradiction to yours.'[118] Lemon juice was sent out from England, but the main source of supply was from Sicily.[119] In this case, Troubridge was correct and large quantities at a good price were secured in Messina from an English merchant named Broadbent by Dr John Snipe, the physician to the fleet.[120]

The blockade continued. Usually the fleet was at the rendezvous, although several forays were made down to Minorca, watching in case the neutral Spanish fleet tried to join the French, and on one occasion they even ventured near the North African coast. Nelson's tactics were to plan raids on the French coast. 'Captain Capel thinks that two corvettes may be taken out of the pond at Marseilles . . . I am willing to give an esprit to the fleet if it is judged practicable.'[121] But in January 1804 the French fleet at Toulon acquired a new commander-in-chief, Admiral Latouche-Tréville, whose careful preparations and energetic leadership at Boulogne had repelled Nelson's attacks. Latouche-Tréville had spent the period of the Peace of Amiens at San Domingo trying to wrest back control of the island after the slave revolt of 1791, and had been taken seriously ill.* He was by now a sick man, but he set about training his fleet systematically. During 1804 the French fleet became a less passive enemy, and their morale and confidence rose.[122]

The entry for 10 April 1804 in the *Victory*'s lieutenant log narrates a typical incident in this game of cat and mouse:

---

* Though seriously ill, Latouche-Tréville left San Domingo for France after the resumption of war, and his passage was authorized by Admiral Duckworth; the two admirals had befriended each other during the peace. On reaching the Strait of Gibraltar, his 'French ship of truce' was intercepted by Captain John Gore (*Medusa*), who gave him provisions and allowed the ship to pass to Toulon (Monarque, 'Latouche-Tréville', 280; NMM, CRK/6/28, 9 Oct. 1803, Gore to Nelson).

Amazon took possession of a Fr. Brig between Cape Sepet and Porquerelles, observed the batteries at Sepet firing at the *Amazon* & that 3 frigates came out of Toulon & stood for the *Amazon* and her prize. *Donegal*'s & *Active*'s signal to close *Amazon*. Observed 4 more of the enemy's ships coming out of Toulon round Sepet, the Prize standing off the land for the Squadron. At 6.30 the enemy ships turned for Toulon. *Superb* closed the *Donegal, Active* & *Amazon*.[123]

'If they go on playing out and in we shall one day get at them,' Nelson wrote to Frere.[124] His thoughts in his private journal on 4 June were much more cautious: 'it was and is my determination to fight the 8 Sail of the Line if they will come from under their batteries but it would be highly improper to fight where [even] if the Courage of the men is ever so conspicuously displayed, all the Enemy's ships can return into their secure harbour.'[125]

A similar provocative tactic four days after he wrote those words did not work so well. This time Nelson approached Toulon with five ships of the line (from his full force of eight) and four frigates, and saw two French frigates anchored in a bay on the north coast of the island of Porquerolles, a dozen miles to the east of Toulon. He detached two frigates and the *Excellent* around the eastern side of the island, while the *Victory* and the other three ships of the line sailed to the west of the island to cut off the escape of the two French frigates. Latouche-Tréville, who had trained and enthused his crews, saw the situation from a high point on Cap Cépet and eight ships of the line put out to sea very quickly, immediately threatening Nelson's four ships and isolating the others. Nelson signalled the *Excellent* and the two frigates, telling them to leave off the chase, and turned his four ships south. Latouche-Tréville's report to Bonaparte ended: 'the English admiral soon renounced his project, called back his ship of the line and two frigates and ran away. I pursued him until night; he ran towards the south-west.'[126]

The report was published in the French newspapers. Nelson was incensed at the way his honour was impugned, but admitted in a letter to the Admiralty that if the French ships had turned towards the land they would also have had the shore batteries to come to their aid, had there been an action.[127] He decided on a sensible retreat, since his force was weak compared to that of the French: had they followed him south, as night fell, he would have led them to the rest of his ships of the line. His anger at Latouche-Tréville's insult continued until the latter died on 18 August 1804. Did the news of his death reach Nelson on 6 September? If so, it caused a show of force. The *Victory*'s log entry for the day reads: 'At 9.45

wore and stood in for Toulon under all sail with the Starboard Division, except the *Spencer*.'[128] What is more certain is that Latouche-Tréville's death caused the morale of the French Mediterranean fleet to sink. The next French commander-in-chief was Pierre Villeneuve. Nelson remarked sharply to a young frigate captain who had been present at the Battle of the Nile: 'It is our old friend Villeneuve that Commands at Toulon, we know he can run away.'[129]

Such incidents were likely to recur given Nelson's seemingly contradictory style of distant blockade, which depended upon provocation as well as giving the French room to tempt them to sea and away from their shore batteries. But this style was criticized by those who believed in close blockade. One of his captains, John Whitby, complained to his mentor Admiral Cornwallis, who was well known for keeping the blockade of Brest as tight as possible:

I write this in Confidence to you, for I would not absolutely dare to give my opinion of the Mediterranean Blockade to any other Person – for doubtless my Ld. Nelson is actuated by a thorough zeal to do right, for he is indeed a great and glorious Officer . . . First he does not cruise upon his Rendezvous; second, I have consequently repeatedly known him from a Week to three Weeks and even a Month unfound by Ships sent to reconnoitre . . . thirdly, he is occasionally obliged to take the whole squadron in to water, a great distance from Toulon; fourthly, since I came away the French Squadron got out in his Absence, and cruised off Toulon several Days.

Whitby went on to criticize John Gore – unfairly, since the circumstances were quite different – in command at Gibraltar: 'so inattentive in my opinion to his Situation at Gibraltar, which I consider the Piquet Guard of you and my Ld. Nelson'.[130] It was the continuation of an argument at least fifty years old, stemming from Hawke's close blockade of Brest in the Seven Years War; Howe was for the more distant system, looking after the wear and tear on his ships. No right or wrong answer existed, as Howe, at the very end of his life, admitted when he wrote to Admiral Sir Roger Curtis: 'Anchorage is inseparable from the best system of Blockades. Tho', when I consider the risks from damage to Hulls, Masts & Yards, by always keeping the sea for the same purpose, I still think (with the spectator to Sir Roger de Coverly) that "much may be said on both sides".'[131]

Nelson, however, nursed his ships and crews through the 'exceedingly bad' weather of the winter months of 1803 and 1804, keeping at sea for most of that time.[132] He noted on 6 February: 'came on one of the heaviest snow storms I have seen which continued without interference all night.'[133]

His carpenters used their ingenuity. Nelson wrote to Nepean: 'The *Kent* is very bad, *Renown* we have just coil'd her with three inch rope. She will soon be ruined. *Superb* we have with large Iron bolts & frappings keep [i.e. kept] her scraf [scarph] of the Stem in its place.'[134] That winter the *Kent* had thirty-two additional bolts put into her hull, most of which were broken by April 1804.[135] When they were off Toulon, the wind came from the direction of the land, and there was rarely a lee shore to endanger his ships, which in high winds sailed very 'free' and frequently with little or no sail. Nelson reported to Commissioner Otway in April 1804: 'we have got well over a very blowing winter and with much less loss of sails and spars than could have been expected, but everybody here is attentive to the weather and furl their sails in due time.'[136] In the worst blows he would go west to shelter near Cape San Sebastián by Barcelona; his distant style of blockading allowed him to leave his station without the enemy knowing where he was. He was able to write to the first lord early in 1805: 'Those Gentlemen [the French] are not used to a Gulph of Lyons gale, which we have buffeted for 21 months and not carried away a spar.'[137] Nelson's ability to read the weather impressed one of his young frigate captains, William Parker: 'Lord Nelson watched the barometer incessantly, and made entries almost hourly in his journal with his own hand.'[138] Nelson had learnt much since the winter of 1794/5 in the *Agamemnon*. In the light of the condition of the hulls and rigging of his ships ten years later, the sea keeping of his ships was impressive.

Periods were also spent at anchor in high wind. From Agincourt Sound on the last day of 1803 he wrote to General Villettes at Malta: 'We have been twice unmoor'd but the western Gales have sett so strong that we cannot move.'[139] The next day he wrote to Bickerton: 'It blows a little hurricane, indeed I think us in high luck to be in such a fine harbour.'[140] As ever, he sought the company of his subordinates when he could.*[141] 'I am always at all times, days & hours glad to see you,' he wrote to Bickerton. To Captain Frank Sotheron when at Agincourt Sound in May, he said,

I would not have you out of any mark of attention take the trouble of rowing round in a boat, but if you and Captain White are inclined for a walk I shall be always very glad to see you, when you are completed in wood & water (but we shall give

---

* The informality of Nelson's dinner table was matched by the excellence of his wines, for he took care to obtain the best: 'they must be very choice wines', he instructed Edward Gayner; and he also secured Hungarian wines, including Tokay, from the English consul in Trieste (BL, Add. MSS 34955, 23 Jan. 1804, to Gayner; 34953, 20 Oct. 1803, to James Anderson, consul in Trieste).

you some coals) and got as many Bullocks as you can carry to sea, you will leave your present anchorage and passing through Agincourt Sound & proceed to anchor in the other large bay to which anchorage as we finish we shall all proceed.[142]

'All the captains and officers of the squadron are delighted with his Lordship,' William Parker wrote home in December 1803, 'and I think I have a good prospect of being very happy under his command.'[143] When George Campbell's nephew arrived in the fleet, Nelson brought together other midshipmen to meet him: 'Captain Conn's son, not 3 feet high, Mrs Lutwidge's élève young Dalton, who is a very fine lad, Sir John Sinclair, Lord William Gordon's nephew and Mr Bulkeley . . . all the Grandees dined with Campbell and I had a midshipman's party.'[144] While this was a privileged group of young men, handpicked from over thirty midshipmen and 'First Class Boys' aboard the *Victory* at this time, Nelson's ability to listen, as well as his accessibility and kindness, makes it easy to understand the loyalty that he engendered.[145] It was the most important facet of his talent as a leader of men.

In London new eyes were looking at the state of the navy. In January 1804 Evan Nepean became disillusioned with his old master St Vincent and resigned on the grounds of ill-health after nine years as secretary to the Board of Admiralty. In May, Addington's government fell, and St Vincent, Troubridge and Markham left the Admiralty. The general relief was palpable. Captain Thomas Bowen wrote to Nelson: 'never was people so Cordially disliked by all kinds of people, their names are execrated by all parties.'[146] Pitt was prime minister again and Henry Dundas, now made Lord Melville, the new first lord of the Admiralty. He complained: 'There is not a day passes on which I do not receive twenty letters, claiming favour from me, because the writers have been ill used by Lord St Vincent.'[147] The mood was bitter among the outgoing administration. Troubridge wrote to Nelson: 'Gross falsehoods which the Faction sent abroad to injure us, but we have now thrown down the Gauntlet, attacking them for their libels . . . respecting that part of a vicious pamphlet which says a Commission was signed to supersede you. I have call[e]d on Lord Melville & through him on Mr Pitt to state if they have any accusation against us the answer is no, that they wish to conciliate but they are not to be trusted, particularly while Nepean has a seat on the board.'[148]

Melville moved fast to repair the damage done by the previous administration. He put in hand the strengthening of old ships with riders ('doubling and cross bracing'), which the previous board had resisted. Troubridge had written to Nelson in May 1803: 'I have long reprobated Riders. Every

Taylor in the Country knows they destroy a ship.'[149] The future Admiralty secretary, John Barrow, thought that reversing this policy was critical to bolstering the numbers of the fleet, which led ultimately to the success of Trafalgar.[150] By July, Melville had analysed the requirements for continuous blockade in a memorandum. 'Wear and Tear ... is a drain on us, but it adds to the skills and alertness of our Seamen'; but, he concluded, 'there must be such a Number of Ships as to admit of the blockading ships being regularly in rotation ... and should not exceed three months ... Improvement and Increase of our Naval Strength [is] more essentially necessary than at the present moment.' And France, according to the latest eyewitness reports, was 'omitting no means of adding to its Naval Strength'.[151] In September, Melville sent Nelson a copy of a secret cabinet paper on his redistribution of ships. 'When I wrote to you last I was not quite aware that so many of your Ships were in so frail a condition,' he told Nelson and sent him the *Tigre* and the *Conqueror*, both 74s. Melville also gently rapped Nelson's knuckles, for Nelson's complaints about his ships had come through Hugh Elliot to the secretary of state. Nelson should in future write to the first lord.[152]

Throughout the second half of 1803 and for all of 1804 Nelson could obtain no coherent picture of what Napoleon was proposing to do with his growing French fleet; nor could he discern Spanish intentions. 'I am so much in the dark respecting the destination of the Toulon fleet', he wrote to Alexander Ball, 'that I must keep my eye on all quarters and all the frigates and vessels are watching them. I have not or ever had a single vessels cruiz[in]g for prizes nor have I a wish but to fulfill the wishes of my Country & friends.'[153] He did his best to collect intelligence; little came from London, and it was slow when it did, usually through Barcelona, to which Nelson sent a frigate 'almost every week' to collect letters, information and newspapers.[154] James Duff in Cadiz was useful as an informant, but the best placed to send information, and the nearest to Toulon, was the Quaker merchant in Rosas, Edward Gayner, whom Nelson asked to procure information. Gayner had contacts in Toulon and, judging by one surviving letter, became experienced in assessing the intelligence that he gathered.[155] Alexander Scott was often ashore in Sardinia to gain information of French activity in Corsica, and Nelson also sent him ashore in Barcelona and Naples, where, according to Nelson in a letter to Hugh Elliot, Scott was 'very anxious to pay his respects in the hotbed of diplomacy'.[156] But, as he commented to Hookham Frere in Madrid in September 1804, 'The only information useful to me would be (when given) a copy of the French Admiral's sailing orders: that would be worth thousands.'[157]

Alexander Scott gives a picture of how intelligence was assessed. 'Day after day might be seen the admiral in his cabin, closely employed with his secretary over their interminable papers. They occupied two black leathern armchairs, into the roomy pockets of which, Scott, weary of translating, would occasionally stuff away a score or two of unopened private letters, found in prize ships, although the untiring activity of Nelson grudged leaving one such document unexamined.'[158]

Nelson's health began to suffer. To Emma he wrote a calm letter in December 1803: 'the constant anxiety I have experienced have shook my weak frame and my rings will hardly keep on my fingers, and what grieves me more than all is that I can perceive a visible (if I may be allowed the expression) loss of sight, a few years must as I have always predicted render me blind.'[159] Ball wrote at that time sympathizing with Nelson's indifferent health, 'no doubt occasioned by your indefatigable and anxious mind'.[160] Nelson freely discussed his intention to go home over the winter with his captains.[161] On 1 July 1804 he first mentioned it lightly to Melville: 'I much fear before the Winter that I shall be obliged to write to the board for some months rest, a half man as I am, cannot expect to be a Hercules.'[162] Nelson speculated with Ball as to who would succeed him, thinking it might be Roger Curtis, or William Young, or Richard Bickerton.[163] 'With my losses and infirmities good health cannot be expected,' he wrote to Melville in November.[164] In two letters to Emma, written on 31 October 1804 and on 14 January 1805, Nelson said that he expected to be home before she received each letter.[165]

By the end of the year he was still hoping for leave, but his second, George Campbell, fell ill and formally requested leave on 3 December 1804.[166] Campbell's departure for England delayed Nelson's return, but, as he informed Melville on 29 December, he still anticipated being relieved, and the rumours that he was coming back to England abounded.[167] Melville was extremely keen to keep Nelson in the Mediterranean, and he invited Alexander Davison to breakfast at his house in Wimbledon to discuss the problem. Davison reported back to Nelson: 'Nothing would give him more real concern than that anything should occur to attend your uneasiness . . . how much he had at Heart a desperation to make your Command the most Respectable.'[168] The first lord eventually sent out Thomas Louis in January 1805 as the replacement for Campbell, but he did not arrive in the Gulf of Palmas until 27 March, by which time much had changed.[169]

In spite of poor health, and the trials of the blockade, Nelson's mind was at rest, in contrast to the anguish in his letters to Emma when he was in the Baltic in 1801. She was, of course, often in his thoughts. When the signal was made that the French squadron were coming out of Toulon in June 1804, his captains were with him; they soon left for their respective ships. William Parker, the most junior of them, 'had to wait till the seniors had left. When he was quite alone with Lord Nelson, who was eager for the battle which he considered to be imminent, the latter returned to the dinner table, filled a bumper of claret and lifting it over his head, and exclaiming, "Here is to Lady Hamilton! She is my Guardian angel!" and drank it off.'[170] His letters to her at Merton were easy and practical. Visitors to Merton wrote to him of her health and well being.[171] One informed him: 'Merton is astonishingly improved . . . even Capability Brown himself could not have laid it out with more taste than her Ladyship.'[172] Samuel Sutton reported back: 'the alterations and improvements are far beyond anything I could have supposed. When finished it will be a delightful spot.'[173] Nelson commissioned the buying of an endless stream of presents for Emma. He wrote fondly to her of Horatia: 'She must be grown very much. How I long to hear her prattle. Heaven keep her. I'm sure she will be mistress.'[174] In January 1804 he sent his daughter a watch, 'which I give you permission to wear on Sundays, and on very particular days when you are dressed and have behaved exceedingly well. I have kissed it and send it with the Affectionate <u>Blessing</u> of <u>Your</u> Nelson and Bronte'. He underlined the words 'Blessing' and 'Your' four times, the nearest he could get to the role of acknowledged parent.[175]

The condition of his estate at Bronte contributed to his anxiety. When Abraham Gibbs visited, 'it was in a sad plight', although Nelson was still optimistic, at least to Emma, that he would soon receive a steady income from it.[176] One exception to the composure of his letters at this time survives, when he wrote in a lonely and reflective mood in May 1804 to the Reverend Dean Allott, the brother of a childhood friend, which cast his mind back to life at Burnham Thorpe thirty-five years earlier: 'my bones will probably be laid with my Father's in the Village that gave me birth . . . the thoughts of former days bring all my Mother into my heart which shews itself in my eyes.'[177]

Still the French did not move. Nelson may have been frustrated, but every day the fleet stayed in port represented a success in Britain's defensive strategy, with Sicily, Malta and, most dear to his heart, Sardinia, protected. This state of affairs underlined British naval ascendancy over the French in the Mediterranean.[178] The frigates and smaller ships were constantly on the move convoying trade and chasing strange sails, but for the ships of the line the blockade continued for weary months through 1804, marked by weeks off Toulon and routine rendezvous with transports. The notebook of the gunner of the *Victory* even records a mathematical problem set him by Nelson: 'A ball 22 inches circumference, what is its weight?'[179] Small excitements were few. In May, in light and variable winds, the *Excellent* struck the Monaci shoal to the north of the eastern entrance to Agincourt Sound, but she was towed off by boats from the rest of the squadron.[180] This was one of few accidents, a reflection of the pilotage and seamanship skills of the officers and men. In August two 68-pound carronades were transferred to the *Victory* from the *Kent*; not for the first time Nelson ensured that he had these powerful weapons aboard his ship.[181] Excitement arose aboard the *Victory* when a midshipman saw his servant fall overboard and jumped in to save him. 'At 955 Jas Archibald fell overboard but was saved by Mr Flinn, Master's Mate, who jumped after him,' ran the log. Nelson witnessed the rescue and made Flinn a lieutenant on the spot, to the cheers of the rest of the midshipmen. Then, according to the Reverend Alexander Scott, 'There was something significant in the tone of their cheer which he immediately recognised, and putting up his hand for silence, and leaning over to the crowd of middies, he said, with a good-natured smile on his face, "Stop, young gentlemen! Mr Flinn has done a gallant thing today – and has done many gallant things before – for which he has got his reward, but mind! I'll have no more making lieutenants for servants falling overboard."'[182]

In spite of Nelson's genial regime for the officers, the monotony of blockade, month after month, much of the time out of sight of land, began to cause discipline problems. In one instance Nelson had to upbraid a lieutenant commanding a brig whose crew had thrown a shot at him. To find the miscreant, he 'had inflicted upon each of your company, by calling them over by watch-bill, and giving them a dozen each . . . I cannot approve of a measure so foreign to the rules of good discipline and the accustomed practice of His Majesty's Navy.'[183] But on board the *Victory* those rules had exceeded regulation and custom. In the first months of the commission, under the captaincy of Samuel Sutton, and in Nelson's time in the *Amphion*, punishments had been relatively few and light, with twelve lashes (the regulation amount) as the norm, and twenty-four for more serious offences. The first 36-lash punishment, for disobedience, was given to two seamen two days before Hardy superseded Sutton at the beginning of August 1803, but from thereon punishments, particularly for drunkenness, increased sharply. By October thirty-six lashes became the standard punishment for this offence, while at the end of the month Peter Blumberry, a Swedish able seaman, was the first to receive forty-eight lashes. On 7 December Charles Donelly, an able seaman from Liverpool, unusually old at forty-eight, received the same; before the month was out he was again given forty-eight lashes. By this time sixty lashes were sporadically ordered for repeated drunkenness.*

Drunkenness, quarrelling and insolence were the main reasons for punishment. A number of petty officers, upon whom day-to-day discipline depended, were themselves punished. A boatswain's mate, William Inwood, from New York, was given forty-eight lashes in December 1803 for insolence; the following May he received twelve for disobedience; and two months later forty-eight for theft. Then he was disrated to able seaman. On 14 August 1804, in the summer heat, nineteen men were given 564 lashes, an average of just under thirty lashes each, the total pushed up by four marines receiving forty-eight lashes for drunkenness. This extraordinarily high level of punishment was by no means exceptional.† Even allowing for the fact that over 800 men were aboard the *Victory*, Thomas Masterman Hardy had raised the severity of punishments to a very high level, well beyond that of any ship in which Nelson had previously served. Nor can Nelson escape responsibility for this regime, for the admiral always set the tone in any flagship; nearly twenty years before, Nelson had written that a flag captain 'is never his own master'.[184] He judged that ruthlessness with his crew was as necessary as ruthlessness in pursuit of the enemy. The contrast between the lot of the officers on the quarterdeck and the men forward was marked. The *Victory* was unquestionably a flogging ship.

Throughout Nelson's time in the Mediterranean confidence in him and his fleet remained high. Troubridge wrote from London at the end of December 1803: 'The account you give of the heartiness of the Fleet and general good order, except Masts and Bottoms, gives us all great pleasure . . . that rage for coming home is worn off . . . I always observe those restless Gents are the first to wish to go out again & is the occasion of many of the meetings when the Captain & officers Growl. Johnny thinks it is right he should do the same.'[185] Ball wrote encouragingly from Malta: 'you have

---

* On 10 December 1803 Nelson remitted the rest of the punishment of 500 lashes for a marine for disobedience and insolence, but warned that punishments for serious offences in future, would 'most certainly be inflicted without Mitigation' ((UK)NA: PRO, ADM 80/141). The warning by Wareham (219–27) on the potential inaccuracy of logs has been heeded by comparing those of the captain, lieutenant and master ((UK)NA: PRO, ADM 51/4514, 51/4515, 51/1482; 52/3711; NMM, ADM/L/V/57). The punishment lists in Goodwin, 250–62, though incomplete, were useful in this analysis.

† Two repeated transgressors were William Petty and James Norgrove, both marines; on 31 October 1804 Norgrove received sixty for drunkenness; the following April, Petty received the same. By late 1804 five to ten men were being flogged each week, averaging between thirty-five and forty lashes each; floggings of twelve and twenty-four lashes had become rare.

had a long and persevering cruise. But I believe the Captains have not felt it, your Lordship's attention to them has made them forget the time – the French will brighten the prospect and change the scene for them soon.'[186] One officer put it well when he wrote to Nelson: 'all England know it is not a Hotham Commands in the Mediterranean, nor is it so long since your Lordship taught the enemy that difficulties only make you more energetic.'[187]

By the summer of 1804 Nelson was still confident, writing to Roger Curtis, 'I command here in every respect, except the hulls of the ships, the very finest fleet I have ever seen.'[188] In October he wrote to Melville, pushing the promotion prospects of his promising young officers: 'I could take two french fleets ... and my followers go but little way towards promoting them all which I ardently wish to do for 60 or 70 finer young Men I never saw than are in the fleet and who have served their time ... No Captain will die or go home (if they can help it): that they assure me, and they are all too valuable for me to wish to part with them.'[189] This no doubt pleased Melville, who had to keep the bulk of the fleet, at one time forty-four ships of the line, with Cornwallis in the Channel to contain the fleet at Brest and guard against invasion.[190] This degree of loyalty was achieved in spite of the Admiralty's centralization of promotion decisions. 'The patronage of Commanders-in-Chief is I fear gone but times may change,' Nelson wrote to a former commander-in-chief who had written to him recommending one of the officers.[191] He wrote regretfully to Captain John Gore: 'how different from the treatment shown Lords Hood, Hotham and St Vincent who made Captains by the dozen.'[192]

Only one matter caused Nelson a sense of prolonged indignation – although it was as nothing compared to his reaction to previous slights. On 2 December 1804 he wrote in his private journal: 'Received an account of Sir John Orde's arrival off Cadiz the 17th Novr with six sail of the Line. It is very extraordinary that no dispatches should be sent me.'[193] Unknown to Nelson, the Pitt government had ordered a pre-emptive strike against four Spanish treasure ships, which had been seized off Ferrol on 5 October. As a result Spain declared war on 12 December. Lord Melville had sent an independent squadron under Orde to guard Cadiz, as ever the most lucrative point for prizes. This position was within Nelson's command, and it had now been effectively cut away from him. Davison, who saw huge amounts of prize money slipping out of his grasp, lamented to Nelson: 'that Man so unaccountably sent off Cadiz to cruise at the very moment when my Dear Lord Nelson ought as his Birth Right to have enjoyed all the Fruits ... Had our Friend Nepean been in England no such appointment would have been made, and He feels most sensibly for you.' Nelson wrote to Emma that Orde 'will get all the money and your Poor Nelson all the hard blows. Am I to take this act as a proof of Lord Melville's regard for me, but I submit patiently, but I feel. I have not had a scrap of a Pen from England 90 days this day. It is rather long in these critical times.' But he ended philosophically to her: 'I send this through Mr F[alconet] at Naples and as it will be read by the French and many others I do not chuse to say anything more than I care for all the World knowing that I <u>love you</u> more than anything in this World, and next my dr H[orati]a.'[194]

On 19 January 1805 everything changed. The *Victory* was anchored in Agincourt Sound, taking bullocks and provisions on board. The weather was miserable, the wind in the north-west; 'Fresh gales and squally with Hail & Rain,' ran the log. Nelson did not miss the opportunity to order the fleet to salute the king's birthday with twenty-one guns.[195] Then through the Bonifacio Strait, before the gale, came two frigates, the *Active* and the *Seahorse*, which had been watching Toulon. Nelson immediately gave the order for the fleet to unmoor. At 4.28, as he records in his journal, he signalled that each ship should carry a light on her stern. In the gloom of a late winter afternoon, the fleet of eleven ships of the line sailed, led by the *Active*, a light shining from each one.* The *Active* was commanded by the Honourable Courteney Boyle, once a midshipman in the *Boreas*.[196] They steered south-east through the Biscie Channel, narrow but free of reefs, a course that all knew since Nelson had already taken the fleet through it in May.[197]

Only at seven o'clock, when all the ships were in the open sea, did the flagship heave to in order to hear the story in detail from the frigate captains. The French had left Toulon in strength on 17 January, and the two frigates, at one point within pistol shot of a superior force of French frigates, had been lucky to escape.[198] Despite the prolonged effort of over a year and a half, and the successful defensive strategy he had pursued, Nelson had failed in his principal aim: to prevent the escape of the French. Nor did he know where they had gone.

---

* They were *Victory* (100), *Royal Sovereign* (100), *Donegal* (74), *Superb* (74), *Canopus* (74), *Spencer* (74), *Tigre* (74), *Leviathan* (74), *Belleisle* (74), *Conqueror* (74) and *Swiftsure* (74).

28

The Long Chase
January–September 1805

Ah, My Emma, June 6th would have been a great day to me had I not been led astray by false information. I cannot help myself, what a loss: what a relief it would have been for the last two years of cares and troubles. Wherever I do get information it is not worth sixpence and I have ever found if I was left and acted as my poor noddle told me was right I should seldom err. My Genius carried me direct to the spot and all would have been as well as heart could wish when comes across me Gen[era]l Brereton's information . . . Nelson to Emma, 16 June 1805[1]

Nelson was convinced that the destination of the French fleet was Egypt. He headed south, pausing at Cagliari to shelter from a fierce north-westerly storm, then steered through the Strait of Messina, setting an easterly course towards Alexandria. As he went, he issued complex orders to his frigate captains, giving them several likely rendezvous: 'But it is recommended for Captains to use their discretion . . . I shall delay nowhere.'[2] At least he did not have to worry about the Adriatic, for the small Russian squadron of three ships of the line and three frigates was now stationed off the Ionian Islands. Commodore Greig, the squadron's commander, assured Nelson that he would inform him if the French were to arrive there.[3]

Nelson's conviction was fuelled by widespread, continuing speculation that domination of Egypt and the North African coast was a long-term French aim. But a more immediate factor was the wind, which had been favourable for a course to the west for two weeks before the French had sailed from Toulon. Those who misinterpret intelligence can be made to look foolish by history, and commentators have criticized Nelson's decision to go east, one suggesting that Nelson had 'an obsessive fear for the eastern Mediterranean' because of the events of 1798.[4] But he was, after all, commander-in-chief of the Mediterranean. If Sicily and Sardinia were lost, a British presence in the Mediterranean would be untenable. Nelson was thus ensuring that his station was clear of a hostile fleet, acting logically within the terms of his orders and in line with defensive British strategy. He had heard nothing from London to act to the contrary. He was not to know that the French had not left Toulon earlier in January because their ships were not ready. When Villeneuve did sail, he attempted to go westwards towards the strait, although his fleet, manned by inexperienced crews and laden with troops, was battered by one of the north-westerly gales that the British had ridden out successfully for nearly two years, and had to return almost immediately to Toulon for repairs.

Napoleon's naval objectives were as much a mystery to the Board of Admiralty as they were to Nelson. The emperor (as he now was) had a number of extravagant schemes in mind, including an expedition to India.* In the twelve months from September 1804, his erratic and imaginative mind conceived as many as eight plans. His decision-making was untram-melled by advisers with maritime knowledge, and he used his minister of marine, Rear-Admiral Denis Decrès, as little more than a secretary. Most orders were issued in sealed envelopes to be opened only when at sea. Napoleon alone could see the whole picture and the ultimate purpose of his plans. He was now swinging towards the invasion of the south coast of England as his principal aim.[5] With the entry of Spain into the war, he controlled a more numerous fleet than Britain, but his ships were dispersed around the coasts of Europe in Toulon, Cartagena, Cadiz, Rochefort, Brest and the Texel. He needed to concentrate them in the Channel in order to create the margin of superiority required to protect an invading force. Napoleon was still undecided about how he was to achieve this, but the concept of the Toulon fleet sailing to the West Indies, thus drawing away British ships from the Western Approaches and the Channel, had become firm. The plan began to unroll in January 1805, when Rear-Admiral Édouard Thomas Burgues, le comte de Missiessy, escaped from Ferrol with a small squadron, steering to the West Indies, pursued by Alexander Cochrane, who had been blockading the port with a small squadron. Still the British government was nonplussed.

Nelson's fleet reached Alexandria on 7 February in the very fast time of seven days, creditable in view of the poor condition of his ships. Only the

---

* In early 1804 the French uncovered a complex émigré network of conspiracy, financed by Britain, to overthrow Bonaparte. The principal conspirator (although probably innocent), the duc d'Enghien, was captured in Germany and brought back to Paris, where he was executed. Thinking to safeguard his regime by making himself an hereditary ruler, the first consul had himself made emperor and proclaimed 'Napoleon I' by the Senate on 18 May 1804 (Sparrow, 291–5; Schroeder, 248–9).

Victory, the *Northumberland*, the *Leviathan* and the *Swiftsure* had been docked and had their copper sheathing renewed within the previous three years, the absolute limit of time for efficiency, sailing performance and, in some cases, safety. The *Belleisle* and the *Donegal* had been sheathed in 1800 and the *Spencer* in 1801. Nelson requested that the 30-year-old *Royal Sovereign* be sent home; her copper had not been renewed since 1799, and she had last been in dockyard hands in January 1801.[6] The *Superb* was in a similar condition, her captain, Richard Goodwin Keats, keeping her going in spite of her wretched condition; she had had trouble from corroded bolts in her hull since late 1803.[7] William Parker of the frigate *Amazon* (38), itself in no great shape, remembered that Keats, 'obtained leave to carry his sail while the other ships communicated, and lashing his studding sail booms to the yard, was always under full sail'.[8] St Vincent's ill-judged and savage attempts at reform caused confusion and loss of morale in the Navy Board and dockyards during the Peace of Amiens, just when these ships should have been properly docked. Ironically, at the very time when Nelson and his officers and crews struggled with their leaky ships, in Parliament St Vincent and his party were attacking the first lord of the Admiralty, Lord Melville, for corruption and inefficiency.

The quality and fitness of the officers and crews went a long way to compensate for this weakness.* By now Nelson knew the captains well, having served with Hardy, William Hargood, Benjamin Hallowell and John Conn before the beginning of the Mediterranean campaign in 1803. Of the newcomers, Mark Robinson in the *Swiftsure* was the son of his old captain in the *Worcester* when Nelson was acting lieutenant nearly thirty years earlier. Richard Goodwin Keats (his star already high in the firmament after his brilliant part in the action off Algeciras), Henry Baytun, Pulteney Malcolm and Robert Stopford were to have long and glittering careers. Malcolm reckoned that William Parker was 'the best frigate captain in the Service'.[9] Nelson rated his officers in the Mediterranean higher than those of the Nile fleet of 1798.[10] Alexander Ball, observing progress from his position as governor of Malta, had similar confidence, reporting to the secretary of state's office in London in late 1804: 'if he should fall in with the French there cannot be a doubt of the event, as most of his captains seem to have been selected for their superior abilities and tried courage.'[11]

The passage back from Egypt took three weeks. On 16 February, Nelson

---

* Of the eleven captains of the ships of the line who steered through the narrow passage on 19 January 1805, eight were to be admirals by the end of the war in 1815. Two would die on active service. Only Thomas Masterman Hardy had to wait until 1825 before reaching flag rank.

was off Malta. Alexander Ball informed Nelson that he could see the fleet at a great distance, 'with a fair wind. I knew your Lordship would not wait a moment after the signal was made of no Intelligence. I attempted to reach the *Superb* but Keats would not wait for me.' Ball and Nelson exchanged letters.[12] Nelson wrote: 'Although I have not yet heard of the French Fleet, and remain in total ignorance of where they are got to, yet to this moment I am more confirmed in my opinion, from communicating with Alexandria, that Egypt was the destination of the French Armament from Toulon.'[13] Ball agreed: 'There can be only one solid approbation respecting the route which your Lordship has pursued. If the French fleet have gone to the Westward of Gibraltar, Sir John Orde and Adm[ira]l Cochrane will have timely notice of their approach from one of your Lordship's ships . . . we must be patient.'[14] The Board of Admiralty also agreed. William Marsden wrote on 17 April that 'the interval was a period of much anxiety, as it is doubtful whether the Enemy's object was to proceed east or west. Their not having gone to the Westward when they might have done so (if their damages were repaired) affords a presumption that your inference was just.' Marsden added that the Egyptian route had been kept a secret: 'even to Lady H's repeated enquiries I thought myself obliged to give obscure answers . . . & I have unfortunately incurred her Ladyship's displeasure as she will probably have told you.'[15] Marsden's cautious assessment of Emma as a security risk was probably sound.

No one in London knew exactly where Nelson was.[16] In any case, few of those in Parliament and Whitehall were concentrating on the progress of the war, for the parties were gripped with political infighting, and the atmosphere was awash with emotion and vitriol. Within a year of the resignation of St Vincent, it was the turn of Lord Melville to be attacked for corruption and he was to resign his office on 2 May 1805. Old Admiral Sir Charles Middleton, now ennobled as Lord Barham, took up the reins as first lord on the same day. There were general misgivings, as Middleton was a relative of Melville. Sir Andrew Snape Hamond, still holding on as comptroller of the Navy Board, felt that 'the cry will be that Lord Melville is still First L[or]d of the Adm[iralty] and Sir Cha[rle]s is a Faggot [slang for a man hired to appear at a muster].'[17] The bitter feelings of this time can be gauged by a letter that Nelson received from Thomas Troubridge, written on 12 February, accusing Pitt's government of dirty tricks: 'Lying & Thieving is the order of the day, & supported openly in the House by Ministers, the Pamphlets which no doubt has reached you were written by the present Minister's instruction & they are now beshitting themselves lest the Printers should Peach . . . the Publick Abuses that are now going on,

I think will soon do the Country up. Whether they will Employ me or not I cannot tell, I never go near the Adm[iralty].'[18]

By the time Nelson had returned to Sardinia from Egypt at the end of February, he knew the French fleet was back in Toulon. From his frigates he received the information that they were nearly ready to depart for a second time. He took the fleet back to the rendezvous off Toulon and attempted to set a trap for the French by sailing to a position off Barcelona, where he made sure he was seen, then quickly withdrew back to the Gulf of Palmas in Sardinia, still guarding the way to the east.[19] He had also placed a frigate between Sardinia and the Barbary coast to ensure that Villeneuve would not slip past him to the south, heading for the east. He hoped that intelligence would reach Villeneuve that he was off Barcelona, thus causing the Frenchman to sail south of Majorca to avoid him. Unfortunately for Nelson's hopes, when Villeneuve left port on 30 March, he met a Ragusan ship, whose master informed him he had seen the British fleet at Palmas. Villeneuve therefore steered north of Majorca and avoided detection, missed by shadowing British frigates. Nelson had lost another game of cat and mouse; it was hardly surprising that he once again complained of a lack of frigates.[20]

During this feint towards the Spanish coast, William Chevallier, Nelson's steward, reported a dramatic incident to Alexander Davison, in which, in spite of his preoccupation with high strategy, Nelson demonstrated that he had lost none of his coolness when danger threatened on board:

Once the *Victory* took fire near the Powder Magazine. The whole of the terrified Crew run[ne]d up the riggin[g] and at that dreadfull moment, when every Man thought it his last hour, Lord Nelson was then as cool and composed as ever I saw him before. He orders every man below to put out the fire, and such is the confidence and respect that the sailors have for him that everyone obied and in twenty Minutes the fire was got under. Thus from the Admiral's fortitude and the readiness his Orders were Obeid, was the *Victory* saved and All Souls on board.[21]

No evidence of this brief incident exists in the logs. It affords a glimpse of the hold that Nelson had over his officers and crew.

The squadron waited in vain from 27 to 30 March in the Gulf of Palmas for a frigate to appear with the news that the French fleet was at sea between Majorca and Sardinia. Nelson then moved for two days to the Pula Roads to water, thence to Palermo, then off Maritimo, sticking cautiously to his defensive plan to protect Sicily but with an increasing sense of foreboding. A short note on 6 April to Davison ended: 'I can neither eat, drink or sleep.'[22]

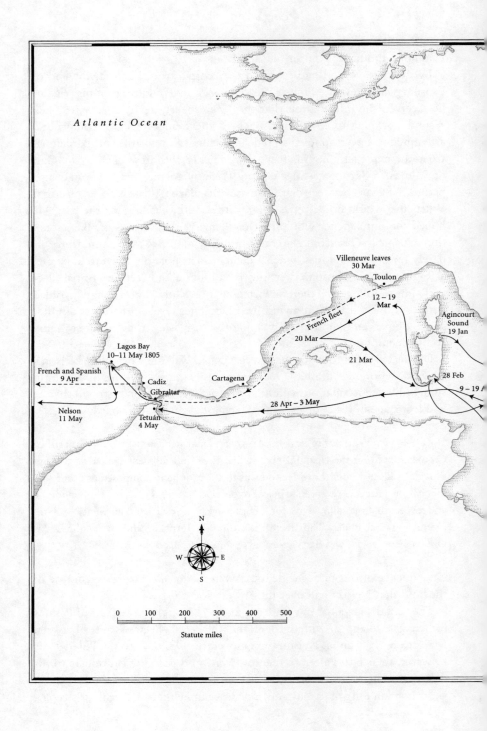

Atlantic Ocean

Villeneuve leaves
30 Mar
Toulon
12 – 19
Mar
Agincourt
Sound
19 Jan
Lagos Bay
10–11 May 1805
French fleet
20 Mar
21 Mar
28 Feb
French and Spanish
9 Apr
Cadiz
Cartagena
9 – 19
Gibraltar
28 Apr – 3 May
Nelson
11 May
Tetuán
4 May

N
W   E
S

0   100   200   300   400   500

Statute miles

The *Victory* seeking the French fleet
in the Mediterranean
January – May 1805

Black Sea

31 Jan

Malta
Feb

Mediterranean Sea

Alexandria
7 Feb

Writing to Ball on the same day he confessed, 'I am, in truth, half dead; but what man can do to find them out, shall be done; but I must not make more haste than good speed, and leave Sardinia, Sicily or Naples for them to take, should I go either for the Eastward or Westward, without knowing some more about them.'[23] Strategically correct, he was carefully maintaining British sea control over the Central Mediterranean. Exercising restraint did not come naturally to him. In many ways he showed resilience and perception of a higher order than required for the momentous events that lay ahead. His decisions during this period were methodical, not impulsive. But he was, as he wrote to Ball on 10 April, 'very, very miserable'.[24]

The days dragged on into the middle of April, and still there was no news. To complicate matters further, he heard indirectly, rather than by official dispatch, of an expedition under Lieutenant-General Sir James Craig about to set out from England for the Mediterranean to protect Naples. Nelson was confronted with the possibility that an unwieldy convoy might encounter a combined French and Spanish fleet. In fact, due to contrary winds, the expedition did not leave Spithead until 19 April.[25] He still had not a shred of information as to Villeneuve's whereabouts. On 10 April he wrote to Acton, no longer in Naples and out of power. 'I can hardly think that they are bound to the westward to give up the Mediterranean, nor can I suppose that any expedition from England is bound into the Mediterranean . . . however, I may be blamed.'[26] 'I am very uneasy,' he confided to his private journal on 16 April, 'although I feel I have done perfectly right in apprising myself that Naples, Sicily, the Morea, Egypt & Sardinia were safe before I proceeded to the westward. I must ever regret my want of frigates which I could have sent to the westward.'[27]

Nelson then decided to sail north to look for news from merchantmen and, off the southern coast of Sardinia, on 19 April, he received the first firm intelligence for weeks. William Parker in the *Amazon* had spoken with a Ragusan merchant ship, which had observed the French passing through the Strait of Gibraltar ten days before on 8 April.[28] Had Nelson known that Sir John Orde had withdrawn northward on the approach of the French fleet through the strait, he would have been even less happy. Orde was outnumbered and his move was strategically sound, but it was not a popular move; nor did Orde send word to Nelson that he was retreating from off Cadiz. Fremantle wrote to his brother from London: 'Orde's conduct is universally censured, and a great source of triumph to Lord St Vincent and his party.'[29] On 9 April, Villeneuve's squadron – twelve ships of the line, a 50-gun ship, five frigates and three corvettes – linked up with the Spanish fleet at Cadiz under Admiral Gravina, the new, young,

Sicilian-born commander-in-chief. Villeneuve did not enter the harbour, setting off into the Atlantic almost immediately. Six Spanish ships of the line and a frigate followed in an untidy straggle.*

Knowing that he had missed Villeneuve by hundreds of miles, Nelson now set a course for the strait, leaving most of his frigates behind to obtain tactical intelligence. He was philosophical, writing a clear and calm letter giving the reasons for his actions to the Admiralty.[30] Bickerton sent him a message of comfort. 'It is [in] vain to torment ourselves because circumstances have not turned out exactly as might have been expected. Your Lordship appears to have taken every precaution in your power to prevent our sly enemy from gaining advantage by appearing when he is not expected.'[31]

During this time Nelson's anxiety drove him hard. According to Chevallier: 'The weather has been very Stormy and had it not been for his astonishing Care not half of his Fleet would have a Standing Mast, in all the bad weather both Night and Day that good man was upon Deck, maimed as he is, sometimes half naked under Such heavy rains as are never Seen in England.'[32] The *Victory*'s surgeon, William Beatty, wrote that Nelson was

seldom enjoying two hours of uninterrupted sleep; and on several occasions he did not quit the deck during the whole night. At these times he took no pains to protect himself from the effects of wet, or the night air; wearing only a thin great coat, and he has frequently, after having his clothes wet through with rain, refused to have them changed, saying that the leather waistcoat which he wore over his flannel one would secure him from complaint. He seldom wore boots, and was consequently very liable to have his feet wet. When this occurred he has often been known to go down to his cabin, throw off his shoes, and walk on the carpet in his stockings for the purpose of drying the feet of them. He chose rather to adopt this uncomfortable expedient, than to give his servants the trouble of assisting him to put on fresh stockings, which, from his only having one hand, he could not himself conveniently effect.[33]

Chevallier thought Nelson's health was reasonable: 'considering the hardships his Lordship undergoes his health is better than could be expected

---

* Admiral Villeneuve and Rear-Admiral Dumanoir: *Bucentaur* (80), *Neptune* (80), *Indomptable* (80), *Formidable* (80), *Aigle* (74), *Swiftsure* (74), *Berwick* (74), *Mont-Blanc* (74), *Intrépide* (74), *Pluton* (74), *Scipion* (74), and *Atlas* (74), with 3,332 troops under General Lauriston. Gravina: *Argonauta* (90), *Firme* (80), *Terrible* (80), *San Raphael* (80), *España* (74) and *Jago del America* (64), with 1,930 Spanish troops (Eastwick, I, 35; James, III, 334; also Keats's intelligence in (UK)NA: PRO, ADM 80/141 [June 1805]).

... for half the time he is deprived of the common necessaries of Life. Yet he seems not to mind it but his body feels it for his Lordship is much thinner than he was, as for his spirits they remain the same.'[34] Nelson, nevertheless, had the physician of the fleet, Leonard Gillespie, write him a medical survey, which included 'severe debilitating perspirations, recurring nightly', 'the complaint in the breast' and 'the impaired condition of your Lordship's eyesight frequent and necessary use of a telescope'. Gillespie's solution was 'a remission from the heavy cares and duties of command'.[35] Nelson had been granted sick leave by the Admiralty, but he never used Gillespie's document.[36]

At no point in his career was he more resolute and calm. His letters to Emma from this time are full of mature love and longing for both her and Horatia. 'You are sure, my Emma, that I am as anxious to see you as you can be to see me for I love and revere you beyond all this world, because I feel you deserve it of me. Therefore I shall say no more upon that subject but shall wait to give you much more efficacious proofs of my love than can be convey'd in a letter. I admire dear Horatia's writing. I think her hand will soon be like her dear mother's, and if she is but as clever, I shall be content.'[37] These letters have a nobility about them, reflecting his security in their relationship and the promise of future happiness. They are much more revealing than the self-centred, hysterical, jealous letters from the Baltic or, indeed, than any of his early love letters.[38]

Nelson described his slow two-week passage westwards out of the Mediterranean as 'a heavy beat'.[39] On 4 May the fleet reached Tetuán Bay, where it obtained water and provisions, then went on to Gibraltar, with the wind still contrary. A few officers (and their laundry) landed at Gibraltar, but Nelson was watching his barometer and, according to Scott, 'perceived an indication of a probable change of wind. Off went a gun from the *Victory*, and up went the Blue Peter, whilst the Admiral paced the deck in a hurry, with anxious steps, and impatient for a moment's delay. The officers said, "Here is one of Nelson's mad pranks." But he was nevertheless right, the wind did become favourable, the linen was left on shore, the fleet cleared the Gut.'[40] By 10 May it was anchored in Lagos Bay.

Over the next two days the naval situation began to clarify. On 10 May, to Nelson's considerable relief, the convoy of the transports carrying the troops commanded by General Craig, destined for Naples, came safely into Lagos Bay, escorted by the *Amphion*. He immediately detached Richard Bickerton, in the worn out *Royal Sovereign*, to escort the convoy to Italy. Off Cadiz, Nelson had no information from Orde's remaining frigates as to where Villeneuve had gone. It was increasingly unlikely that Villeneuve had gone north to the Channel or Ireland. Nelson began to piece together the evidence. A Scotsman in the Portuguese Navy, Donald Campbell, gave him useful intelligence. The *Lively* frigate provided evidence that the French had not gone north; thus they could only have gone to the West Indies.[41] He wrote to Addington, 'notwithstanding my very, very indifferent state of health ... I cannot forego the desire of getting, if possible, at the Enemy; and therefore, I this day steer for the West Indies.'[42] In fact, the decision to follow the French fleet across the Atlantic was not as groundbreaking as legend would have it. For instance, both Rooke in 1704 and Byng in 1756 had given instructions for an escaping Toulon fleet to be followed out of the strait and brought to action wherever it went.[43]

Nelson wasted no time. Through the night of 10 May stores and provisions from the transports that had come with Craig's convoy were loaded into his ships.[44] He set off the next day, escorting the convoy down the Spanish coast, then turned west to the open Atlantic with ten ships of the line and three frigates.* In spite of the state of the *Superb*, Keats volunteered to go with them. They were a month behind the French but made steady progress. The fleet did not stop when orders had to be distributed. Nelson used Parker in the *Amazon*: 'By making sail after each ship in turn, dropping his boat skilfully on the weather bow of each, and picking the boat up on her lee quarter, the progress of the Fleet was delayed as little as possible.'[45] The speed of the ships quickened once they picked up the trade winds. On 19 May they made sixty miles, 'just getting into the Trade Winds', according to Nelson's private journal; by 21 May 'now fairly in the Trade Winds'.[46] Every sail was set. From that point the fleet averaged nearly six knots over fifteen days.† Halfway across the Atlantic, Nelson wrote to Keats to encourage him: the passage was 'not very quick but far from being a bad one'.[47] According to the *Naval Chronicle*, Captain George Murray, whose task as captain of the fleet was to keep it in formation, remarked to Nelson: ' "I suppose, my lord, that, by packing all this canvass on the ships, your Lordship means to engage the enemy, in case you come up with them." "Yes, by G—, Murray, do I," returned the admiral drily and shortly.'[48]

The combined French and Spanish fleet, which had arrived at Martinique on 14 May, proved to be miserably ineffective. Since Napoleon had told

---

* They were: *Victory* (100), *Canopus* (80), *Superb* (74), *Donegal* (74), *Spencer* (74), *Tigre* (74), *Leviathan* (74), *Belleisle* (74), *Conqueror* (74), *Swiftsure* (74), and the frigates *Amazon* (38), *Decade* (36) and *Amphion* (32).
† From 20 May to 3 June the fleet sailed 2,130 miles, averaging 142 miles a day over fifteen days. On 21 May the fleet made 190 miles, the highest day's run. It was a fast crossing (BL, Add. MSS 34968).

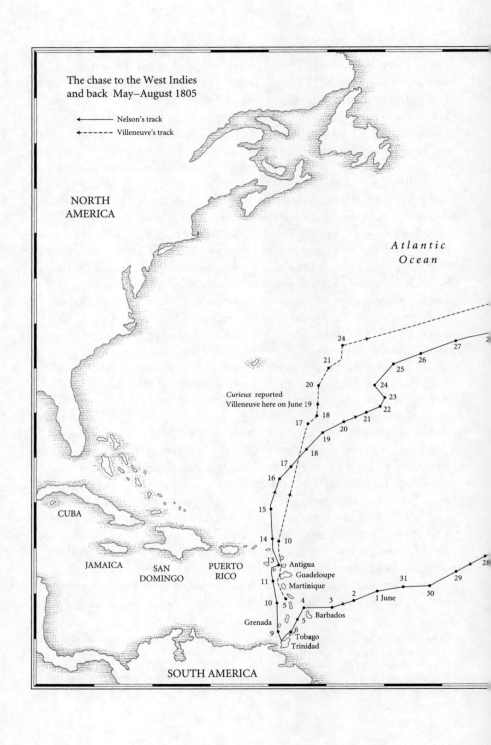

The chase to the West Indies
and back May–August 1805

⟵——— Nelson's track
⟵----- Villeneuve's track

NORTH
AMERICA

*Atlantic
Ocean*

Curieux reported
Villeneuve here on June 19

CUBA

JAMAICA   SAN
              DOMINGO   PUERTO
                            RICO

Antigua
Guadeloupe
Martinique

Grenada

Barbados

Tobago
Trinidad

SOUTH AMERICA

24
21
20
18
17
17
16
15
14   10
13
11
10   5
     5
9

Antigua
Guadeloupe
Martinique

25   26
        27
24   23
   22
21
20
19
18

31   29
2   1 June   30
4   3
5
6

2

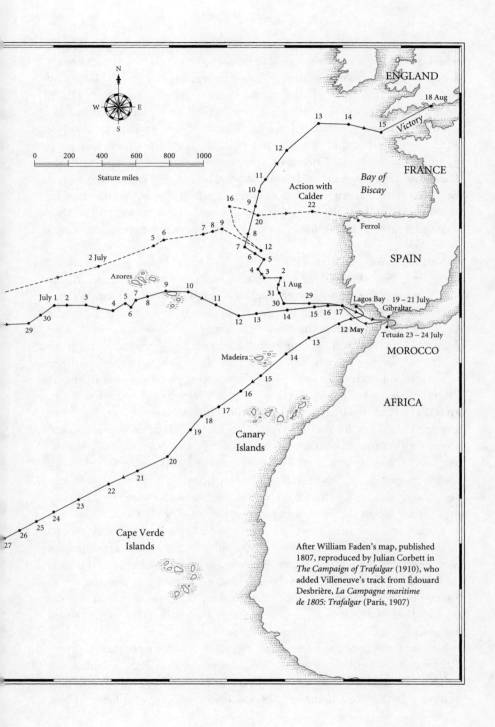

After William Faden's map, published
1807, reproduced by Julian Corbett in
The Campaign of Trafalgar (1910), who
added Villeneuve's track from Édouard
Desbrière, *La Campagne maritime
de 1805: Trafalgar* (Paris, 1907)

no one of his grand design, Villeneuve was unclear about his exact orders, which at present were to wait at Martinique to be joined by another French fleet under Ganteaume from Brest. While he waited, he captured Diamond Rock, a 600-foot lump of basalt a mile off the Martinique coast, which, under the orders of the younger Samuel Hood, had been occupied for eighteen months by a small force of British officers and seamen, armed with, among other things, 18-pounders at the top of the rock and a 24-pounder lower down. Curiously, it was commissioned as a ship (HMS *Diamond Rock*) for legal and administrative reasons. The British force had been annoying French shipping making into Port Royal, Martinique. Its capture was to be Villeneuve's sole conquest.[49] Having waited, he then received a further order from Napoleon to take as many British possessions as he could.

Nelson gained ten days on the French, arriving at Carlisle Bay, Barbados, on 4 June, 'not a little elated at finding he had taken the right road, by the information of the enemy having reached Martinico very sickly', as William Parker reported in a letter to his father.[50] He found Rear-Admiral Alexander Cochrane in a single ship, the *Northumberland*.[51] Cochrane, having chased Admiral Missiessy across from Ferrol, had sailed to Jamaica, it being the great prize for the French, and had left five of his ships of the line there. When Nelson arrived he was given firm intelligence by General Robert Brereton, the governor of St Lucia, that the French had turned south to attack Trinidad or Tobago. Nelson did not think it likely, but he agreed to go, particularly as he was offered 2,000 troops. Once having embarked them, the fleet turned south. Nelson issued 'Fighting Instructions', and the ships were cleared for action. This included making fast a stern cable to an anchor in each ship, for, as William Parker noted, 'every preparation was accordingly made for attacking them at anchor, and the greatest anxiety prevailed through the Fleet, now apparently drawing to a crisis. This was in a great measure heightened when we made Trinidad by observing two or three posts set on fire and were destroyed as we were steering along the island towards the Gulf of P[aria].' Anticipating another Battle of the Nile, on 8 June the fleet turned into the gulf: but no ship of war was in Port of Spain Harbour.[52] 'Judge of our surprise and disappointment at finding they had no intelligence of the enemy, that the out-posts were destroyed supposing our Fleet to be the combined squadrons.'[53]

Nelson's resilience was never more tested, but it was now that Napoleon's elaborate plans began to unravel. On the same day that Nelson went south to Trinidad, Villeneuve sailed from Martinique, steering towards Antigua, and on 9 June took a homeward-bound British convoy of fourteen ships, from which he heard that Nelson and his fleet were, after all, in the West Indies. This news was enough to unsettle the demoralized French admiral. He conferred with Gravina, and they immediately decided to return to Europe. Whatever their difficulties, Villeneuve and Gravina did not add to them by disagreement; the two admirals maintained a mutual respect. The health of the Spanish crews was already giving Gravina cause for concern.[54] The French troops were offloaded into smaller craft on 10 June, and the ships of the line set off east across the Atlantic. Nelson had gained a conscious ascendancy over Villeneuve. One of Nelson's captains wrote to him of the French admiral: 'Your Lordship each night forms part of his dreams.'[55]

Nelson sailed north from Trinidad and soon heard that the French had, as he had suspected, turned north. He was again faced with a difficult decision, but he quickly accumulated enough intelligence to calculate that the enemy had left the West Indies. On 13 June, Nelson landed his troops at St John's, Antigua, which he had known so well twenty years before, saluted Fort Hamilton, and rounded the island, sailing past Barbuda and straight out into the Atlantic.[56] He had been in the West Indies for only two weeks. Although he had missed the enemy, he was none the less confident of his actions. 'I have saved these Colonies, and more than two hundred Sail of sugar-loaded Ships,' he wrote to Alexander Davison.[57] But the next day he wrote in his journal: 'very, very low'.[58] He steered for Gibraltar, back to his station in the Mediterranean. On the destination of the combined fleet he noted that there were 'as many opinions as there are persons'; he thought that the Spanish would go to Havana, and the French to Cadiz and Toulon. He still suspected that the French were heading for Egypt.[59]

Conditions in the fleet were tough on the return journey. Steady breezes prevailed for the first week, after which the log records generally light airs and only moderate breezes.[60] There had been no time to obtain fresh provisions or water in the West Indies.[61] On 17 June, Thomas Atkinson, the master, found that some of the casks in the lowest tier in the fore hold of the *Victory* were rotten: instead of 145 tons of water, only a hundred remained. As the crew were rationed, the daily consumption of water decreased from ten casks (about five tons of water) to six, and then to four.[62] It was the hottest time of the year. Punishments rose sharply, in the main for drunkenness, fighting and quarrelling. On 22 June she made only eighty-two miles; Nelson in his private journal wrote: 'all the afternoon and all the night light airs. Calm and Rainy, very miserable, which is very feverish.'[63] That day fourteen men were given a total of 432 lashes; one man received forty-eight for repeated drunkenness and another the same number for theft; seven received thirty-six lashes.[64] The *Victory* remained a flogging ship.

Progress was slow. On 24 June, Nelson spoke to two American ships and purchased forty-one head of cattle for the fleet. After this, for five days, progress quickened to an average of 159 miles a day, before the weather again gave way to light airs. On 30 June, on a calm afternoon in mid Atlantic, the *Spartiate*, which had joined them in the West Indies, transferred twenty tons of water to the flagship; the diminishing reserve aboard the *Victory* has thus increased to 79 tons. On 8 July, Nelson wrote in his journal, 'We crawled thirty-three miles in the last twenty-four hours; my only hope is, that the Enemy's Fleet are near us, and in the same situation.'[65] Scurvy began to appear. When the fleet reached Gibraltar the *Victory* had only sixteen tons of water left; aboard the *Amazon* the crew was down to five pints of water a day and she reached Gibraltar with only a week's water left.[66] Yet the captain of the *Swiftsure*, William Rutherford, not known to Nelson before the Atlantic crossing, wrote to a friend: 'Coming from the West Indies I was upon salt beef and three quarts of water for a month . . . The privations of this fleet of eleven sail of the line has gone through has been great, but it has been with cheerfulness because Lord Nelson commanded them'; and he added, 'If you do not know Lord Nelson, he is the most gentlemanlike, mild, pleasant creature that was ever seen.'[67]

Villeneuve headed not for Cadiz or the Mediterranean but for northern Spain, in line with Napoleon's grand plan to concentrate French squadrons in the Channel. However, on 7 July, Lord Barham at the Admiralty received priceless information from the 18-gun sloop *Curieux*. She had been sent to England by Nelson with dispatches, but she had happened to chance upon Villeneuve's fleet in mid Atlantic on a course for Ferrol – and not Cadiz. Without delay Barham drafted a far-sighted dispatch to Cornwallis off Brest, the first of several faultless tactical and strategic decisions that he took in the coming months. He directed the British squadron outside Rochefort to join with the one off Ferrol.[68] This formed a squadron of fifteen ships of the line under Sir Robert Calder, Nelson's old protagonist and now a vice-admiral. Calder successfully intercepted Villeneuve on 22 July; heavily outnumbered, he captured two ships, but fog and nightfall prevented decisive action. Though the two fleets were still in contact the next day, Calder did not renew the fight. The Spanish claimed that he retreated. Villeneuve withdrew into Vigo, and two days later into Ferrol, rather than nearer the Channel, rendering Calder's action a minor tactical success.[69] But the British public expected a clear win, not a draw: Nelson had set a new standard for victory. More influential opinion suspected that Calder did not renew the attack the next day because he was too busy shielding his prizes; and they certainly hindered his movements after the action. Upset by adverse comments in the press, Calder demanded a court martial to clear his name, but it was not held until 23 December, during the emotional and confident period after Trafalgar, not the most propitious time for a balanced verdict.[70] Calder was 'severely reprimanded' for not doing all he could to renew the battle on the second day. Later, in September 1806, Sir Robert's fellow Northumbrian Admiral Robert Roddam, long retired, wrote a passionate defence of Calder to the first lord of the Admiralty: 'No officer did go through a task so meritoriously and so difficult, for not only had Sir Robert to Guard himself against these multiplying Squadrons, but he also had to attend to the preservation of Great Britain and Ireland ... eight of the enemy's ships were rendered ineffectual for many Months, two of them captured and a third Struck and only escaped by the darkness of the Night and Extreme fog; nor on the part of Sir Robert Calder was there any loss.'[71] An unpopular officer was unfairly treated.

As early as 30 June, Nelson sent his frigates ahead to prepare the way: the *Amphion* to Tangiers and the *Amazon* to the rendezvous off Cape St Vincent. Of Villeneuve and Gravina's combined fleet there was no news. Samuel Sutton in the *Amphion* had little luck in finding any information from the consul at Tangiers, the blind and disillusioned James Matra, although he made early arrangements for live bullocks, fruit and vegetables to be available at Tetuán.[72] On 17 July, as he approached the Strait of Gibraltar, Nelson entered the distance sailed in his private journal: 3,227 miles out, 3,459 back, 'average, per day, thirty-four leagues, wanting nine miles'. Two days later the *Victory* anchored in Rosia Bay, Gibraltar.[73] On 20 July he entered another statistic: 'I went on shore for the first time since the 16th of June 1803; and from having my foot out of the *Victory*, two years, wanting ten days.'[74] On the same day Alexander Scott wrote to Bickerton: 'I think it probable His Lordship will soon avail himself of his leave of absence.'[75] In London little news had filtered out of the Admiralty. On 9 August the aristocratic Lady Bessborough wrote an impatient letter to Lord Granville Leveson-Gower, the ambassador at St Petersburg: 'Ld. Nelson being pass'd Gibraltar, He seem'd to have a velleite [passing fancy] to pursue the French to Egypt again, where I believe he thinks they grow ... it seems impossible they should escape us everywhere.'[76]

The fleet went to Mazri Bay, Tetuán, for the much needed fresh provisions that had been ordered. Fearful for Malta's food supply, Nelson made rapid rearrangements and dispositions, strengthening Bickerton in the Central

Mediterranean.[77] Here Nelson penned to Emma the frustration he had felt but suppressed in his official dispatches: 'the moment I find the Enemy are safe in Port and out of my reach, that moment I shall sett off for England, but I am dreadfully uneasy. I have reason to hate the name of Gen[era]l Brereton as long as I live and perhaps our Country for ever, but it is in vain to repine & fret myself ill. I know this too well but I cannot help it. The name & circumstance absolutely haunts me.'[78] Hearing that Villeneuve was at Ferrol, he and his squadron set off north on 25 July, swinging well out into the Atlantic because of the northerly wind. The passage was agonizingly slow. On 13 August he met the *Niobe* frigate; having received her intelligence he made for Ushant where he joined Cornwallis's blockading squadron on 15 August. Acting under Barham's instructions, Cornwallis sent over a cutter with orders for the *Victory* to proceed to Spithead with the *Superb*; the rest of Nelson's ships remained with the blockading fleet off Brest.

The appearance and efficiency of Nelson's fleet deeply impressed one of Cornwallis's captains, Edward Codrington of the *Orion*. He wrote to his wife that they 'seem to be of a very high order indeed: and although their ships do not look so handsome as objects, they look so warlike, and show such high conditions, when once I think *Orion* fit to manoeuvre with them, I shall probably paint her in the same manner.'[79] The additional ships enlarged Cornwallis's blockading squadron to a huge fleet. At the same time as Nelson was approaching Spithead, Barham, in another wise strategic move, told Calder to take eighteen of those ships of the line off Ferrol.[80] Collingwood had been off Cadiz with a blockading squadron since June. The moves that would lead to the Battle of Cape Trafalgar were already being made.

At 8 p.m. on 17 August the *Victory* and the *Superb* anchored off Dunnose on the Isle of Wight, and at first light the next day they sailed to Spithead, saluting Admiral Montagu, the commander-in-chief, Portsmouth, in the old flagship *Royal William* with fifteen guns, receiving thirteen in return.[81] The two ships were granted 'pratique', or a clean bill of health, on 20 August, when Nelson struck his flag and went ashore. The news of Nelson's arrival was telegraphed to the Admiralty. The efficient Marsden sent a note to Emma at Clarges Street; it was forwarded to Southend, where she was sea bathing.[82]

Nelson was at home for twenty-five days before he embarked again in the *Victory*, and for a good deal of that time he was conferring with ministers. In his first few days in London, Nelson not only met with Barham but also with Lord Castlereagh, just appointed secretary of state for war and colonies, and with William Pitt.[83] Nelson promoted his ideas for fortifying

Sardinia without success, Castlereagh delivering a decisively negative reply.[84] New weapons in the shape of rockets and submarines were reviewed in Castlereagh's office; present at the meeting were Sidney Smith, William Pitt, William Congreve and 'Mr Francis', an alias for Robert Fulton.[85] Napoleon's next moves dominated discussions, for events in Europe and at sea were now at a critical and anxious stage. Pitt's government was striving to establish another coalition of Continental allies to challenge Napoleon on his land borders. The emperor's threatened invasion of England was still a live political issue, even if the British Navy had privately written it off.

Nelson also met, by chance, when waiting outside Castlereagh's office, Sir Arthur Wellesley, the future duke of Wellington, recently back from India. The recollections of the duke were recorded by John Wilson Croker many years later. When the two men started talking, Wellesley was not impressed: 'If I can call it conversation, for it was almost all on his side, and all about himself, and in, really, a style so vain and silly as to surprise, and almost disgust me.' After some time Nelson went out of the room, presumably to enquire as to who Wellesley was, and, according to the general, 'When he came back, he was altogether a different man, both in manner and matter . . . He talked like an officer and a statesman . . . He really was a very superior man.'[86] When Nelson realized that he did not need to impress Wellesley, who would know his achievements, Nelson relaxed and demonstrated his grasp of events, showing both the uncertain and the confident sides of his character.

As so many meetings were necessary, Nelson often stayed in Gordon's Hotel in Albemarle Street to save the fifty minutes by post-chaise to Merton. As the conventions had to be observed, Emma's official residence was still Clarges Street; thus Nelson spent very little of the time alone with her, and she knew that this leave was to be short. 'He looks very well,' she wrote to Mrs Lutwidge on 3 September, 'but he is not strong and again he is asked to go forth for they cannot go on without his powerfull arm. He will not be many days longer with us, I believe . . . He is adored as he walks the streets, thousands follow him, blessing him & wishing him good luck.'[87] The sense of an impending naval crisis had transmitted itself to the public. Lord Minto 'met Nelson in a mob in Piccadilly and got hold of his arm, so that I was mobbed too. It is really quite affecting to see the wonder and admiration, and love and respect, of the whole world . . . It is beyond anything represented in a play or a poem of fame.'[88]

The quiet of Merton was still to be enjoyed, however, and the family was present for many of these days, even if Nelson's time was much taken up with meetings in London. Visitors were constant. Some were merely well-wishers: the duke of Clarence, Captains Keats, Culverhouse and Thomas Bowen.[89] Some came on business. Sidney Smith recalled his visit 'with the map before us', and Alexander Scott came in September when it was time to leave.[90] With Keats, whom Nelson wanted as 'his right hand man', Nelson walked in the garden; he explained to him what tactics he would employ if he managed to bring the combined fleets together.[91] William Perry, journalist and neighbour, came too, meeting an old political adversary, Minto, who saw Nelson several times.[92] The observant diplomat, more tolerant than two years earlier, reported to his wife: 'Lady Hamilton has improved and added to the house and the place extremely well without his knowing she was about it. He found it already done. She is clever after all: the passion is as hot as ever.'[93] But Emma's situation at Merton was not all that she wished. She used the older Mrs Lutwidge as a confidante: 'He has all his Brothers & Sisters at Merton & I go there to see them but for fear of having all the Cats on my back I am over cautious so as to be completely miserable.'[94]

Nelson took care to meet with opposition politicians, always a useful insurance in case of future disaster. He called on his old friend and supporter William Windham, now a follower of Lord Grenville and in opposition to Pitt. A long conversation ensued, in which Nelson was critical of the capture of the French West Indies islands and observed, intriguingly, that 'Belleisle would, even now, be the best object.'[95] Windham was in the process of gathering information with which to attack the military measures of the government.[96] It was at another opposition dinner party that Lady Elizabeth Foster met Nelson; she had always been an admirer and commented on Nelson's modesty: 'he is delighted with his reception here, "They have received me as if I had done some great feat." And so God knows he has.'[97] According to Lady Bessborough, Lady Elizabeth thought that Nelson

so far from appearing vain and full of himself, as one had always heard, he was perfectly unassuming and natural. Talking of Popular Applause and his having been Mobb'd, L[ad]y Hamilton wanted to give an account of it but he stopped her. 'Why,' said she, 'you like to be applauded – you cannot deny it.' 'I own it,' he answered, 'popular applause is very acceptable and grateful to me, but no Man ought to be too much elated by it, it is too precarious to be depended upon, and it may be my turn to feel the tide set as strong against me as ever it did for me.'

Lady Bessborough herself met Nelson later at a dinner party, where he deftly parried questions about his meeting with Pitt. He demonstrated similar diplomacy when Lady Bessborough 'questioned him about Sir R Calder; he said, "He had great difficulties, and, I hope all this will be forgotten amidst the huzzas and illuminations for a glorious Victory" (and after a pause): "But, by the by, it is Dev—sh disinterested in me to hope so." '[98] Old rivalry was momentarily recalled.

Two weeks after Nelson had landed, the dramatic news arrived that concentrated the minds of ministers. On 2 September, Captain Henry Blackwood of the *Euryalus* hurried from Portsmouth to the Admiralty with the latest reports, calling at Merton on the way. Villeneuve's fleet had left Ferrol, tried to go north but turned south and entered Cadiz on 21 August. Calder, with eighteen ships, had again performed questionably by retreating north to join Cornwallis at Ushant, but later followed Villeneuve to the south and joined Collingwood off Cadiz.[99] In London decisions were taken rapidly. On 4 September, Barham proposed that Nelson, as commander-in-chief, Mediterranean, should go out in the *Victory*. He would be given an extended station up to Cape St Vincent. Other measures were suggested to bottle up the French and Spanish fleet in Cadiz. By the next day he had given Nelson his instructions to take the ships commanded by Collingwood and Calder under his command.[100] Nelson's baggage was simultaneously taken down to Portsmouth.[101]

Farewells and last-minute arrangements absorbed the rest of the time. A backlog of Admiralty business needed attention. Letters went to Davison authorizing him to pay outstanding bills.[102] Nelson went to Richmond Park to see Addington, now Lord Sidmouth, who was ill; his note to Nelson said, 'I am anxious to shake you by the hand once again.'[103] The day before Nelson's departure, according to Minto, 'Lady Hamilton was in tears . . . could not eat, and hardly drink, and near swooning, and all at table.' On 13 September, Nelson took his final leave of the Admiralty and he departed, according to John Barrow, 'more than usually cheerful'.[104] He also delivered a note to Davison to pay Emma £100 a month 'till farther order'.[105] Just before leaving, Nelson was summoned to Carlton House to see the prince of Wales. 'He and Lady Hamilton', Minto related to his wife, 'did not return till half-past five. I stayed till ten at night and took a final leave of him.'[106] Nelson made an emotional entry in his private journal: 'At half-past ten drove from dear, dear Merton, where I left all which I hold dear in this world, to go to Serve my King and Country.' Then, uncharacteristically, he added a brooding and pessimistic prayer, overlaid with premonition: 'May the Great God, whom I adore, enable me to fulfil the expectations of my Country; and if it is His good pleasure that I should return, my thanks will never cease being offered up to the Throne of His Mercy. If it is His good providence to cut short my days upon earth, I bow with the greatest submission.'[107]

From the George Inn at Portsmouth, at 6 a.m. on 14 September, he wrote a short note to Emma: 'My dearest and most beloved of Women, Nelson's Emma, I arrived here this mom[en]t . . . *Victory* is at St Helens and if possible I shall be away at Sea this day. God protect you and My Dear Horatia.'[108] The morning was filled, as usual, with business and final arrangements, rather than, as the legend goes, with heroic gestures. A minor question of aristocratic patronage had to be dealt with by two swift conversations with Lord Egremont, who happened to be in Portsmouth, about a problematic nephew, George Wyndham, a midshipman in the *Colossus*, who had fought a duel in Sardinia. Egremont recalled that Nelson 'sent for me again to explain something which he thought had made an unfavourable impression . . . with great kindness & attention to assure me the Boy had not been in the wrong'.[109] Then Nelson visited the recently constructed steam-powered Block Mills in Portsmouth Dockyard, which were almost fully operational; two years later forty-five machines were turning out 130,000 blocks and pulleys a year for the navy.[110] It is notable that Nelson, in these twenty-five days in England, espoused three developments that were to change Western society and warfare thereafter: rockets, submarines and mass production.

The crowd were pressing, and Nelson, to avoid them, went out of the George Inn through a back door; then he walked down a lane to the beach 'by the Bathing Machines' (rather than to the usual landing place). He was accompanied by two important financial and political figures: George Rose, now joint paymaster of the forces, and George Canning, treasurer of the navy, who went with Nelson out to the *Victory*.[111] He was, according to an American observer,

attended only by Admiral Coffin and a few private gentlemen. But, by the time he had arrived on the beach, some hundreds of people had collected in his train, pressing all around and pushing to get a little before him to obtain sight of his face . . . He was elegantly dressed, and his blue coat was splendidly illuminated with stars and ribbons. As the barge in which he embarked, pushed away from the shore, the people gave him three cheers, which his lordship returned by waving his hat.[112]

Even then he was scribbling a last note to George Murray, his captain of the fleet, who was prevented from sailing by a family death.[113] There was no time for heroic gestures.

29

Trafalgar
14 September–21 October 1805

My heart bleeds every time I think of the irreparable loss of the immortal Nelson. He wrote to me on the 15th of October and sent to me his Plan of Attack which he said was called the Nelson touch and he hoped it would be touch and take. It proves him to have been the most enterprising, judicious and skilful Admiral that ever commanded a British Fleet. Alexander Ball to Granville Penn, 27 December 1805[1]

After the prisoners came on board they sayed that the Devil loded the guns for it was impossible for men to load and fire as quick as we did. Benjamin Stevenson, quartermaster, *Victory*, to his wife, 5 November 1805[2]

The *Victory* sailed immediately from St Helens but soon ran into fog and light winds. Off Dunnose on 15 September the wind picked up: Nelson scribbled a short note to Emma: 'I cannot even read your dear letter, we have a fair wind . . . we go too swift for the boat. May Heavens bless you & Horatia.'[3] But it was to be a frustrating passage: two days later the ship was still east of Portland Bill, with a foul west wind, on a tack that would have taken her near Weymouth, where the king was holidaying. This was 'the place of all others I would wish to avoid,' Nelson wrote to Emma, with his peculiar mixture of loyalty and bitterness; 'but if it continues mod[era]te I hope to escape without anchoring, but should I be forced I shall act as a man and your Nelson neither courting or ashamed to hold up my head before the greatest Monarch in the World.'[4] A week later the ship was only 150 miles south west of the Scillies. Nelson fretted to Emma that he might be too late: 'if the battle has been fought I shall be sadly vext, but I cannot help myself.'[5] On 25 September he wrote: 'now in sight of the Rock of Lisbon, and although we have very little wind I hope to get round the

Cape St Vincent tomorrow. We have only had one day's fair Wind but by perseverance we have done much.'[6]

The passage was irksome as well as slow. The *Victory* had received a thorough refit, her rigging repaired, deck and topsides recaulked, guns taken out, holds emptied and cleaned and restocked.[7] The crew had not rested. Hardy was not well, one captain remarking that he looked twenty years older than the last time he had seen him. Nelson himself remarked to Bickerton, 'I am not very stout, nor is Hardy, but he would come forth.'[8] During the refit, Hardy had continued to dispense punishment, and it was no less hard than it had been in the Mediterranean and West Indies.* Punishment aboard the *Royal Sovereign*, to take the example of only one other ship, was markedly less.[9] Hardy, however, had one admirer, for the crew of *Victory* were healthy and, in the opinion of the surgeon William Beatty, this was to be attributed 'solely to Captain Hardy's attention to their subordination, temperance, warm clothing, and cleanliness'.[10]

The captains of the ships in the fleet assembling under Collingwood off Cadiz were in the main inexperienced in command; only five had commanded a ship of the line in battle before, although three quarters of them had been in at least one fleet battle as a junior officer in the previous two wars.[11] Only eight had previously served with Nelson.[12] Of the flag officers, Collingwood and Thomas Louis were tried and tested. Captains William Hargood and George Hope had been midshipman and lieutenant in the same ship as Nelson many years before in West Indies days. He knew Thomas Fremantle, John Conn and Edward Berry well; William Rutherford had been across the Atlantic with him earlier in the year. The talented frigate captains Thomas Bladen Capel and Henry Blackwood owed much to Nelson. The rest were strangers, although Nelson would have known them by reputation.† Fremantle, now commanding the *Neptune* (98), knew him best, and his letters record the days before Trafalgar in detail. From England Nelson brought to Fremantle news of the birth of a daughter, and the two men slipped into their old comfortable relationship: 'his behaviour to me is just the same as ever,' Fremantle wrote to his brother; 'friendly to

---

* For instance, on 24 September, 552 lashes were given to fourteen men, eleven of them for drunkenness; on 5 October four men were given thirty-six lashes for drunkenness; three days later seven received the same ((UK)NA: PRO, ADM51/4514, 14 Sept.–8 Oct. 1805).

† Those off Cadiz who were strangers to Nelson included Rear-Admiral the earl of Northesk and his captain, Charles Bullen (*Britannia*), George Duff (*Mars*), Israel Pellew (*Conqueror*), Edward Codrington (*Orion*), William Brown (*Ajax*), Charles Mansfield (*Minotaur*), Sir Francis Laforey (*Spartiate*), Henry Digby (*Africa*), Charles Tyler (*Tonnant*), John Cooke (*Bellerophon*), James Morris (*Colossus*), Richard King (*Achille*), Robert Moorsom (*Revenge*), Robert Redmill (*Polyphemus*), William Lechmere (*Thunderer*) and Richard Grindall (*Prince*).

a degree, he has given me my Old Station, his Second, which is very flattering.'[13]

All the captains were, however, looking forward to Nelson's arrival. 'Would to God you were with us, believe me, the loss of you has been much felt,' Thomas Louis had written on 17 August from the *Canopus*.[14] The shy and remote Collingwood, his other qualities so admired by historians, was not appreciated by his captains. Fremantle wrote to his brother: 'we want him [Nelson] or somebody of more consequence and character to command so large a fleet.' And later: 'I hope Lord Nelson will come out as he is the life and Soul of the Squadron he serves with . . . Adm[iral] Collingwood . . . is very much of Cornwallis's way . . . he never invites any one to his table, nor will he allow us to visit each other.'[15] Edward Codrington, captain of the *Orion*, who had not served with Nelson before, wrote to his wife on 4 September: 'Is Lord Nelson coming out to us again? I anxiously hope he may be; that I may once in my life see a commander-in-chief endeavouring to make a hard and disagreeable service as palatable to those serving under him as circumstance will admit of, and keeping up by example that animation so necessary for such an occasion.'[16] Two weeks later his frustration had increased: 'For charity's sake send us Lord Nelson, o ye men of power!'[17]

To the great relief of the captains, Nelson reached the fleet on 29 September. While Collingwood was his second-in-command, the other vice-admiral was Robert Calder. Calder had learnt of the public disappointment in him through the English newspapers and now wanted to go home to clear his name by means of a court martial. Nelson, who was expecting a fleet of forty ships of the line, allowed Calder home in the *Prince of Wales*, a 98-gun ship that, as things turned out, he would have done well to have retained. Nelson showed characteristic generosity to a colleague in trouble, reporting to Emma: 'I have had . . . a very distressing scene with Poor Sir Robert Calder . . . I have given him the advice as to my dearest friend. He is in adversity, and if he ever has been my Enemy he now feels the pang of it, and finds me one of his best friends.'[18] Nelson's gesture to Calder was admired by the officers in the fleet. Fremantle commented: 'Lord Nelson has with much feeling towards Calder, allowed him to take his own Ship to England, contrary to the directions from the Admiralty.'[19] In truth, Nelson did not think much of Calder's determination, commenting to another officer: 'He appears to have had the ships at Ferrol more in his head than the squadron in sight, believing that they would come forth . . . he lays all his stress upon other considerations than fighting the enemy's squadron, if he could have done it, which he denies to be possible.'[20] Nelson even allowed Calder to take two captains to England with him to give evidence on his behalf, leaving their less experienced first lieutenants to command their ships.[21]

Nelson's first move was to withdraw the main fleet over the horizon, leaving the frigates to watch Cadiz, very much in the style of the blockade of Brest. Officers and crews were now able to relax. Collingwood's very close blockade had been a strain; as Fremantle put it: 'we were continually on the stretch, and keeping in close with Cadiz.'[22] The weather was settled, with light airs and breezes, and cloudy, hazy and fine conditions.[23] The combined fleet could hardly move in this windless weather. Codrington reported with relief to his wife that 'The signal is made that boats may be hoisted to buy fruit, stock, or anything from vessels coming into the fleet; this, I trust, will be a common signal hereafter, but it is the first day I have seen it made.'[24] Visits between ships by boat were unimpeded: the *Victory* was busy with visitors. A junior lieutenant wrote home: 'This is a shocking ship for studying, for we are always in a noise; being admiral you know we have a great deal of communication and there is a constant rotation of Boats from one day's end to another.'[25]

Nelson dispersed his ships carefully, all within signal distance. His orders on 4 October to George Duff in the *Mars* (74) started: 'As the Enemy's fleet may be hourly expected to put to Sea from Cadiz . . .' Duff was to keep 'from 3 to 4 leagues between the fleet and Cadiz in order that I may get the information from the frigates stationed off that Port as expeditiously as possible.'[26] The *Mars* was to fire guns by day or night if the combined fleet came out; in thick weather the ships were to close within signal distance of *Victory*. In the meantime the ships in the fleet were busy painting their ships in the style of Nelson's Mediterranean ships to make them more imposing. Codrington was not wholly convinced by the new colour scheme, 'as all small ships are much disfigured by this attempt to look large, like the frog in the fable . . . I shall endeavour to preserve my yellow band, although I intend following our admiral's whim as to the two streaks.'[27] Duff wrote to his wife that his ship's company had 'been employed for this week past to paint the ship à la Nelson, which most of the fleet are doing.'*[28] Only two days before the battle Nelson ordered that the masts of two ships that still had black iron hoops around them were to be painted yellow, to ensure that in the confusion and smoke of battle they would not be mistaken for an enemy ship, all of which had black mast hoops.[29]

---

* It is not exactly clear what this colour scheme was, although it is likely to have been similar to the ochre and black in which the *Victory* is painted today. Benjamin Silliman noted that the *Victory* had 'white sides, and with her three tiers of guns' and 'made a most formidable appearance' (Silliman, II, 11).

Nelson set about getting to know his captains. As usual he used his dinner table as his main means of communication. Fremantle was not included on the first night: 'There were so many seniors to me with the Admiral that I did not dine with him ... because the table could contain no more.' But on 30 September: 'We dined with Lord Nelson – the juniors and I never passed a pleasanter day. I staid with him until eight at night – he would not let me leave him before.'[30] Fremantle was struck by Nelson's healthy appearance: 'He looks better than ever I saw him in my life, and is grown fatter.'[31] George Duff, who first met Nelson when he arrived on 29 September, wrote to his wife: 'I dined with his Lordship yesterday, and had a very merry dinner; he is certainly the pleasantest Admiral I ever served under.'[32] Duff wrote home again ten days later in much the same way: 'He is so good and pleasant a man, that we all wish to do what he likes, without any kind of orders.'[33] Edward Codrington, also at the dinner on 30 September, was well aware of Nelson's motives: 'even you, our good wives, will allow the superiority of Lord Nelson in all these social arrangements which bind his captains to their admiral.'[34]

There was no sign now of Nelson's 'nervous irritability'. He was totally in charge, the only position in which he felt completely happy. He quietly established an atmosphere of confidence and unity, and in a measure that captains who were new to him had never before experienced. Some small quarrels had to be headed off. 'Don't, my dear Blackwood, be angry with anyone,' he wrote about some forgotten difference of opinion on 8 October. 'It was only a laudable anxiety in Admiral Louis and nothing like complaining.'[35] Judging by the speed at which Nelson engendered loyalty and goodwill in a group noted for its independence, he was at the peak of his powers of personal magnetism and inspirational leadership.

Social and professional niceties over, Nelson proceeded to business. At an early meeting of his captains he explained his intended battle tactics, which he called the 'Nelson touch', a term much since debated. As he mentioned 'touch and take' in two letters written in mid September, it is likely that the phrase came to him from 'touch and go', a term used when a ship's keel touched the bottom without lessening its speed.[36] Confusion and uncertainty remain too over Nelson's tactical concepts. These have to be reconstructed, because little documentary evidence from on board the *Victory* survived the battle. George Murray, the first captain, was not on board, and it would have been his job 'to preserve all copies of battle instructions and orders of battle and sailing'.[37] In any case, there was no time for comprehensive and careful drafting.[38]

Speed was the essence of Nelson's plan. The order of sailing was to be

Nelson's sketch showing his intended line of attack through the enemy fleet

the order of battle, to avoid delay in manoeuvring before the action. Instead of hauling in the lower sails, as was customary when the fleet approached the enemy, all sails, including the studding sails, were to be kept aloft and drawing until just before action began. The fleet was to be split into two parallel divisions in line-ahead formation, one led by Nelson and the other by Collingwood, his second-in-command; these divisions were then to sail straight at the enemy.* No firing would take place until the ships were very close. Nelson's division would confuse the enemy by feinting towards the head of the enemy's line, steering at the last minute towards the enemy flagship, which he anticipated would be in the middle of the enemy line. This would have the effect of isolating the van of the enemy's fleet. Collingwood would have independence of action, and his division would attack the rear of the line before the enemy ships ahead could turn back.[39] A short, close-range, decisive, pell-mell battle would result.

The impact on his listeners was dramatic. Nelson described an emotional moment to Emma in a letter of 1 October: 'and when I came to explain the Nelson touch, some shed tears, all approved, as it was new, it was singular, it was simple and from admirals downwards it was repeated, it must succeed if ever they will allow us to get at them. Some may be Judas's, but the majority are much pleased with my commanding them.'[40] Most of Nelson's captains had been young lieutenants when the French wars began; here was

---

* A third column of ships is drawn in the memorandum of 9 October, known as the 'advanced squadron', but soon after Nelson issued his list of the ships in only two squadrons, the 'Van' and the 'Rear' (Nicolas, VII, 94).

the best chance since 1793 to strike a decisive blow, and it was their good fortune to be present, by chance, under a confident and inspiring commander. On 9 October Nelson issued his well-known memorandum containing many of these concepts, which Fremantle mentioned to his brother: 'Lord Nelson has given us secret directions for coming into action if the Weather will allow of their being brought into effect, the event must be decisive.'[41] Nelson, acquainted with every stratum of British seamanship, knew that he could delegate because of the greater fitness and discipline of his seamen, and because of the superiority of their guns and rate of fire. He had to allow initiative if he was to achieve a decisive victory. He told George Rose that it was, after all, 'as Mr Pitt knows, annihilation that the Country wants, and not merely a splendid victory'.[42]

The most often-quoted phrase in the memorandum, 'No captain can do very wrong if he places his Ship alongside that of an Enemy', was both a statement and an instruction. It has been variously interpreted.[43] A long line of commentators have sensed a disdain on Nelson's part towards the French and Spanish warships; a recent historian interprets Nelson's approach to the battle as 'akin to the tactics of contempt'.[44] Nelson's aim was to get an overwhelming result and to get it quickly, within the hours of October daylight. From years of observation Nelson knew of the weaknesses of his enemies and felt able to give his captains the final assurance that he would support any move that led to close-quarter action. It is more likely, however, that this statement stemmed from a lack of knowledge of, and perhaps a lack of confidence in, most of his captains, and that this instruction contained the minimum that he expected from them. From the slow speed at which some of the tail-end ships were to come to action, he was right to suspect that they needed every encouragement.[45]

Not all his concepts were original. Dividing a large fleet into two or three divisions had been current for some years, as admirals had to control constantly growing fleets of increasingly larger ships. As far back as 1794, Lord Howe had written to his first captain: 'I cannot determine whether it would be more suitable to form the Body of the Fleet into two columns, with a detached squadron on the weather quarter; or in three columns.'[46] But Howe, of all people, would not have had the confidence in himself or the trust in others to allow the independence that Nelson gave to Collingwood. In 1797 Duncan had attacked the Dutch at Camperdown in two separate columns. Although the 'Order of Battle and Sailing', issued soon after the memorandum, positioned the *Victory* and the *Royal Sovereign* third in their divisions when sailing, the memorandum makes it clear that the flagships were to lead the fleet into battle.[47] This was indeed new, a measure of the faith that Nelson had in the heavy three-deckers, with the combination of their extra height, heavier guns and, not least, 68-pound carronades on the top decks.[48] Also new was an additional signal issued by Nelson, described as 'Signal Yellow with Blue Fly', which made it clear that each ship was to cut through the enemy's line.[49] The instruction for this signal ran thus:

The Ships being prepared are to make all possible sail (keeping their relative Bearings and close order) so that the whole may pass thro' the Enemy's line as quick as possible and at the same time. It is recommended to cut away the Studding sails if set, to prevent confusion and fire. Each ship will of course pass under the stern of the ship she is to engage, if circumstances permit . . . The Admiral will probably advance his Fleet to the van of theirs before he makes the Signal in order to deceive the Enemy by inducing them to suppose it is his intention to attack their Van.[50]

The plan was daring and exact. By confusing the enemy with a Feint towards the van of their fleet, Nelson intended to lessen the risk to the vulnerable bows of his ships as they approached.[51]

Opinions varied on whether the French and Spanish fleet would leave Cadiz. Fremantle was not confident, writing home to his brother: 'I have much doubt whether the french will ever leave Cadiz until the bad weather obliges us to quit the station . . . we shall soon want all manner of supplies which are not immediately found for so large a fleet.'[52] Another opinion was that the French would 'steal off by small squadrons' to Toulon.[53] For four days from 8 October the wind strength increased, with squalls and rain, giving some hope that the French and Spaniards would move.[54] On 10 October, at six in the morning, thirteen leagues west of Cadiz, Nelson wrote to Henry Blackwood, who had command of the inner squadron of five frigates, as well as the *Weazle* and *Pickle*, used for fast communication. Nelson urged: 'let me know every movement . . . we cannot miss getting hold of them and I will give them such a shaking as they never yet experienced.'[55] On the same day he issued an order to the respective captains: 'It is expected in fine weather that the Ships in Order of Sailing do not keep more than two cables length from each other.'[56] After 12 October, however, the wind fell light again, and Fremantle had not changed his mind: he wrote home on 13 October: '[Nelson] thinks the French fleet <u>must quit</u> Cadiz. I confess I am not of his Opinion.'[57]

Nelson had other reasons to think that he might prise the French and Spanish fleet out of Cadiz, including the new weapons that he had been discussing in London. Lord Castlereagh, the secretary of state for war, made plans for both Mr Francis and the rockets to go out to the fleet. Nelson's letter of 3 October to Castlereagh was guarded: 'I have little faith . . . the rockets must annoy their fleet very much; but I depend more upon hunger for driving them out, and upon the gallant officers and men under my command for their destruction, than any other invention.'[58] Some ten days later, however, he was more optimistic when he took Henry Blackwood into his confidence. 'I expect three stout fireships from England; then, with a good breeze . . . I should hope that, at least, the gentry might be disturbed, and I would not be surprised if Mr Francis and his catamarans were sent, and Colonel Congreve and his rockets. But keep all this to yourself, for officers will talk, and there is no occasion to put the enemy upon their guard. When these things arrive, we will consult how to manage them, and I will have the two bombs ready by that time.'[59]

Still Nelson and his fleet waited. Lacking a first captain of the fleet, Nelson became over-involved with administration, and provisioning and watering were as ever a constant problem. Orders flowed ceaselessly from the *Victory*, most dealing with minor matters such as accounting for provisions and stores.[60] On 2 October, Nelson sent Thomas Louis in the *Canopus* with four ships of the line and a frigate to provision and water, and to escort General Craig's transports deep into the Mediterranean, well beyond the Spanish squadron at Cartagena. Louis protested: 'I feared the Enemy wou'd come out while we were absent. His Reply, "Don't mind, Louis, they won't come out yet and my Fleet must be completed. The Sooner you go the better." '[61] On 9 October he wrote a long letter to Hugh Elliot in Naples, who was concerned that the *Excellent*, the guard ship moored in the bay, was to be withdrawn.[62] But Nelson's fleet was expanding rapidly: between 7 and 13 October it was reinforced by the 74s *Belleisle*, *Defiance* and *Leviathan*, and the 64s *Agamemnon* and *Africa*, but above all by the old *Royal Sovereign*, her three decks and hundred guns particularly welcome.[63] She joined from Plymouth after docking and a rapid refit, her copper sheathing renewed, ready for Collingwood's flag; but she also brought intelligence, confirmation that the French and Spanish combined fleet was directed to the Mediterranean to carry troops to relieve Naples.*

Although hunger was not of itself enough to force out the French and Spanish, their fleet was short of provisions, especially biscuit, and much else. The prices of bread and other provisions were high in Cadiz because of the British blockade. Earlier in 1805 yellow fever had swept along the

---

* Napoleon was countering the Anglo-Russian expedition against Naples. General Craig and his troops had finally reached Malta on 18 July (Mackesy, *Mediterranean*, 75–6).

southern coast of Spain, with many dying in the coastal towns and in the countryside; as a result the harvest was poor. Weak government finance was at the root of the problems of the Spanish Navy. As ever, it was chronically short of money, and, although the navy had recently renewed some of their guns, it generally lost out to the army when it came to resources. The Spanish officers and crew had not been paid for many months and morale was consequently low.[64] Villeneuve's problems, however, lay mainly in the sickliness of his crews. *Algésiras* (74), flagship of Rear-Admiral Magon Charles de Clos-Doré, for instance, had several hundred sick with scurvy, amounting to 37 per cent of the crew. Desertion rates were high.[65] Both Villeneuve and Gravina were conscious that the English fleet was stronger, not least in the preponderance of the heavy three-decked ships. The British had seven; the Spanish four; the French none, although they had some big two-deckers.*

The French and Spanish commands met on 8 October, as the wind got up, to consider how to respond to Napoleon's orders for the fleet to proceed to the Mediterranean.[66] The minutes of the meeting record that the officers 'unanimously recognise that the enemy fleet in the offing is much stronger than ours', and they decided to wait until the British fleet was forced off station by bad weather, 'or from the necessity that may force him to divide his forces in order to protect his commerce in the Mediterranean and the convoys that may be threatened by the squadrons of Cartagena and Toulon'.[67] For a week nothing happened. In that time, Admiral Villeneuve received two pieces of information that were to break the deadlock. The first was the news that Napoleon was sending Villeneuve's replacement, Vice-Admiral François Rosily, to Cadiz, the final insult after years of harassment and inept orders from the emperor. Rosily was now not far from Cadiz. Second, Villeneuve knew that Thomas Louis had sailed eastwards into the Mediterranean with four ships of the line, and two more were still at Gibraltar. For the first time the combined fleet might have a numerical edge.[68] For Villeneuve, it was his only chance to turn the tables on his enemy, who had held such advantage since the Battle of the Nile seven years before, and to redeem his and the French Navy's honour.

Nelson now became less confident that the enemy would leave harbour. He awaited the return of Louis and his six ships, which had reduced his fleet of thirty-three ships to twenty-seven. On 18 October the wind in Cadiz Harbour, which had been north-west, swung to the south-east. Nelson

---

* The three-deckers were the 100- and 98-gun ships: *Victory, Royal Sovereign, Britannia, Neptune, Prince, Dreadnought* and *Temeraire*.

wrote in his private journal: 'Fine weather, wind easterly ... the enemy cannot have finer weather to set sail.'[69] Collingwood's instinct was surer, for he felt they would sail; he wrote to Nelson on 18 October: 'It is very extraordinary the people in Cadiz do not make some movement. If they allow the war to begin in Italy, they cannot hereafter make up for the want of assistance they might give in the first instance.'[70]

On 18 October, at 5.15 p.m., Villeneuve flew the signal to unmoor; French and Spanish ships began to set sail from the harbour on the morning of 19 October. The wind again fell light; some of the French ships had to be towed out of the harbour, and the whole operation took a day and a half. Then the wind freshened from SSW, allowing the rest of the fleet to leave the harbour by the middle of the day on 20 October.[71] The inhabitants of Cadiz watched the fleet leave in total silence. They did not expect victory. They were to watch the dramatic events of the next few days with doubt and fear. The son of one of the captains in the Spanish fleet remembered, 'The numerous towers of Cadiz, and even the flat roofs where part of the sea could be seen, were packed with people, many of them with telescopes.'[72]

Early on 19 October, Nelson, fifty miles to the west, received a signal from the British observing frigates that the French and Spanish ships were preparing to come out of port. Codrington described the moment in a letter written at eight o'clock that evening: 'Lord Nelson had just hoisted his <u>dinner flag</u> to several captains at 9 o'clock this morning, when to my great astonishment he wore ship and made a signal for a general chase to windward. It was nearly calm, and has continued so ever since, till towards evening, but we now have a nice air, which fills our flying kites and drives us along four knots an hour.'[73] The fleet headed south-east. Nelson flew the signal to prepare for battle, expecting the enemy to sail immediately for the strait.

By the middle of the night, when Nelson was between Cape Trafalgar and Cape Spartel, he ordered the fleet to heave to. But at daybreak on 20 October the French and Spanish were nowhere to be seen. British hopes of an action again appeared frustrated. Now the British fleet was under close-reefed topsails 'in a very strong wind with rainy weather'.[74] The immediate fear was that the French and Spanish had returned to Cadiz. Nelson turned back to the north flying an 'Order of Sailing' signal. Not long after, a frigate of the inshore squadron, sent by Henry Blackwood, emerged from the grey horizon flying a signal that the enemy was at sea. At ten that morning Collingwood went on board the *Victory* for a two-hour meeting; also present were the captains of the *Mars*, the *Colossus* and the *Defence*, ships that had special responsibilities for managing the communications between the look-out frigates and the *Victory*.[75] By noon the fleet was twenty miles south-west of Cadiz. In the late afternoon, through another signal from Blackwood, it became clear that the enemy were heading westwards. Nelson entered into his private journal: 'At six o'clock the *Naiad* made the signal for 31 sail of the Enemy NNE.'[76]

John Brown, a 23-year-old Irish able seaman on board the *Victory*, recounted: 'Our look out Ship kept them in Sight all night and every time they wore she burned Blue lights for us to Wear.'[77] According to the surgeon William Beatty, in his *Authentic Narrative*, published in 1807, 'The Enemy wore twice during the night.'[78] But in his copy of the book, Collingwood wrote in the margin: 'I do not believe they ever wore – at 9 at night we were close to them, and when we made the Signal and wore they expecting to be attacked made the signal to prepare for battle, and were not then above 3 or 4 miles from the rear of our fleet.' Beatty's description continued: 'the French fleet's movements made Nelson apprehend that on seeing the British Fleet, they would effect their retreat ... He was, therefore, very careful not to approach their Fleet near enough to be seen by them before morning.' Collingwood wrote in his copy: 'They saw us, and we saw them in the day time.'[79] Villeneuve made it plain that he was confronting Nelson.

Beatty's *Narrative* continues: 'Nelson came upon deck soon after daylight: he was dressed as usual in his Admiral's frock-coat, bearing on the left breast four stars of different orders which he always wore with his common apparel.'[80] Lieutenant George Hewson of the *Royal Sovereign* found it awe-inspiring. 'The human mind cannot form a grander or more awful sight. The morning was remarkably fine, the sea perfectly smooth and the lightness of the wind allowed every sail to be spread.'[81] John Brown recounted: 'On Monday the 21st at day light the French and Spanish Fleets Was like a great wood on our lee bow which cheered the hearts of every british tar in the *Victory* like lions Anxious to be at it.' Both fleets began to form themselves into some sort of order. The combined fleet 'wore in succession about twenty minutes past seven o'clock'; they were now heading towards Cadiz, in line-of-battle formation with Gravina's squadron trying to join.[82] The wind was light south-westerly. A long swell rolled in from the west, the sign of a coming storm; it was to persist all day.[83]

On board the *Neptune* the signal lieutenant, Andrew Green, made his notes: 'At 6.15 the Admiral made the signal to form into two divisions. 6.30: To bear up for the enemy. 6.30: To Prepare for Battle.'[84] Studding sails were set. Officers' cabins were dismantled, messes stowed, surgeons set up their instruments, guns were made ready, rolled hammocks were fixed with netting to the gunwales to afford the crew some protection from musket and pistol fire. In the *Victory* the boatswain William Willmet ordered the hens and turkey coops thrown overboard.[85] At 7.35 the signal was made for 'The captains of the frigates to go on board the *Victory*.' According to Beatty, Nelson 'displayed excellent spirits, and expressed his pleasure at the prospect of giving a fatal blow to the Naval power of France and Spain; and spoke with confidence of obtaining a signal Victory notwithstanding the inferiority of the British fleet, declaring to Captain Hardy, that "he would not be contented with capturing less than twenty Sail of the Line." '[86]

The approach of the two fleets in the light wind was agonizingly slow, the ships not making more than one and a half knots.[87] Nelson's twenty-seven ships, approximately 17,000 men and 2,148 guns faced Villeneuve's thirty-three ships, some 30,000 seamen and soldiers and 2,632 guns.[88] The British fleet, as planned, split into two divisions.* Their slow pace would extend the time when their bows would be exposed to the fire of the waiting enemy. For Nelson there was much to reflect on. He went to his largely dismantled cabin. Pasco witnessed him writing on his knees, there being no chairs. Reflecting his nervous tension, Nelson wrote a prayer of great power in his private journal, as he had done when he left Merton, its sombre, rolling phrases so different to his usual open, practical prose.[89] With the French and Spanish fleet ten miles away, he wrote a codicil to his will, leaving Emma as 'a Legacy to my King and Country' and Horatia 'to the beneficence of my Country', and asked Blackwood and Hardy to witness it.[90] It was a final attempt to get Emma a pension, at which he had so far been signally unsuccessful, to provide for her should he not survive the coming battle.

Little time remained for private affairs, and he remained in his cabin for only a few minutes.[91] Blackwood and the frigate captains had to be briefed.

---

* In the van division, in order of sailing: *Victory* (100), Nelson, Captain Thomas Masterman Hardy; *Temeraire* (98), Eliab Harvey; *Neptune* (98), Thomas Fremantle; *Leviathan* (74), Henry Bayntun; *Conqueror* (74), Israel Pellew; *Britannia* (100), Rear-Admiral the earl of Northesk, Charles Bullen; *Ajax* (74), Lieutenant John Pilford (in the absence of Captain William Brown); *Orion* (74), Edward Codrington; *Minotaur* (74), Charles Mansfield; *Spartiate* (74), Francis Laforey; *Agamemnon* (64), Edward Berry; *Africa* (64), Henry Digby.

In the rear division: *Royal Sovereign* (100), Collingwood, Captain Edward Rotheram; *Belleisle* (74), William Hargood; *Mars* (74), George Duff; *Tonnant* (80), Charles Tyler; *Bellerophon* (74), John Cooke; *Colossus* (74), James Morris; *Achille* (74), Richard King; *Revenge* (74), Robert Moorsom; *Defiance* (74), Philip Durham; *Dreadnought* (98), John Conn; *Swiftsure* (74), William Rutherford; *Polyphemus* (64), Robert Redmill; *Defence* (74), George Hope; *Thunderer* (74), Lieutenant John Stockham (in the absence of William Lechmere); *Prince* (98), Richard Grindall.

Frigates: *Euryalus* (36), Henry Blackwood; *Naiad* (38), Thomas Dundas; *Phoebe* (36), Thomas Capel; *Sirius* (36), William Prowse.

Cutters: *Pickle*, John Richards Lapenotiere; *Entreprenante*, Robert Young.

Then he went round the ship. 'He addressed the crew at their several quarters,' Beatty wrote, 'and admonished them against firing a single shot without being sure of their object.'[92] As John Brown remembered: 'So we cleared away our guns whilst Lord Nelson went round the decks and said, My noble lads, this will be a glorious day for England who ever lives to see it. I Shant be Satisfied with 12 Ships this day I took at the Nile. So we piped to dinner and ate a bit of raw pork and half a pint of Wine.'[93]

Nelson signalled for the ships to form up astern of the *Victory* and the *Royal Sovereign*. He was moving towards the head of the combined fleet. At 10.50 Nelson signalled to the *Royal Sovereign*: 'It is my intention to pass through the Enemy's line and prevent them getting into Cadiz.' At 11.40, only a quarter of an hour before the first gunfire, he sent the famous signal: 'England expects that every man will do his duty.'* He followed it only four minutes later: 'Prepare to Anchor during the ensuing night'; then Signal No. 16, 'Engage the Enemy more closely.' Only a few minutes before the French opened fire, Blackwood left the *Victory* with Nelson's last-minute instructions for the rest of the fleet.

The French and Spanish ships were strung out across the course of two divisions, with the ships of both nations mixed within each division.† Admiral Villeneuve, with his flag in the *Bucentaur*, was eleventh in the line, just astern of the enormous Spanish 140-gun *Santissima Trinidad*. Gravina, the Spanish commander-in-chief, his flag in the *Principe de Asturias* of 112 guns, commanded the 'Squadron of Observation', the other side of the main line of enemy warships, to be used as a strategic reserve. The two British divisions sailed slowly towards the line. The newly coppered *Royal Sovereign*, abreast of the *Victory*, raced ahead of the flagship. She was

---

* Lieutenant John Pasco, the senior lieutenant in the *Victory*, acted as signal lieutenant and the story that Nelson first thought of 'England confides that every man will do his duty' emerged from his evidence given to Sir Harris Nicolas. As there was little time before the beginning of the action, Pasco suggested that 'expects' should be used instead of 'confides', for it would be quicker: one of Popham's numeral flags would transmit the word, and there would be no need to spell out each letter. 'That will do, Pasco, make it directly,' was Nelson's reply (Nicolas, VII, 150).

† The French and Spanish ships were in mixed divisions:

The van: *Neptuno* (84); *Scipion* (74); *Intrépide* (74); *Formidable* (80), Rear-Admiral Dumanoir; *Mont-Blanc* (74); *Duguay Trouin* (74); *Rayo* (100); *San Francisco de Asis* (74).

The centre: *San Agustin* (74); *Heros* (74); *Santissima Trinidad* (140), Rear-Admiral Cisneros; *Bucentaur* (80), Admiral Villeneuve; *Neptune* (80); *San Leandro* (64); *Redoutable* (74); *San Justo* (74); *Indomptable* (80); *Santa Ana* (112); *Fougueux* (74); *Monarca* (74); *Pluton* (74).

'Squadron of Observation': *Algésiras* (74), Rear-Admiral Magon; *Bahama* (74); *Aigle* (74); *Montanez* (74); *Swiftsure* (74); *Argonaute* (74); *Argonauta* (80); *San Ildefonso* (74); *Achille* (74); *Principe de Asturias* (112), Admiral Gravina; *Berwick* (74); *San Juan Nepomuceno* (74).

closely followed by the *Belleisle*, the *Mars* and the *Tonnant*, leading the rear division into action before Nelson in the van. Behind the *Victory* were the *Temeraire* and the *Neptune*. To the watching French and Spanish, it seemed that the British ships were in an untidy straggle.

The French and Spanish line was itself far from tidy. 'They lay in a half moon and going in two divisions towards them, For we formed no line,' wrote John Brown on board the *Victory*, describing the final approach. 'When coming close to the enemy beat to quarters, got our guns double shotted to give them a doce and all ready for Action, when the four-decker fired a broadside into us before We could get a gun to bear on them.'[94] On board the *Orion*, Codrington recalled, 'We all scrambled into battle as soon as we could, and I believe have done our best *in imitation* of the *noble example* before us.'[95] George Hewson thought that 'the enemy . . . seemed rather disconcerted at our mode of attack and not able to penetrate our designs.'[96] At 11.50 Blackwood in the *Euryalus* sailed past the *Neptune*, stationed behind the *Victory*, to shout out instructions to Thomas Fremantle: 'It was the Commander-in-Chief's intention to cut through the enemy about their 13 or 14 ship, then to make sail on the Larbd. Tack for their Van.'

Six minutes later, at 11.56, the French opened fire on Collingwood's ship. Then Villeneuve ran up his flag, and Nelson knew that the French commander-in-chief was in the *Bucentaur* in the centre of the French line. From his course towards the van, Nelson turned head-on in the direction of Villeneuve's flagship. Collingwood's approach was more oblique. Lieutenant Green, aboard the *Neptune*, noted: At '12.[0]5 The *Royal Sovereign* most nobly began to fire and passed through the Enemy's line under the stern of the *Santa Ana*.'[97]

During this phase of the battle the *Victory*, holding her fire, conserving both her ammunition and the energy of her crew, came in for her worst casualties. They were minutes of taut nerves and iron discipline. Twenty men were killed and thirty wounded before the *Victory* fired a shot. John Scott, standing close to Nelson, was cut in pieces by a cannon ball almost immediately, as was Hardy's eighteen-year-old secretary, Thomas Whipple. 'A double-headed shot struck one of the parties of marines on the poop, and killed eight of them.'[98] The steering wheel was shot away, forcing the master, Thomas Atkinson, to rig a tackle to bring the rudder under control. Picking his way slowly through the smoke and the broadsides, Hardy managed to sail the ship through a gap in the wall of French and Spanish ships bunched around the French flagship for her defence.[99] At 12.10 the *Victory's* 68-pounder carronade on the forecastle, 'containing its customary

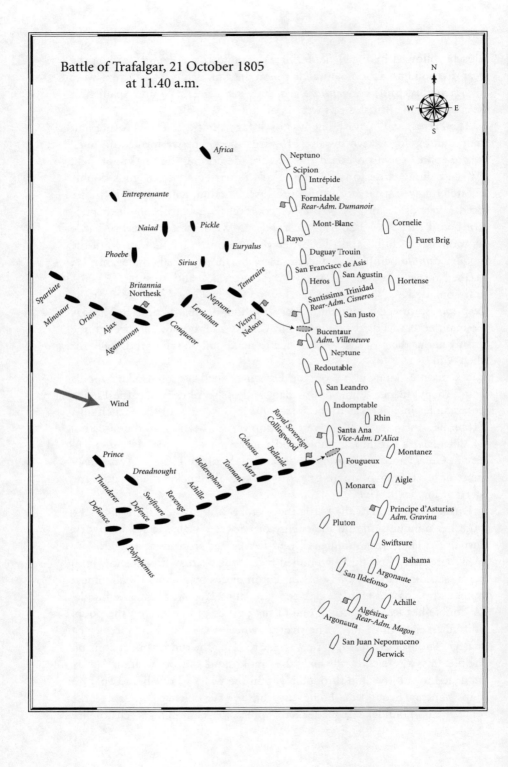

Battle of Trafalgar, 21 October 1805
at 11.40 a.m.

charge of one round shot and a keg filled with 500 musket balls', fired into the stern of the *Bucentaur*.[100] The double-shotted broadside from the *Victory* that followed, raking into the French flagship, was devastating. On the *Victory*'s upper deck it appeared to a young second lieutenant of marines that 'every man appeared a devil'. In the excitement of the action, the marines had thrown off their red jackets: 'in their checked shirts and blue trousers, there was no distinguishing Marine from seaman . . . all were working like horses.'[101]

Twenty minutes after the *Royal Sovereign* opened fire, 'The whole Fleet came up in turn and the Action begun General.'[102] Further up the enemy line, the *Victory* drifted apart from the stricken *Bucentaur*, and was attacked at very close range by the *Redoutable*. The rigging of both ships became hooked together. When the *Victory*'s guns were run out, their muzzles touched the *Redoutable*'s sides.[103] The *Redoutable*'s captain, Jean-Jacques Lucas, brought his crew up to the upper deck; armed with muskets and hand weapons, they had abandoned their guns below in a determined rush to board the upper deck of the *Victory*. Exchange of fire and hand-to-hand fighting was at its most desperate. 'The carnage on the deck of the *Victory* became terrific,' Alexander Scott later reported. The 12-pound guns on her upper deck were only lightly manned because of the slaughter, and the flagship could well have been boarded successfully by the crew of the *Redoutable*. Some were mown down by another supremely destructive blast from the 68-pound carronade on the *Victory*'s starboard forecastle.[104] Then the tables were turned by the arrival of the *Temeraire*, which had come into the action just behind the *Victory*: she ran into the other side of the *Redoutable* and attacked her. The *Victory*'s moment of danger passed.

At the height of this crisis, at 1.15, Nelson was hit in the shoulder by a musket bullet fired from high in the mizzen top of the *Redoutable*. His shoulder was shattered, and the bullet passed through his spine. He knew from the moment he was struck that the wound was fatal,[105] saying, 'Hardy, I believe they have done it at last.'[106] Two sailors took him to the cockpit far down on the orlop deck, where William Beatty was treating the wounded. Nelson was undressed and covered with a sheet.[107]

'He lived about three hours after receiving his wound,' Alexander Scott wrote later, 'perfectly sensible the whole time.'[108] It was a slow and painful death in the dark cockpit, lit only by lanterns, against a backdrop of deafening gunfire, the cries of the wounded, the shouts and the cheers of the *Victory*'s crew whenever a French ship struck – a poignant scene much described.[109] But he was surrounded by friends and close colleagues. The sensitive Scott, who earlier had retreated from the horrors of the wounded in the cockpit, which he later described as 'like a butcher's shambles', never left Nelson's side. With him were William Burke, the purser, and William Chevallier, his steward. Hardy came down from the battle twice. William Beatty, the surgeon, attended him, although Beatty was continually called away, as many others needed treatment. Beatty soon established the seriousness of the wound. Nelson complained of 'pulsations' in his chest and no feeling in the lower part of his body, although his left shoulder was not paralysed.[110] Of the musket ball he said, 'I felt it break my back.' His pulse was weak. Pain and discomfort 'compelled him to speak in broken sentences, which pain and suffering prevented him from connecting'.[111] Beatty told him honestly: 'My Lord, unhappily for our country nothing can be done for you.'[112]

Nelson alternated between calm and agitation. He was given lemonade and water. His most pressing anxiety was that the fleet, on a lee shore, should anchor, and he had flown a signal to this effect before a gun was fired.[113] Hardy was sent for but could not come immediately. The young midshipman Richard Bulkeley came with a message; Nelson said, 'Remember me to your father.' When Hardy still did not come, according to Scott, Nelson again became anxious, 'exclaiming aloud he would not believe he was alive, unless he saw him . . . lamented his being unable to go on deck, and do what was to be done . . . At last the Captain came, and he instantly became more composed, listened to his report about the state of the fleet.'[114] Beatty recorded Nelson's words with Hardy. ' "Well, Hardy, how goes the battle?" – "Very well, My Lord," replied Captain Hardy, "we have got twelve or fourteen of the Enemy's Ships in our possession . . ." – "I hope," said His Lordship, "none of *our* Ships have struck, Hardy." – "No, my Lord, there is no fear of that." '[115] And then Nelson said: 'I am a dead man, Hardy. Come nearer to me. Pray let my dear Lady Hamilton have my hair, and all other things belonging to me.' Hardy returned on deck. Nelson became calm, and confessed to Scott. 'I have not been a great sinner' is all that Scott told the world. Nelson talked of his last worries about Emma and Horatia; his friend George Rose at the Treasury would be Emma's best hope for receiving a pension. Hardy returned some fifty minutes after his first visit, but he prevaricated when Nelson urged him to anchor.* He congratulated Nelson

---

* In view of the ferocity of the storm that followed, it is difficult to calculate whether Nelson's order to anchor the fleet was the correct one. While shallow enough for anchors, the waters around Cape Trafalgar are too exposed for them to have held; it can also be assumed that many anchors and cables were damaged. Edward Codrington, however, had few doubts when he wrote to Lord Garlies: '[Nelson] made the signal to anchor, and had Admiral Collingwood acted upon that hint we might now have secured all our prizes' (Bourchier, I, 71, 4 Nov. 1805).

'on his brilliant victory, which was complete; though he did not know how many of the Enemy were captured, as it was impossible to perceive every Ship distinctly. He was certain however of fourteen or fifteen having surrendered. His Lordship answered, "that is well, but I had bargained for twenty."'[116] Scott, in his account, included some dialogue:

'I shall die, Hardy,' said the Admiral.
'Is your pain great, sir?'
'Yes, but I shall live half an hour yet – Hardy, kiss me.' The Captain knelt down by his side and kissed him.[117]

Unable to move, Nelson felt the sensation and touch of another human being. According to Beatty, Hardy 'kissed him on the cheek, [and] his Lordship said, "Now I am satisfied. Thank God, I have done my duty." Captain Hardy stood for a minute or two in silent contemplation: he knelt down again, and kissed his Lordship's forehead. His Lordship said: "Who is that?" The Captain answered: "It is Hardy"; to which his Lordship replied, "God Bless you, Hardy!"' Two years later Hardy remembered that Nelson's last words to him were: 'Do be kind to poor Lady Hamilton.'[118]

A quarter of an hour after Hardy left the cockpit for the second time, Nelson became quiet. The watchers at first thought he was asleep, but Chevallier fetched Beatty. In Beatty's words, he 'expired without a struggle'.[119] Nelson died at about 4.30 of acute blood loss into his chest, exacerbated by spinal shock.[120] By this time the guns were silent.[121]

The news of Nelson's death spread round the fleet. Exhausted officers and seamen felt an overwhelming sense of sadness and loss, unable to reconcile the completeness of the victory with the loss of their much loved commander-in-chief. On board the *Victory* a boatswain's mate was so overcome that he was unable to pipe the men to quarters.[122] Captains visited each other for comfort. Edward Codrington, in the *Orion*, told his wife: 'Poor Hardy has just been here . . . I feel for him more, perhaps, than our short acquaintance justifies.'[123] The day after the battle two emotional letters were written on board the *Euryalus*. Henry Blackwood sent a long, distressed letter to his wife: 'in my life I never was so shocked or completely upset as upon my flying to the *Victory*, even before the Action was over, to find Lord Nelson was then at the gasp of death . . . such an Admiral has the Country lost, and every officer and man so kind, so good, so obliging a friend as never was. Thank God, he lived to know that such Victory . . . never before was gained.'[124] Cuthbert Collingwood, now in command of the fleet and aboard a frigate because of damage to the *Royal Sovereign*, wrote his dispatch to the Admiralty, his official language heightened by emotion: 'The ever-to-be-lamented death . . . but my heart is rent with the most poignant grief for the death of a friend, to whom by many years intimacy and a perfect knowledge of the virtues of his mind, which inspired ideas superior to the common race of men, I was bound by the strongest ties of affection.'[125]

Nelson had delivered to William Pitt his longed-for battle of annihilation. Over the three days of the battle and the ensuing storm the French lost ten ships and the Spanish ten; the British lost none. The victors, however, took only four prizes. The other French and Spanish ships were wrecked, or foundered, or were destroyed by the British.[126] Two weeks later four ships of the line under Admiral Dumanoir, the remnants of the van, battered by the weather and leaky, were ruthlessly chased and caught in the Bay of Biscay by Sir Richard Strachan. In a brilliant postscript to the main battle, and less well known because of it, all four French ships put up a hard fight; all four struck.[127] It brought to an end a disastrous period for Napoleon and his allies. Before Trafalgar and Strachan's action, the battleship tonnage strength of Britain and her enemies was even. By the end of 1805 Britain had a comfortable superiority over France, Spain and the Netherlands combined.*

Nelson's tactics – confusing the enemy by his feint, isolating the van, using his three-deckers to penetrate the French line – had been successful. The victory was achieved by superior British guns and gunpowder, and by more accurate and faster gunnery. The British had the considerable advantage of the gunlock, the flint-musket mechanism that produced the spark to fire the British guns; this was more exact than the slowmatch of the French, whereby the gunner had to allow delay when aiming his gun. A report to Decrès, the French minister of marine, from the army officer in command of the troops noted that 'the swell took our ships abeam, made them roll heavily and rendered our aim uncertain'.[128] Perhaps the greatest margin of superiority was provided by officers more experienced and crews more disciplined than those of the French and Spanish. 'Ship for ship the British fleet had a clear advantage.'[129]

---

* France and Spain lost twenty-three battleships totalling almost 70,000 tons, of which Britain added eight ships of 23,000 tons to her own navy. In mid 1805 each side had about 330,000 tons each; by the end of the year Britain had 570,000 over the 360,000 tons of France, Spain and the Netherlands (Glete, II, 378). Even so, the comptroller of the Navy Board was concerned about the condition of the fleet: 'he hopes we shall be able to go another year without feeling the loss of our prizes' (Buckingham and Chandos, 448, Thomas Grenville to the marquis of Buckingham).

Total British casualties were 449 killed and 1,241 wounded, with the *Victory*, the *Royal Sovereign*, the *Colossus*, the *Bellerophon* and the *Temeraire* all sustaining over a hundred killed and wounded. The French and Spanish lost perhaps ten times this number.[130] On the *Bucentaur* alone over 200 were killed and wounded.[131] Blackwood reported on the dazed Villeneuve, now a prisoner. 'Admiral Villeneuve is at my elbow, on board the *Euryalus* (whilst I am writing this), and is all amazement, and cannot comprehend how it has happened.'[132]

The scale of the victory, however, masked some deficiencies, for Trafalgar was far from perfect.[133] Nelson's tactics had isolated the van of the Franco-Spanish fleet, and pitted his twenty-seven ships against twenty-three or twenty-four of the enemy. As Blackwood left the *Victory* at the start of the action, Nelson asked him to tell the captains of the British ships 'that he depended upon their exertions; and that if, by the mode of the attack prescribed, they found it impractical to get into Action immediately, they might adopt whatever they thought best, provided it led them quickly and closely alongside an Enemy.'[134] But not all ships got close to the enemy. From the evidence of their logs it is clear that the earl of Northesk in the *Britannia* and John Conn in the *Dreadnought* opened fire too early. Others criticized John Cooke in the *Bellerophon* and Edward Berry in the *Agamem-non*, who blazed away and wasted ammunition long before their shot could have any effect; the same could be said for both the inexperienced lieutenants, John Pilford in the *Ajax* and John Stockham in the *Thun-derer*.[135] Trafalgar was a victory that could have been more complete.

Nelson's death put paid to any undignified bickering among admirals and captains, and Collingwood stifled any criticism. Edward Codrington wrote to his wife: 'I hope we shall hear of no jealousies and reproaches amongst one another, although I fear it is impossible to avoid it.'[136] Letters from the lower deck, however, show that some ill feeling between ships existed, even if their judgements on others were harsh and inaccurate. John Brown of the *Victory* wrote home: 'Out of 27, and 3 sixty-fours among them and only 14 of us to come into action. There is some of our ships to be Kept out of the Land for 7 years for not coming into Action. There Was the most of our heavy Ships sculk't away and the poor little 64 come into action. There is the *Prince* 98 had nobody Killed or Wounded.'[137] A seaman of the *Temeraire* thought little of the *Neptune*, which 'was but of little Service . . . She might as well been laying in Cawsand Bay. I believe they are sent up the Mediterranean as punishment.'[138]

No criticism could be laid at the *Victory*. In the four hours and twenty minutes of firing, she expended a total of 3,041 shot. Her heaviest guns, the 32-pounders, fired 997 shot, the 24-pounders 872, the 12-pounders 800.* As she was engaged on both sides, this implies that an average rate of fire of seven shots an hour per gun was achieved, although the seamen made a greater effort and fired at a faster rate at the start of the battle.† Only 186 double-headed shells were fired; this shot, which was primarily used against rigging and personnel, was of little value in a close engagement. Seven and a half tons of powder were expended, three tons of junk in wads, 3,000 musket balls, 1,000 pistol.[139] She lost seventeen sails, her three mizzenmasts and all their yards, hundreds of yards of ropes and rigging.[140] In his log Thomas Atkinson, the master, noted fifty-four men killed, twenty-five dangerously wounded, twelve badly wounded and forty-two slightly wounded.[141] Marine casualties were high, with twenty dead, including Captain Charles Adair. The young Irish lieutenant William Ram died, as did Quartermaster Thomas Johnson and Midshipman Alexander Palmer. John Pasco, the signal lieutenant, was wounded; Midshipman Rivers, the son of William Rivers, the gunner, lost his foot. The seamen who were killed came from, among other places, Shetland, Sunderland, Deptford, Dublin, Mevagissey, Peterhead, Carmarthen and even Geneva; it was not only London that was to grieve.[142] They were all from the upper deck. Alexander Scott later commented: 'On the quarter-deck, poop and forecastle the slaughter was immense; on the other decks, comparatively nothing; on the lower deck only two wounded, and strange to tell, by musket balls.'[143]

The survivors of the battle, in their battered ships, now had to face a storm of unusual ferocity that lasted several days, the wind from the southwest. By 8 a.m. on 22 October gales and rain struck the fleet. The rain and strong wind persisted through the next day. On the 24th there was a respite, but the wind returned on the 25th and the 26th with even greater force. One meteorologist has recently estimated that at its height the gale 'reached force 10, even 11 is . . . highly probable'.[144] Several used the word 'hurricane', including Edward Codrington: 'the most violent hurricane I was ever in . . . For an hour and a half or two hours we dare not attempt to set even a storm stay sail, although within six miles of a lee shore where we must have been lost'; he was prepared to cut away the *Orion*'s masts and to take his chance with the anchor.[145] The *Victory* lost her main yard on the 25th. The next day Hardy noted in the log: 'the ship laboured very much.'[146] The

---

* These figures from the gunner's accounts did not include 68-pound shot from the large carronades, which were additional to the *Victory*'s establishment of a hundred guns.
† The insoluble problem in calculating the average rate of fire during the battle is to establish when the ship ceased firing. Nevertheless, this rate of fire compares well with what statistics are available for the eighteenth century (Rodger, *Command of the Ocean*, 540–41).

Royal Sovereign's foremast went overboard. The crew rigged a jury-foremast and, with 300 French and Spanish prisoners on board, she slowly crept towards Gibraltar.[147]

Former enemies helped each other. The boats of the *Naiad* frigate rescued 190 men from *L'Achille*, just before she blew up with 300 wounded on board, although hundreds of Frenchmen and Spaniards were killed and drowned.[148] The generosity of the Spanish civilians and authorities was remarkable. The governor of Cadiz offered Collingwood the use of Cadiz Hospital for the British wounded. Spanish civilians cared for British prize crews wrecked on their shores. The Spanish wounded were landed.[149] Prisoners had to be transferred from ship to ship. The *Orion* found herself with an extra hundred men from British ships, as well as 580 French and Spanish prisoners, victualling 1,200 men in all on 29 October.[150] William Rivers recorded that the *Pickle* cutter put nineteen Frenchmen aboard the flagship, as well as 'the Wife of [the] Se[r]jant Major of the *Achille* . . . give her a Pair of Trousers and a Shirt, she did not seem to be the least Conserned . . . she employed her self working her Hair up for the Watch String for the Officers. Having Players on board the *Victory* give her all the Female Dresses.'*[151]

British frigates, sloops and cutters worked ceaselessly. Many anonymous feats of seamanship kept every British ship safe.† The *Naiad* frigate, for instance, towed the *Belleisle* immediately after the battle, but the tow parted when the wind got up again. The two ships collided when they tried to pass another tow rope, after which they lost contact. Then the *Naiad* saw 'the *Belleisle* very near the Shore off Trafalgar seemingly in a perilous situation' and this time managed a successful tow, bringing her to Gibraltar. 'Cast off *Belleisle*'s tow Rope & cam to an anchor in Gibraltar Bay, was received with a feu de joy & Three cheers all Round the Garrison, and that Night an illumination took place in Consequence of the Glorious Action and Victory.'[152]

But in truth there was little cheering. After the storm, an Englishman in Cadiz watched a horrifying stream of dead and wounded Spaniards brought ashore. When he could stand it no longer, he walked out of the town:

As far as the eye could reach, the sandy side of the isthmus bordering on the Atlantic was covered with masts and yards, the wrecks of ships, and here and there the body

---

* Amateur theatricals were encouraged on board some ships.
† The Spanish thought that the reason why the British ships survived the storm was the greater efficiency of their double-action pumps (Zulueta, 313).

of the dead ... I mounted on the cross-trees of a mast which had been thrown ashore, and casting my eyes over the ocean, beheld, at a great distance, several masts and portions of wreck still floating about. As the sea was almost calm, with a slight swell, the effect produced by these objects had in it something of a sublime melancholy, and touched the soul with a remembrance of the sad vicissitudes of human affairs.[153]

The *Neptune* towed the *Victory* to Gibraltar. At seven in the evening on 28 October, with the weather 'fresh breezes and cloudy', the battered flagship anchored in the tiny Rosia Bay, where she was dwarfed by the heights of the Rock. The next morning five able seamen and one ordinary seaman, all under twenty-five, were each given thirty-six lashes for 'contempt and disobedience'. John Matthews was from New York and Richard Collins from Philadelphia; two were from Wales, William Stanford from Brecon and Charles Waters from Monmouth; Michael Griffiths was from Waterford, Ireland, and John Walland from Holland.[154] These men had fought in the most decisive naval battle in modern times, had struggled through a week of violent storms in a leaky and battered ship; but nothing stopped the remorseless discipline of the Royal Navy.

V

The Transfiguration

30

The Funeral

9 January 1806

The Mob assembled here is so very numerous & tumultuous that it is absolutely necessary that your Lordship should apply for a very <u>strong</u> party of Cavalry to line the street on each side from Deptford Bridge to the entrance of the Hospital & to attend the other Gates early on Wednesday morning or it will not be possible for the procession to move from hence – the Mob consisted yesterday of upwards of 30,000 & equally so today and more outrageous – Townsend & the other peace officers say they never saw anything like it before.

Lord Hood, governor of Greenwich Hospital to Lord Hawkesbury, home secretary, 6 January 1806[1]

On 22 October the *Pickle* cutter, commanded by Lieutenant Lapenotiere, took back Collingwood's dispatch reporting the battle to England. The commander-in-chief also ordered that 'a day should be organised of general humiliation before God and thanksgiving' throughout the fleet.[2] One by one the British ships came to anchor off Gibraltar Bay, one of the last being the *Royal Sovereign* on 3 November. Plans were already afoot for a monument to Nelson. In the *Orion* Edward Codrington entered into his log: 'The officers and ship's company being assembled, the Captain read the proposal of the admiral to them that two thousand pounds should be deducted from the prize money of the action on 21 of October, which the officers and ship's company agreed to, and as much as it required.' Codrington added a note: 'The people thought it too little.'[3] On 4 November a patched and battered *Victory*, fitted with jurymasts, embarked her wounded from the hospital ashore and sailed for England with Nelson's body on board in a cask filled with spirits of wine (now known as pure alcohol), which had replaced the brandy in the cask in which he had been placed soon after the battle.[4]

The mood in London before the news of the victory had been dejected and the political establishment remained bitterly divided; Napoleon's victorious progress on the Continent was not to be halted. Lady Elizabeth Foster reported: 'Could anything be done against the Combined Fleet, it would rouse the spirits of the country, which are quite depressed. I have seen nothing like the present moment. You hear nothing else from the drawing room to the steward's room, in every street, and road, and lane; as you walk you hear Bonaparte's name in every mouth.'[5] One veteran politician wrote to Lord Auckland: 'Unless something extraordinary happens, I shall consider the game as up.'[6]

Lieutenant Lapenotiere arrived with the dispatches at the Admiralty at one o'clock in the morning on 6 November. Even the sick and world-weary William Pitt, long used to bad and good news at any time of the day or night, could not 'calm his thoughts, but at length got up, though it was three in the morning'.[7] Lord Barham wrote immediately to Fanny, but his sense of Evangelical rectitude prevented a letter to Emma, so he deputed the comptroller of the navy, Sir Andrew Snape Hamond, to write to her.[8] Collingwood's sombre and dignified dispatch was rushed out in a *London Gazette Extraordinary* and reprinted in every newspaper the next day. The emotional reaction was immediate. Old Admiral Lord Bridport, Lord Hood's brother, admitted that 'I read Vice-Admiral Collingwood's letter with tears in my eyes.'[9] Lady Elizabeth Foster arrived at the Admiralty: 'it was crowded, but every countenance was dejected – nor could one have guessed that it was a victory of twenty ships of the line taken from the enemy, only that defeat would have caused tumult, and this was the silence of sorrow and respect. We were shown into Mr. Marsden's room. He was oppressed with the contradictory feelings of triumph for the country, and sorrow for the loss of the greatest hero we ever had, and his friend. As we came away there was a vast rush of people, but all silent.'[10] When the news arrived in Naples, Samuel Taylor Coleridge was walking in the street: 'and never can I forget the sorrow and consternation that lay on every countenance . . . Numbers stopped and shook hands with me, because they had seen the tears on my cheek, and conjectured, that I was an Englishman; and several, as they held my hand, burst, themselves, into tears.'[11] Politicians took a more pragmatic view. 'The news from Cadiz came like a cordial to a fainting man,' Lord Auckland wrote to a political colleague. 'Nelson is a great loss (I shall not say irreparable) in such times.'[12]

There is no doubting the widespread sense of loss throughout the country. *Bell's Weekly Register* reflected the joy and sorrow: 'The triumph of their arms has been attended with nothing noisy and intoxicating . . . the conduct of the people has been truly manly and decent. With such an oppression as the loss of NELSON upon their heads they could scarcely rejoice – with such a victory achieved by their arms they could scarcely refrain from exultation. This mixed feeling, therefore, has produced something characteristic of itself . . . it is seen on every countenance.'[13] In London, according to Lady Elizabeth Foster, 'Illuminations followed, but the first night, as if unable to rejoice, there were none seen but on public buildings. The next two nights they were general, but chiefly transparencies or mottos relating to the "dear departed hero". Nelson was the only person I ever saw who excited real enthusiasm in the English. Every day makes his victory more precious.'[14] Lady Bessborough commented: 'Almost everybody wears a black crêpe scarf or cockade with Nelson written on it – this is almost general high and low; indeed, the enthusiasm is general beyond anything I ever saw.'[15] Newspaper editors struggled for sufficiently solemn phrases, loyal addresses were composed to the Crown from every conceivable body, Lloyd's Patriotic Fund was unprecedented in its generosity to the combatants. A 'Loyal Musical Impromptu, "Nelson's Glory"', followed the play at the Theatre Royal, Covent Garden. Ten days later the mood had steadied: 'silver favours with black in the centre' were being worn.[16]

By 11 November the king had approved a state funeral. Nelson's will specified that he wished to be buried in Burnham Thorpe, 'unless His Majesty shall signify it to be his pleasure that my body shall be interred elsewhere'.[17] The king wrote to Pitt that the will 'enabled directions to be given for his being buried at St Paul's with military honours, which the brilliancy of the victory seems to call for'.[18] The next day Lord Hawkesbury wrote to William Nelson, who had now been raised to an earldom, that 'in consequence of the shortness of the days, to go through the whole ceremony on one day in a manner suitable to the solemnity of the occasion, that the body be brought by water from Greenwich to Whitehall stairs, and deposited in the Admiralty for that night and should proceed on the ensuing day by land through the Strand and Fleet Street to St Pauls.'[19]

On 6 December the *Victory* arrived at Spithead. The voyage had taken four weeks, for the winds had been contrary and strong, and the ship slow and labouring. Before she passed through the Channel fleet off Brest she had accepted a tow from the 74-gun *Warrior*.[20] At Spithead, Nelson's body was taken from the cask of spirits and embalmed. Beatty extracted the musket ball. The spirits of wine had only partially preserved the body. Nelson was unrecognizable. The young midshipman Richard Bulkeley wrote a letter that evening: 'his body is complete, but his countenance is entirely altered, nor could I perceive any remaining feature that could call him to my recollection, but his upper lip.'[21] The body was placed in a lead coffin, filled with 'brandy holding in solution, camphor and myrrh'.[22] The *Victory* made her way up the Channel on the same day, pausing at Dover for four days for more favourable tides, and then through the Downs, before she moored in the Swin in the Thames estuary on 23 December.[23]

By this time the government and the College of Heralds were making elaborate arrangements for a state funeral, a heraldic ritual of medieval origin, rich in aristocratic precedent, now to be adapted for a commoner.[24] It was a ceremony that was enacted so infrequently that subtle changes of precedent were easily achieved. As Nelson was to be interred in St Paul's, the City's cathedral, complications and arrangements took days to negotiate with the lord mayor of London, discussions that generated high feeling between government and the City.[25] The expectations of the public were fully outlined in the press. Though the king would not attend, the princes, the peers of the realm and the officers of state would be part of the procession.

With the news of the overwhelming French victory over the Austrians at Austerlitz reaching London by mid December, the government decided that the funeral needed to have maximum political impact. Symbolically the navy was to replace the family at the service. It was decided very early that the chief mourner should be either the admiral of the fleet, Sir Peter Parker, or Lord Barham, rather than the heir of the deceased, as decreed by long tradition; the newly ennobled William Nelson was never considered for the position of honour.[26] The assistant mourners were to be senior naval officers, while the pall-bearers and other ceremonial roles were also to be taken by naval officers rather than officers of the College of Heralds. All admirals in attendance were to wear: 'Full dress Uniform Coat, Black Cloth waistcoat & Breeches & crape round the Arm & in the Hat'.[27] Lieutenants from the *Victory* were to be close to the coffin, while seamen from the ship, as well as Greenwich Pensioners, were to process to St Paul's. The procession from the Admiralty in Whitehall to St Paul's was dominated by troops, with the route lined with volunteer regiments. The government wanted to allow full expression to patriotic feelings, but it also sought to insure against any dissension and disorder. Throughout these weeks the establishment and the authorities used the word 'mob' rather than 'crowd'.

It was now that John Tyson, one of the executors of Nelson's will, showed why Nelson had valued his old secretary. Tyson had been single-mindedly trying to ensure that Nelson was buried in the coffin made from *L'Orient*'s mast since the arrival of the *Victory* at Spithead, writing first on the subject to William Haslewood on the same day.[28] Six days later he was still trying to persuade Haslewood to obtain the new Earl Nelson's permission, offering 'to fetch the Coffin and take it in our yacht (belonging to the Dock Yard) to the Nore without any expence . . . I shall then have the pleasing satisfaction of paying the last friendly offices to a man I loved more than a Brother.'[29] Eventually Tyson armed himself with an Admiralty warrant and secured the coffin from the undertakers, Peddison's. Taking with him Joseph Whidby, the master attendant at Woolwich Dockyard, Tyson loaded the coffin into the *Chatham*, one of the yachts belonging to Sheerness Dockyard, and went looking for the *Victory*. He found it, after four days, anchored in the Swin, and went on board on 23 December. The body was again moved from the coffin full of spirits into Nelson's chosen coffin, the lead lining of which was soldered. That evening Tyson left in the yacht for Greenwich, with Nelson's body on board.[30] He was accompanied by Alexander Scott, who was not to leave the coffin until the burial.* The *Victory* sailed the next day up the Medway to Chatham for a refit, mooring in Long Reach on Christmas Day.[31] Able Seaman John Brown wrote to a correspondent from there: 'There is three hundred of us Pict out to go to Lord Nelson Fun[e]ral. We are to wear blue Jackets, white Trowsers and a black scarf round our arms and hats besides gold medal for the battle of Trafalgar, Valued £7–1s, round our necks . . . We scarce have room to move; the Ship is so full of Nobility coming down from London to see the Ship looking at shot holes.'[32]

The *Chatham*, with the coffin on board, sailed up the Thames on the incoming tide, early in the morning on Christmas Eve. Passing ships lowered their flags 'half staff'. Tilbury and Gravesend forts lowered their flags and fired minute guns. Church bells tolled. By 1 p.m. the yacht was moored off the Royal Hospital at Greenwich, where crowds had already gathered. Tyson waited all afternoon until Lord Hood returned to the hospital. Hood wanted the coffin to stay on board, but Tyson persuaded him that it was best to bring it ashore 'at once as the Mob was dispersing and when I went out of the House several enquired of me when the body was to be landed. I told them on Thursday morning for certain, the Beach was very soon cleared after this and at half past 6 we landed the Body without any confusion and I do not believe there were thirty persons besides our own men.' He then had the coffin put in the Record Room, just off the Painted Hall.[33] The room remained closed for eleven days until the public were allowed to view the coffin for three days in the Painted Hall: the lying-in-state took place from 5 to 7 January 1806.

---

* Scott was unable to remain with the body when it was sealed in the Record Room in the Royal Hospital, and took lodgings near by in No. 21 Park Row, Greenwich, since demolished (Monmouth, E474, 26 Dec. 1805, Scott to Lady Lavington).

The size and enthusiasm of the crowds outside the hospital at Greenwich took the authorities by surprise. When 'the gate was thrown open', according to *The Times*, 'above ten thousand persons pressed forward for admittance'. Only a small number managed to enter the Painted Hall. People were rushed past the coffin. The same confusion reigned on the second day. By the third, in response to a request by Hood, a corps of the Life Guards restored some semblance of order.[34] Only the prince of Wales (before the public opening) and the party of sailors from the *Victory* (afterwards) were allowed a private and unrushed viewing of the coffin.

On 8 January the two-day funeral ritual started. Half an hour after noon the procession started from the Painted Hall, and Nelson's body was placed on board the state barge for the journey up the Thames. Five lieutenants from the *Victory* – John Pasco, Edward Williams, Andrew King, John Yule and George Browne – as well as Thomas Atkinson, the master – accompanied the coffin.[35] A grand procession of ceremonial barges and smaller boats escorted the state barge against a stiff wind, but with the tide, and the procession slowly made its way six miles upriver. Thousands lined the river, 'the boats of the River Fencibles firing minute guns the whole way to Whitehall Stairs'.[36] The coffin did not arrive at the Watergate until it was getting dark, at four o'clock. It was then taken to the Admiralty, where Alexander Scott remained by its side all night.

Early in the morning of Thursday, 9 January, the procession assembled in Hyde Park and the troops paraded in the Horse Guards, in St James's Park. At the Admiralty, Nelson's coffin was put on the funeral car, especially designed and built in the style of a ship. In addition to the seamen and the troops, there were fifty mourning coaches. The family was represented by William, Earl Nelson, and his son Horatio, George Matcham and his son George, and four cousins, including two Walpoles. Alexander Davison, William Haslewood and William Marsh shared a coach, as did Alexander Scott and John Tyson. Lady Bessborough described the reaction of the crowd.

Amongst many touching things the silence of that immense Mob was not the least striking; they had been very noisy. I was in a House in Charing Cross, which look'd over a mass of heads. The moment the Car appear'd which bore the body, you might have heard a pin fall, and without any order to do so, they all took off their hats. I cannot tell you the effect this action produc'd; it seem'd one general impulse of respect beyond any thing that could have been said or contriv'd.[37]

The authorities need not have been concerned about disorder; this was an orderly gathering, exhibiting silent, mass grief of a kind rarely seen.[38] This emotion came from gratitude for Nelson's sacrifice from a nation that had placed complete faith in him, but also from a fear that the world was now somehow a more dangerous place. One Bristol clergyman published a sermon that exhorted people not to think that the navy was incapable without Nelson.[39] A former naval chaplain later wrote that the country had sunk into irreligion. 'So long as Lord Nelson was at sea, the fear of ten thousands was quelled, and England was supposed to be in safety under his protection.'[40] The 'cult' of Nelson, as the relationship of the public to the memory of Nelson has been described, now took root.[41]

St Paul's was crowded to bursting point. Those without tickets had been sitting in the bitter cold since seven o'clock that morning, when the doors of the cathedral were opened. The procession, numbering several hundred, consisting of the mourners, Nelson's family, the royal family, peers of the realm, government and opposition politicians, the aldermen and sheriffs of the City of London, took their seats, having accompanied the coffin up to the altar. Over 180 naval officers attended, representing every part of Nelson's life. Of those from the early years, Collingwood and Troubridge were absent at sea: neither would see England again. Collingwood was to remain as commander-in-chief in the Mediterranean until his death in 1810, Troubridge was drowned in the Indian Ocean in 1807. But Sir Peter Parker, now eighty-three, who had given Nelson his first command in the tiny *Badger* in the West Indies twenty-six years earlier, was the chief mourner, swathed in a great black cloak. One of William Locker's protégés, and an early friend of Nelson, Charles Morice Pole, was one of the six assistant mourners. Locker, of course, was dead, as were James Macnamara and Robert Kingsmill. Lord Hood was a supporter of the chief mourner. The duke of Clarence, who had caused Nelson so much trouble in the West Indies, sat among the seven 'Dukes of the Blood Royal'. And two former midshipmen from those times were there, now both captains: George Andrews, who was nearly killed in a duel; and Courtenay Boyle, the charming Irish midshipman who had become the captain of the *Seahorse* and led the fleet out of Agincourt Sound at the beginning of the Long Chase.

Flanking the coffin was the pious William Waldegrave, now Lord Radstock, as the other supporter to the chief mourner; he had helped Nelson gain recognition after the Battle of St Vincent. Commanding the troops in the procession was General Sir David Dundas, who had been one of the cautious generals in Corsica in 1794. Isaac Coffin was there, now a rear-admiral, formerly commissioner of the base at Ajaccio in Corsica, where Nelson's ships had refitted; and Captain Thomas Staines, once a lieutenant in the *Foudroyant*; and John Aylmer, captain of the *Theseus* in 1797, the ship so badly disciplined that Nelson and his officers were transferred to her. Sir John Orde, rival to Nelson, and rich, was a pall-bearer but only as a last-minute substitute. Nelson's other adversary, Sir Robert Calder, was absent, perhaps unsurprisingly, for only a fortnight before he had been reprimanded by his court martial for being overly cautious in his action. Much has been made of St Vincent's absence. He had, however, made it clear before the service that 'he wanted to pay the most liberal and respectful Tribute to the Eminent Services, and rever'd Memory of my late Gallant friend.'[42] To the Board of Admiralty he wrote that he had 'a violent inflammation in my eyes'.[43] Many of his fellow officers would have been uncomfortable had he been there, and, indeed, it would have been very difficult to place him in a ceremony next to officers with whom he was not on speaking terms. And he hated show.

Of Nelson's Nile captains only the younger Samuel Hood was present. Saumarez, Hallowell and Berry were at sea; Thomas Foley was in ill health in Milford Haven; and Ball was in Malta – he too was never to see England again. Ralph Willet Miller had been killed by an exploding shell in 1799. Captain Edward Galwey, the first lieutenant in the *Vanguard*, was there, as was General Sir Thomas Trigge, then governor of Gibraltar, who had received the news of the victory of the Nile in the middle of the night and immediately fired a salute, courteously warning the Spanish Army before he did so. Nelson's time at Copenhagen and in the Baltic was represented by Samuel Sutton, still a captain, and Rear-Admiral William Domett, Hyde Parker's flag captain, though Hyde Parker did not come himself.

Nelson's later colleagues and friends were the most numerous group of mourners. Closest to the coffin were the lieutenants of the *Victory*. Two assisted Thomas Masterman Hardy with the 'Banner of the Emblem'; Thomas Atkinson, the master, bore the bannerols of the family. Henry Blackwood was the trainbearer of the chief mourner. Not all the politicians who knew Nelson well were present, though Henry Addington (now Lord Sidmouth), Lord Hawkesbury, Lord Castlereagh and Sir Evan Nepean were; but Lords Spencer and Melville and Thomas Grenville were absent. Of St Vincent's Board of Admiralty, only John Markham was present. One can surmise that those in office were reluctant to lose at least two days away from their desks, for Lord Barham and Sir Andrew Snape Hamond did not attend: the war at sea was at a critical juncture. William Windham sat between Charles James Fox and Sir William Scott, the Admiralty jurist. William Pitt was gravely ill, and was to die two weeks later.

The service was long and sombre. Anthems were sung, prayers offered; by mid afternoon darkness fell and lights in great candelabras were lit. According to the *Naval Chronicle*, 'During the whole of this solemn ceremony, the greatest order prevailed throughout the metropolis.' Nelson's coffin was lowered into the crypt under the Great Dome of St Paul's. The seamen, who were supposed to lay the flag of the *Victory* in the grave, tore off pieces for themselves as keepsakes. When the body was laid to rest, artillery at Moorfields fired a salute; infantry fired volleys.[44] William Windham noted in his diary: 'Not impressed throughout as I ought. Attention disturbed with the cold.'[45]

Neither Fanny nor Emma was present, as women usually did not attend funerals at this time. Nelson's death made no difference to the intense feeling between them; Emma's cruel nickname for Fanny, 'Tom Tit', was still used in correspondence by the rest of the family.[46] Fanny retained her bitterness. She was very sharp with Alexander Davison five weeks after the news of Trafalgar had reached England, for when she went to meet him his two sons were present, and she wrote to him afterwards: 'recollect I have refused to see some of My Lord's old acquaintances and even my female friends, therefore never bring any person with you, without previously acquainting me.'[47] Although Davison continued to help her, relations were soured between them by his failure to certify Maurice Nelson's death on a deed of trust, and a succession of anxious and imploring letters from Fanny followed for two years.[48]

But Nelson put Fanny first in his will, priority being given to establishing sufficient capital to provide enough interest for her annual allowance. Fanny's financial affairs were looked after by her solicitor, J. W. Western, who informed her early in 1806 that the executors were working to gather enough money to fund her annuity. At his death Nelson had only £15,600 in 3 per cent consols, not enough to generate the income needed for Fanny. Personal items, and 'goods and chattels', went to William Nelson and others in the family, and to Alexander Davison.[49] He also owed Davison £3,000, and the executors had to borrow another £2,000 from Davison before they could start realizing all the assets: but Western assured Fanny that there would be enough. Merton was to be sold. The marquis of Niza's claim for Nelson's prize money was still in the prize courts.[50] 'From the Prize money, which is expected to be received and the produce of the Estate at Merton which is to be sold in the Spring there will be more than sufficient for the payment of all the debts, Legacies and other charges.'[51] Fanny's income was continued, after a gap of six months; in 1806 the executors purchased £33,333. 6s. 8d. in 3 percent consols for her.[52] Together with the consols that Nelson already owned, this would provide her with her comfortable yearly income.

Emma took the news of Nelson's death with a depression of understandable intensity. 'I have been very ill all Day', she wrote to Davison.

My Heart Broken & My Head Consequently weak from the agitations I Suffer – I tell you Truly – I am gone nor do I wish to Live – He that I Loved more than Life, He is gone. Why then shou'd I Live or wish to Live? I Lived but for Him, all now is a Dreary prospect before me. I never Lamented the Loss of a Kingdom (for I was Queen of Naples) for seven years: nor one Sigh ever Escaped me for the Loss I Sustained When I fell from Such a heigtth of grateness & Happiness of Naples to misery and wretchedness . . . nothing gives me a gleam of Comfort but the Hope that I shall soon follow.'[53]

It was rumoured abroad that she never left her bed.[54] Thomas Masterman Hardy could not fulfil Nelson's last wish of being kind to Lady Hamilton, for she would not answer his letters.[55] Three days after the news arrived in London, the ever practical Mrs Cadogan wrote to George Rose: 'Lady Hamilton's most wretched state of mind prevents her imploring her dear good Mr Rose to solicit Mr Pitt to consider the Family of our great & Glorious Nelson, who so gallantly died for his Country leaving behind his favorite Sister with a large family unprovided for . . . They are at this moment surrounding Her Ladyship's bed bewailing their sad loss & miserable estate.'[56]

The problem for Emma and the family was that Nelson, because of Fanny's income and the £4,000 he bequeathed to Horatia, had not left sufficient to keep Emma in the sort of luxury to which she had become accustomed. She was immediately in financial trouble and the slow process of probate made things worse. William Haslewood wrote to Mrs Cadogan in July 1806: 'I am bound to discharge all demands on the estate before anything can be done respecting the legacies.'[57] It was no wonder that Nelson left Emma as a legacy to the nation. Prize money was, as ever to Nelson, a disappointment. There were just over a thousand pounds owing on the St Vincent claim, £4,750 to come from the capture of the Spanish treasure ships, £3,000 from other sources, but William Marsh reckoned at the end of 1805 that no more than £16,250 could be expected.[58] In all, prize money was likely to total about £25,000.

For the rest of her life, Emma was troubled by money problems. In 1811 there were rumours that she was to receive a government pension of £500 a year, but nothing came of it.[59] Emma's spirits sank, her drinking increased and her friends slowly drifted away. Horatia had a miserable life. Two letters of 1813, for instance, from Emma to her daughter, then aged twelve, seem to have been written under the influence of depression or intoxication, or both. On Easter Sunday 1813 Emma wrote: 'if you had grown up as I wished you what a joy, what a comfort might you have been to me ... I have weathered many a storm for your sake but these frequent blows have killed me ... I shall go join your father and my blessed mother and may you on your deathbed have as little to reproach yourself as your once affectionate mother.' In October of the same year: 'Your conduct is so bad, your falsehoods so dreadfull, your cruel treatment to me such that I cannot live under these afflicting circumstances: my poor heart is broken. In two days all will be arranged for your future Establishment ... it is therefore my Command that you do not speak to me till Tuesday.'[60] It was no wonder that Horatia never accepted Emma as her mother. Emma died, in debt, in Calais in January 1815.[61]

But others suffered too. In general, Nelson's protégés in the navy did not flourish. Those to whom he had given a helping hand and who were already connected, such as George Elliot, the young Peter Parker and Frederick Augustus Collier, did well. William Hoste, although he never reached flag rank, gained a frigate squadron victory and a knighthood, while William Bolton performed respectably and had full employment until 1815. But the rest languished. From the *Victory*, Lieutenant John Pasco, though recovered from his wound, was still on half-pay when in February 1807 he pressed his claim on the first lord of the Admiralty, Thomas Grenville: 'I lost my only friend in Lord Nelson.' Pasco was not promoted to captain until 1811 and reached rear-admiral automatically as an old man in 1847.[62] Even Midshipman John Pollard, who had now passed his lieutenant's exam, wrote to Grenville that 'his Lordship's death on that glorious day (however greatly I exult in being the person who shot the Frenchman from whom his Lordship received his wound) has hitherto been fatal to my prospects and promotion.'[63] Pollard was only made commander on retirement nearly sixty years later. Several others were still without employment in 1807, including Thomas Bowen and John Conn; William Layman, who had twice lost his ship, never advanced further than captain.[64] William Nelson too tried his influence with Grenville on behalf of one his wife's family, Lieutenant Charles Browne Yonge, 'for whom my dear Brother had a particular regard ... May I presume once more, to recommend this Orphan young man to your patronage and protection, & humbly hope that the name of Nelson will not plead in vain with the Head of the British Navy ... you will not only confer an obligation on me, but, what is more, evince your regard for the memory of the greatest Naval Character this country ever afforded.'[65] Grenville wrote a prevaricating reply. Lieutenant Yonge was never promoted. Nelson's influence within the navy, always fragile, did not long outlast his death.

31

The Nineteenth and Twentieth Centuries

There was no other way of representing the death of a hero but by an Epic representation of it. It must ... excite awe and veneration ... Wolfe must not die like a common soldier under a bush; neither should Nelson be represented dying in the gloomy hold of a ship, like a sick man in a prison hole ... No boy would be animated by a representation of Nelson dying like an ordinary man. His feelings must be roused and his mind inflamed by a scene great and extraordinary. A mere matter of fact will never produce this effect.

Benjamin West, painter of the *Death of Nelson* (1808) and the
Apotheosis of Nelson (1807), criticizing Arthur Devis's
Death of Nelson (1807)[1]

The naval blockade did not end with Trafalgar. Collingwood still commanded the fleet off Cadiz; the regime he imposed on his captains was as unpopular as ever. In January 1806 Thomas Fremantle wrote to his brother from the *Neptune*: 'The Service here is more wearing than anything you can imagine, worse if possible than before Nelson's arrival. The parsimony or avarice of the Commander in Chief will not allow any social intercourse.'[2] William Cornwallis continued off Brest until relieved in February 1806 by St Vincent, now at the more than advanced age of seventy-two; the old earl remained off Ushant for another year. In order to nurse his worn fleets Lord Barham relaxed the winter Channel blockade, which allowed a French squadron to escape in December 1805 and sail to the West Indies. In the following February off San Domingo five French ships were badly mauled by a slightly larger squadron under Vice-Admiral Duckworth. One of the British ships was the *Superb*, still commanded by Richard Goodwin Keats: as she approached the French, the ship's band played 'Nelson of the Nile' and Keats hung a portrait of Nelson on the mizzenmast. Three French ships were captured and two run ashore.[3]

By degrees the nature of the naval war changed. Using his vast land resources from his conquests, Napoleon built a new, large fleet of ships of the line in ports all over Europe, but it never took to the sea, blockaded for years on end by British fleets and squadrons in a largely forgotten, remorseless effort. Britain built many more smaller warships to convoy trade in European waters. Control of trade routes was contested in many actions by smaller ships, such as the battle of Lissa in 1811 in the Adriatic between two squadrons of frigates. The successful British squadron was commanded by William Hoste: as the battle was joined, Hoste flew the signal 'Remember Nelson.' France and Russia joined forces in 1807, and the anti-British blockade became Europe-wide, formalized by Napoleon when he issued his 'Continental Decrees', by which he extended hostilities to neutral ships 'trading in English merchandise belonging to England or coming from the colonies or of her manufacture'. This was countered by similar measures against France through Britain's 'Orders-in-Council' in the same year.[4] France dominated the land, Britain the sea. A grim total war ensued, with French trade driven from the seas, and for long periods prize money was a thing of the past. Trade and government credit became as much a concern as the condition and performance of the navy.

The Nelson family flourished. By the 'Patent of Creation of the Viscountcy Merton of Trafalgar and of Merton, and Earldom of Nelson', the Reverend William Nelson was raised from viscount to earl. In July 1806 the House of Commons voted £300,000 to purchase an estate, in line with the awards to Marlborough and, in the future, to Wellington, enabling that undistinguished cleric to support his new status.[5] Fanny received £2,000 a year for her life, but £5,000 a year was also voted, for ever, to William's heirs. Nelson's sisters, Susannah and Catherine, received a lump sum of £15,000 each. Eventually in 1815 an estate was found for William Nelson near Salisbury in Wiltshire, for which Parliament agreed an additional sum; it was renamed Trafalgar House.[6] The grant has been called, not without foundation, 'ludicrous over-provision', and it continued until 1948, when it was cancelled by the Labour government of Clement Attlee; the payments ceased in 1951 when the fifth Earl Nelson died.[7] William Nelson also became the second duke of Bronte, and the estate in Sicily, which Nelson never visited, passed down through William's daughter Charlotte to the Bridport side of the family until it was sold to the local commune in the 1980s. The English gardens still bloom, and the naval pictures of eighteenth-century battles and of the admirals of the Bridport and Hood families still hang there, including a full-length portrait of Lord Hood at his most nonchalant. The estate at Bronte remains a small part of England on the side of Mount Etna, a reminder of, rather than a monument to, Nelson's complex relationship with the Kingdom of Naples and Sicily. The final remnants of the story lie in the memorial erected in 1922 to General Viscount Bridport, fourth duke of Bronte, in St George's Anglican Church in the nearby resort of Taormina, on the coast, where the Bridport family spent the winter.[8]

Several monuments to Nelson were built over the next fifty years. Parliament voted money for a statue in St Paul's, and the City of London funded one in the Guildhall.[9] The navy erected an obelisk on Portsdown Hill overlooking Portsmouth, the foundation stone being laid in 1807. Monuments in Hereford, started in 1806, Dublin, completed in 1808, and Glasgow (the foundation stone laid in 1806, but the structure was struck by lightning in 1810) were among the earliest. Birmingham (1809), Liverpool (1813), Yarmouth (1819), Edinburgh (begun in 1823) and Norwich (1852) followed. Others were erected by individuals on their private estates: Alexander Davison built one at his Northumberland estate at Swarland Hall; and Sir William Paxton, a banker, erected a tower, known locally as Paxton's Folly, in Carmarthen in South Wales.[10] Barbados, which Nelson visited briefly in 1805, also honoured him with a statue, now seen as a relic of colonialism, while the monument in Montreal (1808) has been a subject of lively debate in that French-speaking city. It was not until 1843 that the statue of Nelson was finally placed on the great column in the newly laid-out Trafalgar Square in London, but public subscriptions faltered and the government took over the funding the following year. Edwin Landseer's lions at the base were not finished until 1867.[11] Other monuments have been sporadically erected through the twentieth century. Emma Hamilton was finally given a plain memorial in Calais by a more liberal age in 1994.[12]

From the time of Nelson's death pictures, books and even the many mementoes, cheap prints and pottery figures started to transform the image of the successful admiral into the hero.[13] Benjamin West produced the most successful picture of Nelson's death, repeating the composition of his picture *Death of Wolfe* painted thirty years earlier in 1770; West imparted a nobility to the imaginary death scene of the quarterdeck.[14] An alternative vision was provided by Arthur Devis, who talked his way on board the *Victory* when she was at Spithead in December 1805, and who witnessed Nelson's body being transferred to the final coffin. In his *Death of Nelson*, Devis took care to include every detail of the scene in the cockpit, although the deck beams above in the form of a cross faintly echo Christian symbolism.[15] In time this has become the best-known image of Nelson's death, but when the two paintings were first made into prints, West's heightened image of Nelson outsold the realism and pathos of Devis.[16] West went further in his *Apotheosis of Nelson* (1807), a work of the imagination constructed around classical allegory, with Nelson's body rising into heaven and into immortality, about as far from real life as was possible. This painting formed the frontispiece to Clarke and McArthur's *Life of Admiral Lord Nelson* in 1809, appropriately, in view of these authors' airy views on historical accuracy.[17]

Robert Southey's *Life of Nelson*, published in its final form in 1813, came to dominate the biography market. Its strengths were its comparative brevity and the pace and elegance of Southey's prose, but its underlying agenda laid the foundation for more Nelson myths. Southey constructed an early-nineteenth-century hero as a model for the young – in his words, a 'patriotic manual'. He told a friend that he would write 'such a life of Nelson as shall be put into the hands of every youth destined for the navy'. Many illustrated, pocket editions were produced by his publisher, John Murray, for this market.[18] Southey was content to overlook the embarrassment of Nelson's relationship with Emma, claiming that his love for her 'did not pass the bounds of ardent and romantic admiration'.[19] Of more lasting importance was his criticism of Nelson for his conduct at Naples, which, for the time, could hardly have been blunter: he delivered 'a severe and unqualified condemnation of Nelson's conduct'.[20]

However, the tone for the next few decades was set by Thomas Carlyle's *Heroes and Hero Worship* (1841), when the idea of the hero was strengthened in the Victorian mind. In biographies of this period, documents were 'treated cavalierly . . . The biographer might cut out passages or even rewrite them so as to protect the dignity of the subject.' Naval officers were shown with 'a seamless life, and that even as boys they had shown future greatness'.[21] But the predominant aim was to instruct and inspire. One evangelical biography of a naval officer published in 1846 stated on the first page: 'My desire . . . was to do good to others, rather than to do justice to my subject.'[22] Distance from empirical accuracy was further increased in the 1850s and 1860s by the identification of heroes with Christianity, with authors speculating on the inner life of their subject, as well as moralizing at length; often their portraits were in uneasy contradiction with the warlike careers of the heroes, and much ink was spilt on proving the compatibility of the warrior with religious belief. Harris Nicolas published his seven-volume work of Nelson letters between 1844 and 1846, but in 1849 Thomas Pettigrew published his *Memoirs of the Life of Vice-Admiral Lord Nelson*. Up to that point many Victorians had accepted that Nelson had had an illegitimate child, but that Lady Hamilton was not the mother. Pettigrew's book presented evidence to the contrary.[23] Nelson now did not fit easily into the high moral pattern of the Victorians at their most confident.

As Nelson's victories began to fade from living memory, and those who had survived the battles grew fewer, feelings ran high among the survivors that neither soldiers nor seamen had received state recognition for their part in the great war against France. The duke of Wellington opposed the principle of the award of retrospective medals, and he was supported by Admiral Sir George Cockburn. However, after parliamentary debate, support swung to the side of the veterans, and the Royal Approval was given on 27 May 1847 for the distribution of the Naval General Service Medal to all those living who had fought in the battles of the great war. Copenhagen was at last included. On the 'Flag Officers Committee' that awarded the medals were two of Nelson's junior officers, Admiral Sir Thomas Byam Martin and Vice-Admiral the Honourable Sir Thomas Bladen Capel.[24] Soon after, following the military disasters of the Crimean War of 1852–4, the contribution of ordinary seamen and soldiers became established in the public's mind when the idea of 'The Unknown Soldier' took root and the order of the Victoria Cross was created.[25]

The world, however, was changing again by the 1880s when British imperial and naval superiority was perceived to be under threat. A series of articles in the *Pall Mall Gazette* in 1884, entitled 'The Truth about the Navy', contributed to this anxiety.[26] Hot political debate on naval expenditure followed, which led to the Naval Defence Act of 1889, increasing the international tension with France and Russia, and leading to an increased rate of warship building that extended seamlessly into the Anglo-German naval arms race before the First World War. Nelson was immediately brought into the debate, his victories portrayed as the symbol of imperial dominance, underpinning decades of the uncontested supremacy of the British Navy. In 1886 John Knox Laughton published *The Letters and Dispatches of Horatio, Viscount Nelson*, for which he drew almost entirely upon Nicolas, focusing only on Nelson's professional life. Laughton was the propagator of the 'scientific Study of Naval History' and an important figure in the naval thought of the day. Laughton's colleague and friend, Captain Alfred Thayer Mahan of the United States Navy, published his masterly *Life of Nelson* in two volumes in Boston and London in 1897.[27]

Just as Nelson's stock and retrospective fame was being raised by the geopolitical stresses of the day, his reputation came under attack from a quite different direction. From 1889 a group of young Italian liberal historians, led by Benedetto Croce, began to champion the Neapolitan revolution, representing its suppression by reactionary forces in 1799 as the reason for the backwardness of the south of Italy since that time.[28] Nelson's actions were condemned by many Continental historians, and in May 1897 this attack spread to England through the pen of F. P. Badham, a descendant of Captain Foote, whose agreement with the Jacobins Nelson had repudiated. Badham used Italian sources, hitherto unexplored by British historians, and attacked both Laughton and Mahan in an article in the *Saturday Review*, accusing them of bad faith: Laughton in particular was accused of 'patrioti- cally misinterpreting or mutilating the documents'.[29]

Between 1897 and 1908 a bitter controversy took place in the press and academic journals between Badham and Laughton, with the latter helped by Mahan. While Laughton and Mahan were trying to protect Nelson's reputation, they were at the same time defending naval traditions and history as a means of education for the expanding British and American navies of the Edwardian era. Mahan revised the Naples chapter in his *Life of Nelson* for the second one-volume edition of 1898, but the vituperative controversy with Badham continued for more than ten years. Some claim 'victory' for Laughton and Mahan, though Mahan himself was pessimistic, unable in 1905 'to trace any reversal of the verdict obtained by Southey's misstatement'.[30] Badham's second book, *Nelson and Ruffo*, published in 1905, had, in the opinion of one modern Nelson biographer, 'much the better of the argument', and other English historians wrote critically of his months at Naples.[31] For the next twenty years Laughton defended Nelson from every attack. Laughton began, according to his biographer, 'the pro- cess of restoring the lustre of [Nelson's] name by removing the slurs of his contemporaries and the slanders of Southey ... Nelson's name had to be returned, untarnished, to the core of national culture if he was to fulfil Laughton's fondest hopes.'[32] But biographers and modern fictional writers have sided with Badham, producing powerful and widely read indictments of Nelson's actions.[33] The prediction of one of Nelson's young contempor- aries has proved correct: 'in this fatal instance every better feeling was lost sight of, and his character received a stain which the truth of History will make indelible.'[34]

From the early 1880s Victorian painters, with their penchant for scenes of historical fiction, recalled former glories. P. L. Jazet's *Death of Nelson* (1882) was followed by G. W. Joy's *Nelson's Farewell to his Grandmother* (1883) and Edward R. Taylor's *'Twas a Famous Victory* (also 1883). Here a Greenwich Pensioner stands in a gallery of naval victories, regaling two young seamen with stories of victories. Some of these pictures seem faintly ludicrous today, as does William Breakspear's *Nelson and Lady Hamilton in Romney's Studio*, a meeting that never happened. Lady Hamilton sits comfortably in an elegant Victorian dress; only a brooding George Romney in the background strikes a note of reality.[35] Arthur Davidson sounded a more powerful note in *England's Pride and Glory*, painted in about 1890. A widow stands with her naval cadet son, absorbed and inspired, in front of Lemuel Francis Abbott's glamorized portrait of a bemedalled Nelson. With England now coming under threat, Nelson's rehabilitation as a naval hero was under way.

The process continued through the 1890s. In 1891, with rearmament a permanent political issue, the navy put on the extraordinarily well-attended Royal Naval Exhibition, held in the grounds of the Royal Hospital at Chelsea, in which relics of Nelson's life were numerous.[36] The exhibition was designed to help the navy's cause in the rivalry of the army and navy for the greater share of the parliamentary estimates, following the army's successful show the previous year. Laughton founded the Navy Records Society in 1893 to promote naval history by printing historical documents, and at the end of the next year a number of journalists and retired naval officers founded the Navy League, a pressure group that attempted to push British public opinion towards greater expenditure on the navy. One of the means chosen was the promotion of the memory of Trafalgar Day. From 21 October 1895 Nelson and the battle were commemorated in Trafalgar Square, Nelson's Column being garlanded and hung with flags: it was attended by large crowds, and the custom soon became established in many parts of the empire. Thus on 21 October 1905 Trafalgar Square was filled with people for a ceremony of flags at half-mast, bugles, music, prayers and patriotism.[37] In the sombre years of the First World War, Nelson's name and image were used on recruiting posters and in government propaganda.

The most powerful monument of all to Nelson, and to the men who fought at Trafalgar, is the survival and restoration of HMS *Victory* at Portsmouth, still at the time of writing a commissioned ship in the Royal Navy. She served in the Baltic as James Saumarez's flagship between 1808 and 1812, followed by years of passive service in Portsmouth Harbour. Fortunately for her survival, her repairs were undertaken in teak rather than in oak. But by 1922 the ship was in danger of sinking, and public opinion forced the navy to dock her. Among the key people who were engaged in saving the *Victory* were Sir James Caird, a former shipowner who had sold his ships in 1917 at the height of the First World War when prices were astronomically high; the eccentric but knowledgeable Geoffrey Callender, then professor of history at the Royal Naval College and later to be the first director of the National Maritime Museum; and Sir Doveton Sturdee, the victorious admiral at the Battle of the Falkland Islands in 1914.

In September 1922, in a letter to Sturdee, Callender described the ship while she was still afloat: 'I would like to record briefly (a) how shocked I was at the irreverence of the crowds . . . Giggling girls, flirting in Nelson's cabin! Nauseating! and (b) the flippancy of the young "Marine Guides" – "Yuss! This is where Nelson and Lady Hamilton sat canoodling . . . (Shrieks of laughter) . . . Go on, of course they did. Lady Hamilton was always on board when Nelson was. You bet. Not 'arf" – It made me physically sick.'[38] It was a more straightforward task to save the *Victory* than to keep Nelson's reputation intact and respectable, even at the distance of more than a hundred years.

Caird's money and Callender's expertise, and the political assistance of the first lord of the Admiralty, Lord Stanhope, secured the foundation of the National Maritime Museum, which, following the Act of 1934, opened its doors in 1937. Though ostensibly devoted to the history of Britain's relationship with the sea, the museum in its early years was perceived by the public as a shrine to Nelson. During the Second World War, Nelson's memory was most famously used in Alexander Korda's film *That Hamilton Woman*, starring Laurence Olivier and Vivien Leigh. It not only told the story of the affair between Nelson and Emma but showed Nelson resisting tyranny in the form of Napoleon – audiences would equate the emperor in the film with Hitler. Churchill was reputed to have said that the film was worth two divisions.

Nelson was the last admiral in the British Navy to achieve great, set-piece victories, and this has ensured that he has stayed on his pedestal. During the Second World War, Britain was under greater threat of invasion than in 1805, but it was Churchill, rather than a military man who came to epitomize national identity and defiance. Only he, perhaps, has a more powerful claim than Nelson as an historical focus for the defence of British national identity. Nelson's reputation has survived, changed and grown in part because it is many-faceted; as one modern commentator has put it, 'tactician extraordinary, symbol of British courage, monument to the dead, Navy patron saint, morally flawed genius, matinee idol'.[39] Because Nelson lived before the photographic age, his likeness can never be captured entirely. In spite of the 238 portraits catalogued by one modern scholar, and even with the relatively objective evidence of the three 'life masks' that were taken of his face, opinions vary widely on which is the most accurate.[40] We shall never know exactly what he looked like. In spite of the continuous attention of artists and biographers, Nelson remains elusive.

32

The Summing-up

The English method of attack was no doubt daring but it was irresistible. The weather was favourable for the fleet to windward to attempt it and did not permit the fleet to leeward to parry it. But without doubt the greatest misfortune was that the enemy fleet was commanded by a man, uniting genius to daring, who knew how to profit by the rare opportunity of such a situation.

Theodore Contamine, major-general of the expeditionary force aboard the French fleet at Trafalgar, reporting the defeat to the minister of Marine, 20 November 1805[1]

There can be no doubt that Nelson gained an extraordinary psychological ascendancy over his naval adversaries: it is difficult to think of a parallel example, except for Napoleon on land. By the time of Trafalgar that sense of superiority was shared by the rest of the officers and men of the British navy. Perhaps more remarkable was the authority that Nelson exercised over the officer corps, especially his equals and those just junior to him. He took over command of fleets from Bickerton in the Mediterranean and Collingwood off Cadiz, changing routines within hours of his arrival, yet these commanders-in-chief accepted his orders without a murmur. From the mid 1790s, when he was appointed to successive levels of high command, at every stage Nelson found new skills and talents from within himself. This progression was suspended temporarily in 1799 at Naples, when his political and moral judgement erred, and when he risked his career and reputation for his relationship with Emma Hamilton; but he was able to re-establish his position with his peers and superiors after Copenhagen, not only by carrying the day of the battle but also by taking the British fleet into the Baltic, maintaining it virtually unsupported and engaging in forceful diplomacy with complete success. By 1805 one of his Trafalgar captains, William Rutherford, who did not know him well, admired Nelson's all-round abilities, writing: 'Lord Nelson, I believe, is generally thought to be merely a fighting man, but he is a man of amazing resources and abilities, more so, I think, than even Lord St Vincent.'[2]

Not much of this brilliance was obvious in Nelson's early career, nor is there much evidence to distinguish him from many of his contemporaries. Like most of them, he was seeking to improve his station in life. He enjoyed early promotion through the influence of well-placed relatives, and continued to impress senior officers, but made no name for himself with prize money. He was a driven, ambitious young man, with a health record that did not promise longevity. He had self-confidence, but not social confidence, illustrated over several months on the Leeward Islands Station by his sycophancy towards Prince William Henry. This was a period too when he showed his sensitivity to his rank and seniority, which marked him out as a difficult and unpredictable subordinate. For these reasons he was shunned by the Board of Admiralty at the end of the 1780s and not given a ship during the mobilizations of 1790 and 1791.

A shortness of temper stayed with him until the last years of his life. Nelson himself told a court in the late 1780s: 'I know I am hasty.'[3] Alexander Ball told Samuel Taylor Coleridge of Nelson's 'constitutionally irritable and uneven' temper.[4] William Layman recalled his 'petulance at trifles'.[5] Nelson's driven personality did not allow him to put small irritations into perspective, to recognize that smaller things did not matter; it was a shortcoming that led him into difficulties that lesser men avoided. Thirty years after Trafalgar, John Wilson Croker recalled the reflections of 'Old Sir Roger Curtis, a shrewd & observant man, [who] once said to me of his own profession – "[The] better you become acquainted with heroes the less you will think of them & certainly Lord Nelson was, in some respects, as trivial a man as ever made a name." '[6]

But he learnt and he grew wiser, and by the time he was commander-in-chief in the Mediterranean in 1803, although he still had bursts of frenetic energy, he achieved a calmness and maturity that impressed and charmed all around him. During his final command off Cadiz, by the account of his captains, he was happy with the recognition from all except the king, and his kindness had fully displaced any irritability. Thirty years after Nelson's death George Cockburn told John Wilson Croker that Nelson possessed 'a curious compound of weakness, with powers of high exertions of intrepidity and talent whenever great occasions called for the exertion of the nobler qualities and subjection of the former, and blessed with a never failing kindness of heart.'[7]

Nelson's early biographers glossed over his weaknesses as systematically as they overlooked the embarrassment of his liaison with Emma Hamilton. Alfred Thayer Mahan, when he wrote his biography in 1898, could not pass over this liaison because of the documents published by Alfred Morrison, and was fiercely critical.[8] He described Nelson's character 'as a synthesis of personality opposites'.[9] Instead of trying to reconcile Nelson's contradictions, Mahan, a religious man himself, excused them and wrapped them in a blanket of Christianity. The strength of Nelson's Christian conviction, however, is far from clear. Alexander Scott wrote later that Nelson 'was a thorough clergyman's son – I should think he never went to bed or got up, without kneeling down to say his prayers.'[10] This has been taken as proof of the strength of Nelson's religious faith; yet the prayers and sermons, which he learnt at Burnham Thorpe, are the only outward evidence of a strong Christian belief. Nelson always made sure that his ships were plentifully supplied with Bibles and prayer books from societies such as the Society for Promoting Christian Knowledge.[11] They were an important prop in a dangerous and unforgiving life, but Nelson knew well that they were also good as a support to the discipline of his ship.

Many of his fellow officers were more obviously guided by strong religious principles. Waldegrave, Collingwood and Saumarez were well known for their piety, as were the Evangelicals Lord Barham and the younger James Gambier. The religious fervour of the last was so intense that he was known in the fleet as 'Dismal Jimmy'. Before Gambier made his reputation at the Battle of the First of June, he was told by a correspondent, 'it was said in the fleet that the *Defence* had too much preaching and praying on board to be much of a fighting ship.'[12] Barham, the first lord, important in the Evangelical movement and one of the leaders of the anti-slavery movement, would have been displeased had he known that Nelson wrote in 1805 of 'the damnable and cursed doctrine of Wilberforce and his hypocritical allies; I hope my berth in heaven will be exalted as his, who would certainly cause the murder of all our friends and fellow-subjects in the colonies.'[13]

These strong remarks can be construed as political rather than religious sentiments, but Nelson's faith has been overemphasized. He would occasionally copy into his private journal prayers or religious observations when highly relieved after a period of stress, such as after the first action with *La Melpomène* in October 1793 or on his return, low on water, to Gibraltar after chasing Villeneuve across the Atlantic.[14] He did the same when he left Merton for the last time, and in the hour before Trafalgar. Some have stressed the importance that Nelson attached to formal religion, particularly as an aid to firm discipline.[15] Even here he was not consistent.

Early in his career Divine Service was held in the *Seahorse* and on board the *Lowestoffe* under William Locker. A chaplain was aboard during Nelson's brief command of the *Hinchinbroke*, and he had only his brother William as chaplain for a short time during the long cruise of the *Boreas* in the 1780s.[16] No chaplain was aboard the *Agamemnon* or the *Captain*.* Only when the Reverend Stephen Comyn stepped aboard the *Vanguard* on 31 March 1798 was this omission rectified. The myth of Nelson's religiosity was fuelled by his first biographers and the seal put on it by Clarke and McArthur.[17] The last paragraph of their biography begins: 'The whole Character of this great and lamented Admiral was consummated by his uniform sense of the blessed tenets of Christianity. This raised his mind above those mean and ignoble passions which depress the Abilities of so great a portion of mankind.'[18] Nelson's strong religious conviction is one of the most enduring pieces of the emotional scaffolding that his contemporaries and then the Victorians erected around his memory.†

Why, however, was Nelson so admired by contemporaries and later historians? First, he gained a reputation for benevolent paternalism. Many bear testimony to his kindness to junior officers when he was an admiral, such as his dining with midshipmen aboard the *Victory*. His light touch and easy relations with seamen have been noted time and again; perhaps his most singular gesture was to the restless seamen of the *Blanche* in 1797 when he went round the ship shaking them by the hand, congratulating them on their safe arrival at Porto Ferrajo. But there was a limit to this familiarity. Throughout his career, from the *Boreas* to the *Victory*, Nelson could be ruthless in the application of discipline, and insubordination was punished instantly. For two years in the Mediterranean (1803–5), with Thomas Masterman Hardy as flag captain, no ship punished its crew more frequently or severely than the *Victory*.[19]

Another reason for Nelson's enduring popularity was the perception that he remained 'pure' within what the Victorians especially regarded as the

---

* Nelson possibly did not replace William because he hoped that William would get paid for his period of absence. There may also have been a shortage of chaplains during the middle period of Nelson's career. Byrn (105) found that in his sample of ships on the West Indies Station, 1784–1812, 40 per cent of ships held Divine Service.

† Warner, *Diary*, 11, quotes an unreferenced and otherwise untraceable sentence from a letter to Emma, 8 May 1801: 'I own myself a Believer in God, and if I have any merit in not fearing death, it is because I feel his power can shelter me when He pleases and that must fall whenever it is his good pleasure.' Whoever wrote that sentence attributes an untypical degree of Christian fatalism to Nelson, giving rise to the misleading idea that by wearing conspicuous decorations at Trafalgar, Nelson was courting suicide. Warner's opinion was that this was nonsense, but for an example of this reasoning, see the full-page article in *The Times*, 8 Nov. 1969, 'Was Nelson a Suicide?', and ensuing correspondence, 12 Nov. 1969. See also Nicolas, VII, 347–52.

venal late-eighteenth-century system of patronage, and that he reached the top as a result of sheer talent rather than by political favouritism. That his talent shone through is not in doubt, for the generation of admirals above Nelson was weak and in some cases, as the war continued through the 1790s, worn out. In 1796 Jervis wrote to Nepean: 'You and I, and in truth the whole profession are Hero-Makers, and nothing so common among us, as to say, this, that and t'other man is a great Officer, when we really have few Officers on the list of Admirals.'[20] Jervis had a much better opinion of the younger officers.* William Young, always a sharp observer of character, came to the same conclusions ten years later, when he wrote to the new first lord, Thomas Grenville, with advice as to who might be appointed second in command of the Channel fleet under St Vincent. Grenville had no confidence in the incumbent, the worthy but dull Charles Cotton.[21] Charles Morice Pole had declined the post and personality conflict would exclude John Orde, John Borlase Warren, John Colpoys and James Hawkins Whitshed, while James Gambier, as Young put it, 'I should doubt his wishing for it.' Health remained a problem for Richard Bickerton, Roger Curtis and Eliab Harvey, while 'Thornborough's nerves are no longer equal to it.' Young recommended James Saumarez, still at that time a rear-admiral. 'To go down to Saumarez is going very far . . . When one looks at the very long list of Flag Officers,' Young concluded, 'it is wonderful to see how very few there are, especially among the higher classes, that are fitted for situations of importance, some incapable through age, and others from other causes.'[22] Although this list is affected by the great difficulty of finding someone who was willing to serve under St Vincent (and in that respect, Nelson gave no quarter), it indicates that Nelson was indeed exceptional among his peers. Writing after Nelson's death, Minto said, 'The navy is certainly full of the bravest men, but they are mostly below the rank of admiral.'[23]

Unquestionably Nelson was politically independent, and fortunate to be abroad during the three great politically divisive moments during his career. He was in the West Indies with Sir Peter Parker when the Keppel and Palliser courts martial took place in 1779, events that divided the navy by forcing officers to take one side or the other and that poisoned relations for a decade. He was under the wing of St Vincent in the Mediterranean fleet during the mutinies of 1797, which made and unmade reputations, and

---

* Jervis's list of twenty-two 'elite' young captains and commanders, which he sent to Nepean in October 1796, contained seven captains who were to be at Trafalgar: Henry W. Bayntun, Thomas Fremantle, Benjamin Hallowell, George Hope, James Morris, W. G. Rutherford and Charles Tyler (see p. 191n).

unnerved a number of weak officers, such as Duckworth, who, St Vincent thought, was 'not half the man he was before the Mutiny'.[24] Finally, Nelson was in the Mediterranean in 1804 when St Vincent's controversial tenure as first lord erupted on to the political stage. Had he been in London, he would have to have declared himself in the House of Lords. At sea, this independence paid off, as noticed by an old diplomat: '[Nelson] never was a party man himself, and there was never a party in his fleets. All were governed by one mind, and this made them invincible.'[25]

In time Nelson became a skilful political operator. Perhaps the best example of Nelson's developing political guile was after the Battle of St Vincent, when he outmanoeuvred the jealous Robert Calder, responsible for taking home the official dispatch. Guided by Gilbert Elliot, Nelson pulled off a masterstroke of political persuasion by sending his version of events to the secretary-at-war, William Windham, by the hand of Lieutenant Peirson, a message emphasized brilliantly by the gift of the Spanish admiral's sword. For the next four years Nelson's advancement and interests were watched over by Windham and his close friend Lord Spencer, who, just before he resigned as first lord, vitally gave Nelson his second chance in the Baltic after the Naples episode and the scandal over Emma. Nelson supported Addington by personal choice; there is every reason to believe that he did not admire the measures of his first lord of the Admiralty, St Vincent; but Nelson disguised his feelings and refrained from any specific political stance.*

The price of Nelson's political independence was lack of permanent influence and, to some extent, of official recognition. After his first success at the Battle of St Vincent, Nelson shied away from a baronetcy, which was an hereditary honour, 'without a fortune to support the Dignity', as he put it in a letter to Gilbert Elliot.[26] John Jervis, who had just been made Earl St Vincent, disagreed, writing to Nepean: 'Admiral Nelson is the modestest of all human beings, yet the Title of Baronet could not be better applied than on him.'[27] By contrast, the resentment that Nelson felt at only receiving a barony after the spectacular Nile victory never left him, and he felt that his victory was superior in every way to those of Viscount Duncan and Earl St Vincent. For a long period after the Battle of Copenhagen, Nelson unsuccessfully pestered every one in power to recognize the efforts of his officers and men by the awarding of medals. Some historians feel that

---

* For instance, Nelson wrote a long memorandum supporting lightly built gunboats for defence against invasion, against St Vincent's policy, although it remains unclear as to when he wrote it. This issue became of central importance in the last days of Addington's administration (Aspinall, *Prince of Wales*, IV, 535–7).

Nelson 'unsettled the establishment' and judge that 'Nelson was a more compelling symbol than the cult of George III'; ironically so, for the monarch and the court were at the centre of the traditional, stable values for which Nelson fought his battles.[28] As long as Nelson was at sea and not at court, George III approved of him. In early 1805 John Gore related to Nelson that the king had said publicly: '"Nelson had done it and I glory in Him for it. He never loses time in Parlez – it is always a word and a Blow with him – I Glory in him, I Glory in him"', these were the exact words of His Majesty at the Queens House.'[29] But from the time of the conflict surrounding Prince William Henry in 1786, the King never made it easy for Nelson.

Nelson confronted this lack of appreciation in his own way. He rarely appeared without those decorations that were given to him by foreign heads of state, as if to underline his perceived lack of recognition at home. While the political establishment felt uncomfortable with this show, gaining Nelson a reputation for vanity, little criticism came from within the service, and early biographers emphasized his modesty. It was not until 1815 that Nelson was directly described as 'vain' in the *Memoirs of Lady Hamilton*, which contained some of his letters to Emma. This was the start of Nelson's nineteenth-century fall from grace.[30] Biographers since have tended to side with the establishment.[31] But Nelson's penchant for decorations can also be explained as a vital ingredient of his leadership. Admiral Beatty with his six-button non-regulation jacket and jaunty cap angle, Churchill with his cigar and boiler suit, and Montgomery with his many cap badges – all these leaders sported symbols and knew their value when operating outside the rules. Nelson discovered it, even before gazetting and medals established a regular system of recognition of bravery and talent. The possibility of creating the 'Naval and Military Order of Merit' was discussed at the time of the funeral, and would have spread recognition for bravery and skill in battle much more widely, but it never came about.[32] The system itself, or lack of it, forced Nelson to promote and publicize himself.

Nelson, of course, hardly needed decorations to advertise his leadership and his reputation for coolness under fire, when he rapidly calculated the odds and employed his exceptional ability to take successful measures at moments of great stress. He took five supreme battle decisions. At Cape St Vincent he wore the *Captain* out of the line and then boarded the Spanish ships; at the Nile he decided to go straight into Aboukir Bay; at Copenhagen he arranged the ceasefire; at Trafalgar he made his feint and took the French line head-on. Each one was backed by a clear-sighted confidence in British military superiority, except, in the case of Copenhagen, when he realized that it was wearing thin. Any one of these decisions would have gained him naval immortality.

And he had luck too, many times over. Very often Nelson's career was in the hands of others, sometimes momentarily. In 1780 his life was saved by Admiral Parker's order to command another ship when he was desperately ill in his tent outside the fort on the San Juan River. John Sykes saved his life in the boat action off Cadiz in 1797. Later that year in Tenerife he was fortunate not to have been humiliated by the Spanish commander, General Gutierrez, after his failure to take Santa Cruz. The next year Alexander Ball's perseverance saved Nelson's reputation when his ship the *Alexander* towed the *Vanguard* away from the rocks off Sardinia and out of danger. In the autumn of 1803, George Ryves's chart made it possible to bring the Mediterranean fleet, short of water, into Agincourt Sound in the Maddalena Islands for the first time.

Of the many dozens of examples of his physical courage, one might select the boat action off Cadiz, the spectacular point-blank assault and boarding of the Spanish ships at Cape St Vincent and the final frontal attack at Trafalgar.[33] But courage is more than dash and daring. Sir Roger Curtis believed that 'very sharp intellects seldom excel in the technicalities of the profession'; what was needed was 'a constitutional courage, I don't mean against sword or gun merely, but against the elements & against the tempers & passions of mankind, to be the highest of all qualities for a sailor – they are tried under such emergencies, that nerve is, I believe, more valuable than mind.'[34] Here one can remember Nelson facing down the mutiny of the *Blanche* at Porto Ferrajo at the end of 1796, the decision to take his squadron to Alexandria in 1798 with no intelligence to guide him, or doggedly keeping his ships off Sicily in April 1805 when he knew nothing of the whereabouts of the French fleet. He faced the classic intelligence dilemma between timeliness and certainty over the decision to chase the enemy to the West Indies, writing on 4 May 1805 to Commissioner Otway at Gibraltar from Tetuán: 'I cannot very well properly run to the West Indies without something beyond mere surmise; and if I defer my departure, Jamaica may be lost.'[35] How many of his contemporaries would have taken that decision? No officer in the navy was perceived to have had more nerve than Nelson. Decisions made in the quiet of his cabin were often more difficult than the instinctive brilliance that he displayed at the height of battle.

Nor was anyone considered to have possessed a greater professional knowledge. The training from the time he was a young boy to his appointment as a lieutenant could not have been bettered, for he had sailed 45,000 miles before he kept a watch. Seamanship was, and is, of course, many things, including talent at keeping ships at sea, ship handling in confined waters, the ability and perseverance to get a ship to sail fast, and above all knowing how to keep a ship out of danger. In his early career Nelson's driving force sometimes got the better of his seamanship. He lost topmasts like any young captain, and a good many anchors, and later it was not unknown for him to go aground, as in the *Albemarle* in Port Royal Harbour or in the *Medusa* in the Thames estuary.[36] But Nelson continued to learn. In later years he developed a supremely methodical regime; his daily, detailed weather logs, as well as the long periods the Mediterranean fleet spent at sea through all weathers and without the loss of a spar, bear testimony to this. Others have been cited as better all-round seamen – Keats, George Cockburn and the younger Sam Hood, for instance – but it is difficult to see who could have handled a squadron better. Anyone who was able to take eleven ships and several thousand men into Aboukir Bay at sunset, with the minimum knowledge of the depth of water, and to have each ship anchor at stern close by each enemy ship had a very sophisticated appreciation of the seamanlike qualities of his ships, officers and crews, and the limits to which they could be driven.

Throughout the second half of his career, Nelson knew that, ship for ship, a British ship was superior in every way to a French or Spanish one, particularly when yard arm to yard arm, and he exploited this margin ruthlessly. The devastating power of the British carronades, lethal at short range, gave the British a great advantage and was the foundation of Nelson's close-range tactics, particularly as he himself took good care to obtain 68-pound carronades for his own ship. Nelson's risks were often based on forethought. The *Captain*'s sweep into the middle of the great Spanish wooden walls at the Battle of Cape St Vincent was brave but not foolhardy. Her carronades fired 117 68-pound shot into the Spanish ships, one every two and a half minutes.[37] The Spaniards had nothing to match them.

The final proof of Nelson's professional expertise lies in his care in reading and assessing intelligence (although he did not always guess correctly), both of which were critical to the presence of the British fleet in the Mediterranean between 1803 and 1805. From the unsuccessful Vado campaign of 1795–6, when he and his small squadron were often isolated, he was taught early lessons in intelligence, aided by the minister at Genoa, Francis Drake: he learnt the importance of building up a wider picture of information, and of managing the relationship between land and sea forces. After the chase before the Nile, when he was let down by London and French power straddled the Continent, Nelson began to rely on his own efforts, and accordingly he nurtured his consular and other contacts. On his return to the Mediterranean in 1803, he re-established this network; this time he had Alexander Scott to overcome the language problem.

In parallel, Nelson had to find solutions to the problems of food and supplies for his fleet, surrounded as he was in the Mediterranean and, briefly, in the Baltic, by countries that had been cowed by French land power. Although the performance of the supply services from England improved, Nelson, his officers and men, and his agent victualler afloat, Richard Ford, consistently achieved small miracles in feeding the fleet in the Mediterranean and in keeping his men healthy. Between 1803 and 1805 his role in the search for, and procurement of, naval stores for ship maintenance was vital. This plethora of administrative detail contributed to an acute knowledge of the capability of his fleet, which led, in turn, to the development of his strategic grasp in the Mediterranean after 1803.

Nelson's eye for detail was remarkable for an inspirational leader.[38] Numerous examples tell of his detailed concerns, such as maintaining and making good the anchor warps before the Battle of the Nile. These preparations enabled him to take risks in battle. Perhaps the most considered judgement on Nelson was from Cuthbert Collingwood in a letter to Sir Thomas Pasley soon after Trafalgar: 'He possessed the zeal of an enthusiast directed by talents which Nature had very bountifully bestowed on him, and everything seemed, as if by enchantment, to prosper under his direction. But it was the effect of system, and nice combination, not of chance.'[39]

Those who command can be divided into those who control and those who delegate; the minority who can bring themselves to trust their subordinates reap the greater rewards. The core of Nelson's talent for leadership was that he made his officers and men feel as if he had faith in them and depended upon them, taking his captains into his confidence, not only engendering personal loyalty quickly and permanently but also creating an atmosphere of trust and cooperation.[40] What a contrast with the traditions and style of the previous generation of admirals, rent by politics and conflict. St Vincent, from whom in other respects Nelson learnt so much, commanded primarily through fear. The most demonstrable manifestation of this trust and confidence is Nelson's delegation of authority during battle, which encouraged all to use their initiative. No better example can be given than Foley's daring course around the head of the anchored French line in Aboukir Bay on 1 August 1798. In Thomas Byam Martin's opinion, Nelson 'had a most happy way of gaining the affectionate respect of all who had the happiness to serve under his command. I never conversed with any officer who served under Nelson without hearing the most hearty expressions of attachment, and admiration of his frank and conciliating manner to all who showed themselves zealous in the execution of their duties.'[41] Edward Codrington vouched for 'the pains he took to keep the fleet in health and efficiency in every respect, and by his kindness and attention to the wants, wishes, and comforts of those under his command. The predominant feeling was not fear of censure, but apprehension of not gaining his approbation.'[42]

Men follow and are attracted to those who represent certainty, especially in situations that are confusing, dangerous and fast moving. It was a wonderful quality to have had on the quarterdeck of a British warship approaching an enemy fleet. Nelson's extraordinary self-belief brought him to a level of certainty that inspired others and brought constant fighting success. When he arrived at a decision, which he always did quickly, he carried it through ruthlessly. But in more subtle situations certainty becomes a liability. The two shadows that will always fall over him arise from this quality. In Naples, Nelson applied a quarterdeck train of thought to a situation that required political judgement and clear-headedness. In the thrall of the scheming Queen Maria Carolina, he failed to rise above the situation to see the larger picture. Others did. Collingwood, for instance, saw through the Palermo court; Thomas Fremantle was disgusted by it, saying it 'almost ruined, indeed for a time did ruin, the character of Nelson and paralysed all the energy and zeal which distinguished him in every other situation'.[43] The measures that Nelson was called on to take at Naples needed to be legally correct, morally sound and politically possible. Although he acted within the limits of the powers given to him by the king of Naples, his political naivety allowed the use of British ships and men to facilitate executions and cruelty. He did not have to hang his fellow admiral Caracciolo, for he could have waited for of the king. This was Nelson at his most impatient and ruthless. The same qualities governed his treatment of his wife, Fanny. Once he had made up his mind that his future happiness lay with Emma Hamilton, he took every social risk to achieve it; but, although he provided for Fanny with generosity, both during his lifetime and in his will, his personal relations with her after his decision were without sentiment, even savage.

Horatio Nelson was above all the product of the eighteenth-century navy that formed him. With professional if not social advantages, he had to strive – as everyone else in the navy was striving – for recognition and riches within a system in which promotion demanded some advantage and that was not yet designed to distribute fair and systematic reward. Yet he entered the navy at the right time. Had he been born even ten years later, Nelson's advance would have been hindered not only by an increasingly aristocratic and hierarchical service, but by an organization that also stifled individualism and idiosyncrasy. It is difficult to see the young Nelson ever getting to the top of the Victorian navy. But he reached the peak of his career in the first years of the nineteenth century, which were dramatic and special. Britain was under almost continuous threat of invasion. The military success and the autocratic power of the Emperor Napoleon united the country against nearby danger. Nelson personified the naval strength that was its defence; but, as the image of that leader came into being, the truth suffered, especially after his death. Two hundred years later the evidence reveals a driven, flawed, tough-spirited man of exceptional intelligence and talent, whose success can be attributed to reasons far more complex than those represented by an heroic, all-encompassing figure; and he becomes infinitely more understandable and interesting.

Chronology of Nelson's Life

This chronology has been compiled from manuscript sources. For the time when Nelson was ashore, these are often comprised of random references in his letters and those of others. For the journey from Italy through Germany in 1800, I have followed Blumel. Nelson's time can be traced in detail through the occasional use of muster books ((UK)NA: PRO, ADM 36) but principally by ships' logs ((UK)NA: PRO, ADM 51 and 52; NMM, ADM/L).

Log entries at this time began their day at the noon sight and the ensuing twenty-four hours was computed as the nautical day. The nautical day thus ran twelve hours ahead of 'land' time. This can best be illustrated by the Battle of Aboukir Bay, which started at 6.15 in the evening. In 'land' time the date of the battle was 1 August 1798; but because the nautical day began at 12 noon, it is recorded in the various logs as beginning at 6.15 p.m. on 2 August. The discrepancy between sea and land time has not been corrected in this chronology.

During Nelson's lifetime ships in harbour would use civil time, or 'midnight to midnight'. See John Norie, *Practical Navigation* (1864 ed.), 300. Nelson called this 'Natural Day' at the head of one of his journals (NMM, CRK/14/73). Coincidentally, the Admiralty order for changing the start of the nautical day to midnight in ships' logs was dated 21 October 1805 (Bonner Smith, 91).

I   YOUTH AND DISAPPOINTMENT 1758–1793

1   Burnham Thorpe

1758

29 September: Born at Burnham Thorpe, Norfolk

1767

26 December: Catherine Nelson, his mother, dies

1768

Educated at the Royal Grammar School, Norwich

1769

Educated at Sir John Paston's School, North Walsham

1771

1 January: Appointed to the *Raisonable* as midshipman
24 April: Joins *Raisonable* at the Nore

3   Horace Nelson, Midshipman

21 May: Discharged from the *Raisonable*, transferred to the *Triumph*, and is mustered continuously as captain's servant from 24 May while he goes to the West Indies
Summer: Sails to Jamaica and other islands in the merchant ship *Mary Ann*

1772

July: Returns. Rejoins *Triumph*

1773

7 May: Entered on the books of the *Carcass* bound for the Arctic
4 June: *Carcass* sails from the Nore
15 October: Returns from Arctic (last mustered 12 October)
27 October: Entered on books of the *Seahorse*
19 November: Sails from Spithead to East Indies

1774

4–23 March: At Capetown
5 April: Rated as able seaman
16 May: Arrives in Madras, leaves 16 September
16–27 September: Passage to Kedgeree (Kedjeri) on the Hoogly (Hugli) River, near Calcutta
27 September–16 January: Anchors at Kedgeree

1775

16–28 January: Passage to Madras

29–30 January: Anchors in Madras Roads

30 January–17 March: Cruise to Bombay (19 February *Seahorse* chases and fires at two ships of Haider Ali)

17–25 March: Moors at Bombay

25 March–15 August: Convoys to and from Persian Gulf via Surat, Bushire and Muscat

15–25 August: Moors at Bombay

26 August–10 September: Sails to Madras

11–27 September: Anchors in Madras Roads

28 September–8 October: Cruising off Madras

9–14 October: Anchors in Madras Roads

15–22 October: Passage to Trincomalee

23 October–1 November: Anchors at Trincomalee

31 October: Rated midshipman

1–13 November: Passage to Anjenjo (Anjutenga)

14–27 November: Anchors in Anjenjo Road

28 November–7 December: Passage to Goa

8–10 December: Goa

1776

19 December–23 March: Bombay. Falls ill from malaria during this period

14 March: Discharged from *Seahorse*

23 March: Sails in *Dolphin* from Bombay to England

22 May–19 June: Moors in Simon's Bay, South Africa

31 August: *Dolphin* anchors at Spithead

16 September: Last muster on board *Dolphin* (24 September *Dolphin* pays off at Deptford)

26 September: Appointed acting lieutenant of the *Worcester*

5 December–9 January 1777: *Worcester* sails from Spithead with convoy to Gibraltar

1777

9 January–14 February: Anchors at Gibraltar with homebound convoy

15 February–2 April: Sails with convoy via Cadiz

3 April: Anchors at Spithead

9 April: Passes lieutenant's examination

4   Lieutenant to Captain: The West Indies

10 April: Appointed second lieutenant of the *Lowestoffe* (12 April 'appears')
3 May: Sails from Sheerness to Spithead
16 May: Escorts convoy from Spithead to West Indies
30 May–11 June: Funchal, Madeira
4–7 July: Anchors at Carlisle Bay, Barbados
8–10 July: Passage to Antigua
11 July: Anchors at St John's, Antigua
12–18 July: Passage to Port Royal, Jamaica
19 July–8 August: Moors at Port Royal
9 August–30 September: Windward Passage cruise
30 September–6 November: Moors at Port Royal
6–24 November: Second Windward Passage cruise
24 November–10 December: Moors at Port Royal
10 December–31 January: Third Windward Passage cruise

1778

31 January–5 May: *Lowestoffe* refits at Port Royal
6 May–24 June: Fourth Windward Passage cruise (26 May commissioned as third lieutenant of the *Bristol*)
25 June–4 July: The *Lowestoffe* moors at Port Royal (2 July enters and 'appears' on the *Bristol*
5 July–14 August: The *Bristol* cruises in the Windward Passage and Caicos Keys
15 August–4 September: At Port Royal (4 September made first lieutenant of the *Bristol*)
5 September–20 October: The *Bristol* cruises in company in the Windward Passage
20 October–6 November: Refits at Port Royal
6 November–21 December: Second *Bristol* Windward Passage cruise in company (8 December given first command, the *Badger* brig)

1779

1 January: Receives commission and takes command of the *Badger* at Port Royal
25 January: Sets out on cruise to the Mosquito shore
2–21 April: Returns to Port Royal, *Badger* careened
22 April: Starts cruise around the east end of Jamaica
29 April: Takes prize off Cuba, *La Prudente* (80 tons)
24–9 May: Convoys ships to local ports in Jamaica
2 June: Rescues crew of the *Glasgow* when burnt in Montego Bay
11 June: Appointed as post-captain to command the *Hinchinbroke*

19 June: Discharged from the *Badger* but, in the absence of his ship, given charge of the harbour defences of Port Royal

1 September: Takes command of the *Hinchinbroke*, refitting at Port Royal until 4 October

5 October–13 December: Intelligence cruise to South American mainland, then cruises at eastern end of Jamaica

13 December–2 February: Refits at Port Royal

1780

3 February: Sets off from Port Royal with transports on the expedition to the San Juan River, via Mosquito Keys

24 March: Reaches the San Juan River

28 March: Starts up the San Juan River in boats

7 April: Appointed to the *Janus*

9 April: Takes St Bartholomew Island

13 April: Start of the siege of the fortress of San Juan

30 April: Hands over command of the *Hinchinbroke* to Cuthbert Collingwood and is taken back to Port Royal

16 August: Entered on the *Lion*'s books as a supernumerary and resigns command of the *Janus*

5 September: *Lion* leaves for England with convoy

24 November: *Lion* reaches Spithead

26 November: discharged from *Lion*; goes to Bath to recover

5   *Albemarle*

(*November 1780 to August 1781: On half-pay, chiefly at Bath*)

1781

22 January: Arrives at Bath

March: Visits London

May: Visits London (7 May stays at Kentish Town with William Suckling)

15 August: Commissions the *Albemarle* at Woolwich (23 August 'appears')

12 October: Moors in Long Reach, River Thames

15 October: Anchors at the Nore

29 October: Presses men from East Indiaman in the Thames estuary

30 October–November: Passage to Denmark with the *Argo* and the *Enterprise*

4 November–7 December: Moors at Elsinore

8 December: Sails with convoy to England

17–31 December: Anchors in Yarmouth Roads

1782

2 January: *Albemarle* arrives in Downs

26 January: While anchored in Downs, *Albemarle* severely damaged by collision with East India store ship *Brilliant*

7 February: Reaches Spithead under jury-masts

8 February–5 April: Repairs at Portsmouth Dockyard (visits London in early March to see physician)

6 April: Sails for Cork

17–25 April: Anchors in Cork Harbour to pick up convoy

26 April–27 May: Crosses Atlantic with convoy to St John's, Newfoundland

28 May–4 June: Anchors at St John's

5–16 June: Moors in Capillon Bay

17 June–1 July: Passage to St Lawrence with convoy of thirty-two ships

2–4 July: Moors at the Isle of Bic watering, leaves convoy, heads back down the St Lawrence, past Nova Scotia, to cruise off Cape Cod

5–12 July: Passage to cruising area off Cape Cod

13 July to end of August: Cruises off Cape Cod (15 August chased by five French warships over the St George's Banks)

End August–17 September: Passage to Quebec

18 September–15 October: Moors at Quebec

16–19 October: Anchors at the Isle of Bic

20 October: With convoy to New York

11 November: Arrives at Sandy Hook

13–19 November: Anchors at New York (in the East River 13–15 November; in the North River 16–19 November)

20 November: Sails to Sandy Hook, anchors 21 November

22 November: With Hood's fleet to the West Indies

5 December: Arrives off Cap François and cruises

9 December–4 February 1783: With fleet off Monte Cristo

1783

7 January: Captures American prize

25 January: Captures French *Queen of France* mast ship

5–15 February: Repairs at Port Royal (7–8 February aground in the harbour, guns out before *Albemarle* refloats)

16 February–6 April: Cruises off Jamaica and South American mainland (8–9 March attempts to take Turk Island from French; 28 March captures small Spanish prize)

7–25 April: Moors in Port Royal and Kingston

26 April–24 June: With the fleet for England (10–19 May anchors at Havana and in Augustin Roads)

25 June: Arrives Spithead, 26 June in Portsmouth Harbour
3 July: *Albemarle* paid off and Nelson put on half-pay
July: Ill in London
Late August: To Burnham Thorpe
October: To France to learn the language; stays in St Omer

1784

Mid January: Returns to England
End of January: Short visit to his father in Bath

6 *Boreas* and the West Indies

18 March: Appointed to the *Boreas*
24 March: Takes command of the *Boreas* in Long Reach, River Thames
12–13 April: Anchors in the Downs
16–17 April: Passage to Spithead
18 April–17 May: Anchors at Spithead
18–19 May: Anchors at St Helens and sails to Plymouth
20–21 May: Anchors in Plymouth Sound
22 May–25 June: Passage to the West Indies (1–8 June at Funchal, Madeira)
26 June–20 July: In Carlisle Bay, Barbados
21 July: Sails for Martinique
22–3 July: Anchors at Port Royal, Martinique, and in St Piers Roads
25–6 July: Anchors at Prince Rupert Bay, Dominica
27 July: Anchors at Basseterre, St Kitts
28 July–31 October: English Harbour, Antigua, for the hurricane season
1–6 November: Sails to Barbados with the *Mediator* and the *Rattler*
2 November: Boards a vessel bound for St Kitts from Boston
7–20 November: Moors at Carlisle Bay, Barbados (17 November orders several
American ships that came into harbour not to anchor)
21–2 November: Sails to Antigua
23 November: Moors at English Harbour
24 November: Sails to St John, Virgin Islands
25–7 November: Surveys Crawl Harbour, St John, Virgin Islands
28 November–2 December: Cruises towards Antigua
3–5 December: Moors at St John's, Freeman's Bay and English Harbour, Antigua
6–9 December: Cruises towards Barbados
10–22 December: Anchors at Carlisle Bay, Barbados
23 December: Sails for Antigua
24 December–2 January: Anchors in English Harbour

1785

3–4 January: Sails for Montserrat

5 January: Anchors in Montserrat Roads

7–8 January: Anchors in Nevis Roads

9–13 January: Anchors in Basseterre, St Kitts

14 January: Anchors in Nevis Roads

15 January: Anchors in Saltpans, St Kitts, taking in ballast

16–18 January: Anchors at Basseterre, St Kitts

19–20 January: Cruising

23–7 January: Anchors in Prince Rupert's Bay, Dominica, for wood and water

28 January: Passage to St Kitts

29–31 January: Anchors at Basseterre, St Kitts

1–3 February: Anchors in Nevis Roads

4–5 February: Cruising

6–8 February: Moors for repairs in English Harbour; Moutray pennant 'incident'

9–12 February: Passage to Barbados

13–23 February: Anchors in Carlisle Bay

24–5 February: Passage to Antigua

26 February–10 March: Moors in English Harbour

11 March: Passage to St Kitts

12–16 March: Basseterre, St Kitts

17–19 March: Cruises near Nevis and St Kitts

20–21 March: Anchors in Old Road, St Kitts

22–7 March: Basseterre

28–31 March: Cruising

(No log entries survive for 1–19 April 1785)

20–24 April: Carlisle Bay, Barbados

24 April: Passage to Antigua

25 April: Anchors in Freeman's Bay, Antigua

26 April: To St John's, Antigua

27 April: Anchors in St John's

28–30 April: Anchors in Nevis Roads

1–9 May: Anchors in Basseterre Roads, St Kitts (2 May seizes the *Eclipse* of Philadelphia)

10 May: Sails towards Nevis Roads

11 May: Anchors in Nevis Roads

12–13 May: Sails towards St Kitts

13–22 May: Anchors in Basseterre Roads (19 May sends boat to Nevis and 20 May boat returns; 19–20 May seizes four vessels: *Fairview*, *George and Jane*, *Hercules* and *Nancy Pleasants*)

22–4 May: At Nevis (24 May Sir Richard Hughes arrives in Nevis in the *Adamant* and leaves quickly)

25 May: To Basseterre, St Kitts; stays until 28 May

28 May: Sails to Nevis

29 May: To Basseterre, St Kitts; stays until 2 June

3 June: To Nevis

4 June: To Basseterre, St Kitts

5 June: To Nevis; stays until 8 June

9 June: To Basseterre, St Kitts; stays until 11 June

12 June: To Nevis; stays until 20 June

20 June: To St Eustatius, keeping close company with French frigate; stays until 24 June

24 June: Sails to Nevis

25 June: To Basseterre, St Kitts

26 June: To Nevis; stays until 28 June

29 June: Anchors in Basseterre Roads

30 June: Sails to Nevis; stays until 1 July

2 July: Anchors in Basseterre Roads

3 July: Sails to Nevis

4 July: Anchors at Basseterre at 6 a.m.

5 July: Anchors 'in Nevis Road in 4 fathoms at 5 a.m.'; stays until 6 July

6–7 July: Sails to Basseterre, arrives at 4 a.m. on 8 July

8–9 July: Anchors in Basseterre

10–29 July: Anchors in Nevis Roads

30 July: Basseterre Roads

31 July–2 August: Anchors at Nevis

3 August: Anchors in St Kitts Roads

4–8 August: Nevis Roads

9–10 August: Sails to Antigua

10 August–17 October: English Harbour (25 August hurricane)

17–18 October: Sails to Nevis

19 October: Looks into Basseterre

20–31 October: Anchors at Nevis (21 October seizes the brig *Active* for being an American-built vessel)

1 November: Cruising

2–3 November: Anchors in Nevis Roads

4–5 November: Basseterre Roads

6–7 November: Nevis Roads

8–9 November: Cruises towards St Kitts

11 November: Anchors in Basseterre Roads

12–13 November: Anchors in Nevis Roads

14 November: Basseterre Roads and Nevis Roads

17 November: Anchors in Basseterre Roads

20–26 November: Anchors in Nevis Roads
26 November: Sails for Old Road; stays until 27 November
28 November–2 December: Anchors in Nevis Roads
3 December: Anchors at Basseterre
4 December: At Guadeloupe
5–6 December: Anchors at Prince Rupert's Bay
11–12 December: Sails towards Antigua
13–14 December: Freeman's Bay
15–18 December: Passage to Barbados
19–21 December: Anchors in Carlisle Bay
22 December: Passage to Nevis
23 December–8 January: Anchors in Nevis Roads

1786

8 January: Sails to Antigua
9–15 January: Moors at English Harbour
16–18 January: Anchors in Nevis Roads
19 January: Sails towards St Kitts
20 January: Anchors at Basseterre
21 January–12 February: Nevis Roads (2 February seizes the *Sally* of Connecticut)
13–14 February: Cruising
14 February: Anchors at Gustavia, St Barthélémy
15–22 February: Anchors in Nevis Roads
23–4 February: Sails to Antigua
25 February: Moors in Freeman's Bay
26 February–7 March: Cruises towards Barbados
8 March–20 May: Moors in Carlisle Bay, Barbados (15 March Nelson seizes the *Jane and Elizabeth*; 18 March takes possession of American schooner *Brilliant*, alias *Louisa*)
24 May–14 June: Anchors in Nevis Roads
23 June–3 August: Between Nevis Roads and Basseterre (8 July seizes a schooner from Trinidad under Spanish colours on suspicion of being an American – finds American papers, 'most likely the *Eagle*'; 13 July Gustavia, St Barthélémy)

7 Senior Naval Officer, Leeward Islands

1 August: Admiral Hughes leaves for England; Nelson now senior naval officer, Leeward Islands Station
4 August–8 October: Refits in English Harbour
9–17 October: At Nevis and Basseterre
18–26 October: Visit to Dominica

28–31 October: In Antigua
1–23 November: Nevis, Basseterre and St Eustatius
24–5 November: Sails to Antigua
26 November–1 December: Antigua
1 December: Sails to Dominica
2–7 December: Anchors at Roseau, Dominica (3 December meets Prince William Henry)
8–10 December: Anchors in Prince Rupert's Bay
11–12 December: To Antigua
13 December–28 January: Anchors in Freeman's Bay, then English Harbour

1787

29–30 January: Anchors in Nevis Roads
31 January–2 February: Passage to Antigua
3–9 February: Freeman's Bay
10 February: Passage to Montserrat
11–13 February: Anchors in Plymouth Roads, Montserrat
14 February: Passage to Nevis
15 February–18 March: At Nevis and Basseterre
11 March: Marries Frances Nisbet
19–30 March: Sails for Virgin Gorda, St Eustatius, Tortola and back to Nevis
31 March–4 April: Anchors in Nevis Roads
5 April: Sails for Antigua
6–24 April: Alongside the wharf at English Harbour
25–30 April: Cruises near by
1–24 May: Nevis Roads (21 May salutes Prince William Henry as he leaves the Leewards Islands Station)
25 May: Sails to Antigua
26 May–3 June: Anchors in St John's Roads, Antigua
4 June: The *Boreas* sails for England
5 July: Arrives at Spithead, moors there until 17 August
20 August–22 September: Moors at the Little Nore
23 September–21 November: Moors at the Great Nore
22 November: Moves the *Boreas* into Sheerness Harbour
30 November: Ship paid off

8   Half-pay in Norfolk

17 December: Gives evidence at the trial of James Carse
Christmas: Horatio and Fanny stay at Cavendish Square with Arthur Herbert

1788

Early January: To Bath until early April (mid January to Plymouth to visit Prince William Henry, returns 21 January)
Late April–early May: West Country (Plymouth 26 April, Exmouth 30 April and Exmouth Moor 6 May)
Late May – early June: Cavendish Square, London
8 August: Barton, Norfolk
26 August: London

(1789–1792 Burnham Thorpe)

1789

18 May: At Hilborough
Late June: Visits London to be interviewed by the Victualling Board

1790

8 May: Visits London and the Admiralty Office
11 October: London

1793

6 January: Appointed to the *Agamemnon*

II   MATURITY AND TRIUMPH 1793–1798

10   The Commissioning of the *Agamemnon*

7 January: In London
Mid January: To Burnham
7 February: Puts the *Agamemnon* in commission while in dock at Chatham
Mid February: To Burnham
4 March: Nelson travels down to London (12 March still in London)
15 March: At Chatham
16–22 March: *Agamemnon* moors off Princes Bridge at Chatham
23 March–16 April: *Agamemnon* moors at Blackstakes at the mouth of the Medway (4 April Nelson now permanently on board)
17–25 April: *Agamemnon* anchors at the Nore, delayed by gale
25 April: Sails to the Downs
28 April: Escorts convoy to Spithead

29 April: Moors at Spithead

2–6 May: Short cruise to French coast, chases French ships at La Hogue, back to Spithead

12 May: Sails with Hood to the Mediterranean

17 June: Arrives at Cadiz after a very slow passage

18–22 June: At Cadiz, sails on 23 June

24–7 June: Moors in Gibraltar Bay

28 June–17 July: Sails along the coast of Spain to join squadron off Toulon

11   The Western Mediterranean: Frustrated Subordinate

18 July–1 September: Cruises off Toulon and the French coast

2–11 September: Sails south to Naples

12–16 September: Anchors in Naples Bay

17–24 September: Passage from Naples to Leghorn

25–30 September: Moors in Leghorn Roads

1–5 October: Passage from Leghorn to Toulon

6–9 October: At single anchor in Toulon Harbour

10–20 October: Cruises off the north of Corsica

21–2 October: chases the *Melpomène* frigate east of Corsica

23–8 October: Cruises off south of Sardinia with squadron, including a day anchored in Cagliari Bay

29–31 October: Passage south to Tunis with Linzee's squadron

1–15 November: Anchors in Tunis Bay

16–25 November: Cruises off Tunis

26–9 November: Tunis Bay

30 November–21 December: Passage north to blockade ports in north Corsica

22 December–1 January: Anchors in Leghorn Roads

1794

2–28 January: Off north coast of Corsica blockading Calvi (21 January raid on San Fiorenzo)

29–30 January: Leghorn Roads

1–9 February: Cruises off north Corsica (5 February takes Centuri, burns six vessels; 8 February anchors in Rogliano Bay, burns eight vessels in Maginaggio)

10–13 February: Cutting out prize at Capraia

14–17 February: Leghorn Roads

18–19 February: Tower of Miamo, north of Bastia, surrenders to Nelson

20–21 February: Secures the island of Pianosa

23 February–18 March: The *Agamemnon* supports the **Siege of Bastia**, sometimes at anchor, sometimes cruising off

19–24 March: Anchors in San Fiorenzo Bay

25–6 March: Mortello Bay, then to Bastia

27 March–8 June: The *Agamemnon* supports Siege of Bastia (Nelson on shore with besieging forces 6 April–24 May; 22 May surrender of Bastia)

7–17 June: Cruises off the north of Corsica

18–21 June: **Siege of Calvi** – lands troops, seamen and provisions at Galese Bay (Porto Agro) south of Calvi (20 June–11 August Nelson on shore with besieging forces; 12 July wounded in the eye)

22–4 June: The *Agamemnon* cruises off Calvi

25 June–31 July: Anchors in the bay, supporting Siege of Calvi

1–3 August: The *Agamemnon* cruises off Calvi

4–7 August: At anchor at San Fiorenzo during a gale

8–15 August: Cruises off Calvi

11 August: Nelson returns to the *Agamemnon*

16–17 August: Anchors in Mortello Bay

17 August–19 September: Leghorn Roads

20–28 September: Moors in Genoa Mole

29 September–20 October: Cruises off Toulon with squadron

21–31 October: Leghorn Roads

1–13 November: Cruises off Toulon, then north of Corsica

14 November–20 December: Leghorn Roads

21 December–8 January: Cruises off Toulon, then north of Corsica

1795

9–30 January: Moors in Mortello Bay

1–6 February: Moors in San Fiorenzo Bay

7–24 February: Cruises off Toulon in heavy weather

28 February–8 March: Leghorn Roads

9–12 March: Cruises north in Gulf of Genoa

13–14 March: **Hotham's First Action** with the French fleet

16–18 March: Attempts to tow prize into Port Especia (Spezia)

19–24 March: At anchor in Port Especia

25–6 March: Passage to San Fiorenzo

27 March–17 April: Moors in San Fiorenzo Bay

18–27 April: Fleet sails to Leghorn

28 April–8 May: Leghorn Roads

9 May–29 June: Squadron cruises off Minorca

1 June: Appointed a colonel of marines

30 June–4 July: Moors in San Fiorenzo Bay

5–14 July: Fleet off north Corsica, with long pursuit of the French fleet towards the French coast in light airs (8–14 July **Hotham's Second Action**)

15 July: Mortello Bay

12   The Western Mediterranean: Independent Command

16–17 July: Passage to Genoa
18 July: Moors in Genoa Mole
21–2 July: Anchors in Vado Bay
23–4 July: Passage to Leghorn
25–8 July: Leghorn Roads
29–31 July: Passage to Vado Bay
1–25 August: Anchors in Vado Bay
26–7 August: At Alassio captures a French corvette
28 August–4 September: Anchors in Vado Bay
29 August: Orders boat attack at Oneglia; four killed
5–15 September: Squadron cruises towards Genoa
16–19 September: Moors in Genoa Mole
20–23 September: Cruises towards Leghorn
24–8 September: Leghorn Roads
29–30 September: Passage to Vado Bay
1–12 October: Moors in Vado Bay
13–16 October: Cruises towards Leghorn
17–19 October: Leghorn Roads
20 October–5 November: Cruises off French coast around Toulon in heavy weather
6–12 November: Vado Bay
13 November: Passage to Genoa
14–27 November: Moors in a gale in Genoa Roads
28 November–5 December: Cruises towards Leghorn
7 December–15 January: Moors in Leghorn Roads

1796

16–18 January: Passage to San Fiorenzo
19–21 January: Anchors in San Fiorenzo Bay
22 January–5 February: Cruises towards Genoa, with one day at anchor in Port Especia for water
6–8 February: Moors in Genoa Roads
9–11 February: Passage to Leghorn
12–13 February: Moors Leghorn Roads
14 February–2 March: Cruises off Toulon
3–4 March: Moors off Genoa Mole
5–6 March: Passage to Leghorn
7–12 March: Leghorn Roads
13–26 March: Cruises off Toulon

26–9 March: Genoa Mole, getting the *Blanche* out with difficulty

30 March–3 April: Passage to San Fiorenzo Bay

4–5 April: San Fiorenzo Bay

6–8 April: Passage to Genoa

9–10 April: Genoa Mole

9 April: **Appointed commodore** (not confirmed until 29 September)

11–14 April: Covering Austrian troops in operations near Genoa

15–20 April: Genoa Mole

21–9 April: Cruises along French coast (26 April cuts out four vessels from Finale, near Loano)

30 April–3 May: Genoa Mole

4–17 May: Cruises along French coast

17–24 May: Leghorn Roads

25 May–5 June: Cruises along French coast (1 June cuts out French vessels at Port Maurice)

5–10 June: Moors in San Fiorenzo Bay

10 June: Transfers to the *Captain*

11–12 June: Moors in San Fiorenzo Bay

13–21 June: Passage to Genoa (off Toulon 17–18 June)

22–3 June: Off Genoa Mole

24–6 June: Passage to Leghorn

27–9 June: Joins other ships blockading Leghorn in the roads

30 June–1 July: Passage to San Fiorenzo Bay

1–5 July: Anchors storm-bound in San Fiorenzo Bay

6–8 July: Commands convoy of troops to Porto Ferrajo, Elba

9–11 July: Lands troops; at anchor in Porto Ferrajo

12 July: Sails to Port Especia

13–14 July: At anchor in Port Especia

15 July: Sails to Leghorn

16–20 July: Leghorn Roads

21–2 July: Passage to Genoa

23–5 July: Anchors off Genoa Mole

26–7 July: Passage to Leghorn

28 July–15 August: Blockades Leghorn

16 August: Sails to Bastia

16–17 August: Anchors in Bastia Bay

18–20 August: Passage to Leghorn

21–6 August: Blockades Leghorn

27 August–2 September: Passage to the fleet off Toulon and return to blockading ships off Leghorn

3 September: Anchors in Leghorn Roads

4 September: Passage to Genoa

5–10 September: Moors inside Genoa Mole

11 September: Off Genoa Mole, boats pursuing deserters
12–14 September: Passage to Bastia
15–16 September: Bastia Roads, taking on troops and ordnance
17 September: Passage with convoy to Capraia
18 September: Takes possession of Capraia
20–24 September: Passage to Leghorn
25–6 September: Leghorn Roads (25 September: Charles Stuart takes command of the *Captain* under Nelson as commodore)
27 September: Nelson transfers to the *Diadem* (Captain Towry)
27 September–2 October: Passage to Ajaccio
3–10 October: Moors in Ajaccio Bay, replacing *Captain*'s foremast
11–14 October: Passage to Bastia
16–20 October: Bastia Bay, embarking troops in convoy (19 October rejoins *Captain*)
21–4 October: Ferrajo Bay
25 October: Passage to San Fiorenzo
26 October–2 November: San Fiorenzo Bay, evacuating troops
3 November–1 December: Passage to Gibraltar with the fleet
2–10 December: Moors in Gibraltar Bay
8 December: Captain Ralph Willet Miller supersedes Captain Stuart in command of the *Captain*

13   *La Minerve* and the *Blanche* to Porto Ferrajo

11 December: Nelson hoists his broad pennant aboard *La Minerve*
11–14 December: Takes on stores in Gibraltar Bay
15–27 December: Accompanied by the *Blanche*, sails for Porto Ferrajo, Elba. (20 December action with the Spanish frigate *Sabina*; chased by Spanish squadron)
27 December–29 January 1797: Moors in Porto Ferrajo

1797

29 January–9 February: Sets out with convoy back to Gibraltar
10–11 February: Moors in Rosia Bay, Gibraltar
12 February: Sails from Gibraltar, chased by Spanish line of battleships

14   The Battle of Cape St Vincent and the Blockade of Cadiz

13 February: Joins Jervis's fleet
14 February: Shifts his broad pennant back aboard the *Captain*: **Battle of St Vincent**. Transfers when the firing ceases to the *Irresistible*

15 February–23 March: Commands detached squadron cruising off Cape St Vincent

24 March: Shifts his broad pennant back to the *Captain*

2 April: **Hoists his flag as rear-admiral of the Blue** off Cadiz

2–12 April: Cruises with his squadron between Cape St Vincent and Cape St Mary

13 April–18 May: Into the Mediterranean with a squadron to escort the convoy taking the Porto Ferrajo garrison to Gibraltar (21 April meets it north-west of Minorca)

19–22 May: Moors in Gibraltar Bay

22–4 May: Sails to Cadiz

26 May: Hoists flag in the *Theseus* and continues with the blockade of Cadiz

4 July: Incident with the Spanish gunboats off Cadiz

14–22 July: Sails with squadron to Tenerife

15   Disaster at Santa Cruz

23 July: First unsuccessful **attack on Santa Cruz**, Tenerife

25 July: Second unsuccessful attack on Santa Cruz; Nelson wounded in the right arm, which is amputated

27 July–16 August: Squadron sails back to Cadiz

20 August: Nelson embarks on board the *Seahorse*

21 August–1 September: Voyage to Spithead

2 September: Goes ashore (strikes his flag on board the *Seahorse* on 3 September (sea time))

16   Recovery and High Command

c. 2–3 September: Travels to Bath

18 September: Travels to London with Fanny; takes lodgings at No. 141 Bond Street

27 September: Invested as Knight of the Bath at St James's Palace

28 November: Receives the Freedom of the City of London

19 December: Attends St Paul's for celebration of naval victories

c. 25 December: Returns to Bath

1798

Mid February: Travels to London with Lady Nelson, stays at No. 96 Bond Street

28 March: Leaves London for Spithead

29 March: Hoists his flag on board the *Vanguard*

1–9 April: At St Helens, gathering convoy for Lisbon

10 April: Sails for Lisbon
30 April: Joins Lord St Vincent's fleet off Cadiz

17   Chasing the French

3 May: Sails for Gibraltar
4–7 May: Stores and watering at Gibraltar
8–20 May: *Vanguard*'s passage to Toulon with the *Orion*, the *Alexander* and two frigates
21–3 May: Storm dismasts *Vanguard* and she is towed to San Pietro Road at the south of Sardinia
24–6 May: Repairs at anchor
27 May–7 June: Sails towards Toulon, cruises off
8 June: Joined by Troubridge with eleven sail of the line and one 50-gun ship
10–16 June: Sails south down the coast of Italy
17 June: Off Naples
20 June: Through the Strait of Messina
22 June: Sights outlying French frigates south-east of Sicily; consults captains and decides to go for Alexandria
29 June: Reaches Alexandria, then sails north for Turkey (Karamania)
4 July: Reaches Turkey; sails for Italy
20–24 July: Fleet anchors in the harbour of Syracuse, Sicily
25 July: Sails east again

18   The Battle of the Nile

1–2 August: Finds French fleet in Aboukir Bay; **Battle of the Nile**; takes or destroys eleven ships of the line
3–18 August: The *Vanguard* repairs damage in Aboukir Bay
19 August–11 September: The *Vanguard* sails with the *Culloden* and the *Alexander* for Naples in light headwinds
12–13 September: Anchors off Messina in calms
15 September: The *Vanguard* again loses foremast in heavy squall; four seamen killed
16–20 September: Towed by the *Thalia* towards Naples
22 September: Moors in Naples Bay

III PASSION AND DISCREDIT 1798–1801

19 Palermo and Naples

22 September–14 October: The *Vanguard* anchors in Naples Bay

15 October–5 November: Cruises to Malta

6–22 November: Nelson ashore; the *Vanguard* moors in Naples Bay

22–8 November: Sails in heavy winds with small squadron to Leghorn

29 November: Disembarks troops at Leghorn

30 November–5 December: Passage to Naples

6–23 December: Moors in Naples Bay (21 December Sicilian royal family embarks in the *Vanguard*)

24 December: At 7 p.m. leaves Naples for Palermo with Sicilian royal family, accompanied by a Neapolitan ship of the line and merchant vessels

25 December: Struck by sudden heavy squall at 1.30 p.m., with strong gales later that night; arrives at Palermo on 'Christmas Day at night'

26 December–31 January: Nelson ashore; the *Vanguard* moors in Palermo Mole

1799

31 January–13 February: Nelson ashore; hoists flag aboard the *Bellerophon*; moors in Palermo Mole; the *Vanguard* sails to Malta

14 February–22 March: Nelson ashore; the *Vanguard* returns to Palermo, moors in the Mole; Nelson hoists flag in her again

22–31 March: Nelson ashore; hoists flag in the *Culloden* at Palermo; the *Vanguard* sails to Tripoli

31 March–2 April: Nelson ashore; hoists flag in the ship commanded by Lieutenant Philip Lamb, agent for transports

2 April–19 May: The *Vanguard* returns to Palermo; Nelson hoists his flag in her (5 April Nelson receives commission as **rear-admiral of the Red**)

20–30 May: Cruises in *Vanguard* off the island of Maritimo (Marettimo) looking for the French fleet

31 May–8 June: The *Vanguard* in Palermo Roads

8 June: Nelson transfers his flag from the *Vanguard* to the *Foudroyant* at Palermo

9–15 June: Nelson in the *Foudroyant* at Palermo (13 June embarks the crown prince of Naples and his suite; 14 June disembarks the crown prince of Naples and his suite)

16–20 June: Nelson in the *Foudroyant* cruises off Maritimo with the *Alexander* and the *Goliath*

21 June: the *Foudroyant* embarks Sir William and Lady Hamilton in Palermo Bay

21–5 June: Passage to Naples. Eighteen ships of the line anchor at daylight abreast of Naples. Cardinal Ruffo comes aboard the *Foudroyant*
27 June: Thomas Troubridge goes ashore to take command
29 June: Rebel leaders put in confinement in several ships: (shore time 30 June): 'At 9 court martial assembled . . . to try for Rebellion Cavalier Francesco Caracciolo'
30 June: Caracciolo hanged
2 July: Several members of rebel party brought on board for examination
5 July: Several of the rebels brought on board, sent to prison ships
8 July: King of Naples arrives at Naples
11 July: 4 p.m. 'His Sicilian Majesty came on board' the *Foudroyant*
12 July: Neapolitan colours hoisted on Fort St Elmo
15 July: The *Bellona* sails with cartel vessels with French prisoners to Toulon

20   Dalliance and Dishonour

6 August: The *Foudroyant* sails for Palermo
13 August: Nelson ashore at Palermo; shifts his flag to the *Samuel and Jane* transport; the *Foudroyant* sails to Malta, then Sardinia and Leghorn; created duke of Bronte
1 September: Becomes temporary commander-in-chief, Mediterranean
4 October: Nelson hoists flag again in the *Foudroyant*
5–12 October: Passage to Port Mahón, Minorca
13–17 October: Moors in Port Mahón Harbour
18–21 October: Passage from Mahón to Palermo
22–8 October: Moors in Palermo Bay
29 October–15 January 1800: Nelson ashore at Palermo (29 October hoists flag aboard the *Perseus* bomb vessel and the *Foudroyant* sails to Malta; 2 November the *Perseus* sends Nelson's flag aboard the *Samuel and Jane* transport; 18 November the *Foudroyant* returns, Nelson hoists flag in her again; 25 November shifts flag to a transport and *Foudroyant* returns to cruise off Malta)

1800

15 January: The *Foudroyant* returns from Malta; Nelson hoists flag again in her
16–20 January: Nelson takes passage to Leghorn, joining Lord Keith in the *Queen Charlotte*
21–5 January: The *Foudroyant* moors in Leghorn Roads
26 January–3 February: Passage to Palermo with Lord Keith
4–11 February: Moors in Palermo Bay
12–15 February: Passage to Malta with Lord Keith
16–18 February: Cruises off Malta with squadron
19 February: The *Foudroyant* takes *Le Généreux* off Malta

20 February–16 March: Cruises off Malta, sometimes moored in St Paul's Bay

17–24 March: Moors in Palermo Bay

25 March–21 April: Nelson on shore, with flag hoisted in a transport. The *Foudroyant* cruises to Malta (30 March with Edward Berry in command, takes the *Guillaume Tell*; 3–13 April at Syracuse; 14–21 April passage to Palermo)

22–3 April: At Palermo (22 April hoists flag aboard the *Foudroyant*)

24 April–31 May: Cruises in the *Foudroyant* to Malta with Sir William and Lady Hamilton (1–2 May anchors at Syracuse; 3–4 May passage to Malta; 4–9 May moors in St Paul's Bay; 10–11 May off Valetta; 12–19 May moors in Marca Scirocco Bay; 20–31 May passage to Palermo)

1–9 June: Moors in Palermo Bay; appointed a knight grand cross of the Order of St Ferdinand and Merit of the Two Sicilies

10–15 June: The *Foudroyant* sails with the queen of Naples (with a retinue of thirty-six) to Leghorn

10–28 June: Moored in Leghorn Roads

29 June: Nelson transfers his flag to the *Alexander*; the *Foudroyant* to Mahón to refit

10 July: King and queen of Naples embark on board the *Alexander*

12 July: Nelson strikes flag to end Mediterranean commission

17–24 July: Journey from Leghorn with the Hamiltons to Ancona, via Florence, Arezzo and Perugia

24–8 July: At Ancona, embarks on a Russian frigate for Trieste

28 July–1 August: Passage to Trieste by Russian frigate

1–9 August: Stays at Trieste

9–18 August: Trieste to Vienna

18 August–25 September: Stays in Vienna (including a visit to Eisenstadt)

26–7 September: Journey from Vienna to Prague

28–30 September: Stays in Prague

30 September–1 October: Journey from Prague to Dresden, by boat on the River Elbe

2–9 October: Stays in Dresden

10–21 October: Journey by boat on the Elbe from Dresden to Hamburg

22–31 October: Stays in Hamburg

31 October–6 November: Passage from Cuxhaven to Yarmouth in mail packet

7–8 November: Travels to London via Roundwood

21 Separation

8 November–15 December: Stays in London (20 November takes his seat in the House of Lords)

19–26 December: Visits Salisbury and Fonthill

29 December: Returns to London and attends William Locker's funeral

30 December–12 January 1801: Stays in London; separates from Fanny

1801

1 January: Appointed **vice-admiral of the Blue**
13 January: Leaves London for Plymouth via Southampton, arriving 17 January
18 January: Hoists flag on board the *San Josef* in Plymouth
11 February: Hoists flag on board the *St George* in Torbay
20–21 February: Passage from Torbay to Spithead
21 February–2 March: Moors at Spithead
23 February: Admiralty gives Nelson three days' leave in London
24–8 February: Strikes flag
3–4 March: Passage to the Downs
5–7 March: Passage from the Downs to Yarmouth
8–11 March: Moors in Yarmouth Roads

22   Copenhagen

12–21 March: Passage from Yarmouth to the mouth of the Sound
22–9 March: Anchors at mouth of the Sound (27 March shifts flag to the *Elephant*)
2 April: Van division of the fleet sails through passage between the Middle Ground and Seltholm: starts the **Battle of Copenhagen**
3 April: (noon) Battle of Copenhagen

23   Commander-in-Chief, Baltic Fleet

4–16 April: Anchors in Copenhagen Roads (4 April Nelson shifts his flag back to the *St George*)
16 April: Short passage to Køge Bay, south of Copenhagen; shifts flag to the *Elephant*
17–19 April: Passage to Karlskrona
20–21 April: Off Bornholm
22 April: Earthholm. Shifts flag back into the *St George*
26 April–5 May: Anchors in Køge Bay
5 May: Receives commission as commander-in-chief, Baltic
6–13 May: Passage to Reval (Tallinn)
14–15 May: At anchor in Reval Roads
15 May: *London Gazette* announces Nelson's appointment as viscount
17 May–24 May: Passage from Reval to Rostock Roads
24 May–4 June: Anchors in Rostock Roads
5–19 June: At anchor in Køge Bay
19 June: Shifts flag from the *St George* to the *Kite*

19–30 June: Passage to Yarmouth
30 June: Arrives at Yarmouth

24 Boulogne

1 July: Arrives in London
7 July: In London
9 July: With the Hamiltons, Boxhill, Surrey
12 July: With the Hamiltons at Staines
24 July: Appointed commander-in-chief of a squadron employed between Orfordness and Beachy Head to prevent an invasion
27–9 July: At Sheerness; hoists flag aboard *L'Unité*
29 July: Travels to Deal via Faversham
30 July: At Deal, hoists flag aboard the *Leyden* in the Downs
31 July: Shifts flag to the *Medusa* in the Downs
1–2 August: Passage to the squadron off Boulogne
3–6 August: Anchors and sails off Boulogne (4–5 August **bombardment by bomb
vessels of the enemy's gun vessels**)
7–8 August: Passage back to Margate Roads
8–9 August: Passage to Harwich
10 August: Anchors at Harwich
11–14 August: Anchors at the Nore
14–15 August: Sails to Boulogne
16 August: **Second attack on French gunboats at Boulogne**
17 August: Passage to the Downs
18–22 August: Moors in the Downs
23–7 August: Sails to Flushing, then back to Margate
28 August: Moors in the Downs; shifts flag to the *Amazon*
28 August–24 September: Ashore at Deal; *Amazon* moors in the Downs
1–5 October: Cruises in light airs off South Foreland
6–23 October: *Amazon* in the Downs
23 October: Strikes his flag for 'Admiralty leave'

IV ADULATION AND DEATH 1801–1805

25 Peace and the Journey to Wales

22 October: Arrives at Merton for the first time
3 and 12 November: Speaks in the House of Lords

1802

January–July: Mostly at Merton, occasional visits to London
26 April: Edmund Nelson dies at Bath
21 July: Starts the tour to Wales
22–3 July: At Oxford
1–4 August: At Milford
18–20 August: At Monmouth
24–5 August: At Ludlow
5 September: Returns to Merton
21 December: Speaks in the House of Lords

1803

6 April: Sir William Hamilton dies
16 May: Receives commission as commander-in-chief, Mediterranean
19 May: Hoists flag on board the *Victory*
21 May: Sails for Ushant in company with the *Amphion*
24 May: Shifts his flag to the *Amphion* off Ushant

27 Commander-in-Chief, Mediterranean

15–17 June: In Valetta Harbour, Malta
17 June–7 July: Passage to Toulon
8 July: The *Amphion* meets Bickerton's fleet off Toulon; Nelson takes command
9–30 July: Cruises off Toulon
30 July: The *Victory* arrives off Toulon; hoists his flag in her at 5 p.m.
31 July–31 October: Cruises off Toulon and Barcelona
1–9 November: Moors in Agincourt Sound, Maddalena Islands
10 November: Anchors in the Strait of Bonifacio
11–21 November: Passage to rendezvous off Toulon
22 November–8 December: Off Toulon
9–11 December: Passage south to Sardinia
12–18 December: Moors in Gulf of Palma, Sardinia
19–23 December: Cruises around Sardinia, receives provisions off island of Asinara
24 December–1 January 1804: Moors in Agincourt Sound, Maddalena Islands

1804

2–7 January: Passage to rendezvous off Toulon
10 January–3 February: Cruises off Minorca and Majorca
4–7 February: Passage back to Sardinia

8–18 February: Moors in Agincourt Sound
19 February–25 March: Cruises to the west of the Gulf of Lyons, sometimes near Minorca and Majorca
25 March–2 April: Anchors in Agincourt Sound
3–9 April: Passage to rendezvous off Toulon
10 April–10 May: Cruises off Toulon
11–18 May: Anchors in Agincourt Sound
19–27 May: Passage to rendezvous off Toulon
28 May–28 July: Cruises off Toulon
30 July–1 August: Passage to Sardinia
2–8 August: Moors in the Gulf of Palma, Sardinia
9–10 August: Moors in the Pula Roads, Cagliari
11–12 August: Passage to the rendezvous off Toulon
13 August–16 October: Cruises off Toulon
17 October: Passage to Sardinia
18–25 October: Moors in Agincourt Sound
26 October–10 December: Cruises to the west of Toulon (13–15 November off Barcelona)
11–13 December: Passage to Pula Roads, Sardinia
14–18 December: Moors in Pula Roads
19 December: Moors in the Gulf of Palma
20 December–4 January: Cruises to the west of Toulon, off Cap San Sebastian

1805

5–10 January: Cruises off Sardinia
12 January: Anchors in the Strait of Bonifacio
13–19 January: Moors in Agincourt Sound
20 January: Passage out of Agincourt Sound through the Biche (Biscie) Channel

28   The Long Chase

25 January: Gulf of Cagliari
29–31 January: Through the Strait of Messina
1–6 February: Passage to Alexandria
7–8 February: Off Alexandria
11–12 February: Off Gozo, on return passage to Sardinia
16 February: Off Malta
17–27 February: Passage to Sardinia
28 February–3 March: Anchors in Pula Roads
4–8 March: Cruises near Bay of Rousse
9 March: Anchors in the Gulf of Palma

10 March: Passage to rendezvous off Toulon and Barcelona
11–19 March: At rendezvous off Toulon
20–24 March: Cruises off Majorca
25–6 March: Passage to Sardinia
27–30 March: Anchors in the Gulf of Palma
1–2 April: Pula Roads
8 April: Off Maritimo
9–17 April: Cruises near Sicily, then north looking for the French fleet
18 April: Off Toro, south-west Sardinia; learns that French are heading for Gibraltar
19 April–3 May: Passage for the Strait of Gibraltar
4–6 May: Anchors in Mazri Bay, Tetuán
7–9 May: Passage north to Lagos Bay
10–11 May: Anchors in Lagos Bay, Portugal; learns that French fleet are heading for West Indies
11 May–3 June: Passage across the Atlantic to Barbados
4–5 June: Anchors in Carlisle Bay
6–7 June: Passage to Trinidad
8 June: Anchors in the Gulf of Paria, Trinidad
9 June: Passage to Guadeloupe
10 June: At Basseterre, Guadeloupe
11 June: Montserrat
12 June: Passage to Antigua
13 June: At St John's Antigua
14 June–18 July: Passage across the Atlantic
19–21 July: Anchors in Rosia Bay, Gibraltar
22 July: Passage to Tetuán
23–4 July: Anchors in Mazri Bay, Tetuán
25 July–17 August: Passage to England
18 August: Anchors at Spithead, hauls down flag on 20 August; in London and at Merton

29   Trafalgar

14 September: Hoists flag in the *Victory* at St Helens
29 September: Takes command of Collingwood's fleet
30 September–20 October: Cruises off Cadiz
21 October: **Battle of Trafalgar. Nelson killed**
28 October: The *Victory* reaches Gibraltar

30   The Funeral

4 November: The *Victory* sails from Gibraltar to England
6–11 December: The *Victory* anchors at Spithead
25 December: The *Victory* moors in Long Reach, River Medway

1806

5–7 January: Nelson's body lies in state in the Painted Hall, Greenwich Hospital
8 January: Nelson's body taken up the Thames to rest in the Admiralty
9 January: **Nelson's funeral**

General Chronology: Naval, Military and Political Events

1770

10 June: British garrison in the Falklands surrenders to Spanish expeditionary force
19 September: Admiralty ordered to mobilize twenty-two ships of the line against Spain

1771

22 January: Spain recognizes British possession of the Falkland Islands
10 February: Lord North's administration takes office: Lord Sandwich takes over as first lord of the Admiralty (12 January)
6 August: Sir Hugh Palliser made comptroller of the Navy Board

1773

Late June: King reviews the fleet at Spithead
19 November: Commodore Edward Hughes sails for the East Indies

1775

12 April: Captain Maurice Suckling appointed comptroller of the Navy Board
19 April: First shots of the American Revolutionary War fired at Lexington; limited naval mobilization for war against the colonists
17 June: Battle of Bunker Hill, Boston
23 August: Government issues a proclamation declaring the colonists to be in a state of rebellion and begins instituting measures to protect British shipping

1776

27 January: First Admiralty orders for convoy to the Newfoundland trade
4 July: American colonists sign Declaration of Independence

21 July: Lord Sandwich's first request to Lord North for putting more ships of the line into commission
15 September: British capture New York

1777

July: Admiralty first sets up convoy system to Gibraltar due to successful activities of American privateers in European waters
31 July: Admiralty begins planning comprehensive system of coastal convoys in British waters
27 September: British capture Philadelphia
17 October: British Army defeated at Saratoga

1778

6 February: France and the American colonies sign treaty of amity and commerce, and a defensive alliance: war between Britain and France inevitable
27 February: Sir Peter Parker takes over as commander-in-chief, Jamaica
13 March: French ambassador informs British government of the French–American treaty
14 May: Sir Edward Hughes returns to Spithead from the East Indies
17 July: News reaches London of French declaration of war
17 July: Maurice Suckling dies; succeeded as comptroller of the Navy Board by Captain Charles Middleton (later Lord Barham)
18 July: Keppel ordered to attack French shipping
27 July: English and French fleets meet indecisively at the Battle of Ushant

1779

January: Court martial of Admiral Keppel at Portsmouth
21 February: Palliser resigns his seat in Parliament
7 March: Sir Edward Hughes sails to the East Indies, again as commander-in-chief
16 June: Spain declares war on Britain
June–August: Franco-Spanish fleet dominant in the Channel
August: Plymouth 'panic'

1780

16–17 January: Rodney's victory over the Spanish at Moonlight Battle off the Portuguese coast
27 January: Rodney's relief of Gibraltar
17 April: Rodney and Admiral de Guichen meet at the Battle of Martinique
9 July: Denmark–Norway signs the League of Armed Neutrality with Russia

1 August: Sweden joins the League of Armed Neutrality
3 and 10 October: Two devastating hurricanes in the West Indies with loss of life and British ships
1 December: Britain declares war on the Netherlands

1781

4 January: Netherlands joins the League of Armed Neutrality
3 February: Rodney captures St Eustatius
14 April: Second relief of Gibraltar by Admiral Darby
29 April: Hood and de Grasse meet off Martinique
11 May: Spain captures West Florida
5 August: Battle of Dogger Bank against the Dutch
5 September: Battle of the Chesapeake (The Capes)
18 October: Cornwallis surrenders to Washington at Yorktown

1782

5 January: Sir Edward Hughes fights the Battle of Trincomalee
20 March: Fall of Lord North's government; Lord Sandwich ceases to be first lord of the Admiralty on 1 April
1 April: Second administration of Lord Rockingham; Lord Keppel made first lord of the Admiralty
12 April: Rodney wins the Battle of the Saints against de Grasse
13 September: Unsuccessful Spanish attack on Gibraltar with floating batteries
14 October: Third relief of Gibraltar by Lord Howe

1783

30 January: Lord Keppel resigns; Lord Howe made first lord of the Admiralty, with Admiral Hugh Pigot and Captain John Leveson-Gower as commissioners (until 10 April)
10 April: Fox–North coalition government; Lord Keppel made first lord of the Admiralty, with Captain Sir John Lindsay as naval commissioner (until 31 December)
2 July: Order-in-Council proclaimed: American–West Indies trade allowed only in British vessels, owned and built in Britain with British crews.
3 September: Final signing of the Treaty of Versailles ends American Revolutionary War
19 December: Pitt's first administration formed
31 December: Lord Howe again made first lord of the Admiralty, with Captain John Leveson-Gower as Admiralty commissioner (until 16 July 1788)

1784

17 May: Westminster election won by Lord Hood and Charles James Fox

1787

21 April: Death of Wilfred Collingwood
June: Dutch crisis; French intervention possible; naval preparations begin
21 and 25 September: Orders for press and provisioning of fleets against the French
Late September: Navy Office moves from Crutched Friars in the City into Somerset House, followed by the Victualling, Sick and Hurt and Navy Pay Offices
27 October: Declaration and counter-declaration by England and France of non-intervention in the Netherlands; navies back to 1 January 1787 strength

1788

16 July: Lord Howe resigns as first lord of the Admiralty; Lord Chatham succeeds him; Admiral Lord Hood made a naval lord of the Admiralty
12 August: Captain Leveson-Gower resigns from board; succeeded by Vice-Admiral Sir Francis Drake (dies 18 November 1789)
November: Regency crisis until February 1789

1789

14 July: Fall of the Bastille

1790

19 January: Captain Alan Gardner made Admiralty commissioner
30 March: Rear-Admiral Sir Charles Middleton resigns as comptroller of the Navy Board; succeeded by Captain (later Sir) Henry Martin
May–October: Mobilization against Spain over the Nootka Sound crisis; forty-three ships of the line mobilized. Lord Hood commands fleet at Spithead
28 October: Spain backs down to Britain over Nootka Sound

1791

January–May: Ochakov crisis; Hood commands fleet in the Downs

1792

20 April: France declares war on Austria
20 September: Battle of Valmy
September: French army occupies Nice and Savoy
October: French army occupies the Rhine
6 November: Battle of Jemappes; French conquest of the Low Countries
20 December: Supplies granted by Parliament for 20,000 seamen and 5,000 marines

1793

21 January: Execution of Louis XVI
1 February: French declaration of war against Britain. War of the First Coalition (1793–5) begins (Spain, Holland and Britain; and Austria, 22 March)
11 February: Parliament grants supplies for 16,000 extra seamen and 4,000 marines
14 February: British capture Tobago
25 March: Anglo-Russian treaty: twelve ships of line, six frigates to help Royal Navy
April: British attack Martinique; part of San Domingo, Pondicherry (India) and Miquelon (off Newfoundland)
25 April: Anglo-Sardinian treaty
25 May: Anglo-Spanish treaty
12 July: Anglo-Neapolitan treaty
27 August: British capture and occupy Toulon
30 August: Anglo-Austrian treaty
26 November: Jervis–Grey expedition departs for the West Indies
19 December: Evacuation of British forces and refugees from Toulon

1794

7 February: British capture Mortella Bay, Corsica and land troops
19 February: Hood captures San Fiorenzo Bay, Corsica
22 March: British take Martinique
4 April: Capture St Lucia (lost June 1795, recaptured May 1796)
20 April: Surrender of Guadeloupe
12 May: Sir Charles Middleton made an Admiralty commissioner
1 June: Victory of British fleet over the French at the Battle of the First of June
10–14 June: French fleet under Admiral Martin evades Hood's fleet at Gourjean Bay on south coast of France
11 June: Pitt administration joined by the Portland Whigs
26 June: France defeats British and Austrians at Fleurus (Belgium)

25 September: Captain Sir Andrew Snape Hamond succeeds Sir Henry Martin (dies 1 August 1794) as comptroller of the Navy Board; in office until 3 March 1806

19 December: Lord Chatham resigns at first lord of the Admiralty and is succeeded by Lord Spencer

1795

January: Holland in possession of French

5 January: Austro-Prussian treaty

February: Britain finally concludes a formal alliance with Austria after two years of fighting on the same side

3 March: Philip Stephens resigns as secretary to the Admiralty Board (appointed 18 June 1763) and made Admiralty commissioner (until 23 October 1806); succeeded as first secretary by Evan Nepean; second secretary William Marsden

7 March: Lord Hood and Vice-Admiral Sir Alan Gardner resign as Admiralty commissioners; succeeded by Rear-Admiral James Gambier

5 April: Franco-Prussian treaty (Prussia now a second-rate power)

3 May: Lord Hood ordered to strike his flag as commander-in-chief, Mediterranean

22 July: Treaty of Basle between French and Spanish

17 August: Malacca captured from the Dutch

26 August: British take Trincomalee

14 September: Admiral de Richery and six ships of the line escape from Toulon; end September Ganteaume escapes and sails for the Levant to capture trade

23 September: Admiral Sir John Jervis appointed commander-in-chief, Mediterranean Fleet

7 October: Loss of the Levant convoy to the French squadron under de Richery off Cape St Vincent

1 November: Vice-Admiral Hotham goes home, leaving Vice-Admiral Sir Hyde Parker as temporary commander-in-chief, Mediterranean

20 November: Sir Charles Middleton resigns as Admiralty commissioner; succeeded by Rear-Admiral Sir William Young

24 November: French victory at Loano that leads to abandonment of Vado

1 December: Admiral Sir John Jervis reaches San Fiorenzo Bay, Corsica

1796

27 March: Napoleon arrives at Nice to take command of the army of Italy

12–16 April: Napoleon's victories at Montenotte and Dego in Piedmont

April: British capture Dutch Guiana

28 April: Armistice between France and Piedmont (Sardinia); Savoy and Nice ceded to France

10 May: Napoleon takes the bridge at Lodi against the Austrians

15 May: Napoleon enters Milan and occupies Piedmont and Lombardy: during the summer the Austrians driven back to their borders

27 June: French troops capture Leghorn

19 August: Treaty of San Ildefonso; Spain enters offensive alliance with France against England but not yet in a state of war

31 August: Admiralty order for the British forces to evacuate Corsica, and take troops and supplies to Gibraltar

8 October: Spain declares war on England

22 October: Malmesbury peace mission to France arrives in Paris

17 November: Empress Catherine dies; Russian policies reversed and Russian squadron serving with British recalled

1797

15 January: French win at Rivoli

2 February: Fortress at Mantua falls to Napoleon. End of Austrian resistance in Italy

14 February: British victory over the Spaniards at Cape St Vincent

18 February: British capture Trinidad

16 April: Mutiny at Spithead begins

18 April: Peace preliminaries signed between France and Austria at the Peace of Loeben

6 June: Genoa becomes the Ligurian Republic

July: British–French peace negotiations

4 September: *Coup d'état* of Fructidor: the French government controlled by radicals

11 October: Admiral Duncan's victory over the Dutch at Camperdown; eleven ships of the line captured

17 October: Austria signs Treaty of Campo Formio with France. France given Belgium, Lombardy and promise of a frontier on the Rhine, in return for territory in northern Italy to go to Austria

1798

February: War of the Second Coalition – Britain, Austria and Russia, joined by Turkey, Portugal and Naples, against France. French troops enter Rome

April: Outbreak of the 'Quasi-War' between the United States and France

1 April: Austrian request for a fleet to be sent to the Mediterranean; cabinet decides no fleet available until June

6–12 April: First news in London of armament in Toulon and Genoa

28 April: Cabinet decides to send fleet to Mediterranean

29 April–1 May: Orders for reinforcements sent to St Vincent off Cadiz

24 May: Defensive alliance between Austria and Naples signed

11 June: Napoleon seizes Malta

19 June: Napoleon and army leave Malta for Alexandria

30 June: Napoleon's fleet reaches Alexandria

1 July: Napoleon's troops land at Alexandria and take the city the next day

14 July: Union of the Maltese people with the French Republic celebrated in Valetta

21 July: Napoleon's troops defeat main Egyptian Army at the Battle of the Pyramids; enters Cairo 23 July

1 August: Battle of the Nile

6 August: French expedition under General Humbert leaves Rochefort to land in County Mayo, Ireland

15 August: Tsar offers 60,000 troops for the Rhine in return for British subsidies

2 September: Maltese population rises against French occupying force

5 September: Ushakov's fleet appears off Constantinople

8 September: General Humbert defeated in Ireland

9 September: Turkey declares war on France

10 September: Vice-Admiral Robert Man made Admiralty commissioner

16 September: Departure of second French expedition to Ireland

26 September: News of the victory of Aboukir Bay reaches London

12 October: Departure of third French expedition to Ireland

15 November: Surrender of Minorca to the British (under the command of General Stuart and Commodore Duckworth)

29 November: Tsar made grand master of the Knights of St John (Malta)

1 December: Formal treaty between England and Naples signed; army of Naples marches on Rome

29 December: Treaty of alliance between Great Britain, Russia and Naples signed

1799

23 January: French troops under General Championnet enter Naples

26 January: Proclamation of the Parthenopean Republic in Naples

2 March: French forces take offensive on the Rhine

3 March: French forces capitulate in Corfu to Russians and Turks

12 March: French declare war on Austria

19 March: Siege of Acre begins

16 April: Battle of Mont-Thabor, victory of Bonaparte over the Turks

19 April: British confirm subsidy treaty with Russia

26 April: Bruix's squadron evades British blockade of Brest and sails for Mediterranean

27 April: French evacuate Milan

29 April: Russians under Suvorov take the city

3 May: Tippoo Sahib, sultan of Mysore, killed in fighting in Seringapatam

7 May: Prussian offer to Britain of an offensive in return for subsidy

20 May: Bonaparte lifts the Siege of Acre and returns to Egypt

10 June: St Vincent resigns as commander-in-chief, Mediterranean, due to ill health

19 June: French defeat at Trebbia; departure from Piedmont

14 July: Substantial Turkish reinforcements land in Egypt with help of British; defeated by Bonaparte on 25 July

4 August: News in London that Bruix has evaded British in Mediterranean and joined Spanish fleet in Cadiz

5 August: Bruix's squadron returns to Brest

15 August: News that the combined fleet from the Mediterranean has entered Brest

23 August: Bonaparte leaves Egypt, leaving General Kléber in command

27 August: Abercromby's British and Russian troops land at Den Helder in north Holland

30 August: Dutch Navy surrenders

5 September: Duke of York ordered to embark for Holland

9 September: British victory at Zijpe

19 September: Battle of Bergen: Russians and duke of York defeated

9 October: Bonaparte lands at Fréjus in southern France

12 October: Duke of York runs short of supplies; armistice agreed 18 October. British troops to withdraw from Holland

16 October: Capture of the Spanish treasure ships *Santa Brigida* and *El Thetis* near Ferrol by the *Alcmene* (Captain Henry Digby)

9–10 November: *Coup d'état* of 18 Brumaire; founding of the Consulate

15 November: Keith appointed commander-in-chief, Mediterranean; arrives at Gibraltar 6 December

1800

24 January: Convention of El-Arish negotiated by Sidney Smith and the Turks with Kléber for the evacuation of the French Army (not ratified by the British)

March: News reaches England of the Convention of El-Arish

17 March: Loss of Keith's flagship, the *Queen Charlotte*, by fire

20 March: Kléber beats Turkish Army at Heliopolis

April: Second Coalition collapses

5 June: Genoa surrenders to Keith

14 June: Bonaparte's victory over the Austrians at Marengo; General Kléber assassinated in Egypt

26 August: British fail to seize the Spanish Dockyard at Ferrol

5 September: Surrender of Malta to the British

10 September: London hears of failure of expedition against Ferrol

30 September: 'Quasi-War' between France and America ends

3 October: Cabinet decides to send 15,000 troops under Abercromby to Egypt

22 October: Government learns of failure of Abercromby and Keith at Cadiz

3 December: Austrians defeated by Moreau at Hohenlinden

16 December: The Northern Convention (or Armed Neutrality) signed by Sweden, Denmark, Russia, supported by Prussia

1801

13 January: News of signing of Northern Convention reaches London

14 January: Order-in-Council embargoes ships of Baltic powers in British ports

15 January: Armistice between France and Austria

9 February: Treaty of Luneville between France and Austria; confirmation of the terms of the Treaty of Campo Formio recognizing French possession of the left bank of the Rhine.

19 February: End of William Pitt's administration; Addington takes office. Lord Spencer resigns as first lord, Vice-Admiral James Gambier, Vice-Admiral Robert Man and Vice-Admiral William Young resign as Admiralty commissioners. Earl St Vincent succeeds as first lord, with Captain John Markham and Captain Sir Thomas Troubridge as Admiralty commissioners

28 February: Cornwallis appointed to be commander-in-chief, Channel

8 March: Abercromby's army lands at Aboukir Bay, Egypt

19 March: Addington's government decides to sue for peace; also British victory at the Battle of Aboukir

21 March: Treaty of Aranjuez between France and Spain; also Battle of Alexandria, Abercromby's victory over the French (under the command of Menou)

24 March: Assassination of Tsar Paul I

29 March: Peace of Florence between France and Naples; Neapolitan fortresses occupied by French troops and entry to ports by British ships forbidden

30 March: Prussians occupy Hanover

2 April: Battle of Copenhagen

2 April: News reaches London that Abercromby has landed in Egypt

13 April: News of the death of Tsar Paul reaches London

15 April: News of Copenhagen reaches London

21 May: Parliamentary debate on the recall of Sir Hyde Parker

17 June: Britain signs convention with Russia

6 July: Saumarez's unsuccessful action against Linois at Algeciras

12 July: Saumarez's successful night action against French and Spanish off Gibraltar (Battle of the Straits)

2 September: Menou capitulates at Alexandria

20 September: French Army leaves Egypt for France

1 October: Preliminary Articles of Peace with France signed in London

1802

25 March: Definitive treaty signed at Amiens between Britain, France and Holland. Britain returns former French colonies except Trinidad and Ceylon. The French keep their conquests except Rome, Naples and Portugal
August: Napoleon appointed first consul for life
29 December: Bill to set up the Committee of Naval Inquiry passed

1803

8 March: King's message to Parliament threatens Napoleon
18 May: Order-in-Council renews war between Britain and France
May: French retake San Domingo
    British reconquer Tobago, St Lucia, Demerara, Essequibo, Berbice

1804

7 January: British capture of Diamond Rock, Martinique
17 January: Captain Sir Harry Burrard Neale made Admiralty commissioner
20 January: Evan Nepean resigns as first secretary of the Admiralty; succeeded by William Marsden
21 January: Benjamin Tucker made second secretary
15 May: Fall of Addington's administration. Earl St Vincent resigns as first lord of Admiralty, Captain John Markham and Sir Thomas Troubridge resign. Pitt's second administration formed. Lord Melville appointed first lord, with Admiral Sir John Colpoys and Vice-Admiral Philip Patton (until 10 February 1806) as Admiralty commissioners.
18 May: Napoleon becomes emperor of the French
21 May: Benjamin Tucker resigns as second secretary to the Board of Admiralty
13 September: Captain Sir Harry Burrard Neale resigns as Admiralty commissioner
5 October: Spanish treasure ships taken by English frigates off Ferrol
12 December: Spain declares war on Britain

1805

11 January: Britain declares war on Spain
19 April: Troops under Sir James Craig sail for the Mediterranean in convoy commanded by Rear-Admiral John Knight
2 May: Lord Melville resigns as first lord, with Admiral Sir John Colpoys as commissioner; succeeded as first lord by Admiral Lord Barham (Charles Middleton) (until 10 February 1806), with Captain Lord Garlies as Admiralty commissioner (until 10 February 1806)

22 July: Sir Robert Calder's Action
20 October: French victory over the Austrians at Ulm
21 October: Battle of Trafalgar
30 October: French victory over the Austrians in Italy at Caldiero
4 November: Sir Richard Strachan's action against the French survivors of Trafalgar
2 December: French victory against the Austrians and Russians at Austerlitz
26 December: Treaty of Pressburg

1806

23 January: Death of William Pitt

Nelson's Ships: Size, Armament, Complements and a Full Listing of Officers

This appendix has been compiled from Admiralty records in the Public Record Office: ships' muster books (ADM 36) and ships' 'Sailing Qualities' (ADM 95). Building details and dimensions are taken from David Lyon's *The Sailing Navy List*, while Peter Goodwin's *Nelson's Ships 1771–1805* has provided useful evidence since it appeared in 2002. Details of ships that came into the navy on foreign stations, thus never entering an English dockyard, were rarely recorded.

The list of thirty ships consists of those in which Nelson saw active service, but includes three in which he returned to England sick: the *Dolphin* (1776), the *Lion* (1780) and the *Seahorse* (1797).

Nelson was associated with nine other ships, but they are not included in this list because he neither boarded them nor sailed in them. (It is not known in which ship he returned sick from Central America to Jamaica; the *Victor* sloop has been discounted.) He was appointed to the *Janus* (44) in 1780 but never commanded her. In 1799, when ashore at Palermo, he flew his flag in the *Bellerophon* (74), the *Culloden* (74), the *Perseus* bomb vessel and the *Alexander* (74). He also flew it in the *Samuel and Jane* and, in 1800, in another unnamed transport. In 1801, during the opening phases of operations against Boulogne, he flew his flag in *L'Unité* for two days and the *Leyden* (64) for one day.

Raisonable, 64 guns: 24 April–21 May 1771

Building details: Launched Chatham Dockyard 1768. Hulked at Sheerness 1810. Broken up 1815.

Dimensions: 1,376 tons. Length on lower deck: 160 ft. Inside breadth: 44 ft, 4 ins. Depth in hold: 18 ft. Draft: bows 21 ft, 4 ins., aft 22 ft, 3 ins.

Guns: Twenty-six 4-pounders, twenty-six 18-pounders, twelve 9-pounders.

Sailing qualities: (1775) 'Close hauled in a topgallant gale: 7 knots. Stiff gale, a point or two abaft the beam, she runs 11 knots . . . carries her helm about half a turn aweather . . . Will not bear taut rigging . . . Rides well at anchor.'

Men: 500.

Captain: Maurice Suckling, 17 November 1770–15 May 1771. First lieutenant: Matthew Anderson. Second lieutenant: St Alban Roy. Third: William Scott.

Purser: Edward Leigh. Surgeon: Alexander Naismith.

Midshipmen included: Charles Boyles, entered 14 December 1770 as AB; 1 January 1771 midshipman; mustered 15 January, discharged 15 May to the *Triumph*. Horace Nelson entered as midshipman 1 January 1771, appeared 24 April, discharged 15 May 1771 to the *Triumph*.

Triumph, 74 guns: May–Summer 1771; July 1772–6 May 1773

Building details: Launched Woolwich Dockyard 1764. Broken up 1850.

Dimensions: 1,753 tons. Length on lower deck: 171 ft, 3 ins. Inside breadth: 49 ft, 3 ins. Depth in hold: 21 ft, 3 ins. Draft: bows 21 ft, 7 ins, aft 23 ft, 3 ins.

Guns: Twenty-eight 32-pounders, thirty 24-pounders, twelve 9-pounders.

Sailing qualities: (1775) 'Close reefed in a topgallant gale: 7–8 knots . . . best sailing on the beam, rolls very easy.'

Men: 350 (for harbour service only). Borne: 338. Mustered: 333.

Captain: Maurice Suckling, 16 May 1771–1773. First lieutenant: Lambert Brabazon, 10 January–31 August 1771, Thomas Tonken, 1 September 1771. Second: Henry Jackson, 19 January–11 September 1771. Third: John Turner, 17 January–17 July 1771, Robert Shipman, 17 July 1771. Fourth: Samuel Brown, 2 April 1771, John Boyle, 10 March 1772–1 February 1773.

Master: Richard Williams. Purser: Richard Woodmaston. Boatswain: Robert Selby.

Midshipmen included Charles Boyles, entered 22 May as AB; 28 May made midshipman. Horace Nelson, captain's servant, mustered 'in lieu' 24 May 1771– 6 May 1773.

Mary Ann merchant ship: Summer 1771–July 1772

No details extant.

Carcass, bomb vessel: 7 May–12 October 1773

Building details: Launched at Rotherhithe 1759. Sold 1784.

Dimensions: 298 tons. Length on lower deck: 91 ft, 6 ins. Inside breadth: 27 ft, 6 ins. Depth in hold: 12 ft, 1 in. Draft: bows 12 ft, 8 ins., aft 12 ft, 2 ins.

Guns: [One 13, one 10-inch mortar], eight 6-pounders, fourteen swivels.

Sailing qualities: 'Close hauled in a topgallant gale: 5–6 knots . . . Steers well . . . stays [tacks] well unless in a head sea. Under reefed topsails: 4 knots, pitches heavy, otherwise behaves well. Pitches very heavy when close hauled ... Goes very easy with the wind on the beam, ships a good deal of water sometimes in the waist ... pitches much in a hard swell ... Before the wind: goes 10 knots, rolls very deep, but easy.'

Men: 80. Borne: 80. Mustered: 80.

Captain: Skeffington Lutwidge. First lieutenant: John Baird. Second: James Pennington. Third: George Wykham.

Master: James Allen. Purser: John Parry. Boatswain: John Cunningham. Surgeon: William Wallis. Coxswain: Nicholas Beddle.

Midshipmen: John Toms (aged twenty-five at the time of entry), Charles Dean, Rob Hughes (aged eighteen). Horace Nelson (aged sixteen) entered 7 May 1773, paid off 12 October 1773.

Seahorse, 24 guns: 28 October 1773–14 March 1776

Building details: Launched at Ipswich 1748. Sold 1784.

Dimensions: 504 tons. Length on lower deck: 112 ft. Inside breadth: 32 ft. Draft: 10 ft.

Guns: Twenty-two 9-pounders, two 4-pounders.

Men: 160.

Captain: George Farmer. First lieutenant: James Drummond (dismissed service 31 May 1774), Thomas Henery, 1 June 1774.

Midshipmen included: Horatio Nelson (age eighteen) entered 27 October 1773, AB 5 April 1774, midshipman 31 October 1775, discharged 14 March 1776 per order of Sir Edward Hughes (ADM 34/749).

Dolphin, 24 guns: 23 March–16 September 1776

Building details: Launched Woolwich Dockyard 1751. Broken up 1777.

Dimensions: 508 tons. Length on the lower deck: 113 ft. Inside breadth: 32 ft. Depth in hold: 11 ft. Draft: bow 15 ft, aft 14 ft.

Sailing qualities: 'Close hauled in a topgallant gale: 7 and a half knots ... holds a good wind ... find her best going with the wind two points abaft the beam ... before the wind 8 and a half. Rolls a great deal.' Defects, 30 August 1776: 'The ship, in bad weather, complains much in her Upper Works, her sides and decks being very leaky' (ADM 1/2303, James Pigott to Board of Admiralty).

Men: 160.

Captain: James Pigott. Lieutenant: John Jarvis. Horatio Nelson, midshipman, entered 15 March 1776, mustered until 16 September 1776.

Worcester, 64 guns: 1 October 1776–9 April 1777

Building details: Launched at Portsmouth Dockyard 1766. Hulked at Deptford 1788. Broken up 1816.

Dimensions: 1,373 tons. Length on lower deck: 159 ft. Inside breadth: 44 ft, 6 ins. Draft: 19 ft.

Guns: Twenty-six 24-pounders, twenty-six 18-pounders, twelve 9-pounders.

Sailing qualities: 'Stays and wears well, and works as quick as we can attend her, in all moderate winds and sea; has not at any time missed stays; when sailing against a Headswell, she pitches pretty deep, but falls regularly and easily into the sea . . . but I cannot avoid taking notice that she doth not sail near as well in little, or light winds, as she does in fresh or strong gales . . . she is a very stiff ship, and will carry sail in all kinds of Weather, as long as can be expected, or desired' (ADM 95/32, Richard Hughes, 1772).

Men: Peacetime 300 (to 29 October 1776, then 500). Borne: 278–82. Mustered: 256–73.

Captain: Mark Robinson: First lieutenant: D. Shuckforth: Second lieutenant: Robert Pope. Third lieutenant: Geo. Dunn. Fourth lieutenant: Horatio Nelson, 26 September 1776, 'Sir James Douglas's warrant – 9 April 1777', 'appeared' 1 October 1776. Joseph Tobery, fourth lieutenant's servant, entered 1 February.

Master: Kenneth Mackenzie. Purser: Simon Antram. Boatswain: George Hopkins.

Lowestoffe, 32 guns: 12 April 1777–2 July 1778

Building details: Launched at West's Yard at Deptford 1761. Foundered 1801.

Dimensions: 701 tons. Length on lower deck: 130 ft. Inside breadth: 35 ft. Draft: 12 ft. 6 ins.

Guns: Twenty-six 12-pounders, six 6-pounders, twelve swivels.

Sailing qualities: (1773) 'Close hauled in a topgallant gale: 8½ knots . . . Carries a weather helm, gathers to windward very fast and makes but little leeway. Her best sailing is a point, or two, abaft the beam, she runs 10 or 11 knots . . . the most before the wind, 9 & 10 knots, rolls very easy.' 'Trim: one inch or two, afore or abaft, makes no Difference in her sailing.'

Men: 220. Borne: 214.

Captain: William Locker. First lieutenant: Charles Sandys. Second: Horatio Nelson, 10 April 1777–1 July 1778. Cuthbert Collingwood, 1 July 1778–24 December 1778.

Master: Arthur Hill. Purser: Francis Graham. Chaplain: George Rutherford.

Bristol, 50 guns: 2 July–31 December 1778

Building details: Launched Sheerness Dockyard 1775. Hulked 1794.

Dimensions: 1,044 tons. Length on lower deck: 146 ft. Inside breadth: 40 ft, 6 ins. Draft: 17 ft, 6 ins.

Guns: Twenty-two 24-pounders, twenty-two 12-pounders, six 6-pounders.

Men: 367. Borne: 344. Mustered (September 1778): 295.

Commander-in-chief, Jamaica: Rear-Admiral Sir Peter Parker. Captain: Toby Caulfield. First lieutenant: Robert Deans, 7 January–3 September 1778, Horatio Nelson, 4 September–20 December 1778, James Macnamara, 25 December 1778–2 May 1779. Second lieutenant: John Pakenham, James Douglas 2 July–3 September 1778. Third lieutenant: Horatio Nelson, 2 July (per commission of 26 May 1778)–4 September 1778, James Macnamara, 4 September–25 December 1778, Cuthbert Collingwood, 25 December 1778–11 June 1779.

Master: John Holland. Purser: John Williams. Boatswain: Simon Tallack. Chaplain: Thomas Warren. Surgeon: Archibald Bruce.

Badger, 14-gun brig: 1 January–19 June 1779

Building details: Purchased 1777, probably American. Driven ashore in hurricane of 3 October 1780 on north side of Jamaica but refitted.

Dimensions: Not known.

Guns: 14.

Men: 90. Borne: 82–9. Mustered: 79–86.

Captain: Horatio Nelson, 1 January–10 June 1779. Lieutenant: Osborne Edwards.

Master: John Wilson. Purser: John Tyson. Boatswain: Peter Hutton. Surgeon: Francis Forster. Captain's servants: William Sylvan, William Orpwood, John Smith.

AB: Frank Lepee.

Hinchinbroke, 28 guns: 1 September 1779–30 April 1780

Building details: French prize, captured in the West Indies, commissioned as RN ship 7 December 1778. Hull in bad condition, described by Collingwood: 'old French sheathing quite rotten and washed away from the bottom and the seams which it had covered quite open' (ADM 51/442, 12 May 1780). Foundered off Jamaica 1782.

Dimensions: 557 tons. Length on lower deck: 115 ft. Inside breadth: 33 ft, 3 ins.

Guns: 28.

Men: 200. Borne: 180. Mustered: 175

Captain: Horatio Nelson, 11 June ('appeared' 1 September) 1779–30 April 1780. Captain's clerk: Philip Rogers.

First lieutenant: Arthur St Leger, 16 September 1779–9 November 1779, Charles Cunningham, 19 December 1779–13 January 1780, George Harrison, 13 January–24 April 1780 (discharged dead). Second lieutenant: George Harrison, 17 September 1779–13 January 1780, Joseph Bullen, 18 January 1780.

Master: John Walker. Purser: Robert Huggins. Boatswain: William Perry. Surgeon: Francis Foster. Chaplain: Thomas Rees.

Captain's servants included: William Sylvan, John Orpwood, John Smith, William Locker, William Fry, James Hatton.

AB: Frank Lepee.

Lion, 64 guns: August–November 1780

Building details: Launched Portsmouth Dockyard 1777. Sold 1837.

Dimensions: 1,373 tons. Length on lower deck: 159 ft. Inside breadth: 44 ft, 6 ins. Draft 19 ft.

Guns: Twenty-six 24-pounders, twenty-six 18-pounders, twelve 9-pounders.

Men: 500. Borne: 440–42. Mustered: 412–34.

Captain: William Cornwallis. Supernumeraries for victuals only: Horatio Nelson (with Frank Lepee, his servant) entered 16 August 1780, discharged to shore 25 November 1780.

Albemarle, 28 guns: 23 August 1781–3 July 1783

Building details: French ship captured in the Leewards in 1779. Commissioned on 22 November 1779 at English Harbour, served on the station in 1780, dismasted during hurricane of 10 October 1780, returning to Channel and North Sea for early part of 1781. Sold 1784.

Dimensions: 543 tons. Length on lower deck: 125 ft, 3 ins. Inside breadth: 31 ft, 7 ins. Depth in hold: 13 ft, 7 ins. Best sailing draft of water: bows 15 ft., aft 14 ft.

Guns: Twenty-four 9-pounders. Quarterdeck: four 3-pounders.

Sailing qualities: 'Close hauled in a topgallant gale: 6 knots ... steers badly, stays [tacks] well but wears badly: under reefed topsails wears well and runs 5 knots. Goes badly to windward, and carries a good deal of weather helm; goes well with wind on the quarter and when it blows hard, goes 10 or 11 knots.' When anchored in the Downs in the gale of 26 January 1782, she was so 'crank' (heeled or rolled too much) that 'our carpenters were standing by with axes to cut away the mainmast fearing she might overset' (ADM 51/4110). Nelson requested that her masts be shortened. The Portsmouth Dockyard officers reported to the Navy Board that 'the pressure of the sails is so much higher and by that means makes her Tender as she is 6½" narrower than most 24 gun ships' (NMM, POR/D/23, 14 Feb. 1782). Accordingly her masts and yards were shortened.

Men: 200. Borne: 200. Mustered (April 1782): 194.

Captain: Horatio Nelson, 15 August 1781–3 July 1783. First lieutenant: Martin Hinton, 1 September 1781–3 July 1783. Second lieutenant: William Osborn, 1 September 1781–23 April 1782, Joseph Bromwich, 24 April 1782–3 July 1783.

Master: Donald Trail, 30 July 1781–3 July 1783. Purser: Henry Delamain, 23 August 1781–8 October 1781, 9 October post filled by Deputy Purser William Easton. Boatswain: Joseph Pike. Surgeon: James Armstrong.

Captain's servant: Frank Lepee, 7 August 1781, discharged at own request 15 October 1781, ordinary seaman, 16 October 1781.

Boreas, 28 guns: 24 March 1784–30 November 1787

Building details: Launched at Hull 1774. Hulked at Sheerness as a slop ship in 1797 and sold in 1802.

Dimensions: 612 tons: Length on the lower deck: 124 ft. Inside breadth: 33 ft, 6 ins. Depth in hold: 11 ft. Draft with six months' victuals: bows, 16 ft., 4 ins., aft 15 ft, 8 ins. Water capacity 56 tons (ADM 52/2179, 1 June 1785).

Guns: Twenty-four 9-pounders, four 3-pounders, twelve swivels.

Sailing qualities: 'Close hauled in a topgallant gale: 7 knots ... very well in a stiff gale'. In 'a topsail gale' 6 knots; 'the most knots 12 and rolls easy'. Different points of the wind: 'Perfectly easy in every point of sailing: the wind from the quarter to the beam in a topsail gale 10 or 11 knots and when double reefed from 9 to 10 of a constantly Weatherly helm and when in her sailing trim from 13 to 15 inches by the stern.'

Men: 180.

Captain: Horatio Nelson, 24 March 1784–30 November 1787. First lieutenant: James Wallis, 12 December 1783–20 April 1787, Digby Dent, 21 April–29 November 1787. Second lieutenant: Digby Dent, 5 April 1784–21 April 1787, William Hope 10 May 1787–30 November 1787.

First lieutenant of marines: John Thomas Hobbs, 16 October 1786–27 November 1787. Second lieutenant of marines: Theoph. Lane, 21 May 1784–14 April 1786 (invalided in Barbados).

Master: David Reed, 4 November 1783–30 April 1784, James Jameson, 24 March 1784–30 November 1787. Chaplain: William Nelson, 27 June 1784–4 October 1786 (left for England 30 September 1784). Purser: Daniel Lelsome Peers, 10 November 1783–30 November 1787. Boatswain: James Robinson,

15 November 1783–13 August 1784, John Scotland, 21 August 1784–30 April 1786, Joseph King, 1 May 1786–6 February 1787 (discharged to English Harbour), Charles Green, 7 February 1787–3 September 1787, Joseph King, 4 September 1787–30 November 1787. Surgeon: Thomas Graham, 24 March 1784–30 November 1787. Gunner: James Balantine, 13 July 1784–30 November 1787.

Midshipmen (a selective list from thirty-five): Joseph James Beale, midshipman 21 April 1784, master's mate, 2 November 1784, AB, 20 August 1785–30 November 1787 (paid off), Edmund Bishop, midshipman, 14 April 1784, master's mate, 30 September 1785, AB, 30 April 1786–30 November 1787 (paid off), William Oliver, midshipman, 24 March 1784–1 May 1785 (discharged to *Unicorn*), Joseph Bromwich, master's mate, 24 March 1784–20 December 1785 (discharged to the *Adamant*).

AB: Thomas Stansbury, 27 April 1784–1 May 1785 (discharged following duel with Andrews at St Kitts), Thomas Orde, 30 August 1786–30 November 1787 (paid off).

Captain's servants: George Andrews, 24 March 1784 (aged twenty-one), AB, 23 October 1784, master's mate, 21 December 1785, 30 November 1787 (paid off). Hon. Courtenay Boyle, 24 March 1784, midshipman, 10 October 1785, master's mate, 1 May 1786, 30 November 1787 (paid off as midshipman), James Elliott, 14–15 April 1786 (died in Barbados Hospital), Charles Lock, 3 June 1783 (aged twenty), midshipman, 10 October 1785, AB, 1 May 1786–30 November 1787 (paid off), William Man, 28 December 1784–4 February 1786 (discharged), Charles Middleton, 5 October 1785–17 March 1787 (requested discharge), William Shirley, 1 August 1786 (from *Latona*)–30 November 1787, John Talbot, 24 March 1784 (aged twenty-one), midshipman, 2 May 1785, master's mate, 1 April 1786, 30 November 1787 (paid off).

Surgeon's servant: Maurice Suckling (aged twenty), 27 April 1784, captain's servant, 14 August 1784, AB, 28 December 1784, midshipman, 1 January 1786–30 November 1787 (paid off).

Agamemnon, 64 guns: 7 February 1793–10 June 1796

Building details: Launched at Bucklers Hard 1781. At Camperdown, Copenhagen 1801, Calder's Action, Trafalgar, Copenhagen 1807. Wrecked 1809.

Dimensions: 1,376 tons. Length on lower deck: 160 ft. Inside breadth: 44 ft, 4 ins. Depth in hold: 18 ft. Draft: bows, 20 ft, 8 ins., aft, 22 ft, 7 ins., (ADM 52/2632).

Guns: Twenty-six 24-pounders, twenty-six 18-pounders, twelve 9-pounders.

Sailing qualities: (1796) 'Stays indifferent, wears tolerably well . . . pitches much in a head sea . . . rigging slack with safety, nine knots before the wind' (Goodwin, 296). Nelson's opinion: 'We appear to sail very fast: we went, coming out, nearly as fast, without any sail, as the *Robust* did under her topsails' (Nicolas,

I, 304, 18 Apr. 1793, Nelson to William Nelson). '*Agamemnon* sails well' (Nelson to Locker, 20 Aug. 1793, Nicolas, I, 319).

Men: 500. Borne: 483. Mustered (May 1793): 478.

Captain: Horatio Nelson, 7 February 1793–10 June 1796. Captain's clerk: Philip Carstang, 11 February 1793–10 June 1796.

First lieutenant: Martin Hinton, February 1793–17 August 1794 (appointed to *Victory*), George Andrews, 18 August 1794–17 January 1796 (discharged on promotion), Peter Spicer, 17 January 1796–10 June 1796 (discharged to *Captain*), Edward Berry (per commission of 9 November 1795), 16 May 1796–10 June 1796 (discharged to *Captain*).

Second lieutenant: Joseph Bullen, 6 February 1793–8 September 1793 (appointed to *Victory* to a post ashore at Toulon), George Andrews, 10 September 1793–18 August 1794, Wenman Allison, 18 August 1794–4 July 1795 (invalided; died 11 November 1795), Peter Spicer, 4 July 1795–17 January 1796, Maurice William Suckling, 18 January 1796–11 June 1796 (stayed aboard *Agamemnon* and was demoted to third lieutenant by the new captain). Third lieutenant: George Andrews, 12 February–9 September 1793, Wenman Allison, 10 September 1793–18 August 1794, Thomas Edmonds, 18 August 1794–3 April 1795 (discharged per order of Admiral Hotham), Peter Spicer, 18 April 1795–4 July 1795, Maurice William Suckling, 6 July 1795–17 January 1796, James Summers, 17 January 1796–10 June 1796 (discharged to *Captain*). Fourth lieutenant: Wenman Allison, February–9 September 1793, Thomas Edmonds, 10 September 1793–28 August 1794, Maurice William Suckling, 28 August 1794–5 July 1795, James Summers, 4 July 1795–17 January 1796, James Noble, 17 January 1796–10 June 1796 (discharged to *Captain*). Fifth lieutenant: Thomas Edmonds, February 1793–9 September 1793, Wm. Lucas, 5 October 1793–5 April 1794, Maurice William Suckling, 6 April–28 August 1794, Edward Cheetham, 16 August 1794–July 1795 (invalided), James Noble (acting), 13 October 1795–16 January 1796, Henry Compton, 22 January 1795–10 June 1796 (discharged to *Captain*).

Master: John Wilson, 7 February 1793 (returns to England in *Agamemnon*). Boatswain: Alexander Moffat, 31 January–27 June 1793, Joseph King, 28 June 1793–10 June 1796 (discharged to *Captain*). Surgeon: John Roxburgh, Michael Jefferson. Purser: Thomas Fellowes.

Schoolmaster: Thomas Withers, joined at sea from *Victory*, schoolmaster to 1 October 1794, then midshipman to 15 August 1795, master's mate to 11 June 1796. AB: Maurice William Suckling, 6 April 1794, Francis Lepee, AB to 18 April 1793, then coxswain (discharged to *Zealous*, 20 October 1795), John Sykes, AB, 12 April–15 July 1793, then ship's corporal, 10 June 1796 (discharged to *Captain*), William Fearney, AB, 6 March 1793–1 January 1796, then yeoman to 10 June 1796 (discharged to *Captain*).

Midshipmen included: Josiah Nisbet, midshipman 30 March 1793–10 June 1796 (discharged to *Captain*), John Weatherhead, AB, February–3 March 1793, midshipman to 28 June 1793, then master's mate (10 June 1796 discharged to

Captain), William Bolton, captain's servant, 6 March 1793–1 February 1794, midshipman 1 February 1794–10 June 1796 (discharged to *Captain*), William Hoste, captain's servant, 11 April 1793–1 February 1794, midshipman 1 February 1794–10 June 1796 (discharged to *Captain*), Thomas Lund, 20 March–26 May 1796 (discharged to *Captain*).

Captain, 74 guns: 11 June–26 September, 19 October–10 December 1796, 14 February, 24 March–25 May 1797

Building details: Launched at Limehouse 1787. Hulked 1809. Burnt accidentally in 1813.

Dimensions: 1,632 tons. Length on lower deck: 170 ft. Inside breadth: 46 ft, 7 ins. Depth in hold: 20 ft, 6 ins. Draft: bows 21 ft, 9 ins., aft 23 ft, 8 ins.

Guns: Twenty-eight 32-pounders, twenty-eight 18-pounders, twenty-eight 9-pounders.

Sailing qualities: (1806) 'Sails as fast as most line of battleships, but when blowing fresh in general is crank [heels easily], makes little or no leeway, wears and stays in less room than any large ship. Steers very easy . . . is always more Weatherly than most ships; in a head sea pitches, but does not strain or carry away anything . . . will go twelve knots or more five points from the wind.'

Men: 590. Borne: 533. Mustered: 510.

Commodore (Rear-Admiral, 20 February; hoisted flag, 2 April) Horatio Nelson, 11 June–11 December 1796, 13 February–26 May 1797.

Captain: (acting) Edward Berry, 12 August–27 September 1796, Charles Stuart, 24 September–8 December 1796, Ralph Willet Miller, 9 December 1796–26 May 1797.

Lieutenants (not listed in order in muster book): Edward Berry, 11 June–11 August 1796, 27 September 1796–2 March 1797, Peter Spicer, 11 June 1796–22 March 1797, James Summers, 11 June 1796–26 May 1797, James Noble, 11 June–11 December 1796, 13 February–2 March 1797, Henry Compton, 11 June 1796–26 May 1797, Josiah Nisbet, 8 April–26 May 1797.

Captain 69th Regiment: Alex Sanderson, 4 July 1796–10 December 1796.

Master: Philip Thomas. Purser: William Williams. Boatswain: Joseph King, 11 June–12 December 1796 on promotion to Gibraltar Yard. Commodore's secretary: Philip Carstang.

Midshipmen: Josiah Nisbet, 11 June 1796–8 April 1797, then promoted to lieutenant, William Bolton, William Hoste, John Weatherhead 11 June 1796–26 May 1797, Thomas Withers, 11 June 1796–18 February 1797 (discharged to *San Nicolas*), Thomas Lund 11 June 1796–14 February 1797 (died of wounds).

Gunner's mate: John Sykes, 11 June 1796–26 May 1797. AB: William Fearney, 11 June 1796–26 May 1797.

Diadem, 64 guns: 27 September–18 October 1796

Building details: Launched Chatham Dockyard 1782.

Dimensions: 1,369 tons. Length on lower deck 159 ft, 6 ins. Inside breadth: 44 ft, 4 ins. Depth in hold: 19 ft.

Guns: Twenty-six 24-pounders, twenty-six 18-pounders, twelve 9-pounders.

Men: 500.

Commodore: Horatio Nelson. Flag lieutenant: James Noble.

Captain: Henry Towry.

La Minerve, 38 guns: December 1796–February 1797

Building details: Launched at Toulon 1794. Captured by *Dido* and *Lowestoffe* on 24 June 1795. Stranded near Cherbourg in 1803 and retaken by the French.

Dimensions: 1,101 tons. Length on lower deck: 154 ft, 4 ins. Inside breadth: 39 ft, 11 ins. Depth in hold: 13 ft. Draft: bows 18 ft, 3 ins., aft 19 ft, 8 ins.

Guns: Twenty-eight 18-pounders, twelve 9-pounders, two 18-pound carronades.

Sailing qualities: (1797) 'Stays and wears very well . . . sails about nine or ten knots when the wind is abaft the beam . . . iron ballast 160 tons, stows her provisions very well, 100 tons of water with four months provisions' (Goodwin, 296).

Men: 300.

Commodore: Horatio Nelson, 12 December 1796–13 February 1797. Flag lieutenant: James Noble, 12 December 1796–13 February 1797.

Captain: George Cockburn, 20 August 1796–February 1802.

First lieutenant: John Culverhouse, 20 August 1796–26 February 1797. Second Lieutenant: Thomas Masterman Hardy, 20 August 1796–28 May 1797, Charles Gill (per acting order of Commodore Nelson), 12 January–10 February 1797.

Irresistible, 74 guns: 15 February–23 March 1797

Building details: Launched at Harwich in 1782.

Dimensions: 1,634 tons. Length on lower deck: 168 ft. Inside breadth: 47 ft. Depth in hold: 18 ft, 10 ins.

Guns: Twenty-eight 32-pounders, twenty-eight 18-pounders, twenty-eight 9-pounders.

Men: 550.

Commodore: Horatio Nelson. Flag lieutenant: James Noble. Secretary: P. J. Carstang.

Captain: George Martin
AB: William Hoste, 3–15 March 1797.

Theseus, 74 guns: 27 May–19 August 1797

Building details: Launched at Blackwall 1786. Broken up in 1814.

Dimensions: 1,658 tons. Length on deck: 170 ft. Inside breadth: 46 ft, 6 ins. Depth in hold: 19 ft, 4 ins. Draft: bows, 20 ft, 6 ins., aft 22 ft, 10 ins. '110 tons iron ballast, 130 tons shingle, stows 230 tons water and eight months' bread' (Goodwin, 298).

Guns: Twenty-eight 32-pounders, twenty-eight 18-pounders, eighteen 9-pounders.

Sailing qualities (1800): Wind aft of the beam: 'with a Stiff Gale and everything set she will go from 10 to 11 knots.' To windward: 'sails very fairly on the wind – we have beat more ships than have beat us . . . is naturally a stiff ship.' Running: 'eight to ten knots, is very easy in the Sea . . . is a very easy ship to every Situation' (Goodwin, 298).

Men: 550.

Rear-Admiral: Horatio Nelson, 27 May–19 August 1797. Secretary: P. J. Carstang, 27 May–11 July 1797 (to *Ville de Paris* on promotion), Thomas Allen, 27 May–19 August 1797 (to *Seahorse*).

Captain: Ralph Willet Miller, 27 May 1797–14 May 1799 (died).

Lieutenants: Richard Hawkins, Henry Compton (to *Seahorse*, 20 August 1797), James Summers, John Davies, John Weatherhead (discharged dead, 29 July 1797), Josiah Nisbet (to *Dolphin* hospital ship, 21 August 1797).

Master: Thomas Atkinson, 26 May 1797. Surgeon: Thomas Eshelby, 26 May–18 August 1797 (to *Seahorse*). Louis Remonier, surgeon's first mate. Coxswain: John Sykes.

Midshipmen included: William Bolton, 27 May–18 June 1797 (to *Ville de Paris*), William Hoste, Thomas Knight, George Kippin, Sam Shillington (25 July 1797 killed at Santa Cruz), William Fearney.

Seahorse, 38 guns: 20 August–4 September 1797

Building details: Launched at Rotherhithe 1794. Broken up 1819.

Dimensions: 983 tons. Length on lower deck: 146 ft. Inside breadth: 39 ft. Depth in hold: 13 ft, 9 ins.

Guns: Twenty-eight 18-pounders, eight 9-pounders.

Men: 270.

Rear-Admiral: Sir Horatio Nelson, 20 August–2 September 1797, accompanied by Lieutenant Henry Compton.

Captain: Thomas Fremantle.
Surgeon: Thomas Eshelby.
Admiral's servant: Thomas Allen.

Vanguard, 74 guns: 28 March 1798–7 June 1799

A small discrepancy exists between the log and muster books. The muster notes that Nelson 'made his appearance' on 28 March; the logs note that his flag was hoisted on 29 March a.m., i.e., during the morning of 30 March (Monmouth E986; NMM, ADM/L/V/28; (UK)NA: PRO, ADM 52/3516).

From 31 January 1798 to 13 February 1800 Nelson flew his flag in the *Bellerophon* (74), moored within Palermo Mole.

Building details: Launched at Deptford Dockyard 1787. Broken up 1821.

Dimensions: 1,604 tons: Length on lower deck: 168 ft. Inside breadth: 46 ft, 9 ins. Depth in hold: 19 ft, 9 ins. Draft: bows 20 ft, 11 ins., aft 22 ft, 8 ins. (22 ft, 11 ins. loaded, ADM 52/3516, 10 Mar. 1798). Iron ballast 124 tons, shingle 225 tons. Water 200 tons with four months provisions on board.

Guns: Twenty-eight 32-pounders, twenty-eight 18-pounders, eighteen 9-pounders.

Sailing qualities: (1800) 'Most she runs before the wind 11 knots, stiff' (Goodwin, 298). 'The *Vanguard* is an exceedingly clever ship. We found her best sailing was her main mast raking, rigging not too tight . . . among that class of 74 I don't know any I would so soon have' (BL, Add. MSS 34906, 11 Dec. 1797, Charles Thompson to Nelson). 'Steers easy, but is long in wearing; does not make so much leeway as Ships in general; before the wind Rolls much and does not exceed 8 or 9 knots (NMM, ADM/L/V/28, qualities signed by Captain Simon Miller, 27 Aug. 1797).

Men: 595. Borne: 598. Mustered (April 1798): 553.

Rear-Admiral: Sir Horatio Nelson, 28 March 1798–7 June 1799. Secretary: John Campbell, 28 March–14 August 1798, John Tyson, 14 August 1798–7 June 1799. Admiral's servant: Thomas Allen, 29 March 1798.

Captain: Edward Berry, 29 December 1797–5 August 1798, Thomas Masterman Hardy, 4 August 1798–7 June 1799.

First lieutenant: Edward Galwey, 28 December 1797–4 January 1799 (promotion), Nathaniel Vassall, 5 January–14 April 1799 (discharged on promotion), William Parkinson, 15 April–7 June 1799 (discharged to *Foudroyant*). Second lieutenant: Nathaniel Vassall, 28 December 1797–4 January 1799, William Parkinson, 5 January–14 April 1799, Henry Compton, 15 April–7 June 1799 (discharged to *Foudroyant*). Third lieutenant: William Parkinson, 24 December 1797–5 January 1799, Henry Compton, 5 January–14 April 1799, William Bolton, 15 April 1799–7 June 1799 (discharged to *Foudroyant*). Fourth lieutenant:

Henry Compton, 3 February 1798–4 January 1799, William Bolton, 20 January–12 April 1799, Edward Thornborough Parker, 12 April–7 June 1799 (discharged to *Foudroyant*). Fifth lieutenant: John Miller Adye, 28 December 1797–5 October 1798 (invalided), William Bolton, 6 October 1798–20 January 1799, John Lecky, 20 January–7 June 1799 (discharged to *Foudroyant*).

Acting: Thomas Bladen Capel, 5 April 1798, per order of Sir Horatio Nelson (nomination of Lord Spencer), discharged 13 August 1798 on promotion.

Captain of marines: William Faddy, 4 January–1 August 1798 (killed in action).

Master: Wales Clodd, 21 December 1797–7 June 1799. Purser: Alexander Sheppard, 24 December 1797–7 June 1799. Boatswain: Michael Austin, 24 January 1798–7 June 1799. Surgeon: Michael Jefferson, 23 December 1797–7 June 1799. Chaplain: Geo. Huddersford, 14 February–17 March 1798 (discharged at own request), Stephen G. Comyn, 31 March 1798–7 June 1799. Gunner: William Dawson. Carpenter: John Cooper.

Midshipmen/first-class boys included: Thomas Seymour (killed 1 August 1798), Thomas Meek (impressed man recommended by John Weatherhead's father (Nicolas, III, 4), killed 21 May 1798), John Henry Kramer (discharged 30 March 1798, and arrested on shore at Portsmouth), James Quick entered 6 March 1798 as coxswain, 30 March midshipman, Thomas Plaford, AB to 30 March, then midshipman. First-class boy: Francis Augustus Collier, 21 March 1798.

Foudroyant, 80 guns: 8 June 1799–29 June 1800

During Nelson's time in the *Foudroyant*, he was frequently ashore at Palermo while she was on active service. He therefore flew his flag in ships in Palermo Harbour: the *Samuel and Jane* transport (13 August–3 October 1799); *Perseus* bomb vessel (Captain Henry Compton, 29 October–2 November 1799); *Samuel and Jane* (2–18 November 1799); and an unnamed transport (25 November 1799–15 January 1800). For two weeks before he returned to England in July 1800, he flew his flag in the *Alexander* (74) in the Leghorn Roads.

Building details: Designed by John Henslow. Launched May 1798. Hulked 1861. Refitted as a training ship and wrecked on Blackpool Sands 1897.

Dimensions: 2,054 tons. Length on lower deck: 184 ft. Inside breadth: 50 ft, 6 ins. Depth in hold: 22 ft, 6 ins. Draft in sailing trim: bows, 24 ft, 4 ins., aft, 23 ft, 3 ins.

Guns: Thirty 32-pounders, thirty-two 24-pounders, eighteen 12-pounders, two 32-pound carronades, six 18-pound carronades.

Sailing qualities: (1812) 'Weatherly; best point of sailing about two points off the beam; rolls easy but deep, pitches easy and quick' (Goodwin, 299). In a fresh gale, 'went eleven miles an hour, sometimes more' (Nicolas, IV, 251, 15 June 1800, Nelson to Sir John Acton).

Men (8 June 1799): 724. Borne: 741. Mustered: 733.

Rear-Admiral: Lord Nelson 'and Retinue' John Tyson, Thomas Spencer, Thomas Allen, Angelo Melone, 8 June 1799–28 June 1800 (to the *Alexander*, striking his flag on 12 July 1800).

Captain: Thomas Masterman Hardy, 8 June–12 October 1799 (transferred to the *Princess Charlotte*), Edward Berry, 13 October 1799–2 November 1800.

Lieutenants (transferred with Nelson and Hardy from *Vanguard*): William Standway Parkinson, 8 June–15 July 1799 on promotion, Henry Compton, 8 June–4 August 1799 on promotion, William Bolton, 8 June 1799–22 August 1800 (to *Guillaume Tell*), Edward Thornborough Parker, 8 June–22 September 1799 on promotion, John Lackey, 8 June–9 August 1799, Archibald Duff, 1 January 1799–25 February 1800 (to *Queen Charlotte*), Andrew Thomson, 3 August 1799–21 May 1800 on promotion (to *Stromboli*), Frederick Langford, 10 August 1799–27 August 1800 (to *Guillaume Tell*), John Aitken Blow, 14 October 1799–22 August 1800 (to *Guillaume Tell*), Thomas Staines, 17 October 1799, still on board in January 1802, George Langford, 20 February 1800–14 February 1801, Thomas Cole, 27 March–25 August 1800.

First lieutenant of marines: Richard Bunce, 25 May 1798.

Master: William James, 1 January 1799–1 May 1800. Purser: George Unwin, 1 May 1798–8 July 1800. Boatswain: Philip Bridge, 24 December 1799–6 July 1800. Surgeon: Michael Jefferson, 8 June 1799–15 December 1800 (to *Guillaume Tell*). Chaplain: Reverend Stephen Comyn, 8 June 1799–28 August 1800 (to *Guillaume Tell*). Gunner: Owen Phillips, June 1798–23 January 1800, Joseph Hall, 20 December 1799–28 February 1800, Richard Hill, 1 March 1800, still on board in January 1802.

Midshipmen included (transferred from *Vanguard*): George Antrim 8 June–22 July 1799 (to *Mutine* as lieutenant), Hon. Granville Leveson Proby, 8 June 1799, Clement Ives, 8 June 1799–2 November 1800 (to *Princess Charlotte*), Edward West, 8 June 1799–20 July 1800 (to *Anson* from sick quarters), Hon. William Walpole, 29 July 1799–18 October 1800, Fred. Augustus Collier, 16 August 1799–29 October 1800 (to *Greyhound*), William Fearney, 15–25 November 1799 (to *Courageux* on promotion).

Supernumeraries for victuals only (23 April–15 June 1800, ashore at Leghorn) Sir William and Lady Hamilton, Miss Knight, Madame Julie, Mr Merchett, Michele Strepino, Andrea Placoto (23 April–1 June 1800, ashore at Palermo), Mrs Graeffer, Mr Bernard, Nicolo Giorgi.

(9–16 June 1800, Palermo to Leghorn) Queen Maria Carolina, Prince Leopold, Princesses Maria Christiana, Maria Amelia, Maria Antoinette, Princes Luggia, Castelcicala, Belmonte, General Ruffo, Countess Snell (Lady of the Bedchamber), three maids of honour, Abbé L'Eblan (priest) and twenty-three servants (total thirty-seven).

San Josef, 112 guns: 18 January–10 February 1801

Building details: Built Ferrol in 1797. Captured by the *Captain* under Nelson's command at the Battle of St Vincent (called the *San Jose* before its capture). Broken up in 1849 (Goodwin, 196).

Dimensions: 2,456 tons. Length on lower deck: 194 ft, 3 ins. Inside breadth: 54 ft, 3 ins. Depth in hold: 24 ft, 3 ins. Draft when stores and provisioned: bows 27 ft, aft, 26 ft, 4 ins. Iron ballast 130 tons, 80 tons of limestone. Stowed provisions well with 536 tons of water.

Sailing qualities: 'Rather leewardly but forereaches in proportion . . . requires a good stiff gale, she will run nine, ten or eleven knots' (Goodwin, 295).

Guns: Thirty-two 32-pounders, thirty-two 24-pounders, thirty-two 12-pounders, eighteen 9-pounders.

Men: 839.

Vice-Admiral: Lord Nelson, 7 January–10 March 1800: Secretary: J. P. Rance. Domestics: James Bell, Thomas Allen, George Sullivan, Samuel Paston.

Captain: Thomas Masterman Hardy.

Lieutenants: Philip Lyne, William Bolton, Robert Pettet, Hon. Whitworth Pearse, William Layman, Hon. George Elliot, Frederick Langford, John Stockham (all discharged to *St George*, 10 February 1800).

Master: Thomas Atkinson. Purser: Nicolas Rathey. Chaplain: Stephen Comyn.

Midshipmen included: Henry Portbury, Thomas Todd, Thomas Evans, John Peyton, Benjamin Rippon, James Brooks. Volunteer: Richard Bulkeley (all transfered to *St George*, 10 February 1800).

St George, 90 guns: 11 February–1 April, 2–16 April, 22 April–19 June 1801

Building details: Launched 1785 at Portsmouth Dockyard. Wrecked 1811.

Dimensions: 1,931 tons. Length lower deck: 177 ft, 6 ins. Inside breadth: 50 ft. Depth in hold: 21 ft, 2 ins. Draft when victualled for six months: bows, 23 ft, 2 ins., aft 24 ft, 9 ins. Iron ballast 160 tons.

Guns: Twenty-eight 32-pounders, thirty 18-pounders, thirty 12-pounders, two 6-pounders.

Sailing qualities: 'She sails heavy always, but in Smooth Water may be said to keep company very well with Ships of the same class. Stands up well under her sail and has gone six knots or more close hauled . . . is long in Wearing in a swell' (Goodwin, 300). St Vincent to Spencer: 'well adapted to serve in the Baltic being of an easy draft of water, sailing well, and remarkably handy' (BL, Add. MSS 75847, 9 Dec. 1800).

Men: 750.

Officers: As *San Josef*.

Elephant, 74 guns: 27 March–3 April, 16–21 April 1801

Building details: Launched 1786 at Burlsedon, Hampshire. Broken up 1830.

Dimensions: 1,604 tons. Length on lower deck: 168 ft. Inside breadth: 46 ft, 9 ins. Depth in hold: 19 ft, 9 ins. Draft when stored: bows 22 ft, aft 23 ft, 6 ins. Iron ballast 195 tons, shingle 100 tons. Water 200 tons.

Guns: Twenty-eight 32-pounders, twenty-eight 18-pounders, eighteen 9-pounders.

Sailing qualities: 'Topgallant gale: 8 or 9 knots . . . wears quick and stays the same . . . the most knots she runs before the wind 11 knots.'

Men: 590.

(20 February 1801) Borne: 533. Mustered: 510.

Vice-Admiral: Lord Nelson, 27 March–3 April, 16–21 Apr 1801. Secretary: Thomas Wallis, 16–21 April, Thomas Allen, Lieutenant Frederick Langford. Eight signalmen.

Captain: Thomas Foley.

Kite sloop, 16 guns: 19–30 June 1801

Building details: Launched at Deptford in 1795. Built of fir. Sold 1805.

Dimensions: 365 tons. Length 96 ft. Breadth 30 ft, 6 ins. Depth in hold: 12 ft, 9 ins.

Guns: Sixteen carronades.

Men: 121. Borne: 93. Mustered: 89.

Vice-Admiral: Lord Nelson. Secretary: Thomas Wallis, Lieutenant Frederick Langford, 19–30 June 1801.

Captain: Thomas Digby.

Master: Robert Neave. Purser: Henry W. Nelson. Boatswain: John Courtney.

Medusa, 38 guns: 31 July–28 August 1801

Building details: Launched at Northfleet 14 April 1801. Broken up 1816.

Dimensions: 909 tons. Length on gun deck: 144 ft. Extreme breadth: 37 ft, 8 ins. Depth in hold: 12 ft, 5 ins. Draft when victualled for six months: bows, 18 ft, 9 ins, aft, 19 ft, 11 ins.

Guns: Twenty-six 18-pounders, four 6-pounders, twelve 24-pound carronades.

Sailing qualities: 'Goes fast to windward . . . her leeway is never very good . . . She always sails very fast off the wind from the Beam to the Quarter: in light winds with all sails set she has frequently gon [*sic*] 11 knots' (Goodwin, 302).

Men: 256.

(August 1801) Borne: 253. Mustered: 247.

Vice-Admiral: Lord Nelson. Secretary: Thomas Wallis, Lieutenant Frederick Langford, 30 July–27 August 1801.

Captain: John Gore. Lieutenants: Edward Williams, John Stuart, Hon. William Cathcart.

Master: William Kirby. Purser: James Baker.

Amazon, 38 Guns: 28 August–23 October 1801

Building details: Launched at Woolwich Dockyard 1799. Broken up 1817.

Dimensions: 1,038 tons. Length on deck: 150 ft. Extreme breadth: 39 ft, 5 ins. Depth in hold: 13 ft, 9 ins.

Guns: Twenty-eight 18-pounders, ten 9-pounders, eight 32-pound carronades.

Men: 284.

Vice-Admiral: Lord Nelson and retinue. Secretary: Thomas Wallis. Domestics: Joseph Webb, Thomas Allen, Berry Cook, Sam. Parton.

Captain: Samuel Sutton.

Lieutenants: John Quilliam, David Johnston, Geo. Walpole (acting).

Master: Pike Channel. Purser: John Goldsmith. Boatswain: John Eddy.

Amphion, 32 Guns: 24 May–30 July 1803

Building details: Launched Mistleythorn 1798. Sunk for use as a breakwater at Woolwich 1820.

Dimensions: 909 tons. Length on deck: 144 ft. Extreme breadth: 37 ft, 6 ins. Depth in hold: 12 ft, 6 ins.

Guns: Twenty-six 18-pounders, six 6-pounders, four 24-pound carronades.

Sailing qualities: 'The *Amphion* is one of the nicest Frigates I have seen – not so large as *Amazon*, but has every good quality' (Nelson to Sutton, 18 June 1803, Nicolas, V, 91).

Men: 254. Borne (20 May): 233 + 43 supernumeraries = 276. Mustered: 224 + 43 supernumeraries = 267.

Supernumeraries (24 May–30 July 1803): Vice-Admiral Lord Nelson and retinue, including Captain George Murray, captain of the Mediterranean fleet, John Scott, secretary, John McArthur, purser of the *Victory*; Captain the Honourable George Elliot; Hugh Elliot, ambassador to Naples, 24 May–11 June (transferred to the *Maidstone* at sea (PRO, ADM 51/1446)); William Mack, able seaman, 11 June–30 July 1803 (to *Victory*).

Captain: Thomas Masterman Hardy, 25 January–30 July 1803, Samuel Sutton, 31 July 1803.

Lieutenants: W. Bennett, Robert B. Yates, Charles Phillott, George Matthew Jones, 25 January 1803.

Master: John Hole, 26 February–13 May 1803, Edward George Napier, joined 14 May 1803. Purser: John Hodge. Boatswain: Rose Fuller. Surgeon: George McGrath. Gunner: James Banks. Chaplain: William Humphries, joined 25 January.

Midshipmen included: Richard Bulkeley, Sir John Gordon Sinclair, Bt, Hon. Ralph Neville. Volunteers first class: William Benjamin Suckling (all transferred to the *Victory*, 30 July 1803).

Victory, 100 guns: 31 July 1803–19 August, 14 September– 21 October 1805

Building details: Launched Chatham Dockyard 1765.

Dimensions: 2,162 tons. Length of gun deck: 186 ft. Extreme breadth: 51 ft, 10 ins. Depth in hold: 21 ft, 6 ins. Draft fully laden: fore, 23 ft, 11 ins, aft, 25 ft, 1 in. Height of ports above water: bow 5 ft, midship, 4 ft, 0 ins., aft, 5 ft, 2 ins. (PRO, ADM 52/3711, 7 May 1803, Thomas Atkinson, master, measured at Chatham). Will stow 380 tons of water, but during 1803 and 1804 usually 310 tons. Bread Room will just stow six months' bread loose, suppose six months' provisions to be 300 tons (Goodwin, 303).

Guns: Thirty 42-pounders, twenty-eight 24-pounders, thirty 12-pounders, twelve 6-pounders, two 68-pound carronades put on board 17 August 1804 (NMM, ADM/L/V/57).

Men: Complement 837.

(5 Aug 1803) Borne: 798 + 100 supernumeraries = 898. Mustered: 693 + 100 supernumeraries = 793.

(5 January 1804) Borne: 875 + 72 supernumeraries = 947. Mustered: 752 + 65 supernumeraries = 817.

(31 January 1805) Borne: 875 + 47 supernumeraries = 922. Mustered: 791 + 47 supernumeraries = 838.

Sailing qualities: 'She steers remarkably well, Wears very quick, and Seldom misses Stays . . . in sailing with Other ships, she holds her wind very well with them, and forereaches upon most, or all Ships of three decks we have been in Company with . . . Rolls easy and Strains nothing. Will run 10 or 11 knots Large She is thought to be a stiff ship. She rides rather heavy on her anchor' (Goodwin, 303, quoting PRO, ADM 95/76). 'The weather off Toulon is not mended . . . but this ship is so easy in a sea that we scarce feel a gale' (BL, Add. MSS 34953, 4 Oct. 1803, Nelson to Charles Pole). '. . . we rolled rather heavily last night, at a time when I observed that the *Victory* to be quite steady' (NMM, CRK/2, 13 Mar. 1804, Bickerton to Nelson).

Supernumeraries: Vice-Admiral Lord Nelson and retinue (all entered 20–23 May, then 31 July 1803), John Scott, secretary (killed 21 October 1805), William Hasleham (discharged 20 August 1805), W. Lewis Chevalier, Gaetano Spedillo, William Brest, Henry Nicholls, Thomas Bartlett, Robert Drummond (all discharged 22 December 1805), George Murray, captain of the fleet, 31 July 1803–August 1805, Frederick Peters, 31 July 1803–3 September 1805, Thomas Whipple, clerk, 31 July 1803–21 October 1805 (killed), William Mark, clerk, rated as AB, 30 July 1803–13 August 1803 (promotion to *Halcyon*), Hugh Elliot, ambassador to Naples, and retinue, Captain the Hon. George Elliot, 20–23 May 1803 (transferred to *Amphion*), Richard Ford, agent victualler, and John Geoghegan, secretary, 12 February 1804–September 1805. Leonard Gillespie, physician of the fleet, 3 January 1804–14 September 1805, John Conn, acting captain, 25 August (discharged to *Royal Sovereign*).

Captain: Samuel Sutton, 9 April–30 July 1803, Thomas Masterman Hardy, 31 July 1803–6 January 1806 (Admiralty leave November–December 1805).

Lieutenants: Robert Pettet, 4 April–1 August 1803 (promoted to *Termagant*), John Pasco, 7 April 1803–23 December 1805 (half-pay); William Layman, 4 April–5 October 1803 (promoted to *Weazle*), John Quilliam, 4 April 1803–3 November 1805 (to *Aeolus*), John Lackey, 4 April 1803–24 April 1804 (invalided), George Miller Bligh, 4 April–29 December 1805 (to *Ocean*), John Yule, 4 April–23 December 1805 (promotion, half-pay), Andrew King, 13 April 1803–1 January 1806 (to *Ocean*), Frederick William Pearse, 16 May–13 August 1803 (on promotion to *Halcyon*), John William Hussey, 26 August 1803–15 January 1805 (invalided), Peter Parker, 7 October 1803–29 July 1804 ('promoted to the rank of Master and Commander'), Edward Williams, 9 October 1803–23 December 1805 (promoted, half-pay), George Browne, 2 August 1804–[?1806], George Granville Waldegrave, 25 April 1804–11 April 1805 (promoted to the *Hydra*), Alexander Hills, 10 January 1805–19 November 1804 (discharged to *Conqueror*), entered again [?1805]–29 December 1805 (to *Ocean*), William Ram, 12 April 1805–21 October 1805 (killed).

Marines: Charles William Adair, captain, 14 April 1803–21 October 1805 (killed). First lieutenants: William Crockett, 14 April 1803–14 May 1804 (to *Niger*), James J. Peake, 30 April 1803–15 January 1806. Second lieutenants: George Keith, 17 April 1803–20 April 1803 (to *Gelykheid*), Lewis Buckle Reeves, 19 May 1803–15 January 1806, John Bunce, 21 April 1803–15 January 1806, Lewis Roatley, 3 September 1805–15 January 1806.

Master: Thomas Atkinson, 7 April 1803–last muster 31 December 1805. Purser: John McArthur, 9 April 1803–17 April 1804, William Burke, 18 April 1804–last muster 31 December 1805. Boatswain: Mel Jones, 9 April 1803–30 November 1804. George Lockhart, 1 December 1804–27 March 1805 (transferred to *Superb*), W. Willmet, 29 March 1805–last muster 31 December 1805. Surgeon: Edward Williams, 22 April–30 July 1803 (transferred to *Amphion*), George McGrath, 31 July 1803–30 December 1804, William Beatty, 31 December 1804 (entered from *Spencer*) – last muster 12 January 1806. Chaplain: Alexander John Scott, 26 May 1803 – last muster 31 December 1805. Gunner: William Rivers, 4 April 1803 – last muster 31 December 1805, William Bunce, 9 April 1803–31 December 1805.

Midshipmen and volunteers first class included: Richard Bulkeley, 31 July 1803–15 January 1806 (to *Ocean*), John McArthur (2), 18 May–26 August 1804 (to *Leviathan*), William Rivers (2), 9 April 1803–1 January 1806 (to *Princess of Orange*), Hon. Ralph Neville, 31 July 1803–4 November 1805 (to *Phoebe*), Sir John Gordon Sinclair, Bt, 31 July 1803–last muster 31 December 1805, Charles Connors, 27 May 1804–1 October 1804 (to *Niger*), Samuel Bolton, 31 July–12 October 1805 (to *Eurydice*).

Biographical Sketches

Acton, Sir John, Bt (1736–1811) Of English descent, former naval officer in the Tuscan Navy, reorganized and built the Neapolitan Navy from 1779, later promoted to prime minister of the Kingdom of Naples and Sicily; pro-British and supportive of Nelson and a frequent correspondent; in May 1804 forced out of office by French pressure and retired to Sicily, when Queen Maria Carolina took over the reins of the government.

Addington, Henry, later **Viscount Sidmouth** (1757–1844) A doctor's son who became Speaker of the House of Commons, then unexpectedly British prime minister from March 1801 to March 1804. Nelson became a personal friend and political supporter, writing to Addington on 4 October 1801: 'You may rely on my feeble support in the Senate as I have strove to support your honest principles' (DRO, 152/M/c1801/OP/46). When Addington was out of office, Nelson wrote to him: 'Friend I may call thee now, without suspicion of adulation to a Minister; but believe me, that my opinion of your honourable abilities as a Minister, and your constant friendship for me as a man, have ever held the same place in my heart' (23 June 1804, Nicolas, VI, 89). Nelson made a particular point of seeing Addington in September 1805: 'Lord Nelson came on that day & passed some Hours at Richmond Park. This was our last meeting' (8 Sept. 1805 DRO, 152/M/1805/ON-6).

Ali Pasha (1741–1822) Turkish ruler based in what is now Greece. His rule extended into the southern part of modern Albania. He was largely independent of the Porte in Constantinople. Known as the butcher of Yanina because of his cruelty. Nelson wrote to Addington that 'you will see the good disposition of Ali Vizir towards us' (Nicolas, V, 173, 24 Aug. 1803); and to the consul in the Ionian Islands, 'he has always been a staunch friend to the English ... I shall certainly, if he is within a few days' reach, go and see him' (Nelson to Foresti, 22 Oct. 1803, Nicolas, V, 270).

Allen, Tom (1764–1838) Servant to Nelson, who called him a 'Norfolk ploughman' (Naish, 190). Illiterate and simple but loyal, 'This affectionate domestic watched his lordship with unceasing attention, and many times have I seen him persuade the admiral to retire from a wet deck, or a stormy sea, to his bed'

(Parsons, 250). He left Nelson's service in February 1802 (Nelson to Sutton, 9 Feb. 1802, Nicolas, V, 4).

Allison, Wenman, Lieutenant (d. 1795) Lieutenant in the *Agamemnon* who was sent home and died soon after. 'I am not surprised at it. His drinking must sooner or later, I knew, carry him off, and . . . considering the derangement of intellect it may be considered a mercy' (Nelson to Fanny, 25 Dec. 1795, Naish 233).

Andrews, George, Captain (d. 1810) Midshipman in *Boreas*; 'he was forced . . . to fight a duel, which terminated fatally for the poor lad: the ball is lodged in his back' (Nelson to William Nelson, 20 Feb. 1785, Nicolas, I, 125); but Andrews survived, becoming a lieutenant in the *Agamemnon* under Nelson and captain in 1796, though he lost Nelson's good opinion: 'I should have been much distressed had Captain Andrews been appointed to my ship. He has taken to hard drinking, which would not have suited me' (Nelson to Fanny, 14 Dec. 1796, Naish, 311).

Atkinson, Thomas (1771–*c.* 1836) A Yorkshireman from Halifax ((UK)NA: PRO, ADM 36/15901); served as master of the *Theseus*, then with Nelson in the Baltic as master in the *San Josef* and *St George*; surveyed the Great Belt; later served as master of the *Victory*, 1803–5, keeping a meticulous log. Nelson described him as 'an élève of Hallowell's' (Nelson to Troubridge, 21 Dec. 1803, Nicolas, V, 320); Atkinson surveyed the Gulf of Palma, Sardinia ((UK)NA: PRO, ADM 2/923). Atkinson came ashore and became third and then first master attendant at Portsmouth Dockyard, 4 November 1823–16 July 1836.

Ball, Sir Alexander, Rear-Admiral (1756–1809) Captain of the *Alexander* at the Nile. Recommended to St Vincent by Evan Nepean, who had once served as a midshipman with Ball (St Vincent to Nepean, 3 Apr. 1797, NMM, NEP/4). St Vincent described him as 'A thinking, judicious man without pomp or display' (to Spencer, 30 Nov. 1800, Richmond, *Spencer Papers*, IV, 21). In 1799 Nelson sent him to blockade Malta, writing to St Vincent, 'Captain Ball has the important command of the blockade of Malta, and is as eminently conspicuous for his conciliating manners as he is for his judgment and gallantry' (30 Dec. 1798, Nicolas, III, 215). On the fall of Valetta, Ball was left out of the negotiations and returned home in April 1801. He returned to the island in June 1802, when he was *de facto* governor. Samuel Taylor Coleridge served as one of his secretaries and called him 'a very extraordinary man – indeed a great man. And he is really the abstract Idea of a wise & good Governor' (Holmes, II, 18). Nelson wrote: 'I hope to see you again afloat' but Ball never went back to sea (16 Sept 1803, Nicolas, V, 205). He found time for academic pursuits, writing to Nelson on 20 November 1803: 'I am translating Leibnitz memoirs into Italian to circulate throughout the continent' (NMM, CRK/1). He died in Malta in 1809, honoured by the Maltese.

Barham, *see* **Middleton, Sir Charles**

Beatty, Sir William, MD (d. 1842) Surgeon of the *Victory* in December 1804, transferring from the *Spencer*. Beatty performed a full autopsy on Nelson after Trafalgar (11 Dec. 1805, Nicolas, VII, 257), in which he included detailed observations on Nelson's health and his life during his last year. In 1806 he was appointed physician to Greenwich Hospital, where he remained until 1840. He was knighted in 1831.

Beckford, William Thomas (1760–1844) MP and eccentric collector, with great wealth from inherited West Indies estates; related to Sir William Hamilton. He built a folly at Fonthill, visited by Nelson and the Hamiltons in December 1800. Nelson refused a second invitation to visit Fonthill: 'Nothing could give me more pleasure than paying my respects at Fonthill, but I cannot move at present as all my family are with me, and my stay is very uncertain; and besides I have refused, for the present, all invitations' (Nelson to Beckford, 31 Aug. 1805, Nicolas, VII, 22).

Bedford, William, Admiral (1764?–1827) With Nelson at Boulogne commanding the *Leyden*; obtained intelligence on Flushing and was asked to 'keep every thing as secret as possible, relative to my intentions . . . be particularly careful not to let a word drop of what is now passing' (Nelson to Bedford, 10 Aug. 1801, Nicolas, IV, 452). Nelson wrote to him from Merton with his views on the peace: 'We may be wanted in 7 years but I do not think there is a probability of it being very soon. The French wish for peace if possible perhaps more than ourselves' and thanking him for 'your kind attention to my venerable father' (13 Feb. 1802, BL, Add. MSS 30182).

Bedingfield, John (fl. 1792–1802) From 1792 inspector of the office of treasurer of the navy. Probably came from Norfolk, was a friend of William Marsh and looked to Nelson for preferment for his son Thomas, a lieutenant.

Berry, Sir Edward, Rear-Admiral (1768–1831) Served with Nelson in the Mediterranean in 1796 and 1797 as lieutenant in the *Agamemnon* and *Captain*, and chosen by Nelson as captain of the *Vanguard*, in which Berry fought at the Nile. Nelson thanked him with the following words: 'I shall never forget your support for my mind on the 1st of August' (10 Dec. 1798, Nicolas, III, 192). After the battle he was sent home with dispatches but was captured in the Adriatic by the French. As captain of the *Foudroyant*, he captured the *Généreux* with Nelson and the *Guillaume Tell* without him. After a period of unemployment, he commanded the *Agamemnon* at Trafalgar, opening fire far too early and ineffectively; his leadership and seamanship, though not his bravery, were questionable, although he saved the *Colossus* in the storm after Trafalgar by towing her for eight days (Berry to Thomas Grenville, 1 Oct. 1806, Huntington, STG 135 (48)). Berry's final appointment before the end of his active service in 1815 was to command one of the royal yachts; he was made rear-admiral in 1821.

Bethune, *see* **Drinkwater, John**

Bexley, *see* **Vansittart, Nicholas**

Bickerton, Sir Richard Hussey, Admiral, Bt (1759–1832) Remained in the Mediterranean during the Peace of Amiens as commander-in-chief and served there as second in command under Nelson, 1803–5. Although St Vincent had no time for him, Nelson came to a different opinion: 'Sir Richard Bickerton is a very steady, good Officer, and fully to be relied upon' (to St Vincent, 12 Dec. 1803, Nicolas, V, 308). Sent home with a liver complaint before Trafalgar (Louis to Nelson, 31 Aug. 1805, Warren R. Dawson, *Nelson Collection*, 214). He then served on the Board of Admiralty until 1812.

Blackwood, Sir Henry, Vice-Admiral (1770–1832) Captain of the *Penelope* during the blockade of Malta, took part in the capture of the *Guillaume Tell*; of his action, Nelson wrote: 'Is there a sympathy which ties men together in bonds of friendship without having a personal knowledge of each other? If so (and, I believe, it was so to you) I was your friend and acquaintance before I saw you. Your conduct and character on the late glorious occasion stamps your fame beyond the reach of envy' (5 Apr. 1800, Palermo, Nicolas, VII, cxcv). But Blackwood's hasty temper got him into repeated trouble with authority. Captain John Markham to Lord Keith: 'Blackwood is a spirited young man, but wants judgement very much, and all his letters to the Board, and most particularly those to Lord St V—, are highly disrespectful, to say no worse of them . . . I wish he had not been so flippant with his pen' (19 Dec. 1803, Lloyd, *Keith*, III, 59). As captain of *Euryalus*, Blackwood was sent by Nelson in October 1805 to watch the French in Cadiz: 'I am gratified (because it shows your soul is in your business). I see you feel how much my heart is set on getting at these fellows, whom I have hunted so long' (Nelson to Blackwood, 8 Oct. 1805, Nicolas, VII, 88). He followed Nelson's instructions to 'watch all points, and all winds and weathers for I shall depend upon you' (Nelson to Blackwood, 9 Oct. 1805, Nicolas, VII, 96). Before Trafalgar, Blackwood was convinced that Villeneuve would not venture out of Cadiz, and he thus chose to remain in his frigate rather than to command on one of the ships of the line vacated by the captains who went home with Robert Calder. Blackwood witnessed the codicil to Nelson's will and left the deck of *Victory* to return to the *Euryalus* as the battle of Trafalgar began.

Bolton, Susannah (1755–1813) Elder sister of Nelson. Married a Norfolk merchant, Thomas Bolton, in 1780 and had twin daughters and a son, Thomas, who succeeded to the title as second Earl Nelson. Nelson sent £100 for Tom's education: 'I hope to be able to keep Tom at College without one farthing's expense to Mr Bolton and . . . I would do more, if in my power'. (Nelson to Mrs Bolton, 9 May 1805, Nicolas, VI, 429).

Bolton, Thomas (1752–1834) Unsuccessful merchant, married to Nelson's sister Susannah; settled as a farmer at Cranwich, Norfolk: 'Mr B's glaring impropriety in taking so large a farm, makes everybody talk' (Fanny to Nelson, 7 June 1799, Naish, 529). Nelson constantly and unsuccessfully tried to find a government place for Bolton, writing to Lord Melville from the Mediterranean (29 Sept. 1804, NAS, GD51/2/1082/35) and to George Rose (29 Aug. 1805,

Nicolas, VII, 18; Monmouth, E366, 3 Sep 1805) asking them to intercede with William Pitt.

Bolton, Sir William, Captain (d. 1830) Son of the brother of Nelson's brother-in-law, Thomas Bolton, William was married to Nelson's niece Catherine; he acted as a proxy for Nelson at his installation of the Bath, thus gaining his knighthood. Served as a lieutenant in both the *Vanguard* and the *Foudroyant*; later commanded the *Childers* sloop in the Mediterranean, 1803–5. Nelson was frustrated that he was not more active, writing to Emma of his laziness (9 Mar. 1805, Nicolas, VI, 350); and three weeks later, 'he is a very good young man, but he will never do any good for himself, he has no activity' (Nelson to Emma, 30 Mar. 1805, Morrison, II, 256); and again, 'that Goose Sir William Bolton has lost his frigate' (Monmouth, E445, 4 Apr. 1805). Appointed by Nelson to the *Amphitrite* frigate, he did not appear and Nelson could not wait for him, but five days before Trafalgar Nelson appointed Bolton to the *Eurydice* (Nicolas, VII, 99). Bolton had a respectable career as a frigate captain, taking his first prize in 1809 (Morrison, II, 323); his final command in 1814 was the *Forth* (40), in which he took a small United States privateer. One of the few members of the Nelson family who could be said to have done well.

Bowen, Richard, Captain (d. 24 July 1798) Highly regarded young officer, one of five brothers in the navy; brought up through the service by Jervis, who in 1796 put him in command of the Gibraltar squadron (NMM, MS/95/001); his career was cut short by his death in the attack on Santa Cruz. Nelson was upset by his death: 'a more enterprising, able and gallant Officer does not grace his Majesty's Naval Service' (Nelson to Jervis, 27 July 1797, Nicolas, II, 423). St Vincent and Nelson tried to persuade the government to erect a monument to Bowen in Westminster Abbey but with no success (Nicolas, II, 433).

Bowen, Thomas, Captain (d. 1809) Brother of Richard Bowen; as lieutenant wounded at St Vincent; after the Nile, Nelson gave him the command of the captured French 74, *Aquilon*, which he brought to England; according to Bowen, Nelson wanted him for the Danish expedition and 'made particular application that I should accompany him' (Bowen to Thomas Grenville, 5 Dec. 1806, Huntington, STG 136 (29)); but Bowen was appointed to the *Courageux* in 1801, serving under Calder. St Vincent wrote to Nepean, 'you could not have appointed a more useful man to command . . . than Tom Bowen, besides being very near an ideal, is the most [good] hearted fellow in the whole list' (27 Jan. 1801, BL, Add. MSS 36908). Bowen visited Merton, but after the Peace of Amiens had difficulty getting another ship, writing to Nelson: 'I made several attempts to have a conference with the Old Jesuit [St Vincent] but could not succeed' (24 Sept. 1804, NMM, CRK/2/105); after Nelson's death appointed to the *Ocean* (90), got her ready for sea and was then superseded. Nelson's support had not been effective.

Boyle, Sir Courtenay, Vice-Admiral (d. 1844) Third son of the earl of Cork and Orrery, a midshipman in the *Boreas* in the West Indies; Nelson called him 'amiable in the truest sense of the word' (15 July 1787, Nicolas, I, 247); later captain of the *Seahorse* frigate in the Mediterranean, 1803–5, leading the fleet out of the Maddalena Islands at the beginning of the Long Chase; a commissioner of the Navy Board, 1823–9, retiring as superintendent of transports in March 1831.

Boyles, Charles, Vice-Admiral (*c.* 1756–1816) Son of the collector of customs at Wells, Norfolk; entered the navy at the age of fifteen; in 1771 joined the *Raisonable* at the same time as Nelson; he was home in Wells when Nelson wrote to his brother William: 'Remember me kindly to Charles Boyles. The Wells Club must be strong this winter. Noisy, I'll answer, with you and him' (20 Feb. 1785, Nicolas, I, 126); reached flag rank in 1809.

Brame, Joseph (*fl.* 1794–9) Consul at Genoa, elderly and ill. His son-in-law James Bird conducted most of the victualling business for him. 'The Consul is very ill; and if he ever had any sense, it is all gone. Beef, lemons, and onions may be had here in abundance, but proper people must be sent to provide: the Consul is incapable' (Nelson to Jervis, 23 July 1796, Nicolas, VII, xciii).

Bromwich, Joseph, Lieutenant (d. 1829) Served as second lieutenant under Nelson in the *Albemarle* in the West Indies. Nelson described him as 'A brave and good Officer' (Nelson to Keppel, 20 Aug. 1783, Nicolas, I, 82), but, owing to a clerical slip, he was not confirmed and appears never to have been made a lieutenant. In 1801 he sought Nelson's patronage for 'a place in the dockyard, Adm[ira]l Holloway pressed me to write again' (8 Sept. 1801, NMM, CRK/2/118 and, at Nelson's request, St Vincent appointed Bromwich warden of Portsmouth Dockyard in October 1802. He remained there until his death in April 1829.

Buckinghamshire, *see* **Hobart, Robert**

Bulkeley, Richard (*fl.* 1781–1805) An army officer who met Nelson in the West Indies during the expedition to San Juan and remained a friend for life, writing scurrilous and bawdy letters about a fellow officer (NMM, CRK/2/86). He visited Merton; and in return Nelson visited him – on the return from Wales, at Bulkeley's home in Ludlow. Bulkeley later wrote supportively to Emma, 'You say it is a sin to love him, – I say, sin on, it is a crime worth going to hell for' (26 Oct. 1804, Houghton, pf MS Eng. 196.5 (118)).

Bulkeley, Richard, Lieutenant (d. 1809) Son of Nelson's friend, he served in the *Victory* in the Mediterranean as a midshipman, 1803–5; marked in the muster book as coming from America ((UK)NA: PRO, ADM 36/15895); at one time requested permission of Nelson to attempt to infiltrate Toulon to get intelligence on the French fleet ([n.d.], NMM, CRK/2/92). Nelson commented to Emma that Bulkeley was 'one of the finest and active young men I ever saw. I only regret he has not served his time' (13 Dec. 1803, NMM, MAM/28); wounded at Trafalgar, he was one of the last people to speak to Nelson.

Bullen, Joseph, Admiral (*c.* 1761–1857) Served with Nelson as second lieutenant on the *Hinchinbroke* on the expedition to San Juan and on the *Lion* under Cornwallis; with Nelson on the *Agamemnon* in 1793 and transferred to the

Victory under Hood, where he was one of the last out of Toulon. Captain in 1796, participated in the attacks on Calvi and Bastia in 1797.

Cadogan, Mrs (d. 1810) Mrs Lyon, mother of Emma Hamilton. Assumed the name Cadogan; lived with her at Naples, travelled across Europe with the Hamiltons and later managed Merton; executor of Emma's will.

Caffarena, Frances (*fl.* 1794–1801) An elderly Englishwoman married to a Genoese merchant. Her family supplied the fleet in the Mediterranean with bullocks and other goods in the mid 1790s; she provided Nelson with intelligence on French activity at the court of Genoa and on developments on the Continent and further afield through her network of merchant informants (BL, Add. MSS 34904, fol. 262). Nelson forwarded her reports to Jervis: 'I send you a packet . . . and one from Mrs Caffarena. I find Mr Wilson, purser of the *Meleager*, is her very old friend . . . she wishes he had a larger Ship' (Nelson to Jervis, 11 Sept. 1796, Nicolas, VII, cxi). Most important were her reports on Cadiz: 'letters from Cadiz mention orders from the French minister at Madrid for the French squadron to sail from there' (Caffarena to Nelson, 20 Aug. 1796, NMM, CRK/3/1).

Calder, Sir Robert, Admiral (1745–1818) One of his midshipmen described him as 'a very strict disciplinarian. We dared not appear on deck without our full uniform.' Calder was known to order a visiting officer off his ship when improperly dressed (Gardner, 80–81); captain of St Vincent's flagship, *Ville de Paris*, surprisingly, since St Vincent was even ruder about him than about many others, describing Calder to Nepean as 'violent, impracticable, ignorant, and illiterate beyond description' (3 Sept. 1798, NMM, NEP/4), and to John Markham, 'I hope Sir Robert Calder will have more confidence than when he served with me; his dread of approaching the shore at that time was truly ridiculous' (3 Nov. 1803, Markham, 30–31). Betsey Fremantle wrote of Lady Calder, 'she talks of nothing but ships and sea service and of the red ribbon that was given to Admiral Nelson, instead of the great Sir Robert' (25 Oct. 1797, Fremantle (1952), 289). After his failure to bring the French to action in 1805, Nelson wrote, 'I am glad Sir Robert Calder is gone; and from my heart I hope he will get home safe, and end his inquiry well' (Nelson to Collingwood, 14 Oct. 1805, Nicolas, VII, 121), sending him home in the *Prince of Wales*: 'however great the loss of such a ship . . . may be to me . . . I could not desert Calder in Adversity. But I cannot alter my first opinion of the great necessity of an enquiry taking place; he thinks he can prove that he did all which was possible – I hope it will turn out so' (Nelson to Gambier, 2 Oct. 1805, Chatterton, II, 4). Fremantle wrote more sympathetically: 'he is not a wise man [but] He is so fair a man to serve with and so accommodating, that I am much interested in his getting off with credit' (30 Sept. 1805, Buckingham and Chandos, III, 446). Best summarized by Thomas Byam Martin: 'Poor Calder, who was a wrong-headed, and consequently often a wrong judging man' (R. V. Hamilton, *Byam Martin*, I, 73–4). His court martial ended his seagoing career, although he served as commander-in-chief, Plymouth, between 1810 and 1812.

Campbell, Donald, Admiral (d. 1819) Admiral in the Portuguese Navy; carried out an important mission at Tripoli under Nelson's orders, which 'interfered with his Portuguese promotion'; when Campbell burnt ships in Naples Harbour in 1799 contrary to his orders, Nelson wrote, 'I am satisfied you thought that the time was proper for that destruction, not understanding, from the translation, that I had fixed a particular epoch, when it was to take place ... no stain on your character' (2 Jun 1804, Clements, Melville Papers, memorial by Campbell to George III).

Campbell, Sir George, Rear-Admiral (d. 1821) Joined Nelson in the Mediterranean in the *Canopus* on 17 Aug. 1803 (Nelson to Nepean, Nicolas, V, 168) but was invalided home, 'very ill with debility, hectic fever etc., but he cheered up on going away' (Nelson to Ball, 5 Dec. 1804, Nicolas, VI, 286). He was 'as good a fellow as ever lived' (Gardner, 107).

Campbell, John (d. 1799) Served as Nelson's secretary in *Vanguard* and was transferred as a purser to the *Franklin* immediately after the Nile: 'he has not activity for me' (Nelson to Maurice Nelson, 12 Aug. 1798, Nicolas, VII, clxii).

Caracciolo, Francesco, Admiral (d. 1799) Neapolitan admiral, served with the British fleet under Hotham in the *Tancredi*. After he sided with the Republican cause in Naples, he was tried by a Neapolitan court martial; Nelson allowed the execution.

Carew, Sir Benjamin Hallowell, Admiral (1760–1834) Known as Hallowell until he changed his name in 1828 on inheriting land; born in Boston, Mass.; with Nelson in the Mediterranean, 1794–6, and at the Nile as captain of the *Swiftsure*; energetic but outspoken: Ball wrote of him to Nelson: 'If I were an admiral I would rather have him than any officer I know' (27 Aug. 1803, NMM, CRK/1); after the Nile Hallowell presented Nelson with a coffin made out of the mast of *L'Orient*, 'that you may be buried in one of your trophies' (23 May 1799, Nicolas, III, 89). Nelson wrote: 'His spirit is certainly more independent than almost any man's I ever knew; but, I believe, he is attached to me. I am sure he has no reason to be so to either Troubridge, or any one at the Admiralty' (Nelson to Emma, 23 Apr. 1804, Nicolas, V, 513). He accompanied Nelson at the blockade of Toulon, and across the Atlantic after Villeneuve, but his ship *Tigre* was detached before Trafalgar.

Chatham, *see* **Pitt, Sir John**

Chevallier, William (*fl.* 1803–05) Nelson's steward on the *Victory*, on the recommendation of Davison, who wrote to Nelson, 'I am extremely happy to hear my friend Chevallier pleases. I have had proof of his integrity and Honesty, and whatever is better for you, he will take care that no-one else shall be Dishonest about you' (26 Dec. 1803, NMM, CRK/3/150). In March 1804 Chevallier claimed to be 'disagreeably situated' and asked to be released, Nelson writing to Davison, 'I can have no conception to what this is owing. I never said a harsh thing to him, nor any one else, I am sure. He is very much respected and an excellent servant' (28 Mar. 1804, Nicolas, V, 475). To Davison, Chevallier claimed that 'many disagreeable treatments' were 'never once from his Lordship, but from another quarter' (14 Mar. 1805, RNM MS 2002/76). He stayed aboard the *Victory* and was present at Nelson's death.

Clanricarde, *see* **De Burgh, John Thomas**

Clarence, *see* **William Henry, Prince**

Cockburn, Sir George, Admiral (1772–1853) Highly competent and combative, driven not least by the fact that his father was a bankrupt; served with Nelson in the Mediterranean, 1794–7, as captain of the *Meleager* and *La Minerve*, in which Nelson returned to relieve the garrison at Porto Ferrajo. 'I wish you to be impressed with a favourable opinion of Captain George Cockburn, than whom a more able gallant young captain does not serve His Majesty' (Nelson to Spencer, 28 Mar. 1797, Nicolas, VII, cxxxii). *La Minerve* brought home Gilbert Elliot and Colonel Drinkwater, who transferred to the *Lively* to watch the Battle of Cape St Vincent. Helped Nelson to sort out prize-money claims on his return to England. A very long and distinguished career followed, in which he was known for burning the White House and for taking Napoleon to St Helena; member of the Board of Admiralty, 1818–30, and first naval lord, 1834–5, 1841–6. Sir Roger Curtis commented many years later that of all the admirals, 'Cockburn [was] the cleverest altogether that I ever knew' (Croker to Peel, 31 Aug. 1845, BL, Add. MSS 40573).

Coffin, Sir Isaac, Admiral (1759–1839) Born in Boston, Massachusetts, Coffin was an idiosyncratic, aggressive officer who could not serve afloat after an injury in 1794; commissioner of the naval dockyard at Ajaccio in Corsica, and later in Lisbon and Minorca. Betsey Wynne wrote of him: 'very good humoured and pleasant but sometimes makes a fool of himself' (23 Jan. 1796, Fremantle, *Wynne*, II (1937), 164). St Vincent wrote of him to Gilbert Elliot that 'it is a matter of astonishment that, with my impatient temper, we could have kept on reasonable terms so long' (10 Dec. 1796, NMM, ELL/1141), and he recommended him to Spencer for the commissionership at Halifax 'as the only Man thoroughly qualified . . . his powers and exertions going much beyond any other persons in that Department' (2 Aug. 1797, BL, Add. MSS 75812). St Vincent, when first lord, used Coffin to carry through reforms in the dockyards as resident commissioner of Sheerness and Portsmouth.

Coke, Thomas William, later earl of Leicester (1754–1842) Whig MP who inherited the estate at Holkham in Norfolk in 1776 and experimented with agricultural reform; the Nelsons as Tories kept their distance, but Coke and Nelson had some social contact as Nelson's fortunes rose. According to Stirling (*Coke*, 288), Coke took Nelson's part in the betting book at Brooks's Club (dated 30 Apr. 1801): 'Mr. Coke bets Sir Thomas Miller 50 guineas that Nelson is neither taken prisoner or capitulated.'

Collier, Sir Francis Augustus, Rear-Admiral (1783?–1849) Midshipman in the *Vanguard* and the *Foudroyant* after entreaties from his mother, Lady Collier.

She wrote to Nelson: 'he has had the good fortune . . . to have stood near you in the ever memorable and never to be forgotten Victory of the Nile' (28 Dec. 1800, NMM, CRK/3/83); wounded in the capture of the *Guillaume Tell*. Lady Collier continued to write an extraordinary number of letters on her son's behalf to Lord Barham (see his weary reply, NMM, LBK/77, 11 Aug. 1805) and to Thomas Grenville (4 Dec. 1806, Huntington, STG/139 (9)). Collier had a long active career, dying in Hong Kong as commander-in-chief, China Station.

Collingwood, Cuthbert, Vice-Admiral Lord (1748–1810) One of Nelson's earliest and closest friends. They met in 1773 when Nelson was a midshipman in the *Triumph* and Collingwood was in the *Portland* at Sheerness. They were both at Portsmouth in November of that year when Nelson was in the *Seahorse* and Collingwood in the *Lenox* (Owen, 190); and they served together in the West Indies under Peter Parker. In 1798 Collingwood was very disappointed when St Vincent prevented him from joining Nelson in the Mediterranean: 'as my going would have interfered with the command of his great favourite Captain Troubridge, who is junior to me and who he meant should be second to Nelson. But Nelson having no such partiality kept Sir James Saumarez with him, and so the Chief was doubly defeated – for Sir James and he were on the worst possible terms' (Collingwood to Edward Collingwood, 14 Dec. 1798, Owen, 167). Collingwood was shy and, when an admiral, was not popular among his captains. Thomas Fremantle described his style as 'very much of Cornwallis's way in one respect namely that he never invites any one to his table, nor will he allow us to visit each other' (12 Sept. 1805, Parry, 70). He was notably easy on his crew: 'well might Lord Collingwood say that when a mutiny took place on board a ship, it must be the fault of the captain or officers' (Richardson, 79). When he took command after Trafalgar, Fremantle was again critical: 'Our Admiral is never of the same opinion four hours together consequently little can be expected from a man of so undecided a character' (Fremantle to his brother, 28 Oct. 1805, Parry, 75). But Collingwood's humane treatment of his crew and the care that he took over training were remarkable, and his light punishment regime, which became lighter as he grew older, contrasted with Nelson's (Lavery, *Trafalgar*, 128–9). His long and patient command of the Mediterranean Station was relatively uneventful and successful; he was recalled in 1810 but died off Minorca on his way home. He had spent only one year ashore in seventeen years of war.

Comyn, Stephen, Reverend (*fl.* 1798–1805) Chaplain who served with Nelson on the *Vanguard*. Nelson assured him of his support, writing from Sheerness to Long Parish, Hants, 'until you are better provided on shore, you may rely that I shall not pass you by' (28 July 1801, Monmouth, E94). In 1803 Comyn was still seeking Nelson's patronage for a better-funded rectory and reporting his attendance 'at an elegant entertainment given by Lady Hamilton . . . in commemoration of Dr Nelson's Birthday' (30 Oct. 1803, NMM, CRK/3/90).

Conn, John, Captain (*c.* 1773–1810) First served with Nelson at Boulogne as captain in command of the mortar gunboats; recommended by Nelson to St Vincent for promotion: 'You know Captain Conn's worth . . . he deserves whatever can be done for a very able Officer' (8 Sept. 1801, Nicolas, IV, 486). Served in the Mediterranean as captain of the *Canopus*, where he was superseded by Francis Austen (brother of Jane) in March 1805. In October 1805 he brought the *Royal Sovereign* out of Portsmouth but transferred to the *Dreadnought* before the Battle of Trafalgar. Drowned when captain of the *Swiftsure* in 1810.

Cornwallis, Sir William, Admiral (1744–1819) Nelson first met Cornwallis in the West Indies, writing to Locker, 'our mess is broke up. Captain Cornwallis and myself live together. I hope I have made a friend of him, which I am sure from his character you will be glad to hear' (23 Jan. 1780, Nicolas, I, 33). Cornwallis brought the sickly Nelson home from the West Indies in the *Lion*. Commander-in-chief of the Channel fleet blockading Brest, 1803–6; Nelson considered that Cornwallis had great merit for 'his persevering cruise' (11 Mar. 1804, Nicolas, V, 438). Cornwallis's strength of character and strategic sense were fully tested by his command off Brest, where he met every challenge.

Correglia, Adelaide (*fl.* 1794–7) Nelson's mistress during his time in the Mediter-ranean, introduced to him by the consul at Leghorn, John Udney. After the fall of Leghorn to the French in June 1796, she lived at Pisa. Nelson arranged for Thomas Pollard, a merchant at Leghorn, to send her money for rent on his behalf (Christie's catalogue, 1989).

Cracraft, William Edward, Captain (*c.* 1770–1810) Captain of the *Anson* with Nelson in the Mediterranean, sent into the Adriatic in mid 1803 with five frigates and sloops on several missions including watching the French Army in the heel of Italy and the Russians in Corfu, and protecting trade from the Levant. Described by Nelson as a 'very intelligent officer' (Nelson to Lord Hawkesbury, 20 Oct. 1803, Nicolas, V, 258). He was given secret orders to investigate the potential for naval stores from the Morea and to consult with Ali Pasha at Yanina.

Culverhouse, John, Captain (d. 1809) First lieutenant on board *La Minerve* with Nelson and Cockburn when the *Sabina* was taken, described as 'an old Officer of very distinguished merit' (Nelson to Jervis, 20 Dec. 1796, Nicolas, II, 313); with Nelson as a lieutenant at the Battle of Cape St Vincent. Described as a 'very active and able officer . . . He was an excellent signal officer, a good sailor, and agreeable messmate, and in every respect a very clever fellow'. He was made a post-captain, but was unfortunately drowned at the Cape of Good Hope (Lloyd, *Gardner*, 47).

Cumby, William Pryce, Captain (d. 1837) First lieutenant of the *Bellerophon* at Trafalgar when his captain was killed; after the battle unemployed for eighteen months; later captain of the *Polyphemus* and in 1837 superintendent, Pembroke Dockyard (Warren R. Dawson, *Nelson Collection*, 454).

Curtis, Sir Roger, Admiral (1746–1816) Captain of the fleet to Howe at the First of June in 1794, when he made many enemies; commanded the squadron that relieved Troubridge at Cadiz to enable St Vincent to reinforce Nelson in the Mediterranean before the Nile. St Vincent commented to Nepean that he 'has no fortiter in him, although he abounds in the suavities', and that he 'sacrificed discipline to the popularity of the moment' (16 Apr. 1799, NMM, NEP/5). In 1800 he was appointed commander-in-chief, Cape of Good Hope Station, which, in a letter to Nelson, he called 'an abominable station' (12 Nov. 1803, NMM, CRK/3/11). He returned in ill health and did not serve at sea again.

Cutforth, James (*fl.* 1803–5) Victualling agent at Gibraltar; Nelson met him on board the *Amphion* and described him to Emma thus: 'his character is excellent' (9 Mar. 1804, Morrison, II, 225); supplied Nelson with wine and provisions; instructed by him to deal with the prizes left at Gibraltar in 1805. Richard Ford, the agent victualler afloat, was asked to consult Cutforth about dealing with the Barbary States 'upon the best mode of keeping those gentry in good humour, and that the Fleet may get liberal supplies without any further trouble' (Nelson to Ford, 2 Oct. 1805, Nicolas, VII, 65).

Darby, Henry D'Esterre, Admiral (d. 1823) St Vincent described him as 'a good humoured blundering Irishman' (27 Feb. 1799, Pettigrew, I, 204); commanded the *Bellerophon* at the Nile, where he was wounded. Cornelia Knight records in her journal that Troubridge wrote to Darby with condolences on his wounds, saying, 'he had rather have been in his place than have borne the anguish he felt from running aground, and being kept from the Action – that he had found great difficulty in keeping from shooting himself, and that he even then frequently shed tears. Captain Darby . . . wept' ([n.d.], Nicolas, III, 476); with Nelson in Palermo, where he was busy on convoy duties; sent to Minorca: 'I'm sure Duckworth could not have left any one who will take better care of Minorca than yourself' (Nelson to Darby, 13 Sept. 1799, Nicolas, IV, 15).

Davison, Alexander (1750–1829) A government contractor for army supplies who was Nelson's prize agent after the Nile and later handled many of his financial affairs. They first met in Canada in 1782; Davison was pushing for prize agency through Nelson's brother Maurice as early as 1797. Nelson explained his appointment to his brother: 'Davison was the only man I knew who answered the description' (2 Feb. 1799, Monmouth, E667); handled Nelson's dispute with St Vincent over the share of prize money. Davison was found guilty in April 1804 of bribing voters in the Ilchester by-election, spending a year in the Marshalsea Prison: 'An ignoramus like me could only warn him not to touch Boroughs. He has, poor fellow, been completely duped . . . I am most sincerely sorry for him . . . he must not kill himself, that his enemies would rejoice at, and I hope he will live to plague them' (Nelson to Emma, 27 June 1804, Morrison, II, 232). Davison re-established himself in another banking firm. He broke to Nelson the news 'of the Death of your valuable and ever to be lamented brother Maurice' (24 Apr. 1801); and he wrote to Nelson regularly with news and gossip and handled correspondence with both Fanny and Emma.

Nelson's brother William was wary of him: 'I am afraid this is some sharp trick of Davison's to secure himself. I don't half like his cunning' (14 May 1802, Morrison, II, 190). Nelson still owed him money when he left for Trafalgar (Nelson to Davison, 6 Sept. 1805, Nicolas, VII, 30). Davison again found himself in prison for twenty-one months after a trial in 1808 concerning army contracts. Davison was a man 'of great energy, efficiency and ambition, and his friends regarded him as a man of probity' (DNB); like many contractors, he benefited from loosely drawn contracts and paid the price of the jealousy of his fellow merchants.

Day, William, Captain (d. 1806) Served in Corsica; Nelson wrote, 'A more zealous active Officer as Agent for Transports I never met with. General de Burgh also speaks of him in the highest terms . . . [for what] Lieutenant Day has not only done at Bastia but at Porto Ferrajo' (Nelson to Jervis, 1 May 1797, Nicolas, II, 385). He provided critical information on the French armament at Toulon in 1798.

De Burgh, John Thomas, Lieutenant-General, later **earl of Clanricarde** (d. 1808) Army officer commanding operations in Corsica; who, together with Nelson, was the last to leave the shore on its evacuation in November 1796; left in command at Porto Ferrajo, Elba, and refused to leave with Nelson in January 1797, arguing that he had to wait for orders from London. Thomas Fremantle, who could be scathing at times, described him as 'a most Gentlemanlike good man' (Parry, 45).

Despard, Edward, Colonel (d. 1803) Army officer who served with Nelson in the West Indies. In 1803 accused of leading a Republican plot to assassinate the king; 'I was at Colonel Despard's trial, subpoenaed by him for a character. I think the plot deeper than was imagined' (Nelson to Davison, 8 Feb. 1803, Nicolas, V, 42). He was executed.

Dickson, Sir Archibald, Admiral (d. 1803) Commodore of the convoy when Nelson sailed from the Baltic in 1781. Fanny wrote to Nelson, 'Admiral Dickson is going to marry an 18 year old' (23 Sept. 1799, Naish, 533).

Drake, Francis (1764–1821) British minister plenipotentiary in Genoa, 1793–7, who corresponded with Nelson on diplomatic and intelligence matters, particularly in 1795 when trying to encourage the Austrian general de Vins to move against the French along the south coast of France. Drake provided Nelson with two cipher books for secret correspondence (Warren R. Dawson, *Nelson Collection*, 57). He and John Trevor sailed from Genoa with Nelson in the *Agamemnon* to meet with de Vins (Nelson to Hotham, 22 July 1795, Nicolas, II, 58). Fremantle wrote to his brother from Genoa, 'They have a tolerable Opera here . . . I have been twice and am well accommodated, the [British] Minister having given me a seat in his box . . . we dined with Mr Drake' (10 Sept. 1793, Parry, 26). On the arrival of the French in Genoa, Drake moved to the headquarters of the Austrian Army: 'I shall always remember, with the most lively gratitude, your kind expressions about me' (Nelson to Drake, 22 June 1796, Nicolas, VII, lxxxv).

Drinkwater, John, Colonel, later **Drinkwater-Bethune** (1762–1844) Author and army officer who served on Corsica, accompanied Gilbert Elliot back to England and witnessed the Battle of Cape St Vincent from the deck of the *Lively* frigate; published *A Narrative of the Battle of St Vincent* (1797).

Drummond, Sir William (1770?–1828) MP, scholar and diplomat, serving as chargé d'affaires at Copenhagen in 1801 when Nelson arrived in the Baltic, then sent as minister plenipotentiary to Sicily and Naples in 1801, moving to be ambassador to the Ottoman Porte in September 1803, succeeding Lord Elgin. In the last appointment he does not seem to have made much impact, Nelson writing, 'I do not know Mr Drummond, but I am told he is not likely to make the Porte understand the purity of our Cabinet' (Nelson to Ball, 16 Jan. 1804, Nicolas, V, 374). Drummond returned from Constantinople after only a few months, in November 1803, perhaps discouraged by the burning down of the British Embassy.

Duckworth, Sir John Thomas, Admiral (1748–1817) Commodore of the squadron that secured Minorca in November 1798. He did not impress St Vincent: 'Duckworth is a very artful, sly, impudent, pushing fellow' (to Nepean, 23 July 1797, NMM, NEP/4). Nelson sent his stepson, Josiah Nisbet, to Duckworth, hoping that he could improve his behaviour and performance as a naval officer. Nelson was concerned when Duckworth did not come to his aid when Nelson was expecting the French fleet to attack Sicily: 'Why D. should have not made haste to join I cannot conceive. If he shelters himself under nice punctilios of orders, I do not approve of an Officer's care of himself' (Nelson to Emma, 21 May 1799, Nicolas, VII, clxxxii); Duckworth hoped to get home during the peace, but was sent to the Leeward Islands, as he complained to Nelson: 'an officer that has been above forty out of forty-four years' servitude on board ship, and for these last ten years never had a moment to attend to his private affairs, or see a favourite daughter for six years, has a full claim to relief' (16 Jan. 1803, Morrison, II, 205). He was never close to Nelson, and missed Trafalgar, joining Collingwood off Cadiz on 15 November. 'Brave and reliable, eager for glory because anxious for recognition, Duckworth also remained curiously uncertain of himself' (*DNB*).

Duff, George, Captain (*c.* 1759–1805) Served briefly with Nelson at Trafalgar as captain of the *Mars*, when he engaged the *Fougeux*, but was killed. His letters to his wife describe his first meeting with Nelson: 'I dined with his Lordship yesterday, and had a very merry dinner. He certainly is the pleasantest Admiral I ever served under'; and later: 'He is so good and pleasant a man, that we all wish to do what he likes, without any kind of orders. I have been myself very lucky with most of my Admirals but I really think the present the pleasantest I have met with' (1, 10 Oct. 1805, Nicolas, VII, 71).

Duff, James (*fl.* 1776–1803) Long-serving consul at Cadiz: 'next January is 27 years since our first acquaintance' (Nelson to Duff, 4 Oct. 1803, BL, Add. MSS 34953); supplied Nelson with wines and provisions, arranged the dispatch of specie to England, as well as giving Nelson information on the Spanish fleet in Cadiz.

Dundas, Henry, later **Viscount Melville** (1742–1811) Powerful Scottish politician, close to William Pitt, who became secretary of state for war, 1794–1801, later becoming Lord Melville and briefly first lord of the Admiralty, 1804–5. He had a great interest in India and became a governor of the East India Company, as a consequence of which he advocated a maritime, imperial strategy rather than military intervention on the Continent. He had a sharp lawyer's mind, but he made enemies among Scottish Whigs. Described by his friend Glenbervie as 'an affectionate heart as a parent, a husband and a friend, and an unparalleled good temper' (quoted in Mackesy, *War without Victory*, 93). Lady Spencer wrote to him disarmingly: 'the more I know of you the better I like your Good old fashioned downright manner – never, never change for any other' (27 Dec. 1796, Clements, Melville Papers, XII). When appointed first lord some suspected that Melville would 'introduce some more of the Northern Heroes into the Navy. He is rather popular and judging of his abilities he is well received by the public' (Captain Robert Reynolds to Nelson, 18 May 1804, NMM, CRK/10/115). Early in his career Melville had attacked his rival Warren Hastings when he was brought to trial, and he suffered a similar fate when attacked for abuses: 'Time has now brought the poisn'd chalice to his own lips and they will make him drink its contents to the dregs' (Burges to Croker, 3 July 1804, Clements, Croker Papers). Nelson wrote, 'I believe Lord Melville would have been a good friend to the Navy; and therefore, am sorry he is out' (to Davison, 14 May 1805, Nicolas, VI, 440). William Windham, long an opponent, disagreed: 'It is a separate piece of good fortune that the Admiralty is to be taken out of hands that would soon have given us a Scotch Navy' (Baring, 444). He resigned office after his impeachment, although acquitted in June 1806, but never again held office.

Elliot, Sir George, Admiral (1784–1863) Second son of Gilbert Elliot; went to sea in 1794 under Thomas Foley, present at Hotham's Action, Cape St Vincent and the Nile: 'Foley tells me that he is one of the most active and best youths he has ever met with' (Nelson to Minto, 29 Aug. 1798, Nicolas, III, 113); Elliot was made lieutenant in 1800, and was with Nelson in the Baltic in the *St George*. In 1803, when a volunteer on *Victory*, Elliot was made captain of the *Maidstone* by Nelson: 'George is gone down the Mediterranean, as I wish to put £10,000 in his pocket' (Nelson to Hugh Elliot, 8 Sept. 1803, Nicolas, V, 198). Nelson described him to Minto as 'one of the best officers in our Service, and his ship in high order' (11 Jan. 1804, NMM, ELL/163); but, later that year, less flatteringly to Emma: 'Geo. Elliot is grown so proud that he scarcely deigns to own them [Hugh Elliot's children] for his cousins and would scarcely speak to a very fine lad which Mr E. has sent to sea . . . Captain Hardy says Geo. Elliot will turn out an ungrateful wretch although he may be a good officer' (Nov. 1804, Houghton, pf MS Eng. 196.5 (185)). Elliot had a long career serving until 1851, including service on the Board of Admiralty. He was knighted in 1862.

Elliot, Sir Gilbert, later **Lord Minto** (1751–1814) Scottish politician, diffident and modest, who was sent out as civil governor of Toulon, but when the town was retaken by the French he was appointed minister to the Italian states and in June 1794 viceroy of Corsica, which he ruled controversially for two years and four months. He was a friend and vitally important patron of Nelson, whom he described as 'without exception one of the most pleasing and least assuming men . . . gentle to a degree in his manner, but firm in his purpose, with a great deal of that indifference to danger that belongs, chiefly from habit, to a military life' (Stirling, *Pages and Portraits*, I, 65); used his influence to secure the command for Nelson in 1798 by calling on Lord Spencer and telling him Nelson was 'the fittest man in the world for the command', finding 'Lord Spencer . . . his opinion was already exactly the same as mine (I mean what relates to you)' (Elliot to Nelson, 25 Apr. 1798, Nicolas, III, 25). Minister in Vienna, 1799–1801, where he met Nelson again; became Baron Minto. He ended his career as governor-general of India.

Elliot, Hugh (1752–1813) Diplomat, soldier and adventurer, younger brother of Gilbert Elliot. Minister in Naples, 1803–6, sailed to the Mediterranean at short notice with Nelson in the *Victory*: 'Mr Elliot is happy, has quite recovered his spirits: he was very low at Portsmouth' (Nelson to Emma, 22 May 1803, Nicolas, V, 72). John Scott thought him 'a pleasant, well-informed man' (to Emma, 8 July 1803, Morrison, II, 214); 'a very active man & has his eyes open to everything & is considered an excellent minister in every respect' (Falconet to Nelson, 24 Sept. 1803, NMM, CRK/5/50). Nelson wrote extensively to Elliot on the security of Sicily and Naples, asking him to pass his assurances to the king and queen. Nelson wrote to Emma, 'Mr Elliot cannot bear Naples. I have no doubt, but that it is very different to your time' (1 Aug. 1803, Nicolas, V, 150). Nelson agreed to take Elliot's son William into the fleet. However, a Neapolitan courtier was hostile: Elliot was 'unscrupulous and unprincipled; in short, he is as dangerous in public affairs as he is amusing in society' (quoted in Mackesy, *Mediterranean*, 39). Elliot too fell under the spell of Maria Carolina, leaving Naples for Palermo with the court on the approach of the French in February 1806. It was his last diplomatic posting, although he became governor-general of the Leeward Islands and of Madras. He proved an erratic diplomat, 'enterprising and ambitious', but with 'a flawed personality' (*DNB*).

Elphinstone, Thomas, Captain (d. 1821) Served in the Mediterranean squadron in 1795–6; Jervis described him to Spencer optimistically as 'a child of the Service, son of an old Captain and the brother in law of Commissioner Hartwell' (19 Apr. 1797, BL, Add. MSS 75812); and, more realistically, to Nepean: 'tho' a dull man, has been industrious and worked hard, for his father, mother and sister I have not much to say, nor of Comm[issione]r. Hartwell, or his father, who possessed as small a share of real merit considering them in a seaman or military point of view as any two gentlemen I ever met with & can at best be considered negative characters. Yet I always have made a point to provide for the Children of the Profession, therefore I hope Lord Spencer will confirm him' (20 Apr. 1797, Houghton, pf MS Eng. 196.5 (126)). Elphinstone is mentioned cryptically by Fremantle in his diary: he was said to be carrying 'dolly on shore at one o'clock. Found Elphinstone with his brat on the chair' (27 Dec. 1796, Fremantle (1952), 259).

Eshelby, Thomas (*fl.* 1796–8) Surgeon in the *Captain* in 1796, who transferred to the *Theseus*. After the attack on Santa Cruz, amputated Nelson's arm: 'I am fortunate in having a good surgeon on board' (Nelson to Fanny, 5 Aug. 1797, Naish 333). Nelson noted in his accounts: 'paid Thomas Eshelby for amputating my arm, quitting the *Theseus* and attending me to England in the *Seahorse* frigate, £36.0.0' (1 Mar. 1798, Naish, 378).

Falconet, John (*fl.* 1799–1805) Merchant in Naples, and banker in partnership with Abraham Gibbs until the latter moved to Sicily (Falconet to Nelson, 18 June 1803, NMM, CRK/5/45). He looked after Nelson's financial affairs there and also purchased presents and forwarded mail to and from Emma when Nelson was commander-in-chief, Mediterranean: 'this [letter] goes by Naples. Mr Falconet, I think, will send it; although, I am sure, he feels great fear from the French Minister, for having anything to do with us' (Nelson to Emma, 31 Aug. 1804, Nicolas, VI, 181).

Farmer, George, Captain (d. 1779) Captain of the *Seahorse*, 1773–7, in which Nelson sailed to the East Indies; previously a midshipman with Nelson's uncle, Captain Maurice Suckling, in the *Dreadnought* in the West Indies during the Seven Years War.

Fearney, William (*fl.* 1793–7) A volunteer seaman from Newcastle, who served in the *Agamemnon* and transferred with Nelson to the *Captain*; promoted to midshipman in *Theseus* and later served in the *Foudroyant* and the *Courageux*, but was never made lieutenant.

Fellowes, Thomas (*fl.* 1793–1801) Purser of the *Agamemnon*, about whom Nelson wrote, 'I am very much disposed to like Mr Fellowes . . . He seems perfectly to understand me, and I dare say we shall do very well together' (Nelson to Locker, 21 Feb. 1793, Nicolas, I, 301); later had difficulty in clearing his accounts through the Navy Board and was imprisoned for debt. 'I am truly concerned about Mr Fellowes but what can I do? I have signed every paper for the victualling those men which he says stop his accounts . . . I would lend him money but I have it not' (Nelson to Berry, 26 Jan. 1801, Nicolas, IV, 277). Nelson subsequently wrote to St Vincent on his behalf to secure an appointment at Chatham for him: 'Mr Fellowes is a man of strictly honest principles' (26 Nov. 1801, Nicolas, IV, 531).

Foley, Sir Thomas, Admiral (1757–1833) A large, quiet, confident Welshman, who entered the navy a year before Nelson in 1770; with Nelson in the Mediterranean in 1793–6, where he was, according to Fremantle, 'violently

Rear-Admiral Sir Horatio Nelson by Lemuel Francis Abbott, commissioned by John
McArthur in 1799, who deplored Abbott's efforts to 'adonize' the picture by softening
Nelson's features. Abbott painted many versions of this portrait.

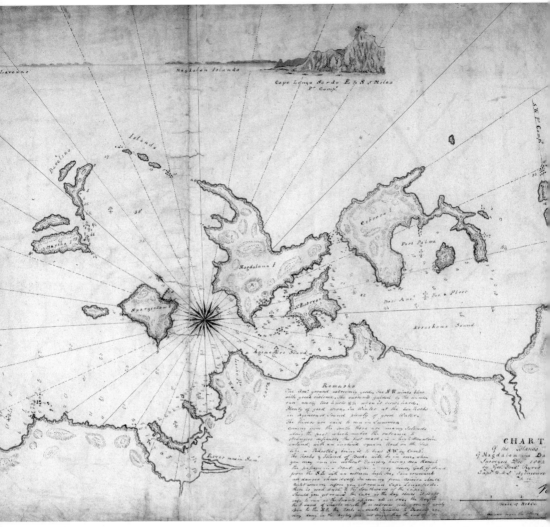

Chart of the Maddalena Islands, at the north-eastern end of Sardinia, 1802, drawn by Captain George Ryves. Agincourt Sound was used regularly by Nelson's Mediterranean fleet as an anchorage.

(*top*) The British fleet forcing the passage of the Sound, 30 March 1801, by Robert Dodd. Kronborg Castle is in the backgound, although the narrowness of the Sound is exaggerated by the artist.

(*bottom*) The Battle of Copenhagen by Dominic Serres. To the right, the *Bellona* and the *Russell* are aground; the spires of the city can be seen in the background.

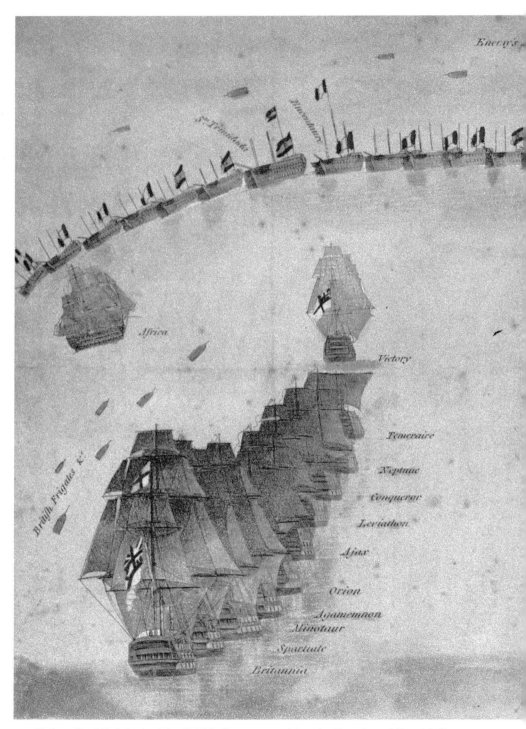

Enemy's

St Trinidada

Bucentaure

Africa

Victory

Temeraire

Neptune

Conquerer

Leviathon

British Frigates &c

Ajax

Orion

Agamemnon

Minotaur

Spartiate

Britannia

Robert Dodd's 'plan' of the British fleet approaching the French and Spanish line at Trafalgar, published immediately after the news of the victory reached London.

Ste Anne

Prince gesAsturias

Royal Sovereign

Mars

Belleisle

Tonnant

Bellerophon

Collossus

Achille

Polyphemus

Revenge

Swiftsure

Defence

Thunderer

Defiance

Prince

Dreadnought

The Death of Nelson, after Benjamin West, a print that follows the artist's low-key painting of 1809. This picture, with its small scale and sense of the ordinary, conveys the anguish of Nelson's death better than West's great quarterdeck scenario painted soon after Trafalgar, or the expansive and staged-below-decks death scene by Arthur Devis.

Nelson's funeral procession on the Thames, 9 January 1806 (*top*, by Daniel Turner), showing the barge with Nelson's coffin approaching the Watergate. Nelson's funeral in St Paul's (*bottom*, after A.C. Pugin). Seven thousand people were said to be in St Paul's.

Thomas Davidson's *England's Pride and Glory*, painted in about 1890 when Britain again felt threatened by the growth of foreign navies. Abbott's portrait of Nelson provides inspiration for the young naval cadet.

smitten' with Betsey (18 Oct. 1796, Fremantle (1952), 258); Nelson placed the young George Elliot with him, who later recalled the 'kindness of Captain Foley – I never left him until I was a lieutenant' (Elliot, *Memoirs*, 5). As captain of the *Goliath* at the Nile, he led the first five ships around the anchored French to attack them from the landward side; commanded the *Elephant* at Copenhagen; host to Nelson and the Hamiltons at Milford Haven. Foley married during the Peace of Amiens but was too ill to join Nelson in the Mediterranean in 1803, 'my health though mending very much does not yet prompt me to be very forward' (to Nelson, 25 Aug. 1803, NMM, CRK/5/105). He hoped Nelson would help his nephew Richard Foley. After Copenhagen, Foley did not serve at sea again, although his last command was as commander-in-chief, Portsmouth, when he died in 1833. Foley was made KCB in 1815.

Foote, Sir Edward James, Admiral (1767–1833) In the *Seahorse*, was left in command of the ships remaining in Naples Bay when Nelson sailed for Palermo in May 1799, leaving decisions 'entirely to your judgement' (Nelson to Foote, 18 June 1799, Nicolas, III, 381). Foote signed the capitulation agreed with the Republicans, which Nelson subsequently repudiated. Foote remained on good terms with Nelson, but in 1810, a year after the pubication of Clarke and McArthur's *Life*, he published his *Vindication*. Foote was knighted in 1831.

Ford, Richard (*fl.* 1790–1804) Agent victualler afloat in the Mediterranean, 1803–4, previously 'several years in the Victualling office & was chosen to accompany Commr. Towry to Lisbon to assist the concerns there of Mr Heatly – in every situation he has conducted himself with ability & honor' (William Marsh to Nelson, 23 Nov. 1803, NMM, CRK/8/184). Lord Hood wrote of him to Nelson: 'he was many years ago recommended by me to be a clerk in the Victualling Office ... his real character beyond everything I can say, & have therefore no doubt but you will find him usefull' (21 Nov. 1803, NMM, CRK/6/167). Nelson sent him ahead to the West Indies in the *Martin* sloop, but there was no chance to replenish the fleet while there.

Foresti, Spiridion (*fl.* 1801–13) Consul at Corfu, appointed resident to the Republic of the Seven Isles. Nelson approved of intelligence he provided: 'The more I hear of you, the more I am impressed with your extraordinary attention to the business of your office. Never have I seen anything to equal it' (29 Oct. 1799, Nicolas, IV, 75).

Fremantle, Sir Thomas, Vice-Admiral (1765–1819) A well-connected, competent officer, rather critical of others in his correspondence; served with Nelson in the Mediterranean in 1794–6 in command of the *Inconstant*, where he kept an intimate diary of his exploits; took a leading role in the capture of the *Ça Ira*. Married Betsey Wynne, who was among the English residents he evacuated from Leghorn in June 1796; Jervis praised his 'unparalleled exertions' in that endeavour (Nicolas, II, 194). Transferred to the *Seahorse*, wounded at Tenerife; served again with Nelson at Copenhagen in the *Ganges* and was sent to

St Petersburg with a message for the new tsar. When appointed to the *Neptune* in July 1805, he wrote to Betsey: 'I am in hopes of getting a very famous band, who have offered themselves to me; they are the 2nd Devon Militia band, the Regiment being reduced ... I shall indeed be en grand Seigneur' (Fremantle (1952), 395, 24 July 1805). Fought at Trafalgar in the *Neptune* (90). He ended his career afloat as a successful commander-in-chief, Mediterranean.

Frere, John Hookham (1769–1846) Diplomat and author, was under-secretary of state in the Foreign Office in April 1799, after which he was appointed minister at Lisbon, 1800–1802, transferred as minister to Madrid, 1802–4. Nelson did not trust his dispatches: 'Mr Frere has created some little alarm that the French Fleet has escaped us. My letter to him was intended to do away any such fears' (Nelson to Lord Hobart, 17 Mar. 1804, Nicolas, V, 451). Frere returned to Spain as minister in 1809, when he was blamed for advice given to Sir John Moore before the retreat to Corunna, after which his public career ended.

Gaetano, *see* **Spedillo**

Gallo, Marquis de (*fl.* 1798) Neapolitan nobleman and politician, disliked by Nelson: 'This Marquis de Gallo I detest. He is ignorant of common civility' (to Spencer, 29 Sept. 1798, Nicolas, III, 137). He later confided to Sir William Hamilton: 'I do not understand him. We are different men. He has been bred in a court, and I in a in a rough element, but I believe my heart is susceptible of the finer feelings as his' (27 Oct. 1798, Nicolas, III, 162).

Galloway, *see* **Garlies, George Stewart**

Galwey, Edward, Rear-Admiral (d. 1844) Following his service in the *Seahorse* as third lieutenant in 1797; chosen by Nelson as his first lieutenant in the *Vanguard*. In May 1798 Nelson subsequently told St Vincent he 'is one of the best officers' (Nicolas, III, 15); he was promoted from the *Vanguard* in early 1799.

Gardner, Alan, Admiral Lord (1742–1809) Sea officer and MP. Nelson had a high opinion of Gardner, whom he met in the West Indies: 'There is not a better Officer, or more of a gentleman this day in the Service' (Nelson to William Nelson, 8 Feb. 1782, Nicolas, I, 58). He had 'a countenance rather stern, but though an irritable, he was a good natured man' (Stirling, *Pages and Portraits*, I, 40). He famously lost his temper with the mutineers at Spithead when in conference with them on the *Queen Charlotte* in April 1797. Gardner was passed over for the Channel fleet in 1800, though he was appointed to it in 1807, declining because of poor health. St Vincent considered that Gardner had 'a deficiency of nerve under responsibility' (*DNB*).

Garlies, George Stewart, Admiral Lord, later **earl of Galloway** (1768–1834) An independent-minded Scot who in 1797 served with Nelson in the Mediterranean as captain of the frigate *Lively*; 'Lord Garlies is active, and I feel a real pleasure in having him with me' (Nelson to Jervis, 22 Aug. 1797, Nicolas, II, 249); served on the Board of Admiralty, May 1805 to February 1806, where he was described by Sir John Barrow as 'an excellent man, but of a warm and sanguine temperament' (Barrow, *Autobiography*, 2).

Gayner, Edward (1764–1846) Merchant at Rosas, north of Barcelona, who supplied wines and onions, as well as occasional information, to Nelson. Nelson called him 'an honest Quaker' who went on board the *Victory* and was 'quite delighted with our regularity and he went to our church on Sunday' (Nelson to Emma, 7 Dec. 1803, NMM, MAM/28); assisted after the loss of the *Hindostan* in 1804 by arranging the ransom of the crew taken prisoner by the Spanish and was rewarded with a silver cup worth a hundred guineas (Nicolas, V, 513); provided a personal postage service for Nelson and his captains; handled deserters. Nelson instructed William Bolton: 'deliver my letter, herewith transmitted, to Mr. Edward Gayner, Merchant at [Rosas] who will give you such letters and papers as he may have for me, with any Political information he may be able to obtain' (30 Aug. 1804, Nicolas, VI, 180); moved to Minorca, probably in 1808.

Gibbs, Abraham (*fl.* 1799–1804) Merchant from Naples who moved to Palermo in 1799 and lived with the Hamiltons in the Palazzo Palagonia; later looked after Nelson's business affairs, including the administration of his estate at Bronte: 'Good and great good, must come to me if you will take the business for me' (Nelson to Gibbs, 12 Aug. 1803, Nicolas, V, 164). Nelson undertook to send Gibbs's daughter to England: 'I shall be glad of so good an opportunity of obliging him, as it will naturally tie him to my interest' (Nelson to Emma, 18 Oct. 1803, Nicolas, V, 253). Nelson recommended him to Hugh Elliot: 'He was lately the partner of Mr Falconet, and was always the intimate household friend of dear Sir William and Lady Hamilton, and give me leave to add, my friend' (Nelson to Elliot, 19 Oct. 1803, Nicolas, V, 256).

Gibert, J. B. (*fl.* 1803–5) British consul at Barcelona, who supplied Nelson with wine, provisions and information, and forwarded letters to and from Madrid. 'I am very much obliged by your sending the Gazette and Newspapers, and will feel particularly thankful for the most early information respecting our situation with Spain' (Nelson to Gibert, 10 Oct. 1803, Nicolas, V, 242). Nelson thanked him for 'information respecting the King's recovery and the political circumstances of news from Paris' (26 Apr. 1804, Nicolas, V, 517).

Gibson, John, Lieutenant (d. 1797) Commanded the *Fox* cutter in the Mediterranean, 1796–7; described as 'a truly fine specimen of the old English seaman without having contracted their vulgarity' (Parsons, 312–13); drowned when the *Fox* was sunk at Tenerife.

Gillespie, Leonard, Dr (1758–1842) Served for many years in the West Indies before being appointed physician of the fleet in the Mediterranean in 1804; described as 'an able professional Man, and of an admirable and humane Disposition' (Dr Harness to Nelson, 20 Oct. 1804, NMM, CRK/6/115); in his journal Gillespie describes Nelson's 'noble frankness of manners, freedom from vain formality and pomp necessary to the decoration of empty little men', also

St Petersburg with a message for the new tsar. When appointed to the *Neptune* in July 1805, he wrote to Betsey: 'I am in hopes of getting a very famous band, who have offered themselves to me; they are the 2nd Devon Militia band, the Regiment being reduced ... I shall indeed be <u>en grand Seigneur</u>' (Fremantle (1952), 395, 24 July 1805). Fought at Trafalgar in the *Neptune* (90). He ended his career afloat as a successful commander-in-chief, Mediterranean.

Frere, John Hookham (1769–1846) Diplomat and author, was under-secretary of state in the Foreign Office in April 1799, after which he was appointed minister at Lisbon, 1800–1802, transferred as minister to Madrid, 1802–4. Nelson did not trust his dispatches: 'Mr Frere has created some little alarm that the French Fleet has escaped us. My letter to him was intended to do away any such fears' (Nelson to Lord Hobart, 17 Mar. 1804, Nicolas, V, 451). Frere returned to Spain as minister in 1809, when he was blamed for advice given to Sir John Moore before the retreat to Corunna, after which his public career ended.

Gaetano, *see* **Spedillo**

Gallo, Marquis de (*fl.* 1798) Neapolitan nobleman and politician, disliked by Nelson: 'This Marquis de Gallo I detest. He is ignorant of common civility' (to Spencer, 29 Sept. 1798, Nicolas, III, 137). He later confided to Sir William Hamilton: 'I do not understand him. We are different men. He has been bred in a court, and I in a in a rough element, but I believe my heart is susceptible of the finer feelings as his' (27 Oct. 1798, Nicolas, III, 162).

Galloway, *see* **Garlies, George Stewart**

Galwey, Edward, Rear-Admiral (d. 1844) Following his service in the *Seahorse* as third lieutenant in 1797; chosen by Nelson as his first lieutenant in the *Vanguard*. In May 1798 Nelson subsequently told St Vincent he 'is one of the best officers' (Nicolas, III, 15); he was promoted from the *Vanguard* in early 1799.

Gardner, Alan, Admiral Lord (1742–1809) Sea officer and MP. Nelson had a high opinion of Gardner, whom he met in the West Indies: 'There is not a better Officer, or more of a gentleman this day in the Service' (Nelson to William Nelson, 8 Feb. 1782, Nicolas, I, 58). He had 'a countenance rather stern, but though an irritable, he was a good natured man' (Stirling, *Pages and Portraits*, I, 40). He famously lost his temper with the mutineers at Spithead when in conference with them on the *Queen Charlotte* in April 1797. Gardner was passed over for the Channel fleet in 1800, though he was appointed to it in 1807, declining because of poor health. St Vincent considered that Gardner had 'a deficiency of nerve under responsibility' (*DNB*).

Garlies, George Stewart, Admiral Lord, later **earl of Galloway** (1768–1834) An independent-minded Scot who in 1797 served with Nelson in the Mediterranean as captain of the frigate *Lively*; 'Lord Garlies is active, and I feel a real pleasure in having him with me' (Nelson to Jervis, 22 Aug. 1797, Nicolas, II, 249); served on the Board of Admiralty, May 1805 to February 1806, where he was

you do not want any of his kindness; nor will he give you justice' (Nelson to Emma, 31 Aug. 1804, Nicolas, VI, 181). Greville's collection of minerals was one of the finest in the world, and he brought several varieties of flowers into Britain.

Hallowell, *see* **Carew, Sir Benjamin Hallowell**

Hamilton, Emma, Lady (1765–1815) Born Emma Hart at Neston in Cheshire. Went to London as a housemaid and became a kept woman, first by Sir Harry Featherstonehaugh, then by Charles Greville. Went to Naples, where she became mistress of Greville's maternal uncle, Sir William Hamilton, whom she married in September 1791. Met Nelson briefly in 1793. Betsey Wynne met her in 1797, noting in her diary that 'she makes no secret of the meanness of her birth, and is a little intoxicated by the splendour of her present situation, that her mother is always with her, and that she loudly says to all those who will hear her, that before she married Sir William she had not a gown to put on her back' (18 Jan. 1797, Fremantle (1937), II, 153). Became emotionally involved with Nelson in 1799 and his mistress not long afterwards; mother of Horatia, born in January 1801 (possibly Horatia had a twin, who was stillborn). A third child, who was short-lived, may have been born in 1803 or 1804. Full details of her passionate relationship with Nelson are not known, since Nelson destroyed her letters. Emma was one of the beauties of the age. Even when older, her 'Attitudes' drew reluctant admiration from society: 'L[ad]y Hamilton did her attitudes beautifully notwithstanding her enormous size – at least the grave ones; she is too large for Bacchante' (Lady Bessborough to Leveson Gower, 5 Mar. 1805, Granville, II, 35; also Sichel, 141). After Nelson's death, she took to drink and, unable to manage money, died in debt in Calais. The *Morning Post* obituary ran: 'in private life she was a humane and generous woman, intoxicated with the flattery and admiration which attended her in a rank of life so different from the obscure condition of her early days' (quoted in Fraser, 372–3).

Hamilton, Sir William (1731–1803) Minister at Naples for thirty-seven years, vulcanologist and connoisseur of Italian paintings and Greek vases. At the age of sixty, married Emma in 1791. According to his friend Nathaniel Wraxall, Hamilton was 'tall and meagre, with a dark complexion, a very aquiline nose' (*DNB*). Nelson first met him in 1793 when he called at Naples in the *Agamemnon*. Nelson stayed with the Hamiltons after his return from the Nile, and they sailed to Palermo with the king and queen of Naples. Hamilton returned when 'their majesties requested me to accompany Ld Nelson, who did not know the language & had not the long experience of the country, & of which I was perfectly master' (Hamilton to Greville, 14 July 1799, Morrison, II, 54). Travelled across Europe in 1801 with Emma and Nelson as the 'trio juncto in uno'. In spite of his embarrassing position, he wanted to avoid trouble: 'I know how very uncomfortable it would make his L[ordshi]p, our best friend, if a separation shou'd take place . . . which would be essentially detrimental to all parties, but wou'd be more sensibly felt by our dear friend than by us . . . I hope I may be allow'd sometimes to be my own master, & pass my time according to my own inclination, either by going on my fishing parties on the Thames or by going to London to attend the Museum, R[oyal] Society, the Tuesday Club, & Auctions of pictures' (Hamilton to Emma [n.d. but 1802], Morrison II, 197).

Hamond, Sir Andrew Snape, Captain, (1738–1828) Entered the navy in 1753 and earned a distinguished reputation in the American Revolutionary War, which not many officers did; comptroller of the Navy Board, 1794–1806; MP for Ipswich 1796–1806. His family were friendly with Fanny, but Nelson was also on good terms with him. 'I feel very much obliged by your kindness to my brother [Maurice] and I trust he will get one rise more in the Navy Office – I mean a Seat at the Board' (Nelson to Hamond [n.d. but 1801], Nicolas, IV, 356). Hamond was very sorely tried by St Vincent as first lord, and Nelson's sympathies were with the comptroller. When the Addington government fell, Davison wrote to Nelson: 'Sir And[re]w Hamond is now in Clover, and his son's success in taking the Spanish Frigates with Treasure is a codicil to his Soul' (7 Jan. 1805, NMM, CRK/3/159). Political attacks were renewed, but, as Hamond wrote to another enemy of St Vincent, John Orde, 'nothing shall make me yield to the machinations of that arch fiend L[or]d St Vincent or his juncto' (23 Apr. 1805, NMM, ORD/18). Hamond was called before the Commission of Inquiry into naval abuses; Nelson wished him luck: 'I rely . . . that you will pass the fiery ordeal without a singe' (17 Sept. 1805, Nicolas, VII, 41). Nelson refers to Hamond's son, Graham Eden, 'a better or more diligent Officer is nowhere to be found' ([n.d.], Nicolas, IV, 356).

Hampden, *see* **Trevor, John**

Hardy, Sir Thomas Masterman, Vice-Admiral, Bt (1769–1839) Served in the Mediterranean, 1793–7, as a lieutenant in the *Meleager* and *La Minerve* under Cockburn; taken prisoner with John Culverhouse during the capture of the *Sabina* but later exchanged, earning the praise of Nelson (Nelson to Jervis, 20 Dec. 1796, Nicolas, II, 315). Given command of the *Mutine* brig, captured as a prize, in which he served at Santa Cruz and the Nile, until promoted captain in the *Vanguard* in place of Berry. Thereafter, Nelson always asked for Hardy to serve with him, in 1801 exchanging William Wolseley for him after Copenhagen; served as flag captain in the *Victory* throughout 1803–5. He was a practical seaman, Whitby commenting to Nelson: 'Hardy who I doubt not is up to his elbows in rigging and reefing' (4 Sept. 1804, NMM, CRK/13/151). A month before Trafalgar, Fremantle commented on how well Hardy's character complemented Nelson's: 'No man is so well calculated to serve with Lord Nelson as he is, and I believe that whilst Hardy has health to carry on the business, he will not have a first Captain' (to the marquis of Buckingham, 30 Sept. 1805, Buckingham and Chandos, III, 445). Edward Codrington was very complimentary: 'From the first day that I saw him on board the *Victory*, I was captivated by his manner, so unusual and yet so becoming to his station as confidant of Lord Nelson; and I gave in to the general opinion of the fleet. He has not beauty or those accomplishments which attract sometimes on shore above all other qualities; but he is very superior in his situation' (Codrington, I, 68/9). In the *Victory*, Hardy was an unceasingly hard disciplinarian. He had a distinguished career, notable for a long and successful command of the South American Station, 1819–24, becoming first naval lord, November 1830 to August 1834. He then became governor of Greenwich Hospital, where he died.

Hargood, Sir William, Admiral (1762–1839) Son of a purser, he was midshipman in the *Bristol* in 1778–9 when Nelson was a lieutenant. In 1804 joined Nelson in the Mediterranean, replacing John Whitby as captain of the *Belleisle*: 'a very old acquaintance and shipmate of mine, and an élève of the Duke of Clarence, and, what is better than all, a very good man' (Nelson to Hugh Elliot, 23 Mar. 1804, Nicolas, V, 474). Fought at Trafalgar, where the *Belleisle* was in Collingwood's division: in the thick of the battle, she was totally dismasted, losing thirty-seven men and ninety-four wounded. His last post was as commander-in-chief, Plymouth, 1833–6.

Haslewood, William (*fl.* 1801–46) Nelson's solicitor in the firm Booth and Haslewood of Craven Street, The Strand, who handled Nelson's prize-money claim against St Vincent, for which Nelson congratulated him: 'You have acted not only as able lawyers, but a most friendly part throughout the whole business' and enclosing a codicil to his will, 'which you will not communicate to any person breathing' (6 Sept. 1803, Nicolas V, 197); he also handled the purchase of Merton and administered Nelson's estate after his death.

Heatly, John (*fl.* 1796–1805) Agent victualler to the navy at Lisbon; in 1796 in the Mediterranean, where he was active in acquiring bullocks: 'Mr Heatly the great victualler, writes me that the supply he is now procuring will be the first and last for the port of Genoa will be shut' (Nelson to Elliot, 20 Aug. 1796, Nicolas, II, 248). But in 1801 the victualling commissioners discovered to their 'astonishment and disappointment' that Heatly had not submitted accounts and that 'imprests to the amount of Four hundred thousand pounds and upwards are standing out against you in this office' (3 Mar. 1801, NMM, ADM/D/P/21). When Heatly requested to 'resign his employment and to return to England for the purpose, he alleges of passing his accounts with this office', it was noted that 'he had been appointed 11 March 1797 with a salary of £400 per annum and 15 shillings per diem table money' (Victualling Board to Nepean, 7 May 1801, NMM, ADM/D/P/21). Nelson in 1803 regretted 'there being no Agent-Victualler like Mr Heatly, who would find the Fleet in everything, in all parts that we used to send to' (Nelson to St Vincent, 12 July 1803, Nicolas, V, 133), though within months he had Richard Ford as his agent victualler afloat.

Hinton, Martin, Captain (*c.* 1759–1814) First lieutenant in the *Albemarle* in 1782 and in the *Agamemnon* in 1793, before being appointed second lieutenant in Hood's flagship *Victory*. Nelson wrote to Fanny in December 1795: 'Mr Hinton formerly 1st lieutenant of the *Agamemnon* is now Capt Hinton' (Naish, 231). Commanded the *Modeste* (36) 1800; to Sea Fencibles, Yarmouth, 1803.

Hobart, Robert, Baron Hobart, later **fourth earl of Buckinghamshire** (1760–1816.) Secretary of state for the colonies and the War Department under Addington, who asked Nelson to write to Hobart with his views on political issues in the Mediterranean (Hobart to Nelson, 23 Aug. 1803, Nicolas, V, 220). Nelson addressed a series of letters to him on the value of Sardinia, the importance of retaining Sicily, the activities of Barbary privateers, the treatment of the Maltese by the bey of Algiers and the problem over the consul at Algiers, John Falcon. The capital of Tasmania was named after him.

Hood, Samuel, Admiral Viscount (1724–1816) Nelson's patron from 1782: 'The Lord is very good friends with me, he is certainly the best Officer I ever saw. Everything from him is so clear it is impossible to misunderstand him' (Nelson to Locker, 1 Dec. 1793, Nicolas, I, 339). Collingwood did not share this enthusiasm: 'Lord H's ambition far exceeding his abilities gives rise to many unpleasant circumstances' (Collingwood to Sir Edward Blackett, 2 Mar. 1794, Hughes, 43). His personal courage was observed by Colonel John Moore, when Hood was called to the deck of a transport when it was in danger. 'I turned round to observe his countenance. It was not in the least discomposed. I could see him dress himself with the greatest deliberation . . . Lord Hood went upon deck and remained there two hours, during which the ship weathered the land' (5 Feb. 1794, Godfrey, 366). Hood continued to write to Nelson after becoming governor of Greenwich Hospital. 'Great pleasure to receive your affectionate letter . . . look forward to seeing Mrs Nelson and your father in Bath' (Hood to Nelson, 4 July 1797, BL, Add. MSS 34906). Sided with Fanny after the split. Hood was a long-lived governor of the Royal Hospital at Greenwich, dying at Bath after a fall.

Hood, Sir Samuel, Vice-Admiral (1762–1814) Cousin of Lord Hood, captain of the *Zealous* at Santa Cruz, and at the Nile. Jervis described to Spencer how Hood found the *Zealous* in such 'an undisciplined disorderly state . . . the captain whose whole soul is wrapped up in the profession . . . establishing discipline and good order' (29 Dec. 1796, Corbett, *Spencer Papers*, II, 84). Hood was left in command of the ships blockading the French in Egypt after Nelson sailed for Naples, and later took Salerno, prompting Nelson to say, 'I never expect any but the most useful services where he commands' (Nelson to Troubridge, 8 May 1799, Nicolas, III, 348). Hood's role was to keep the peace in Naples after the fall of the St Elmo Castle. 'Naples . . . was never more quiet than under his directions' (Nelson to Nepean, 3 Sept. 1799, Nicolas, III, 426). A fine seaman, in January 1804, in a remarkable operation, he took Diamond Rock, off Fort Royal, Martinique, which he equipped with a crew and guns. This annoyed French shipping for over a year. Hood died of a fever in Madras when commander-in-chief, East Indies.

Hoste, Sir William, Captain (1780–1828) Son of the Reverend Dixon Hoste of

Godwick and Tittleshall in Norfolk. Nelson took him to sea in the *Agamemnon* and was particularly fond of him, writing to his father: 'your son is everything which his dearest friends can wish him to be, and there is strong proof that the greatest gallantry may be under the gentlest behaviour' (4 Feb. 1794, Monmouth, E300). Nelson describes how he met with an accident: 'I am sorry to tell you poor little Hoste has very near broke his leg . . . He was prize master of a vessel and fell down a scuttle' (Nelson to Fanny, 1 Sept. 1795, Naish, 221). He saw action at the Battle of Cape St Vincent: 'Hoste is with me here, in the action he made me promise never to leave him again' (Nelson to Fanny, 3 Mar. 1797, Naish, 318); served as a lieutenant in the *Theseus* under Ralph Willet Miller at the Nile, after which he was promoted to the command of the *Mutine* brig. He missed Trafalgar but when in command of the frigate squadron at the action off Lissa in March 1811 he flew the signal 'Remember Nelson.' He was made KCB in 1815.

Hotham, William, Admiral Lord (1736–1813) Commander-in-chief in the Mediterranean, 1794–5, after the departure of Lord Hood and before the arrival of Jervis. Hotham was cautious and indecisive, and, judging by the shakiness of his handwriting, far from well. After the action on 14 March 1795 Nelson commented to Fanny: 'He is much cooler than myself and said "We must be contented. We have done very well" . . . I could never call it well done' (1 Apr. 1795, Naish, 204); and after the action on 13 July 1795 Nelson complained, '[we] were just again getting into close Action, when the Admiral made our signals to call us off' (Nelson to Locker, 14 July 1795, Nicolas, II, 51). 'Our Admiral, entre nous, has no political courage whatever, and is alarmed at the mention of any strong measure' (Nelson to Collingwood, 31 Aug. 1795, Nicolas, II, 78). After his Mediterranean command he saw no further service.

Hughes, Sir Richard, Admiral (1729–1812) Commander-in-chief, Leeward Islands, 1783–6. Nelson, like most other naval officers, thought little of him. Hughes also played the violin, Nelson commenting to Locker, 'Sir Richard . . . is a fiddler, therefore his time is taken up tuning that instrument, you will consequently expect the squadron is cursedly out of tune' (5 Mar. 1786, Nicolas, I, 156). Nelson was glad to see the admiral and his wife depart for England: 'I had rather have their room than their company' (Nelson to William Nelson, 28 June 1785, Nicolas, I, 134). Hughes was commander-in-chief, Halifax, 1789–92, after which he saw no further service.

Hunter, John (*fl.* 1802–3) Consul-general in Madrid. Provided Nelson with intelligence on the Spanish capabilities and intentions: 'The Spanish Squadron at Ferrol, dropped down the Harbour, having on board a number of Spanish Troops, intending to carry them to the Province of Biscay, then in insurrection' (Nelson to Gore, 13 Oct. 1804, Nicolas, VI, 240).

Inglefield, John Nicholson, Captain (1748–1828) A survivor of the sinking of the *Centaur* off Newfoundland in 1782, one of eleven out of 600. Captain of the *Aigle* in the Mediterranean, 1793–4; as acting first captain of Lord Hood's fleet, returned to England with Hood. Thereafter became resident commissioner of the navy in Corsica, Malta, Gibraltar and Halifax until 1811. Hood described him as 'A most experienced and very excellent officer' (Hood to Hamilton, 25 Aug. 1793, NMM, CRK/7/21). Fremantle did not like him: 'his hectoring manner, more like the bully of a bawdy house than a gentleman' (29 Apr. 1794, Fremantle (1952), 253). St Vincent's opinion was: 'tho' pompous is an honest man, and well acquainted with his business' (St Vincent to Nepean, 12 Jan. 1800, NMM, NEP/8).

Jefferson, Michael (*fl.* 1797–1805) Surgeon's mate in the *Agamemnon* who attended to Nelson's eye on Corsica; in the *Vanguard* in the Mediterranean in 1797. Later that year in London Jefferson looked after Nelson in the painful weeks when the ligature would not come away from the stump of his amputated arm. Jefferson later held a post in Malta Hospital but appears to have had some sort of breakdown and was replaced: 'He must now begin again and act with much more attention and sobriety, than he has done, to ever get forward again' (Nelson to Emma, 14 Mar. 1804, Nicolas, V, 439).

Jervis, Sir John, Admiral of the Fleet, from 1797 **Earl St Vincent** (1735–1823) Took command of the fleet in the Mediterranean, arriving at Corsica 29 November 1795. A disciplinarian, he treated mutineers in 1797 with harsh reprisals and commanded his captains through fear; he also wrote shrewd letters about his fellow officers to Evan Nepean, rarely far from the mark, though they are sometimes savagely uncharitable. Nelson was one of few junior officers to stand up to him. Though the two men were opposites in temperament and style, Jervis probably had more influence on Nelson and his career than any other man. Jervis was a controversial reforming first lord of the Admiralty under Addington, 1801–4. Nelson distanced himself from St Vincent because of their prize-money dispute, and because of the intense political controversy surrounding the first lord; but when at sea St Vincent, a centralizer and controller, made an exception in Nelson's case, gave him his head in the Mediterranean and enabled him to understand the principles and problems of high command. At the age of seventy-one, and not in good health, St Vincent accepted command of the Channel fleet, finally coming ashore in April 1807.

Keats, Sir Richard Goodwin, Admiral (1757–1834) An early favourite of Prince William Henry. When commanding the *Superb* in July 1801 in Saumarez's Action, Keats won fame from his night attack on a fleeing Spanish squadron when two enemy battleships blew one another up. He served under Nelson in the Mediterranean in the *Superb*, 1803–5, earning Nelson's praise: 'His health has not been very good but . . . I esteem his person alone as equal to one French 74, and the *Superb*, and her Captain equal to two 74-gun Ships' (Nelson to Hugh Elliot, 11 July 1803, Nicolas, V, 130). After recovering from illness at Naples, Nelson sent 'my right trusty friend' Keats to treat with the bey of Algiers over the reinstatement of the consul, John Falcon, for which he earned Nelson's praise: 'the stamp of whose character (if it was not so well known by

Godwick and Tittleshall in Norfolk. Nelson took him to sea in the *Agamemnon* and was particularly fond of him, writing to his father: 'your son is everything which his dearest friends can wish him to be, and there is strong proof that the greatest gallantry may be under the gentlest behaviour' (4 Feb. 1794, Monmouth, E300). Nelson describes how he met with an accident: 'I am sorry to tell you poor little Hoste has very near broke his leg . . . He was prize master of a vessel and fell down a scuttle' (Nelson to Fanny, 1 Sept. 1795, Naish, 221). He saw action at the Battle of Cape St Vincent: 'Hoste is with me here, in the action he made me promise never to leave him again' (Nelson to Fanny, 3 Mar. 1797, Naish, 318); served as a lieutenant in the *Theseus* under Ralph Willet Miller at the Nile, after which he was promoted to the command of the *Mutine* brig. He missed Trafalgar but when in command of the frigate squadron at the action off Lissa in March 1811 he flew the signal 'Remember Nelson.' He was made KCB in 1815.

Hotham, William, Admiral Lord (1736–1813) Commander-in-chief in the Mediterranean, 1794–5, after the departure of Lord Hood and before the arrival of Jervis. Hotham was cautious and indecisive, and, judging by the shakiness of his handwriting, far from well. After the action on 14 March 1795 Nelson commented to Fanny: 'He is much cooler than myself and said "We must be contented. We have done very well" . . . I could never call it well done' (1 Apr. 1795, Naish, 204); and after the action on 13 July 1795 Nelson complained, '[we] were just again getting into close Action, when the Admiral made our signals to call us off' (Nelson to Locker, 14 July 1795, Nicolas, II, 51). 'Our Admiral, entre nous, has no political courage whatever, and is alarmed at the mention of any strong measure' (Nelson to Collingwood, 31 Aug. 1795, Nicolas, II, 78). After his Mediterranean command he saw no further service.

Hughes, Sir Richard, Admiral (1729–1812) Commander-in-chief, Leeward Islands, 1783–6. Nelson, like most other naval officers, thought little of him. Hughes also played the violin, Nelson commenting to Locker, 'Sir Richard . . . is a fiddler, therefore his time is taken up tuning that instrument, you will consequently expect the squadron is cursedly out of tune' (5 Mar. 1786, Nicolas, I, 156). Nelson was glad to see the admiral and his wife depart for England: 'I had rather have their room than their company' (Nelson to William Nelson, 28 June 1785, Nicolas, I, 134). Hughes was commander-in-chief, Halifax, 1789–92, after which he saw no further service.

Hunter, John (*fl.* 1802–3) Consul-general in Madrid. Provided Nelson with intelligence on the Spanish capabilities and intentions: 'The Spanish Squadron at Ferrol, dropped down the Harbour, having on board a number of Spanish Troops, intending to carry them to the Province of Biscay, then in insurrection' (Nelson to Gore, 13 Oct. 1804, Nicolas, VI, 240).

Inglefield, John Nicholson, Captain (1748–1828) A survivor of the sinking of the *Centaur* off Newfoundland in 1782, one of eleven out of 600. Captain of the *Aigle* in the Mediterranean, 1793–4; as acting first captain of Lord Hood's

a less than successful protégé of Nelson, who asked Layman to serve in the Baltic in both the *San Josef* and the *St George*. In the Mediterranean in 1803, took charge of *Victory*'s prize, the *Ambuscade*, leaving $1,000 at Gibraltar, which prompted an inquiry. Nelson gave him the command of the *Weazle*, which was wrecked near Gibraltar, March 1804, though he was exonerated by the court martial. Described by Nelson as 'a most zealous, able, active and brave officer' (Huntington, STG 1334(40)). Nelson had written, 'I hope the Admiralty have confirmed Layman; for he is not only attached to me, but is indeed a very active Officer. It was his venturing to know more about India than Troubridge did, that made them look shy upon him. His tongue runs too fast. I often tell him neither to talk nor write so much' (2 Apr. 1804, Nicolas, V, 487). In January 1805 his ship the *Raven* was again wrecked in Cadiz Bay. 'Captain Layman arrived – to my great surprise – not in his Brig, but in a Spanish Cartel; he having been wrecked off Cadiz' (9 Mar. 1805, Nicolas, VI, 349). This time the court martial 'censured Captain Layman for not approaching the shore with greater caution' (Nelson's private journal, 8 Mar. 1805, BL, Add. MSS 34968). According to Layman, he withheld evidence at his court martial to protect another man, at Nelson's request: 'It is all my fault but leave it to me. I'll get you over it' (Foster Barham to Thomas Grenville, Huntington STG 134(40)). Nelson's death deprived him of further support and Layman was never employed again. He committed suicide.

Leicester, *see* **Coke, Thomas William**

Lepee, Frank (*fl.* 1785–95) Probably from Norfolk. A servant to Nelson during the American Revolutionary War, on shore and in the 1780s. Suffered from epileptic fits: 'poor Frank is better in health but that there are no hopes the surgeon tells me of his judgments returning' (Nelson to Fanny, 5 Dec. 1794, Naish, 190) to which Fanny replied: 'Poor Frank! I own something was the matter – that he was not so good as formerly: I am sorry that he is in so deplorable a way. I hope he never is with you: you may be able to get him into Greenwich hospital. You are sure of Captain Locker'. (10 Dec. 1794, Naish, 262). Discharged to the *Zealous* in October 1795; Nelson wrote to his father that he had 'parted with Frank for drunkenness, and when so, mad; never will keep a drunkard another hour' (29 Sept. 1795, Nicolas, II, 90).

Linzee, Robert, Admiral (d. 1804) Lord Hood's brother-in-law, commodore in the Mediterranean in the *Alcide* when Nelson first arrived in the *Agamemnon* in 1793. Nelson thought he was too cautious. Rear-admiral in April 1794. He faced a mutiny in his ship the *Windsor Castle* in November 1794 and returned to England in May 1796.

Lock, Charles (d. 1804) Consul at Naples, who witnessed the events in Naples and accused the pursers and captains of colluding with merchants over prices, which Nelson challenged; died of plague at Malta en route to Egypt (where he had been appointed consul-general) with his secretary, Lambton Este.

Locker, William, Captain (1731–1800) Distinguished service under Hawke in the

Channel during the Seven Years War. Wounded in the leg in 1757, from which he never completely recovered. An early patron of Nelson. According to his son, 'in the selection of his earlier naval friends he had shewn great discernment, for they became some of the most distinguished officers in the service. When in his turn he became a patron, his example as a commander drew around him a number of young officers whose brilliant career richly repaid the obligation they received from him' (Locker, 34). His son described him as 'the most natural [of] people . . . he hated nothing in the world except hypocrisy' (Locker, 35). Finished his career as lieutenant-governor of Greenwich Hospital, to which he was appointed in February 1793. At his death, Nelson wrote of him to his son John: 'a man whom to know was to love, and those who only heard of him honoured . . . he has left a character for honour and honesty which none can surpass, and very, very few attain' (27 Dec. 1800, Nicolas, IV, 271).

Louis, Sir Thomas, Admiral (1758–1807) Served under Nelson when commanding the *Minotaur* at the Nile. Nelson took Louis's son with him to the Mediterranean in 1803; Louis complained that St Vincent at the Admiralty 'played the Jesuit with me' and delayed his son's promotion (Louis to Keith, 18 Aug. 1804, Clements, Melville Papers). Joined Nelson in the Mediterranean in 1805 and in the *Canopus* took part in the chase to the West Indies. In October 1805 he protested to Nelson at being sent to Gibraltar for provisions: 'You are sending us away, My Lord – the enemy will come out, and we shall have no share of the battle.' To which Nelson replied: 'My dear Louis, I have no other means of keeping my fleet complete in provisions and water, but by sending them in detachments to Gibraltar. The enemy will come out, and we shall fight them; but there will be time for you to get back first. I look upon *Canopus* as my right hand . . . and I send you first to insure your being here to help to beat them' (Sir Francis Austen, captain of *Canopus*, quoted in Nicolas, VII, 63). But Louis missed Trafalgar, and died off the coast of Egypt of an illness picked up in the West Indies.

Lucas, Simon (*c.* 1766–1800) A merchant, Lucas was captured and pressed into the service of Morocco. On his return to England was appointed as Oriental interpreter to the British court, after which he attempted an exploration of the Sahara. He was appointed in 1793 as consul-general at Tripoli; Nelson dealt through him with the bashaw of Tripoli, threatening 'to sink all vessels attempting to carry supplies' if Tripoli continued its alliance with the French (20 Mar. 1799, Nicolas, III, 301). St Vincent had a very unfavourable opinion of Lucas and placed no reliance on his statements about the bashaw (St Vincent to Nelson, 30 Apr. 1799, Nicolas, III, 302). Nelson replied: 'The Consul is exactly as you describe him; but as I am not apt to be led by such gentry, he could do me little harm, and when put on my guard, by your just description of him, I troubled not my head about him' (5 June 1799, Nicolas, III, 374). Lucas wrote to Nelson: 'should he [the bashaw] make peace with Naples, he must declare war with some other nation, or lay up his cruisers.' On the envelope Nelson wrote: 'very good reason for being at war – well said bashaw' (14 Oct. 1799, Nicolas, IV, 117).

Lutwidge, Skeffington, Admiral (d. 1814) Captain of the *Carcass* on which Nelson sailed to the Arctic in 1773, who 'has continued the strictest friendship to this moment' (Nelson, in his 'Sketch of My Life', 15 Oct. 1799, Rawson, 9). Admiral in the Downs during the attack on Boulogne: 'I came on shore; for my business lays with the Admiral who lives in a Ship hauled on shore' (Nelson to Emma, 11 Aug. 1801, Nicolas, IV, 454). He and his wife became friends with Emma, dining with her regularly.

McArthur, John (1755–1840) (sometimes spelt M'Arthur) Purser, prize agent, author and skilled swordsman, author of *A Treatise of the Principles and Practice of Naval Courts Martial* (1792). Met Nelson in 1782; purser in the *Victory*, 1793–4. Secretary to Lord Hood, when he handled the prize money gained from the Toulon operation of 1793, and afterwards to Hyde Parker. McArthur wrote: 'having served 24 years as purser & having risen by progressive steps in the civil line from the lowest class of vessels, the cutter of which I was first made purser, from being her clerk, & one of the bourders [*sic*] in an action with two French privateers each of superior force' (McArthur to Nelson, 16 May 1803, NMM, CRK/8/152). When McArthur was appointed purser of the *Victory* in 1803, Nelson told him: 'I went to the Admiralty yesterday to ask about the *Victory* and Sir Evan Nepean assured me that it had for some time been a regulation of the Board that no Purser of a ship in which the Admiral was should be his secretary. I can only say that I shall oppose nothing in your arrangement for the *Victory* which you can settle at the Admiralty; at all events I would not give her up till War is certain' (11 Apr. 1803, Monmouth, E524). Went out to the Mediterranean as purser in the *Victory* in 1803 but left the ship in April 1804. According to a critic, William Young, who objected to McArthur's 'exorbitant charges', McArthur made £13,000 from Toulon: 'I believe he had no thoughts of going to sea as Purser again. The late Admiralty determined that he should go to sea, or give up the *Victory* and he gave her up ... I should observe that the money of captors never ought to be visited by the speculation of Agents making use of it for their own emolument' (Young to Pole, 31 May 1805, NMM, WYN/104). Wrote the *Life of Nelson* (1809) with James Stanier Clarke.

Macnamara, James, Captain (d. 1802) Accompanied Nelson on his trip to France in 1783. He describes how the journey was prolonged: 'I must do Captain Mac the justice to say it was all my doings, and in a great measure against his advice; but experience bought is the best; all mine I have paid pretty dearly for' (Nelson to Locker, 2 Nov. 1783, Nicolas, I, 84). When ashore at Portsmouth wrote to Nelson after the Nile – 'an old shipmate of yours, I've no interest' – asking for help in getting a post in a yacht or promotion (15 Dec. 1798, BL, Add. MSS 34905, fol. 211). (Not to be confused with the James Macnamara who served as a young captain with Nelson in the Mediterranean in the 1790s, and for whom Nelson appeared as a character witness after he had killed an army officer in a duel over a quarrel over their dogs.)

Magra, Perkin (*fl.* 1793–1803) Consul at Tunis, brother of James Matra, consul at Tangier. Nelson conducted negotiations through Magra with the bey of Tunis: 'your arduous task in keeping the Bey in good humour, and inducing him to act with vigour against the common Enemy, deserves more praise and approbation than it is in my powers to bestow' (Nelson to Magra, Feb. 1799, Nicolas, III, 273). Nelson rated highly both Magra and Spiridion Foresti at Corfu: 'These two gentlemen are the only ones I have found who really and truly do their duty' (Nelson to Nepean, 28 Nov. 1799, Nicolas, IV, 115).

Man, Robert, Admiral (d. 1813) Served in the Mediterranean in 1793–6 in the *Victory*, 'a better man could not have been found' (Nelson to Pollard, 8 July 1795, Warren R. Dawson, *Nelson Collection*, 239). Dogged by ill health: 'Poor Admiral Man has been afflicted with such a distempered mind, during the last nine months' (Jervis to Spencer, 27 July 1796, Corbett, *Spencer Papers*, II, 42). 'Man [has] been really ill, we had fears for [him]' (Nelson to Locker, 20 Aug. 1793, Nicolas, I, 319); later Jervis reported to Nepean that Man 'appeared to us here quite broke up, and becoming an old man fast' (29 Aug. 1796, NMM, NEP/7). But Man served on Lord Spencer's Board of Admiralty from September 1798 to February 1801.

Maria Carolina, Queen (d. 1814) Queen of Naples, wife of King Ferdinand IV, daughter of the Empress Maria Theresa and sister of Marie Antoinette, the executed queen of France. Maria Carolina was a fierce anti-Jacobin who wielded great power at the Neapolitan court. Befriended Lady Hamilton and through her persuaded Nelson to rescue the court in 1799, from which point Nelson was completely dominated by the queen. Ambitious and strong-willed, she impressed young midshipman Parsons, who described her as an 'energetic woman, whose slender and perfect form seemed to tread on air, while the tender animation of her sparkling eyes expressed a warmth of heart that prompted her (at least in my imagination) to embrace all around her' (Parsons, 46). Her energy is apparent in her letters, 'lacking in clearness and method . . . the words literally flowed from her mind on to paper in a chaotic stream . . . she often breaks off in the middle of a sentence and rushes off on another train of thought, leaving the reader to imagine what it was she meant in the first place' (Gutteridge, cix–cx). When Collingwood met her in 1809, he was unimpressed: 'She is a weak woman, and fancies she is conducting all the affairs of Europe. Her vanity blinds her, she cannot conduct anything' (to his sister, 19 Feb. 1809, Hughes, 268).

Marsden, William (1754–1836) A distinguished orientalist and numismatist, he started his career in the East India Company, becoming principal secretary to the government in Sumatra. Returning to England, he established an East India agency before becoming second secretary to the Admiralty in 1795 (Warren

R. Dawson, *Nelson Collection*, 289). Succeeded Nepean as secretary to the Admiralty in 1804. Marsden survived the political upheavals between 1804 and 1806, but retired in 1807.

Marsh, William (1755–1846) Nelson's banker, and senior partner in the firm Marsh and Creed of Norfolk Street, The Strand. Nelson empowered Davison to pursue his prize money claim against St Vincent 'jointly with my agents Messrs Marsh, Page and Creed . . . to support my just and undoubted claim by due course of law' (Nelson to Davison, 9 May 1800, Nicolas, IV, 234). The firm was ruined when one of its partners was hanged for forgery and fraud in 1824 (Warren R. Dawson, *Nelson Collection*, 289).

Martin, Sir George, Admiral of the Fleet (1764–1847) Knew Nelson in the West Indies during the American Revolutionary War; at the Battle of St Vincent as captain of the *Irresistible*, to which Nelson transferred when the *Captain* was damaged. Commanded the *Northumberland* in the Mediterranean at the capture of the *Généreux*. Nelson sent him off Genoa, 'relying on your well known abilities and judgment' (Nelson to Martin, 3 Aug. 1799, Nicolas, III, 432). Later served in the *Barfleur*: 'I'm sorry to hear George Martin has quitted his Ship from ill-health' (Nelson to Sutton, 14 Mar. 1805, Nicolas, VI, 362). Missed Trafalgar, being relieved by 'Sir Robert Barlow in *Barfleur* vice George Martin very ill' (Nelson to Blackwood, 8 Oct. 1805, Nicolas, VII, 88). However, Martin was active until 1815, when he received the KCB.

Matcham, George (d. 1833) Husband of Nelson's younger sister Catherine. Married in 1787 and had a large family. An East India merchant, Matcham helped Nelson with the purchase of Merton by providing a mortgage from money he had in the funds.

Matra, James (*c*. 1745–1806) Brother of Perkin Magra (Matra changed his name by deed poll), consul at Tangier, 1787–1806. Corresponded with Nelson on provisioning in 1805 (Matra to Nelson, 17 July 1805, NMM, CRK/9/38). Even in the highly mobile late eighteenth century, Matra had an extraordinary career. Born in New York; an able seaman in the navy in 1762; on the voyage of the *Endeavour*, where he managed to fall out with Cook, who called him 'good for nothing'; wrote a long detailed proposal to Joseph Banks for the establishment of a settlement at Botany Bay; filled various consular and diplomatic posts at Tenerife, Constantinople and finally Tangier (Frost, 12–13). By 1804 his sight had almost totally failed. Nelson was far from pleased with him (Nelson to Marsden, 1 Nov. 1804, Nicolas, VI, 255–6).

Melville, *see* **Dundas, Henry**

Messer, Thomas, Rear-Admiral (Russian Navy) (*fl.* 1783–1806) An Englishman who joined the Russian Navy as a midshipman in 1783, and he fought in the Black Sea against the Turks in 1788. Transported Nelson and the Hamiltons from Ancona to Trieste in his ship on their journey home from the Mediterranean. In 1804 Messer wrote asking Nelson for a letter of recommendation when commanding a 64 in the Russian squadron in the Adriatic (3 July 1804,

NMM, CRK/9/38). Messer was made rear-admiral in February 1806 as commandant at the port of Sevastopol.

Middleton, Sir Charles, Admiral, from 1805 **Baron Barham** (1726–1813) When comptroller of the navy, 1776–90, Middleton met Nelson in 1787 over the corruption allegations in the West Indies. Clearly Nelson did not admire him, for when Middleton resigned from the Admiralty Board to which he was appointed in November 1794, Nelson wrote to Fanny: 'I rejoice as do many at Sir Charles Middleton being out' (18 Dec. 1795, Naish, 230). Middleton's bureaucratic ways were the subject of a longer than usual tirade from Jervis: 'That damned Fellow . . . with his cant, Imposture, loads of precedents, and scraps of stay Tape & Buckram and makes you all believe that he is the only man capable of regulating your proceedings; when he really truly is fit for nothing . . . for he neither possesses a mind to direct great features, nor was ever in a situation, as an officer, to acquire knowledge or experience' (to Nepean, 5 May 1797, BL, Add. MSS 36708). Middleton was created first lord (when he was made Lord Barham) in April 1805 on the resignation of Lord Melville. Nelson wrote to Berry, who had asked for help in getting a ship, 'Lord Barham is an almost entire stranger to me' (31 Aug. 1805, Nicolas VII, 23); but subsequently he told Richard Bickerton, 'You will find Lord Barham a wonderful man' (20 Sept 1805, Monmouth, E187).

Miller, Ralph Willet, Captain (1762–99) A New Englander by birth (Buckland, vii), served as Nelson's flag captain in the *Captain* at Cape St Vincent. Nelson gave him a topaz ring for 'those four glorious hours became more than years in affection' (Miller to his father, 3 Mar. 1797, White, *Destiny*, Appendix 1, 154). Captain of the *Theseus* at the Nile; Saumarez thought him 'an excellent man' (26 Aug. 1798, Ross, I, 248) and Nelson called him 'the only truly virtuous man that I ever saw' (Nelson to Dixon Hoste, Sept. 1797, Nicolas, II, 443). Killed in an explosion aboard the *Theseus* off D'Acre. His brother officers from the Nile contributed to the erection of a memorial to him by Flaxman in St Paul's: 'if you think the £200 is enough for poor dear Miller's monument that you will direct Flaxman to instantly proceed about it, and as far as that sum, if no one subscribes, I will be answerable . . . The language must be plain, as if flowing from the heart of one of us Sailors who have fought with him' (Nelson to Berry, 26 Jan. 1801, Nicolas, IV, 276). However, no statue was erected.

Minto, *see* **Elliot, Sir Gilbert**

Moira, Francis Rawdon Hastings, second earl of Moira, General (1754–1826) Inherited his father's title in 1793; a general who gave employment to Nelson's brother Maurice, 1793–5, when he commanded the unsuccessful expedition to Flanders. During Nelson's absence at sea, 1803–5, Moira exercised Nelson's proxy vote in the Lords. Nelson wrote to Davison: 'I have signed the Proxy for Lord Moira and in doing it, I have broke through a resolution I made, never to give a Proxy; nor could anything have induced me to swerve from it, but to

R. Dawson, *Nelson Collection*, 289). Succeeded Nepean as secretary to the Admiralty in 1804. Marsden survived the political upheavals between 1804 and 1806, but retired in 1807.

Marsh, William (1755–1846) Nelson's banker, and senior partner in the firm Marsh and Creed of Norfolk Street, The Strand. Nelson empowered Davison to pursue his prize money claim against St Vincent 'jointly with my agents Messrs Marsh, Page and Creed . . . to support my just and undoubted claim by due course of law' (Nelson to Davison, 9 May 1800, Nicolas, IV, 234). The firm was ruined when one of its partners was hanged for forgery and fraud in 1824 (Warren R. Dawson, *Nelson Collection*, 289).

Martin, Sir George, Admiral of the Fleet (1764–1847) Knew Nelson in the West Indies during the American Revolutionary War; at the Battle of St Vincent as captain of the *Irresistible*, to which Nelson transferred when the *Captain* was damaged. Commanded the *Northumberland* in the Mediterranean at the capture of the *Généreux*. Nelson sent him off Genoa, 'relying on your well known abilities and judgment' (Nelson to Martin, 3 Aug. 1799, Nicolas, III, 432). Later served in the *Barfleur*: 'I'm sorry to hear George Martin has quitted his Ship from ill-health' (Nelson to Sutton, 14 Mar. 1805, Nicolas, VI, 362). Missed Trafalgar, being relieved by 'Sir Robert Barlow in *Barfleur* vice George Martin very ill' (Nelson to Blackwood, 8 Oct. 1805, Nicolas, VII, 88). However, Martin was active until 1815, when he received the KCB.

Matcham, George (d. 1833) Husband of Nelson's younger sister Catherine. Married in 1787 and had a large family. An East India merchant, Matcham helped Nelson with the purchase of Merton by providing a mortgage from money he had in the funds.

Matra, James (*c.* 1745–1806) Brother of Perkin Magra (Matra changed his name by deed poll), consul at Tangier, 1787–1806. Corresponded with Nelson on provisioning in 1805 (Matra to Nelson, 17 July 1805, NMM, CRK/9/38). Even in the highly mobile late eighteenth century, Matra had an extraordinary career. Born in New York; an able seaman in the navy in 1762; on the voyage of the *Endeavour*, where he managed to fall out with Cook, who called him 'good for nothing'; wrote a long detailed proposal to Joseph Banks for the establishment of a settlement at Botany Bay; filled various consular and diplomatic posts at Tenerife, Constantinople and finally Tangier (Frost, 12–13). By 1804 his sight had almost totally failed. Nelson was far from pleased with him (Nelson to Marsden, 1 Nov. 1804, Nicolas, VI, 255–6).

Melville, *see* **Dundas, Henry**

Messer, Thomas, Rear-Admiral (Russian Navy) (*fl.* 1783–1806) An Englishman who joined the Russian Navy as a midshipman in 1783, and he fought in the Black Sea against the Turks in 1788. Transported Nelson and the Hamiltons from Ancona to Trieste in his ship on their journey home from the Mediterranean. In 1804 Messer wrote asking Nelson for a letter of recommendation when commanding a 64 in the Russian squadron in the Adriatic (3 July 1804,

grasping, second eldest brother of Nelson. Rector of Hilborough; married Sarah Yonge. Became first Earl Nelson but, as his son, Horatio, predeceased him, the title passed to the eldest son of his sister Susannah Bolton. William was disliked intensely by Fanny and criticized by his father: 'The various passions that torment the Rector discomposes our good father who has been describing them to me. First of all ambition, pride and a selfish disposition' (Fanny to Nelson, 7 June 1799, Naish, 529). Nelson referred to him witheringly as 'the paltry prebendary' in a letter to his sister Susannah (11 Jan. 1804, Nicolas, V, 363). Nelson was extraordinarily patient with William, but even he became disillusioned: 'My brother hopes I shall meet the Enemy's fleet that somehow or other he may be a Lord' (quoted by Abbé Campbell to Emma, 8 Dec. 1805, Monmouth, E216). William constantly pressed Nelson to seek preferment for him, finally succeeding in gaining a stall at Canterbury: 'as from the situation I am now in I am in some measure obliged to give dinners & good wine, it is required & expected of me in ye double capacity of Prebendary of Canterbury & Lord Nelson's brother' (William to Nelson, 26 May 1804, NMM, CRK/9/33). William's daughter Charlotte married Samuel Hood, later Lord Bridport, who succeeded to the estates at Bronte. After the death of his first wife, Sarah, William married again.

Nepean, Sir Evan (1751–1822) First entered the navy as a clerk in 1773 and was appointed purser in 1775. At some point he was embroiled in 'a boxing fight with Prince William Henry, after which they became good friends' (Broadley and Bartelot, 77). In 1780 he was appointed to the *Foudroyant*, commanded by John Jervis. He then received 'an astonishing promotion' (*DNB*) when Lord Shelburne appointed him as under-secretary of state to the Home Office, during which he began to specialize in intelligence. In March 1794 he was made secretary of the Admiralty, where he served until January 1804: 'I really do not know a life of more importance to the public than his, and we are all interested in the preservation of it' (St Vincent to Gilbert Blane, 17 Mar. 1799, BL Add. MSS 31166). Nepean had political enemies. 'I trust you will not be thwarted by the routine Oracle who presides over our Naval Operations, by having got the ear of our First Lord . . . this self important little gentleman' (Huskisson to Home Popham, 16 July 1799, Clements, Melville Papers); Nepean received a baronetcy in July 1802 after a brief and unsuccessful spell in Ireland. When he returned, Davison reported to Nelson: 'Nepean arrived yesterday from Ireland to the great joy of Lord Melville and will instantly take his Seat at the Admiralty Board. He will relieve the First Lord of much anxiety and Trouble, as he will take the Labouring Oar. The principal business will now all be done by him' (7 Jan. 1805, NMM, CRK/3/159). 'Nepean says "he is the packhorse of all the departments"' (Davison to Nelson, 11 Feb. 1805, NMM, CRK/3/161). Nelson did not trust Nepean, writing to Emma: 'Our friend, Sir Evan, is a great courtier; whilst we are in prosperity, or that your face or voice may please him, he will be our admirer in different ways – me to feed his ambition, you to please his passion. But I can, and so can you, see into such friends' (1 Oct. 1805, Morrison, II, 267). Nevertheless, this tough, political civil servant broke down before Nelson's funeral, as A. J. Scott related to Emma; he 'cried very much – most sincerely: had the man not been in office, I would have taken him by the hand – nay, embraced him' (8 Jan. 1806, Morrison, II, 274).

Nisbet, Josiah, Captain (d. 1830) Stepson of Nelson, who went to sea with him as midshipman in the *Agamemnon* in 1793, but was never a success. Nelson worked hard to get him early promotion as a lieutenant, and successfully secured the command for him of the frigate *Thalia*. Nelson reported to Duckworth that George Martin thought that Nisbet was 'uncouth, he thinks the Master, who is a very clever man has by far too much Influence over him & there are two Women in the *Thalia*'s Gun Room who do no good . . . my wish is only that he would let me be kind to him' (16 Oct. 1799, NMM, PST/39). Nisbet continued to disappoint Nelson: 'Josiah is to have another ship, and to go abroad, if the *Thalia* cannot soon be got ready. I have done <u>all</u> for him, and he may again, as he has often done before, wish me to break my neck, and be abetted in it by his friends, who are likewise my enemies; but I have done my duty as an honest, generous man' (Nelson to Fanny, 4 Mar. 1801, Morrison, II, 125). Nisbet later made a good deal of money, suggesting that he was in the wrong career all along, and lived, and died, in Paris.

Niza, Marquis de (*fl.* 1797–1805) Rear-admiral of the Portuguese squadron in the Mediterranean. Nelson described the squadron as 'totally useless. The Marquis de Niza has certainly every good disposition to act well; but he is completely ignorant of sea affairs' (29 Nov. 1798, Nicolas, III, 180) and to St Vincent he wrote: 'Niza is a good tempered man not worth —. We are apparently the very best of friends' (25 Jan. 1799, Nicolas, III, 239). Niza later claimed a share of the prize money that Nelson won after his long case with St Vincent.

Noble, Edmund (*fl.* 1799–1805) Merchant who accompanied the Hamiltons to Palermo in 1799; Nelson assured him of 'my regard for your person and character, both as a Gentleman and as a Merchant in both of which lights I do not believe any man in Italy stands higher' (Nelson to Noble, 2 June 1800, Nicolas, VII, cxcvi). Settled in Malta 14 June 1803 to establish his commercial business there, leaving his brother George to handle the business at Naples (George Noble to Nelson, 7 July 1803, NMM, CRK/9/125). Took care of the Hamiltons' effects that had been left behind at Palermo and Naples. Hoped to rent a warehouse from Ball and to set up as a prize agent, although he confessed: 'I have little time . . . being well employed in Mercantile commerce, & in the privateering line' (Noble to Nelson, 16 Nov. 1803, NMM, CRK/9/114). He also offered to help Nelson with the estate at Bronte.

Noble, James, Vice-Admiral (*c.* 1776–1851) Lieutenant in the *Agamemnon*, *Captain* and *La Minerve*; flag lieutenant to Nelson when commodore: 'A most worthy and gallant Officer' (Nelson to Jervis, 25 Apr. 1796, Nicolas, II, 162);

wounded by a musket ball through his throat in an attack on a French convoy, and again in Dec. 1796 in an attack on the *Sabina*. Jervis wrote of Nelson's lieutenants: 'One at least will be made a Captain immediately and I think Spicer and Noble cannot be long with it' (to Nelson, 29 Sept. 1796, NMM, CRK/11/79). After the battle of St Vincent recommended again by Nelson for promotion, but commanded the Sea Fencibles in Sussex from March 1798. Applied unsuccessfully for active service, writing 3 October 1806 to Thomas Grenville, 'The death of Lord Nelson deprived me of the Friend on whom I relied for employment' (Huntington, STG 158 (49)).

Notter, William, Lieutenant (?Edward) (*fl.* 1780–1804) Commander of the *Queen* packet and twenty-four years in the navy. On learning of the death of his wife, sent for his children to join him in Malta, then disobeyed an order to join the *Agincourt*. He petitioned Nelson: 'All I beg of your Lordship is that I may be allowed to remain on the spot until the children arrive' (17 Mar. 1804, NMM, CRK/9/136); Nelson granted permission immediately. Notter replied: 'I return my most grateful thanks for the very feeling way in which your Lordship was pleased to express yourself about my family, I know that I took a very great liberty in not complying with your Lordship's orders, I had little reason to expect an exertion of your generosity in my behalf, but from your Lordship's natural disposition to relieve the distress of your fellow creatures I had everything to hope . . . in which I have not been mistaken' (15 May 1804, NMM, CRK/9/137). Included here as an instance of Nelson's instinctive kindness and willingness to break the rules on behalf of a junior officer of no consequence.

Orde, Sir John, Admiral, Bt (1751–1824) A universally unpopular officer, 'of a haughty disposition' (Dillon, I, 191). Orde was appointed governor of Dominica in February 1783, a post that he held until 1790 and for which he was given a baronetcy; his time there led to 'tedious and expensive litigation' (Melville to Orde, 19 June 1803, NMM, ORD/17). Friction with St Vincent started in earnest in 1798 after Nelson's appointment to the Mediterranean, when he called Orde 'a vain ignorant supercilious creature' (to Nepean, 6 Sept. 1798, NMM, NEP/4); he commented to Lord Spencer soon after: 'The removal of a certain baronet [Orde] from this squadron has produced a wonderful effect, and all are returning to good sense and good manners' (28 Sept. 1798, Corbett, *Spencer Papers*, II, 473). Collingwood thought 'Sir [John] Orde is proud and carries himself very high' (to Sir Edward Blackett, 3 Dec. 1798, Hughes, 90). St Vincent also complained that Orde was 'in the habit of making [minutes] from the disputes he had with the colonists at Dominica, of every conversation he hears . . . and this same Gossip . . . is at times both inconvenient and weaning' (to Lord Keith, 13 Apr. 1799, BL, Add. MSS 31166). Orde's challenge to St Vincent followed. When Orde was given command at Cadiz in 1805, he was a 'martyr to gout, was then in bed and had not quitted his cabin since he left England' (Lambton Este, journal, 4 Nov. 1804, Nicolas, VI, 258). Characteristically Nelson tried to heal wounds (25 July 1801, NMM, ORD/11, 16 Dec.

1804, 6 Apr. 1805, NMM, ORD/16) through correct but conciliating letters, and was philosophical about the Cadiz appointment: 'when he has made money enough he will be removed and the responsibility left where it was before' (to Sutton, 14 Mar. 1805, Clements, Smith Collection, fol. 32), but Davison, who stood to lose prize business, was more angry: 'he is without exception the most unpopular admiral in the Navy. I cannot bear the name' (to Nelson, 11 Feb. 1805, NMM, CRK/3/162). When the Board of Admiralty ordered Orde to share prize money with Nelson off Cadiz, he protested. His active career was ended by perhaps the most crushing letter that an eighteenth-century officer ever received from their lordships: 'I am commanded to express their dissatisfaction that so much of their Time should of late have been employed in the perusal of correspondence in which competition for Prize Money seems to be the chief if not the only subject of discussion' (Marsden to Orde, 11 Jan. 1805, NMM, ORD/18). Orde was never employed again. He was a pall-bearer at Nelson's funeral, although only as a last-minute substitute (*Naval Chronicle*, XV, 1806, 143). Orde's resentment at his treatment was unabated by the end of 1806, as demonstrated in a letter to the first lord, Thomas Grenville, at the end of 1806 (20 Dec. 1806, Huntington, STG/159 (8)).

Otway, Sir Robert Waller, Admiral, Bt (1770–1846) Popular and much respected Irish officer who sailed as flag captain in the *Royal George* and the *London* with Hyde Parker in 1801 to the Baltic. He is said to have persuaded Hyde Parker (and informed Nelson) of the decision to sail through the Sound rather than through the Great Belt. Otway also persuaded the captain of the Danish ship *Holsten* to surrender after Nelson had recommended sending him for that purpose (Nelson to Sir Hyde Parker, 3 Apr. 1801, Nicolas, IV, 331). Returned to England with dispatches after the Battle of Copenhagen, but not rewarded because of the king's illness: 'in my judgment there is not an officer in His Majesty's Navy of greater zeal and promise ... and I foretell that if justice is done him, he will rival all the heroes of the last two wars' (St Vincent [n.d.], in Rolfe, 35). Otway married the daughter of Admiral Holloway, Nelson providing a recommendation: 'Otway is as good as an Angel' (8 July 1801, Nicolas, IV, 422). Served under Cornwallis off Brest from 1804 in the *Culloden* and was part of Sir Richard Strachan's squadron when it took the remaining four French ships after Trafalgar. Created a baronet in 1831.

Otway, William Albany, Admiral (d. 1815) Commissioner of the Gibraltar Dockyard to whom Nelson wrote: 'I suppose Malta is equally under your control as Gibraltar yard' (25 Aug. 1803, Nicolas, V, 179). Nelson complained to the Navy Board: 'Commissioner Otway informs me, that they are so bare of stores at Gibraltar as to be unable to supply the ships cruising in that vicinity, who are consequently much distressed for almost every article' (10 Jan. 1804, Nicolas, V, 354). Nelson was nevertheless pleased with the service provided by Otway: 'The whole of your conduct is so correct, that I can have no doubt but it must always give me satisfaction' (14 Aug. 1804, Nicolas, VI, 154).

Owen, Sir Edward William Campbell Rich, Admiral (1771–1849) Between 1797 and 1798 Owen had command of a division of gun brigs off the Nore; he served with Nelson at Boulogne as captain of the *Nemesis*, was familiar with the coast, conducted reconnaissance close to Flushing and was privy to Nelson's plans: 'I cannot but admire Captain Owen's zeal in his anxious desire to get at the Enemy' (Nelson to Nepean, 25 Aug. 1801, Nicolas, IV, 480). His distinguished and active career ended in 1845. His brother William Fitzwilliam Owen, as lieutenant of the *Nancy* fire brig, was to have sailed her into Boulogne to set fire to ships in the harbour in the planned third attack, which did not take place (Nelson to Owen, 1 Oct. 1801, Nicolas, IV, 501).

Paget, Sir Arthur (1771–1840) A diplomat of 'easy charm', also prone to extravagance (*DNB*). Minister who succeeded Sir William Hamilton at Naples in 1800: 'I have either (after thirty six years service at this Court) been either kicked up or down out of my post; and Mr Paget, Lord Uxbridge's son, is named Envoy Extraordinary and Plenipotentiary . . . and is on his way here in a Frigate . . . I suppose it is a cabinet job, wishing to provide for Paget' (Hamilton to Nelson, 7 Feb. 1800, Nicolas, IV, 185). Paget moved to Vienna in 1801, where he stayed through the war of the Third Coalition and the disaster of Austerlitz, being recalled in 1806. He left the diplomatic service after a scandal when he eloped with a married woman.

Parker, Edward Thornborough, Captain (1780–1801) Served on the *Princess Royal* under Orde: 'Captain Thornborough's nephew, Mr Parker, a very fine young man' (St Vincent to Nepean, 23 Aug. 1798, NMM, NEP/4); a favourite of Nelson, who treated him as a son. Served on the *Medusa*, severely wounded at Boulogne. Nelson wrote: 'Dear little Parker, his thigh very much shattered; I have fears for his life' (Nelson to St Vincent, 16 Aug. 1801, Nicolas, IV, 464); and to Doctor Baird: 'he is my child, for I found him in distress. I am prepared for the worst although I still hope' (20 Sept. 1801, Nicolas, IV, 491). After his death: 'I beg that his hair may be cut off and given to me; it shall remain and be buried with me. What must the poor father feel when he is gone!' (26 Sept. 1801, Nicolas, IV, 497).

Parker, Sir Hyde, Admiral, Bt (1739–1807) Second son of Admiral Sir Hyde Parker, who commanded the British fleet at the Battle of the Dogger Bank in 1781. Parker served in the Mediterranean in 1793, when Fremantle wrote of him: 'I still keep in with my old friend Sir Hyde who is really a staunch friend, tho' sometimes very vinegar, but I cannot say he has ever been so to me' (Fremantle to his brother, 12 Dec. 1793, Parry, 27). (Parker's father had had the nickname 'Vinegar' when in the navy.) 'My good friend Sir Hyde is cruising off Toulon . . . nothing can equal the acrimony and ill humour of Lord Hood towards him' (Fremantle to his brother, 13 Apr. 1794, Parry, 31). When Parker was appointed to the command of the squadron for Copenhagen, he delayed sailing to humour his new, young wife. After the battle Nelson explained his differences with Sir Hyde's tactics: 'what Sir Hyde thought best

... was to stay in the Cattegat, and there wait the time when the whole Naval force of the Baltic might choose to come out and fight – a measure, in my opinion, disgraceful to our Country' (Nelson to Vansittart, 12 May 1801, Nicolas IV, 368). Nelson wrote in a confidential postscript to Davison: 'we all respect and love Sir Hyde; but the dearer his friends, the more uneasy they have been at his idleness, for that is the truth – no criminality' (15 June 1801, Nicolas, IV, 416). After his return from the Baltic, Parker was not employed again.

Parker, Sir Peter, Admiral of the Fleet (1721–1811) Patron of Nelson in the 1770s in the West Indies, where Collingwood and Fremantle benefited from his wife's kindness. Later Betsey Fremantle called on them: 'Lady Parker who is I think the most civil kind woman I ever saw. Sir Peter very kind likewise, but the oddest figure in the world, and would make a most excellent caricature' (7 Sept. 1797, Fremantle (1952), 284). Nelson wrote: 'I owe my present situation in life to your and good Sir Peter's partiality for me, and friendly remembrance of Maurice Suckling' (Nelson to Lady Parker, 21 May 1801, Nicolas, IV, 377) and 'This day 22 years I was made a Post Captain by Sir Peter Parker as good a man as ever lived, if you meet him again say that I shall drink his health in a bumper' (Nelson to Emma, 11 June 1801, BL, Egerton 1614). Parker was deputy grand master of the Freemasons in England (Downer, *Nelson's Purse*, 144).

Parker, Sir William, Admiral (1743–1802) As commodore Parker relieved Nelson as senior naval officer in the Leeward Islands command in 1787 (3 June 1787, (UK)NA: PRO, ADM 51/120); married to Jane, daughter of Edward Collingwood, a cousin of Cuthbert Collingwood (Hughes, 86). St Vincent thought Parker 'though a gallant man, has certainly much low, vulgar manner' (31 Oct. 1798, NMM, NEP/4, 171). Parker sided with Orde in the dispute with St Vincent over Nelson's appointment in 1798; St Vincent reported to Nepean: 'I do verily believe if Sir William's feelings had not been worked upon by Sir Robert Calder and Sir J Orde, more particularly by the former, he would have sat down quietly until his wife and connexions in England had spurred him on to some act of indiscretion, he is brave and honest, but weak, gossiping and made to be play'd upon' (6 Oct. 1798, NMM, NEP/4). Six months later St Vincent was scathing: 'The weakness of Sir William Parker, in the character of President of a Court Martial, exceeds that of Sir Roger Curtis, if possible' (to Nepean, 15 Mar. 1799, NMM, NEP/5). Nevertheless, Parker remained with the fleet until 1799, after which he was appointed to be commander-in-chief, Halifax, in March 1800. He was recalled by St Vincent when the latter was first lord, asking for a court martial and receiving a reprimand. He died suddenly in 1802, a very rich man.

Parker, Sir William, Admiral of the Fleet (1781–1866) Served under Foley, who applied to Nelson in 1799 for him to be examined for lieutenant (Foley to Nelson, 20 June 1799, Wellcome, 3670). It was on promoting Parker captain

Owen, Sir Edward William Campbell Rich, Admiral (1771–1849) Between 1797 and 1798 Owen had command of a division of gun brigs off the Nore; he served with Nelson at Boulogne as captain of the *Nemesis*, was familiar with the coast, conducted reconnaissance close to Flushing and was privy to Nelson's plans: 'I cannot but admire Captain Owen's zeal in his anxious desire to get at the Enemy' (Nelson to Nepean, 25 Aug. 1801, Nicolas, IV, 480). His distinguished and active career ended in 1845. His brother William Fitzwilliam Owen, as lieutenant of the *Nancy* fire brig, was to have sailed her into Boulogne to set fire to ships in the harbour in the planned third attack, which did not take place (Nelson to Owen, 1 Oct. 1801, Nicolas, IV, 501).

Paget, Sir Arthur (1771–1840) A diplomat of 'easy charm', also prone to extravagance (*DNB*). Minister who succeeded Sir William Hamilton at Naples in 1800: 'I have either (after thirty six years service at this Court) been either kicked up or down out of my post; and Mr Paget, Lord Uxbridge's son, is named Envoy Extraordinary and Plenipotentiary . . . and is on his way here in a Frigate . . . I suppose it is a cabinet job, wishing to provide for Paget' (Hamilton to Nelson, 7 Feb. 1800, Nicolas, IV, 185). Paget moved to Vienna in 1801, where he stayed through the war of the Third Coalition and the disaster of Austerlitz, being recalled in 1806. He left the diplomatic service after a scandal when he eloped with a married woman.

Parker, Edward Thornborough, Captain (1780–1801) Served on the *Princess Royal* under Orde: 'Captain Thornborough's nephew, Mr Parker, a very fine young man' (St Vincent to Nepean, 23 Aug. 1798, NMM, NEP/4); a favourite of Nelson, who treated him as a son. Served on the *Medusa*, severely wounded at Boulogne. Nelson wrote: 'Dear little Parker, his thigh very much shattered; I have fears for his life' (Nelson to St Vincent, 16 Aug. 1801, Nicolas, IV, 464); and to Doctor Baird: 'he is my child, for I found him in distress. I am prepared for the worst although I still hope' (20 Sept. 1801, Nicolas, IV, 491). After his death: 'I beg that his hair may be cut off and given to me; it shall remain and be buried with me. What must the poor father feel when he is gone!' (26 Sept. 1801, Nicolas, IV, 497).

Parker, Sir Hyde, Admiral, Bt (1739–1807) Second son of Admiral Sir Hyde Parker, who commanded the British fleet at the Battle of the Dogger Bank in 1781. Parker served in the Mediterranean in 1793, when Fremantle wrote of him: 'I still keep in with my old friend Sir Hyde who is really a staunch friend, tho' sometimes very vinegar, but I cannot say he has ever been so to me' (Fremantle to his brother, 12 Dec. 1793, Parry, 27). (Parker's father had had the nickname 'Vinegar' when in the navy.) 'My good friend Sir Hyde is cruising off Toulon . . . nothing can equal the acrimony and ill humour of Lord Hood towards him' (Fremantle to his brother, 13 Apr. 1794, Parry, 31). When Parker was appointed to the command of the squadron for Copenhagen, he delayed sailing to humour his new, young wife. After the battle Nelson explained his differences with Sir Hyde's tactics: 'what Sir Hyde thought best

I, 338). But Pole did well, including early appointment as commander-in-chief, Newfoundland, in 1800. Succeeded Nelson as Commander-in-chief, Baltic, in June 1801. Pole came ashore during the Peace of Amiens and went into politics; he was MP for Newark in 1802 and for Plymouth in 1806.

Pollard, Thomas (*fl.* 1795–7) Merchant based in Leghorn who acted as an agent for Nelson, including paying money to his mistress Adelaide. Fremantle noted in his diary: 'Dine with Pollard, stupid enough' (26 July 1795, Fremantle (1952), 255). When the French took Leghorn, Pollard and his wife were among those taken off to safety to San Fiorenzo, Corsica. He moved to Naples and wrote to Nelson of the problems of doing business in Naples (3 Jan. 1796, BL, Add. MSS 34904). 'If I had any interest in naming Agents, I should certainly name Pollard as one' (Nelson to Mrs Pollard, 25 Jan. 1797, Nicolas, II, 327).

Pringle, Thomas, Vice-Admiral (d. 1803) Scottish captain of the *Daedalus*, under whose orders Nelson sailed in the *Albemarle* in April 1782 with a convoy to Newfoundland. Nelson, who was in London, had an invitation to visit Pringle in Edinburgh but was unable to take it up: 'he is my particular friend, and a man of great honour' (Nelson to Hercules Ross, 9 Aug. 1783, Nicolas, I, 80).

Quilliam, John, Captain (1771–1839) Served in the *Amazon* in 1801 under Riou, who was killed at Copenhagen after engaging the Trekroner batteries. When Quilliam found himself left in command, after all senior officers had been killed, it is alleged that Nelson asked: 'How are you getting on?', to which Quilliam, a Manxman, is said to have answered: 'Middlin'.' (*Trafalgar Chronicle*, 12, 2002, 144). Lieutenant on the *Victory* in 1803 and at Trafalgar, where he had the good fortune (because Nelson wanted the senior lieutenant, John Pasco, as signal lieutenant) to act as first lieutenant during the battle, and thus secured promotion to post-captain; this 'produced much mortification to those of Nelson's followers who were senior to himself' (Nicolas, VII, 140, quoting Marshall, *Naval Biography*, II, 963).

Radstock, *see* **Waldegrave, William**

Robinson, Mark, Rear-Admiral (d. 1799) Captain of the *Worcester* in which Nelson served as acting lieutenant, October 1776 to April 1777.

Rose, Sir George (1744–1818) Briefly in the navy as a midshipman, 1758–62. Served as a junior secretary to the Treasury, 1783–1801; confidant of George III and Pitt. Nelson applied through Rose to Pitt for advancement for his brother-in-law, Thomas Bolton, and corresponded with him about his pension (29 Aug. 1805, Nicolas, VII, 18). On the death of Pitt, Rose wrote in his diary: 'This afflicting stroke follows close on the loss of Lord Nelson, for whom I had also a cordial love and affection' (26 Jan. 1806, Harcourt, 233). Later tried to help the Nelson family, and Emma, though he lost patience with her.

Ryves, George Frederick, Rear-Admiral (1758–1826) Served with Nelson in the Mediterranean in 1803. Surveyed the Maddalena Islands in the *Agincourt*, earning Nelson's thanks and praise; he transferred to the *Gibraltar*, on the Naples Station, being awarded a diamond ring by the king of Naples, and a gold snuffbox for conveying the prince of Sardinia to Cagliari. When his wife died, Nelson wrote: 'for the sake of your dear children, you must bear up against the heavy misfortune. To attempt consolation at this time is, I know, out of the question' (10 Feb. 1804, Nicolas, V, 411). Ryves returned to England in the *Gibralta*r in August 1804, remarried, and saw active service again only briefly in 1810.

St Vincent, *see* **Jervis, Sir John**

Sandys, Charles, Rear-Admiral (d. 1814) Captain of the *Latona* in the West Indies. Nelson liked him but had no respect for him, writing to Locker: 'The little man Sandys, is a good-natured laughing creature, but no more of an Officer as a Captain than he was as a Lieutenant' (24 Sept. 1784, Nicolas, I, 110) and 'he is not fit to command a Man of War. His ship is the merest privateer' (5 Mar. 1786, Nicolas, I, 156). Nelson feared his heavy drinking would harm him.

Saumarez, Sir James, Admiral, later **Baron de Saumarez** (1757–1836) An officer from Guernsey, sensitive, though urbane and more than usually courteous, with strong Christian beliefs. With Nelson at the Nile in the *Orion*. In spite of Nelson working very hard to win Saumarez over, the latter never quite succumbed to Nelson's charm; and he was professionally and personally hurt that Nelson did not acknowledge him as second in command at the Nile (Ross, I, 24, 227, 230, 273). According to his biographer, when Saumarez was receiving the congratulations of brother officers on being the second in command, 'Captain Ball came on deck, and interrupted the conversation by observing, "Nelson says there is to be no second-in-command; we are all to be alike in his despatches."' Saumarez received no honour for the battle, but generously took the lead in arranging for Egyptian swords and a portrait to be 'hung up in the room belonging to the Egyptian Club now established, in commemoration of that glorious day' (Ross, I, 227–8, 231). Saumarez distinguished himself against a French and Spanish squadron off Algeciras, but is chiefly known for his skilful and lengthy diplomacy as commander-in-chief, Baltic, 1808–12; he was and is much revered in Sweden, for his fleet enabled that country to resist Napoleon's pressure and guaranteed its neutrality.

Schomberg, Isaac, Captain (1753–1813) Arrested by Nelson in 1786 when lieutenant of the *Pegasus* after requesting a court martial over a dispute with Prince William Henry, and was sent home. A similar dispute also arose in 1790 when Schomberg served in the East Indies. But he distinguished himself at the Battle of the First of June, came ashore in 1795, wrote a history of the navy and became a Navy Board commissioner, 1808–13.

Scott, Alexander John, Reverend (1768–1840) Chaplain with a talent for languages; went to the Mediterranean in 1793 as chaplain to the *Berwick* when he first met Nelson (Scott, 78). 'Our chaplain was a learned gentleman, and always going onshore to make researches after antiquities' (Gardner, 113); appointed to a living in Jamaica. Nelson wrote in a testimonial: 'I have such a high opinion of Mr Scott's ability and honour that if he is well enough, I should feel happy, on being appointed to a foreign command, to have him as my foreign secretary, and to be confidentially employed with business to foreign ministers' (Scott, 97); and, writing from the Mediterranean to Emma in 1803, 'He is a very sober, unassuming man, very learned, very Religious and very Sickly and he reads which is more I dare say than any of our proud churchmen, the lessons for the day in German, Latin, Greek and English every day . . . poor fellow, once or twice every moon his head is gone. At this moment he is abed not scarcely knowing anyone, owing to the dreadful stroke of lightning', an accident that had happened some years before (7 Dec. 1803, NMM, MAM/28; Scott, 85–6). Joined Nelson in 1803 in the *Victory* at short notice: 'It had for several years been my intention whenever I was appointed to the Mediterranean Command to request Mr Scott to go with me. It was only on the Sunday that . . . I was to go, on the Tuesday Mr S[cot]t was informed of it and Friday we sailed from Portsmouth' (Nelson to the bishop of London, 6 Apr. 1804, BL Add. MSS 34955). Nelson also described him in the same letter as 'one of the most learned men of the age and a great observer of men and manners. He is my confidential Private Foreign Secretary.' Nelson wrote asking Nepean for a salary for Scott's extra duties, since he had to deal with 'correspondence from several quarters that requires knowledge of the different languages' (27 July 1803, Monmouth letter book, 18); Nepean allowed Scott £100 per annum (to Nelson, 22 Dec. 1803, (UK)NA: PRO, ADM/2/923). Ball met him in Malta: 'I have had a great deal of conversation with Dr Scott who reasons better on Political subjects than any person I have met here – he appears an excellent man and I regret his short stay' (Ball to Nelson, 20 Feb. 1805, NMM, CRK/1). After Trafalgar the Admiralty refused to acknowledge his services, and Scott settled down as vicar of Southminster in Essex, and after 1816 with a crown living in Catterick in Yorkshire.

Scott, John (d. 1805) Purser in the *Royal Sovereign*. Nelson had him transferred to the *Victory* as his secretary (6 Apr. 1803, Nicolas, V, 56). Recommended by William Marsh: 'I am happy to learn from Mr Creed that Mr Scott appears to give your Lordship satisfaction as a secretary . . . if I had not most seriously thought and believed he would, I should never have mentioned him' (Marsh to Nelson, 10 May 1803, NMM, CRK/8/183). Nelson wrote: 'he is a very excellent good man; and I am very fortunate in having such a one' (Nelson to Emma, 26 Aug. 1803, Nicolas, V, 183); he thanked her for her 'news of Mrs Scott's being brought to bed . . . he was very uneasy.' Like Tyson before him, he acted as a prize agent: 'if he was satisfied to do all the business in this Country, that the Agency being five per cent. on the nett proceeds, two per cent should go to him for his trouble, and three per cent to you for making the distribution' (Nelson to Davison, 12 Dec. 1803, Nicolas, V, 305). Killed by a shot early in the Battle of Trafalgar while conversing with Hardy (Nicolas, VII, 155).

Shirley, Sir Thomas, General, Bt (1727–1800) Army officer and colonial governor, third son of William Shirley, governor of Massachusetts, 1741–57. Thomas Shirley was made governor of the Leeward Islands in 1781 and given a baronetcy in 1786, at the same time that Nelson tangled with him. He was promoted to lieutenant-general in 1793 and general in 1798.

Sidmouth, *see* **Addington, Henry**

Smith, Sir [William] Sidney, Admiral (1764–1840) Impulsive, egotistical but talented, who irritated all his fellow officers. His career peaked at the successful defence of Acre against Napoleon in 1799. Judged by Spencer as 'certainly an odd eccentric man but he is very clever' (to Windham, 12 Aug. 1794, BL, Add. MSS 37845). Referring to his acceptance of foreign honours, Nelson wrote 'the Swedish Knight . . . forgets the respect due to his senior officer' (Nelson to St Vincent, 31 Dec. 1798, Warren R. Dawson, *Nelson Collection*, 117) and 'I despise such frippery and nonsense as he is composed of' (Nelson to St Vincent, 6 Mar. 1799, Nicolas, III, 281). St Vincent complained of 'the romantic colouring of Sir Sidney Smith who has been in a continual maze of errors and imposture' (to Nepean, 16 Jan. 1799, Dawson, 117); the Admiralty Board was also not impressed: 'Thompson will not give you a very favourable account of the Knight, who I suppose you will not trust out of sight' (Young to Pole, 4 July 1798, NMM, WYN/104). Eventually Nelson recognized his qualities.

Snipe, Dr John, MD (d. 1805) A physician to the Naval Hospital in Plymouth; appointed physician to the fleet in the Mediterranean in 1803. He investigated the possibility of a naval hospital on Malta for Nelson; this was established in December 1803; recommended treatment for seamen sent ashore for water in marshy areas of Sardinia (wine mixed with Peruvian bark), asking to see information on its effects (Nicolas, V, 318). When he visited Naples, Nelson recommended him to Elliot: 'He is not only a very able Professional gentleman, but a man of most excellent private character' (30 Mar. 1804, Nicolas, V, 479). He became ill: 'we have been very near losing Dr Snipe . . . by a consumptive complaint . . . spitting blood etc' (Nelson to Dr Baird, 22 Sept. 1804, Nicolas, VI, 202). Snipe returned home in February 1805 and died in London in August.

Spedillo, Gaetano (*fl.* 1799–1805) Servant of the Hamiltons, who returned to England with them. Mr Falconet in Naples promised to 'supply his family with the monthly allowance on the pension given him by Mr Greville' (Falconet to Nelson, 18 June 1803, NMM, CRK/5/45); described as 'old Gaetano, his Italian steward' (Lambton Este, 4 Nov. 1804, Nicolas, VI, 258). Gaetano sailed in the *Victory* and revisited Naples 'in very high spirits', according to John Scott (to Emma, 8 July 1803, Morrison, II, 214), despite Nelson's concern that he might stay 'once he gets with his wife and family' (to Emma, 10 June 1803, Morrison, II, 213). But 'Gaetano returned in the Frigate. I believe he saw enough of Naples. He carried his family money' (Nelson to Emma, 8 July 1803, Nicolas, V, 119).

Spencer, George John, second Earl Spencer (1758–1834) Politician, younger brother of Georgiana, duchess of Devonshire, the radical Whig political hostess, who so outraged society by appearing on the hustings at the 1784 election. Spencer was, however, a book collector. A member of the Portland Whigs, he was appointed to be first lord of the Admiralty in December 1794, 'without any administrative experience or knowledge of the Navy' (*DNB*). Lord Howe's first impressions were good: 'Lord Spencer is a young man of singular probity and worth. Has much application, and I believe intelligent capacity. And those that have business or intercourse with him will find him to be of a most pleasing character' (to Curtis, 20 Dec. 1794, Huntington, HO 209). Spencer was instrumental in selecting Nelson for independent command in the Mediterranean in 1798. St Vincent, as usual, was more critical: 'There is an irritability & jealousy ab[ou]t Lord Spencer that lessens his character very much, upon the whole I am inclined to think him a just man, he certainly is a very laborious one' (to Nepean, 28 Nov. 1800, BL, Add. MSS 36708). He served as first lord until February 1801. He placed his second son on board the *Tigre* with Captain Hallowell. Spencer wrote to Nelson, 'I cannot resist the opportunity which his sailing to join you offers me of recalling myself to your Remembrance & of recommending my boy to your protection . . . a great advantage to him to have belonged to a fleet commanded by you & to be under the more immediate superintendence of one of the Companions of your glory at Aboukir' (25 Aug. 1804, NMM, CRK/11/48). When he retired from public life, Spencer amassed the greatest private library in Europe.

Stephens, Sir Philip, Bt (1723–1809) Shadowy but powerful figure in the navy, secretary of the Admiralty from 1763 to 3 March 1795, writing skilful letters of reprimand to the young Nelson. He was made a baronet in 1795. He then served on the Board of Admiralty until October 1806. In all, he served the navy for sixty-seven years.

Stewart, William, Lieutenant-General (d. 1827) Served as a lieutenant-colonel with Nelson in the Baltic in the *St George* and wrote a narrative of the battle of Copenhagen (Nicolas, IV, 299). '. . . if Nelson is Commander in chief, I care not how long I serve as marine – if he don't – I may again look for land service' (Stewart to Colonel Sir William Clinton, 6 Apr. 1801, NMM, AGC/27). Nelson planned to include Stewart in the share of prize money as a junior flag officer (memorandum, July 1802, Nicolas, V, 22).

Stuart, Sir Charles, General (1753–1801) Irascible but talented major-general in Corsica, 1794–5. Cooperated with Nelson at the Siege of Calvi: 'he is an extraordinary good judge of ground' (Nelson to Lord Hood, 11 July 1794, Nicolas, I, 431); but Stuart quarrelled with both Hood and Gilbert Elliot. With Duckworth in 1798 he secured Minorca, where he became governor. Nelson wrote of 'the very highest [opinion] from experience, of General Stuart, who, by his abilities would make a bad Army a good one' (Nelson to Duckworth, 7 Jan. 1799, Nicolas, III, 226). He captured Valetta in September 1800, and later reinforced Sicily. St Vincent complained to Spencer that, although Stuart had many good points, 'He is a niggard in his praise to the Navy and there are very few seamen who could act with him' (6 Dec. 1798, Corbett, *Spencer Papers*, II, 487); yet he also praised him: 'Good Lord deliver us from all conjunct expeditions unless they are commanded by Sir Charles Grey or Sir Charles Stuart' (to Spencer, 7 Sept. 1800, Richmond, *Spencer Papers*, III, 368). Stuart resigned over the government's policy on Malta, returned to England and died suddenly.

Suckling, Maurice, Captain (d. 1778) Nelson's elder maternal uncle and comptroller of the navy, 1775–8; captained the *Raisonable*, Nelson's first ship. Nelson hoped 'I shall prove myself, by my actions, worthy of supplying that place in the Service of my Country, which my dear Uncle left for me' (Nelson to William Suckling, 5 July 1786, Nicolas, I, 187).

Suckling, William (c. 1729–98) Nelson's uncle, who played a critical role in securing Nelson's command of the *Albemarle* in 1781; 'Clerk of Foreign Entries' and later deputy collector of customs. 'He is a person who has been in that Office since a boy, and is consulted in all doubtful cases relative to that board' (Nelson to Collingwood, 28 Sept. 1785, Nicolas, I, 143). Married Miss Rumsey of Hampstead on 26 October 1786: 'It will add to his felicity for had he not done that, he must have kept a woman, which you will allow would have been very disagreeable' (Nelson to William Nelson, 29 Dec. 1786, Nicolas, I, 204). Suckling died on 15 December 1798, leaving Nelson a legacy of £100 and appointing him one of his executors. Nelson only learnt of this much later, writing to his widow: 'My dear uncle, God only knows with what disinterested affection I loved him' (22 Aug. 1799, Nicolas, III, 458).

Sutton, Samuel, Admiral (1765–1832) Commanded the *Alcmene* at Copenhagen and succeeded Riou in the *Amazon*; at Boulogne, Nelson asked Sutton to arrange Parker's funeral. Addington wrote to Nelson: 'Captain Sutton has relieved you, in a great degree, from the pressure of some of the most laborious parts of your duty' (8 Oct. 1801, Nicolas, IV, 507), allowing Nelson to go on shore. In 1803 fitted out the *Victory* and sailed in her with Nelson; later brought her into the Mediterranean, capturing the *Ambuscade* en route; transferred to the *Amphion* when the *Victory* became Nelson's flagship. Nelson had assured him that 'The *Amphion* is one of the nicest frigates I have seen – not so large as *Amazon*, but has every good quality' (Nelson to Sutton, 18 June 1803, Nicolas, V, 91). Sutton wrote: 'I hope it will turn out a good thing for that great & good man Lord Nelson, as well as for myself' (Sutton to Emma, 20 Oct. 1804, Morrison, II, 242). By arrangement, Sutton and Hardy agreed to share any prize money; 'For your and Hardy's sake, I wish you had been more fortunate' (Nelson to Sutton, 14 Dec. 1804, Nicolas, VI, 287); Hardy wrote later, 'I fear our Galeons will not turn out so well as we expected, as it is said you are to have only one-fifth of the money, and all the hulls' (25 Sept. 1805, Nicolas, VII, 49). Sutton visited Merton: 'I wish I could have changed with you when you went to Merton, but I hope to see it very soon' (Nelson to Sutton, 14 Mar. 1805, Nicolas, VI, 362); after the chase to the West Indies, Nelson wrote to James Matra, consul at Tangier: 'I have sent the *Amphion*, Captain Sutton, to Tangier Bay in order to receive such intelligence of the Enemy's fleet as you may be able to give him' (30 June 1805, Nicolas, VI, 466). Invalided before Trafalgar and succeeded in the *Amphion* by William Hoste.

Sykes, John (*fl.* 1792–7) Served with Nelson as able seaman in the *Agamemnon*; as gunner's mate in the *Captain*; and as coxswain in *Theseus*. Saved Nelson's life in the gunboat action off Cadiz in 1791. Miller wrote to Nelson from Lisbon, 'Nothing has turned up for Sykes or Remonier, the former does duty as Mate and if he had serv'd time sufficient I would have endeavour'd to make him a lieutenant, for his manners and conduct are so entirely above his station that nature certainly intends him for a gentleman' (17 Oct. 1797, BL, Add. MSS 34904). Nelson wrote to his parents: 'your son . . . is quite recovered of his wounds & is now on board Lord St Vincent's ship the *Ville de Paris* by whom he will be made a gunner – & if he is not before he comes to England I will take care & provide for him' (Nelson to Thomas Huddlestone, fishmonger, Waterside, Lincoln, 23 Sept. 1797, NMM, AGC 18/5). According to Oman (692), Sykes died aged eighty, the proprietor of a fishmonger's shop in Church Passage, Greenwich.

Thompson, Sir Charles, Vice-Admiral, Bt (*c.* 1740–1799) Second in command at Cape St Vincent, for which he was made a baronet. 'Our Captain was as gruff as the devil, and had a voice like a mastiff whose growling would be heard superior to the storm' (Gardner, 48). Thompson opposed the hanging of four mutineers on a Sunday in July 1797, for which St Vincent demanded he be sent home. At Thompson's death St Vincent commented acidly: 'a report says had accumulated about £60,000 a proof that Foote's Maxim was just, viz. By living poor any man can die rich' (to Nelson, 13 Apr. 1799, BL, Add. MSS 31166); and to Nepean he wrote that Thompson 'was a gallant man but the most timid officer, as it related to Rocks, Sands, Shores . . . he had however the manners of a rough Seaman' (16 Apr. 1799, NMM, NEP/5, 31). Thompson cultivated the image of the rough seaman by often appearing in sailor's dress and a straw hat.

Thompson, Sir Thomas Boulden, Vice-Admiral (1766–1828) Served at Tenerife, then distinguished himself at the Nile in the *Leander*: 'with a degree of skill and intrepidity highly honourable to his professional character, advanced towards the Enemy's line on the outside and most judiciously dropped his anchor athwart hause of *Le Franklin*, raking her with great success' (Tracy, *Naval Chronicle*, I, 277). Later commended for his 'gallant and almost unprecedented defence' against the *Généreux* in 1799 (Nicolas, III, 90), when he was severely wounded, taken prisoner and almost died because the French robbed his surgeon of his medical instruments (Tracy, *Naval Chronicle*, I, 280, quoted in Nicolas, III, 191). Captain of the *Bellona*, which went aground during the approach to the Battle of Copenhagen, where he lost a leg. He was created a baronet in 1806, the same year in which he was appointed comptroller of the Navy, an office that he held until 1816.

Totty, Thomas, Rear-Admiral (d. 1802) Briefly with Nelson in the Baltic: possessed 'a sound judgment with much industry, and precision,' (St Vincent to Spencer, 9 Dec. 1800, BL, Add. MSS 75847). Nelson was pleased with him: 'I feel indebted to you as an Admiral, for your truly Officer-like manner of conducting the King's service, and also, for the truly kind and handsome manner you have ever expressed yourself towards myself' (Nelson to Totty, 15 [?18] June 1801, Nicolas, IV, 419).

Trail, Donald (*fl.* 1782–94) Master of the *Albemarle*. Nelson wrote to Locker: 'He is the best Master I ever saw since I went to sea' (12 July 1783, Nicolas, I, 77). Trail was later master of the *Neptune* transport in the second fleet which went to Botany Bay; 150 men and eleven women died, forty-six between England and the Cape. Trail was brought to trial for a private charge of wilful murder of one of his crew on 9 June 1792, but acquitted. He has been called 'avaricious and unscrupulous' and 'inexcusably lax and incompetent' (Charles Bateson, *The Convict Ships* (1959), 128).

Trevor, John, later **Viscount Hampden** (1748–1824) Diplomat who served as minister at Turin, 1783–97; sailed from Vado Bay to Genoa with Nelson and Francis Drake, after consulting with General de Vins on an Austrian attack (Nelson to Hotham, 28 July 1795, Nicolas, II, 62); 'every day since I first had the honour of seeing you has been marked by some fresh proof of your zeal and ability' (25 Sept. 1795, Nicolas, VII, xxii). Trevor retired in 1797, succeeding his brother as Viscount Hampden in 1824.

Trigge Sir Thomas, Lieutenant-General (d. 1814) Governor of Gibraltar, 1803–4, succeeded in January 1805 by General Fox; became lieutenant-general of the ordnance. Nelson kept him informed on the dispositions of his frigates.

Troubridge, Sir Thomas, Rear-Admiral (1758–1807) An officer from a humble background who first knew Nelson when both were midshipmen in the *Seahorse* in 1773. A man of great courage, short temper and extreme views; his relationship with Nelson always had an edge to it. Hardy once remarked of Troubridge, 'tho' a particular friend of mine, I do not think we should make it out so well together in the same ship as he is extremely hasty on duty' (Hardy to Manfield, Jan. 1802, Broadley and Bartelot, 84). Troubridge went to the Mediterranean in the *Culloden* at the same time as Sir John Jervis, under whom Troubridge's prospects flourished. He was present at Cape St Vincent, Tenerife and the Nile; at the last he missed the battle through going aground, which mortified him. Cornelia Knight said that he 'wrote to condole with Captain Darby of the *Bellerephon* for his wounds . . . but added that had his suffering been fifty times as much, he had rather been in his place than have borne the anguish he felt from running aground, and being kept out of the Action – that he had found great difficulty in keeping from shooting himself, and that he even then frequently shed tears' ([n.d.], Nicolas, III, 475–6). St Vincent considered Troubridge superior to Nelson in the late 1790s, writing to Spencer, 'the ablest adviser and best executive officer . . . with honour and courage bright as his sword' (22 May 1797, Corbett, *Spencer Papers*, II, 403); and he told Nepean that 'Troubridge wou'd make by far the best comptroller of the Navy . . . he possessing a greater extent of knowledge, industry, of sterling integrity than any man I ever met with' (20 Apr. 1797, Houghton, pf MS Eng. 196.5 (n6)). In the Mediterranean, Nelson depended upon him, writing to St Vincent, 'I trust you will not take him from me. I well know he is my superior and I want so often his advice and assistance' (27 Sept. 1798, NMM, PAR/251). After Naples, Troubridge returned to the Channel fleet, and in 1801 became a member of St Vincent's Board of Admiralty. At this point Nelson turned against him, writing sharp letters, causing Troubridge to reply: 'Your letter of yesterday quite upset me . . . I never meant to give offence. I really feel so much hurt . . . where you say you never had but one real friend' (17 Aug. [1801], NMM, CRK/13/65). Nevertheless Nelson took Troubridge's son to sea: 'I feel most sensibly your kind acquiescence in his being received on the *Victory*' (Troubridge to Nelson, 27 June 1803, NMM, CRK/13/86). Troubridge's lack of judgement was demonstrated by his selling stock when a member of the Board of Admiralty in March 1803 'just before the press sent prices down: he was accused of corruption in the House, but the matter was dropped' (Thorne, V, 416). In 1805 Troubridge was appointed commander-in-chief, East Indies, and was lost at sea on his return journey.

Tyson, John (d. 1816) Met Nelson as purser in the *Badger*, 1778–9, and became his secretary after the Battle of the Nile in 1798, having transferred from Alexander Ball. Nelson depended upon him for drafting letters: 'Tyson wrote the above. I will send him to you for 2 days when I can spare him, a difficult thing' (Nelson to Ball, 31 Jan. 1799, Nicolas, III, 248). In Naples he was fêted alongside Nelson: 'to Mr Tyson, my Secretary, [the king] has also presented a diamond ring' (Nelson to Nepean, 24 Sept. 1799, Nicolas, IV, 28). He managed victualling and prize money and was appointed prize agent for the *Généreux*. Ball wrote to Nelson from Malta: 'Poor Tyson at my particular request went to the Morea three months since to purchase corn for this garrison . . . he has lost the place of storekeeper at Minorca . . . [I hope for] . . . your friendly interest for him to obtain or secure some place at home, he will feel happy in his retirement after such fagging and vicissitudes as he has experienced' (29 Jan. 1801, NMM, CRK/1). After he returned to England, Ball helped to get him recompense: 'I am glad to hear the Tyson's are well: have the goodness to tell honest John that I have written to the Treasury' (to Emma, 8 Nov. 1802, Morrison, II, 201). Appointed clerk of the survey of Woolwich Dockyard on 20 October 1802; he wrote to Nelson a year later when commanding the dockyard volunteers: 'Little did I think after serving Thirty Years at Sea to have turned Soldier in my old Age. We have four companies in this yard and I have the <u>Honor</u> to be Captain of them' (13 Sept. 1803, NMM, CRK/13/45). Mrs Tyson visited Merton, thanking Emma for the happy time spent there (28 Dec. 1802, Morrison, II, 203), and the visit was reciprocated (Tyson to Nelson,

26 Nov. 1803, NMM, CRK/13/46), though clearly Mrs Tyson's cooking was lacking, for Catherine Bolton wrote to Emma: 'I hope you liked your visit better this time . . . and that you had more to eat' (12 May 1805, Morrison, II, 257). In 1803 Tyson attended the installation of the order of the Bath to Nelson, acting as an esquire, and after Nelson's death he took care of his body, ensuring that Nelson was buried in the coffin that Hallowell had made from the mast of *L'Orient*. He accompanied the coffin to Greenwich (Nicolas, VII, 259; Coleman, 350). Tyson retired from Woolwich Yard on 5 December 1808.

Udney, John (*fl.* 1793–8) Consul at Leghorn and member of the English Factory; evacuated to Corsica when the French took the city in June 1796; anxious to return to secure his house and possessions within the twenty days promised by Nelson. He wrote to England of his concern that the object of the French armament was Egypt (April 1798, BL, Add. MSS. 34906). 'I flatter myself that you will still continue me as one of the Agent Victuallers for your fleet united with Messrs Littledale & Broderick and to enjoy a share with them and others in the profits of the Agency' (Udney to Nelson, 19 Aug. 1798 BL, Add. MSS 34907, 181).

Ushakov, Fedor Fedorovich (*fl.* 1799–1800) Russian admiral at Naples who withdrew to Corfu. Nelson disliked him, writing to Ball: 'I hate the Russians, and if she [the ship] came from their Admiral at Corfu, he is a blackguard' (21 Jan. 1799, Nicolas, III, 236). Nevertheless, he wrote to Ushakov congratulating him on the capture of Corfu (23 Mar. 1799, Nicolas, III, 304).

Vansittart, Nicholas, Baron Bexley (1766–1851) Sent to Denmark by Addington as minister plenipotentiary on a special mission in 1800, leaving in March 1801. Chosen to succeed George Rose as a joint secretary to the Treasury, 1801–4. Davison thought highly of him, writing to Nelson, 'Your friend Vansittart has given me employment enough and has discovered that I can do more for government than those he has been in the habit of employing . . . I find him very prompt and civil' (24 Nov. 1803, NMM, CRK/3/145). Vansittart subsequently had a long political career.

Villettes, William, Lieutenant-General (1754–1808) A 'popular and capable' army officer (*DNB*); organized the Siege of Bastia in Corsica in 1794. Nelson called him 'a most excellent officer' (to Dixon Hoste, 3 May 1794, Nicolas, I, 393). His 'unremitting zeal, exertion, and judicious conduct' were praised by Hood as 'never was either more conspicuous' (Lord Hood's dispatch, 24 May 1794, Nicolas, I, 399). Commander of troops on Corfu in 1800 and in Malta in 1801. Nelson asked Villettes to keep 2,000 troops in readiness for Sicily to deter the French from invading, but the general felt he could only spare fewer. He served in Malta until 1807.

Waldegrave, William, Admiral, later **Baron Radstock** (1753–1825) Second son of the third Earl Waldegrave, third in command at Cape St Vincent (*Barfleur*) and a supporter of Nelson's achievement in the battle. Betsey Wynne thought he was 'a gentleman-like pleasant man but I think rather too serious' (Fremantle,

Wynne (1952), 226). 'The admiral was a polished, good natured gentleman' (Parsons, 319). St Vincent could not stand him, writing to Nepean, 'the most assuming and wearing companion I ever met with, and my deliverance from him, is the greatest blessing I ever met with' (22 Mar. 1797, BL, Add. MSS 36708) and asking Spencer to remove him: 'he writes me volumes from the *Barfleur* to the *Victory* upon trifles light as air' (29 July 1796, Corbett, *Spencer Papers*, II, 43). In 1797 Waldegrave was appointed commander-in-chief, New-foundland, which did not stop St Vincent complaining to Nepean that Waldeg-rave's squadron was cruising off the Azores (i.e., looking for prizes) when he should have been protecting the Newfoundland fishery (5 Oct. 1797, NMM, NEP/4). Waldegrave had no further service after the Newfoundland command, and was made Lord Radstock in December 1800. His son Granville served as a lieutenant in the *Victory*, 1804–5. He was having difficulty getting his pro-motion, but Nelson considered him an excellent young man (15 Mar. 1805, Waldegrave Papers, NMM, Box 5). Nelson assured him: 'the sons of Brother Officers have an undoubted claim to our protection and when to that is added the son of a very old friend, nothing can . . . weigh stronger with me' (Nelson to Radstock, 22 Aug. 1803, Nicolas, V, 171). His son was finally promoted to the command of the frigate *Hydra* in 1806.

Wallis, James, Captain (*c.* 1769–1808) First lieutenant in the *Boreas*, 1783–7. Nelson appointed him to temporary command of the *Rattler*, but Wallis was not confirmed as commander; captain of the *Gorgon* store ship during the Corsica operations, 1794; an eccentric who to one of his officers 'at times appeared half mad' (Gardner, 123–40).

Warren, Sir John Borlase, Admiral (1753–1822) Sea officer, MP and diplomat, 'a man of fashion and elegant manners' (*DNB*). St Vincent wrote: 'he is a good fellow in the presence of an enemy but runs a little wild in other matters when detached; he cannot bear being confined to a fleet, no more than our friend Nelson, and will be miserable when he is obliged to serve en masse' (St Vincent to Man, 13 Oct. 1800, Richmond, *Spencer Papers*, IV, 14). This view was endorsed by others: 'I am not surprised at your account of Warren, who though very zealous and active, is not always pleased when subjected to control' (Young to Pole, 13 June 1806, NMM, WYN/104). Another critic said he was 'good for nothing but fine weather and easy sailing' (*DNB*).

Westcott, George Blagdon, Captain (*c.* 1753–98) From a poor family in Honiton, Devon; rose through the ranks and promoted captain in 1790. At the Nile he was captain of the *Majestic*, but his anchoring left his ship exposed and he was killed. Collingwood called him 'a good Officer and a worthy man' (Nicolas, III, 87). According to Oman (417), his mother was a baker's widow, his brother a tailor. Nelson went out of his way to visit Westcott's widow in January 1801 on his way to Plymouth, presenting her with his own Nile medal (*DNB*).

Whitby, John, Captain (d. 1806) As captain of the *Minerva* in the East Indies in the 1790s introduced penalties for swearing, which 'displeased the men very much who had not had time to divest themselves of this new crime they had long been accustomed to', a petty measure that was countermanded by Admiral Cornwallis (Richardson, 105, quoted in Rodger, *Command of the Ocean*, 444). Whitby was captain of the *Belleisle* in 1803 in the Mediterranean, when Nelson thought highly of him, writing to Cornwallis, 'I have with me an élève of yours whom I esteem most highly, not only as an active officer, but as a gentleman; his ship is always perfectly ready for any service, and he executes in the best style, and I am sure that Capt Whitby will give me support in the true Cornwallis style should the French come out' ([?] July 1803, Cornwallis-West, 390). Cornwallis requested Whitby as his captain of the fleet off Brest; when he returned to England, he sent Cornwallis a detailed critique of Nelson's method of blockading Toulon: 'Tho' Ld Nelson is indefatigable thro' the Mediterranean in keeping the Sea, there are so many Reasons that make it possible for the French to escape' (Whitby to Cornwallis, 11 June 1804, Cornwallis-West, 419).

Whitworth, Charles, Earl Whitworth (1752–1825) Ambassador in St Petersburg from 1786 who, when expelled by Tsar Paul, moved to Copenhagen in July 1800. Nelson wrote to him to solicit honours from Russia of the order of the Knights of Jerusalem, for Ball and Emma, who replied that his recommendations had been approved (Whitworth to Nelson, 4 Jan. 1800, Nicolas, IV, 192). When posted to Paris as ambassador during the Peace of Amiens, Whitworth had the unrewarding task of negotiating with Napoleon over Malta.

Wilkie, Patrick (*fl.* 1796–1805) Consul at Cartagena, 1796; became the agent victualler at Malta, 1803–5; his inability to supply the fleet adequately in 1803 led Nelson to complain to St Vincent: 'Troubridge told me, when I asked him for a floating Agent-Victualler, who would pay all things in all places, "Mr Wilkie is a very clever man; he will arrange everything; he will get you things from everywhere." Now the direct contrary is the fact. Mr Wilkie will have nothing to do with supplying the Fleet anywhere but at Malta' (12 July 1803, Nicolas, V, 133). By 28 December, Troubridge had changed his mind, writing to Nelson: 'Wilkie I know is but a poor creature, & D—d job of Marsh's sending him out, if he does not exert himself we will remove him' (NMM, CRK/13/95). This led directly to the appointment of Richard Ford as agent victualler afloat.

William Henry, Prince, from 1788 **duke of Clarence,** then **William IV** (1765–1837) Went to sea in 1779 and by 1782 was a midshipman in Hood's flagship *Barfleur* in the West Indies; befriended Nelson and acted as best man at his wedding, but he was a baleful influence and led Nelson into a situation over the Schomberg court martial that could have ended Nelson's career. The prince's other role in this story is as a useful correspondent, for almost throughout his career Nelson wrote comprehensive letters to him in the hope that the prince would further his career. He did not. Nelson was always over-impressed, writing to Locker: 'he is a seaman, which you could hardly suppose. Every other qualification you may expect from him. But he will be a disciplinarian, and a strong one: he says he is determined every person shall serve his time before they shall be provided for, as he is obliged to serve his . . . With the best temper, and great good sense, he cannot fail of being pleasing to every one' (25 Feb. 1783, Nicolas, I, 72). Prince William Henry pleased very few naval officers.

Windham, William (1750–1810) Linguist, scholar and politician; MP for Norwich, 1784–1802, secretary-at-war with a seat in the cabinet, July 1794, when the Portland Whigs joined Pitt's administration; described by Fanny Burney as 'one of the most agreeable, spirited, well bred conversers I have ever spoken with' and by the duchess of Devonshire as 'a great genius [with] talents for conversation and discussion' (Thorne, V, 608). An admirer of Nelson, he wrote to Spencer: 'As a Norwich Hero, he has a claim upon me to urge his honours to the extent to which I think they are justly due' (Windham to Spencer, 4 Oct. 1798, Richmond, *Spencer Papers*, III, 7); supported Nelson's appointment to command of the Nile squadron and corresponded with him. Resigned with Pitt in February 1801 over Catholic Emancipation. Secretary of state for war and the colonies, February 1806 to March 1807. Windham described himself as 'a little of two characters and good in neither: a politician among scholars and a scholar among politicians' (*DNB*).

Wolseley, William, Admiral (1756–1842) Captain of the *Lowestoffe* in the Mediterranean in 1795, where he shared some prize money with Nelson; later in the *Impérieuse* at Bastia; in 1801 appointed to the *St George* but transferred when it became Nelson's flagship and was replaced by Hardy before sailing to the Baltic; appointed to the *San Josef*. Nelson was disappointed at the last ship's condition: 'he may be a clever young [man] for a small [vessel] but if he stays in the *San Josef* a week longer, I believe she will be ruined. This ship has not been cleansed down below since last November . . . I should hardly think her masts safe . . . in my life I never saw such an alteration' (Nelson to St Vincent, 20 Feb. 1801, Nicolas, IV, 287). Wolseley came ashore at the Peace of Amiens.

Young, Sir William, Admiral (1751–1821) Nelson first met him in France: 'Captain Young visited me today, and tomorrow we meet at dinner; I shall certainly deliver your compliments; he is come over to place his brother, who is a Lieutenant, in a French family' (Nelson to Locker, 26 Nov. 1783, Nicolas, I, 89). With Hood in the Mediterranean in 1795 as captain of *Fortitude*; at the occupation of Toulon, and took part in Hotham's two Actions. Young was appointed to Lord Spencer's Board of Admiralty, serving 1795–1801. 'He was, in more than ordinary degree, calculated for office – was diligent in application, clear in method, and generally informed. He had been very much in good society and availed himself of this great advantage. He had a strong natural talent and was a good linguist' (Stirling, *Pages and Portraits*, I, 59). St Vincent disliked him: 'I shall tell Lord Spencer bluntly, if Admiral Young continues at the Admiralty Board, I will cease to command the Channel Fleet' (to Nepean, 28 Aug. 1800, BL, Add. MSS 36708). Young wrote to his friend Charles

Morice Pole: 'You are right in not considering the Admiralty a bed of roses, I never was in one that had so many thorns' (1 Sept. 1799, NMM, WYN/104). Sir Roger Curtis recalled in old age that 'Admiral Young was also a very able man, but not so much of a technical sailor' (quoted by J. W. Croker to Sir Robert Peel, 31 Aug. 1845, BL, Add. MSS 40573); yet his efficient command of the blockade of the Scheldt from 1811 to the end of the war was commendable.

Glossary

Blackstakes: The lower reach of the River Medway by Sheerness.

Blue Peter: Flag flown to alert the fleet preparatory to sailing.

Bower anchors: The main working anchors in the bow of a ship, the best bower being on the starboard and the small bower on the port side of the ship, there being no difference in size.

Brig: A vessel square rigged on two masts.

Bring to: To check the way of a ship by bringing her head into the wind to take off speed.

Captain of the fleet, or first captain: A senior captain or rear-admiral who assists the commander-in-chief of a large fleet aboard a flagship.

Carcass: An iron incendiary shell filled with combustible material, pierced with holes through which the flame blazes. Generally fired from a mortar.

Careen: To heave the ship down by her masts to expose the bottom for cleaning; used only on smaller warships when no dry dock was available.

Cartel: A ship commissioned in wartime to exchange prisoners or to carry proposals for an exchange.

Caulking: A means of keeping a vessel watertight by forcing material made of oakum (old rope untwisted) and covered with tar into the seams between the planks of the hull or deck.

Close hauled: To sail against the wind, when the head of a ship is near enough to the direction of the wind to fill the sails when they are hauled close.

Close reefed: When, in a high wind, all the topsails are reefed to the maximum.

Condemned: A captured ship declared by sentence of an admiralty court to be a lawful prize; also used in surveys of unserviceable stores and victuals.

Country ship: A private merchant ship, i.e., one not belonging to the East India Company, trading in the Indian Ocean or Eastern Seas.

Cross-bracing: A general term for strengthening a ship by means of riders.

Double: (1) To attack an enemy from both sides. (2) To cover a ship with thick extra planking, either internally or externally, which strengthens the ship without driving out the original fastenings.

The Downs: The anchorage inside the Goodwin Sands off the east Kent coast at Deal, sheltered from westerly winds.

Gun brig: A small brig-rigged war vessel.

Gut: The main part of a strait or channel, such as the Gut of Gibraltar.

Factor: An agent overseas commissioned by merchants to purchase or sell goods on account by letter of attorney.

Factory: An association of factors, as at Lisbon, Leghorn or Calcutta; also a business or firm such as the East India Company.

Faggot: Slang for a man hired to appear at a muster.

Felucca: A small vessel of six or eight oars, found in the Mediterranean; or a narrow-decked galley-built vessel with lateen sails.

First-class boys or volunteers: A rating introduced by the Admiralty in 1794 for young gentlemen. It was intended to supplant midshipmen selected by a captain.

Fishing a mast: To repair a sprung mast with two pieces of shaped, concave wood that are bound around the mast with tightly wound rope, known as woolding.

Flog around the fleet: *See* **Punished through the fleet**.

Fore-and-aft rig: A rig used in smaller ships where the sails are set parallel to the ship's centre line, in contrast to square-rigged ships.

Freight money: Money earned by a ship's captain for carrying specie.

Frigate: A single-decked, smaller, fast warship of up to thirty-six or thirty-eight guns but usually thirty-two or twenty-eight guns (1805).

Head money: Prize money awarded for every person on board a captured enemy warship.

Junk: Remnants or pieces of old rope cable, untwisted and put to various uses, particularly for the wads that were placed between cannon balls and the gunpowder charge.

Ketch: A small two-masted vessel, rigged 'fore and aft' or with square sails.

Knot: A measure of speed of a vessel, one nautical mile an hour.

Lateen: A long triangular sail attached at its foremost edge to a yard that is hoisted at an oblique angle to the mast. Most small Mediterranean vessels were lateen rigged.

Ligature: A thread used to bind up a bleeding artery.

Luff: The order to the helmsman to bring the ship's head up more to windward.

Mast ship: A merchant ship with a cargo of masts to replace those damaged in warships.

Master's mate: A petty officer assisting the master of a ship.

Mess: Any company of the officers or crew of a ship who eat, drink and associate together.

Nautical mile: Equivalent to 6,075.6 feet. Sixty nautical miles constitute a degree of latitude. A nautical mile is 15 per cent longer than a statute mile (5,280 feet).

Orlop deck: The lower deck of a warship laid over the beams in the hold, used in the main for coiling cables or storing goods.

Pinnace: A small vessel propelled by oars and sails, often attending to a larger vessel, although French pinnaces of up to 60–80 tons could be armed and carry 100 men.

Polacre: A ship of the Levant with three masts carrying square sails on the main and lateen rig on the mizzenmast, the masts usually formed from one spar.

Port: An opening in the side of a ship of war through which artillery is ranged in battery on the decks above and below. They are closed when sailing by hanging doors (the port lids).

Post-captain: The rank of a captain of a sixth-rate ship or above.

Pratique: The licence to trade or to enter harbour, after a period of quarantine, or upon production of a clean bill of health.

Privateer: A vessel of war of any nation armed and equipped by merchants with a letter of marque or military commission from the country's admiralty to cruise against the enemy to capture shipping.

Prize money: The profits arising from the sale of prizes, either cargo or vessel and distributed in a specific system.

Prove: To test the soundness of firearms by trying them with greater charges than those used on service.

Punished through the fleet: A large number of lashes, authorized by a court martial, administered to a seaman or marine by a petty officer from each ship of the fleet or squadron present.

Rate: The six orders into which ships of war were divided, according to their size and weight of armament. Their rate determined their complement of men and officers.

Rated time: The period of time served on board a ship that counted towards eligibility for promotion.

Receiving ship: A moored warship at the Nore, Spithead or Plymouth that held seamen pressed into service before they were assigned to a ship at the beginning of a commission, or when changing ship.

Regulating captain: A captain or commander in charge of a district of the Impress Service.

Riders: Additional internal ship timbers laid, usually athwartships, to strengthen an old or weakened vessel.

Sails sleeping: A sail sleeps when, steadily filled with wind, it bellies to the breeze.

Scorbatic or scorbutic: Afflicted with scurvy.

Scurvy: Illness causing bleeding and sponginess of the gums, often suffered by seamen on long voyages. Brought about by vitamin deficiency through lack of fresh meat and vegetables.

Sea Fencibles: A volunteer force of fishermen and seamen gathered for defence of the south and east coasts of Britain during the time of Napoleon's invasion threats.

Shore: A prop fixed under a ship's side or bottom, to keep a ship upright when aground or in dock; or to reinforce a ship's hull or deck.

Shot: Material discharged from guns. Usually solid metal in various forms such as ball shot, bar shot, chain shot, case shot and grape shot.

Sloop: A small warship with one internal deck and main batteries on the upper deck.

Spar: A general term for a mast, yard, boom, gaff, etc.

Specie: Coin, or gold and silver bars.

Spring: A rope reaching diagonally from the stern of a ship to the bow of another alongside, or to a quay or rope attached to an anchor cable to allow the ship to be moved sideways.

Studding sails: A light sail used in light airs, supported by a boom run outboard of one of the main yards.

Supernumerary: A member of a ship's crew additional to her established complement, e.g., Nelson's 'retinue' of clerks and stewards when he was commander-in-chief; also people taking passage.

Table money: An entertainment allowance for ships' commanders, graded by rank.

Tack: To change the direction of the ship by pointing the ship through the wind so that the wind is on the other side of the sail, allowing the ship to progress to windward in a zigzag direction.

Taken aback: When the sails are headed by the wind to deaden her way. Brought about by an unexpected change in the direction of the wind or by inattention of the helmsman.

Topgallant mast: The highest mast above the deck, fixed to the topmast, which in turn is fixed to the lower mast.

Topman: A selected, young able seaman stationed in the topmasts to attend to the taking in or setting of the upper sails.

Twice-laid rope: Rope made from the best yarns of old rope; not as strong as that made from new hemp.

Unbend: To undo ropes that have been tied together or to release a sail from its yard.

Van: The foremost division or position within the fleet, which advances first in the order of sailing.

Victualling: Conveying or providing food and similar provisions to a ship or fleet. The victualling scale set out the basic provisions per man, as a ration per day or week.

To warp: To move a vessel by ropes attached to buoys, other ships, anchors or fixed objects on shore.

Wear: To change direction by turning the head of the vessel away from the wind and, without strain on a square-rigged ship, to bring it to the wind on the opposite tack. The modern equivalent term in fore-and-aft rigged vessels is to gybe.

Xebec: A small three-masted vessel of the Mediterranean sea found along the coasts of Spain, Portugal and the Barbary States.

Yard: A long piece of timber suspended from the masts of a ship on which the sails are hung.

Yawing: The motion of the ship when it deviates from its course by swinging to the port or starboard in steering.

Bibliography

PRIMARY SOURCES

United Kingdom

All Saints Church, Burnham Thorpe

Nelson to Dean Allot, 14 May 1804

Bodleian Library, University of Oxford

Montagu MSS
MS Eng. Hist.

British Library

Egerton MSS 1614, Nelson letters to Lady Hamilton

Additional Manuscripts

Ball Papers: 37268
Bridport Papers: 35194
Croker Papers: 40573
Grenville Papers: 58908
Liverpool Papers: 38307–8
Nelson Papers
   In-letters 1762–99: 34903–10
   Official correspondence 1781–99: 34933–6
   Hood to Nelson, to 1794: 34937
   St Vincent to Nelson: 34938–40
   Foreign correspondence 1798–1800: 34941–51
   Pressed letter copies 1804–5: 34953–60
   Letter books 1781–6, 1795: 34961–2
   Private journals 1803–5: 34966–8

Nelson family correspondence: 34988
Nepean Papers: 36708
Northwick Papers: 30999
St Vincent Papers: 31166
Spencer Papers: 75801–37, 75847, 75853–68
Windham Papers: 37845–52

Colindale Newspaper Library
Bath Chronicle and Weekly Gazette 1797
Bath Herald and Register 1797
Bath Journal 1797

Devon Record Office

Sidmouth Papers: DRO, 152/M/C1801–C1805

Holkham Archives, Wells-next-the-Sea, Norfolk

Game books 1793–8, 1797–8
Papers relating to the 1788 Fête: F/TWC 27; 28/N (10)

Centre for Buckinghamshire Studies, Aylesbury

Fremantle Papers: D/FR/33/11, 45/4–39

National Archives: Public Record Office

Admiralty In-letters
Commander-in-chief, Mediterranean 1797–8: ADM 1/396–7
Commander-in-chief, Baltic 1801: ADM 1/4
Commander-in-chief, Mediterranean 1802–3: ADM 1/406–7
Commander-in-chief's dispatches, Admiral Parker 1778–9: ADM 1/241
Senior officers' dispatches 1779–86: ADM 1/242
Captain's In-letters
  'S' 1771: ADM 1/2481
  'P' 1776: ADM 1/2303
  'R' 1776: ADM 1/2389
  'R' 1777: ADM 1/2390
  'L' 1777: ADM 1/2054
  'D' 1781: ADM 1/1709
  'N' 1781: ADM 1/2222
  'N' 1793–6: ADM 1/224–6
  'M' 1799: ADM 1/2137

Courts martial
    Minorca 1799: ADM 1/5352
    Tygress 1801: ADM 1/5356
    Invincible 1801: ADM 1/5355
Letters from secretary of state 1801–3: ADM 1/1487–90
Letters from secretaries of state 1801: ADM 1/4186–7
Alphabetical list of intelligence 1801–6: ADM 1/6038

Admiralty Out-letters
Secretary to Admiral Parker 1779–1780: ADM 2/563
Secretary to Admiral Hughes 1784–5: ADM 2/583, 585
Commander-in-chief Mediterranean 1795–1800: ADM 2/922
Admiral Bickerton 1802–3: ADM 2/923
Secret instructions to commander-in-chief, Mediterranean 1798: ADM 2/1353
'Most Secret Orders' 1803: ADM 2/1360

Admiralty Minutes
Jan.–June 1801: ADM 3/144
Jul.–Dec. 1802: ADM 3/146

Papers of Admiral Sir Edward Hughes
Letter book 1775: ADM 7/746

Ship Lists
1784: ADM 8/60
1789: ADM 8/65
1790: ADM 8/66

Courts Martial Records
ADM 12/27B 1774 (Index)

Ships' Pay Books
Seahorse 1773–7: ADM 34/749
Victor 1780: ADM 34/831

Muster Books
Raisonable 1770: ADM 36/7669
Triumph 1771–72: ADM 36/7689
Carcass 1773: ADM 36/756
Dolphin 1776: ADM 36/7583
Worcester 1776–7: ADM 36/8677
Lowestoffe 1777: ADM 36/10047
Lowestoffe's prize 1777: ADM 36/8254

Bristol 1778: ADM 36/8118
Badger 1778–79: ADM 36/9882
Hinchinbroke 1779–80: ADM 36/9510, 36/9511
Lion 1780–81: ADM 36/9202, 36/9203
Albemarle 1781–1783: ADM 36/10081, 36/10082
Boreas 1783–7: ADM 36/10524, 36/10525, 36/10526, 36/10528
Agamemnon 1793–5: ADM 36/11358, 36/11360, 36/11362
Captain 1796–7: ADM 36/11799
Diadem 1796: ADM 36/11823
Irresistible 1797: ADM 36/11775
Theseus 1797: ADM 36/12648
Vanguard 1798–9: ADM 36/15356, 36/15357
Foudroyant 1799–1800: ADM 36/14946
San Josef 1801: ADM 36/14012
Elephant 1801: ADM 36/15432
Kite 1801: ADM 36/13958
Medusa 1801: ADM 36/15155
Amazon 1801: ADM 36/14681
Amphion 1803: ADM 36/16645
Victory 1803–5: ADM 36/15895, 36/15898–15901

Admirals' Journals
Richard Hughes 1785–6: ADM 50/100
Samuel Hood 1793–4: ADM 50/125
John Jervis 1796–9: ADM 50/79, 50/93
Horatio Nelson 1805: ADM 50/38

Captains' Logs
Raisonable 1770–71: ADM 51/763
Triumph 1772–3: ADM 51/1015
Seahorse 1773–5: ADM 51/883
Dolphin 1776: ADM 51/259
Worcester 1776–7: ADM 51/1085
Lowestoffe 1777–9: ADM 51/4247, 51/557
Badger 1779: ADM 51/78
Hinchinbroke 1779–80: ADM 51/442
Lion 1778–81: ADM 51/540
Albemarle 1781–3: ADM 51/4110
Boreas 1784–7: ADM 51/125, 51/120
Agamemnon 1793–6: ADM 51/1104, 51/1126
Captain 1796–7: ADM 51/1267, 51/1194
La Minerve 1796–7: ADM 51/1204
Irresistible 1797: ADM 51/1212

Theseus 1797: ADM 51/1221
Seahorse 1797: ADM 51/1190
Vanguard 1798–9: ADM 51/1288
Bellerophon 1799: ADM 51/1281
Culloden 1799: ADM 51/1294
Foudroyant 1799–1800: ADM 51/1279, 51/1330
Perseus 1799: ADM 51/1323
San Josef 1801: ADM 51/1317
St George 1801: ADM 51/1371
Elephant 1801: ADM 51/1356
Leyden 1801: ADM 51/13
Medusa 1801: ADM 51/1437
Amazon 1801: ADM 51/4409
Amphion 1803: ADM 51/1446
Victory 1803–5: ADM 51/4514, 51/1482
Kent 1802–3: ADM 51/1453
Anson 1804: 51/1483
Royal Sovereign 1805: ADM 51/4494

Masters' Logs

Carcass 1773: ADM 52/1639
Boreas 1785: ADM 52/2179
Agamemnon 1793–6: ADM 52/2710, 52/2707, 52/2632
Captain 1796–7: ADM 52/2825
La Minerve 1796–7: ADM 52/3223
Blanche 1796–7: ADM 52/2765
Vanguard 1797–9: ADM 52/3516
Zealous 1798: ADM 52/3550
Goliath 1798: ADM 52/3055
Elephant 1801: ADM 52/2968
Medusa 1801: ADM 52/3208
Kent 1802–3: ADM 52/3142
Victory 1803–5: ADM 52/3711

Logs and Journals of Ships on Exploration

Carcass 1773: ADM 55/12

Greenwich Hospital Records

R. G. Keats letter book 1804: ADM 80/141

Ships' Sailing Qualities
'A–G' 1763–80: ADM 95/30
'H–P' 1763–80: ADM 95/31
'Q–Z' ADM 1765–80: 95/32
1791–6: ADM 95/38
1795–1802: ADM 95/39

Surgeons' Journals
Seahorse 1797: ADM 101/120/6
Theseus 1797: ADM 101/121/2

Lieutenants' Passing Certificates
ADM 107/6

Victualling Board Records
In-letters 1789: ADM 114/26

Upnor Armaments Supply Depot
Proportion tables of ordnance stores for HM ships 1781–1828: ADM 160/150
Returns of ordnance on HM Ships 1803–12: ADM 160/154

Progress and Dimensions Books
1st to 3rd rates: 1759–1820: ADM 180/6
3rd to 6th rates 1765–1818: ADM 180/7

English Harbour, Antigua
Resident commissioners and senior naval officer, Leeward Islands, to the dockyard officers 1779–87: ADM/241/1

Non-Admiralty Records
Foreign Office Out-letters 1801: FO/22/40
'Advices, Intelligences, etc., from Vice-Consul James Bird' 1798–1803: FO/28/18
William Pitt Papers: PRO/30/8
Audit Office, Declared Accounts 1811: AO/1/850/5
War Office, ordnance artillery letter books 1801: WO/55/1072

National Maritime Museum

Records of the Central Administration of the Navy
Victualling Board to Admiralty 1800–1801: ADM/DP/20

Lieutenants' Logs

Triumph 1772–3: ADM L/T/268

Seahorse 1773–4: ADM L/S/222

Lowestoffe 1777–8: ADM L/L/220

Bristol 1778–80: ADM L/B/137, L/B/175B, L/B/174

Victor 1780: ADM L/V/133

Albemarle 1781–3: ADM L/A/72

Boreas 1786: ADM L/B/136

Agamemnon 1793–6: ADM L/A/51

Captain 1796–7: ADM L/C/51

Vanguard 1797–8: ADM L/V/28

Kite 1801: ADM L/K/54

Victory 1803–5: ADM L/V/57

Dockyard Papers

Portsmouth yard officers to Navy Board 1782: POR/D/23

Navy Board to the Chatham yard officers 1793, 1797–8: CHA/E/40, CHA/E/59

Navy Board to the Chatham Dockyard commissioner 1797–8: CHA/F/3

Personal Collections

Lord Barham (Admiral Sir Charles Middleton): MID/ and MS 94/010

Captain Richard Bowen: MS95/001

Admiral Lord Bridport: BRP/

Admiral Lord Collingwood: COL/

Admiral Sir William Cornwallis: COR/

Alexander Davison: DAV/

Sir Gilbert Elliot (Lord Minto): ELL/

Admiral Sir Thomas Foley: FOL/

Vice-Admiral Sir Thomas Fremantle: FRE/

William Haslewood: HAS/

Admiral Lord Hood: HOO/ and MKH/

Admiral Sir John Jervis (Lord St Vincent): JER/

Admiral Lord Keith: KEI/

John Montagu, fourth earl of Sandwich: SAN/

Sir Evan Nepean: NEP/

Admiral Sir John Orde: ORD/

Admiral Sir William Parker: PAR/251 (letters from Nelson to Jervis 1796–1805)

Admiral Charles Morice Pole: WYN/

Vice-Admiral Robert Roddam: ROD/

Admiral William Waldegrave (later Lord Radstock): MS 82/007

BIBLIOGRAPHY

Artificial Collections
(Inherited collections of manuscripts, formed by collectors or accumulated by institutions)

De Coppet: (Nelson letters 1799–1805, collected by André De Coppet): COP/
Girdlestone: (Bolton family papers inherited by Miss Girdlestone): GIR/
Monsarrat: (Nelson letters 1786–1805, collected by Nicholas Monsarrat): MON/
Nelson-Ward: (letters of Nelson and Emma Hamilton, inherited from Horatia by Reverend Nelson-Ward): NWD/
Phillipps – Croker: (letters to and by Nelson purchased by John Wilson Croker, later owned by Sir Thomas Phillipps): CRK/
RUS: (miscellaneous papers formerly owned by the Royal United Services Institution): RUSI/
Stewart: (miscellaneous Nelson items collected by Sir Malcolm Stewart): STW/
Sutcliffe-Smith: (Nelson letters to other naval officers 1799–1804): SUT/
Tunstall: (signal books collected by Brian Tunstall): TUN/
Trafalgar House: (family and service papers purchased from Earl Nelson in 1947): TRA/
Walter: (domestic papers and the Merton sketchbook): WAL/

Individual Volumes
Letters from Lieutenant Thomas Wilkes to Henry Clarke 1798–1801: AGC/W/2
Fifth Report of the Commissioners on Fees and Gratuities 1786: CAD/D/11
'Remarks Taken on Board HM Ship *Swiftsure* in the Action of 1 August 1798 ... by J.L. Davis, Lieutenant': HIS/35
In- and Out-letter and order book, Prince William Henry 1786–8: LBK/33
Nelson's copy of Chambaud's *Grammar of the French Tongue* (1779): REC/33
Signal Book 1799: SIG/B/76
Nelson's journal and codicil to his will written before Trafalgar: JOD/14

Individual Letters
Autograph Collection: AGC/

Microfilm, Etc.
Matcham Papers: MAM/
French reports on the attacks on Boulogne, August 1801, from the Archives Nationale, France: MRF/181
Copies of Nelson letters presented by Lady Lenanton (Carola Oman): PST/39
Transcripts from the Spiro Collection: XAGC/8

Nelson Museum, Monmouth

Llangattock Collection (letters): E25–987
Foudroyant's signal log 1799–1800: E986
Volumes of out-letters 1796–7, 1799–1801, 1803–4: E987–92

Norfolk Record Office

Parish records, Burnham Thorpe: PD 571/2
Levett Hanson to Nelson, 29 Sept. 1802: MC 20/48

Royal Naval Museum, Portsmouth

'A Family Historical Register by Edm. Nelson, Rector of Burnham Thorpe': 85/57
'William Bolton's Journal of Proceedings of HMS *Agamemnon*. 2 Mar. 1793–24 June 1795': 1983/1069
Nelson to Emma Hamilton, 27 Oct. 1798: 1964/49
Gunner's notebook, *Victory* 1804–5: 1998/41/1
William Chevallier letters to Alexander Davison 1803–5: 2002/76
Account of boatswains' and carpenters' stores, *Victory* 1805: 1983/1064

Archives and Manuscripts, Wellcome Library for the History and Understanding of Medicine, London

Nelson Collection:
 Prizes, finance 1780–1803: Western MSS 3676
 Secret rendezvous, signalling, etc. 1794–1805; Western MSS 3677
 In-letters from captains: Western MSS 3667-3675

United States

William L. Clements Library, University of Michigan

Hubert Smith Naval Collection
Croker Papers
Kemble Papers
Melville Papers
Sydney Papers
Correspondence of Lieutenant General Sir John Vaughan
Charts and views of the Arctic voyage 1773 by Philip D'Auvergne: MSS Maps 8-0-9

Houghton Library, Harvard University

Joseph Husband Collection: pf MS Eng. 196.5
Lowell Collection: f MS Lowell 10

Huntington Library, San Marino, California

Nelson to Thomas Troubridge 1801–2: HM 34208–83
Nelson to William Locker 1777–1800: HM 34098–178
Nelson to Lady Hamilton 1798–1803: HM 34077–96
Nelson to Hood, Otway and others: HM 34180–207
Howe–Curtis correspondence: HO 1–408
Stowe–Grenville Collection (in-letters to Thomas Grenville 1806–7): STG 102–85
Nelson miscellaneous: EA 372

SECONDARY SOURCES

(*Place of publication London, unless otherwise stated*)
Acerra, Martine, 'Le redéploiement français en Méditerranée 1789–1815' in
    Français et Anglais en Méditerranée 1789–1830 (Vincennes, 1992), 121–8
Acerra, Martine, and Meyer, Jean, *Marines et Révolution* (Rennes, 1988)
Anderson, R. C., 'The Lee Line at Trafalgar', *Mariner's Mirror*, 57, 1971, 157–61
Aspinall, A. (ed.), *The Later Correspondence of George III*, 5 vols. (1962–70)
    The Correspondence of George, Prince of Wales 1770–1812, 5 vols.
    (1963–71)
Baker, H. A., *The Crisis in Naval Ordnance* (1983)
Baker, Mike, 'Lord Nelson and John Bowsher', *Mariner's Mirror*, 86, 2000,
    310–12
Baring, Mrs Henry (ed.), *The Diary of the Right Honourable William Windham
    1784–1810* (1866)
Barker, Rosalin, *Prisoners of the Tsar: East Coast Sailors Held in Russia 1800–
    1801* (Beverley, Humberside, 1992)
Barker, T. C., 'Transport: The Survival of the Old Beside the New' in Peter Mathias
    and John A. Davis (eds.), *The First Industrial Revolution* (1981), 86–100
Barnett, Richard D., 'Richard Barnett: An Anglo-Jewish Sailor at the Battle of the
    Nile', *Mariner's Mirror*, 71, 1985, 185–200
Barras, T. C., 'Vice-Admiral Lord Nelson's Lost Eye', *Transactions of the
    Ophthalmology Society*, 105, 1986, 351–5
    'Nelson's Injury at the Battle of the Nile', *Nelson Dispatch*, 2, 1987, 217
Barrett, Mark, 'Nelson and the Theatre', *Nelson Dispatch*, 7, 2000, 151–60
Barritt, M. K., 'Nelson's Frigates: May to August 1798', *Mariner's Mirror*, 58,
    1972, 281–95

Barrow, Sir John, *Life of George, Lord Anson* (1839)
  An Autobiographical Memoir (1847)
Bath and Wells, Bishop of (ed.), *The Journals and Correspondence of William, Lord Auckland*, 4 vols. (1860–62)
Battesti, Michèle, *La Bataille d'Aboukir 1798: Nelson contrarie la Stratégie de Bonaparte* (Paris, 1998)
Baugh, Daniel A., 'The Politics of British Naval Failure 1775–1777', *American Neptune*, 52, 1992, 221–46
  'The Eighteenth-century Navy as a National Institution 1690–1815' in J. R. Hill (ed.), *The Oxford Illustrated History of the Royal Navy* (Oxford, 1995)
  'Maritime Strength and Atlantic Commerce' in Lawrence Stone (ed.), *An Imperial State at War* (1994), 185–223
  'Naval Power: What Gave the British Navy Superiority?' in Leandro Prados de la Escosura (ed.), *Exceptionalism and Industrialization: Britain and Its European Rivals 1688–1815* (Cambridge, 2004), 235–57
Beatty, William, *The Authentic Narrative of the Death of Lord Nelson* (1807)
Bennett, Geoffrey, *Nelson the Commander* (New York, 1972)
Beresford, John (ed.), *Woodforde: Passages from the Five Volumes of the Diary of a Country Parson 1758–1802* (1935)
Berry, Edward, *An Authentic Narrative of the Proceedings of His Majesty's Squadron . . .* (1798)
Bickley, Francis (ed.), *The Diaries of Sylvester Douglas*, 2 vols. (1928)
Bindoff, S. T., Malcolm Smith, E. F., and Webster, C. K., *British Diplomatic Representatives 1789–1852* (Royal Historical Society, 1934)
Black, Jeremy, 'Eighteenth-century Intercepted Dispatches', *Journal of the Society of Archivists*, 11, 1990, 138–43
Blanning, T. C. W., *The French Revolutionary Wars 1787–1802* (1996)
Blumel, Thomas, 'Nelson's Overland Journey', *Nelson Dispatch* 7, 2000, 82–96, 162–81
Bonner-Smith, D. (ed.), *Letters of Admiral of the Fleet the Earl of St Vincent whilst First Lord of the Admiralty 1801–1804*, 2 vols. (Navy Records Society, 55, 61, 1922, 1927)
  'The Evacuation of Naples, *Mariner's Mirror*, 16, 1930, 91
Bourchier, Jane, Lady (ed.), *Memoir of the Life of Admiral Sir Edward Codrington*, 2 vols. (1873)
Bradford, Gershon, 'Nelson in Boston Bay', *American Neptune*, 11, 1951, 239–44
Breihan, John R., 'The Addington Party and the Navy in British Politics 1801–1806' in Craig L. Symonds (ed.), *New Aspects of Naval History* (Annapolis, Maryland, 1981), 163–89
Brenton, Edward Pelham (ed.), *Life and Correspondence of John, Earl of St Vincent*, 2 vols. (1838)
Brewer, John, *The Sinews of Power: War, Money and the English State 1688–1783* (1989)

Broadley, A. M., and Bartelot, R. G., *Nelson's Hardy: His Life, Letters and Friends* (1909)

Buchet, Christian, 'Les Préparatifs de l'expédition d'Éygpte' in *Français et Anglais en Méditerranée 1789–1830* (Vincennes, 1992), 55–68

Buckingham and Chandos, duke of, *Memoirs of Court and Cabinets of George III*, 4 vols. (1853–5)

Buckland, Kirstie, *The Miller Papers* (1805 Club, 1999)

Bullocke, J. G. (ed.), *The Tomlinson Papers* (Navy Records Society, 74, 1935)

Burrows, Edwin G., and Wallace, Mike, *Gotham: A History of New York City* (New York, 1999)

Byrn, John D., *Crime and Punishment in the Royal Navy: Discipline in the Leeward Islands Station 1784–1812* (Aldershot, Hants, 1989)

Callender, Geoffrey, 'Collingwood's Copy of Beatty's *Authentic Narrative*', *Mariner's Mirror*, 24, 1938, 237

Caruana, Adrian B., *The History of English Sea Ordnance 1523–1875*, Vol. II, *The Age of the System 1715–1815* (1997)

Chalus, Elaine, 'Elite Women, Social Politics, and the Political World of the Late Eighteenth Century', *Historical Journal*, 43, 2000, 688

Chatterton, Henrietta Georgiana, Lady (ed.), *Memorials, Personal and Historical, of Admiral Lord Gambier . . .*, 2 vols. (1861)

Childers, Spencer (ed.), *A Mariner of England, An Account of the Career of William Richardson . . .* (1908, repr. 1970)

Chisholm, Henry, 'Nelson at Port Agro', *Mariner's Mirror*, 65, 1979, 269

Christie, A. B., *Infectious Diseases: Epidemiology and Clinical Practice* (1987)

Clark, John D., *The Men of HMS* Victory *at Trafalgar* (1999)

Clark, S. G., 'The Lad Who Caught Nelson's Eye', *Mariner's Mirror*, 64, 1978, 347–8

Clarke, James Stainer, and McArthur, John, *The Life of Admiral Lord Nelson, KB, from His Lordship's Manuscripts*, 2 vols. (1809)

Clayton, Tim, and Craig, Phil, *Trafalgar* (2004)

Coad, Jonathan, *The Royal Dockyards 1690–1850* (Aldershot, Hants, 1989)

Colchester, Charles Lord (ed.), *The Diary and Correspondence of Charles Abbott, Lord Colchester*, 3 vols. (1861)

Coleman, Terry, *Nelson: The Man and the Legend* (2001, paperback ed. 2002)
'Nelson, the King and His Ministers', *Trafalgar Chronicle*, 13, 2003, 6–11

Coleridge, Samuel Taylor, *The Friend*, (ed.) Barbara Rooke, 2 vols. (1969)

Colley, Linda, 'The Apotheosis of George III: Loyalty, Royalty and the British Nation 1760–1820', *Past and Present*, 1984, 94–129
'Class and Class Consciousness in Britain 1750–1830', *Past and Present*, 1986, 97–117
Britons: Forging the Nation 1707–1837 (1992)

Collingwood, G. Newnham (ed.), *Selections from the Public and Private Correspondence of Vice-Admiral Lord Collingwood* (1828)

Constantine, David, *Fields of Fire: A Life of Sir William Hamilton* (2001)

Corbett, J. S., *The Private Papers of George, Second Earl Spencer*, Vols. I and II (Navy Records Society, 46, 48, 1913, 1914)
The Campaign of Trafalgar (1919, repr. 1976)

Cordingly, David, *Billy Ruffian: HMS* Bellerophon *and the Downfall of Napoleon – The Biography of a Ship of the Line 1782–1836* (2003)

Cormack, William S., *Revolution and Political Conflict in the French Navy 1789–1794* (Cambridge, 1995)

Cornwallis-West, G., *The Life and Letters of Admiral Cornwallis* (1927)

Coutau-Begarie, Hervé, 'Seapower in the Mediterranean from the Seventeenth to the Nineteenth Centuries' in J. B. Hattendorf (ed.), *Naval Strategy and Policy in the Mediterranean* (2000), 30–47

Cowie, L. C., *Lord Nelson 1758–1805: A Bibliography* (1990)

Crimmin, P. K., 'Letters and Documents Relating to the Service of Nelson's Ships 1780–1805', *Historical Research*, 70, 1997, 52–69
'Petition of the Crew of HMS *Royal Sovereign*', *Mariner's Mirror*, 59, 1973, 100–101
'John Jervis, Earl of St Vincent' in Richard Harding and Peter Le Fevre (eds.), *The Precursors of Nelson* (2000), 325–49

Crook, Malcolm, *Toulon in War and Revolution: From the Ancien Régime to the Restoration 1750–1820* (Manchester, 1991)

Cross, Anthony, 'An Offence against the Nation: An Account of the Theft of Lord Nelson's Relics from the Painted Hall, December 1900', *Trafalgar Chronicle*, 23, 2003, 92–110

Cryer, H. L., 'Horatio Nelson and the Murderous Cooper', *Mariner's Mirror*, 60, 1974, 3–7

Czisnik, Marianne, 'Nelson and the Nile: The Creation of Admiral Nelson's Public Image', *Mariner's Mirror*, 88, 2002, 41–60
'Nelson at Naples: A Review of the Events and Arguments', *Trafalgar Chronicle*, 12, 2002, 84–121.
'Nelson at Naples: The Development of a Story', *Trafalgar Chronicle*, 13, 2003, 35–55
'Nelson: Image and Icon' (Ph.D., University of Edinburgh, 2004)
'El consejo de Guerra antes de la batalla de Trafalgar', *Revista de Historia Naval*, 81, 2003, 49–60
'Admiral Nelson's Tactics at the Battle of Trafalgar', *History*, Oct. 2004, 549–59
'La interpretactión del combate de Trafalgar más conocida: la novella *Trafalgar* de Benito Pérez Galdós' in Agustín Guimerá, Alberto Ramos, and Gonzalo Butrón (eds.), *Trafalgar y el mundo Atlántico* (Madrid, 2004), 359–74

Damer-Powell, J. W., 'Abraham Parsons: Mariner and Merchant', *Mariner's Mirror*, 42, 1956, 94–100

Dancer, Thomas, *A Brief History of the Late Expedition against Fort Juan So Far as It Relates to the Diseases of the Troops* (Kingston, Jamaica, 1781)

Dann, John C., *The Nagle Journal: A Diary of the Life of Jacob Nagle, Sailor, from the Year 1775 to 1841* (New York, 1988)

Dawson, L. S., *Memoirs of Hydrography* (1885)

Dawson, Warren R., *The Nelson Collection at Lloyd's* (1932)

The Banks Letters (1958)

Denham, H. M., *The Tyrrhenian Sea: A Sea-guide to Its Coasts and Islands* (1969)

Deuchar, Stephen, 'The Immortal Memory' in Pieter van der Merwe (ed.), *Nelson: An Illustrated History* (1995), 141–67

Donaldson, David, 'Edward Gayner and the Nelson Legend in Minorca', *Nelson Dispatch*, 5, 1996, 430–35

Douglass-Morriss, Kenneth, *The Naval General Service Medal 1793–1840* (1982)

Downer, Martyn, *Nelson: The Alexander Davison Collection* (Sotheby's catalogue, 2002)

Nelson's Purse (2004)

Drinkwater (later Drinkwater-Bethune), John, *A Narrative of the Proceedings of the British Fleet off Cape St Vincent* (1797)

Dropmore, Historical Manuscripts Commission, *Report on the Manuscripts of J. B. Fortescue, Esq. Preserved at Dropmore*, 9 vols. (1892–1915)

Duffy, Michael, *Soldiers, Sugar and Seapower: The British Expeditions to the West Indies and the War against Revolutionary France* (1987)

'British Naval Intelligence and Bonaparte's Egyptian Expedition of 1798, *Mariner's Mirror*, 84, 1998, 278–90

'Samuel Hood, First Viscount Hood' in Richard Harding and Peter Le Fevre (eds.), *The Precursors of Nelson* (2000), 249–77

' "Science and Labour": The naval Contribution to Operations Ashore in the Great Wars with France' in Peter Hore (ed.), *Sea Power Ashore* (2001), 39–52

'The Gunnery at Trafalgar: Training, Tactics or Temperament', *Journal of Maritime Research*, May 2005

Dull, Jonathan, 'Why Did the French Revolutionary Navy Fail?', *The Consortium on Revolutionary Europe. Proceedings for 1989* (Athens, Georgia, 1990)

Dupont, Maurice, 'Peut-on sauver l'armée d'Égypte?' in *Français et Anglais en Méditerranée 1789–1830* (Vincennes, 1992), 91–118

Duro, Cesáreo, *Armada Espagnola desde la Union de los Reinos de Castilla y Aragón*, 9 vols. (Madrid, 1895–1902)

Eastwick, C. L. (ed.), *The Naval Campaign of 1805: Trafalgar by Édouard Desbrière*, 2 vols. (Oxford, 1933)

Eastwood, David, 'Patriotism Personified: Robert Southey's *Life of Nelson* Reconsidered', *Mariner's Mirror*, 77, 1991, 143–9

Edgcumbe, Richard (ed.), *The Diary of Frances Lady Shelley 1787–1817*, 2 vols. (1912)

Edwards, Lesley, 'Horatio Nelson and Lady Hamilton's Twins', *Mariner's Mirror*, 86, 2000, 313–15

Ehrman, John, *The Younger Pitt. Vol. I: The Years of Acclaim* (1969); *Vol. II: The Reluctant Transition* (1983); *Vol III: The Consuming Struggle* (1996)

Elliot, Sir George, *Memoir of Admiral the Honourable Sir George Elliot* (1863, repr. 1891)

Ellis, K. L., 'British Communications and Diplomacy in the Eighteenth Century', *Bulletin of the Institute of Historical Research*, 31, 1958, 159–61

Emsley, Clive, 'The Recruitment of Petty Offenders during the French Wars 1793–1815, *Mariner's Mirror*, 66, 1980, 199–208

Falconer, William, *The Shipwreck* (1811 ed.)

Fawcett, Nigel, 'Did Nelson Ever Come Ashore in Simonstown?', *Nelson Dispatch*, 2, 1985, 35–7

Feldbæk, Ole, 'The Anglo-Danish Conflict of 1800', *Scandinavian Journal of History*, 2, 1977, 161–82

'Humanity or Ruse de Guerre? Nelson's Letter to the Danes', *Mariner's Mirror*, 73, 1978, 339–49

The Battle of Copenhagen 1801 (1985, English trans. 2002)

Finamore, Daniel, 'Sailors and Slaves on the Wood-cutting Frontier: Archaeology of the British Bay Settlement, Belize' (Ph.D., Boston, 1994)

Findlay, Alexander, G., *A Sailing Directory for the Mediterranean Sea* (1868)

Fisher, Susanna, 'Captain Thomas Hurd's Survey of the Bay of Brest during the Blockade in the Napoleonic Wars', *Mariner's Mirror*, 79, 1993, 293–304

Flayhart, William Henry, *Counterpoint to Trafalgar: The Anglo-Russian Invasion of Naples 1805–1806* (University of South Carolina Press, 1992)

Foster, Vere (ed.), *The Two Duchesses* (1898)

Fraser, Flora, *Beloved Emma: The Life of Emma, Lady Hamilton* (1986)

'If You Seek His Monument' in Colin White (ed.), *The Nelson Companion* (1997), 129–51

Fremantle, Anne (ed.), *The Wynne Diaries*, 3 vols. (1935–40); 1 vol. (1952; repr. 1982)

Frost, Alan, *Convicts and Empire: A Naval Question* (Melbourne, 1980)

Galiano, Antonio Alcalá, *Recuerdos de un anciano* (Madrid, 1878)

Gardiner, Robert, *Frigates of the Napoleonic Wars* (2000)

Gardner, James Anthony, *Above and under Hatches: Being Naval Recollections in Shreds and Patches* (ed.) Christopher Lloyd (1955)

Gentleman's Magazine, 1801

[Gilbert, Arthur N.], 'Buggery and the British Navy 1700–1861', *Journal of Social History*, 10, 1976, 72–88

Gilbert, Arthur N., 'The Nature of Mutiny in the British Navy in the Eighteenth Century' in Daniel M. Masterman, *Naval History: The Sixth Symposium of the US Naval Academy* (1987), 111–20

Gill, Edward, *Nelson and the Hamiltons on Tour* (Gloucester and Monmouth, 1987)

Glete, Jan, *Navies and Nations: Warships, Navies and State Building in Europe and America 1500–1800* (Stockholm, 1993)

Godfrey, J. H., 'Corsica 1794' in Christopher Lloyd (ed.), *The Naval Miscellany*, IV (Navy Records Society, 92, 1952), 360–422

Gonzalez-Aller, Ignatio José, and O'Donnell, Hugo, 'The Spanish Navy in the Eighteenth Century' in Stephen Howarth (ed.), *Battle of Cape St Vincent: Two Hundred Years* (Shelton, Notts. 1998), 67–83

Goodwin, Peter, *Nelson's Ships 1771–1805* (2002)

Grant, N. H. (ed.), *The Letters of Mary Nisbet of Dirleton, Countess of Elgin* (1926)

Granville, Countess, *Lord Granville Leveson-Gower: Private Correspondence 1781–1821*, 2 vols. (1916)

Gray, Peter, 'Turning a Blind Eye', *Trafalgar Chronicle*, 11, 2001, 38–51

Green, Geoffrey L., *The Royal Navy and Anglo-Jewry 1740–1820* (1989)

Gregory, Desmond, *Malta, Britain and the European Powers 1793–1815* (Cranbury, New Jersey, 1996)

Guimerá, Agustín, *Tenerife 1797: La Victoria de la Isla sobre la Escuadra de Nelson* (Santa Cruz de Tenerife, 1998)

Nelson and Tenerife (1805 Club, 1999)

'Gravina y el liderazgo naval de su tiempo' in Agustín Guimerá, Alberto Ramos, and Gonzalo Butrón, *Trafalgar y el mundo Atlántico* (Madrid, 2004), 233–56

Guimerá, Agustín, Ramos, Alberto, and Butrón, Gonzalo (eds.), *Trafalgar y el mundo Atlántico* (Madrid, 2004)

Gutteridge, H. C., *Nelson and the Neapolitan Jacobins* (Navy Records Society, 25, 1903)

Gwyther, John, 'Nelson in St Omer', *Trafalgar Chronicle*, 1999, 112–16

'Nelson's Gifts to La Maddalena', *Trafalgar Chronicle*, 10, 2000, 47–56

'Nelson in Carloforte', *Trafalgar Chronicle*, 13, 2003, 35–55

Hague, Douglas B., *Lighthouses: Their Architecture, History and Archaeology* (1972)

Hamilton, C. I., 'Naval Hagiography and the Victorian Hero', *Historical Journal*, 23, 1980, 381–98

Hamilton, R. V. (ed.), *Journal and Letters of Admiral of the Fleet Sir Thomas Byam Martin 1773–1854*, Vols. I and III (Navy Records Society, 1902, 1900)

Hampson, Norman, *The Perfidy of Albion: French Perceptions of England during the French Revolution* (1998)

Hannay, David (ed.), *Letters of Lord Hood 1781–1782* (Navy Records Society, 3, 1895)

Hansard, *Parliamentary History of England*, 38, 1801–3

Harbron, John D., *Trafalgar and the Spanish Navy* (1988)

Harcourt, Reverend Leveson Vernon, *The Diaries and Correspondence of the Right Honourable George Rose* (1860)

Hardin, Craig, 'Lord and Lady Nelson: Some Unpublished Letters', *Huntington Library Quarterly*, 11, 1947–8, 81–6

Harding, Richard, *Amphibious Warfare in the Eighteenth Century: The British Expedition to the West Indies 1740–1742* (1991)

Seapower and Naval Warfare 1630–1830 (1999)

Harland, John, *Seamanship in the Age of Sail* (1984)

Harlow, Vincent T., *The Founding of the Second British Empire 1763–1793*, Vol. I (1952)

Harmon, Susan, 'The Serpent and the Dove: Studying Nelson's Character', *Mariner's Mirror*, 75, 1989, 43–51

Harrison, John, *The Life of the Right Honourable Horatio Viscount Nelson . . .* (1806)

Hattendorf, John B., 'Sea power as Control: Britain's Defensive Naval Strategy in the Mediterranean, 1793–1815' in *Français et Anglais en Méditerranée 1789–1830* (Vincennes, 1992), 203–20

St Barthélémy and the Swedish West India Company: A Selection of Printed Documents (New York, 1994)

Hattendorf, John B., and Hattendorf, Lynn C., *A Bibliography of the Works of Alfred Thayer Mahan* (Newport, Rhode Island, 1986)

Hattendorf, John B., Knight, R. J. B., Pearsall, A. W. H., Rodger, N. A. M., and Till, Geoffrey, *British Naval Documents 1204–1960* (Navy Records Society, 131, 1993)

Hay, M. D. (ed.), *Landsman Hay: The Memoirs of Robert Hay 1789–1847* (1953)

Hayward, Joel, 'Horatio Lord Nelson's Warfighting Style and the Maneuver Warfare Paradigm', *Defence Studies*, 2001, 15–27

For God and Glory: Lord Nelson and His Way of War (Annapolis, Maryland, 2003)

Heath, Charles, *Descriptive Account of the Kymin Pavilion and Beaulieu Grove with Their Various Views: Also the Naval Temple; to which is Now Added Lord Nelson's Visit* (Monmouth, 1808, repr. 2002)

Herbert, John Beresford, *Life and Services of Sir Thomas Foley, GCB* (Cardiff, 1884)

Hibbert, Christopher, *Nelson: A Personal History* (1994)

Hildebrand, Ingegerd, *Den svenska kolonin S:t Barthélémy och västindiska kompaniet fram till 1796* (Lund, Sweden, 1951)

Hill, Richard, *The Prizes of War: The Naval Prize System in the Napoleonic Wars 1793–1815* (Stroud, Gloucs., 1998)

Hills, A-M. E., 'His Belly off Cape St Vincent' in Stephen Howarth (ed.), *Battle of Cape St Vincent: Two Hundred Years* (Shelton, Notts., 1998), 84–9

'Nelson's Illnesses', *Journal of the Royal Naval Medical Service*, 86, 2000, 72–80

'Nelson's Illnesses 1780–1782', *Trafalgar Chronicle*, 12, 2002, 128–40

Hogg, O. F. G., *The Royal Arsenal: Its Background, Origin and Subsequent History*, 2 vols. (1963)

Holland Rose, J., 'British Rule in Corsica' in *Pitt and Napoleon: Essays and Letters* (1912), 60–78

Lord Hood and the Siege of Toulon (1922)

Holmes, Richard, *Coleridge: Darker Reflections* (1998)

Hoock, Holger, *The King's Artists: The Royal Academy of Arts and the Politics of British Culture 1760–1840* (Oxford, 2003)

Hood, Dorothy, *The Admirals Hood* (1941)

Hoon, E. E., *The Organization of the English Customs System 1696–1786* (1938, repr. 1968)

Horn, Pamela, *The Rural World 1780–1850: Social Change in the English Countryside* (1980)

Horsburgh, James, *The India Directory*, 2 vols. (1841 ed.)

Horsfield, John, *Art of Leadership in War: The Royal Navy from the Age of Nelson to the Second World War* (Westport, Conn., 1980)

Howarth, David, 'The Man Who Lost Trafalgar', *Mariner's Mirror*, 57, 1971, 361–77

Hughes, Edward (ed.), *The Private Correspondence of Admiral Lord Collingwood* (Navy Records Society, 98, 1957)

Hughes, Wayne P., *Fleet Tactics: Theory and Practice* (Annapolis, Maryland, 1986)

Hutchinson, William, *A Treatise on Naval Architecture* (Liverpool, 1794, repr. 1970)

Hydrographer of the Navy, *Baltic Pilot* (2001)

Africa Pilot (1982)

Ilchester, the Earl of (ed.), *The Journal of Elizabeth Lady Holland*, 2 vols. (1908)

Ingram, Edward, 'Illusions of Victory: The Nile, Copenhagen and Trafalgar Revisited', *Military Affairs*, 48, 1984, 140–43

Isaacson, Cecil J., *Nelson's Five Years on the Beach* (Fakenham, Norfolk, 1991, repr. 1996)

Jackson, Hilary W., *Cumby of the Bellerophon: A Hero of Trafalgar* (Durham, [n.d.])

James, William, *The Naval History of Great Britain*, 6 vols. (1878 ed.)

Jamieson, Alan, 'War in the Leeward Islands 1775–1783' (Ph.D., Cambridge, 1981)

A People of the Sea: The Maritime History of the Channel Islands (1986)

Jane, Charles W. E., *Shirley Heights: In Defence of Nelson's Dockyard* (Antigua, 1982)

Jenks, Timothy, 'Contesting the Hero: The Funeral of Admiral Lord Nelson', *Journal of British Studies*, 39, 2000, 422–53

Jennings, Louis J. (ed.), *The Croker Papers: Correspondence and Diaries of the Late Right Honourable John Wilson Croker* (1884)

Jesse, J. Heneage, *Memoirs of the Life and Reign of King George III*, 3 vols. (1867)

Jordan, Gerald, 'Mahan's *Life of Nelson*', *Northern Mariner*, 8, 1988, 39–49

Jordan, Gerald, and Rogers, Nicholas, 'Admirals as Heroes: Patriotism and Liberty in Hanoverian England', *Journal of British Studies*, 28, 1989, 201–4

Keevil, J. J., 'Leonard Gillespie, MD, 1758–1842', *Bulletin of the History of Medicine*, 28, 1954, 303–32

Kemble, James, *Idols and Invalids* (1933)

Kennedy, Ludovic, *Nelson and His Captains* (1951, rev. 1975)

Kent's *Shopkeepers' and Tradesmen's Assistant* (1799)

King, Dean, and Hattendorf, John B., '*Every Man Will Do His Duty*': An Anthology of First-hand Accounts from the Age of Nelson (New York, 1997)

Kirby, Brian S., 'Nelson and American Merchantmen in the West Indies 1784–1787', *Mariner's Mirror*, 75, 1989, 137–47

Knight, Carlo, 'The British at Naples in 1799', *Trafalgar Chronicle*, 11, 2001, 15–34

Knight, Cornelia, *Autobiography of Miss Cornelia Knight*, 2 vols. (1861)

Knight, Jane, 'Nelson and the Eastern Mediterranean 1803–1805', *Mariner's Mirror*, 91, May 2005

'Nelson's Old Lady: Merchant News as a Source of Intelligence, June–October 1796', *Journal for Maritime Research*, May 2005

Knight, Roger, 'Nelson and the Forest of Dean', *Mariner's Mirror*, 87, 2001, 88–92

Knox, Dudley (ed.), *Naval Documents Related to the Quasi-War between the United States and France: Naval Operations from February 1797 to October 1798* (Washington, DC, 1935)

Krajeski, Paul C., *In the Shadow of Nelson: The Naval Leadership of Admiral Sir Charles Cotton 1753–1812* (Westport, Conn., 2000)

Lambert, Andrew, *The Foundations of Naval History: John Knox Laughton, the Royal Navy and the Historical Profession* (1998)

'Sir William Cornwallis' in Richard Harding and Peter Lefevre (eds.), *The Precursors of Nelson* (2000), 353–75

(ed.), *Letters and Papers of Professor Sir John Knox Laughton 1830–1915* (Navy Records Society, 143, 2002)

Nelson: Britannia's God of War (2004)

Langford, Paul, *A Polite and Commercial People: England 1727–1783* (1989)

Laughton, J. K. (ed.), *Journal of Rear-Admiral Bartholomew James 1752–1828* (Navy Records Society, 6, 1896)

The Nelson Memorial: Nelson and His Companions in Arms (1896)

(ed.), *The Naval Miscellany*, I and II (Navy Records Society, 20, 40, 1901, 1912)

(ed.), *The Letters and Papers of Charles, Lord Barham*, 3 vols. (Navy Records Society, 32, 38, 39, 1907–11)

Laughton, L. G. Carr (ed.), *The Life of a Sea Officer: Jeffrey Baron de Raigersfeld, Rear-Admiral of the Red* (1929)

Lavery, Brian, *The Arming and Fitting of English Ships of War 1600–1815* (1987)
    'Carronades and Blomefield Guns: Developments in Naval Ordnance 1778–1805' in Robert D. Smith (ed.), *British Naval Armaments* (1989), 15–27
    Nelson's Navy: The Ships, Men and Organization 1793–1815 (1989)
    'The British Navy and Its Bases 1793–1815' in *Français et Anglais en Méditerranée 1789–1830* (Vincennes, 1992), 159–67
    (ed.), *Shipboard Life and Organization 1731–1815* (Navy Records Society, 138, 1998)
    Nelson and the Nile: The Naval War against Bonaparte 1798 (1998)
    'George Keith Elphinstone, Lord Keith' in Richard Harding and Peter Le Fevre, *The Precursors of Nelson* (2000), 377–399
    Nelson's Fleet at Trafalgar (2004)
Le Fevre, Peter, 'Little Merit will be Given to Me': Admiral Sir Hyde Parker (1739–1807) and the Diplomatic Build-up to the Battle' in Stephen Howarth (ed.), *Battle of Copenhagen: The Bicentennial International Naval Conference, Portsmouth, England 19 May 2001* (Shelton, Notts., 2003), 1–29
Le Fevre, Peter, and Harding, Richard (eds.), *The Precursors of Nelson* (2000)
Le Quesne, L. P., *Nelson Commemorated in Glass Pictures* (Woodbridge, Suffolk, 2001)
Lewis, Michael (ed.), *A Narrative of My Professional Adventures (1790–1839) by Sir William Henry Dillon, KCH, Vice-Admiral of the Red*, 2 vols. (Navy Records Society, 93, 97, 1956)
    A Social History of the Navy 1793–1815 (1960)
Lewis-Jones, Huw, 'Displaying Nelson: Navalism and "The Exhibition" of 1891', *Trafalgar Chronicle*, 14, 2004, 53–86
Lincoln, Margarette, *Representing the Royal Navy: British Sea Power 1750–1815* (2002)
Lindsay-MacDougall, K. F., 'The Nelson Manuscripts at the National Maritime Museum', *Mariner's Mirror*, 41, 1955, 227–32
Linebaugh, Peter, and Rediker, Marcus, *The Many-Headed Hydra: The Hidden History of the Revolutionary Atlantic* (2000)
Littlewood, Kevin, and Butler, Beverly, *Of Ships and Stars: Maritime Heritage and the Founding of the National Maritime Museum, Greenwich* (1998)
Lloyd, Christopher, *The Keith Papers*, Vols. II and III (Navy Records Society, 90, 96, 1950, 1955)
    'St Vincent and Nelson's Funeral', *Mariner's Mirror*, 53, 1967, 160
Lloyd, Christopher, and Anderson, R. C. (eds.), *A Memoir of James Trevenen* (Navy Records Society, 101, 1955)
Lloyd, Christopher, and Coulter, Jack S., *Medicine and the Royal Navy. Vol. III: 1714–1815* (1961)
Locker, Edward Hawke, *Memoirs of Celebrated Naval Commanders Illustrated from Original Pictures in the Naval Gallery* (1832), Chapter 16, 'William Locker'

Lockwood, Allison, 'Nelson as Seen by an American just before Trafalgar', *Nelson Dispatch*, 2, 1985, 33–5

Lodey, Joy, 'Joseph Emerson', *Nelson Dispatch*, 6, 1999, 434–5

Lovenorn, P. de, *Directions for the Kattegat* (Copenhagen, 1800)

Lowe, J. A., *Records of the Portsmouth Division of Marines 1764–1800* (Portsmouth Record Series, 1990)

Lyon, D. J., *The Sailing Navy List: All the Ships of the Royal Navy, Built, Purchased and Captured 1680–1860* (1993)

McCaig, A. D., ' "The Soul of Artillery": Congreve's Rockets and Their Later Effectiveness in Warfare', *Journal of the Society for Army Historical Research*, 78, 2000, 252–63

McCord, Norman, 'The Impress Service in North-east England during the Napoleonic War', *Mariner's Mirror*, 54, 1968, 163–80

MacDonald, Janet, 'Victualling the British Mediterranean Fleet, May 1803–June 1804' (MA, University of Greenwich, 2003)

Feeding Nelson's Navy: The True Story of Food at Sea in the Georgian Era (2004)

MacDougall, Philip, 'The Formative Years: Malta Dockyard 1800–1815', *Mariner's Mirror*, 73, 1987, 205–13

Mackay, Ruddock F., *Admiral Hawke* (1965)

'Lord St Vincent's Early Years', *Mariner's Mirror*, 76, 1990, 51–65

Mackesy, Piers, *War in the Mediterranean 1803–1810* (1957)

The War for America (1964)

Statesmen at War: The Strategy of Overthrow 1798–1799 (1974)

War without Victory: The Downfall of Pitt 1799–1802 (Oxford, 1984)

Macmillan's Magazine, June 1895

McNeil, Ian, *An Encyclopaedia of the History of Technology* (1990)

Madariaga, Salvador de, *The Fall of the Spanish Empire* (1947)

Maffeo, Steven E., *Most Secret and Confidential: Intelligence in the Age of Nelson* (2000)

Mafit, Burdett, and Bennett, Leslie H. (comps.), *Nelson's Watchdog: The Life of Sir Henry Blackwood* (Eugene, Oregon, 1998)

Mahan, A. T., *The Life of Nelson, the Embodiment of the Sea Power of Great Britain* (1899)

Malcolmson, Tom, 'An Aid to Nelson's Victory? A Description of the Harbour of Aboukir 1798', *Mariner's Mirror*, 84, 1998, 291–7

'The Visit to Fonthill: Nelson's Immersion in Folly', *Nelson Dispatch*, 7, 2000, 223–37

Malmesbury, Earl of (ed.), *Diaries and Correspondence of James Harris, First Earl of Malmesbury*, 4 vols. (1844)

Manning, Helen Taft, *British Colonial Government after the American Revolution 1782–1820* (New Haven, Conn., 1933, repr. 1966)

Marione, Patrick, 'A Great Coxcomb', *Trafalgar Chronicle*, 12, 2002, 8–38

Markham, Clements, *Correspondence of Admiral John Markham 1801–1807* (Navy Records Society, 28, 1904)

Mark-Wardlaw, W. Penrose, *At Sea with Nelson: Being the Life of William Mark, a Purser Who Served under Nelson* (1929)

Masefield, John, *Sea Life in Nelson's Time* (1905, 1937 ed.)

Matcham, M. Eyre, *The Nelsons of Burnham Thorpe: A Record of a Norfolk Family, Compiled from Unpublished Letters and Notebooks* (1911)

May, W. E., 'Nelson's Appointment to the Command of the *Albemarle*', *Mariner's Mirror*, 62, 1976, 133–4

Mead, H. P., 'Descriptions of Royal and Naval Signal colours 1702–1937', *Mariner's Mirror*, 37, 1951, 143–64; 38, 1952, 53–64

Merwe, Pieter van der, 'Nelson's Last Provision for Lady Hamilton 1805', *Mariner's Mirror*, 68, 1982, 42

Minto, Countess of, *Life and Letters of Sir Gilbert Elliot, First Earl of Minto, from 1751 to 1806*, 3 vols. (1874)

Monaque, Rémi, 'Latouche-Tréville: The Admiral Who Defied Nelson', *Mariner's Mirror*, 86, 2000, 272–84

'On Board HMS *Alexander* (1796–1799)', *Mariner's Mirror*, 89, 2003, 207–12

'Trafalgar 1805: estrategia, táctica y resultados' in Agustín Guimerá, Alberto Ramos, and Gonzalo Butrón (eds.), *Trafalgar y el mundo Atlántico* (Madrid, 2004), 161–75

Monk, W. F., *Britain in the Western Mediterranean* (1953)

Moriconi, Emilio J., 'Jervis and Nelson', *Nelson Dispatch*, 4, 1992, 84–91

'St Vincent, Pitt and the Libellers', *Nelson Dispatch*, 4, 1993, 188–96

Morrison, Alfred, *The Collection of Autograph Letters and Historical Documents Formed by Alfred Morrison: The Hamilton and Nelson Papers*, 2 vols. (privately printed, 1893–4)

Morriss, Roger, *The Royal Dockyards during the Revolutionary and Napoleonic Wars* (Leicester, 1983)

'Problems Affecting the Maintenance of the British Fleet in the Mediterranean 1793–1815' in *Français et Anglais en Méditerranée 1789–1830* (Vincennes, 1992), 171–80

Guide to British Naval Papers in North America (1994)

Nelson: The Life and Letters of a Hero (1996)

Cockburn and the British Navy in Transition: Admiral Sir George Cockburn 1772–1853 (1997)

(ed.), *The Channel Fleet and the Blockade of Brest 1793–1801* (Navy Records Society, 141, 2001)

'Practicality and Prejudice: The Blockade Strategy and Naval Medicine during the French Revolutionary War 1793–1801' in Pieter van der Merwe (ed.), *Science and the French and British Navies 1700–1850* (2003), 77–87

Naval Power and British Culture 1760–1859 (Aldershot, Hants, 2004)

Moseley, Benjamin, *A Treatise on Tropical Diseases and on the Climate of the West Indies* (1787)

Mulvey-Roberts, Marie, 'A Physic against Death: Eternal Life and the Enlightenment' in Marie Mulvey-Roberts and Roy Porter (eds.), *Literature and Medicine in the Eighteenth Century* (1994), 153–67

Naish, G. P. B. (ed.), *Nelson's Letters to His Wife and Other Documents 1785–1831* (1958)

Namier, Lewis, and Brooks, John, *The House of Commons 1754–1790*, 3 vols. (1985)

Nash, Michael, 'Building a Nelson Library' in Colin White (ed.), *The Nelson Companion* (1995)

Nicolas, Nicholas Harris, *The Dispatches and Letters of Vice-Admiral Lord Viscount Nelson*, 7 vols. (1846, repr. 1998)

O'Byrne, William P., *A Naval Biographical Dictionary* (1849)

Oman, Carola, *Nelson* (1946, repr. 1996)

Orde, Denis A., *Nelson's Mediterranean Command: Concerning Pride, Preferment and Prize Money* (Edinburgh, 1997)

O'Shaughnessy, Andrew Jackson, *An Empire Divided: The American Revolution and the British Caribbean* (Philadelphia, 2000)

Ostergard, Derek E., *William Beckford 1760–1844: An Eye for the Magnificent* (2001)

Owen, C. H. H., 'Letters from Vice-Admiral Lord Collingwood 1794–1809' in Michael Duffy (ed.), *The Naval Miscellany*, VI (Navy Records Society, 146, 2003), 149–219

Oxford Dictionary of National Biography (2004)

Padfield, Peter, *Maritime Power and the Struggle for Freedom: Naval Campaigns that Shaped the Modern World* (2003)

Paget, Sir Augustus, *The Paget Papers: Diplomatic and Other Correspondence of the Right Honourable Sir Arthur Paget, GCB, 1794–1807* (1896)

Palmer, M. A. J., 'Sir John's Victory: The Battle of Cape St Vincent Reconsidered', *Mariner's Mirror*, 77, 1991, 31–46

'The Soul's Right Hand: Command and Control in the Age of Fighting Sail', *Journal of Military History*, 61, 1997, 679–705

Panzac, Daniel, *Les Corsaires barbaresque: La Fin d'une épopée* (1999)

Pares, Richard, *War and Trade in the West Indies 1739–1763* (1936)

Parkinson, C. Northcote (ed.), *The Trade Winds: A Study of British Overseas Trade during the French Wars 1793–1815* (1948)

Britannia Rules: The Classic Age of Naval History 1793–1815 (1977, repr. 1987)

Parry, Ann, *The Admirals Fremantle 1788–1920* (1971)

Parson, Abraham, *Travels in Asia and Africa* (1808)

Parsons, George, *Nelson Reminiscences: Leaves from Memory's Log* (1843, repr. 1976)

Pasley, Rodney M. S. (ed.), *Private Sea Journals 1778–1782* (1931)

Pearsall, Alan, 'British Convoys in the North Sea 1781–1782' in W. Minchinton (ed.), *Britain and the Northern Seas: Some Essays* (1988), 105–12

Perrin, W. G. (ed.), *Letters and Papers of Admiral Viscount Keith*, Vol. I (Navy Records Society, 62, 1927)

'Letters of Lord Nelson 1804–5', *The Naval Miscellany*, III (Navy Records Society, 63, 1928), 175–90

Pettigrew, Thomas, *Memoirs of the Life of Vice-Admiral Lord Nelson*, 2 vols., (1849)

Phillimore, Rear-Admiral Augustus, *The Life of Admiral of the Fleet Sir William Parker, Bart., GCB, from 1781 to 1866*, 3 vols. (1876)

Phillips, Ivan Lloyd, 'Lord Barham at the Admiralty 1805–6', *Mariner's Mirror*, 64, 1978, 217–33

Phipps, Constantine John, *A Voyage towards the North Pole, Undertaken by His Majesty's Command, 1773* (1774)

Tom Pocock, *Remember Nelson: The Life of Captain Sir William Hoste* (1977)

The Young Nelson in the Americas (1980)

Horatio Nelson (1987)

A Thirst for Glory: The Life of Admiral Sir Sidney Smith (1998)

Nelson's Women (1999)

'Lady Hamilton's Twins', *Mariner's Mirror*, 87, 2001, 97

'The Summer of 1801: Nelson at Deal and Boulogne', *Nelson Dispatch*, 7, 2001, 451–9

The Terror before Trafalgar (2002)

Pope, Dudley, 'News of Trafalgar', *Mariner's Mirror*, 54, 1968, 303

The Great Gamble: Nelson at Copenhagen (1972)

Prentice, Rina, *A Celebration of the Sea* (1994)

Pritchard, James, *Louis XV's Navy 1748–1762. A Study of Organization and Administration* (Kingston and Montreal, 1987)

Pryce-Lewis, O., 'Horatio Nelson and Simons Bay', *Mariner's Mirror*, 72, 1986, 355–9

Pugh, P. D. Gordon, *Nelson and His Surgeons* (Edinburgh, 1968)

Quennell, Peter (ed.), *Memoirs of William Hickey* (1975)

Rahn Phillips, Carla, 'Recruiting Sailors in Eighteenth-century Spain', *Mariner's Mirror*, 2001, 87, 420–45

Ralfe, J., *Sir Robert Waller Otway, Bart., KCB, 1771–1840: Historical Memoir* (1840)

Ram, Charley, 'Letters of William Andrew Ram, Killed at Trafalgar', *Nelson Dispatch*, 6, 184–7

Ramsay, Malcolm, 'Nelson, Carse and Eighteenth-century Justice', *Mariner's Mirror*, 69, 1979, 177

Ranft, Bryan McL., 'Prince William and Lieutenant Schomberg' in Christopher Lloyd (ed.), *The Naval Miscellany*, IV (Navy Records Society, 92, 1952), 267–93

Rawson, Geoffrey (ed.), *Letters from Lord Nelson* (1949)
  (ed.), *Nelson's Letters from the Leeward Islands* (1953)
Rees, J. F., *The Story of Milford (Milford Haven)* (Cardiff, 1954)
Richardson, Patricia, 'Captain William Locker, Royal Navy', *Nelson Dispatch* 3,
  1998, 52–8
Richmond, H. W., *The Private Papers of George, Second Earl Spencer*, Vols. III
  and IV (Navy Records Society, 58, 59, 1924)
  The Navy in India (1931)
Robertson, E. Arnot, *The Spanish Town Papers* (1959)
Robertson, F. L., *The Evolution of Naval Armament* (1921, repr. 1968)
Robertson, John, 'Enlightenment and Revolution: Naples 1799' in *Transactions
  of the Royal Historical Society* (2000), 17–44
Robinson, D. E., 'Secret of British Power in the Age of Sail: Admiralty Records
  of the Coasting Fleet', *American Neptune*, 48, 1988, 5–21
Rodger, N. A. M., *The Wooden World: An Anatomy of the Georgian Navy* (1986)
  'The Inner Life of the Navy 1750–1800: Change or Decay?' in *Les Empires en
  Guerres et Paix 1660–1815* (Vincennes, 1987), 171–9
  'Lieutenant's Sea-time and Age', *Mariner's Mirror*, 75, 1989, 269–72
  '"A little navy of your own making." Admiral Boscawen and the Cornish
  Connection in the Royal Navy' in Michael Duffy (ed.), *Parameters of British
  Naval Power 1650–1850* (Exeter, 1992), 82–92
  The Insatiable Earl: A Life of John Montagu, Fourth Earl of Sandwich (1993)
  'The Naval Chaplain in the Eighteenth Century', *British Journal for Eighteenth-
  century Studies*, 18, 1995, 33–45
  'Commissioned Officers' Careers in the Royal Navy 1690–1815', *Journal for
  Maritime Research*, July 2001, 1–29
  'Honour and Duty at Sea 1660–1815', *Bulletin of the Institute of Historical
  Research*, 75, 2002, 425–47
  'Navies and the Enlightenment' in Pieter van der Merwe (ed.), *Science and the
  French and British Navies 1700–1850* (2003)
  'Image and Reality in Eighteenth-century Naval Tactics', *Mariner's Mirror*, 89,
  2003, 280–96
  The Command of the Ocean (2004)
Rodriguez, Gonzáles, Agustín, 'Los españols en Trafalgar: navíos, cañones,
  hombres y una alianza problemática' in Agustín Guimerá, Alberto Ramos,
  and Gonzalo Butrón (eds.), *Trafalgar y el mundo Atlántico* (Madrid, 2004),
  195–214
Rosebery, Earl of (ed.), *The Windham Papers*, 2 vols. (1913)
Ross, Sir John, *Memoirs and Correspondence of Admiral Lord de Saumarez*,
  2 vols. (1838)
Rowbotham, W. B., 'The West Indies Hurricanes of October 1780', *Journal of
  the Royal United Services Institution*, 1961, 573–84
Russell, Jack, *Nelson and the Hamiltons* (1969)

Russell, W. Clark, *Horatio Nelson and the Naval Supremacy of England* (1890)

Rutherford, J. H. (ed.), *The Rutherfords of That Ilk and Their Cadets* (Edinburgh, 1884)

Ryan, A. N., 'The Royal Navy and the Blockade of Brest 1689–1815: Theory and Practice' in Martine Acerra, Jose Merino, and Jean Meyer (eds.), *Les Marines de Guerre Européennes XVII–XVIII siècles* (Paris, 1985), 175–93

'An Act of Parliament Cannot Make Men: The Quota Acts of 1795–1796', in *Les Empires en Guerre et Paix 1793–1860* (Vincennes, 1990), 103–4

'In Search of Bruix 1799' in *Français et Anglais en Méditerranée 1789–1830* (Vincennes, 1992), 81–90

Sartori, Claudio, *I Libretti italiani a stampa dalle origini al 1800: Catalogo analitico con 16 indici: Indice dei cantanti* (Cuneo, Italy, 1994)

Savours, Ann, 'A Very Interesting Point in Geography: The 1773 Phipps Expedition towards the North Pole', *Arctic*, 1984, 402–28

Schofield, Philip, 'British Politicians and French Arms: The Ideological War of 1793–1795', *History*, 77, 1992, 183–201

Schom, Alan, *Trafalgar: Countdown to Battle 1803–1805* (1990)

Schroeder, Paul W., *The Transformation of European Politics 1768–1848* (Oxford, 1994)

Scott, A. J., *Recollections of the Life of the Reverend A. J. Scott, D D, Lord Nelson's Chaplain* (1842, repr. 2003 as *Nelson's Spy? The Life of Alexander Scott*)

Sermoneta, Duchessa di, *The Locks of Norbury: The Story of a Remarkable Family in the Eighteenth and Nineteenth Centuries* (1940)

Le Service historique de la Marine, *Pierres de Mer: La Patrimoine immobilier de la Marine nationale* (Vincennes, 1996)

Shannon, David, ' "God Blessed our Endeavours with a great Victory": The story of Nelson's Nile Dispatches to Bombay', *Nelson Dispatch*, 6, 1998, 285–8

Sheffield, A. M., 'In Defence of Man', *Mariner's Mirror*, 20, 1934, 187–98

Sichel, Walter (ed.), *The Glenbervie Journals* (1910)

Simms, Brendan, 'Continental Analogies with 1798: Revolution or Counter-revolution?' in Thomas Bartlett *et al.*, *1798: A Bicentenary Perspective* (Dublin, 1998), 577–95

Slope, Nick, 'The Trials of Nelson: Nelson's "Camel" ', *Nelson Dispatch*, 7, 2001, 436–45

'The Trials of Nelson: Nelson and the *Emerald*', *Nelson Dispatch*, 8, 2002, 612–17

Southey, Robert, *The Life of Nelson* (1831, 1873 eds.)

Sparrow, Elizabeth, *Secret Service: British Agents in France 1792–1815* (Woodbridge, Suffolk, 1999)

Spinney, J. D., 'Nelson at Santa Cruz', *Mariner's Mirror*, 45, 1959, 207–23

'By God, I'll Not Lose Hardy', *Mariner's Mirror*, 55, 1969, 115–16

'Nelson at Port Agro', *Mariner's Mirror*, 65, 1979, 90–91

Stammers, Michael, 'The Handmaiden and Victim of Agriculture: The Port of

Wells-next-the-Sea, Norfolk, in the Eighteenth and Nineteenth Centuries', *Mariner's Mirror*, 86, 2000, 60–63

Starkey, David J., 'War and the Market for Seafarers in Britain 1736–1792', in Lewis R. Fischer and Helge W. Nordvik, *Shipping and Trade 1750–1950: Essays in International Economic History* (1990), 25–42

Steel, David, *Original and Correct List of the Royal Navy* (1796)

Steele, Sir Robert, *The Marine Officer; or, Sketches of Service* (1840)

[Stewart, Sir William], *Cumloden Papers* (privately printed, Edinburgh, 1871)

Stirling, A. M. W., *Coke of Norfolk and His Friends* (1907)

   The Hothams (1908)

   Pages and Portraits from the Past: Being the Private Papers of Sir William Hotham, GCB, Admiral of the Red (1919)

Sturges Jackson, T., *Logs of the Great Sea Fights 1794–1805*, 2 vols. (Navy Records Society, 16, 18, 1899, 1900)

Sugden, John, 'Lord Nelson and the Film Industry', *Nelson Dispatch*, 2, 1986, 83–8

   'Captain George Andrews, *c.* 1767–1810: A Protégé of Nelson', *Mariner's Mirror*, 81, 1995, 85–8

   Nelson: A Dream of Glory (2004)

Sutton, P. C., 'Nationalistic Controversy over Nelson Monuments', *Nelson Dispatch*, 2, 1987, 191–8

Syrett, David, *Shipping and the American War 1775–1783: A Study of British Transport Organization* (1970)

   'The Organization of British Trade Convoys 1775–1783', *Mariner's Mirror*, 62, 1976, 169–81

   The Royal Navy in European Waters during the American Revolutionary War (1998)

   'Admiral Rodney, Patronage and the Leeward Islands Station Squadron 1780–1782', *Mariner's Mirror*, 85, 1999, 411–20

   'Nelson's Uncle: Captain Maurice Suckling, RN', *Mariner's Mirror*, 88, 2002, 33–40

Syrett, David and Dinardo, Richard, *The Commissioned Sea Officers of the Royal Navy 1660–1815* (Navy Records Society, Occasional Publication 1, 1994)

Talbott, John E., *The Pen and Ink Sailor: Charles Middleton and the King's Navy 1778–1813* (1998)

Taylor, Ernest, *The Taylor Papers: Being a Record of Certain Reminiscences, Letters, and Journals in the Life of Lieutenant-General Sir Herbert Taylor, GCB, GCH* (1913)

Thorne, R. G., *The House of Commons 1790–1820*, 5 vols. (1980)

Thursfield, H. G. (ed.), *Five Naval Journals 1789–1817* (Navy Records Society, 91, 1951)

Tooke, Thomas, *Thoughts and Details on the High and Long Prices of the Last Thirty Years, from 1793 to 1822* (1824 ed.)

Tracy, Nicholas, *Navies, Deterrence and American Independence: Britain and Seapower in the 1760s and 1770s* (1988)

'Sir Robert Calder's Action', *Mariner's Mirror*, 77, 1991, 259–70

Nelson's Battles: The Art of Victory in the Age of Sail (1996)

(ed.), *The Naval Chronicle: The Contemporary Record of the Royal Navy at War*, 5 vols. (1998–9)

The Battle of Copenhagen 2 April 1801 (Shelton, Notts., 2003)

Trench, R. Chevenix, *Remains of the Late Mrs Richard Trench* (1862)

Tunstall, Brian, *Naval Warfare in the Age of Sail: The Evolution of Fighting Tactics 1650–1815* (ed.), Nicholas Tracy (1990)

Unsworth, Barry, *Losing Nelson* (1999)

Vane, Charles (ed.), *Memoirs and Correspondence of Viscount Castlereagh, Second Marquis of Londonderry* (4 vols. first series, 1848; 4 vols., second series, 1851)

Vaughan, H. R. H., 'The Old Dockyard at English Harbour', *Mariner's Mirror*, II, 1925, 301–6

Vigo, Pietro, *Nelson a Livorno: Episodio della guerra tra Francia e Inghilliterra sul finire del XVIII secolo* (Sienna, 1903)

Vincent, Edgar, *Nelson: Love and Fame* (2003)

Walder, David, *Nelson* (1978)

Walker, Richard, *The Nelson Portraits* (1998)

Ware, Chris, 'Toulon 1793' in *Français et Anglais en Méditerranée 1789–1830* (Vincennes, 1992), 23–37

Wareham, Tom, *The Star Captains: Frigate Command in the Napoleonic Wars* (2001)

Warner, Oliver, *A Portrait of Lord Nelson* (1958)

'Nelson's Leghorn Friend', *Mariner's Mirror*, 46, 1960, 63

The Life and Letters of Vice-Admiral Lord Collingwood (Oxford, 1968)

(ed.), *Nelson's Last Diary: A Facsimile* (Kent State University Press, Ohio, 1971)

Watt, Sir James, 'Naval Surgery in the Time of Nelson' in Nicholas Tracy (ed.), *The Age of Sail* (2002), 25–33

Webb, Paul, 'The Naval Aspects of the Nootka Sound Crisis', *Mariner's Mirror*, 61, 1975, 133–54

'The Rebuilding and Repairing of the Fleet 1783–1793', *Bulletin of the Institute of Historical Research*, 50, 1977, 194–209

'Construction, Repair and Maintenance in the Battle Fleet of the Royal Navy 1793–1815' in Jeremy Black and Philip Woodfine (eds.), *The British Navy and the Use of Naval Power in the Eighteenth Century* (Leicester, 1988), 207–19

'British Squadrons in North American Waters 1783–1793', *Northern Mariner*, 5, 1995, 19–34

'The Frigate Situation of the Royal Navy 1793–1805', *Mariner's Mirror*, 82, 1996, 28–40

Wheeler, Dennis, 'The Weather of the European Atlantic Seaboard during October 1805: An Exercise in Historical Climatology', *Climatic Change*, 48, 2001, 361–85

White, Colin, *The Nelson Companion* (1995)

'An Eyewitness Account of the Battle of Cape St Vincent, *Trafalgar Chronicle*, 7, 1997, 52–8

1797: Nelson's Year of Destiny (Stroud, Glos., 1998)

'The Battle of Cape St Vincent, 14 February 1797' in Stephen Howarth (ed.), *Battle of Cape St Vincent: Two Hundred Years* (Shelton, Notts., 1998) 52–68

'Nelson Ashore' in Peter Hore (ed.), *Seapower Ashore: Two Hundred Years of Royal Naval Operations on Land* (2001), 53–78

The Nelson Encyclopaedia (2002)

'Nelson's Tour of South Wales and the Midlands 1802', *Trafalgar Chronicle*, 12, 2002, 1–7

'The View from Nelson's Quarterdeck' in Stephen Howarth (ed.), *Battle of Copenhagen 1801: Two Hundred Years* (Shelton, Notts., 2003), 43–62

'The Public Order Book of Vice-Admiral Lord Nelson, Commander-in-Chief of a Squadron of Ships and Vessels Employed on a Particular Service, July– October 1801' in Michael Duffy (ed.), *The Naval Miscellany*, VI (Navy Records Society, 146, 2003), 221–55

'A Public Argument: Nelson and His Captains Discuss the Fate of the Neapolitan Jacobins', *Trafalgar Chronicle*, 13, 2003, 57–60

' "El toque Nelson": la evolución de las tácticas de Nelson en Trafalgar' in Agustín Guimerá, Alberto Ramos and Gonzalo Butrón (eds.), *Trafalgar y el Mundo Atlántico* (Madrid, 2004), 145–60

White's *Norfolk Directory* (1845)

Wilkinson, Clive, 'The Nelson Network', *Nelson Dispatch*, 4, 1993, 231–4; 5, 1994, 37–42

Willan, T. S., *The English Coasting Trade 1600–1750* (1961)

Williamson, Tom, *The Transformation of Rural England: Farming and the Landscape 1700–1870* (Exeter, 2002)

Zulueta, Julian de, 'Trafalgar – The Spanish View', *Mariner's Mirror*, 66, 1980, 293–318

Notes

ABBREVIATIONS

BL	British Library
Bucks.	Centre for Buckinghamshire Studies, Aylesbury
Clements	William L. Clements Library, University of Michigan
DRO	Devon Record Office
Houghton	Houghton Library, Harvard University
Huntington	Huntington Library, San Marino, California
Monmouth	Nelson Museum, Monmouth
NAS	National Archives of Scotland
NMM	National Maritime Museum, Greenwich
NRO	Norfolk Record Office
RNM	Royal Naval Museum, Portsmouth
(UK)NA: PRO	National Archives, Public Record Office
Wellcome	Wellcome Library for the History and Understanding of Medicine, London

Introduction

1. Barrow, *Anson*, 404; quoted in C. I. Hamilton, 388.
2. Heath, unpaginated.
3. Nash, 178.
4. Cowie, *Lord Nelson 1758–1805: A Bibliography* (1990).
5. Lewis, *Dillon Narrative*, II, 52.
6. Czisnik, 'Image and Icon'. Chapters 1, 3 and Appendix B contain the most rigorous analysis of these sources.
7. Aspinall, *Correspondence of Prince of Wales*, V, 342–3, Earl Nelson's memorandum, 16 Feb. 1806.
8. Coleman, 2–3, 338.
9. James, II, 204.
10. James, II, 347. James includes Robert Southey in this criticism; see Chapter 31.

11. Steele, 141. I owe this amusing reference to Professor Nicholas Rodger.
12. C. I. Hamilton, 382.
13. Czisnik, 'Image and Icon', 456–9; Nash, 183–5.
14. BL, Add. MSS 40560, 18 Feb. 1845, Croker to Peel; 21 Feb. 1845, Peel to Croker.
15. Lambert, *Foundations*, Chapter 7; *Laughton Papers*, Section 4.
16. Lindsay-MacDougall (1955).
17. Southey, 19; Clark Russell, 5; Oman, 11; Warner, 12; Pocock, 7; Hibbert, 9.
18. Harrison, *Life*, 1, 12, gives the most accurate account.
19. (UK) NA: PRO, ADM 51/763, *Raisonable*'s log.
20. (UK) NA: PRO, ADM 36/7669, muster book.
21. Barker, 95.
22. Carr Laughton, xi.
23. Michael Lewis in Geoffrey Rawson, *Leeward Islands Letters* (1953), 18.
24. Unsworth, *Losing Nelson* (1999), 304.

Prologue

1. NMM, CRK/9/65.
2. (UK) NA: PRO, ADM 52/3055.
3. NMM, TUN/20.
4. Ross, I, 215n.
5. James, II, 182.
6. Lavery, *Arming and Fitting*, 44–7.
7. Lavery, *Nile*, 59, quoting (UK)NA: PRO, ADM 95/70; also ADM 160/150, table of the 'Weight of Metal' of French and English guns.
8. Tracy, *Naval Chronicle*, II, 266n., following the description of Captain Hallowell of the *Swiftsure*.
9. See Chapter 18.
10. Stirling, *Pages and Portraits*, 240.
11. Parsons, *Reminiscences*, 12.
12. Rodger, 'Honour and Duty', 445; *Command of the Ocean*, 439.
13. Stirling, *Pages and Portraits*, 240.
14. Wareham, 162–3, describes this quality of detachment in action in the elite frigate captains in the 1790s.
15. Tracy, *Naval Chronicle*, II, 160.
16. Coleridge, I, 572.

I YOUTH AND DISAPPOINTMENT 1758–1793

1 Burnham Thorpe

1. Rawson, *Letters from Lord Nelson*, 9.
2. White's *Norfolk Directory*, 662–3.
3. (UK)NA: PRO, ADM 1/5358, 8 Sept. 1801, Nelson to Maurice William Suckling's court martial; NMM, CRK/12/59, 29 Aug. 1801, Captain Shire of the *Lynx* to Nelson.
4. Williamson, 6, estimates from 25 to 50 bushels an acre between 1720 and 1840.
5. Stammers, 61. Exports of malt from Wells doubled between 1727 and 1750, when it stood at 106, 690 quarters.
6. Kent's *Shopkeepers' and Tradesmen's Assistant* (1799) notes that the Wells packet left from Symond's and Harrison's wharves, regularity not recorded.
7. Willan, 116, 144.
8. Langford, 396–403.
9. Beresford, 117.
10. NRO, PD 571/2 Burnham Thorpe records.
11. White's *Norfolk Directory*, 663; in 1841 Burnham Thorpe had a population of 396.
12. Williamson, 80, 83.
13. White's *Norfolk Directory*, 665. Sainfoin (modern spelling) is a herb grown for forage.
14. Horn, 34–5.
15. Davidoff and Hall, 24.
16. RNM, MS 1957/85, fol. 7.
17. M. Eyre Matcham, 20.
18. Oman, 39–40.
19. Morrison, II, 188 [3 May 1801], William Nelson to Nelson.
20. RNM, MS 1957/85.
21. NRO, PR Burnham Thorpe records.
22. Williamson, 169–70.
23. Nicolas, I, 294, 10 Dec. 1792, Nelson to Prince William Henry, included a detailed analysis of a farm labourer's wages.
24. NMM, CRK/12/57, 29 Aug. 1801, Alex Shire, captain of the *Lynx*, to Nelson.
25. Beresford, 127, 22 May 1779; 171, 14 Aug. 1783.
26. Beresford, 322. Woodforde's entry for 20 Mar. 1791: 'The small-Pox being at present in every part of the Parish by inoculation etc.'
27. *Royal Kalendars*; Hoon, 131.

28. Oman, 26.

29. RNM, MS 1957/85.

30. Syrett, 'Suckling', 33–6.

31. Nicolas, I, 15–17.

32. Eyre Matcham, 20.

33. NRO, MC 20/48, 29 Sept. 1802, Levett Hanson to Nelson.

34. Nicolas, V, 238, 8 Oct. 1803, to Hugh Elliot; Burnham Thorpe parish church [Nicolas, VI, 18], 14 May 1804, Nelson to Dean Allott.

35. Vincent, 10–13.

36. NMM, DAV/2, Apr. 1801, Frances Nelson to Alexander Davison.

2   The Navy in 1771

1. Rodger, 'Honour and Duty', quoting Nicolas, VII, ccxiv.

2. Tracy, *Navies and Deterrence*, 95–8.

3. Beaglehole, *Cook Journals*. I, 477n.

4. Baugh, 'Navy as Institution', 121, 123; Rodger, *Insatiable Earl*, 131–3; Tracy, *Navies and Deterrence*, 100–117.

5. Baugh, 'Navy as Institution', 156.

6. Rodger, 'Commissioned Officers', 14.

7. Rodger, 'Honour and Duty', 425.

8. Rodger, 'Inner Life of the Navy', 172.

9. NMM, SAN/V/3, 4; SAN/3.

10. Analysis in Rodger, *Insatiable Earl*, 191.

11. Barrow, *Life of Howe*, 182.

12. Falconer, xxiv.

13. Nelson wrote an interesting letter when a junior captain about his problems with his midshipmen on board the *Albemarle* (Nicolas, I, 52–3); see also L. G. Carr Laughton, *Raigersfeld*, 26.

14. Masefield, *Sea Life*, 79.

15. Wareham, 203; Lavery, *Shipboard Life*, 263, quoting from 'A Captain in the Royal Navy' [John Davie], *Observations and Instructions* (1804).

16. An order by Howe of 1776, quoted in Lavery, *Shipboard Life*, 72.

17. Huntington Library, HO 121, 19 Dec. 1792.

18. Huntington Library, STG 156 (49), Sir Frederick Maitland to Thomas Grenville, 4 Nov. 1806.

19. Carr Laughton, *Raigersfeld*, 36.

20. NMM, BRP/6, 31 Dec. 1785, 20 Dec. 1787.

21. Nicolas, I, 249, 22 July 1787, Nelson to the earl of Cork.

22. They were *Raisonable, Triumph, Worcester, Bristol*. See 'Nelson's Ships' section.

23. Rodger, *Insatiable Earl*, 172, quoting John Brown, *An Estimate of the Manners and Principles of the Times* (1757–8), I, 58.

24. Lowe, lvii.

25. Rodger, 'Honour and Duty', 346, quoting Richmond, *Spencer Papers*, IV, 23, 24 Dec. 1800, St Vincent to Spencer.

26. Rodger, 'Honour and Duty', 431.

27. Hill, *Prizes of War*, 9.

28. Wareham, 136.

29. Mahan, 31–2; Oman, 49.

30. Nicolas, I, 56, 28 Jan. 1781, to William Nelson.

31. Nicolas, I, 290, 5 Feb. 1792, to William Nelson.

32. NMM, HOO/2, 2 Aug. 1784, Hood to Prince William Henry. I owe this reference to Daniel Baugh.

33. BL, Add. MSS 34903, 18 June 1773.

34. Baugh, 'Navy as Institution', 154. For the resentments, duels and insults in the French Navy, and the attempts to stop the problem, see Pritchard, Chapters 3 and 4.

35. Syrett, 'Suckling', 36–9.

36. NMM, SAN/3, fol. 53.

37. NMM, CAD/D/11, 88.

38. Hoon, 290–91; Brewer, 101–34.

39. Baugh, 'Maritime Strength', 195, quoting Thomas Lediard, *The Naval History of England* (1735), Preface.

40. Starkey, 'Seafarers', 40; Robinson, 'Coasting Fleet', 5–21.

41. Acerra and Meyer, 28; Cormack, 25.

42. Rahn Phillips, 436.

43. Starkey, 39.

44. (UK)NA: PRO, ADM 1/241, 23 Sept. 1778, Admiral Parker to Admiralty. One of them was the *Minerva* frigate.

45. Rodger, *Wooden World*, 206–7.

46. Byrn, 186.

47. Mahan, 85; Pocock, 104. See Chapter 9.

48. Rodger, in Duffy, *Parameters*, 82–92. Local recruiting by captains began to die out by the end of the century.

49. See Chapter 4.

3 Horace Nelson, Midshipman

1. Rawson, *Letters*, 10.

2. NMM, ADM/L/R/20, 23 Sept. 1771.

3. Hague, 198.

4. For the accidental burning of the *Glasgow* and Nelson's role in saving her crew, see Chapter 4.

5. NMM, ADM L/R/20, 23–25 Apr. 1771.

6. (UK) NA: PRO, ADM 36/7669.

7. Syrett, 'Suckling', 37.

8. (UK) NA: PRO ADM 36/7689; *Lloyd's List*, 21 July 1772. Rathbone is spelt 'Rathborne', but there is no other master's name remotely similar.

9. RNM, MS 1957/850.

10. 'Sketch of My Life', Rawson, *Letters*, 9.

11. NMM, ADM/L/T/268, lieutenant's log of the *Triumph*.

12. NMM, SAN/V/3. Suckling requested that the *Raisonable* be kept at Chatham as a guard ship.

13. NMM, ADM/L/T/268.

14. 'Sketch of My Life', Rawson, *Letters*, 9.

15. NMM, ADM/L/T/268, 29 Sept., 16 Oct., 23, 26 Nov. 1772, 21 Jan. 1773; 'Sketch of My Life', Rawson, *Letters*, 9–10.

16. (UK) NA: PRO ADM 2/98, 16 Apr. 1773, quoted in Savours, 408.

17. (UK)NA: ADM 36/7567, 11 May 1773.

18. Rosebery, I, 11.

19. (UK) NA: ADM 51/167, 2 June 1773, quoted in Savours, 411.

20. (UK) NA: PRO, ADM 52/1639, 8–10 July 1773.

21. Phipps, 42.

22. Anonymous *Journal*, published in 1774, 55–6; quoted in Savours, 414–15; this author thinks that the most likely author was the *Carcass*'s surgeon, William Wallis.

23. Quoted in Savours, 415–16.

24. (UK)NA: PRO, ADM 55/12, 1 Aug. 1773.

25. (UK)NA: PRO, ADM 55/12, 5 Aug. 1773.

26. (UK)NA: PRO, ADM/1639, 6–8 Aug. 1773.

27. (UK) NA: PRO, ADM 51/167, quoted in Savours, 418.

28. 'Sketch of My Life', Rawson, *Letters*, 10.

29. Savours, 420, quoting the anonymous *Journal*, 86.

30. (UK) NA: PRO, ADM 36/7567.

31. Savours, 419, quoting the anonymous *Journal*, 78–9.

32. NMM, SAN/F/34/6, 11 Mar. 1774.

33. (UK) NA: PRO, ADM 51/883, 28 Apr. 1774.

34. NMM, SAN/F/34/6, 11 Mar. 1774, Hughes to Sandwich.

35. (UK) NA: PRO, ADM 51/883, 4–23 Mar., 21 Oct., 29 Nov. 1774.

36. NMM, SAN/F/34/6, 11 Mar. 1774, Hughes to Sandwich.

37. (UK) NA: PRO, ADM 12/27B, 30 May 1774, court martial records; more remarkable are the deadpan entries made by Drummond himself in the lieutenant's log (NMM, ADM/L/S/222, 26 Apr., 31 May 1774).

38. Richmond, *Navy in India*, 76.

39. (UK) NA: PRO, ADM 51/883, 19 Nov. 1773–31 Mar. 1776. On 16 Feb. a three-hour eclipse of the moon was noted in the log: 'this eclipse was not visible in England.'

40. (UK) NA: PRO, ADM 51/883, 19 Feb. (nautical day), 20 Feb. 1775.

41. 'Sketch of My Life', Rawson, *Letters*, 10.

42. Parsons, 201–5; Damer-Powell, 98.

43. Nicolas, III, 475, Appendix, extract from Cornelia Knight's journal.

44. (UK) NA: PRO, ADM 34/749. After Nelson's departure the *Seahorse* went further east, calling at Macao and Canton, reaching Madras in January 1777 and England later that year.

45. 'Sketch of My Life', Rawson, *Letters*, 10.

46. (UK) NA: PRO, ADM 36/5783.

47. Steel's *Navy List* (1787). In the same list, by coincidence, Nelson was 175 places from the top of the list.

48. (UK) NA: PRO, ADM 51/259, 16 Sept. 1776; ADM 36/7583.

49. Syrett, 'Organization of Convoy', 170–73.

50. (UK) NA: PRO, ADM 107/6, fol. 386, Nelson's Lieutenant's Passing Certificate. It is printed in full in Nicolas, I, 21.

51. (UK) NA: PRO, ADM 1/952, 29 Sept. 1776.

52. Nicolas, I, 6, n. 3.

53. Nicolas, I, 6, n. 3. Suckling was MP for Portsmouth 18 May 1776 to his death, 14 July 1778 (Namier and Brooke, III, 508).

54. (UK)NA: PRO, ADM 36/8677.

55. (UK) NA: PRO, ADM 1/2389, 19 July 1776, Robinson to Philip Stephens.

56. Baugh, 'British Naval Failure', 242–3.

57. (UK) NA: PRO, ADM 1/2389, Robinson to the Admiralty, list of ships in the convoy.

58. (UK) NA: PRO, ADM 51/1085.

59. Nicolas, I, 6, n. 3, diary entry for 11 Jan. See also BL, Add. MSS 34953, 4 Oct. 1803, Nelson to Duff, 'Next January is 27 years since our first acquaintance . . .'

60. (UK) NA: PRO, ADM 1/2390, 2 Apr. 1777, Robinson to Stephens.

61. (UK) NA: PRO, ADM 51/1085, 15–16 Feb.

62. (UK) NA: PRO, ADM 1/2390, 2 Apr. 1777.

63. (UK) NA: PRO, ADM 1/2390, 2 Apr. 1777.

64. (UK) NA: PRO, ADM 107/6.

65. (UK) NA: PRO, ADM 36/10047. The day after that he wrote his first official letter to the Admiralty, requesting that he be paid as fourth lieutenant of the *Worcester* (PRO, ADM 1/242, 11 Apr. 1777).

66. (UK)NA: PRO, ADM 36/10047, 12 Apr. 1777.

67. Nicolas, I, 21–2, 14 Apr. 1777.

68. Rodger, 'Lieutenant's Sea Time', 271. He was referring to Sir John Knox Laughton, particularly his entries in the old *Dictionary of National Biography*, and Michael Lewis.

69. e.g., Mahan, 14; Oman, 22; Pocock, *Nelson*, 22. By contrast, Coleman, 20–21, describes the circumstances accurately.

4 Lieutenant to Captain: The West Indies

1. BL, Add. MSS 34903, 29 June 1780.
2. NMM, ADM/L/L/220.
3. Locker, 35.
4. When the two men had first met, Locker employed a struggling artist, Robert Cleveley (1747–1809), on board the *Thames* as a servant.
5. Nicolas, I, 89, 26 Nov. 1783.
6. Nicolas, I, 23, 12 Aug. 1777, Nelson to Locker. These letters survived and are now in the Huntington Library.
7. (UK) NA: PRO, ADM 1/2054, 29 Apr. 1977, Locker to Philip Stephens.
8. (UK) NA: PRO, ADM 51/4247, 3 May 1777. It was replaced at Portsmouth on 12 May by a cutter.
9. Syrett, 'Organization of convoys', 175–8.
10. O'Shaughnessy, 158.
11. O'Shaughnessy, 157, quoting PRO, CO 152/56, Governor Burt to Lord George Germain, 30 July 1777.
12. See Chapter 4.
13. Rawson, *Letters*, 11.
14. Parkinson, *Trade Winds*, 186–7.
15. (UK) NA: PRO, ADM 1/241, 21 June 1778, Parker to the Admiralty. Figures from 5 Mar. to 6 June.
16. (UK) NA: PRO, ADM 51/4247, 11 Sept. 1777.
17. (UK)NA: PRO, ADM 51/4247.
18. (UK)NA: PRO, ADM 1/241, 19 Apr. 1778, Parker to the Admiralty; also 20 May 1780 and a private letter to Sandwich, 17 Feb. 1781 (NMM, SAN/F/26/69).
19. A. Lambert, 'Cornwallis', *Precursors of Nelson*, 357. This was a running and inconclusive action in light airs off Monte Cristo; La Motte Picquet was the French commander.
20. (UK)NA: PRO, ADM 2/564, 9 Oct. 1779, Stephens to Parker, referring to 'the difficulty of procuring White Artificers . . . contemplation of bringing up some Negro Boys as Artificers'.
21. Hughes, *Collingwood*, 164, 1 Nov. 1805.
22. (UK)NA: PRO, ADM 1/241, 21 June 1778, received 18 Sept. 1778.
23. (UK)NA: PRO, ADM 1/241, 23 Sept. 1778.
24. Pares, 100–104. There had been Spanish attacks on the settlements in 1745, 1747 and 1754.
25. Finamore, Chapter 2.
26. Pocock, *Young Nelson*, 35–6.
27. 'Sketch of My Life', Rawson, *Letters*, 10.
28. Laughton, *Bartholomew James*, 71.

29. (UK)NA: PRO, ADM 36/9882.

30. (UK)NA: PRO, ADM 51/78, *Badger*'s log, 1 Apr. 1779.

31. (UK)NA: PRO, ADM 51/78, 29, 30 Apr. 1779.

32. Nicolas, I, 26, 30 Apr. 1779, to Locker.

33. E. Arnot Robertson, 42.

34. Manning, 262.

35. E. Arnot Robertson, 43.

36. (UK)NA: PRO, ADM 1/241, list of vessels taken 9 Mar.–26 July 1779.

37. Wellcome 3676.

38. (UK)NA: PRO, ADM 51/78, 2 June 1779.

39. (UK)NA: PRO, ADM 1/241, 14 June 1779, Parker to Stephens.

40. (UK)NA: PRO, ADM 1/241, 23 Aug. 1779, Parker to Stephens.

41. Nicolas, I, 32, 23 Jan. 1780.

42. E. Arnot Robertson, 41.

43. Laughton, *Bartholomew James*, 72–7; Pocock, *Young Nelson*, 47–8.

44. Clements, Sydney Papers, unsigned intelligence report from Peru, 30 July 1781; De Madariaga, *Spanish Empire*, 210–17.

45. Moseley, 77.

46. NMM, MON 1/1, 8 Jan. 1780, Nelson to Parker.

47. Nicolas, I, 33, 23 Jan. 1780.

48. Dancer, 8.

49. Quoted in Linebaugh and Rediker, 263, from BL, King's 214, Campbell's 'Memoir Relative to the Island of Jamaica'.

50. (UK)NA: PRO, ADM 51/442, Log of the *Hinchinbroke*, 3 Feb. 1780; Pocock, *Young Nelson*, 68.

51. (UK)NA: PRO, ADM 51/442, 17 Feb.–3 Mar. 1780.

52. Dancer, 10.

53. Dancer, 12–13.

54. Dancer, 17; Moseley, 86.

55. Dancer, 18.

56. Some have asserted that Nelson returned to Jamaica in the *Victor* sloop (e.g., Pocock, 46), but the evidence from logs and muster books is inconclusive (NMM, ADM/L/V/133; (UK)NA: PRO, ADM 34/831).

57. Collingwood, 7.

58. (UK)NA: PRO, ADM 51/442, Collingwood's *Hinchinbroke* log, 1 May–23 Aug. 1780; ADM 1/242, 23 Sept. 1780, Parker to Stephens.

59. *Naval Chronicle*, 25, 1810, 380–81.

60. Moseley, 89–90.

61. NMM, CRK/10/130, 8 Dec. 1800, Benjamin Rogers to Nelson.

62. Harding, *Amphibious Warfare*, 83–4, 206.

63. O'Shaughnessy, 205.

64. Nicolas, I, 30, 28 July 1779; 33, 23 Jan. 1780, Nelson to Locker.

65. Linebaugh and Rediker, 259.

66. Hills, 'Nelson's Illnesses' (2000), 73–6; (2002), 131. This author attributes Nelson's illness to Tropical Sprue, a gastro-intestinal infection, although this seems unlikely.

67. (UK)NA: PRO, ADM 1/242, 1 Sept. 1780, signed Robert Wood, Archibald Bruce and James Melling.

68. BL, Add. MSS 34903, 1 Sept. 1780, Parker to Nelson; PRO, ADM 1/242, 5 Sept. 1780, Parker to Philip Stephens, secretary to the Admiralty.

69. Quennell, *Hickey.* 189.

70. (UK)NA: PRO, ADM 51/540. On 31 Oct., in mid-Atlantic, the convoy came upon Nelson's first ship, the *Raisonable*, after which she accompanied the convoy.

71. Rowbotham, 573–84.

72. BL, Add. MSS 34903, 18 July 1780, letter from Captain Polson.

73. BL, Add. MSS 34903, 29 June 1780, Dalling to Germain.

74. Nicolas, I, 27–8, 13 May 1779, Nelson to Locker.

75. (UK)NA: PRO, ADM 1/242, 5 Sept. 1780, Parker to Stephens.

5 *Albemarle*

1. Nicolas, I, 71.

2. *Bath Journal*, 29 Jan. 1781; Nicolas, I, 36, 23 Jan. 1781, Nelson to Locker. Nelson lived at No. 2 Pierrepoint Street, at the house of Dr Spry, and was attended by Dr Woodward (NMM, AGC/N/9, 8 June 1802, Nelson to Messrs Brooke and Hayward, note on the letter).

3. Nicolas, I, 38–40, 15 Feb.–9 Mar. 1781, to William Locker.

4. Nicolas, I, 42, 7 May 1781, to William Nelson.

5. Nicolas, I, 38, 39: 15, 21 Feb. 1781.

6. NMM, SAN/6, fols. 5, 7.

7. Namier and Brooke, II, 675, 677.

8. BL, Add. MSS 38308, fol. 81.

9. BL, Add. MSS 38308, fol. 113; W. E. May, 133.

10. Five years later Nelson wrote to his uncle, suggesting, in order to settle a point, that 'you can ask Mr Stephens', then secretary to the Board of Admiralty (Nicolas, I, 162, 9 Mar. 1786).

11. NMM, ROD/4/4, out-letter book, 13 Sept. 1781.

12. Hills, 76.

13. Nicolas, I, 41–2, 7 May 1781.

14. (UK)NA: PRO, ADM 51/4110.

15. See 'Nelson's Ships' section.

16. NMM, SAN/6, fol. 15.

17. (UK)NA: PRO, ADM 1/242, 3, 6, 24 Sept. 1781, Nelson to Stephens.

18. NMM, ROD/4/4, 15 Oct. 1781, to the captain of the *Conquestadore*.

19. Nicolas, I, 47, 21 Oct. 1781.

20. NMM, ROD/9/39, in-letters, 20 Oct. 1781, George Jackson to Roddam; Nicolas, I, 47.

21. BL, Add. MSS 34961, 22 Oct. 1781, Nelson to Roddam.

22. NMM, ADM/L/A/72, 29 Oct. 1781; Nelson's log, PRO, ADM 51/4110, 29 Oct. 1781.

23. Syrett, *European Waters*, 122–32.

24. BL, Add. MSS 34961, 5 Nov.; PRO, ADM 1/242, 5 Nov. 1781, to Stephens.

25. (UK)NA: PRO, ADM 51/4110, 13 Nov. 1781.

26. (UK)NA: PRO, ADM 1/1709, 18 Dec. 1781, Dickson to the Admiralty; Pearsall, 111; Nelson claimed there were 350 ships in his convoy in a letter to Locker (Nicolas, I, 50, 22 Dec. 1781).

27. Nicolas, I, 50, 22 Dec. 1781; VII, Addenda, iv. There is a useful copy of the *Albemarle*'s log, 15 Aug. 1781–7 Mar. 1783, included in the last volume of Nicolas.

28. (UK)NA: PRO, 1/2222, 6 Dec. 1781, Captain Thomas Newnham to the Admiralty.

29. (UK)NA: PRO, ADM 1/242, 18 Dec.; BL, Add. MSS 34961, 18 Dec. 1781, to Stephens.

30. (UK)NA: PRO, ADM 1/1709, Dickson to the Admiralty.

31. (UK)NA: PRO, ADM 1/242, 18 Dec. 1781.

32. Nicolas, I, 54, 28 Jan. 1782, to William Nelson.

33. BL, Add. MSS 34961, 4 Jan. 1782, to Stephens.

34. BL, Add. MSS 34961, 11 Jan. 1782, Hughes to Nelson; 12 Jan., Nelson to Hughes.

35. I am grateful to Dr Huw Bowen for this information from BL, Oriental and Office Collections # L/AG/1/6, Vol. 18.

36. Nicolas, I, 55, 28 Jan. [1782], to William Nelson. For a dramatic description of a similarly destructive winter gale in the Downs in 1775, see Quennell, *William Hickey*, 173–9.

37. (UK)NA: PRO, ADM 51/4110, 2, 11 Feb.; BL, Add. MSS 34961, 24 Jan. 1782, Drake to Nelson.

38. NMM, STW/2, 8 Mar., to Edmund Nelson; Nicolas, I, 60, 29 Mar. 1782, to William Nelson.

39. Nicolas, I, 61–2, 2 Apr. 1782, Nelson to Locker.

40. Rodger, *Command of the Ocean*, 354.

41. Nicolas, I, 63, 20 Apr. 1782, to Locker.

42. (UK)NA: PRO, ADM 51/4110, 6–7 May, 21 May 1782.

43. Nicolas, I, 64, 1 June 1782, to Locker.

44. Nicolas, I, 77, 12 July 1783, to Locker; for further details of the voyage, see Goodwin, 102–3. Trail later was master of the *Neptune* transport in the second fleet, which went to Botany Bay in 1790; 150 men and eleven women died, forty-six between England and the Cape. Trail was brought to trial for a private charge of wilful murder of one of his crew on 9 June 1792 but acquitted. Charles

Bateson in *The Convict Ships* (1959) called Trail 'avaricious and unscrupulous' and 'inexcusably lax and incompetent'.

45. Nicolas, I, 64, 1 June 1782, to Locker.
46. (UK)NA: PRO, ADM 51/4110, 17 June–4 July 1782.
47. Mackesy, *War for America*, 492.
48. Nicolas, I, 65; Bradford, 239–44.
49. Nicolas, I, 66, 19 Oct. 1782, to Locker.
50. Oman, 46–7; Pocock, *Nelson's Women*, 26–8; Coleman, 40–41; Downer, *Nelson's Purse*, 64–6.
51. (UK)NA: PRO, ADM 51/4110, 18 Sept.–15 Oct. 1782.
52. Syrett, *Shipping and the American War*, 238–41.
53. Burrows and Wallace, 258.
54. Nicolas, I, 70, 17 Nov. 1782, to Locker.
55. Mackesy, *War for America*, 494.
56. Nicolas, I, 67, 19 Oct. 1782, to Edmund Nelson.
57. Michael Duffy, 'Samuel Hood, First Viscount Hood' in Le Fevre and Harding, *Precursors of Nelson*, 258–65.
58. Nicolas, I, 339, 1 Dec. 1793.
59. Duffy, 'Hood', 268.
60. Rodger, *Command of the Ocean*, 354.
61. Pasley, 273.
62. Nicolas, I, 68, 17 Nov. 1782, to Locker.
63. Hannay, *Hood Papers*, 22 Nov. 1782, Hood to Pigot.
64. (UK)NA: PRO, ADM 51/4110, 5–9 Dec. 1782; Jamieson, 327.
65. (UK)NA: PRO, ADM 51/4110, 1–20 Jan. 1783.
66. (UK)NA: PRO, ADM 51/4110, 25 Jan. 1783.
67. Nicolas, I, 71, 25 Feb. 1783, to Locker.
68. (UK)NA: PRO, ADM 51/4110, 8–9 Mar. 1783.
69. Nicolas, I, 74, 9 Mar. 1783, to Hood.
70. Jamieson, 323–6.
71. (UK)NA: PRO, ADM 51/4110, 26 Apr.–19 May 1783.
72. Oman, 41.
73. Nicolas, I, 80, 9 Aug. 1783.
74. (UK)NA: PRO, ADM 51/4110, 30 Apr. 1782.
75. Nicolas, I, 76, 12 July 1783.
76. BL, Add. MSS 34988, 23 July 1783, Nelson to William Nelson.
77. BL, Add. MSS 34988, 20 Aug. 1783, Nelson to William Nelson.
78. Nicolas, I, 84–5, 2 Nov. 1783, Nelson to Locker.
79. Nicolas, I, 84, 2 Nov. 1783, Nelson to Locker.
80. Gwyther, 'St Omer', 113–14, finds it impossible to discover where Nelson stayed, since Lamoury owned three houses.
81. Nicolas, I, 85, 2 Nov. 1783.
82. NMM, REC/33.

83. Nicolas, I, 92, 4 Dec. 1783.

84. Nicolas, I, 89, 26 Nov. 1783, to Locker; Stirling, *Pages and Portraits*, 59.

85. Coleridge, I, 547; Marione, 9. Nelson also disapproved of the newly fashionable epaulettes worn by Ball.

86. Nicolas, II, 479; Oman, 58–9.

87. Nicolas, I, 94, 19 Jan.; 93, 3 Jan. 1784, to William Nelson.

88. Nicolas, I, 91, 4 Dec. 1783, to William Nelson.

89. Nicolas, I, 97, 23 Jan. 1784, Nelson to Locker; 99, 19 Mar. 1784, Nelson to William Nelson.

6   *Boreas* and the West Indies

1. Nicolas, I, 136.

2. Quoted in Rodger, 'Commissioned Officers', 2, from House of Commons, 1833, XXIV, 279; (UK)NA: PRO, ADM 8/60, Ship Lists 1784.

3. Coleman, 57, suggests that Nelson's political support for the government in the Westminster election secured him his captaincy, but this is doubtful, particularly since Howe regarded party politics as a disagreeable necessity. Hood's professional recommendation would have carried weight.

4. (UK)NA: PRO, ADM 180/7.

5. (UK)NA: PRO, ADM 36/10525, *Boreas*'s muster book.

6. Wellcome 3676, 20 Mar. 1784.

7. Nicolas, I, 126, 20 Feb. 1785.

8. Nicolas, I, 101, 29 Mar. 1784, Nelson to William Nelson; PRO, ADM 51/125, 22 Aug., 5, 19 Sept. 1784; Nicolas, I, 123–6, 20 Feb. 1785.

9. Nicolas, I, 106, 23 Apr. 1784; 125, 20 Feb. 1785.

10. A captain was allowed four captain's servants for every 100 of the ship's company; the *Boreas*'s complement was 180; see Rodger, *Wooden World*, 27, Appendix 1, 348–9; Lavery, *Nelson's Navy*, 328.

11. BL, Add. MSS 34903, 3 Dec. 1788, Nelson to the Navy Board. It is unclear to which of several Douglas's Nelson was referring.

12. Nicolas, I, 247, 249, 15 July; 249, 22 July 1784.

13. NMM, COR/58, 28 Oct. 1784.

14. Nicolas, I, 142, 25 Sept. 1785. Cuthbert Collingwood too took great care of the training of young midshipmen, detailed in a wonderfully observant journal kept at this time by one of them (Carr Laughton, *Raigersfeld*, 34, 36).

15. BL, Add. MSS 34903, 3 Dec. 1788, Nelson to Navy Board.

16. BL, Add. MSS 35194, 29 Jan. 1783, Hood to George Jackson, deputy secretary to the Admiralty until 1782.

17. BL, Add. MSS 34903, 3 Dec. 1788.

18. BL, Add. MSS 34990, 25 Mar. 1787; Rawson, *Leeward Islands Letters*, 54. Lady Hughes published a much quoted letter after Nelson's death about his

training for the midshipmen on board the *Boreas*, concluding 'which made the young people adore him' (Nicolas, I, 125n.).

19. BL, Add. MSS 34903, 3 Dec. 1788.
20. Wellcome MSS 3668, 13 Apr. 1785; Nicolas, VII, Addenda, viii.
21. Nicolas, I, 125, to William Nelson, 20 Feb. 1785.
22. Nicolas, I, 104, 21 Apr. 1784, to Locker, but there is no mention of the grounding in the *Boreas*'s log.
23. (UK)NA: PRO, ADM 51/125, 15, 20 Apr.; BL., Add. MSS 34961, 15 Apr., Philip Stephens, secretary of the Board of Admiralty, to Nelson; ADM 36/10526, 20 Apr. 1784.
24. Nicolas, I, 105, to Locker, 21 Apr. 1784.
25. Nicolas, I, 107–8, 30 May 1784.
26. (UK)NA: PRO, ADM 51/125, log; NMM, COR/58, 25 Oct. 1784.
27. (UK)NA: PRO, ADM 8/60, Ship Lists 1784.
28. Nicolas, I, 112, 156; 23 Nov. 1784, 5 Mar. 1786, to Locker; 125, 127, 131, 20 Feb., 16 Mar., 3 May 1785, to William Nelson. Nelson was wrong: Sandys lived for another thirty years, dying as a superannuated rear-admiral in 1814.
29. NMM, COR/58, 25 Oct. 1784.
30. R. V. Hamilton, *Byam Martin*, I, 83.
31. Vaughan, 303–4; Jane, 21–31.
32. Naish, 21, 13 Dec. 1785, to Frances. Nelson established a captains' mess at English Harbour 'for the Hurricane months' (Nicolas, VII, Addenda, vii, 3 Aug. 1784, to Mr Kerr).
33. See p. 20.
34. BL, Add. MSS 34961, 6 Feb. 1785, Nelson to Sandys.
35. Nicolas, I, 120, 15 Feb. 1785.
36. BL, Add. MSS 34961, [n.d. but filed between letters of 7–9 Jan. 1785].
37. (UK)NA: PRO, ADM 2/584, Stephens to Hughes, 5 May 1785.
38. Mahan, *Nelson*, 43; Naish, 25–6, 31, to Frances, 25, 29 Mar., 23 Apr. 1786.
39. Nicolas, I, 126, 131, 16 Mar., 3 May 1785, to William Nelson. For a detailed and sympathetic portrait of Mary Moutray, see Sugden, 278–81.
40. Harlow, *Second British Empire*, 476.
41. Quoted in O'Shaughnessy, 239–40.
42. O'Shaughnessy, 238–48.
43. 26 Geo III, c. 60; see also (UK)NA: PRO, ADM 2/585, 3 Nov., 8 Dec. 1785, 4 Jan. 1786, Stephens to Hughes.
44. Manning, 258–9, 261; (UK)NA: PRO, ADM 1/243, 7 Apr. 1786, Gardner to Stephens, enclosing letter from the governor of New Providence.
45. Kirby, *American Merchantmen*, 139.
46. Nicolas, I, 173–4, 12 Nov. 1784, 'Captain Nelson's Narrative of His Proceedings . . . Apparently Written towards the End of June 1786'.
47. (UK)NA: PRO, ADM 51/125.
48. Nicolas, I, 175, 29 Dec. 1784.

49. BL, Add. MSS 34961, 29 Jan. 1785; quoted in Rawson, *Leeward Islands Letters*, 34.

50. Rawson, *Leeward Islands Letters*, 34, 5 Feb. 1785.

51. Nicolas, I, 157, 5 Mar. 1786.

52. (UK)NA: PRO, ADM 2/585, 10 May 1785.

53. Nicolas, I, 176–8, 'Narrative'.

54. (UK)NA: PRO ADM 52/2179, 19–20 May 1785; Nicolas, I, 178, 'Narrative'.

55. Rawson, *Leeward Islands Letters*, 52, 'Wallis's Memoir'.

56. Nicolas, I, 129–31.

57. Nicolas, I, 134–6, 29 June 1785.

58. (UK)NA: ADM 52/2179, 5 [6] July 1785.

59. BL, Add. MSS 34903, 29 July 1785. 'I do hereby release the said Horatio Nelson . . . from all . . . damages.'

60. The cargo of oak barrel staves and corn from the *Fairview*, one of the ships seized on 19 May, was valued by the Court of Admiralty at Nevis on 8 Aug. 1785. Total value was £776. 14s. 6d. Nelson, his officers and crew shared £388. 7s. 3d., Hughes £97.1s. 9d. (BL, Add. MSS, 34903).

61. Nicolas, I, 178, 'Narrative'; also 1, 144, 28 Sept. 1785, Nelson to Collingwood. Over ten years later Hughes was trying to retrieve this prize money (Nicolas, I, 317–18, 7 Aug. 1793, Nelson to Charles Long, joint secretary to the Treasury; NMM, CRK/7/85, 8 Sept. 1796, Hughes to Nelson).

62. Rawson, *Leeward Islands Letters*. 45, 46; BL, Add. MSS, 34961, 4 Aug., 29 Sept. 1785.

63. Nicolas, I, 144–7, 14 Nov. 1785, Nelson to William Suckling; see also Sugden, 300.

64. (UK)NA: PRO, ADM 2/585, 3 Nov.; 8 Dec. 1785, Stephens to Hughes.

65. NMM, ADM/L/B/136, 15, 18 Mar. 1786; Kirby, 145.

66. (UK)PRO, ADM 51/120, 21 May 1786; Kirby, 145. The legal proceedings are examined in detail by Sugden, 316–20, 29–35.

67. (UK)NA: PRO, ADM 51/125, 25–7 Nov. 1784; ADM 2/583, 21 July 1784, Stephens to Hughes.

68. (UK)NA: PRO, ADM 52/2179, 20–21, 29 June 1785; also 51/125, 22 Dec. 1784.

69. Hildebrand, 126ff. 979 ships were reported to have called at Gustavia carrying American products in 1786.

70. NMM, ADM/L/B/136 (i), 14 Feb. 1786; Nicolas, VII, Addenda, ix.

71. Hattendorf, *St Barthélémy*, 24.

72. Nicolas, I, 150, 15 Dec. 1785, to William Nelson.

73. Naish, 30, 23 Apr. 1786, Nelson to Fanny.

74. Naish, 49 [4 Mar. 1787].

75. Naish, 33, 19 Aug. 1786, Nelson to Fanny.

76. Naish, 31–2, 4 May 1786, Nelson to Fanny.

77. Naish, 34, 35, 19, 31 Aug. 1786, Nelson to Fanny.

78. Naish, 40, 24 Dec. 1786.

79. For examples, see NMM, WYN/104, 1 Dec. 1788, 11 June 1792, Young to Charles Morice Pole; John Jervis's opposition to early naval marriage was well known; see Brenton, II, 338, 353.

80. Oman, 73–82; Pocock, *Nelson's Women*, 50–57.

81. Nicolas, I, 160–63; also NMM, MON/1, 9 Mar. 1786, Nelson to Suckling.

82. (UK)NA: PRO, ADM 52/2179. It seems extraordinary that lower masts should be cut away.

83. (UK)NA: PRO, ADM 2/585, 2 Nov. 1785, Stephens to Hughes; Nicolas, I, 138, 24 Aug. 1785.

84. (UK)NA: PRO, ADM 52/2179, 20–22 Sept. 1785.

85. Naish, 21, 13 Dec. 1785.

86. NMM, ADM/L/B/136, 9–16 Jan. 1786.

87. (UK)NA: PRO, ADM 51/125, 27 Apr. 1784.

88. (UK)NA: PRO, ADM 52/2179, 29–30 Apr. 1785 for examples of maintenance and trimming the ship.

89. For a sample of victuals taken on at Carlisle Bay, Barbados, see the master's log (UK)NA: PRO, ADM 52/2179, 20–24 Apr. 1785.

90. Clements Library, Hubert Smith Naval Collection, *Boreas*'s purser's accounts, 4 Nov. 1783–31 Oct. 1785.

91. Carr Laughton, *Raigersfeld*, 15.

92. Carr Laughton, *Raigersfeld*, 17, 23.

93. Byrn, 131. The sailors' rum ration, instituted in 1844, lasted until 1970.

94. *Boreas*'s log appears to be detailed and accurate and accords with the master's, but the same cannot be said for all eighteenth-century logs. See Rodger, *Wooden World*, 228; Wareham, 219–20.

95. Coleman, 90. A list of the *Boreas*'s punishments 5 Oct. 1786–10 Oct. 1787 appears in Goodwin, 116.

96. (UK)NA: PRO, ADM 52/2179, 20 Aug. 1785. This phrase represented urinating.

97. (UK)NA: PRO, ADM 36/10528, muster book; ADM 51/125, 29 June 1784; 52/2179, 15 Sept. 1785; 51/120, 10 Apr., 25 Dec. 1786, 11 Feb. 1787.

98. At the end of the commission the *Boreas* was kept at the Nore for three months, during which there occurred a plummeting of morale and consequent heavy punishment.

99. (UK)NA: PRO, ADM 51/125, 17 Dec. 1784.

100. (UK)NA: PRO, ADM 51/125, 12 Oct. 1784.

101. (UK)NA: PRO, ADM 51/120, 12 Apr. 1786.

102. (UK)NA: PRO, ADM 2/587, 14 Sept. 1786, Stephens to Hughes.

103. Nicolas, I, 258, 30 Sept. 1787, Nelson to Philip Stephens.

104. Byrn, 221–28. Punishments are measured by the average per month, rather than by the length of the commissions.

105. Warner, *Collingwood*, 24–5, quoting Carr Laughton, *Raigersfeld*, 33, 35–6.

106. BL, Add. MSS 34961, 10 Oct. 1785.

107. Rawson, *Leeward Islands Letters*, 54.

108. Nicolas, I, 111, 24 Oct. 1784, to William Nelson.

109. (UK)NA: PRO, ADM 51/125, 9 June, 7 Oct. 1784; NMM, ADM/L/B/ 136, 21 Feb. 1786; PRO, ADM 51/120, 30 July 1786.

110. Nicolas, I, 175–6, June 1786; Rawson, *Leeward Islands Letters*, 16.

111. Nicolas, I, 159, 5 Mar. 1786, Nelson to Locker.

7 Senior Naval Officer, Leeward Islands

1. (UK)NA: PRO, ADM 2/581.

2. The French West Indies squadron at Hughes's departure consisted of three frigates and three smaller ships, with a 64 expected ((UK)NA: PRO, ADM 50/ 100, July 1786).

3. (UK)NA: PRO, ADM 241/1, 17, 26 Sept. 1785, Hughes to yard officers.

4. (UK)NA: PRO, ADM 241/1, 1 Mar. 1785, Moutray to yard officers.

5. (UK)NA: PRO, ADM 241/1, 5 Sept. 1786, Nelson to yard officers.

6. (UK)NA: PRO, ADM 51/120.

7. NMM, HOO/1, 30 Oct. 1782, Hood's draft to George III.

8. Laughton, *Miscellany*, I, 227, 16 Apr. 1783.

9. Naish, 39, 24 Dec. 1786, Nelson to Fanny.

10. NMM, LBK/33, 15 Dec. 1786, Prince William Henry to Archibald Dow.

11. NMM, LBK/33, 9 Mar. 1787, Philip Stephens to Prince William Henry.

12. (UK)NA: PRO, ADM 2/581, 9 Mar. 1787, Stephens to Nelson; Nicolas, I, 240, 4 July 1787, Nelson to Stephens.

13. (UK)NA: PRO, ADM 241/1, 7, 8, 9 Feb. 1787, Nelson to yard officers; Nicolas, I, 255, 257, 29 Aug., 21 Sept. 1787, Nelson to Stephens.

14. Nicolas, I, 255, 29 Aug. 1787, Nelson to Stephens.

15. Aspinall, I, 291, 20 May 1787.

16. Naish, 56–7; BL, Add. MSS 34902, fol. 1.

17. Naish, 57.

18. Aspinall, I, 291, 20 May 1787.

19. Naish, 57; BL, Add. MSS 34902 [n.d.]. The prince's letters home displeased the king (NMM, HOO/1, 16 Apr. [1787], Bude to Hood).

20. R. V. Hamilton, *Byam Martin*, I, 67.

21. Naish, 57: BL Add. MSS 34902 [n.d.].

22. Nicolas, I, 213, 9 Feb. 1787.

23. (UK)NA: PRO, ADM 1/243, 5 June 1787, Gardner to Philip Stephens, Enclosure No. 1.

24. Nicolas, I, 235, 13 May, Nelson to Gardner.

25. Nicolas, I, 224, 26 Apr. 1787.

26. NMM, LBK/33, 3 May 1787, Prince William Henry to Nelson.

27. Nicolas, I, 215, 13 Feb. 1787.

28. NMM, ORD/10, 20 June 1787, Howe to Orde.

29. Aspinall, I, 293, 20 May 1787.

30. Ranft, 288–9; NMM, LBK/33, 11 May, Prince William Henry to Nelson.

31. (UK)NA: PRO, ADM 1/243, 5 June 1787; also R. V. Hamilton, *Byam Martin*, I, 84.

32. (UK)NA: PRO, ADM 1/243, 22 Sept. 1787, Gardner to Stephens.

33. Hood, 94, 18 Apr. 1787.

34. R. V. Hamilton, *Byam Martin*. I, 67.

35. Coleman, 78.

36. BL, Add. MSS, 34903, 21 July 1786, Sholto Archibald to Nelson.

37. NMM, HOO/2, 5 Oct. 1787.

38. R. V. Hamilton, *Byam Martin*, I, 67.

39. Stirling, *Hotham*, I, 27.

40. BL, Add. MSS 34903, 30 May 1787.

41. NMM, CRK/6/78, 19 Nov. 1800, Graham to Nelson.

42. (UK)NA: PRO, ADM 50/100, 22 Aug., 19 Sept. 1786.

43. NMM, LBK/33, 15 Apr. 1787; Byrn, 60–63.

44. Byrn, 62.

45. (UK)NA: PRO, 2/588, 27 July, 7 Sept. 1787.

46. Byrn, 62, quoting Admiralty minutes, ADM 3/103, 27 July, 7 Sept. 1787.

47. (UK)NA: PRO, ADM 2/588, 3 May 1787.

48. (UK)NA: PRO, ADM 51/120, 1, 2 Feb. 1787.

49. BL, Add. MSS 34903, 30 May 1787, James Young to Nelson.

50. (UK)NA: PRO, ADM 51/120, 3 June 1787.

51. Stirling, *Hotham*, I, 27.

52. Monmouth, E540, 8 Nov. 1789.

53. NMM, HOO/14, 19 July 1787.

54. (UK)NA: PRO, ADM 2/588, 11 Sept. 1787, Stephens to Nelson.

55. NMM, HOO/2, 30 July 1787, Howe to Hood.

56. Nicolas, I, 240, 241, 4, 11 July 1787.

57. NMM, HOO/7, 17 Aug. 1787, Hood's out-letter book; Nicolas, I, 259, 3 Oct. 1787, Nelson to Locker.

58. (UK)NA: PRO, ADM 51/120.

59. BL, Add. MSS 34903, 17 Aug. 1787.

60. Naish, 62.

61. NMM, HOO/2, 2 July 1787; Ranft, 287.

8 Half-pay in Norfolk

1. NMM, COR/58.

2. Mahan, 78.

3. Nicolas, I, 261–2, Huntington, HM 34152, 27 Nov. 1787 to Locker; Oman, 97.

4. Rodger, *Wooden World*, 209.

5. Nicolas, I, 263, 29 Dec. 1787, to Philip Stephens.

6. Nicolas, I, 260, 29 Oct. 1787; 265, 3 Jan. 1788, to William Nelson.

7. Nicolas, I, 266, Huntington HM 34153, 27 Jan. 1788, to Locker.

8. NMM, LBK/33, 19 Feb. 1788.

9. M. Eyre Matcham, 52; Nicolas, I, 267; Huntington, HM 34153, 27 Jan. 1788.

10. Mahan, 74.

11. Naish, 54, 74; Pocock, *Nelson*, 87.

12. Wellcome 3676, 22 July 1788–27 Oct. 1790.

13. Huntington, HM 34011, 29 Sept, 1 Oct. 1787, to Peers; BL, Add. MSS 34903, 30 Aug. 1790, 25 May 1791, Marsh and Creed to Nelson.

14. BL, Add. MSS 34903, 12 July 1789, George Forbes to Nelson.

15. Nicolas, I, 274–5 [May 1788].

16. M. Eyre Matcham, 64, 65, 77.

17. Nicolas, I, 290, 5 Feb. 1792, Nelson to William Nelson.

18. Holkham Archives, F/TWC 27, 'List of Persons', 5 Nov. 1788, notebook, loose letters, 31 Oct. 1788. See Stirling, *Coke of Norfolk*, 216.

19. Isaacson, 7–8.

20. M. Eyre Matcham, 80, 65.

21. BL, Add. MSS 34903, 14 Nov. 1790, Collingwood to Nelson; Huntington, HM 34012, 8 June 1790, Nelson to Graham.

22. Nicolas, I, 277, 26 Dec. 1788, Nelson to Philip Stephens.

23. BL, Add. MSS 34903, 22 Sept. 1788.

24. NMM, HOO/2, 26 Dec. 1787, 1 Jan. 1788.

25. Huntington, HM 34153; Nicolas, I, 267, 27 Jan. 1788.

26. BL, Add. MSS 34903, 4 May 1788.

27. Huntington, HM 34012, 8 June 1790.

28. Nicolas, I, 226–9, 2 May 1787, to Middleton; [n.d.] to Howe.

29. (UK)NA: PRO/30/8/187, 4 May 1787, Nelson to William Pitt.

30. Nicolas, I, 264–5, [Nov or Dec 1787], Nelson to Middleton.

31. BL, Add.MSS 34903, 14 Nov. 1787, 25 July, 9 Oct. 1788; Nicolas, I, 269–73, 26 Apr. 1788, Nelson to Wilkinson and Higgins [Apr. 1788], Nelson to the commissioners of Sick and Hurt; 279–80, 24 Jan., 1 Feb. 1789; 283, 28 Nov. 1789, Nelson to Wilkinson and Higgins.

32. BL, Add. MSS 34903, 17 Aug. 1787, Middleton to Nelson.

33. BL, Add. MSS 34903, 30 May 1787.

34. (UK)NA: PRO, ADM 114/26, 21, 26 June 1789. I am grateful to Janet McDonald for this reference.

35. (UK)NA: PRO, ADM 114/26, 19 Dec. 1789, Stephens to the Victualling Board; 12 Jan. 1790, Wilkinson to the Board; BL, Add. MSS 34903, 11, 12 Sept. 1789, Wilkinson to Nelson.

36. Morriss, *Naval Power and Culture*, 118.

37. NMM, CAD/D/15, 9th Report, Commission on Fees, Appendices 4 and 5.
38. Ehrman, *Pitt*, I, 316-17. *Reports of the Commissioners Appointed by Act 25 Geo. III, cap. 19., to Inquire into the Fees, Gratuities, Perquisites and Emoluments, which were or have been lately Received into the Public Offices Therein Mentioned, 1786-1788; 1806* (309).
39. Morriss, *Naval Power and Culture*, 261.
40. Nicolas, I, 276-7, 8 Aug. 1788.
41. Naish, 51, 26 Aug. 1788.
42. (UK)NA: PRO, ADM 8/66, Ship Lists 1790.
43. NMM, COR/58, 8 Oct. 1788; Nicolas, I, 277n.; 291, 5 Feb. 1792.
44. BL, Add. MSS 34903, 24 Mar. 1789.
45. Nicolas, I, 282, 10 Sept. 1789.
46. BL, Add. MSS 34903, 30 Aug. 1790.
47. Monmouth, E540, 8 Nov. 1789, Hood to Nelson.
48. NMM, GIR/1/b, 14 Dec. 1789.
49. BL, Add. MSS 34903, 29 Apr. 1790.
50. BL, Add. MSS 35194, 10 Aug., Chatham to Bridport.
51. Nicolas, I, 288, 24 June 1790, Nelson to Prince William Henry.
52. BL, Add. MSS 34988, 1 Oct. 1790, William Suckling to Nelson.
53. Hughes, 21, 23, 24.
54. Nicolas, I, 294n.
55. Naish, 62.
56. Nicolas, I, 289, 26 Sept. 1790; BL, Add. MSS 34903, 17 Nov. 1790, Mulgrave to Nelson.
57. Private collection, communicated by Colin White.
58. (UK)NA: PRO, ADM 8/66, 1 Nov. 1790; Syrett and Dinardo, *passim*.
59. Southey, 68-73; Clark Russell, 39-41; Oman, 94-118; Pocock, 75-99.
60. NMM, MAM/1, 13 Oct.; MAM/2, 15 Dec. 1792, Nelson to Kitty Matcham.
61. NMM, GIR/1/b, 11 Dec. 1791, Nelson to Thomas Bolton.
62. NMM, MAM/1, 13, 23 Oct. 1792, Nelson to Kitty Matcham.
63. NMM, GIR/1/b, 23, 30 Apr. 1792, Nelson to Bolton.
64. Nicolas, I, 291, 5 Feb. 1792.
65. Sugden, 399-400, is the first to draw attention to the connection of Nelson with this trial.
66. Nicolas, I, 292-7, 3 Nov., 10 Dec. 1792.
67. Nicolas, I, 294, 10 Dec. 1792.
68. Naish, 72, 7 Jan. 1793.
69. Naish, 51, 26 Aug. 1788, Nelson to Fanny.

II   MATURITY AND TRIUMPH 1793–1798

9   The Navy in 1793

1. BL, Add. MSS 34903.
2. Webb, 'Rebuilding and Repairing', 196–7.
3. Ehrman, I, 184, 315–6.
4. Namier and Brooke, I, 114; Thorne, I, 314.
5. Thorne, I, 314.
6. Namier and Brooke, III, 12.
7. Huntington, HO 158, 14 June 1793.
8. R. V. Hamilton, *Byam Martin*, III, 300.
9. Nicolas, I, 98, 31 Jan. 1784.
10. Duffy, 'Hood' in Le Fevre and Harding, *Precursors of Nelson*, 264.
11. Nicolas, I, 128, 16 Mar. 1785.
12. Monmouth, E638, note by Fanny, Dec. 1793, 'I was then at Lord Walpole's'.
13. Monmouth, E619, 11 Apr. 1796.
14. Thorne, IV, 143.
15. Namier and Brooke, II, 258.
16. Rodger, 'Commissioned Sea Officers', 14.
17. Huntington, HO 79, 1 Jun 1790, to Roger Curtis.
18. Rodger, *Insatiable Earl*, 183.
19. Locker, 36.
20. Nicolas, I, 69, 17 Nov. 1782; 71, 25 Feb. 1783.
21. Nicolas, I, 68, 17 Nov. 1782, Nelson to Locker.
22. Wilkinson, 'Nelson Network' (1993), 232.
23. Richardson, 56.
24. Glete, I, 272, 276, 313; Harding, 244, 251, 254.
25. Webb, 'Rebuilding and Repairing', 201–3.
26. NMM, Middleton Papers, MID/1/145, 'Observations on the Estimates of 21 March 1786'.
27. Morriss, *Royal Dockyards*, 80, 81, 86.
28. Lavery, *Nelson's Navy*, 244.
29. Webb, 'The Navy and British Diplomacy', 143; Talbott, 104–111.
30. Caruana, II, 262.
31. Hogg, 1, 471; Baker, 2.
32. Caruana, II, 354, lists two gun bursts in 1794, one in 1795, one in 1796, one in 1798 and one in 1801.
33. Corbett, *Trafalgar*, 53; Rodger, *Command of the Ocean*, 421. The French introduced the carronade experimentally in 1793 and made them standard in 1799 (Clayton and Craig, 109).

34. West, 185–6. The French had difficulty in obtaining saltpetre.

35. Rodger, *Command of the Ocean*, 420.

36. Caruana, II, 353–4.

37. F. L. Robertson, 128–9.

38. (UK)NA: PRO, ADM 160/150, 'Establishment of Carronades for a Ship of Every Class in the Royal Navy'.

39. Lavery, 'Carronades', 15–16.

40. Clements, Melville Papers, 22 Feb. 1801.

41. F. L. Robertson, 137–8; Rodger, *Command of the Ocean*, 568.

42. Cormack, 44–8.

43. Cormack, 25–6.

44. Laughton, *Barham Papers*, II, 255–7, 18 Aug. 1787, McBride to Middleton; Huntington Library, HO 68, 1 Dec. 1788, Howe to Sir Roger Curtis.

45. Service Historique de la Marine, *Pierres de mer*, 27; Cormack, 30.

46. Baugh, 'British Navy Superiority', 236.

47. Acerra and Meyer, *Marines*, 71, 74; Cormack, 291–302; Dull, 'French Navy', 121–37.

48. Webb, 'Nootka Sound', 133, 147; 'Ochakov', 22.

49. (UK)NA: PRO, 8/66, Ship Lists 1790.

50. Schofield, 184.

51. (UK)NA: PRO, ADM 8/65, Ship Lists 1789.

52. Schofield, 192, quoting the *Parliamentary Register*.

53. Hampson, ix, xiii, 94–7.

54. Schofield, 198; Oman, 7; Warner, *Portrait*, 9; Pocock, *Nelson*, 6.

55. Starkey, 40–41.

56. Ehrman, II, 496.

57. Lewis, 86–127; Baugh, 'Navy as an Institution', 135; Ryan, 'Quota Acts', 103–4.

58. Rodger, *Command of the Ocean*, 378–9; Baugh, 'Naval Superiority', 1–31; Glete, I, 276–94, 369.

10   The Commissioning of the *Agamemnon*

1. Wellcome 3677.

2. Stammers, 61; Naish, 76, 9 Apr. 1793, Nelson to Fanny.

3. Naish, 72, 7 Jan. 1793, to Fanny.

4. NMM, CHA/E/40, 12 Jan. 1793.

5. (UK)NA: PRO, ADM 36/11362; Nicolas, II, 89–90, 24 Sept. 1795, to Edmund Nelson; PRO, ADM 36/11362, 20 Oct. 1795.

6. Nicolas, I, 300, 10 Feb. 1793, to William Nelson.

7. Naish, 93, 12 Oct. 1793, Nelson to Fanny. Clarke and McArthur omit this detail, but Naish prints the whole letter; see Nicolas, I, 333, for the mangled version.

8. Naish, 234, 6 Jan. 1796, Nelson to Fanny.

9. Pocock, *Hoste*, 26–32.

10. Naish, 220, 25 Aug. 1795.

11. Lodey, 434–5, Joseph Emerson to his brother, 9 May 1793.

12. Nicolas, I, 299, 10 Feb. 1793, Nelson to William Nelson.

13. Nicolas, I, 298, 26 Jan. 1793, Nelson to Locker; Starkey, 32.

14. Nicolas, I, 299, 10 Feb. 1793.

15. Naish, 76, 9 Apr. 1793.

16. Naish, 76, 9, 14 Apr. 1793.

17. Naish, 80, 6 May 1793.

18. Nicolas, I, 303 [Apr. 1793], Nelson to George Rose; BL, Add. MSS 34903, 20 Apr. 1793, Charles Long, Treasury, to Nelson. The cases were those of the *Hercules* and the *Nancy Pleasant*.

19. (UK)NA: PRO, ADM 51/1104, 16 Mar. 1793.

20. (UK)NA: PRO, ADM 51/1104, 52/2710.

21. (UK)NA: PRO, ADM 36/11358.

22. (UK)NA: PRO, ADM 36/11358.

23. Naish, 77, 18 Apr. 1793.

24. NMM, CHA/E/40, 12 Mar. 1793.

25. Nicolas, I, 304, 18 Apr. 1793, to William Nelson.

26. Naish, 78, 29 Apr. 1793. Nicolas, I, 304, prints a typically embellished Clarke and McArthur version in which Nelson states that 'it is now certain' that he was going with Lord Hood; this phrase is omitted in Naish.

27. (UK)NA: PRO, PRO 30/8/163, 5 May 1793, Nelson to Hood.

28. Naish, 80, 6 May 1793, to Fanny.

29. (UK)NA: PRO, 30/8/163, 5 May 1793, Nelson to Hood.

30. (UK)NA: PRO, ADM 52/2710, 4 May 1793. There is no mention of this incident in either the captain's or the lieutenant's log.

31. Hughes, 26, 14 June 1790, Collingwood to his sister.

32. See Wareham, *Star Captains*, Chapter 2, 'The Lure of Frigate Command'.

33. Wellcome 3676, 8 Apr. 1793; NMM, CHA/E/40, 14 Mar. 1793.

34. Jamieson, *Channel Islands*, 209, 372.

35. Wellcome 3667, 7 May, 18 June 1793; 3676, 2 Nov. 1796.

36. Wellcome 3676, 1 Apr. 1793.

37. Naish, 80, 11 May 1793, Nelson to Fanny.

38. Naish, 80–81, 18 May 1793, 12 leagues NW of Guernsey, to Fanny.

39. (UK)NA: PRO, ADM 51/1104, 28 May 1793.

40. NMM, CRK/7/16, 23 June 1793, 'A List of Ships and Vessels under the Command of Admiral Lord Hood'.

41. (UK)NA: PRO, ADM 50/125, 30 May–9 June 1793.

42. Bourchier, I, 15.

43. NMM, CRK/7/16, 23 June 1793.

44. Ehrman, II, 274–87; Schroeder, 125–60.

45. Panzac, 129–31.
46. Naish, 83, 23 June 1793; White, 1797, 29–30.
47. Naish, 84, 23 June 1793.
48. Wellcome 3667, 20 June 1793.
49. R. V. Hamilton, *Byam Martin*, I, 177.

11   The Western Mediterranean: Frustrated Subordinate

1. Naish, 86.
2. Monmouth, E428.
3. Crook, 12–47.
4. Crook, 138–9. For a vivid account of how that contact was made, see Tracy, *Naval Chronicle*, I, 37–9.
5. Crook, 140; see also 13–21; Ware, 23–37. Violence on the same scale had taken place at Brest in 1790–91 (Cormack, 78–108).
6. NMM, CRK/14/1, 23–6 Aug. 1793.
7. Monmouth, E598, 20 Aug. 1793, Nelson to Edmund Nelson.
8. J. Holland Rose, *Toulon*, 51; Godfrey, 361.
9. Vane, III, 475, Hood to Sir John Coxe Hippersley, 7, 19 Oct. 1793; Crook, 143.
10. Naish, 90, 7–11 Sept. 1793.
11. BL, Add. MSS 34903, 25 Aug. 1793.
12. NMM, CRK/14/1, 12–16 Aug. 1793.
13. Bodleian, Montagu, d. 18, fol. 26, printed in Nicolas, I, 331–2.
14. Parsons, 46.
15. Nicolas, I, 328, 27 Sept. 1793, to William Nelson.
16. Constantine, xiv–xx, 37–9, 98–9, 194–7.
17. Holland Rose, *Toulon*, 39; Naish, 91, 92, 14, 27 Sept. 1793; Constantine, x, 192; Fraser, I, 190. The exact year of Emma's birth is not known.
18. Naish, 91, 14 Sept. 1793.
19. (UK)NA: PRO, ADM 51, 1104, 15 Sept. 1793.
20. NMM, CRK/14/1, journal, 16 Aug. 1793.
21. (UK)NA: PRO, ADM 51/1104, 19 Sept. 1793; his first-recorded letter to Pollard is 31 Jan. 1794 (Nicolas, I, 350).
22. Naish, 92, 27 Sept. 1793. Sidney Smith reported a similar incident in Leghorn Harbour (NMM, CRK/11/7, 2 Dec. 1793, Smith to Sir William Hamilton).
23. (UK)NA: PRO, ADM 51/1104, 6–9 Oct. 1793.
24. (UK)NA: PRO, 52/2710, 22 Oct. 1793, master's log; the entry of the first lieutenant's log is identical (NMM, ADM/L/A/51).
25. Nicolas, I, 334–6, 22 Oct. 1793.
26. Naish, 99, 16 Jan. 1794.

27. Naish, 99, 16 Jan. 1794; PRO, ADM 51/1104, NMM, ADM/L/A/51, 22 Oct. 1793.

28. Naish, 138–9. The prayer was from the *Spectator*, 8 Mar. 1711:

When I lay me down to sleep I recommend myself to the care of Almighty God, when I awake I give myself up to his direction, amidst all the evils that threaten me, I will look up to him for help, and question not but that he will either avert them, or turn them to my advantage, though I know neither the time nor the manner of my death, I am not at all solicitous about it, because I am sure that He knows them both, and that he will not fail to support and comfort me under them.

29. Monmouth E602, Nelson to Maurice Nelson, 8 Nov. 1793.

30. Nicolas, I, 334n.

31. (UK)NA: PRO, ADM 51/1104, 1 Nov. 1793.

32. Holland Rose, *Toulon*, 53.

33. Naish, 95, 1 Dec. 1793.

34. Holland Rose, *Toulon*, 15–16; R. V. Hamilton, *Byam Martin*, I, 178, 'Reminiscences and Notes'.

35. (UK)NA: PRO, ADM 51/1104, 23, 30 Nov. 1793. Nicolas, I, 337n., quoting the *Memoirs of Sir William Hoste*, I, 18, 27 Nov. 1793, records that Nelson was dispatched on a mission with the *Lowestoffe*.

36. Godfrey, 365, quoting the diary of Sir John Moore.

37. NMM, CRK/7/49, 24 Dec. 1793, Hood to Sir William Hamilton.

38. NMM, CRK/7/51, Hood to Sir William Hamilton, 25 Dec. 1793.

39. Crook, 148.

40. Nicolas, II, 46, 22 June 1795.

41. Acerra, 26.

42. Crook, 147.

43. Crook, 159; Acerra, 127. In 1793 and 1794 the French laid the keels of nineteen ships of the line (Glete, II, 386).

44. Naish, 97, 27 Dec. 1793.

45. (UK)NA: PRO, ADM 1/2224, Nelson to Chatham, 26 Dec. 1793 [read 13 Jan. 1794]. This is a curiously phrased letter: the sense of his intelligence report conveys the idea that it was Nelson himself who observed the burning of Toulon.

46. NMM, CRK/7/56, 6 Feb. 1794, Hood to William Hamilton.

47. Lloyd, 'Gardner', 101, 110. This was the *Berwick*.

48. Nicolas, I, 348, 17 Jan. 1794, to Locker; also Duffy, 'Hood', 272; for the weakness of the *Berwick*'s commanding officer, see PRO, ADM 50/125.

49. Nicolas, I, 347, 17 Jan. 1794.

50. (UK)NA: PRO, ADM 51/1104. This was the *Armée de L'Italie*, ten guns, eight swivels.

51. Naish, 16 Jan. 1794, to Fanny. In a letter dated 1 Mar. he wrote that 'Myself and one frigate are the only ships who kept their station' (Naish, 104).

52. (UK)NA: PRO, ADM 51/1104; Nicolas, I, 349.

53. (UK)NA: PRO, ADM 51/1104; Nicolas, I, 354, 13 Feb. 1794, Nelson to Hood. The French had a garrison on the island that was not dislodged for some months. The *Courageux* (Captain Waldegrave) was detailed to lie off Capraia throughout the Siege of Bastia (Tracy, *Naval Chronicle*, 1, 34).

54. Duffy, 'Science and Labour', 44–5; Holland Rose, 'Corsica', 62.

55. NMM, CRK/7/57, 19 Feb. 1794, Hood to Hamilton.

56. (UK)NA: PRO, ADM 52/2707.

57. Nicolas, I, 364.

58. Nicolas, I, 402, 30 May 1794.

59. NMM, CRK/7/59, 26 Feb. 1794.

60. Godfrey, 382, 1 Apr. 1794.

61. Monk, 102–3.

62. Stirling, *Pages and Portraits*, I, 66.

63. Nicolas, I, 357, 366, 3, 4 Mar. 1794; Hood, 130–33.

64. Godfrey, 377, 382, 402, 19 Mar., 1 Apr., 31 May 1794.

65. (UK)NA: PRO, ADM 51/1104, 23 Feb.–14 Mar. 1794. Denham, 51, gives the same advice to modern vessels.

66. NMM, AGC/8/3, 24 Feb. 1794, Nelson to Udney.

67. Nicolas, I, 366–7, 371, 3, 12 Mar. 1794, journal; I, 372, 16 Mar. 1794, letter to Hood.

68. (UK)NA: PRO, ADM 51/1104, 2 Apr. 1794; Nicolas, I, 386, 24 Apr. 1794.

69. Nicolas, I, 382, journal.

70. Nicolas, I, 376, 27 Mar. 1794, to Captain William Paget, *Romney*.

71. (UK)NA: PRO, ADM 51/1104, e.g., 28, 29 Apr. 1794.

72. Nicolas, I, 395, 12 May, journal.

73. Nicolas, I, 394–6, journal.

74. (UK)NA: PRO, ADM 51/1104, 24 May 1794.

75. Nicolas, I, 398, 23 May 1794.

76. Nicolas, I, 387, 25 Apr. 1794.

77. Godfrey, 419, 7 Feb. 1795.

78. Monmouth, E25, Hood to Sir John Coxe Hippersley, 15 June 1794; James, I, 213–15.

79. Godfrey, 404, 19 June 1794.

80. Hood, 139.

81. Spinney, 'Port Agro', 90–91; Chisholm, 269.

82. Houghton, pf MS Eng. 196.5(2), Nelson's journal at Calvi, 10 June–6 July 1794.

83. (UK)NA: PRO, ADM 51/1104, 7–25 June 1794; Nicolas, I, 405–10, 429. The log gives a detailed account of the attempts to retrieve it four days later, with exact bearings.

84. Nicolas, I, 412 n.

85. Godfrey, 405, 406, 13 July 1794.

86. Nicolas, I, 433, 12 July 1794.

87. Nicolas, I, 439, 16 July 1794.

88. Gray, 38–41; Barras, 351–2.

89. Nicolas, I, 476, 6 and 10 Aug. 1794, to Prince William Henry.

90. Godfrey, 407–8, 409, 18, 19 July 1794.

91. Monmouth, E25, 15 June 1794, Hood to Sir John Coxe Hippersley.

92. Nicolas, I, 462, 31 July 1794, Nelson to Hood.

93. Holland Rose, 'Corsica', 64–7.

94. Nicolas, I, 427–9, 9–10 July 1794.

95. (UK)NA: PRO, ADM 51/1104.

96. (UK)NA: PRO, ADM 52/2707, 4 Aug. 1794.

97. Ajaccio was made the main naval base (Warren R. Dawson, *Nelson Collection*, 52–6, Aug. 1794).

98. (UK)NA: PRO, ADM 51/1104, 1–12 Aug. 1794.

99. NMM, Waldegrave Papers, Box 5, Waldegrave to Spencer, 11 June 1794; Nicolas, I, 476, 6, 10 Aug. 1794, to Prince William Henry.

100. (UK)NA: PRO, ADM 51/1104, 15 Aug. 1794; Nicolas, I, 477–9.

101. (UK)NA: PRO, ADM 52/2707, master's log.

102. Monmouth, E675, Josiah Nesbit to Fanny, 20 Aug. 1793, reports seizing a brig and sending her to Leghorn, with young Maurice Suckling as her prize master; PRO, ADM 51/1104, 29–30 Aug., 9 Sept. 1793. Naish, 91, 93, 27 Sept., 12 Oct. 1793. Nelson was beginning to have success, however; the letter to Pollard quoted above quotes £7,000 to be shared between the *Agamemnon* and the *Lowestoffe*.

103. Warren R. Dawson, *Nelson Collection*, 51, Nelson to Pollard, 27 June 1794; e.g., Wellcome 3676, 4 July, 8 Oct. 1793; 2 May, 15 July 1794.

104. Nicolas, II, 98, 12 Nov. 1795, Nelson to the prize agents John McArthur, John Udney and Thomas Pollard; Hill, 212.

105. Naish, 115, 27 June 1794.

106. Nicolas, I, 363, 1 Mar. 1794.

107. Nicolas, I, 350, 31 Jan. 1794, to Thomas Pollard; Morrison, II, 383, Marsh and Creed's accounts, 1795.

108. Nicolas, I, 483–4, 20 Sept. 1794, to Hood.

109. Nicolas, I, 481–2.

110. Naish, 215, 9 July 1795.

111. Nicolas, I, 491, 10 Oct. 1794, to Locker.

112. See pp. 183–5.

113. (UK)NA: PRO, ADM 51/1104, 26 Dec. 1794. The chain plate secured the shrouds, which supported the mast from the side of the ship; when it broke the mast was thus immediately endangered.

114. (UK)NA: PRO, ADM 52/2632, 18 Feb. 1795.

115. Findlay, 80, 124.

116. Naish, 187, 31 Oct. 1794.

117. BL, Add. MSS 34903, 1 Dec. 1794, Hood to Nelson; 34904 [n.d.], copy of a letter from Spencer to Hood in Hood's hand.

118. Naish, 256, 2 Nov. 1794, Fanny to Nelson, from Kentish Town.

119. Duffy, 'Hood', 271; Rodger, *Command of the Ocean*, 433.

120. Lloyd, *Gardner*, 110.

121. Nicolas, II, 31 Aug. 1795.

122. Huntington, HO 252, 4 Oct. 1795, Howe to Sir Roger Curtis.

123. James, I, 215, 10 Nov. 1794.

124. NMM, ADM/L/A/51, 13–14 Mar. 1795.

125. Gardiner, 162.

126. James, I, 287–8.

127. BL, Add. MSS 37852, 2 Apr. 1795, Elliot to William Windham.

128. NMM, ADM/L/A/51, 16–19 Mar. 1795.

129. Tracy, *Naval Chronicle*, I, 147.

130. Hotham, *Pages and Portraits*, I, 74.

131. Nicolas, II, 27, 5 Apr. 1795, to Gilbert Elliot.

132. Nicolas, II, 20–24, 21–24 Mar. 1795.

133. Fremantle, *Wynne* (1952), 254.

134. BL, Add. MSS 37852, 2 Apr. 1795, Elliot to William Windham.

135. Monmouth, E428, 26 Feb. 1795.

136. NMM, ADM/L/A/51, 15 June 1795.

137. Tracy, *Naval Chronicle*, 151.

138. NMM, ADM/L/A/51, 8 July 1795.

139. Tracy, *Naval Chronicle*, I, 152.

140. Tracy, *Naval Chronicle*, I, 149–51.

141. (UK)NA: PRO, ADM 52/2632.

142. Stirling, *Pages and Portraits*, I, 79–80.

143. Naish, 216, 9 July 1795.

144. Nicolas, II, 63, 29 July 1795, to William Nelson. The historian William James appropriated the phrase (James, I, 299n.).

145. Steel's *Navy List*, 1796.

146. Nicolas, II, 34, 24 Apr. 1795.

147. Monmouth, E428, 26 Feb. 1795.

148. Nicolas, II, 32, 24 Apr. 1795.

149. Naish, 218, 2 Aug. 1795, Nelson to Fanny.

150. The other two captains were Thomas Pakenham and George Berkeley (BL, Add. MSS 34904, 6 June 1795).

151. Morrison, II, 383, 385, accounts with Marsh and Creed, 1795–6. See also Naish, 320, 14 Mar. 1797.

152. Naish, 216, 18 July 1795.

153. Monmouth, E611, 5 Aug. 1795.

12 The Western Mediterranean: Independent Command

1. Naish, 225.
2. Naish, 339.
3. Naish, 217, 24 July 1795.
4. Corbett, *Spencer Papers*, II, 18n.
5. BL, Add. MSS 34962, 22 July 1795, Nelson to Hotham.
6. De Richery broke out of Toulon in Sept. when Hotham and his ships were provisioning at San Fiorenzo (Corbett, *Spencer*, II, 14).
7. Morriss, *Cockburn*, 28.
8. Wellcome 3667, 1 July 1795, P. P. Brill to Nelson.
9. Naish, 216, 18 July 1795.
10. Nicolas, II, 77, 31 Aug. 1795.
11. BL, Add. MSS 34962, 26 Aug., Nelson's orders to Cockburn; 26 Aug., letter to Drake; Nicolas, II, 72–3, 27 Aug. 1795, report to J. Harriman, clerk to Udney. The *Ariadne* went on shore during the operation and had to be towed off by the ships' boats ((UK)NA: PRO, ADM 52/2632, 26 Aug. 1795). Earlier in the month a previous attempt to cut out the convoy had failed (BL, Add. MSS 34904, 12 Aug. 1795, affidavit by George Andrews).
12. (UK)NA: PRO, ADM 52/2632, 30 Aug.; Nicolas, II, 76–7, 30 Aug. 1795.
13. Private collection, 10 Sept. 1795; draft in BL, Add. MSS 34962.
14. NMM, CRK/7/78, 4 Sept. 1795, Hotham to Nelson.
15. BL, Add. MSS 34962, 1 Aug. 1795; NMM, CRK/4/65, 19 Sept.; CRK/4/80, 26 Oct.; CRK/4/84, 7 Nov. 1795, Drake to Nelson.
16. NMM, CRK/4/64, 18 Sept. 1795, Drake to Nelson.
17. e.g., BL, Add. MSS 34904, 10 Sept. 1795, draft.
18. BL, Add. MSS 34904, 3 Jan. 1796, Pollard to Nelson; private collection, 3 Sept. 1796; Nicolas, II, 25 Jan. 1797, Nelson to Mrs Pollard.
19. (UK)NA: PRO, ADM 51/1126, 25–28 July 1795.
20. (UK)NA: PRO, ADM 51/1104, 3 Dec. 1794.
21. NMM, ADM/L/A/51, 25 Feb.–8 Mar. 1795; (UK)NA: PRO, ADM 51/1126, 7–15 Jan. 1796.
22. Naish, 190, 5 Dec. 1794.
23. Gardner, 103–6.
24. (UK)NA: PRO, ADM 36/11358, 11360.
25. Fremantle, *Wynne* (1952), 254.
26. Fremantle, *Wynne* (1952), 255–6.
27. Scott, 25, 28.
28. BL, Add. MSS 34906, 24 July 1797, Cockburn to Nelson.
29. Christie's catalogue, 21 June 1989, lot 214. The letter is published in Nicolas, II, 4, but without the postscript.
30. Fremantle, *Wynne* (1952), 255, 21, 27 Aug. 1795.

31. She does not appear in Sartori's *I Libretti italiani a stampa dalle origini al 1860: Catalogo analitico con 16 indici.*

32. The 'Centurion' English Tavern in Genoa, kept by a Mrs Walsh, was well known, as her grandson reminded Nelson (NMM, CRK/12/63 [n.d.], Robert Smith to Nelson).

33. e.g. BL, Add. MSS 34904, 3 Sep. 1796, Brame to Nelson.

34. Sparrow, 57, 63–4.

35. BL, Add. MSS 34904, 17 Mar. 1796. See also Warren R. Dawson, *Nelson Collection*, 56–62, for a version of their numeral code.

36. Naish, 241 [Dec. 1795] referring to 18–21 July 1795.

37. NMM, CRK/4/79, 10 Oct. 1795, Drake to Nelson; NMM, PST/39, 16 Aug. 1795, Nelson to Drake.

38. BL, Add. MSS 34904, 11, 23 May 1796.

39. e.g., BL, Add. MSS 34962, 8 Aug.; NMM, CRK/4/49, 3 Aug., CRK/4/55, 10 Aug.; Bucks., D/FR/33/11, 8 Aug. 1795, Nelson to Fremantle.

40. NMM, CRK/4/48, 29 July 1795.

41. e.g., BL, Add. MSS 34904, 15 July 1796, Nelson to Jervis; also NMM, PAR/251, 2 Aug. 1796.

42. e.g., NMM, CRK/4/44, 25 July 1795, Drake to Nelson.

43. BL, Add. MSS 34903, 3 Jan. 179[4], Udney to Nelson.

44. NMM, FRE/3, 4 Aug. 1796.

45. Morriss, *Cockburn*, 33, quoting from Cockburn's papers, 2 Oct. 1796.

46. Morriss, *Cockburn*, 23–6.

47. Private collection, 1 Aug. 1795, Nelson to Drake.

48. BL, Add. MSS 34904, 28 Mar. 1796.

49. Wellcome 3676, 9 Oct. 1793, 25 Apr. 31 May 1796; Warren R. Dawson, *Nelson Collection*, 51–2, 27 June 1794; BL, Add. MSS 34904, 6 July 1796.

50. BL, Add. MSS 34962, 6 Nov. 1795, Nelson to Trevor.

51. Morrison, II, 383, 385.

52. Nicolas, II, 93, 27 Oct. 1795; see Hill, 149, quoting Nicolas, II, 178–9.

53. James, I, 304–6.

54. (UK)NA: PRO, ADM 51/1126, 29, 30 Oct. 1795.

55. NMM, ADM/L/A/51, PRO, ADM 52/2632, 51/1126, 3–5 Nov. 1795.

56. (UK) NA: PRO, ADM1/2225, 13 Nov. 1795, Nelson to Evan Nepean. The admiral was Hyde Parker.

57. Monmouth, E37, 12 Nov. 1795, Nelson to Drake; he also wrote to the foreign secretary, Lord Grenville (Nicolas, II, 103–5, 23 Nov. 1795).

58. NMM, CRK/11/36, 15 Jan. 1796, Spencer to Nelson.

59. NMM, CRK/11/37, 4 May 1796; CRK/11/38, 12 May 1786; CRK/11/39, 26 May 1796, Spencer to Nelson. Whether he wrote to Spencer with the knowledge and agreement of Jervis is not known.

60. BL, Add. MSS 34904, 4 Sept. 1795, Thomas Jackson to Nelson.

61. (UK) NA: PRO, ADM 51/1126, 23–4 Nov. In the entry for 29 Nov. is an

indication of the strength of the weather: 'Hove one bullock overboard which died of bruises received in the Gale off Genoa.'

62. NMM, ADM/L/A/51, 29–30 Nov. 1795; Drake tried to retrieve them through an exchange, which was done eventually (NMM, CRK/4/92, 1 Dec. 1795, Drake to Nelson).

63. Crimmin, 'Jervis', 349.

64. Mackay, 'St Vincent', 60–66.

65. NMM, NEP/4, 5 Oct. 1797, Jervis to Nepean.

66. Fremantle, *Wynne* (1952), 282.

67. NMM, NEP/4, fol. 137, 15 Aug. 1798, to Nepean.

68. Crimmin, 'Jervis', 330.

69. NMM, CRK/11/71, 23 Aug. 1796.

70. Naish, 230, 2 Dec. 1795.

71. Naish, 290, 24 Apr. 1796; NMM, CRK/11/57, 11 May 1796, Jervis to Nelson.

72. Nicolas, II, 256–7, 27 Aug. 1796 and n.; Sheffield, 198.

73. NMM, NEP/4, 15 June 1798, to Nepean. Lack of discipline on Knight's ships was notorious (Stirling, *Pages and Portraits*, II, 53).

74. Corbett, *Spencer Papers*, II, 84, 29 Dec. 1796.

75. Corbett, *Spencer Papers*, II, 42, 27 July 1796.

76. Houghton, pf MS Eng. 196.5 (126), 22 Sept. 1796.

77. BL, Add. MSS 31166, 24 Mar. 1799, St Vincent to Keith.

78. Nicolas, II, 22, 26 Dec. 1795, Nelson to Edmund Nelson.

79. Naish, 271, repeats Harrison's story that Locker had introduced Nelson to Jervis in London. Nelson had taken a midshipman recommended by Jervis in the *Boreas*.

80. (UK) NA: PRO, ADM 51/1126, 19 Jan. 1796.

81. Naish, 282, 27 Jan. 1796.

82. NMM, NEP/7, 29 Aug. 1796, Jervis to Nepean.

83. NMM, PAR/251, 27 Sept. 1798; also Nicolas, III, 132–3.

84. Corbett, *Spencer Papers*, II, 43, 27 July 1796, Jervis to Spencer.

85. NMM, CRK/11/52, 13 Jan. 1796, Jervis to Nelson.

86. Naish, 281, 20 Jan. 1796.

87. NMM, CRK/11/53, 21 Mar. 1796.

88. Corbett, *Spencer Papers*, II, 21, 28 Mar. 1796. Nelson received the news on 15 Aug. (Naish, 301).

89. NMM, NEP/4 [n.d.], Jervis to Nepean.

90. NMM, ELL/141, 1 Apr. 1796.

91. (UK) NA: PRO, ADM 51/1126, 8 Apr. 1796.

92. Naish, 301, 15 Aug.; Corbett, *Spencer Papers*, II, 57, 29 Sept. 1796.

93. Naish, 286, 25 Mar. 1796.

94. Monmouth letter book, E987, 24 Feb. 1796.

95. (UK)NA: PRO, ADM 51/1126.

96. NMM, ELL/141, 28 Feb. 1796, Jervis to Elliot.

97. (UK) NA: PRO, ADM 51/1126, 1–2 Mar.; 52/2632, master's log; NMM, ADM/L/A/51, first lieutenant's log.

98. NMM, ELL/141, 5 Apr. 1796.

99. Monmouth, E987, 11 Apr. 1796.

100. (UK) NA: PRO, ADM 51/1126, NMM, ADM/I/A/51, 26 Apr. 1796. Lieutenant James Noble was wounded.

101. Morriss, *Cockburn*, 28, quoting Cockburn Papers and Brenton's *Naval History*, II, 223.

102. (UK) NA: PRO, ADM 51/1126, 1 June 1796, though it was noted that two large cables were lost in getting the prizes off.

103. Nicolas, II, 176, 31 May 1796. Jervis had originally intended William Hotham to have *La Minerve* (Stirling, *Pages and Portraits*, II, 31). Jervis wrote to Nelson that 'the exchange of captains of the *Meleager* and *La Minerve* shall be made under my Eye, which will prevent any discontent on either side' (NMM, CRK/11/65, 1 July 1796).

104. Dann, *Nagle Journal*, 200. Napoleon was not with these troops.

105. NMM, CRK/11/59, 1 June 1796, Jervis to Nelson.

106. NMM, CRK/11/59, 1 June 1796, Jervis to Nelson.

107. NMM, CRK/11/57, 11 May 1796, Jervis to Nelson.

108. NMM, CRK/11/58, 22 May 1796, Jervis to Nelson.

109. NMM, CRK/11/60, 7 June 1796, Jervis to Nelson.

110. (UK) NA: PRO, ADM 52/2632, 27 May 1796, master's log.

111. Naish, 295, 13 June 1796.

112. Naish, 293, 20 May 1796, Nelson to Fanny.

113. NMM, CRK/11/58, 22 May 1796, Jervis to Nelson.

114. (UK) NA: PRO, ADM 36/11360, *Agamemnon*'s muster book.

115. (UK) NA: PRO, ADM 51/1267, 12 June 1796.

116. NMM, CRK/11/66, 13 July 1796, Jervis to Nelson.

117. Naish, 11 May 1796.

118. (UK) NA: PRO, ADM 180/6. *The Agamemnon* did not require a repair, but was refitted quickly at Chatham between Oct. and Dec. 1796.

119. NMM, ELL/141, 5 July 1796, Jervis to Elliot.

120. Bucks., DFR 33/11, 23 June 1796.

121. Nicolas, II, 194n. Nelson was occupied with a complaint from the Genoese government that accused him of breaching neutrality.

122. Naish, 297, 7 July 1796, Nelson to Fanny.

123. NMM, CRK/11/64, 30 June 1796, Jervis to Nelson.

124. Naish, 300, 11 Aug. 1796.

125. Morrison, II, 222, 1 Aug. 1796.

126. NMM, CRK/10/70, accounts of 7 Jan. 1797.

127. Fremantle, *Wynne* (1952), 256.

128. NMM, CRK/11/66, 13 July 1796; BL, Add. MSS 34904, 18, 23 July 1796.

129. BL, Add. MSS 34904, fol. 231. Casa Turbati is in Via Carlo Fedeli in Pisa, near the Church of San Torpe and the Roman baths now known as the Bagno di Nerone, for which information I am indebted to Susie Nesso. Jervis gave Nelson permission to 'take your twenty days leave at Pisa Baths' (NMM, CRK/11/58, 22 May 1796).

130. NMM, ELL/159, 30 July, 10 Aug. 1796, Elliot to Nelson.

131. NMM, PAR/251, 2 Aug. 1796, Nelson to Jervis.

132. Nicolas, II, 233–42, 5–15 Aug., Nelson to Elliot; 6 Aug. 1796, Elliot to Nelson.

133. BL, Add. MSS 34904, 21, 22 Aug. 1796.

134. Huntington, HM 34180.

135. NMM, CRK/11/63, 29 June 1796.

136. Brenton, II, 338–44.

137. Fremantle, *Wynne* (1937), II, 112, 29 July 1796.

138. (UK) NA: PRO, ADM 36/11799. The soldiers were from the 69th Regiment.

139. BL, Add. MSS 34904, 7 July 1795.

140. BL, Add. MSS 34906, 12 May 1797, General de Burgh to Nelson.

141. Monmouth, E415, 28 Oct. 1798; Coleman, 179.

142. BL, Add. MSS 34904, 30 July, 1 Aug. 1796, Frances Caffarena to Nelson.

143. NMM, CRK/11/87, 16 Oct. 1796, Jervis to Nelson; NMM, ELL/11/59, Elliot to Jervis.

144. BL, Add. MSS 34904, 16 Jan. 1797. Nelson was to receive a further sad letter from Madame Caffarena in 1802, but full of news: 'Consul Brame is reduced to childhood in Pisa . . .' (NMM, CRK/3/3, 28 Dec. 1801).

145. Nicolas, II, 232, 3 Aug. 1796; several authors confuse Madame Caffarena with Adelaide Correglia; but see Jane Knight, 'Nelson's Old Lady'.

146. NMM, MS 95/001, 15 Aug. 1796, Jervis to Richard Bowen.

147. Fremantle, *Wynne* (1937), II, 104.

148. Fremantle, *Wynne* (1952), 257.

149. Nicolas, II, 209, 10 July 1796.

150. For a vivid lower-deck account in Aug. 1796 by Jacob Nagle of the *Blanche*, see Dann, 200–202.

151. NMM, CRK/11/75, 17 Sept. 1796.

152. e.g., NMM, ELL/141, 6 Oct. 1796, Jervis to Elliot; Nicolas, II, 259–64.

153. (UK) NA: PRO, ADM 51/1267, 11 Sept. 1796.

154. NMM, CRK/11/72, 25 Aug. 1796, Jervis to Nelson. The earl of Bute was the ambassador in Madrid.

155. NMM, ELL/141, 31 Aug. 1796, Admiralty Order.

156. NMM, ELL/141, 12, 15 Aug. 1796.

157. Naish, 301, 15 Aug. 1796, to Fanny.

158. (UK) NA: PRO, ADM 36/11823.

159. Nicolas, II, 282–6; James, I, 348.

160. Nicolas, II, 199, Nelson to Elliot.
161. King and Hattendorf, Chapter 5, reprint of 'Nelson at Bastia' by 'M. C.', *United Service Journal*, Feb. 1841, No. 147.
162. Naish, 306, 24 Oct. 1796, Nelson to Fanny.
163. Naish, 308, 22 Nov. 1796, Nelson to Fanny, off Ibiza, at night.
164. Ehrman, *Younger Pitt*, II, 610–11.
165. Corbett, *Spencer Papers*, I, 317–39, Aug. 1796–Jan. 1797; Holland Rose, 'Corsica', 77.
166. Corbett, *Spencer Papers*, II, 71, 11 Nov. 1796.
167. BL, Add. MSS 34904, 29 Oct. 1796.
168. Corbett, *Spencer Papers*, II, 72, 11 Nov. 1796.
169. NMM, ELL/141, 11 Nov. 1796, Jervis to Elliot; James, I, 398–9.
170. Monmouth, 1 Oct. 1796, Nelson to William Hamilton.
171. Houghton, pf MS Eng. 196.5(1a), 3 Sept. 1796; see also Monaque, 'Alexander', 208–10.
172. Corbett, *Spencer Papers*, II, 78, 10 Dec 1796
173. Naish, 305, 13 Oct. 1796.
174. NMM, CRK/11/68, 11 Aug. 1796.
175. Corbett, *Spencer Papers*, II, 400–401, 5 May 1797.
176. BL, Add. MSS 31166, 11 Feb. 1796.
177. Naish, 303, 10 Sept. 1796.
178. Naish, 304, 30 Sept. 1796.
179. Naish, 308, 22 Nov. 1796.
180. 'My complaint is as if a girth was buckled taut over my breast . . . If the Service will admit of it, perhaps I shall at a future day take your leave' (Nicolas, VII, lxxviii, 3 Jun. 1796, Nelson to Jervis).
181. Naish, 309, 22 Nov. 1796.

13 *La Minerve* and the *Blanche* to Porto Ferrajo

1. Naish, 310.
2. NMM, CRK/11/71, 22 Aug. 1796.
3. NMM, ELL/141, 10 Dec. 1796.
4. NMM, ELL/141, 11 Nov., 10 Dec. 1796.
5. Dann, 204.
6. Morriss, *Cockburn*, 34–5, 287.
7. Nicolas, VII, cxviii, 30 Sept. 1796.
8. NMM, CRK/11/79, 29 Sept. 1796, Jervis to Nelson; Morriss, *Cockburn*, 34–6.
9. Fremantle, *Wynne* (1952), 234, 6 Dec. 1796.
10. NMM, CRK/11/79, 29 Sept. 1796. Jervis had served with Sawyer's father, now an admiral, early in his career, in the same ship as Maurice Suckling, Nelson's uncle.

NOTES TO PP. 208–16

11. Dann, 206, 366; (UK)NA: PRO, ADM 51/1204, 19 Dec. 1796. Cockburn entered in his log that the vessel was a Genoese polacre from Cartagena bound for Malaga, though he counted eight rather than seven bales; the silk was Spanish property.

12. (UK)NA: PRO, ADM 51/1204, 20 Dec. 1796. In subsequent letters Nelson corrected the name of the Spanish ship, which was the *Sabina* and not the *Santa Sabina*. *Sabina* is confirmed by Spanish sources, e.g., Duro, VIII, 78.

13. Nicolas, II, 312–14, 314–15, 20 Dec. 1796, Nelson to Jervis; see also Monmouth, E599, 1 Jan. 1797, Nelson to Edmund Nelson, and Tracy, *Naval Chronicle*, I, 179n.

14. (UK)NA: PRO, ADM 1/396, 24 Dec. 1796, unknown correspondent to Admiralty; Duro, VIII, 78, gives two killed and forty-eight wounded.

15. Nicolas, II, 313–14, 20 Dec. 1796, Nelson to Jervis.

16. Dann, 206.

17. Monmouth, E988, 20 Dec. 1796.

18. Rahn Phillips, 439–40.

19. Nicolas, II, 446, 18 Sept. 1797, Nelson to Jervis. (Clarke and McArthur letter).

20. Dann, 207.

21. Nicolas, II, 326, 13 Jan. 1796, Nelson to William Nelson. Nicolas speculates that the 'particular tune' might have been 'See the Conquering Hero'.

22. Fremantle, *Wynne* (1937), II, 144–5.

23. BL, Add. MSS 34906, 24 July 1797, Cockburn to Nelson.

24. Fremantle, *Wynne* (1937), II, 162–3.

25. Slope, 437–4. The other captains were George Cockburn, the Hon. Philip Wodehouse, Richard Retalick and Bartholomew James.

26. Fremantle, *Wynne* (1952), 259, 28 Jan. 1797.

27. BL, Add. MSS 34905, 30 Dec. 1796, 'Account of a Court Martial'.

28. NMM, PAR/251, 5 Mar. 1797, Nelson to Jervis.

29. (UK)NA: PRO, ADM 1/396, 7 Feb. 1797, Jervis to Nepean.

30. (UK)NA: PRO, ADM 51/1204, 1 Jan. 1797.

31. Dann, 209.

32. Gilbert, 'Mutiny', 116–18; e.g., Gardner, 103.

33. When the *Blanche* was paid off in July 1798 the crew still disliked Hotham and they petitioned the Admiralty to be drafted to other ships (Dann, 211).

34. (UK)NA: PRO, ADM 1/396, 13 Feb. 1797, Jervis to Nepean.

35. Nicolas, VII, cxxviii, 16 Jan. 1797, Nelson to Spencer.

36. Nicolas, II, 322, 29 Dec. 1796, Nelson to de Burgh.

37. (UK)NA: PRO, ADM 1/396, 30 Dec. 1796, de Burgh to Jervis.

38. (UK)NA: PRO, ADM 1/396, 22 Jan. 1797, de Burgh to Jervis; Minto, II, 374, 24 Jan. 1797, Elliot to his wife.

39. Nicolas, VII, cxxvii, 4 Jan. 1797, Nelson to Spencer.

40. Nicolas, II, 324, 30 Dec. 1796, Nelson to de Burgh.

41. (UK)NA: PRO, ADM 1/396, 13 Feb. 1797, Jervis to de Burgh.

42. The *Mignonne* (32) was a French prize, later burnt at Porto Ferrajo.

43. Laughton, *Bartholomew James*, 323, 387–8.

44. Fremantle, *Wynne* (1937), II, 164. Mr Hardman was the private secretary to Sir Gilbert Elliot, presumably in charge of civil matters in Porto Ferrajo.

45. They were *Inconstant*, *Blanche*, the sloops *Peterel*, *Speedy*, *L'Utile*, the gunboats *Rose* and *Venom*, and the *Mignonne* (Nicolas, II, 330, 25 Jan. 1797, Nelson to Jervis).

46. (UK)NA: PRO, ADM 51/1204, 4 Feb.; ADM 52/3223, 5 Feb. 1797.

47. (UK)NA: PRO, ADM 1/396, 14 Jan. 1797, Jervis to William Parker.

48. (UK)NA: PRO, ADM 51/1204, 12 Feb. 1797.

49. (UK)NA: PRO, ADM 52/3223, 12 Feb. 1797.

50. Spinney, 'Hardy', 116. Spinney was quoting from unpublished memoirs.

51. (UK)NA: PRO, ADM 51/1204, 12 Feb. 1797; Morriss, *Cockburn*, 30–31.

52. Bethune, 13–15.

53. Harland, Chapter 21.

54. Morriss, 33, quoting NMM, Croker Papers, CKE/6 (microfilm), 11 Apr. 1845, Cockburn to J. W. Croker.

14   The Battle of Cape St Vincent and the Blockade of Cadiz

1. NMM, CRK/10/103, 14 Feb. 1805.

2. NMM, NEP/4.

3. (UK) NA: PRO, ADM 51/1204, 12 Feb. 1797.

4. (UK)NA: PRO, ADM 50/79. He arrived with five sail of the line, *Prince George* (98) and *Namur* (90), and three 74s (*Orion*, *Irresistible* and *Colossus*).

5. (UK)NA: PRO, ADM 50/79, signal of 2.10 p.m., 12 Feb. 1797.

6. (UK)NA: PRO, ADM 50/79, 13 Feb. 1797; Corbett, *Spencer Papers*, II, 402, 22 May 1797, Jervis to Spencer.

7. (UK)NA: PRO, ADM 51/1204; Goodwin, 137. The *Blanche* also joined the fleet at this time.

8. White, 'Eyewitness Account', 55: Miller to his father, 3 Mar. 1797.

9. (UK)NA: PRO, ADM 51/1204, 23–28 Jan. 1797.

10. e.g., (UK)NA: PRO, ADM 51/1204, 14 Dec. 1796: 'Water expended 1½ tons. Remains 121¼ tons. Rainwater 5 tons.'

11. White, 'Eyewitness Account', 55.

12. Parsons, 324.

13. (UK)NA: PRO, ADM 51/1204.

14. Parsons, 323.

15. Gonzalez-Aller and O'Donnell, 80.

16. Gonzalez-Aller and O'Donnell, 73.

17. Parsons, 321–2.

18. (UK)NA: PRO, ADM 50/79, 14 Feb. 1797; Palmer, 32; Tunstall, 217.

19. Corbett, *Spencer Papers*, I, 343; Cordova's Account, *Madrid Gazette*, 10 Mar. 1797; Gonzalez-Aller and O'Donnell, 76; Tunstall, 218.

20. Rodger, 'Tactics', 282-88.

21. White, 'Eyewitness Account', 56.

22. (UK)NA: PRO, ADM 52/2825, 14-15 Feb. 1797. The *Captain*'s master, Philip Thomas, has left a coherent and timed account of the battle in his log. It is strikingly similar to Captain Miller's long letter to his father of 3 Mar. 1797 (White, 'Eyewitness Account', 53-7).

23. (UK)NA: PRO, ADM 50/79; ADM 52/2825; NMM, ADM/L/C/51.

24. (UK)NA: PRO, ADM 52/2825.

25. Palmer, unpublished, longer and referenced version of 'Sir John's Victory', 27; I am grateful to Professor Palmer for sending me this copy. His detailed analysis of the battle appeared in the *Mariner's Mirror* in 1991. The impact of this fine piece of work has been blunted by that journal's policy of the time not to include footnotes.

26. Sturges Jackson, 235.

27. White, 'Eyewitness Account', 55.

28. BL, Add. MSS 34905, 15 Feb. 1797, Collingwood to Nelson.

29. Tunstall, 218.

30. Palmer, 'Sir John's Victory', 40.

31. Palmer, 'Sir John's Victory', 42.

32. (UK)NA: PRO, ADM 50/79.

33. Sturges Jackson, 218.

34. (UK)NA: PRO, ADM 52/2825.

35. (UK)NA: PRO, ADM 52/2825.

36. (UK)NA: PRO, ADM 1/396, 16 Feb. 1797.

37. Tracy, *Naval Chronicle*, I, 187. Fearney transferred to the *Theseus* with Nelson and was made a midshipman, but was promoted no further.

38. (UK)NA: PRO, ADM 50/79.

39. (UK)NA: PRO, ADM 50/79.

40. BL, Add. MSS 34905, fol. 326, Culverhouse to Nelson, 23 Mar. 1797.

41. (UK)NA: PRO, ADM 51/1212; Sturges Jackson, 247.

42. (UK)NA: PRO, ADM 50/79.

43. Houghton, pf MS Eng. 196.5 (10), gunner's stores fired away and expended, 14 Feb. 1797, William Colnutt, gunner. The majority were round shot: only 5 per cent was grape shot and 6 per cent double-headed. Twenty-eight 18-pounders fired 973, eighteen 9-pounders, 587.

44. James, II, 42; Nicolas, II, 338-9. William James's opinion that Nelson's action was 'not a spontaneous act, but arose from a signal made by the Commander-in-Chief' provoked an emotional response by Sir Harris Nicolas. James uses the evidence of 'an entry in the log book of a flag-ship then at no great distance from her'.

45. Palmer, 39; White, *Year of Destiny*, 55–6. Edgar Vincent's recent account takes an unusually critical view of Jervis's role, achievement and mental state (Vincent, 189–92).

46. White, *Year of Destiny*, 59.

47. Mackay, 245; Brenton, I, 289. The *Poder* was a 64-gun Spanish ship.

48. (UK)NA: PRO, ADM 1/396, 16 Feb. 1797, Jervis to Nepean.

49. BL, Add. MSS 34905, 15 Feb. 1797.

50. Nicolas, II, 335–6, 16 Feb. 1797; an unorthodox view of this letter is in Vincent (191), where it is described as 'bizarre and a travesty of events' written by 'a Jervis disorientated and overwhelmed by the emotional and mental overload of the battle'.

51. (UK)NA: PRO, ADM 1/396, 4 Apr. 1797, Jervis to Nepean.

52. See Nicolas, II, 340–43; Tracy, *Naval Chronicle*, I, 186–7.

53. BL, Add. MSS 75803, 14 Feb. 1797.

54. NMM, NEP/4, fol. 147, 3 Sept. 1798.

55. BL, Add. MSS 34905, 17 Mar. 1797.

56. Baring, 354, 15 Mar. 1797.

57. BL, Add. MSS 37845 [n.d.], fols. 150–54. Letters and drafts to and from the Assembly at Norwich are also among Windham's papers (Add. MSS 37877, 3 May; 1 Aug. 1797).

58. BL, Add. MSS 75814, 14 Feb. 1797, a memorandum entitled: 'Let the scoffer at Providence attend to the following incidents and then doubt if can.'

59. BL, Add. MSS 34905, Locker to Nelson, 17 Mar. 1797.

60. Spicer and Noble met Maurice Nelson, who reported to Fanny: 'they both speak in raptures and look upon my Brother as their Father' (Monmouth, E664, 10 May 1797); BL, Add. MSS 75812, 17 Mar. 1797, St Vincent to Spencer).

61. BL, Add. MSS 34905, 17 Mar. 1797.

62. Naish, 351, 11 Mar., Fanny to Nelson; Monmouth, E625, 6 Mar. 1797, Edmund Nelson to Nelson.

63. Nicolas, II, 341, 'A Few Remarks Relative to Myself in the *Captain*'.

64. For instance, the evidence of *Orion*'s master's log (Sturges Jackson, 232).

65. NMM, MID/1/70, 18 Feb. 1797. There is no obvious reason why this letter should be among Middleton's papers.

66. Nicolas, II, 471–3, Parker to Nelson, 25 July; Nelson to Parker, 19 Aug. 1797.

67. Corbett, *Spencer Papers*, II, 98–100, Parker to Spencer, 1 Sept.; Spencer to Parker, 22 Sept. 1797.

68. Tracy, *Naval Chronicle*, I, 190–92.

69. BL, Add. MSS 34938, 21 Mar. 1797, Jervis to Nelson.

70. Nicolas, II, 350, 16 Feb., Nelson to Minto; 368, 2 Apr. 1797, Nelson to Spencer.

71. NMM, Box 3, Waldegrave Papers, 7 Mar. 1797.

72. NMM, NEP/4, Jervis to Nepean, 29 Mar. 1797.

73. Naish, 348n.

74. BL, Add. MSS 34905, 17 Mar., Spencer to Nelson; (UK)NA: PRO, ADM 50/93, 2 Apr. 1797.

75. Steel's *Navy List*, June 1798.

76. BL, Add. MSS 34905, Elliot to Nelson, 15 Feb. 1797; Hoste to Nelson, 17 Mar.

77. BL, Add. MSS 34905, 15 Mar. 1797.

78. Monmouth, E627, 22 May 1797.

79. I am indebted to Tim Voeleker for these two references from Shrubland, Ipswich, SA 3/1/2, 25 Feb., 17 Mar. 1797, Lady Saumarez to Sir James Saumarez.

80. Tracy, *Naval Chronicle*, I, 188.

81. (UK)NA: PRO, ADM 1/396, 16 Feb. 1797, Jervis to Nepean.

82. Duro, VIII, 92-9; this sentence (Duro, VIII, 95) is translated in a version in Corbett, *Spencer Papers*, I, 346.

83. (UK)NA: PRO, ADM 1/396, 8 Mar. 1797. 'The Isla' is most likely to be the island fortress of San Sebastian, rather than the Isla de Leon where the dockyard is situated.

84. BL, Add. MSS 34938, 31 Mar. 1797, St Vincent to Nelson; Gonzalez-Aller and O'Donnell, 78-81; Guimera, 'Gravina'.

85. Monmouth, E45, 17 Feb. 1797, Nelson to Vice-Admiral Thompson; Nicolas, II, 350, 15 Feb. 1796, Nelson to Elliot.

86. Nicholas, II, 356, 23 Feb. 1797, to William Suckling.

87. Hills, 'St Vincent', 88. Nelson to Emma: 'My cough is very bad, and my side, where I was struck on 14th February, is very much swelled; at times a lump as large as my fist, brought on by violent coughing' (Pettigrew, II, 437, 25 Nov. 1804).

88. BL, Add. MSS 75814, Waldegrave's memorandum.

89. (UK)NA: PRO, ADM 50/79, 2 Mar. 1797.

90. (UK)NA: PRO, ADM 51/1212, 20 Apr. 1797.

91. (UK)NA: PRO, ADM 1/396, 5 Mar. 1797.

92. NMM, MAM/1, 3 Mar. 1797, Nelson to Kitty Matcham. Endorsed: 'The last letter I rec[eive]d from the best of brothers written with his right hand.'

93. (UK)NA: PRO, ADM 1/396, 11 Apr. 1797. By 10 Apr. he had seven ships of the line blockading the port (PRO, ADM 50/93, 10 Apr. 1797). Knox, 20.

94. Houghton, pf MS Eng. 196.5 (126), 20 Apr., Jervis to Nepean; BL, Add. MSS 34938, 7 May 1797, Jervis to Nelson.

95. (UK)NA: PRO, ADM 1/396, 8 Apr. 1797, Fremantle to St Vincent.

96. (UK)NA: PRO, ADM 1/396, 22 Mar. 1797, St Vincent to Nepean.

97. Parsons, 312; (UK)NA: PRO, ADM 1/396, 22 Mar. 1797, St Vincent to Nepean.

98. Brenton, I, 323-4, 14 Mar. 1797, St Vincent to Fremantle.

99. (UK)NA: PRO, ADM 50/93.

100. BL, Add. MSS 75812, 13 Apr. 1797, St Vincent to Spencer.

101. (UK)NA: PRO, ADM 1/396, 1 May 1797, Nelson to St Vincent.

102. (UK)NA: PRO, ADM 1/396, 5 May, 1797, St Vincent to Nepean, Fremantle's enclosure of 8 Apr. 1797.

103. (UK)NA: PRO, ADM 1/396; ADM 51/1194, 21 Apr. 1797.

104. (UK)NA: PRO, ADM 1/396, 12 May 1797, St Vincent to Nepean.

105. (UK)NA: PRO, ADM 51/1194.

106. NMM, LBK/51, 19 May 1797. Petty officers and able seamen were to receive 4s. a month, ordinary seamen 3s. and landsmen 2s. Wounded seamen were also to continue in pay until their wounds healed.

107. BL, Add. MSS 34948, 17 June 1797, St Vincent to Nelson; BL, Add. MSS 75812, 20 Mar. 1797, St Vincent to Spencer.

108. Goodwin, 157; (UK)NA: PRO, ADM 1/396, 21 May 1797, St Vincent to Nepean.

109. (UK)NA: PRO, ADM 51/1194; 51/1221; 36/12648.

110. Nicolas, VII, cxliv, 23 June 1797, Nelson to St Vincent.

111. Naish, 326, 15 June 1797.

112. (UK)NA: PRO, ADM 51/1221, 31 May, 6, 26 June 1797.

113. BL, Add. MSS 34906, 3, 10 June, 12 July 1797, Calder to Nelson; PRO, ADM 51/1221, 3, 12, 20, 23 June 1797; Nicolas, VII, Addenda, cxlvii, 15 July 1797, Nelson to St Vincent; Buckland, 15.

114. Fremantle, *Wynne* (1937), II, 184, 22 July 1797.

115. Nicolas, VII, Addenda, cxlv, 3 July 1797.

116. Dann, 210.

117. NMM, NEP/4, fol. 17, 5 Apr. [1797].

118. Corbett, *Spencer Papers*, II, 401, 5 May 1797, St Vincent to Spencer.

119. Fremantle, *Wynne* (1937), II, 182, 29 June 1797.

120. Corbett, *Spencer Papers*, II, 406, 15 June 1797, St Vincent to Spencer.

121. Fremantle, *Wynne* (1937), II, 183, 5 July 1797.

122. Nicolas, VII, Addenda, cxlv, 3 July 1797.

123. Nicolas, VII, Addenda, cxlvii, 13 July 1797; Corbett, *Spencer Papers*, II, 393, 19 Apr. 1797, St Vincent to Spencer; (UK)NA: PRO, ADM 1/396, c. 18 Apr. 1797, St Vincent to Nepean.

124. Naish, 328, 30 June 1797, Nelson to Fanny.

125. BL, Add. MSS 34906, 15 June 1797, Saumarez to Nelson.

126. BL, Add. MSS 34906, 9 June 1797. The cargoes were valued at £348 and the agent inquired whether it would be possible to have bills drawn on London for the amount.

127. BL, Add. MSS 34938, 5, 13 June 1797, St Vincent to Nelson.

128. BL, Add. MSS 34906, 2 June–12 July 1796. On 4 June, for instance, the challenge was 'Anson' and the answer 'Boscawen'; on 5 June it was 'Hawke' and 'Saunders'.

129. (UK)NA: PRO, ADM 51/1221, 4 July 1797.

130. Nicolas, II, 404, 5 July 1797, Jervis's dispatch. One of the British launches was sunk, but raised the next day by the *Culloden*.

131. NMM, PAR/251, 5 July 1797.

132. (UK)NA: PRO, ADM 51/1221.

133. Nicolas, VII, Addenda, cxlv, 3 July 1797.

134. Buckland, 8–10. Miller's account took the form of a detailed letter to his father.

135. NMM, PAR/251, 5 July 1797.

136. Nicolas, VII, Addenda, cxlv, 6 July 1797, Nelson to St Vincent.

137. (UK)NA: PRO, ADM 51/1221, 9 July 1797.

138. Fremantle, *Wynne* (1937), II, 183, 6 July 1797.

139. Nicolas, VII, Addenda, cxlvi–cxvii, 13 July 1797, Nelson to St Vincent. This mutiny is not confirmed by Spanish sources.

140. Corbett, *Spencer Papers*, II, 410, St Vincent to Nepean; 411, to Spencer, 9 July 1797.

141. Gilbert, 'Buggery', 81; for the outcome of the Sawyer case, see Morriss, *Cockburn*, 34–6; NMM, CRK/11/79, 29 Sept., CRK/11/80, 1 Oct.; CRK/11/83, 10 Oct.; CRK/11/89, 17 Oct. 1796, Jervis to Nelson.

142. Gilbert, 'Buggery', 84–5, 97. He was Henry Allen, commander of the *Rattler*, on 15 May 1797.

143. Slope, '*Emerald*', 612–15.

144. Lincoln, 124–5; Rodger, 'Naval Chaplain', 41; Scott, 192.

145. Nicolas, II, 409–10, 9 July 1797, Nelson to Calder.

146. Naish, 328, 30 June 1797.

15   Disaster at Santa Cruz

1. Taylor, 53.

2. BL, Add. MSS 75805; Aspinall, *George III*, II, 1,613.

3. (UK)NA: PRO, ADM 1/396, 19 Apr. 1797, Bowen to St Vincent.

4. Spinney, 'Santa Cruz', 207.

5. Tracy, *Naval Chronicle*, 1, 194, in Troubridge's 'Memoir of Public Services', quoting letter of 12 Apr. 1797.

6. BL, Add. MSS 34938, 6 June 1797.

7. BL, Add. MSS 34948, 17 June 1797.

8. Nicolas, II, 412–13n.

9. Buckland, 16.

10. (UK)NA: PRO, ADM 51/1221.

11. Horsburgh, I, 11; Hydrographer, *Africa Pilot*, 104. Guimerá, *Tenerife 1797*, 7; Nicolas, II, 430, Nelson's journal. These winds are known today as 'katabatic' winds.

12. BL, Add. MSS 34906, fol. 125 [n.d.]. Nelson drew a larger sketch for Lord Keith in 1800 (Lloyd, *Keith Papers*, opposite 91).

13. Guimerá, *Tenerife 1797*, 34, Appendix 2.

14. Guimerá, *Tenerife 1797*, 1, 5.

15. Buckland, 17.

16. Tracy, *Naval Chronicle*, 196–7. Nelson also drafted on 20 July the terms of surrender of the town, the first paragraph of which covered the terms of surrender of the Manila galleon (Nicolas, II, 419–20).

17. Buckland, 18.

18. Naish, 372.

19. Guimerá, *Tenerife 1797*, 8.

20. Nicolas, II, 417. The average July temperature is 34 degrees C (Hydrographer, *Africa Pilot*, Appendix).

21. Buckland, 19.

22. Nicolas, II, 443, 8 Sept. 1797, Nelson to Sir Andrew Snape Hamond.

23. Buckland, 23.

24. Nicolas, II, 443, 8 Sept. 1797, Nelson to Sir Andrew Snape Hamond.

25. Nicolas, II, 421; Naish, 374, 'Lady Nelson's memorandum', written about 1806; there is every reason to think that this account is based on Josiah Nisbet's recollection of the incident.

26. Fremantle, *Wynne* (1952), 278.

27. Buckland, 24.

28. Guimerá, *Tenerife 1797*, 12.

29. (UK) NA: PRO, ADM 51/1221.

30. Buckland, 31.

31. BL, Add. MSS 34906, 25 July 1797.

32. Naish, 374.

33. (UK)NA: PRO, ADM 101/123/2, 25 July 1797.

34. Watt, 28.

35. (UK) NA: PRO, ADM 101/121/2.

36. BL, Add. MSS 34906, fol. 215 [Aug.] 1797, 'Translation of a Spanish despatch by Revd. Mr Mangold found among the papers of a Spanish schooner captured off the Coast of Barbary by frigates *Alcmene* and *Andromache*'.

37. Buckland, 27–30.

38. BL, Add. MSS 34906, fol. 215.

39. Buckland, 30. This is largely based on Miller's account (Buckland, 27–30). See also White, *Year of Destiny*, 117–25.

40. Nicolas, II, 424; (UK) NA: PRO, ADM 1/396, 16 Feb. 1797, Jervis to Nepean.

41. Nicolas, II, 433.

42. (UK) NA: PRO, ADM 51/1221.

43. Fremantle, *Wynne* (1952), 279.

44. (UK) NA: PRO, ADM 51/1221, 26 July–16 Aug. 1797.

45. Fremantle, *Wynne* (1952), 281, 13 Aug. 1797.

46. Lloyd and Coulter, *Medicine and the Navy*, 143–4.

47. Fremantle, *Wynne* (1952), 280.

48. BL, Add. MSS 75813, 16 Aug. 1797.

49. Nicolas, II, 435, 16 Aug. 1797.

50. BL, Add. MSS 75813, 16 Aug. 1797.

51. Nicolas, II, 435–6n., 16 Aug. 1797, St Vincent to Nelson.

52. Nicolas, II, 436, 3 Aug. 1797.

53. (UK) NA: PRO, ADM 50/93, 20 Aug. 1797.

54. (UK) NA: PRO, ADM 101/120/6, 20 Aug. 1797.

55. Fremantle, *Wynne* (1937) II, 20–1 Aug. 1797, 188–9.

56. Nicolas, II, 444, 18 Sept. 1797, Nelson to St Vincent.

57. (UK) NA: PRO, ADM 101/120/6.

58. Fremantle, *Wynne* (1952) 282, 23 Aug. 1797.

59. Fremantle, *Wynne* (1937) II, 189; 26, 31 Aug. 1797; (UK) NA: PRO, ADM 51/1190.

60. (UK) NA: PRO, ADM 101/120/6, 1 Sept. 1797.

61. NMM, WYN/104, 2 Sept. 1797, Young to Pole.

62. NMM, WYN/104, 6 Oct. 1797, Young to Pole.

63. NMM, NEP/4, 24 Oct. 1797, St Vincent to Nepean.

64. BL, Add. MSS 34906, 3 Sept. 1797, Spencer to Nelson.

65. NMM, PAR/251, 18 Sept. 1797, Nelson to St Vincent.

66. Duffy, 'Science and Labour', 40, quoting from Captain A. Crawford, *Reminiscences of a Naval Officer* (1851, repr. 1999), 213.

67. Nicolas, II, 435, 16 Aug. 1797; Addison, *Cato*, I, ii, 43: ' 'Tis not in mortals to command success/But we'll do more, Sempronius; we'll deserve it.'

16   Recovery and High Command

1. *Bath Journal, Bath Herald* and *Bath Chronicle and Weekly Gazette*.

2. NMM, PAR/251, 18 Sept. 1797.

3. Naish, 332–3, 5 Aug. 1797. Oman (251) asserts that the letter was delivered on Sat., 2 Sept. The *London Gazette* published the news of Santa Cruz on 2 Sept.; Nelson arrived in Bath on 3 Sept.

4. Naish, 378; Lloyd and Coulter, III, 144.

5. *Bath Journal*, 11 Sept. 1797.

6. Bodleian MS Montagu d. 16 fol. 28, 6 Sept. 1797, Fanny to William Suckling.

7. BL, Add. MSS 34906, 3 Sept. 1797.

8. BL, Add. MSS 34906, 17 Oct. 1797.

9. BL, Add. MSS 34906, 19 Sept. 1797, Thomas Coke to Nelson.

10. NMM, AGC/18/15, 6 Oct. 1797, Nelson to St Vincent.

11. BL, Add. MSS 75813, 29 Sept. 1797.

12. BL, Add. MSS 34906, 22 Sept. 1797.

13. *Bath Journal*, 2 Oct. 1797.

14. Nicolas, II, 448n. Although this is a Clarke and McArthur story, Nicolas checked it with Lady Berry and cites Lord Eldon in support.

15. William Locker was the first to call on the Nelsons (NMM, PAR/251, 18 Sept. 1797).

16. Naish, 379.

17. BL, Add. MSS 34906, 28 Sept. 1797, Marsh, Sable and Stracey to Nelson.

18. BL, Add. MSS 34906, 27 Sept. 1797, Galwey to Nelson.

19. Huntington, HM 34017, 2 Oct. 1797, Nelson to Fellowes; BL, Add. MSS 34906, 3 Mar. 1798, Fellowes to Nelson.

20. Lloyd and Coulter, 145.

21. NMM, MON/1/8, 1 Oct. 1797, Nelson to Commissioner Hope.

22. BL, Add. MSS 34906, 22 Sept. 1797, Man to Nelson; fol. 268, 288, 6 Dec. 1797; Charles Thompson thought that it would be quicker to go to law about the matter (BL, Add. MSS 34906, 11 Dec. 1797, Thompson to Nelson).

23. BL, Add. MSS 34906, 10, 12 May 1798, Heseltine (prize agent) to Maurice Nelson; 34907, 1 June 1798, Cockburn to Nelson.

24. Monmouth, E629, 12 Oct., Edmund Nelson to Nelson; E655, 11 Nov.; 646, 30 Nov. 1797, William Nelson to Nelson.

25. Naish, 380.

26. Naish, 378.

27. Lloyd and Coulter, III, 145.

28. Naish, 378.

29. Huntington, HO 209, 20 Dec. 1794, Howe to Curtis.

30. Edgcumbe, II, 77.

31. Minto, II, 2, 5 Oct. 1797, Minto to his wife.

32. NMM, WYN/104, 6 Oct. 1797, Young to Charles Morice Pole.

33. Nicolas, II, 449, 11 Oct. 1797, Fanny to William Locker.

34. Holkham Gun Book, 3, 12 Nov. 1797. On 3 Nov., for instance, Coke sent six partridges and a pheasant.

35. BL, Add. MSS 34906, 22 Nov. 1797, Galwey to Nelson.

36. Nicolas, II, 449–50, 12, 23 Oct. 1797, Nelson to Loughborough.

37. Baring, 382, entry for 28 Nov. 1797.

38. Nicolas, II, 453. The keel of the *Foudroyant* had been laid nine years earlier at Plymouth Dockyard and was not to be launched until Aug. 1798.

39. BL, Add. MSS 34906, 25 Feb. 1798, Berry to Nelson: 'There's eternal reports about our destination but I regard them not.'

40. BL, Add. MSS 34906, 8 [Dec.] 1797.

41. *Bath Journal*, 4 Dec. 1797.

42. Nicolas, II, 453n.; Namier and Brooke, III, 640.

43. Baring, 384.

44. Colley, 'Apotheosis', 104, 96–106.

45. BL, Add. MSS 34933, 12 Dec. 1797.

46. Pasley, 33.

47. BL, Add. MSS 34906, 19 Dec. 1797, printed instructions for the ceremony;

Bath Journal, 25 Dec.; *Bath Chronicle*, 21 Dec. 1797; also Oman, 269–70; Colley, 'Apotheosis', 110; Jordan and Rogers, 213.

48. (UK)NA: PRO, ADM 180/6. The *Vanguard* had been in dock a little short of four months. She had been recoppered. The total cost of the refit was computed at £19,121, of which rigging and stores cost £8,369 and hull and yards £10,752.

49. (UK)NA: PRO, ADM 52/3516, 26 Dec. 1797–22 Jan. 1798; two Mediterranean station ships, the *Victory* and the *St George*, were paid off in Oct. (NMM, CHA/F/3, 24 Oct. 1797).

50. NMM, CHA/E/59, 13, 16 Jan., 17 Feb. 1798, Navy Board to the Chatham yard officers.

51. BL, Add. MSS 34906, 25 Feb. 1798.

52. *Bath Journal*, 19 Feb. 1798.

53. Nicolas, III, 4–5, 29 Jan. 1798, to Thomas Lloyd. Nicolas identifies him as the captain of the *Glasgow*, rescued by Nelson when his ship burnt in 1779 (Nicolas, III, 17n.). This letter has been much copied to a high standard in facsimile. During the author's time as custodian of manuscripts at the National Maritime Museum, examples of the facsimile were often brought in to the library by owners for inspection, hoping to be told that they owned an original letter.

54. BL, Add. MSS 34906, 12 Mar. 1798.

55. See p. 337.

56. BL, Add. MSS 34906, 14 Mar., Joseph Chapman to Nelson; 14 Mar., Thomas Rumsey (whose son did not accompany Nelson); 29 Mar. 1798, James Hawkins Whitshed; four [n.d.] from Lady Collier. There is also a copy of an angry letter to Lady Collier from Berry, who discovered that a bill for £10 to cover the expenses of Francis Augustus Collier was not honoured (24 Apr. 1798). Collier was to have a distinguished naval career.

57. BL, Add. MSS 34906, 16 Mar. 1798, Campbell to Nelson.

58. BL, Add. MSS 34906, 13 Mar. 1798, Parker to Nelson.

59. Baring, 389, 6 Mar. 1798. Fanny was to dine with Phillip and his wife in Bath; Nelson described him as 'a good man' (Naish, 421, 4 Apr., Fanny to Nelson; 392, 7 Apr. 1798, Nelson to Fanny).

60. Edgcumbe, 77–8.

61. Coleman, 146, points to the inaccuracies of this often-related story.

62. Coleman, 148, quoting NMM, PAR/251.

63. BL, Add. MSS 34906, 17 Mar. 1798.

64. Duffy, 'Naval Intelligence', 279.

65. *Bath Journal*, 19 Mar. 1798; Huntington, HM 34018, 31 Mar. 1798, Nelson to Fanny. See his farewell note to Sir Peter Parker and his family (Houghton, pf MS Eng. 196.5 (13), 9 Apr. 1798).

66. Corbett, *Spencer Papers*, II, 445, Spencer to St Vincent.

67. Duffy, 'Naval Intelligence', 280–83; see Warren R. Dawson, *Nelson Collection*, 292–5, 28 Apr. 1798, Lord Grenville's minute.

68. Corbett, *Spencer Papers*, II, 231, dated by Sir Julian Corbett as Feb. 1797 but, as corrected by Piers Mackesy, Apr. 1798 (Mackesy, *Statesmen*, 17n.).
69. Corbett, *Spencer Papers*, II, 240, 29 Jan. 1798, Dundas to Spencer; Mackesy, *Statesmen*, 16. Dundas was secretary of state *for* war, not to be confused with the secretary-*at*-war, William Windham. Both were in cabinet.
70. Corbett, *Spencer Papers*, II, 441, 1 May 1798.
71. NMM, NEP/4, 30 Oct. 1797, St Vincent to Nepean; ORD/11, 19 Jan. 1798, Orde to Lady Orde.
72. NMM, NEP/4, 19 Feb. 1798.
73. BL, Add. MSS 34906, 11 May 1798; Barritt, 289.
74. NMM, WYN/104, 4 July 1798, Young to Charles Morice Pole.
75. Corbett, *Spencer Papers*, II, 439, 29 Apr. 1798; see also NMM, CRK/7/8, 25 Apr. 1798, transcript of a letter from Minto to Nelson.
76. NMM, ORD/11, 16 June 1798, Orde to Lady Orde.
77. NMM, ORD/11, 8 July 1798, Orde to Lady Orde.
78. This extraordinary episode has been bravely chronicled by Sir John Orde's descendant, His Honour Judge Denis A. Orde (Orde, 1–7).
79. Huntington, STG 159 (8), 20 Dec. 1806, Orde to Thomas Grenville.
80. Steel's *Navy List*, June 1798, lists the promotion of rear-admirals as follows: 1791, 0; 1792, 0; 1793, 13; 1794, 27; 1795, 23; 1796, 0; 1797, 9; 1798, 0. Up to Jan.–June 1799, 34 (Steel, June 1799).
81. NMM, WYN/104, 19 Mar. 1799, Young to Pole.
82. NMM, WYN/104, 21 July 1798, Young to Pole.
83. Morrison, 156–7 [11 July, 1801], Nelson to Orde.
84. Huntington, HM 34020, 11 Jan. 1799.
85. NMM, NEP/4, 19 June 1798. St Vincent also wrote to Nelson to warn him of the feelings of Parker and Orde (BL, Add. MSS 31166 [?] June 1798).

17   Chasing the French

1. (UK)NA: PRO, ADM 2/1353.
2. NMM, NEP/4.
3. Naish, 395, 4 May 1798.
4. Naish, 431, 435, 439, 28 May, 18 June, 16 July 1798.
5. Naish, 395.
6. Naish, 423 [5 Apr.] 1798.
7. Naish, 433, 11 June; 439, 2, 16 July 1798.
8. UK(NA): PRO, ADM 52/3516, 3, 5 May; NMM, ADM/L/V/28, 6 May 1798.
9. NMM, NEP/4, 2 May 1798.
10. Fremantle, *Wynne* (1937), II, 183.
11. BL, Add. MSS 34906, 11 May 1798, 'Substance of the Commander-in-Chief's Orders'.

12. UK(NA): PRO, ADM 52/3516.

13. UK(NA): PRO, ADM 52/3516; NMM, ADM/L/V/28, 20–23 May 1798.

14. NMM, CRK/3/90, 30 Oct. 1803.

15. Lavery, *Nile*, 60–61.

16. Berry, 5.

17. BL, Add. MSS 34906, 11 Dec. 1797.

18. Lavery, *Nile*, 51.

19. James, II, 170, 201.

20. Harland, 208.

21. Coleridge, I, 548.

22. Naish, 396–7, 24 May 1798.

23. NMM, ADM/L/V/28, 27 May 1798; Gwyther, 'Carloforte', 19–23.

24. Gwyther, 'Carloforte', 24.

25. UK(NA): PRO, ADM 52/3516; NMM, ADM/L/V/28, 23–8 May 1798.

26. Gwyther, 'Carloforte', 27–8.

27. Barritt, 284–95; Lavery, *Nile*, Chapter 15. Both authors analyse the complicated rendezvous system set up by St Vincent and Nelson that failed to take into account a long foray into the Eastern Mediterranean.

28. Nicolas, III, 27, 11 June, Nelson to St Vincent; ADM 52/3516, 8 June 1798.

29. William Young at the Admiralty doubted that the reinforcement would meet up with Nelson (NMM, WYN/104, 22 June 1798, Young to Pole).

30. Mackesy, *Statesmen*, 22.

31. Clements Library, Melville Papers, 'Precis of correspondence and intelligence relating to Napoleon's expedition to Egypt', 20 Apr. 1798–10 May 1799. It contains a list of fifty-one pieces of intelligence received by the British government before the destination of Egypt was confirmed incontrovertibly.

32. Corbett, *Spencer Papers*, II, 437–41.

33. Tracy, *Deterrence*, 72–3, 100–103.

34. Schroeder, 179.

35. NMM, NEP/4, 15 June 1798, St Vincent to Nepean.

36. The Foreign Office acted without telling Dundas. (Clements, Melville Papers, 'Precis of correspondence').

37. Clements Library, Melville Papers, 'Memorandum by Evan Nepean, 29 Apr–24 July 1798'.

38. See Lavery, *Nile*, 93–8, for a detailed consideration of the cabinet decision Warren R. Dawson, *Nelson Collection*, 292–312, prints some lesser known and useful documents.

39. BL. Add. MSS 34906, 24 May 1798.

40. NMM, NEP/4, 19 May 1798.

41. Huntington HM 34023, 29 Sept. 1798, to Roger Curtis.

42. Hughes, 90, 3 Dec. 1798, Collingwood to Sir Edward Blackett.

43. Clements Library, Melville Papers, 18 June 1798, Dundas to Lord Macartney.

44. Corbett, *Spencer Papers*, II, 446, 19 May 1798. The problems of victualling

and watering were outlined in a long memorandum from David Heatley to St Vincent (BL, Add. MSS 34906, 29 May 1798).

45. Lavery, *Nile*, 13–24; Holland Rose, *Hood and Toulon*, 81; Battesti, 217–18.

46. Battesti, 217–18. This author calculates that the full complement of the French warships should have been 9,976, but that effective seamen amounted to only 7,750, while soldiers amounted to 7,850.

47. e.g., BL, Add. MSS 34906, 9, 16, 17 June 1798; Monmouth, E 417, 418, 15, 16, 26, 30 June 1798. These letters also related to the efforts of Hamilton to persuade Naples to supply Nelson's ships with stores and provisions. Emma Hamilton's later exaggerated account of her role in persuading the king and queen of Naples to supply Nelson's fleet should be discounted (Houghton, pf MS Eng. 196.5 (72), 7 Feb. 1813).

48. BL, Add. MSS 34906, 20 Apr. 1798. In a letter of 28 May, Udney revised his opinion, postulating the objective as Naples or Sicily.

49. Berry, 9.

50. Lavery, *Nile*, 124–5, 134–5. Lavery believes that Hamilton may have mentioned the possibility of Egypt as Napoleon's objective outside the meeting with Acton, but as he did not believe it, failed to put the possibility over with any emphasis; as a result, the unsubtle Troubridge dismissed and forgot the remark.

51. Naish, 410, 29 June 1798, Nelson to St Vincent.

52. Monmouth, E986, 22 June 1798; Lavery, *Nile*, 126.

53. Naish, 407–8.

54. NMM, ADM/L/V/28.

55. Lavery, 229–235, especially the track charts of the frigates (229, 234).

56. Berry, 15.

57. BL, Add. MSS 34907, 28 June 1798, Hamilton to Nelson. St Vincent was now able to send some more frigates after Nelson, including on 9 July *L'Aigle* with Joseph Nisbet aboard. She, however, was wrecked ((UK) NA: PRO, ADM 50/93, 9 July 1798; Lavery, *Nile*, 239).

58. NMM, ADM/L/V/28, 20–27 June 1798.

59. Naish, 411–12, 23 Jan. 1802.

60. HMC, *Dropmore*, IV, 328, Dundas to Lord Grenville, 28 Sept. 1798.

61. Naish, 409–11, 29 June 1798, draft.

62. NMM, AGC/W/2, Thomas Wilkes to his cousin Henry Clarke, 15 Aug. 1798; also Lavery, *Nile*, 131.

63. Lavery, *Nile*, 140.

64. Battesti, 70, 66–7.

65. Lavery, *Nile*, 142–50.

66. NMM, ADM/L/V/28, 4 July 1798.

67. BL, Add. MSS 34907, 3 July 1798.

68. NMM, ADM/L/V/28, 4–15 July 1798.

69. Lavery, *Nile*, 134, quoting BL, Add. MSS 34974.

70. Berry, 17–18.

71. Lavery, 156, 132.
72. NMM, ADM/L/V/28.
73. Ross, I, 244.
74. Palmer, 'Command and Control', 702; Rodger, 'Tactics', 293–4.
75. Ross, I, 214.
76. Ross, I, 210.
77. Ross, 207.
78. NMM, ADM/L/V/28.
79. Sturges Jackson, II, 19, 10 Aug. 1798, Hood to Viscount Hood.
80. Nicolas, III, 47, 22 July 1798.
81. Nicolas, III, 46, 22 July 1798.
82. BL, Add. MSS 34907, 1 July 1798, Curtis to Nelson.
83. BL, Add. MSS 34907, 22 June 1798, Tough to Nelson.
84. BL, Add. MSS 34907, 16 June 1798.
85. NMM, WYN/104, 22 June 1798.
86. BL, Add. MSS 34907, 18 July 1798, Thomas Jackson to Nelson.

18   The Battle of the Nile

1. Clements Library, Melville Papers.
2. Lavery, *Nile*, 166.
3. NMM, ADM/L/V/28, 28–31 July 1798.
4. Lavery, *Nile*, 167.
5. (UK) NA: PRO, ADM 52/3550, 2 Aug. 1798.
6. Malcolmson, 291–7, confirms the story of Hallowell's chart as told in Clarke and McArthur (Nicolas, III, 55).
7. Sturges Jackson, II, 20, 10 Aug. 1798, Hood to Viscount Hood.
8. NMM, AGC/W/2, 15 Aug. 1798.
9. Minto, III, 150, 7 Sept. 1800, Lady Minto to Lady Malmesbury.
10. Battesti, 88–9.
11. Battesti, 80–84, 88–9.
12. BL, Add. MSS 34907, fol. 107, translation of 'Rear-Admiral Blanquet's account of the Battle of the Nile'; printed in Tracy, *Naval Chronicle* (1, 271–6).
13. BL, Add. MSS 34907, fo. 107
14. Elliot, 17.
15. Elliot, 11–12, also attested by Thomas Browne, 27 Apr. 1845 (Nicolas, III, 474); but see Lambert, *Laughton* (2002), 132–4, for Sir J. K. Laughton's denial of Foley's role.
16. Herbert, 43.
17. Sturges Jackson, II, 21, 10 Aug. 1798, Hood to Viscount Hood.
18. (UK) NA: PRO, ADM 52/3055.
19. See pp. xxxii–xxxiii.

20. NMM, ADM/L/G/64; Elliot, 12.

21. Elliot, 10.

22. Elliot, 18.

23. Sturges Jackson, II, 23, 10 Aug. 1798, Hood to Viscount Hood.

24. BL, Add. MSS 34907, fol. 105 [1 Aug. 1798].

25. Ross, I, 217.

26. Nicolas, VII, clx, R. W. Miller's account of the battle.

27. Monmouth, E986, 2 Aug. 1798.

28. Lloyd and Coulter, 147, quoting BL, Add. MSS 37076; Barras, 'Nile', 217.

29. Barras, 'Nile', 217.

30. Coleridge, I, 549.

31. NMM, HIS/35, fol. 10.

32. NMM, HIS/35. As at the Battle of St Vincent, none of these timings correlate exactly, as timepieces then did not have the accuracy of the watches of today.

33. Lavery, *Nile*, 204.

34. NMM, AGC/W/2; see Lavery, *Nile*, 243.

35. NMM, HIS/35.

36. Monmouth, E986.

37. BL, Add. MSS 34954, 21 Oct. 1803, Nelson to Troubridge, extolling the quality of his fleet then, which 'I never saw exceeded, it is like the Nile fleet without Davidge Gould'.

38. Nicolas, VII, clvii, Miller's account of the battle to his wife.

39. NMM, AGC/W/2.

40. Monmouth, E986.

41. Monmouth, E986.

42. Lavery, *Nile*, 204–10.

43. Tunstall, 224–7.

44. Calculated from data from Syrett and Dinardo.

45. Rodger, 'Tactics', 293.

46. Hughes, *Fleet Tactics*, 16–25, and Hayward, 15–37, are two examples.

47. Huntington, Howe Papers, HO 382, 1 Jan. 1799, Howe to Curtis.

48. Tracy, *Naval Chronicle*, II, 11.

49. Nicolas, II, 22, 21 Mar. 1795.

50. Elliot, 19.

51. Cornelia Knight, I, 114.

52. Granville, II, 134, 10 Nov. 1805, Lady Bessborough to Lord Leveson-Gower.

53. McNeil, 990. Considerable effort to improve the destructive power of ordnance was made by both sides and not without cost: Ralph Willet Miller and forty-five seamen were to lose their lives in examining a captured French shell on board the *Theseus* in 1799 (James, II, 218).

54. Corbett, 52.

55. 11,183 has been cited (Lloyd and Coulter, III, 147, quoting BL. Add. MSS 37076); 895 killed and wounded, 'or about 10 per cent of those engaged' (Lavery,

Nile, 217). The complements of the British ships, as distinct from the numbers of those mustered and borne, total 8,193.

56. Battesti, 116–17.

57. BL, Add. MSS 34907, 2 Aug.; also Foley, 2 Aug. 1798.

58. Ross, I, 231.

59. James, II, 465–6, Appendix 14; Shannon, 285–8.

60. Nicolas, III, 92, 3 Aug. 1798.

61. Nicolas, VII, clxi–clxii, 11 Aug., to Davison; enclosure to Maurice Nelson. See also the Davison papers sold recently at Sotheby's (Downer, 32).

62. Nelson regretted that he had no bomb vessels with him to destroy Napoleon's transports in Alexandria and tried to urge the Turks to do so (Nicolas, III, 110, 29 Aug. 1798, Nelson to Minto).

63. NMM, AGC/W/2, 15 Aug. 1798.

64. RNM, 48/64, 13 Aug. 1798.

65. Nicolas, III, 7 Sept. 1798, Nelson to William Hamilton.

66. Sturges Jackson, II, 25, 10 Aug. 1798, Hood to Viscount Hood.

67. Monmouth, E666, 4 Oct. 1798, Maurice Nelson to Frances Nelson, quoting Campbell: 'these were his very words.'

68. Ross, I, 234. When Nelson landed in Naples, he wrote to his father that his 'head was quite healed' (Nicolas, III, 131, 25 Sept. 1798).

69. Naish, 416. Professor Le Quesne has observed that as Nelson seems to have suffered no loss of consciousness or retrograde amnesia from his head wound, his injury was not likely to have been as serious as some writers have imagined.

70. Morrison, II, 94, 23 Mar. 1800, Tyson to Lady Hamilton.

71. Nicolas, III, 128, 20 Sept. 1798, Nelson to St Vincent. This is a Clark and McArthur letter, II, 100, subject to the usual suspicion.

72. Huntington, HO 381, 15 Nov. 1798, Howe to Curtis.

73. BL, Add. MSS 37845, 24 July 1798, Lady Spencer to William Windham.

74. NMM, ELL/165; Elliot was interested not only in Nelson but in the well-being of his son, George Elliot, serving on board the *Goliath*. See also Harcourt, 10 Aug. 1798, Pitt to George Rose.

75. NMM, WYN/104, 22 Aug., 1 Sept. 1798, William Young to Charles Morice Pole; Clements, Melville Papers, 26 Aug. 1798, William Huskisson to Lord Macartney.

76. NMM, ELL/165, 30 Aug., 1, 11 Sept. 1798, Drinkwater to Minto; Lavery, *Nile*, 245.

77. Coleman, 155.

78. Naish, 448.

79. NMM, WYN/104, 20 Sept. 1798, Young to Morice Pole. The message was headed 'Redactum', suggesting that part of the message had been omitted; to redact, or to take out sensitive material, is a term still used in intelligence.

80. Barnett, 134.

81. NMM, ADM/L/V/8, 15 Sept. 1798.

82. BL, Add. MSS 34907, fol. 144 [n.d.], copy.

83. BL, Add. MSS 34907, 26 Sept. 1798, Inglefield to Nelson.

84. Edgcumbe, I, 80, Lady Shelley's account.

85. BL, Add. MSS 39407, 2 Oct. 1798.

86. BL, Add. MSS 34907, 27 Sept., 2, 9 Oct. 1798. It seems likely that Nelson received many more letters of congratulation than there are preserved in the British Library.

87. Huntington, STG Box 185 (20), 14 June 1799.

88. NMM, RUSI/199, *The Times*, 3 Oct. 1798.

89. Aspinall, *Prince of Wales*, III, 477, 4 Oct. 1798, queen to prince of Wales.

90. Clements, Pitt Papers, 4 Oct. 1798, Pitt to Marquis Cornwallis.

91. Leveson-Gower, I, 226.

92. Beresford, 461.

93. Colley, *Britons*, 190.

94. Aspinall, *George III*, III, letter 1844, 3 Oct. 1798; see also Coleman, 'King and Ministers', 6–11.

95. Aspinall, *George III*, III, letter 1845, 4 Oct. 1798.

96. BL, Add. MSS 34907, 15 Oct. 1798, Hood to Nelson.

97. BL, Add. MSS 34907, 7 Oct. 1798.

98. Baring, 403, 3 Oct.; Rosebery, II, 78, 9 Oct., William Windham to Captain Lukin; Richmond, *Spencer Papers*, III, 7, 4 Oct. 1798, Windham to Spencer.

99. BL, Add. MSS 31166, 7 Mar. 1799.

100. Minto, III, 25–6, 21 Nov. 1798.

101. Czsinik, 'Nile', 42–7. This article describes the dramatic increase in British public interest in Nelson as expressed in prints, caricatures, pottery, enamelled boxes and poems.

102. Blanning, 183–4.

103. Mackesy, *Strategy*, 42.

104. Knox, 484–5, 2 Oct. 1798, David Humphreys to the US secretary of state. He noted in particular the blow it dealt the Dutch carrying trade in the Mediterranean.

105. Glete, II, 378, calculates a British advantage of 550,000 against 470,000 tons. The *Conquérant*, *Aquilon*, *Peuple Souverain*, *Spartiate*, *Franklin* and *Tonnant* were taken into the Royal Navy, but only the last three saw active service. The *Guerrier* was hulked at Gibraltar. The *Franklin* (renamed *Canopus*) lasted sixty years and ten other ships were built to her design (Lavery, 302; Battesti, 116–17).

106. Acerra and Meyer, 215 (translation).

III PASSION AND DISCREDIT 1798–1801

19 Palermo and Naples

1. BL, Add. MSS 37852, fol. 288–90, 9 Nov. 1799, Lady Elliot to Windham, forwarding letter of 9 Aug. 1799, William Daniels to Lord Minto.
2. Naish, 417, 419, 29 Sept., 5 Oct. 1798.
3. Naish, 417, 29 Sept. 1798.
4. Warren R. Dawson, *Nelson Collection*, 115, 9 Oct. 1798.
5. Ross, I, 276, 11 Oct. 1798.
6. Naish, 404, 1, 6 Oct. 1798. To control the carriages attending his party, Hamilton asked the Neapolitan Army for a subaltern, four cavalry and four infantry soldiers (Warren R. Dawson, *Nelson Collection*, 150–51, 28 Sept 1798, Hamilton to the prince of Trabia).
7. Nicolas, III, 129, 25 Sept. 1798.
8. Nicolas, III, 131, 25 Sept. 1798.
9. Nicolas, III, 114–15, 7 Sept. 1798.
10. Naish, 400, 16 Sept. 1798, to Fanny.
11. (UK) NA: PRO/30/8/163, 4 Oct. 1798, Nelson to Pitt.
12. Monmouth, E606, 11 Nov. 1799.
13. Huntington, HM 24023, 29 Sept. 1798, to Roger Curtis.
14. Naish, 479, 11 Dec. 1798; also quoted by Nicolas in a shortened and garbled version from Clarke and McArthur (III, 194).
15. Nicolas, III, 320, 10 Apr. 1799.
16. Constantine, 231.
17. Constantine, 290.
18. Dropmore, V, 78, 3 June 1799, Grenville to Thomas Grenville.
19. Fraser, 7–8.
20. Mulvey Roberts, 155. The description of Graham is Roy Porter's.
21. Morrison, I, 78–9, 10 Jan. 1782, Greville to Emily [Emma] Hart; Fraser, 12–17.
22. Cornelia Knight, 144.
23. Naish, 401, 25 Sept. 1798.
24. RNM MS 1964/49, 27 Oct. 1798.
25. Nicolas, III, 140, 3 Oct. to Lady Hamilton; III, 195, 11 Dec., Nelson to Spencer; Naish, 478, 11 Dec. 1798, Nelson to Fanny.
26. John Robertson, 24–40.
27. Gutteridge, xiv.
28. (UK) NA: PRO, ADM 2/1353, 3 Oct. 1798.
29. e.g., (UK) NA: PRO, ADM 2/922, 13 Oct. 1796; Gutteridge, xxv.
30. BL, Add. MSS 34907, 7 Oct. 1798; Pocock, *Smith*, 71.

31. Nicolas, III, 169, 11 Nov. 1798, Troubridge's orders.

32. Nicolas, III, 163, 27 Oct. 1798, Nelson to Simon Lucas.

33. Nicolas, III, 152, 24 Oct. 1798 to William Hamilton.

34. Nicolas, III, 157, 25 Oct. 1798, orders to Ball.

35. Clements, Smith Collection, 26 Oct. 1798, Hamilton to Nelson.

36. Schroeder, 207.

37. Nicolas, III, 170, 13 Nov. 1798, to Spencer; 187, 6 Dec. 1798, to Stuart. Lord Hood came to the same conclusion about Sicilian officers during the Toulon operation in 1793.

38. (UK) NA: PRO, ADM 51/1288, log of the *Vanguard*.

39. Clements, Smith Collection, Vol I, 1 Dec. 1798, Nelson's account of the capture of Leghorn (also Morrison, II, 26). He also had an altercation with William Wyndham, the British minister on shore, but finally got his way over the privateers (Nicolas, III, 189–90, 9 Dec. 1799, Nelson to Troubridge).

40. Nicolas, III, 227, 7 Jan. 1799, Nelson to General Stuart.

41. Nicolas, III, 201, 15 Dec. 1798.

42. Cornelia, Knight, 125.

43. Nicolas, III, 212, 28 Dec. 1798, Nelson to St Vincent; 200, 14 Dec. 1799, Nelson to Lieutenant Philip Lamb, agent of transports.

44. Morrison, II, 35, 7 Jan. 1799, Emma Hamilton to Charles Greville.

45. Barnett, 196.

46. Monmouth, E65, 17 Jan. 1799, St Vincent to Lady Hamilton.

47. NMM, MON/1/11 [n.d.], 'on voyage from Naples to Palermo'.

48. Barnett, 196–7.

49. BL, Add. MSS 37852, 20 Aug. 1799, Daniels to Lady Minto, then forwarded to William Windham.

50. Morrison, II, 48, 16 May 1799, Nelson to William Hamilton.

51. Nicolas, III, 247, 31 Jan. 1798, Nelson to Ball; Gutteridge, xxvii; Coleman, 224–6. Commanders-in-chief were soon to live ashore to control their fleets, e.g., St Vincent in the Channel and Keith in 1803 in the North Sea.

52. Nicolas, III, 180, 29 Nov. 1798, Nelson to Spencer.

53. Nicolas, III, 300; Warren R. Dawson, *Nelson Collection*, 120, 20 Mar. 1799, Nelson to Lucas; Houghton, pf MS Eng. 196.5 (153a), 28 Mar. 1799, Lucas to William Hamilton.

54. Huntington, EA 372, 28 Apr. 1799, Nelson to the bashaw of Tripoli.

55. NMM, PST/39, 13 Apr. 1799, Nelson to Stuart. Nelson had written pleading for troops, but did not expect them to be sent (e.g., NMM, MON/1/12, 16 Feb. 1799, Nelson to Duckworth).

56. Nicolas, III, 320, 10 Apr. 1799.

57. Richmond, *Spencer Papers*, IV, 43, 13 Feb. 1799.

58. NMM, WYN 104, 19 Mar. 1799, Young to Charles Morice Pole.

59. NMM, NEP/5, 13 Feb. 1799.

60. NMM, WYN/104, 15 June 1799, Young to Charles Morice Pole.

61. Pocock, *Sidney Smith*, 71–4; NMM, NEP/4, 13 Aug. 1798, St Vincent to Nepean. Smith enjoyed no support from the rest of the Admiralty Board; William Windham noted in his diary how disparaging Young was about Smith (Windham, *Diary*, 388, 4 Feb. 1798).

62. BL, Add. MSS 34907, 9 Oct. 1798.

63. Richmond, *Spencer Papers*, IV, 60, 16 Jan. 1799.

64. e.g., Warren R. Dawson, *Nelson Collection*, 118–19, 31 Jan., to Ball; Nicolas, III, 281, to St Vincent, 6 Mar. 1799.

65. Dropmore, V, 475, 18 Oct. 1799. Letters between naval officers reflecting irritation at Smith's behaviour are common at this time.

66. Gutteridge, xxxviii.

67. Huntington, HM 34020, 11 Jan. 1799.

68. Nicolas, III, 248, 1 Feb. 1799.

69. Morrison, II, 49, 27 May 1799.

70. Naish, 485, 17 June 1799.

71. Gutteridge, xli–xlii.

72. Huntington, HM 34031, 21 May 1799, Nelson to Hamilton.

73. Clements Library, Melville Papers, 10 June 1799, St Vincent to Keith.

74. Gutteridge, xxxvii.

75. Huntington, HM 34033, 25 May 1799; also HM 34031, 21 May 1799.

76. Richmond, *Spencer Papers*, III, 68–9, 5 May 1799, Young to Spencer.

77. BL, Add. MSS 31166, 27 Mar. 1799, St Vincent to Nelson.

78. NMM, CRK/17/1, 10 June 1799, contemporary English translation of the 10 June Instructions. The version given by Gutteridge, 67–71, is taken from Harcourt, I, 231, and several important paragraphs are omitted. Croker's papers were not available to Gutteridge, since they were out of the public domain between 1858, when they were purchased at Sotheby's by Sir Thomas Phillipps, and 1946, when they were acquired by the National Maritime Museum. The original instructions in Italian from Ferdinand are not there; conceivably they were destroyed by Croker.

79. NMM, CRK/17/1, 10 June 1799, translation of Acton's letter to Nelson; not in Gutteridge.

80. Nicolas, VII, clxxxv, 12 June 1799, Nelson to St Vincent.

81. BL, Egerton 1614, 18 June 1799.

82. BL, Add. MSS 37852, fol. 288, 9 Aug. 1799, William Daniels to Lady Minto, sent on to Windham.

83. BL, Add. MSS 37852, 9 Nov. 1799, Daniels to Lady Minto.

84. Houghton, pf MS Eng. 196.5 (145), 25 June 1799.

85. Nicolas, VII, clxxxv, 20 June 1799; Gutteridge, 145.

86. (UK) NA: PRO, ADM 51/1279.

87. Nicolas, III, 385, 24 June 1799; Gutteridge, 197.

88. BL, Add. MSS 30999, fol. 75.

89. Gutteridge, 231, 26 June 1799, Hamilton to Ruffo.

90. NMM, CRK/12/63 [n.d.], Robert Smith to Nelson.

91. Richmond, *Spencer Papers*, III, 90, 15 July 1799.

92. (UK) PRO: ADM 51/1279, 29 June 1799.

93. White, 'Public Argument', 59; BL, Add. MSS 30999, fol. 82; also fol. 75. Lock was later a critic of Nelson, a distant cousin by marriage to Charles James Fox and probably the source of information with which Fox attacked Nelson in the House of Commons. In the opinion of Jack Russell, Rushout (later Lord Northwick) was 'a society gossip who could make a pound of lies out of half an ounce of truth' (127), but presents no evidence to back up this strong assertion. However, Rushout's evidence here is too detailed to discount, and it accords with the outspoken characters of each of these three officers.

94. Gutteridge, 269; Czisnik, 'Naples' (2002), 117.

95. Gutteridge, xcii.

96. Carlo Knight, 21–9.

97. Czisnik, 'Naples' (2002), 116.

98. Coleman, 345–50; Between the first publication of his biography and the 'Revised' edition (both 2001) Coleman, 215, hardens his judgement by adding four lines, concluding that Nelson was 'duplicitous and politically inept'.

99. Parsons, 2.

100. Gutteridge, 288, 30 June 1799, Nelson to King Ferdinand.

101. BL, Add. MSS 30999, fol. 82, 'Particulars as to the Trial & Execution of Caracciolo from an eyewitness . . .'

102. Sermoneta, 166. This author was a descendant of Caracciolo.

103. BL, Add. MSS 30999, fol. 82.

104. Parsons, 5.

105. Stirling, *Pages and Portraits*, 242.

106. Gutteridge, xciii.

107. Coleman, 209, calls the hanging 'hasty' and 'pitiless' and 'unnecessary'; but see Czisnik, 'Naples' (2002), 118–19. The idea that a factor in the treatment of Caraccioli was Nelson's dislike of the admiral from the time that they served together in 1795 is discounted here (Stirling, *Pages and Portraits*, I, 74, 243; *The Hothams*, 327–9; Czisnik, 118, n. 218).

108. Parsons, 6–7; Stirling, *Pages and Portraits*', 243.

109. (UK) NA: PRO, ADM 51/1279.

110. NMM, WYN/104, 10 Aug. 1799, Young to Charles Morice Pole.

111. (UK) NA: PRO, ADM 51/1279. Alexander Ball went immediately back to Malta, where he found that the French had not managed to resupply their garrison in Valetta in his absence (NMM, CRK/4/158, 10 Aug. 1799, Duckworth to Nelson).

112. (UK) NA: PRO, ADM 51/1279, 2, 5 July 1799.

113. Morrison, II, 56, 17 July 1799.

114. NMM, GIR/3. One of the lists is signed by Samuel Hood.

115. Parsons, 7–8.

116. Granville, I, 249, 11 Aug. 1799, Lady Bessborough to Granville Leveson-Gower.

117. Lloyd, *Keith Papers*, II, 49–50, 13, 15 July; 53–4, 24 July 1799, Keith to Nelson; Nicolas, III, 414, 19 July 1799, Nelson to Keith.

118. Nicolas, III, 401, 402, 6, 9 July 1799, Nelson to Troubridge; IV, 240, 22 May 1800. Coleman, 207, quoting NMM CRK/22, 6 July 1799, Jolly to Emma Hamilton. See Chapter 20 for further examples.

119. Nicolas, III, 420–21 [n.d]; Sermoneta, 172–7.

120. Sermoneta, 164–5, 172. The inquiry found the pursers guiltless (NMM, CRK/12/63, Robert Smith to Nelson [n.d.]).

121. Sermoneta, 181–200.

122. Granville, I, 250, Aug. 1799, Lady Bessborough to Granville Leveson-Gower. I disagree in part with Coleman, 199, when he states that Emma Hamilton did not have 'a mistress's power' over Nelson; I believe that she influenced him at this time.

123. Ilchester, II, 12–13, 21 Aug. 1799.

124. BL, Add. MSS 37852, 9 Aug. 1799, Daniels to Lady Minto, sent on to Windham.

125. Morrison, II, 68, 14 Sept. 1799, Matthew Wade to Emma Hamilton.

126. Lloyd, *Keith Papers*, II, 173, 30 May 1800.

127. Robertson, 19.

128. Richmond, *Spencer Papers*, III, 97, 18 Aug. 1799; 99, 19 Aug. 1799, Spencer to Nelson.

129. Morrison, II, 322–3, 20 Aug. 1799, 'Minutes of Instructions to Lord Nelson'.

130. See Czisnik, 'Naples: The Development of the Story', 35–55, for the impact of the news of Naples in England and the slow build-up of the controversy. I am grateful to Dr Czisnik for her help on this difficult issue.

131. e.g., Coleman, 191, quoting BL, Add. MSS 34910, 4, 12 Apr. 1799, in which Troubridge threatens 'to piss on the d—d Jacobins carcass'.

132. Simms, 590. The lowest estimates for deaths in Ireland in 1798 are below ten thousand.

133. BL, Add. MSS 37852, quoted at the head of this chapter.

134. Coleman, 212, quoting (UK) NA: PRO, FO 70/12, 4 Aug. 1799, Hamilton to Charles Greville.

20 Dalliance and Dishonour

1. Minto, III, 114.

2. NMM, DAV/2/10, 22 Apr. 1799, Fanny to Alexander Davison.

3. NMM, CRK/9/88, 15 Mar. [1799].

4. Naish, 10 Apr. 1799.

5. NMM, DAV/2/6, 21 Feb., Fanny to Davison; Naish, 481–94, 2 Feb. 1799–25 Jan. 1800, Nelson to Fanny.

6. Naish, 487–8, 4 Aug. 1799.

7. NMM, GIR/1/C, 29 Oct. 1799, Edmund Nelson to Sarah Bolton; Monmouth, E657 [2 Nov. 1799], William Nelson to Edmund Nelson; see also NMM, COP/2, 27 Feb. 1800, Nelson to William Marsh, 'I care not for money for myself but as it may be useful to my friends, and it is this alone which drains my pocket.'

8. NMM, DAV/2/3 [n.d.], Fanny to Davison.

9. NMM, DAV/2/7, 11 Apr. 1799, Fanny to Davison.

10. NMM, DAV/2/10 & 11, 22, 29 Apr., 8 May 1799.

11. NMM, DAV/2/17, 18 July 1799.

12. NMM, DAV/2/14 and 16, 23 [June], 18 July 1799, Fanny to Davison.

13. NMM, DAV/2/17, 6 Aug. 1799. Berry had been made a baronet, having finally reached London with the news of the Battle of the Nile; he had been captured when taking back dispatches in the *Leander*.

14. NMM, DAV/2/18, 29 Aug. 1799.

15. NMM, DAV/2/19 [n.d., 1799], Fanny to Davison.

16. Naish, 492, 593, 15, 26 Dec. 1799.

17. Naish, 319, 3 Mar., 323, 12 Apr. 1797, Nelson to Fanny.

18. Corbett, *Spencer Papers*, II, 477, 14 Sep. 1798; Nicolas, III, 305, 25 Mar. 1799, Nelson to Ball.

19. NMM, PAR/251, 19–26 Aug. [1798], Nelson to St Vincent; Naish, 484, 4 May [1799], Nisbet to Nelson.

20. Nicolas, III, 333, 21 Apr. 1799.

21. Nicolas, III, 375, 5 June 1799, Nelson to St Vincent.

22. BL, Add. MSS 34907, fol. 218 [n.d.], Troubridge to Nelson.

23. Nicolas, IV, 50, 14 Oct. 1799.

24. NMM, CRK/4/166, 12 Nov.; CRK/4/167, 4 Dec. 1799, Duckworth to Nelson.

25. Naish, 516–19, the master of the *Thalia* to John Tyson, Nelson's secretary.

26. Nicolas, IV, 63, 24 Oct. 1799, Nelson to Minto.

27. Naish, 490, 23 Sept. 1799, Nelson to Fanny.

28. Nicolas, IV, 53, 15 Oct. 1799, Nelson to John McArthur.

29. Clements Library, Smith Collection, 13 Oct. 1799, Nelson to William Hamilton.

30. Clements Library, Smith Collection, 20 Aug. 1799, Nepean to Nelson (copy); Richmond, *Spencer Papers*, IV, 30.

31. Dropmore, VI, 91, 29 Dec. 1799, Lord Elgin to Lord Grenville.

32. Vane, III, 246, 6 Mar. 1800, J. King to Castlereagh; Feldbaek, *Copenhagen*, 19–20.

33. Nicolas, IV, 119–21, 29 Nov. 1799, Nelson to Spencer.

34. Hattendorf *et al.*, *Naval Documents*, 344–50, Dundas's memorandum, 31 Mar. 1800.

35. Richmond, *Spencer Papers*, III, 103, 7 Oct. 1799.

36. Mackesy, *War without Victory*, 80–92, 95.

37. Houghton, pf MS Eng. 196.5 (144), 4 Sept. 1799, Acton to Nelson.

38. Nicolas, IV, 70, 26 Oct. 1799, Nelson to Troubridge.

39. Nicolas, IV, 140–41, 14 Dec. 1799, Nelson to Nepean. In Sept. two 74s, one 64, one 32 and three smaller ships were off Malta (Nicolas, IV, 25, 21 Sept. 1799); they were later joined by Troubridge in the *Culloden*. For Nelson's system of 'Private Distinguishing Signals . . . during the night', see Monmouth, E988, a loose page tipped into the volume at 4 July 1797.

40. NMM, AGC/N/38, 27 Sept. 1799, Nelson to Ball.

41. Nicolas, IV, 78–9, 31 Oct. 1799, Nelson to the tsar.

42. Nicolas, IV, 145, 18 Dec. 1799, Nelson to de Niza.

43. Nicolas, IV, 155, 22 Dec., to Troubridge; 159, 23 Dec. 1799, Nelson to Spencer.

44. Nicolas, IV, 181, 16 Jan. 1800, Nelson to Nepean.

45. Nicolas, IV, 166, 5 Jan. 1800.

46. (UK)NA: PRO, ADM 2/922, 11 Oct. 1799, Nepean to Nelson; ADM 1/2137, 'Occurrences on His Majesty's Ship *Charon*', Captain McKellar.

47. Nicolas, IV, 110, 26 Nov. 1799, Nelson to Nepean.

48. Nicolas, IV, 113, 27 Nov. 1799, Nelson to Duckworth.

49. Nicolas, IV, 116, 28 Nov. 1799, Nelson to Spencer.

50. (UK)NA: PRO, ADM 2/922, 22 Oct., 13 Dec. 1799.

51. Monmouth, E989, 14 Dec. 1799, Nelson to Spencer.

52. Grant, 24.

53. Grant, 25.

54. NMM, AGC/N/38, 27 Sept. 1799, Nelson to Ball.

55. Lloyd, *Keith Papers*, II, 59.

56. Nicolas, IV, 194, 26 Feb. 1800.

57. Stirling, *Pages and Portraits*, II, 32.

58. Laughton, *Miscellany*, I, 257, Nov. 1800, Samuel Hood to Viscount Hood.

59. NMM, KEI/18/5, 30 Mar. 1800. Young to Keith. Keith wrote on 6 Jan. from Minorca that he would come first to Palermo, but changed his mind (Lloyd, *Keith Papers*, II, 69).

60. Paget, I, 200, 6 May 1800, Keith to Paget.

61. Huntington, HM 34034, 12 Feb. 1800.

62. Huntington, HM 34200, 27 Jan. 1800, Hamilton to Sidney Smith.

63. NMM, KEI/18/5, 30 Mar. 1800, Young to Keith.

64. Parsons, 13.

65. Monmouth, E986, 19 Feb. 1800.

66. Nicolas, IV, 193–4, 26 Feb. 1800, Nelson to Minto.

67. (UK)NA: PRO, ADM 51/1330; Monmouth, E986, 19 Feb. 1800.

68. Nicolas, IV, 194, 26 Feb. 1800.

69. Morrison, II, 95, 29 Mar. 1800, Fanny to Nelson.

70. Morrison, II, 87–8, 21 Feb. 1800, Tyson to Emma Hamilton.

71. Nicolas, IV, 188, 20 Mar. 1800.

72. (UK)NA: PRO, ADM 51/1330, 21 Feb.; 1/5352, 21 Feb. 1800, Captain Miller of the *Minorca*.

73. Lloyd, *Keith Papers*, II, 164–6, Captain Manley Dixon of the *Lion* to Troubridge.

74. (UK)NA: PRO, ADM 51/1330.

75. Parsons, 41.

76. Monmouth, E989, 20 Mar. 1800.

77. NMM, KEI/18/5, 11 May 1800, Young to Keith.

78. NMM, KEI/18/4, 3 Apr. 1800, Nelson to Keith.

79. Constantine, 244–6.

80. Dropmore, VI, 324; Paget, I, 218–19, 13 May 1800.

81. Morrison, II, 100, 22 Apr. 1800.

82. Minto, III, 114, 23 Mar. 1800.

83. Morrison, II, 89, 27 Feb. 1800, Ball to Emma Hamilton.

84. Vincent, 340, quoting BL, Althorp Papers, 15 Aug. 1799, to Dowager Lady Spencer.

85. (UK)NA: PRO, ADM 1/1522, 21 July 1800. The letter also raised the issue of the loss of Ball's prize money because of his position as governor ashore; curiously he also requested the post of the resident commissioner of Halifax Dockyard.

86. NMM, KEI/18/4, 23 Apr. 1800, Nelson to Keith.

87. Coleman, 224–6, correctly attributes the letter of '29 Jan.' from Nelson to Emma, which describes his erotic dream, to 1800, when Nelson was on passage from Leghorn to Palermo ((UK)NA: PRO, ADM 51/1330, 26 Jan.–3 Feb. 1800).

88. Morrison, II, 142, 23 Apr. 1801, Nelson to Emma Hamilton.

89. (UK)NA: PRO, ADM 51/1330, 10–11 May 1800; Parsons, 61–4.

90. Morrison, II, 100, 19 May 1800.

91. (UK)NA: PRO, ADM 36/14946.

92. *Paget Papers*, I, 232, 256, 20 June, 23 July 1800, Keith to Paget; Constantine, 247.

93. NMM, CRK/8/41, 10 May, Keith to Nelson; *Paget Papers*, I, 196, 200, 20 Apr., 6 May 1800, Keith to Paget.

94. Morrison, II, 100, 22 Apr. 1800, William Hamilton to Charles Greville.

95. Nicolas, IV, 263, 2 July 1800, Cornelia Knight to Berry.

96. (UK)NA: PRO, ADM 51/1362, 12 July 1800.

97. Lloyd, *Keith Papers*, II, 62, quoting the *Diary of Sir John Moore*, I, 367.

98. NMM, KEI/18/5, 15 Sept. 1800, Young to Keith.

99. Nicolas, IV, 262, 26 June 1800.

100. Nicolas, IV, 264, 24 July 1800, Cornelia Knight to Berry.

101. Nicolas, IV, 265, 8 Aug. 1800, Cornelia Knight to Berry.

102. Minto, III, 147 [n.d.], 1800. Lady Minto confirms her husband's earlier role in lobbying on Nelson's behalf, for she reported Nelson as saying but for 'the interest he took about him he should have had no reward for his services in the

first action [St Vincent], nor have been placed in a situation to [obtain] the second [the Nile]'.

103. NMM, KEI/18/5, 30 Aug. 1800, Minto to Keith.

104. Nelson was informed that Fuger would finish the paintings in two or three months and de Hertz promised to send them on (NMM, CRK/6/157, 19 Nov. 1800, Leopold de Hertz to Nelson).

105. Cornelia Knight, 152.

106. NMM, KEI/18/5, 30 Aug. 1800, Minto to Keith.

107. Naish, 526–7: NMM, CRK/6/157, 19 Nov. 1800, Leopold de Hertz to Nelson. Nelson paid 76s. for thirty-eight baths and 13s. for the use of a 'Forte Piano'. By contrast, Thomas Masterman Hardy had taken a similar overland route earlier in the year, but was only allowed £145 by the Admiralty ((UK)NA: PRO, ADM 1/1922, 13 Jan. 1800, Hardy to Nepean).

108. Minto, III, 147 [n.d.], 1800, Lady Minto to her sister.

109. Malmesbury, II, 222.

110. Houghton (97), 1 Sept. 1800, Greville to Joseph Banks. 'Unprofitable curiosities' because the expense would lessen William Hamilton's estate, which Greville stood to inherit.

111. Blumel, 165, 167 quoting Trench, 105–112.

112. The distance by river from Dresden to Hamburg at this time was 601 kilometres, 35 longer than today because of cuts made in the nineteenth century. For this information, and that of the customs stations, I am grateful to Dr Boyer Meyer Friese.

113. Blumel, 165–74.

114. Blumel, 181.

115. Cornelia Knight, 163.

116. Tracy, *Naval Chronicle*, II, 118.

117. Nicolas, IV, 267, 7 Nov. 1800, Nelson to Marsh and Creed; NMM, AGC/17/8, 7 Nov. 1800, Nelson to Warmington [?].

118. Tracy, *Naval Chronicle*, II, 118.

119. Naish, 496, 20 Sept., Nelson to Fanny.

120. NMM, DAV/2/24, 20 Oct. 1800, Fanny to Nelson. Fanny decided that a house could not be afforded and substituted a hotel instead.

121. Broadley and Bartelot, 51, Hardy to John Callard Manfield, 30 Oct. 1800. He too thought that a frigate would have met Nelson in Hamburg.

122. Naish, 496, 6 Nov. 1800, Nelson to Fanny. The letter was readdressed to 'Nerotts Hotel, King Street, London'.

123. Tracy, *Naval Chronicle*, II, 118.

124. Broadley and Bartelot, 53, 8 Nov. 1800, Hardy to Manfield.

21 Separation

1. NMM, DAV/2/30.
2. NMM, DAV/2/32.
3. Tracy, *Naval Chronicle*, II, 118.
4. Scott, 192.
5. Laughton, *Miscellany*, II, 329.
6. NMM, AGC/J/6/1; Nicolas, IV, 278, quoting from the *Memoirs of Lord Collingwood*, I, 110.
7. Colley, *Britons*, 189.
8. Nicolas, IV, 283, 5 Feb. 1801.
9. Naish, 571.
10. Naish, 572.
11. Barrett, 153.
12. Cornelia Knight, 162.
13. Tracy, *Naval Chronicle*, II, 118.
14. Baring, 434.
15. BL, Add. MSS 58908, 11 Dec. 1800; also printed in Dropmore, VI, 406.
16. DRO, 152/M/c1800/0234, Addington to General Simcoe.
17. Edgcumbe, 78–9.
18. *Gentleman's Magazine*, Mar. 1801, 207.
19. Ostergard, 17.
20. It was to fall down again after Beckford sold it.
21. *Gentleman's Magazine*, Apr. 1801, 298.
22. Nicolas, IV, 270–71, 27, 29 Dec. 1800, Nelson to John Locker.
23. Monmouth, E89, 3 Jan. 1801, W. H. Bowne to Spencer Smith.
24. Nicolas, IV, 267, 6 Nov. 1800.
25. NMM, DAV/2/29, 20 Feb. 1801, Fanny to Davison.
26. Laughton, *Miscellany*, II, 329, 9 Nov. 1800.
27. Richmond, *Spencer Papers*, IV, 273, 28 Nov. 1800, Spencer to St Vincent.
28. Richmond, *Spencer Papers*, IV, 21, 30 Nov. 1800, St Vincent to Spencer; also NMM, AGC/J/1, 23 Jan. 1801, St Vincent to Nelson.
29. Feldbæk, *Copenhagen*, 19.
30. Tracy, *Naval Chronicle*, II, 96–8, 'Journal of the Proceedings of Vice-Admiral Dickson's Squadron'.
31. NMM, MS 94/010 Middleton Papers; Tooke, 27, 30.
32. Ehrman, III, 395–400.
33. Barker, Rosalin, 12, 44.
34. NMM, MS 94/010, Middleton Papers. The committee, set up between 15 and 22 Dec., came up with some optimistic ideas and papers, but no solutions were found.
35. Richmond, *Spencer Papers*. IV, 274, 7 Dec.; 275, 18 Dec., Whitworth to Spencer; BL, Add. MSS 75847, 9 Dec. 1800, St Vincent to Spencer.

36. For an example of this nickname, see NMM, CRK/2, 24 Sept. 1804, Thomas Bowen to Nelson.

37. Hughes, 116-17, 16 Nov. 1800, Collingwood to his sister.

38. NMM, XAGC/8, 30, 9 Jan. 1801.

39. Nicolas, VII, 391-2, 13 Apr. 1846, William Haslewood to Sir Harris Nicolas.

40. Hardin, 81-6; Naish, 618-20.

41. Nicolas, VII, ccix, 23 Apr. 1801, Nelson to Davison.

42. NMM, AGC/18/26, 14 Jan. 1801, Nelson to Emma.

43. Nicolas, IV, 273, 17 Jan. 1801. Oman records (unreferenced) a stop at Honiton to see the mother of George Westcott, who had been killed at the Nile (Oman, 417).

44. NMM, AGC/J/6/2, 17 Jan. 1801, St Vincent to Nepean; Laughton, *Miscellany*, II, 332, 17 Jan. 1801, St Vincent to Nepean. Nelson also met General John Graves Simcoe, who commanded the army in Plymouth, who reported to Henry Addington, 'He received me from your kindness with all the frankness of an old acquaintance, so perfectly congenial to my own sentiments as becoming the military character' (DRO, 152/M/c1801/oN2, 26 Jan. 1801).

45. Nicolas, VII, cci, 2 Feb. 1801.

46. Nicolas, IV, 274, 17 Jan. 1801, Nelson to Spencer.

47. The decision was confirmed by the Board of Admiralty on 26 Jan. ((UK)NA: PRO, ADM 3/144).

48. NMM, AGC/J/1, 21 Jan. 1801, St Vincent to Nelson.

49. (UK)NA: PRO, ADM 51/1317.

50. NMM, AGC/J/1, 23 Jan. 1801, St Vincent to Nelson.

51. Hardin, 81-6; Naish, 618-19, 20, 21 Jan., 3 Feb. 1801. On 25 Jan. Nelson wrote to Davison about 'nonsensical rumours' that Davison was to buy him a fine house; he considered that Fanny when in town should live in lodgings or a ready furnished house (Nicolas, VII, cxcix).

52. Morrison, II, 108, 25 Jan. 1801.

53. Morrison, II, 110, 1 Feb. 1801.

54. Morrison, II, 110 [3 Feb. 1801].

55. NMM, DAV/2/27, 5 Feb. 1801, Fanny to Davison.

56. Morrison, II, 111, 4 Feb. 1801.

57. Morrison, II, 112, 6 Feb. 1801. Firm evidence of Horatia's first two years is non-existent, but see p. 435 and p. 478.

58. NMM, CRK/11/43, 30 Jan. 1801, Spencer to Nelson.

59. Morrison, II, 112, 6 Feb. 1801, Nelson to Emma. Edward Thornborough Parker was by now a commander and Nelson was trying to find him a ship (NMM, CRK/11/43, 30 Jan. 1801, Spencer to Nelson).

60. Morrison, II, 114 [14 Feb. 1801], Nelson to Emma.

61. (UK)NA: PRO, ADM 51/1371, 11-19 Feb. 1801.

62. Morrison, II, 115 [17 Feb. 1801].

63. NMM, CRK/9/161, 13 Feb. 1801, Hyde Parker to Nelson.

64. (UK)NA: PRO, ADM 3/144, 12, 18 Feb. 1801.

65. RNM, 1990/199 [n.d.], Nelson to Mrs Thompson. A short letter not in Morrison, in which he observes that 'children bring their cares and pleasures with them.'

66. Morrison, II, 114–15 [14 Feb. 1801].

67. Morrison, II, 117 [18 Feb. 1801].

68. Morrison, II, 118–20.

69. Morrison, II, 120, 20 Feb. [1801].

70. Naish, 576, 19 Feb. 1801.

71. Morrison, II, 115 [17 Feb. 1801].

72. NMM, DAV/2/28, 13 Feb. [1801].

73. NMM, DAV/2/29, 20 Feb. 1801.

74. (UK)NA: PRO, ADM 51/1371, 21 Feb. 1801.

75. (UK)NA: PRO, ADM 3/144, 23 Feb. 1801.

76. NMM, DAV/2/30, 24 Feb. 1801, Fanny to Davison.

77. Nelson struck his flag from 24 to 28 Feb. ((UK)NA: PRO, ADM 51/1371).

78. Naish, 24 Feb. 1801, to Mrs William Nelson.

79. NMM, DAV/2/31, 2 Mar. [1801].

80. NMM, DAV/2/32, 15 Mar. 1801.

81. Morrison, II, 121, 27 Feb. 1801.

82. Morrison, II, 123, no. 531 [1 Mar. 1801].

83. Morrison, II, 123, no. 532, 1 Mar. 1801. This letter was delivered personally by William Oliver, who had worked as a general factotum since they met him in Vienna: 'I can give full scope to my feelings, for I daresay Oliver will faithfully deliver this letter.'

84. Morrison, II, 124; also Houghton, pf Eng. 196.5 (22), 2 Mar. 1801; another letter where the violence of Nelson's anger is obvious from the condition of the paper and the raggedness of the writing.

85. Bonner Smith, *St Vincent*, I, 84.

86. Naish, 580. Nelson made generous allowance for Fanny at £1,800 a year, consisting of £400 a quarter and 5 per cent interest on the £4,000 that had been given to him by her uncle and that he later returned to her.

87. Monmouth, E669, 8 Mar. 1801.

88. Monmouth, E673, 'Sunday morning' [1801].

89. Fremantle, *Wynne* (1953), 310.

90. Coleman, 251, quoting *Morning Post*, 31 Jan. 1801.

91. Bucks., D/FR/45/1/4, 11 Mar. [1801].

92. Nicolas, VII, ccii, 11 Mar. 1801.

93. Bucks., D/FR/45/1/4, 11 Mar. [1801].

94. The correspondence between William Young and Charles Morice Pole is an example; Lord Bridport when commanding the Channel fleet was very angry about it (NMM, WYN/104, 12 Oct. 1799).

95. Laughton, *Miscellany*, I, 417–18, 10 Mar. 1801.

96. Minto, III, 219, 19 May 1801.
97. Morrison, II, 126, 127, 6, 9 Mar. 1801.
98. BL, Egerton 14, 11 Mar. 1801.
99. Morrison, II, 128, 11 Mar. 1801.
100. Bonner Smith, *St Vincent*, I, 86, 11 Mar. 1801.
101. Laughton, *Miscellany*, I, 419, 11 Mar. 1801, Nelson to Troubridge.
102. (UK)NA:PRO, ADM 51/1371, 13 Mar. 1801.
103. Monmouth, E607, 11 Mar. 1801, Nelson to William Marsh.

22   Copenhagen

1. Broadley and Bartelot, 63.
2. NMM, AGC/14/27.
3. Glete, II, 398–9.
4. (UK)NA: PRO, ADM 1/4186, 9 Jan. 1801, Dundas to Nepean.
5. Feldbæk, *Copenhagen*, 16.
6. (UK)NA: PRO, FO 22/40, 17 Feb. 1801, Hawkesbury to Vansittart. Hawkesbury was the son of Charles Jenkinson, previously Lord Hawkesbury; the father was now the earl of Liverpool. Vansittart was appointed on 20 Feb. (Bindoff, *et al.*, 42).
7. (UK)NA: PRO, ADM 1/4186, 23 Feb. 1801, Dundas to the Admiralty.
8. Feldbæk, 32–9; Pope, 208–15.
9. Feldbæk, 221.
10. (UK)NA: PRO, ADM 1/4186, 14 Mar. 1801, Dundas to the Admiralty.
11. (UK)NA: PRO, ADM 1/4186, 17 Jan. 1801, Edward James to Lord Grenville, from Bristol.
12. (UK)NA: PRO, ADM 1/4186, 14 Mar. 1801, Dundas to the Admiralty.
13. (UK)NA: PRO, ADM 1/4186, 14 Feb. 1801, letter of 30 Jan. from John Mitchell at Khristiansand (Kristiansund, now in southern Norway). It is clear from this volume how fast intelligence was then moving around Whitehall; e.g., 20, 23, 28 Jan. 1801.
14. Le Fevre, 17. Denmark and Norway were united under the same crown.
15. Clements, Smith Collection, 8 Apr. 1801; Morrison, II, 136.
16. NMM, NEP/2, 13 Jan. 1801.
17. (UK)NA: PRO, ADM 1/4186, 14 Mar. 1801, Dundas to the Admiralty.
18. Bullocke, 300.
19. Laughton, *Miscellany*. I, 420, 16 Mar. 1801, Nelson to Troubridge.
20. NMM, CRK/14/13, 12 Mar. 1801, Nelson's journal, which he marked 'natural day' rather than the noon-to-noon timing of the official logs.
21. NMM, CRK/14/73, Nelson's journal, 12 Mar. 1801.
22. NMM, MON/1/18, 17 Mar. 1801.
23. Nicolas, VII, cciii, 19 Mar. 1801, Nelson to Davison.

24. Fremantle, *Wynne* (1937), III, 31, 17 Mar. 1801.

25. NMM, CRK/14/73, Nelson's journal, 13 Mar. 1801.

26. NMM, CRK/14/73, Nelson's journal, 14 Mar. 1801; Tracy, *Naval Chronicle*, II, 161.

27. NMM, MON/1/18, 17 Mar. 1801, Nelson to Emma Hamilton. Pope, 215, makes this date 19 Mar., quoting (UK)NA: PRO, FO 22/40, 19 Mar. 1801; Le Fevre, 18.

28. NMM, CRK/14/73, Nelson's journal, 19 Mar. 1801.

29. Pope, 242.

30. NMM, CRK/14/73, Nelson's journal, 21 Mar. 1801.

31. NMM, CRK/14/73, Nelson's journal, 21 Mar. 1801.

32. (UK)NA: PRO, ADM 51/1371, 21 Mar. 1801; Laughton, *Miscellany*, I, 423, 23 Mar. 1801.

33. NMM, NEP/8, 4 Apr. 1801, St Vincent to Nepean.

34. Monmouth, E473, 23 Mar. 1801, Scott to Lady Lavington.

35. Scott, 69, 23 Mar. 1801, Scott to Rear-Admiral Scott.

36. Pope, Chapters 21–3, is justifiably critical of Parker's hesitation and unwillingness to take risks. It has been more recently implied that he knew from British agents that the assassination of the tsar was imminent and that this accounted for the delay (Sparrow, 223, 226). This suggestion is not backed by sufficient evidence (Le Fevre, 15–16).

37. Lovenorn, 15. It was compiled by P. de Lovenorn, director of the archives, commodore and adjutant-general in the navy, chief for the coasting pilots in Denmark, translated by Frederick Schneider, teacher at the Royal Military Academy for the Danish Navy.

38. (UK)NA: PRO, ADM 1/4, 4 Mar. 1801. Parker to Nepean; Scott, 68, 21 Mar. 1801, Scott to Rear-Admiral Scott.

39. NMM, CRK/14/73, Nelson's journal.

40. Parry, 54, 23 Mar. 1801, Fremantle to his brother William.

41. Bullocke, 306, 4 June 1801, Tomlinson to Nepean.

42. NMM, CRK/14/73, Nelson's journal, 23 Mar. 1801.

43. Nicolas, IV, 368, 12 May 1801, Nelson to Vansittart. He wrote this letter from the Gulf of Finland, and he regretted the delay, reckoning that he could have been off Reval rather than Copenhagen on 2 Apr.

44. Bonner-Smith, *St Vincent*, I, 63–4, 23 Mar. 1801.

45. A crowded voyage in a small vessel that took forty-three passengers, including Vansittart, Drummond and Talbot and merchant families (NMM, ADM/L/K/54).

46. Clements, Hubert Smith Collection, 8 Apr. 1801, Vansittart to Nelson; Morrison, II, 135–6.

47. Le Fevre, 29, quoting Hyde Parker Papers F76/2, 6 Apr. 1801, Parker to his wife.

48. NMM, CRK/14/73, Nelson's journal, 24 Mar. 1801.

49. Feldbæk, 86.

50. Pope, 274, makes a valid point that Parker does not appear to have asked either the captain of the *Blanche*, Graham Eden Hamond, or Lieutenant McCulloch, who had been to Copenhagen; their opinions would have been more valuable than those of a diplomat.

51. Nicolas, IV, 295–8, 24 Mar. 1801, Nelson to Hyde Parker. On 8 July, Nelson wrote to Parker: 'I took the liberty of writing you a letter on the 24th the rough copy of which I read to you' (NMM, CRK/14/90, Nelson to Parker).

52. NMM, CRK/14/65, 'Remarks of masters of ships on board the *Kite* in the Great Belt' [n.d.]: 'the small chart layed down by Compass by Laurie & Whittle very correct and the others equally so.'

53. NMM, CRK/9/164, 24 Mar. 1801.

54. Ralfe, 20; the captain of the fleet, William Domett, also claimed to have changed Parker's mind (Le Fevre, 11, quoting BL, Add. MSS 35201, 4 May 1801, Domett to Lord Bridport).

55. NMM, CRK/14/73, Nelson's journal.

56. (UK)NA: PRO, ADM1/4, 6 Apr. 1801.

57. Fremantle, *Wynne* (1937), III, 37, 29 Mar. 1801, Fremantle to his wife.

58. Tracy, *Copenhagen*, 17.

59. Le Fevre, 12.

60. Le Fevre, 18, quoting Hyde Parker Papers, F 76/2, 27 Mar. 1801, Sir Hyde to Fanny Parker.

61. Bullocke, 308, 4 June 1801, Tomlinson to Nepean.

62. Pope, 292–3, quoting NMM, Nelson's order book, 26 Mar. 1801.

63. (UK)NA: PRO, ADM 51/1356, 28 Mar. 1801.

64. NMM, CRK/14/73, Nelson's journal, 26 Mar. 1801. Pope, 293, erroneously, has 'arguing and convincing' rather than 'arranging and explaining'.

65. Nicolas, IV, 301, Stewart's narrative.

66. Morrison, II, 132, 30 Mar. 1801, Nelson to Emma.

67. NMM, CRK/14/73, Nelson's journal, 27 Mar. 1801.

68. NMM, CRK/9/167, 29 Mar. 1801.

69. (UK)NA: PRO, ADM 51/1356, 30 Mar. 1801.

70. NMM, CRK/14/73, Nelson's journal, 30 Mar. 1801.

71. Bullocke, 308, 4 June 1801, Tomlinson to Nepean.

72. Feldbæk, 112. The Swedes were criticized and later issued a communiqué defending their decision (Bonner-Smith, *St Vincent*, I, 80–81).

73. Morrison, II, 132, 30 Mar. 1801, Nelson to Emma.

74. (UK) NA: PRO, ADM 51/1356, 30 Mar. 1801; Sturges Jackson, II, 88, Parker's journal.

75. Morrison, II, 132, 30 Mar. 1801.

76. Rodger, *Command of the Ocean*, 469, points out how much more effective the Danish defence would have been had it been across, rather than parallel with the channel. It is possible that the Danes did not feel that they could safely moor their ships athwart (sideways on to) the current, flowing north at a considerable rate.

77. Feldbæk, 121–2.

78. James, III, 46–7; Tracy, *Naval Chronicle*, II, 150–54.

79. Parker should have had a second rear-admiral, Thomas Totty, but his ship, the *Invincible*, was wrecked on the sands outside Yarmouth three days after the main part of the squadron had departed (Nicolas, IV, 301).

80. Lyon, 241.

81. Nicolas, IV, 384, 23 May 1801, Nelson to Nepean. Both these ships set off two days before the *Kite* sloop on their way from Yarmouth and the *Glatton* arrived two days after the *Kite* (NMM, ADM/L/K/54, 19 June–3 July 1801).

82. White, 'Copenhagen', 48, quoting BL, Add. MSS 46356, fol. 37, 4 Apr. 1801.

83. (UK)NA: PRO, ADM 51/1371, 28 Feb. 1801.

84. Nicolas, IV, 303, Colonel Stewart's narrative. Nicolas took this verbatim from Clarke and McArthur, but contrast the account in Stewart, *Cumloden Papers*. Stewart died in 1827 (Nicolas, IV, 298n.).

85. Nicolas, IV, 304–7, 'Orders for the Attack'.

86. Tracy, *Naval Chronicle*, III, 172–3; also Pope, 331–4.

87. Feldbæk, 79, 85.

88. Pope, 319, quoting Millard, *Macmillan's Magazine*, June 1895. Millard never received a commission as a lieutenant.

89. Bullocke, 309. Tomlinson was highly critical of this in his report to Evan Nepean. The current is almost always north flowing because of the 'great influx of residual fresh water'; only a northerly gale causes a south-flowing stream (Hydrographer of the Navy, *Baltic Pilot*, 21). Nelson noted 'a strong current setting out of the Sound' on 29 Mar. (NMM, CRK/14/73, journal).

90. Sturges Jackson, II, 89, Parker's journal.

91. Stewart, *Cumloden Papers* [unpaginated].

92. Pope, 353, quoting the *Alcmene*'s master's log (UK)NA: PRO, ADM 52/2652.

93. The times of the stages in the battle are taken from White, *Copenhagen*. 'The Inshore Squadron's Timeline'.

94. Pope, 364, quoting *Macmillan's Magazine*, June 1895.

95. Fremantle, *Wynne* (1937), III, 42, 4 Apr. 1801, Fremantle to the marquis of Buckingham.

96. Nicolas, IV, 348 [n.d.], 'Memoranda Respecting the Battle of Copenhagen'.

97. Stewart's description of events hereafter is taken from a long letter to a fellow officer, Colonel Sir William Clinton, 'Aide de Camp to the RH the Commander-in-Chief (NMM, AGC/14/27, 6 Apr. 1801), rather than the usual diary extracts quoted by Clarke and McArthur, and Nicolas.

98. Stewart estimated 500 yards (NMM, AGC/14/27, 6 Apr. 1801, Stewart to Clinton).

99. Feldbæk, 148.

100. Nicolas, IV, 347–8 [n.d.], 'Memoranda Respecting the Battle of Copenhagen'.

101. NMM, AGC/14/27, 6 Apr. 1801, Stewart to Clinton.

102. (UK)NA: PRO, ADM 51/1371.

103. NMM, AGC/14/27, Stewart to Clinton.

104. Ralfe, 21. In 1900 Sturges Jackson pronounced this theory as 'incredible' (II, 84) and there is no reason to disagree with this judgement.

105. See Coleman's detailed analysis of how the story developed through Clarke and McArthur, and Southey (Coleman, 258–60; also Nicolas, IV, 309, Stewart's narrative; Pope, 411).

106. White, *Copenhagen*, 56.

107. Pope, 415–16.

108. Fremantle, *Wynne* (1952), 312, 4 Apr. 1801, Fremantle to Betsey.

109. Fremantle, *Wynne* (1937), III, 43, 4 Apr. 1801, Fremantle to the marquis of Buckingham.

110. Broadley and Bartelot, 62–3, 5 Apr. 1801, Hardy to Manfield.

111. Thursfield, 110.

112. NMM, AGC/14/27, 6 Apr. 1801, Stewart to Clinton.

113. Nicolas, IV, 360 [8 May 1801], Nelson to Addington.

114. Houghton, pf MS Eng. 196.5(186), 9 Apr. 1801, Nelson to Emma [photograph of letter with the words 'original not located 6 Nov. 1935'].

115. Feldbæk, opposite 113.

116. Feldbæk, 199–200.

117. Feldbæk, 183–4.

118. NMM, CRK/5/170, 12 Sept. 1801, Fothergill to Nelson; (UK)NA: PRO, ADM 51/1356; 52/2968, 3 Apr. 1801.

119. Ralfe, 24.

120. NMM, AGC/14/27, 6 Apr. 1801, Stewart to Clinton.

121. Nicolas, IV, 316–19 [n.d.], 'List of Killed and Wounded'.

122. NMM, AGC/14/27, 6 Apr. 1801, Stewart to Clinton.

123. NMM, AGC/W/2, 3 Apr. 1801, Wilkes to Henry Clarke.

124. Feldbæk, 205.

125. Fremantle, *Wynne* (1937), III, 43, 4 Apr. 1801, Fremantle to the marquis of Buckingham.

126. Feldbæk, 205; Clements, Smith Collection, 7 May 1801, signed by two captains in the Danish Navy. This was to ensure that Nelson's officers and men gained the 'head money' to which they were entitled.

127. NMM, AGC/W/2, 3 Apr. 1801, Wilkes to his cousin, Henry Clarke.

128. Coleman, 162, quoting Kathleen Coburn (ed.), *The Notebooks of Samuel Taylor Coleridge* (New York and London, 1962), II, item 2,188.

129. NMM, CRK/14/73, Nelson's journal, 2 Apr. 1801.

130. NMM, AGC/14/27, 6 Apr. 1801, Stewart to Clinton.

131. BL. Add. MSS 75849, 5 Apr. 1801, Nelson to Spencer.

132. NMM, CRK/11/47, 19 Apr. 1801, Spencer to Nelson.

133. NMM, CRK/1, 20 Apr. 1801, Addington to Nelson.

134. NMM, AGC/14/27, 6 Apr. 1801, Stewart to Clinton.

135. Bonner-Smith, *St Vincent*, I, 91, 17 Apr. 1801.

136. Nicolas, IV, 524, 20 Nov. 1801, Nelson to the lord mayor.

137. NMM, AGC/14/27, 6 Apr. 1801, Stewart to Clinton.

138. (UK)NA: PRO, ADM 1/5355, 31 Mar. 1801, court martial; also James, III, 481.

23   Commander-in-Chief, Baltic Fleet

1. NMM, CRK/14/73.

2. Nicolas, VII, ccv, 4 Apr. 1801.

3. NMM, CRK/14/73, Nelson's journal, 3 Apr. 1801.

4. Clements, Smith Collection, 3 Apr. 1801, Nelson to Addington; Morrison, II, 133–4.

5. Nicolas, VII, ccv, 4 Apr. 1801, Nelson to Robert Fancourt.

6. Feldbæck, 216.

7. Fremantle, *Wynne* (1937), III, 48, 6 Apr. 1801, Fremantle to the marquis of Buckingham.

8. NMM, NEP/8, 4 Apr. 1801. William Marsden informed Spencer that when Otway reached London he praised Nelson: 'he speaks in raptures of his conduct and presence of mind' (BL, Add. MSS 75849, 15 Apr. 1801).

9. NMM, CRK/14/73, Nelson's journal, 7 Apr. 1801.

10. NMM, CRK/14/73, Nelson's journal, 8 Apr. 1801; Feldbæk, 224.

11. Clements, Smith Collection, Apr. 1801, signed copy, Nelson and Bronte, 'to be given out in general orders'. For the full text of the armistice, see Tracy, *Naval Chronicle*, II, 170–71.

12. Laughton, *Miscellany*, I, 427, 9 Apr. 1801.

13. NMM, CRK/14/73, Nelson's journal, 10 Apr. 1801.

14. (UK)NA: PRO, ADM 51/1371, 12 Apr. 1801.

15. Clements, Smith Collection, 9 Apr. 1801, Nelson to Emma; Morrison II, 136–7.

16. BL, Egerton 1614, 11 Apr. 1801, Nelson to Emma.

17. On 16 April, Alexander Davison tried to make peace between St Vincent and Nelson by suggesting that the first lord make Maurice Nelson a commissioner of the Navy Board, which 'would be more gratifying to Lord Nelson than any Mark of attention that possibly could be bestowed' (Downer, 82).

18. Clements, Smith Collection, 14 Apr., Lindholm to Nelson; 15 Apr. 1801, Nelson to Lindholm; Morrison, II, 137.

19. NMM, CRK/14/73, Nelson's journal, 25 Apr. 1801. Even so, when the fleet was moving in and out of the bay to anchor, gun brigs were positioned at the outer end of the shoals to act as markers (NMM, AGC/N/18, 31 May 1801, Graves's orders).

20. (UK)NA: PRO, ADM 51/1356, 13 Apr. 1801.

21. 14 Apr. 1801, Nelson to Isaac Preston. This letter is in the possession of a descendant of Preston, Commander Peter Jermy Gwyn, RCN, and I am grateful to his brother, Professor Julian Gwyn, for obtaining a transcript for me.

22. NMM, CRK/14/13, 73, Nelson's journal, 13–15 Apr. 1801.

23. Tracy, *Navy Chronicle*, II, 182, letter from Alexander Briarly, 19 Apr. 1801.

24. NMM, CRK/14/73, Nelson's journal, 15 Apr. 1801; James, III, 62.

25. BL, Egerton 1614, 8 June 1801, Nelson to Emma.

26. NMM, CRK/14/73, Nelson's journal, 19 Apr. 1801.

27. NMM, AGC/W/2, 22 Apr. 1801, Wilkes to his cousin.

28. NMM, CRK/9/169, 21 Apr. 1801, Parker to Nelson.

29. (UK)NA: PRO, ADM 51/1371, 21, 22 Apr. 1801.

30. Clements, Smith Collection, 13 Apr. 1801; Morrison, II, 137.

31. NMM, AGC/W/2, 22 Apr. 1801.

32. BL, Egerton 1614, 25 Apr. 1801, Nelson to Emma.

33. Laughton, *Miscellany*, I, 430, 25 Apr., Nelson to Nepean; 431, 28 Apr. 1801, to Troubridge.

34. Laughton, *Miscellany*, I, 432, 2 May 1801.

35. NMM, CRK/9/172, 29 Apr. 1801, Parker to Nelson.

36. Bonner-Smith, *St Vincent*, I, 67, quoting Nepean's letter of 16 Apr. 1801. Parker was also criticized for failing to mention his captain of the fleet, William Domett, in his dispatches, as was the custom. To Hood, 'it was a matter of astonishment'. (NMM, CRK/6/165, 1 June 1801, Hood to Nelson).

37. Bonner-Smith, *St Vincent*, I, 63, quoting George Rose's diary entry of 6 Apr. 1801.

38. Lloyd, *Keith Papers*, II, 373, 21 May 1801, Young to Keith.

39. Bucks., D/FR/451/12, 3 July 1801, Fremantle to William Fremantle.

40. Nicolas, VII, ccv, 13 Apr. 1801.

41. Aspinall, *George III*, 24 May 1801, St Vincent to the king.

42. Morrison, II, 144, 2 May 1801.

43. Laughton, *Miscellany*, I, 432–3, 7 May 1801.

44. (UK)NA: PRO, ADM 1/4187, 16 Apr. Hawkesbury to the Admiralty; 12 June 1801, Hobart to the Admiralty.

45. (UK)NA: PRO, ADM 1/4187, 5 May 1801, Hobart to the Admiralty.

46. Barker, Rosalin, Chapters 6–10.

47. Tooke, 19.

48. NMM, CRK/5/111, 23 May 1801, Fremantle to Nelson; see also Thomas Messer's account to Nelson of this period (NMM, CRK/9/38, 3 July 1804).

49. Nicolas, IV, 363, 8 May 1801.

50. NMM, CRK/14/73, Nelson's journal, 9 May 1801; Nicolas, IV, 364–5, 9 May 1801.

51. Monmouth, E990, 8 May 1801.

52. Hyde Parker informed Nelson that he was 'more likely to procure water at

the Island of Ertholmene than at Bornholm' (NMM, CRK/9/169, 21 Apr. 1801). Ertholmene is a group of islands of which Khristiansø and Fredericksø are the largest.

53. Nicolas, IV, 375, 17 May 1801, Nelson to Nepean; Clements, Smith Collection, 15 May 1801, Totty to Nelson; Morrison, II, 148.

54. Clements, Smith Collection, 12 May 1801, draft, Nelson to 'My dear Admiral'.

55. Nicolas, IV, 369, 12 May 1801, Nelson to Davison.

56. NMM, CRK/5/111, 23 May 1801, Fremantle to Nelson.

57. Clements, Smith Collection, 12 May 1801, A. Balaschoff to Nelson; Morrison, II, 146 (in French).

58. BL, Egerton 1614, 15 May 1801, Nelson to Emma.

59. Stewart, *Cumloden Papers*, Table of Letters, II, 22 May 1801, Nelson to St Vincent; NMM, ADM/L/K/54, 13, 14 May 1801.

60. Nicolas, IV, 371–2, 13 May 1801, Pahlen to Nelson; 371–3, 16 May, Nelson to Pahlen.

61. NMM, AGC/N/2, [17] May 1801.

62. (UK)NA: PRO, ADM 3/144, 31 May 1801, draft letter, Nepean to Nelson; also Morrison, II, 150.

63. Nicolas, IV, 377, 20 May 1801; NMM, ADM/L/K/54, 20 May 1801.

64. Nicolas, IV, 376–7, 20 May 1801, Nelson to Panin.

65. Nicolas, IV, 385–7, 23 May, Nelson to Admiral Cronstedt; 24 May 1801, Nelson to Nepean.

66. NMM, ADM/L/K/54, 18 May 1801.

67. Fremantle, *Wynne* (1952), 330–31, 21 May 1801, Fremantle to Betsey.

68. NMM, CRK/11/49, 5 June 1801, St Helens to Nelson; Schroeder, 221.

69. NMM, CRK/11/50, 20 June 1801, St Helens to Nelson.

70. NMM, AGC/N/19, 15 June 1801, 'Nelson's Farewell Message to the Fleet'.

71. Morrison, II, 150, 31 May 1801, Nepean to Nelson; Nicolas, IV, 405, 11 June 1801, Nelson to Totty.

72. Fremantle, *Wynne* (1952), 325, 22 Apr. 1801, Fremantle to marquis of Buckingham.

73. When in Køge Bay water was available at 'Stephens Point' (Stevns Klint), at the south of the bay. Graves ordered the fleet to water, junior captains first: 'watering is not to be interrupted by any partys of Pleasure' (NMM, AGC/N/18, 31 May 1801, Graves's orders).

74. Nicolas, IV, 400, 2 June 1801, Nelson to Totty.

75. Nicolas, IV, 398, 29 May 1801, Nelson to Totty: NMM, CRK/1, 27 Jan. 1803, Baird to Nelson.

76. Morrison, II, 148, 15 May 1801, Totty to Nelson; Nicolas, IV, 23 May 1801, Nelson to Nepean.

77. NMM, CRK/3/80, 10 Apr. 1801, Cockburn to Nelson.

78. Monmouth, E990, 8 May 1801, Nelson to Cockburn.

79. Nicolas, IV, 392, 26 May 1801, Nelson to Totty.

80. NMM, CRK/3/81, 29 May 1801, Cockburn to Nelson.

81. Nicolas, IV, 396–7, 28 May 1801, Nelson to Booth.

82. NMM, CRK/3/24, 26 May 1801, Lord Carysfort to Nelson.

83. NMM, ADM DP/21, Victualling Board to the Admiralty, 20 Oct. 1801. The total cost of the live cattle was £8,851; the returned hides were valued at £259. I am grateful to Janet McDonald for this reference.

84. NMM, CRK/12/132, 19, 26 May 1801, Totty to Nelson.

85. Laughton, *Miscellany*, I, 435, 1 June 1801.

86. Nicolas, IV, 23 May 1801, Nelson to Holloway.

87. Aspinall, III, 545, 30 May 1801, St Vincent to the king.

88. Bonner-Smith, *St Vincent*, I, 99, St Vincent to Lord Chatham; 100, 31 May 1801, St Vincent to Nelson.

89. NMM, AGC/N/18, 30 May 1801, Nelson to Graves.

90. Morrison, II, 153–5, 10–13 June 1801.

91. Clements, Smith Collection, 10 June 1801; Morrison, II, 153–4.

92. NMM, CRK/8/74, 27 May 1801, Lindholm to Nelson.

93. Clements, Smith Collection, 13 July 1801; Morrison, II, 157.

94. BL, Egerton 1614, 11 June 1801, Nelson to Emma.

95. BL, Egerton 1614, 10 June 1801, Nelson to Emma.

96. Dawson, 166, 4 June 1801, Nelson to Ball.

97. Bucks., D/FR/45/1/12, 3 July 1801.

98. NMM, AGC/N/19, 15 June 1801, 'Farewell to the Fleet'; see also Nicolas, IV, 420, 18 June 1801.

99. (UK)NA: PRO, ADM 51/1371; NMM, ADM/L/K/54, 19–30 June 1801.

100. Broadley and Bartelot, 68–9, 8 July 1801, Hardy to Manfield.

101. Bucks., D/FR/45/1/12, 3 July 1801, Fremantle to William Fremantle.

102. Tooke, 15, 19, 55.

103. DRO, 152M/c1801/0284, 29 Apr. 1801.

104. NMM, CRK/6/94, 5 May 1801, Sir Andrew Snape Hamond to Nelson.

105. Nicolas, IV, 378, 22 May 1801.

106. NMM, DAV/2/7 [n.d.], Fanny to Davison.

107. Naish, 585–6 [Apr. 1801], Fanny to Nelson, Edmund Nelson to Nelson. 'I have written My Lord a Congratulatory letter' (NMM, DAV/2/44, 7 May 1801, Fanny to Davison).

108. Naish, 586–7, 23 Apr. 1801, Nelson to Davison.

109. NMM, DAV/2/37, 26 Apr. [1801], Fanny to Davison.

110. NMM, DAV/2/40 [?] May 1801, Fanny to Davison.

111. NMM, DAV/2/46, 24 May; DAV/2/47, 27 May 1801, Fanny to Davison.

112. NMM, DAV/2/37, 26 Apr. [1801], Fanny to Davison.

113. NMM, DAV/2/40 [n.d.], Fanny to Davison.

114. Monmouth, E670, 14 May 1801, Susannah Bolton to Fanny.

115. Naish, 592–3 [Sept. 1801], Emma to Mrs William Nelson.

116. Naish, 585, 16 Apr. 1801, William Hamilton to Nelson.
117. NMM, DAV/2/36 [?] Apr. 1801, Fanny to Davison.
118. NMM, DAV/2/42, 1 May 1801, Fanny to Davison.
119. NMM, DAV/2/43, 3 May 1801, Fanny to Davison.
120. NMM, DAV/2/43, 3 May 1801, Fanny to Davison.
121. NMM, DAV/2/51, 27 June 1801, Fanny to Davison.
122. NMM, DAV/50, 26 June 1801, Fanny to Davison.

24 Boulogne

1. NMM, MON/1/19, 27 July 1801.
2. NMM, CRK/13/71, 2 Sept. [1801].
3. (UK)NA: PRO, ADM 1/4187, 10 Apr. 1801, George Hammond to Nepean, extract of intelligence.
4. (UK)NA: PRO, ADM 1/4187, 21, 25 Apr. 1801, duke of Portland to St Vincent, 'from the usual source': 'L'allure générale des expéditions maritimes qui ne sont pas dans leur beau.' This source is possibly Bayard, identified by Sparrow, 246.
5. Mackesy, *War without Victory*, 212.
6. Mackesy, *War without Victory*, 203.
7. Bonner-Smith, *St Vincent*, I, 119.
8. (UK)NA: PRO, ADM 1/4187, 18 May, 12, 22 June 1801, extracts of intelligence.
9. Bonner-Smith, *St Vincent*, I, 121; Monaque, 'Latouche-Tréville', 276.
10. NMM, ADM/L/K/54, 30 June, Nicolas, IV, 421, 1 July 1801, Nelson to St Vincent.
11. Nicolas, V, 21, 9 July [1801], Nelson to Davison (Nicolas prints it as a letter of 1802); see Vincent, 441–2; Nicolas, IV, 423, 12 July 1801, Nelson to St Vincent; Monmouth, E685, 12 July 1801, Davison to Fanny.
12. NMM, CRK/1, 11, 13 July 1801, Addington to Nelson.
13. Nicolas, IV, 423–4, 18 July 1801, Nelson to Addington; Aspinall, *George III*, 2489, 27 July, Addington to the king; NMM, CRK/13/106, 30 July 1801, Vansittart to Nelson. See also Catherine Matcham's thanks for this honour, 'but I hope the Title will never be in the possession of any of my children though I should be very unhappy to have been forgotten by you' (NMM, CRK/9/17, 11 Aug. 1801).
14. White, 'Public Order Book', 221.
15. Bonner-Smith, *St Vincent*, I, 121, 125–6, 24 July 1801.
16. Morrison, II, 157–9, 26 July 1801, Board of Admiralty to Nelson.
17. NMM, CRK/11/105, 5 Aug.; 11/112, 14 Aug.; 11/118, 28 Aug. 1801, St Vincent to Nelson.
18. NMM, CRK/13/49, 28 July 1801, Troubridge to Nelson; also Bonner-Smith, *St Vincent*, I, 130, St Vincent to General Simcoe.

19. NMM, CRK/2/25, 1 Aug. 1801, William Bedford to Nelson. They demanded £20 for the first month and thereafter 6s. a day.

20. NMM, CRK/13/51, 1 Aug. 1801, Troubridge to Nelson.

21. Bonner-Smith, *St Vincent*, I, 127, 29 July 1801, St Vincent to Nelson.

22. NMM, CRK/6/123, 6 Aug. 1801, Harvey to William Bedford of the *Leyden*.

23. NMM, CRK/13/58, 10 Aug. 1801, Troubridge to Nelson.

24. Nicolas, IV, 429, 26, 27 July 1801, Nelson to Nepean.

25. Nicolas, IV, 429–30, 28 July 1801, Nelson to Nepean.

26. Nicolas, IV, 431, 28 July 1801, Nelson to Berry.

27. Houghton, pf MS Eng. 196.5 (110), 30 July 1801, Parker to Lady Hamilton.

28. Monmouth, E95, 29 July 1801, Nelson to Emma.

29. White, 'Public Order Book', 253–5.

30. NMM, KEI/18/4, 14 Sept. 1801, Nelson to Keith.

31. (UK)NA: PRO, WO/55/1072, 31 July 1801, George Bean to Lieutenant-Colonel McLeod.

32. (UK)NA: PRO, ADM 1/1437, 3 Aug. 1801.

33. NMM, MRF/181, 2 Aug. 1801.

34. Monaque, 'Latouche-Tréville', 276.

35. Laughton, *Miscellany*, I, 292, 7 Aug. 1801, William Cathcart to Lord Cathcart.

36. Huntington, HM 34051, 7 Aug. 1801.

37. NMM, CRK/13/106, 30 July 1801, Vansittart to Nelson. The average depth of the inside hold of the bomb vessels was between 12 and 13 feet (Lyon, 254–5).

38. Bonner-Smith, *St Vincent*, I, 130, 3 Aug. 1801.

39. NMM, RUSI/NM/202, 3 Aug. 1801.

40. Laughton, *Miscellany*, I, 292, 7 Aug. 1801, William Cathcart to Lord Cathcart; Monarque, 'Latouche-Tréville', 278; NMM, MRF/181, Latouche-Tréville to the minister of marine, 5 Aug. 1801.

41. Nicolas, IV, 441, 4 Aug. 1801, Nelson to Nepean; Monaque, 'Latouche-Tréville', 276, 278; NMM, CRK/13/58, 10 Aug. [1801], Troubridge to Nelson.

42. Downer, 122, 3–4 Aug. 1801, Edward Parker to Davison.

43. NMM, CRK/13/52, 4 Aug. 1801, Troubridge to Nelson. The speed of this information was near to the modern-day 'real-time' intelligence.

44. White, 'Public Order Book', 226; Monaque, 'Latouche-Tréville', 277–8.

45. (UK)NA: PRO, WO/55/1072, 7 Aug. 1801, Fryer to McLeod.

46. NMM, CRK/9/140, 7 Aug. 1801, William Nowell of the *Isis* to Nelson.

47. Nicolas, IV, 441, 4 Aug. 1801, Nelson to Nepean.

48. Nicolas, I, 440, 4 Aug. 1801, Nelson to Berry.

49. Huntington, HM 34051, 7 Aug. 1801, Nelson to Lutwidge.

50. Bonner-Smith, I, 131, 7 Aug. 1801.

51. (UK)NA: PRO, ADM 1/4188, 13 Aug. 1801, 'extract of intelligence' sent from the Foreign Office to the Admiralty.

52. Houghton, pf MS Eng. 196.5 (22a), 4 Aug. [1801].

53. Downer, *Davison*, 122, 9 Aug. 1801, Parker to Davison.

54. NMM, AGC/J/1, 8 Aug. 1801, St Vincent to Nelson.

55. NMM, CRK/13/54, 7 Aug. [1801], Troubridge to Nelson.

56. NMM, CRK/13/62, 14 Aug. 1801, Troubridge to Nelson.

57. NMM, CRK/13/59, 12 Aug. 1801, Troubridge to Nelson.

58. Nicolas, IV, 443, 6 Aug. 1801, Nelson to Captains Shields, Hamilton, Schomberg and Edge.

59. NMM, KEI/18/4, 14 Sept. 1801. Although the phrase 'half seas over' came to mean 'half or almost drunk', Nelson was more likely to use the phrase in its older sense, 'half way across the sea'.

60. Bonner-Smith, *St Vincent*, I, 133, 10 Aug. 1801, St Vincent to Nelson.

61. Bonner-Smith, *St Vincent*, I, 131–2, 7 Aug. 1801.

62. Nicolas, IV, 442, 6 Aug., Nelson to Lutwidge; (UK)NA: PRO, ADM 51/1437, 7 Aug. 1801.

63. Bonner-Smith, *St Vincent*, I, 7 Aug., St Vincent to Nelson; Nicolas, IV, 449, 10 Aug. 1801, Nelson to Captain Owen of the *Nemesis*. Dickson was a lieutenant of 1759, thus over sixty, and had married a girl of eighteen at Yarmouth in 1799, an example Sir Hyde Parker was to follow. Fanny gleefully repeated the story to Nelson in happier times (Naish, 533, 23 Sept. 1799, Fanny to Nelson). Dickson had commanded the convoy from Elsinore in 1781 when Nelson was in the *Albemarle*, but Nelson did not know him well.

64. Nicolas, IV, 437, 3 Aug. 1801, Nelson to Nepean.

65. NMM, CRK/13/56, 8 Aug. [1801], Troubridge to Nelson; Bonner-Smith, *St Vincent*, I, 135, 12 Aug. 1801, St Vincent to Nelson.

66. (UK)NA: PRO, WO/55/1072, 7 Aug. 1801, George Bean to McLeod.

67. (UK)NA: PRO, ADM 52/3208, 8–9 Aug. 1801.

68. Nicolas, IV, 451, 10 Aug. 1801, Nelson to Nepean.

69. Dawson, *Hydrography*, 14–15.

70. (UK)NA: PRO, ADM 52/3208, 10 Aug. 1801.

71. Nicolas, IV, 450–51, 10 Aug. 1801. The *Medusa*'s draft was 19′ 11″.

72. Bonner-Smith, *St Vincent*, I, 134, 11 Aug. 1801, St Vincent to Nelson.

73. (UK)NA: PRO, ADM 52/3208; 51/1437, 11 Aug. 1801.

74. NMM, CRK/13/56, 8 Aug. 1801, Troubridge to Nelson.

75. (UK)NA: PRO, ADM 1/4188, 9 Aug. 1801.

76. NMM, MRF/181, 14 Aug. 1801, Latouche-Tréville to the minister of marine, Citizen Forfait.

77. Tracy, *Naval Chronicle*, II, 250. This state of affairs was in stark contrast to the disciplined days of the Mediterranean when Sir William Hamilton had written frustratedly to Sidney Smith: 'You Gentlemen of the Sea Service are so very secret in respect to your destination' (Huntington, HM 34200, 27 Jan. 1800).

78. (UK)NA: PRO, ADM 51/1437, 16 Aug. 1801.

79. Nicolas, IV, 468, 'An account of losses . . .'; James, III, 65–7.

80. NMM, MRF/181, 16 Aug. 1801, reports to the minister of marine.

81. (UK)NA: PRO, ADM 51/1457, 18–22 Aug. 1801.

82. Nicolas, IV, 460–63, 15 Aug. 1801, 'Plan of Attack'.

83. (UK)NA: PRO, WO/55/1072, 16 Aug. 1801, William English to McLeod.

84. Nicolas, IV, 459, 14 Aug. 1801.

85. Bonner-Smith, *St Vincent*, I, 135, 14 Aug. 1801, St Vincent to Nelson. See the prince of Bouillon's (Philip d'Auvergne) dispatch in Addington's papers, 2 June 1801, 'from a confidential person at Bernadotte's headquarters . . . Ireland is certainly a primary object of the preparations at Brest if the Fleet can get out' (DRO/ c1801/OM/11).

86. NMM, CRK/1, 19 Aug. 1801, Addington to Nelson.

87. NMM, CRK/13/66, 19 Aug. 1801.

88. Coleman, 271–2.

89. NMM, COR/60, 31 Aug. 1801.

90. NMM, CRK/14/116, 6 Sept. 1801; printed in Nicolas, IV, 485, 6 Sept., Nelson to Nepean.

91. Coleman, 273, 398.

92. Bonner-Smith, *St Vincent*, I, 143, St Vincent to Nelson.

93. Nicolas, IV, 495, 20, 24 Sept. 1801, Nelson to Dr Baird.

94. Nicolas, IV, 465, 16 Aug. 1801.

95. NMM, CRK/13/107, 24 Aug. 1801, Vansittart to Nelson.

96. (UK)NA: PRO, ADM 51/4409, 5 Sept. 1801.

97. Bonner-Smith, *St Vincent*, I, 141, 5 Sept. 1801.

98. NMM, CRK/9/153, 21 Aug. 1801, Captain Owen of the *Nemesis*, off Flushing, to Nelson.

99. NMM, CRK/13/72, 7 Sept. 1801, Troubridge to Nelson.

100. (UK)NA: PRO, WO/55/1072, 20 Aug. 1801, William English to McLeod.

101. Nicolas, IV, 479, 25 Aug. 1801, Nelson to Nepean.

102. Nicolas, IV, 479–80, 25 Aug. 1801, Nelson to Nepean.

103. NMM, CRK/13/69, 28 Aug. [1801], Troubridge to Nelson.

104. Nicolas, IV, 488, 14 Sept., Nelson to Nepean; NMM, AGC/J/1, 14 Sept. 1801, St Vincent to Nelson.

105. NMM, BRP/3, 27 Aug., Sarah Nelson to William Nelson.

106. NMM, BRP/3, 27 Aug., 7 Sept. 1801, Sarah Nelson to William Nelson.

107. Monmouth, E96, 27 Aug. 1801.

108. NMM, BRP/3, 7 Sept. 1801, Sarah Nelson to William Nelson.

109. Nicolas, IV, 497, 27 Sept. 1801, Nelson to Davison.

110. RNM, MS 1973/334, 30 Sept. 1801, Nelson to Emma.

111. NMM, CRK/13/81, 25 Sept. [1801], Troubridge to Nelson.

112. Mackesy, *War without Victory*, 213; Owen, 176. Eleven men were hanged, seven sentenced to hard labour.

113. NMM, CRK/13/78, 20 Sept. 1801, Troubridge to Nelson.

114. Nicolas, VII, ccxxx, 23 Sept. 1801, Nelson to St Vincent.

115. (UK)NA: PRO, ADM 51/4409, 9 Sept. 1801.

116. NMM, CRK/13/78, 20 Sept. 1801, Troubridge to Nelson.

117. Coleman (2002), 359 [?] Sept. 1801, Nelson to Nepean.

118. NMM, CRK/13/73, 5 Sept. 1801, Troubridge to Nelson.

119. NMM, AGC/17/11, 24 Sept. 1801.

120. NMM, CRK/13/78, 20 Sept. [1801], Troubridge to Nelson.

121. NMM, CRK/13/80, 24 Sept. [1801], Troubridge to Nelson.

122. NMM, CRK/13/74, 9 Sept. [1801].

123. Broadley and Bartelot, 74, 16 Oct. 1801, Hardy to Manfield.

124. Mackesy, *War without Victory*, 215; Nicolas, IV, 507, 8 Oct. 1801, Addington to Nelson.

125. NMM, MAM, 1–49, 10 Oct. 1801, Nelson to Emma.

126. Monmouth, E112, 13 Oct. 1801, Nelson to Emma; Ehrman, III, 544.

127. Nicolas, IV, 511, 14, 19 Oct. 1801, Nelson to Lutwidge.

128. (UK)NA: PRO, ADM 51/4409, 23 Oct. 1801. He did not strike his flag until 10 Apr. 1802.

129. Lambert, 'Cornwallis', 365.

130. Mackesy, *War without Victory*, 215.

131. Schroeder, 225–8.

132. Clements, Melville Papers, 22 Feb. 1801, Sir Alexander Hope to Dundas.

133. Clements, Pitt Papers, 2 Oct. 1801.

134. Owen, 174, 13 Aug. 1801, Collingwood to Edward Collingwood.

135. NMM, KEI/18/4, 14 Sept. 1801, Nelson to Keith. Rodger, *Command of the Ocean*, 471, remarks that Nelson had been downgraded to what was 'essentially a captain's command'.

IV   ADULATION AND DEATH 1801–1805

25   Peace and the Journey to Wales

1. Morrison, II, 185.

2. Minto, III, 283–4.

3. Monmouth, E96, 98, 99, 27 Aug. 1801, Nelson to Haslewood.

4. Morrison, II, 175, 16 Oct. 1801.

5. Constantine, 257.

6. Minto, III, 242–3, 22 Mar. 1802, Minto to Lady Minto.

7. Houghton, FMS Lowell 10, 2 Oct. 1801, Nelson to Emma.

8. Morrison, II, 397, 13 Jan. 1802, accounts with Marsh and Creed; Nicolas, V, 47, 6 Mar. 1803, Nelson to Addington.

9. NMM, XAGC/8, 30, transcript of document signed by Nelson and Fanny, 9 Jan. 1801.

10. Nicolas, IV, 489, 14 Sept. 1801, Nelson to Davison; Morrison, II, 396,

Nelson's account with Marsh and Creed, 26 Jan. 1802. As a prize agent, Tyson would be able to advance money, at least for a short time.

11. NMM, MAM/19, 14 July 1802, Nelson to George Matcham; Naish, 601, 9 Jan. 1803, George Matcham to Nelson. Nelson also used some of his father's legacy to purchase Axe's farm.

12. (UK)NA: PRO, AO/1/850/5, 3 Sept. 1811, 'Declaration of the Account of the Right Honourable Charles Francis Greville Executor to His Excellency the Late Right Honourable Sir William Hamilton . . .' Much of this money had gone to support the royalist émigrés in Naples.

13. Morrison, II, 404, 21 Sept. 1802, 'Statement of account between Sir William Hamilton and Myself . . .'

14. Morrison, II, 406–17, Appendix D; Huntington, HM 21718, 2 Feb. 1802, William Hamilton to Emma Hamilton; Morrison, II, 173, 9 Oct. 1801, Hamilton to Greville; Constantine, 258–62.

15. Morrison, II, 177–8, 5 Dec. 1801, Hamilton to Greville.

16. Dawson, 177–8, 14 June 1802, Hamilton to Greville.

17. Morrison, II, 167, 27 Sept. [1801], Greville to Hamilton; Constantine, 267; Morrison, II, 182, 24 Jan. 1802, Hamilton to Greville; Houghton, Husband Collection (84), 31 July [1801], William Hamilton to Emma.

18. Houghton, pf MS Eng. 196.5 (84), 31 July 1801.

19. Naish, 580 [4 Mar. 1801], 'Memorandum'.

20. Nicolas, IV, 489, 14 Sept. 1801.

21. He planned to pay Fanny £1,800 a year, £200 of which would be paid as interest on her legacy of £4,000 from her uncle (Naish, 580, 'Memorandum' [4 Mar. 1801]). Nelson, as the husband, legally controlled his wife's capital.

22. Morrison, II, 406–17, 'Weekly Accounts' 21 June 1802–4 Apr. 1803.

23. Nicolas, IV, 533, 28 Nov. 1801, Nelson to Davison.

24. NMM, GIR/1/A, 11 June 1802, Nelson to Susannah Bolton.

25. Nicolas, V, 11–12, 13–14, 15, 28 Apr., 7 May, 11 June 1802, Nelson to John McArthur.

26. Monmouth, E137, 1 Aug. 1803, Nelson to Booth and Haslewood, from the Victory off Toulon.

27. Naval Chronicle, V, 254–6, 'Earl St Vincent v. Mr Tucker, Prize Agent'; Hill, 82, 176–8.

28. NMM, PST/39, 10 Jan. 1802.

29. NMM, XAGC/8, 13 Feb. 1802, Nelson to Duckworth.

30. Hill, 81–2; Naval Chronicle, V, 254–6.

31. Broadley and Bartelot, 77, 7 Nov. 1801, Hardy to Manfield.

32. Morrison, II, 166–7, 26 Sept. 1801, Graefer (from Bronte) to Nelson.

33. Warren R. Dawson, Nelson Collection, 178–9, 30 July 1802, Graefer to Emma Hamilton.

34. NMM, CRK/1, 8 Nov. 1802, Ball to Nelson; Warren R. Dawson, Nelson Collection, 179.

35. BL, Add. MSS 34953, 16 Sept. 1803, Nelson to Edmund Noble at Malta.

36. NMM, CRK/9/114, 16 Nov. 1803, Edmund Noble to Nelson.

37. NMM, GIR/1B, 10 June 1802, Nelson to Bolton.

38. NMM, CRK/2/68, 20 Dec. 1802, Thomas Bolton to Nelson; Naish, 600–601.

39. Morrison, II, 219, 6 Oct. 1803, Nelson to Emma; NMM, CRK/13/103, 28 Jan. 1804, George Unwin to Nelson.

40. NMM, PST/81, 19 Dec., Edmund to Nelson; 21 Dec. 1801, Edmund to Emma Hamilton; Naish, 596.

41. Naish, 597 [n.d. but 1802], Horatio Nelson (Nelson's nephew) to his mother, Mrs William Nelson.

42. NMM, GIR/1/B, 10 June 1802, Emma to Thomas Bolton.

43. NMM, MAM/27, 4 Jan. 1803.

44. Morrison, II, 203–4, 28 Dec. 1802, Mrs Tyson to Emma.

45. e.g., Addington's invitation to call on 26 Oct. 1801 (DRO, 152M/c1801/ON/16).

46. Brenton, 2, 48.

47. NMM, PST/39, 15 July 1802, Nelson to William Marsh.

48. Minto, III, 275, 28 Feb. 1802, Minto to Lady Minto.

49. Nicolas, V, 13, 6 May 1802, Nelson to Hercules Ross; Morrison, II, 203, 26 Dec. 1802, Richard Bulkeley to Nelson.

50. Nicolas, V, 23, 21 Jan., 12 July 1802, Nelson to Samuel Sutton; Tracy, *Naval Chronicle*, II, 160; Naish, 597 [n.d. but 1802], Emma's postscript to Mrs William Nelson; Scott, 78.

51. Morrison, II, 178–9, 16 Dec. 1801, Walterstoffe to Nelson.

52. Broadley and Bartelot, 90, 5 Apr. 1802, Hardy to Manfield.

53. Hughes, 138–40, 20 Apr., Collingwood to his sister; 9 May 1802, to Mrs Stead.

54. Parsons, 11. There is no corroboration for this story, and it may be embroidered by memory in old age, for Parson's *Nelsonian Reminiscences* were not published until 1843; but a number of points in the story ring true, including the confirmation of Parsons as lieutenant on 25 Mar. 1802.

55. Broadley and Bartelot, 82–3, 6 Jan. 1802, Hardy, from the *Isis* at Sheerness, to Manfield.

56. Morrison, II, 192, 2 July 1802, William Hamilton to the marquis of Douglas.

57. Constantine, 255, quoting Anson, Elizabeth and Florence eds., *Mary Hamilton* (1925), 325–7, Lady Frances Harpur to Mary Dickenson.

58. Morrison, II, 182, 24 Jan. 1802, Hamilton to Charles Greville.

59. Naish, 598, 20 Apr. 1802, Edmund Nelson to Fanny.

60. NMM, DAV 2/54, 56, 57, 3 Sept., 3 Nov., 27 Dec. 1801, Fanny to Davison.

61. Monmouth, E689 [?] Oct. 1801, Fanny to Edmund Nelson.

62. Monmouth, E650, 17 Oct. 1801.

63. Morrison, II, 173, 8 Oct. 1801.

64. NMM, DAV 2/56, 3 Nov. 1801, Fanny to Davison.

65. Naish, 596, 18 Dec. 1801.

66. Naish, 597, 23 Mar. 1802, Edmund Nelson to Nelson.

67. NMM, MAM/10, 12, 13, 26, 28, 29 Apr. 1801, Nelson to George Matcham.

68. NMM, MAM 12, 28 Apr. 1801, Nelson to Matcham.

69. NMM, MAM/10, 26 Apr. 1802, Nelson to George Matcham.

70. NMM, MAM/12, 28 Apr. 1802, Nelson to George Matcham.

71. Naish, 599 [15 May 1802], Susannah Bolton to Fanny.

72. Naish, 599 [15 May 1802], Susannah Bolton to Fanny.

73. Naish, 9 Jan. 1803, George Matcham to Nelson.

74. Naish, 606, 7 Nov. 1805, Lady Walpole to Captain Nisbet.

75. Broadley and Bartelot, 94, 24 June 1802, Hardy to Manfield.

76. Nicolas, V, 23, 12 July 1802, Nelson to Samuel Sutton.

77. White, 'Tour of South Wales', 5, 12 July 1802, Nelson to Dr Goodall (from a private collection).

78. NMM, MAM/20, 16 July 1802.

79. Heath [unpaginated].

80. Gill, 34–7; Gardiner, 45, 94; Rodger, *Command of the Ocean*, 421–2. The keels of the ships were laid down in 1798. They were the *Milford* (74), launched 1809; *Lavinia* (44), launched 1806; and *Nautilus* (18), launched 1804. The last was one of the sloops to bring back the news of Trafalgar.

81. NMM, CRK/6/84 [n.d.], Greville to Nelson, outlining his plans for Milford; Rees, 28.

82. Morriss, *Dockyards*, 54.

83. Baker, 'John Bowsher', 310–12; Roger Knight, 88–9.

84. One of the plaques on the wall commemorates the undistinguished Admiral Sir Charles Thompson, who had been an absentee MP for Monmouth from 1796 to 1799 (Heath [unpaginated]; Thorne, V, 366).

85. Morrison, II, 401–4, Appendix C, 'Sheets of Accounts'.

86. Morrison, II, 197, 30 Sept. 1802, Banks to Greville.

87. Morrison, II, 197 [n.d. but 1802].

88. NMM, AGC/18/21, 26 Oct. 1802, Nelson to Moseley; also Morrison, II, 207, 17 Feb. 1803, Bulkeley to Nelson.

89. Nicolas, V, 23, 8 Feb. 1803, Nelson to Davison.

90. Nicolas, V, 47–9, 8 Mar. 1803, Nelson to Addington; also to George Rose, 'on the extraordinary thing of my not receiving an Irish Pension' (Nicolas, V, 65, 15 May 1803).

91. Ehrman, III, 575.

92. Warren R. Dawson, *Nelson Collection*, 180, 21 Nov. 1802, Nelson to Nepean.

93. Minto, III, 258, 26 Nov. 1802, Minto to his wife.

94. NMM, MAM/23, 23 Dec. 1802, Emma to Kitty Matcham.

95. Linebaugh and Rediker, 272–86.

96. NMM, CRK/2/84, 12 Feb. 1803, Bulkeley to Nelson.

97. Nicolas, V, 42, 8 Feb. 1803, Nelson to Davison.

98. NMM, CRK/4/8, 15 Feb. 1803, Despard to Nelson; CRK/4/9, Despard's petition to the king.

99. Minto, III, 274, 23, 28 Feb. 1803, Minto to his wife.

100. Morrison, II, 297, 17 Feb. 1803, Bulkeley to Nelson.

101. NMM, CRK/4/10 [n.d.], Despard to Nelson.

102. Linebaugh and Rediker, 248–50.

103. NMM, CRK/2/85, 1 Mar. 1803, Bulkeley to Nelson.

104. Malmesbury, IV, 214, 21 Feb. 1803.

105. Constantine, 282.

106. NMM, CRK/13/43, 7 Apr. 1803, Tyson to Nelson.

107. NMM, MAM/25, 8 Apr. 1803, Nelson to Kitty Matcham. The 3 April death was that of Maurice Nelson in 1801.

108. Morrison, II, 418–24, Appendix E. He also left Nelson the two guns he kept at Merton.

109. Minto, III, 283, 18 Apr. 1803, Minto to his wife; NMM, AGC/18/27, 21 Apr. 1803, Nelson to [Addington].

110. Broadley and Bartelot, 105, 6 Apr. 1803, Hardy to Manfield.

111. Monmouth, E134, 12 May 1803, Nelson to William Haslewood.

112. Naish, 590–91, 26 Sept. 1801, Nelson to Emma; Oman, 488, 493.

113. Morrison, II, 226 [n.d.], [?] Mar. 1804, Nelson to Emma; also 225–6 [n.d.]; Fraser, 306–7.

114. Stirling, *Pages and Portraits*, I, 245, the view of Sir William Hotham, at this time a captain.

115. NMM, MAM/23, 23 Dec. 1802, Emma to Kitty Matcham.

116. NMM, PST/39, 3 Sept. 1805, Emma to Mrs Lutwidge, wife of Admiral Skeffington Lutwidge.

26   The Peace of Amiens

1. (UK)NA: PRO, ADM 1/406, Bickerton to Nepean, enclosure. Bickerton ordered a court martial on Edward Hicks, seaman, suspected of writing it.

2. (UK)NA: PRO, ADM 3/146, 6 Apr. 1802; Glete, II, 382–4, calculates tonnage captured up to 1800 as 250,000 tons.

3. (UK)NA: PRO, ADM 1/4189, 3 Apr. 1802, Hobart to Admiralty.

4. Rodger, *Command of the Ocean*, 476.

5. NMM, NEP/5, 15 Mar. 1799, St Vincent to Nepean. St Vincent was referring to the 1750s and the 1760s, when George Jackson was assistant clerk of the acts (1758–1766) and George Cockburne was comptroller of the Navy Board (1756–70). Jackson moved to the Admiralty in 1766 as deputy secretary and was judge advocate to the fleet when St Vincent made the remark.

6. See, for instance, the failure to purchase Riga masts between April and June 1803 ((UK)NA: PRO, ADM 2/1360, 28–9 June 1803, Nepean to the Navy Board).

7. Rodger, *Command of the Ocean*, 478.

8. Rodger, *Command of the Ocean*, 476–7.

9. NMM, CRK/2/88, 5 Nov. 1803, Richard Bulkeley to Nelson.

10. Keevil, 324.

11. Morriss, *Dockyards*, 194–5; Tracy, *Naval Chronicle*, II, 283–4.

12. (UK)NA: PRO, ADM 1/407, 1 Apr. 1803; Nicolas, V, 53–4.

13. Nicolas, V, 44–6, Feb. 1803; see p. 431 for the memorandum on timber.

14. DRO, 152/M/c1802/ON 7 and 8, 25 Oct. 1802, Nelson to Addington, and enclosure.

15. DRO, 152/M/c1802/ON1, 17 Feb. 1802, Nelson to Addington.

16. DRO, 152/M/c1802/ON4, 2 July 1802, Nelson to Addington.

17. Thorne, II, 286.

18. DRO, 152M/c1802/ON/6, 29 Dec. 1802, Nelson to Addington.

19. Hansard, 38, 1801–3, 186, 3 Nov. 1801.

20. Morrison, II, 202 [4 Dec. 1802], draft; Nicolas, V, 36–7, 4 Dec. 1802, memorandum to Addington. Compare this with his view of the desirability of a British Malta in his letter to Spencer of 6 Apr. 1799 (NMM, PST/10).

21. Tracy, *Naval Chronicle*, II, 276–9.

22. NMM, KEI/16/1, 5 July 1803, St Vincent to Keith.

23. (UK)NA: PRO, ADM 2/1360, 23 June 1803, St Vincent to Hobart.

24. NMM, CRK/13/86, 27 June 1803; see also Melville's confidence as the new first lord in his secret naval memorandum of 14 June 1804: 'The Naval force of this Country already afloat is perfectly adequate to repel the Attempts of the Enemy' (Clements, Melville Papers).

25. NMM, CRK/10/104, 15 Dec. [1803].

26. Hansard, 38, 1801–3, 687, 3 Nov. 1802.

27. (UK)NA: PRO, ADM 2/1360, 19 June 1803.

28. DRO, 152M/c 1803/ON 20, 6 Oct. 1803, Sir John Dalrymple to Nepean; McCaig, 252–3.

29. Aspinall, *Prince of Wales Correspondence*, IV, 535–7. The memorandum is endorsed by Nelson as 'April 1804', but this is more likely to refer to the date when the matter was debated, rather than the date of writing, since he was then cruising off Toulon. It opposed the view of St Vincent. Why the document should be among the papers of the prince of Wales is unexplained.

30. (UK)NA: PRO, ADM 3/146 [Dec.] 1802.

31. (UK)NA: PRO, ADM 1/406, 31 May 1802, survey on *Kent*.

32. (UK)NA: PRO, ADM 1/406, 7 Dec. 1802; 1/407, 26 Jan. 1803, Bickerton to Nepean.

33. (UK)NA: PRO, ADM 1/407, 24 Apr. 1803, Bickerton to Nepean.

34. (UK)NA: PRO, ADM 1/407, 19 Mar. 1803, Bickerton to Nepean.

35. (UK)NA: PRO, ADM 51/1453, 52/3142, 6 Nov. 1802; Tracy, *Naval Chronicle*, II, 285–6.

36. (UK)NA: PRO, ADM 2/1360, 7 Mar. 1803, Admiralty to Bickerton; see also ADM 1/1490, 1 Feb., 5 Mar. 1803, Hobart to Admiralty.

37. (UK)NA: PRO, ADM 1/406, 13 Sept. 1802. Oristano Bay turned out to be a disappointment as an anchorage, for during the summer months it was unhealthy and there was no water (BL, Add. MSS 37268, 6 Oct. 1802, Ball to Granville Penn).

38. NMM, ADM/L/V/47, 31 Oct. 1803; Admiralty Chart 1213.

39. Schroeder, 243.

40. Tracy, *Naval Chronicle*, II, 291.

41. (UK)NA: PRO, ADM 2/1360, 1 Apr. 1803, St Vincent to Hood.

42. (UK)NA: PRO, ADM 2/1360, 7 May 1803.

43. (UK)NA: PRO, ADM 1/407, 8 Apr., 26 June 1803, Bickerton to Nepean.

44. DRO, 152/M/c1803/ON/39.

45. NMM, KEI/16/1, 11 Mar. 1803, Keith to St Vincent.

46. NMM, KEI/16/1, 14 Mar. 1803, St Vincent to Keith.

47. NMM, KEI/16/1, 17 Mar. 1803, Keith to St Vincent.

48. Minto, III, 273–4, 23 Feb. 1803, Minto to his wife.

49. Tracy, *Naval Chronicle*, II, 291–2; Nicolas, V, 70; the British declaration of war is usually dated 18 May, the day by which the various proclamations were complete.

50. (UK)NA: PRO, ADM/180/6 (NMM, photocopy, Vol. III). The total cost of repair was £70,922; she had also had an eighteen-month repair between 1787 and 1789, costing £36,782.

51. BL, Add. MSS 34953, 4 Oct. 1803, Nelson to Charles Morice Pole; see also 'Nelson's Ships' section.

52. Nicolas, V, 64–5, 12 May 1803.

53. (UK)NA: PRO, ADM 52/3711, Apr. and May 1803; 16 May was sea time; by land time this would have been the afternoon of 15 May.

54. Schroeder, 231.

55. Mackesy, *Mediterranean*, 21.

56. (UK)NA: PRO, ADM 2/1360, 18 May 1803, Board of Admiralty to Nelson; Nicolas, V, 68–9.

57. Nicolas, V, 66, 17 May 1803, Nelson to Sutton.

58. (UK)NA: PRO, ADM 51/1446, Jan–Mar. 1803.

59. (UK)NA: PRO, ADM 52/3711, 17 May 1803; this was 2.30 in the afternoon of 16 May by land time.

60. Houghton, pf MS Eng. 196.5 (33), 18 May 1803.

61. Nicolas, V, 67, 18 May 1803, 3 p.m.

62. (UK)NA: PRO, ADM 2/923, 18 May 1803, Nepean to Nelson.

63. NMM, CRK/13/84, 19 [May 1803], Troubridge to Nelson.

64. (UK)NA: PRO, 36/16645.

65. NMM, MAM/26, 19 May 1803, Nelson to Emma.

66. Nicolas, V, 68, 20 May 1803, Nelson to Gardner; (UK)NA: PRO, ADM 36/15895, 7 June 1803. The *Victory*'s complement was 837; she had 834 borne and 779 mustered.

67. Mark-Wardlaw, 180–81. This description was recorded by William Mark, but he was not a witness as he was already in the Mediterranean.

68. DRO, 152/M/c1803/ON28, 23 May 1803, Nelson to Addington.

69. (UK)NA: PRO, ADM 36/16645; 36/15895. A similar number transferred from the *Amphion* to the *Victory*.

70. Mark-Wardlaw, 181.

71. Broadley and Bartelot, 107, 20 May 1803.

27 Commander-in-Chief, Mediterranean

1. NMM, CRK/5/105.

2. Cornwallis-West, 397–8, dated from internal evidence: see Houghton, pf MS Eng. 196.5 (36), 13 Jan. 1804, Nelson to Thomas Trigge, on the arrival of the *Excellent*.

3. Mackesy, *Mediterranean*, 32–7.

4. Nicolas, V, 90, 17 June 1803, Nelson to Nepean.

5. Nicolas, V, 93, 19 June 1803, Nelson to Elliot.

6. (UK)NA: PRO, ADM 51/1446, 17 June 1803.

7. (UK)NA: PRO, ADM 52/3711, 28, 30 May 1803; RNM MS 2002/76, 12 June 1803, William Chevallier to Alexander Davison; Nicolas, V, 130, 11 July 1803, Nelson to Elliot.

8. Nicolas, V, 94, 28 June 1803, Nelson to Addington; (UK)NA: PRO, ADM 51/1446.

9. Nicolas, V, 107.

10. Nicolas, V, 116, 4 July 1803, Nelson to St Vincent.

11. NMM, MAM/28, 7 Dec. 1803, Nelson to Emma.

12. NMM, CRK/1, 23 July 1803, Ball to Nelson.

13. (UK)NA: ADM 51/1446, 14 July 1803.

14. Warren R. Dawson, *Banks Letters*, 632, 9 July 1803; NMM, CRK/2/3, 8 Aug. 1803, Banks to Nelson. Davison reported to Nelson that the king wanted to see the items (NMM, CRK/3/141, 15 Aug. 1803).

15. NMM, ADM/L/V/57, 31 July 1803.

16. Nicolas, V, 153, 8 Aug. 1803, Nelson to the commanding admiral of the fleet of the French Republic, proposing an exchange of prisoners.

17. Nicolas, V, 161, 12 Aug. 1803, Nelson to Captain Moubray of the *Active*.

18. NMM, AGC/18/23, 31 July 1803, Nelson to Nepean.

19. Mark-Wardlaw, 179, 183; (UK)NA: PRO, ADM 36/16645; 36/15895.

20. Mark-Wardlaw, 179. On 12 Aug. 1803 Mark was promoted to be purser of the *Halcyon*.

21. (UK)NA: PRO, ADM 52/3711, 31 July 1803. Bickerton in the *Kent* had gone back to Malta to replenish.

22. Nicolas, V, 291–2, 22 Sept. 1803, Hobart to Nelson.

23. Nicolas, V, 179–80, 25 Aug. 1803, Nelson to Nepean.

24. It was this period that defeated Nicolas's aim to publish Nelson's entire correspondence. In Vols. V and VI Nicolas prints as many as a dozen letters for each day, but he omitted many more, particularly those of a more administrative – though vital – nature.

25. NMM, CRK/7/106, 26 Sept. 1804, John Hunter from Madrid to Nelson. The *Decade* and the *John Bull* took twenty-three and twenty-one days respectively, while the *Martin* sloop was also very fast, reaching the fleet off the coast of Spain in thirteen days (BL, Add. MSS 34967, 13 Oct. 1804; 34968, 1 May 1805).

26. BL, Add. MSS 34955, 19 Apr. 1804; Tracy, *Naval Chronicle*, III, 21–2.

27. NMM, CRK/9/2, 13 Jan. 1805.

28. Nicolas, VI, 73, 18 June 1804, general order.

29. NMM, MAM/28, 7/13/25 Dec. 1803.

30. BL, Add. MSS 34953, 4 Oct. 1803, Nelson to James Duff.

31. Nicolas, V, 171, 7 Jan. 1800, Nelson to Keith. Foresti is better known for his contact with Lord Byron in 1809.

32. BL, Add. MSS 34953, 17 Aug. 1803, Nelson to Ball; 34955, 17 Jan. 1804, Nelson to Keats; NMM, CRK/5/42, 23 Mar. 1804, Falcon to Nelson; Nicolas, VI, 322–3, 16 Jan. 1805, Nelson to Earl Camden, secretary of state for the War Department; Tracy, *Naval Chronicle*, III, 88–9.

33. e.g., NMM, CRK/10/23, 10 Apr. 1804, Pellew to Nelson; CRK/3/62, 3 June 1804, Cochrane to Nelson.

34. NMM, CRK/13/95, 28 Dec. [1803], Troubridge to Nelson.

35. Nicolas, V, 472–3, 23 Mar. 1804.

36. NMM, CRK/10/82, 29 Oct. 1803, Price to Nelson.

37. NAS, GD51/2/1082/31, 23 Nov. 1804, Nelson to Melville.

38. Jane Knight, 'Eastern Mediterranean', typescript, 13–16.

39. Nicolas, V, 290, 24 Nov. 1803, Nelson to Nepean.

40. BL, Add. MSS 34953, 7 Oct. 1803, Nelson to William Drummond. In early 1804 Benjamin Hallowell in the *Argo* transported the Egyptian ruler Elphi Bey and his suite back to Alexandria after a diplomatic mission to London: 'I do not think I was in so uncomfortable position in my life' (NMM, CRK/6/90, 25 Jan. 1804, Hallowell to Nelson, from Gibraltar).

41. Nicolas, V, 214, 27 Sept. 1803, Nelson to St Vincent.

42. Grant, 22 May 1802, Lady Elgin to her mother.

43. BL, Add. MSS 34953, 7 Oct. 1803, Nelson to Cracraft; Nicolas, V, 237, 6 Oct. 1803, Nelson to Elliot.

44. (UK)NA: PRO, ADM 51/1483, 12–31 July 1804; Wellcome, Western MSS 3681, 30 Aug. 1804, Cracraft to Nelson; Jane Knight, 'Eastern Mediterranean', (typescript) 8.

45. BL, Add. MSS 34953, 20 Oct. 1803, Nelson to Lord Hawkesbury.

46. Mackesy, *Mediterranean*, 37.

47. Monmouth, E139, 5 Aug. 1803.

48. e.g., NMM, CRK/4/143, 12 Sept. 1803, Drummond to Nelson; CRK/13/148, 24 Aug. 1804, Wherry to Nelson.

49. Nicolas, V, 226, 6 Oct. 1803, Nelson to Ball.

50. Nicolas, V, 413, 11 Feb. 1804, Nelson to Ball.

51. Nicolas, V, 223, 261, 5 Oct., to Davison; 21 Oct. 1803, to St Vincent.

52. Nicolas, V, 219, 4 Oct. 1803.

53. BL, Add. MSS 34953, 9 Sept. 1803, Nelson to the Reverend Dr Garkin of Bartholomew Buildings, Holborn.

54. BL, Add. MSS, 34966, list of 'Prizes and Supposed Value'.

55. Huntington, HM 34064, 11 Jan. 1804; Nicolas, V, 363–4.

56. Nicolas, V, 178–9, 25 Aug. 1803, Nelson to Addington.

57. Nicolas, V, 194, 3 Sept. 1803.

58. Nicolas, V, 266, 22 Oct. 1803, Nelson to victualling commissioners.

59. Nicolas, V, 206–7, 21 Sept. 1803, Nelson to Nepean.

60. Nicolas, V, 244, 13 Oct. 1803, Nelson to Sir Thomas Pasley.

61. BL, Add. MSS 34966, 24 Oct. 1803.

62. BL, Add. MSS 34953, 1 Nov. 1803, Nelson to Thomas Jackson; Mahan, 576.

63. BL, Add. MSS 34966, 24, 29 Oct. 1803.

64. NMM, ADM/L/V/57, 31 Oct. 1803.

65. (UK)NA: PRO, ADM/80/141, 1 Aug. 1803, 'Report of the *Superb*'s passage through the Straits of Bonifacio'.

66. BL, Add. MSS, 34966, 31 Oct. 1803.

67. Nicolas, V, 277–8, 2 Nov. 1803, Nelson to Ryves.

68. Nicolas, V, 290, 24 Nov. 1803.

69. NMM, CRK/10/162, 5 Nov. 1803, Ryves to Nelson; Denham, 63–6.

70. NMM, ADM/L/V/57, 2 Nov. 1803; Scott, 134–5.

71. BL, Add. MSS 34956, 9 Nov. 1803.

72. Gwyther, 'Maddalena', 47–56; Denham, 61. For the account of how A. J. Scott purchased the gifts in Barcelona, see Scott, 145–51.

73. NMM, MON/2/36, 10 Feb. 1803, Nelson to General Villettes.

74. Broadley and Bartelot, 112, 25 Dec. [1803], to Manfield; see MacDonald, *Feeding Nelson's Navy*, 26.

75. NAS, GD51/2/1082/30, 2 Nov. 1804, Nelson to Melville.

76. BL, Add. MSS 34967, 7, 10 Aug., 13 Dec. 1804.

77. Nicolas, V, 399, 31 Jan. 1804, Nelson to Captain Thomas Staines.

78. BL, Add. MSS 34955, 26 Jan., Nelson to 'Your Royal Highness [?]'; 30 Jan. 1804, to Sir John Acton.

79. BL, Add. MSS 34955, 17 Feb. 1804, Nelson to the duke of Genovese.

80. Nicolas, V, 399, 31 Jan. 1804, Nelson to Captain Robert Pettet, *Termagant*.

81. e.g., BL, Add. MSS 36953, 1 Nov. 1803, to Thomas Jackson; 34853, Sept. 1803, to duke of Clarence; 34954, 25 Dec. 1803, to Hobart; 34955, 17 Mar. [1804], to Troubridge; NMM, ELL/163, 11 Jan. 1804, Nelson to Minto.

82. BL, Add. MSS 34955, 19 Mar. 1804.

83. Mackesy, *Mediterranean*, 15, 41–2.

84. Mark-Wardlaw, Chapter 10.

85. Morrison, II, 227, 19 Mar. 1804, Nelson to Baird.

86. Nicolas, V, 133–4, 12 July 1803, Nelson to St Vincent.

87. MacDougall, 205–7.

88. NMM, CRK/1, 25 Sept. 1803, Ball to Nelson.

89. Houghton, pf MS Eng. 196.5 (36), 13 Jan. 1804.

90. NMM, CRK/13/86, 27 June [1803], Troubridge to Nelson.

91. BL, Add. MSS 34954, 20 Oct. 1803, Nelson to Troubridge.

92. BL, Add. MSS 34955, 18 Apr., Nelson to Ball; NMM, CRK/1, 16 May 1804, Ball to Nelson.

93. BL, Add. MSS 37268, 24 Jan. 1804, Ball to Granville Penn.

94. NMM, MS 78/093, 6 Jan. 1804, Nelson to Fremantle.

95. Huntington, HM 34191, 34192, 15 Jan. 1805, Nelson to William Otway.

96. Monmouth, E991, 12 July 1803; also Nicolas, V, 233.

97. NMM, CRK/13/92, 22 Sept. [1803], Troubridge to Nelson.

98. MacDonald, *Feeding Nelson's Navy*, 163–4.

99. BL, Add. MSS 34954, 8 Jan. 1804, Nelson to Gayner; Donaldson, 432. Wine was also purchased from Gibert at Barcelona (Clements, Smith Collection, 28 Oct. 1804, Nelson to victualling commissioners). See also (UK)NA: PRO, ADM 80/141, 4 Sept. 1803.

100. Gayner was paid £2,555 for his efforts (MacDonald, 'Victualling', 46–7, quoting (UK)NA: ADM 114/55, 17, 22 Mar. 1804).

101. NMM, CRK/6/96, 28 Nov. 1803, Sir Andrew Snape Hamond to Nelson.

102. NMM, CRK/13/88, 26 Aug. [1803], Troubridge to Nelson.

103. BL, Add. MSS 34954, 24 Nov. 1803, Nelson to Cracraft; also 34955, 31 Jan. 1804.

104. NMM, CRK/5/128, 31 Jan. 1804, Foresti to Nelson.

105. Nicolas, VI, 313, 2 Jan. 1805, Nelson to Otway.

106. Nicolas, V, 502, 18 Apr. 1804, Nelson to Nathaniel Taylor, naval store-keeper, Malta.

107. NMM, CRK/4/152, 11 Aug. 1803, Commander William D'Urban of the *Weazle* to Nelson.

108. NMM, CRK/9/150, 5 Nov. 1804, Otway to Nelson.

109. Nicolas, VI, 280, 24 Nov. 1804, Nelson to Otway.

110. BL, Add. MSS 34956, 9 Aug. 1804, Nelson to Andrew Snape Hamond.

111. Nicolas, V, 470, 21 Mar.; VI, 249, 20 Oct. 1804, Nelson to Woodman; NAS, GD51/2/1082/21, 1 Nov. 1804, Nelson to Melville; Bodleian, MS Eng. Hist. c. 237, fols. 43–51, 18 Nov. 1804, to Sir Rupert George, copy to Nelson.

112. e.g., BL, Add. MSS 34954, 21 Oct. 1803, Nelson to Captain Donelly, *Narcissus*; Nicolas, V, 272, 24 Oct. 1803.

113. BL, Add. MSS 34954, 1 Jan. 1804, Nelson to Bickerton.

114. NMM, ADM/L/V/57, 15 Feb. 1804.

115. BL, Add. MSS 34967, 27 Oct. 1804.

116. MacDonald, 'Victualling', 66.

117. Nicolas, V, 133, 12 July 1803, Nelson to St Vincent; Macdonald, *Feeding Nelson's Navy*, 164.

118. Houghton, pf MS Eng. 195.6 (40), 22 Sept. 1804, Nelson to Baird; BL, Add. MSS 34955, 23 Mar. 1804, Nelson to Elliot. A shortened version of the letter to Baird is in Nicolas, VI, 202. See also MacDonald, 'Victualling', 58–9.

119. NMM, CRK/13/92, 22 Sept. [1803].

120. Nicolas, VI, 142, 7 Aug. 1804; 334–5, 4 Feb. 1805, Nelson to Marsden.

121. BL, Add. MSS 34953, 15 Sept. 1803, Nelson to Bickerton.

122. Monaque, 'Latouche-Tréville', 281.

123. NMM, ADM/L/V57, 10 Apr. 1804.

124. BL, Add. MSS 34955, 10 Apr. 1804.

125. BL, Add. MSS 34966, 4 June 1804.

126. Monaque, 'Latouche-Tréville', 283.

127. Nicolas, VI, 150–51, 12 Aug. 1804, Nelson to Marsden.

128. NMM, ADM/L/V/57, 6 Sept. 1804.

129. NMM, PST/39, 7 Nov. 1804, Nelson to Thomas Bladen Capel.

130. Cornwallis-West, 420–1, 11 June 1804, Whitby to Cornwallis.

131. Huntington, HO 401, 13 July 1799, Howe to Curtis.

132. BL, Add. MSS 34954, 25 Dec. 1803, Nelson to Sir John Acton.

133. BL, Add. MSS 34966, 6 Feb. 1804.

134. Warren R. Dawson, *Nelson Collection*, 499, 14 Jan. 1804.

135. (UK)NA: PRO, ADM 80/141, 25 Apr. 1804, 'Survey of the *Superb, Victory* and *Canopus*'.

136. BL, Add. MSS 34955, 5 Apr. 1804.

137. NAS, GD51/2/1082/40, 22 Feb. 1805, Nelson to Melville.

138. Phillimore, I, 226, 25 Dec. 1803.

139. BL, Add. MSS 34954, 31 Dec. 1803, Nelson to General Villettes.

140. BL, Add. MSS 34954, 1 Jan. 1804.

141. The account by Leonard Gillespie of the leisurely way of life on board the flagship is much quoted (e.g., Mahan, 594–6; Keevil, 327–8).

142. Monmouth, E451, 19 Oct. 1804, Nelson to Bickerton; NMM, MON/2/42, 12 May 1804, Nelson to Sotheron.

143. Phillimore, I, 226, 25 Dec. 1803.

144. NMM, MAM/28, 7 Dec. 1803, Nelson to Emma.

145. (UK)NA: PRO, ADM 36/15895.

146. NMM, CRK/2/105, 24 Sept. 1804, Thomas Bowen to Nelson.

147. Clements, Melville Papers, 25 Sept. 1804, Melville to Sir John Colpoys.

148. NMM, CRK/13/98, 13 Nov. 1804.

149. NMM, CRK/13/84, 19 May [1803].

150. Barrow, 263. Barrow wrote a handsome letter after Trafalgar to Melville to say so (Clements, Melville Papers, 2 Feb. 1806; see also Sir John Sinclair to Melville, 20 Nov. 1805. Melville also quickly appreciated that 'The Naval force of this Country already afloat is perfectly adequate to repel the Attempts of the Enemy' (Clements, Melville Papers, secret naval memorandum of 14 June 1804).

151. Clements, Melville Papers, 3 July 1804, secret naval memorandum; see also 14 June and 12 Sept. 1804.

152. Clements, Melville Papers, 22 Sept. 1804.

153. BL, Add. MSS 34955, 20 Mar. 1804, Nelson to Ball.

154. Chatterton, II, 2, 1 May 1804, Nelson to Sir Edward Pellew.

155. Morrison, II, 222, 13 Jan. 1804, Gayner to Nelson; Donaldson, 430–35.

156. BL, Add. MSS 34957, 28 Aug. 1804, Nelson to Elliot; NMM, CRK/11/5, 19 Oct. 1804, Scott to Nelson from Cagliari.

157. BL, Add. MSS 34957, 9 Sept. 1804, Nelson to Frere.

158. Scott, 121.

159. NMM, MAM/28, 7 Dec. 1803.

160. NMM, CRK/1, 9 Jan. 1804, Ball to Nelson.

161. e.g., BL, Add. MSS 34955, 5 Apr. 1804, to John Gore.

162. NAS, GD51/2/1082/7, 1 July 1804.

163. Nicolas, VI, 135, 5 Aug.; 162, 10 Aug. 1804, Nelson to Ball.

164. NAS, GD51/2/1082/30, 2 Nov. 1804, Nelson to Melville.

165. Houghton, FMS Lowell 10, 31 Oct. 1804; Clements, Smith Collection, 14 Jan. 1805.

166. NMM, CRK/3/18, 15 Dec. 1804, Campbell to Nelson.

167. NAS, GD51/2/1082/36, 29 Dec. 1804, Nelson to Melville; NMM, CRK/13/101, 12 Feb. 1805, Troubridge to Nelson.

168. NMM, CRK/3/159, 7 Jan. 1805, Davison to Nelson.

169. NMM, ADM/L/V/57, 27 Mar. 1805.

170. Phillimore, I, 229.

171. NMM, CRK/3/145, 24 Nov. 1803, Davison to Nelson; CRK/5/42, 23 Mar., CRK/5/43, 17 Oct. 1804, John Falcon to Nelson.

172. NMM, CRK/2/105, 24 Sept. 1804, Thomas Bowen to Nelson.

173. NMM, CRK/12/125, 6 Feb. 1805. Sutton returned to England with Spanish prizes in Oct. 1804 (Nicolas, VI, 267 n.).

174. NMM, MAM/28, 7 Dec. 1803, Nelson to Emma.

175. Monmouth, E161, 20 Jan. 1804.

176. BL, Add. MSS 34955, 30 Jan. 1804, Nelson to Falconet; Houghton, pf MS Eng. 196.5 (39), 27 Aug. 1804, Nelson to Emma.

177. Letter in the possession of the rector and churchwardens of Burnham Thorpe, 14 May 1804; the usual abbreviated version appears in Clarke and McArthur, reproduced by Nicolas in VI, 18.

178. Hattendorf, 'Sea Power as Control', 214.

179. RNM, MS 1998/41/1.

180. NMM, ADM/L/V/57, 20 May 1804.

181. NMM, ADM/L/V/57, 17 Aug. 1804.

182. NMM, ADM/L/V/57, 12 Sept. 1803; Scott, 126.

183. Nicolas, VI, 211, 4 Oct. 1804, Nelson to Lieutenant Harding Shaw.

184. Naish, 30, 23 Apr. 1786, Nelson to Fanny.

185. NMM, CRK/13/95, 28 Dec. [1803], Troubridge to Nelson.

186. NMM, CRK/1, 29 Oct. 1803, Ball to Nelson.

187. NMM, CRK/10/115, 18 May 1804, Captain Robert Reynolds to Nelson.

188. Huntington, HM 34068, 4 Aug. 1804, Nelson to Curtis.

189. NAS, GD51/2/1082/23, 10 Oct. 1804, Nelson to Melville.

190. Clements, Melville Papers, 3 July 1804, Melville's secret memorandum; Rodger, *Command of the Ocean*, 530; Cornwallis-West, 480.

191. BL, Add. MSS 34955, 17 Mar. 1804, Nelson to Lord Bridport.

192. BL, Add. MSS 34955, 5 Apr. 1804, Nelson to Gore.

193. BL, Add. MSS 34967, 2 Dec. 1804, private journal.

194. Monmouth, E159, 19 Dec. 1804, Nelson to Emma; also Morrison, II, 251.

195. NMM, ADM/L/V/57, 19 Jan. 1805.

196. Tracy, *Naval Chronicle*, III, 142, 'Biographical Memoir of the Captain Courtenay Boyle'.

197. NMM, ADM/L/V/57, 18 May 1804; BL, Add. MSS 34967, 19 Jan. 1805; Nicolas, VI, 324–5, 19 Jan. 1805.

198. Corbett, *Trafalgar*, 35.

28 The Long Chase

1. Monmouth, E416.

2. Clements, Smith Collection 29 Jan. 1805, 'Intended Route which may be altered by Information obtained.' The numbers of the rendezvous were '103, 55, perhaps 79 or 110, then 82', but to which areas these numbers refer is not clear. See Corbett, *Trafalgar*, 60.

3. NMM, CRK/6/86, 9 Feb. 1805, Greig to Nelson: also CRK/5/151, 9 Feb. 1805, Foresti to Nelson.

4. Mackesy, *Mediterranean*, 42.

5. Rodger, *Command of the Ocean*, 529–30, Corbett, *Trafalgar*, 38–46.

6. Nicolas, VI, 343–4, Nelson to Marsden.

7. (UK)NA: PRO, ADM 80/141, 23 Nov. 1803, Keats to Nelson; 23 May 1804, master shipwright, Malta, to Keats.

8. Phillimore, I, 288.

9. Phillimore, I, 193, 267–8.

10. BL Add. MSS 34954, 21 Oct. 1803, Nelson to Troubridge.

11. BL, Add. MSS 37268, 23 Feb. 1804, Ball to Granville Penn.

12. NMM, CRK/1, 21 Feb. 1805, Ball to Nelson.

13. Nicolas, VI, 11 Feb. 1805, Nelson to Ball; also Monmouth E162, 11 Feb. 1805, Nelson to General Villettes.

14. NMM, CRK/1, 13 Feb. 1805, Ball to Nelson.

15. NMM, CRK/9/4, 17 Apr. 1805, Marsden to Nelson.

16. Clements, Melville Papers, [late] Mar. 1805, John Barrow, memorandum on the Mediterranean.

17. NMM, ORD/18, 23 Apr. 1805, Hamond to Orde.

18. NMM, CRK/13/101, 12 Feb. 1805, Troubridge to Nelson.

19. Corbett, *Trafalgar*, 61–2; (UK)NA:PRO, ADM 51/1482, 10–30 Mar. 1805.

20. e.g., Monmouth, E367, 28 Mar. 1805, Nelson to Charles Arbuthnot, going out as minister in Constantinople.

21. RNM, MS 2002/76, 14 Mar. 1805, Chevallier to Davison.

22. Nicolas, VI, 400, 6 Apr. 1805.

23. Nicolas, VI, 399, 6 Apr. 1805.

24. Nicolas, VI, 402, 10 Apr. 1805.

25. Corbett, *Trafalgar*, 80.

26. NMM, MON/3/49, 10 Apr. 1805, Nelson to Acton.

27. BL, Add. MSS 34968. 16 Apr. 1805.

28. (UK)NA: PRO, ADM 1/6038, alphabetical list of intelligence, Sept. 1801–Feb. 1806; Phillimore, I, 284; Corbett, *Trafalgar*, 102.

29. Parry, 66, 28 May 1805, Fremantle to his brother William; Corbett, *Trafalgar*, 68–70.

30. Nicolas, VI, 407, 18 Apr. 1805, Nelson to Marsden; 407, 18 Apr. 1805 to Hugh Elliot.

31. NMM, CRK/2/60, 26 Apr. 1805.

32. RNM MS, 2002/76, 14 Mar. 1805, Chevallier to Davison.

33. Nicolas, VII, 260–61, Beatty's narrative.

34. RNM, MS 2002/76, 14 Mar. 1805, Chevallier to Davison.

35. NMM, CRK/6/51, 12 Apr. 1805, Gillespie to Nelson.

36. NMM, CRK/3/20, 4 Apr. 1805, George Campbell to Nelson.

37. Monmouth, E437, 30 Mar. 1805, also in Morrison, II, 255.

38. Monmouth, E445, 4 Apr. 1805; they are certainly of more interest than the 'erotic' letter of 29 Jan. [1800] to Emma, sold at Christie's on 3 Dec. 2003 for £117,250.

39. Nicolas, VI, 428, 7 May 1805, Nelson to Marsden.

40. Scott, 171–2.

41. Phillimore, I, 292; Corbett, *Trafalgar*, 115, 117.

42. Nicolas, VI, 436, 10 May 1805, Nelson to Addington.

43. Corbett, 83.

44. Without these substantial stores the fleet could not have crossed the Atlantic.

The *Victory*, for instance, took in 285 bags of bread, over 4,000 pounds of flour, pork, sugar, wine, coals ((UK)NA: PRO, ADM 52/3711, 11 May 1805).

45. Phillimore, *Parker*, I, 289.

46. BL Add. MSS 34968, 19-21 May 1805.

47. Nicolas, VI, 443, 19 May 1805, Nelson to Keats.

48. Tracy, *Naval Chronicle*, II, 303.

49. Monmouth, E460, 6 June 1805, Commander James Wilkes Maurice to Nelson.

50. Phillimore, I, 292, 12 June 1895.

51. (UK)NA: PRO, ADM 51/1482, 4 June 1805.

52. (UK)NA: PRO, ADM 51/1482, 8 June 1805.

53. Phillimore, I, 293, 12 June 1805, Parker to his father.

54. Zulueta, 304-5.

55. Corbett, *Trafalgar*, 231, quoting BL, Add. MSS 34930, 21 June 1805, Henry Bayntun to Nelson; for the French opinion of Nelson's ascendancy over Villeneuve, see General Lauriston to Napoleon (Eastwick, II, 113-17).

56. (UK)NA: PRO, ADM 51/1482, 13 June 1805; Corbett, 183-6.

57. Nicolas, VI, 454, 12 June 1805.

58. BL, Add. MSS 34968, 13 June 1805.

59. Nicolas, VI, 469, 10 July 1805, Nelson to Otway. Corbett makes the harsh comment that Nelson was suffering from what he called the typical 'station bias' of a commander-in-chief: that his station was the main objective of the enemy (Corbett, *Trafalgar*, 232).

60. Nicolas, VI, 463, 19 June 1805, Nelson to Keats; (UK)NA: PRO, ADM 51/1482, late June and early July 1805.

61. Nicolas, VI, 479, 21 July 1805, Nelson to Sir John Acton.

62. (UK)NA: PRO, ADM 52/3711, 16-17 June 1805.

63. BL, Add. MSS 34968.

64. (UK)NA: PRO, ADM 51/1482, 22 June 1805.

65. BL, Add. MSS 34968.

66. (UK)NA: PRO, ADM 52/3711, 20 July 1805; Phillimore, I, 296, 299.

67. Rutherford [no continuous pagination]; also in the *Navy League Journal*, Aug. 1897, 241, 30 Aug. 1805, Captain William Rutherford of the *Swiftsure* to J. C. Beresford of Dublin.

68. Laughton, *Barham*, III, 257-9, 9 July 1805, Barham to Cornwallis.

69. Corbett, *Trafalgar*, 225.

70. Tracy, 'Calder', 267.

71. Huntington, STG 161 9680, 18 Sept. 1806, Roddam to Thomas Grenville.

72. NMM, CRK/9/15, 17 July 1805, Matra to Nelson.

73. (UK)NA: PRO, ADM 51/1482, 19 July 1805.

74. BL, Add. MSS 34968, 20 July 1805.

75. Houghton, pf MS Eng. 196.5 (114), 20 July 1805.

76. Granville, II, 98, 9 Aug. 1805.

77. Corbett, *Trafalgar*, 233.

78. NMM, XAGC/8, Spiro Collection, 24 July [1805]; also Nicolas, VI, 478, 20 July 1805, Nelson to Marsden.

79. Bourchier, I, 4, 21 Aug. 1805, Codrington to his wife.

80. Corbett, *Trafalgar*, 274.

81. (UK)NA: PRO, ADM 51/4514, 18–20 Aug. 1805.

82. NMM, CRK/9/5, 18 Aug. 1805, Marsden to Nelson.

83. Nicolas, VII, 16, 24 Aug. 1805, Nelson to Keats; 18, 29 Aug. 1805, Nelson to George Rose.

84. Vane, second series, V [?] Sept. 1805, Castlereagh to Nelson. Typically, Nelson never gave up hope (Nicolas, VII, 112, 11 Oct. 1805, Nelson to Ball).

85. BL, Add. MSS 37852, 12 Feb. 1806, Sidney Smith to Windham.

86. Jennings, II, 233–4.

87. NMM, PST/39, 3 Sept. 1805, Emma to Mrs Lutwidge.

88. Minto, III, 363, 26 Aug. 1805, Minto to his wife.

89. Nicolas, VII, 16, 24 Aug. 1805, Nelson to Keats; NMM, PST/39, 3 Sept. 1805, Emma to Mrs Lutwidge.

90. DRO, 152/1805/ON1 [n.d.], Smith to Addington; Scott, 177.

91. Houghton, pf MS Eng. 196.5 (33), 22 Mar. 1824, memorandum by William Pearce; Nicolas, VII, 241, Keats's account transcribed by Edward Hawke Locker, 1 Oct. 1829.

92. Minto, III, 370–71, 13 Sept. 1805, to his wife.

93. Minto, III, 363, 26 Aug. 1805, Minto to his wife.

94. NMM, PST/39, 3 Sept. 1805.

95. Baring, 452–3.

96. Rosebery, II, 265, 30 Aug. 1805, Charles James Fox to Windham; Thorne, III, 523.

97. Foster, 238, 31 Aug. 1801, Lady Elizabeth Foster to Augustus Foster.

98. Granville, II, 110–12 [?] Sept., 12 Sept. 1805, Lady Bessborough to Lord Leveson-Gower.

99. Corbett, *Trafalgar*, 296–9.

100. Laughton, *Barham*, III, 312–15, 4 Sept., Barham to Pitt, with memorandum; 5 Sept. 1805, Barham to Nelson.

101. Nicolas, VII, 28, 5 Sept. 1805, Nelson to Robert Rolfe.

102. BL, Add. MSS 34968; Nicolas, VII, 30, 6 Sept. 1805.

103. DRO, 152M/c1805/ON/6, 8 Sept. 1805, Nelson to Sidmouth; 152M/c1805/ON/2(1) [undated note], Sidmouth to Nelson.

104. Barrow, *Autobiography*, 281.

105. Merwe, van der, 42.

106. Minto, III, 370, 13 Sept. 1805.

107. Nicolas, VII, 33–4, 13 Sept. 1805.

108. Monmouth, E180, 14 Sept. 1805.

109. Huntington, STG, 169 (16), 2 Jan. 1807, Egremont to Thomas Grenville.
110. Coad, 232; I am grateful to Jonathan Coad for the reference to Nelson's visit from the Goodrich Papers in the Science Museum (journal and memoranda book, 10, 14 Sept. 1805).
111. BL, Add. MSS 34968; Nicolas, VII, 35.
112. Lockwood, 34.
113. Nicolas, VII, 36, 14 Sept. 1805.

29 Trafalgar

1. BL, Add. MSS 37268.
2. RNM, MS 1963/1.
3. NMM, AGC/17/18, envelope marked 15 Sept. postmarked 17 Sept. 1805.
4. Monmouth, E429, 16 Sept. 1805, Nelson to Emma.
5. Monmouth, E436, 20 Sept. 1805, Nelson to Emma.
6. Monmouth, E183, 25 Sept. 1805, Nelson to Emma.
7. Goodwin, 255–6.
8. Buckingham and Chandos, III, 445, 30 Sept. 1805, Fremantle to the marquis of Buckingham; Monmouth, E187, 20 Sept. 1805, Nelson to Bickerton.
9. (UK) NA: PRO, ADM 51/4494. Curiously, no marine on board the *Victory* was flogged in this period for drunkenness, in contrast to the previous two years, although two were punished for theft, one with as many as seventy-two lashes.
10. Beatty, 20. '*Victory*'s casualties from 29 Dec. 1804 to 20 Oct. 1805 were only five fatal cases (one of these by accidental injury), and two patients sent to a naval hospital.' At Trafalgar, Beatty had only ten convalescents, 'all of who attended their respective quarters' (Beatty, 20–21).
11. Lavery, *Trafalgar*, 123.
12. Duffy, 'Gunnery', typescript, 13. I am very grateful to Dr Duffy for an early sight of this paper, to be published in the spring of 2005.
13. Bucks., D/FR/45/1/34, 2 Oct. 1805, Fremantle to his brother William; Parry, 71.
14. Clements, Hubert Smith Collection, 17 Aug. 1805.
15. Bucks., D/FR/45/1/32, 31 Aug., 12 Sept. 1805, Fremantle to his brother William; Parry, 69–70, 70–71.
16. Bourchier, I, 47, 4 Sept. 1805.
17. Bourchier, I, 49, 30 Sept. 1805.
18. Monmouth, E438 [Oct. 1805], Nelson to Emma; Morrison, II, 267.
19. Parry, 72, 13 Oct. 1805, Fremantle to his brother William.
20. Chatterton, II, 4, 2 Oct. 1805, Nelson to Lord Gambier.
21. Nicolas, VII, 119–20, 13 Oct. 1805, Nelson to Marsden.
22. Buckingham and Chandos, III, 445, 30 Sept. 1805, Fremantle to the marquis of Buckingham.

23. Wheeler, 372.

24. Bourchier, I, 51, 30 Sept. 1805.

25. Ram, 187, 13 Oct. 1805, Lieutenant William Ram to his sister.

26. Houghton, pf MS Eng. 196.5 (48), 4 Oct. 1805.

27. Bourchier, I, 52, 30 Sept. 1805, Codrington to his wife.

28. Tracy, *Naval Chronicle*, III, 192, 10 Oct. 1805, Duff to his wife; also Fremantle, *Wynne* (1952), 413, 1 Oct. 1805, Fremantle to Betsey. The captain of a ship had much more latitude in dictating the appearance of his ship at this time than later.

29. Beatty, 7–8.

30. Buckingham and Chandos, III, 445–6, 29/30 Sept. 1805, Fremantle to the marquis of Buckingham.

31. Buckingham and Chandos, III, 445, 30 Sept. 1805, Fremantle to the marquis of Buckingham.

32. Tracy, *Naval Chronicle*, III, 191, 1 Oct. 1805, Duff to his wife.

33. Tracy, *Naval Chronicle*, III, 192, 10 Oct. 1805, Duff to his wife.

34. Bourchier, I, 51, 30 Sept. 1805.

35. NMM, CRK/7/11, 8 Oct. 1805, Nelson to Blackwood.

36. BL, Add. MSS 37268, quoted at the head of the chapter; it is also mentioned in John Barrow's *Autobiography*, 282, in a letter to George Rose, 17 Sept. 1805. Nelson first used the phrase in a letter to Emma on 25 Sept. (Monmouth, E183).

37. Tunstall and Tracy, 251.

38. Czisnik, 'Trafalgar', 549–50. The historical controversy is summarized in this article.

39. Czisnik, 'Trafalgar', 551–3.

40. BL, Egerton 1614, 1 Oct. 1805, Nelson to Emma.

41. Bucks., D/FR/45/1/35, 13 Oct. 1805, Fremantle to his brother William; Parry, 72.

42. Nicolas, VII, 80, 6 Oct. 1805.

43. Nicolas, VII, 89–92, 9 Oct. 1805.

44. Padfield, 228. The idea that over-risky audacity had defeated a weak enemy has a long history, held by critics as diverse as Thomas Byam Martin, Thomas Cochrane and Julian Corbett, and is reviewed in Czisnik, 'Icon and Image', 88–99.

45. Duffy, 'Gunnery'.

46. Huntington, HO 181, 27 Feb. 1794, Howe to Roger Curtis.

47. Czisnik, 'Trafalgar', 552–3.

48. Corbett, *Trafalgar*, 51–2.

49. The importance of this signal, which was printed only for the first time in 1990 by Tunstall and Tracy (251), has been recently pointed out by Czisnik, 'Trafalgar', 553–4.

50. NMM, SIG/B/76, Signal Book 1799, issued between 2 May 1805 and 10 Feb. 1806, marked 'Exd TMH' (Examined T.M. Hardy); reproduced in Tunstall and Tracy, 251; NMM, TUN/61, quoted as 'Appendix to the Signal

Book', 'Signals from Senior Officers to Junior Officers by Lord Nelson, 26 Sept. 1805'.

51. See Czisnik, 'Trafalgar', 549–55. The influential Sir Julian Corbett criticized the attack in line ahead as 'extremely risky' and 'mad'; he did not believe that Nelson had the idea of the 'feint' (Czisnik, 549–50).

52. Bucks., D/FR/45/1/33, 22 Sept. 1805, Fremantle to his brother William.

53. Bourchier, I, 54, 7 Oct. 1805.

54. Wheeler, 374.

55. NMM, CRK/7/13, 10 Oct. 1805, Nelson to Blackwood.

56. Nicolas, VII, 107, 10 Oct. 1805.

57. Bucks., D/FR45/1/35, 13 Oct 1805, Fremantle to his brother William; Parry, 72; also Fremantle, *Wynne* (1952), 11 Oct. 1805, to Betsey.

58. Vane, second series, V, 3 Oct. 1805, Nelson to Castlereagh.

59. NMM, CRK/7/14, 14 Oct. 1805, Nelson to Blackwood.

60. e.g., Nicolas, VII, 104–5, 10 Oct. to the respective captains; 115, 12 Oct. to Collingwood; 123–4, 15 Oct. 1805, to the boatswains of the *Victory, Ajax* and *Thunderer* to survey the stores of the former boatswain of the *Thunderer*, who had 'run' from the ship.

61. Houghton, pf MS Eng. 196.5 (129), 9 Nov. 1805, Louis to Emma; also Nicolas, VII, 63n.

62. NMM, MON/3/54, 9 Oct. 1805, Nelson to Hugh Elliot.

63. Beatty, 5.

64. Zulueta, 303; Eastwick I, 169; Rodriguez, Gonzáles, 208–11.

65. Eastwick, I, 167–9; Monarque, 'Trafalgar', 170–71.

66. Flayhart, 115.

67. The notion that sharp differences were revealed between the French and Spanish in this meeting has recently been refuted in Czisnik, 'El consejo de Guerra', 49–60. For the traditional view, see Zulueta, 308; Corbett, *Trafalgar*, 360–61.

68. Corbett, *Trafalgar*, 368–9, quoting Eastwick, 101–2.

69. Nicolas, VII, 126; Wheeler, 376.

70. Corbett, *Trafalgar*, 368, quoting BL. Add. MSS 34968, 18 Oct. 1805.

71. Wheeler, 376; Corbett, *Trafalgar*, 375.

72. Galiano, 34. I am grateful to Agustín Guimerá of Madrid for this reference and for his translation.

73. Bourchier, I, 57, 19 Oct. 1805, Codrington to his wife.

74. Bourchier, I, 57, 20 Oct. 1805, Codrington to his wife.

75. (UK) NA: PRO, ADM 51/4494, 20 Oct. 1805; Beatty, 8–9.

76. Nicolas, VII, 137.

77. Thursfield, 364, 28 Oct. 1805, to William Windever; for Nelson's instructions for burning lights, see Nicolas, VII, 136.

78. Beatty, 10.

79. Callender, 237.

80. Beatty, 12. As can be clearly seen on display in the National Maritime Museum, the stars of the orders were sewn into the coat, and this, Beatty is saying, was his usual practice. The still current idea that Nelson deliberately dressed in full uniform to draw attention to himself is countered by this statement.

81. Houghton, pf MS Eng. 196.5 (134), 8 Nov. 1805, George Hewson to [?].

82. Beatty, 18; Czisnik, 'Trafalgar', 556–9.

83. Wheeler, 377.

84. Huntington STG/150 (1), 'Copy of minute kept on board H. M. Ship *Neptune* by Lieutenant Andrew Green, signal officer', also printed in Fremantle, *Wynne*, (1952), 419–21. As usual, the exact timing of the events and phases of battle varies from account to account; compare with Beatty's *Narrative*, for these two orders of 6.40 and 6.50 (quoted in Nicolas, VII, 137).

85. RNM, MS 1983/1064.

86. Beatty, *Narrative*, quoted in Nicolas, VII, 137–8.

87. Lavery, *Trafalgar*, 155, estimates 2 or 3 knots. If the two fleets were eight or nine miles apart at dawn (Corbett, *Trafalgar*, 379) this would seem too fast.

88. Goodwin, 257. This calculation does not include frigates and smaller ships.

89. 'May the Great God, whom I worship, grant to my Country, and for the benefit of Europe in general, a great and glorious Victory; and may no misconduct in any one tarnish it; and may humanity after Victory be the predominant feature in the British Fleet. For myself, individually, I commit my life to Him who made me, and may his blessing light upon my endeavours for serving my country faithfully. To Him I resign myself and the just cause which is entrusted to me to defend. Amen. Amen. Amen.' (NMM, JOD/14; Nicolas, VII, 139–40).

90. NMM, JOD/14; Nicolas, VII, 140–41.

91. Beatty, 14.

92. Beatty, 18.

93. Thursfield, 364. Meat would have been uncooked since the stoves would have been extinguished.

94. Thursfield, 364–5.

95. Bourchier, I, 60, Codrington to Lord Garlies.

96. Houghton, pf MS Eng. 196.5 (134), 8 Nov. 1805.

97. Huntington, STG/150 (1), Lieutenant Green's minute.

98. Beatty, 28–9.

99. (UK) NA: PRO, ADM 51/4514. *The Victory*'s log records the gap as being between the eleventh and twelfth ships; it is more likely to have been between the thirteenth and fourteenth.

100. James, III, 399.

101. Goodwin, 259, quoting Royal Marines Museum, 11/12/1, diary of Lieutenant Lewis Roatley, RM.

102. (UK)NA: PRO, ADM 51/4494, 21 Oct. 1805; Callender, 237.

103. Beatty, 32–3.

104. According to James, III, 402, it was fired by William Willmet, the boatswain.

105. Some weeks earlier a seaman had fallen to the deck, broken his back and slowly died; Nelson had discussed this with Beatty (Beatty, 43–4).

106. Nicolas, VII, 240, quoting *Correspondence of Lord Collingwood*, I, 234, 12 Dec. 1805, Collingwood to the duke of Clarence. From this letter it is clear that Collingwood heard this directly from Hardy.

107. Beatty, 37.

108. Scott, 185, 188.

109. Czisnik, 'Image and Icon', Chapter 6, reviews the idealizing of Nelson's death by early biographers, including those claims that he wished to die.

110. He shook hands with Hardy (Beatty, 41, 42).

111. Scott, 188.

112. Beatty, 44–5.

113. Beatty, 47.

114. Scott, 189.

115. Nicolas, VII, 248–9.

116. Nicolas, VII, 248–51.

117. Scott, 190.

118. Scott, 213, 10 Mar. 1807, Hardy to Scott.

119. Beatty, 70.

120. Specifically bleeding from the severing of his left pulmonary artery (Beatty, 70), which led to loss of blood from circulation, significantly increased by injury to his spinal cord. I am grateful to Professor Leslie Le Quesne for this opinion.

121. Hardy's log noted that 'the Action continued general until 3.0 pm' and that firing continued until 3.40 ((UK) NA: PRO, ADM 51/4514).

122. Rodger, *Command of the Ocean*, 542.

123. Bourchier, I, 68–9.

124. Mafit and Bennett [unpaginated], 22 Oct. 1805.

125. *The Times*, 7 Nov. 1805.

126. James, III, 458; Harbron, 119; Eastwick, I, 296–7, 300–301. Spanish losses are undisputed but discrepancies exist between these sources on the fate of French ships.

127. Corbett, *Trafalgar*, 443–9.

128. Eastwick, II, 145, 20 Nov. 1805, Theodore Contamine to Decres.

129. Corbett, *Trafalgar*, 53.

130. James, III, 443; Rodger, *Command of the Ocean*, 542.

131. Duffy, 'Gunnery', estimates the *Bucentaur*'s casualties at between 209 and 287; Eastwick, II, 146, gives over 400.

132. Bath and Wells, IV, 253, 10 Nov. 1805, Mr Hatsell to Lord Auckland.

133. Duffy, 'Gunnery'.

134. Nicolas, VII, 150.

135. Duffy, 'Gunnery', collects evidence of logs and critical captains, particularly Edward Codrington in the *Orion*.

136. Bourchier, I, 63, 30 Oct. 1805, Codrington to his wife.

137. Thursfield, 365.

138. Thursfield, 363.

139. RNM, MS 1998/41/1. This averages 11.7 a minute, but the majority of the broadsides were in the first two hours of the battle, so that it is difficult to estimate the rate of broadsides.

140. RNM, MS 1983/1064.

141. (UK)NA: PRO, ADM 52/3711.

142. (UK) NA: PRO, ADM 36/15901.

143. Corbett, *Trafalgar*, 50n., quoting an unpublished letter of A. J. Scott, 27 Oct. 1805; Beatty, 28-9.

144. Wheeler, 379.

145. Bourchier, I, 67 [?], Oct. 1805, to his wife.

146. (UK) NA: PRO, ADM/51/4514.

147. RNM, MS 1983/1064; (UK) NA: PRO, ADM 51/4494.

148. The most detailed and graphic account of the storm is in James, III, 452-8.

149. Clayton and Craig, 345-50.

150. Bourchier, I, 63, 30 Oct. 1805, Codrington to his wife.

151. RNM MS 1998/41/1, fols. 155-6.

152. Warren R. Dawson, *Nelson Collection*, 221, 'Remarks etc H. M. Ship *Naiad* off Cadiz Commencing at 7 A.M. of 19th October 1805'.

153. Tracy, *Naval Chronicle*, III, 238.

154. (UK) NA: PRO, ADM 51/4514; ADM 36/15901. The ages given in the muster book are ages on entry in the ship's books.

V   THE TRANSFIGURATION

30   The Funeral

1. Monmouth, E387.

2. *The Times*, 7 Nov. 1805.

3. Bourchier, I, 69. The fleet subscribed £3,000 for a monument on Portsdown Hill, and Thomas Fremantle chaired the overseeing committee (Fremantle, *Wynne* (1952), 434, 31 Dec. 1805, Fremantle to Betsey.

4. (UK)NA: PRO, ADM 51/4514.

5. Foster, 244, Oct. 1805, to Augustus Foster.

6. Bath and Wells, IV, 250-51, 29 Oct. 1805, Lord Sheffield to Lord Auckland.

7. Malmesbury, IV, 341.

8. Naish, 605-6, 6 Nov. 1805, Barham to Fanny; Morriss, *Papers in North America*, 210. I am grateful to Mr Karpeles of Santa Barbara for a sight of Hamond's letter.

9. Monmouth, E386, 9 Nov. 1805, Lord Bridport to an unnamed correspondent.

10. Foster, 251, 29 Nov. 1805, Lady Elizabeth Foster to Augustus Foster.

11. Coleridge, I, 575.
12. Colchester, II, 23, 8 Nov. 1805, Lord Auckland to Lord Colchester.
13. NMM, RUSI/199, 10 Nov. 1805.
14. Foster, 251, 29 Nov. 1805, Lady Elizabeth Foster to Augustus Foster.
15. Granville, II, 133, 10 Nov. 1805, Lady Bessborough to Leveson-Gower.
16. Foster, 249, 20 Nov. 1805, earl of Aberdeen to Augustus Foster.
17. Nicolas, VII, ccxxi, Nelson's will dated 10 May 1803.
18. Jesse, III, 447, 11 Nov. 1805, George III to Pitt.
19. Monmouth, E218, 12 Dec. 1805, Hawkesbury to William Nelson.
20. (UK)NA: PRO, ADM 51/4514.
21. *Naval Chronicle*, XVI, 1812, 202, 12 Dec. 1805 to Captain Thomas Bertie.
22. Beatty, *Narrative*, quoted Nicolas, VII, 258.
23. (UK)NA: PRO, ADM 51/4514, 13–17 Dec.; Monmouth, E471, 14 Dec., Scott to Lady Lavington.
24. Czisnik, 'Image and Icon', 234–7.
25. Jenks, 429–31; Czisnik, 'Image and Icon', 225–49.
26. Jenks, 427–9; Monmouth, E218, 12 Dec. 1805, Hawkesbury to William Nelson.
27. NMM, Waldegrave Papers, Box 3.
28. Monmouth, E214, 6 Dec. 1805.
29. Monmouth, E217, 12 Dec. 1805.
30. Monmouth, E222, Christmas Day 1805, Tyson to William Haslewood; see Tracy, *Naval Chronicle*, III, 250, for official accounts; also Coleman, 330–31.
31. (UK)NA: PRO, ADM 51/4514, 25 Dec. 1805.
32. Thursfield, 364, 28 Dec. 1805, Brown to Thomas Windever. The number of seamen and marines was no more than sixty (Tracy, *Naval Chronicle*, III, 250).
33. Monmouth, E217, 12 Dec. 1805, Tyson to Haslewood.
34. Jenks, 434, quoting *The Times*.
35. *Naval Chronicle*, XV, 1806, 143. Another lieutenant, Lieutenant James Purches, is listed, but he does not appear in the *Victory*'s muster list.
36. Tracy, *Naval Chronicle*, 252–3.
37. Granville, II, 155, 9 Jan. 1806, to Leveson-Gower.
38. Arguably this level of public emotion was not seen in Britain again until 1997, at the funeral of Diana, princess of Wales.
39. Lincoln, 114, quoting from Reverend J. Bouquet, *Thanksgiving Sermon on Account of the Victory . . . 21st October 1805* (Bristol, 1805).
40. Lincoln, 114, quoting from [R. Marks], *Nautical Essays: or . . . with Reflections on the Battle of Trafalgar . . .* (London, 1818).
41. Jenks, 447; Colley, *Britons*, 182, calls attention to a wider cult of 'elite heroism'.
42. Huntington, HM 34205, 12 Nov. 1805, St Vincent to his second cousin Thomas Jervis, then MP for Great Yarmouth.
43. Lloyd, 'St Vincent', 160.
44. Tracy, *Naval Chronicle*, III, 255.

45. Baring, 455.

46. e.g., Morrison, II, 258, 7 July 1805, Miss Bolton to Emma.

47. NMM, DAV/2/65, 14 Dec. 1805.

48. NMM, DAV/2/60, 14 Jan., 2/61, 30 Jan. 1805; 2/62, 28 July; 2/63, 18 Aug. 1805; 2/68, 20 Jan. 1807, Fanny to Davison.

49. Nicolas, VII, ccxxi–ccxl, Nelson's will, dated 10 May 1803, and eight codicils, the last one dated 21 Oct. 1805. The estate at Bronte was left to the family. Hardy received Nelson's telescope and £100.

50. NMM, HAS/1, 24 Jan. 1806, Haslewood to Earl Nelson.

51. Monmouth, E714, 4 Feb. 1806, J. W. Western to Fanny.

52. Monmouth, E726, 17 Oct. 1806, J. W. Western to Fanny. She purchased another £1,000 in 3 per cent stock at that time (20 Oct. 1806, Fanny to Western).

53. Downer, 175 [n.d.].

54. Granville, II, 143, 6 Dec. 1805, Lady Bessborough to Lord Granville Leveson-Gower.

55. Houghton, pf MS Eng. 196.5 (113), 14 May 1806, Hardy to Emma.

56. Monmouth, E212, 9 Nov. 1805, Mrs Cadogan to George Rose.

57. NMM, HAS/1, 2 July 1806, Haslewood to Mrs Cadogan.

58. Monmouth, E219, 16 Dec. 1805, Marsh and Creed to Haslewood; considerable discontent was generated among the captains about the level of prize money after Trafalgar (NMM, DAV/1/1–27, Davison's correspondence with Collingwood, Hardy, etc., 1806). This contrasted with one estimate of Nelson's share of £100,000 (Bath and Wells, IV, 259, 18 Dec. 1805, Lord Henley to Lord Auckland).

59. Morrison, II, 345, 2 Jan. 1811, Mrs Matcham to Emma.

60. Houghton, FMS Lowell 10, 18 Apr., 31 Oct. 1813, Emma to Horatia.

61. Fraser, 362–71.

62. Huntington, STG 159 (45), 1 Feb. 1807, John Pasco to Grenville.

63. Huntington, STG 160 (49), 10 Oct. 1806, Thomas Pollard to Grenville.

64. Huntington, STG 136 (23), 5 Dec. 1806, Thomas Bowen to Grenville; STG 139 (60), 30 Oct. 1806, John Conn to Grenville; STG 158 (25), 6 Feb. 1807; STG 134 (40), 26 Dec. 1806, J[oseph] Foster Barham to William Windham, on behalf of Layman. Bowen died in 1809 and Conn was drowned in 1810.

65. Huntington, STG 158 (52), 24 Feb. 1807, William Nelson to Grenville.

31   The Nineteenth and Twentieth Centuries

1. Deuchar, 156, reported by Joseph Farington, quoted in Charles Mitchell, 'Benjamin West's *Death of Nelson*' in Douglas Fraser *et al.* (eds.), *Essays in the History of Art Presented to Rudoph Wittkower* (1967), 270. Devis's great painting is in the National Maritime Museum (BHC, 2894), as is a later one by West of 1808, when he painted a poorly finished *Death of Nelson* scene in the cockpit (NMM, BHC 0566).

2. Bucks. D/FR/45.1/39, 3 Feb. 1806, Fremantle to William Fremantle.

3. James, IV, 103.

4. Hattendorf *et al.*, *Naval Documents*, 351–4.

5. NMM, HAS/1, 4 July 1806, William Haslewood to William Nelson.

6. Nicolas, VII, 340, 419–21.

7. Walder, 510, 512–13.

8. I am grateful to the Reverend Donald Thorpe for his notes on the memorials in the church.

9. Nicolas, VII, 352–3. It was an age of monument building. Parliament funded thirty-six national monuments in St Paul's and Westminster Abbey between 1794 and 1823 (Hoock, 259–61).

10. Fraser, 'Monument', 140.

11. Czisnik, 'Image and Icon', 260, and Chapter 11 generally.

12. Fraser, 'Monument', 150.

13. Prentice, Chapter 2; Le Quesne, *Glass Pictures*; Czisnik, Chapter 13.

14. West's first *Death of Nelson* is in the Walker Art Gallery in Liverpool.

15. Walker, 159–62; Czisnik, 'Image and Icon', 277–8; Colley, *Britons*, 180.

16. Deuchar, 155.

17. Czisnik, 'Image and Icon', Chapter 12 generally.

18. Eastwood, 145. For instance, a leather-bound edition of 1831.

19. Southey (1873), 317; Hamilton, 392. Southey dedicated the book to John Wilson Croker, who four years later was to use government money to purchase letters to Nelson to keep them out of the public domain.

20. Southey (1873), 228.

21. Hamilton, 382–3.

22. Hamilton, 384, quoting Henry Raikes, *Memoir of the Life and Service of Vice-Admiral Sir Jahleel Brenton* (1848), i.

23. Hamilton, 392–3.

24. Douglas-Morris, xvii.

25. Deuchar, 158.

26. Hattendorf, *Naval Documents*, 604–7.

27. Hattendorf and Hattendorf, section A6. *The Life of Nelson* went through a number of editions and was later translated into Swedish and Japanese.

28. John Robertson (2000), 19–20, points out: 'Not surprisingly, modern histori-cal scholarship, much of it by Neapolitans, has questioned and qualified this judgement.'

29. Lambert, *Foundations*, 175. For a sophisticated analysis of French, German and Italian sources, see Czisnik, 'Image and Icon', Chapter 4, 107–21. Dr Czisnik makes a strong case for Nelson's legal position, demonstrating the weakness of Badham's arguments.

30. Lambert, *Laughton* (2002), 231, 31 Dec. 1905, Mahan to Laughton; see also 120–92, 201, 203, 205, 209–11, 222, 227.

31. Coleman (2000), 347. He devotes nearly a fifth of the pages of his biography

to the weeks at Palermo and Naples. John Robertson, 20, cites books influenced by Croce published in 1903 (by Constance H. D. Giglioli (née Stocker)) and 1925 (by Lucy Collison-Morley).

32. Lambert, *Foundations*, 173, also 76–8.

33. For example, Susan Sontag, *The Volcano Lover* (1992), and Barry Unsworth, *Losing Nelson* (1999).

34. William Hotham in Stirling, *Pages and Portraits*, 242.

35. Deuchar, 160.

36. Lewis-Jones, 74–5.

37. Czisnik, 378–85.

38. Littlewood and Butler, 34, quoting NMM, SNR/7/2, 10 Sept. 1922, Society for Nautical Research Collection.

39. Deuchar, 163.

40. Walker, *Nelson Portraits*, xix.

32   The Summing-up

1. Eastwick, II, 147.

2. Rutherford [no pagination]; *Navy League Journal* (Aug. 1897), 4 Aug. 1805, Rutherford to J. C. Beresford.

3. Cryer, 6.

4. Coleridge, I, 572.

5. Tracy, *Naval Chronicle*, II, 160.

6. BL, Add. MSS 40573, 31 Aug. 1845, Croker to Sir Robert Peel. I am indebted to Iain Hamilton for this reference.

7. Morriss, *Cockburn*, 33, quoting NMM, CKE/6, 11 Apr. 1845.

8. Mahan, 452–55.

9. Jordan, 40.

10. Scott, 191.

11. e.g., NMM, AGC/17/3, 26 Jan. 1798, Nelson to Dr Gaskin.

12. Chatterton, I, 248. When Gambier and the *Defence* drifted mastless past the *Invincible*, her captain, the irreverent Irishman Edward Pakenham, 'seized a speaking trumpet and called out to him, "Whom the Lord loveth, he chasteneth"' (Chatterton, I, 5). For Saumarez, see Matcham, 142.

13. Laughton, *Miscellany*, I, 438–9, 11 June 1805, Nelson to Simon Taylor, an old Jamaica friend. See Talbott, 129–32, for Barham's religious views.

14. Naish, 138–9; BL, Add. MSS 34968, 4 July 1805.

15. Even Alexander Scott's evidence on Nelson's religious feeling emphasizes Nelson's concern that Scott's sermons should be understandable to the crew (Scott, 191–2).

16. e.g., (UK)NA: PRO, ADM 51/883, 1 May 1774; ADM 51/4247, 15 June 1777; ADM 51/557, 14, 21, 28 June 1778; ADM 51/4110, 20 Feb., 5 Mar. 1780.

17. Czisnik, 'Image and Icon', 179-80.

18. Clarke and MacArthur, II, 470.

19. Lavery, *Trafalgar*, 25, quoting Kathrin Orth's unpublished paper 'Crime and Punishment in the Royal Navy', 1995.

20. NMM, NEP/7, 29 Aug. 1796, St Vincent to Nepean; also quoted in Horsfield, 60.

21. Krajeski, 43-6.

22. Huntington, STG 169 (43), 29 Nov. 1806, William Young to Thomas Grenville.

23. Minto, III, 374.

24. NMM, NEP/4, 3 July 1798, St Vincent to Nepean.

25. Malmesbury, IV, 342.

26. Nicolas, II, 350, 16 Feb. 1797, Nelson to Gilbert Elliot.

27. BL, Add. MSS 36708, 23 Mar. 1797, St Vincent to Nepean.

28. Jordan and Rogers, 223.

29. NMM, CRK/6/49, 1 Feb. 1805, Gore to Nelson.

30. Czisnik, 'Image and Icon', 181.

31. Czisnik, 'Image and Icon', 183-7, reviews those writers who have emphasized Nelson's vanity.

32. Jenks, 431-3.

33. St Vincent, in choleric old age, and infuriated by the *Memoirs of Lady Hamilton*, wrote in a postscript of a letter in 1814: 'Animal courage was the sole merit of Lord Nelson' (Coleman, *Nelson* (2001), 343, quoting NMM, PAR/167c, 18 Oct. 1814). Coleman also draws attention to a similar reference to the phrase, written on 30 Jan. 1807 (NMM, AGC/J/3); for a gentler view of St Vincent's last years, see Crimmin, 'Jervis', 348; see Czisnik, 'Image and Icon', 45n.

34. BL, Add. MSS 40573, 31 Aug. 1845, Croker to Peel.

35. Nicolas, VI, 419, 4 May 1805, Nelson to Otway, quoted in Corbett, *Trafalgar*, 108.

36. e.g., (UK)NA: PRO, ADM 51/78, 1 Apr. 1779, topmast in the *Badger*; 51/4110, 7-8 Feb. 1783, in light airs the *Albemarle* ran aground in Port Royal Harbour and only got off two days later after some guns and ballast were offloaded.

37. See p. 226.

38. Walder, 140.

39. Nicolas, VII, 241, 16 Dec. 1805, Collingwood to Sir Thomas Pasley.

40. Coleman accentuates the untypical dissatisfaction of those who served under Nelson at Boulogne, but they were not regulars, and peace was about to be signed after eight years of war (Coleman, *Nelson* (2002), 358-60). See chapter p. 416.

41. R. V. Hamilton, *Byam Martin*, III, 307-8.

42. Bourchier, I, 32-3.

43. Fremantle (1952), III, 94.

Text and Illustrations Permissions

The publisher would like to thank the following institutions and individuals for their kind permission to reproduce the copyright material in this book:

The Bodleian Library, University of Oxford; British Library; Devon Record Office; Centre for Buckinghamshire Studies; National Archives; National Archives of Scotland; National Maritime Museum, London; Nelson Museum, Monmouth; Norfolk Record Office; Royal Naval Museum, Portsmouth; Wellcome Library for the History and Understanding of Medicine; William L. Clements Library, University of Michigan; Houghton Library, Harvard University; Huntington Library, San Marino, California; Lord Sidmouth; the Earl of Leicester; Lord de Saumaurez

1. *Racehorse* and *Carcass* in the ice, 1773, watercolour by John Cleveley. © National Maritime Museum, London, PY3970
2. View of Bastia from the *Victory*, May 1794, watercolour by Lieutenant Ralph Willet Miller. © National Maritime Museum, London, PY2326
3. Frances, Lady Nelson, 1798, pencil drawing by Daniel Orme. © National Maritime Museum, London, A0094
4. Emma Hamilton, 1800, pastel by Johann Heinrich Schmidt. © National Maritime Museum, London, A4288
5. Nelson leading the boarding party on to the *San Nicolas* at the Battle of Cape St Vincent, after James Daniell, print of 1 Nov. 1798. Warwick Leadlay Gallery, Greenwich
6. Nelson before the attack on Santa Cruz, July 1797, watercolour by an unknown artist. Nelson Museum, Monmouth
7. Nelson's reception at Fonthill, December 1800, hand-coloured print from the *Gentleman's Magazine*, 1801. © National Maritime Museum, London, PU3988
8. *A Jig round the Statue of Peace; or, All Parties Reconciled* by W. Holland, 6 Oct. 1801. Royal Naval Museum, Portsmouth, 1973/275(2)
9–12. Four coloured prints of the Battle of the Nile, 'At Evening', '10 O'Clock', 'Midnight', 'The Ensuing Morning', by Robert Dodd. Warwick Leadlay Gallery, Greenwich

13. Merton, watercolour by Thomas Baxter. © National Maritime Museum, London, Manuscript Collection WAL/1

14. Captain Horatio Nelson, 1781, oil painting by Jean Francis Rigaud. © National Maritime Museum, London, BHC2901

15. Reverend Edmund Nelson, 1800, oil painting by Sir William Beechey. © National Maritime Museum, London, BHC2881

16. Captain William Locker, oil painting by Gilbert Stuart. Greenwich Hospital Collection, © National Maritime Museum, London, BHC2846

17. *Midshipmen Studying between Decks On Board the 'Pallas', May 1775*, watercolour by Gabriel Bray. © National Maritime Museum, London PT2026

18. Cuthbert Collingwood, unattributed print. © National Maritime Museum, London, PU3141

19. Prince William Henry, later the duke of Clarence, *c.* 1791, miniature by Richard Cosway. Private collection, on loan to the National Portrait Gallery, London, L176

20. Admiral Viscount Hood, oil painting by James Northcote. © National Maritime Museum, London, BHC2774

21. Rear-Admiral Thomas Fremantle, engraving of 1810, from a painting by Pellegrini. © National Maritime Museum, London, BHC2289

22. The *Agamemnon* cutting out French vessels at Port Maurice, 1 June 1796, watercolour by Nicholas Pocock. © National Maritime Museum, London, PW5874

23. The French Army enters Leghorn, 30 June 1796, engraving by Duplessix-Bertaux and Daubrun (after Carl Vernet, artist). © National Maritime Museum, London, PX8938

24. The sword of Rear-Admiral Don Francisco Winthuysen surrendered to Nelson at the Battle of Cape St Vincent. Norwich Castle Museum and Gallery

25. Gilbert Elliot, later Lord Minto, by Sir Thomas Lawrence, 1794. Private collection, courtesy of the Witt Library, Courtauld Institute, London

26. William Windham by Sir Joshua Reynolds, 1787. National Portrait Gallery, London, 704

27. Admiral Sir John Jervis, before 1797, oil painting, by Lemuel Francis Abbott. National Portrait Gallery, London, 936

28. Earl Spencer, mezzotint by Reynolds, after a painting by John Hoppner. National Portrait Gallery, London, RN33347

29. Rear-Admiral Sir Alexander Ball, oil painting by Henry Pickersgill. Greenwich Hospital Collection. © National Maritime Museum, London, BHC2528

30. The dismasted *Vanguard* off Sardinia being towed by the *Alexander*, 21–3 May 1798, watercolour by Nicholas Pocock. © National Maritime Museum, London, PW5876

31. The arrival of the *Vanguard* at Naples, 22 September 1798, gouache drawing by Giacomo Guardi. © National Maritime Museum, London, PX9746

32. Rear-Admiral Sir Thomas Troubridge, oil painting by Sir William Beechey. © National Maritime Museum, London, BHC3168

33. Captain Thomas Foley, miniature on ivory, attributed to Robert Bowyer or William Grimaldi. © National Maritime Museum, London, MNT0164

34. Captain Sir Edward Berry, engraving after Daniel Orme. © National Maritime Museum, London, PU3435

35. Captain Thomas Masterman Hardy, oil painting by Domenico Pellegrini. © National Maritime Museum, London, BHC2352

36. Rear-Admiral Sir Horatio Nelson, 1799, by Lemuel Francis Abbott. © Greenwich Hospital Collection © National Maritime Museum, London, BHC2889

37. Chart of the Maddalena Islands, 1802, drawn by Captain George Ryves. By permission of the Controller of Her Majesty's Stationery Office and the UK Hydrographic Office, n56Ry

38. The British fleet forcing the passage of the Sound, 30 March 1801, oil painting by Robert Dodd. © National Maritime Museum, London, BHC0522

39. The Battle of Copenhagen by Dominic Serres. © National Maritime Museum, London, BHC0528

40. Diagram of the British fleet approaching the French and Spanish line at Trafalgar by Robert Dodd. © National Maritime Musuem, London, PW4741

41. *The Death of Nelson*, print of 1809, after Benjamin West. © National Maritime Museum, London, PAF4733

42. Nelson's funeral procession on the Thames, 9 January 1806, oil painting by Daniel Turner. © National Maritime Museum, London, BHC0569

43. Nelson's funeral in St Paul's, after A. C. Pugin. © National Maritime Museum, London, PY7333

44. *England's Pride and Glory* by Thomas Davidson. © National Maritime Musuem, London, BHC1811

MANUSCRIPT REPRODUCTIONS

A page from Nelson's journal, 17–21 October 1793. © National Maritime Museum, London, CRK/14/1

Nelson's draft note to Adelaide Correglia. Huntington Library, San Marino, California, HM34180

The coast at Santa Cruz, Tenerife, sketched by Nelson for Lord Keith, *c.* early 1800. © National Maritime Museum, London, KEI/19/5

Nelson's first letter written with his left hand, 27 July 1797, to Earl St Vincent © National Maritime Museum, London, PAR/251

Nelson's questions to his captains as to the course to set to find the French fleet, 22 June 1798. © National Maritime Museum, London, CRK/14/43

Nelson's sketch of his plan for Copenhagen. © National Maritime Museum, London, CRK/14/68

Nelson's note to Henry Addington, 9 March 1803. Devon Record Office, DRO, 152/M/c1803/ON39
Nelson's sketch of his intended tactics before Trafalgar. © National Maritime Museum, London, BRP/6

Index